NEW

WITHDRAWN

NEW

ENCYCLOPEDIA OF WORLD BIOGRAPHY

10

ENCYCLOPEDIA OF WORLD BIOGRAPHY
SECOND EDITION

Love
Micah

10

GALE

DETROIT · NEW YORK · TORONTO · LONDON

Staff

Senior Editor: Paula K. Byers
Project Editor: Suzanne M. Bourgoin
Managing Editor: Neil E. Walker

Editorial Staff: Luann Brennan, Frank V. Castronova, Laura S. Hightower, Karen E. Lemerand, Stacy A. McConnell, Jennifer Mossman, Maria L. Munoz, Katherine H. Nemeh, Terrie M. Rooney, Geri Speace

Permissions Manager: Susan M. Tosky
Permissions Specialist: Maria L. Franklin
Permissions Associate: Michele M. Lonoconus
Image Cataloger: Mary K. Grimes

Production Director: Mary Beth Trimper
Production Manager: Evi Seoud
Production Associate: Shanna Heilveil
Product Design Manager: Cynthia Baldwin
Senior Art Director: Mary Claire Krzewinski

Research Manager: Victoria B. Cariappa
Research Specialists: Michele P. LaMeau, Andrew Guy Malonis, Barbara McNeil, Gary J. Oudersluys
Research Associates: Julia C. Daniel, Tamara C. Nott, Norma Sawaya, Cheryl L. Warnock
Research Assistant: Talitha A. Jean

Graphic Services Supervisor: Barbara Yarrow
Image Database Supervisor: Randy Bassett
Imaging Specialist: Mike Lugosz

Manager of Data Entry Services: Eleanor M. Allison
Data Entry Coordinator: Kenneth D. Benson

Manager of Technology Support Services: Theresa A. Rocklin
Programmers/Analysts: Mira Bossowska, Jeffrey Muhr, Christopher Ward

Copyright © 1998
Gale Research
835 Penobscot Bldg.
Detroit, MI 48226-4094

ISBN 0-7876-2221-4 (Set)
ISBN 0-7876-2550-7 (Volume 10)

Library of Congress Cataloging-in-Publication Data

Encyclopedia of world biography / [edited by Suzanne Michele Bourgoin and Paula Kay Byers].
    p. cm.
    Includes bibliographical references and index.
    Summary: Presents brief biographical sketches which provide vital statistics as well as information on the importance of the person listed.
    ISBN 0-7876-2221-4 (set : alk. paper)
    1. Biography—Dictionaries—Juvenile literature. [1. Biography.]
I. Bourgoin, Suzanne Michele, 1968- . II. Byers, Paula K. (Paula Kay), 1954- .
CT 103.E56 1997
920′ .003—dc21
                                    97-42327
                                         CIP
                                         AC

Printed in the United States of America
10 9 8 7 6 5 4 3 2

ENCYCLOPEDIA OF
WORLD BIOGRAPHY

10

L

Nat Love

Nat Love (1854-1921), African American champion cowboy known as Deadwood Dick, was famous for his great skill as a range rider and cattle-brand reader.

Nat Love was born a slave on a plantation near Nashville, Tenn., in June 1854. He had no formal education but, with help from his father, he learned to read and write. When the slaves were freed following the Civil War, Love worked on the small farm that his father rented from his former owner. After his father's sudden death, he became the sole support of his mother and younger brother and sister. He was able to obtain work on various plantations, where he displayed great skill in breaking horses.

In 1869, at the age of 15, Love was strong and alert and looked older than his years. He left his family in an uncle's charge and, with $50 in his pocket, headed west for Kansas, walking most of the way. When he reached Dodge City (a shipping center for the cattle industry), he got his first job, as a cowboy with the Duval Ranch. In the course of his 3 years with the Duval Ranch, Love became their buyer and chief brand reader. He made many trips into Mexico in this capacity and in the process learned to speak Spanish fluently.

In 1872 Love went to work for the Gallinger Ranch in Arizona, where he remained for many years. He became a master range rider and traveled over all the important western trails between the Gulf of Mexico and Montana. His dangerous work involved him numerous times in gun battles with Native Americans, cattle rustlers, and bandits, and he became an expert marksman. In one encounter with Indians he was wounded but taken captive rather than killed because the Indians were impressed with his bravery. He came to know many of the famous men of the West, including Billy the Kid, Bat Masterson, and Pat Garrett.

Love acquired the name Deadwood Dick as a result of winning a shooting contest in Deadwood, S. Dak., on July 4, 1876. He became a champion rifleman by placing 14 out of 14 shots in the center of a target at 250 yards.

Love married in 1889, and a year later he left the range to work as a Pullman porter on the Denver Rio Grande Railroad. In 1907 he published his autobiography, which contains photographs of him wearing his western gear. He died in Los Angeles in 1921.

Further Reading

The best book about Love is his autobiography, *The Life and Adventures of Nat Love* (1907; repr. with new introduction, 1968). A well-written source of general information about the Afro-American cowboys is Philip Durham and Everett L. Jones, *The Negro Cowboys* (1965). Also useful is William H. Leckie, *The Buffalo Soldiers: A Narrative of the Negro Cavalry in the West* (1967). □

Susan M. Love

Susan M. Love (born 1948) feels that too many women succumb to breast cancer every year. A breast cancer specialist, Love believes women are losing control over their condition due to the male centered medical community.

D r. Susan Love believes too many women fall victim to breast cancer each year. And just as disturbing, many of those women are further victimized by the male-dominated medical establishment, losing control of how their condition is treated. Love, a surgeon specializing in breast cancer, is out to change both issues.

A leading authority in her field, Love was director of the UCLA Breast Center, a haven for patients who come for consultation and treatment of the disease that ranks second only to lung cancer as America's leading killer of women. Love is also the author of *Dr. Susan Love's Breast Book,* a straightforward, no-nonsense and nontechnical look at the hows and whys of breast diseases.

"What drives Love in all this is more than a sense of urgency—she also has profound hope, believing that given adequate funds and intelligent research priorities, the fight against breast cancer can be won, and soon," commented Beth Horner in *Technology Review.* In an interview with Love, Horner noted that advice given to women about mammograms seems to change almost yearly. "The basic problem," replied Love, "is that no one quite understands the disease yet. We're just beginning to fill in the gaps in our knowledge, and as we do, doctors naturally find themselves reevaluating some of their recommendations."

But Love is certain of one thing: "Breast cancer does send incredible fear through women's hearts, but I don't think that's because it's had too much publicity. I don't even think it's entirely because breast cancer can be fatal." What keeps women fearful—even of examinations—is the pros-

pect of a mastectomy, the removal of one or both breasts. "The breast," Love explained, "has some special psychological baggage—for one thing, there are all the associations of breastfeeding and nurturing the next generation. Then, too, the breast is the most obvious identifying feature of femaleness."

Another problem is that the doctor recommending treatment is invariably male. "Even when the patient has got over the shock of diagnosis, doctors can make it hard for her to come to a good, clear-headed decision about what kind of surgery she wants," Love told Horner. "They'll say things like, 'Well, you're elderly and you're widowed—you don't need your breast anymore. Why don't you just have a mastectomy? It'll be easier.' In my experience, though, older women aren't any more likely than younger ones to want a mastectomy."

Love has come by her insight as both a doctor and a woman. Ironically, the specialty she ended up with was not her first choice. In fact, "when Love became the first female general surgeon on staff at Boston's prestigious Beth Israel Hospital in 1980," Elizabeth Gleick stated in a *People* article, "she swore that she would not allow herself to get pigeonholed into women's medicine. 'I am not going to let them turn me into a breast surgeon,' she remembers thinking of her fellow doctors."

But the very fact that Love *was* a female surgeon in a medical field dominated by men led breast cancer patients to seek her out. As Love related in her book: "For any other form of surgery, they might have chosen, even preferred, a male doctor—but for breasts, they wanted someone they instinctively felt would understand their bodies and respect the particular meaning their breasts had for them. I soon realized that I could make a particular contribution in this area: I could combine my experience as a woman with my medical knowledge. I decided to specialize in breast problems."

In 1987 Love was appointed assistant clinical professor in surgery at Harvard Medical School; a year later she founded the Faulkner Breast Center, employing additional women as surgeons, oncologists, nurse specialists, radiologists, and more. Combining research with her political agenda, Love in 1990 cofounded the National Breast Center Coalition, an advocacy group dedicated to awareness of, and funding for, women's health issues.

With the publication of her book and the opening of the UCLA center, Love became a widely sought out figure. In *People* she detailed a schedule of surgery twice a week, lecturing to women's groups, and the frequent trips from her home base in California to Washington, D.C., to meet with U.S. Health and Human Services Secretary Donna Shalala. Spare time is spent with the family—daughter Katie and Love's companion, Helen Cooksey, herself a surgeon. Love, who has made no secret of her sexual orientation, drew headlines in 1993 when Katie, born to Love of donated sperm, was jointly adopted by the two women—a groundbreaking custody case ensuring the pair will share full parental responsibility.

Having worked so extensively in the name of women's health, Love has some words of encouragement for those who have—or fear getting—breast cancer. "The first message I try to get across is that a diagnosis of breast cancer is not an emergency," she told *Technology Review.* "The typical notion is that you're a time bomb and the cancer is going to take over your body unless you do something tomorrow. Well, that's just not true. By the time they're diagnosed, most breast cancers have been around for years, which means it's unlikely that anything too dramatic will happen right away. You really do have a few weeks to research the subject, get second opinions, sort out your feelings and so on. I also think it's vital to treat women like intelligent human beings who are capable of all that."

In April 1996 Love announced her resignation from the UCLA Breast Center and received a position as professor of surgery at UCLA. She also published two more books on women's health. They include *Dr. Susan Love's Hormone Book: Making Informed Choices About Menopause* (1996) and *To Dance with the Devil: The New War on Breast Cancer* (1997).

Further Reading

Love, Susan, *Dr. Susan Love's Breast Book,* Addison-Wesley, 1990.
Love, Susan, *Dr. Susan Love's Hormone Book: Making Informed Choices About Menopause,* 1997.
Love, Susan, *To Dance with the Devil: The New War on Breast Cancer,* 1997.
People, July 25, 1994, p. 147.
Technology Review, May 1993, p. 45. □

H. P. Lovecraft

H. P. Lovecraft (1890-1937) is widely considered the most important literary supernaturalist of the twentieth century. He is one of the greatest in a line of authors that originated with the Gothic novelists of the eighteenth century and was perpetuated throughout the nineteenth century by such figures as Edgar Allan Poe, Ambrose Bierce, J. Sheridan LeFanu, and Arthur Machen.

Lovecraft was born August 20, 1890, in Providence, Rhode Island, at the home of his maternal grandfather, Whipple V. Phillips, a prosperous industrialist and New England gentleman who was the dominant intellectual influence on his grandson's early life, both personally and through his extensive library of works by eighteenth- and nineteenth-century authors. Of the Victorian mansion on Angell Street, Lovecraft wrote: "Here I spent the best years of my childhood. The house was a beautiful and spacious edifice, with stable and grounds, the latter approaching a park in the beauty of the walk and trees." A precocious child whose delicate health allowed him only sporadic attendance at school, Lovecraft flourished in a world of cultured adults who fostered his interest in Greco-Roman antiquity, astronomy, eighteenth-century literature and history, and Gothic tales of terror. This milieu, and the traditions on which it was founded, served as the prime mental and emotional coordinates of Lovecraft's life, whose auspicious beginnings gradually devolved into a lethargic procession of loss and unfulfilled promise: Lovecraft's father, a handsome, syphilitic traveling salesman who was effectively a stranger to his son, died in 1898 after spending the last five years of his life institutionalized with general paresis; Lovecraft's grandfather died in 1904, and subsequent ill-management of his financial holdings forced Sarah Phillips Lovecraft and her only child to move from their family home into a nearby duplex. In his published letters, Lovecraft unfailingly celebrates his mother's refinement and cultural accomplishments; in biographies of Lovecraft, his mother is portrayed as an intelligent and sensitive woman, a neglected wife, and an overprotective parent who instilled in her son a profound conviction that he was different from other people.

In 1908 Lovecraft suffered a nervous breakdown that prevented his attaining enough credits to graduate from high school, and, rather than entering Brown University to pursue the professorship that he had formerly assumed would occupy the rest of his life, he continued his program of self-education. During this period Lovecraft in large part existed as a semi-invalid recluse. In 1914 his isolation was alleviated when he joined the United Amateur Press Association, a group of nonprofessional writers who produced a variety of publications and exchanged letters. A voluminous writer from an early age, Lovecraft now directed his efforts toward these amateur journals, with his own magazine, the *Conservative,* appearing from 1915 to 1923. He also became involved in a network of correspondence which for the rest of his life provided a major outlet for personal and artistic expression. In these letters, Lovecraft discussed an encyclopedic range of subjects in essay-like length and depth; here he also vented his lifelong obsessions, most prominently his love of the past and of scientific truth, and his aversion to the modern world and to all peoples who were not of the Anglo-Nordic cultural stream, although several biographers maintain that he moderated some of his extremist views later in his life. Lovecraft's contributions to amateur journals were almost exclusively in the form of poems and essays, the former being imitations of such eighteenth-century poets as Alexander Pope and James Thomson, and the latter displaying a style strongly influenced by such eighteenth-century prose writers as Joseph Addison and Samuel Johnson. Although Lovecraft wrote several horror stories after his first reading in 1898 of the tales of Poe, he destroyed most of these efforts and wrote no fiction from 1908 to 1917. In the latter years he was encouraged by editor W. Paul Cook to resume fiction writing, resulting in the successive composition of *"The Tomb"* and *"Dagon,"* the first of what are considered Lovecraft's mature works. After further encouragement from other friends, these two stories, along with three others, were submitted to the pulp magazine *Weird Tales,* which afterward became the principal publisher of Lovecraft's fiction during his lifetime.

Beginning around 1919, Lovecraft began to socialize with other amateur journalists, and through these channels in 1921 he met Sonia H. Greene, a Russian Jewish businesswoman from New York City. They married in 1924 and Lovecraft went to live with his wife in New York, where he hoped to find employment that would enable him to abandon the disagreeable and insubstantial living he previously earned as a literary reviser and ghostwriter. Ten months later the couple separated for reasons that Lovecraft described as largely financial, although the situation was aggravated by Lovecraft's hatred of a city with such a conspicuously mixed racial and ethnic population. In 1926, Lovecraft returned to Providence, where he lived for the remainder of his life. To supplement his dwindling inheritance he was forced to continue his revision work. Despite his nearly destitute financial state, Lovecraft managed to travel extensively, documenting these excursions in his letters and in such essays as "Vermont: A First Impression," "Charleston," and *A Description and Guide to the City of Quebeck.* During the last ten years of his life, he also produced what are considered his greatest works, including "The Call of Cthulhu," *The Case of Charles Dexter Ward,* "The Colour out of Space," "The Shadow over Innsmouth," and *At the Mountains of Madness.* Lovecraft died of intestinal cancer March 15, 1937, at the age of forty-six.

While an account of the outward events of Lovecraft's life may suggest some of the character traits that critics have found immensely valuable in explicating his works, it fails to convey the full range and intensity of his convictions, preoccupations, and eccentricities. As revealed in his letters, Lovecraft's most important experiences were those of a self-sustaining and isolated imagination. The solitary worlds that he inhabited in childhood—based on his reading of the

Arabian Nights, classical mythology, and Georgian authors—were fortified and augmented throughout his life, providing him with a well-defined set of interrelated roles which he sometimes facetiously, sometimes tenaciously assumed: the Anglophile gentleman who upheld the most staid conventionality and lamented the "tragic rebellion of 1775-83," the Nordic warrior who reveled in dreams of adventure and blood, the proud citizen of the Roman Empire, the anemic decadent immersed in every form of human and metaphysical abnormality, the frigid scientist seeking truth by the strictest criteria of logic, the generous and brilliantly humorous friend, the xenophobic admirer of *Mein Kampf* who evolved into a quasi-socialist supporter of Franklin Roosevelt's New Deal, and the "cosmic-minded" dreamer of imaginary spheres that transcend the brief and aimless episode of human history. The last-named quality of cosmic-mindedness was perhaps less a discrete component of Lovecraft's temperament than the relatively stable foundation upon which his numerous personae were constructed. Philosophically, Lovecraft was a strict scientific materialist who held that the universe is a mechanical assemblage of forces wherein all values are simply fabrications having no validity outside the context of human imagination and that humanity itself is merely an evanescent phenomenon without any special dimension of soul or spirit to distinguish it from other forms of animate or inanimate matter. At the same time Lovecraft wrote that his strongest feelings were connected with a sense of unknown realms outside human experience, an irrationally perceived mystery and meaning beyond the world of crude appearances. It is particularly this tension between Lovecraft's sterile scientism and mystic imagination—whose contradictory relationship he always recognized and relished—that critics find is the source of the highly original character of his work.

Lovecraft's stories are commonly divided into three types: those influenced by the Irish fantasist Lord Dunsany, a diverse group of horror narratives set in New England, and tales sharing a background of cosmic legendry usually referred to as the "Cthulhu Mythos," a term coined by August Derleth and never used by Lovecraft himself. The Dunsanian stories begin with "Polaris," which Lovecraft actually wrote the year before his first reading of Dunsany's works. Nevertheless, his discovery of Dunsany was a crucial impetus to continue developing narratives more or less related to a tradition of fairy tales and typified by wholly imaginary settings and characters with otherworldly names. Stories in this vein are "The White Ship," "The Doom That Came to Sarnath," "The Cats of Ulthar," and *The Dream-Quest of Unknown Kadath.* Contrasting with these dreamlike romances are tales in which the central element of supernatural horror originates and is circumscribed in a realistic New England setting. Throughout his life Lovecraft was captivated by the architecture, landscape, and traditions of New England. In a letter of 1927, he wrote: "Sometimes I stumble accidentally on rare combinations of slope, curved street-line, roofs & gables & chimneys, & accessory details of verdure & background, which in the magic of late afternoon assume a mystic majesty & exotic significance beyond the power of words to describe. . . . All that I live for is to capture some fragment of this hidden & unreachable beauty; this beauty which is all of dream, yet which I feel I have known closely & revelled in through long aeons before my birth or the birth of this or any other world." To some extent, the fantasy realms of the Dunsanian stories are transfigurations of this New England of ideal beauty. On the other hand, Lovecraft simultaneously perceived and devoted much of his work to depicting a different side of his native region: the degeneracy and superstition that flourish in isolated locales, as described in "The Picture in the House" and "The Unnameable;" the survival of unearthly rites practiced in a quaint, colonial town in "The Festival;" the clan of ghouls that inhabits modern Boston in "Pickman's Model;" the horror interred beneath "The Shunned House," which was inspired by an actual home in the district of Providence where Lovecraft resided; and the foul aspirations of an eighteenth-century wizard which are recapitulated in twentieth-century Providence in *The Case of Charles Dexter Ward*. In other stories, those of the Cthulhu Mythos, Lovecraft provided literary travelogues to a New England that departed even further from the sites of his antiquarian wanderings, revising the geography so familiar to him to create the fictional world of Arkham, Innsmouth, and Dunwich. As he wrote to one of his correspondents: "Yes—my New England is a dream New England—the familiar scene with certain lights and shadows heightened (or meant to be heightened) just enough to merge it with things beyond the world." Among these "things" are the primeval and extrastellar pantheon of a body of myth that, although irregular in its details, is highly consistent as Lovecraft's expression of humanity's insignificant and unsteady place in the universe.

One of the most important and controversial issues in Lovecraft criticism is that regarding nomenclature for his Mythos stories. Various labels have been employed, from the broad designations of "horror" and "Gothic" to more discriminating terms such as "supernormal" and "mechanistic supernatural." At the source of this diverse terminology is the fact that, while these works clearly belong to the tradition of Gothic literature, Lovecraft did not make them dependent on the common mythic conceits associated with this tradition—such as ghosts, vampires, witches, werewolves, and other figures of folklore—and even when they do appear in his work, these entities are often modified to function against a new mythical background, one whose symbolism emphasizes the philosophical over the psychological. For example, Keziah Mason in "Dreams in the Witch-House" has all the appearance and appurtenances of a seventeenth-century New England witch; but instead of serving the demonic forces of Christian mythology, she is in league with extraplanetary forces wholly alien to the human sphere and ultimately beyond good or evil, superterrestrial entities blind to either the welfare or harm of the human species. This order of alien existence and its imposing relationship to human life is similarly displayed in such works as "The Call of Cthulhu," "The Dunwich Horror," "The Whisperer in Darkness," and "The Shadow over Innsmouth," while *At the Mountains of Madness* and "The Shadow out of Time" offer more elaborate development of cosmic civilizations whose nonhuman

nature violates all earthly conceptions of reality, forcing upon the protagonists of these narratives an esoteric knowledge which they can neither live with nor disregard. The question of how to describe tales whose effect derives from the violation of the laws of nature rather than those of personal or public morality was somewhat resolved by Lovecraft himself when he applied the term "weird" to such works. In a letter of 1926, he wrote: "As to what is meant by 'weird'—and of course weirdness is by no means confined to horror—I should say that the real criterion is *a strong impression of the suspension of natural laws or the presence of unseen worlds or forces close at hand*." The literary consequences of this distinction between weirdness and horror may be noted in the remarks of critics who find horrific effects minimal in Lovecraft's stories, their power relying more on an expansive and devastating confrontation with the unknown.

Critical reaction to Lovecraft's work displays an unusual diversity, from exasperated attacks upon what are judged to be the puerile ravings of an artistic and intellectual incompetent to celebrations of Lovecraft as one of the greatest writers and thinkers of the modern era. His severest detractors regard him as an isolated neurotic, and even something of an imbecile, whose writings merely betray a pathetic estrangement from the concerns of adult society. For the most part admitting Lovecraft's eccentricity, his defenders find in his fiction, and more obviously in the five volumes of his *Selected Letters,* a complex vision of reality which could only be formed by a mind of exceptional independence. Summarizing his perception of existence and the implications this had for the outward aspect of his life, Lovecraft explained: "I preach & practice an extreme conservatism in art forms, society, & politics, as the only means of averting the ennui, despair, & confusion of a guideless & standardless struggle with unveiled chaos." While this reaction has been called pathological, and its manifestation as literature uninteresting for readers whose psychic functions remain sound, it has also inspired empathy, even admiration, as an existential ploy not without relevance for a world in which "chaos" has become a key word. With regard to the literary consequences of Lovecraft's character, a great deal of controversy has persisted over his prose style which, reflecting the division between his reactionary code and his sense of universal discord, varies from a highly formal, essay-like discourse to manic outbursts wherein rationality is sacrificed for poetic effect. Briefly, Lovecraft's prose has been derided as labored and archaic by critics who regard plain-spoken realism as the modern standard for fiction; at the same time, it has been praised by those who perceive its calculated suitability for the idiosyncratic nature of Lovecraft's fictional universe, which demands artificiality and a remoteness from the familiar as paradoxical requisites for a vivification of the unreal and the impossible.

The debate concerning the value of Lovecraft's work is, of course, hardly unique in the history of literature. Lovecraft himself was the first to argue both sides of this controversy, which often extends beyond his own work and calls into question the validity of all weird literature. As he described his position to one correspondent: "Doubtless I am the sort of shock-purveyor condemned by critics of the urbane tradition as decadent or culturally immature; but I can't resist the fascination of the *outside's* mythical shadowland, & I really have a fairly respectable line of literary predecessors to back me up." Elsewhere Lovecraft defended the weird tradition when he noted shared traits in his fiction and that of his contemporaries, contending that this similarity "illustrates the essential parallelism of the fantastic imagination in different individuals—a circumstance strongly arguing the existence of a natural & definite (though rare) mental world of the weird with a common background & fixed laws, out of which there must necessarily spring a literature as authentic in its way as the realistic literature which springs from mundane experience." For most of those concerned with this "world of the weird," Lovecraft has long taken his place among its most dedicated explorers and supreme documentarians.

Further Reading

Burleson, Donald, *H. P. Lovecraft: A Critical Study,* Greenwood Press, 1983.
Carter, Lin, *Lovecraft: A Look Behind the "Cthulhu Mythos,"* Ballantine, 1972.
Carter, Paul A., *The Creation of Tomorrow: Fifty Years of Magazine Science Fiction,* Columbia University Press, 1977.
Davis, Sonia H., *The Private Life of H. P. Lovecraft,* Necronomicon, 1985.
de Camp, L. Sprague, *Lovecraft: A Biography,* Doubleday, 1975.
Derleth, August, *H. P. L.: A Memoir,* Ben Abramson, 1945.
Faig, Kenneth W., Jr., *H. P. Lovecraft: His Life, His Work,* Necronomicon, 1979. □

Arthur Oncken Lovejoy

Arthur Oncken Lovejoy (1873-1962), American philosopher, helped establish the history of ideas as a separate scholarly field.

Born in Berlin, Germany, on Oct. 10, 1873, Arthur Lovejoy emigrated to the United States. He received a bachelor of arts degree from the University of California in 1895. In 1897 Harvard awarded him a master of arts degree. After studying at the Sorbonne in Paris, he organized a department of philosophy at Stanford University in California. However, he resigned to protest what he felt was an unfair dismissal of a colleague. From 1901 to 1908 Lovejoy taught at Washington University in St. Louis. After 2 years at the University of Missouri, he moved to Johns Hopkins University, where he spent the rest of his teaching career, with occasional trips to Harvard as visiting lecturer.

For many years Lovejoy's primary influence came through his teaching and short articles, as well as through the History of Ideas Club he helped organize at Johns Hopkins. Not until relatively late in life did he publish book-length expositions. *The Revolt against Dualisms* (1930) reflected his desire to establish a philosophical position somewhere between the popular extremes of "idealism" (which

made the universe dependent upon consciousness) and "realism" (which argued for an objective existence independent of consciousness). His philosophical focus on the transitional dimension of being and knowledge coincided with his interest in intellectual history.

In numerous essays and two books, *Primitivism and Related Ideas in Antiquity* (1935) and *The Great Chain of Being* (1936), his most important work, Lovejoy elaborated a scholarly discipline best described as the study of the history of ideas. Whereas most intellectual historians had emphasized the external relationship of thought to environment, Lovejoy stressed internal analysis to demonstrate how the meaning of ideas changes through the ages and how "unit-ideas" manifest themselves in the thought of men outside the philosophical profession. Essentially, his was a philosopher's method, which may explain why historians and literary experts in the field did not often attempt to duplicate his approach. *The Great Chain of Being* evoked much admiration but little imitation; the *Journal of the History of Ideas,* which Lovejoy helped found and edit, maintained his high standards of philosophical analysis. He died on Oct. 30, 1962.

Further Reading

For a succinct statement of Lovejoy's philosophical position see his essay in George P. Adams and William Pepperell Montague, eds., *Contemporary American Philosophy: Personal Statements,* vol. 2 (1930). Some of his most important contributions to intellectual history appear in his *Essays in the History of Ideas* (1948). There is little biographical information on Lovejoy. A good background work on modern philosophy is John Passmore, *A Hundred Years of Philosophy* (1957; rev. ed. 1960)

Additional Sources

Wilson, Daniel J., *Arthur O. Lovejoy and the quest for intelligibility,* Chapel Hill: University of North Carolina Press, 1980. □

Elijah Parish Lovejoy

The death of the American newspaper editor and abolitionist Elijah Parish Lovejoy (1802-1837) at the hands of a mob in Illinois gave the antislavery cause its first martyr.

Elijah P. Lovejoy was born at Albion, Maine, on Nov. 9, 1802, the son of a Presbyterian minister. He graduated from Waterville College (renamed Colby) in 1826 and, after a brief period of schoolteaching and newspaper work in St. Louis, Mo., studied for the ministry at Princeton. On receiving his license to preach he returned to St. Louis to edit a Presbyterian weekly, the *Observer.* His editorials on slavery soon brought protests from his readers, for even the gradual abolition of slavery that Lovejoy proposed was controversial. A meeting of citizens in 1835 warned him to desist, but Lovejoy refused to modify his position. On March 4, 1835, he married Celia Ann French.

In early 1836 Lovejoy published a full account of the brutal lynching of a free African American in St. Louis, including a report of the trial that acquitted the mob leaders. Threats of personal harm and lack of support by the Presbyterian General Assembly soon led him to move to Alton, Ill., 25 miles away. When the *Observer*'s press, left unguarded on the Alton dock, was smashed and thrown into the Mississippi River, local citizens pledged money for a new one.

Lovejoy's abolitionism, however, grew increasingly aggressive, and his press was destroyed again in 1837, 2 months before he helped form the Illinois auxiliary of the American Antislavery Society. When his third press was thrown into the river, Lovejoy wrote in his paper, "We distinctly avow it to be our settled purpose, never, while life lasts, to yield to this new system of attempting to destroy, by means of mob violence, the right of conscience, the freedom of opinion, and of the press." By this time his uncompromising abolitionism and defense of free speech had received national attention.

At the request of Alton's mayor the *Observer*'s fourth press was placed in a warehouse for safekeeping. Lovejoy's friends gathered about 50 armed men to guard it. On the evening of November 7 some 20 or 30 local citizens surrounded the warehouse. Responsibility for the first shot was never fixed, but one from within the building killed a member of the attacking group. There was more firing from both

sides, and when several defenders rushed out to extinguish a fire on the roof, Lovejoy, standing in an open doorway, fell with five bullets in his body. He died within the hour. After his supporters surrendered, the mob burned the warehouse.

The fact that Lovejoy died defending the freedom of speech and press was the subject of hundreds of sermons and editorials throughout the North. His death, wrote John Quincy Adams, "gave a shock as of an earthquake throughout this continent."

Further Reading

The best modern sources are John Gill, *Tide without Turning: Elijah P. Lovejoy and Freedom of the Press* (1958), and Merton L. Dillon, *Elijah P. Lovejoy: Abolitionist Editor* (1961). William S. Lincoln, *The Alton Trials* (1838), written by the court reporter at the trials, remains the best account of the Alton mob.

Additional Sources

Dillon, Merton Lynn, *Elijah P. Lovejoy, abolitionist editor,* Westport, Conn.: Greenwood Press, 1980, 1961.
Simon, Paul, *Freedom's champion—Elijah Lovejoy,* Carbondale: Southern Illinois University Press, 1994. □

Richard Lovelace

English Cavalier poet Richard Lovelace (ca. 1618-ca. 1657) is famous for a handful of often-anthologized lyrics.

Richard Lovelace began as Fortune's darling but ended as her victim. Born probably in the Netherlands, he belonged to a prosperous Kentish family noted for professional soldiers: Sir William, his father, died fighting for the Dutch; one of his brothers became governor of New York. After Richard left Charterhouse School, his comedy, *The Scholar,* written at the age of 16, was performed at his college, Gloucester Hall, Oxford, and "with applause" in London. The influence of one of the Queen's ladies is said to have accounted for his receiving an honorary master of arts degree after 2 years in the university. He was "the most amiable and beautiful person that ever eye beheld, a person also of innate modesty, virtue, and courtly deportment, which made him . . . much admired and adored by the female sex." He did not neglect them.

After a few months at Cambridge, Lovelace rejoined the somewhat decadent but ceremonious and cultured court of Charles I in 1638; as a schoolboy, he had gained entry to it as an honorary servitor to the King. The glitter of being young, brilliant, and charming, a dabbler in polite behavior and learning, a promising poet, and a noteworthy ornament in royal pageantry soon faded. The Scots rebelled, and Lovelace participated in two inglorious campaigns against them. But he did not abandon the pen for the sword. Though his tragedy, *The Soldier,* has not survived, his exquisitely disciplined lyric "To Lucasta, Going to the Wars" won him lasting fame, especially its concluding resolution of the

and "To Lucasta from Prison." Lines of extraordinary felicity redeem even his second-rate work. He had potentialities for greatness but preferred the role of an amateur versifier characterized by *sprezzatura*—graceful nonchalance. The real Lovelace seems to have been a player of roles unwilling to sustain responsibilities; even as a soldier he lacked the "industrious valor" of his brothers. He is better known by the myth of him which his better poems created—that of an ideal Cavalier in amour and war, a second Sir Philip Sidney.

Further Reading

The standard edition, *The Poems of Richard Lovelace,* edited by Cyril Hackett Wilkinson (1925), provides the most authoritative life and commentary. Robert Guy Howarth, *Minor Poets of the Seventeenth Century: Suckling, Lovelace, Carew and Herbert* (1931; rev. ed. 1953), is readily available and provides the poems in a modernized text but without commentary. Cyril Hughes Hartmann, *The Cavalier Spirit and Its Influence on the Life and Work of Richard Lovelace* (1925), is partly superseded by Wilkinson and by Manfred Weidhorn, *Richard Lovelace* (1970), which comprehensively and readably surveys the life, the works, and all the publications about them.

Additional Sources

Hartmann, Cyril Hughes, *The Cavalier spirit, and its influence on the life and work of Richard Lovelace (1618-1658),* Folcroft, Pa.: Folcroft Library Editions, 1974; Norwood, Pa.: Norwood Editions, 1976; Philadelphia: R. West, 1977. □

love-honor conflict: "I could not love thee, Dear, so much/ Loved I not Honor more."

With the restoration of peace and his coming of age, Lovelace became a Kentish country gentleman. But his defiant royalist sympathies and his presenting Parliament with a pro-Episcopal petition, when it had abolished Episcopacy and had already ordered the petition burned, led to his being jailed for 7 weeks. It was probably then that he achieved the classical perfection of "To Althea from Prison" and its much-quoted "Stone walls do not a prison make,/ Nor iron bars a cage."

After the Puritan Revolution exploded in 1642, Lovelace sold most of his lands, spent several years in Holland, and in 1646 was wounded while fighting for the French against the Spaniards. In 1646 parliamentary troops arrested him in Kent as a dangerous royalist. During a half year in prison he prepared his best poems for publication, and in 1646 they appeared as *Lucasta:* this pseudonymous mistress has not been identified. A decade later his brother's edition of *Lucasta, Posthume Poems* brought the total of his published original poems to just over a hundred; they were accompanied by some verse translations. Nothing is known of his whereabouts in the years preceding his death about 1657; but there is no sound basis for the notion that he was reduced to penury. During this period he published two complimentary poems, celebrated a friend's wedding in verse, and seems to have revised other compositions.

Lovelace's literary reputation rests on the lyrics mentioned above and a few others, notably "The Grasshopper"

Sir Alfred Charles Bernard Lovell

The English astronomer Sir Alfred Charles Bernard Lovell (born 1913) pioneered in radio astronomy and founded the Jodrell Bank Laboratory.

B ernard Lovell was born Aug. 31, 1913, in the village of Oldland Common (Gloucestershire), Great Britain. At the age of 20, he received his bachelor's degree in physics from Bristol University; three years later, in 1936, he received his doctorate, also in physics. He was appointed assistant lecturer in physics at the University of Manchester. In 1937 he married Mary Joyce Chesterman, a teacher, who collaborated with her husband in writing popular books on astronomy. They had two sons and three daughters.

At the outbreak of World War II Lovell joined the Air Ministry Research Establishment and soon became head of the blind-bombing and antisubmarine groups; in this capacity, he helped develop the use of airborne radar systems in Great Britain. At the end of the war, in 1945, Lovell returned to the University of Manchester as lecturer in physics. He rose rapidly through the academic ranks, becoming senior lecturer in 1947 and reader in 1949. His researches during these years were a direct outgrowth of his wartime researches on radar detection techniques combined with his desire to resume his prewar cosmic-ray studies.

Early Meteor Studies

When bouncing radio waves off cosmic-ray showers and detecting the echoes, Lovell observed many transient (short-term) echoes, which he concluded were from meteor trails. Carefully choosing a known comet with desirable characteristics, Lovell, in October 1946, directed his radar equipment skyward and proved beyond question that the transient meteor-trail echoes he had observed earlier were signals bounced off the tails of comets. His meteor studies lead to the discoveries that meteors orbited within the solar system (and did not come from beyond it), and that science was underestimating the number and intensity of daytime meteor showers.

Technical disturbing effects from the city of Manchester during this work convinced Lovell of the need for a country location, and he received permission to establish the Jodrell Bank Laboratory in Cheshire, of which he became director in 1951. That same year, a special academic chair was created for him at Manchester University: he became professor of radio astronomy. Using Michelson stellar interferometric techniques, Lovell proved that radio sources are constantly emitting "point sources" of energy, and not, as had been previously thought, diffuse interstellar clouds of ionized hydrogen. The previously detected fluctuations in radio sources were shown to be imposed on them by the earth's ionosphere, in much the same way as the earth's atmosphere causes the twinkling of a star at optical wavelengths.

Development of Telescope at Jodrell

The potentialities of radio astronomy were therefore clear, and in 1952 Lovell convinced the British government and the Nuffield Foundation to jointly finance the construction of the largest, completely steerable radio telescope in the world at Jodrell Bank, now part of the Nuffield Radio Astronomy Laboratory. As it developed, the huge telescope, 250 feet in diameter, was completed in time to track the first artificial earth satellite, the Russian Sputnik, in October 1957. Communications work and future trackings, including that of the American manned moon landing in July 1969, gained for Lovell and Jodrell Bank a great deal of publicity. His work in radio astronomy led to the 1963 discovery of quasars and the development of knowledge about pulsars and red dwarf stars.

Beginning in 1958, Lovell carried out much research on the characteristics of flare stars. In 1960, he began collaborating with Fred Whipple of the Smithsonian Astrophysical Observatory in this work. In 1955 he was elected a fellow of the Royal Society; in 1960 he received the Royal Medal of the society; and in 1961 he was knighted.

Further Reading

Sir Bernard Lovell, in collaboration with his wife, wrote a number of books on astronomy, one of the later being *Discovering the Universe* (1967). For his work on the radio telescope and for biographical information see Otto Struve and Velta Zebergs, *Astronomy of the Twentieth Century* (1962), and Colin A. Ronan, *Astrnomers Royal* (1969).

Additional Sources

The Biographical Dictionary of Scientists, New York: Peter Bedrick Books, 1984, p. 101-102.

The Cambridge Dictionary of Scientists, New York: Cambridge University Press, 1996, p. 210.

Lovell, Bernard, *Astronomer by Chance,* New York: Basic Books, 1990.

Lovell, Bernard, *Emerging Cosmology,* New York: Praeger, 1985.

Lovell, Bernard, *In the Center of Immensities,* New York: Harper and Row, 1978.

Lovell, Bernard, *The Jodrell Bank Telescopes,* New York: Oxford University Press, 1985.

Lovell, Bernard, *Man's Relation to the Universe,* San Francisco, Freeman, 1975.

Lovell, Bernard, *The Origins and International Economics of Space Exploration,* Edinburgh: Edinburgh University Press, 1973.

Lovell, Bernard, *Out of the Zenith: Jodrell Bank 1957-1970,* London: Oxford University Press, 1973.

Lovell, Bernard, *Voice of the Universe: Building the Jodrell Bank Telescope,* New York: Praeger, 1987.

Graham-Smith, Francis and Bernard Lovell, *Pathways to the Universe,* New York: Cambridge University Press, 1988.

Saward, Dudley, *Bernard Lovell: A Biography,* London: R. Hale, 1984. □

Juliette Gordon Low

American reformer Juliette Gordon Low (1860-1927) was the founder of the Girl Scouts of the United States of America. With a mission of providing healthy activities for girls while instilling a sense of good citizenship, the Girls Scouts has grown to include millions of members in troops across the country.

Juliette Gordon Low was a wealthy socialite of the United States and Great Britain who spent most of her life enjoying the recreations of the privileged classes. However, after meeting the founder of the Boy Scouts, Sir Robert Baden-Powell, she discovered a social cause to which she would devote the rest of her days—the formation of a similar organization for girls in the United States. An enthusiastic organizer and fundraiser, she led the formation of the Girl Scouts of the United States of America in 1915, using her own fortune as the primary source of financial support for the group in its early years. By the time of her death, the Girl Scouts had become a successful national organization with thousands of members.

Low was born Juliette Magill Kinzie Gordon in Savannah, Georgia, on October 31, 1860. The second of six children, Low was part of a distinguished and wealthy family. Her mother, Eleanor Lytle Kinzie Gordon, hailed from Chicago and had written a book about the experiences of her adventurous father, a government agent who had worked on the western frontier among Native Americans. Low's father, William Washington Gordon II, had made his fortune as a cotton trader in the South. During Low's childhood, her father served in the Civil War as a Confederate officer; he later served the reunited nation as a general in the Spanish-American War. Low, who was known to her family as "Daisy," inherited traits from the personalities of both parents: like her mother, she possessed a great deal of charm and wit, but she also had her father's instinct for organization and leadership. Her talents were apparent in the active summers she would spend with her sisters and cousins at her aunt's estate in northern Georgia, where she took the lead in organizing camping and hunting trips. She also had a gift for artistic pursuits and enjoyed writing and acting in the plays that the children would put together.

Entered Elite Social Circles

Low was sent to private schools in Georgia, Virginia, and New York. In New York, Low pursued her artistic interests by continuing to write plays and act in dramatic productions; she also studied painting. After completing her schooling, she traveled to Europe, where she would spend part of each year for the rest of her life. It was on a trip to England that she began a courtship with the English millionaire William Mackay Low. For four years, the two carried on a romance, despite the disapproval of William Gordon, who considered his daughter's suitor to be a libertine. The couple was eventually married in Savannah, in December of 1886. As the wife of a wealthy landowner, Low was introduced to the highest levels of British society. Her husband was a friend of the Prince of Wales and Low had the honor of being presented to Queen Victoria at the royal court. The Lows entertained frequently at their Scottish estate as well as in England and the United States.

Over the coming years, however, Low found herself becoming increasingly lonely and frustrated. Her husband frequently traveled to exotic spots around the world for hunting expeditions and other adventures while Low remained at home. A back injury prevented Low from horseback riding, one of her favorite pursuits, so she returned to art to fill her days. She took up painting again and began working on larger projects such as carving a mantelpiece for one home and designing a set of iron gates for another. She also continued traveling, taking a female companion when her husband did not join her. By the early 1900s, the marriage was coming to an end. William Low's affair with another woman had become well-known, and in 1902 his wife agreed to begin divorce proceedings. Complications arose when William Low died before the divorce was settled and left his entire estate to his mistress. After months of legal negotiations, Low was finally awarded $500,000. That amount provided her with the means to continue her previous style of life, spending part of the year in London and Scotland and the colder months in the United States, particularly Savannah.

Inspired by Boy Scouts Founder

In 1911, when she was 51, Low's social circles brought her into contact with Sir Robert Baden-Powell, a hero of the Boer war who had founded the Boy Scouts organization. The two became good friends and Baden-Powell introduced Low to his sister, who had founded a similar group for girls known as the Girl Guides. The social aims of the Boy Scouts and Girl Guides—to provide healthy activities for children while instilling a sense of responsible citizenship—struck a chord in Low, who soon founded her own Girl Guide troops in Scotland and England. Her enthusiasm for the cause quickly evolved into a desire to introduce the Girl Guides program in the United States.

Returning to Savannah, she established the first U.S. unit of the Girl Guides on March 12, 1912. Her group included two small troops of girls that met in the carriage house behind Low's home. The Girl Guides, dressed in a uniform of a sailor-style blouse, blue tie, navy skirt, and dark stockings, engaged in a variety of sports and outdoor activities such as camping. Other girls in Savannah were eager to join in the fun, and the response convinced Law that a nationwide organization should be formed. Her plans were interrupted, however, by the death of her father, to whom she had been greatly devoted. She spent the following year with her mother in England before returning to her work on the Girl Guides.

Founded Girl Scouts of America

Low had hoped to form a group known as the Girl Scouts through a partnership with an already existing American group, the Campfire Girls, which had been founded in

1910. When this arrangement failed to materialize, Low sprang into action to make her dreams of a Girl Scouts organization a reality. She drafted several prominent Americans to serve on a board of directors, created a national headquarters, personally traveled to a number of states to launch organization efforts, and used her own money as the main source of funding. Her efforts came to fruition in 1915, when the Girl Scouts of America officially incorporated. Low began serving as the Girl Scouts' first president, a position she would hold for five years. By 1916, there were more than 7,000 girls participating in Girl Scouts.

The World War I years saw an enormous amount of growth in the Girl Scouts, which participated in a number of activities to help support the war effort. The public notice that this drew brought in new members and increased donations. But the rapidly expanding organization soon overtook Low's ability to adequately finance the group. While continuing to encourage generous donations from others, she also began instituting cost-cutting measures in her own home in order to provide money to her scouts. Some friends felt that her measures, such as not turning on the electric lights in the house until after five each day, would never save her enough to make up for the large amounts she spent on her girls' organization; other acquaintances suggested that such "hardships" were just an act to solicit more donations. Whatever the truth was behind these stories, Low's ultimate concern was always the Girl Scouts.

Remembered as "the Best Scout"

By 1920, the Girl Scouts had become so large that it required a full-time administrative staff to manage the duties that had previously been handled by volunteers. Low, expressing confidence in the new leaders, retired from her post as president with the title of "Founder," but continued many of her activities within the Girl Scouts. Although she was losing her hearing and was diagnosed with cancer a few years later, she traveled to England to attend the World Camp of the Girl Scouts in 1924 and volunteered to bring the event to New York state in 1926. She could barely disguise the pain she was suffering as she hosted the week-long World Camp in New York. Knowing that she did not have long to live, Low made a final trip to England to say goodbye to friends and then came home to Savannah. In tribute to her unflagging efforts to bring the Girl Scouts to children across the country, organization executives sent a telegram to her stating that she was "the best scout of them all." She died in Savannah on January 18, 1927. The Girl Scouts organization has continued to prosper since the death of Low, bringing her ideals to millions of girls in an organization that has reached every state in the nation.

Further Reading

Choate, Anne Hyde, and Helen Ferris, editors, *Juliette Low and the Girl Scouts: The Story of an American Woman, 1860-1927,* Doubleday, 1928.

Saxton, Martha, "The Best Girl Scout of Them All," *American Heritage,* June/July, 1982, pp. 38-47.

Schultz, Gladys D., and Daisy Gordon Lawrence, *The Life of Juliette Low,* J. B. Lippincott, 1958. □

Seth Low

The American civic leader and college president Seth Low (1850-1916) was a distinguished crusader for urban reform.

S eth Low was born into a wealthy Brooklyn, N.Y., family on Jan. 18, 1850. His grandfather had been a prosperous merchant in the China trade, and his father continued the business. Seth graduated with distinction from Columbia College in 1870 and then entered his father's business.

Low soon turned to civic affairs. By the time the family business was liquidated in 1887, he had become active in several community activities. He was the first president of the Brooklyn Bureau of Charities. In 1880 he served as president of the Young Republican Club in Brooklyn. He was elected mayor of Brooklyn in 1881 and in 1883. Although a Republican, he established independence from the party. Making use of a new charter that concentrated power in the hands of the mayor, he provided the city with an excellent administration and introduced the merit system.

Low served on the commission that prepared the first charter for Greater New York under its new consolidation. In 1897 the Citizens Union selected him to run for mayor of New York, but he was defeated.

Despite his political involvement, most of Low's time was spent on educational matters. In 1889 (the year President William McKinley named him a delegate to the First Hague Conference) Low was asked to become president of Columbia. Starting in 1890, he gave the school bold and effective leadership for 11 years. He also contributed money for the Low Library, named after his father. He served on the Rapid Transit Board in 1899, which was established to plan New York's first subway.

In 1901, Low resigned from Columbia when he was elected mayor of New York on the Fusion and Republican ticket. However, his attempt to provide New York with the same type of administration he had given Brooklyn was less successful, and he lost his bid for reelection in 1903.

Low continued his civic activities until the end of his life. In 1907 he served both as president of the National Civic Federation and as chairman of the Board of Trustees of Tuskegee Institute. Seven years later he was chosen president of the New York Chamber of Commerce. He also was active as a labor arbitrator. He died on Sept. 17, 1916.

Further Reading

One short biography of Low is by his nephew Benjamin R. C. Low, *Seth Low* (1925). Low is mentioned in several works, including Joseph Lincoln Steffens, *The Autobiography of Lincoln Steffens* (1931), and R. Gordon Hoxie and others, *A History of the Faculty of Political Science, Columbia University* (1915). □

of the annual report of the American Historical Association), a work whose ideas and data political scientists still find valuable. His best known book was *The Government of England* (2 vols., 1908), which won praise on both sides of the Atlantic for its detailed and sensitive description of the way the political life of England actually functioned.

Lowell was active in university affairs and, on the retirement of Charles W. Eliot in 1909, was chosen president of Harvard, serving until 1933. Concentrating on the college, he modified Eliot's elective system by reintroducing some required courses; established a tutorial system to encourage individual work; introduced the "house system," which divided the undergraduates into smaller residential and social units, modeled after English universities; and encouraged changes in the admission and scholarship practices that opened Harvard to public school graduates from the entire country, making it a truly national educational institution. A strong believer in academic freedom, he vigorously defended his faculty against attack during and just after World War I.

In the 1920s Lowell aroused great controversy when appointed by the governor of Massachusetts to a committee to review the murder conviction of Sacco and Vanzetti, because he strongly affirmed the justice of that decision. He died on Jan. 16, 1943.

Further Reading

Lowell detailed his educational ideas in *At War with Academic Traditions in America* (1934) and *What a University President*

Abbott Lawrence Lowell

The American college president and political scientist Abbott Lawrence Lowell (1856-1943) strengthened the Harvard undergraduate college during his presidency at the university. As a political scientist, he stressed the role of parties in government.

On Dec. 13, 1856, Abbott Lawrence Lowell was born into one of the leading families of Boston society. When he received his bachelor's degree from Harvard University in 1877, he was the sixth in an unbroken series of generations of alumni.

Although he earned a degree from the Harvard Law School in 1880 and opened a law office in Boston, Lowell found this profession uninteresting and began writing articles on political science, collected into a book, *Essays on Government* (1889). He went on to compose a two-volume comparative study, *Government and Parties in Continental Europe* (1896), which led to his appointment to the Harvard faculty in 1897.

Lowell insisted on the value of careful observation of actual political practice rather than theoretical speculation, and his studies convinced him that political parties played a greater role in government than did constitutional forms. This approach dominated his *The Influence of Party upon Legislation in England and America* (1902; published as part

Has Learned (1938). The only full-scale biography of Lowell is Henry A. Yeomans, *Abbott Lawrence Lowell, 1856-1943* (1948). His life is sketched in the context of his family background in a chapter of Ferris Greenslet, *The Lowells and Their Seven Worlds* (1946). His services at Harvard are analyzed in two books by Samuel Eliot Morison, *The Development of Harvard University since the Inauguration of President Eliot, 1869-1929* (1930) and *Three Centuries of Harvard, 1636-1936* (1965).

Additional Sources

Pusey, Nathan March, *Lawrence Lowell and his revolution,* Cambridge, Mass.: Harvard University, 1980.

Yeomans, Henry Aaron, *Abbott Lawrence Lowell, 1856-1943,* New York: Arno Press, 1977, 1948. ☐

Amy Lowell

Amy Lowell (1874-1925), American poet, critic, biographer, and flamboyant promoter of the imagist movement, was important in the "poetic renaissance" of the early 20th century.

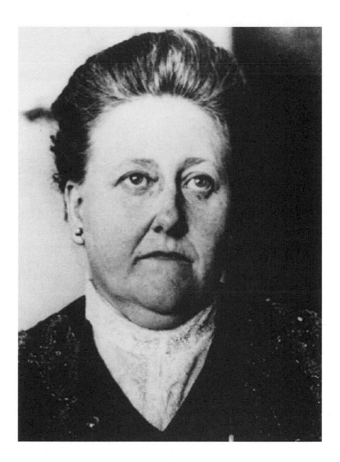

Amy Lowell was born in Brookline, Mass., of the prominent and wealthy Lowell family of Boston and counted among her ancestors the famous 19th-century poet James Russell Lowell. After being privately educated, she spent many years traveling abroad. Rebelling against her genteel, respectable upbringing, she delighted in smoking a big black cigar while expounding the most advanced and revolutionary esthetic theories of the pre—World War I avant-garde. Endowed with a remarkable flair for organization, she was highly influential in stimulating interest in the poetic experiments of the time. From 1915 through 1917 she edited an annual anthology of imagist poets.

Lowell published her first volume of verse, *A Dome of Many-coloured Glass,* in 1912. *Sword Blades and Poppy Seed* (1914), her second volume, first showed the influence of imagist ideas. Curiously enough, in her critical comments she seemed to prefer the work of midwestern "nonimagists," such as Carl Sandburg, Edgar Lee Masters, and Vachel Lindsay, to the more image-centered and cosmopolitan poetry of T. S. Eliot and Ezra Pound. Though she borrowed often from Eliot in her poetry, she slighted him in her criticism and carried on a bitter feud with Pound.

Despite her enthusiasm for imagism, Lowell's best poems are closer in style to symbolist poetry than to imagist verse. "Patterns," her best-known poem, protests against puritan inhibitions and the repressive conventions of society. A moving feeling for the New England past pervades "Lilacs." Her unsigned *Critical Fable* (1922) was a contemporary redoing of James Russell Lowell's "Fable for Critics" and attempted to reproduce that earlier work's vernacular humor in judging contemporary poets. In this, Lowell was the first critic to note the "madness" of the characters in Robert Frost's *North of Boston.* She achieved another "first"

by including a discussion of Wallace Stevens, who would not be recognized as a major poet until much later. Her denigration of Pound and Eliot as expatriates seems based more on patriotic than on literary principles. Perhaps her finest overall work was her biography of John Keats (1925).

A few of Lowell's separately published volumes of verse are *Men, Women, and Ghosts* (1916), *Pictures of the Floating World* (1919), *What's o'Clock* (1925), *East Wind* (1926), and *Ballads for Sale* (1927). Also of value are her *Complete Poetical Works* (1955) and *Six French Poets* (1915), a critical study.

Further Reading

Studies of Amy Lowell's life and work are S. Foster Damon, *Amy Lowell: A Chronicle with Extracts from Her Correspondence* (1935), and Horace Gregory, *Amy Lowell* (1958). She figures prominently in the critical study by Glenn Hughes, *Imagism and the Imagists: A Study in Modern Poetry* (1931). Hyatt H. Waggoner, *American Poets: From the Puritans to the Present* (1968), contains a section on her. ☐

Francis Cabot Lowell

The American merchant and manufacturer Francis Cabot Lowell (1775-1817) introduced the power loom and the integrated factory system to American cotton textile manufactures.

Francis Cabot Lowell was born in Newburyport, Mass., the son of John Lowell, a prominent lawyer, and Susanna Cabot, the daughter of a wealthy family of merchant shippers. Lowell earned a Harvard degree in 1793 and shortly afterward went to sea on family ships. His marriage in 1798 to Hannah Jackson joined him to two other substantial shipping families. By 1810 he was a major merchant in his own right; his trade encompassed Europe, Canada, India, and China.

In 1810 Lowell made an extended visit to England, where he was fascinated by the power loom, not yet available in America. Since it was illegal to export either models or designs, he studied the looms so thoroughly that with the help of a skilled mechanic, Paul Moody, he was able to have them reproduced from his memory and drawings on his return to Boston. The power loom was pivotal in the American attempt to compete in textile manufactures at a time when capital and technological superiority still belonged to the English.

The Boston Manufacturing Company was chartered in 1812 with an authorized capital of $400,000. Lowell, five brothers-in-law, and others in the mercantile community provided the large sums of capital necessary for what quickly became a major enterprise. In 1814 a mill was in operation at Waltham, Mass., which not only exploited the power loom but also, and for the first time, contained all of the processes of spinning and weaving cotton cloth under one roof. The Waltham mill was the parent of the famous mills at Lowell, Mass. Lowell was one of the first American company towns, characterized by a paternalism that has been both praised and damned.

Lowell was an active lobbyist for the protective tariff and in 1816 was influential in achieving the first American tariff that acknowledged an "infant industries" principle and provided a substantial duty on foreign cotton goods. Lowell died at the early age of 42, leaving a daughter and three sons, one of whom, Francis Cabot Lowell II, was to inherit his father's managerial abilities and a leading position in the expanding textile industry. After Lowell's death in 1817, the interrelated family firms produced textile machinery too.

Further Reading

Ferris Greenslet, *The Lowells and Their Seven Worlds* (1946), provides a popular account of several generations of the Lowell family. Kenneth Wiggins Porter, *The Jacksons and the Lees* (1937), contains both family and business history. A scholarly analysis of the textile interests Lowell helped to build is in George Sweet Gibb, *The Saco-Lowell Shops* (1950). Still important as a source is Nathan Appleton, *Introduction of the Power Loom, and Origin of Lowell* (1858). □

James Russell Lowell

The versatility of American poet, editor, and diplomat James Russell Lowell (1819-1891) made him an influential figure in 19th-century America.

James Russell Lowell was born in Cambridge, Mass., on Feb. 22, 1819, of a well-established New England family. Following family tradition, he attended Harvard, graduating in 1838 and taking a law degree there in 1840. Soon after the publication of his first volume of poems, *A Year's Life* (1841), he gave up law to devote himself to literature.

Encouraged by the success of his second volume, *Poems* (1844), Lowell married Maria White, a poet and abolitionist whose zeal for attacking social injustices Lowell soon absorbed. For a year he was an editorial writer for the abolitionist journal the *Pennsylvania Freeman*.

Lowell's reputation as a social critic was soundly established with the publication of the *Biglow Papers* (first series, 1848). Speaking in dialect through the homespun Yankee character Hosea Biglow, Lowell attacked the war with Mexico as an attempt to extend slave territory. He revived Biglow in 1862 in support of the Union cause against the Confederacy (second series, 1867). The year 1848 also saw the publication of *The Vision of Sir Launfal, Poems: Second Series,* and *A Fable for Critics,* humorous (and often barbed) verse which offered Lowell's estimation of a number of contemporary writers—himself included.

A trip abroad in 1851-1852 was followed by the death of Lowell's wife. He married Frances Dunlap in 1857. In 1855 Lowell began his career as a teacher by succeeding Henry Wadsworth Longfellow as professor of modern lan-

Heymann, C. David (Clemens David), *American aristocracy: the lives and times of James Russell, Amy, and Robert Lowell,* New York: Dodd, Mead, 1980.
Hudson, William Henry, *Lowell & his poetry,* Norwood, Pa.: Norwood Editions, 1975; Philadelphia: R. West, 1977.
Scudder, Horace Elisha, *James Russell Lowell; a biography,* New York, AMS Press, 1974. □

Josephine Shaw Lowell

Josephine Shaw Lowell (1843-1905), American social reformer and philanthropist, influenced legislation and organizations creating modern programs for the poor and needy.

Josephine Shaw was born in West Roxbury, Mass., on Dec. 16, 1843, into a family marked by social and intellectual distinction. She was raised on Staten Island, N.Y. During 1851-1855 the family lived and traveled in Europe, where "Effie" proved brilliant in her absorption of cultures and languages. She continued her education in New York and Boston.

When the Civil War broke out, Josephine Shaw worked intensively for a branch of the U.S. Sanitary Commission. On Oct. 31, 1863, she married Col. Charles Russell Lowell of Massachusetts and joined him on the fighting front in Virginia. She had already lost her brother, Col. Robert Gould Shaw, in the war. On Oct. 19, 1864, her husband died in the Battle of Cedar Creek, Va. Six weeks later their daughter, Carlotta Russell Lowell, was born.

Lowell returned to Staten Island and began a new career, seeking to advance African American education. She visited schools as well as hospitals, jails, and asylums. She later moved to Manhattan with her mother and daughter in order to be nearer the scene of her activities. Her work with the State Charities Aid Association and her impressive reports on the need for more adequate facilities for the poor and defenseless, as well as better investigatory processes, caused Governor Samuel J. Tilden in 1876 to appoint her to the State Board of Charities. She was the first woman to be so honored. As a result of her unremitting labors, the first custodial asylum in the country for mentally disabled women was established in 1878. In 1881 legislation was passed which resulted in state reformatories for women.

Lowell's reports, speeches, and correspondence—models of clarity and fact—affected dependent children, the insane, almshouses, prison conditions, the unemployed, and civil service reform. Although she concentrated on New York, her work affected national services. Her greatest achievement was the founding of the Charity Organization Society of the City of New York, which gave form and direction to all the efforts of distinguished philanthropists in that city and beyond.

The thoughts of Lowell went beyond charity to the causes of crime and injustice. In 1889 she left the State Board of Charities to move more freely in other directions. Her interests included the Woman's Municipal League and

guages at Harvard, a position he held with distinction until 1876, when he retired. During this period he also served as editor of the newly founded *Atlantic Monthly* (1857-1861) and the *North American Review* (1864-1872), wrote books, and took an active interest in politics. In the final phase of his career Lowell served ably as ambassador to Spain (1877-1880) and England (1880-1885).

In addition to the *Biglow Papers* and *A Fable for Critics,* Lowell's best-known works include the *Ode Recited at the Harvard Commemoration* (*1865*), *The Cathedral* (1870), and the collections of essays *Fireside Travels* (1864), *Among My Books* (first series, 1870; second series, 1876), *My Study Windows* (1871), and *Democracy and·Other Addresses* (1887). He died in Cambridge on Aug. 12, 1891.

Further Reading

Lowell's *Complete Writings,* edited by Charles Eliot Norton (16 vols., 1904), includes a valuable early biography by Horace E. Scudder. *The Complete Poetical Works of James Russell Lowell,* edited by Scudder (1897), is the best one-volume edition. Martin Duberman's biography *James Russell Lowell* (1966) is excellent, as is Leon Howard, *Victorian Knight-Errant: A Study of the Early Literary Career of James Russell Lowell* (1952). See also Edward Everett Hale, *James Russell Lowell and His Friends* (1899), and Richmond Croom Beatty, *James Russell Lowell* (1942).

Additional Sources

Hale, Edward Everett, *James Russell Lowell and his friends,* New York: Chelsea House, 1980.

the National Consumers' League (of which she was a principal founder), as well as the study of methods and practical experiments for mediating labor-management conflicts. She died Oct. 12, 1905.

Further Reading

A collection of Mrs. Lowell's major papers, some correspondence, and a bibliography are in William Rhinelander Stewart, ed., *The Philanthropic Work of Josephine Shaw Lowell, Containing a Biographical Sketch of Her Life together with a Selection of Her Public Papers and Private Letters* (1911). See also *In Memoriam: Josephine Shaw Lowell* (1906). □

Robert Trail Spence Lowell Jr.

American poet Robert Trail Spence Lowell, Jr. (1917-1977) was one of the most highly esteemed and honored poets of his day. Many still acclaim his work for its mastery of diverse literary form, intense expression of personal concern, and candid commentary on social and moral issues.

obert Lowell, winner of three Pulitzer Prizes, was the only child of Commander R.T.S. Lowell, U.S. Navy, and Charlotte Winslow Lowell, born on March 1, 1917, in Boston, Massachusetts. His was a famous family, including James Russell Lowell, 19th-century poet and ambassador to England; Amy Lowell, another notable New England poet; and A. Lawrence Lowell, president of Harvard. On his mother's side, Robert was descended from early New England colonists, including Edward Winslow, one of the Pilgrim Fathers; the key masculine figure in young Lowell's life was his maternal grandfather, Arthur Winslow. His troubled childhood is candidly pictured in "91 Revere Street," an autobiographical prose memoir included in *Life Studies* (1959).

Following graduation from the St. Mark preparatory school, he attended Harvard for two years, where he encountered the poetry of William Carlos Williams, which later influenced his switch in the 1950s to what critics refer to as his confessional verse (his friend Elizabeth Bishop once called him the leading poet of the "anguish school"). His passion for poetry took him to Kenyon College, where poet John Crowe Ransom was teaching a generation of critics and creators. Lowell studied classics, graduated *summa cum laude,* Phi Beta Kappa, and class valedictorian. He had just married Jean Stafford, a novelist and short-story writer.

For a while Lowell supported himself by teaching and then working in publishing in New York City. Throughout 1942, he attempted to enlist, hoping to go officer's school, but when he was drafted in September of 1943, he "regretfully declined to serve," writing to President Roose-

velt about how painful it was "for an American whose family traditions, like your own, have always found their fulfillment in maintaining . . . our country's freedom and honor." Lowell was sentenced to a year in prison, five months of which were spent in Danbury, Connecticut and the rest on work-release parole.

Lowell's first book, *Land of Unlikeness,* was published in 1944. Some of these poems were included in his second volume, *Lord Weary's Castle* (1946), which won him, at the age of 29, the Pulitzer Prize. It was immediately apparent that a poet of unusual stature had emerged, one who combined rebellion and tradition, formalism and experiment, to achieve what some called "a disciplined wildness." Poet and critic Randall Jarrell said that "the degree of intensity of his poems is equalled by their degree of organization. . . . It is hard to exaggerate the strength and life, the constant richness and surprise of metaphor, and sound and motion, of the language itself. It is impossible not to notice the weight and power of his lines. . . . One or two of these poems, I think, will be read as long as men remember English."

With succeeding volumes Lowell became widely regarded as the most important poet of the period. Before he turned 30, he had won a Guggenheim fellowship and a grant from the National Institute of Arts and Letters. He also received the Bollingen Prize. In 1947-1948 he was consultant in poetry at the Library of Congress.

The title poem of *The Mills of the Kavanaughs* (1951) consisted of long, dramatic monologues, which most critics regarded as convoluted and burdensome. In *Life Studies* (1959), Lowell turned to free verse in the confessional manner; it became one of the most influential volumes of post-World War II poetry, and won the National Book Award for the best book of poetry published that year. One of the poems, "Skunk Hour," is perhaps Lowell's best known.

In his forties, Lowell began writing for the theater; *The Old Glory* (1965), which was successfully produced off-Broadway, consisted of three one-act plays based on stories by Nathaniel Hawthorne and Herman Melville. He also made a free adaptation of Jean Racine's *Phèdre* and an even more individualistic rendering of Aeschylus's tragedy *Prometheus Bound* (1969). In addition, he wrote critical essays.

But it was Lowell's poetry that made the deepest impression. *Imitations* (1961) was a book of free translations ranging from the classic Greek of Homer to the modern Russian of Boris Pasternak translations that are re-created poems rather than literal renderings. *For the Union Dead* (1964), has been considered the most powerful and direct of Lowell's books. *Near the Ocean* (1967) contained, among its 13 poems, some of his darker meditations. *Notebooks, 1967-68* (1969) consists of some 260 conversational sonnets (some polished verse, some unrhymed), presenting pictures of himself and his family, private associations, and social criticism. Lowell revised and expanded much of this material into three separate volumes of unrhymed sonnets, published in 1973 as *For Lizzie and Harriet, The Dolphin,* and *History.*

Lowell had great powers of concentration, closeting himself in New York or Maine for ten- and twelve-hour stretches of reading and writing. He taught intermittently at Harvard, Cambridge, and several other American colleges. He suffered numerous severe breakdowns from a bipolar disorder and was hospitalized frequently. In his school days his nickname was "Cal," after the infamous Roman emperor, because of his manic behavior. For much of his adult life Lowell was subjected to electroshock therapy, psychotherapy, and chemical therapy, although sometimes he added alcohol to the mix and couldn't remember to take his drugs. His personal and family relations were often turbulent. His marriage to Jean Stafford ended in 1948; he was then married to the writer and critic Elizabeth Hardwick for over 20 years, and then to Lady Caroline Blackwood, a writer as well, for four. There were also numerous other women in his life. A mercurial person, he once declined President Lyndon Johnson's invitation to the White House Festival of the Arts in 1965, after having agreed to attend. He then agreed not to publicize his refusal to attend, but changed his mind and sent his letter of refusal to the *New York Times,* which made it into a front page story. Among other problemmatic traits, Lowell had a capacity for cruelty. In *The Dolphin,* he quoted directly from letters Elizabeth Hardwick had written him as he was leaving her for Caroline Blackwood. Some notable poets agreed that this use of personal material was in poor taste. W.H. Auden threatened to not speak to Lowell again because of the book, and Elizabeth Bishop pled with him to forego publication. Poet and critic Adrienne Rich, an old friend, told Lowell it was "a poor excuse for a cruel and shallow book," and Miss Hardwick herself called it "inane, empty, unnecessary . . . so many fatuities, indiscretions, bad lines still there on the page." One critic noted that *The Dolphin* is a self-conscious depiction of the poet ordering material and trying to come to terms with his actions, a process reflecting Lowell's emotional candor and "the confessional nature of his verse." Despite these criticisms, Lowell was awarded his third Pulitzer Prize for this work.

By his late fifties, Lowell was a sickly man with a weakened heart. In his last book of poems, *Day by Day,* Lowell adds up the sadness of a painful life coming to its close. He died of a heart attack at age 60, in a New York taxi cab, on his way to see Elizabeth Hardwick. To a friend, Lowell had written, "I think in the end, there is no end, the thread frays rather than is cut," and to another he said he never quite comprehended his own life: "it is addition not to be understood, just completed."

Further Reading

For a brief view of Lowell's life and work, see Joseph Epstein, "Mistah Lowell He Dead" *The Hudson Review* (September 1996), pp. 185-202. For fuller treatments, see Ian Hamilton, *Robert Lowell: A Biography* (1982); Paul Mariani *Lost Puritan: A Life of Robert Lowell* (1994); Richard Tillinghast, *Damaged Grandeur* (1995). See also William Doreski, *The Years of Our Friendship: Robert Lowell and Allen Tate* (1990); Patrick K. Miehe (comp.), *The Robert Lowell Papers at the Houghton Library, Harvard University: A Guide to the Collection* (1991). □

Robert Harry Lowie

The Austrian-born American anthropologist Robert Harry Lowie (1883-1957) specialized in the culture of the Plains Indians in North America.

Robert H. Lowie was born on June 12, 1883, in Vienna. His parents emigrated to the United States in 1893, and Lowie entered the City College of New York in 1897, studying classics and reading randomly in natural science. After receiving his bachelor's degree in 1901, he taught in New York public schools until 1904, when he began graduate study in psychology at Columbia. Lowie soon became involved with the anthropological program taught by Franz Boas and changed his professional aspirations. He received his doctorate in 1908.

Lowie's fieldwork began in 1906, when he studied the heavily acculturated Lemhi Shoshoni for the American Museum of Natural History. He also made a survey of Plains Indians over several consecutive summers and was one of the first to do intensive fieldwork with a single tribe. His focus on Crow ethnology grew out of fieldwork during part of each summer between 1907 and 1916 and again in 1931; he reported his results in many technical papers and in *The Crow Indians* (1935). Lowie's *Indians of the Plains* (1954) summarized the survey fieldwork, adding later results by other workers, in a popular form.

In 1921 Lowie became associate professor at the University of California; in 1925 he was promoted to full professor. From 1922 to 1946 he served as cochairman of the anthropology department and from 1946 to 1950 as sole chairman.

Lowie's major contributions to American anthropology were theoretical, although his own fieldwork provided examples. He was familiar with European, particularly German, philosophy, history, and literature and served as American interpreter of German anthropological and psychological theories. In his first book, *Culture and Ethnology* (1917), he tried to relate ''culture,'' the integrating concept of American anthropology under Boas, to race, psychology, and environment. *Primitive Society* (1920), again primarily Boasian, was intended to popularize the American approach to anthropology. *Primitive Religion* (1920) was a more personal statement and had less effect. *Introduction to Culture Anthropology* (1934) provided a topical exposition of anthropology as then taught in the United States. *The History of Ethnological Theory* (1937) summarized Lowie's views on the development of his profession. *Social Organization* (1948) attempted to update *Primitive Society* with the addition of examples from more recent and sophisticated ethnographic reports. These books were in some ways closer to Lowie's teaching than to his fieldwork since they attempted to place anthropology as he saw it in a meaningful context for students and interested laymen as well as for his colleagues.

Politics and political philosophy concerned Lowie. His works in this field included *The Origin of the State* (1927)

and *Are We Civilized?* (1929). During World War II he helped with Army training courses. His concept of anthropology made that science relevant to politics and to the study of modern society as well as of primitive tribes in transition from their old ways of life to modern civilization.

Lowie received numerous professional honors, including membership in the National Academy of Sciences. He was president of the American Folklore Society in 1916, the American Ethnological Society in 1920, and the American Anthropological Association in 1935. He edited the *American Anthropologist* briefly in 1912 and again from 1924 to 1933. He died of cancer on Sept. 21, 1957, in Berkeley, Calif.

Further Reading

Lowie's autobiography, *Robert H. Lowie, Ethnologist,* was published posthumously in 1959. The development of Boasian anthropology has been discussed in detail by Marvin Harris, *The Rise of Anthropological Theory* (1968); George Stocking, *Race, Culture and Evolution: Essays in the History of Anthropology* (1968); and Regna Darnell, *The Development of American Anthropology, 1879-1920: From the Bureau of American Ethnology to Franz Boas.* □

Ernst Lubitsch

The German-American film director Ernst Lubitsch (1892-1947) is recognized as one of the comic masters of the cinema. A brilliant craftsman, he is chiefly admired for his witty political satires and inventive bedroom farces.

Ernst Lubitsch was the son of a Berlin storekeeper. As a young man, he worked as assistant to the noted theatrical director Max Reinhardt and later established himself as a talented actor in silent films, many of which he directed. Beginning in 1913, Lubitsch played the role of a clothing store salesman in a series of short movies, achieving a popularity with German audiences comparable to that of Charlie Chaplin in America. *The Eyes of the Mummy* (1918) was Lubitsch's first feature-length film; that same year he directed his own version of *Carmen,* called *Gypsy Blood.* The popularity of his two large-scale historical productions, *Passion* (1919), the story of Madame de Pompadour starring Pola Negri, and *Deception* (1920), about Anne Boleyn and Henry VIII, brought him numerous offers from American motion picture studios. In 1924 he left for Hollywood.

Coming under the influence of Chaplin and of Cecil B. DeMille's sophisticated comedies, Lubitsch established his creative independence by hiring his own German staff and embarking on a series of hilarious, visually imaginative bedroom farces. The most memorable were *The Marriage Circle* (1924), *Kiss Me Again* (1925), and *So This Is Paris* (1926). In 1924 Lubitsch directed a scathing satire of the Hollywood film industry, *Forbidden Paradise.*

Lubitsch's facility with the camera and his love of slapstick made him an ideal silent-film director, and his rapport with actors and his gift for verbal subtleties rendered him equally adept with the sound medium. His first talking movies, the Maurice Chevalier-Jeanette MacDonald series, were stylishly entertaining. However, his later work gained in wit and intellectual sophistication. *Monte Carlo* (1930) and *Trouble in Paradise* (1932) are superior, the latter considered by most critics to be his finest film.

In 1939 Lubitsch directed Greta Garbo in his most popular production, *Ninotchka. Shop around the Corner* (1940), a modest drama notable for its atmosphere and vivid characterization, and *To Be or Not To Be* (1942), a controversial comedy described by Lubitsch as "a satirization of the Nazi spirit and the foul Nazi humor," are among the director's most creative efforts. His last production, *Heaven Can Wait* (1943), is an intelligent exploration of a rogue's life while he waits at the gates of hell.

Further Reading

An excellent full-length study of Lubitsch's career is Herman G. Weinberg, *The Lubitsch Touch: A Critical Study* (1968). For briefer but equally perceptive analyses see John Grierson, *Grierson on Documentary,* edited by Forsyth Hard (1947; rev. ed. 1966); Andrew Sarris, *The American Cinema, 1929-1968* (1968); and Dwight Macdonald's "Notes on Hollywood Directors" in his *Dwight Macdonald on Movies* (1969).

Additional Sources

Ernst Lubitsch, Paris: Cahiers du cinema: Cinematheque francaise, 1985.
Eyman, Scott, *Ernst Lubitsch: laughter in paradise,* New York: Simon & Schuster, 1993.
Nacache, Jacqueline, *Lubitsch,* Paris: Edilig, 1987.
Poague, Leland A., *The cinema of Ernst Lubitsch,* South Brunswick N.J.: A. S. Barnes, 1978. □

Luca della Robbia

The Florentine sculptor Luca della Robbia (1400?-1482) is usually remembered for his singularly lovely images of the Madonna and Child in glazed terracotta.

L uca della Robbia was praised by his compatriot Leon Battista Alberti for genius comparable to that of the sculptors Donatello and Lorenzo Ghiberti, the architect Filippo Brunelleschi, and the painter Masaccio. By ranking him with contemporary artists of this stature, Alberti reminds us of the interest and strength of Luca's work in marble and bronze, as well as in the terra-cottas always associated with his name.

There are no certain details of Luca della Robbia's youth, training, or early sculpture, and many of his most popular later works cannot be dated absolutely. He was born in Florence. His first documented commission, the marble *Singing Gallery* (1431-1438) for the Cathedral of Florence, proves that he must have been an accomplished artist long before joining the Sculptors' Guild in 1432. The *Singing Gallery* shows children singing, dancing, and making music to "praise the Lord" in the words of Psalm 150. Their figures are at once lively, finely observed, and gracefully combined in groups designed to fit the 10 panels of the gallery.

In the next 2 decades Luca executed important commissions in marble and bronze: a series of marble reliefs (1437) for the bell tower of the Cathedral of Florence; a marble and enameled terra-cotta tabernacle (1443), now in S. Maria in Peretola; bronze angels to enrich the *Singing Gallery;* and, in collaboration with Michelozzo, the large project of bronze doors for the Sacristy of the Cathedral. These doors were not finished until 1469; their reliance on a few figures placed in simple, orderly compositions against a flat ground contrasts sharply with the elaborate pictorial effects of Ghiberti's more famous Baptistery doors.

Although the data of Luca's first work in colored, glazed terra-cotta is not known, his control of this medium was clearly enough recognized to justify two major commissions for the Cathedral of Florence: the large reliefs *Resurrection* (1445) and *Ascension of Christ* (1446). The pliant medium of baked clay covered with a "slip" of vitrified lead and refined permitted a lustrous, polished surface capable of reflecting light and using color that was beautifully appropriate for architectural sculpture. Whether animating the vast, somber space of the Cathedral or in the series *Twelve Apostles* gracing the pristine surfaces of the small Pazzi Chapel (1443-1450) in Florence, Luca's reliefs in this medium achieved a perfection never before or since attained.

Working with assistants, including members of his own family, Luca produced a number of decorative reliefs and altarpieces until the end of his life. One of the finest and richest examples is the enameled terra-cotta ceiling (1466) of the Chapel of the Cardinal of Portugal in S. Miniato, Florence. Luca della Robbia died in Florence in February 1482.

Further Reading

Allan Marquand, *Luca della Robbia* (1914), remains the most important and readable monograph on the artist. The earliest account of Luca della Robbia, in Giorgio Vasari, *Lives of the Most Eminent Painters, Sculptors and Architects,* vol. 2, translated by Gaston De Vere (1914), is sympathetic but should be supplemented by Charles Seymour's more recent *Sculpture in Italy, 1400-1500* (1966).

Additional Sources

Gaeta Bertela, Giovanna, *Luca, Andrea, Giovanni Della Robbia,* London: Constable, c. 1979.
Pope-Hennessy, John Wyndham, Sir, *Luca della Robbia,* Ithaca, N.Y.: Cornell University Press, 1980. □

Cyril Lucaris

The Greek Orthodox theologian Cyril Lucaris (1572-1637), who was patriarch of Constantinople, aroused a storm of controversy by interpreting the doctrines of his Church along Calvinistic lines.

Cyril Lucaris, or Lukar, was born on the island of Crete on Nov. 13, 1572. He was a bright young man who displayed a great deal of personal initiative as well as a strong religious faith. He spoke fluent Greek and learned Latin thoroughly, profiting by his student years in Venice, Padua, and especially Geneva. Cyril came in contact with the faith of the Reformers in Geneva toward the end of the 16th century. He was greatly impressed by John Calvin's teachings, especially his view that some men are clearly predestined by God to heaven and his interpretation of a decent, upright life as a sign of God's favor.

In 1602 the brilliant young theologian was elected patriarch of Alexandria in Egypt, which had traditionally been a center of the Orthodox faith. He filled the position with dedication for 19 years. Cyril began to exercise his greatest influence in the Orthodox Church in 1621, when he became patriarch of Constantinople. The city, which had been under Moslem domination for centuries, was not prepared for him. Cyril's articulate preaching and penetrating writings upset the city's religious peace. Several times he was deposed, but each time the Sultan was forced to reinstate

him to calm the indignant Orthodox population, who loved him.

Cyril attempted to inject new life into the Orthodox faith by reshaping its teachings in the spirit of Calvin. He arranged for a number of promising theologians to study in the Calvinist centers of Europe, especially in Switzerland and Holland. Not everyone appreciated his efforts. He met with a great deal of opposition in his own Church from those who thought that he was misinterpreting instead of reinterpreting the faith. In 1629 Cyril published his *Confession,* a declaration of his beliefs about God and man in language that was traditional but expressing ideas that were derived from the Reformation. This work served as the focal point of a controversy that stirred the Orthodox Church for decades, until the patriarch of Jerusalem called a synod in 1672 which condemned Cyril's teachings, long after his death.

Cyril disappeared suddenly and permanently in June 1637. A story emerged that he had been ordered killed by the Sultan, who was about to embark on a war with Persia and wanted to avoid the trouble Cyril would cause while he was away. Reportedly Cyril was strangled by a contingent of soldiers who threw his body into the sea.

Further Reading

Cyril Lucaris's controversial *The Confession of Faith* reveals his major religious ideas. A study of his life is Georgios A. Chatzeantoniou, *Protestant Patriarch: The Life of Cyril Lucaris, 1572-1638, Patriarch of Constantinople* (1961). Cyril's influence on the history of his Church is examined in Adrian Fortescue, *The Orthodox Eastern Church* (1907; 3d ed., 1920), and R. M. French, *The Eastern Orthodox Church* (1951). □

Lucas van Leyden

The Dutch engraver and painter Lucas van Leyden (1494-1533) was the leading graphic artist in the Netherlands in the early 16th century.

Because Lucas van Leyden showed such a highly developed graphic talent in engravings dated 1508, his birth date has been thought by some to be as early as 1489. Generally, however, scholarly opinion has accepted Karel van Mander's statement (1604) that Lucas was born in Leyden (Leiden) in 1494. His father, Hughe Jacobsz, was his first teacher, followed by the mannerist painter Cornelis Engelbrechtsz. In 1515 Lucas was married in Leyden, where he worked all his life. In 1521 he traveled to Antwerp. There he met Albrecht Dürer, whose works provided the most important artistic influence on his graphic oeuvre.

Lucas's engraving *Mohammed and the Monk Sergius* (1508) confirms Van Mander's story of his precocity. His technical mastery and compositional skill at this early age presuppose considerable training and experience as well as a formidable natural talent. It is not unlikely that, as Van

Mander says, Lucas had learned his craft in the shops of a specialist in inlaying metal in weapons and of a goldsmith.

Graphic Works

Much of Lucas's large production of engravings and woodcuts and a few etchings bear dates, from 1508 to 1530, so that it is possible to follow his development and to establish a probable chronology for his paintings, only five of which are dated.

In 1510 Lucas produced several masterpieces of engraving, including the large *Ecce Homo* and the *Return of the Prodigal Son,* both of which impressed Rembrandt more than a century later. Lucas's *Triumph of Mordecai* (1515) was the basis for a painting by Rembrandt's teacher, Pieter Lastman. Lucas's close observation of nature, delight in landscape, and grotesque physiognomies were in the Dutch tradition. His best works are the early ones, in which these features predominate. Later he was so overawed by the achievements of Dürer and by the prints of the Italian engraver Marcantonio Raimondi that he attempted to emulate them at the expense of his personal bent.

Lucas was commissioned to make woodcuts to illustrate a number of books. A series of seven large woodcuts, *Pernicious Women* (ca. 1513), show his power in this medium, which he used for admirable independent subjects as well as sets. His graphic works dealt mainly with religious subject matter. A few were genre subjects, such as the engraving *The Dentist* (1523), which pointed out a moral in

an ironic way, a form of art that became very popular in Holland in the 17th century.

His Paintings

We know of no painting that can with certainty be identified as a youthful work by Lucas. The most likely candidate is a small *Adoration of the Magi.* Certainly awkward enough to be early is the *Beheading of John the Baptist,* which is thought to date from about 1512, in which the belated Gothic flavor of Engelbrechtsz is sharply reflected.

Lucas's portraits have a forthright quality that is characteristically Dutch. This sense of unsparing veracity can be seen in his painted *Self-portrait* (ca. 1508) and in the chalk drawing *Portrait of a Young Man* (1521).

The *Last Judgment* triptych, which was commissioned in 1526, is Lucas's masterpiece. Groups of nude figures realized in a broad, painterly style are arranged in a field of vast depth that depends for its sense of distance mainly on aerial perspective. *Moses Striking Water from the Rock* (1527) is confused in composition, but it displays very well Lucas's genre–like way of treating a religious theme. The *Worship of the Golden Calf* triptych is a better-composed work of his maturity in which his natural bent for genre and for a Northern specificity of detail tends to submerge the Old Testament subject. In the foreground families that represent all the ages of man eat, drink, quarrel, and cuddle, and in the far distance one can descry with difficulty the Golden Calf, which is the ostensible occasion for the celebration.

Lucas was a transitional figure rather than a major innovator, despite his exceptional gifts. He appreciated Renaissance developments but failed in his efforts to adapt them in his native idiom.

Further Reading

A detailed study is F. W. H. Hollstein, *The Graphic Art of Lucas van Leyden* (Amsterdam, 1955). Reproductions of all the graphic works are provided in Jacques Lavalleye, *Pieter Bruegel the Elder and Lucas van Leyden: The Complete Engravings, Etchings, and Woodcuts* (1967). On the paintings, see Max J. Friedländer, *Early Netherlandish Painting* (trans., 5 vols., 1967-1969).

Additional Sources

Vos, Rik., *Lucas van Leyden,* Bentveld: Landshoff; Maarssen: G. Schwartz, 1978. □

Clare Boothe Luce

Playwright and U.S. congresswoman Clare Boothe Luce (1903-1987) was hailed as one of the most able and outspoken women in public life. She became ambassador to Italy in 1953, the first American woman to represent her country to another major world power. Her marriage to publisher Henry Luce

gave Clare Boothe an opportunity to compete also for journalistic acclaim.

Ann Clare Boothe was born on April 10, 1903, in New York City to Anna Snyder and William F. Boothe. Although her father, a violinist, deserted the family when Clare was nine, he instilled in his daughter a love of music and literature. In 1912 Clare became understudy to Mary Pickford in David Belasco's *The Good Little Devil.* She subsequently obtained similar understudy parts. In 1915 Clare entered St. Mary's, an Episcopal school on Long Island, where she met the daughter of journalist Irvin Cobb. A frequent visitor to the Cobb home, Clare was awed by such celebrities as Flo Ziegfeld, Kathleen Norris, and Richard Harding Davis.

A bright student, in 1917 Boothe enrolled in the Castle School at Tarrytown, New York, from which she graduated at the head of her class. After graduation in 1919 she went to New York City to find work.

Her mother had married physician Albert E. Austin of Greenwich, Connecticut, later a Republican Congressman from Fairfield County. Soon the three journeyed to Europe, where she met Alva Smith Vanderbilt Belmont, the women's suffrage leader.

In New York Alva Belmont offered Clare a secretarial position. During her employment she was introduced to George T. Brokaw. At 43, Brokaw was a millionaire bachelor much sought after. Smitten, he courted Clare, and they were married on August 10, 1923, at a ceremony attended by 2,500 guests.

After a European honeymoon, the couple returned to a Fifth Avenue mansion where they lived with Brokaw's mother. Their daughter Ann was born in August 1924, and the family lived at the epicenter of society until Brokaw began to lose his long battle with alcoholism. Marriage became intolerable, and Clare divorced Brokaw on May 20, 1929.

Determined to apply her writing talents, Clare appealed to Conde Nast, owner of *Vogue.* After a brief trial she was hired, but soon went to *Vanity Fair.* By early 1930 Clare was hard at work, dazzling staff and readers of *Vanity Fair* with her sharp intelligence and barbed wit.

In 1934 Clare met Henry Luce, publisher of *Time* and *Fortune.* Although married, he soon divorced his wife and married Clare on November 23, 1935. About that time Clare produced a play, *Abide with Me,* which met mixed reviews. When Henry started *Life* magazine, Clare wrote another play, *The Women,* a biting satire on modern life. It opened in New York on December 26, 1936, to wide critical acclaim.

Clare dabbled in left-wing politics during the 1930s but was ultimately as repelled by Communism as she was by Fascism. In the face of war, in 1939 Clare left for Europe as a *Life* correspondent. She interviewed Winston Churchill and visited the doomed Maginot Line in France. She was in Brussels May 10, 1940, when the Germans crossed the border, an experience described in her book *Europe in the Spring.*

Clare's work as *Life* correspondent carried her to the Philippines, where she interviewed Gen. Douglas MacArthur. The resulting article was a *Life* cover story on December 8, 1941, the day the Japanese attacked in the Far East. Throughout World War II she produced many *Life* stories, often at peril to her safety.

Clare Boothe Luce ran for office in 1942, winning the same Republican congressional seat from Fairfield County, Connecticut, held by her step-father in 1938. Sadly, her daughter Ann Brokaw was killed in an auto accident in January 1944. This misfortune led her to take religious instruction from Rev. Fulton J. Sheen. Later that year Luce won reelection to her congressional seat, but a growing spiritual unease prompted by her daughter's death caused her to resign from politics in 1946. She at that time announced her conversion to the Roman Catholic faith.

Luce plunged into writing: screenplays, articles, a movie script, and a monthly column for *McCall's.* Drawn again to the political arena, she was a delegate to the Republican National Presidential Convention in 1952.

In 1953 President Eisenhower named her U.S. ambassador to Italy. Her well-known opposition to Communism and her relentless energy, as well as the rocky nature of Mediterranean diplomacy at that time, made her tenure a stormy one. But Luce was respected and admired, and at her departure in 1956 she was given the Order of Merit of the Italian Republic.

Clare and Henry Luce moved to Arizona where she took up painting. She also became absorbed with scuba diving and travelled to Bermuda, writing an article for *Sports Illustrated.* In 1957 she was awarded the Laertare Medal as an outstanding Catholic layperson. She also received honorary degrees from both Fordham and Temple universities.

In 1959 Clare Boothe Luce was considered for assignment as the U.S. ambassador to Brazil, but due to Senate debate over her outspoken views, she withdrew her name. She continued to speak out vehemently against Communism and joined the unsuccessful 1964 presidential campaign to elect Barry Goldwater.

Henry Luce died on March 7, 1967, and Clare was left with a substantial income from $30 million worth of Time, Inc. stock. She settled in Honolulu, Hawaii, but in 1983 moved to Washington, D.C. Taking up residence at the Watergate apartments, she served for a time as a member of the President's Foreign Intelligence Advisory Board and maintained a position in the capital's social scene until her death from cancer October 9, 1987.

Further Reading

The most timely biography to date of Clare Boothe Luce is *Rage for Fame: The Ascent of Clare Boothe Luce* by Sylvia Jukes Morris (1997). Another useful reference is an earlier portrait by Stephen Shadegg entitled *Clare Boothe Luce* (1970). Other insight may be gained by reading Luce's articles and stories that appeared in *Life* magazine. ☐

combination of news reporting, interpretation, and departmentalized coverage of a dozen other fields—all in a distinctive writing style, originated by Hadden, that featured brevity, brashness, and shock. Luce excelled as the editorial executive.

In February 1930 Luce's new project, *Fortune,* appeared, addressed to business executives. He encouraged talented writers to develop civilized expositions of America's business world. Archibald MacLeish, J. K. Galbraith, Dwight MacDonald, and Louis Kronenberger contributed to *Fortune,* while *Fortune* contributed to their own professional development. In 1932 Luce purchased *Architectural Forum.*

Few journalistic executives of Luce's generation could match his ability to organize and to gratify his curiosity and ambitions. None possessed the sense of moral purpose that sustained Luce in his Americanism, Republicanism, anti-communism, and anti-McCarthyism. In 1935 Luce divorced his first wife to marry the brilliant, talented Clare Boothe Brokaw. It was said they planned *Life* magazine on their honeymoon. Luce bought the name and subscription list of the humorous weekly *Life* and transformed it into a fresh and stunning experiment in photographic journalism. *Life* took only 2 years to reach a circulation of over 2 million.

Luce had pioneered new techniques of team journalism—in *Time,* the reporter-researcher-writer team; in *Life,* the photographer-writer team. In 1954 he launched *Sports Illustrated.* Retiring as editor in chief of all Time, Inc. publi-

Henry Robinson Luce

Henry Robinson Luce (1898-1967), American magazine editor and publisher, was the most powerful journalistic innovator of his generation because of his insatiable curiosity and consuming sense of moral purpose.

Born of American Presbyterian missionary parents at Tenchow, China, Henry Luce attended a British school from the age of 10 to 14 and then went to Hotchkiss Academy in the United States as a scholarship student. He entered Yale in 1916 and joined the Army in 1917. He graduated from Yale in 1920 *summa cum laude* and a member of Phi Beta Kappa. He had formed a close friendship with Briton Hadden; editing the *Yale Daily News,* Hadden and Luce determined to found a weekly newsmagazine.

Luce studied for a year at Oxford University and then worked with Hadden on the *Baltimore News.* They left in 1922 to raise $86,000, with which they launched *Time* magazine in March 1923. By 1928 *Time's* profits came to $125,000. In 1929 Hadden died of a streptococcus infection. His obituary in *Time* concluded: "To Briton Hadden, success came steadily, satisfaction never."

Time was successful because its creators had captured the growing college-educated public with a frankly biased

cations in 1964, Luce remained the company's principal owner.

By the time of Luce's death, *Life* had a circulation of 750 million and *Time* a circulation of 350 million. *Life* had more than twice the advertising revenue of any American magazine; *Time* ranked second.

Further Reading

Background on Luce is in Robert T. Elson, *Time, Inc.: The Intimate History of a Publishing Enterprise, 1923-1941* (1968); John Kobler, *Luce: His Time, Life and Fortune* (1968); and John K. Jessup, ed., *The Ideas of Henry Luce* (1969). See also Noel F. Busch, *Briton Hadden: A Biography* (1949), and T. S. Matthews, *Name and Address: An Autobiography* (1960). ☐

Lu Chi

The Chinese poet and critic Lu Chi (261-303) is best known for his *Wen-fu,* one of the finest works of criticism and esthetics by a Chinese, and a masterpiece in the poetic style of the fu.

L u Chi, with the courtesy name Shih-heng, was of a distinguished family in the service of the Wu kingdom (south of the Yangtze) during the Three Kingdoms period. Both his grandfather Lu Sun and father, Lu K'ang, were brilliant military leaders and statesmen-scholars for the kingdom of Wu, but soon after Lu K'ang's death its fortunes rapidly declined. Both Lu K'ang's sons, Lu Chi and the year-younger Lu Yün, carried on the martial tradition of the family but a achieved greater fame as men of letters.

When Wu fell before the invading forces of the Chin, Chi, then 19, and Yün escaped to their family estate at Hua-t'ing in the Yangtze delta, where they lay low for some 10 years. Lu Chi studied hard and wrote an essay on the causes of the fall of the Wu kingdom. In 290 the two brothers went to the Chin capital, Loyang, to seek the patronage of Chang Hua, a high official and the leading writer of his time. Chang Hua appreciated the wit and talent of the brothers, and they soon rose in literary fame as well as official rank.

Military Career

During the reign of the Western Chin emperor Hui-ti (290-306), there arose a civil war known as the Rebellion of the Eight Princes, each prince either using the weak emperor as a hostage or trying to supplant him. In 301 Lu Chi got involved in one of these princes' plots to overthrow Hui-ti and narrowly escaped execution. After leaving the service of another rebel prince in disgust, he finally threw in his lot with Ssu-ma Ying, the prince of Ch'eng-tu.

In 302 the prince started a war with Ssu-ma I, the prince of Ch'ang-sha. Lu Chi was appointed rear general, and he suffered a disastrous defeat in a battle. The prince of Ch'eng-tu listened to slander, believing Lu Chi had turned traitor, and had him executed along with his two sons and his brother Yün. Chi was only 42 years old.

Poetry and Poetics

Lu Chi excelled in both the *shih* and *fu* forms of poetry. Of his some hundred extant *shih* poems many are direct and moving, but the majority are imitative, devoid of content, and given to rhetoric. It is on his *Wen-fu* (*Essay on Literature*) that his fame mainly rests. Comprising 131 distichs and a short prose introduction, it was the most brilliant disquisition on literary creation by a Chinese up to its time. Though Liu Hsieh's *Wen-hsintiao-lung* far exceeds it in length and comprehensiveness, it remains unsurpassed among Chinese works of criticism for its penetrating insights into the nature of poetic creation. In its best passages one gets the impression of a true poet using dazzling metaphors to indicate the kind of dejection and ecstasy inherent in his attempt to capture the world through words.

Further Reading

There are three translations of Lu Chi's *Wen-fu* available: E. R. Hughes, *The Art of Letters: Lu Chi's "Wen Fu"* (1951); Chen Shih-hsiang, "Lu Chi: Essay on Literature" (1953), reprinted with excisions in Cyril Birch, ed., *Anthology of Chinese Literature,* vol. 1 (1965); and Achilles Fang, "Rhymeprose on Literature: The *Wen-fu* of Lu Chi," in John L. Bishop, ed., *Studies in Chinese Literature* (1965). The translations by Fang and Chen are far more accurate than Hughes's. Archibald MacLeish discusses Lu Chi's poetic theory in his interesting book *Poetry and Experience* (1961). ☐

Lu Chiu-yuan

Lu Chiu-yuan (1139-1193) was a Chinese thinker, public official, and man of letters. He is regarded as the representative of the idealistic wing, as distinct from the rationalistic wing, of Sung-dynasty Neo-Confucianism.

L u Chiu-yuan, better known in China by his literary name as Lu Hsiang-shan, had a remarkably original mind which was noticeable from his childhood. At the age of 4 he asked his father, "Where would one find the limit of heaven and earth?" Later he detected a difference between the Neo-Confucianism of Ch'eng I and classical Confucianism and raised the query, "Why is it that Ch'eng I's words do not seem to agree with those of Confucius and Mencius?"

In the course of his study of the ancient classics when Lu Chiu-yuan was 13 years of age, he came across the term *yü-chou* (universe), on which the commentary said, "The four directions together with what is above and what is below are called *yü;* the bygone past and the coming future are called *chou.*" With a sudden enlightenment, he came to the realization of the great infinitude which man shares with the universe, and he recorded: "The universe is nothing other than my mind and my mind is nothing other than the universe. . . . Whenever sages were to appear they would still have nothing other than this same mind and this same Truth. . . . This Truth manifests itself as *yin* and *yang* in relation to heaven, as firm and pliable in relation to earth, and as benevolence and righteousness in relation to man. Hence benevolence and righteousness are the original mind of man."

Neo-Confucian Debate

The first meeting between Lu Chiu-yuan and Chu Hsi, spokesman of the rationalistic wing of Neo-Confucianism, took place in 1175 at the Goose Lake Monastery in northern Kiangsi. At the outset a poem by Lu Chiu-yuan was presented, and Chu Hsi felt greatly displeased, particularly with the following couplet: "The endeavor in the easy and the simple will forever increase; while the pursuit of the piecemeal will after all prove ephemeral." Here lay the central difference between the two thinkers. The objective of both was to achieve enlightenment and sagehood. However, to Chu Hsi the procedure called for patient investigation of individual things and affairs, leading to a gradual understanding of the truth, while to Lu Chiu-yuan, on the other hand, the one and only important thing was to "let a man first firmly establish the nobler part of his constitution," as "Truth is nothing other than the mind and the mind is nothing other than the Truth." Consequently Chiu-yuan advocated the procedure of personal cultivation through contemplation and reflection, leading to sudden enlightenment—a procedure which Chu condemned as copying Ch'an Buddhism (Zen). The participants at the 10-day debate parted friends, but their philosophical positions remained unreconciled.

Lu Chiu-yuan was so convinced of the unitary principle of the mind that he put little value on book learning and scholarship. He said, "The Six Classics are but footnotes of my mind," and he did not write a single book. He was, however, a brilliant lecturer and conversationalist. At the invitation of Chu Hsi, Lu Chiu-yuan delivered a lecture to the students at the White Deer Grotto Academy, and all listeners, including his host, were genuinely moved by his eloquence, sincerity, and penetration.

Contrary to expectation, Lu Chiu-yuan was also a man of affairs. He cultivated horsemanship and archery in his youth, when he learned about the national humiliation at the hands of the Chin invaders. In 1191 Lu Chiu-yuan was appointed magistrate of the strategic and populous Ching-men district of the present Hupei Province. During his administration of less than 2 years many improvements were introduced—reduction of taxes and official extravagance, easy access by the people with their grievances and speedy settlement of lawsuits, building of the city walls, and suppression of lawlessness and banditry. In the midst of all these activities, he still found time to deliver lectures on civic duties to the people and minor government officials. In 1217 the posthumous title of Wen-an was conferred on him, and in 1530 his tablet was admitted in the Confucian Temple.

Further Reading

The only volume devoted completely to Lu Chiu-yuan is Siu-chi Huang, *Lu Hsiang-shan: A Twelfth Century Chinese Idealist Philosopher* (1944), a doctoral thesis that contains translations from the Chinese, with explanatory introductions, of selected passages of the *Complete Works of Lu Hsiang-shan*. Chapters on Lu Chiu-yuan are in Fung Yu-lan, *A History of Chinese Philosophy,* vol. 2 (trans. 1953); Chia-sên (Carsun) Chang, *The Development of Neo-Confucian Thought* (2 vols., 1957-1962); and Wing-tsit Chan, comp. and trans., *A Source Book on Chinese Philosophy* (1963). □

Lucian

The Greek satirical writer Lucian (ca. 120 A.D.-ca. 200 A.D.) is noted for his mastery of Greek prose and satirical dialogue. He was an unrelenting but delightful critic of mythological and philosophical doctrines.

Most of what we know about Lucian comes from his own works. He was born at Samosata in Syria, and his native language was probably Syriac, though he thoroughly mastered Greek. He practiced the profession of a sophistic rhetorician in Greece, Italy, and Gaul. About 165 A.D. he settled in Athens but later, apparently in desperate need of funds in his old age, accepted a governmental position in Roman Egypt. Never a philosopher in the technical sense, he knew the schools of the Academics, Skeptics, and Cynics and seemed to have leanings toward the Epicureans.

Lucian wrote about 80 works, which are principally in dialogue form. They can be divided into five periods and categories: rhetorical, literary, philosophical, satirical, and miscellaneous.

The rhetorical output of Lucian includes two speeches: in *Phalaris I* the tyrant Phalaris of Akragas sends his famous bull as an offering to Delphi; in *Phalaris II* one of the Delphians suggests accepting the offering. The *Tyrannicide* and the *Disowned Son* also belong in this category. Later in date are the *Apology for a Wrong Greeting* and some other works.

Lucian's literary work varies in significance and length. *Lexiphanes* and *Trial before the Vowels* make fun of extreme Atticizing; *How to Write History* contains advice on historiography that is still valuable; and *The True History* is a hilarious account of man's trip to the moon, which is remarkably modern in tone.

The philosophical category owes much to the satirist Menippus, who appears in a number of the works. Lucian himself also appears, thinly disguised. The most impressive work is probably the *Hermotimus,* a critique of stoicism, but *Cock, Sale of Lives, Icaromenippus, Demonax, Charon, Fisher, Zeus Cross-examined,* and *Voyage to the Lower World* are worthy of note.

In his satirical writings, Lucian attacks the philosophers. Common life (*Dialogues of Courtesans*) and contemporary life (*Against an Ignorant Bookbuyer* and *Concerning Hired Companions*) are described, but most notable are the attacks on religious movements (*Dialogues of the Gods* and

the biographies of Alexandros of Abonuteichos and Peregrinos).

Miscellaneous writings by Lucian include *Tragopodagra* (*Tragic Gout*) and *Ocypus* (*Swift Foot*), mock tragedies in poetic form. The novel *Lucius; or The Ass* is often assigned to him.

Lucian was a versatile writer with a highly developed sense of the ridiculous. He sensed what often seems the futility of human life, but he also showed real sympathy for the poor and down-and-out. He subjected the institutions of his day to a scrutiny they deserve but cannot always survive. The classical scholar Gilbert Murray (*The Literature of Ancient Greece,* 3d ed. 1956) well describes Lucian's significance: "He is an important figure, both as representing a view of life which has a certain permanent value for all ages, and also a sign of the independent vigour of Eastern Hellenism when it escaped from its state patronage or rebelled against its educational duties."

Further Reading

Francis G. Allinson, ed., *Lucian: Selected Writings* (1905), includes some information about Lucian. A study of his life, works, and beliefs is Allinson's *Lucian: Satirist-Artist* (1926). See also Basil L. Gildersleeve's "Lucian" in Richard C. Jebb, *Essays and Studies* (1907), and John Jay Chapman, *Lucian, Plato and Greek Morals* (1931). □

Lucretius

Lucretius (ca. 94–ca. 55 B.C.), full name Titus Lucretius Carus, was a Latin poet and philosopher. His one work, *De rerum natura,* a didactic poem in hexameters, renders in verse the atomistic philosophy of Epicurus, forerunner of the modern-day atomic theory.

Almost nothing is known of the life of Lucretius. The medieval chronicler Jerome is the only source of information. After giving his subject's birth date, Jerome declares that Lucretius was made insane by a love potion and composed his poetry during intervals of lucidity, with later emendations by Cicero. Lucretius committed suicide, according to Jerome, in the forty-fourth year of his life (50 B.C.)

Despite Jerome, the date of Lucretius's death is more commonly assigned to 55 B.C., because Donatus, the 4th-century biographer of Virgil, says that the poet assumed the toga of manhood on the very day Lucretius died. Cicero also comments in a letter to his brother Quintus in 54 B.C. that "The poems of Lucretius are, as you say in your letter, touched by flashes of genius and all the same composed with great skill." It is assumed that Cicero would have had Lucretius's poem in hand only after the letter's death. If Jerome is correct as to Lucretius's age at death (44 B.C.) and Donatus as to the year, the poet was born in 99 B.C.

Lucretius is generally considered to have belonged to one of Rome's old aristocratic families, although some scholars have concluded from the name Carus that he was a slave in a Lucretian household or, at best, a freedman.

As to the story of Lucretius's insanity from a love potion, it is supported by a passage at the end of book 4 of *De rerum natura* (*On the Nature of the Universe*) in which the poet violently attacks the lovemaking of men and women—which he describes rather fully. No other direct or indirect evidence exists. The work itself is dedicated to Memmius, a patron of literature who dabbled in verse. Memmius was a Roman magistrate in 58 B.C. and afterward governor of the province of Bithynia.

His Work

De rerum natura, some 7,400 lines long, is divided into 6 books. The title translates the *Peri Physeos* of Epicurus, whom Lucretius acknowledges as his master and praises in the most lavish terms.

Book 1 begins by invoking Venus, appealing to Memius, praising Epicurus, and listing the wrongs committed in the name of religion, the reasons for accepting Epicurus, and the difficulty of treating Greek philosophy in Latin verse. Next, the poet sets forth the atomic theory of Epicurus (derived from Democritus). Nothing comes from nothing and nothing can be destroyed. Matter exists in imperceptible particles (atoms) separated from one another by space. The atoms are solid, indivisible, and eternal. Lucretius then refutes the rival systems of Heraclitus,

Empedocles, and Anaxagoras and proves that the universe is infinite and that its two components are also infinite, atoms in number, space in extent.

Book 2 contains Lucretius's most explicit reference to the moral theory of Epicurus. It also deals with the motion of the atoms, maintaining that their "slight swerve" (*exiguum clinamen,* book 2: line 292) causes free will. Lucretius passes to the shape of the atoms and the effects their various forms create. The number of shapes is not infinite, but the number of any given shape is. The atoms lack secondary qualities, that is, color, heat, and sound, and are without sensation. Finally, Lucretius shows that there is an infinite number of worlds and describes their formation and destruction.

Book 3 treats of the soul, its nature, composition, and fate. In the first two books Lucretius's purpose is to dispose of human fear of the intervention of gods into the world by proving that the universe is material and all events are due to the movement and combination of atoms. In book 3 he counteracts the fear of death and of punishment after death by proving that the soul, too, is composed of matter and is dissolved at death into atoms. The book ends with a triumphant passage on the mortality of the soul and the folly of the fear of death.

In book 4 the poet deals with the nature of sensation and thought: sight is the result of emanations of atoms from an object which pass into the eye. The remaining senses and the mental processes function in an analogous way. Next, the poet refutes the teleological view of creation, treats of the will, sleep, and dreams, and ends the book with a violent attack on the passion of love (which makes men do unreasonable things).

Books 5 and 6 are an appendix in which the atomic principle is applied in detail. Book 5, after praise of Epicurus and an attack on the religious view, describes the beginning and end of this world and certain problems of astronomy. The poet then accounts for the origin of life on earth, the creation of man, and the development of civilization.

Book 6 begins with a eulogy to Epicurus. It deals with miscellaneous celestial and terrestrial phenomena and proves that they have physical causes, thus opposing popular superstition, which interpreted unusual occurrences as divine signs. A treatment of pestilences leads him to a long (150 lines) description of the plague at Athens in 430 B.C. on which the work closes.

His Philosophy

Throughout his work Lucretius attacks religion and the fear of death, for him the causes of all evils on earth. He upholds the powerful light of intellect, which has discovered the true nature of the universe. Specifically, it is Epicurus who, through the "living force of his mind" (1:72), penetrated beyond the "flaming walls of heaven," traversed the measureless universe in his imagination, and then set forth what can and cannot come into being and how each thing has its powers limited (1:62-79).

Religion, says Lucretius, has been responsible for such monstrous acts as the sacrifice at Aulis of the pitiful Iph-

igenia, young daughter of King Agamemnon. The fear of death and of punishment after death is the cause of avarice, ambition, cruelty, and other forms of wickedness. This fear can be dispelled only by an understanding of the "outer appearance and inner working of nature" (3:31-93). Lucretius maintains that it is necessary to use the charm of poetry to explain the nature of the universe just as doctors, when attempting to persuade children to drink bitter medicine, smear the rim of the cup with honey (1:933-950, 4:6-25).

Liberated by philosophy from superstitious fears and the fear of death, man achieves *ataraxia,* a state in which he is free of disturbances of all kinds. He has gained, Lucretius says, a lofty and serene sanctuary, well fortified by the teaching of the wise, from which he may view others in their futile struggle to reach the top in human affairs.

The fervor of Lucretius's arguments, especially the violence of his attack on love at the end of book 4, does not seem to stem from a completely tranquil mind. Yet his poetry is at times magnificent, his hexameters, although not as lithe and graceful as Virgil's, have a powerful and austere majesty. Above all, Lucretius's effort to free men, by science and the power of intellect, from the dark and irrational fears which enslave and torture them has earned him a place among the benefactors of humankind.

Further Reading

Works on Lucretius include George Santayana, *Three Philosophical Poets: Lucretius, Dante and Goethe* (1910); George D. Hadzsits, *Lucretius and His Influence* (1935); E. E. Sikes, *Lucretius, Poet and Philosopher* (1936); Henri Bergson, *The Philosophy of Poetry: The Genius of Lucretius,* edited and translated by Wade Baskin (1959); Alban D. Winspear, *Lucretius and Scientific Thought* (1963); Donald R. Dudley, *Lucretius* (1965); and David West, *The Imagery and Poetry of Lucretius* (1969). □

Erich Friedrich Wilhelm Ludendorff

The German general Erich Friedrich Wilhelm Ludendorff (1865-1937), a brilliant strategist and successful field commander, directed Germany's total war effort during the last 2 years of World War I. He later promoted the rise of Hitler.

Erich Ludendorff was born on April 9, 1865, in Kruszewnia in the chiefly Polish-populated Prussian province of Posen. He was the son of an impoverished former cavalry officer. Educated in military schools, Ludendorff entered the German army in 1882, where his fine performance earned him an assignment to the general staff in 1894. He at once gained the confidence of its chief, the younger Count Moltke, and as chief of mobilizations from 1908 to 1912 Ludendorff was largely responsible for Germany's preparations for war.

The first month of World War I witnessed the meteoric rise of the young staff officer. As deputy chief of staff of the 2d Army, Ludendorff immediately made a name for himself by taking the key Belgian fortress of Liège by means of a bold coup. This move earned him the highest German military award. Weeks later Ludendorff won his greatest victory as chief of staff for 8th Army commander Paul von Hindenburg at Tannenberg on the Eastern front against the advancing Russians. During the next 2 years Ludendorff remained in the East, overseeing a series of German victories, yet frustrated in his hopes of launching a decisive campaign against the Russians.

After the failure of Erich von Falkenhayn's Supreme Command in the murderous battle for the key French fortress of Verdun (1916), Hindenburg and Ludendorff were called to the Supreme Command, the latter as first quartermaster general. In this position Ludendorff gained increasing control of the German war effort, not only in its military phases but also in its economic and political ones. In January 1917 Ludendorff ordered unrestricted submarine warfare over the objections of Chancellor Theobald von Bethmann Hollweg. This move soon brought the United States into the war against Germany. After peace moves began in the German Parliament in the summer of 1917, Ludendorff brought about Bethmann Hollweg's dismissal, replaced him with a nonentity, and began a program of total mobilization (Hindenburg Program) and national emergency service. In February 1918 Ludendorff dictated the harsh Treaty of Brest-Litovsk to the defeated Russians. After the German position in the war had become hopeless in the West in the summer of 1918, Ludendorff suddenly demanded armistice negotiations and a democratization of the government. In the face of President Woodrow Wilson's reply, however, Ludendorff called for a last-ditch national resistance. He resigned when he was overruled by the new chancellor, Prince Max von Baden, and thereby he shirked all responsibility for Germany's defeat.

In the postwar years Ludendorff vociferously spread the "stab in the back" legend that blamed German Socialists and Democrats for the defeat. Ludendorff then became active in "folkish" ultranationalist movements, and he participated in the Nazis' Beer Hall Putsch of 1923. Ludendorff entered Parliament as a Nazi in 1924, and he ran for president on the Nazi ticket in 1925.

With his second wife, Dr. Mathilde von Kemnitz, Ludendorff later founded the mystico-religious Aryan-German Tannenberg League, which actively campaigned against Jews, Marxists, Freemasons, and Jesuits. Ludendorff set down his political views in numerous writings, particularly in his openly militarist *The Nation at War* (1936). Highly acclaimed by the Nazi regime but isolated in his own mystical politics, Ludendorff died in Munich on Dec. 20, 1937.

Further Reading

Ludendorff's autobiographical accounts include *My War Memoirs, 1914-1918* (trans. 1919) and *The General Staff and Its Problems,* translated by F. A. Holt (2 vols., 1920). The memoirs of his first wife, Margarethe Ludendorff, *My Married Life with Ludendorff* (1930), were translated by Raglan Somerset; those of his second wife are unavailable in English. The standard biography in English is D. J. Goodspeed, *Ludendorff: Genius of World War I* (1966).

Additional Sources

Parkinson, Roger., *Tormented warrior: Ludendorff and the Supreme Command,* London: Hodder and Stoughton, 1978; New York: Stein and Day, 1978, 1979.

Venohr, Wolfgang., *Ludendorff: Legende und Wirklichkeit,* Berlin: Ullstein, 1993. □

Robert Ludlum

Robert Ludlum (born 1927) is a prolific author of best-selling spy and thriller novels noted for their complicated plots and high-powered suspense. The diverse settings and time periods are embellished by his protagonists, who are ordinary people either accidentally propelled or manipulated into participating in acts of espionage and political machination.

While some critics find Ludlum's plots formulaic and his prose overwritten, others commend his ability to create plausible situations, evoke foreign milieus, and sustain reader interest.

The Scarlatti Inheritance (1971), *The Rhinemann Exchange* (1974), and *The Holcroft Covenant* (1978) are all set in the World War II era and depict the attempts of the Third Reich to gain world dominance. *The Scarlatti Inheritance,* which takes place during the early years of World War II, details the financial backing of the fledgling Nazi party by a group of Western business executives whose leader is an American expatriate and Nazi sympathizer. A Corrupt military-industrialist faction is central to *The Rhinemann Exchange,* a tale of international double-dealing during the last year of World War II. *The Holcroft Covenant,* set in present-day Europe, revolves around the fruition of a scheme devised forty years earlier by German army leaders, who secretly bankrolled a large sum of money to be used by their descendants in reestablishing the Third Reich.

In several of his works, Ludlum unfolds speculative accounts of conspiracy in various facets of American society. In *The Osterman Weekend* (1972), the CIA enlists the aid of a television reporter to dissolve a conspiracy aimed at economic insurgency in which several of his close friends may be involved. *The Matlock Paper* (1973) centers on the criminal activities of a group of New England college professors and the reluctance of the school's dean to assist a government bureau in exposing the teachers. In *The Chancellor Manuscript* (1977), Ludlum alters history in his story of the assassination of J. Edgar Hoover by a group of government officials who seek control of his private files.

International terrorism is a prominent feature in many of Ludlum's novels. In *The Matarese Circle* (1979), several multinational corporations attempt to undermine govern-mental restrictions and regulations by using the services of a terrorist group. *The Bourne Identity* (1980) centers on a Vietnam veteran named David Webb, alias Jason Bourne, who is maneuvered by American intelligence officials into becoming a counter-assassin in an effort to eliminate a notorious terrorist. In *The Aquitaine Progression* (1983), military leaders from several powerful nations conspire to destabilize and usurp their respective governments. *The Bourne Supremacy* (1986), a sequel to *The Bourne Identity,* revolves around a plot to destroy the People's Republic of China with the aid of a terrorist who masquerades as Jason Bourne.

Ludlum has also written novels under pseudonyms: *Trevayne* (1973) and *The Cry of the Halidan* (1974) as Jonathan Ryder, and *The Road to Gandolfo* (1975) as Michael Shepherd. *The Osterman Weekend* and *The Holcroft Covenant* have been adapted for film.

Further Reading

Bestsellers 89, Issue 1, Gale, 1989.
Bestsellers 90, Issue 3, Gale, 1990.
Christian Science Monitor, March 31, 1977, p. 31.
Contemporary Literary Criticism, Gale, Volume 22, 1982, Volume 43, 1988.
Library Journal, October 1, 1974, p. 2504; April 1, 1975, pp. 694-695.
Los Angeles Times, March 1, 1997, p. F17.
Los Angeles Times Book Review, March 11, 1984, p. 3; March 23, 1986, p. 3; March 18, 1990, p. 8. □

Daniel Keith Ludwig

Daniel Keith Ludwig (1897-1992) was an entrepreneur who amassed his fortune in shipping, building a fleet of tankers for government use during World War II and later a fleet of super tankers. Other endeavors included oil refining, saltwater conversion, agriculture, finance and banking, and an ambitious development project in the Amazon basin that eventually fell through.

Daniel Ludwig was born in South Haven, Michigan, on June 24, 1897, the only child of a real estate agent. Little is known of his early years, except that he left school after the eighth grade and at age 19 went into the chartering business with $5,000, raised mostly on his father's credit. With this money he bought an old steamer and converted it into a barge for hauling molasses on the Great Lakes. During the 1920s and 1930s Ludwig struggled to keep one old tanker after another running while searching for cargoes and charters. He moved into an office in New York City where, according to a friend, "he didn't have a desk; he was working from a windowsill."

Ludwig's persistence was finally rewarded in the late 1930s. At that time he developed a unique financing routine. Correctly foreseeing a great expansion in the world oil trade, Ludwig would line up a long-term charter with a major oil company, turn it over to a bank or insurance company as collateral for a loan, and then cover the entire cost of building a tanker without having put up a cent of his own money. Then, during World War II, Ludwig built a tiny shipyard near Norfolk, Virginia, where he developed a process for welding rather than riveting tankers. At these yards he built a fleet of tankers for the government, which was graciously returned to him after the war.

All of this served as a basis for the vast fortune Ludwig would build during the post-war years. He was one of the first to foresee the advantages of using inexpensive foreign labor, and in 1950 he rented the Kure naval yards from the Japanese government at bargain rates. Using this cheap labor source, Ludwig soon began building larger and larger ships, and when the closure of the Suez Canal in 1956 made these bigger ships a necessity, he became known as the "father of the supertanker." In a race with his Greek rivals, Onassis and Niarchos, Ludwig pulled ahead in 1968 with a fleet of six 335,000-ton crude carriers to transport oil from the Persian Gulf to Ireland. In the mid-1970s he had a deadweight tonnage of five to six million tons in the fifty odd tankers and bulk carriers operating under his Universe Tankships Subsidiary, flying the Liberian flag and registered in Panama. By 1980 he ranked third in tonnage, following Chinese shipowners Y. K. Pao and C. Y. Tung.

Ludwig's shipping base, constructed entirely on credit, served both as collateral and as a huge flow of cash for his other mammoth enterprises. Although he was largely unknown to the American public, the *New York Times* estimated in 1979 that he was, with the recent deaths of J. Paul Getty and Howard Hughes, the richest man in America. He had major interests in six areas: oil refining, coal mining, salt water conversion, agriculture, real estate, and finance and banking.

In oil refining, Ludwig until 1971 owned a 75,000 barrel a day refinery in Panama, and in 1973 he built a $300 million refinery in Scotland to process North Sea oil. He owned the United Pocahantas Coal Company in West Virginia, which had an annual output of one million tons of high grade, low sulfur coal, and his Australian Clutha Mines produced five million tons of high grade coking coal, mostly for Japan's steel industry. In 1973 he sold what was then the largest solar salt water plant in the world to Mitsubishi Industries. He developed large scale agricultural ventures and constructed more than 100,000 units of low-cost housing in Latin America, South Africa, and the United States under the patented Con-Tech System. Ludwig also developed a small empire of savings and loan companies in the American Southwest, which if combined would rank as the nation's ninth largest, with assets of nearly $4 billion. Ludwig also owned a luxury hotel chain, the Princess Hotels.

Planned an Ambitious Project

Ludwig's greatest adventure—and biggest disaster—was Jari Florestale Agropecuria, a massive project on the Jari River, some 48 hours by boat from the Amazon River port of Belem, deep in the Amazon jungle. The project, which ultimately cost him over one billion dollars, was said to be the largest and most costly entrepreneurial effort ever undertaken by one man. The project had its genesis in 1967, when Ludwig paid just $3 million to a group of Brazilian families for some 6,000 square miles of dense rain forest in the country's most remote Amazon region. He then set in motion a bold plan for developing the area to help meet anticipated world shortages of food, lumber, and wood pulp for papermaking.

In vast stretches of virtually unpopulated jungle, Ludwig built a string of airstrips, thousands of miles of roads, a private railway to haul freight, a deep water port, hospitals, schools, and a giant service depot stocked with spare parts and equipment. His original goal was to develop a 3.5 million acre tree plantation in the area, growing the so called gmelina or "super-trees" from Burma, which reach full height for timber purposes in just a fraction of the time of normal trees. He soon found, however, that this was not feasible and had to move into pine and eucalyptus. To mill this lumber, Ludwig built a 60,000 ton pulp mill in Japan which stood 17 stories high and three blocks long and cost $200 million. He floated it 17,000 miles across the Indian and Atlantic oceans and up the Amazon. But Ludwig misjudged the world pulp market. Pulp supplies turned out to be far more plentiful than he had estimated, and then the world-wide recession of the 1970s dealt a heavy blow to the project.

Then too, there were managerial and political problems. Ludwig was always somewhat of a loner and an eccentric. He insisted on making all the important practical decisions himself from his office in New York. He was also temperamental, which resulted in 30 changes in project directors in 14 years. Ludwig's penchant for secrecy ultimately created much public hostility toward the project in Brazil, making it—fairly or unfairly—a veritable symbol of "Yankee imperialism." Such backlash ultimately convinced Ludwig to turn the project over to a Brazilian consortium.

Finally, there was the jungle itself. Like Henry Ford, who attempted to grow rubber in the Amazon, Ludwig found his dreams sabotaged by the merciless climate and physical obstacles. As one American executive recalled: "From the time you arrived till you flew out again you worried about what kind of disease you'd get. You'd be brushing your teeth with Coke. In the guesthouse cockroaches and lizards crawled around. Ludwig showed us the riverside site for the pulp mill. It was nothing but jungle. That he could ever put a modern industrial complex in there boggled our minds." Ludwig brought in giant bulldozers, only to find that they damaged the topsoil. In 1981 he asked the Brazilian government for financial assistance to offset his infrastructure expenses, but was refused. This rejection caused Ludwig to refuse to repay loans given him by the country's National Economic Development Bank. Combined with his failing health, these difficulties put an end to his Jari project in early 1982.

Business success brought Ludwig everything he ever wanted, and he asked for no other recognition. Once, when the emperor of Japan wanted to award him Japan's highest national honor, the Order of the Chrysanthemum, Ludwig refused, asking that it be given to his shipyard manager instead. A secretive, reclusive man, Ludwig wore cheap suits, shoes, and eye glasses bought at bargain prices in department stores. He usually traveled alone, economy class, carrying his own baggage, arriving at tropical airports a few hours before dawn. All of his foreign assets, totaling some $1.5 billion, although run by Ludwig, were owned by his principal heir, his Zurich cancer institute. He retained in his own name some $500 million in U.S. assets. Despite the massive losses of the Jari project, *Forbes* magazine in 1984 estimated Ludwig's worth at $2 billion. However, six years later the magazine reported that the shipping operations of National Bulk Carriers, a New York-based shipping concern that was Ludwig's main corporate vehicle, had significantly diminished. When Ludwig died of heart failure on August 27, 1992, R. Palmer Baker, Jr., Ludwig's executor, estimated the endowment of the cancer institute at about $700 million but did not disclose the amount of Ludwig's own worth.

Further Reading

Ludwig is the subject of a single book-length biography, Jerry Shields, *The Invisible Billionaire: Daniel Ludwig* (1986). Shields reports several questionable practices on Ludwig's path to success, particularly the damage to the ecology of the Amazon basin in the failed jungle project.

Ludwig's plans for the Jari Project are discussed in "One Man's Brazilian Empire," A. Machado, *World Press Review,* February, 1981; and "End of a Billion-Dollar Dream," *Newsweek,* January 25, 1982.

His obituary, by Eric Pace, was in the August 29, 1992 edition of *New York Times.* □

Karl Friedrich Wilhelm Ludwig

The German physiologist Karl Friedrich Wilhelm Ludwig (1816-1895) was one of the leading experimental physiologists of the 19th century and invented a number of important pieces of laboratory equipment.

On Dec. 29, 1816, K. F. W. Ludwig was born at Witzenhausen, Hessen. He was educated at the universities of Erlangen and Marburg and received his doctorate from Marburg in 1839. He was appointed lecturer in physiology at Marburg in 1842 and associate professor of comparative anatomy in 1845. In 1843-1844 Ludwig put forward his theory that urine was formed by a filtration process in the kidneys. Later (1870) Ludwig modified the original theory to give the basis of the modern theory about the formation of urine. While still at Marburg he developed the kymograph, an instrument used to record physiological variables in graphical form. This invention was one of a number which helped him live up to his aim to place "physiology on a chemicophysical foundation, and give it equal rank with physics."

In 1849 Ludwig was appointed to the chair of anatomy and physiology at the University of Zurich. At Zurich he and his pupils studied the formation of lymph, the mechanism of glandular secretion, and the nervous control of blood vessels. In 1855 Ludwig left Zurich to take a chair of physiology and zoology in Vienna. Here he continued his studies of the blood and the way in which the nervous system controlled its circulation. At Vienna he also invented the mercurial blood-gas pump for separating gases from the blood.

In 1865 Ludwig accepted a chair in physiology at the University of Leipzig. Here he was the foundation director of the Institute of Physiology, which under his direction became a renowned graduate school that attracted students from many countries. Ludwig investigated capillary blood pressure, introduced techniques to keep individual organs "alive" outside the body, and invented the stromuhr, which measured the flow of blood in a vessel.

It was Ludwig's custom to allow his students to publish under their own names work to which he had made substantial contributions. Frequently he not only designed the experimental procedure but also did much of the laboratory work and wrote the final draft of the paper. Ludwig's contributions to science were acknowledged when he was elected a foreign member of the Royal Society in 1875 and when he was awarded the society's Copley Medal in 1884. He died in Leipzig on April 23, 1895.

Further Reading

There is no full-scale biography of Ludwig readily available in English. A full account of much of his work is in Alfred P. Fishman and Dickinson Richards, eds., *Circulation of the Blood: Men and Ideas* (1964), which can be supplemented with Fielding H. Garrison, *An Introduction to the History of Medicine* (1913; 4th ed. 1929). □

Frederick John Dealtry Lugard

Frederick John Dealtry Lugard, 1st Baron Lugard (1858-1945), was a British imperialist and colonial administrator in Africa. He made significant contributions to the theory and practice of the British colonial policy of indirect rule.

Frederick Lugard was born on Jan. 22, 1858, of missionary parents in India. He attended the Royal Military College, Sandhurst, England. He obtained a commission in 1878 and returned to India, where he participated in the Afghan War of 1879-1880. In 1885 he accompanied the Indian contingent to the Sudan, joining the Suakin campaign to relieve Khartoum; in 1886 he joined military operations in Burma.

Stationed in East Africa

In 1887 Lugard returned to England, but unable to resume his commission for medical reasons and despairing over an unhappy love affair, he set out for the east coast of Africa. In 1888 he arrived in Mozambique, where he entered the employ of the African Lakes Company, for whom he commanded a mission to Lake Nyasa to relieve a trading station besieged by Arab slave traders.

In 1890 he went to Mombasa, where he was employed by the Imperial British East Africa Company to open a trade route to Buganda. Lugard remained in the interior of East Africa for 2 years, where, through a combination of diplomatic skill and military force, he established the suzerainty of the company over the region of present-day Uganda. During this time the company decided to withdraw from Buganda, a decision Lugard chose to ignore. He returned to England and launched a political campaign designed to convince the government to annex Uganda. In England, Lugard was criticized for his activities in Buganda, particularly for his treatment of French missionaries. Therefore, in defense of himself and in advocacy of his imperial vision, he published his first book, *The Rise of Our East African Empire* (1893), an autobiographical account of his activities in Nyasaland and Uganda.

Creation of Nigeria

In 1894 Lugard visited West Africa for the first time. Employed by the Royal Niger Company, he led an expedition to forestall a French effort to establish a position on the lower Niger River. After a brief tour to Bechuanaland for the British West Charterland Company, he returned to the Niger in 1897 as commissioner for the hinterland of Nigeria and commander of the West African Frontier Force, a military contingent designed to aid the Royal Niger Company in defending its territorial claims.

When the charter of the Royal Niger Company was revoked in 1900, the British government assumed administrative responsibility for former territories of the company, and Lugard became high commissioner for Northern Nigeria. At that time, Northern Nigeria existed in name only, since the company had never extended any form of administration beyond the banks of the Niger. During his tenure Lugard laid the foundations of British rule in the North, first establishing British sovereignty by conquest of the Moslem states which had resisted alien domination and then by developing the forms of administration whereby the British would rule.

In 1906 Lugard resigned as high commissioner and the following year accepted an appointment as governor of Hong Kong, where he remained until 1911. Then, in 1912, he returned to Nigeria as governor of both the Northern and Southern protectorates, charged with amalgamating the two territories into a single unit.

Lugard's plans for amalgamation provided for the extension into the Southern Protectorate of the policy of indirect rule which he had developed in the North. Indirect rule was designed to allow for the administration of colonized peoples through the agency of indigenous institutions. Al-though indirect rule was not uniformly effective among peoples of very diverse traditional institutions, Lugard pushed hard for its adoption and as a guide published his *Political Memoranda*, earlier directives he had circulated in establishing the Northern administration. By 1919, when Lugard retired as governor general, Nigeria had been set well on its way to becoming a unified territory administratively.

Upon his return to England, Lugard set to work on his second book, *The Dual Mandate in British Tropical Africa* (1922). In this book he set out in detail his conceptions of indirect rule and expressed his belief that Britain as an imperial power was responsible for aiding in the social, political, and economic development of its African dependencies. The book was hailed as an authoritative statement of British policy and became a guide to the administration of British dependencies.

Lugard never resumed his service abroad but remained an active public figure until his death in 1945. He was appointed to the Privy Council in 1920 and was a member of the Permanent Mandates Commission of the League of Nations from 1922 to 1936; he also served on several other national and international commissions dealing with Africa. In 1928 he was raised to the peerage. His wife, the former Flora Shaw, was the author of *A Tropical Dependency*, a history of Nigeria.

Further Reading

Margery Perham edited *The Diaries of Lord Lugard* (4 vols., 1959-1963), which offers an intimate view of Lugard's activities. Perham is also author of an authoritative biography, *Lugard* (2 vols., 1956-1960). I. F. Nicolson, *The Administration of Nigeria, 1900-1960: Men, Methods, and Myths* (1970), is an unfavorable description of Lugard's role in Nigeria. □

Mabel Dodge Luhan

Mabel Dodge Luhan (1879-1962), American writer, salon hostess, patron saint, and inspiration to an assortment of talented artists, writers, and political radicals in the early decades of the 20th century, was a leading symbol of the "New Woman."

M abel Dodge Luhan was born on February 26, 1879, in Buffalo, New York, to Charles and Sara (Cook) Ganson. The Gansons were an affluent family living on inherited wealth. Both of Mabel's grandfathers had made fortunes in banking. Her father Charles was trained as a lawyer, but his weak, nervous disposition, coupled with violent and unpredictable temper tantrums, made him unfit for this or any other profession. When he was not shouting at his wife in jealous "fits," he spent hours alone in his study doing absolutely nothing at all. He lavished affection on his dogs but had no interest in his only daughter. Mabel knew he did not love her. "To him," she recalled, "I was something that made a noise sometimes in the house and had to be told to get out of the way." Her mother Sara was strong and decisive where her father was weak, but Sara was a cold woman, unfeeling and entirely self-centered. Bored with the endless routine of Victorian social life and finding few outlets for her abundant energy, Sara became indifferent to both her husband and child. Mabel could not remember her mother ever giving her a kiss or an affectionate look. In her nursery, Mabel kissed the Mother Goose figures on the walls.

Mabel's need for emotional and intellectual sustenance was not met by her conventional education at Saint Margaret's School for Girls, where the class motto was "They also serve who only stand and wait," or at Miss Graham's School in New York City, or at the fancy finishing school she attended in Chevy Chase, Maryland.

Mabel Ganson was educated to be a charming and decorative wife, which she became in 1900 at the age of 21. Her husband, Karl Evans, was a member of her social set whose chief attraction for Mabel was that he was engaged to another woman. Emotionally deprived as a child, she would continue to believe that she had a right to "steal" love whenever the opportunity presented itself.

In 1903, shortly after the birth of their son, Karl Evans died in a hunting accident. Mabel, who had as much interest in her child as her parents had had in her, suffered a nervous breakdown. Her family sent her to Europe in 1904 to recover. This was the first of three journeys—the second would be to Greenwich Village and the third to Taos, New Mexico—which marked her search for both a personal identity and a place where she could feel "at home."

On her way to Paris Mabel met "a nice young man in tweeds"—Edwin Dodge, a wealthy architectural student from Boston. Dodge became her second husband, and together they moved to Florence in 1905. There, depressed and trapped in another loveless marriage, Mabel decided to devote herself to the love of art for its own sake. She and Dodge purchased a magnificent Medician estate which they named Villa Curonia, and for the next eight years Mabel spent enormous amounts of money, energy, and creative intelligence transforming her surroundings and herself into works of Renaissance art.

Filling her home with objets d'art and artists, Mabel began her apprenticeship as a salon hostess in Florence. She entertained lavishly, and at her table sat the rich, the famous, the colorful, and the noteworthy of the international set: French novelist André Gide, actress Eleanor Duse, painter Jacques-Emile Blanche, Gertrude and Leo Stein, Lord and Lady Acton, and an Indian swami, to name only a few. Mabel, dressed in Renaissance costume, became celebrated for her role as Muse. Unwilling or unable to create in her own right, she wanted at least to serve as the inspiration for genius.

Bored with her life in Florence by 1912 and greatly influenced by the Gertrude and Leo Stein's philosophy that the individual could overcome the ill effects of both heredity and environment and create herself anew, Mabel returned to New York. Separated from her husband, Mabel moved to an apartment in Greenwich Village, the heartland

of America's avant-garde. There, at 23 Fifth Avenue, she launched the most successful salon in American history. For the next three years Mabel entertained the "movers and shakers" of pre-war America, men and women who were sweeping in their condemnation of bourgeois values and industrial capitalism. Gathered together at one of Mabel's "Wednesday evenings" one might find artists, philosophers, writers, reformers, and radicals of all stripes: Margaret Sanger, Walter Lippmann, Lincoln Steffens, Emma Goldman, "Big Bill" Haywood, and Hutchins Hapgood. Mabel was determined to make herself the mistress of the spirit of her age by embracing its most idealistic and committed men and women.

Mabel Dodge gave generously of her time and money to support the various causes she believed would liberate Americans from the shackles of their Victorian past. She helped to sponsor the watershed Armory show which introduced postimpressionist art to a largely unfamiliar American audience; contributed to *The Masses,* the leading left-wing literary and political journal of her day; wrote a syndicated newspaper column popularizing Freudian psychology; and supported a host of organizations, among them the Women's Peace Party, the Heterodoxy Club, the Women's Birth Control League, and the Twilight Sleep Association.

Heralded by her friends and the public as the "New Woman," Mabel experimented with free love, having several unsatisfactory affairs, the most famous of which was with radical journalist John Reed. Mabel, who was never able to rid herself of the belief that women could only achieve through men, realized the tremendous gap that existed between the radical, emancipated image she projected and the reality that she was intellectually and emotionally dependent on men.

In 1916 Mabel and her third husband, artist and sculptor Maurice Sterne, moved to Taos, New Mexico. There she finally found the "cosmos" she had been searching for all her life. In the 600-year-old Pueblo culture she saw a model of permanence and stability; a total integration of personality achieved through the organic connection of work, play, community, and environment. Soon she fell in love with Tony Luhan, a fullblooded Pueblo Indian. Divorcing Sterne and marrying Luhan, her fourth and final husband, Mabel viewed their alliance as a bridge between Anglo and Native American cultures.

For the rest of her life Mabel took a leading role in calling "great souls" to Taos to help her create "a city upon a hill." The American Southwest was destined, she believed, to serve as a source of social and psychic renewal for the dying, decadent, and disillusioned postwar white civilization. Among the "great souls" she called to Taos to help her spread her gospel of American regeneration were D. H. Lawrence, Robinson Jeffers, Georgia O'Keeffe, Willa Cather, John Collier, Thomas Wolfe, Andrew Dasburg, Edna Ferber, Leopold Stowkowski, and Mary Austin.

In the 1920s Mabel wrote her four-volume memoirs: *Background, European Experiences, Movers and Shakers,* and *Edge of Taos Desert.* She wrote numerous articles on behalf of the integrity of Native American culture, health, and the protection of tribal lands. She died in Taos of a heart attack on August 13, 1962. Although she never fulfilled her messianic vision for the American Southwest, she herself remained, as one reporter described her in the early 1920s, "the most peculiar common denominator that society, literature, art, and radical revolutionaries ever found in New York and Europe." In attempting to alter the direction of American civilization, she captured the imaginations of her generation's most talented writers, artists, and thinkers, and profoundly influenced their understanding of modern America.

Further Reading

There are three biographies, Winifred L. Frazer's *Mabel Dodge Luhan*, Emily Hahn's *Mabel* and Lois Palken Rudnick's *Mabel Dodge Luhan: New Woman, New Worlds*. For comments on her character and influence see: Christopher Lasch, *The New Radicalism in America* (1965); Hutchins Hapgood, *A Victorian in the Modern World* (1939); *The Autobiography of Lincoln Steffens*, vol. II (1931); Robert Crunden, *From Self to Society, 1919-1941* (1972); Joseph Foster, *D. H. Lawrence in Taos* (1972); Maurice Sterne, *Shadow and Light* (1952); and Claire Morrill, *A Taos Mosaic* (1973).

Additional Sources

Frazer, Winifred L., *Mabel Dodge Luhan,* Boston: Twayne, 1984.

Hahn, Emily, *Mabel: a biography of Mabel Dodge Luhan,* Boston: Houghton Mifflin, 1977.

Luhan, Mabel Dodge, *Movers and shakers,* Albuquerque: University of New Mexico Press, 1985, 1936.

Rudnick, Lois Palken, *Mabel Dodge Luhan: new woman, new worlds,* Albuquerque: University of New Mexico Press, 1984.

□

Niklas Luhmann

A prominent German sociologist, Niklas Luhmann (born 1927) developed a general sociological systems theory, which he applied to a wide range of problems.

Niklas Luhmann was born on December 8, 1927, in Lüneburg, Germany. He studied law at the University of Freiburg/Breisgau in the years 1946-1949 and pursued further legal studies in preparation for the German state exam in 1953. He entered the civil service in 1954 and from 1956 to 1962 worked in the ministry of culture of the state of Lower Saxony, overseeing educational reform. He spent 1960-1961 on leave at Harvard University, studying sociology and administrative science. The teaching of the famous Harvard sociologist Talcott Parsons would prove to be an especially important influence on Luhmann's later work.

After returning to Germany, Luhmann decided to turn to social science and an academic career. He held research and teaching positions at institutions in Speyer and Dortmund from 1962 until 1968. Having started to publish at a rapid pace in the early 1960s—mostly on topics in the sociology of organizations and of law—he received the doctorate and the so-called "habilitation" (a standard postdoctoral certificate) in sociology from the University of Münster in 1966. In 1968 he became professor of sociology at the University of Bielefeld, a position he held thereafter, with periodic interludes as a visiting professor at several institutions in Germany and the United States.

Holder of a number of honorary degrees, Luhmann received the prestigious Hegel Prize of the City of Stuttgart in 1988. Articles in German newspapers and numerous speaking engagements at professional meetings enabled him to broaden his audience. Although primarily occupied with his own research after 1968, he served as an occasional political adviser on matters of public policy in Germany.

Largely working independently, Luhmann became one of the most prolific and original sociological theorists in the world. His works, which for the most part were written in a relatively dense and scholarly style, drew on disciplines ranging from philosophy to linguistics to information science. They covered a wide spectrum of subjects, including law and love, politics and religion, education and the environment. Based as they were on a thorough familiarity with the tradition of Western thought, Luhmann's writings were often considered unusually complex and abstract by conventional sociological standards. Yet this complexity and abstractness can be reduced considering the basic themes and methods which ran through Luhmann's work and gave it systematic coherence. The proper starting point was the central idea of a "system," which referred to any entity selecting certain possibilities available in its environment, thus becoming less complex and more stable than the environment. This term can be applied to any number of things, ranging from large organizations to brief conversations. Luhmann's general question, then, was: What makes different systems work? How can they maintain themselves and relate to other systems?

Luhmann was especially interested in systems which operate on the basis of "meaning," in particular, systems of human communication. He regarded society not as a network of individuals united by shared beliefs, but rather as the totality of all communications. But in modern societies many kinds of communication were highly "differentiated," which meant essentially they operated independently according to the specific functions they served. The bulk of Luhmann's work consisted of systematic analyses of these kinds of communication (especially those organized in the form of full-fledged institutions, such as education and law) using a set of basic conceptual tools he developed beginning in the 1960s. Economic communication by means of money (rather than exchange in kind) was a case in point; it made possible interaction between buyers and sellers and laid the foundation for a whole economic system with its own specifically economic functions.

Like money, trust also served as a specific medium in modern societies, for example in interaction between professionals and laypersons: on some issues we had to accept the judgment of competent experts without checking its validity. Without some such trust, many social relationships would break down very quickly. Even love was now a specialized kind of communication, made possible by the passion exchanged between individuals who were supposed to treat each other as lovers without regard to their other social roles.

Like many social theorists before him, Luhmann analyzed the implications of the transition from traditional to modern society. In older, stratified societies the various functions that had to be performed were arranged in a hierarchy, from the aristocracy down to the peasantry. By contrast, modern societies have separated various social tasks in a "horizontal" fashion, a pattern Luhmann called functional differentiation. This had many advantages; for example, institutions handled more complex problems and individuals generally enjoyed greater opportunities. But it also raised new problems. Institutions (such as religious ones) that in the past played a broad role must now redefine and limit that role. Also, since all institutions now focused on their own function and performance, certain societal problems may be neglected because everyone can claim it was "none of their business"; according to Luhmann, this was one source of the current environmental crisis.

Although Luhmann suggested various applications of his ideas, he did not think sociological theory should assume a political role. He concentrated on developing a deliberately open-ended way of analyzing the world rather than formulating formal models and easily testable propositions. While his work often seems highly technical, it was usually based on simple empirical observations and existing historical materials that Luhmann "translated" into his own abstract theoretical language. Only by means of abstraction, he suggested, could social scientists grasp the complexity of modern society and reduce that complexity at the same time.

The (translated) titles of Luhmann's main publications in German convey the focus and range of his work: *Functions and Consequences of Formal Organization* (1964), *Fundamental Rights as an Institution: A Contribution to Political Sociology* (1965), *The Goal Concept and System Rationality: On the Function of Goals in Social Systems* (1968), *Theory of Society or Social Technology* (1971; a famous debate with the German social theorist Jürgen Habermas), *Societal Structure and Semantics* (3 volumes; 1980, 1981, 1989); *Social Systems: Outline of a General Theory* (1984; perhaps Luhmann's theoretical masterpiece, in which he developed the concept of "autopoietic" or self-producing systems, to be published in English by Stanford University Press), and four volumes of essays under the general title *Sociological Enlightenment*.

To his credit, Luhmann's biography listed 377 works he had written; the last as late as 1996; twelve of which have been translated into English. He and his work was cited in The Graduate Journal of the Program in Comparative Literature, Emory University, Atlanta, Georgia as late as April 1997. The article includes an interview with his friend and colleague, Friedrich A. Kittler.

Luhmann married Ursula von Walter in 1960; she died in 1977. They had two sons and one daughter. He has been a Professor of Sociololgy, University of Bielefeld since 1968.

Further Reading

Some of Luhmann's key works are now available in English translation: *Trust and Power* (1979), the essay on trust is a good entry point into Luhmann's work; *The Differentiation of Society* (1982), an excellent collection of essays with a good introduction; *Religious Dogmatics and the Evolution of Societies* (1984), contains Luhmann's main ideas on religion and a good introduction; *A Sociological Theory of Law* (1985), an extended treatment of one field in Luhmannian terms; *Love as Passion* (1986), an intriguing and readable historical and sociological study of love; *Ecological Communication* (1989), an application of systems theory to environmental problems; *Political Theory in the Welfare State* (1990), and *Essays on Self-Reference* (1990). Other translated works included *Soziologie des Risikos. English Risk: A Sociological Theory* (1993) and *Soziale System, English Social Systems* (1995). □

Lu Hsün

Lu Hsün (1881-1936) was the pen name of Chou Shu-jen, a Chinese author and social critic. Best known for his pioneering short stories in the modern style and his prolific output as a polemic and personal essayist, he was a prominent man of letters and cultural leader.

Modern Chinese literature began with the literary revolution of 1917, initiated by Hu Shih and his friends. It aimed to replace the classical styles of poetry and prose with the vernacular form of writing (*pai-hua*). The new literature became a reality with the so-called May Fourth movement of 1919, when students held nationwide demonstrations against their government's feeble stand at the Paris Peace Conference in response to their newly awakened national consciousness. Lu Hsün achieved instant fame for his articulation of this new consciousness in a disciplined vernacular prose which has remained unmatched for its verve and trenchancy. He was also noted for his scholarship, especially in the field of Chinese fiction, for his voluminous translations of European and Japanese works, and for his occasional poetry in the classical style.

Lu Hsün was born in Shaohing, Chekiang Province, the eldest son of an impoverished family which had nevertheless retained the tradition of learning. Like so many youths of the declining Ch'ing dynasty, he took to practical studies to strengthen his nation despite his earlier training in, and personal liking for, literature. In 1902 he sailed for Japan on a government scholarship after spending some 5 years in Nanking as a student in the Kiangnan Naval Academy and the School of Railways and Mines.

In 1904, having completed 2 years of language study in Tokyo, Lu Hsün entered the Sendai Provincial Medical School, believing that medicine would enable his countrymen to strengthen themselves. Early in 1906, however, he came to the conclusion that their spiritual health was more vital than their physical health and that only with his pen could he combat their apathy and backwardness. All along, of course, he had been reading Western literature through Japanese and German translations: Charles Darwin, Friedrich Nietzsche, and such Russian writers as Nikolai Gogol, Anton Chekhov, and Leonid Andreyev would remain influential throughout his writing career.

Early Literary Ventures

After an abortive attempt to launch a magazine, Lu Hsün wrote a series of didactic essays in the classical style subsequently collected in the volume called *Fen* (*Tomb*). Chou Tso-jen, his younger brother also studying in Japan on a government scholarship, was then his literary collaborator; they translated two volumes of European short stories, mainly by Russian authors.

Lu returned to China in 1909 and taught science in middle schools. In 1912, following the establishment of the republic, he accepted a post in the ministry of education and moved to Peking, where he engaged in antiquarian research in a state of apparent discouragement. But his literary ambition revived with the Literary Revolution. In May 1918 his story *K'uang-jen jih-chi* ("A Madman's Diary") appeared in the leading intellectual journal of the time, *Hsin Ch'ing-nien* (The New Youth). It was a sensation not only because it was the first Chinese story in the Western manner but because it indicated the Chinese tradition as one of inhumane cannibalism, despite its supposed respect for the Confucian virtues.

The brilliance of this story was sustained by many of Lu Hsün's stories written during the period 1919-1926, collected in two volumes entitled *Na-han* (*A Call to Arms*) and *P'ang-huang* (*Hesitation*). This period also marked the flowering of the author's genius in other forms: a book of somber prose poetry called *Yeh-ts'ao* (*Wild Grass*); a volume of childhood reminiscences, *Chao-hua hsi-shih* (*Morning Flowers Picked in Evening*); and several essay collections containing his random thoughts on all aspects of the Chinese psyche and the Chinese scene.

Short Stories

Though Lu Hsün was claimed by the Communists as their hero, the stories in his first two collections are remarkably free of the cant of revolutionary optimism in their cautious affirmation of a kind of hope rooted in a profound despair over China's inability to change toward a better future. Most of these stories are about Shaohing and its rural environs, about the people Lu Hsün remembered from his childhood and his subsequent visits there. The most personal among the best stories is *Kuhsiang* ("My Old Home"), which records the author's awareness of the pointed contrast between the robust peasant companion of his childhood and what he subsequently becomes—a careworn family man given to superstition.

A more tragic story, *Chu-fu* ("The New Year's Sacrifice"), traces the fate of a peasant woman in a feudalistic setting which denies her even the illusion of happiness in an after world. *Ah Q cheng-chuan* ("The True Story of Ah Q"), the longest and most celebrated of the author's stories, presents in its hero a ubiquitous national type who lives in a slaphappy world of self-deception by pretending to have achieved "spiritual victory" when under manifest defeat. Its tragic and satiric thesis notwithstanding, the story is told with a great deal of humor. The most urbanely satiric of Lu Hsün's stories is *Fei-tsao* ("Soap"), which makes fun of the pretended righteousness of a Confucian gentleman.

Career after 1926

Along with many other intellectuals, Lu Hsün left Peking (and his professorship at National Peking University) when the city became a stronghold of reaction under warlord rule. He served briefly in universities in Amoy and Canton and eventually settled in Shanghai, where he stayed until he died of tuberculosis and various other illnesses in October 1936, at the age of 55. A staunch individualist, he had come under attack from the Communist writers soon after his escape from Peking. After a series of spirited debates with them, Lu Hsün finally joined the Communist cause and became the nominal leader of the League of Left-wing Writers when it was formed in 1930. An idol of the youth, he was now mainly a miscellaneous essayist, dissipating his creative energy in an endless series of polemics. He also translated a great deal and refrained from writing fiction except for a volume of satiric fables, *Ku-shih hsin-pien* (*Old Legends Retold*), which sadly marked the decline of his talent.

Judging from his letters, Lu Hsün was definitely unhappy during the middle 1930s despite the constant care provided by his second wife, Hsü Kuang-p'ing: his health had deteriorated, and he was finally facing an enemy, the Communist cultural leadership in Shanghai, that he could not openly attack without betraying his basic pessimism and his superficial allegiance to the Communist cause. He was irked by that leadership, which had formulated policies without consulting him, and he also found these new policies incomprehensible. But he could no longer contain his anger following the dissolution of the League of Left-wing Writers, and shortly before his death he published an open letter exposing the duplicity of that leadership.

In his later life Lu Hsün wore a traditional Chinese gown, cropped hair, and a thick mustache. With all his irritability and irascibility, he was nevertheless extremely kind to young writers. Many of his disciples and protégés have written lovingly of his kindness and personal integrity.

Further Reading

An official translation sponsored by the Foreign Languages Press of Peking is *Selected Works of Lu Hsün*, translated by Yang Hsien-yi and Gladys Yang (4 vols., 1956-1960). Published by the same press is *Selected Stories of Lu Hsün*, by the same translators (1960; 2d ed. 1963). See also *Ah Q and Others: Selected Stories of Lusin*, translated by Chi-chen Wang (1941). Huang Sungk'ang, *Lu Hsün and the New Culture Movement of Modern China* (1957), though undistinguished, remains the only monographic study of Lu Hsün in English. The best discussions of him are in C.T. Hsia, *A History of Modern Chinese Fiction, 1917-1957* (1961), and Tsi-an Hsia, *The Gate of Darkness: Studies on the Leftist Literary Movement in China* (1968).

Additional Sources

Lyell, William A., *Lu Hsün's vision of reality,* Berkeley: University of California Press, 1976.

Wang, Shih-ching, *Lu Hsün, a biography,* Beijing: Foreign Languages Press: Distributed by China International Book Trading Corp., 1984. ☐

Gyorgy Lukács

The Hungarian literary critic and philosopher Gyorgy Lukács (1885-1971) was one of the foremost Marxist literary critics and theorists. His influence on criticism has been considerable in both Western and Eastern Europe.

Gyorgy Lukács was born April 13, 1885, in Budapest, into a wealthy, intellectual, Jewish banking family. He was a brilliant student and was given a cosmopolitan education in Hungary and Germany. Until 1917 he devoted himself to art and esthetics and was not interested in politics. Writing primarily in German, he achieved his first fame as a literary critic with *The Soul and the Forms* (Hungarian, 1910; German, 1911) and *The Theory of the Novel* (1916 as an article; 1920 as a book), a study of the spiritual aspects of the novel. During World War I he taught in a German university.

Because of the shock of the war and the impressions made on him by the Russian Revolution, Lukács completed a move from Neo-Kantianism through Hegelianism to Marxism and joined the Hungarian Communist party. Despite the party's often official displeasure with his intellectual work, he remained faithful to it. In 1919 he served as deputy commissar of culture in the revolutionary Béla Kun Communist government in Hungary. After the government was overthrown, he had to emigrate to Vienna and for about a decade participated actively in party affairs and disputes.

In 1923 he wrote *History and Class Consciousness.* This complex, theoretical, sociological work explored important but, until then, little-emphasized aspects of Marx's work: the strong connection with Hegel, the importance of the dialectic, and the concept of alienation. He also examined the nature of the working class's own self-consciousness. Lukács argued that genuine Marxism was not a body of rigid economic truths but a method of analysis which could enable the revolution to be created. His interpretation of Marxism influenced many European intellectuals but was attacked as dangerously revisionist by Soviet dogmatists, and his career in party politics was over by the late 1920s.

With the danger of fascism growing in Europe, Lukács emigrated to the Soviet Union in 1933. He worked as a literary editor and critic, emphasizing the relationship between a work of art and its sociohistorical period. Several times he publicly repudiated all his previous work and occasionally shifted his views to conform to the official party line and paid lip service to official Soviet socialist realism, but he later regarded this as a tactical necessity to survive physically in Stalin's Russia and still get his ideas heard. Despite occasional Marxist-Leninist dogmatisms, he wrote perceptive criticism and concentrated on realistic 19th-century literature. Whether through personal predilection or the exigencies of the Communist party line, he became cold to almost the entire modernist movement in literature.

Returning to Hungary in 1945, Lukács was active in cultural affairs and as a professor of esthetics and cultural philosophy, but he was again stigmatized for his heterodox views. Deeply affected by Nikita Khrushchev's revelations of Stalin's crimes, he spoke out publicly against Stalinist dogmatism in Hungary, and in 1956, joined the short-lived Imré Nagy government. After the Soviet invasion of Hungary, he was exiled to Romania, allowed to return in 1957, and forced to retire and go into seclusion. However, after 1965 he was again publicly honored in Hungary. Lukács died on June 4, 1971, in Budapest.

Further Reading

For a fairly complete bibliography of Lukács's work in Western European languages see G. H. R. Parkinson, ed., *Georg Lukács: The Man, His Work and His Ideas* (1970), which also has extensive biographical material. George Lichtheim, *George Lukács* (1970), is a study of Lukács's ideas; Lichtheim's *The Concept of Ideology and Other Essays* (1967) contains a generally favorable discussion of Lukács's early career and considers that his later career was an intellectual disaster. Victor Zitta, *Georg Lukács's Marxism: Alienation,*

Dialectics, Revolution; A Study in Utopia and Ideology (1964), is a detailed study of Lukács and his thought up to the 1920s. An interesting critique of Lukács is in Susan Sontag, *Against Interpretation, and Other Essays* (1966).

Additional Sources

Lukács, Gyorgy, *Record of a life: an autobiographical sketch,* London: Verso, 1983.

Kadarkay, Arpad, *Gyorgy Lukács: life, thought, and politics,* Cambridge, Mass., USA: B. Blackwell, 1991.

Congdon, Lee, *The young Lukács,* Chapel Hill: University of North Carolina Press, 1983. □

St. Luke

St. Luke (active 50 A.D.) was one of the four Evangelists. Since the 2nd century he has been regarded as the author of the Third Gospel and its sequel, the Acts of the Apostles.

L uke's name—of Latin origin—indicates that he apparently was not of Jewish derivation. The earliest surviving testimony describes him as a Syrian from Antioch. His abundant acquaintance with the Antiochean Church, as well as his knowledge of literary Greek, both illustrated in his writings, supports this testimony. Tradition and one text of St. Paul's (Colossians 4:14) say that Luke was a trained physician. His Gospel exhibits a Greek literary style absent from the other Gospels and documents of the New Testament. Luke, apparently, was a well-educated man. His Greek was as polished as that of such classical writers as Xenophon.

Luke's association with the disciples of Jesus probably began after Christ's death, in the early 30s of the 1st century. His Gospel reveals a special acquaintance with Mary, the mother of Jesus, and tradition describes him as a friend and companion of Paul and of Mark. When Paul began his second missionary journey, about 49 A.D., Luke became a member of the party, joining Paul at the town of Troas and traveling to Macedonia with him (Acts 16: 11-12). Luke then probably remained at Philippi, rejoining Paul when he had finished his third missionary journey and was returning to Jerusalem (Acts 20:5, 26:18). The Acts further say that Luke accompanied Paul when Paul was taken as a prisoner to Rome to be judged by Caesar (Acts 27:1, 28:26). The contents of Paul's letters to Philemon (24) and Timothy (II, 4:11) reveal that Luke probably stayed with Paul until Paul's death. A document called the Anti-Marcionite Prologue, which dates from the end of the 2nd century, says that Luke died unmarried in Boeotia or Bithynia at the age of 84 toward the end of the 1st century.

Luke's authorship of the Third Gospel has not been seriously disputed. Nor has the attribution of the Acts of the Apostles to him been questioned. Luke's Gospel is clearly related to the Gospels of Mark and Matthew both in content and in structure; all three drew on a common source. Luke, however, used a second source unknown to either Matthew or Mark. Scholars have surmised that this source may have been Mary, the mother of Jesus, and her closest friends, all of whom knew Jesus intimately.

The story of Jesus is presented by Luke within a tripartite view of human history. According to his view, the lifetime of Jesus occupied the central position, being preceded by the time of the Law and the Prophets and being followed by the time of the Christian Church. Scholars have assigned the composition of Luke's Gospel to between 70 and 80. Both internal and external evidence indicates that it was composed outside Palestine and intended for use by non-Jews.

Further Reading

Works dealing with Luke include Henry Joel Cadbury, *The Style and Literary Method of Luke* (1919-1920); Vincent Taylor, *Behind the Third Gospel* (1926); Alfred R. C. Leaney, *A Commentary on the Gospel According to St. Luke* (1958); and Hans Conzelmann, *The Theology of St. Luke* (1960). □

George Benjamin Luks

American painter George Benjamin Luks (1867-1933) was a pioneer realist, a member of "The Eight," and a vigorous opponent of academic and conservative standards in subject matter.

George Luks was born in Williamsport, Pa., on Aug. 13, 1867. About 1884 he entered the Pennsylvania Academy of Fine Arts but soon made his way to Europe, where he remained for several years. His chronology and many details of his life remain obscure because of the extravagant claims he made about exploits which seem to have been wholly fictitious. At Düsseldorf he acquired a taste for somber colors. He may have worked in London and Paris as well. He admired Rembrandt and Frans Hals.

On his return to Philadelphia in the early 1890s, Luks supported himself precariously by all kinds of commercial jobs—by painting signs, circus and band wagons, campaign portraits, and houses and floors. Frequent references to activities as a professional prizefighter (under a variety of picturesque names) do not seem to be founded on fact. Like Glackens, Sloan, and Shinn, he was employed as a newspaper artist, and he was sent by the *Bulletin* to cover the Spanish-American War in 1895. His illustrations were lively and exciting but apparently largely imaginary, as was the story that he had been captured, sentenced to death, and deported. He returned, penniless, to New York, where he was employed by the *World*. He was one of the earliest comic strip artists and continued R. F. Outcault's "The Yellow Kid," created in 1895, when Outcault moved to another paper. For 15 years most of his work was in black and white; it was only in 1898 that Luks started painting. He was married three times.

Luks was fascinated with the characters and environment of the Lower East Side and consciously attempted to portray these with the explicitness and vitality of Hals. Beggars, drunks, actors, street urchins, prizefighters, the whole range of urban activity, are presented with sharp observation and gusto. Street scenes and landscapes are rarer subjects.

The rejection of one of Luks's paintings from the 1907 exhibition of the National Academy of Design was one of the causes for the formation and exhibition of "The Eight" in 1908. Luks's work in this show had a kind of raw strength and even brutality which offended academic patrons and critics but brought him into attention. From this time on his work was increasingly exhibited, received a number of prizes, and was acquired by the more daring contemporary collectors. For a time, he taught at the Art Students League.

Luks was a radical only in subject matter, not in style or technique. He was involved in the formation of the 1913 Armory Show, in which he was well represented. However, he was unable to understand or accept the genuinely radical European art, which was shown in America for the first time, and resigned from the society which had formed the show.

Luks, always lusty and belligerent, was apparently killed as the result of a tavern fight on Oct. 29, 1933, dying in New York on the streets which he had immortalized on many canvasses.

Further Reading

There is no comprehensive study of Luks. Elisabeth Luther Cary, *George Luks* (1931), is a brief but useful picture book. There are interesting personal sidelights in Bennard P. Perlman, *The Immortal Eight: American Painting from Eakins to the Armory Shows 1870-1913* (1962). □

Raymond Lull

A Spanish theologian, poet, and missionary to the Arabs, Raymond Lull (C. 1232-1316) was one of the foremost apologists for the Christian faith in his time.

Raymond Lull was born at Palma in Majorca. Through family connections and his own ability he began a career as a courtier, first at the court of King James I of Aragon and then at the court of King James II of Majorca. Lull's love of poetry seems to date from this period, when he came under the influence of the troubadour tradition. In 1263 he experienced a religious conversion. He left his wife (whom he had married in 1256), and began the study of Arabic and philosophy with the intention of helping to convert Moslems to Christianity and fighting Averroistic tendencies in Western philosophy.

Lull's study of philosophy and his religious experience culminated in a vision which he had on Mt. Randa in 1272. In that vision he saw a system for the reduction of all knowledge to a series of basic principles associated with the nature of God. Beginning in 1274, he described his system in a series of works, many of which bear the title *The Art*. He stressed that certain principles of philosophy and theology (which for Lull could never contradict each other) are self-evident and common to all sciences. By a combination of these principles (represented by symbols or numbers) one could be led to the principles of every science and even to the discovery of new truths. For Lull, this method, especially as it used symbols representative of these basic principles in various combinations to express the basic truths, was an aid for exposition and explanation or a device to aid the memory. It did not constitute a means of deducing the universal truths according to algebraic signs, as it did later for Gottfried Wilhelm von Leibniz.

In 1276 Lull founded the College of Miramar in Majorca, which trained men in the study of Arabic and prepared missionaries for service in Islamic lands. He made repeated missionary trips to these lands and also continued writing. Altogether, he wrote some 150 or 200 works in Latin, Arabic, and Catalan on such diverse subjects as theology, philosophy, logic, and poetry. Most of them were apologies for the faith and indicate not only his primary desire to convert the infidel but also his attempt to make philosophy subordinate to theology in order to obtain that goal. The Augustinian elements in his thought are quite strong: his rejection of the concept of creation from eternity and his adoption of the ideas of the universal hylomorphic composition of all creatures, the plurality of substantial forms in man, and the primacy of the will over the intellect.

Lull's reputation was so great that he was allowed to teach his system at the University of Paris from 1287 to 1289

Raymond Lull (far left)

without holding a degree in theology. In Paris again, from 1297 to 1299, he lectured against the adoption of pagan concepts by Christian thinkers and, in particular, the total separation of philosophy and theology. In 1298 he wrote a book on the errors of Boethius of Dacia and Siger of Brabant, two of the leading Latin Averroists at Paris, and refuted 219 propositions that had been condemned in Paris in 1277.

After missionary activity in Armenia (1302) and Africa (1306), Lull returned to Paris in 1309 and for another 2 years continued his attack on the Latin Averroists, this time on the teaching of Averroës and a contemporary exponent of Averroism, John of Jandun. During this period he wrote 17 tracts against the teaching of the Averroists.

In search for more official support for his program, Lull attended the Council of Vienne in 1311, where he presented a petition calling for the prohibition of Averroistic teaching, the beginning of another crusade, a fusion of the military orders, and the creation of a college for the study of Oriental languages. In 1314 he returned to his missionary activity in North Africa, and while preaching in Tunisia he was stoned by a crowd at Bougie and later died aboard a ship that had rescued him. His mutilated body returned to Majorca on that same ship.

Further Reading

The best general study of the life and works of Lull is E. Allison Peers, *Ramon Lull: A Biography* (1929). Peers is also author of a shorter, popular biography, *Fool of Love: The Life of Ramon Lull* (1946). Some aspects of the literary side of Lull's career were the subject of a study by Miriam T. Olabarrieta, *The Influence of Ramon Lull on the Style of the Early Spanish Mystics and Santa Teresa* (1963). □

Jean Baptiste Lully

Jean Baptiste Lully (1632-1687), Italian-born French composer, established the basic form of French opera, which remained virtually unchanged for a century.

Jean Baptiste Lully was born in or near Florence on Nov. 28, 1632. At the age of 12 he went to Paris, where he received his musical training. He performed successfully as violinist, dancer, and conductor. He started his own orchestra of stringed instruments and trained it to play with exceptional precision; it was famous throughout Europe for the quality of its performance.

At the same time, Lully was writing music and achieving a reputation as a composer. He was very much favored at the French court, particularly by King Louis XIV. In 1661 Lully was appointed Superintendent of Music; the following year he was named Master of Music of the Royal Family. These prestigious appointments carried high salaries, and Lully built up a large fortune. He was ambitious to the point of ruthlessness and seems to have had no scruples when it came to advancing his own interests. He gained a monopoly over French opera and virtually eliminated any possible rivals in this field. Lully had many enemies, along with many admirers, when he died in Paris on March 22, 1687.

Apart from a small body of sacred music, Lully's work belongs to the realm of theater music. He composed the music for over 40 ballets and other entertainments in the theater. Among his collaborators was the great dramatist Molière. Molière's comedy *Le Bourgeois gentilhomme* was performed in 1670 with incidental music by Lully. This music, which is still used occasionally in performances of the Molière play, is a brilliant complement to the spoken drama.

Italian Traditions

Lully's main achievement, however, was his composition of 14 operas between 1673 and 1687. He was provided with excellent French librettos, mainly by Philippi Quinault, on a variety of subjects: classical, pastoral, and heroic. Musically, Lully modeled his operas to a large extent upon Italian operas of a slightly earlier period. Italian operas had been performed in Paris in the 1640s to the 1660s, and he had taken part in some of the performances.

When Lully came to write his own operas, he took over the essential features of these Italian operas: a flexible, expressive kind of recitative and a contrasting musical style in the arias. His recitative is somewhat different, being set to French words; but it is expressive in its own way and notable for its correct declamation of the words. Lully was

particularly careful in setting words to music. He listened to the best actors at the Comédie Française and aimed to reproduce in music the inflections of spoken French drama. His arias are usually quite short and quite simple structurally, but in performance the singers decorated them with graceful ornaments. The art of ornamentation was part of the training of 17th-century singers; it was expected that they would embellish their solo arias in a skillful, tasteful manner.

French Traditions

Other elements in Lully's operas are derived from French traditions. The ballet had been a favorite entertainment in itself, and it now became an important element in French opera. The chorus was equally important to Lully. In many of his scenes the chorus is treated in rondo fashion: it performs a refrain and thus serves to unify the opera.

To accompany the choral passages and ballets in Lully's operas, there was an orchestra of strings and woodwinds, supplemented by brass and percussion instruments when the situation called for them. Sometimes the orchestra played alone, in separate instrumental pieces. Many long scenes are devoted to dancing and to other kinds of stage spectacles; in them the orchestra has a most important function.

Lully cannot strictly be called the creator of French opera, since other French composers had already written a few operas. He was, however, the first composer of genius to write French operas, and he proved that opera in French could be a viable art form. His operas were immensely popular and continued to be performed long after his death. Today they are almost never presented in their complete form because of their great length. They contain much beautiful music, for Lully was a master of the operatic form and, at his best, a composer of rare inspiration.

Further Reading

Lully's operas are discussed by Manfred F. Bukofzer, *Music in the Baroque Era: From Monteverdi to Bach* (1947); Donald J. Grout, *A Short History of Opera* (1947; 2d ed. 1965); and Claude V. Palisca, *Baroque Music* (1968). Bukofzer also describes the background to French opera and mentions Lully's contribution to sacred music.

Additional Sources

La Laurencie, Lionel de, *Lully,* New York: AMS Press, 1978. ☐

The Lumière Brothers

The French inventing team of brothers Auguste Lumière (1862-1954) and Louis Lumière (1864-1948) was responsible for a number of practical improvements in photography and motion pictures. Their work on color photography resulted in the Autochrome process, which remained the preferred method of creating color prints until the 1930s. They

also applied their technological talents to the new idea of motion picture photography, creating the first projection system that allowed a film to be seen by more than one person at a time.

Auguste and Louis Lumière were pioneers in the improvement of photographic materials and processes in the late 1800s and early 1900s. Using their scientific abilities and business talents, they were responsible for developing existing ideas in still photography and motion pictures to produce higher quality products that were practical enough to be of commercial value. Their initial business success was manufacturing a "dry" photographic plate that provided a new level of convenience to photographers. The brothers later turned to less viable experiments with color photography, producing a more refined, but expensive, method known as the Autochrome process. The best-known of the Lumières' achievements, however, was the Cinematograph system of projected motion pictures. Their 1895 screening of a series of short films created with the Cinematograph at a Paris cafe is considered the first public cinema performance in history.

Auguste Marie Louis Lumière was born on October 19, 1862, in Besançon, France. His younger brother and future collaborator, Louis Jean Lumière, was born October 5, 1864, in the same town. The brothers also had two other siblings, a sister, Jeanne, and a brother, Èdouard, who was killed while serving as a pilot in World War I. The Lumière children were influenced by the artistic and technological interests of their father, Claude-Antoine (known as Antoine) Lumière, a painter and award-winning photographer. In 1860, Antoine had established his own studio in Besançon, where he met and married Jeanne-Josèphine Costille. He entered into a partnership with another photographer in Lyons in 1871, and over the coming years won medals in places such as Paris and Vienna for his photographs. His sons Auguste and Louis would also be avid photographers throughout their lives.

Produced New Photographic Plates

Antoine Lumière encouraged the scientific interests of his sons, and over the years the brothers developed their own specialities. Both had a firm grasp of organic chemistry, an asset that would become valuable in their later photographic work. But while Auguste had a preference for topics in biochemistry and medicine, Louis was more interested in the subject of physics. While attending Martinière Technical School, Louis distinguished himself as the top student in his class in 1880. It was during his school years that Louis began working on an improved photographic plate. Originally, "wet" photographic plates had been the only available medium for photography; these were very inconvenient, however, because they required treatment in a dark room immediately before and after the exposure of the plate. A new, more convenient, "dry" plate had been developed and marketed in the 1870s. Louis developed a better version of the dry plate that became known as the "blue label" plate.

The Lumière brothers and their father saw the potential for marketing such a product, and so, with financial backing from Antoine Lumière, the brothers began producing the plates in 1882. The following year, the venture opened a manufacturing facility in Lyons as the Antoine Lumière and Sons company. As the "blue label" plate became more popular among photographers, production increased from a few thousand a year to more than one million a year by 1886 and 15 million a year by 1894. The contributions of each brother to the success of the company and its products are difficult to isolate, because throughout their careers, the brothers both engaged in refining scientific techniques and they shared all credit on their works and patents. Although their interests varied as the focus of the company changed, a profound professional respect was always obvious between the two and certainly played a major role in their fruitful research and business partnership.

The Problem of Color Photography

The financial security the Lumière brothers enjoyed, from their booming sales of the dry plate, allowed them to carry out experiments in other aspects of photography. In the early 1890s, they turned to the problem of color photography. Since the advent of photography in the 1830s, numerous attempts had been made to create color photographs, with mixed success. The British scientist James Clerk Maxwell had devised a method in which a color reproduction could be created by using variously colored filters to photograph a subject; the resulting picture, however, could only be viewed by projecting the image—no prints were possible. This obstacle was overcome in the 1860s by the French researcher Louis Ducos du Hauron, who produced a color image by superimposing positive and negative shots taken through colored filters. While a print could be produced in this way, it was a complicated and time-consuming process that never gained much popularity. The Lumières set themselves to the task of creating a more practical application of color photography, but they eventually set the topic aside in favor of pursuing the exciting new field of motion pictures. Their early experiments in color photography, however, provided the groundwork for later innovations.

The interest in film technology had begun as a sort of hobby for the brothers, but soon they realized that work in this area could have great commercial value. Beginning in the summer of 1894, they began to look for a way to project motion pictures. The moving picture had been pioneered more than a decade earlier by the English photographer and bookseller Eadweard Muybridge. In an attempt to find a way to analyze the movement of a horse, around 1880 Muybridge had taken a series of photos of a horse in motion and placed the images on a glass disc that allowed him to project the images in quick succession. The result was a moving image, but one that was limited by the number of pictures that could fit on the disc. The idea was taken up later in the 1880s by French physiologist Étienne-Jules Marey and U.S. inventor Thomas Edison. Edison led experiments that resulted in the 1889 creation of his kinetograph, a machine that used strips of photographic paper to take motion pictures. In 1893 Edison and his researchers produced the kinetoscope, a device also known as a ''peep box,'' which allowed a single person to view the moving image. The Lumière brothers' goal was to improve on Edison's ideas by finding a way to project motion picture films for a larger audience.

Created First Projected Motion Pictures

Louis realized that the main obstacle to their goal of projection was finding a way to automatically create a continuous movement of the film containing the images. Part of the answer to the problem was found by Louis, who suddenly was inspired while lying awake one night. He realized that the same ''presser foot'' mechanism that drives a sewing machine could be adapted to move small sections, or frames, of film across the lens in quick succession, allowing a short period of time for each frame to be stationary to allow for exposure. Louis drew up the plans for a prototype camera, which was constructed by one of his technicians at the family factory. This machine, known as the Cinematograph, underwent a number of further developments that made it an extremely versatile tool. Not only could it create the negatives of an image on film, but it could also print a positive image as well as project the results at a speed of 12 frames per second.

Louis made the first use of his new camera in the summer of 1894, filming workers leaving the Lumière plant. He presented the film to the Société d'Encouragement pour l'Industrie Nationale on March 22, 1895. He and Auguste then made arrangements to bring a series of short films to a public audience. They rented a room at the Grand Café in Paris, and on December 28, 1895, held the first public show of projected moving pictures. The audience wasn't quite sure what to make of the new technology. Louis's creative use of the camera had led him to photograph an approaching train from a head-on perspective; some people in the audience were frightened at the image on the oncoming locomotive and in a panic tried to escape—others simply fainted. Despite their surprise, even shock, at the sight of moving pictures, audiences flocked to the Lumières' demonstrations and the Cinematograph was soon in high demand all around the world.

Autochrome Process Invented

Both Auguste and Louis created films for a while, but eventually they handed this work over to others so they could pursue other interests. Louis returned to research on color photography, developing the Autochrome process in 1904. His method, although still fairly expensive, provided a level of convenience similar to the dry plate. Autochrome achieved recognition as the best means of producing color images at that time and remained the favored means of color photography for the next 30 years. In later years, Louis would continue his interest in visual reproduction by developing a photographic method for measuring objects in 1920 and inventing relief cinematography techniques in 1935. Auguste spent the early 1900s investigating medical topics such as tuberculosis, cancer, and pharmacology. He joined the medical profession in 1914 as the director of a hospital radiology department. In 1928, Auguste published a medical book entitled *Life, Illness, and Death: Colloidal Phenomena.*

The Lumière brothers were each recognized for their numerous technological and scientific achievements: Auguste was named a member of the Legion of Honor, and Louis was elected to the French Academy of Sciences. At the age of 83, Louis Lumière died in Bandol, France, on June 6, 1948. His older brother lived to the age of 91 and died in his long-time home of Lyons, France, on April 10, 1954. For their work together in creating improvements in both photography and motion pictures, the Lumière brothers are recognized as symbols of an age of technological creativity and growth. They are also remembered for their lifelong aims of bringing such technology to a wider marketplace, a value seen most clearly in their contributions to the motion picture industry, which has become a popular form of entertainment in countries around the world.

Further Reading

Lumière, Louis, ''The Lumière Cinematography,'' in *A Technological History of Motion Pictures and Television,* compiled by Raymond Fielding, University of California Press, 1967.

Macgowan, Kenneth, *Behind the Screen: The History and Techniques of the Motion Picture,* Delacorte Press, 1965.

Sadoul, Georges, ''Louis Lumière: The Last Interview,'' in *Rediscovering French Film,* edited by Mary Lea Bandy, Museum of Modern Art (New York), 1982.

Walter, Claude, ''The Story of Lumière,'' *Ciba Journal,* spring, 1964, pp. 28-35. □

Patrice Emery Lumumba

Patrice Emery Lumumba (1925-1961) was the first prime minister of the Republic of the Congo. His fame rests on the manner of his death and on the symbolic character of his short public life.

Patrice Lumumba was born on July 2, 1925, at Onalua near the town of Katako-Kombe in the Sankuru district of northeastern Kasai. His tribe, the Batetela, is a peripheral but dynamic branch of the Mongo-Nkutshu family of central Congo. He attended Protestant and then Catholic missionary schools and, after completing his secondary education, found a job as a postal clerk in the provincial capital of Statesville (now Kisangani) in 1954.

Political Leader

Lumumba rapidly emerged as a leader of the *évolué* community and organized a postal workers' union. He also became a protégé of local sympathizers of the Belgian Liberal party at a time when the policy of the Liberal minister of colonies Auguste Buisseret toward mission schools was raising violent conflicts between Catholic and non-Catholic members of the colonial establishment. This patronage led to an extensive interview with King Baudouin when he visited the Congo in 1955 and helped minimize the legal aftereffects of an embezzlement charge raised against Lumumba in 1956.

In 1957, having been appointed to the much better paid position of sales director for an important brewery, Lumumba left Stanleyville for Léopoldville just in time to witness the first manifestation of organized political activity in the form of a bitterly fought municipal election that was won by Joseph Kasavubu's ABAKO. Lumumba's debut on the Léopoldville political scene was in the relatively modest role of leader of a tribal association which took part in an alliance of non-Bakongo elements in the capital.

Lumumba soon became involved, however, in a less parochial endeavor—namely, the foundation of a supraethnic movement called Movement National Congolais (MNC), a group initially dominated by educated Congolese linked to Catholic circles who wanted to broaden their appeal. Lumumba's dynamism and oratorical talents soon won him prominence in the party. He led an MNC delegation to the December 1958 All-African Peoples' Conference in Accra, where he met Kwame Nkrumah, with whom he remained in touch during the rest of his own short political career.

Rise in National Politics

The year 1959 saw the emergence of Patrice Lumumba as the sole truly national figure on the Congo political scene. His persuasive, magnetic personality dominated the Luluabourg congress of April 1959, where all those political formations favoring a unitary form of government for the

Congo attempted to establish a common front. Lumumba's growing prestige as well as his comparative radicalism, however, antagonized other MNC leaders, and the outcome was a split in the ranks of the party (July 1959), as a result of which most of the original founders of the party rallied behind Albert Kalonji while Lumumba retained the bulk of the rank and file.

Lumumba was briefly imprisoned in November 1959 on charges of inciting riots in Stanleyville, but he was set free in time to attend the Round Table Conference in Brussels, where his dramatic appearance stole the show from other Congolese leaders. Lumumba's efforts throughout this period were directed more steadfastly than those of any other Congolese politician toward the organization of a nationwide movement. To this effect, he took full advantage of local political situations, of his earlier connections in Stanleyville, and of his own ethnic background, which provided him with an initial foothold in many districts of the Congo. His linguistic abilities—unlike Kasavubu or Moïse Tshombe, Lumumba was an effective speaker in each of the Congo's major vehicular languages as well as in French— also helped his campaigning.

Head of Government

In the May 1960 general elections, Lumumba and his allies won 41 of 137 seats in the National Assembly and held significant positions in four of six provincial governments. As leader of the largest single party (the MNC's nearest competitor had only 15 seats), Lumumba was somewhat reluctantly selected by the Belgians to form a coalition cabinet and became the Congo's first prime minister (and minister of defense) a week before independence, and Kasavubu, leader of the Bakongo, became president of the republic with Lumumba's tacit support.

During his brief incumbency, Lumumba had to face a conjunction of emergencies such as has seldom been met by a newly independent country: the mutiny of the army and the secession of Katanga and then of Southern kasai, aided and abetted by Belgian interests and the unilateral intervention of Belgian forces. Lumumba turned to the United Nations for support, only to discover that they had no intention of accepting his definition of the Congo's national interest and insisted on opposing the use of force whether by legal or illegal authorities. In desperation, Lumumba asked for Soviet logistical support to mount an offensive against the break away regimes of Southern Kasai and Katanga but was stopped in his tracks when President Kasavubu dismissed him from office on Sept. 5, 1960.

The National Assembly reconfirmed Lumumba in power, but a fraction of the army, led by Col. Mobutu, took power, and Lumumba was confined to de facto house arrest under the protection of Ghanaian troops of the UN force. His political associates had meanwhile withdrawn to Stanleyville to organize a rival government. Lumumba slipped out of the capital and tried to make his way toward Stanleyville, but he was arrested by an army patrol and incarcerated in a military camp at Thysville.

His Murder and Legacy

Even then, Lumumba's prestige and the strength of his followers remained a threat to the unstable new rulers of the Congo. This was demonstrated when Lumumba nearly managed the incredible feat of persuading his military jailers to help him recapture power. This incident only confirmed the Léopoldville authorities' determination to get rid of the deposed premier. The decision to transfer him to either one of the secessionist states of Southern Kasai or Katanga (where he was sure to be put to death) had been debated for some time as a possible prelude to reconciliation with these two breakaway regions. On Jan. 18, 1961, Lumumba was flown to Elisabethville, capital of Katanga, where, despite the presence of UN troops, he was picked up by a small Katanga task force led by Interior Minister Godefroid Munongo and including white mercenaries, taken to a nearby house, and murdered.

The Katanga government made clumsy attempts to conceal and then to disguise the murder, but the shock waves caused by the assassination reverberated around the world and generated enough international pressure to ensure passage of a Security Council resolution permitting the use of force as a last resort by UN forces in the Congo (Feb. 21, 1961). This resolution itself unleashed a train of events which led to the restoration of a civilian regime in Léopoldville and to the eventual liquidation of all secessionist movements.

Lumumba had not been a Communist, had little interest in ideologies, and was more opportunistic than truly radical, but this has not prevented his name from being invoked after his death from a number of different quarters. The most legitimate use of Lumumba's memory is probably that which associates it with an attitude of intransigent nationalism and opposition to neocolonialism.

Further Reading

Studies of Lumumba are R. Lermachand's "Patrice Lumumba" in W. A. E. Skurnik, ed., *African Political Thought: Lumumba, Nkrumah, and Touré* (1968), and G. Heinz and H. Donnay, *Lumumba: The Last Fifty Days* (1970). Profiles of Lumumba are in Catherine Hoskyns, *The Congo since Independence, January 1960—December 1961* (1965), and Crawford Young, *Politics in the Congo: Decolonization and Independence* (1965). □

Benjamin Lundy

Benjamin Lundy (1789-1839) nurtured the antislavery movement in the United States during the 1820s through his newspaper, the *Genius of Universal Emancipation*.

Benjamin Lundy was born into a New Jersey Quaker family on Jan. 4, 1789. Although he had little formal education, he acquired the traits of activism and concern for oppressed people. At the age of 19 he moved to Wheeling, Va., where he learned saddle–making and first saw slaves being marched southward. In St. Clairsville, Ohio, he married Esther Lewis. In 1815 he founded the Union Humane Society, devoted to using legal and political means to free slaves and to assist free blacks. When an antislavery newspaper was started in a nearby town in 1817, Lundy found that he could write effectively. Henceforth, antislavery journalism became his primary interest.

Witnessing slavery firsthand in Missouri in 1819, Lundy realized that economic and political pressures, not just moral attack, would be needed to eliminate slavery. In 1821, back in Ohio, he founded his own newspaper, the *Genius of Universal Emancipation,* which more or less continuously for the next 18 years described the evils of slavery, the superiority of free labor, the need for political pressure, and the basic equality of blacks and whites. Moving about the country, he published the *Genius* whenever and wherever he could.

During the 1820s the *Genius* served as a national link between scattered groups of abolitionists. Lundy's interest in black emigration was not widely shared. He believed that, though blacks had every right to remain in the United States and could be a useful part of society, emigrant colonies would demonstrate to slave owners the economic superiority of free labor. To find suitable places for such colonies, Lundy visited Haiti in 1825 and 1829, Canada in 1832, and the Mexican province of Texas three times in the 1830s.

On a lecture tour in 1828-1829, Lundy persuaded a young journalist named William Lloyd Garrison to join the *Genius* at Baltimore. During Lundy's absence Garrison libeled local slave dealers in the pages of the *Genius,* and both Lundy and Garrison were sued and physically attacked. Garrison left to found his own journal, the *Liberator,* and replaced Lundy as the leading voice of abolitionism in the 1830s. The *Genius* ceased publication in 1839.

After Texas won its independence, Lundy vigorously opposed efforts to annex the Republic of Texas to the United States as slave territory. In 1836 he published an effective booklet, *The War in Texas,* which detailed the Texas slave owners' conspiracies. Former President John Quincy Adams, then in Congress, used Lundy's information to mobilize northern opinion and delay annexation. Lundy also published the *National Enquirer* from 1836 to 1838.

Although overshadowed by the Garrisonian abolitionists after 1831, Lundy's achievements were acclaimed by both white and black reformers. He died in Illinois on Aug. 22, 1839.

Further Reading

The Life, Travels and Opinions of Benjamin Lundy (1847), compiled from Lundy's writings by Thomas Earle, contains the Mexican diary and various pieces, mostly from the period after 1830. Merton L. Dillon, *Benjamin Lundy and the Struggle for Negro Freedom* (1966), includes rich detail and sympathetic analysis. □

Joseph Luns

West European political leader Joseph Luns (born 1911) played an essential role among European foreign policy figures in creating and maintaining the alliance and community structures of the post-World War II era. His most visible position was as secretary-general of the North Atlantic Treaty Organization (NATO) from 1971 until 1984.

Born on August 28, 1911, in Rotterdam, The Netherlands, Joseph Marie Antoine Hubert Luns grew up in a family with six children and a father who was a painter, teacher, author of art books, and finally a museum director. Luns moved to Amsterdam at a young age and was educated in a Roman Catholic high school, St. Ignatius College in Amsterdam, as well as in the Institut St. Louis in Brussels, Belgium. He read law at the University of Leyden and the University of Amsterdam, taking his degree at the latter school in 1937. He subsequently took courses at the London School of Economics (in political economy) and at the "Deutsche Institute fur Auslander" at the University of Berlin. The only interruption in his education came in a year's service with the Royal Netherlands Navy in 1931, when he was drafted into the military to be a signalman.

In 1938 Luns entered the Dutch foreign service. He rose through the customary grades, his last being that of counselor of embassy (1950). His early career was rudely interrupted by the German invasion and occupation of The Netherlands in 1940, at which time Luns joined the government-in-exile, based in Britain, and he spent the war years fulfilling assignments for that resistance effort. He was posted to Berne (1940-1941), Lisbon (1941-1943), and London, where he served out the remainder of the war and later at the reconstituted embassy until 1949. His final position with the foreign service was as a member of the Dutch delegation to the United Nations from 1949 until 1952.

Luns's remarkable career as leader of Dutch foreign policy blossomed in 1952, with the creation of a coalition government in the wake of elections that year. The sharing of power between the Labor Party and the Catholic People's Party (to which Luns belonged) not only created a broad-based cabinet, but also the sharing of certain posts among more than one person. In the case of the Ministry of Foreign Affairs, Luns shared the position with J. W. Beyen until 1956. Subsequently, Luns was appointed to the position in his own right after successive elections in 1959, 1963, 1967, and 1971. In each case, Luns stood for election to a parliamentary seat and, according to Dutch law specifying that a person may not be both a member of Parliament and a minister for more than three months, resigned his parliamentary seat within months of being elected. In the process Luns served under seven different prime ministers and lent a remarkable degree of continuity to Dutch foreign policy during the period of construction of the European Community and of transition through decolonization for European countries.

Having been a signatory of the Treaty of Rome, Luns was one of the initiators of the scheme to allow African countries that were not former colonies of member states to establish relations with the European Economic Community. His attention to the problems of Africa, Asia, and Latin America was only one theme he carried over from his Dutch responsibilities to his broader European and alliance responsibilities. Luns also argued strongly for expansion of the European Community to include Britain and other European countries. His efforts in this direction were constantly frustrated by the position of President Charles de Gaulle of France, especially in the consideration of expansion in the early 1960s. Luns left the foreign ministry when the European Community was expanded in 1973.

It was a natural transition for Luns to move to the work of the North Atlantic Treaty Organization when he was invited to take up the position of secretary-general by vote of the NATO foreign ministers on June 4, 1971. His view of the importance of Western unity made NATO a natural pulpit from which he could preach the necessity for joint planning and action. Luns had, of course, an extensive background in NATO affairs from his Dutch service: he had represented The Netherlands on the NATO Council for many years and, indeed, had presided over the celebration of the tenth anniversary of NATO in 1959 in Washington and Norfolk.

Luns's views as secretary-general were only occasionally controversial. He was solidly pro-American, even during the period of the Vietnam War, and entered into public disagreement with the United States only over issues of diplomatic style. He faced major internal problems in NATO during his tenure, including the sometimes violent disagreements between Greece and Turkey, the challenges of increasing defense spending levels, and the dissension caused by disarmament and arms control talks with the Soviet Union and the Eastern bloc. He supported modernization of NATO weapons and deployments to meet Soviet military growth, particularly in the debates over Pershing II missiles, enhanced radiation warheads, and cruise missiles. Over time his political conservatism cost him some popularity, but that did not deter him from saying what he considered right.

In October of 1983 Luns announced his retirement as secretary-general of NATO. One of his last accomplishments before turning over the reigns to Lord Peter Carrington of England was a general agreement to update technology for conventional weapons so NATO would be less reliant on nuclear arms.

For his work Luns received awards from countries all over Europe, among them the Charlemagne Prize of the City of Aix-la-Chapelle for his efforts to promote European unity and the Gustav Stresemann medal for 1968 for his promotion of the rule of international law. In his own country he was awarded a Knight Grand Cross of the Order of the Netherlands Lio and an Officer of the Order of Orange-Nassau. Luns was also an Honorary Fellow of the Royal Geographic Society and the London School of Economics and had honorary degrees from Harvard University, Oxford University, and other universities. He was married to Baroness Elisabeth van Heemstra and had one son and one daughter.

Further Reading

Luns has not been the subject of a biography, but his own views can be discerned in a great variety of speeches and policy-statement articles published over the years. Such articles include "NATO," in *World Affairs* (Fall 1983) and "NATO and Intermediate Range Nuclear Forces" in *Millenium* (Spring 1984); For articles about NATO and issues involving Luns, see journals such as the *Atlantic Community Quarterly* or *The Washington Quarterly;* Other information on Luns can be found in "NATO Urges Soviets to Join 'Dialogue' in a New Relationship," by John Vinocur, *New York Times* (October 12, 1983). □

Isaac ben Solomon Ashkenazi Luria

The Jewish mystic Isaac ben Solomon Ashkenazi Luria (1534-1572) founded a Cabala which profoundly influenced central European Judaism of the 18th and 19th centuries.

Isaac ben Solomon Ashkenazi Luria was born in Jerusalem. His parents were German, hence the title Ashkenazi (German) in his name. He was called Ari Ha-qodesh (The Holy Lion) or simply Ari (Lion) by his followers. After his father's death, he lived with an aunt in Cairo. After several years of rabbinic studies, at the age of 17 he found a Cabalistic manuscript and was fascinated by its contents. He retired from all his friends for 6 years to study Cabala and to concentrate especially on the *Book of Zohar*. After this period he retired to a hut on the Nile where he underwent further study and practiced extreme asceticism. In 1570 he returned to Palestine and settled at the Palestinian center of Cabala at Safed. He drew a large and enthusiastic group of followers and students. But he spent only a year and a half there; a plague broke out, and he died on Aug. 5, 1572, at the early age of 38.

Luria is best known as the founder of the Lurianic Cabala. He wrote only a commentary on certain parts of the *Book of Zohar,* but his doctrine became known through the works of his disciples, particularly Joseph in Tabal and Hayyim Vital, and through the letters of a certain Shlomel Dresnitz of Moravia, which were published under the title *Shivhe Ha-Ari* (The Praises of the Lion).

Luria had mystic experiences of visions and communications, and he expressed his thought in complex imagery. He taught three basic tenets. First, creation came about through *tzimtum. Tzimtum* was a withdrawal or retraction of God from Himself, thereby making existence outside Himself possible. Second, evil was created through *shevirat ha-kelim* (breaking of the vessels); once the divine spilled over into creation, some sparks of being fell into demonic spheres, and thereby evil was produced. Third, he preached the *tikkun* (restoration of God's unity). This restoration was to be effected by the life of holy men and their observance of the commandments. This doctrine of redemption of the world by men had never before been prominent in Jewish thought.

The teaching of the 15th-century Jewish mystic Joseph Alkastiel of Játiva, Spain, deeply impressed Luria. He also used themes and motifs drawn from earlier rabbinic sources. His genius, however, lay in the synthesis he made of traditional Jewish teaching with a mystical outlook.

Luria provided consolation for those who had lost loved ones or had misspent their lives. He did this by his doctrine of *gilgul* (transmigration of souls). For Luria this was not a mode of punishment but a chance to cleanse and perfect oneself. Lurianic teaching heightened the ethical value of each individual action because he taught that each action helped to redeem the world. His doctrines greatly influenced Jewish piety and ritual and provided the Hasidic movement of the 18th and 19th centuries with its main tenets.

Further Reading

Studies of Luria are found in Solomon Schechter, *Studies in Judaism: Second Series* (1908), and Gershom G. Scholem, *Major Trends in Jewish Mysticism* (1941; 3d rev. ed. 1954). □

Martin Luther

The German reformer Martin Luther (1483-1546) was the first and greatest figure in the 16th-century Reformation. A composer of commentaries on Scripture, theology, and ecclesiastical abuses, a hymnologist, and a preacher, from his own time to the present he has been a symbol of Protestantism.

Martin Luther was born at Eisleben in Saxony on Nov. 10, 1483, the son of Hans and Margaret Luther. Luther's parents were of peasant stock, but his father had worked hard to raise the family's status, first as a miner and later as the owner of several small mines, to become a small-scale entrepreneur. In 1490 Martin was sent to the Latin school at Mansfeld, in 1497 to Magdeburg, and in 1498 to Eisenach. His early education was typical of late-15th-century practice. To a young man in Martin's circumstances, only the law and the church offered likely avenues of success, and Hans Luther's anticlericalism probably influenced his decision that his son should become a lawyer and increase the Luther family's prosperity, which Hans had begun. Martin was enrolled at the University of Erfurt in 1501. He received a bachelor of arts degree in 1502 and a master of arts in 1505. In the same year he enrolled in the faculty of law, giving every sign of being a dutiful and, likely, a very successful son.

Religious Conversion

Between 1503 and 1505, however, Martin experienced a religious crisis which would take him from the study of law forever. His own personal piety, fervently and sometimes grimly instilled by his parents and early teachers, and his awareness of a world in which the supernatural was perilously close to everyday life were sharpened by a series of events whose exact character has yet to be precisely determined. A dangerous accident in 1503, the death of a friend a little later, and Martin's own personal religious development had by 1505 started other concerns in him.

Then, on July 2, 1505, returning to Erfurt after visiting home, Martin was caught in a severe thunderstorm in which he was flung to the ground in terror, and he suddenly vowed to become a monk if he survived. This episode, as important in Christian history as the equally famous (and parallel) scene of St. Paul's conversion, changed the course of Luther's life. Two weeks later, against the opposition of his father and to the dismay of his friends, Martin Luther entered the Reformed Congregation of the Eremetical Order of St. Augustine at Erfurt. Luther himself saw this decision as sudden and based upon fear: "I had been called by heavenly terrors, for not freely or desirously did I become a monk, much less to gratify my belly, but walled around with the terror and agony of sudden death I vowed a constrained and necessary vow."

Luther's early life as a monk reflected his precipitate reasons for entering a monastery: "I was a good monk, and kept strictly to my order, so that I could say that if the monastic life could get a man to heaven, I should have entered." Monastic life at Erfurt was hard. Monks had long become (with the friars and many of the secular clergy) the targets of anticlerical feeling. Charged with having forsaken their true mission and having fallen into greed and ignorance, monastic orders made many attempts at reform in the 15th and 16th centuries. The congregation at Erfurt had been reformed in 1473. The year before Luther entered the Augustinian order at Erfurt, the vicar general Johann Staupitz (later Luther's friend) had revised further the constitution of the order.

Luther made his vows in 1506 and was ordained a priest in 1507. Reconciled with his father, he was then selected for advanced theological study at the University of Erfurt, with which his house had several connections.

Luther at Wittenberg

In 1508 Luther was sent to the newer University of Wittenberg to lecture in arts. Like a modern graduate student, he was also preparing for his doctorate of theology while he taught. He lectured on the standard medieval texts, for example, Peter Lombard's *Book of Sentences;* and he read for the first time the works of St. Augustine. In 1510 Luther was sent to Rome on business of the order and in 1512 received his doctorate in theology. Then came the second significant turn in Luther's career: he was appointed to succeed Staupitz as professor of theology at Wittenberg. Luther was to teach throughout the rest of his life. Whatever fame and notoriety his later writings and statements were to bring him, his work was teaching, which he fulfilled diligently until his death.

Wittenberg was a new university, founded in 1502-1503, strongly supported by the elector Frederick the Wise. By 1550, thanks to the efforts of Luther and his colleague Philip Melancthon, it was to become the most popular university in Germany. In 1512, however, it lacked the prestige of Erfurt and Leipzig and was insignificant in the eyes of the greatest of the old universities, that of Paris. It was not a good place for an ambitious academic, but Luther was not ambitious in this sense. His rapid rise was due to his native ability, his boundless energy, his dedication to the religious life, and his high conception of his calling as a teacher.

The intellectual climate which shaped Luther's thought is difficult to analyze precisely. The two competing philosophic systems of the late Middle Ages—scholasticism (derived from the Aristotelianism of St. Thomas Aquinas) and nominalism (derived from the skepticism of William of Ockham and his successors)—both appear to have influenced Luther, particularly in their insistence on rigorous formal logic as the basis of philosophic and theological inquiry. From Ockhamism, Luther probably derived his awareness of the infinite remoteness and majesty of God and of the limitation of the human intellect in its efforts to apprehend that majesty.

Luther's professional work forced him further to develop the religious sensibility which had drawn him to monasticism in 1505. In the monastery and later in the university Luther experienced other religious crises, all of

which were based upon his acute awareness of the need for spiritual perfection and his equally strong conviction of his own human frailty, which caused him almost to despair before the overwhelming majesty and wrath of God. In 1509 Luther published his lectures on Peter Lombard; in 1513-1515 those on the Psalms; in 1515-1516 on St. Paul's Epistle to the Romans; and in 1516-1518 on the epistles to the Galatians and Hebrews. Like all other Christians, Luther read the Bible, and in these years his biblical studies became more and more important to him. Besides teaching and study, however, Luther had other duties. From 1514 he preached in the parish church; he was regent of the monastery school; and in 1515 he became the supervisor of 11 other monasteries: "I . . . write letters all day long," he wrote, "I am conventual preacher, reader at meals, sought for to preach daily in the parish church, am regent of studies, district Vicar, inspect the fish-ponds at Leitzkau, act in the Herzberg affair at Torgau, lecture on St. Paul, revising my Psalms, I seldom have time to go through my canonical hours properly, or to celebrate, to say nothing of my own temptations from the world, the flesh, and the devil."

Righteousness of God

Luther's crisis of conscience centered upon the question of his old monastic fears concerning the insufficiency of his personal efforts to placate a wrathful God. In his own person, these fears came to a head in 1519, when he began to interpret the passage in St. Paul's Epistle to the Romans which says that the justice of God is revealed in the Gospels.

Luther, the energetic monk and young theologian, felt himself to be "a sinner with an unquiet conscience." After an intense period of crisis, Luther discovered another interpretation of St. Paul's text: "I began to understand that Justice of God . . . to be understood passively as that whereby the merciful God justifies us by faith. . . . At this I felt myself to be born anew, and to enter through open gates into paradise itself." Only faith in God's mercy, according to Luther, can effect the saving righteousness of God in man. "Works," the term which Luther used to designate both formal, ecclesiastically authorized liturgy and the more general sense of "doing good," became infinitely less important to him than faith.

The doctrine of justification, taking shape in Luther's thought between 1515 and 1519, drew him into further theological speculation as well as into certain positions of practical ecclesiastical life. The most famous of these is the controversy over indulgences. In 1513 a great effort to dispense indulgences was proclaimed throughout Germany. In spite of the careful theological reservations surrounding them, indulgences appeared to the preachers who sold them and to the public who bought them as a means of escaping punishment in the afterlife for a sum of money. In 1517 Luther posted the 95 Theses for an academic debate on indulgences on the door of the castle church at Wittenberg. Both the place and the event were customary events in an academic year, and they might have gone unnoticed had not someone translated Luther's Latin theses into German and printed them, thus giving them widespread fame and calling them to the attention of both theologians and the public.

News of Dr. Luther's theses spread, and in 1518 Luther was called before Cardinal Cajetan, the papal legate at Augsburg, to renounce his theses. Refusing to do so, Luther returned to Wittenberg, where, in the next year, he agreed to a debate with the theologian Johann Eck. The debate, originally scheduled to be held between Eck and Luther's colleague Karlstadt, soon became a struggle between Eck and Luther in which Luther was driven by his opponent to taking even more radical theological positions, thus laying himself open to the charge of heresy. By 1521 Eck secured a papal bull (decree) condemning Luther, and Luther was summoned to the Imperial Diet at Worms in 1521 to answer the charges against him.

Diet of Worms

A student of Luther's described his teacher at this period: "He was a man of middle stature, with a voice which combined sharpness and softness: it was soft in tone, sharp in the enunciation of syllables, words, and sentences. He spoke neither too quickly nor too slowly, but at an even pace, without hesitation, and very clearly. . . . If even the fiercest enemies of the Gospel had been among his hearers, they would have confessed from the force of what they heard, that they had witnessed, not a man, but a spirit."

Luther throughout his life always revealed a great common sense, and he always retained his humorous understanding of practical life. He reflected an awareness of both the material and spiritual worlds, and his flights of poetic theology went hand in hand with the occasional coarseness of his polemics. His wit and thought were spontaneous, his interest in people of all sorts genuine and intense, his power of inspiring affection in his students and colleagues never failing. He was always remarkably frank, and although he became first the center of the Reform movement and later one of many controversial figures in it, he retained a sense of self-criticism, attributing his impact to God. He said, in a characteristic passage: "Take me, for example. I opposed indulgences and all papists, but never by force. I simply taught, preached, wrote God's Word: otherwise I did nothing. And then, while I slept or drank Wittenberg beer with my Philip of Amsdorf the Word so greatly weakened the papacy that never a prince or emperor did such damage to it. I did nothing: the Word did it all. Had I wanted to start trouble . . . I could have started such a little game at Worms that even the emperor wouldn't have been safe. But what would it have been? A mug's game. I did nothing: I left it to the Word."

Great personal attraction, absolute dedication to his theological principles, kindness and loyalty to his friends, and an acute understanding of his own human weakness—these were the characteristics of Luther when he came face to face with the power of the papacy and empire at Worms in 1521. He was led to a room in which his collected writings were piled on a table and ordered to repudiate them. He asked for time to consider and returned the next day and answered: "Unless I am proved wrong by the testimony of Scripture or by evident reason I am bound in conscience and held fast to the Word of God. Therefore I cannot and will not retract anything, for it is neither safe nor salutary to act against one's conscience. God help me. Amen." Luther left Worms and was taken, for his own safety, to the castle of Wartburg, where he spent some months in seclusion, beginning his great translation of the Bible into German and writing numerous tracts.

Return to Wittenberg

In 1522 Luther returned to Wittenberg, where he succeeded in cooling the radical reforming efforts of his colleague Karlstadt and continued the incessant writing which would fill the rest of his life. In 1520 he had written three of his most famous tracts: *To The Christian Nobility of the German Nation,* which enunciates a social program of religious reform; *On the Babylonian Captivity of the Church,* on Sacraments, the Mass, and papal power; and *Of the Liberty of a Christian Man,* a treatise on faith and on the inner liberty which faith affords those who possess it.

The Lutheran Bible, which was "a vehicle of proletarian education" as well as a monument in the spiritual history of Europe, not only gave Luther's name and views wider currency but revealed the translator as a great master of German prose, an evaluation which Luther's other writings justify.

Besides these works, Luther had other matters at hand. His name was used now by many people, including many with whom he disagreed. The Reformation had touched society and its institutions as well as religion, and Luther was drawn into conflicts, such as the Peasants' Rebellion of 1524-1525 and the affairs of the German princes, which drew from him new ideas on the necessary social and political order of Christian Germany. Luther's violent antipeasant writings from this period have often been criticized. His fears of the dangerous role of extreme reformers like Karlstadt and Thomas Münzer, however, were greater than his hope for social reform through revolution. Luther came to rely heavily upon the princes to carry out his program of reform. In 1525 Luther married Katherine von Bora, a nun who had left her convent. From that date until his death, Luther's family life became not only a model of the Christian home but a source of psychological support to him.

Luther's theological writings continued to flow steadily. Often they were written in response to his critics or in the intense heat of debate with Protestant rivals. Among those great works not brought about by conflict should be numbered the *Great Catechism* and the *Small Catechism* of 1529 and his collection of sermons and hymns, many of the latter, like *Ein Feste Burg,* still sung today.

Debates with Theologians

In 1524-1525 Luther entered into a discussion of free will with the great Erasmus. Luther's *On the Will in Bondage* (1525) remained his definitive statement on the question. In 1528 Luther turned to the question of Christ's presence in the Eucharist in his *Confession concerning the Lord's Supper,* which attracted the hostility of a number of reformers, notably Ulrich Zwingli. In 1529 Luther's ally Melancthon arranged a discussion between the two, and the Marburg

Colloquy, as the debate is known, helped to close one of the early breaches in Protestant agreement.

In 1530, when Charles V was once again able to turn to the problems of the Reformation in Germany, Luther supervised, although he did not entirely agree with, the writing of Melancthon's Augsburg Confession, one of the foundations of later Protestant thought. From 1530 on Luther spent as much time arguing with other Reformation leaders on matters of theology as with his Catholic opponents.

Luther's disputes with other theologians were carried out with the same intensity he applied to his other work: he longed for Christian unity, but he could not accept the theological positions which many others had advanced. He was also fearful of the question of a general council in the Church. In 1539 he wrote his *On Councils and Churches* and witnessed in the following years the failure of German attempts to heal the wounds of Christianity. On the eve of his death he watched with great concern the calling of the Council of Trent, the Catholic response to the Reformation.

In the 1540s Luther was stricken with diseases a number of times, drawing great comfort from his family and from the lyrical, plain devotional exercises which he had written for children. In 1546 he was called from a sickbed to settle the disputes of two German noblemen. On the return trip he fell sick and died at Eisleben, the town of his birth, on Feb. 18, 1546.

Further Reading

The Writings of Martin Luther (1958) provides 55 volumes of selected works in good translations. A shorter selection is *Martin Luther: Selections from His Writings,* edited by John Dillenberger (1961). There is a vast literature on Luther and the Reformation. An old but still useful work, of interest because it was written almost a decade before the "Luther Renaissance" of the 1920s, is Preserved Smith, *The Life and Letters of Martin Luther* (1911; repr. 1968). But it needs to be supplemented by more recent studies.

Roland H. Bainton, *Here I Stand: A Life of Martin Luther* (1950), is one of the most comprehensive biographies. Other biographies are Gordon Rupp, *Luther's Progress to the Diet of Worms, 1521* (1951); Robert H. Fife, *The Revolt of Martin Luther* (1957); Erik H. Erikson, *Young Man Luther: A Study in Psychoanalysis and History* (1958); V. H. H. Green, *Luther and the Reformation* (1964); Gerhard Ritter, *Luther: His Life and Work,* translated by John Riches (1964); and Arthur Geoffrey Dickens, *Martin Luther and the Reformation* (1967), half of which is devoted to the Reformation itself. A popular account is Edith Simon, *Luther Alive: Martin Luther and the Making of the Reformation* (1968).

A specialized study dealing with doctrinal issues is Erwin Iserloh, *The Theses Were Not Posted: Martin Luther between Reform and Reformation* (1968). Two brief and good accounts of Luther's theology are Philip S. Watson, *Let God Be God: An Interpretation of the Theology of Martin Luther* (1947), and Gordon Rupp, *The Righteousness of God: Luther Studies* (1953). An interesting account of later interpretations of Luther is Jaroslav Pelikan, ed., *Interpreters of Luther: Essays in Honor of Wilhelm Pauck* (1968). The best general accounts of Luther and the Reformation are Roland H. Bainton, *The Reformation of the Sixteenth Century* (1953); *The New Cambridge Modern History* (14 vols., 1957-1970), vol. 2: G. R. Elton, ed., *The Reformation, 1520-1559;* A. G. Dickens, *Reformation and Society in Sixteenth-century Europe* (1966); and H. G.

Koenigsberger and George L. Mosse, *Europe in the Sixteenth Century* (1968). □

Albert John Luthuli

Albert John Luthuli (1898-1967) was a South African statesman and the first African to win the Nobel Prize for peace. His leadership of black resistance to apartheid helped to focus world opinion on South Africa's race policies.

Albert Luthuli was born in Solusi mission station, Rhodesia, where his father served American missionaries as an interpreter. The Luthulis had originally come from Groutville, a Zulu mission station about 40 miles to the north of Durban. Young Albert attended school in Groutville and trained as a teacher at Adams College, where he later taught. It was while he was teaching at Adams that the Groutville community requested him to become its chief. Sugarcane production, which was the reservation's main source of income, had run into difficulties. Luthuli accepted the invitation and saved the community's economy from collapse.

Luthuli's thinking was influenced as much by the Zulu's view of life as by his Christian background and by race segregation. These made his regard for the sacredness of the person and his commitment to nonviolence and the creation of a nonracial democracy in South Africa the dominant features of his leadership.

Luthuli regarded the traditional evaluation of the person as transcending all barriers of race because the infinite consciousness has no color. Black and white are bound together by the common humanity they have. He believed that Christian values can unite black and white in a democratic coalition. Apartheid's preoccupation with color and the particular experience of the Afrikaner outraged him because it gives a meaning to Christian values which uses race to fix the person's position in society and sets a ceiling beyond which the African cannot develop his full potential as a human being. In this setting the black man (or any other person of color) is punished for being the child of his parents. Luthuli rejected violence not only because it militates against the coalition he had in mind but also because it offends the Golden Rule.

For holding these views Luthuli was later to be deposed, banned, and brought to trial for treason. The law under which he was charged (1956) was the Suppression of Communism Act. South African law recognizes two forms of communism: the Marxist-Leninist and the statutory. Whoever opposes apartheid with determination or advocates race equality seriously is a statutory Communist.

Luthuli was interested in the human experience as a totality. He translated his beliefs into action by supporting the nonracial Christian Council of South Africa, which sent him to the conference of the International Missionary Council held in India in 1938. Ten years later he was in the

United States representing his Congregational Church at the synod of the North American Missionary Conference.

In the meantime Luthuli had involved himself directly in his people's political struggle and, in 1946, had been elected to the Natives Representative Council, a body set up by James Munnik Hertzog to advise the government on African affairs. Luthuli became president of the Natal section of the African National Congress (ANC) in 1951. In this capacity he led the 1951-1952 campaign for the defiance of six discriminatory laws. For doing this he was deposed as chief. In a statement issued after his dismissal he said, "I have joined my people in the spirit that revolts openly and boldly against injustice and expresses itself in a determined and nonviolent manner."

The Africans replied to the dismissal by electing him president general of the ANC. The government countered with a ban which confined him to Groutville for two years. A second ban restricted his movements when the first expired in 1954. Two years later a charge of treason, which collapsed in court after a year's trial, was brought against him and some of his colleagues. Three years later he was banned for five years under the Suppression of Communism Act.

By 1959 Luthuli was coming under criticism from the militants for both his insistence on nonviolence and his form of collaboration with non-Africans. The final split came when Robert Mangaliso Sobukwe broke away from the ANC and formed the Pan-Africanist Congress (PAC). On March 21, 1960, Sobukwe called the Africans out in a national demonstration against the Pass Laws. The police opened fire on the demonstrators in Sharpeville, Cape Town, Clermont Township near Pinetown, and Durban. Luthuli proclaimed a day of mourning and was subsequently arrested during the state of emergency which followed the shootings.

The Swedish Parliament nominated Luthuli for the Nobel Peace Prize, which he received at Oslo University on Dec. 10, 1961. In his acceptance speech he stressed the element of continuity in his people's struggle and reaffirmed his hopes for Africa. "I did not initiate the struggle to extend the area of human freedom in South Africa; other African patriots—devoted men—did so before me." He continued, "Our goal is a united Africa in which the standards of life and liberty are constantly expanding . . . a nonracial democratic South Africa which upholds the rights of all who live in our country." He invited "Africa to cast her eyes beyond the past and to some extent the present" to the "recognition and preservation of the rights of man and the establishment of a truly free world."

The United States offered Luthuli sanctuary if he decided not to return to South Africa. He did not accept the offer. He was involved in a train accident and died in Stanger on July 21, 1967.

Further Reading

In his autobiography, *Let My People Go* (1962), Luthuli describes the influences that shaped his thinking. Edward Callan, *Albert John Luthuli and the South African Race Conflict* (1962), is an informative monograph on Luthuli's public life. For further background consult Anthony Sampson, *The Treason Cage: The Opposition on Trial in South Africa* (1958); Gwendolen M. Carter, *The Politics of Inequality: South Africa since 1948* (1958); and two works by Mary Benson, *Chief Albert Luthuli of South Africa* (1963) and *The African Patriots: The Story of the African National Congress* (1963). A chapter on Luthuli is in Melville Harcourt, *Portraits of Destiny* (1966). □

Witold Lutoslawski

Witold Lutoslawski (1913-1994) was the leader of the group of Polish composers who came into prominence in the 1950s. His work was performed and honored worldwide throughout his lifetime.

Witold Lutoslawski was born in Warsaw, Poland, and spent all of his formative years there. He received his musical education at the Warsaw Conservatory and also attended the university as a mathematics student. During World War II he served in the military radio section of the occupying German army in Warsaw.

Lutoslawski was active in reorganizing Polish cultural life after the war. He formed the Union of Polish Composers and the Society for the Publication of Polish Music, and he helped to organize the first Warsaw Festival in 1956. These annual festivals served as a showcase for Poland's young composers, whose number and originality astounded the musical world. Before the war Poland had not been strong in creative musicians, and during the war it had been cut off from the rest of Europe.

Musical Work and Influence

Lutoslawski's early compositions show the influences that helped to form his style. His *Symphonic Variations on a Theme by Paganini* (1938) for two pianos is a brilliant piece, strongly influenced by Igor Stravinsky's neoclassicism in its sharp dissonance and use of jazz. Lutoslawski's First Symphony (1947) is also a neoclassic work. His *Concerto for Orchestra* (1954) shows a new influence: the music of Béla Bartók. It has a strong folk-music basis, not in the manner of the 19th-century nationalists but in Bartók's forthright dissonant manner. The brilliance of the orchestral writing equals that found in Bartók's *Concerto for Orchestra*. Lutoslawski acknowledged his debt to Bartók in one of his most powerful compositions, *Trauermusik* (1958; Mourning Music). In this piece he uses a modified twelve-tone technique, showing his awareness of Arnold Schoenberg and the second Viennese school of composers, but this was not to be a permanent influence. "My music," Lutoslawski said, "has no direct relationship to the traditions of the Viennese school. I am much more strongly tied to Claude Debussy, Stravinsky, Bartók, and Varèse."

In *Venetian Games* (1961), *Three Poems by Henri Michaux* (1963), and the Second Symphony (1969) Lutoslawski uses controlled aleatory effects, giving the individual orchestra members freedom to play some passages as

they choose with respect to notes and rhythm. In *Poems,* written for 23 instruments and a chorus of 20, each singer has an individual part, which they speak, whisper, moan, and shout as well as sing. Lutoslawski's use of such devices is always for expressive purposes. No matter how experimental and advanced these works are, his musical vitality, combined with his discipline of traditional craftsmanship, gives his compositions a seriousness, dignity, and power of communication rarely found among contemporary composers.

Award and Honors

Lutoslawski won a UNESCO prize in composition in 1959 and was elected to the presidency of the International Society for Contemporary Music that year. He taught at the Berkshire Music Center in Lenox, Massachusetts, the Dartmouth Congregation of the Arts in Hanover, New Hampshire, the Dartington Summer School in England, and in Stockholm, Sweden. In 1985 he was invited to the dedication ceremony of the Polish Music Reference Center at the University of Southern California at Los Angeles. During his two-week stay there, he presented five original manuscripts to the Center.

He and his work were recognized many times in his lifetime. Lutoslawski's awards included the University of Louisville Grawemeyer Award in 1985 for his Third Symphony; the 1993 Kyoto (Japan) Prize in Creative Arts and Moral Sciences; the Grammy Award, Cecilia Prize, Koussevitsky Award and Grammaphone Award, all in 1986, for the Los Angeles Philharmonic Recording of his Third Symphony, and Britain's Classical Music Award in January, 1997, for his Fourth Symphony. He also received several honorary degrees.

Upon presenting the Kyoto Prize, the Inamori Foundation said, "His works have had a powerful effect on the postwar musical world. A new method of atonality, the distinctive aleatoric music, and development of contemporary forms of musical expression have made him a master of music in the 20th century."

Lutoslawski died Feb. 7, 1994, in Warsaw, at the age of 81. He is survived by his wife, Danuta.

Further Reading

Ove Nordwall, ed., *Lutoslawski* (1968), contains analyses of each of Lutoslawski's compositions up to 1967 as well as a biographical sketch, a complete catalog of his works, and an essay by the composer; see also David Ewen, *The World of Twentieth-century Music* (1968); and Peter S. Hansen, *An Introduction to Twentieth Century Music* (3d ed. 1971).

Additional Sources

Wilk, Wanda, "Poland Loses a Great Son, A Great Loss to the World," *Polish-American Journal.* April 1, 1994.

Kaczynski, Tadeusz, *Conversations with Witold Lutoslawski,* London: Chester Music, c1984.

Stucky, Steven, *Lutoslawski and His Music,* New York: Cambridge University Press, c1981. □

Edwin Landseer Lutyens

Edwin Landseer Lutyens (1869-1944) was one of England's most prominent and inventive architects working in a traditional manner during the late 19th and early 20th centuries.

Edwin Landseer Lutyens was born on March 29, 1869, in London, England, the 11th of 14 children of an army captain who retired from service to study art with the English animal painter Edwin Landseer, after whom the young Lutyens was named. As a boy he wandered the Surrey countryside where he developed an appreciation for the local crafts traditions and a special admiration for the complex interlocking shapes of the vernacular cottages and barns found in the region.

At age 16 Lutyens attended the South Kensington School of design to study architecture. He then joined the office of Ernst George (1839-1922), a talented pupil of Norman Shaw (1831-1912). The influence of Shaw, Philip Webb (1831-1915), and the English Arts and Crafts Movement became the foundation for Lutyens' creative career. Upon establishing his own office in 1889, at age 20, Lutyens embarked on a long career that included every kind of commission, from cottage design through commercial and ecclesiastical buildings to town planning. His work can for the most part be divided into three general stylistic categories: Romantic Vernacular, Neo-Georgian, and Neo-Classical.

Lutyens established a national reputation early in his career by designing houses for the English nouveau riche in a rambling, picturesque vernacular style derived from Shaw. These houses, like the majority of his work, reveal his mastery of spatial play with rooms flowing together in a loose, coherent manner. His designs are characterized by their incorporation of traditional vernacular styles and an honest use of local materials. An important feature of these houses is their careful integration with romantically conceived gardens, frequently designed in collaboration with the famous garden designer Gertrude Jekyll (1843-1932). In fact, his first major house, Mustead Wood, Godalming, Surrey, was designed for Jekyll, a close personal friend of Lutyens who did much to promote his career. In Mustead Wood, tile roofs come right down to the tops of the doors and large gables with windows that are treated as strips made of oak-framed casements with leaded lights.

One of Lutyens' most inventive houses is Deanery Gardens, Sonning, Berkshire (1899), designed for Robert Hudson, founder of *Country Life,* a magazine to which Jekyll contributed numerous articles. Lutyens created a rambling, picturesque composition with the complex interlocking of architectural elements that characterizes so many of his house designs. His delight in the interplay of spaces is displayed here in the southeastern corridor, which runs straight through the house, becoming partly open and covered passage for the family from entrance to garden. Lutyens, who believed architecture should sometimes exhibit a bit of hu-

mor or wit, often exaggerated dominant features such as tall brick chimneys, mullioned windows, and deep gables.

Lutyens' Neo-Georgian work, which he jokingly referred to as his "Wrenniassance Style" (after the great English baroque architect Christopher Wren) is typified by the use of English baroque forms and details. Characteristic examples of this stylistic approach include his much copied design for Middlefield, Great Helford, Cambridge (1908), with its symmetrical plan, classical details, sweeping roofs, and tall chimney stacks. The alternating planes of the chimneys, the outer chimney planes projecting outward and reversed for the central chimney, reveal Lutyens' inventive love of form. This same inventive spirit is found in his Neo-Georgian design for Ednaston Manor, Brallsford, Derbyshire (1912). Here the simple brick facade, symmetrically organized with a central pedimented facade that features an elaborate broken scroll pediment for the central doorway, is divided by plain pilaster strips. The carved panels in the coved cornice, placed above each pilaster, create the witty allusion of classical capitals.

Lutyens' controlling sense of proportion and organizational principles eventually led him to explore the harmony, strength, and repose of classical design. Counter to the romantic, rambling plans of his earlier houses, Lutyens increasingly began to incorporate a strong sense of balance, symmetry, and order in his designs. Lutyens viewed the manipulation and organization of the classical vocabulary as a great intellectual game to be played by the architect to create unique, individual designs. His first exercise in this Neo-Classical idiom came with the commission for

Heathcoate, Ilkley, Yorkshire (completed in 1906). Here the plan is strictly symmetrical—a large central block with two rectangular side wings. Lutyens created a pseudo-Italian villa with smooth grey Gulseley stone walls, red pantiled roofs, and a full range of Roman Doric elements, including columns, pilasters, metopes, guttea, and triglyphs.

The crowning achievement of Lutyens' Neo-Classical work is his Viceroy's House (1912-1932) and related planning of the new colonial capital in New Delhi, India. The Viceroy's House is an excellent example of Lutyens' interest in abstract classical design and rich use of materials. The large structure, surmounted by a huge dome, displays slightly battered walls constructed of pink and cream Dholpur sandstone. The design exhibits a strong abstract quality achieved by the organization of mass and geometry rather than through the inclusion of classical details or ornament. Through intense study and thought Lutyens attempted to distill the classical vocabulary down to its pure essence or, as the architect stated, "They have to be so well digested that there is nothing but essence left." This approach to classicism recalls the work of the revolutionary French 18th-century architects Étienne-Louis Boullée (1728-1799) and Claude Ledoux (1736-1806).

Lutyens creatively blended particular Moghul features into his monumental design. These include the *chattris*, or roof pavilions, and the *chujjas*, or pronounced projecting cornices, which produce much needed shadows. The lower part of the dome is also derived from traditional Indian architecture, being patterned on such monuments as the circular palisade of the Great Stupa at Sanchi in India. Lutyens selected this feature not only for its Indian association but for its grid-like form, which harmonizes with the geometrical basis of the entire design. The dome, therefore, is a hybrid of classical and Moghul emblems of authority producing the desired imperial associations for the British Raj.

The interior also displays the architect's sensitivity to the dry, hot climate of the region. Everywhere unsuspected spaces open up to the sky, bringing fresh air and breezes to the interior. Water plays an important role in the interior and exterior, where Lutyens created a formal garden with fountains and radiating paths that blend traditional elements of Moghul design and English garden schemes.

Although Lutyens did not study at the Ecole des Beaux-Arts in France, his strictly formal plan for the city of New Delhi reflects basic French planning principles. The city was laid out along a dominant central axis terminating with the Viceroy's House. Radiating avenues connect this central structure with the secretariats, designed by Herbert Baker (1862-1946), which symbolically link the division of power, recalling the formal scheme for Washington, D.C. that inspired it.

The success of the New Delhi commission led to Lutyens' selection to design memorials for those who died in World War I. Again Lutyens turned to the abstract classical language that he had explored in his New Delhi designs. The greatest of these monuments was the Memorial to the Missing of the Somme at Thiepval near Aaras, France (1927-1932). Lutyens selected the classical triumphal arch as the

basis for his design but manipulated this precedent to produce a highly inventive composition. The memorial does not glorify war and triumph, but with its sense of interlocking parts becomes a sublime reminder of the senseless slaughter of the war. The large blank surfaces provided area for the inscription of the names of over 70,000 missing men.

Throughout his career Lutyens received numerous awards and honors, beginning with his knighthood in 1918. This was followed by his election as a Royal Academician in 1920 and his award of the Royal Gold Medal for Architecture in 1921. He became president of the Royal Academy in 1938, and when he died on January 1, 1944 his ashes were honorably interred in St. Paul's Cathedral, London.

Further Reading

The best biography of Lutyens is Christopher Hussey's book *The Life of Sir Edwin Lutyens* (London, 1950), which includes an extensive analysis of his buildings. Later studies of Lutyens' work include Roderick Gradidge, *Edwin Lutyens: Architect Laureate* (London, 1981). Other sources which are particularly good for their illustrations are A. S. G. Butler's book *The Architecture of Sir Edwin Lutyens* (3 vols., London, 1950), which includes a magnificent compilation of Lutyens' main works in drawings, photographs, and descriptions, and the exhibition catalogue by Colin Amery *et al.*, *Lutyens: The Work of the English Architect Sir Edwin Lutyens (1869-1944)* (London, 1981), includes an excellent bibliography. For the creative relationship between Lutyens and the garden designer Gertrude Jekyll see Jane Brown, *Gardens of a Golden Afternoon. The Story of a Partnership: Edwin Lutyens and Gertrude Jekyll* (London, 1982).

Additional Sources

Brown, Jane, *Gardens of a golden afternoon: the story of a partnership, Edwin Lutyens & Gertrude Jekyll,* New York: Van Nostrand Reinhold, 1982; New York: Penguin Books, 1994.

Gradidge, Roderick, *Edwin Lutyens: architect laureate,* London; Boston: Allen & Unwin, 1981.

Hussey, Christopher, *The life of Sir Edwin Lutyens,* Woodbridge, Suffolk: Antique Collectors' Club, 1989.

Lutyens, Mary, *Edwin Lutyens,* London: Murrary, 1980; London: Black Swan, 1991. □

Rosa Luxemburg

Rosa Luxemburg (1870-1919) was a Polish revolutionary and theorist. She led the German workers' uprisings which followed World War I and is considered one of the pioneer activists and foremost martyrs of the international Communist movement.

Rosa Luxemburg was born in Zamo in Russian Poland and brought up in Warsaw. She was the daughter of a middle-class, Polish-speaking Jewish merchant. Dainty, almost tiny, she walked with a limp as the result of a childhood disease.

From her earliest years Rosa possessed "one of the most penetrating analytical minds of her age." In a period when the czarist government was increasing its religious and political oppression in Poland, especially of the Jews, she gained admission to the best girls' high school in Warsaw, usually reserved for Russians. There she joined a revolutionary cell and began a lifelong association with the socialist movement. When she was 18, her activities came to the attention of the Russian secret police, and she fled to Switzerland to avoid arrest.

Luxemburg continued her interests in socialist and revolutionary activities there. She earned a doctorate of laws at the University of Zurich in 1898. Her thesis on industrial development in Poland later served as a basis for the program of the Social Democratic party of Poland. She decided to go to Germany and attach herself to the large, vital, and well-organized Social Democratic party (SPD). In Berlin she obtained German citizenship through a fictitious marriage and quickly became one of the most effective, respected, and even beloved leaders of the international socialist movement.

With Karl Kautsky, Luxemburg headed the revisionist wing of the SPD in opposition to its major theorist, Eduard Bernstein. She wrote articles in socialist newspapers increasingly critical of Bernstein's political and economic theories. Gradually, in a series of works published before the outbreak of World War I, she drifted apart from Kautsky and established herself as the acknowledged leader of the left, or revolutionary, wing of the SPD. She gave new life and theoretical form to the revolutionary goals of the party in a period when most factions were oriented toward parliamentary reform.

During World War I Luxemburg, now dubbed the "Red Rose" by police, was imprisoned for her revolutionary activities. Released for a short time in 1916, she helped to found the revolutionary Spartacus Union with Karl Liebknecht. When she again emerged from prison, in 1918, dissatisfied with the failure to effect a thoroughgoing socialist revolution in Germany, she helped to found the German Communist party (KPD) and its newspaper, the *Rote Fahne,* and drafted its program. She and Liebknecht urged revolution against the Ebert government, which came to power after the armistice, and were largely responsible for the wave of strikes, riots, and violence which swept across Germany from the end of 1918 until June 1919.

In January 1919 one of the most violent outbreaks occurred in Berlin. Luxemburg and Liebknecht, in spite of their doubts as to the timing, supported the Berlin workers in their call for revolution. The troops that were called in acted with extreme violence and brutality, crushing the revolt in a few days. On January 15 Liebknecht and Luxemburg were caught and murdered by the soldiers who held them prisoner.

Further Reading

A good study of Rosa Luxemburg in English is the abridged version of J. P. Nettl, *Rosa Luxemburg* (1966). Nettl presents an exhaustive, scholarly analysis of her life, work, and influence. A shorter but older and more partisan treatment is Paul Frölich, *Rosa Luxemburg: Her Life and Work* (trans. 1940). Luxemburg is discussed in the personal account of Bertram D. Wolfe, *Strange Communists I Have Known* (1965).

Additional Sources

Abraham, Richard, *Rosa Luxemburg: a life for the International,* Oxford England; New York: Berg; New York: Distributed excusively in the US and Canada by St. Martin's Press, 1989.

Bronner, Stephen Eric, *A revolutionary for our times: Rosa Luxemburg,* London: Pluto Press, 1981; New York: Columbia University Press, 1987.

Ettinger, Elzbieta, *Rosa Luxemburg: a life,* Boston: Beacon Press, 1986.

Luxemburg, Rosa, *Comrade and lover: Rosa Luxemburg's Letters to Leo Jogiches,* Cambridge, Mass.: MIT Press, 1979.

Nettl, J. P., *Rosa Luxemburg,* New York: Schocken Books: Distributed by Pantheon Books, 1989, 1969.

Shepardson, Donald E., *Rosa Luxemburg and the noble dream,* New York: P. Lang, 1995. □

Arturo Rogerio Luz

Arturo Rogerio Luz (born 1926) was a Philippine painter and sculptor. His paintings are marked by meticulous simplicity and restraint, with subdued colors and understated form. Luz himself described them as "semirepresentational, semiabstract."

Arturo Luz was born on Nov. 20, 1926, in Manila, Republic of the Phillipines. He studied painting at the School of Fine Arts at the University of Santo Tomas in Manila, the Art School of the Brooklyn Museum in New York, and the Académie Grade Chaumière in Paris; he received a diploma from the California College of Arts and Crafts in Oakland in 1994. He married artist Tessie Ojeda Luz.

Worldwide Recognition

While still in college Luz began exhibiting his works and won his first prize in the annual art competition of the Art Association of the Philippines. Other outstanding awards included the first prize at the First International Art Salon in Saigon, Vietnam, in 1962; an award from the California Art Association; and the Republic Cultural Heritage Award for painting of the Philippine Republic in 1966. He was chosen the "Outstanding Young Man in Art" by the *Manila Times* in 1955.

Luz's works have been exhibited in all major art centers of the world. His design "Harana" (Serenade) was engraved in Steuben glass and displayed as one of two Philippine representatives in the much-heralded exhibit "Asian Artists in Crystal" in 1955. He also represented the Philippines in an exhibition entitled "Arte de America y Espana," organized in Madrid and exhibited in the major cities of Europe.

Some of Luz's better-known paintings are *Street Musicians, Venezia, City,* and *Cyclists No. 2.* A book of his drawings, with an introduction by Emmanuel Torres, was published in 1956.

Luz was much admired by his fellow painters, one of whom, Fernando Zobel de Ayala, called him "a painter's painter" and noted that, when a Luz painting was offered for sale, which was seldom because of the painstaking nature of the artist's work, the buyer was often another painter. "Where other painters shout at the top of their voices," Zobel wrote, "Luz speaks in a whisper and, insidiously, gets a great deal more said."

From Painting to Sculpture

Luz began working with sculpture rather late. Like his painting, it is characterized by simplicity of line and geometry of form. Although *Figura II* stands 6 feet high, most of Luz's sculptural pieces are relatively small. He worked in Philippine hardwoods, marble, and metal and exhibited his sculptures chiefly in Manila. His work has been described as sparse and spatial.

Luz was a founding director of the Metropolitan Museum of Manila, and served in that position from 1976 to 1986. He owned the Luz Gallery in Makati, Philippines. His work, which includes paintings, sculpture, graphics and photographs, is in private and institutional collections.

In 1995, his work was on exhibit at the Metropolitan Museum. At that time, Filipino art critic Rod Paras-Perz said, "The Luz retrospective is still one of the most significant and major shows ever attempted on a contemporary artist."

Further Reading

Information on Luz is sparse, but there is some biographical material in *The Two Thousand Men of Achievement* (1970). A useful background study is W. S. Smith, *Art in the Philippines* (Manila, 1958).

Additional Sources

Yotoko, Marla, "Letter from Manila: Arturo Luz Retrospective at Manila Metropolitan," *Filipino Reporter,* May 4, 1995. □

Moses Hayyim Luzzato

The mysticism of the Jewish mystic and poet Moses Hayyim Luzzato (1707-1747) was based on the coming of the Messiah and the ethical cleansing of men's consciences in preparation for that day.

Moses Luzzato was born in Padua, Italy, and received his early education there. His earliest works were lyrical poems and at least one drama, called *Migdal Oz* (Tower of Strength). Early in his life he took up Cabalistic studies, which were more suited to his poetic sensitivity and intuitive understanding of the world than strictly rabbinic studies. Very soon he claimed to have received communications from angelic voices during mystic trances. Based on these experiences, he composed mystic meditation and Cabalistic theories.

The circle of Luzzato's followers provoked such an impression on the rabbinic authorities that they were reminded of the pseudo-Messiah Sabbatai Zevi, who had shaken world Jewry of his time. They censured Luzzato and exacted a promise from him that he would abstain from Cabalistic writing and surrender his manuscripts to the authorities. It is not clear at this distance whether Luzzato had any conscious intention of proclaiming himself as the Messiah. The messianic fervor created by Sabbatai Zevi in the previous century had not yet died down; many of his followers still believed Sabbatai to be alive and well in a distant country. Indeed, such personal messianism would not really die out in Judaism until the full force of the 18th-century Enlightenment overtook Judaism and concentrated its attention on more worldly interests. At any rate, Luzzato's popularity with his adherents and his mystical explorations seem to have continued even after his censure and abjuration.

Luzzato did not succeed in placating his rabbinic critics, and he was finally forced to leave Padua. He proceeded to Frankfurt and then to Amsterdam. There he became a diamond polisher, but he continued to write his poetry and to meditate on the Cabala. It was here that he composed his most famous works. He wrote a morality play called *La-Yesharim Tehillah* (Praise for the Upright), in which ethical excellence is illustrated and praised, its good effects lauded, and its redemptive value emphasized. In his well-known poem *Mesillat Yesharim* (Path of Upright Ones), he treated the same themes but elaborated on them poetically. Happiness and redemption are tied to an ethically good life. The poem rapidly became a classic in Jewish literature and is one of the most widely read of its kind.

Luzzato decided to go to Palestine, and he settled in Acre in 1744. It is not known whether his move was due to his pursuit of messianic ideals or to pressure from the rabbis. He perished in the plague of 1747.

Further Reading

A study of Luzzato is Simon Ginzburg, *The Life and Works of Moses Hayyim Luzzato: Founder of Modern Hebrew Literature* (1931). Useful background studies with information on Luzzato are Nahum Slouschz, *The Renascence of Hebrew Literature* (trans. 1909); Shalom Spiegel, *Hebrew Reborn* (1930); and Meyer Waxman, *A History of Jewish Literature,* vol. 3 (1936).

Additional Sources

Bindman, Yirmeyahu, *Rabbi Moshe Chaim Luzzatto: his life and works,* Northvale, N.J.: J. Aronson, 1995.

Ginzburg, Simon, *The life and works of Moses Hayyim Luzzatto, founder of modern Hebrew literature,* Westport, Conn.: Greenwood Press, 1975.

Isaacs, A. S. (Abram Samuel), *The life and writings of Moses Chaim Luzzatto: a modern Hebrew poet,* Washington, D.C.: Institute for Jewish Bibliography, 1989. □

Mondino de' Luzzi

The Italian anatomist Mondino de' Luzzi (ca. 1265-1326) prepared an anatomical treatise that has been considered the first modern work on anatomy.

The date and place of birth of Mondino de' Luzzi, as well as other aspects of his life and writings, have long been subjects of scholarly debate. Certain authorities claim that he was a native of Florence or Milan, but it seems likely that he was born in Bologna, where he lived during his boyhood, studied, and, during his adult years, taught and became famous.

Mondino, also known as Mundinus, whose name was probably a diminutive for Raimondo or Rimondo, registered at the College of Medicine of the University of Bologna in 1290 and also is known to have studied in the College of Philosophy. His academic ability is reflected in the fact that he had become a public lecturer at the university by 1314 and that he remained in that capacity until 1324.

During the first decades of the 14th century, Bologna was world-renowned as a center for anatomical studies based on human dissection. The first such recorded anatomical exploration occurred for medicolegal reasons at Bologna in 1302, but it is generally believed that academic dissections had been carried out previously. In any event, Mondino reports that in January 1315 he conducted such a procedure on the body of a woman, affording him the opportunity to examine and study human uterine anatomy.

Before the end of the following year, Mondino completed his *Anathomia.* Despite its title, his treatise resembles less a modern anatomical textbook that describes structures in relation to the systems of the body than it does a dissecting manual. In the *Anathomia,* organs are discussed in the order they appeared to the dissector, and as preservatives were unknown, dissections were performed as rapidly as possible upon the most perishable parts of the body first. Hence, Mondino's work deals with structures in the abdominal cavity initially, then with those of the thoracic cage, and finally with the head and the extremities.

Professors who succeeded Mondino conducted anatomical demonstrations by reading statements, appropriate or not, from classical texts while an assistant actually performed the procedure, but Mondino has been commended for having dissected cadavers himself. Evidence in the *Anathomia* of his firsthand experience is rare, however, and the work abounds with accounts of structures found not in the human body but only in authoritative writings. His descriptions of a five-lobed liver, a seven-celled uterus, and of three cardiac ventricles illustrate that often Mondino dissected in order to prove rather than to test the truth of statements in his sources.

These limitations notwithstanding, the *Anathomia* enjoyed considerable success and was acclaimed as a significant work even before Mondino's death. It was the most popular textbook on anatomy during the period between 1470 and 1530, being replaced only when new texts were written by men who also undertook to study the structure of the human body by means of direct observation and dissection.

Further Reading

Material in English on Mondino is scarce. Perhaps the best account of his *Anathomia* is in Charles Singer, *A Short History of Anatomy from the Greeks to Harvey* (2d ed. 1957; first published as *The Evolution of Anatomy,* 1925). Biographical facts on Mondino are in the English edition of Arturo Castiglioni, *A History of Medicine,* translated by E. B. Krumbhaar (1941; 2d ed. rev. 1947). For background see Ralph H. Major, *A History of Medicine,* vol. 1 (1954), and Benjamin Lee Gordon, *Medieval and Renaissance Medicine* (1959). □

André Lwoff

The French microbiologist, protozoologist, and geneticist André Lwoff (1902-1994) was influential in the creation of the European Organization of Molecular Biology in 1964.

André Lwoff, born May 8, 1902, at Ainay-le-Château (Allier), was the son of Russian parents recently settled in France. He studied science and medicine at the University of Paris and was attached to the Pasteur Institute from 1921, becoming head of the department of microbic physiology and later a professor. He performed services for which he was awarded the Médaille de la

Resistance in 1964 and became *commandeur* of the Légion d'Honneur in 1966. He shared the Nobel Prize for physiology or medicine in 1965 for his research on episomes.

Early bacteriologists had considered bacteria to be primitive forms of life, (protista) more closely akin to animals than plants, because bacteria lacked chlorophyll and were believed to be devoid of such defined structures as nuclei and chromatin. The view that they did not possess specificity and could at times produce various diseases was disproved by Robert Koch, who established the specific lesions of pathogenic microorganisms such as *Bacillus anthracis* and *B. tuberculosis*.

When more refined and powerful methods of investigation became available and the chemistry of nucleoproteins was clarified, it became clear that certain hitherto neglected observations required attention. Among them were the spontaneous clearing of colonies of micrococci found in certain cultures recovered from a vaccine lymph by F. W. Twort (1917) and the clearing of suspensions of dysentery bacilli in an apparently sterile filtrate of the feces from a patient who had the disease by H. d'Hérelle (1917). An astonishing discovery was that when a minute quantity of the clear filtrate was added to a suspension of a fresh subculture of the same organisms, the bacteria under the microscope were seen after a short time to swell and burst, setting free tadpolelike objects that D'Hérelle considered a virus (bacteriophage or phage). According to D'Hérelle, a virus phage became adsorbed by the bacterium, penetrating and dissolving it while multiplying in the process and generating a solvent.

Lwoff adopted a suggestion of Eugène Wollman that the manifestations might be due to the action of genes. A large band of workers was attracted—over 50 are included in Lwoff's list of contributors—and he recorded and analyzed many remarkable findings in his review (1953).

In the United States, particularly, much research was stimulated.

Lwoff speaks of "lysogeny" as the faculty of certain strains of bacteria to produce phage. The production of phage is a lethal process that is survived only if the bacteria do not produce it in their hereditary constitution. The experimental evidence on which the conclusions rest is complex and need not be extended here. As it is expressed by Lwoff: "The unitary concept. . .provides a model to which all the properties of lysogenic bacteria are ascribed. This unitary concept is accounted for by the *presence* and *position* of a specific structure representing the genetic material of the phage, the properties of a lysogenic bacterium being the consequence of the right particle at the right place. Position is the 4th dimension of the prophage. Although the unitary concept has the advantage of explaining lysogeny, lysogenization, incompatibility, immunity and induction—all the properties of lysogenic bacteria—it is only a hypothesis and not a dogma."

Apart from the practical use of Lwoff's conclusions in "typing" strains of organisms recovered in epidemics, a justification of his views appeared later in developments such as those obtained by Shapiro and coworkers (1969), who isolated a complex of genes controlling a single function representing lactose operon.

Lwoff was professor of microbiology at the Sorbonne from 1959 to 1968. In 1968, he left the Pasteur Institute to become head of the Cancer Research Institute at Villejuif, near Paris. He retained that post until 1972.

Lwoff died in Paris on September 30, 1994, at the age of 92. He was the last surviving member of the triad that had shared the 1965 Nobel Prize. Writing in *Le Monde* shortly after Lwoff's death, his colleague, Dr. Claudine Escoffier-Lambiotte, praised Lwoff for his opposition to capital punishment, his love of painting, sculpture, music, and "those things that awaken the spirit." Dr. Escoffier-Lambiotte also noted that Lwoff's "total absence from conformity and diplomacy" often earned the enmity of his colleagues.

Further Reading

A biographical sketch of Lwoff is in Theodore L. Sourkes, *Nobel Prize Winners in Medicine and Physiology, 1901-1965 1901-1965* (rev. ed. 1967); An interesting discussion of Lwoff's personality and career is in Leonard Engel, *The New Genetics* (1967); The book *Of Microbes and Life* (1971) consists of essays by former students and colleagues in celebration of the 50th anniversary of Lwoff's immersion in biology; Lwoff's obituary appeared in *the New York Times* on 4 October 1994. □

Abdoulaye Ly

Abdoulaye Ly (born 1919) was an African historian and Senegalese political leader. He was a key leader of the post-World War II African student generation and among the first to demand independence from France as a legitimate political goal.

Abdoulaye Ly was born in Saint-Louis, Republic of Senegal. He received his higher education in Paris, where he was awarded a doctorate in history and was president of the African Students' Association. Upon his return to Senegal in the middle 1950s, he was appointed head of the historical museum at Gorée and assistant director of the French Institute of Black Africa (Institute Française d'Afrique Noire).

Striving for Independence

A man of great principle and courage, Ly did not hesitate to enter into a minority opposition, even at great peril to his own career, when he thought conditions so warranted. At a time when almost all the established African leaders wanted to continue their membership within the colonial establishment, Ly, as leader of the returning students and technicians, demanded that all of the countries of West Africa leave the French orbit. At a time when France was conducting a war against the Algerians, the idea of seeking increased African representation in the French National Assembly was particularly abhorrent to him.

Political Career

At the same time, Ly and his followers felt that to be effective they could not afford to be isolated. Hence, they decided that their best opportunities lay in bringing about reforms within the governing party rather than remaining on the outside. In 1956 the "young intellectuals" were welcomed into Léopold Senghor's party in power, and Ly was made a minister and party secretary. By September 1958, however, Ly left the government to form a new opposition party over the issue of accepting France's offer of complete and immediate independence, an offer that could also have meant the end of all economic aid. Finally, in 1966, confronted with new issues and trying to raise the standard of living of all the people, Ly brought his followers back into the government, accepting another ministry in order to help in the task of national reconstruction.

According to the Senagalese Embassy in Washington, DC, Ly has been living a quiet life in Saint-Louis for the past several years.

Further Reading

Ruth Schacter Morgenthau presents the best history of Ly's role in the politics of the immediate post-World War II period in *Political Parties in French West Africa* (1964). See also Michael Crowder, *West Africa under Colonial Rule* (1968), for historical background and Irving Leonard Markovitz, *Léopold Sedar Senghor and the Politics of Negritude* (1969), for a discussion of the politics of contemporary France and Senegal.

Among Ly's numerous books, none translated into English thus far, *Les Masses Africaines et l'Actuelle Condition Humaine* (1956), which discusses the theory of modern economic expansionism and anti-imperialism, is the most important; He also published *La Compagnie du Sénégal* (1958), on the mechanics of French exploitation of the colonies; and *Mercenaires Noires* (1957), in which he asserted that black troops were the cannon fodder and instruments of European rivalries. □

Louis Hubert Gonzalve Lyautey

The French marshal and colonial administrator Louis Hubert Gonzalve Lyautey (1854-1934) is famed for the pacification and colonization of Morocco.

On Nov. 17, 1854, L. H. G. Lyautey was born at Nancy to a family with strong military traditions. He was educated at the military academy of Saint-Cyr and the Staff College and was then commissioned as a cavalry officer. He served in Algeria from 1880 to 1887. In 1894 he was transferred to Indochina under Gen. Joseph Simon Gallieni, who first inspired his interest in colonial affairs. When Gallieni was transferred to Madagsgar as governor general, he took Lyautey along as his chief of staff. Together they were very successful in pacifying the island and in applying new methods of government.

In 1900 Lyautey was appointed colonel and, after a short period in France, was given command of the AinSefra territory in Algeria. In 1903 he was promoted to general and, as commander of the Oran division in Algeria, was entrusted with enforcement of international agreements concerning Morocco. He restored order on the border and then served briefly as commander of the X Corps at Rennes.

In April 1912 Lyautey was sent as resident general and high commissioner to Morocco, which had recently been declared a protectorate. He first relieved Fès and then began the tasks of pacification and colonization which were to occupy his attention for the next 13 years. Lyautey's work in Morocco has come to be recognized as a masterpiece of French colonization. He believed that pacification should be achieved with a demonstration of force and as little fighting as possible. To him, colonization was, above all, a creative work. Although he endeavored to preserve the political, social, and economic traditions of Morocco, he wished the country to progress through adopting some of the material civilization of Europe and by acquaintance with its spirit. Medicine, education, public works, and agricultural colonization were the chief means by which he hoped to accomplish these ends.

Although Lyautey was ordered to withdraw from the interior of Morocco at the beginning of World War I, to free as many of his forces as possible, he maintained his ground during the war and even extended the subjugated territory.

He served as minister of war for 3 months, from December 1916 to March 1917, and then returned to Morocco, where he remained until his retirement in 1925, successfully subduing the Riff rebellion under Abd el-Krim. He was elected to the French Academy in 1912 and was made marshal of France in 1921. He wrote many articles on colonial administration. Lyautey died on July 27, 1934, at Thorey, in Lorraine, where he had spent his last years.

Further Reading

A vivid portrayal of Lyautey's thought and personality is in the interesting and literate André Maurois, *Lyautey* (trans. 1931). His career is discussed at length in Eleanor Hoffmann, *Realm of the Evening Star: A History of Morocco and the Land of the Moors* (1965), and John P. Halstead, *Rebirth of a Nation: The Origins and Rise of Moroccan Nationalism, 1912-1944* (1967).

Additional Sources

Hoisington, William A., *Lyautey and the French conquest of Morocco,* New York: St. Martin's Press, 1995. □

John Lydgate

The English poet John Lydgate (ca. 1370-1449) ranks as one of the most prolific, versatile writers of the Middle Ages.

ittle is known of John Lydgate's life. He was a professed disciple of Geoffrey Chaucer, and for many years his fame rivaled Chaucer's. Lydgate became a Benedictine monk at Bury St. Edmund's about 1385, and he was ordained a priest in 1397. He studied at Oxford. His early poems, written before 1412, include *The Temple of Glas,* perhaps composed to be read at a wedding ceremony, and *Reson and Sensuallyte,* an adaptation of part of a long French allegory.

Lydgate's first major poem was his *Troy Book* (1412-1420), based on the *Historia Troiana* of Guido delle Colonne (1287). It contains more than 30,000 lines and was dedicated to Henry V. The poet became associated with Chaucer's son Thomas, who entertained a number of prominent persons, including Humphrey of Gloucester, John Tiptoft, Thomas Montague, and William de la Pole, at his estate not far from Oxford. Between 1420 and 1422 Lydgate wrote *The Siege of Thebes,* a tribute to Geoffrey Chaucer and, in form, a continuation of *The Canterbury Tales.* Probably at the request of Humphrey, Lydgate wrote *The Serpent of Division* (1422), a prose life of Julius Caesar designed as a warning against division in the kingdom.

In 1423 Lydgate became prior of Hatfield. During the next few years he wrote a number of "mummings," or allegorical performances, in which various figures appeared and performed symbolic actions while a narrator described the proceedings in verse. About 1426 the poet went to Paris for a visit of about 2 years. There he wrote his verse adaptation of Deguileville's *Pelerinage de la vie humaine* (original revised about 1355) for Thomas Montague, Earl of Salis-

bury. This long allegory of salvation contains more than 24,000 lines. He also composed an English version of the *Danse macabre.*

Between 1431 and 1439 Lydgate worked on his masterpiece, *The Fall of Princes,* written for Duke Humphrey. Giovanni Boccaccio had written a series of "tragedies," or stories of great men who through a weakness subjected themselves to fortune and thus fell, in a collection called *De casibus virorum illustrium* (1355-1360). These stories had been adapted into French prose by Laurent de Premierfait. Lydgate turned Laurent's version into an enormously long and popular English poem in nine books.

In addition to these works, Lydgate also wrote saints' lives, devotional poems, and occasional pieces. Generally, artificial diction and obvious moralizing mark his poetry, but it represents the attitudes and tastes of his time.

Further Reading

An interesting study of the poet and his work is Derek Pearsall, *John Lydgate* (1970).

Additional Sources

Schirmer, Walter F. (Walter Franz), *John Lydgate: a study in the culture of the XVth century,* Westport, Conn.: Greenwood Press, 1979, 1961. ☐

Sir Charles Lyell

The Scottish geologist Sir Charles Lyell (1797-1875) established the uniformitarian view of geology.

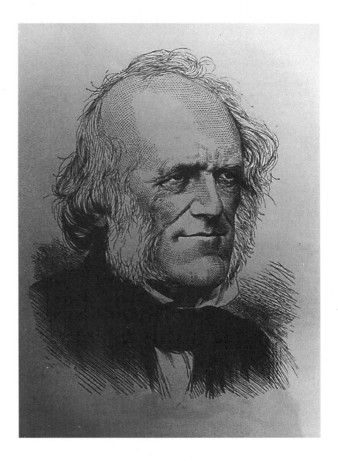

Charles Lyell, the eldest son of Charles Lyell, was born at Kinnordy, Forfar, the family estate, on Nov. 14, 1797. During his early childhood, the family moved to Lyndhurst, Hampshire, where he received his early education. He showed a keen interest in collecting moths, a hobby he pursued throughout his life. At age 15 Lyell read Robert Bakewell's *Introduction to Geology* (1813), which aroused his interest in geology. Entering Exeter College, Oxford, in 1816, he studied classics and attended geology lectures with William Buckland.

Lyell earned his bachelor's degree in 1819 and then entered Lincoln's Inn to study law. However, eye trouble interrupted his law study, and he developed an even greater affinity for geological study. He joined the Geological Society, becoming its secretary in 1823 and later president for two terms.

Beginning with Rome in 1820, Lyell made several geological tours on the Continent as well as in England and Scotland. Returning to law in 1825, he was called to the bar and practiced intermittently for 3 years, during which time he also wrote many papers on geological subjects, published primarily in the proceedings of the Geological Society.

In *Principles of Geology* (3 vols., 1830-1833) Lyell attempted to explain the former changes of the earth's surface by reference to causes now in operation. The continuous revision and expansion of the *Principles,* his main object in life, form a record of 40 years' progress in geology through the 12 editions. The twelfth edition was published posthumously in 1875. In these volumes, through his wide-ranging synthesis of geological phenomena observed in Europe and America, Lyell established the uniformitarian view of geology; that is, contemporary processes, long continued, of land erosion and deposition coupled with slow uplift of sea floors were a sound basis for reconstructing the earth's past. The wasting land of one age becomes the rocks of later ages. This view, set out with forensic skill, opposed and displaced the catastrophist view of sudden violent occurrences, the last of which was believed to be Noah's flood.

Lyell served as the first professor of geology at King's College, London, from 1831 to 1833. In 1832 he married Mary Horner; they had no children. He stopped teaching to devote his time to research and writing. In addition to the *Principles,* he wrote *Manual of Elementary Geology* (1838), two accounts of his North American travels (1845, 1849), and *Geological Evidence of the Antiquity of Man* (3 eds., 1863-1873).

Lyell was elected a fellow of the Royal Society in 1826; was knighted in 1848; was awarded the Copley Medal in 1858; and was created baronet in 1864. He died on Feb. 22, 1875, in London and was buried in Westminster Abbey.

Further Reading

Important biographical material is in *Life, Letters and Journals of Sir Charles Lyell, Bart,* edited by his sister-in-law, Katherine Lyell (2 vols., 1881). The two major studies of Lyell are Thomas G. Bonney, *Charles Lyell and Modern Geology* (1901), and Edward Bailey, *Charles Lyell* (1962). □

Helen Merrell Lynd

Sociologist and educator Helen Merrell Lynd (1896-1982) was a coauthor of the classic sociological study *Middletown: A Study in Contemporary American Culture.* With her husband, Robert S. Lynd, she studied the beliefs and practices of the residents of a small industrial town to provide a unique portrait of American life in the 1920s. They returned to the town during the Great Depression of the 1930s to observe changes in the community, a study which was published as *Middletown in Transition: A Study in Cultural Conflicts.*

Helen Merrell Lynd, with her husband, Robert S. Lynd, coauthored the classic sociological work *Middletown: A Study in Contemporary American Culture.* A study of the lives of the citizens of an average American town in the 1920s, the book became a best-seller and a standard text for sociology students. The Lynds followed up on Middletown residents in the 1930s, producing the volume *Middletown in Transition: A Study in Cultural Conflicts.* In addition to these collaborative works with her husband, Lynd also had a successful independent career in academia. A longtime member of the staff of Sarah Lawrence College, she wrote a number of books on education, history, philosophy, and sociology.

Lynd was born Helen Merrell on March 17, 1896, in La Grange, Illinois. She was one of the three daughters of Edward Tracy Merrell, the editor of the Congregationalist Church publication *The Advance,* and Mabel Waite Merrell. Her parents maintained a strong emphasis on religion in their home, passing along to their daughters a commitment to humanitarian and social issues. Lynd spent her primary school and high school years attending classes in La Grange. After she had graduated from high school, her father took a new job and the family moved to Framingham, Massachusetts. There, Lynd enrolled in Wellesley College, where she developed an interest in philosophy. She excelled in her studies and was elected to the Phi Beta Kappa honor society before she graduated with a bachelor of arts degree in 1919.

Studied Small Town Life

After leaving Wellesley, Lynd taught for a year at the Ossining School for Girls in Ossining, New York. It was while on a mountain climbing trip during this time that she met Robert S. Lynd, who was then in the publishing busi-ness. The next year she worked as a teacher at Miss Master's School in Dobbs Ferry, New York. In September of 1922, she and Robert Lynd were married; that same year she received a masters degree in history from Columbia University in New York. Robert Lynd had also decided to pursue advanced studies and was enrolled in Union Theological Seminary at the time of the couple's marriage. After he received his doctor of divinity degree in 1923, he and Lynd traveled to oil fields in the western United States where Robert Lynd worked as a missionary. After viewing the poor conditions of workers in the oil drilling business, the Lynds became interested in sociological aspects of small industrial towns. In the mid-1920s, Robert Lynd organized a series of studies on small towns for the Institute of Social and Religious Research. The institute then hired the Lynds to conduct a thorough examination of the religious life of an average small industrial town in America. The couple selected the town of Muncie, Indiana, as their subject.

The Lynds arrived in Muncie with a small team of researchers in January of 1924. They found it impossible to study just the religious aspects of the town; instead they spent the next one and a half years studying every aspect of town life. They used strategies familiar to anthropologists studying an unfamiliar culture, analyzing the activities the community engaged in to ensure its survival. These included employment, housing, education and training of children, religion, leisure, and community events. The Lynds, who coauthored the study, did not impose any evaluation or judgement on their subject, but simply presented objective observations. Their work did, however, reveal distinct class differences in the city. While the upper classes enjoyed habits of conspicuous consumption, the working class struggled to meet material needs, but maintained an optimism that hard work would allow them to change their social and economic position.

Middletown Praised for Research

Concluding their study in 1925, the Lynds submitted it to the Institute of Social and Religious Research and received a chilly response. The research was not what they had expected, and the organization refused to publish the work. The Lynds searched around for a publisher, and their work was finally accepted by the Harcourt, Brace Company. In order to keep the identity of their subject anonymous, they renamed Muncie as "Middletown" in their book. But upon the publication of *Middletown: A Study in Contemporary American Culture* in 1929, the residents of Muncie immediately recognized their town and charged that the book was overly critical of the community. Others around the country praised the work, however, and it went through six printings in its first year. Sociologists found a successful technique in the Lynds' research that was soon emulated in studies of other cities. Social critics saw *Middletown* as providing evidence of the vacuousness of American culture.

Because of gender inequities in academia at that time, Robert Lynd received much of the acclaim for *Middletown's* success. He was named professor of sociology at Columbia University in 1931, receiving his Ph.D. in the subject by submitting a copy of *Middletown* under only his name as his dissertation. Helen Lynd joined the faculty of the new Sarah Lawrence College in 1928; she would remain with the institution until her retirement in 1964. During her tenure there, she helped to institute many of the nontraditional educational methods for which the women's college became renowned. In the early years of their college teaching careers, the Lynds had two children, their son Staughton, born in 1929, and their daughter, Andrea, born in 1934.

Studied Effects of Great Depression

With the Great Depression of the 1930s, the Lynds were curious to see how the nation-wide economic strife was affecting the town of Muncie. They returned for a follow-up study in 1935. The resulting book, *Middletown in Transition: A Study in Cultural Conflicts,* found that the family that owned the local factory had gained even more power in the local economy, creating a starker division between the classes. The tone of this second study was markedly different from the first; the Lynds no longer made any attempt to hide their leftist sympathies and expressed disappointment that the town citizens still felt that the hard work of the individual, rather than the solidarity of workers, was the key to a better life. Throughout the 1930s and 1940s, the Lynds would become more outspoken on leftist and liberal ideas, leading them to support the position of the Soviet Union in the early days of the Cold War after World War II, even though they were never aligned with the Communist Party. Helen Lynd was particularly vocal in her criticisms of the American attacks on Communism that were highlighted by the McCarthy era trials of accused Communists. This led to Lynd herself being called before a Senate investigating committee during that time.

In the 1940s, Lynd returned to her work in history and philosophy, earning a Ph.D. in both subjects from Columbia University in 1944. Her dissertation was published in 1945 as *England in the Eighteen-Eighties: Toward a Social Basis for Freedom.* The work studied social and material changes among the upper and lower classes of England during a period of industrial and economic growth. It was hailed as a powerful book marked by its thorough research and flowing prose. A 1958 work by Lynd also displayed her continuing interest in sociological topics. In *On Shame and the Search for Identity,* she compared the idea of guilt, a feeling created by breaking a rule of society, with the concept of shame, the sense of having betrayed the self. Psychologists and psychiatrists saw the work as a valuable reevaluation of the ideas of identity presented by Sigmund Freud. The book also helped to link the areas of sociology and psychology by showing that they each played a role in creating the personality of the individual. Lynd also wrote a number of books on education during her career, including *Field Work in Education* in 1945 and *Toward Discovery* in 1965.

After retiring from Sarah Lawrence College in 1964, Lynd continued to teach there on a part-time basis until just before her death. She died in Warren, Ohio, on January 30, 1982. Although best known for her collaboration with her husband on the Middletown studies, Lynd also left her mark as an outstanding academic. Through her teaching and writ-

ings, she contributed a number of new ideas that had an important influence on the fields of education and sociology.

Further Reading

Deegan, Mary Jo, editor. *Women in Sociology: A Bio-Bibliographical Sourcebook,* Greenwood Press, 1991.

Horowitz, Irving Louis, "Robert S. and Helen Merrell Lynd," in *International Encyclopedia of the Social Sciences: Biographical Supplement,* edited by David L. Sills, Free Press, 1979.

Madge, John, *The Origins of Scientific Sociology,* Free Press, 1962. □

Robert Staughton Lynd

The American sociologist Robert Staughton Lynd (1892-1970) greatly influenced American sociology through his "Middletown" studies.

Robert S. Lynd was born in Indiana. He wrote a sensitive account of the influence of his background in *Middletown in Transition:* "Although reared during his first 18 years in a city of 18,000 population in the same state as Middletown, the investigator came to Middletown in 1924 after fourteen years spent in the East. Accordingly, he may have had an outlook somewhat different from the modal outlook of Middletown, even though the culture of the East North Central and Middle Atlantic States are fundamentally overwhelmingly alike. The fact that he came from ten years of residence in New York City to a city of 36,000 in 1924 may have emphasized latent differences. The fact that, despite several years of business experience, he came as an 'academic' person undoubtedly made a difference."

The first book, *Middletown,* by Lynd and his wife, Helen Merrill Lynd, was the first elaborate study of an American community from a scientific rather than from a social-reform perspective. This is of special interest in the case of the Lynds because they were not trained previously in sociology. Lynd had been associated with the Commonwealth Fund, and *Middletown* was one of a series of social and religious surveys. Unlike the usual survey, *Middletown* was a study of an average American city with reference to the six main-trunk activities of a community: getting a living, making a home, training the young, using leisure, engaging in religious practices, and engaging in community activities. The Lynds described in some detail the nature of bureaucratic organization and the structure of power in Middletown. It was one of the first sociological analyses of bureaucracy and power in a local community setting.

Perhaps owing to its departure from the usual social survey format (and perhaps owing to the candor with which the Lynds discussed certain personalities in Middletown, which later was identified as Muncie, Ind.), there is reported to have been some doubt as to whether the study should be published until Clark Wissler, a highly regarded anthropologist, was obtained to write an introduction placing the study in the frame of reference of the anthropological method of studying a community and its culture. The success of Lynd's approach can be seen from a survey made in 1950 of 47 introductory textbooks, in which 304 sociology authors were indexed. Lynd was in the top 30 for number of times cited.

The publication of *Middletown* in 1929 was followed in 1937 by that of a follow-up study, *Middletown in Transition,* an unusual practice in itself even today among social scientists.

In 1938 Lynd delivered the Stafford Little Lectures at Princeton, which were published under the title *Knowledge for What?* He emphasized that man's biology imposes certain needs and rhythms on him and that social institutions reflect needs and rhythms insofar as man is able to make them do so. Another contribution by Lynd was his attempt to view power as a major social resource instead of chiefly as a concomitant of conflict of interests. Even today this approach still merits exploiting.

From a beginning as a nonsociologist, Lynd came to occupy a professor's chair in sociology at Columbia University, was elected president of the Eastern Sociology Society in 1944, and was elected to membership in the Sociological Research Association.

Further Reading

For information on Lynd see Robert Bierstedt, *The Social Order* (1957; 3d ed. 1970); Irwin Taylor Sanders, *The Community: An Introduction to a Social System* (1958); Alvin and Helen Gouldner, *Modern Sociology: An Introduction to the Study of Human Interaction* (1963); and Ritchie Plowry and Robert P. Rankin, *Sociology: The Science of Society* (1969). □

Staughton Lynd

One of the most outspoken opponents of the Vietnam War, rebellious historian Staughton Lynd (born 1929) became a leading peace militant, and as a result he was shunned by academe and turned to the practice of law.

Staughton Lynd was the son of two of America's most famous sociologists, Helen Merrell Lynd and Robert S. Lynd, the authors of *Middletown.* In their pioneering study of an industrial American city (Muncie, Indiana), the senior Lynds concluded that the gap between middle-class and working-class people was crucial in determining their different life styles. Staughton Lynd never forgot this lesson.

He was born in Philadelphia, Pennsylvania, on November 22, 1929. When he was two years old his father was appointed professor of sociology at Columbia University, and Lynd grew up in the urban intellectual environment of New York City. His family played a vital role in the molding of his mind. His father had originally planned on a religious career. When he moved into academic work, his study of sociology tended to sustain the "class struggle" theory of

Karl Marx. Thus Lynd's family was not only interested in events around them, it was eager to play some role in shaping those events.

Lynd had difficulty discovering what he wanted to do with his life. After earning both Bachelor's and Master's degrees at Harvard University he worked on a farm, made toys in a utopian community, organized tenants to combat rent-gouging landlords, and served as a non-combatant conscientious objector in the army. In 1958 he decided on a career in the study and teaching of history. In 1962 he received his doctorate from Columbia University. He wanted to follow somewhat in his father's footsteps by being) a student, author, and participant in contemporary American radical history. His decision was certain to cause problems for him, because most older historians then took the posture of "objectivity." This meant that they approved the idea of study and authorship, but frowned upon young scholars who sought to play an active role in history.

Moreover, the United States in the 1960s did not lend itself to objective contemplation. It was a polarizing society divided between youth and age, between Black people and white, and between "hawks" who favored military solutions in international situations (particularly in Vietnam) and "doves" who preferred peaceful solutions. Lynd was a young Quaker and a member of Students for a Democratic Society (SDS) who opposed U.S. involvement in the war in Asia. Lynd's sympathies were with the southern segregated Blacks who were fighting for voting rights and education. Lynd joined the Student Non-violent Coordinating Committee (SNCC) which had been formed while he was in graduate school. SNCC was committed to the mass education and political organization of the poorest southern Blacks. Lynd's first teaching job was at a Black school in Atlanta, Georgia—Spelman College. Thus he was an obvious choice to serve in the summer of 1964 as a SNCC education project director in Mississippi. There he hired teachers, wrote curricula, located whatever classroom buildings he could, and began to teach reading and writing to illiterate working class people.

In the fall of 1964 Lynd returned to New England to teach history as an untenured assistant professor at Yale University. By the spring of 1965 the First Marine Division had landed at Danang Air Base in South Vietnam, and the United States had started bombing enemy targets in Laos and North Vietnam. Lynd found his attention drawn away from the classroom and into active anti-war activity. During the summer of 1965 he refused to pay his taxes, and he openly advocated non-violent civil disobedience by those who opted to refuse draft induction. In August 1965 Lynd, David Dellinger, and 350 other protesters were summarily arrested in front of the Capitol in Washington, D.C., for attempting to read a "Declaration of Peace" to the U.S. Congress. The conservative faculty members and administrators at Yale were not pleased with their young colleague's behavior.

In December 1965 Herbert Aptheker, an American Communist historian, was invited to visit North Vietnam and to bring two non-Communist Americans with him. He chose as his travelling companions Tom Hayden, one of the founders of SDS, and Staughton Lynd. As soon as the university semester ended, the three men flew in defiance of U.S. travel regulations and without American passports to the Communist capital cities of Prague, Moscow, Peking, and Hanoi. They returned in early January and wrote a book appealing to Americans to look at the war through the eyes of the Asian peoples. Lynd started looking for another job as it became apparent that his Yale contract would not be renewed.

During the 1960s Lynd's fame in the resistance movement made him a favored speaker at rallies and demonstrations. A man of inexhaustible energy, he authored a succession of books and articles on history and radical politics. He was invited to teach at four different universities in Illinois, but at the last moment each time he was rejected. There was no question in his mind that he had been blacklisted by academe after the Hanoi trip.

By the beginning of the 1970s it was clear that Lynd could not stand up actively for what he believed and at the same time be hired to teach history at any first-rank American university. He graduated from the University of Chicago Law School in 1976 and soon afterward joined the staff of a Youngstown, Ohio, law firm specializing in labor law. Later he was hired by the National Legal Services Corporation to take legal cases for people too poor to pay for court representation. Lynd then began the next phase of his intellectual journey-towards a leftist critique of American capitalism, somewhere in that space which his father and Karl Marx said lay between middle and working class. In an interview with Jane Slaughter of the *Progressive,* Lynd said he found himself "in an odd position about Marxism. . .to the Marxists I seem like some sort of middle-class sentimentalist. To everyone else I seem like a hardcore Marxist." During the recession of the early 1980s—the worst economic downturn since the Great Depression of the 1930s—he joined with steelworkers in Youngstown to fight the closings of their plants, and wrote a book about their efforts, *The Fight Against Shutdowns—the Youngstown Steel Mill Closings.*

Throughout the 1980s and 1990s, Lynd continued to battle against injustice by corporate America, writing books and articles and seeking to mobilize workers in defense of their rights. He proclaimed in the *Progressive* interview that "Since coming to Youngstown, I've become more of a Marxist. I've seen. . .capital at work when U.S. Steel felt it could make more money by buying another company than by rebuilding its own steel mills." While others on the left urged the support of President Clinton, Lynd said that the President was a hypocrite who made "compassionate noises" while not having any intention to actually do anything about economic injustice.

Further Reading

Lynd's writings fall into three categories. His outstanding contribution to historical analysis is *Intellectual Origins of American Radicalism* (1968). His best-known books on the politics of the 1960s are *The Other Side* (co-authored with Tom Hayden) (1967) and *The Resistance* (co-authored with Michael Ferber) (1971). Among his many works on the U.S. labor movement are *American Labor Radicalism* (1973); *Rank and File* (1981); *The Fight Against Shutdowns—The Youngstown Steel Mill Closings* (Singlejack Books, 1982); *Empty Promise—Quality of Live Programs and the Labor Movement* (Monthly Review Press, 1987); and *Solidarity Unionism: Rebuilding the Labor Movement from Below* (1994). An interview with Staughton Lynd by Jane Slaughter was in the February, 1994, issue of the *Progressive.* □

Sir David Lyndsay

The Scottish poet and courtier Sir David Lyndsay (ca. 1485-1555) was probably the best-known Scottish poet from his death until the mid-18th century. He was widely credited with effecting the reformation of the Scottish Church.

David Lyndsay was the eldest son of Sir David Lyndsay of the Mount, a Scottish nobleman. Nothing is known of his youth, although his poetry suggests that he had a sound formal education. He first appears in court records as a participant in a play performed in 1511. In 1512 he was appointed "usher," or personal attendant, to the infant prince, who would become King James V. He later reminded the King in one of his poems of how he cared for him, played the lute for him, told him stories, and entertained him. In 1522 Lyndsay married Janet Douglas, a royal seamstress.

In 1524 young James fell under the control of the Queen Mother and the Douglases, and Lyndsay lost his position at court. But in 1528 the Douglases fell from power, and Lyndsay was restored. He acted as chief herald to the King from 1529 until 1542, when he was knighted and made Lyon king, or chief herald, officially. His earliest attack on the evils of the times appears in "The Testament and Compleynt of Our Soverane Lordis Papyngo" (1530). The clergy here suffers heavily, for the dying parrot (papyngo) is ill-treated by a magpie (regular canon), a raven (Benedictine), and a kite (friar). After abusing the poor parrot, these "birds" devour him.

His official position at court took Lyndsay overseas at various times in the capacity of an ambassador. Thus he accompanied the envoys sent to arrange a marriage between King James V and Marie de Bourbon. But James, who followed his ambassadors, preferred Magdalen, eldest daughter of the King of France. She was of frail constitution, however, and died before her coronation. Lyndsay wrote an elegy for her in which he describes in detail the pageantry that was to have accompanied the ceremony. James married Mary of Lorraine in 1538. She was welcomed at St. Andrews with an elaborate and instructive pageant designed by Sir David.

Shortly after the marriage of the King, Lyndsay composed his most famous work, *A Pleasant Satyre of the Thrie Estaits,* an interlude or play faintly reminiscent in substance and technique of the "Vision" of *Piers Plowman* attributed to William Langland. But the reforming doctrines are now more extreme, and there are direct attacks on the Pope. The clergy is revealed to be sensual, ignorant, grasping, and generally corrupt, and there are unmistakable traces of the traditional attacks on the friars that also appear in Geoffrey Chaucer and William Dunbar. The play is vigorous and effective. It was performed again in 1552 and in an expanded version in 1554.

The English invaded Scotland in 1542, and King James died late in the year. As Lyon king, Sir David visited the courts of Charles V, Francis I, and Henry VIII to return the Order of the Golden Fleece, the Order of St. Michael, and the Order of the Garter held by his late master. Lyndsay's interest in chivalry is evident in his biography in the form of a romance, *Squyer Meldrum,* written about 1550. The young hero, who was an actual person, distinguishes himself in both war and love. The same interest appears in different form in the satirical poem "The Justing betwix James Watsoun and Jhone Barbour."

It is difficult to estimate Lyndsay's exact position with reference to the Church. He is said to have encouraged John Knox, but he can hardly be called a follower of Knox. His last work, *The Monarchie,* completed about 1553, is a poem of religious instruction. In it he recommends that the Bible be read in the language of the people and that ordinary prayers also be conducted in that language.

Further Reading

A good account of Lyndsay's life and work is by William Murison, *Sir David Lyndsay: Poet and Satirist of the Old Church in Scotland* (1938). A biography of Lyndsay appears in Henry Morley, *English Writers* (11 vols., 1887-1895), and a brief scholarly study of his work in James Kinsley, ed., *Scottish Poetry: A Critical Survey* (1955), Kurt Wittig, *The Scottish Tradition in Literature* (1958), contains a chapter on Lyndsay.

☐

Mary Lyon

Mary Lyon (1797-1849) was the founder of Mount Holyoke Female Seminary and a pioneer in women's education.

In the midst of the panic of 1837, an economic depression which left many Americans jobless, homeless, and helpless, Mary Lyon opened a new school to educate young women. Though the institution, known as Mount Holyoke Female Seminary, was not filled to capacity, she would not be discouraged. She was determined to offer women the kind of education available only—until then—in men's colleges.

A descendent of hardy New England pioneers, Lyon saw examples of courage on both sides of her family. After completing his studies at Cambridge University, her maternal ancestor, the Reverend Henry Smith, journeyed across the Atlantic to become a minister in Connecticut. Lyon's great-grandfather, Chileab Smith, staged a successful battle to avoid paying taxes for the support of the Anglican Church in Massachusetts; a devout Baptist, he took his case all the

way to London. Chileab lived to see the birth of his great-granddaughter Mary Lyon on February 28, 1797, in Buckland, Massachusetts. As the sixth child of Jemima Shepard Lyon and Aaron Lyon, a Revolutionary War veteran and farmer, she enjoyed a happy childhood. The bright, inquisitive blue-eyed girl was described by an early biographer as:

> possessed of an energy that was volcanic and of a sweet teachableness that won hearts. Through glad eyes she looked at the world and found it good, and the people in it. . . . Her laugh lay very near her lips. . . .

Lyon's delightful sense of humor became troublesome, however, when she began teaching, at age 17. In an age when children's conduct was considered more important than their academic achievements, Lyon's tendency to laugh along with her pupils, combined with the fact that she was a less-than-perfect disciplinarian, was looked on as an impediment. Realizing that besides improving her style of classroom management she needed to acquire more education, at age 20 Lyon began studying in earnest at Sanderson Academy in Ashfield, Massachusetts. "In that quiet retreat among the hills," she recalled later, "the intellect was stirred, the taste refined, and intensity given to the desire for knowledge. To mind and heart that institution was what the mountain airs are to the physical powers."

At Sanderson, Lyon studied mathematics, logic, speech, grammar, and geography. When she wasn't drawing maps, or acting in school plays, she was learning

etiquette in the home of attorney Thomas White where she boarded. White's daughter Amanda became Lyon's lifelong friend, and in 1821 they went off to the Byfield Massachusetts Female Seminary together. By this time, having alternated between teaching and attending school at both Sanderson and Amherst Academy, Lyon was ready to devote herself to full-time study.

The experience at Byfield was intellectually rewarding. She forged close ties with Zilpah Grant, a faculty member who would later invite Lyon to become a teacher at the Ipswich Female Seminary where Grant would serve as principal. Lyon also underwent a religious conversion and joined the Congregational Church; religion, together with learning and family, thereafter played an important role in her life. She was exposed to the Reverend Joseph Emerson's advanced views on education for women. As both head of the school and a gifted teacher, Emerson was very influential, telling his students: "It is thinking, close thinking that makes the scholar." In class, he posed many questions, encouraging students to find the relationships between the various subjects they discussed. He also encouraged the diverse student body, which included a minister's widow in her 30s, to converse among themselves and learn from one another. The use of discussion as a teaching tool appealed to Lyon, and in 1824, when she established her own school, the Buckland Female Seminary, she had her students discuss articles from contemporary magazines. She became a popular and gifted teacher.

In 1833, Lyon embarked upon what was then considered a long journey, traveling to Philadelphia, Detroit, and western New York, where she was reunited with a brother she had not seen in many years. During her travels, Lyon stopped at various schools, including Emma Willard's famous Troy Female Seminary. When she returned to Massachusetts, she was determined to open a new school.

Now 36, Lyon possessed an impressive resume. Though her Buckland Female Seminary had closed after her departure for Zilpah Grant's Ipswich Academy, she continued her education by studying part-time at Amherst College and at the school known later as Rensselaer Polytechnic Institute. Both her education and teaching career were interrupted by typhoid fever in 1828 but, once recovered, she devoted her energy to helping Zilpah Grant raise funds for the Ipswich Academy and for a seminary they hoped to create for the training of teachers. These efforts were unsuccessful; the seminary was never established, and Ipswich Academy was ultimately forced to close in 1839. With the exception of a brief assignment as acting principal in Grant's absence, Lyon had severed her ties with Ipswich in 1834 and was then hired to finalize plans for the institution known today as Wheaton College.

In 1836, the year after Wheaton opened, Lyon's own Mount Holyoke Female Seminary was chartered. Envisioned as a nonprofit Christian institution charging tuition and fees low enough for "the daughters of the common people" to obtain a liberal education, Mount Holyoke was endorsed by New England ministers, but the seed money for the new school was furnished by women. In keeping with the concept of "republican motherhood," well-educated women were deemed better able to raise the next generation of citizens, and Lyon hoped to see the influence of such women spread beyond the household. But first, a considerable amount of money would be required for her new school. To raise the initial $1,000, Lyon made personal visits to the homes of Ipswich women. Her enthusiasm and a rapid-fire explanation of her new educational venture caused donors to loosen their purse strings.

Besides raising money, Lyon oversaw the construction of the school's first building. The sizable contribution made by the community of South Hadley, Massachusetts, convinced the institution's trustees to choose that city for the site. But the discovery of quicksand at the location and the collapse of a brick wall slowed construction of the four-story Georgian style building. Finally, in the fall of 1837, Mount Holyoke Female Seminary, which derived its name from a geographic feature of the area, was completed. Contemplating the official opening of her experiment in women's education, Lyon noted in September 1837:

> When I look through to November eighth it seems like looking down a precipice of many hundred feet, which I must descend. I can only avoid looking at the bottom, and fix my eye on the nearest stone, till I have safely reached it.

The excitement of opening day was tempered by the panic of 1837. Initially only 80 students enrolled, but a few months later there were over 100 girls, age 17 and above, in attendance. To keep costs low and create a family atmosphere, students, along with the founder, performed the domestic work. According to Lyon's friend, Edward Hitchcock, president of Amherst College:

> During that first cold winter, Miss Lyon's powers of body and mind were in constant service from sixteen to eighteen hours out of the twenty-four.... From basement to attic she was in constant request. The celebrity of her movements was almost equal to the gift of multipresence, and yet she could hardly answer the calls for her aid and counsel.

While her dedication set the tone for life at Mount Holyoke, both outside and inside the classroom, it was in the academic area that she made her most important contribution. Striving to give students an intellectual experience comparable to that of men's colleges, Lyon included natural science, mathematics, philosophy, and economics in a constantly evolving curriculum. When the school first opened, she taught chemistry and logic herself. In time, visiting professors were added to the faculty and students were encouraged to stretch themselves intellectually, culturally, and physically.

At the same time, they were urged to cooperate with one another. Out of this came something known as the "Holyoke spirit," consisting of "alertness, democracy, sincerity and an unobtrusive helpfulness." This spirit made itself felt beyond South Hadley as Mount Holyoke graduates—responding to Lyon's advice: "Do what nobody else wants to do, go where nobody else wants to go"—went out to become teachers in far-flung places.

Others became missionaries, a calling Lyon praised in her book, *A Missionary Offering,* published in 1843. Two of her favorite nieces went off to the Far East as missionaries; their departure from South Hadley saddened Lyon, who had also lost her mother in 1840 and a nephew to suicide in 1849. At the time of her nephew's death, Lyon herself was ill with erysipelas, an infectious skin disease resulting in fever, chills and inflammation. Within a few months, she died.

Lyon's passing on March 5, 1849, saw the termination of a brilliant career and the end of the first phase of Mount Holyoke's development. But, in accordance with her original plan, the school continued to prosper, for unlike earlier institutions with which she had been associated, Mount Holyoke was not dependent upon any one individual. It was a nonprofit corporation with a board of trustees who could ensure a smooth transition from one administration to the next. This was exactly what Mary Lyon had envisioned when she wrote:

Uncommon talents are very convenient, but they are so rare an occurrence that any establishment, so organized that it be sustained and prosper only by such talents, would ever be in danger of falling by its own weight, and of being crushed by its own ruins.

Yet, Lyon was a person of uncommon talents. An extraordinarily effective teacher, she was warm, encouraging, and readily accessible to her students and the many visitors to Mount Holyoke; she was also a first-rate administrator who created the illusion that the operation of the seminary was effortless. In reality, careful planning and strenuous efforts characterized her undertakings, setting a supreme example for those who followed her at Mount Holyoke and the numerous other schools that derived inspiration from her achievements.

Further Reading

Gilchrist, Beth Bradford. *The Life of Mary Lyon.* Houghton Mifflin, 1910.
Green, Elizabeth Ann. *Mary Lyon and Mount Holyoke Opening the Gates.* University Press of New England, 1979.
Hitchcock, Edward. *The Power of Christian Benevolence Illustrated in the Life and Labors of Mary Lyon.* The American Tract Society, 1858.
Lansing, Marion, ed. *Mary Lyon Through Her Letters.* Bruce Humphries, 1937.
Stow, Sarah. *History of Mount Holyoke Seminary.* Mount Holyoke Seminary, 1887.
Boynick, David K. *Women Who Led the Way: Eight Pioneers for Equal Rights.* Thomas Y. Crowell, 1959
Cole, Arthur C. *A Hundred Years of Mount Holyoke College: The Evolution of Educational Ideal.* Yale University Press, 1940.
Fenner, Mildred S. and Eleanor Fishburn. *Pioneer American Educators.* Kennikat, 1968.
Goodsell, Willystine. *Pioneers of Women's Education in the United States.* AMS Press, 1970. □

Joseph Aloysius Lyons

The Australian statesman Joseph Aloysius Lyons (1879-1939) was a Labour stalwart in Tasmania and later moved to the federal sphere just as the Depression took hold. As leader of the new United Australia party, he served as prime minister from 1932 to 1939.

The son of a farmer, Joseph Lyons was born in Stanley, Tasmania, on Sept. 15, 1879. At 17 he qualified as a teacher with the education department. He was an active advocate of educational reform, and in 1907 he resigned from his post to run for Tasmania's State Assembly as a Labour candidate dedicated to improvement of school facilities and the establishment of high schools.

In 1914 Lyons became minister for railways, minister for education, and state treasurer. Opposed to the raising of conscript forces for overseas service, he remained faithful to the Labour party when the state premier broke away to side with William Morris Hughes in 1915, and he moved up to leadership in Tasmania. After the election of 1923 Labour was the largest party (12 in a House of 30). As state premier, Lyons pursued cautious but constructive policies. The election of 1926 gave him a clear majority, and he legislated to encourage mining and the wood pulp industry. He initiated plans for expanding rural settlement and updated Tasmania's laws on labor conditions and social welfare.

Labour leader James Scullin encouraged Lyons to run for the Federal House of Representatives. Elected in 1929, Lyons immediately joined Scullin's new Cabinet. In the deepening financial crisis of 1930 he became acting treasurer but early in 1931 resigned from the Cabinet and was expelled from the Labour party. Political opponents at once accepted Lyons as the ablest leader of their cause, creating a new party—the United Australia party—around him. His honesty, political shrewdness, common sense, and humor were acknowledged assets.

Labour was quickly defeated (December 1931), and Lyons became prime minister and treasurer. His government was soon aided by improved returns from exports following devaluation, which, with higher tariffs, also sharply checked imports. The Ottawa Agreement (1932), consolidating British Commonwealth preferential trade, and new commodity marketing legislation were adopted. Unemployment remained at high levels, but in 1934 Lyons was returned. Holding fewer seats, he had to rely on a coalition with the Country party to remain in office. In 1935 he handed over the treasurership to Richard Gardiner Casey.

Lyons was reelected in 1937, and his government soon faced serious defense issues. After the 1937 Imperial Conference in London, heavy defense expenditure was pledged, and factional struggles were rending his Cabinet. Lyons died in Sydney on April 7, 1939. His widow, Dame Enid Lyons, remained actively associated with politics. In 1943 she became the first woman to be elected to the House of Representatives and in 1949 the first woman Cabinet member. She retired in 1951.

Further Reading

Enid Lyons, *So We Take Comfort* (1965), is a memoir by Lyons's widow. The political background to Lyons's career is explained in Leslie F. Crisp, *The Australian Federal Labour Party, 1901-1951* (1955). His estrangement from Labour is covered in Warren E. Denning, *Caucus Crisis: The Rise and Fall of the Scullin Government* (1937). Political aspects of Lyons's administration are dealt with in Louise Overacker, *The Australian Party System* (1952), and Earle Page, *Truant Surgeon: The Inside Story of Forty Years of Australian Political Life* (1963). Economic factors are considered in E. O. G. Shann and D. B. Copland, *The Crisis in Australian Finance, 1929 to 1931* (1931); and Lyons's handling of some of these financial problems is outlined in Douglas Copland, *Australia in the World Crisis, 1929-1933* (1934). For general background on Australia's international relations in Lyons's time see H. V. Hodson, ed., *The British Empire: A Report on Its Structure and Problems* (1937; 2d ed. 1938). □

Lysander

Lysander (died 395 B.C.) was a Spartan military commander and statesman who defeated Athens in the Peloponnesian War and was responsible for establishing a Spartan administration in the conquered territories.

Lysander son of Aristocritus, was appointed naval commander in 407 B.C., when the Peloponnesian fleet had become demoralized by several defeats, and after previous Spartan commanders had quarreled with their Persian allies. Lysander restored confidence. He assembled a fleet at Ephesus and ingratiated himself with the Persian viceroy, Cyrus, who had received secret orders to support Sparta. Lysander hired mercenary rowers with high wages, manned 90 ships, and organized a network of personal supporters, who were to establish themselves as oligarchic rulers or dictators in any liberated states. He waited until the Athenian fleet was divided, and then early in 406 he defeated an Athenian flotilla at Notium.

When his term as commander expired, Lysander could not be reappointed by Spartan law. His successor was killed in a disastrous defeat at Arginusae. His friends and Cyrus clamored for the reappointment of Lysander, and he was sent as nominal second-in-command but with actual full power.

With Cyrus's subsidies Lysander manned 200 ships and advanced to the Dardanelles, where his threat to Athens's supplies from the Black Sea brought the Athenian fleet to a beach two miles away at Aegospotami. For four days in August 405 B.C. the Athenians offered battle, but Lysander declined. He noted, however, that each evening the Athenians disembarked and scattered. On the fifth evening Lysander attacked and caught 171 ships empty or half manned. Only nine ships escaped destruction.

Lysander sought total victory and personal power. He executed 3,000 Athenian prisoners and advanced to blockade Piraeus harbor. In April 404 B.C. Athens surrendered, and Lysander demolished Athens's fortifications. He established oligarchies or tyrannies in Athens and throughout the conquered and liberated areas. When reaction set in and democrats at Athens seized Piraeus, Lysander got himself appointed to suppress the rising. But the two Spartan kings, distrusting him, persuaded the Spartan authorities to supersede Lysander, reverse his policies at Athens, and modify them elsewhere.

Back in Sparta, Lysander planned unsuccessfully to convert the hereditary monarchy into an elective monarchy, banking on his own prestige. When Agis II died in 398, Lysander secured the election of Agesilaus, who took command in Asia Minor. Lysander accompanied him as chief of staff, but Agesilaus soon dismissed him. In 395, when Boeotia and Athens rose against Sparta, Lysander was killed in action at Haliartus.

Further Reading

Ancient sources on Lysander include Xenophon, Diodorus Siculus, and Plutarch, In modern works, accounts of Lysander are in John Bury, *History of Greece* (1902; 3d ed. 1951); Humfrey Michell, *Sparta* (1952); and Nicholas G. L. Hammond, *History of Greece to 322 B.C.* (1959; 2d ed. 1967), all of which are also useful for historical background. □

Trofim Denisovich Lysenko

The Soviet agronomist Trofim Denisovich Lysenko (1898-1976) developed a number of theories dealing with heredity and variability, species formation, intraspecific and interspecific relationships, and plant nutrition.

Trofim Lysenko was born on Sept. 30, 1898, in the Ukrainian village of Karlovka in Poltava Province. He studied at the Poltava Primary School for Horticulture and Gardening (1913-1917) and at the Uman School for Horticulture (1917-1921), after which he was assigned to the Belotserkovsky Experimental Station and went on to the Kiev Agricultural Institute, continuing his studies until 1925.

Genetics vs. Environment

Lysenko accepted a position at the Kirovabad experimental station in Azerbaijan, where he worked out his theory on the stages of plant development. In 1929 he described a process known as vernalization which involved a pre-sowing treatment of seeds to induce plants to flower sooner than usual, and enable them to adapt to different climates. According to initial reports from Soviet collective farms, vernalization was something of a sensation, and Lysenko was appointed director of the Odessa Plant Breeding-Genetics Institute.

Lysenko's theory to explain the process of vernalization was challenged in 1934 by Soviet scientists as a repudiation of the classical Mendelian theory of heredity and variation, which is based on the idea that genes are the carriers of hereditary characteristics. Lysenko defended his theory, known as "Lysenkoism," and launched a vicious attack on Soviet geneticists. It took him and his followers three contrived conferences and a dozen years (1936-1948) to topple Soviet geneticists from leading positions in research centers and educational institutions. Outstanding geneticists were vilified as "enemies of the people." Lysenko's meteoric rise to power and prestige is evidenced by his becoming a full member of the Soviet Academy of Sciences in 1935, full director of the All-Union Institute of Selection and Genetics in 1936, president of the Lenin's All-Union Academy of Agricultural Sciences, an active member of the Presidium of the Soviet Academy of Sciences in 1938, and director of the academy's institute of Genetics in 1940. His school of "genetic" thought also received the personal endorsement of Joseph Stalin. During his heyday, he received many awards and prizes, including three Stalin prizes and six orders of Lenin.

Reigning as the supreme authority in practical and theoretical agriculture, Lysenko advised the hierarchy of the Communist party on land reclamation and reforestation, the use of fertilizers, and methods of increasing crop and animal yields. Between 1954 and 1968 Lysenko's theories and contributions came under increasing scrutiny, but he managed to hold on to most of his positions mainly because of the intervention of Premier Nikita Khrushchev. By 1963 the Central Committee of the Communist party and the U.S.S.R. Council of Ministers became alarmed that Soviet Russia was lagging dangerously behind the West in several critical branches of biology and medicine.

Later Years

When Khrushchev was replaced, the monopolistic position of Lysenko and his followers in biology ended. Lysenko was charged with being oblivious to the recent advances in contemporary biology and with employing "administrative methods" to gain support for his theories and programs. Scientists both inside and outside the then Soviet Union were never able to validate his theories. In 1965 the new scientific journal *Genetics* appeared, sponsored by the Soviet Academy of Sciences; this marked the restoration of genetics to a respectable position in Soviet science. Lysenko was nevertheless permitted to head a laboratory at the Institute of Genetics, and his popularity with the Soviet Union's collective farmers hardly diminished—they understood his language, methods, and ideas.

Lysenko died in Moscow on Nov. 20, 1976, at the age of 78.

Further Reading

For a brief biographical sketch and evaluation of Lysenko's theories see Maxim W. Mikulak, "Trofim Denisovich Lysenko," in George W. Simmonds, ed., *Soviet Leaders* (1967); Of special interest is Zhores A. Medvedev, *The Rise and Fall of T. D. Lysenko* (trans. 1969); Accounts of the Soviet biological controversies can be found in Julian Huxley, *Soviet Genetics and World Science: Lysenko and the Meaning of Heredity* (1949); Conway Zirkle, ed., *Death of a Science in Russia: The Fate of Genetics as Described in Pravda and Elsewhere* (1949); Theodosius Dobzhansky, "The Crisis of Soviet Biology," in Ernest J. Simmons, ed., *Continuity and Change in Russian and Soviet Thought* (1955); and David Joravsky, *The Lysenko Affair* (1970), the best study to date.

Additional Sources

"Lysenko, Science Overlord Under Stalin, Dead at 78," *New York Times,* Nov. 24, 1976, p 36.

Rossianov, Kirill, "Biology Under Lysenko and Stalin," *Science,* Nov. 11, 1994, p. 1085-1086.

Sakharov, Andrei D., "The Poisonous Legacy of Trofim Lysenko," *Time,* May 14, 1990, p. 61.

Soifer, Valerii, *Lysenko and the Tragedy of Soviet Science,* New Brunswick, NJ: Rutgers University Press, c1994. □

Jean Mabillon

The French monk and historian Jean Mabillon (1632-1707) made an important contribution to the science of historical investigation by discovering a way of dating ancient manuscripts.

Jean Mabillon was born on Nov. 23, 1632, the son of a peasant who lived close to Reims. He was a capable student and a religiously devout young man. After spending a year in the diocesan seminary, he became a novice in 1653 in the Benedictine monastery in Reims. He was ordained a priest in 1660, and his quiet scholarly competence prompted his abbot to send him to the abbey of St-Germain-des-Prés in Paris in 1664 to take part in the work of historical research in which the monks there were engaged.

The abbey belonged to a group of reformed Benedictine monasteries called the Congregation of St. Maur. The Maurists were beginning to establish a reputation in Paris for sound historical scholarship. Mabillon's first major project at St-Germain-des-Prés was to collect documents pertaining to the lives of Benedictine saints and to edit these manuscripts into a nine-folio *Acta* (1668-1701). His grasp of history showed itself in a series of introductions in which he connected each saint's life with the ecclesiastical and civil events that were taking place at that particular time. Mabillon's sensitive interpretations, particularly of the early Middle Ages, received wide attention in French historical circles outside the Benedictine order.

When a Jesuit scholar named Daniel Papebroch attacked the validity of the ancient charters supposedly given by the Merovingian kings to the Benedictine monks for the land on which the Maurist monasteries were built, Mabillon spent 8 years working on a reply: *De re diplomatica* (1681; On Diplomatics). In it he showed that the age of a manuscript could be determined from its handwriting. With this important work Mabillon established the principles for the modern science of determining manuscript authenticity by means of dating. Later Mabillon was again called upon, this time to defend the legitimacy for monks to do scholarly work. This resulted in his *Traité des études monastiques* (1691; Treatise on Monastic Studies).

Mabillon traveled widely in Europe in search of manuscripts, but the most profitable trip was to Italy, which led to the publication of *Museum Italicum* (1687-1689). Throughout his life Mabillon was a monk and a scholar first, and only secondly did he allow himself to become a man of fame and controversy. When he died in St-Germain-des-Prés on Dec. 27, 1707, he had established his place as the greatest historical scholar of the 17th century.

Further Reading

There are no biographies of Mabillon in English. His importance is described in works on the science of history. James Westfall Thompson, *A History of Historical Writing*, vol. 2 (1942), is especially good. □

Apolinario Mabini

Apolinario Mabini (1864-1903) was a Filipino political philosopher and architect of the Philippine revolution. He formulated the principles of a democratic popular government, endowing the historical strug-

gles of the Filipino people with a coherent ideological orientation.

Apolinario Mabini was born in Talaga, Tanauan, Batangas, on July 22, 1864. His parents belonged to the impoverished peasantry. He studied at the Colegio de San Juan de Letran in 1881 and at the University of Santo Thomas, where he received the law degree in 1894. During this time he earned his living by teaching Latin and then serving as copyist in the Court of First Instance in Manila.

In 1896 Mabini contracted an illness, probably infantile paralysis, that deprived him of the use of his legs. When the Katipunan revolt broke out late that year, the Spanish authorities arrested him. Unknown to many, Mabini was already a member of José Rizal's reformist association, the Liga Filipina. And though as a pacifist reformist, he was at first skeptical of Andres Bonifacio's armed uprising, Mabini later became convinced of the people's almost fanatical desire for emancipation. Subsequently, he turned out subversive manifestos appealing to all Filipinos to unite against Spain.

In May 1898 Emilio Aguinaldo summoned Mabini to act as his adviser. Mabini formulated the famous decree of June 18, which reorganized the local government under Filipino control. His policy throughout the struggle can be epitomized by a statement in that decree: "The first duty of the government is to interpret the popular will faithfully."

Mabini was also instrumental in supervising the proper administration of justice, the election of delegates to the revolutionary congress, and the establishment of the mechanism of the revolutionary government itself.

When the revolutionary congress was convoked in Barasoain, Malolos, Bulacan, on Sept. 15, 1898, Mabini found himself opposed to the plans of the wealthy bourgeoisie to draft a constitution. He believed that, given the emergency conditions of war, the function of the congress was simply to advise the president and not to draft a constitution. Defeated by the majority, Mabini then submitted his own constitutional plan, based on the Statutes of Universal Masonry. It was rejected in favor of a composite draft submitted by Felipe G. Calderon, which became the basis of the Malolos Constitution of the first Philippine Republic.

Mabini's conflict with the conspiracy of property owners and the landlord class in the congress led to his eclipse in 1899 as Aguinaldo's trusted adviser—the only competent thinker and theoretician in the Aguinaldo Cabinet. Mabini succeeded in exposing the vicious opportunism of the Paterno-Buencamino clique, who were trying to gain control over, and to profit from, the financial transactions of the revolutionary government. When the Aguinaldo camp fled from the advancing American forces, Mabini was captured on Dec. 10, 1899. Still refusing to swear an oath of allegiance to the U.S. government and continuing to support the insurgents in their ideological struggle, he was deported to Guam in 1901. He died on May 13, 1903.

Mabini's chief work, *La Revolution Filipina,* a reasoned analysis and cogent argument concerning the ideological implications of the revolution against Spain and the resistance to the American invaders, reveals the progressive and democratic impulse behind his thinking. He always tried to mediate between the people's will and the decisions of their leaders. He was a selfless and dedicated patriot.

Further Reading

The best critical study of Mabini's life and works is Cesar Adib Majul, *Mabini and the Philippine Revolution* (1960). See also Majul's *The Political and Constitutional Ideas of the Philippine Revolution* (1957) and Teodoro A. Agoncillo, *Malolos: The Crisis of the Republic* (1960). For the general historical background the most reliable text to consult is Teodoro A. Agoncillo and Oscar Alfonso, *A Short History of the Filipino People* (1969).

Additional Sources

Majul, Cesar Adib, *Apolinario Mabini revolutionary,* Ermita, Manila: National Historical Institute, 1993 printing.
Villarroel, Fidel, *Apolinario Mabini, his birth date and student years,* Manila: National Historical Institute, 1979. ☐

Kamo Mabuchi

Kamo Mabuchi (1697-1769) was a Japanese writer, poet, and scholar and one of the major figures in the school of National Learning.

Kamo Mabuchi was born Masanobu, or Masafuji, the son of the superior (*Kannushi*) of the Kamo shrine in Totomi, and later took the name Mabuchi. He was chosen by a hosteler in Hamamatsu as son-in-law (the custom was not unusual). His father-in-law was disappointed though, if he expected help in the family business, for Mabuchi spent the greater part of his time with his books. Finally he obtained permission to go to Kyoto and study with Kada Azumamaro, a lay priest at the Inari shrine in Kyoto who had underwritten the Shinto revival.

Later Mabuchi went to Edo and became a teacher of considerable fame in his own right. The middle counselor (*chunagon*) Tayasu Munekata, a son of the Tokugawa shogun Yoshimune, was his patron. In 1760, however, Mabuchi left his teaching position to his adopted son Sadao and devoted himself to poetry and the study of antiquity.

A neo-Shintoist, Mabuchi was the first scholar of national importance in the movement called National Learning (*kokugaku*), which was an attempt to discover what was Japanese in Japanese literature and culture. Mabuchi insisted, not entirely correctly, that the 8th-century *Manyoshu*, an anthology of poetry, had been free of foreign influence and that it represented the true expression of national sentiments. He maintained that the *Manyoshu* poems were spontaneous, vigorous, and guileless. He said that they had a "manly style" (*masuraoburi*), by which he meant that the poems had strong feeling which stemmed from deep emotion. This sincerity and strength of emotion, he upheld, distinguished the *Manyoshu* from the *Kokinshu*, a 10th-century collection of poetry renowned for its elegance. Mabuchi himself composed poems in the *Manyoshu* style and urged others to follow his example.

The National Learning movement needed more than poetry for scripture, and in 1765 Mabuchi wrote *A Study of the Idea of the Nation*. It was written in almost pure Japanese, not the usual ornamental Chinese thought necessary in serious works for reasons of prestige. It was an attack on Chinese Confucian thought but was conceived largely in Taoist terms with direct and indirect references to Lao Tzu. Indeed, Taoist intuitive, anti-intellectual ideas were congenial to Shinto scholars.

Some of his other works were *Kojiki shiki* (Private Notes on the *Kojiki*), *Manyo-ko* (Treatise on the *Manyoshu*), *Genji monogatari shinyaku* (A New Interpretation of the Tale of Genji), and *Saibara-ko* (A Treatise on the *saibara*).

Mabuchi died on Oct. 31, 1769, at the age of 72. In 1883 he was awarded the court status of senior fourth rank and in 1905 junior third rank.

Further Reading

Short excerpts of Mabuchi's *A Study of the Idea of the Nation* may be found in Ryusaku Tsunoda and others, eds., *Sources of the Japanese Tradition* (1958). A study of Mabuchi is in Tsunetsugu Muraoka, *Studies in Shinto Thought* (trans. 1964). See also Robert N. Bellah, *Tokugawa Religion: The Values of Pre-industrial Japan* (1957), and Herschel Webb, *The Japanese Imperial Institution in the Tokugawa Period* (1968). □

Diosdado P. Macapagal

Diosdado P. Macapagal (1910-1997) was the fifth president of the Republic of the Philippines. He was instrumental in initiating and executing the Land Reform Code, which was designed to solve the centuries-old land tenancy problem, the principal cause of the Communist guerrilla movement in central Luzon.

Diosdado Macapagal was born on Sept. 28, 1910, the son of poor tenant farmers. In 1929 he entered the University of the Philippines, where he received an associate in arts degree in 1932. Meanwhile he worked part time with the Bureau of Lands.

Macapagal was constantly forced to interrupt his schooling for lack of funds. His brother-in-law Rogelio de la Rosa, with whom he acted in and produced Tagalog operettas, helped him continue his education. Macapagal entered the University of Santo Tomas in Manila, receiving his bachelor of laws degree in 1936, his master of laws degree in 1941, and doctor of laws degree in 1947. He also received a doctorate in economics in 1957.

Early Career and Government Service

In 1941 Macapagal worked as legal assistant to President Quezon and as professor of law in the University of Santo Tomas. A claim is made that he served as an intelligence agent for the guerrillas during the Japanese occupation, but this period of his life has not been well documented.

In 1946 Macapagal served as assistant and then as chief of the legal division in the Department of Foreign Affairs. In 1948 he was second secretary to the Philippine embassy in Washington and in 1949 became counselor on legal affairs and treatises in the Department of Foreign Affairs. In 1949 he was elected representative of the first district of Pampanga Province on the ticket of the Liberal party. In 1953 he was the only Liberal party member to win reelection.

Macapagal attained worldwide distinction in 1951, when, as chairman of the Philippine UN delegation, he conducted a debate with Soviet foreign minister Andrei Vishinsky. In November 1957 Macapagal was elected vice president, receiving 116,940 more votes than the total received by the elected president, Carlos P. Garcia. In December Macapagal became the titular head of the Liberal party. In spite of his rank as vice president and because he belonged to the opposition party, Macapagal was treated as a complete outsider; he was barred from Cabinet meetings and was assigned routine ceremonial duties. Consequently, Macapagal denounced the graft and corruption in the Garcia administration and toured the country campaigning for the next election.

On Jan. 21, 1961, Macapagal was chosen as Liberal party candidate for president. Rallying the masses in the

villages and towns, he elaborated a familiar motif in his speeches: "I come from the poor. . .Let me reap for you the harvest of the poor. Let us break the chain of poverty. . ."

Performance as President

Macapagal became president on Nov. 14, 1961, defeating Garcia. In his inaugural statement he declared: "I shall be president not only of the rich but more so of the poor. We must help bridge the wide gap between the poor man and the man of wealth, not by pulling down the rich to his level as Communism desires, but by raising the poor towards the more abundant life." With his naiveté and paternalistic attitude, Macapagal vowed to open Malakanyang Palace, the presidential residence, to all the citizens. He canceled the inaugural ball and issued a decree forbidding any member of his family or of his wife's to participate in any business deals with the government. He dismissed corrupt officials and started court action against those who could not explain their sudden acquisition of wealth. He changed the date that Filipinos celebrate their independence to June 12 from July 4. In 1898, Filipino revolutionaries had declared independence from Spain on June 12; July 4 was the date the Philippines were declared independent by the United States after World War II.

Macapagal aimed to restore morality to public life by concentrating on the elevation of the living standard of the masses. Addressing Congress in 1962, he formulated the objectives of his socioeconomic programs as, first, the immediate restoration of economic stability; second, the alleviation of the common man's plight; and third, the establishment of a "dynamic basis for future growth." Unfortunately, Macapagal's friends in the oligarchy and the privileged minority in Congress and business soon began parading their lavish wealth in conspicuous parties, junkets, and anomalous deals.

On Jan. 21, 1962, Macapagal abolished the economic controls that had been in operation since 1948. He devalued the Philippine peso by setting its value according to the prevailing free market rate instead of by government direction. He lifted foreign exchange controls and reduced tariff rates on essential consumer goods. Seeking to remedy the problem of unemployment, he took steps to decentralize the economy and at the same time encourage commerce and industry in the provinces. He also proposed decentralization in government by investing greater power in provincial and local governments as a step essential to the growth of democratic institutions. He also suggested the establishment of eight regional legislatures with power to levy taxes.

Land Reform Program

To ameliorate the plight of the Filipino peasant in the face of vast population growth, Macapagal instituted a public land clearance program to make new farmlands available for immediate use. The product of his concern for the impoverished majority was the Land Reform Code of Aug. 8, 1963, which sought to replace the abusive and unjust tenancy system inherited from colonial times by the leasehold system, affording full government protection to the leaseholder. The positive result obtained in 1966 demonstrated the value of the land reform program in materially improving the local living conditions of the rural poor.

Foreign Policy

Macapagal's foreign policy displayed an eccentric course. On the one hand, he affirmed that he would never recognize Communist China despite what the United States or other nations might decide. On the other, he criticized in May 1962 the United States support of Laos neutralists as "a species of sophistry that can only weaken the defense of the free world."

In June 1962 Macapagal registered a claim of Philippine sovereignty over British North Borneo (Sabah). In July he proposed the establishment of a greater Malayan confederation which would supersede the British-sponsored plan for the Federation of Malaysia. This would be a step toward ultimate establishment of a Pan-Asian Union. Macapagal initiated the Manila Accord of July 31, 1963, signed by himself, President Sukarno of Indonesia, and Abdul Rahman of Malaya; on August 6 the three chiefs of state issued the Manila Declaration toward the establishment of Maphilindo, designed to set up closer ties between the three countries in their collective fight against neocolonialism. This plan broke up with the formation on Aug. 1, 1964, of the Federation of Malaysia by the Malayan and British governments.

Although Macapagal prided himself in being the "conscience of the common man," he failed in preventing his administration from being wrecked by the Stonehill scandal of 1962, which revealed massive government corruption and racketeering that involved almost the whole bureaucracy and Congress. Despite Macapagal's so-called incorruptibility, he failed to solve decisively the major social and economic problems of the nation. He lost his bid for re-election in 1965 to Ferdinand Marcos, who ruled for the next 20 years. However, Macapagal's political legacy lives on in his daughters, both of whom followed him into politics: Gloria Macapagal-Arroyo is a Filipino senator, and Cielo Macapagal-Salgado is vice-governor of Pampanga, her father's home province. Macapagal also had two sons, Arturo and Diosdado, Jr.

He died in Manila on April 21, 1997 of heart failure. He was 86.

Further Reading

The only official biography of Macapagal in print is Quentin J. Reynolds and Geoffrey Bocca, *Macapagal, the Incorruptible* (1965). For a just estimate of Macapagal's administration see Teodoro A. Agoncillo and Oscar Alfonso, *A Short History of the Filipino People* (1969).

Additional Sources

"Diosdado Macapagal, ex-Philippine Leader," *Newsday,* April 23, 1997, p. 13.
Reuters News Service, April 21, 1997.
Macapagal, Diosdado, *A Stone for the Edifice; Memoirs of a President,* Quezon City, Philippines, Mac Publishing, c1968.
□

Rising Military Career

Returning to the United States, MacArthur began his meteoric rise through the military ranks. In 1906 he was appointed aide-de-camp to President Theodore Roosevelt and in 1913 became a member of the general staff. As colonel of the "Rainbow Division" during World War I, MacArthur emerged as a talented and flamboyant military leader, returning from combat with a wide assortment of military decorations. Following the war, he became a brigadier general and superintendent of West Point, where he remained until 1922. After another sojourn in the Philippines, MacArthur was appointed chief of staff of the U.S. Army in 1930, a post he held through 1935.

The interwar years were frustrating ones for professional soldiers, and MacArthur led a troubled existence. In 1922 he married Louise Cromwell Brooks; in 1929 they were divorced. Gloomy about the social unrest of the 1930s, he warned a Pittsburgh, Pa., audience in 1932: "Pacifism and its bedfellow, Communism, are all about us. . . . Day by day this cancer eats deeper into the body politic." His uneasiness perhaps explains his savage assault in June 1932, in the midst of the Great Depression, on the thousands of ragged veterans of World War I who had massed in Washington, D.C., to petition Congress for early payment of their war service bonuses. Camped with their wives and children in a miserable shantytown, they were set upon by tanks, four troops of cavalry with drawn sabers, and a column of steel-helmeted infantry with fixed bayonets— all led by MacArthur. He sought to justify this action by

Douglas MacArthur

The American general Douglas MacArthur (1880-1964) attained widespread fame through his military activities in the Pacific during World War II and the cold war.

D ouglas MacArthur was born in Little Rock, Ark., on Jan. 26, 1880, the descendant of a long line of military men. His father, Arthur MacArthur, was a well-known general. Educated in a haphazard fashion on Western frontier posts, Douglas MacArthur recalled, "I learned to ride and shoot even before I could read or write." A poor-to-average student, MacArthur began to excel upon entering the military academy at West Point, N. Y., in 1899. Under the watchful eye of his mother, who followed her son to the military academy, he compiled an outstanding record. Proud, and convinced of his destiny as a military leader, MacArthur graduated first in his class in 1903, with the highest scholastic average at the academy in 25 years.

MacArthur sailed to the Philippines for his first military assignment. In 1904 he was promoted to first lieutenant and that October was ordered to become his father's aide-de-camp in Japan. Shortly thereafter he embarked upon a tour of the Far East, which he later termed the "most important preparation of my entire life."

contending that he had narrowly averted a Communist revolution.

MacArthur found a more appropriate field for his endeavors in 1935, when President Franklin Roosevelt dispatched him to the Philippines to develop a defensive strategy for the islands. In 1937 he married Jean Marie Faircloth. Retiring from the U.S. Army, he continued his work for the government of the Philippines. With the heightening crisis in Asia, he was recalled to active duty as a lieutenant general and commander of U.S. forces in the Far East in July 1941.

Despite advance warning, the Japanese invasion of December 1941 badly defeated MacArthur's forces in the Philippines. In part, this reflected Japanese military superiority, but it also followed from MacArthur's assessment of Japan's unwillingness to attack the Philippines. The American and Filipino forces were forced to retreat to Bataan. MacArthur was determined to hold the Philippines but the situation was hopeless, and he was ordered to withdraw to Australia to take command of Pacific operations. Reluctantly MacArthur agreed, and accompanied by his wife and child, he set out on a daring escape by PT boat. Dismayed by the bitter American defeat and by the apparent abandonment of the men at Bataan, he vowed upon arrival, "I came through and I shall return."

Success in the Pacific

After the Philippine debacle, MacArthur began the long campaign to smash Japanese military power in the Pacific. Hampered in the early months by shortages of men and supplies, MacArthur's forces eventually won substantial victories. Although his personal responsibility for the battles and the extent of the casualties inflicted by his command were inflated by the skillful news management of his staff, there can be little question of the general's success in New Guinea and in the Philippines. Despite the urgings of other military leaders to bypass the Philippines in the drive on Tokyo, MacArthur convinced President Roosevelt that an invasion was necessary. In October 1944 MacArthur waded onto the invasion beach at Leyte and delivered his prepared address into a waiting microphone: "People of the Philippines: I have returned. . . . Rally to me." For MacArthur, as for millions of Americans, it was an inspiring moment—one that even eclipsed in drama his acceptance of the Japanese surrender in Tokyo Bay on Sept. 2, 1945.

With the end of World War II, President Harry Truman appointed MacArthur supreme commander of the Allied Powers in Japan. MacArthur set out in the next 6 years to remold Japanese society. His rule proved unexpectedly benevolent. The Occupation successfully encouraged the creation of democratic institutions, religious freedom, civil liberties, land reform, emancipation of women, and formation of trade unions. It did little, however, to check the monopolistic control of Japanese industry.

The outbreak of fighting in Korea in 1950 resulted in MacArthur's appointment as commander of the United Nations forces in July. Engaged in a desperate holding action against North Korean forces in the first months of combat, MacArthur launched a brilliant counterattack at Inchon which routed the North Korean armies. Advancing his troops to the Yalu River, the boundary between North Korea and China, MacArthur inexplicably discounted the possibility of Chinese intervention and assured his troops that they would be home for Christmas dinner. In November, however, massive Chinese armies sent the UN forces reeling in retreat. Angered and humiliated, MacArthur publicly called for the extension of the war to China. President Truman, who wanted to limit American involvement in Korea and had repeatedly warned MacArthur to desist from issuing inflammatory statements on his own initiative, finally relieved the general of his command in April 1951.

"Old Soldiers Never Die"

MacArthur's return to the United States was greeted by massive public expressions of support for the general and condemnations of the President. On April 19, 1951, he presented his case to a joint session of Congress, attracting a tremendous radio and television audience. His speech ended on a sentimental note that stirred millions of Americans, "I now close my military career and just fade away. . . ." But MacArthur became more active than he had predicted. After testifying at great length before the Senate Armed Services and Foreign Relations committees, he barnstormed across the country, lambasting the Truman administration and assuming the leadership of those Americans who believed that the President and his advisers had "sold out" Asia to communism.

In December 1952 president-elect Dwight Eisenhower met with MacArthur to hear the general's views on ending the Korean War. MacArthur advocated a peace conference which, if unsuccessful, would be followed by "the atomic bombing of enemy military concentrations and installations in North Korea and the sowing of fields of suitable radioactive materials," the bombing of China, and the landing of Chinese Nationalist troops in Manchuria to overthrow the Communist government. To his chagrin, MacArthur was not consulted again.

Perhaps aware that his political appeal was ebbing, MacArthur had accepted a job as chairman of the board of the Remington Rand Corporation in August 1952. Thereafter, shaken by illness, he retreated to a life of relative obscurity. A soldier to the end, he died in the Army's Walter Reed Hospital on April 5, 1964.

Further Reading

MacArthur's own evaluation of his life is in his *Reminiscences* (1964). For his speeches see *A Soldier Speaks,* edited by Vorin E. Whan, Jr. (1965). D. Clayton James, *The Years of MacArthur,* vol. 1: *1880-1941* (1970), is a scholarly portrait of the general. A penetrating study of MacArthur's career is Richard Rovere and Arthur M. Schlesinger, Jr., *The MacArthur Controversy and American Foreign Policy* (1965). An objective treatment of MacArthur's generalship is Gavin Long, *MacArthur as Military Commander* (1969). John Gunther, *The Riddle of MacArthur: Japan, Korea and the Far East* (1951), is helpful for understanding the general's personality, as are the adulatory books of Clark Gould Lee and Richard Henschel, *Douglas MacArthur* (1952); Charles Willoughby and John Chamberlàin, *MacArthur, 1941-1951* (1954); and Courtney Whitney, *MacArthur: His Rendezvous with History* (1956). A useful collection of writings by and about the general is Lawrence S. Wittner, ed., *MacArthur* (1971). □

John Macarthur

John Macarthur (ca. 1767-1834) was an Australian merchant and sheep breeder. He became a powerful political leader and was a spokesman for the free settlers.

The date of John Macarthur's birth is uncertain, but he was baptized on Sept. 3, 1767, at Stoke Damerel near Plymouth, Devon, England, the second son of Scottish parents, Alexander and Katharine Macarthur. In 1782 he became an ensign in the army but the following year retired on half pay, as the American War had ended. In 1788 he rejoined the army in the 68th Regiment and in 1789 transferred as a lieutenant to the New South Wales Corps for service in the new colony. With his wife and son he arrived in Sydney on June 28, 1790.

Sheep Farmer

Almost at once Macarthur set the standard for a lifetime of turbulence by quarreling with Governor Arthur Phillip. But in 1792 he became regimental paymaster, and the next year he became inspector of public works and was in a position to advance his own interests in the rudimentary settlement. He established Elizabeth Farm at Parramatta and with additional land grants soon became a leading farmer and sheep breeder. In 1795 he was promoted to captain and consolidated his position as the chief trader among the army officers in the colony.

Trouble with the second governor, John Hunter, was followed by more serious differences with the third, Philip Gidley King. After a duel with his commanding officer, William Paterson, in 1801, Macarthur was arrested and sent to England for court-martial. He took some samples of his own wool with him and, because of the wartime problems of the British wool industry, was able to interest some textile manufacturers in the colonial product. Macarthur astutely capitalized on this situation, resigned his commission, obtained a grant of 5,000 acres of the best land in the colony, and returned in 1805 with the blessing of the British government to concentrate on the growing of fine wool.

Rum Rebellion

Macarthur took up his grant at the Cowpastures near Camden and between 1805 and 1808 expanded and developed not only his wool production but also his merchant interest. But the replacement of Hunter with Governor William Bligh brought a determined attempt to restrict illegal trading, especially in rum, as part of a plan to restore order to the colony.

Macarthur emerged as the chief leader of the private enterprise group adversely affected by Bligh's policy; the governor, in many ways as irascible and uncompromising

as Macarthur, also provoked other elements in the settlement including some of the senior army officers. When Macarthur was arrested in January 1808 for an alleged breach of mercantile regulations, the senior officer, Maj. George Johnston, released him and deposed Bligh in the so-called Rum Rebellion. Macarthur was colonial secretary until July. The next year he sailed for England to support Johnston at his court-martial. In 1817 he returned to New South Wales.

In his absence Macarthur's wife had carefully nurtured his Merino sheep, in a period of increased demand for fine wool that coincided with a commercial depression. Macarthur continued this process, and when Commissioner John Thomas Bigge recommended in 1822 that fine wool production be encouraged in the colony, Macarthur was able to take rapid advantage of the increasing opportunities.

In 1824 Macarthur helped to promote the Australian Agricultural Company. He had become one of the wealthiest and most influential of the free colonists, or "exclusives," of New South Wales. He was appointed as one of three to the first Legislative Council in 1825 but was removed in 1832, "pronounced a lunatic." He died on April 11, 1834, and was buried at Camden Park.

Further Reading

Sibella Macarthur-Onslow, ed., *Some Early Records of the Macarthurs of Camden* (1914), gives a useful selection from the many papers left by Macarthur and his sons. The biography by M. H. Ellis, *John Macarthur* (2d ed. 1967), offers an idiosyncratic and approving view of Macarthur and has an extensive bibliography. A wellbalanced general account is in Charles M. H. Clark, *A History of Australia* (2 vols., 1962-1968). S. J. Butlin, *Foundations of the Australian Monetary System, 1788-1851* (1953), provides an erudite survey of the mercantile and financial background against which Macarthur operated.

Additional Sources

Ellis, Malcolm Henry, *John Macarthur*, Sydney: Angus & Robertson, 1978, 1969. □

Herbert Macaulay

Herbert Macaulay (1864-1945) was a Nigerian political leader. One of the first leaders of the Nigerian opposition to British colonial rule, he was also a civil engineer, journalist, and accomplished musician.

Born in Lagos, Herbert Macaulay was the son of the Reverend Thomas Babington Macaulay, prominent Lagos missionary and educator, and the maternal grandson of Samuel Ajayi Crowther, first African bishop of the Niger Territory. Receiving his early education in the mission schools of Lagos, Macaulay in 1881 became a clerk in the Public Works Department in Lagos. He was recognized as a promising civil servant and in 1890 was awarded a government scholarship to study civil engineering in England, where he spent 3 years. Upon his return to Lagos he was appointed surveyor of crown lands for the colony of Lagos, a position he held until 1898, when he resigned the post.

Macaulay's resignation seems to have been precipitated by his growing resentment for the racial discrimination practiced by Europeans in the civil service. He established himself as a private surveyor in Lagos and slowly over the ensuing years emerged as a spokesman for opposition to British rule in Lagos and all Nigeria. Macaulay addressed himself to numerous issues, usually in articles he contributed to the *Lagos Daily Times*. He opposed every attempt by the British authorities to expand their administration, interpreting these developments as detrimental to the interests of indigenous Nigerians, who inevitably would be forced to pay the bills in taxes. He agitated against the payment of water rates in 1915 and, as a leader of the Lagos auxiliary of the Antislavery and Aborigines Protection Society, led the opposition against government plans to reform land tenure arrangements in Lagos and Yorubaland.

Through his antigovernment activities Macaulay rose to preeminence in Lagos politics. In 1921 he was sent to London by the *eleko,* or king, of Lagos to represent him in the legal appeal of a local land tenure case. In London, Macaulay proclaimed that the British colonial government was eroding the power and authority of the *eleko,* who, he said, was recognized by all Nigerians as the rightful king of Lagos. This episode embarrassed the British, although it did not deter their activities, and established Macaulay as a leading advocate of the rights of traditional leadership in Lagos.

In 1922 a new Nigerian constitution was introduced providing for limited franchise elections in Lagos and Calabar. In order to contest the three elective seats in Lagos, Macaulay organized the Nigerian National Democratic party (NNDP). The platform of the NNDP sought self-government for Lagos, the introduction of institutions of higher education into Nigeria, compulsory primary school education, the Africanization of the civil service, and non-discrimination in the development of private economic enterprise.

Macaulay's political activities were limited to Lagos affairs until the very end of his life, when the quest for independence began to pervade all Nigeria. He presided in 1944 at the meeting of the Nigerian Union of Students, from which ultimately emerged the National Council of Nigeria and the Cameroons (NCNC), Nigeria's first national political party. Macaulay was elected president of the NCNC and was engaged in a national tour for the party in 1945, when he was taken ill. Returning to Lagos, he died in the same year.

Further Reading

Isaac B. Thomas, *Life of Herbert Macaulay* (1948), is a biography which is difficult to obtain. An excellent discussion of Macaulay and the early nationalist movement in Lagos is in James Smoot Coleman, *Nigeria: Background to Nationalism* (1958). Robert July, *The Origins of Modern African Thought* (1968), contains a chapter on the intellectual underpinnings of Macaulay's activities.

Additional Sources

Tamuno, Tekena N., *Herbert Macaulay, Nigerian patriot,* London: Heinemann Educational, 1975 i.e. 1976. ☐

Thomas Babington Macaulay

The English essayist, historian, and politician Thomas Babington Macaulay, 1st Baron of Rothley (1800-1859), was the most popular and dazzling English historian of the 19th century. He was an eloquent spokesman for the liberal English middle classes.

The views of the Tory ascendancy, which had dominated England in the later 18th and early 19th centuries, also gave color to David Hume's *History of England,* the leading text on the subject after its publication between 1754 and 1761. The growing power of the Whigs, as the party of the middle-class industrialists and businessmen, created the need for a reinterpretation of English history that emphasized the role of the civil war of the 17th century, the Glorious Revolution, and the Hanoverian Settlement as the cornerstones of English freedom, prosperity, and social progress. More than any other writer, Macaulay promulgated this "Whig view of history" and trusted to the maintenance of this tradition for continued national advancement. Macaulay was, therefore, the spokesman for Victorian material advancement; but he was correspondingly somewhat blind to the social and economic evils that followed upon the industrial revolution.

Thomas Babington Macaulay was born at Rothley Temple, Leicestershire, on Oct. 25, 1800. His father, Zachary Macaulay, a Scotsman, had been a governor of Sierra Leone and was a leading figure in the "Clapham sect," a group of Evangelical reformers and abolitionists. The young Macaulay was educated at a private school and then went to Trinity College, Cambridge, where he became a fellow. In 1826 he was called to the bar.

His Essays

At Cambridge, Macaulay's brilliant reputation attracted the attention of Francis Jeffrey, editor of the *Edinburgh Review,* the leading organ of Whig opinion and the most authoritative literary periodical of the day. He was invited to become a contributor, and his first publication in the *Edinburgh* was the famous essay on Milton (1825). In it Macaulay's main concern was to defend Milton as a champion of civil and intellectual liberty against tyranny and despotism. The essay was an immediate success and inaugurated a long connection with the magazine.

Macaulay's essays are immensely readable and vigorous. They dispose judgment with majestic ease, but their inability to perceive subtle qualifications and shades of character diminishes their critical value. They are all laced with partisan zeal. The essay on Dr. Johnson, for instance, is

unsympathetic to his Tory leanings and violently hostile to John Wilson Croker, the editor of Boswell's *Life of Johnson,* who was associated with the High Tory *Quarterly Review.* The essays do, however, show a shrewd awareness of the social context of literature.

Macaulay admitted the occasional and transient value of his essays. However, he did feel that the later ones were markedly superior to the earlier ones. Although the style does improve and the bias becomes less obvious, the point of view is essentially unchanged.

Career in Politics

The essays were composed in the midst of an active political life. In 1830 Macaulay entered Parliament, first as a member for Calne and then for Leeds. He delivered memorable speeches in support of the 1832 reform bill. His brilliant conversational powers and lively social gifts made him popular in the fashionable world. He was appointed a commissioner of the Board of Control and devoted himself to a study of Indian affairs. In 1834 he became a member of the Supreme Council of India. During his 4-year stay in India he helped found a system of national education and was the chief architect of the criminal code.

On his return to England, Macaulay was elected to Parliament to represent Edinburgh (1839-1847). He also had a seat in the Cabinet as secretary of war from 1839 to 1841. But Macaulay's interests had now turned more fully to writing. In 1842 his *Lays of Ancient Rome* appeared. He continued to write essays, including those on Warren Hast-

ings and Robert Clive, which derived from his Indian experience; one on Addison; and one on William Pitt the Elder.

History of England

However, the principal labor of Macaulay's later years was the celebrated *History of England,* to which he sacrificed both his political career and his life in society. The first two volumes of the *History* appeared in 1848, volumes 3 and 4 in 1855, and the last installment posthumously in 1861. The success of the *History* was enormous.

Macaulay intended to write the history of England from the accession of James II (1685) through the reign of George IV. However, it was also his aim to emphasize the art of narrative and evoke the drama and scenic quality of historical events. His methods prevented the realization of his plan, for despite the rapidity with which he worked and notwithstanding the help of a miraculous photographic memory, he could barely bring his work to 1700. The common taste of today is unlikely to respond to the oratorical style of the work or to its optimistic presentation of the historical origins of Victorian prosperity and the grandeur of its imperial power. Nevertheless, the discerning reader will still admire the vigor of the work. And, finally, the *History* remains a valuable index of the style and values of its age.

In 1857 Macaulay was raised to the peerage. He died on Dec. 28, 1859, and was buried in Westminster Abbey.

Further Reading

The standard biography of Macaulay is by his nephew, Sir George Otto Trevelyan, *The Life and Letters of Lord Macaulay* (2 vols., 1876; repr. 1932). Other useful introductions to his life and work are Arthur Bryant, *Macaulay* (1933), and Richmond C. Beatty, *Lord Macaulay, Victorian Liberal* (1938). Recommended for general historical and intellectual background are George Peabody Gooch, *History and Historians in the Nineteenth Century* (1913; rev. with a new intro., 1961); George Macaulay Trevelyan, *British History in the Nineteenth Century, and After, 1782-1919* (1938); David Churchill Somervell, *English Thought in the Nineteenth Century* (1929); and Walter Houghton, *The Victorian Frame of Mind, 1830-1870* (1957).

Additional Sources

Bryant, Arthur, Sir, *Macaulay,* New York: Barnes & Noble, 1979, 1932.

Clive, John Leonard, *Macaulay, the shaping of the historian,* Cambridge, Mass.: Belknap Press, 1987, 1973.

Edwards, Owen Dudley, *Macaulay,* New York: St. Martin's Press, 1988.

Hamburger, Joseph, *Macaulay and the Whig tradition,* Chicago: University of Chicago Press, 1976.

Roberts, S. C. (Sydney Castle), *Lord Macaulay, the pre-eminent Victorian,* Philadelphia: R. West, 1977.

Trevelyan, George Otto, Sir, *The life and letters of Lord Macaulay,* Oxford; New York: Oxford University Press, 1978.

Young, Kenneth, *Macaulay,* Harlow Eng.: Published for the British Council by Longman Group, 1976. □

Macbeth (left)

Macbeth

Macbeth (died 1057) was king of Scotland from 1040 to 1057. Although he is best known through the Shakespearean drama bearing his name, his historical importance lies in the fact that he was the last Celtic king of Scotland.

The career of Macbeth is hidden in obscurity, but certain facts make it clear that Shakespeare's portrayal of the character of the man is at marked variance with reality. Macbeth was a person of great importance before he became king. As holder of the office of mormaer of Moray by virtue of inheritance from his father, he was a district chieftain and one of a handful of the most important men of the realm. His own ancestry could be traced back to royalty, and he was cousin to Duncan I (reigned 1034-1040), whom he served as commander of the royal army. His wife, Gruoch, was also descended from royalty. Macbeth came to represent opposition to the king at several points: in him northern and Celtic sentiments found a defender against southern and Saxon influences supported by Duncan; and Macbeth had personal claims to kingship in his own name and in that of his stepson, Lulach.

There was some question about the right of Duncan to be king since, as grandson of Malcolm II, he represented the first instance of the rule of primogeniture in the history of the Scottish crown. The usual principle of succession required that the crown pass to a collateral of the king, not to heirs of the direct line. As Macbeth pressed his claim, he had tradition on his side; he won the crown by slaying Duncan at Bothgowanan in 1040.

During Macbeth's reign there was only one native uprising, that led by Abbot Crinan, Duncan's father. The realm was peaceful enough for Macbeth to make a pilgrimage to Rome in 1050. An invasion from Northumberland in the name of Duncan's son, Malcolm (later, Malcolm III), was repulsed in 1054. A second invasion, in 1057, led by Malcolm was successful, and Macbeth fell in battle; but rather than accept the "Saxon" Malcolm, Macbeth's supporters took Lulach for their king. Within a few months Lulach was defeated, and Malcolm was able to inaugurate the Canmore dynasty.

This dynastic revolution seems to be the basis for the identification of Macbeth as a monster and usurper. When later Canmore kings fought Celtic forces of decentralization, they exalted their ancestor Duncan and developed a hostile vision of Macbeth, the last Celtic king, so as to discredit the Celtic cause. The first written picture of Macbeth in this new light came in the *Scotichronicon* of John of Fordun (ca. 1380). From this base the legend grew until it reached its fullest statement in the writing of Raphael Holinshed, the immediate source for Shakespeare.

Further Reading

William Henry Gregg, *Controversial Issues in Scottish History* (1910), contains a valuable chapter on Macbeth's place in the chronicles of Scotland and England. An excellent bibliography on the career of Macbeth is in William Croft Dickinson, *A New History of Scotland* (1965). A readable general account is in Gordon Donaldson, *Scottish Kings* (1967).

Additional Sources

Ellis, Peter Berresford, *MacBeth, High King of Scotland, 1040-57 AD,* London: F. Muller, 1980. □

Dwight Macdonald

Dwight Macdonald (1906-1982) was an editor, journalist, essayist, and critic of literature, popular culture, films, and politics.

Dwight Macdonald was born in New York City on March 24, 1906, the son of Dwight and Alice (Hedges) Macdonald. Macdonald attended Phillips Exeter Academy, an elite private school in Exeter, New Hampshire, and Yale University, from which he graduated in 1928. After trying his hand at becoming a merchandiser in a training program at Macy's, Macdonald, with the help of a friend from Yale, became an associate editor in 1929 of Henry Luce's *FORTUNE,* the first issue of which appeared in 1930. Macdonald worked on *FORTUNE* until 1936, when he resigned to protest alterations that the pro-business magazine made in a series of articles he had written about U.S. Steel Corporation.

Macdonald devoted himself in the mid-1930s to discovering his own political philosophy. He read Marx, Lenin, and Trotsky; became an enthusiastic anti-Stalinist; and, in 1937, became an editor of the radical *Partisan Review.* Macdonald joined the Trotskyist Party in 1939 and contributed articles to its monthly periodical, the *New International.* By 1941 Macdonald had broken with the Trotskyists, who had themselves split apart in a bitter factional dispute. In 1943, declaring himself a pacifist and objecting to World War II, he resigned from *Partisan Review* because of disagreements with its editor, Philip Rahv.

Magazine Editor and Writer

In 1944 Macdonald founded *Politics,* which appeared first monthly, then quarterly, until Macdonald abandoned it in 1949 to devote more of his time to writing. *Politics* published essays on politics and culture and included among its contributors James Agee, John Berryman, Bruno Bettelheim, Albert Camus, Paul Goodman, Mary McCarthy, Marianne Moore, and Simone Weil. As editor of *Politics* Macdonald began to refer to his own politics as "essentially anarchist."

In 1951 Macdonald became a staff writer for the *New Yorker.* From 1960 to 1966, while retaining his role on the

staff of the *New Yorker,* Macdonald was movie critic for *Esquire.*

Many of Macdonald's essays on culture and politics have been collected in books that are interesting both for their intrinsic merits and because they record and reflect the ferment of a generation of American intellectuals whose work spanned the Depression, the "Red Decade" of the 1930s, the New Deal, World War II, the Cold War, McCarthyism, and the birth and death of the New Left in the confusions of the civil rights movement, the Vietnam War, the Watergate affair, and the rise of neo-conservatism. Macdonald's *Henry Wallace: The Man and the Myth* (1948) is a polemic arguing, in effect, that the former New Deal secretary of agriculture and vice president did not deserve the support of the American Left, primarily because of Henry Wallace's professed admiration for Stalinist Russia. (Wallace was the 1948 presidential candidate of the Progressive Party.) *Memoirs of a Revolutionist* (1957) includes many of Macdonald's most important political essays, including a brief political memoir, "Politics Past," in which Macdonald comments on his Trotskyist period: "What strikes me most, looking back, is the contrast between the scope of our thought and the modesty of our actions."

The Ford Foundation: The Men and the Millions (1956), which originally appeared as a series in the *New Yorker,* describes the "philanthropoid" as an institutional type and the Ford Foundation itself as "a large body of money completely surrounded by people who want some."

A Sharp Critic in Many Areas

Against the American Grain (1962) contains Macdonald's celebrated attacks on James Gould Cozzens' *By Love Possessed,* on the Revised Standard Version of the Bible, and on the third edition of *Webster's New International Dictionary. Against the American Grain* also contains the famous essay on "Masscult & Midcult," in which Macdonald argues that mass culture is a parody of high culture and that mass culture serves modern industrial society by transforming "the individual into mass man," turning culture into an "instrument of domination" and making "a pluralistic culture impossible." Midcult, on the other hand, is a more recent and sophisticated phenomenon, according to Macdonald. Midcult is as formulaic and predictable as masscult, but pretends to be high culture, which it waters down and displaces.

Macdonald had by now clearly articulated his own fascination with popular culture and his own unwillingness to abandon high culture as a standard against which to judge it. *Against the American Grain* contains Macdonald's admiring review of Richard Ellman's biography of James Joyce and displays Macdonald's characteristic suspicion of academic students of literature—but a suspicion overcome by a genuine and generous celebration of Professor Ellman's work and a convincing perspective on the place of biography in literary studies. Despite his frequent invocations of high culture as a standard of judgment and the wide range of literary learning that is frequently evident in his work, Macdonald produced no large body of critical writing on serious or "high" culture and literature, such as was produced, for example, by Philip Rahv or Edmund Wilson.

Macdonald's film criticism, collected in *On Movies* (1969), continued to work out his lifelong admiration for movies and his unwillingness to overlook or forgive the mediocre or meretricious. Still, as he said in the introduction to *On Movies*, "I wouldn't want to see a movie made by a director who had to learn to make movies from my reviews."

Macdonald's writing is learned, conversational, sometimes even chatty, digressive, personal, witty, constantly seeking the apt judgment, the appropriate attitude. William Barrett recalls the New York literary culture in which Macdonald moved as a band of passionate debaters. Macdonald, though he had left the core of intellectuals who formed the *Partisan Review* crowd, stayed in the debate, but, says Barrett, "he was not very good at argument, for he stammered. In his case the pen—or, rather, the typewriter—was mightier than the tongue; and where in written polemic he could spear his victim with a single deadly phrase or sentence, in oral argument he would become excited and reduced to an incoherent stammer" (William Barrett, *The Truants*, 1982).

Macdonald cheerfully conceded to Paul Goodman's criticism that he "thought with his typewriter," discovering what he thought by writing it down and revising it. And, as he also cheerfully admitted, he tried to reconcile a fascination for popular culture with a taste formed by high culture and a passionate interest in politics with a growing conviction that collective actions led to diminishments of humankind's essential individualism.

Further Reading

Macdonald's books include *Henry Wallace: The Man and the Myth* (1948), *The Ford Foundation: The Men and the Millions* (1956), *Memoirs of a Revolutionist: Essays in Political Criticism* (1957), *Against the American Grain* (1962), *On Movies* (1969), and *Discriminations* (1974). Greenwood Reprint Corporation reissued *Politics* in 1968 with an introduction by Hannah Arendt. For discussion of the tradition within and against which Macdonald worked, see William Barrett, *The Truants: Adventures among the Intellectuals* (1982), and John P. Diggins, *Up from Communism: Conservative Odysseys in American Intellectual History* (1975).

Additional Sources

Whitfield, Stephen J., *A critical American: the politics of Dwight Macdonald*, Hamden, Conn.: Archon Books, 1984.
Wreszin, Michael, *A rebel in defense of tradition: the life and politics of Dwight Macdonald*, New York: Basic Books, 1994.
□

Eleanor Josephine Macdonald

Eleanor Josephine Macdonald (born 1906) has been a pioneer in the field of cancer epidemiology. Over the course of forty years, she made several significant contributions to the understanding of cancer and was a strong advocate for early treatment of cancer symptoms.

Macdonald was the first cancer epidemiologist; previously, epidemiologists had only researched communicable diseases. While working at the Massachusetts Department of Public Health, she was the first to precisely determine incidence rates for cancer. In Connecticut, Macdonald developed the first population-based cancer registry. Later, she proved that there is a connection between sunlight and malignant melanoma of the skin. Many of the cancer programs in existence today are due to her efforts, or are patterned after programs she developed.

Macdonald, the third of six children, was born on March 4, 1906, in West Somerville, Massachusetts, to Angus Alexander, an engineer of Scottish descent who worked for the American Telephone and Telegraph Company, and Catharine Boland Macdonald, a concert pianist of Anglo-Irish descent. She was educated at Radcliffe College and graduated with a degree in music and history of literature and English. She performed as a professional cellist for two years after graduation. Around this time, a physician friend of her father's requested her help writing a research paper; this work inspired her to become an epidemiologist.

Macdonald took a job with the Massachusetts Department of Public Health, beginning a series of studies on cancer, a subject which would become the focus of her lifetime's work. At the Massachusetts agency, the first cancer program in the country was set up. Here Macdonald studied the incidence of cancer and other chronic diseases occurring in people older than age 40. For a period of five years, she and her colleagues went house-to-house in Massachusetts seeking information on the residents' health. When she presented her results, the medical community hailed it as the first accurate calibration of cancer incidence in the country. Macdonald felt that although cancer was a pervasive problem, with early detection people would fare better. She collaborated with a group of physicians who went out to every one of the 355 communities in Massachusetts to raise people's awareness of cancer. The physicians provided outpatient diagnostic clinics and encouraged individuals to see a doctor when the symptoms of cancer first appeared. The physicians also explained cancer symptoms to community physicians who were unlikely to have seen many cancer patients. Coming to a doctor sooner enabled many people to have their cancer treated while it was still in an early stage and helped more people recover or live longer. Macdonald's approach to the problem of cancer made her the first epidemiologist in the cancer research field. She also approached the issue on another level, speaking about public health and cancer awareness on a radio program that aired every week for a number of years. During this time, Massachusetts became the first state to have a cancer awareness week.

From 1940 to 1948, Macdonald worked for the Connecticut State Health Department. There she created a population-based cancer record registry and follow-up program for the state of Connecticut, the first such program in the world. Over a six-year period, she and a volunteer checked all hospital records for patients with cancer. They then traced each case to find what had become of the patients. They found 1,800 were still alive, although physicians who had treated them earlier had assumed they had died. "This was the beginning of follow-up for cancer patients," Macdonald commented in an interview for *NTCS*. Cancer registries that have been created since have used this system as a model. This aspect of her career was only a part of her work at the time. For about 10 years, Macdonald worked weekends to set up and run the statistical department at Memorial Sloane Kettering in New York, a hospital that specializes in cancer. In addition, she served as a consultant to the National Advisory Cancer Council in Washington, D.C.

Macdonald's next major opportunity to further her work arose when she was asked to set up and run the cancer epidemiology program at the University of Texas M. D. Anderson Hospital in Houston. Macdonald was made a full professor of epidemiology in 1948, a position she held for 45 years. In her years with the University of Texas, Macdonald created a pilot cancer registry and follow-up program in El Paso with data compiled from 1944 onward. This pioneering program was very comprehensive and included data from hospitals, clinics, laboratories, nursing homes, private group practices, and dermatologists' offices—places where cancer patients would have been seen. The study included follow-up in 56 counties for 23 years. This survey yielded the first cancer incidence data for Hispanics, which turned out to be lower than in whites. From her research, Macdonald determined that intense exposure to sunlight was linked directly to a rise in the occurrence of skin cancer, including melanoma. Part of her evidence was the fact that individuals who live closer to the equator have a higher incidence of skin cancer than those who live farther away.

Macdonald's work resulted in clinical trials to check the effectiveness of cancer treatments. She also helped to organize the first southwestern chemotherapy trials for leukemia patients. She stepped down from her position as professor in 1974, but has remained on call for the University of Texas M. D. Anderson Hospital. "It has been marvelous to be a pioneer. Everyone encouraged me in my work, and I did not feel that they discriminated against me because I was female," Macdonald stated in her interview. Macdonald was awarded the Myron Gordon award in 1973 for research into pigment cell growth in melanoma. That year she also won several other awards, including an Outstanding Service Award from the American Cancer Society. During her career, she was a member of the American Association for the Advancement of Science and the American Public Health Association; in 1946 she was elected a member of the American Association for Cancer Research. Now retired and living in Texas, she remains active by taking classes and pursuing her hobbies of playing the cello and writing.

Further Reading

Macdonald, Eleanor J., Interview with Barbara Proujan, conducted on January 13, 1994. □

James Ramsay MacDonald

The British politician James Ramsay MacDonald (1866-1937), three time prime minister of Great Britain, was one of the great architects of the British Labour party. In 1924 he formed the first Labour government.

Ramsay MacDonald, born in October 1866 in the little peasant and fishing village of Lossiemouth in Morayshire, Scotland, was the illegitimate son of Anne Ramsay, a farm servant, and John MacDonald, a plowman and a Highlander from the Black Isle of Ross. He was reared by his mother and his grandmother, Isabella Ramsay, a woman of strong religious convictions, remarkable intelligence, and character. He attended first the Free Kirk School in Lossiemouth and then, the Drainie Parish School, where at 15 he was the leading pupil and at 16 became a pupil-teacher. Politics fascinated him, and he became an ardent Gladstonian.

In 1885 MacDonald went south to Bristol to a position in a Church-sponsored guild for young men. He associated with the Bristol branch of the Social Democratic Federation (SDF), a Marxist-oriented society. His employment soon proved unsatisfactory, and, after a brief return to Lossiemouth, he went to London in 1886. There he became an invoice clerk in a warehouse. More significant was his prompt membership in the London Trades Council and in the Fabian Society, whose intellectual and non-revolutionary approach to socialism he found more congenial than the SDF. Secretaryships with the Scottish Home Rule Association in 1888 and with the Fellowship of the New Life in 1892, as well as membership on the executive of the Fabian Society from 1894 to 1900, made him known and respected. In 1894 he joined the Independent Labour party (ILP), whose advocacy of both socialist doctrine and labor representation in Parliament attracted him. In 1895 he was an unsuccessful ILP candidate for Parliament. All these years he was educating himself by voracious reading.

In 1896 MacDonald married Margaret Gladstone, daughter of John Hall Gladstone, a prominent scientist and one of the founders of the YMCA. His marriage made him less skeptical and brought an income sufficient for independence. They lived in London and raised a family of six children. With his wife by his side, MacDonald, it has been said, readily acquired the manners, though not the prejudices, of the ruling class. Their home became a focal point for the labor and socialist world in London. The MacDonalds travels, so important for his later role as diplomat, included a trip around the world in 1906 and a trip to India in 1909. Margaret MacDonald died in 1911.

recognized the Soviet Union but fell in October, when proposed trade agreements with the Soviet Union brought attacks. He drafted, in large part, "Labour and the Nation," the party manifesto in the election of 1929, which gave Labour a plurality in the Commons. In his second government (1929-1931) his main achievements were again in foreign policy; his talks with President Herbert Hoover were a successful preliminary to the Five Power Naval Conference in London, over which he presided with great skill. But the world economic situation steadily worsened, with mounting unemployment placing unprecedented demands on the Unemployment Insurance Fund and rendering precarious the finances of the country. Failure of his Cabinet to agree on measures brought MacDonald's resignation in August 1931.

Under pressure from the King and with the support of other party leaders, MacDonald formed a national government, an action soon repudiated by his party. The new government stabilized the financial situation and won an overwhelming mandate from the electorate in October, MacDonald remaining as prime minister until 1935, though with little Labour support. In general he accepted Conservative policies, notably a return to a general tariff in 1932, but failing health greatly reduced his effectiveness. After inaugurating rearmament in March 1935, he resigned and took the honorary post of lord president of the Council. Though defeated in 1935, he was returned to Parliament in 1936 by a by-election from the Scottish Universities. He died in November 1937, while on a holiday trip to South America.

Labour Party

In the meantime, MacDonald's career developed quickly. He wrote for labor and socialist journals. He opposed the Boer War and resigned from the Fabian Society over the issue. When the Labour Representation Committee (LRC; later the Labour party) was organized in 1900, MacDonald was unanimously elected its first secretary. In 1903 he negotiated with the Liberals an agreement whereby in 35 parliamentary constituencies the Liberals would not oppose Labour. In 1906 the LRC was victorious in 29 constituencies, including Leicester, where MacDonald was elected. He at once became the party's most effective spokesman in the Commons. In 1911 he became chairman of the parliamentary Labour party.

When party differences over the war developed, MacDonald resigned his chairmanship. He condemned the British entry, but he was no pacifist and believed that the war must be won, with peace coming as soon as possible. He was one of the founders in 1914 of the Union of Democratic Control, which sought parliamentary control over foreign policy. Repudiation of secret diplomacy was also a main theme of the Labour party statement on war aims in December 1917, drafted largely by MacDonald.

Defeated in 1918, MacDonald returned to the Commons in 1922 and was elected chairman of the parliamentary Labour party. As such, he formed the first Labour government, in January 1924. His major achievement was the acceptance by France and Germany of the Dawes Plan for the payment of German reparations. His government

Further Reading

There is no adequate biography of MacDonald. Lord Godfrey Elton, *The Life of James Ramsay MacDonald* (1939), is useful but incomplete. Other studies are L. MacNeill Weir, *The Tragedy of Ramsay MacDonald* (1938), a sympathetic account of MacDonald's political career, and Benjamin Sacks, *J. Ramsay MacDonald in Thought and Action: An Architect for a Better World* (1952). MacDonald's association with the early history of the Labour party is fully presented in Philip R. Poirier, *The Advent of the British Labour Party* (1958), and the high points of his career are treated in detail in Richard W. Lyman, *The First Labour Government* (1924), and in Reginald Bassett, *Nineteen Thirty-one* (1958). □

Sir John Alexander Macdonald

Sir John Alexander Macdonald (1815-1891) was a leading Canadian politician and Cabinet minister, serving as premier in the Province of Canada and twice as prime minister of the Dominion.

John Alexander Macdonald, although his name was to become the core of a Canadian legend, was born in Glasgow, the son of a merchant who migrated to British North America in 1820. The family settled in the Kingston area of what is now Ontario, and Macdonald was educated in Kingston and Adolphustown. In 1830 he was articled to a prospering lawyer with connections that were to prove helpful to Macdonald, who rose rapidly in his profession.

Macdonald began his own practice in 1835 in Kingston, actually before he had been called to the bar, and for several years lived the usual active life of a young professional man, active in local political and social affairs. Since Kingston was a border town, it was inevitably involved in the border incidents of the late 1830s, and Macdonald's first celebrated case found him in 1838 defending a captured invader from the United States on a charge of murder. Kingston's location kept it immediately free of the abortive Upper Canada Rebellion of 1837, but Macdonald's sympathies were from the first on the side of constituted authority, and the rebellions and the coincidental border incidents gave him a lasting concern for the military vulnerability of the colonies.

Start of a Political Career

Macdonald was elected to the Assembly of the Province of Canada (created in 1840) in 1844 as the member for Kingston, beginning a public career that spanned half a century. At a time when party lines were loose, Macdonald regarded himself as a moderate conservative and always remained one, serving for the rest of his life in the Liberal Conservative party. His abilities brought him rapid promotion, and he became receiver general in W. H. Draper's Cabinet in 1847; thereafter he was without public office only when his party was in opposition. He worked indefatigably to conciliate the dissident elements in his party and by

1851 was the recognized leader of its Canada West (now Ontario) wing.

By 1856, when Macdonald was, as attorney general for Canada West, the recognized leader in the Assembly of a Cabinet whose titular head was in the upper house, his position had been confirmed, and his leadership was never seriously challenged in his lifetime. He was premier of the Province of Canada in all but name while his party was in power (and actually so for the first time in 1857), simultaneously holding major portfolios, which included Militia Affairs.

The politics of the Province of Canada, in which Canada East and West had equal legislative representation, was extremely unstable, and successive administrations in the colony, in the absence of reliable party lines, broke down; an impasse was reached in 1864, when Macdonald was one of the leading protagonists in arranging what became the Great Coalition, which led to confederation in 1867. In 1858, although federation was an older idea than that date, he had been a member of the first Canadian Cabinet to announce officially its interest in a federal union for the British North American colonies.

Champion of Confederation

Once he had taken up confederation, Macdonald threw all his energies into the task of persuading the colonists of its soundness as a solution to their economic and military weaknesses. In 1864, he led the delegation from Canada to the conference at Charlottetown, Prince Edward Island and continued to lead when the conference adjourned to Quebec in the same year. In 1865, he went to London to discuss military arrangements for Canada in the light of the outcome of the American Civil War and resulting British-American relations. Macdonald was back in London in 1866, though disturbed by Fenian raids on Canada from American soil. He presided over the conference which worked its way through several drafts of the British North America bill before its final enactment by the United Kingdom Parliament as the written basis of the Canadian constitution.

The final act bore all the marks of Macdonald's influence. Canada was to be a monarchy in North America, with a quasi-federal system in which a strong central government would have several instruments of control over the provinces, and with a parliamentary government modeled clearly on the British, not any American, model. He never wavered in his belief that this was the proper sort of government if Canada were to survive as an independent entity. He never wavered either in his conviction that the United States, whose government he never trusted, posed the real long-run threat to Canada's survival.

Consolidation of Canada

In 1867 Macdonald became the first prime minister of the Dominion of Canada. He set about consolidating into reality his vision of Canada as a northern transcontinental nation whose nerve center was always to be the national government. He immediately pacified Nova Scotia, the least satisfied member of the new federation. He gradually gathered into federal hands control of the election machinery, giving the country a unified national electoral system which still exists. He used freely the federal power of disallowing provincial statutes which he considered to be against the national interest. He worked hard to enlarge Canada's boundaries, first helping to acquire the Northwestern Territory and then obtaining the admission of Manitoba, British Columbia, and Prince Edward Island.

Macdonald never relinquished his interest in the defense of British North America and was indeed frequently exasperated by what seemed to him British indifference not only to Canada's military needs but to its economic relations with the United States; he often saw that British and American authorities were, in their own interests, only too ready to make concessions to each other at Canada's expense.

Macdonald consolidated Canada's continental position in more than territorial ways. Through two great policies—the building, under incredible financial and technical difficulties, of a transcontinental railway; and the establishment of a national policy of protective tariffs for the stimulation of industry—he sought to build the national economy clearly envisaged in the British North America Act. The railway cost him his only major electoral defeat, for in 1873, in a well-meant and undoubtedly customary move, he turned to potential backers of the Canadian Pacific Railway for election funds; and the opposition caught him out. Facing certain parliamentary defeat, he then resigned and lost the general election of 1874.

But in opposition, Macdonald was as wily as in office: he gave his Liberal opponents a couple of years in which to fall out among themselves and then produced his national policy, which he discussed widely at great public picnics, beginning in 1876. In 1878 he returned triumphantly to the prime ministership and held it until his death.

Macdonald was fortunate in his political career, as his opponents never really produced a fighter who could challenge him. Even in his most trying problems, as in the Riel Rebellions of 1870 and 1885, his opposition seemed unable to exploit his undoubted difficulties; and even after the execution of Louis Riel in 1885—an act which, despite careful judicial decisions, outraged some Roman Catholic and considerable French-Canadian opinion—he won his last two general elections. He was defeated as the candidate for Kingston only once, in 1878, but in the same election he won two other seats and sat for one of them.

Personal Life

Macdonald's brilliant public career was not matched by an equally felicitous private life. He enjoyed many honors, including degrees, and a knighthood conferred in 1867. But his first wife, his cousin Isabella Clark, whom he married in 1843, was an invalid almost all their life together and died in 1857; their first son died in his second year, but their second son, Hugh John, lived to become a lawyer-politician with modest success.

In 1867 Macdonald married Susan Agnes Bernard, and they were very happy; but their only child, Mary, was a hydrocephalic who never approached normalcy. Mac-

donald was also plagued until his later years by what would now be recognized as alcoholism: he was a sporadic heavy drinker, often at inconvenient times for his public duties. Yet his colleagues never lost faith in him, and successive able governors general, who had to report on his activities to their home government, treated his intemperance as merely an unfortunate weakness in an otherwise remarkable man.

That he was. A cheerful, convivial person who loved stories, a crafty partisan who enjoyed discomfiting his opponents by any means, and a voracious and perceptive reader of a wide range of literature, Macdonald had a vast capacity for arousing the affection of his colleagues. When he died in 1891, after a last exhausting campaign which appeared to have induced a series of paralyzing strokes, his chief opponent said of him that "for the supreme art of governing men, Sir John Macdonald was gifted as few men in any land or in any age were gifted."

Further Reading

Joseph Pope edited *Memoirs of the Right Honourable Sir John Alexander Macdonald* (1894) and *Correspondence of Sir John Macdonald* (1921). The best works on Macdonald are Donald Creighton's superb *John A. Macdonald: The Young Politician* (1952) and *John A. Macdonald: The Old Chieftain* (1956), moving and affectionate studies which are also works of profound scholarship.

Additional Sources

Newman, Lena, *The John A. Macdonald album,* Montreal: Tundra Books of Montreal; Plattsburgh, N.Y.: Tundra Books of Northern New York, 1974.

Kingston Historical Society (Ont.), *Sir John A. Macdonald, 1815-1891: a remembrance to mark the centennial of his death, 6 June 1891,* Kingston, Ont.: Kingston Historical Society, 1991.

Swainson, Donald, *Macdonald of Kingston: first prime minister,* Toronto: T. Nelson & Sons (Canada), 1979.

Swainson, Donald, *Sir John A. Macdonald: the man and the politician,* Kingston, Ont.: Clayton, N.Y.: Quarry Press, 1989.

Waite, Peter B., *Macdonald: his life and world,* Toronto; New York: McGraw-Hill Ryerson, 1975. □

Edward Alexander MacDowell

Edward Alexander MacDowell (1861-1908), pianist and composer, was among the first American musicians to win an international reputation. In the late 19th century he was considered the greatest composer of the United States.

Edward MacDowell was born on Dec. 18, 1861, into an upper-middle-class family in New York City. His father was Scottish; his mother was Irish. The boy early showed promise as a musician and received every encouragement from his family. At the age of 8 he began piano lessons, and when he was 15 his mother took him to Paris for study. For a year he was a pupil of Antoine François

Marmontel. In 1877 MacDowell won a scholarship to the Paris Conservatory. After 2 years he grew disenchanted with the conservatory and left for Germany.

For a brief time MacDowell was a student at the Stuttgart Conservatory and then went to the Frankfurt Conservatory, where he studied piano with Karl Heymann and composition with Joachim Raff. By 1880 MacDowell had decided to devote himself primarily to composition, although he continued private piano lessons and began taking pupils himself. His first published work was *First Modern Suite,* which had been written between lessons.

In 1882 MacDowell called on Franz Liszt at Weimar. Liszt not only encouraged the American to devote himself to composition but helped him secure publication of his early works. Two years later MacDowell married Marian Nevins, one of his pupils.

In 1888 MacDowell returned to the United States permanently, spending 8 years in Boston as a composer, teacher, and concert pianist. He made a number of concert tours, specializing in his own music, which by then was much in demand. In 1896 he was invited to head the new department of music at Columbia University. MacDowell was not temperamentally suited for either an administrative position or the routine aspects of academic life. He resigned in 1904 after a public disagreement with the faculty over the position of music and the fine arts in the university curriculum. He did some private teaching for a year, but by 1905 mental deterioration had become evident. He died in New York City on Jan. 23, 1908.

His Works

Although MacDowell's compositions are not as highly regarded today as they once were, they are still among the most frequently performed American works. In style MacDowell has much in common with the Norwegian composer Edvard Grieg, and his smaller piano pieces are generally superior to his larger orchestral works. MacDowell wrote two piano concertos (1884, 1890). The Second Concerto has maintained a consistent popularity, but neither shows the imaginative depth of his later works. He wrote four sonatas: the *Tragica,* the *Eroica,* the *Norse,* and the *Keltic,* but not until the *Twelve Virtuoso Studies* for piano (1894) did MacDowell demonstrate his maturity as a composer. Of his *Woodland Sketches* (1896) the most popular are *To a Wild Rose* and *To a Water Lily,* both quite excellent. The *Sea Pieces* (1898) reveal him at the height of his lyric and dramatic ability.

MacDowell's first purely orchestral work was the tone poem *Hamlet and Ophelia* (1885). *Lancelot and Elaine* (1888), the First Suite for Orchestra (1891), and the Second (*Indian*) Suite (1896) conclude his orchestral writing. The *Indian Suite* ranks among his best compositions for orchestra, although MacDowell insisted that he was not intending to write American music simply by employing Indian themes. Besides his choruses, he published over 40 songs, some set to his own poems and all reflecting his remarkable gift for melody.

At heart MacDowell was a romantic, essentially in the German tradition. He was probably at his best when expressing the moods of nature. In these smaller, impressionistic pieces he caught much of the American spirit, blending romantic techniques with an intimate feeling for the American scene. "If a composer is sincerely American at heart," MacDowell said, "his music will be American."

Further Reading

MacDowell's *Critical and Historical Essays,* edited by W. J. Baltzell (1912), is an interesting collection of lectures. The best biographies of MacDowell are Elizabeth Fry Page, *Edward MacDowell: His Work and Ideals* (1910), and John F. Porte, *Edward MacDowell, a Great American Tone Poet: His Life and Music* (1922). There is a comprehensive chapter on MacDowell in Gilbert Chase, *America's Music from the Pilgrims to the Present* (1955; 2d ed. 1966).

Additional Sources

Porte, John Fielder, *Edward MacDowell: a great American tone poet, his life and music,* Boston: Longwood Press, 1978. □

Antonio Maceo

Antonio Maceo (1845-1896) was a Cuban mulatto patriot who rose to the rank of general in Cuba's Independence Army and became a hero of the wars which ended Spanish domination over Cuba.

Antonio Maceo was born in Santiago de Cuba on June 14, 1845. He was the son of Marcos Maceo, a Venezuelan mulatto émigré and of a free Cuban black, Mariana Grajales, one of the outstanding women in Cuba's history. Young Maceo spent his early years on his father's small farm in Oriente Province and received most of his education at home from private tutors. He also worked on his father's farm, making occasional trips to Santiago de Cuba to sell agricultural products.

The island was then experiencing revolutionary turmoil as Cuban patriots conspired to rid themselves of Spanish control. Unhappy with Spanish domination and horrified by the exploitation of the black slaves, Maceo entered the Masonic lodge of Santiago in 1864 and started to conspire with Cuban revolutionaries. When, on Oct. 10, 1868, Carlos Manuel de Céspedes and other leaders began Cuba's Ten Years War, Maceo joined the rebellion.

Guerrilla Leader

Maceo soon showed superior ability in guerrilla fighting. Under the instructions of Máximo Gómez, a Dominican guerrilla expert who had joined the Cuban forces, Maceo developed into one of the most daring fighters of the Cuban army. He defeated the Spanish forces in numerous battles and was soon promoted to the rank of captain. By January 1869 he was made lieutenant colonel. His incursions into the sugar zones not only helped to disrupt the sugar harvest but also were the principal means of freeing the slaves, who soon joined the ranks of the Cuban army.

By 1872 Maceo had achieved the rank of general. His prominent position among revolutionary leaders soon gave rise to intrigue and suspicion. Conservative elements who supported the war efforts began to fear the possibility of the establishment of a Negro republic with Maceo at its head. The example of Haiti still loomed in the minds of many, and when Gen. Gómez advocated an invasion of the west to cripple sugar production and liberate the slaves, he met determined opposition. Maceo was ordered to remain in Oriente Province, and the invasion of the west had to be postponed until 1875.

Even after the invasion got under way, it reached only to Las Villas Province in central Cuba. The destruction of the sugar estates increased the opposition from landed and sugar interests. Supplies, weapons, and money failed to arrive from exiles in the United States. Dissension in the revolutionary ranks and fear of the blacks again slowed down the revolutionary efforts. After a prolonged silence, Maceo finally answered those who accused him of attempting to establish a black republic. "In planting these seeds of distrust and dissension," he wrote on May 16, 1876, "they do not seem to realize that it is the country that will suffer. . . . I must protest energetically that neither now nor at any other time am I to be regarded as an advocate of a Negro Republic. . . . This concept is a deadly thing to this democratic Republic which is founded on the basis of liberty and fraternity."

Continued Fight for Independence

The war dragged on with neither the Cubans nor Spaniards able to win a decisive victory. Finally, on Feb. 11, 1878, the Peace of Zanjón was signed, which ended the Ten Years War. Most of the generals of the Cuban army accepted the pact. Yet Maceo refused to capitulate and continued to fight with his now-depleted army. He held a historic meeting, known as the Protest of Baraguá, with the head of the Spanish forces, Marshal Arsenio Martínez Campos, requesting independence for Cuba and complete abolition of slavery. When these two conditions were rejected, he again resumed the fighting.

It was, however, a futile effort. Years of bloodshed and war had left the Cuban forces exhausted. Exile aid decreased, and Maceo now faced the bulk of the Spanish forces. Realizing the hopeless situation, Maceo left for Jamaica. From there he traveled to New York to raise money and weapons necessary to continue fighting. He soon joined the activities of Maj. Gen. Calixto Garcia, then organizing a new rebellion. This uprising, known as La Guerra Chiquita (Little War, 1879-1880), ended in disaster. Maceo was retained in exile for fear of antagonizing the conservative elements in Cuba, and Garcia was captured soon after he landed in the island.

Exile for Maceo

Disappointed and disillusioned, Maceo traveled to the Dominican Republic and finally settled in Honduras. There he joined Gen. Gómez and was appointed to an army post in Tegucigalpa. But Maceo saw his exile as only a temporary interruption in the struggle to liberate Cuba. He and Gómez soon began to organize a new rebellion. Maceo visited different exile centers in the United States seeking support. However, the leadership was totally in military hands, thus alienating such revolutionary leaders as José Martí. Then, weapons that were to be used for the uprising were either confiscated in the Dominican Republic or lost in Jamaica when the captain of the ship *Morning Star,* which was transporting the weapons, dumped them in the sea for fear of being arrested. Finally, dissensions, mistrust, and prejudice among the revolutionary leaders dealt a mortal blow to this new effort.

For the next several years Maceo wandered throughout the Caribbean and Central America and finally settled in Costa Rica, where he engaged successfully in tobacco and sugar production. There he received a call from Martí in 1893 for a final effort to liberate Cuba. Martí had organized a revolutionary party in exile and now offered Maceo an important position in the movement. Maceo joined Martí and Gómez in organizing the Cubans in and out of the island until finally, on Feb. 24, 1895, the War for Independence began. One month later, Maceo and a group of expeditionaries landed in Oriente Province to join the rebellion.

Now Gómez and Maceo were able to implement their plan to invade the western provinces and thus carry the war to that part of the island. The two generals and Martí met on Cuban soil to map the war strategy. Maceo advocated a strong military junta rather than civilian control to direct the effort. Although the question of civilian versus military control was not resolved, Gómez was made commander in chief of the army, Maceo military commander of Oriente, and Martí head of the revolution abroad and in nonmilitary matters.

Martí's tragic death only days after the meeting, on May 19, 1895, dealt a strong blow to the morale of the Cuban forces. Yet Maceo and Gómez did not waver. In repeated attacks the two generals undermined and defeated the Spanish troops. For the next 3 months Maceo and Gómez carried the war to the western provinces. From January to March 1896 Maceo waged a bitter but successful campaign against larger Spanish forces in the provinces of Pinar del Río and Havana. On Dec. 7, 1896, while preparing their next campaign, near the small town of San Pedro in Havana, Maceo's troops were attacked, and the courageous general was killed in a minor battle with Spanish forces.

Further Reading

The major works on Maceo are in Spanish. Much valuable information on Maceo and Cuba's wars for independence can be found in Philip S. Foner, *A History of Cuba and Its Relations with the United States* (2 vols., 1962-1963), and Hugh Thomas, *Cuba: The Pursuit of Freedom* (1971).

Additional Sources

Foner, Philip Sheldon, *Antonio Maceo: the "bronze titan" of Cuba's struggle for independence,* New York: Monthly Review Press, 1977.
Pando, Magdalena, *Cuba's freedom fighter, Antonio Maceo, 1845-1896,* Gainesville, Fla.: Felicity Press, 1980. □

Ernst Mach

Ernst mach (1838-1916), an Austrian physicist and philosopher of science, made important contributions in several sciences but especially in the areas of the history and theory of science and of perception.

Ernst Mach was born on Feb. 18, 1838, in Turas in Moravia, then part of Austria and subsequently a province of the former Czechoslovakia. His father, Johann, was a high school teacher, and Ernst was tutored at home until he entered the University of Vienna, from which he graduated in 1860. In 1864 he became professor of mathematics at Graz; in 1867 he became professor of physics at Prague, a post he held until 1895, when he was appointed to the chair of the history and theory of the inductive sciences at Vienna. He was active in academic and political affairs, and after his retirement he was appointed to the upper house of the Austrian Parliament. He died near Munich on Feb. 19, 1916.

Mach is generally credited with establishing the study of the philosophy of sciences as a separate discipline. He brought to this study, in his words, "an incorruptible skepticism and independence." One of his most important works, *The Science of Mechanics* (1883), is an attack upon the "objective descriptions" of nature which in Newtonian physics produce such concepts as the "absolute" nature of space and time. Demonstration is a misplaced rigor which mistakes experiential summation for prediction. The relativism of his empiricism was an important corrective for modern science by its insistence that all concepts be traced to the objects to which they refer together with an explanation of the rules by which they are applied. For example, atomic theory is an explanation in physics and chemistry. But if such tools are taken to be unobservable realities rather than "theoretical models" for summarizing facts, then science has made the fatal error of identifying description with explanation.

Obviously Mach's views on the nature of science derived from his analysis of human knowledge. He acknowledged his indebtedness to the English empiricists, especially George Berkeley and David Hume. To him "the world consists only of our sensations," and this phenomenalism follows the empiricist tradition of deriving "ideas" from "impressions." Knowledge consists in communicating the observed distinctions of our sensations. From Mach's views has come the tradition of distinguishing between the public and private data of sensation, that is, that part of man's sensory experience which can be confirmed by others and man's individual perceptions. On this basis Mach proposed a unified theory of the sciences. The difference between physics and psychology, material and mental, is relative to the perspective of the observer. Color can be considered physically in terms of its dependencies or psychologically in terms of its receptivity. This scientific theory consists of coherent, concise descriptions of observed phenomena.

The Vienna Circle of contemporary positivism was originally founded as the Ernst Mach Society. Mach also

gave his name to the Mach number, the standard scale for gradations of supersonic speed.

Further Reading

For discussions of Mach consult: Karl R. Popper, *The Logic of Scientific Discovery* (1935; trans. 1959); Carlton Berenda Weinberg, *Mach's Empirio-pragmatism in Physical Science* (1937); Richard Von Mises, *Positivism: A Study in Human Understanding* (1939; trans. 1951); Morris Raphael Cohen, *Reason and Nature: An Essay on the Meaning of Scientific Method* (1953); A. J. Ayer's introduction to his anthology, *Logical Positivism* (1959); and Brand Blanshard, *Reason and Analysis* (1962).

Additional Sources

Ernst Mach-a deeper look: documents and new perspectives, Dordrecht; Boston: Kluwer Academic Publishers, 1992. □

Joaquim Maria Machado de Assis

The Brazilian novelist Joaquim Maria Machado de Assis (1839-1908), although only recently "discovered" outside Brazil, ranks among major world authors of the 19th century. His works are notable for their pessimistic view of human nature and their sophisticated psychological insights.

Joaquim Maria Machado de Assis never left Rio de Janeiro, where he was born. His father was a mulatto house painter, and the future novelist received most of his "formal" education in the kitchen of a girls' school where his stepmother was a dishwasher. At 17 he became a typographer's apprentice and later a proofreader. For most of his life he supported himself—and later his cultured Portuguese wife, 5 years his senior—from his earnings as a middle-ranking bureaucrat. He was sickly from childhood, suffered from epilepsy, and lived in fear that he would suffer an attack in public. As a poor mulatto, he considered himself inferior even when lionized by a public that, to be sure, never really understood him.

Although Machado de Assis began writing early and was widely acclaimed by the time he was 25 years old, it was not until a serious bout with illness and a long convalescence in the late 1870s that he developed his great insight into the human soul. Some critics note his intuitive awareness of the subconscious, his references to what would later be called fetishism, and his belief in man's irrationality, and they consider him a depth psychologist ahead of his time. In any case, his illness stripped from him the last vestiges of romanticism. During this period of illness he also had the opportunity for much reading in English, French, and German, although his artistic development is firmly rooted in the Brazilian milieu.

Machado de Assis' first novel in this new period was *Epitaph for a Small Winner* (1881). Told in the first person by a character who has already died, it recounts the petty concerns and meaningless acts of selfishness that typify the

lives of ordinary men. Ten years later he wrote *Philosopher or Dog?*, a novel about a man who goes—or has always been—insane; one critic has dubbed Machado de Assis an encomiast of lunacy. The next novel of prominence was *Dom Casmurro* (1900), the theme of which is man's inability to love.

Machado de Assis also wrote many short stories, some of which have been translated into English. Apart from the potboilers he turned out for serialized publication in Sunday supplements, he left a substantial collection of novels and stories that are rich, perceptive, and humane.

Further Reading

Four of Machado de Assis' novels and a collection of short stories are available in English. José Bettencourt Machado, *The Life and Times of Machado de Assis* (1953), is adulatory. Helen Caldwell studied one of his novels in *The Brazilian Othello of Machado de Assis: A Study of Dom Casmurro* (1960) and wrote the biography *Machado de Assis: The Brazilian Master and His Novels* (1970). Dorothy Scott Loos pays him much attention in *The Naturalistic Novel of Brazil* (1963). □

Gerardo Machado y Morales

Gerardo Machado y Morales (1871-1939) was a general in Cuba's War for independence of 1895-1898 against Spain. Later elected president, he developed into a harsh dictator.

Gerardo Machado was born in Santa Clara, Las Villas Province, on Sept. 28, 1871. He spent his childhood on his family's cattle estate, attended private schools, and in his early 20s engaged in growing and selling tobacco. During Cuba's Ten Years War (1868-1878) against Spain, Machado's father had joined the Cuban rebels, attaining the rank of major. Machado followed in his father's steps, and when the Cubans resumed the war in 1895, he enrolled, rising to the rank of brigadier general.

After the war ended, Machado turned to politics and business. He became mayor of Santa Clara and during José Miguel Gómez's administration (1909-1913) was appointed inspector of the armed forces and later secretary of interior. Soon after, he engaged in farming and in business and, together with American capitalists, invested in public utilities. He grew wealthy, returning to politics in the early 1920s. He won control of the Liberal party and, with his slogan "Water, roads, and schools," was elected president in 1924.

Reform President

Machado's first administration coincided with a period of prosperity. Sugar production expanded, and the United States provided a close and ready market. Machado embarked on an ambitious public works program which included the completion of the Central Highway, the construction of the national capital, the enlargement of the University of Havana, and the expansion of health facilities. He also sponsored a tariff reform bill in 1927 providing protection to certain Cuban industries. Despite these accomplishments, Cuba's dependence on sugar continued, and United States influence and investments increased.

Before his first administration ended, Machado sought reelection. Claiming that his economic program could not be completed during his 4-year term and that only he could carry it out, Machado announced his decision to have himself reelected and to extend the presidential term to 6 years. He prevented the growth of political opposition by controlling the Conservative party and the small Popular party. Through bribes and threats he subordinated Congress and the judiciary to the executive will, and in 1928 he was reelected over virtually no opposition.

Repression and Reaction

Machado's second term was fraught with problems. Affected by the shock waves of the world depression and oppressed by an increasingly ruthless dictator, many Cubans, led primarily by university students, organized resistance to the regime. In 1931 former president Mario García Menocal led a short-lived uprising in Pinar del Río Province. That same year an anti-Machado expedition landed in Oriente Province, only to be crushed by the army.

As urban violence increased, so did repression. Machado's police raided secret meeting places, arresting students and opposition leaders, whom they tortured or killed.

The United States, attempting to find a peaceful solution to Cuba's political situation, sent special envoy Sumner Welles to mediate between government and opposition. The mediation was supported by most political factions and leaders with the exception of the conservatives and, particularly, the students. Welles's efforts finally led to a general strike and an army revolt which forced Machado to leave the country on Aug. 12, 1933. Machado settled in the United States and died in Miami Beach, Fla., on March 29, 1939.

Further Reading

There is no biography of Machado in English. Background information is in Robert F. Smith, *The United States and Cuba: Business and Diplomacy 1917-1960* (1960); Wyatt MacGaffey and Clifford R. Barnett, *Cuba* (1962; repr. 1965 as *Twentieth Century Cuba*); Robert F. Smith, *Background to Revolution: The Development of Modern Cuba* (1966); Ramon E. Ruiz, *Cuba: The Making of a Revolution* (1968); and Hugh Thomas, *Cuba: The Pursuit of Freedom* (1971). □

Guillaume de Machaut

Guillaume de Machaut (ca. 1300-1377) was the greatest French composer of his century, the creator of the first complete polyphonic Mass setting, and a renowned poet.

Guillaume de Machaut (far left)

Guillaume de Machaut was born in the village of Machault in Champagne, near Reims. He became a cleric, and in 1323 he joined the household of King John of Bohemia as a secretary. John was the son of one German emperor and the father of another; his ancestral castle was Luxembourg. He was also the brother-in-law of one French king and later became the father-in-law of another, and his closest associations were with the French court. One of the most traveled noblemen of Europe and involved in numerous military campaigns, John took his secretary with him to Bohemia, Prussia, Poland, Lithuania, and Italy.

Later John settled Machaut at Reims with a canonicate. There Machaut lived from about 1340 on, quietly and peacefully, except for frequent trips to Paris and hunting expeditions; he was joined by his brother in 1355 and by his student, the poet Eustache Deschamps, who may have been his nephew. Machaut always kept in close touch with the royal family, and his last patron was Jean de France, Duke of Berry, the grandson of King John and brother of King Charles V of France. The Duke of Berry was one of the greatest art patrons of all time. The most beautiful of the five manuscripts that contain all Machaut's works was written for the duke under Machaut's personal supervision. Because of this "complete edition," Machaut's output reaches us fully and is the most voluminous of any composer before the 15th century.

In 1374 Machaut's brother died, and in April 1377 Guillaume followed him. Two poems written by Deschamps in May commemorate his death; shortly thereafter they were set to music by a composer of the younger generation, Andrieu, and they constitute the earliest such "complaint" about a poet or composer.

His Works

In his poetry and in his life Machaut shows himself conscious of his lowly origin but also of his worth. He is dignified, but he can be rollicking and rustic; he is realistic and honest rather than formal. Machaut describes nature as he saw it, responds to the events of his day as a poet-historian, and gives a very honest account of his last love affair, that with Peronne, a girl of 18 or 20, with whom he fell in love during his early 60s; elsewhere he records the names of some eight other girls he had loved. But the majority of his poetry deals with love in the manner of the *trouvères,* whose style he sought to revive. In fact, he was the last composer outside of Germany to write monophonic songs like those of the *trouvères.*

Machaut's works can be divided into four categories. The first consists of larger poetic works: seven historical poems (dits); *Le Remède de fortune,* in part a textbook of poetry; *Le Veoir dit* (1362-1365), the story of his last love; *La Prise d'Alexandrie* (ca. 1370), chronicling the sack of Alexandria by the king of Cyprus in 1365; and seven others. Several of these works contain poems set to music. The second group comprises his shorter poems: *La Louange des dames,* some 270 poems in praise of women; and about 50 complaints and other poems. The third category includes poems set to his own music: 19 lais; 23 motets, with 2 texts each; and 101 pieces in the standard forms of the period (*formes fixes*) —ballade, virelai, and rondeau. The fourth group consists of two large musical works: the hocket *David* and a Mass. Many of these works reappear in manuscripts other than the five of his "complete edition," proving the composer's widespread fame. They are all available in modern editions.

Musical Technique

Machaut's musical technique represents the *ars nova,* or new music, of the 14th century, championed by Philippe de Vitry in the preceding generation. It employs duple meter alongside the previously explored triple meter; the triad; isorhythm, that is, a lengthy rhythmic pattern applied to changing melodic phrases; and complex, often syncopated rhythm. Machaut also seems to have introduced such artifices as reading a melody backward; and his accompanied songs—a melody accompanied· by two instruments—are the first of the genre to reach us, since those of Philippe de Vitry are lost.

In his *Remède de fortune,* Machaut teaches several form types, among them the lai, the complaint, the chanson royale, and the *formes fixes.* His lais are in 12 stanzas, each subdivided into two or four pairs of lines, sung to the same melody; all line pairs differ in length and rhythm, and therefore melodically, except that the last stanza is sung to the music of the first one. Of Machaut's 25 lais 19 are set to music, monophonically (for one unaccompanied voice only), but in two of them monophonic stanzas alternate with canonic ones (of the type of the modern round, then called a chace).

The complaint is a poem of many (30-50) stanzas of 4X4 lines each. When sung—only one of some 15 by Machaut is set to music (monophonically)—all stanzas are sung to the same music, each stanza falling into two repeated sections.

The chanson royale is a poem of 5 stanzas of 8-11 lines and a refrain of 3-4 lines. Only one of Machaut's eight chansons royales is set to music (monophonically).

Ballade, virelai, and rondeau are related forms, all derived from the dance, though only some rondeaux were still connected with dancing at the time. All involve a refrain which is repeated in all stanzas and may comprise 6-20 lines or more. Most of these poems are set to music: 20 of the 21 rondeaux, each for one sung part and one to three instrumental parts; 32 of 38 virelais, most of them monophonically, but some for voice plus one or two instruments; and 42 ballades, mostly for voice and one or two instruments.

To these types must be added the motet, the hocket, and the Mass. The motet, created shortly before 1200 as a liturgical work, soon became the chief type of serious secular art music. Machaut's motets are among the most artful of the century. Whereas isorhythm appears infrequently in the ballades and rondeaux and not at all in the other form types described above, it is ubiquitous in the motets. They are all written for two sung parts—sung to different texts, two, indeed, to one French and one Latin text simultaneously— and either one or two instrumental parts. The majority are secular, but some are liturgical.

The hocket *David* is one of the last works, and the longest, of a type created during the 13th century. In a hocket two parts alternately give out snatches of a melody, here above an isorhythmic *cantus firmus* (preexisting melody).

Machaut's Mass is probably the outstanding musical work of the entire 14th century. It is a polyphonic setting of the entire Mass Ordinary (the portions sung at every Mass except at the Requiem Mass, the Mass for the Dead), consisting of six sections: Kyrie, Gloria, Credo, Sanctus, Agnus Dei, and Ite Missa Est (the last section is rarely set by other composers). Only one such complete setting, the Mass of Tournai (ca. 1300), compiled from various composers, antedates Machaut's, and it is artistically not comparable. Machaut's Mass may have been composed for the Marian Feasts at a chapel served by the Machaut brothers in the 1350s (but it was not, as is often said, written for or sung at the coronation of King Charles V in 1364). The long texts of the Gloria and Credo are set simply in chordal style, each followed by an elaborate Amen. All the other sections are composed in the style of the isorhythmic motet. Almost the entire work is written in four melodic lines, for voices and instruments, and all the sections are unified by a pervasive motif, a technique not employed before or within the following 60 years or so.

There was no one in France during the second half of the 14th century and the first quarter of the 15th to even remotely approach Machaut's musical eminence. In fact, all composers followed his lead and adopted his style, developing it only with respect to an increasingly mannered complexity, which parallels the late Gothic, or mannered, style of architecture prevailing during the period.

Further Reading

The fullest account in English of Machaut's life is in Siegmund Levarie, *Guillaume de Machaut* (1954), and of his works in Donald Jay Grout, *A History of Western Music* (1960). All of Machaut's music is available in modern transcriptions and much of it on records. □

Samora Moises Machel

A dedicated military man and socialist revolutionary, Samora Moises Machel (1933-1986) presided over the independence of Mozambique from Portugal in 1975 and became its first president.

Samora Moises Machel was born on September 29, 1933, in a village in the District of Gaza in the south of Mozambique. Like the great majority of Mozambicans of his generation, he grew up in an agricultural village and attended mission elementary school. Machel completed the fourth class—the prerequisite certificate for any higher education. Most youngsters aspired to complete elementary school and perhaps learn a skill, but most found it difficult. Machel's hopes for higher education were frustrated by Catholic missionaries who refused to grant him a scholarship. Without financial assistance it was difficult for most Africans to pay school fees, room, and board. Many families needed the income earned by all family members just to survive.

Machel hoped to train as a nurse—one of the few professions which had been open to blacks, albeit on a subordinate basis, since the early 20th century. Unable to secure the fees to complete formal training at the Miguel Bombarda Hospital in Lourenco Marques (today Maputo), he got a job working as an aide in the hospital and earned enough to continue his education at night school. He worked at the hospital until he left the country to join the nationalist struggle.

The Progress of a Revolutionary

Machel, like so many others, suffered under colonial rule. He saw the fertile lands of his farming community on the Limpopo river appropriated by white settlers. His family worked unprofitable and arduous cotton plots to comply with the colonial government's cotton cultivation scheme, and they lost loved ones to work accidents and illness resulting from the unsafe and unhealthy work conditions prevailing in the mines, farms, and construction companies which employed thousands of Mozambicans. As an educated black working in the capital city in the heyday of colo-

nialism, Machel faced the arrogance and racism despised by black workers throughout the country.

The visit of Eduardo Mondlane to Lourenco Marques and Gaza in 1961 was a turning point for Mondlane and many others. Samora Machel, among others, urged the educator Mondlane to dedicate himself to the nationalist cause. Since the late 1950s Mozambicans from many backgrounds had left the country to organize an offensive. Mondlane accepted the challenge to unite the many currents of Mozambican nationalism into a front with a better chance for success. In June 1962 Mondlane accepted Tanzanian President Nyerere's invitation to convene the principal nationalist groups in Dar es Salaam. The leaders of these groups agreed to form the Front for the Liberation of Mozambique (Frelimo) under Mondlane's leadership. Thereafter, the stream of Mozambicans making their way to Tanzania to take up arms became a river. By August 1963 Samora Machel had made his way to Tanzania to join the insurgents.

Machel was a member of the first group of Frelimo soldiers sent to Algeria for military training. Upon completion of training, Machel returned to Tanzania to serve as an instructor at Frelimo's Kongwa military training camp. By September 25, 1964, when Frelimo launched the armed struggle, 250 guerrillas had been trained for combat. Machel coordinated guerrilla strategy for the Niassa campaign. Two years later, upon the death of Frelimo's Secretary of Defense Filipe Magaia, Machel became secretary of defense and then commander-in-chief of the army—positions he held throughout the war.

Machel developed Frelimo strategies from his positions within the war zone, propagandizing revolutionary values among the population of areas held by the guerrillas. Machel firmly held that political and social issues were as fundamental to the viability of the guerrilla war as were military tactics. His qualities as a tough soldier and a persuasive speaker won him favor among his cadres. He also enjoyed the confidence and respect of Frelimo President Mondlane. By 1968, when tension due to conflicting political visions among competing factions within the leadership reached crisis proportions, Mondlane, sensing the imminent danger of assassination, remarked to a close friend: "They are determined to kill me. . . . But I am not worried any more. We really do have a collective leadership, a good leadership. Frelimo—the movement—is greater than one man. They don't understand that. . . . That Samora, they don't know him. That man is brilliant. He understands."

On February 3, 1969, Mondlane was killed by a parcel bomb. It was then nearly impossible to maintain unity among factions. In April 1969 a presidential council was elected comprised of Uria Simango (former vice president), Samora Machel, and Marcelino dos Santos (former secretary for foreign affairs). In November 1969 Simango was suspended from the council, and in February 1970 he was expelled from Tanzania. Machel became acting president and dos Santos acting vice president. At the fourth session of Frelimo's Central Committee in May 1970 their positions were confirmed and Simango was formally expelled from the party. The faction within Frelimo which opposed the emphasis on a prolonged guerrilla struggle in favor of combining military action with the establishment of socialism left with Simango and eventually organized an opposition movement.

Machel, like Mondlane, was committed to the transformation of Mozambican society. He claimed: "Of all the things we have done, the most important—the one that history will record as the principal contribution of our generation—is that we understand how to turn the armed struggle into a Revolution; that we realized that it was essential to create a new mentality to build a new society." As Frelimo president he continued his efforts to instill new attitudes among the Mozambican people in the war zones. Observers quipped that he travelled " . . . with the headquarters in his pocket." Machel had a special colleague in the person of his wife and comrade-in-arms Josina Abiatar Muthemba Machel. They were married in May 1969.

Josina Muthemba Machel first tried to leave Mozambique to join Frelimo forces in Tanzania in March 1964, but was apprehended and imprisoned by the Portuguese. She finally escaped to Tanzania and in August 1965 she was assigned to organize political education within the women's unit on the Niassa front. From 1965 to 1971 she continued as a guerrilla and political organizer. By 1970 it was clear that her health was deteriorating. Nonetheless, in March 1971 she undertook a march into Cabo Delgado, but was ultimately evacuated to a hospital in Dar es Salaam where she died on April 7, 1971. Today she is remembered as a revolutionary heroine. In 1975 Machel married Graca Simbine, also a Frelimo militant. Simbine became Mozambique's minister of education.

Under Machel's leadership Frelimo's military made some key inroads and suffered some devastating setbacks. He emphasized the expansion of the military effort, but insisted that it proceed hand in hand with the political effort. The armed struggle gained momentum in 1973-1974. In 1974 a combination of factors—not the least of which was Frelimo's tenacious military drive—led to the 25th of April military coup in Portugal and the subsequent collapse of Portuguese colonialism.

Independence and First President

At this key juncture Machel and the Frelimo leadership held out for full independence and progress toward socialism, rejecting overtures toward compromise. They increased military pressure, and by September 1974 Portugal agreed to grant Mozambique independence under Frelimo rule on June 25, 1975.

During Mozambique's first decade of independence Samora Machel—President Samora, as he was popularly known in Mozambique—faced the immensely difficult task of national reconstruction. He spearheaded socialization of services and nationalization of wealth and oversaw the transformation of Frelimo into a Marxist-Leninist party in 1977. By the early 1980s, however, increasing guerrilla war waged by a somewhat motley collection of opposition groups, a period of destructive floods followed by a devastating regional drought, strategic errors in the state economic planning sector, and a world-wide economic recession combined to create a crisis situation in Mozambique. The government found itself increasingly unable to feed, defend, and service its people.

Machel remained characteristically pragmatic—taking responsibility for both popular and unpopular decisions. He imposed economic sanctions on the Rhodesian government, a popular act even though it caused severe economic consequences for the Mozambican economy. He also signed the unpopular Incomati Accord, a non-aggression pact with Mozambique's principal foe, the Union of South Africa. He signed the accord hoping to alleviate the combination of economic and military pressure which was increasingly undermining the viability of the Mozambican economy.

Machel remained committed to realizing a revolution from the armed struggle, but not wedded to any single means for achieving that end. He consistently emphasized the need to retain—and in some cases regain—the confidence of the people. He remained popular, in part because Mozambicans related to Machel's personal experience as a peasant, a worker, a guerrilla, and a political militant. His resilience may be due to something highlighted by political observer John S. Saul: "What is impressive about the Mozambican leadership . . . is that the awareness of the need to sustain a genuinely dialectical relationship between leadership and mass action remains very alive. . . ."

Unhappily for Mozambique Machel was killed in an airplane crash October 20, 1986. He was succeeded by Foreign Minister Joaquin Chissano (born 1939).

Further Reading

Biographical material in English on Machel is scarce. Journalist Iain Cristie's "Portrait of President Machel," in the Mozambique Independence issue of *Africa Report* 20 (May-June 1975), is the most accessible. *Mozambique, Sowing the Seeds of Revolution* (London, 1974) is a translation of some of Machel's most important speeches. Machel's "The Task of National Reconstruction in Mozambique," in *Objective: Justice* 7 (January-March 1975), and his interview with Allen Isaacman in *Africa Report* 24 (July-August 1979), also reveal his political views. Several general studies explore Mozambique's experience during Machel's lifetime. The following are among the best: John S. Saul, *A Different Road: Socialism in Mozambique* (1983); Allen and Barbara Isaacman, *Mozambique: From Colonialism to Revolution* (1983); and Thomas Henriksen, *Revolution and Counterrevolution: Mozambique's War of Independence, 1964-1974* (1983). Students will find a valuable annual update of events in Mozambique in *Africa Contemporary Record: Annual Survey & Documents*, edited by Colin Legum and published in New York by Africana Publishing Company.

Additional Sources

Christie, Iain, *Samora Machel, a biography*, Atlantic Highlands, N.J.: Panaf, 1989. □

Niccolò Machiavelli

The Italian author and statesman Niccolò Machiavelli (1469-1527) is best known for *The Prince*, in which he enunciated his political philosophy.

Niccolò Machiavelli was born in Florence of an aristocratic, though by no means wealthy, family. Little is known of the first half of his life, prior to his first appointment to public office. His writings prove him to have been a very assiduous sifter of the classics, especially the historical works of Livy and Tacitus; in all probability he knew the Greek classics only in translation.

In 1498 Machiavelli was named chancellor and secretary of the second (and less important) chancellery of the Florentine Republic. His duties consisted chiefly of executing the policy decisions of others, carrying on diplomatic correspondence, digesting and composing reports, and compiling minutes; he also undertook some 23 missions to foreign states. His embassies included four to the French king and two to the court of Rome. His most memorable mission is described in a report of 1503 entitled "Description of the Manner Employed by Duke Valentino [Cesare Borgia] in Slaying Vitellozzo Vitelli, Oliverotto da Fermo, Signor Pagolo and the Duke of Gravina, Orsini"; with surgical precision he details Borgia's series of political murders, implicitly as a lesson in the art of politics for

Florence's indecisive and timorous gonfalonier, Pier Soderini.

In 1502 Machiavelli married Marietta Corsini, who bore him four sons and two daughters. To his grandson Giovanni Ricci we owe the preservation of many of his letters and minor works.

In 1510 Machiavelli, inspired by his reading of Roman history, was instrumental in organizing a citizen militia of the Florentine Republic. In August 1512 a Spanish army entered Tuscany and sacked Prato. The Florentines in terror deposed Soderini, whom Machiavelli characterized as "good, but weak," and allowed the Medici to return to power. On November 7 Machiavelli was dismissed; soon afterward he was arrested, imprisoned, and subjected to torture as a suspected conspirator against the Medici. Though innocent, he remained suspect for years to come; unable to secure an appointment from the reinstated Medici, he turned to writing.

In all likelihood Machiavelli interrupted the writing of his *Discourses on the First Ten Books of Titus Livius* to write the brief treatise on which his fame rests, *Il Principe* (1513; *The Prince*). Other works followed: *The Art of War* and *The Life of Castruccio Castracani* (1520); three extant plays, *Mandragola* (1518; The Mandrake), *Clizia,* and *Andria;* the *Istorie fiorentine* (1526; History of Florence); a short story, *Belfagor;* and several minor works in verse and prose.

In 1526 Machiavelli was commissioned by Pope Clement VII to inspect the fortifications of Florence. Later that year and the following year his friend and critic Francesco Guicciardini, Papal Commissary of War in Lombardy, employed him in two minor diplomatic missions. He died in Florence in June 1527, receiving the last rites of the Church that he had bitterly criticized.

The Prince

Machiavelli shared with Renaissance humanists a passion for classical antiquity. To their wish for a literary and spiritual revival of ancient values, guided by such authors as Plato, Cicero, and St. Augustine, he added a fierce desire for a political and moral renewal on the model of the Roman Republic as depicted by Livy and Tacitus. Though a republican at heart, he saw as the crying need of his day a strong political and military leader who could forge a unitary state in northern Italy to eliminate French and Spanish hegemony from Italian soil. At the moment that he wrote *The Prince* he envisioned such a possibility while the restored Medici ruled both Florence and the papacy. He had taken to heart Cesare Borgia's energetic creation of a new state in Romagna in the few brief years while Borgia's father, Alexander VI, occupied the papal throne. The final chapter of *The Prince* is a ringing plea to his Medici patrons to set Italy free from the "barbarians." It concludes with a quotation from Petrarch's patriotic poem *Italia mia:* "Virtue will take arms against fury, and the battle will be brief; for the ancient valor in Italian hearts is not yet dead." This exhortation fell on deaf ears in 1513 but was to play a role 3 centuries later in the Risorgimento.

The preceding 25 chapters of *The Prince* are written in a terse, analytical, and frequently aphoristic style. Preceding political writers, from Plato and Aristotle in ancient times and through the Middle Ages and the 15th-century humanists, had all concurred in treating politics as a branch of morals. Machiavelli's chief innovation was to break with this long tradition and to confer autonomy upon politics. In chapter 15 of *The Prince* he writes: "My intent being to write a useful work for those who understand, it seemed to me more appropriate to pursue the actual truth of the matter than the imagination of it. Many have imagined republics and principalities which were never seen or known really to exist; because how one lives is so far removed from how one ought to live that he who abandons what one does for what one ought to do, learns rather his own ruin than his preservation." Like Galileo in astronomy at the end of the 16th century, Machiavelli in politics chooses to describe the world as it is, rather than as people are taught that it should be. Although his longest work, the *Discourses on Livy,* takes the familiar humanistic form of a commentary on a classical text, his approach to political theory marks a sharp break with tradition.

Fundamental to Machiavelli's conception of history and politics is the binomial of *fortuna* and *virtù.* Abandoning the Christian view of history as providential, Machiavelli views events in purely human terms. Often it is fortune that gives—or terminates—the political leader's opportunity for decisive action. Borgia, though a virtuoso politician, succumbed to an "extreme malignity of fortune" when he fell ill just as his father died. Moses, Cyrus, Romulus, and Theseus alike received their occasions from fortune. Sacred history implicitly is reduced to the same plane as secular history. In some passages it seems that fortune itself hinges upon human habits and institutions: "I believe that the fortune which the Romans had would be enjoyed by all princes who proceeded as the Romans did and who were of the same virtue as they." Like others in the Renaissance, Machiavelli believed in man's capacity for determining his own destiny in opposition to the medieval concept of an omnipotent divine will or the crushing fate of the ancient Greeks. *Virtù* in politics—unlike Christian virtue—is an effective combination of force and shrewdness, the lion and the fox, with a touch of greatness.

The kernel of *The Prince* is found in chapters 17, "On Cruelty and Clemency, and Whether It Is Better To Be Loved or Feared," and 18, "How Princes Should Keep Their Word." As Machiavelli frequently says also in other works, the innate badness of men requires that the prince instill fear rather than love in his subjects and break his pledge, when necessary, with other princes, who in any case will be no more honest than he. Moralistic critics of Machiavelli have sometimes forgotten that he is attempting to describe rather than to invent the rules of political success. For him the state is an organism, greater than the sum of its citizens and individual interests, subject to laws of growth and decay; its health consists in unity, but even in the best of circumstances its longevity is limited.

The founding of a state is the work of one man; its continuance, however, is better trusted to many than to one (*Discourses,* I, 9 and 58). If this maxim is kept in mind, much of the alleged discrepancy between the monarchical *Prince*

and the republican *Discourses* vanishes. The two books differ little in their teachings; the *Discourses* is more leisurely and somewhat fragmentary, *The Prince* more "scientific," absolute, revolutionary, and exciting. Both works are excessively exemplary; unlike Guicciardini, Machiavelli thought it possible to find in his Roman ideal a practical guide to contemporary Italian politics. Particularly in *The Prince,* he combines recent examples with ancient ones to illustrate his axioms.

Other Works

Certain passages in the *Discourses* (I, 11 and 12; II, 2) set forth Machiavelli's quarrel with the Church: by the bad example of the court of Rome, Italy has lost its devotion and religion; the Italian states are weak and divided because the Church, too feeble politically to dominate them, has nevertheless prevented any one state from uniting them. He suggests that the Church might have been destroyed by its own corruption had not St. Francis and St. Dominic restored it to its original principles by founding new orders. However, in an unusual if not unique departure from traditional anticlericalism, Machiavelli contrasts favorably the fiercely civil and militaristic pagan religion of ancient Rome with the humble and otherworldly Christian religion.

The *Mandragola,* the finest comedy of the Italian Renaissance, is not unrelated to Machiavelli's political writings in its comic indictment of contemporary Florentine society. In a well-knit intrigue the simpleton Nicia contributes to his own cuckolding. Nicia's beautiful and virtuous wife, Lucrezia (so named by the author with an eye to Roman history), is corrupted by those who should be her closest protectors: her mother, her husband, and her unscrupulous confessor, Fra Timoteo, all pawns in the skillful hands of the manipulator Ligurio.

Although not equaling Guicciardini as a historian, Machiavelli in his *History of Florence* nevertheless marks an advance over earlier histories in his attention to underlying causes rather than the mere succession of events as he tells the history of the Florentines from the death of Lorenzo de' Medici in 1492.

Machiavelli closely adhered to his maxim that a servant of government must be loyal and self-sacrificing. He nowhere suggests that the political morality of princes is a model for day-to-day dealings between ordinary citizens. His reputation as a sinister and perfidious counselor of fraud is largely undeserved; it began not long after his death. His works were banned in the first printed Index (1559). In Elizabethan England, Machiavelli was represented on the stage and in literature as diabolically evil. The primary source of this misrepresentation was the translation into English by Simon Patericke in 1577 of a work popularly called *Contre-Machiavel,* by the French Huguenot Gentillet, who distorted Machiavelli and blamed his teachings for the St. Bartholomew Night massacre of 1572. A poem by Gabriel Harvey the following year falsely attributed four principal crimes to Machiavelli: poison, murder, fraud, and violence. Christopher Marlowe's *The Jew of Malta* (1588) introduces "Machiavel" as the speaker of an atrocious prologue; Machiavellian villains followed in works by other playwrights.

Many of Machiavelli's authentic values are incorporated into 19th-century liberalism: the supremacy of civil over religious power; the conscription of citizen armies; the preference for republican rather than monarchical government; and the republican Roman ideals of honesty, work, and the people's collective responsibility for values that transcend those of the individual.

Further Reading

Recommended translations of Machiavelli's works are *The Prince and the Discourses,* translated by Luigi Ricci, E. R. P. Vincent, and Christian E. Detmold (1940); *Mandragola,* translated by Anne and Henry Paolucci (1957); *Literary Works,* edited by J. R. Hale (1961); and *The Chief Works and Others,* edited and translated by Allan Gilbert (3 vols., 1965). Among the many works about Machiavelli are Pasquale Villari, *Life and Times of Niccolò Machiavelli* (2 vols., 1877-1883; trans., rev. ed. 1892); Federico Chabod, *Machiavelli and the Renaissance* (1926; trans. 1958); Mario Praz, *Machiavelli and the Elizabethans* (1928); Ralph Roeder, *The Man of the Renaissance* (1933); D. Erskine Muir, *Machiavelli and His Times* (1936); Leonardo Olschki, *Machiavelli the Scientist* (1945); J. H. Whitfield, *Machiavelli* (1947); Roberto Ridolfi, *The Life of Niccolò Machiavelli* (1954; trans. 1963); and Giuseppe Prezzolini, *Machiavelli* (1966). □

Alasdair Chalmers MacIntyre

An influential American philosopher, Alasdair Chalmers MacIntyre (born 1929) wrote widely on such diverse topics as Marxism, the concept of the unconscious, the history of ethics, and the concepts of virtue and justice. He made a vital contribution to the revival of contemporary interest in the ethical systems of Aristotle and Aquinas and many significant contributions to the history of philosophy and ethical theory.

Alasdair Chalmers MacIntyre was born on January 12, 1929, in Glasgow, Scotland, to John and Emily (Chalmers) MacIntyre. He was educated at the University of London and Oxford University and began his teaching career in Great Britain at Manchester University in 1951. He also taught at Leeds University, Essex University and Oxford. In 1969 he came to the United States and took a position as professor of the history of ideas at Brandeis University. In 1972 he was appointed dean of the College of Liberal Arts and professor of philosophy at Boston University. In 1980 he was awarded the Henry Luce Professor at Wellesley College, in 1982 the W. Alton Jones Professor at Vanderbilt University and in 1984 he was president of the Eastern Div. of the American Philosophy Association. He took a position as professor of philosophy at the University

of Notre Dame in 1985. He went to Vanderbilt University in Nashville, Tennessee later in 1985. He was a professor of philosophy until 1988 when he became a visiting scholar at the Whitney Humanities Center at Yale University (1988-1989). He accepted the position of McMahon-Hank Professor of Philosophy at Notre Dame (1989 to 1994). From 1995-1997 he was the Arts & Sciences Professor of Philosophy at Duke University.

Relevance of the History of Philosophy

Alasdair MacIntyre believed the history of philosophy was profoundly relevant to contemporary life and thought; and the philosophical systems of such figures as Aristotle and Aquinas could and ought to be used as viewpoints from which contemporary thought itself can be criticized. For MacIntyre, the history of philosophy was not necessarily a history of progress in which our grasp of truth was improving. Rather, he argued earlier traditions within philosophy were, in many respects, far more intellectually adequate than contemporary systems of thought and people ought to in some significant ways return to these earlier systems for first principles. In this respect, he may be referred to as a philosophical conservative.

To illustrate his strategy, he conceived the major intellectual defect within contemporary Western civilization as: the absence of a coherent tradition which assisted us in resolving our moral dilemmas. He argued contemporary ethics were characterized by insolvable moral problems, precisely because the philosophical founders of Western civilization attempted to ground philosophy on something pure, solid, unchangeable and certain—namely, *the mind.* The mind was, for the British, French, and German Enlightenment philosophers, a storehouse of truth, not in the sense of containing sets of *facts,* but in containing the *general principles of method* by which the truth could be acquired. The mind was the foundation for growth in knowledge.

The fathers of the Enlightenment gave this foundation many names, but Kant's was perhaps the most familiar. He claimed the part of the mind providing us with the foundation upon which all further science could develop was pure reason. *Pure reason,* according to Kant, could liberate men and women by separating us from the dictates of tradition. One could, according to Kant, transcend the tradition into which one was accidentally born by following the methods dictated by pure reason. Furthermore, by following these dictates one could resolve the fundamental difficulties one encountered within one's moral life. In short, pure reason could answer and resolve our moral conflicts and, thus, the science of ethics could be founded by deriving our moral principles from pure reason alone.

According to MacIntyre, the main difficulty with the notion that ethics ought to be based on something standing over and above social traditions is *it cannot be done.* His argument for this sweeping claim was rather simple, but anything but simpleminded. He argued somewhat pragmatically the sign of an adequate philosophy was its ability to resolve practical, moral problems experienced by ordinary people; for example, should the active killing of terminally ill patients who are in states of persistent and unremitting pain be permitted? This was sometimes called active euthanasia. The abortion issue represented another such problem. According to MacIntyre, examples could multiply interminably. The common thread which united these problems was society was unable to answer any of them, and this inability was derived from the Enlightenment assumption—ethical problems can only be solved by pure reason. But since pure reason was silent on all of these questions, our society was at a loss to resolve any of the major dilemmas that it faced. In short, if the mark of adequacy of a philosophy was its ability to resolve practical ethical problems, then the philosophy of contemporary society was a bankruptcy.

MacIntyre's assault on the concept of pure reason was based on the notion that pure reason was simply not universal. As many anthropologists and sociologists (and later many feminist thinkers) have pointed out, there was no shared set of intellectual assumptions all men and women in all cultures shared. MacIntyre argued the empirical absence of such shared ideas indicating pure reason was another name for Western reason, not reason itself. It cannot be universalized without coming into conflict with the empirical facts of sociology and anthropology.

Does this mean ethical problems are unresolvable? MacIntyre argued moral problems can be addressed within the broader confines of a cultural or religious tradition containing substantive principles concerning the meaning and purpose of individual and social life. In short, to solve moral problems one needed a set of principles richer than what pure reason can supply. More important, he argued these traditions are somewhat immunized against rational critique since reason itself was not pure and isolated from tradition. Reason itself was, and needed to be, defined in terms of a broad context and, given the dependence of reason on tradition, it seemed impossible to use reason to undermine a cultural or religious tradition.

Traditional Christian Ethics

MacIntyre's rejection of the spirit of modernity left one with a fundamental question: To what tradition does he ascribe? His answer was quite straightforward. He was a Christian with the traditions of Augustine and Aquinas. When, therefore, he faced a moral difficulty, he faced it not as a pure reasoner but as a traditional Christian influenced by the ethics of Aquinas and Augustine.

Contemporary critics of MacIntyre emphasized some of the difficulties in his position. Three difficulties are prominent. First, given his objections to universalism, it would seem he could not ascribe to traditional Christianity since Christians of all denominations believe the gospel is directed to everyone. In short, it is a religion intrinsically universal. Secondly, our society is a pluralistic society in which there was a deep and binding commitment to individual autonomy or liberty. It was also a society deeply committed to the principles of social welfare. These principles went a long way toward defining our culture and, thus, they may be construed as the tradition of the West. A modern pluralistic society was based on a tradition which MacIntyre criticized. This culture was obviously very different from the cultures which spawned Aristotle, Augustine, and Aquinas. While these cultures were rich in many respects, they had little respect for individual freedom. Individuals were, for the most part, forced into social roles and could do little to determine the course of their own lives.

Personal

Throughout his career he penned 33 books on philosophy, theology and religion. His book *Whose Justice? Whose Reason?* (1988) was published by the University of Notre Dame Press. He received a Metcalf Prize in 1974 and a D.H.A. from Swarthmoure College in 1983. Other honorary degrees include: D. Lit. Queens University of Belfast (1988); D.U.E. University of Essex (1990); D. Lit. Williams College (1993) and DHL for the New School for Social Research (1996).

He married Ann Peri in 1953 (divorced in 1963) and they had two daughters. Also in 1963 he married his second wife, Susan Margery Willans, and had one son and one daughter. They divorced in 1977. He married Lynn Sumida Joy later the same year. They had no children.

Further Reading

MacIntyre's style of writing was clear and straightforward and was, with patience, accessible to readers. His three most influential books were *Marxism and Christianity* (1953, 1984), *After Virtue* (1981), and *Whose Justice, Whose Reason?* (1988). In addition, see *Against the Self Images of the Age* (1971), *A Short History of Ethics* (1983), and, with Stanley Hauerwas as co-editor, *Revisions: Changing Perspectives on Moral Philosophy* (1983). Commentary on his work was widespread. Among the recommended sources were Charles Larmore's review of *Whose Justice? Whose Reason?* in the *Journal of Philosophy* (August 1989). Richard Bernstein's *Beyond Objectivism and Relativism* (1983) has an excellent discussion of many of the issues that MacIntyre's philosophy addresses. □

Robert Morrison MacIver

Robert Morrison MacIver (1882-1970) was a Scottish-American sociologist, political philosopher, and educator. He was a leading theorist of the interaction between the operation of society and the political institution.

Robert M. MacIver was born in Stornoway, Scotland, on April 17, 1882. His education was in classics at the University of Edinburgh and at Oxford University. He lectured in political science and sociology at Aberdeen University (1907-1915). At the University of Toronto (1915-1927) he was professor and head of the department of political science and served as vice-chairman of the Canadian War Labor Board (1917-1919). After heading the department of economics and sociology at Barnard College (1927-1929), he was Lieber professor of political philosophy and sociology at Columbia University (1929-1950).

During the next decade MacIver was successively director of research for the Jewish Defense Agencies, the Assault on Academic Freedom, the United Nations, and the Juvenile Delinquency Evaluation Project for New York City. He was president of the American Sociological Society (1940) and president and then chancellor of the New School for Social Research (1963-1966).

Beginning as a political philosopher with broad social interests, MacIver viewed the state as a social institution that is necessarily interdependent with other institutions and the prevailing class system. These themes formed the basis of his *Community* (1917) and *The Modern State* (1926). But in several editions of his *Society* (particularly the 1937 edition), he came to regard society as a network of acquired interests expressed in groups or associations and in legitimate value systems called institutions. Interests differ sociologically by emphasis either on goals (culture or myth) or on means and techniques (civilizational interests). *The Web of Government* (1947) analyzed the two forms of interest in promoting social change and gave special attention to the critical role of government in facilitating or moderating varied effects of innovations. In a related work, *Social Causation* (1942), he analyzed social change as a complex process of social causation in which a key aspect is the shared evaluation of cultural and technical innovation.

MacIver also had a continuing and judicious interest in many public issues. In *The More Perfect Union* (1949) he warned about the vicious circle of discrimination, deprivation, and accentuated racial prejudice. In *Academic Freedom in Our Time* (1955) he exposed contemporary assaults on academic freedom and convincingly demonstrated the importance of such freedom for a viable society. He directed a thorough investigation of delinquency programs in New York City which was summarized in one of his last books, *The Prevention and Control of Delinquency* (1966). He died on June 15, 1970.

Further Reading

MacIver's autobiography, *As a Tale That Is Told* (1968), is informative. Morroe Berger and others, *Freedom and Control in Modern Society* (1954), contains discussions of some aspects of MacIver's work by former students. ☐

John William Mackay

John William Mackay (1831-1902), American miner and business leader, controlled the richest ground in the Comstock mining area of Nevada and founded the Postal Telegraph Company.

John William Mackay was born on Nov. 28, 1831, in Dublin, Ireland. In 1840 his family emigrated to New York City. On his father's death 2 years later, Mackay had to leave school and find employment. He worked at temporary jobs in New York and in Louisville, Ky., and for 4 years served as an apprentice to a builder of clipper ships.

Caught up in the gold fever then sweeping the nation, Mackay went to California in 1851.

For 8 years Mackay labored in the diggings along the Yuba and American rivers and in the Sierra Nevada foothills. In 1860 he joined the miners going to test their luck in the new mines of the Comstock Lode in Nevada.

Mackay became a mining contractor, accepting shares in mines in exchange for driving tunnels and constructing timber shorings. When the value of these shares soared, Mackay had enough capital to broaden his activities. Realizing that as much money could be made by processing ore as by mining it, he built a profitable mill in the heart of the Gold Hill mining district. In the late 1860s he formed a partnership with James C. Flood, James G. Fair, and William S. O'Brien. Their firm soon gained control of the most valuable properties on the Comstock. Their wisdom in acquiring properties was demonstrated in 1873, when they struck the Big Bonanza, a shelf of ore that produced more than $100 million worth of gold and silver.

Mackay used his Comstock profits to broaden his business ventures. With Flood and Fair he established the Bank of Nevada, thus controlling the finances of the Comstock as well as its mining operations. Mackay also bought mines in Colorado, Idaho, and Alaska and timber lands and ranches in California. He owned part of the Spreckels Sugar Company and part of the Sprague Elevator and Electrical Works, and he served as a director of the Canadian Pacific and the Southern Pacific railroads.

By the 1880s the Comstock Lode was near exhaustion. Mackay liquidated his interests. At this time the transatlantic cable was monopolized by Jay Gould. In 1883 Mackay and James Gordon Bennett, publisher of the *New York Herald,* organized the Commercial Cable Company and soon succeeded in laying a second cable across the Atlantic. The ensuing rate war between the Mackay and Gould interests resulted in a reduction of charges to a third of the established figure. When Gould attempted to cripple the Commercial Cable Company by denying it the right to use Western Union lines in the United States, Mackay consolidated numerous small telegraph companies into a new nationwide organization, the Postal Telegraph Company.

His successes induced Mackay to try to establish service between San Francisco and Manila. While the transpacific cable was being laid, its owner died in London on July 20, 1902. Mackay, ever mindful of his humble beginnings and lack of education, had remained throughout his life an unassuming man and had twice declined a seat in the U.S. Senate.

Further Reading

A complete biography of Mackay is Ethel H. Manter, *Rocket of the Comstock: The Story of John William Mackay* (1950). Other pertinent works include Dan De Quille, *The Big Bonanza* (1876; rev. ed. 1947); Oscar Lewis, *Silver Kings: The Lives and Times of Mackay, Fair, Flood, and O'Brien, Lords of the Nevada Comstock Lode* (1947); and James W. Hulse, *The Nevada Adventure: A History* (1965).

Additional Sources

Lewis, Oscar, *Silver kings: the lives and times of Mackay, Fair, Flood, and O'Brien, lords of the Nevada Comstock lode,* Reno: University of Nevada Press, 1986. □

August Macke

August Macke (1887-1914) was a German painter whose harmonious and simple scenes of everyday life made a unique contribution to Expressionism.

Born on January 3, 1887, in Meschede, Germany, August Macke attended the Arts and Crafts School as well as the Academy of Fine Arts in Düsseldorf from 1906 to 1908. His career as an artist spanned only eight short years. He was killed on September 26, 1914, as a soldier in the first weeks of World War I. As a student he contributed costume and stage designs for the Düsseldorf theater (famous for its director and outstanding actress, Louise Dumont). Trips to Italy, Holland, and Belgium culminated in the first visit to Paris, financed by Bernhard Koehler, a famous collector and the uncle of Macke's future wife.

In 1908 Koehler went with Macke to Paris, visiting exhibits and artists, thus providing Macke with an introduction to Cubism and Fauvism, the works of Paul Cezanne and Robert Delaunay. Koehler—through Macke—was also in-

strumental in providing funds for one of the most important contributions to modern art, the publication of the *Blue Rider Almanac* in 1911, to which Macke also contributed an article. Koehler also financed in part the largest European avant-garde art exhibit ever held in Germany at that time, the *Erster Deutscher Herbst Salon* (First German Fall Salon) at the Sturm Gallery of Herwarth Walden in Berlin in 1913.

Macke's half year of study with the famous painter Lovis Corinth was of less importance to his artistic development than his friendship with Franz Marc (after 1910) and his subsequent participation with Wassily Kandinsky in the Blue Rider Group. Macke was not very interested in the theoretical concepts of either Kandinsky or Marc; his vitality, his love for life, led him to experiment with various forms on his own, developing a variance of Cubism based on his special relations to colors. From early on, Macke chose as his main themes simple, everyday scenes from the life he loved so much. Neither the speed of modern life nor the tranquility of rural sites held any fascination for him. He painted modern, often elegantly dressed, human figures in quiet, harmonious, man-made surroundings: in parks, in the zoo, on the banks of rivers, or in front of shop windows, as well as scenes from the circus. There is no haste in the movements of his figures: quiet conversations, people reading or watching animals or the river flow by, scenes rarely found elsewhere in German Expressionism.

Macke was fascinated by the power of color to construct space and distance, permitting him to make figures and surroundings equally important. He ordered his abbreviated forms in carefully balanced color variations, avoiding the frequently apocalyptic and fantastic forms of his friends of the Blue Rider Group. The influence of Delaunay's ''orphic'' colors is easily recognized in Macke's work, but his vigorous and strong temperament translated the various influences into paintings which are independent and unique and—in strong contrast to most expressionistic works of the period—closely allied to the French developments in the arts.

Macke also produced small sculptures, designed stained-glass windows, and made designs for embroideries. He actively participated in two important modern exhibitions: the exhibition of Rhenish Expressionists in Bonn as well as the First German Fall Salon in Berlin in 1913. His greatest artistic achievements, promising even more succinct accomplishments, were made in 1914. Again with the help of Bernhard Koehler, he travelled with Paul Klee and an old Swiss friend, the painter Louis Moilliet, to North Africa, Tunis, and Kairouan. Paul Klee remarked later that it was this trip which provided him with the true understanding of color, probably in part under Macke's influence. Macke's many watercolors and sketches show strong response to the Mediterranean light, the different forms of North Africa, and the appreciation of the extraordinary local colors.

Macke's simple and direct approach to everyday life, his carefully balanced compositions, and his lively colors all enhanced his images of the column-like figures. The serene and balanced visions show a world of visual poetry which separates him from the more forceful works of his expressionist friends and establish for him a special position in this early development of modern art.

Further Reading

Macke's oeuvre catalogue has been published by Gustav Vriesen (2nd edition, Stuttgart, 1967). His letters exchanged with Franz Marc were published, edited by Wolfgang Macke (Cologne, 1964) and recollections were made public by his widow, Elisabeth Erdmann-Macke (Stuttgart, 1962). Valuable contributions were made in the books by Günter Busch (Cologne, 1956), M. T. Engels (2nd edition, Recklinghause, 1958), and Walter Holzhausen (Munich, 1956). As in all cases of the German Expressionists, the various exhibition catalogues are of importance. An important exhibit was held in 1979 at the Citymuseum of Bonn, "Die Rheinischen Expressionisten" (The Rhenish Expressionists), edited by Dierk Stemmler, which places Macke in the midst of his contemporaries. A small monograph on Macke's painting, "Das Russische Ballett" (The Russian Ballet) (Stuttgart, 1966), by Günter Busch is a useful interpretation. Günter Busch also published an evaluation of Macke's drawings (Hamburg, 1966). The Westfälisches Landesmuseum für Kunst und Kulturgeschichte, Münster, holds 78 sketchbooks of Macke. A large collection of Macke's works is in the Städtische Kunstmuseum, Bonn. □

Sir Alexander Mackenzie

The Scottish explorer, fur trader, and businessman Sir Alexander Mackenzie (ca. 1764-1820) was perhaps the most venturesome of all the explorers of the Northwest of North America. He was the first to travel overland to the Pacific Coast.

Alexander Mackenzie was born near Stornoway on Lewis Island. Upon the death of his mother, his father took him to New York in 1774. During the American Revolution his father fought as a loyalist, and he sent Alexander to safety in Montreal. A brief period of schooling was followed by his entry as a clerk into the trading firm of Gregory and McLeod. He remained there for 5 years and in 1784 went to Detroit as a trader for the company.

The next year Mackenzie was offered a partnership in the XY Company if he would go to the Saskatchewan River to join the competition with the North West Company in the fur trade. Two years of sharp hostility, which included at least two killings, led to a merger of the two companies. Mackenzie now became a wintering partner in the Nor'Westers and, in 1788, was placed in charge of the Athabasca Department. He took his cousin Roderick with him to oversee the trade, which left him free to indulge his ambition to explore.

Descent of the Mackenzie River

It was Mackenzie's passion to reach the Pacific Ocean overland. In the summer of 1789 he set out, hoping to discover a passage westward by way of a river, described to

him by the Indians, which flowed out of Great Slave Lake. After 3 weeks exploring the north shore of the lake, they found the outlet. Unknown to Mackenzie, of course, it was one of the great rivers of the continent and led to the Arctic Ocean. He embarked optimistically on this river to which he would give his name, as its original course was westward. He became more and more gloomy, however, as the direction of the river swung to the north. He persevered in his search, visiting previously unknown Indian tribes little beyond a Stone Age culture. They reached the sea in early July but realized it only by the movement of the tides.

Mackenzie established a post on Whale Island, north of the delta of his river, to mark the limit of his journey. The arduous return brought the party back to Lake Athabasca by mid-September. They had traveled almost 3,000 miles in a little over 3 months, along the Mackenzie River to the sea and back. The feat brought little satisfaction to Mackenzie or his employers because of the lack of trading possibilities in the north and his own disappointment in not finding a westward route through the mountains.

Mackenzie spent the next 3 years in company affairs. In 1791 he went to Montreal. He spent the next winter in London studying, especially longitude calculation, and collecting instruments. He had not abandoned his hope of reaching the Pacific. By the fall of 1792, he was once again in the west, where he met cousin Roderick and planned his second, and greatest, expedition.

Land Route to the Pacific

Mackenzie set out in October and wintered up the Peace River in order to have an early start in the spring in his assault on the Rockies. Fur trading during the winter discharged his duty to the company, and on May 9, 1793, with six voyageurs, he began his quest for the Pacific again. By the end of the month they reached the forks of the Peace, deep in the mountains. They followed the south fork (Parsnip River) to its source and, on June 17, crossed over to the turbulent Fraser.

After a difficult week descending this river they abandoned the attempt, retraced their route, and struck overland on July 4. Eighteen days later they reached the Pacific near the mouth of the Bella Coola River. A simple inscription was painted on a rock face: "Alexander Mackenzie, from Canada, by land, July 22, 1793." He was the first to cross the continent north of the Spanish possessions.

Mackenzie retired from the company in 1799 and published his *Voyages* in 1801 in England. He reentered the fur trade, first in competition with his old company and then again as a member of it. But his interest was waning. He was knighted in 1802. In 1805 he was elected as a member of the Lower Canada Assembly. Three years later he returned to Scotland. He married in 1812 and died on his estate on March 12, 1820.

Further Reading

Several editions of Mackenzie's own accounts have been published; but W. Kaye Lamb, Dominion Archivist of Canada, is preparing what probably will be the definitive edition of Mackenzie's writings. Of the several good studies of Mackenzie and his travels in the west, the most recent are Phillip Vail (pseudonym for Noel Bertram Gerson), *The Magnificent Adventures of Alexander Mackenzie* (1964), and Roy Daniells, *Alexander Mackenzie and the North West* (1969). Older but still useful are M. S. Wade, *Mackenzie of Canada, The Life and Adventures of Alexander Mackenzie, Discoverer* (1927); Arthur P. Woolacott, *Mackenzie and His Voyageurs: By Canoe to the Arctic and the Pacific, 1789-93* (1927); and Hume Wrong, *Sir Alexander Mackenzie, Explorer and Fur Trader* (1927).

Additional Sources

Hing, Robert J., *Tracking Mackenzie to the sea: coast to coast in eighteen splashdowns,* Manassas, Va.: Anchor Watch Press, 1992.

Mackenzie, Alexander, Sir, *First man West: Alexander Mackenzie's journal of his voyage to the Pacific coast of Canada in 1793,* Westport, Conn.: Greenwood Press, 1976, 1962.

A narrative or journal of voyages and travels through the northwest continent of America in the years 1789 & 1793, Fairfield, Wash.: Ye Galleon Press, 1979. □

Alexander Mackenzie

Alexander Mackenzie (1822-1892) was a Scottish-born Canadian political leader. He was head of the Liberal party and the first Liberal prime minister of Canada.

On Jan. 28, 1822, Alexander Mackenzie was born near Dunkeld. His parents were poor, and young Mackenzie left school to apprentice himself to a stone mason. At the age of 20 Mackenzie emigrated to Canada, where he soon found work in his trade at Kingston, Upper Canada. Prospering, Mackenzie moved to Sarnia, further west, as builder and contractor. He was also a concerned citizen, and in 1852 he became the editor of the *Lambton Shield,* a tiny newspaper that nonetheless served to give him access to the world of politics. In 1861 he ran successfully for the Assembly as a Reformer, and in 1867 he was elected to the first Parliament of Canada, where he became the leader of the opposition to the government of Sir John Alexander Macdonald. For a time in 1871/1872 he was treasurer of Ontario, but in 1872 he determined to devote his time to federal politics.

The Macdonald government was pressing ahead with plans for a transcontinental railroad but had unfortunately become too close in its relations with financiers and contractors. The resulting "Pacific scandal" drove the government from office in disgrace, and Mackenzie became prime minister on Nov. 7, 1873. The Mackenzie administration had some able men in it, but the Liberals had bad luck in taking power at the onset of a long business depression. Mackenzie's only remedy was to trim expenses to the bone and to halt the construction of the railway. The depression continued unabated.

There were some real successes, however. As a convinced democrat, Mackenzie extended the right to vote and introduced the secret ballot. A Supreme Court was established, the Royal Military College of Canada was founded, and the nation was pushed toward independence after Mackenzie and his attorney general, Edward Blake, trimmed the powers of the governor general to interfere in affairs of state.

For all these accomplishments, however, the nation was unhappy, and when the Conservatives began to advocate a protective tariff to encourage the development of Canadian industry, they found ready audiences. Mackenzie, as a free-trade Liberal, regarded the tariff as an abomination, but not enough of the electorate agreed with him and the Liberals were defeated in 1878. For 2 years more the dour Scot led the Liberals. He remained in Parliament until his death on April 17, 1892, in Toronto.

Further Reading

A study of Mackenzie is Dale Thomson, *Alexander Mackenzie: Clear Grit* (1960). There is also substantial material on him in J. M.S. Careless, *Brown of the Globe* (2 vols., 1959-1963). An excellent study of the history of liberalism in Canada, in which Mackenzie is discussed, is Robert Kelley, *The Transatlantic Persuasion: The Liberal-Democratic Mind in the Age of Gladstone* (1969). □

William Lyon Mackenzie

William Lyon Mackenzie (1795-1861) was a Scottish-born Canadian journalist, politician, and rebel.

He became the leader of the radical Reformers, and the refusal of the authorities to institute certain reforms finally led him to open rebellion.

Williamilliam Lyon Mackenzie was born on March 12, 1795, at Springfield, Dundee. After completing his formal education at the parish school, he entered business, becoming in 1817 managing clerk of a canal company in Wiltshire.

In 1820 Mackenzie emigrated to British North America. In 1824 he began to publish the *Colonial Advocate* and before the year was out had moved its place of publication from Queenston to York (Toronto). Through his newspaper he attacked the men of privilege and power within the colony so vigorously that on June 8, 1826, a number of young Tories smashed his printing press. This was an error on the part of the ruling clique, known as the Family Compact, for it publicized Mackenzie, his paper, and his reformist views more fully than he himself had been able to accomplish.

In 1828 Mackenzie won election to the Upper Canada Legislative Assembly for the county of York and was reelected in 1830. In 1831 he attacked the government so vigorously that he was expelled from the Assembly. He was repeatedly reelected and expelled, until in 1834 the Reform party won a majority of the Assembly seats, enabling Mackenzie to take his place once more. In 1835 he was elected

to be the first mayor of the newly incorporated city of Toronto.

Mackenzie was the driving force in compiling the "Seventh Report of the Committee on Grievances," issued in 1835, which detailed the reform case in the province. In November 1835 Mackenzie visited Louis-Joseph Papineau and strengthened the alliance between the reformist groups in the two Canadas.

In the general election of 1836 Mackenzie lost his seat, and the Reformers their control of the Assembly. He was outraged at the open politicking of the new governor, Sir Francis Bond Head, and at the general intransigence of the Tory faction. Mackenzie became the center of a group of men advocating radical measures. In July 1837 a vigilance committee was appointed under his direction with the task of establishing centers for possible future revolution. Mackenzie and his followers moved toward open rebellion until, on Nov. 25, 1837, he proclaimed a provisional government.

Rebellion and Exile

It was not Mackenzie and his followers who moved to the attack, however, but rather the Tories, led by Governor Bond Head. On Dec. 7, 1837, the rebels were attacked by the loyal Tory forces; the rebels were soon in disarray, and Mackenzie fled to the United States. He proclaimed a provisional government from the sanctuary of Navy Island in the Niagara River but soon withdrew. In 1839 he was arrested by American authorities and sentenced to 12 months' imprisonment for breaking the neutrality laws.

For the next decade Mackenzie supported his family through journalism and, for a time, employment in the New York Customs House. In 1849 the Legislative Assembly of the United Province of Canada passed a general amnesty, and Mackenzie returned to Canada. In 1850 he was elected to the legislature for the Riding of Haldimand and sat in the Assembly until his retirement from politics in 1858. But he little understood responsible government and the institutions that had been fashioned to make that principle operative in the political life of the United Province of Canada, and he played no leading part in its political life henceforth, as he had prior to rebellion in 1837.

Though Mackenzie had failed to bring about those reforms which he had believed desirable, his actions and the abortive rebellion he led acted as catalysts for change, and much of the subsequent political history of the Canadas was influenced by what he had written and done. He died at Toronto on Aug. 28, 1861.

Further Reading

Mackenzie was a prolific writer. Of particular interest is *Mackenzie's Own Narrative of the Late Rebellion* (1838). Margaret Fairley, ed., *The Selected Writings of William Lyon Mackenzie, 1824-1837* (1960), offers an excellent selection of his work. The best book on Mackenzie's life is William Kilbourn, *The Firebrand* (1958), although Charles Lindsey's earlier biography, *The Life and Times of Wm. Lyon Mackenzie* (2 vols., 1862), is still useful. See also Stephen Leacock, *Mackenzie, Baldwin, La Fontaine, Hincks* (1926), and Edwin C. Guillet, *The Lives and Times of the Patriots* (1938).

Additional Sources

Gates, Lillian F., *After the rebellion: the later years of William Lyon Mackenzie,* Toronto: Dundurn Press, 1988.

William Lyon Mackenzie: a reinterpretation, Toronto: Macmillan of Canada; Ottawa: Institute of Canadian Studies, Carleton University, 1979.

1837: revolution in the Canadas, Toronto: NC Press, 1974.

Raible, Chris, *Muddy York mud: scandal & scurrility in Upper Canada,* Creemore, Ont.: Curiosity House; Toronto: Dundurn Press distributor, 1992.

Salutin, Rick, *1837: William Lyon Mackenzie and the Canadian revolution,* Toronto: J. Lorimer, 1976. □

Mary MacKillop

The first Australian candidate for sainthood in the Roman Catholic Church, Mary MacKillop (1842-1909), known in the convent as Mother Mary of the Cross, was the foundress of the Sisters of St. Joseph of the Sacred Heart.

Mary MacKillop, the eldest of eight children of Scottish immigrants Alexander and Flora Mac-Killop, was born in Melbourne, Australia, on January 15, 1842. She had an unsettled childhood. Her father dabbled in politics and business and experienced mixed fortune. The family often moved, and formal schooling was disrupted. When aged 14 she worked as a nursery governess and later with the stationers Sands and Kenny.

In 1860 Mary left Melbourne for the small isolated town of Penola in South Australia to act as governess for the two daughters of her father's sister, Margaret Cameron. In Penola she met the local priest, Julian Tenison Woods. This was to change her life.

Australia had been settled originally as a penal colony in 1788, but by the middle of the 19th century immigrants from the British Isles were settling new farming areas. There were few schools, and children were deprived of an education. Father Woods wanted to do something to help these children.

Father Woods thought about an order of Australian nuns, unhampered by formal convent structures, who could move to remote areas and provide schooling. He saw in Mary MacKillop someone who could help him achieve his dream. On March 19, 1866, the feast of St. Joseph, she discarded her secular clothing and put on a simple religious habit. She was the first of the Sisters of St. Joseph.

The first school was established in Penola in an old stable. Soon other young women joined her. Father Woods composed a Rule to direct their lives, emphasizing poverty and simplicity. By the end of 1869 there were 72 sisters teaching in 21 schools as well as an orphanage and a refuge for women in distress.

Word spread to other parts of Australia, and Mary was asked to send sisters to begin schools. However, not everyone accepted this new type of religious community with its emphasis on helping the most needy in society. The sisters were denounced to Bishop Sheil in Adelaide, who responded by changing the Rule and putting himself in charge. Mary protested his interference. On September 22, 1871, the bishop imposed on Mary a sentence of excommunication—excluding her from the sacraments of the Catholic Church. Mary's response to this was one of calm acceptance and firm trust in God. Five months later, on February 23, 1872, only six days before he died, Bishop Sheil removed the excommunication and admitted his mistake in listening to bad advice.

The dispute about central government or control by each diocesan bishop continued for many years. The sisters were frequently the target of suspicion and opposition and were sometimes accused of incompetence as teachers. Some accused Mother Mary of drinking to excess. Bishop Reynolds, who succeeded Bishop Sheil in Adelaide, established a commission of inquiry in 1883. This prompted Mother Mary to move her motherhouse (headquarters) to Sydney, where Cardinal Moran was more supportive.

In 1888 Cardinal Moran returned from Rome with a decree from the Vatican settling the dispute. Central government was accepted as well as separate diocesan congregations. The two groups were to have different religious dress. Those who remained affiliated with the Sydney motherhouse wore brown habits, and those under the jurisdiction of the bishops wore black. From that time on the two groups have generally been known as "Brown Josephites" or Black Josephites."

The work of the sisters continued to expand, and there were new foundations throughout Australia and New Zealand. At a time when state education was becoming secular, the work of the Sisters of St. Joseph helped lay the foundations for the extensive system of Catholic schools that still exists in Australia.

Mother Mary suffered a stroke in 1902. Over the next few years her health gradually deteriorated. On August 4, 1909, Cardinal Moran visited her sick room at the motherhouse in Mount St., North Sydney. He left with the comment, "I consider this day I have assisted at the death bed of a saint." Mother Mary of the Cross died on Sunday, August 8, 1909. At her funeral, before an enormous crowd, Cardinal Moran quoted from the Bible, from the Book of Daniel: "They that instruct many unto justice shall shine as stars for all eternity." Soon after her death people commented about her sanctity. Such was the devotion that, on January 27, 1914, her remains were reburied in the motherhouse of the Sisters of St. Joseph, where a special shrine and place of pilgrimage were constructed.

The official Vatican Decree for her canonization sums up the meaning of Mother Mary's life:

Mary's public achievement is a historical fact in Australia, but for those who knew her personally the most striking thing about her was her kindness. She was a great believer in encouragement, urging people to be kind and united. In everything she said or did, she showed respect and love for those around her, making no distinction between the rich, the high-born, and the influential on the one hand, and the lowly, the jailbirds, and the outcasts of society on the other.

The Vatican accepted the biographical details of Mother Mary as evidence of exceptional virtue. It accepted a miraculous cure in Sydney in 1961 of a young woman who was dying of leukemia and prayed to Mother Mary. Mother Mary MacKillop is now called "Blessed," the second-to-last step before formal recognition as a saint. Someone who has been "blessed" can be canonized by the pope as a saint only after evidence of one additional miracle.

Further Reading

The most authoritative biography of Mother Mary MacKillop is that of Paul Gardiner, S.J., the promoter of her cause for canonization: *An Extraordinary Australian Mary MacKillop* (Sydney, 1993). Other worthwhile biographies include William Modystack, *Mary MacKillop A Woman Before Her Time* (Dee Why, NSW, 1982); and Felicity O'Brien, *Called to Love: Mary MacKillop* (Sydney, 1992). A set of two audio tapes, *Mary MacKillop No Plaster Saint,* were produced by the Australian Broadcasting Corporation. A video, *Long Have I Loved You The Story of Mary MacKillop,* was produced by Catholic Communications, Greenwich, NSW, Australia. Further information can be obtained from the Mary MacKillop Secretariat, Mount St., North Sydney, NSW, 2060, Australia. □

Charles Rennie Mackintosh

Charles Rennie Mackintosh (1868-1928) was a Scottish artist, architect, and interior/furniture/textile designer who had a professional influence on the development of the Modern movement. He worked to create totally integrated art/architecture.

Charles Rennie Mackintosh was born in Glasgow, Scotland, on June 7, 1868. He gained entry to the Glasgow School of Art where he studied principally architecture and design and was recognized as a remarkable talent by the school's director, Fra Newbery. Mackintosh joined the architectural practice of Honeyman and Keppie (1889) as a draftsman and won the competition to design and build a new School of Art for his mentor, Newbery, in 1896: this was his first major building commission and was a revolutionary design quite unlike anything erected in Europe to that date. Austere, elegant, defiantly "modern," it was shorn of almost all decoration and made historical references to Scottish vernacular architecture and to Japanese arts, a culture in which Mackintosh had an abiding interest. The building established Mackintosh from the outset as a radical architect determined to find a new design language appropriate for the coming 20th century. It has been said that modern architecture began when Mackintosh built the Glasgow School of Art.

While generally associated with the *art nouveau* style, Mackintosh rejected such comparisons and did not feel part of the 19th-century *art nouveau* European style represented by Guimard, Horta, van der Velde, or Gaudi, and little of their sinuous "whiplash" curvilinear expression is to be seen in Mackintosh's work. He sought to unite natural forms, especially those deriving from plants and flowers, with a new architectural and design vocabulary that set him well apart from the mainstream of architects who looked to Greece, Rome, and Egypt for inspiration from the antique. His marriage to a talented artist-designer, Margaret Macdonald (1864-1933), and the marriage of her sister, Frances, to Mackintosh's close friend Herbert McNair led to the formation of a brilliantly creative group, clearly led by Mackintosh, known variously as "The Four" or "The Spook School."

Considerable attention was focussed on the work of Mackintosh and the "Glasgow Style" artists and designers who had come from the School of Art. In 1900 Mackintosh and his friends were invited to create a room complete with furnishings at the Vienna Seccession exhibition. This created huge interest, and the Mackintoshes were lionized when they went to Vienna. Their exhibition display had a direct influence on the development of the Wiener Werkstatte formed shortly thereafter by Josef Hoffmann. Hoffmann and Mackintosh were close friends, and Hoffmann visited Glasgow twice to see Mackintosh's work, as did the influential critic Hermann Muthesius and the Werkstatte's patron, Fritz Wärndorfer. "The Four" exhibited widely in Europe, both together and individually, and Mackintosh received commissions for furniture from patrons in Berlin, Vienna, and elsewhere in Europe.

In Glasgow Mackintosh's greatest public exposure was through the creation of a number of restaurants, the tea rooms of his most enduring patron, Kate Cranston. The tea rooms provided a wonderful opportunity for Mackintosh to put into practice his belief that the architect was responsible for every aspect of the commissioned work. At The Willow Tea Room (1903) he converted an existing interior into a remarkable dramatic and elegant series of contrasting interiors with furniture, carpet, wall decor, light fittings, menu, flower vases, cutlery, and waitresses' wear all designed by Mackintosh to create a harmonious whole, implementing the idea of totally integrated art-architecture. It is said that Mackintosh used to go to the Room de Luxe at The Willow just before it opened for morning coffee to arrange the flowers and ensure the perfection of his creation!

Surprisingly, despite Mackintosh's fame in Europe and the numerous articles in, for example, *The Studio* magazine devoted to his work, he never became a dominant force in Glasgow architecture. He created the private house Windyhill in 1901, a number of tea rooms, many works of decorative art and furniture, and other architectural conversions but never had the opportunity to create a second masterpiece after the School of Art and in the manner of Hoffmann's success with the Palais Stoclet in Brussels (1905) which owes so much to Mackintosh's influence. The dramatic designs for the huge International Exhibition in Glasgow in 1901 were rejected as too radical, and his entries for other competitions—for example, Liverpool Cathedral—were unsuccessful. His direct influence on European architecture came not by examples but by suggestions, notably the distribution of a full-color lithographic portfolio of "Designs for the House of an Art-Lover" (1901), which was never built.

The Hill House of 1902 is the best example of Mackintosh's domestic architectural style and interior (open to the public: National Trust for Scotland) and has survived virtually intact. The Mackintoshes' own house, complete with its furnishings, has been brilliantly recreated at the Hunterian Art Gallery, University of Glasgow (open to the public), while his Glasgow School of Art has undergone extensive restoration of its interiors and collection (open to the public).

Mackintosh left Glasgow in 1915 for reasons never exactly clear but associated with a notable lack of commissions and the general building slump occasioned by the onset of World War I. He moved to England and journeyed to France and created a sumptuous series of watercolors of the landscape and flowers. Opportunities for a stylized series of flower forms to become widely-distributed printed textiles failed to materialize.

The famous flowing white-on-white interiors of the Glasgow period were replaced by geometric black-on-black interiors which clearly anticipated Art Deco in his final architectural commissions: 78 Derngate, Northampton, England, in 1915/1916, and the "Dug-Out" additions to the Willow Tea Room in Glasgow.

Mackintosh was a visionary designer and architect who had a professional influence on the development of the Modern movement. Although prolific during the height of his most creative years, 1896-1916, much of his work has been lost and the remainder is essentially confined to the city of Glasgow and surrounding region. Although completely neglected and largely ignored in the middle decades of this century, he has now been the subject of intense scrutiny and rediscovery. His furniture and textile designs are being produced with notable success, and in 1979 a writing desk he designed in 1901 for his own use reached the then world record price paid at auction for any piece of 20th-century furniture, 89,200 pounds. Now much admired and copied, he is seen as a central figure in the development of integrated art-architecture at the turn of the century and a seminal influence on many architects and designers of the Post Modern movement in the 1970s and 1980s. Charles Rennie Mackintosh died in distressed circumstances in London in 1928; his wife Margaret in 1933.

Further Reading

Additional information on the work of Mackintosh can be found in "Charles Rennie Mackintosh and the Modern Movement" (1977) by Thomas Howarth; "Charles Rennie Mackintosh Artist and Architect" (1983) by Robert McLeod; "Charles Rennie Mackintosh Architecture" (1980) by Jackie Cooper; and "Mackintosh Textile Designs" (1982), "Mackintosh Watercolours" (1979), and "The Complete Mackintosh Furniture, Drawings and Interiors" (1979), all by Roger Billcliffe. A thriving CRM Society devoted to the preservation of his work and to scholarship on the period publishes a quarterly newsletter and is based at Mackintosh's Queen's Cross Church, Glasgow.

Additional Sources

Crawford, Alan, *Charles Rennie Mackintosh,* New York: Thames and Hudson, 1995.
Howarth, Thomas, *Charles Rennie Mackintosh and the modern movement,* London: Routledge & Kegan Paul, 1977.
Charles Rennie Mackintosh Society. *Mackintosh & his contemporaries in Europe and America,* London: J. Murray, 1988.
Macleod, Robert, *Charles Rennie Mackintosh: architect and artist,* New York: Dutton, 1983.
Moffat, Alistair, *Remembering Charles Rennie Mackintosh: an illustrated biography,* Lanark: C. Baxter Photography, 1989.
□

George Maclean

George Maclean (1801-1847) was a Scottish solider and agent of British imperial expansion. As an administrator of the British-owned Gold Coast forts, he was instrumental in extending British influence in the interior of present-day Ghana.

Born on Feb. 24, 1801, George Maclean spent his early years primarily in idleness and aimlessness. Eventually he obtained a military commission and was gazetted to the Royal African Corps, considered at the time to be a most undesirable billet. His first assignment was to Freetown, Sierra Leone, where he arrived in 1826. The ensuing 2 years were spent in Freetown and the Gold Coast (now Ghana), where he began to reveal his potential as a leader. But illness in 1828 forced him to return to England.

In the same year conditions in the Gold Coast had led the British government to withdraw from the area. British merchants on the coast strongly opposed this decision, and an agreement was reached whereby the British government would provide a subsidy to a committee of merchants who would be responsible for administration of the forts. In 1829 Maclean was appointed by the committee as president of the Council of Government in the Gold Coast, where he arrived in 1830.

Maclean's duties were strictly limited to directing the internal affairs of the forts, and he was to avoid any involvements with the interior. But as an agent for the merchants, Maclean believed that trade would improve only in conjunction with improved relations with the numerous neighboring African states. He therefore entered into negotiations with the Ashanti government and in 1831 concluded a treaty with them which provided for several decades of relative peace in the region. Concurrently he entered into negotiations with the states which lay between Ashanti and the coast.

In time, Maclean became widely respected in the interior for his ability to settle diplomatic and judicial disputes. His success in regularizing the tangled affairs of the Gold Coast has been attributed to his strong sense of justice, respect for African institutions and custom, and tenacity in upholding British commitments in agreements and treaties. His success is clearly documented by the dramatic increase in trade volume during the first decade of his administration.

Maclean's activities did not escape criticism, however. In 1843 a parliamentary select committee was appointed to investigate charges that although Maclean had increased trade he had ignored local slave-trading activities and that his relations with the interior far exceeded the limits of his responsibility. The select committee recommended that the British government resume direct responsibility for the Gold Coast, and in 1844 Maclean was relieved of his duties. The newly arrived governor immediately sought to legalize, in the view of British law, the informal jurisdiction over the interior which Maclean had developed. The rulers of about 20 African states signed the Bond of 1844, an agreement which provided for the extension of British standards of law into their territories. Maclean remained in the Gold Coast as judicial assessor with the responsibility of enforcing the conditions of the bond. He died there 3 years later.

Further Reading

The only biography of Maclean is George Edgar Metcalfe, *Maclean of the Gold Coast* (1962). ☐

Archibald MacLeish

Archibald MacLeish (1892-1982) was an American poet, playwright, teacher, and public official and a Pulitzer Prize winner.

Archibald MacLeish was born in Glencoe, Ill. on May 7, 1892. He graduated from Yale University in 1915. After serving in World War I as a field artillery officer, he received a degree from the Harvard Law School in 1919 and practiced law in Boston for 3 years. In 1923 he departed for Europe to travel and write. He lived mainly in France for the next 5 years, publishing several books of poetry during this period, including *The Pot of Earth* (1925), which echoed T. S. Eliot's *The Waste Land*, and *The Hamlet of A. MacLeish*, an expression of MacLeish's disillusionment with the postwar scene.

During the 1930s MacLeish was a reporter on the staff of *Fortune* magazine. A strong supporter of the New Deal, he served as adviser to President Franklin D. Roosevelt while working as librarian of Congress (1939-1944). A vigorous defender of democracy in many articles and speeches, he revealed a growing awareness of the dangers of both fascism and communism. From 1944 to 1945 MacLeish was assistant secretary of state. In 1949 Harvard offered him the Boylston professorship in rhetoric and oratory; he continued to teach at that university until his retirement in 1962.

MacLeish served as a sort of poetic weather vane; for more than 40 years his work reflected the thought and feeling, the poetic environment, of its time. Responding more to the outside world than to any abiding philosophic or esthetic commitment within himself, he expressed, from his earliest published verse to *The Wild Old Wicked Man and Other Poems* (1968), the cultivated man's changing sense of a rapidly changing world. The conclusion of his poem *Ars Poetica* (1926) has become the universal motto of New Critical poetic theory: "A poem should not mean/ But be." "You, Andrew Marvell" (1930) expressed for the entire generation of modernist poets who came of age with Eliot their debt to 17th-century metaphysical verse.

MacLeish's lengthy poem *Conquistador* (1932) was, in effect, a summation of the poetic fashions of the 1920s, in style and plan derived from Ezra Pound, in attitudes indebted to Eliot. It won a Pulitzer Prize. *Frescoes for Mr. Rockefeller's City* (1933) might have served as campaign poetry for the New Deal. His Pulitzer Prize-winning verse drama, *J. B.*, reflected the 1950s concern with existential absurdity in its retelling of the biblical story of Job.

MacLeish's most important critical work, *Poetry and Experience* (1961), treats esthetic theory and practice. The body of his poetry is included in *The Collected Poetry of Archibald MacLeish* (1963). His criticism and commentary are in *Poetry and Journalism* (1958) and *The Dialogues of Archibald MacLeish and Mark Van Doren* (1964). He died in Boston on Apr. 20, 1982.

Further Reading

Useful for information on MacLeish are Signi Lenea Falk, *Archibald MacLeish* (1966), and the section on MacLeish in Hyatt

H. Waggoner, *American Poets: From the Puritans to the Present* (1968). □

Hugh MacLennan

Hugh MacLennan (1907-1990) was a widely respected Canadian novelist and academic. He wrote primarily of Canadian themes and was credited with being the first writer to establish a national literary identity for Canada. Although MacLennan was known first and foremost as a novelist, he published several collections of essays and has himself been the subject of academic study. The National Film Board (NFB) of Canada has paid tribute to MacLennan by dramatizing his life and work.

Born March 20, 1907, in Glace Bay, Cape Breton Island, Nova Scotia, (John) Hugh MacLennan grew up in Halifax, where he was educated at Dalhousie University. He received his bachelor's degree there in 1929, and won a Rhodes scholarship, which took him to Oxford University. The Oxford years were invaluable, for they provided MacLennan with the opportunity to travel extensively and test his left-wing convictions against firsthand impressions and personal observations.

He returned to Canada in the mid-30s, taking a teaching job at Lower Canada College near Montréal. He later failed to publish a novel based on his earlier travels.

Earned Ph.D. at Princeton

Unable to find suitable employment, MacLennan enrolled in the graduate school at Princeton University and studied Roman history. He obtained a doctorate in 1935 with a dissertation titled *Oxyrhynchus: An Economic and Social Study* (1940).

Writing Career Took Off

MacLennan was inspired, by his earlier literary failures, to write *Barometer Rising* (1941), a novel based on the 1917 explosion of a munitions ship in Halifax Harbor. This disaster symbolized a traumatic break for Canada from its colonial, pre-World War I past—while embodying a conflict of generational attitudes. With the success of this work, MacLennan staked out a national identity and continued to write, producing *Two Solitudes* (1945); *The Precipice* (1948); *Each Man's Son* (1951); *The Watch That Ends the Night* (1959); and *The Return of the Sphinx* (1967). He worked with themes that mirrored major national concerns and the moral and social issues of his time, as well as a growing self-awareness in Canada. He said, however, that he never lost sight of Canada as part of the world community.

Storylines Spoke of His Culture

As a novelist, MacLennan deliberately undertook to forge a Canadian consciousness in literature, an endeavor which appears to have left him little time or opportunity to experiment with different literary techniques—but which enabled him to master traditional techniques and the economies of an honest and forthright style. Because he was adept at using narrow storylines as springboards to broader statements about his country and his culture, he became a widely translated and respected writer.

MacLennan also wrote nonfiction, including: *The Colour of Canada* (1972); *Rivers of Canada* (1974); *Voices in Time* (1980); and *On Being a Canadian Writer* (1991).

Essays Were Notable

MacLennan was an essayist of considerable skill. He published several collections of essays, including *Cross Country* (1949); *Thirty and Three* (1954); *Scotchman's Return and Other Essays* (1960); *Seven Rivers of Canada* (1961); and *The Other Side of Hugh MacLennan* (1978).

He wrote for a 1965 issue of *American Heritage* that focused on Canada. The Winter 1979-80 issue of *Journal of Canadian Studies* was the Hugh MacLennan issue. In 1995, his essay titled "French is a Must for Canadians" appeared in the anthology *Influential Writing,* edited by W. Connor and M. Legris.

His Keen Perception Won Awards

In his role as essayist, MacLennan showed a keen perception of Canada's history, environment, and character. He wrote in a lucid, conversational style which was not without its passion, its moods, and its ironic insights. In 1951 MacLennan accepted an appointment to McGill University. He taught in the English department until 1981, publishing *McGill: the Story of a University* in 1960. In 1952 he received the Lorne Pierce Medal from the Royal Society of Canada; in 1953 he was elected to the Society. In 1967 MacLennan was named a companion of the Order of Canada. He contributed the foreword to Gertrude Katz, *The Time Gatherers; Writings from Prison* (1970).

MacLennan won the Governor General's Literary Award more than any other Canadian author: three times for fiction (*Two Solitudes, The Precipice, The Watch that Ends the Night*) and twice for nonfiction (*Cross-Country* and *Thirty and Three*). In 1987 he became the first Canadian to be awarded the James Madison Medal by Princeton University. The medal is given annually to a distinguished graduate.

MacLennan died Nov. 7, 1990, at the age of 83.

Further Reading

There have been several book-length studies of MacLennan, of which the most ambitious is Robert H. Cockburn, *The Novels of Hugh MacLennan* (Harvest House, 1969). Also of considerable interest are: George Woodcock, *Hugh MacLennan* (Copp Clark Publishing Co., 1969); Patricia Morley, *The Immoral Moralists: Hugh MacLennan and Leonard Cohen* (Clarke, Irwin, 1972); Paul Goetsch, *Hugh MacLennan* (McGraw-Hill Ryerson, 1973); Elspeth Cameron, *Hugh MacLennan: a Writer's Life* (University of Toronto Press, 1981); Thomas Donald MacLulich, *Hugh MacLennan* (Twayne, 1983); and Frank M. Tierney, ed., *Hugh MacLennan* (University of Ottawa Press, 1994).
MacLennan has often been featured in *Canadian Literature, a quarterly of Criticism and Review,* including Nos. 3 ("The Story of a Novel"), 6 ("The Defence of Lady Chatterley"), 33 (Questionnaire and Answers section), 41 ("Reflection on Two Decades"), 68-69 (interview with Ronald Sullivan), and 90 (review of Elspeth Cameron's *Hugh MacLennan: a Writer's Life*), 99 and 112 (review of *On Being a Maritime Writer*).
MacLennan's work with Marian Engel, who wrote her master's thesis under his direction, is documented in a collection of letters called *Dear Marian, Dear Hugh: The MacLennan-Engel Correspondence* (1995), edited by Christl Verduyn and published by University of Ottawa Press; *The Hugh MacLellan Papers* (May, 1986) describes the University of Calgary's archival holdings of the author's personal and professional papers as well as correspondence, news clippings, scrapbooks and miscellaneous writings.
The National Film Board (NFB) of Canada has produced at least three documentaries featuring the life and work of Hugh MacLennan; The first, *Hugh MacLennan: Portrait of a Writer* (1982), is described by the NFB as a tribute to MacLennan for paving the way for a thriving national literary movement; the second, *View from the Typewriter* (1983), discusses the work of MacLennan and nine other prominent Canadian writers; *Each Man's Son* was dramatized in 1954. □

Donald Baxter MacMillan

The American explorer and scientist Donald Baxter MacMillan (1874-1970) surveyed and mapped unknown land and water in the Arctic.

Donald MacMillan was born in Provincetown, Mass., on Nov. 10, 1874, the son of a ship captain. He was orphaned at an early age. He attended Bowdoin College in Maine, graduating in 1898. For the next few years he taught school and conducted a summer camp at Casco Bay, Maine, where he met explorer Robert Peary. MacMillan signed on for the expedition that became Peary's first, after 2 decades of effort, to reach the North Pole (April 6, 1909). The intrepid explorer's eventual success was dependent upon capable support parties, one of which MacMillan led.

MacMillan's initial Arctic experience inspired him to make northern exploration his life's work. After exploring the interior of Labrador in 1910, he began postgraduate work in anthropology at Harvard University. In 1911 and again in 1912 MacMillan returned to northern Labrador to conduct ethnological studies of the Eskimos and Indians there. The following year MacMillan left on an extended 4-year expedition into the Arctic, seeking to find final evidence as to the existence of a large landmass north of Greenland that Peary believed he had seen. Establishing its base at Etah, northwestern Greenland, the MacMillan party's exploration of thousands of square miles proved that Crocker Land did not exist. The party did, however, confirm the existence of coal in Ellesmere Land, discover two islands, and obtain valuable museum specimens and other items before returning to the United States in 1917.

After brief wartime service MacMillan taught anthropology at Bowdoin College, but he made trips north in 1920, 1921-1922, and 1923-1924, sailing in a small, specially designed and constructed vessel which he christened the *Bowdoin*.

During the next 15 years MacMillan made repeated trips northward, surveying and mapping unknown land and water, collecting zoological and geological specimens, studying Eskimo life and language, and establishing a school for Eskimo children in Labrador. He interspersed his trips with fund-raising articles and lecture tours throughout the country. In 1935 MacMillan married Miriam Look, who subsequently accompanied him on voyages. During World War II, MacMillan lent his expertise to the U.S. Navy, consulting on Arctic work and compiling an Eskimo-English conversational dictionary for the military. Following the war, the aged explorer reacquired and refitted the *Bowdoin* and resumed his northward sailings. MacMillan was highly honored in his later years for his Arctic service. He died in Provincetown, Mass., on Sept. 7, 1970.

Further Reading

MacMillan's writings include *Four Years in the White North* (1918); *Etah and Beyond* (1928); *Kah-da* (1930); and *How Peary Reached the Pole* (1934), an account of the 1908-1909

expedition and an outspoken defense of Peary. Everett S. Allen, *Arctic Odyssey: The Life of Rear Admiral Donald B. MacMillan* (1962), is the only biography of the explorer; but see also the account by MacMillan's wife, Miriam MacMillan, *Green Seas and White Ice* (1948). □

Harold Macmillan

The British politician and prime minister (Maurice) Harold Macmillan (1894-1986) was one of the outstanding Conservative leaders of the 20th century in terms of achieving both unity in his party and electoral success.

Harold Macmillan was born on Feb. 10, 1894, in London, England. He was educated at Eton and at Balliol College, Oxford. During his World War I service in the Grenadier Guards he was wounded three times. From 1919-1920 he was an aide to the governor general of Canada. In 1920 he married into one of the most deeply rooted Conservative aristocratic families—the Cavendishes (Lady Dorothy Cavendish, daughter of the 9th Duke of Devonshire). She died in 1966. They had three daughters and one son.

Early Career

This impeccable upper-class background served Macmillan in good stead in his prime ministerial career (January 1957-October 1963) when he wished to lead his party in directions that it would have found difficult to take from another leader. But in the early phase of his career this background could be seriously misleading. As member of Parliament for Stockton-on-Tees after 1924, he was no orthodox Conservative. He was deeply moved by mass unemployment; in such works as *Reconstruction: A Plea for a National Policy* (1933) and *The Middle Way* (1938) he advocated neo-Keynesian solutions to the economic crisis of those years that were by no means fashionable.

As an opponent of Neville Chamberlain's appeasement policy toward Hitler's Germany, and as a Conservative rebel, he was an obvious choice for Winston Churchill's wartime administration. Macmillan served as parliamentary secretary to the Ministry of Supply from 1940 to 1942, as undersecretary of state for the colonies in 1942, and his most important office, as minister resident at Allied Headquarters in Northwest Africa from 1942 to 1945. In the latter capacity he came close to Churchill and acted as an effective link between quarreling Allied military and political commanders.

Political Service

After the war, he was made secretary of state for air in the caretaker government. In the Conservative government of 1951, Macmillan served first, and most successfully, as

minister of housing and local government (1951-1954). He was then minister of defense, foreign secretary, and chancellor of the Exchequer (December 1955-January 1957) before succeeding Anthony Eden as prime minister in January 1957, a position he held until his resignation in October 1963.

As prime minister, Macmillan took over after the Suez operation, when President Abdul Nasser of Egypt nationalized the Suez Canal, and his party's morale and fortunes were at a low ebb. By 1959 the Conservatives had recovered enough to win a large electoral victory. His period in office was associated with developments that only Macmillan's public relations skills made acceptable to large sections of his own party: the acceptance of the move toward black African independence (1960), the initiation of formal government planning through the National Economic Development Council, and the approach to joining the European Common Market (now the European Union) in 1961. Macmillan was also instrumental in negotiating the Nuclear Test Ban Treaty that was signed by the former Soviet Union, England, and the United States in 1963.

Speaking to the South African Parliament in 1960, Macmillan said, "A wind of change is blowing through this continent. Whether we like it or not, the growth of national consciousness is a political fact."

In 1963 a downturn in the economy coupled with a sex scandal involving one of the prime minister's aides resulted in Macmillan's resignation from office. When he left public life, Macmillan returned to his family's publishing business, Macmillan Ltd., of which he became president in 1974. After years of refusing his peerage, he was created Earl of Stockton in 1984. Macmillan died of pneumonia, December 29, 1986, in Haywards Heath, West Sussex, England.

Further Reading

MacMillan, Harold, *Winds of Change 1914-1939* (1966); *The Blast of War 1939-1945* (1967); *Tides of Fortune 1945-1955* (1969).
"Earl of Stockton: British Politician," *Annual Obituary 1986*, New York: St. Martins Press, c1986, p. 736-739.
Horne, Alistair, *Harold Macmillan*, New York: Viking, c1989.
Hughes, Emrys, *Macmillan: Portrait of a Politician* (1962).
Sampson, Anthony, *MacMillan: A Study in Ambiguity* (1967).
Turner, John, *Macmillan*, New York: Longman, c1994.
Davenport-Hines, R.P.T., *The Macmillans*, London: Heineman, c1992. ☐

Louis MacNeice

The British poet Louis MacNeice (1907-1964) claimed himself to be not a theorist but a poetic empiricist. His unfinished autobiography was posthumously published as *The Strings Are False*.

Louis MacNeice was born on September 12, 1907, in Belfast, Ireland. Educated at Merton College, Oxford, he taught Greek for a short time in London, lectured in classics at Birmingham University from 1930 to 1936, and lectured in Greek at Bedford College for women from 1936 to 1939. During the first year of World War II (1939) he was a lecturer at Cornell University in the United States.

MacNeice returned to London in 1940. In 1941 he joined the British Broadcasting Company (BBC) as a staff script writer and producer to illustrate Britain's war effort. He continued in these capacities, with the exception of an 18-month hiatus during 1950-1951 when he served as director of the British Institute in Athens; his knowledge of Greek language and culture served him well.

MacNeice was twice married. His first wife was Giovanna Marie Therese Ezra. This marriage began in 1930 and ended in divorce in 1946. He had a son by his first marriage and a daughter by his second. In 1954, with his second wife, vocalist Hedli Anderson, he conducted a reading and concert tour in the United States. Before his death, in London, he travelled extensively abroad in France, Norway, Italy, and India.

MacNeice rarely read novels. His favorite was Tolstoy's *War and Peace*. MacNeice himself wrote three novels in his youth, all of which he considered poor attempts. He published his first poetic collection, *Blind Fireworks*, in 1929.

In politics, MacNeice distrusted the established parties; in economics, he predicted the inevitable fall of capitalism. On a visit to Barcelona in 1939, he pronounced that the Republican government was in the right in the Spanish Civil War. He was in opposition to partition in Ireland and voted for the Labour Party in England in spite of his opposition to the party leaders, whom he regarded as reactionary.

As poet, MacNeice's early work derives from the forms and traditions of classic poetry. He confessed that he proceeded by trial and error, attempting to achieve Wordsworth's "Real Language of Men," an objective he sought not only in diction but in rhythm as well. MacNeice acknowledged that his imagistic propensity for the topical and visual led him to diffuse composition, in which one descriptive passage led to another.

Eventually growing bored with description for its own sake, MacNeice began to experiment with traditional lyrics, in which he sought to express a single, strong personal feeling. He employed symmetrical but intricate verse patterns and rhymes to this purpose. Again, stylistic boredom set in as his content grew too narrow and his rhythm too predictable.

Seeking escape in structure, MacNeice subordinated semantic and other elements of his poems, preferring dull interdependent to brilliant independent images. His attention was given to sheer syntax rather than to the relations between sentence structures and verse patterns. In his later works he strove for economy. Especially in imagery he pursued the *multam in parvo* of poetic compression. MacNeice quoted himself to exemplify this "much in little" compression which he sought. He described a prostitute sitting at the end of a long bar as "Mascara scrawls a gloss on a torn leaf."

In spite of his claim to empiricism and denial of theoretically derived poetics, MacNeice was nonetheless identified in the 1930s with a group of young poets of social protest (an occupational hazard of poets). The group included his friends Stephen Spender and W. H. Auden. In later years he returned from political to moral themes. As his obsession shifted from the political to the moral his compositional complexity and aesthetic intensified.

Collaborating with a scholar of German in 1951, Mac-Neice provided an abridged translation of the poetic rather than literal linguistic aspects of Goethe's Faust for a radio presentation. During the late 1950s it was Robert Lowell, in reference to his own translations from Italian, who appropriately observed that poetic translation requires not so much translation *per se* as the composition of a new poem based upon an original in another language. If MacNeice's linguistic collaborator translated that which was German, it was MacNeice who translated that which was Faust.

With W. H. Auden, MacNeice co-authored *Letters from Iceland* (1936). Co-authorship is rare in the 20th century, and in this endeavor he again revealed his divergency. His originality knew no "Mass-production of neat thoughts," and he was never afraid to take the poetic leap into " . . . Fates great bazaar."

Some critics regard MacNeice as an undeveloped poet; but in art, as in life, his invocation was:

> . . . O fill me/
> With strength against those who would freeze
> my humanity, would dragoon me into a lethal
> automaton, would make me a cog in a machine,
> a thing with one face. . . .

MacNeice was connected with the English Group Theatre in London, which produced his translation of the *Agamemnon* by Aeschylus in 1936 and his experimental play, *Out of the Picture* (1937), which he, himself, judged a bad play. At this time he began a trilogy of one-act plays with the intention of having them produced by the Abbey Theatre in Dublin, because he considered the London West End Stage moribund.

His later works included *The Roman Smile,* a book of literary criticism; a verse translation of the *Hippolytus* by Euripedes; and a quasi-autobiographical book. In addition to his own publications, MacNeice contributed articles to several anthologies of literary criticism. Most of his work was published in the United States.

MacNeice was made C.B.E. (Commander of the British Empire) in 1957. He died on September 3, 1964, from viral pneumonia.

Further Reading

The best source of information about his life is his *The Strings Are False: An Unfinished Autobiography,* published by Oxford University Press in 1966 under MacNeice's pseudonym, Louis Malone. His *Collected Poems* was published the following year.

Additional Sources

Coulton, Barbara, *Louis MacNeice in the BBC,* London; Boston: Faber and Faber, 1980.
Stallworthy, Jon, *Louis MacNeice,* New York: W.W. Norton, 1995. □

Nathaniel Macon

Nathaniel Macon (1758-1837), American statesman, was Speaker of the U.S. House of Representatives and a senator.

Nathaniel Macon was born in Edgecombe (now Warren) County, N.C., on Dec. 17, 1758. In 1774 he entered the College of New Jersey at Princeton and remained until 1776, when he joined the New Jersey militia. He returned to North Carolina late in 1777 to study law but rejoined the army in 1780 after the British invasion of the South. He served in the North Carolina Senate from 1781 to 1786. He joined the Antifederalists in their opposition to the Constitution in 1788. After serving in the North Carolina Legislature in 1790, Macon was elected to the U.S. House of Representatives in 1791. He served until 1815, when he was elected to the Senate, where he remained until 1828.

From 1791 to 1801 Macon vigorously opposed Federalist policies, especially Alexander Hamilton's financial program, Jay's Treaty, the quasi-war with France, and the Alien and Sedition Acts. In general he opposed any broad constitutional interpretation that expanded Federal power, whether it supported Federalist policies in the 1790s or Democratic-Republican policies after 1801. In opposing the restrictive Sedition Law of 1798, he argued that "the people suspect something is not right when free discussion is feared by government."

When Thomas Jefferson was elected president in 1800 (carrying Congress with him), Macon was chosen Speaker of the House. He held the post until 1807. As Speaker, he appointed all of the House's standing committees and played a notable role in fixing Republican leadership in the House. However, when John Randolph, Macon's appointee as chairman of the House Ways and Means Committee, broke openly with Jefferson's administration, Macon's influence slipped, and he was removed as Speaker.

This estrangement from the President was temporary, and Macon remained influential. As chairman of the House Foreign Relations Committee, he supported Jefferson's policy of commercial coercion as an alternative to war with Great Britain or France. Although he finally favored the War of 1812, he opposed taxation to support it or naval construction and manpower conscription to prosecute it.

Macon fought attempts to recharter the Bank of the United States in 1811 and 1816 and consistently opposed protective tariffs and internal improvements. An ardent defender of slavery, he opposed the Missouri Compromise because "to compromise is to acknowledge the right of

Congress to interfere" with states' rights. When he reached the age of 70, Macon resigned from the Senate. He presided over the North Carolina constitutional convention (1835) but would not vote for the amended constitution. He died on June 29, 1837.

Further Reading

Some of Macon's correspondence was edited by Kemp P. Battle in *Letters of Nathaniel Macon, John Steele and William Barry Grove* (1902). The only biography is by William E. Dodd, *The Life of Nathaniel Macon* (1903). See also D. H. Gilpatrick, *Jeffersonian Democracy in North Carolina, 1789-1816* (1931). □

Lachlan Macquarie

Lachlan Macquarie (1762-1824), British officer and governor of New South Wales, sought to improve the status of emancipists and undertook a major public works program.

Lachlan Macquarie, born on Jan. 31, 1762, came from a poor Scottish family in the Inner Hebrides. The American War of Independence offered him an opportunity to rise in the world, and he joined a Highland regiment commanded by a cousin. In 1784 Macquarie returned to Scotland as a lieutenant and 3 years later embarked upon 16 years of military service in India and Egypt.

Promotion to major, prize money, and an inheritance from his first wife, a West Indian heiress, enabled Macquarie to accumulate a competent fortune, and in 1803 he returned home to take possession of a 10,000-acre estate which he had acquired from his uncle on the island of Mull. The outbreak of war with France led to his appointment as assistant adjutant general of the London District, and Lt. Col. Macquarie soon came into contact with the country's leading politicians. When Maj. Gen. Miles Nightingall declined to become governor of New South Wales following the deposition of Capt. William Bligh in 1808, Macquarie successfully volunteered for the position.

Macquarie's administration, which began in January 1810, lasted for 12 years. He set out to improve the material and moral condition of the colony, and wide experience as a staff officer made him a vigorous administrator. The public service and financial arrangements of the colony were remodeled; a hospital, barracks, and roads were constructed; the Bank of New South Wales was established under his patronage in 1817; he encouraged exploration across the Blue Mountains, and accompanied by his second wife, he frequently toured the settled parts of the colony.

Champion of Emancipation

Believing that convicts who had been reformed by their prison sentences should be reincorporated into society with

full civil rights, Macquarie appointed emancipists to public office and invited them to Government House. By 1815 not only was his expenditure on public works causing concern in London, but his charitable attitude toward emancipists was alienating officers and free settlers within the colony.

Objecting to Macquarie's emancipist policy and authoritarian style of government, a faction of "exclusives" sought representative government and a separation of powers. Opposed to them was an "emancipist" faction, which regarded the country as belonging to former convicts and opposed their relegation to a permanently inferior status.

A campaign was mounted against Macquarie in Parliament which resulted in an inquiry under John Bigge between 1819 and 1821. Macquarie returned to England in 1822, when the Bigge reports, which favored the "exclusive" cause, were published. Macquarie's reply was not made public by the government until 1828. Bitterly disappointed, sick, and in debt, he was promised a pension but died in London on July 1, 1824.

Macquarie was an ambitious, vain and humorless man who interpreted criticism as disloyalty. Arbitrary acts robbed him of the public acclaim which he craved, and Australian society did not develop along the lines he anticipated.

Further Reading

The Public Library of New South Wales published a well-illustrated edition, *Lachlan Macquarie, Governor of New South Wales: Journals of His Tours in New South Wales and Van Diemen's Land, 1810-1822* (1956). The standard biography is M. H. Ellis, *Lachlan Macquarie: His Life, Adventures, and Times* (1947); it is a large-scale and colorful study, rich in detail and with flashes of insight, but on the whole the interpretation is weak. Marjorie Faith Barnard, *Macquarie's World* (1946), is more systematic in its portrayal of a benevolent despot sacrificed by a British government determined to introduce a new policy. Basil Holmes Travers, *The Captain-General* (1953), deals sympathetically with Macquarie's administration in New South Wales, concluding that he was a model governor.

Additional Sources

The Age of Macquarie, Carlton, Vic.: Melbourne University Press in association with Historic Houses Trust of New South Wales, 1992.

Ellis, Malcolm Henry, *Lachlan Macquarie: his life, adventures and times,* Sydney: Angus & Robertson, 1978.

Ritchie, John, *Lachlan Macquarie: a biography,* Carlton, Vic.: Melbourne University Press; Beaverton, OR: International Specialized Book Services, 1986. □

John Macquarrie

John Macquarrie (born 1919) was professor of divinity at Oxford University. His authoritative study, *Twentieth Century Religious Thought,* **was a high point of modern scholarship. His later work,** *Principles of Christian Theology,* **was characteristic of the Anglican tradition.**

John Macquarrie was born on June 27, 1919, in Scotland. Educated at Paisley Grammar School, his scholarly degrees (M.A.; B.D.; Ph.D.; D.Litt.) were all from the University of Glasgow. Before his appointment as Lady Margaret Professor of Divinity at Oxford University in 1970, he was with the Royal Army Chaplains Department (1945-1948), minister of St. Ninian's Church, Brechin (1948-1953), lecturer in theology at the University of Glasgow (1953-1962), and professor of systematic theology at Union Theological Seminary in New York City (1962-1970).

Macquarrie's reputation in the scholarly world was established with the publication of two books: *An Existentialist Theology* (1955) and *The Scope of Demythologizing* (1960), both interpretations of the thought of the German theologian Rudolf Bultmann. Macquarrie was also translator of the German philosopher Martin Heidegger's major work, *Being and Time,* and wrote a book introducing Heidegger's philosophy. For awareness of the thought of others and for analysis that is scrupulously fair and clear, his *Twentieth Century Religious Thought* (1963, 1981) is without equal in modern scholarship. In the mid-1960s he left the Church of Scotland for the Church of England, being more comfortable with its broadly catholic and richly symbolic theology. Macquarrie's own religious beliefs were systematically stated in *Principles of Christian Theology* (1966, 1977).

Part One of *Principles* discusses the inevitability of grounding theology in some philosophy or other. Confessing his indebtedness to Wilhelm Dilthey and to Edmund Husserl, Macquarrie's methodology emphasizes *description* of human experience rather than *deduction* from supposedly logical premises. Such description always has a bi-polar quality, moving between the existential pole of personal life and the larger ontological pole in which we live and move and have our being. The analysis is clearly and openly indebted to Heidegger, but not uncritically and with a far more profound appreciation of and respect for the value of religious symbols.

For purposes of summary, it is easier to begin with the ontological pole. Macquarrie believed that the proper issue for religion is not whether some god or other exists as a super being among but above other beings. Rather, the issue is what is always implicit, though seldom explicit, whenever we say that something *is.* "God" is our name for the power that gives the verb "to be" its meaning, the power of *is*-ness in everything that is and without which we would have to say that it isn't, the power of being in everything that has being and without which it would not be, the power of reality in everything real and without which it would have no reality. So understood, the traditional issue of the "existence" of God becomes meaningless; but a new issue arises. Is this power of being, or Being itself, good? Only if Being is gracious is it worthy of the title God.

Macquarrie believed that there remains a critical difference between people of faith and people who lack faith. It does not really have to do with belief in a supernatural being. Rather, it has to do with the experience and conviction that Being itself is good, gracious, supportive. The true atheist affirms that Being is simply indifferent, leaving human existence without good will or support, whereas the religious person trusts in and is committed to the graciousness of Being.

The *existential* pole of Macquarrie's theology analyzes these attitudes of faith or doubt. The *ontological* pole argues faith's reasons for trusting in the goodness of life. Human beings are authentically religious when they trust in and are committed (the existential pole) to the goodness or graciousness of the power that lets things be or Being itself (the ontological pole). The word "God" is therefore not a neutral designation, as is "Being." Properly speaking, to say "God" is to assume the attitude of faith—of trust and commitment—toward Being.

Part Two is titled "Symbolic Theology" and covers much of what is traditionally considered the essentials of Christian doctrine. Macquarrie was convinced that *all* language about God is symbolic and must not be taken literally, though it must be taken seriously. Human language is constructed to describe individual beings and is therefore inadequate for describing Being itself. Hence, all language about God is symbolical, analogical, paradoxical, and mythological. Theological statements are to be honored insofar as they symbolize the experienced character of Being, but they are to be denied as literal descriptions.

Macquarrie used this approach to interpret the doctrine of God, of Creation, of Providence, of the Spiritual Presence, and of Personal and Cosmic Destiny. Perhaps his most instructive chapters concern the person and work of Jesus, who is known in the New Testament as both "Lord" and "Word." The title "Lord" describes the *existential* pole in which individual persons value and commit themselves to following Jesus. A person who says "Jesus is Lord" is primarily saying something about himself or herself—that he or she is committed to obeying Jesus, to discipleship. The title "Word" describes the *ontological* pole in which it is claimed that Jesus reveals the final "Word" (Greek *logos*) about the nature of reality. A person who says that Jesus is "the Word of God" is primarily expressing a belief about the way the world is made and works—that the character of creation is focused for us in Jesus, and therefore that Being is gracious.

Part Three is titled "Applied Theology" and deals with such practical matters as the church, its ministry and mission; preaching and sacraments; worship and prayer; and hope for the transformation of the world. Perhaps no work of modern theology moves with such comfort from philosophical abstraction to practical application. Throughout, Macquarrie's thought is ecumenical or catholic, evidencing both knowledge and appreciation of the broad spectrum of Christian thought—from Quaker to Roman Catholic, from conservative to liberal, from Baptist to Orthodox.

Jesus Christ in Modern Thought (Philadelphia, Trinity Press International,1991) is the conclusion of a trilogy of books examining a treatment of Christ as both human and divine. The book is divided into three parts: theologies of Christ from the Bible through the 16th century, the theologies of Christ over the last three hundred years, and his own theology as it relates to Christ. Macquarrie treats the identity of Jesus as inseparable from the community of his followers, and Jesus as a man who received God's spirit and through his free will and obedience was raised to the status of Christ and achieved divinity. The Gospels ultimately portray Jesus "as truly man, or even the true man, who simply by being man in the fullest sense is also Son of God."

Further Reading

In addition to the books cited in the text, important works are: *The Faith of the People of God* (for lay readers) (1972); *God Talk* (1979); *The Humility of God* (1978); *Christian Hope* (1978); *In Search of Humanity* (1983), the first of a trilogy which includes *In Search of Deity* (asdkads) and the aforementioned *Jesus Christ in Modern Thought*. An evaluative study of Macquarrie's thought can be found in *Existence, Being and God* by Eugene Thomas Long (1985), (Oxford, Harold Copeman, 1994); and *Mediators Between Human and Divine: From Moses to Muhammad* (Oxford,1997). Another book is *Mary for All Christians* (Grand Rapids, W.B. Eerdsmans,1991); Macquarrie's book. *Jesus Christ in Modern Thought* is discussed in "Reviving Adamic Adoptionism: The Example of John Macquarrie" by Charles Hefling Jr., *Theological Studies* (September, 1991). ☐

Carlo Maderno

The Italian architect Carlo Maderno (1556-1629) was the creator of the early baroque style in architecture.

Carlo Maderno was born at Capolago on Lake Lugano. He went to Rome before 1588 and worked for his uncle, Domenico Fontana, the architect to Pope Sixtus V. Not until 1596 did Maderno receive an important architectural commission—the church of S. Susanna; until then he lived as a stuccoworker and decorator.

The facade of S. Susanna was completed in 1603 and is considered the first baroque facade. Maderno started from the type established by Giacomo da Vignola's design for, and Giacomo della Porta's executed version of, the Church of the Gesù in Rome, but the significance of Maderno's contribution lies in his reversal of Della Porta's alterations to Vignola's design. In its original form the Gesù facade had a slight emphasis on the center, building up from the pilasters at the edges to attached columns in the middle. But, Della Porta made a more complex design in which no really dominant accent is felt: Maderno returned to the concept of a facade as something simple but building up to a climax at the center, and he used both sculpture and decorative elements to create a simple, uncluttered, but rich impression. This is the hallmark of early baroque.

St. Peter's

S. Susanna was a great success, and in 1603 Maderno was appointed, with another uncle, Giovanni Fontana, to succeed Della Porta as architect to St. Peter's. Here he made the most significant contribution since Michelangelo, because he pulled down the remaining parts of Old St. Peter's and proceeded to transform Michelangelo's centralized Greek-cross design into a Latin cross with a long nave and chapels. This extension of the basilica was undoubtedly necessary from the point of view of practical requirements, but it destroyed Michelangelo's great conception and substituted something less impressive, since the great dome can no longer be appreciated from every point of view.

As a result of these alterations, Maderno had to design a facade which would not detract too much from the dome and, at the same time, would be worthy of its setting and also contain a central feature, the Benediction Loggia, to provide a frame for the figure of the pope when he appeared in public. These conflicting requirements were met as far as possible by Maderno's adaptation of a typical Roman palace facade, with decorative motives taken from Michelangelo's works. The plan to provide bell towers at the ends to enframe the dome in distant views had to be abandoned because the foundations gave trouble. The work, including the decoration, was completed and consecrated on Nov. 18, 1626.

Among Maderno's other works are the church of S. Maria della Vittoria (1605; facade by G. B. Soria, 1626) and the church of S. Andrea della Valle (1608-1628; facade completed by Carlo Rainaldi in 1665), which has the largest dome in Rome after St. Peter's. In 1628 he designed the huge Palazzo Barberini, altered and completed by others. He died in Rome on Jan. 30, 1629.

Further Reading

The best account of Maderno in English is in Rudolf Wittkower, *Art and Architecture in Italy, 1600-1750* (1958; 2d ed. 1965).

☐

Francisco Indalecio Madero

Francisco Indalecio Madero (1873-1913) was a Mexican political leader who led the rebellion which overthrew Porfirio Díaz and made possible the later far-reaching social revolution.

Francisco Madero was born in Parras, Coahuila, on Oct. 30, 1873, the son of a wealthy landowning and industrialist family. After studying in the United States and France, he settled on a farm in San Pedro de las Colonias, where he introduced modern farming techniques and improved the educational, housing, and health facilities of his workers. A devotee of homeopathy and spiritism, Madero was influenced by the latter system of beliefs to enter politics at first locally and then nationally as the means of serving his fellowmen. Beginning in 1905, he backed several local candidates and supported journalists opposing the Díaz regime.

The Creelman interview, in which President Díaz promised free elections, encouraged Madero to write his book *Presidential Succession in 1910* and to participate in the organization of independent political groupings—both

efforts being directed toward assuring the return of Mexico to the path of democracy. At first willing to compromise with Díaz if an acceptable vice-presidential choice could be obtained, Madero moved first to a political and then a military challenge of the aging dictator.

Rebellion against Díaz

Madero's courageous campaign, in which he was aided by his wife, Sara Pérez de Madero, earned him the title "Apostle of Democracy." Imprisoned, he escaped to the United States and initiated the armed movement under the Plan of San Luis Potosí (dated Oct. 5, 1910). The document was directed principally at political change, containing but a single paragraph on the land problem and nothing on labor. November 20 was set as the date for initiating the armed movement.

After several months of sporadic and ineffective efforts, the forces of Pascual Orozco in the north and those of Emiliano Zapata in the south began to force the Díaz regime to negotiate. Finally, the fall of Ciudad Juárez in May 1911 brought the relinquishment of power by Díaz, and a provisional, compromise government was set up under Francisco de la Barra. Venustiano Carranza warned that the "revolution that compromises, must be refought."

A Presidency Beset by Troubles

Madero was elected president in a truly popular election and took office on Nov. 6, 1911. His 15 months in office were marred by serious political opposition, the effort

to accommodate both revolutionaries and the old regime in the government, the excessive influence of Madero's family, and four serious rebellions which threatened the existence of the regime, absorbed its attention and resources, and finally destroyed it.

In the south Zapata and his agrarians impatiently rebelled under the Plan of Ayala 3 weeks after Madero took office. In the north Gen. Bernardo Reyes headed a still-born movement, and the revolutionary Orozco, with conservative backing, posed a serious military threat for 5 months. Félix Díaz seized the port of Veracruz in an abortive move, and he and Reyes initiated the uprising in Mexico City on Feb. 9, 1913, which after the "Ten Tragic Days" and the betrayal by Gen. Victoriano Huerta brought the first revolutionary government to an end.

Despite the hectic conditions, under the Madero government press and political freedom was maintained, reform proposals were freely discussed in the Chambers, an agrarian commission began to study the land problem, and an important labor organization, the Casa del Obrero Mundial, was established. However, freedom bred license. Mexico was not ready for political democracy, but fundamental reforms were urgently needed. Internal disorder, vested interests, the opposition of U.S. ambassador Henry Lane Wilson, and the betrayal by Huerta, who had been given command against the rebels in Mexico City, brought defeat and tragedy to the Madero government.

The diminutive, bearded Madero and his vice president Pino Suárez were forced to resign their posts and while being transferred from the palace to prison were shot by their escort (Feb. 22, 1913). The martyred Madero became a symbol for revolutionary unity against the usurper Huerta. He had achieved in death what he had been unable to do while alive.

Further Reading

The standard English-language biography of Madero is Stanley R. Ross, *Francisco I. Madero: Apostle of Mexican Democracy* (1955). A fine companion work is Charles C. Cumberland's monographic study of the initial phase of the Mexican Revolution, *Mexican Revolution: Genesis under Madero* (1952). There are a number of works written with a different focus which constitute useful reading on the *maderista* period and on those who opposed Madero: the revisionist effort of William L. Sherman and Richard E. Greenleaf, *Victoriano Huerta: A Reappraisal* (1960); Michael C. Meyer, *Mexican Rebel: Pascual Orozco and the Mexican Revolution, 1910-1915* (1967); John Womack, *Zapata and the Mexican Revolution* (1969); and Kenneth J. Grieb, *The United States and Huerta* (1969). Madero is discussed in a popular history of the period by Ronald Atkin, *Revolution! Mexico, 1910-1920* (1970). Useful for the precursory period is James D. Cockcroft, *Intellectual Precursors of the Mexican Revolution, 1900-1913* (1968). □

Dolly Madison

Dolly Payne Madison (1768–1849) was highly respected by some of history's greatest politicians during an age when it was considered appropriate for women to be seen and not heard, and was accepted equally by both men and women.

Dorothea Payne Todd Madison, wife of former United States President James Madison, protegee of George and Martha Washington, and the friend of the reserved John and Abigail Adams, was once described by President Andrew Jackson as a "national institution." She withstood personal tragedies to become a popular First Lady who was devoted to her family and country.

Dolly Payne Madison was born May 20, 1768 on a farm in New Garden, North Carolina to John Payne, Jr. and Mary Coles Payne, who were aristocratic, Quaker Virginians. She grew up in Virginia on the Payne Plantation called Scotchtown. Madison claimed both states as her home and later in life would refer to herself as being a native of North Carolina, Virginia, and Pennsylvania.

Moved to the North

In 1783, when Dolly Payne was 15 years old, her parents made the decision to sell their plantation, free their slaves, and move the family north. Dolly's father did not believe in slavery and decided to use the money made from selling the plantation to set up business in Philadelphia. With this in mind, he and Mrs. Payne moved Dolly and her seven siblings, Walter, William Temple, Isaac, Lucy, Anna,

Mary and John to a large and thriving city. This move coincides with a significant event in United States history, as 1783 marked the end of the Revolutionary War.

For several years, Madison adjusted well to city life. Her father had set up an office and shop in the front room of their home and was working in the starch business. Madison eventually became a very beautiful woman, and was considered to be the greatest beauty of her era. However, she remained a modest person who did not take her attributes for granted.

Constitutional Convention

When Madison was 19 years old, the Constitutional Convention assembled in Philadelphia in May of 1787. There she watched with others as the prestigious delegates arrived, among them George Washington, Alexander Hamilton, and Benjamin Franklin. She also saw for the first time a man from Virginia who was known to be a brilliant political thinker, James Madison, and who would later be called the "Father of the Constitution."

The year 1789 marked a drastic change in the Payne household, as Madison's father was forced into bankruptcy. Although John Payne had been a successful farmer in Virginia, he did not know how to be a successful businessman. After his failure in business, Madison's father sank into despair and her mother was forced to take in boarders.

Husband and Child Died

During this time, Madison had many suitors and was very popular. At the age of 21, many of her friends were already married, but she was in no hurry to settle down. The most persistent of her suitors was a man by the name of John Todd, a religious Quaker and lawyer. Eventually, Madison said yes to his proposal and the two were married in January of 1790. Two years later they had their first son, and a year after that, their second.

August of 1793 brought about a horrific change in many Philadelphians' lives. An epidemic of yellow fever swept over the city, and it was the worst epidemic to strike any American city at that time. A great number of people died, including Madison's husband and second born child. Although she also became ill, Madison eventually recovered after a long, slow fight. She then found herself a widow who had to care for her remaining son, Payne.

Met James Madison

In the spring of 1794, Madison experienced what would later affect the rest of her life; she was notified that James Madison would like to meet her. He was a highly ambitious man, and well known in Philadelphia. He helped draft the Constitution and was responsible for proposing the Bill of Rights, the first ten constitutional amendments which safeguard an individual's civil liberties. Within a few weeks after the two met, it was widely rumored that they were engaged, and Martha Washington even questioned Madison about the matter. Although she emphatically denied this rumor, it proved to be true, as Dolly Payne Todd and James Madison were married in September of 1794.

Over the next several years, Dolly and James observed, and at times were directly involved in some of the most important events in the history of the United States. They saw John Adams inaugurated as President in 1797; Thomas Jefferson served two terms as a United States President beginning in 1801, and James Madison was made Secretary of State at that time; in 1800, the capital was moved to Washington, D.C.; and Napoleon gained Louisiana from Spain. Then in 1803, the United States bought the Louisiana Territory from France. As a result of this Purchase, the United States had suddenly doubled in size.

When Jefferson decided not to run for a third term, his first choice for a successor was Madison. So in 1809, James Madison was inaugurated as President and Dolly Madison became the First Lady. Some say she took on the job as if she had been born to fill it. At times, she was affectionately referred to as "Lady Presidentess" or "Queen Dolly"; she was widely known for her caring and loving nature, her fashion consciousness, her impeccable manners, and discreetness. Many commented on the good food Madison always served her guests. There were many kinds of cakes, jellies, macaroons and fruits, but the one thing Madison served, which was new to most, was a delicious cold treat referred to as "ice creams" by her guests.

The year 1812 brought about a Declaration of War and James Madison's re-election. America was soon at war with the British, and in the beginning, much of the battling was done at sea, with many American victories until about 1814. During this time, the British would take the offensive in the land war. Madison's actions on August 24, 1814 would cause her to be remembered forever in American history. On that date, as the British troops advanced upon the city and Madison had been advised to flee, she first took the time to decide what precious possessions would be stowed away in wagons and what would be sacrificed to the enemy forces. Madison made certain that her husband's important and secret papers were saved, along with the silver and a few small portable treasures and a portrait of George Washington, yet she left all of her own frivolities behind. Once Madison left the city, the British were there within two hours of her departure. The destruction that was caused included the burning of the Capitol Building and the torching of the President's House. All the contents remaining in the home had been destroyed forever. With Madison's foresight and quick actions, future generations would be able to view the Washington portrait which had hung over the fireplace.

In the following years, Madison witnessed the end of the war and James Monroe's inauguration as president. After leaving office, the Madisons returned to Montpelier, Virginia, to stay. Montpelier, in Orange County, had been James's home long before he and Dolly were married. The Madisons found peace in Virginia during those retirement years and all energies were spent on improving James's beloved home. Here Dolly Madison would remain for the next 20 years.

In their final years, the Madisons came to realize their increasing poverty. This was largely due to the fact that they were "land poor," and constant visitors to their home were very expensive. Also, Madison's son Payne proved to be extravagant, unproductive, and self-indulgent, while his expenses seemed endless. He spent more money than he had, and James Madison was forced to pay his gambling debts repeatedly. Despite Payne's troubles, Madison displayed constant love and devotion for her son.

James Madison's Death

James Madison died in 1836, and the Madison papers were his last preoccupation. He willed them to Dolly Madison so she might have them published and perhaps be comfortable financially. These papers were James's testimony and reflections on many years of significant historical events. After his death, Madison decided to move back to Washington, and at this time, she sold some of his papers to Congress and received $30,000 for them.

In the remaining years of Madison's life, she would see four different presidents enter office, the rest of the Madison papers sold to Congress, the laying of the cornerstone of the Washington Monument, and the introduction of the first telegraph. She had led a full, active, and productive life and witnessed and participated in a whole span of history. In 1849, Dolly Madison died and would be remembered with respect, admiration, and affection.

Further Reading

Mayer, Jane, *Dolly Madison,* 1954.
Gerson, Noel B., *The Velvet Glove, A Life of Dolly Madison,* 1975. □

under President John Witherspoon, whose intellectual independence, Scottish practicality, and moral earnestness profoundly influenced him. Madison also had gained a wide acquaintance with the new thought of the 18th century and admired John Locke, Isaac Newton, Jonathan Swift, David Hume, Voltaire, and others who fashioned the Enlightenment world view, which became his own.

American Revolution

From his first consciousness of public affairs Madison opposed British colonial measures. He served on the Orange County Committee of Safety from 1774, and two years later he was elected to the Virginia convention that resolved for independence and drafted a new state constitution. His special contribution was in strengthening the clause on religious freedom to proclaim "liberty of conscience for all"—an exceptionally liberal view. Elected to the governor's council in 1777, he lived in Williamsburg for two years, dealing with the routine problems of the Revolutionary War. He also began a lifelong friendship with Governor Thomas Jefferson.

Madison's skill led to his 1780 election to the Continental Congress, where he served for nearly four years. During the first year he became one of the leaders of the so-called nationalist group, which saw fulfillment of the Revolution possible only under a strong central government. Madison thus supported the French alliance and Benjamin Franklin's policies in Europe. He also worked persistently to strengthen the powers of Congress. By the end of his service in 1783, after ratification of the peace treaty and demobili-

James Madison

James Madison (1751-1836), the fourth president of the United States, was one of the principal founders of America's republican form of government.

James Madison lived all his life in the county of Orange, Va., on a 5,000-acre plantation that produced tobacco and grains and was worked by perhaps 100 slaves. Though Madison abhorred slavery and had no use for the aristocratic airs of Virginia society, he remained a Virginia planter, working within the traditional political system of family-based power and accepting the responsibility this entailed. Like his neighbors and friends Thomas Jefferson and James Monroe, Madison worked creatively if not always consistently to make republican government a reality amid a social system and a slave economy often deeply at odds with principles of self-government and individual fulfillment.

After learning the fundamentals at home, Madison went to preparatory school and then to the College of New Jersey at Princeton. The bookish boy got a thorough classical education as he learned Latin and Greek. Since all of his teachers were clergymen, he was also continually exposed to Christian thought and precepts. He received his bachelor of arts degree in 1771 and remained for six months studying

zation of the army, Madison was among the half dozen leading promoters of stronger national government. He had also earned a reputation as an exceedingly well-informed and effective debater and legislator.

Constitution Making

After three years in Virginia helping enact Jefferson's bill for religious freedom and other reform measures, Madison worked toward the Constitutional Convention, which gathered in Philadelphia in May 1787. There, Madison spent the most fruitful months of his life. He advocated the Virginia plan for giving real power to the national government, guided George Washington and other Virginia delegates to support this plan, worked with James Wilson and other nationalists, accepted compromises, and—altogether—became the most constructive member of the convention.

Madison's basic theoretical contribution was his argument that an enlarged, strengthened national government, far from being the path to despotism its opponents feared, was in fact the surest way to protect freedom and expand the principle of self-government. His concept of "factions" in a large republic counteracting each other, built into a constitution of checks and balances, became the vital, operative principle of the American government. In addition to taking part in the debates, Madison took notes on them; published posthumously, these afford the only full record of the convention.

Establishment of the New Government

Madison shared leadership in the ratification struggle with Alexander Hamilton. He formulated strategy for the supporters of the Constitution (Federalists), wrote portions of the *Federalist Papers,* and engaged Patrick Henry in dramatic and finally successful debate at the Virginia ratifying convention (June 1788). Then, as Washington's closest adviser and as a member of the first Federal House of Representatives, Madison led in establishing the new government. He drafted Washington's inaugural address and helped the President make the precedent-setting appointments of his first term.

In Congress, Madison proposed new revenue laws, ensured the President's control over the executive branch, and proposed the Bill of Rights. From the Annapolis Convention in 1786, when he had assumed leadership of the movement for a new constitution, through the end of the first session of Congress (October 1789), Madison was the guiding, creative force in establishing the new, republican government.

Growth of the Party System

However, Hamilton's financial program, presented in January 1790, and Madison's quick opposition to it marked the beginning of Madison's coleadership, with Jefferson, of what became the Democratic-Republican party. Madison opposed the privileged position Hamilton accorded to commerce and wealth, especially when it became apparent that this power could awe and sometimes control the organs of government.

Madison and Jefferson saw republican government as resting on the virtues of the people, sustained by the self-reliance of an agricultural economy and the benefits of public education, with government itself remaining "mild" and responsive to grass-roots impulses. This attitude became the foundation of their political party, which was fundamentally at odds with Hamilton's centralized concept of government, requiring strong leadership.

As Madison and Jefferson organized opposition to Hamilton, they seized on widespread public sympathy for France's expansive, revolutionary exploits to promote republican sentiment in the United States. The Federalists, on the other hand, cherished America's renewed commercial bonds with Britain and feared disruptive, entangling involvement with France. Madison opposed Jay's Treaty, feeling that it would align the United States with England in a way that was dependent and betrayed republican principles. Thus, the final ratification of Jay's Treaty (April 1796), over Madison's bitter opposition, marked his declining influence in Congress. A year later he retired to Virginia.

Madison viewed with alarm the bellicose attitude toward France of John Adams's administration. He felt that the "XYZ" hysteria, resulting in the Alien and Sedition Acts, severely threatened free government. With Jefferson, he executed the protest against these acts embodied in the Kentucky and Virginia Resolutions of 1798. Madison's drafts of the milder Virginia Resolutions and the Report of 1800 defending them are his most complete expression of the rights of the states under the Constitution. He did not, however, advocate either nullification or secession, as some later claimed. The political frustrations of the years 1793-1800 were relieved by Madison's happy marriage in 1794 to the vivacious widow Dolley (or Dolly) Payne Todd, whose name became a symbol for effusive hospitality in Washington social life.

Secretary of State

Madison worked hard to secure Jefferson's election as president in 1800 and was appointed secretary of state. With the President and the new secretary of the Treasury, Albert Gallatin, he made up the Republican triumvirate that guided the nation for eight years. Madison skillfully took advantage of Napoleon's misfortune in the West Indies to purchase Louisiana in 1803 and supported suppression of the Barbary pirates by American naval squadrons (1803-1805). The renewed war between France and Britain, however, became a major crisis, as both powers inflicted heavy damage on American shipping. Britain also engaged in the outrageous impressment of American sailors. Finding appeals to international law useless, and lacking power to protect American trade, Madison promoted the 1807 embargo, which barred American ships from the high seas. However, an unexpected capacity by the belligerents to replace American trade, and substantial smuggling and other evasions by Americans, prevented the embargo from having real force. Madison therefore accepted its repeal at the end of Jefferson's administration.

The President

Elected president in 1808, Madison continued his struggle to find peace with honor amid world war. Republican doctrine, which he shared in part, precluded a heavy military buildup, so Madison's administration lurched from one ineffective commercial policy to another. At the same time, interparty squabbling, Cabinet shuffles, and powerful opposition in Congress undermined his authority. Finally, in November 1811, receiving only insults and deceit from Europe and most heavily injured by Britain, Madison asked Congress for war. "War Hawks," led by Henry Clay and John C. Calhoun, spurred Congress to some inadequate defense measures, and, as final peace attempts failed, war with England was declared in June 1812. Bitter, active opposition to the war by virtually all New England preachers and politicians (near treasonable in Madison's eyes) severely hindered the war effort and added to the President's difficulties. He nonetheless was reelected easily in 1812.

War of 1812

Madison hoped that American zeal and the vulnerability of Canada would lead to a swift victory. However, the surrender of one American army at Detroit, the defeat of another on the Niagara frontier, and the disgraceful retreat of yet another before Montreal blasted these hopes. Then victories at sea, and the 1813 defeat of the British by Commodore O. H. Perry on Lake Erie and by Gen. W. H. Harrison on the Thames battlefield, buoyed American hopes. Yet the chaos in American finance, Napoleon's debacles in Europe, and another fruitless military campaign in New York State left Madison disheartened. His enemies gloated over his nearly fatal illness in June 1813. New England threatened secession, and the republican government seemed likely to fail the test of survival in war.

The summer of 1814 brought to the American battlefields thousands of battle-hardened British troops. They fought vastly improved American armies to a standstill on the Niagara frontier and appeared in Chesapeake Bay intent on capturing Washington. Madison unwisely entrusted defense of the city to a sulking secretary of war, John Armstrong, and to an inept general, William H. Winder. A small but well-disciplined British force defeated the disorganized Americans at Bladensburg as Madison watched from a nearby hillside. His humiliation was complete when he saw flames of the burning Capitol and White House while fleeing across the Potomac River. However, after he returned to Washington 3 days later, he was soon cheered by news of the British defeat in Baltimore Harbor. News also arrived that two American forces had driven back a powerful British force coming down Lake Champlain.

Thus, with Armstrong dismissed and a new secretary of the Treasury, Alexander J. Dallas, restoring American credit, Madison felt that his peace commission in Ghent could demand decent terms from Britain. On Christmas Eve, 1814, a peace treaty was signed restoring the prewar boundaries and ensuring American national self-respect. Andrew Jackson's victory at New Orleans achieved on the battlefield what the treaty makers recognized at Ghent: Britain had lost any remaining hope of dominating its former colonies or blocking United States expansion into the Mississippi Valley.

In his last two years as president, Madison urged a sweeping program of internal development. Madison's program, though only partially enacted by Congress, showed that republican principles were not incompatible with positive action by the Federal government. He retired from office in March 1817, enjoying a popularity unimaginable a few years earlier.

Years of Retirement

In happy retirement at Montpelier, Madison practiced scientific agriculture, helped Jefferson found the University of Virginia, advised Monroe on foreign policy, arranged his papers for posthumous publication, and maintained wide correspondence. He returned officially to public life only to take part in the Virginia constitutional convention of 1829. However, informally, he wrote influentially in support of a mildly protective tariff and the national bank, among other issues. Most important, he lent intellectual leadership and vast prestige to the fight against nullification, which in Madison's eyes betrayed the benefits of the union for which he had fought all his life. But his health slowly declined, forcing him more and more to be a silent observer. By the time of his death on June 28, 1836, he was the last of the great founders of the American Republic.

Further Reading

Madison's writings are collected in W.T. Hutchinson and others, eds., *The Papers of James Madison* (6 vols. to date, 1962-1969). The standard biography is Irving Brant, *James Madison* (6 vols., 1941-1961); a one volume abridgment of this is *The Fourth President: The Life of James Madison* (1970). Another account is Ralph Ketcham, *James Madison* (1971). Adrienne Koch, *Jefferson and Madison: The Great Collaboration* (1950), discusses Madison's views on selected topics. On the elections of 1808 and 1812 see Arthur M. Schlesinger, Jr., ed., *History of American Presidential Elections*, vol. 1 (1971). □

Madonna

Singer and dancer Madonna (Madonna Louise Veronica Ciccone, born 1958) was a master marketer and sensational self-promoter who propelled herself to stardom, dominating pop charts, concert halls, film, and music video. She has been called "an outrageous blend of Little Orphan Annie, Margaret Thatcher, and Mae West," and "narcissistic, brazen, comic . . . the Goddess of the Nineties."

Born in August 1958, Madonna Ciccone was the third child of six in a Catholic family living in Bay City, Michigan. Her father, Tony, a design engineer for Chrysler/General Dynamics, was a conservative, devout Roman Catholic and a first-generation Italian American. Madonna's mother and namesake was of French-Canadian descent. She died of breast cancer when Madonna was five years old.

Tony Ciccone moved the family to Pontiac, Michigan, and married one of the women hired to care for the Ciccone household. The adjustment was difficult for Madonna as the eldest daughter. She had considered herself the "lady of the house" and had received much of her father's affection and attention.

In her younger school years Madonna acted in school plays. As she entered adolescence, Madonna discovered her love and talent for dancing, an activity she pursued under the direction and leadership of Christopher Flynn, her private ballet instructor. Dedicated and disciplined, Madonna worked hard, but played hard as well, something Flynn made easy by introducing her to the disco nightlife of downtown Detroit.

Despite the glamour and sophistication she developed with Flynn, who was more than 20 years older than she, neither Madonna's extracurricular activities nor her father's disapproval kept her from caring for her younger siblings and working hard in school. She graduated early from high school with mostly "A's" and was awarded a dance scholarship to the University of Michigan. She stayed two years before going to New York City in 1978 with $37 and a wealth of determination and ambition.

An apartment in an East Village tenement building surrounded by crime and drugs was the place from which she began her steady and focused climb to superstardom. Her first jobs included figure modeling for artists and acting in low budget movies. She danced briefly with the Alvin Ailey American Dance Theater, studied for a time with Pearl Lang of the Martha Graham Dance group, and went to Paris as a short-lived singer/dancer with French disco artist Patrick Hernandez.

Talent, Determination, and Unbridled Ambition

Before she left for Paris, Madonna had developed a fascination with the music field. It started with rock and roll, playing drums and singing backup in several small bands. When she returned to New York she spent a lot of time writing songs, making demonstration tapes, and hanging out in such popular lower-Manhattan nightclubs as the Roxy and Danceteria. It was a simple, four-track demo called "Everybody" that earned Madonna a recording contract with Sire Records in October 1982.

The album *Madonna* sold few copies when it was first released in July 1983. However, repeated club performances and radio air-play of several cuts from the album eventually earned her three huge hits with "Holiday," "Lucky Star," and "Borderline." A flurry of chart-busting hits, videos, concert tours, and films followed. She seemed to have a Midas-like quality with most everything she did. Even a brief singing performance in a largely forgettable film, *Vision Quest,* resulted in the top-five love ballad "Crazy for You."

Her second album, *Like a Virgin,* released in late 1984, produced two number one hits—the title track and

"Material Girl." Madonna was becoming an accomplished songwriter; she had written five of the songs herself. During the spring of 1985 she embarked on her first concert tour, which was so successful that she had to switch to larger venues as the tour progressed. On the heels of *Like a Virgin* came the detective/comedy film *Desperately Seeking Susan* in 1985 (directed by Susan Seidelman and co-starring Madonna and Rosanna Arquette), which spawned another popular single and video, "In the Groove."

The tour had thousands of teenage girls all over the country tying lace bows on top of their heads, wearing underwear as outerwear, and walking the halls of schools and shopping malls as "Madonna wannabees." Madonna had become an icon as much as a singer to her fans.

Controversial Behavior Shared Center Stage

Madonna was married briefly to actor Sean Penn from August 1985 to early 1989; it was a marriage with many well chronicled ups and downs. In 1986 she released her third album, *True Blue,* from which three singles topped the charts: "Papa Don't Preach," about a pregnant teen who wants to keep her child; the title track, a light "girl loves boy" tune; and "Live to Tell," a soulful ballad from the soundtrack of *At Close Range* starring Sean Penn. In 1987 a movie starring Madonna called *Who's That Girl* was largely ignored, unlike the accompanying soundtrack and concert tour.

The release of *Like A Prayer* coincided with the breakup of her marriage, and included a fare-thee-well written by Madonna entitled "Till Death Do Us Part." However, it was the video of the title song portraying Madonna's confession to a priest followed by engaging in sexually suggestive behavior with him that caused a stir in the Catholic Church. The controversy resulted in a disagreement over a $5 million endorsement contract with the Pepsi company. Controversy again surrounded Madonna in 1990 when she was banned from M-TV before 11 p.m. with the sexually explicit video "Justify My Love."

Other films featuring Madonna include *Shanghai Surprise* (1986), in which she co-starred with then-husband Sean Penn; *Dick Tracy* (1989), the film that launched her short-lived affair with Warren Beatty and also was accompanied by a Madonna-sung soundtrack; and *Truth or Dare,* her own feature-length video/documentary compiled of footage from her Blonde Ambition Tour of 1990-1991. Madonna also appeared in Penny Marshall's *A League of Their Own* (1992); and she co-starred with Willem Dafoe in *Body of Evidence* (1993). Each work contained some form of "out-there" sexuality that titillated her fans, and kept the press and critics focused on her.

Created and Cashed In on Era of Voyeurism

By 1992 Madonna had established herself as a worldwide entertainer and a sharp, confident business woman. In April of that year she signed a $60 million contract with Time-Warner, which included a multi-media package with her own record company (under the Maverick label), HBO specials, videos, films, books, merchandise, and more than six albums.

The announcement of the seven-year deal was timed with the combined release of the album *Erotica,* an extended video, and a coffee table picture book called *Sex.* The book can only be purchased by adults and comes in a Mylar, vacuum-sealed cover. It has scores of black and white photographs by fashion photographer Steven Meisel. Madonna appears mostly without clothes in compromising positions with everything from men and women (in all combinations, positions, and numbers) to chairs, dogs, and slices of pizza. She was even shown hitch-hiking in Miami wearing nothing but high heels. The book was a sellout across the country.

A perfect example of the paradox represented by the serious and the playful Madonna all in one, *Sex* was published at the same time as *The Madonna Connection,* a series of scholarly essays by academics who had been tracking the phenomenon of the Material Girl for several years.

Madonna's career evolved with phases and images distinct and carefully planned. There was her lacy underwear, big hair, and black jewelry phase (her self-described "chubby" phase, as she referred to it in an M-TV anniversary program); then the 1940s and 1950s sultry, sleek glamour phase reminiscent of Rita Hayworth and Marilyn Monroe; the lean dancer; the businesswoman; and the unashamed, uninhibited sex goddess. Each phase seemed to be accompanied by a different lover, including Chicago Bulls' bad boy Dennis Rodman in the spring of 1994.

Madonna Reincarnated

Part of Madonna's genius was to recognize when the mood of her audience changed. In the late 1994 release of *Bedtime Stories,* written primarily by Madonna, a new image emerged projecting a softer eroticism and more soulful sound. By the mid-1990s she seemed more intent on establishing herself as a serious artist than making headlines with yet another boyfriend. She set her sights on playing the leading role in Andrew Lloyd Webber's movie musical *Evita,* and after repeated auditions convinced producers that she would bring a unique understanding to the portrayal of Eva Peron. Like Eva Peron, Madonna was a strong, willful woman who mesmerized her followers and also felt misunderstood by her critics.

Madonna was in the midst of personal as well as professional change. In her personal life, she settled into a relationship with Carlos Leon, her personal trainer. Meanwhile, in 1995, she accepted an industry award for Most Fashionable Artist as well as VH1's Viewer's Choice award for Most Fashionable Artist, and in December of 1996, *Billboard* magazine's Artist Achievement Award.

A New Propriety

Her determination to play the staring role in *Evita* paid off. While the film—and her performance—received mixed reviews, no one could take away her dedication, hard work, or box office success. In January 1997 Madonna was nominated for and won the Best Actress Award at the 54th Annual Golden Globe Award Ceremony. Later that spring, the song "You Must Love Me" from *Evita* won the Academy Award for Best Song. The film's premier in late 1995 was upstaged in October when Madonna gave birth to a girl named Lourdes Maria Ciccone Leon. Madonna described the event to *People* magazine as, "the greatest miracle of my life." She even traded in her pink Hollywood mansion for a home in a low key suburb of Los Angeles.

The Material Girl turned serious actress, singer, song writer and mom appeared to have it all in the late 1990s. She accepted it all—including the stress of living a fishbowl existence—with characteristic calm, as if she were planning the next phase. She told *Time* magazine, "I never wish I had a different life. I am lucky to be in the position of power that I am in and to be intelligent. . . . It's not my nature to just kick back."

Further Reading

Most of the published information on Madonna is found in newspapers and magazines. See *New York Daily News* (May 31, 1985); *People* (May 13, 1985); *The Encyclopedia of Pop, Rock and Soul* (1989); *USA Today* (April 21, 1992); *New Yorker* (October 26, 1992); *New York Times Book Review* (October 25, 1992); *Newsweek* (November 2, 1992); *Nation* (December 14, 1992); *Entertainment Weekly* (April 15, 1994; September 22, 1995); *Esquire* (August, 1994); *People* (April 29, 1996; October 28, 1996; December 30, 1996); *Billboard* (November 16, 1996; December 16, 1995); *New York Times* (March 24, 1997); and *Forbes* (September 23, 1996). □

Count Maurice Maeterlinck

The Belgian poet, dramatist, and essayist Count Maurice Maeterlinck (1863-1949) is known for his symbolist dramas and for his writings on insects, flowers, and man's mystical inner life. He was awarded the Nobel Prize for literature in 1911.

Maurice Maeterlinck was born in Ghent on Aug. 29, 1863. He was destined by his family for a career in law but turned early to the world of letters. In 1886 he went to Paris, where he met Villiers de l'Isle-Adam, Saint-Paul Roux, and Catulle Mendès. Three years later he published a volume of verse, *Serres chaudes* (Hothouses), and a five-act play, *La Princesse Maleine,* the first in a long series of dramatic works, among the most notable being two one-act plays, *L'Intruse* (1890; *The Intruder*) and *Les Aveugles* (1890; *The Blind*); *Pelléas et Mélisande* (1892); *Intérieur* (1894); *La Mort de Tintagiles* (1894); *Aglavaine et Sélysette* (1896); *Monna Vanna* (1902); and *L'Oiseau bleu* (1909; *The Blue Bird*). Other plays are *Les Sept Princesses* (1891), *Alladine et Palomides* (1894), *Joyselle* (1903), *Ariane et Barbe Bleu* (1907), *Marie Magdeleine* (1910), *Le Miracle de Saint Antoine* (1919), *Le Bourgmestre de Stilmonde* (1919), *Les Fiancailles* (1922), *La Princesse Isabelle* (1935), and *Jeanne d'Arc* (1948).

Maeterlinck's preoccupation with man's inner life and spiritual mystery is evident in *Le Trésor des humbles* (1896; The Treasure of the Humble), a collection of essays whose chapters "Silence," "The Awakening of the Soul," "The Tragic in Everyday Life," "The Inner Life," and "The Beauty Within" afford a rich introduction to Maeterlinck's thought and provide a very helpful background for his symbolist plays, where unseen forces are at work beyond the ordinary levels of human consciousness. *The Intruder* and *The Blind* show Maeterlinck's effective technique of suggestion and creation of mood or emotion by repetition, oversimplified vocabulary, and the use of symbols and periods of silence—a technique employed to remarkable advantage in *Pelléas et Mélisande.*

In Maeterlinck's characteristic symbolist plays, the individuals who sense most profoundly the spiritual mystery in which they move are those at the extremes of life—the very young and the very old, the blind, and those in love. Other characters tend to exist unperceiving. But even the most sensitive seem incapable of comprehending their situations or resolving their destinies, so that in watching them one seems to be observing figures in a dream allegory rather than living beings.

Maeterlinck wrote books and collections of speculative essays on a variety of subjects, among them *The Life of the Bees* (1901), *The Intelligence of Flowers* (1907), *Death* (1913), *The Great Secret* (1921), *The Life of Space* (1928), *The Life of the Ants* (1930), *Before the Great Silence* (1934), *The Shadow of the Wings* (1936), *Before God* (1937), and *The Great Portal* (1939). He died in Nice on May 7, 1949.

Further Reading

Useful studies of Maeterlinck and his work include Edward Thomas, *Maurice Maeterlinck* (1911); Jethro Bithell, *Life and Writings of Maurice Maeterlinck* (1913); Una Taylor (Lady Troubridge), *Maurice Maeterlinck: A Critical Study* (1914); and W. D. Halls, *Maurice Maeterlinck: A Study of His Life and Thought* (1960).

Additional Sources

Halls, W. D., *Maurice Maeterlinck: a study of his life and thought,* Westport, Conn.: Greenwood Press, 1978, 1960.
Leblanc, Georgette, *Souvenirs: my life with Maeterlinck,* New York: Da Capo Press, 1976, 1932.
Mahony, Patrick, *Maurice Maeterlinck, mystic and dramatist: a reminiscent biography of the man and his ideas,* Washington, D.C.: Institute for the Study of Man, 1984. □

Ferdinand Magellan

While in the service of Spain, the Portuguese explorer Ferdinand Magellan (1480-1521) led the first European voyage of discovery to circumnavigate the globe.

Ferdinand Magellan was born in Oporto of noble parentage. Having served as a page to the Queen, Magellan entered the Portuguese service in the East in 1505. He went to East Africa and later was at the battle of Diu, in which the Portuguese destroyed Egyptian naval hegemony in the Arabian Sea. He went twice to Malacca, the Malayan spice port, participating in its conquest by the Portuguese. He may also have gone on an exploratory mission to the Molucca Islands (Spice Islands), the original source of some of the most valuable spices.

In 1513 Magellan was wounded in one of the many frustrating battles against the Moors in North Africa. But all of his services brought him little favor from the Crown, and in 1517, accompanied by his friend the cosmographer Ruy Faleiro, he went to Seville, where he offered his services to the Spanish court.

The famous Treaty of Tordesillas (1494) had divided the overseas world of the "discoveries" between the two powers. Portugal acquired everything from Brazil eastward to the East Indies; the Spanish hemisphere of discovery and conquest ran westward from Brazil to 134°E meridian. This eastern area had not yet been explored by the Spaniards, and they assumed that some of the Spice Islands might lie within their half of the globe. They were wrong, but Magellan's scheme was to test that assumption.

In addition it must be recalled that Columbus had made a terrible mistake, brought home by his "discovery" of America. Accepting the academic errors of learned geographers, ancient and modern, he had grossly underestimated the distance between Europe and the East (sailing westward from the former). Balboa's march across the Panamanian Isthmus had subsequently revealed the existence of a "South Sea" (the Pacific) on the other side of Columbus's

and it was only on March 6, 1521, that the fleet finally anchored at Guam.

Magellan then passed eastward to Cebu in the Philippines, where, in an effort to gain the favor of a local ruler, he became embroiled in a local war and was slain in battle on April 27, 1521; Barbosa and Serrão were killed shortly thereafter. With the crew wasted from sickness, the survivors were forced to destroy the *Concepción,* and the great circumnavigation was completed by a courageous former mutineer, the Basque Juan Sebastián del Cano. Commanding the *Victoria,* he picked up a small cargo of spices in the Moluccas, crossed the Indian Ocean, and traveled around the Cape of Good Hope from the east. With a greatly reduced crew he finally reached Seville on Sept. 8, 1522. In the meantime the *Trinidad,* considered unfit to make the long voyage home, had tried to beat its way against contrary winds back across the Pacific to Panama. The voyage revealed the vast extent of the northern Pacific, but the attempt failed, and the *Trinidad* was forced back to the Moluccas. There its crew was jailed by the Portuguese, and only four men returned after 3 years to Spain.

Magellan's project brought little in the way of material benefit to Spain. The Portuguese were well entrenched in the East, their trans-African route at that time proving to be the only feasible maritime connection to India and the Spice Islands. Charles V acknowledged the political and economic facts by selling his vague East Indian rights to Portugal, rights that were later in part resumed with the Spanish colonization of the Philippines. Yet though nearly destroying itself in the process, the Magellan fleet for the first time revealed in a practical fashion the full extent of humanity's inheritance upon this globe. And in this, its scientific aspect, it proved to be the greatest of all the "conquests" undertaken by the gold-, slave-, and spice-seeking overseas adventurers of early modern Europe.

"mainlands in the Ocean Sea." Thereafter, explorers eagerly sought northern and southern all-water passages across the stumbling block of the Americas; Magellan, too, sought such a passage.

Major Voyage

King Charles V of Spain (the emperor Charles V) endorsed the design of Magellan and Faleiro, and on Sept. 20, 1519, after a year's preparation, Magellan led a fleet of five ships out into the Atlantic. Unfortunately the ships—the *San Antonio, Trinidad, Concepción, Victoria,* and *Santiago*—were barely seaworthy, and the crews, including some officers, were of international composition and of dubious loyalty to their leader. With Magellan went his brother-in-law, Duarte Barbosa, and the loyal and able commander of the *Santiago,* João Serrão. Arriving at Brazil, the fleet sailed down the South American coast to the Patagonian bay of San Julián, where it wintered from March to August 1520. There an attempted mutiny was squelched, with only the top leaders being punished. Thereafter, however, the *Santiago* was wrecked, and its crew had to be taken aboard the other vessels.

Leaving San Julián, the fleet sailed southward; on Oct. 21, 1520, it entered the Strait of Magellan. It proceeded cautiously, taking over a month to pass through the strait. During this time the master of the *San Antonio* deserted and sailed back to Spain, and so only three of the original five ships entered the Pacific on November 28. There followed a long, monotonous voyage northward through the Pacific,

Further Reading

A primary source is the narrative of Antonio Pigafetta, principal chronicler of the expedition, *Magellan's Voyage around the World by Antonio Pigafetta,* translated by James A. Robertson (2 vols., 1906). The Pigafetta translation and other source narratives are included in Charles E. Nowell, ed., *Magellan's Voyage around the World: Three Contemporary Accounts* (1962). The best works on Magellan, by Jean Denuce and Jose Toribio Medina, are in Spanish. In English, Francis H. H. Guillemard, *The Life of Ferdinand Magellan* (1890), is still good. Another study is Charles M. Parr, *So Noble a Captain: The Life and Times of Ferdinand Magellan* (1953; 2d ed. entitled *Ferdinand Magellan, Circumnavigator,* 1964). George E. Nunn, in *The Columbus and Magellan Concepts of South American Geography* (1932), shows the Magellan voyage to have been a logical consequence of the final views of the Columbus brothers. ☐

Alessandro Magnasco

The Italian painter Alessandro Magnasco (1667-1749) is best known for his scenes of disembodied, flamelike figures in stormy landscapes or cavernous

interiors and for the vitality of his nervous, open brushwork.

Alessandro Magnasco, called Lisandrino, was born in Genoa. His father, Stefano, also a painter, died when Alessandro was young, leaving his family in poverty. His mother remarried, and Alessandro's position in the new family seems to have been precarious. When he was about 10 years old, he was sent off to Milan in the care of a merchant of that city. His new guardian arranged for him to be trained as a painter in the workship of Filippo Abbiati.

Magnasco learned rapidly. His first independent work was in portraiture, but he made his reputation with the landscape and genre paintings for which he is famous today. He painted them for private patrons. A marked increase in the size and secular orientation of the middle class in northern Italy during the first part of the 18th century made it possible for him to sell enough not merely to survive but even to become well-to-do without painting either frescoes or altarpieces.

Having found an appreciative audience in Milan, Magnasco stayed there most of his life, but at heart he was Genoese. In Florence, where he worked for the Medici (ca. 1709-1711), he married a Genoese girl. In 1735, when he was an old man, he moved back to the city he had had to leave as a child. He found that the Genoese did not care much for his radical new style. Besides, palsy made it harder and harder for him to hold a brush. Not long after he arrived he stopped painting altogether. On March 12, 1749, he died.

Magnasco's manner is Genoese. This painterly technique, in which loose, free brushwork becomes a major vehicle of expression, was brought to Genoa (via Venice) by Peter Paul Rubens and Anthony Van Dyck and flowered in the work of such masters as Bernardo Strozzi, Giovanni Benedetto Castiglione, and Valerio Castello (the teacher of Magnasco's father). It reached its fullest fruition with Magnasco.

Friars by a Stormy Sea exemplifies Magnasco's landscapes. A ruined tower against the darkening sky reminds us of the romantic landscapes of Salvator Rosa. But nothing in Rosa prepares us for waves so wild they seem about to tear off sections of the shore and pull them into the sea. Amplification comes from interaction, in our own mind, between the movement of the wave and the signs of how the painter's hand moved when he painted it: strong staccato strokes slashed one beside another, all sweeping the same way, like the water. The little figures in the landscape are minor accents, signposts of impotence.

In Magnasco's *Synagogue* it is the background that is neutral and the figures that provide the fire. The figures, wrote Carlo Giuseppe Ratti (1759), who had known Magnasco well, "are painted with rapid, seemingly careless, but telling strokes, that are strewn about with a certain bravura that cannot be imagined by those who have not seen it." The people who populate Magnasco's synagogue are fragile, weightless, ghostlike. They are composed of short nervous strokes that combine into zigzags and corkscrew patterns. These in turn set up an overall agitation. Whether these disturbed visions, and the many other canvases like them, were painted by Magnasco as quaint decorations (*bizarie* some of his contemporaries called them) or as mystical affirmations or as savage satires, no one now knows.

Further Reading

The standard work on Magnasco, lavishly illustrated but with an Italian text, is Benno Geiger, *Alessandro Magnasco* (1949). An abridged English translation of Carlo Giuseppe Ratti's "Life of Magnasco" (1759) appears in Robert Enggass and Jonathan Brown, *Italy and Spain, 1600-1750: Sources and Documents* (1970). See also Rudolf Wittkower, *Art and Architecture in Italy, 1600-1750* (1958; 2d rev. ed. 1965), and Mario Monteverdi, *Italian Art to 1850* (1965). □

René Magritte

The Belgian artist René Magritte (1890-1967) was a Surrealist painter famous for bizarre images depicted in a realistic manner. Many of his paintings showed a dignified gentleman in a bowler hat.

The Belgian painter René François Chislain Magritte in 1940 praised "that pictorial experience which puts the real world on trial," and his career bore out this aesthetic strategy. Born in Lessines, Belgium, on November 21, 1890, he would become a chief proponent of representational Surrealism. By the age of 12 he began drawing and painting and attended informal art classes in Chatelet, where his family then resided. A chance encounter with a plein-air painter inspired the budding artist.

In 1912 Magritte's mother drowned herself, and the family moved to Charleroi shortly after the tragedy. At age 15, at the local fair, he met a girl named Georgette Berger, and though he would not see her again until 1920 the two eventually married in 1922. In the intervening years Magritte enrolled at the *Academie des Beaux-Arts* in Brussels, where he studied intermittently from 1916 to 1918. In 1919, in association with several young artists, poets, and musicians in Brussels, he helped publish the review *Au Volant!* That same year he exhibited his first canvas, *Three Women,* a Cubistic picture.

The early 1920s found Magritte using a generally abstract idiom based on Cubo-Futurist principles. After brief military service in 1921 and his marriage to Georgette the following year, he supported himself by working in a wallpaper factory, as well as by designing posters. Around this time Magritte saw a reproduction of Giorgio de Chirico's painting *The Song of Love* (1914), and the image, illustrated in the Roman periodical *Valori Plastici,* is said to have moved him to tears. The strange juxtaposition of objects in de Chirico's work revealed to Magritte the poetic possibilities of painting, and thereafter his pictures challenged expectations.

Rene Magritte (center)

The images and techniques of the movies were an influence on Magritte, especially the French film anti-hero Fantômas, a master of crime and disguise. Many of Magritte's works at this time, in keeping with Surrealist practices, disclosed a sinister side of human personality, as in *Pleasure* (1926) or *The Threatened Assassin* (1926-1927). In 1930 Magritte, never much one for political endeavors, broke with the Surrealists in a dispute over their dogmatic aims, burned most of his possessions associated with this time in his life, and returned to his native Brussels.

The following decade Magritte developed his mature style, first introduced in 1925. He was represented at major international exhibitions of Surrealist art and wrote on art's potential, though he offered no explanations—choosing instead to maintain its mysterious aura. Though an admirer of Max Ernst, he did not adopt that artist's novel methods of rubbing and blotting. He also persisted with his painstakingly literal approach. He took care to distinguish between an object and its image. Magritte had first presented this lesson in his teasing *The Use of Words I* (1928-1929), in which the inscription "this is not a pipe" is written beneath a painted image of one.

This semantic investigation of the connection between language and visual source is evident in his *Key of Dreams* series of the 1930s in which objects depicted do not necessarily conform with the labels below them. Contextual correspondence and associative meaning are at the heart of Magritte's pursuits, and around 1936 he reversed his (and the general Surrealist) tact by exploring similar rather than dissimilar things.

Magritte's definitive work also shows an interest in the coexistence of opposite states of being. Interior is confused with exterior (*The Human Condition I,* 1933), night fuses with day (*The Empire of Lights,* 1954), and a human face is comprised of body parts (*The Rape,* 1945). Though Magritte's method is one of utmost clarity, he confounds imagined and "real identities," commenting on the relativity of perception.

In the 1940s Magritte experimented briefly with Impressionism (1940-1945) and a brash Fauve-inspired style (1948) dubbed "*Vache*" (literally, cow). Thus, working from his home in Brussels, he forever kept the critics off guard. His sedate bourgeois way of life masked his creative unpredictability. At times he resembled the staid bowler-hatted gentlemen who peopled many of his paintings.

Magritte minimized the importance of his achievements: " . . . life obliges me to do something so I paint." Yet he raised profound aesthetic issues of much importance for future generations, including the Pop artists of the 1960s. The fantastic content of his art had great appeal for the general public and became widely disseminated in commercial advertising and posters in the 1960s and 1970s. Magritte, who died in Brussels on August 15, 1967, created a world of enchantment with far-reaching consequences.

Magritte's pictures of the early 1920s already explored thematic ambiguity, and by the mid-1920s he and E. L. T. Mesens helped form a Belgian Surrealist group that included Paul Nougé, Camille Goemans, and Louis Scutenaire, an early chronicler of Magritte's art. The Surrealists, who included writers and composers too, overturned conventional notions by exercising their unconscious impulses for creative effect, and Magritte's paintings often took on a bizarre, dream-like quality. Working at a rapid rate, he investigated these new non-formalist concerns. One subject, *The Lost Jockey,* typically explored in a sequence of pictures (sometimes collage), contrasted oversized balusters with a horse and rider. Magritte's first one-man show, in Brussels in 1927, was a critical failure, and that year he moved to the Surrealist center, Paris, befriending poet Paul Eluard and André Breton, spokesman for the movement.

Breton released his two Surrealist manifestoes in 1924 and 1929, and between these years the movement was perhaps at its most exuberant. One main inspirational source for the Surrealists was the literature of Isidore Ducasse, alias the Comte de Lautréamont, who around 1870 had written that nothing is "as beautiful as . . . the chance encounter of a sewing machine and an umbrella on a dissecting table." Later, in 1948, Magritte illustrated Lautréamont's complete works with 77 drawings which rivaled the text in strangeness.

Further Reading

William Rubin, *Dada, Surrealism and Their Heritage* (1967) locates Magritte in art history and is a fine introduction to Surrealism. Jose Vovelle, *Le Surréalisme en Belgique* (1972, in

French), is a comprehensive look at Surrealism in Belgium. Numerous monographs on the artist exist, among these Suzi Gablik, *Magritte* (1970, reprint 1985) and James Thrall Soby, *René Magritte* (1965). □

Ramon Magsaysay

Ramon Magsaysay (1907-1957) was the third Philippine president. Credited with restoring peace, law, and order during the Philippine crisis of the 1950s and the Hukbalahap rebellion, he was the first Philippine president from the landless lower middle class, the petit bourgeois stratum of society.

R amon Magsaysay was born in Iba, Zambales, on Aug. 31, 1907, to Exequiel Magsaysay, a blacksmith, and Perfecta del Fierro, a schoolteacher. He entered the University of the Philippines in 1927. He worked as a chauffeur to support himself as he studied engineering; later, he transferred to the Institute of Commerce at José Rizal College (1928-1932), where he received a baccalaureate in commerce. He then worked as automobile mechanic and shop superintendent. When World War II broke out, he joined the motor pool of the 31st Infantry Division of the Philippine army.

When Bataan surrendered in 1942, Magsaysay escaped to the hills, organized the Western Luzon Guerrilla Forces, and was commissioned captain on April 5, 1942. For 3 years Capt. Magsaysay operated under Col. Merrill's famed guerrilla outfit and saw action at Sawang, San Marcelino, Zambales. Magsaysay was among those instrumental in clearing the Zambales coast of the Japanese prior to the landing of American liberation forces on Jan. 29, 1945.

After the war Magsaysay was appointed by the U. S. Army as military governor of Zambales on Feb. 4, 1945. On Feb. 8, 1946, Maj. Magsaysay was discharged from the army. He was elected representative of Zambales on April 23, 1946, and reelected in November 1949 under the banner of the Liberal party.

Government Service

In Congress, Magsaysay served as chairman of the House Committee on National Defense and belonged to numerous other committees. In April 1948 President Manuel Roxas appointed Magsaysay to head a veterans' mission to Washington which lobbied for the passage of the Rogers bill. In 1950 Magsaysay attacked the Liberal party-dominated administration for corruption and called for reforms of the deplorable social conditions which had produced the Hukbalahap rebellion (the rebels were peasants fighting for democratic rights, equality, and justice). *Time* (Nov. 26, 1951) reported that "when politicians kept him from buying Quonset huts he needed as schoolhouses for Zambales, he gathered some of his wartime guerillas, raided a surplus dump, and made off with 140 huts. Later he paid for them— 50 centavos (25 cents) apiece, the price he figured the

profiteer who owned them had paid in the first place." Prompted by his American advisers, President Elpidio Quirino appointed Magsaysay secretary of national defense on Sept. 1, 1950.

From 1950 to 1953 Magsaysay revitalized the army with vast American aid; the army had been demoralized, politics-ridden, and virtually defeated by the mass revolution under way. Within 83 days Magsaysay retired three generals, discharged and demoted many erring and inefficient officers, and gave the 18,000 enlisted men better food, quarters, and pay. He also reorganized the vicious Philippine Constabulary and created the Scout Ranger Battalions, whom he commanded to "kill Huks." Magsaysay sent civilian officers to the barrios to propagandize in support of the government. He gathered $500,000 from the oligarchic ruling class—the big landlords, compradors, and bureaucrat-capitalists—to pay as reward for any information leading to the capture of the Huk leaders. This policy led to the arrest and conviction of 29 top leaders of the People's Liberation Army and 6 members of the Politburo of the Communist party of the Philippines. Labor leaders, professors, diplomats, and many other innocent citizens were arrested and deprived of their right to due process of law under a repressive martial law.

As head of the Defense Department, Magsaysay encouraged Huk surrenders by offering medical treatment, parole, and homesteads in the Mindanao jungle. The Economic Development Corps, an agency of the government, then built farmhouses, schools, hospitals, and other facilities in Mindanao under Magsaysay's initiative. He also tried to rehabilitate the Huks by offering vocational training and loans to aid in establishing small businesses. From a later perspective, these measures (including anti-Communist indoctrination) had practically no result; the reestablished Communist party (Marxist-Leninist) reoccupied and liberated large areas of central Luzon and rapidly gained ground in other parts of the country.

In November 1951 Magsaysay sought to keep the elections clean by employing his 40,000-man army and 5,500 reserves to police the land. The opposition Nacionalista party won a decisive victory against the ruling Liberals. In the summer of 1952 Magsaysay was also responsible for the military solution to the protesting Moslems, who had been victims of Christian chauvinism, land-grabbers, and government malfeasance. Magsaysay also sent forces to fight under the United Nations command in Korea.

Accession to the Presidency

For his reputation of energy and honesty, Magsaysay was idolized by the electorate, which voted him to succeed Quirino. Magsaysay had earlier resigned from the Liberal party and was subsequently chosen candidate for president by the Nacionalista party. On Nov. 10, 1953, Magsaysay won by a landslide victory.

During Magsaysay's term the Huk leader Taruc surrendered. In 1954 Magsaysay's government renegotiated the iniquitous Bell Trade Act of 1946 into the Laurel-Langley Agreement, which maintained the economic subservience of the nation to United States monopolies. The peso currency, controlled by the United States dollar, declined in value. Magsaysay also signed the first Agricultural Commodities Agreement with the United States in 1957, thus perpetuating the colonial pattern of the nation's economy, and was also responsible for the passage of the Antisubversion Law, which curtailed the citizens' democratic rights of assembly, free speech, and belief.

In line with his position as America's "staunch friend in Asia," Magsaysay was the chief sponsor in forming the Southeast Asia Treaty Organization (SEATO). He was killed in a plane crash on March 17, 1957.

Further Reading

Carlos P. Romulo and Marvin M. Gray, *The Magsaysay Story* (1956), is a full-length biography. A more specialized study is Frances Lucille Starner, *Magsaysay and the Philippine Peasantry: The Agrarian Impact on Philippine Politics, 1953-1956* (1961). Reliable information on Magsaysay is in Eufronio Melo Alip, ed., *The Philippine Presidents from Aguinaldo to Garcia* (1958); Teodoro A. Agoncillo and Oscar M. Alfonso, *History of the Filipino People* (1960; rev. ed. 1967); Jésus V. Merritt, *Our Presidents: Profiles in History* (1962); Hernando J. Abaya, *The Untold Philippine Story* (1967); and Pedro A. Gagelonia, *Presidents All* (1967).

Additional Sources

Barranco, Vicente F., *The man who lived a hundred years,* 1983 (Manila: UST Press). □

Alfred Thayer Mahan

Alfred Thayer Mahan (1840-1914), American naval historian and strategist, provided the intellectual and historical foundations for American imperial expansion.

Alfred Thayer Mahan was born on Sept. 27, 1840. His father was an officer at the U.S. Military Academy at West Point and a professor of civil and military engineering. Young Mahan evidently intended a military career from the beginning. After 2 years at Columbia College he entered the U.S. Naval Academy at Annapolis in 1856, graduating second in his class in 1859.

During the Civil War, Mahan spent most of his time on blockade duty and in the years after the war received a variety of assignments. He became increasingly interested in writing and in 1883 published his first book, *The Gulf and Inland Waters,* part of the naval history of the Civil War.

Almost immediately thereafter occurred what was probably the decisive event of Mahan's life. He was invited in 1884 to lecture on naval tactics and history at the newly established Naval War College. In outlining his lectures he first formulated the ideas that became the basis of *The Influence of Sea Power upon History, 1660-1783* (1890). Up to this point in his life, Mahan had believed that the United States should avoid international involvement and concentrate solely on defense. But his study of the influence of sea power changed his views, and he came to the conclusion that strong naval power was essential to maintain national strength. His book attracted favorable attention and established him as an important military thinker. His other major work was *The Influence of Sea Power upon the French Revolution and Empire, 1793-1812* (2 vols., 1892).

Mahan retired in 1896, but during the Spanish-American War he was called to serve on the Naval War Board, an informal advisory body to the secretary of the Navy. After the war he was one of the American representatives to the Hague Disarmament Conference.

Mahan's major influence came from his association with such politicians as John Hay, Henry Cabot Lodge, and Theodore Roosevelt, all of whom were committed to American imperial expansion. In his writings Mahan argued that expansion was a military necessity for the United States. It was largely on the basis of Mahan's ideas, for instance, that President Theodore Roosevelt took steps to acquire the Panama Canal for the United States.

In 1912 Mahan accepted a position at the Carnegie Institution in Washington, D.C. He died on Dec. 1, 1914.

Further Reading

Mahan's autobiography, *From Sail to Steam: Recollections of Naval Life* (1907), is essential. The basic biography of Mahan is William D. Puleston, *Mahan: The Life and Work of Captain Alfred Thayer Mahan* (1939). The author, however, is a Navy captain, and his exclusively naval viewpoint should be supplemented with William E. Livezey, *Mahan on Sea Power*

(1947), which contains the essential biographical information while placing Mahan's ideas more correctly in the context of the times.

Additional Sources

Mahan, A. T. (Alfred Thayer), *Letters and papers of Alfred Thayer Mahan,* Annapolis: Naval Institute Press, 1975.

Seager, Robert, *Alfred Thayer Mahan: the man and his letters,* Annapolis, Md.: Naval Institute Press, 1977.

Turk, Richard W., *The ambiguous relationship: Theodore Roosevelt and Alfred Thayer Mahan,* New York: Greenwood Press, 1987. □

Maharishi Mahesh Yogi

The Indian guru Maharishi Mahesh Yogi (born ca. 1911) came to the West as a missionary of traditional Indian thought in popular form and founded the Transcendental Meditation Movement, which reached its height of popularity in the 1960s and 1970s.

Indian sources say Maharishi Mahesh Yogi was born Mahad Prasad Varma on October 18, 1911, the son of a local income tax official in the northern state of Uttar Pradesh, India. His official biography says he graduated from Allahabad University in 1942 with a degree in physics. After working in a factory, he turned to an Indian guru of the Jyotir Math, Swami Brahmananda Saraswati Shankaracharya (1869-1953), whom he would call Guru Dev, "divine teacher." Brahmananda was of the Indian school of religious thought known as Advaita Vedanta, whose major exponent was the eighth century thinker Shankara. Maharishi received the Guru's training for 13 years and as a result of Brahmananda's encouragement dedicated his life to spreading his master's teachings.

After what is officially called a period of meditation in the Himalayas, he decided to develop a popular form of traditional Advaita Vedanta and yogic practices. His first mission to Madras in southern India met with little success, so he decided to bring it to Americans, "the people who are in a habit of adopting things quickly." He arrived in the United States in 1959, after settling first in London where he founded the Spiritual Regeneration Movement, whose goal was to change the world through the practice of Transcendental Meditation (TM).

At first the movement met with little success, but when the British rock group The Beatles announced in 1967 that they had spent some months at his International Academy of Meditation at Rishikesh in the Himalayan foothills, a decade of growth followed. Other actors, actresses, athletes, and politicians began TM in the hope of benefiting from its claims for a life of "success without stress." The early scientific claims, later mostly discounted as based on poorly controlled experiments, were presented to high school and college students through the Students' International Meditation Society, founded in 1966, with phenomenal success.

In 1968 Maharishi announced that his ten-year period of public activity had ended, and the training of meditators was entrusted to a staff of advanced teachers. After tax problems with the Indian government the movement shifted its international headquarters from India, where it was never as popular as it was abroad. After locating in a number of countries, its international headquarters was firmly established in Seelisberg, Switzerland. In 1971 Maharishi International University opened in Los Angeles, and in 1974 it moved to the site of the former Parsons College in Fairfield, Iowa.

In the mid 1970s interest among professionals replaced dwindling campus attraction. TM promised "increased creativity and flexibility, increased productivity, improved job satisfaction, improved relations with supervisors and co-workers." At the same time the movement was organized on multinational corporate lines, and Maharishi began to adopt the life of a corporate executive with conferences, foreign travel, and chauffeured limousines. The movement announced a "World Plan" to change the world through the propagation and practice of TM, and in 1975 Maharishi announced that the "Age of Science" had risen to "The Age of Enlightenment." Thus began the demonstration of the "full significance" of TM.

Though it often denied that it was yoga, "The Age of Enlightenment Course" promised that its students, through untapped abilities, could experience the "siddhis," supernormal powers traditionally identified with yogis in India. TM claimed that its meditators could have "the ability to perceive things which are beyond the reach of the senses, the development of profound intimacy and support from one's physical environment, and even such abilities as disappearing and rising up or levitating at will."

Accepting the movement's claims that TM was nonreligious and beneficial for reducing crime and drug use, a number of government agencies began efforts to involve TM. The U.S. Department of Health, Education and Welfare awarded the World Plan Council of the United States a $40,000 grant. TM's theoretical foundation, called "The Science of Being" and later "The Science of Creative Intelligence" (SCI), was adopted in 1975-1976 as the basis for an elective course in five New Jersey public high schools taught by World Plan trained teachers. But in 1977 a U.S. District Court declared TM/SCI religious, and an appeal to the U.S. Court of Appeals in 1978-1979 upheld that decision.

TM claimed that one does not have to understand the theories behind the practice in order to benefit from it, but as one progresses beyond the introductory level, the metaphysical basis becomes more important. Central to this theory is the traditional Advaita Vedanta (from Shankara) doctrine that the true self is the highest and ultimately the only Reality. Sometimes this Reality is called "God," though it is not a personal being but an unchanging Absolute, an impersonal state of consciousness. The meditational technique is meant to put one in touch with the essential Self, the eternal Being within, by moving one's attention away from the surface consciousness of change, suffering, and stress. One then becomes one with the Absolute Being, an experience which Maharishi calls "God-consciousness."

Introductory sessions which present the "benefits" of TM are followed for the inquirer by a mandated *puja* or service of offering. The student brings a small offering to a room prepared with a table with candles; dishes for water, rice, and sandalpaste; incense; and camphor. On the table is a picture of Guru Dev. The offerings are placed on the table while the student stands before it and the teacher sings a chant in Sanskrit which expresses thanks to the authorized line of teachers and to some of the gods of Hinduism. At the conclusion of the chant, the student is given a secret *mantra* or syllable for the mind and instructed in the technique for using it. Meditators are instructed to meditate for 20 minutes twice a day. Further education may follow and is encouraged, for changing the world requires the spiritual influence of a large number of meditators.

The Maharishi's followers established the Maharishi International University in 1974 in Fairfield, Iowa, where they mixed courses in TM and academic curriculum. The next several years resulted in difficulties for Maharishi and the TM movement. In 1986 the University was sued for $9 million by a former student, Robert Kropinski, and six other people on the grounds of "fraud, neglect, and intentionally inflicting emotional damage." Kropinski charged that although he had taken the course, none of the promised benefits had resulted, and that when he tried to discontinue the university, Maharishi had used "fear and intimidation"

to prevent him from leaving. Maharishi was not a defendant because he could not be found to be served with the papers. Kropinski was eventually awarded $138,000 by a Washington D.C. jury.

In 1992 Maharishi and magician Doug Henning (a follower of TM) announced plans for establishing Maharishi Veda Land, by Niagara Falls, Ontario, Canada. This would have been a $1.5 billion theme park which would combine recreation with "spiritual enlightenment," including a thousand residential units in a "Heaven on Earth" housing development, a Tower of World Peace, and an International Summit Conference Center in addition to 33 rides and attractions and an indoor water park. However, the park never materialized. In 1995 another college, the former Nathaniel Hawthorne College in Antrim, New Hampshire, was purchased by the Maharishi's followers, who said they intended to make it the eastern headquarters for the TM movement. In the 1990s the TM movement turned to politics, forming a new political party, the Natural Law Party. Sponsoring candidates in the United States, Great Britain, Canada, and Australia, the party sought to combine practical politics with Transcendental Meditation. However, they experienced little success electorally.

Further Reading

The TM movement has produced a large body of literature, but Maharishi's writings are found in only three books: an introductory text called *Transcendental Meditation: Serenity Without Drugs* (1968), which was previously published as *The Science of Being and Art of Living* (1963); a commentary on a popular Indian scripture, *On the Bhagavad-Gita: A New Translation and Commentary: Chapters 1-6* (1967); and a collection of the *Meditations of Maharishi Mahesh Yogi* (1968).

Most introductions to the TM movement are either the uncritical approach of believers or the critical and often inaccurate approaches of other religious perspectives. For a scientific perspective on these movements see David G. Bromley and Anson D. Schupe, *Strange Gods* (1981); on TM in particular, see William S. Bainbridge and Daniel H. Jackson, "The Rise and Decline of Transcendental Meditation" in Bryan Wilson, editor, *The Social Impact of New Religious Movements* (1981); an example of a highly critical look at TM is a chapter in James Randi's *Flim-Flam: The Truth About Unicorns, Parapsychology and Other Delusions* (New York, Lippincott & Crowell, 1980); *Celebrating the Dawn-Maharishi Yogi and the TM Movement* by Robert Oates Jr. (Putnam, 1976) is a sympathetic look at the Maharishi and his Activities; articles dealing with the TM movement and its activities in recent years are "University'd Degree Comes with Heavy Dose of Meditation" by Anthony DePalma, *New York Times* (April 26th, 1983); "Trial Under Way for Lawsuit Brought by Maharashi Follower," *New York Times* (December 14th, 1986); "Veda Land-Theme Park for Ontario," *New York Times* (March 22nd, 1992); "Antrim Resets Its Sights for Future from Prison Cells to Free Spirits," by Ralph Jimenez, *Boston Globe* (February 12th, 1995); "Perot's Party Is Not Alone," *New York Times* (June 2nd, 1996). □

Datuk Seri Mahathir Mohamad

Despite a controversial career in politics, Datuk Seri Mahathir bin Mohamad (born 1925) became prime minister of Malaysia in 1981 and then won three consecutive elections. He is listed as the 41st oldest office-holders among the worldwide leadership.

One of the most distinctive of Prime Minister Mahathir's characteristics, his imposing titles notwithstanding, was that he was the first chief executive of Malaysia to come from a modest social background. Whereas the first three prime ministers were members of the "royal families" which gave Malay society its elitist—some would say feudal—quality, Mahathir was the son of a school teacher. His childhood experiences in Alor Star, the provincial capital of Kedah state, included selling fried bananas in the public market.

Just as his relatively humble origins probably would explain his failure to qualify for legal studies in Great Britain, they also may help account for his aggressive, even abrasive, approach to politics. And even though his style was notably "un-Malay," it was used by Mahathir to champion more pro-Malay policies than those advocated by his predecessors. In a political system dominated by conflict between large Chinese and Indian minorities and an "indigenous" Malay majority, it was above all Mahathir's commitment to Malay interests which shaped his career as physician, author, and party and government leader.

Born on December 20, 1925, Datuk Seri Mahathir Mohamad attended a Malay school in Sebrang, Perak, before enrolling in Sultan Abdul Hamid College in Alor Star. When subsequently he went to Singapore for medical studies, at the University of Malaya he already had established a pattern of participation in literary and nationalist study and discussion groups, and he soon developed a reputation as a bold and skillful debater. Nevertheless, he devoted the first decade of his post-graduate life to medicine, first in government service on Langkawi Island and then in private practice beginning in 1957. His status as one of very few Malay doctors contributed to his popularity and success when he first won a seat in the national parliament in 1964.

Even before that first campaign, and certainly after, Mahathir's political identity was closely associated with the United Malay National Organization (UMNO), the dominant political party in Malaysia. It was thus a particularly crucial moment in his career when he was expelled from the party in 1970. The forced vacation from politics gave Mahathir time to complete a controversial book, *The Malay Dilemma,* in which he advanced provocative generalizations about the temperament and character of Malay and Chinese populations. It also greatly elevated his political profile.

Although Mahathir previously had been associated with the "ultra" faction of youthful and chauvinistic UMNO members of Parliament, the immediate cause of the expulsion was his harsh criticism of Prime Minister Tengku Abdul Rahman in the aftermath of serious interethnic violence in May 1969. A personal but widely distributed letter calling on the Tengku to resign was more than party leaders could bear. But at the same time the party was forcing Mahathir out, it was formulating a 20-year economic program, the New Economic Plan, which emphasized nurturance and protection of Malay interests along lines Mahathir already favored.

Before his standing in UMNO was restored in early 1972, Mahathir published *The Malay Dilemma.* The book was widely interpreted as a brief for Malay privilege, but its message included some sweeping cultural and even genetic arguments which were not always clear and convincing. He contended the Malays are the "definitive race" in Malaysia, and they had a right to expect the other ethnic groups to assimilate linguistically and, to some extent, culturally. Shortly after the book appeared it was banned on the ground it might rouse communal antagonism; the book and its author thus gained in notoriety, even though the book's message was at times contradictory and confusing.

After his rehabilitation in the party, Mahathir began a rapid ascent through the ranks of the government. In June 1972 he was the leading vote-getter in the election of UMNO's Supreme Council. Two years later he was named to the cabinet as minister of trade and industry and then as minister of education, a position that each previous prime minister had occupied. When he became deputy prime minister in 1976 his prospects to succeed Tun Hussein Onn as chief executive improved even as his extremist image subsided somewhat.

Mahathir's succession to the leadership of UMNO and the government occurred in 1980 when Tun Hussein Onn resigned for reasons of ill health. Parliamentary elections in the next year consolidated his victory. Because he displayed a close working relationship with his deputy prime minister and former "ultra" associate, Musa Hitam, his administration initially, and generally approvingly, was labeled the "Two-M" administration. Their strong personalities and differences on some policy issues, however, led to Musa's vexed resignation from the government in 1986. UMNO and its United Front allies did quite well in elections held later in the year, but Musa's defection foretold growing discontent within UMNO. In 1988 another former Mahathir ally, Tunku Razaleigh Hamzah, formed a rival Malay party which loomed as a significant challenger to UMNO.

Dissidence with UMNO and in Malaysian politics in general is complex, involving personalities as well as disagreements over various issues. While many of Mahathir's policies were controversial, most withstood the scrutiny and criticism of opponents rather well. The Malaysian economy rebounded from a slow period in the early 1980s. Malays continued to benefit from the implementation of the New Economic Policy, but its application was pragmatic enough to allow a continuing substantial role for Chinese entrepreneurs and, especially at the end of the 1980s, foreign investment. In exhorting Malaysians to "look east" Mahathir was asking them to emulate the Japanese, Koreans, and Taiwanese more than some wanted. And his harsh denial of the legitimacy of some forms of dissent and opposition, as expressed especially in the draconian arrest and detention of 106 varied political and social activists in 1987, prompted considerable domestic and foreign criticism.

Said criticism was reflected in the July 1997 visit of US Secretary of State Madeleine Albright to Kuala Lumpur by his decrying of the United Nations' Universal Declaration of Human Rights. This Declaration was one of the founding documents of the world body and states the inalienable rights of the individual and equal protection before the law.

The Universal Declaration, he told the *New Straits Times* on the eve of the meeting of the Association of Southeast Asian Nations, was an "oppressing" instrument by which the United States and other countries tried to impose their values on Asians, who would prefer to be undisturbed while they concentrate on economic development. Referring to his and other poor nations, the prime minister said, "We need a government which is stable to develop our country and provide the basic needs of our people."

Mahathir was only the latest Asian leader to defend so-called Asian values against the West's supposedly universal principles. Singapore's patriarch, Lee Kwan Yew, is fond of similar pronouncements, which have won him admiration in Beijing especially. In 1993 Asian leaders banded together to issue the Bangkok Declaration, which said they should be free from outside pressure to democratize. "All countries have the right to choose their own systems and values, and other countries have no right to interfere," said a Chinese official at the time.

Mahathir didn't specify which practices condemned by the Universal Declaration were needed for economic growth. The real flaw in Mahathir's argument was the idea that democracy and human rights were bizarre Western fetishes with no appeal to Asians. As an example, Aung San Suu Kyi was a threat to the Burmese military junta not because she was popular in the West but because she had a large following of Burmese who wanted a voice in governing themselves. The Chinese Communists imprisoned prodemocracy dissidents out of fear that those values would resonate with ordinary Chinese. Asians were naturally drawn to the idea they should be allowed to read uncensored books and newspapers, discuss political issues among themselves, worship according to their own faith and be entitled to a fair trial. They had no trouble comprehending the idea of the consent of the governed. Even so, Mahathir Mohamad's ruling coalition was swept back into power in the elections of 1990.

In 1956 Mahathir married another medical doctor, Siti Hasmah binti Haji Mohamad Ali. They had three sons and two daughters. A heart bypass operation in 1989 at age 63 was successful, and Prime Minister Mahathir continued to be an expansive, activist leader of his party and government in the late 1990s.

Further Reading

While there is some doubt as to the continuing relevance of the book *The Malay Dilemma*, published in Singapore (1970), it provides some insight into Mahathir's thinking. Malaysian politics during the period of that book's prominence are covered in Karl von Vorys, *Democracy Without Consensus* (1975). Another treatment is provided by John Funston, *Malay Politics in Malaysia: A Study of UMNO and PAS* (1980). Mahathir's policies are reviewed in *Ethnicity and the Economy: The State, Chinese Business, and Multinationals in Malaysia* (1989) by James Jesudason. □

Vardhamana Mahavira

Vardhamana Mahavira (ca. 540-470 B.C.), called the Jina, was an Indian ascetic philosopher and the principal founder of Jainism—one of the major religions of the Indian subcontinent.

Vardhamana Mahavira was born in northern India during the turbulent religious and political upheavals of the middle of the 1st millennium B.C. He was a contemporary of the Buddha, and in many respects their lives are similar. Mahavira's father was chief of the Jnatrika clan, an indigenous oligarchical tribe. Mahavira's tribal affiliation is reflected in one of his later epithets, Nigantha Nataputta, which means literally "the naked ascetic of the Jnatrika clan."

Despite his royal upbringing, his religious sensibilities drove Mahavira inexorably to renounce his worldly ties at the age of 30 and embark on a search for ultimate spiritual truth. Traditional religious practices were centered in an archaic magical and sacrificial cult dominated by a hereditary priestly elite. But for Mahavira and for many others the external rites could not solve the basic spiritual enigmas defined by the problem of transmigration: the soul of every sentient creature is entrapped in the phenomenal world, suffering an endless round (*samsara*) of deaths and rebirths as a result of inward moral defilements engendered through perverted attitudes and acts (*karma*).

The goal was to obtain spiritual release from this karmic bondage through an inward self-discipline (the yoga) designed to eliminate its libidinal and material causes. For 12 years Mahavira lived a life of radical physical asceticism, mortifying the flesh and struggling to purify his soul of its Karmic burden. Finally, at the age of 42, he achieved spiritual purification and enlightenment; he was now the Jina (conqueror)—the source of the traditional name applied to his followers, the Jains. He preached for another 30 years, founding an increasingly wide circle of monastic and lay followers, and died about the age of 72.

His Teaching

In Jain tradition Mahavira is represented as the twentyfourth—the last and most influential—of the great teachers of Jainism. Mahavira's teachings reflect a very ancient indigenous tradition. Every discrete natural phenomenon has a life-force (*jiva*), a soul which is a substantial entity. This includes gods, demons, human beings, animals, insects, plants, and even inanimate objects like stones. All contain souls, originally pure and translucent, entrapped in the material stuff of the phenomenal universe, moving up and down the scale of life-forms, from birth to birth—higher or lower—as the result of *karma.*

Furthermore, *karma* is not understood simply as a causal system. It is in itself a kind of malevolent and defiling substance which adheres to the soul like dirt. Every debased act or thought will bring in more karmic contamination, weighing the soul down like ballast and sweeping it into the rebirth process and a worldly status appropriate to the degree of moral contamination. To attain salvation the soul must be freed from these burdensome defilements, first by preventing the influx of fresh *karma,* principally through the practice of noninjury (*ahimsa*) to all creatures, and second, by rigorous physical asceticism in which the wasting away of the body is regarded as an outward sign of the sloughing off of karmic matter.

The greatest ascetic discipline in the tradition is the rite of *sallekhana*—voluntary self-starvation conducted systematically over a 12-year period. It combines the mandates of both asceticism and noninjury, since the eating of food, even of plants, and the drinking of water entail the ingestion and killing of vegetable and microorganic life. The fully committed Jain monk is obliged to sweep the path before him lest he step on an insect, to strain his water, and to avoid movement in the dark and even bathing since both actions might harm insects and organic life. But when final and complete purification is attained, the soul rises to a transcendental realm of pure omniscience far above the highest heavens—even of the gods.

Monastic Order and Laity

The Jina's teaching appears to be profoundly pessimistic and in certain respects highly irrational; but in fact it is, given its presuppositions, supremely optimistic and has therapeutic consequences for the human personality and social organization. First, it is a basic tenet of the teaching that in the transmigratory process the soul attains rebirth in human form only once in a vast spectrum of cosmic time; and it is in this human state that one is privileged to hear and practice the Jina's message of salvation; consequently this lends immense dignity and urgency to the human life.

The monk is described as joyful and cheerful, enduring all hardships for the sake of this extraordinary blessing. Second, the believer abides by the rules of a generalized ethical system which has—like Buddhism—universal potential for social reconstruction. Third, the extreme emphasis on noninjury to sentient creatures, even inanimate objects, had an unusual consequence for the laity: occupations involving manual labor, cultivation, cutting, sawing, hammering, and so on, were excluded; and consequently the Jain laity found its social grounding chiefly among the mercantile and banking classes.

Added to this was the fact that the ascetic yoga promoted an economic ethic in which disciplined control over economic resources (analogous to the Puritan work ethic) resulted in capital accumulation and mastery for their own sake—not for self-indulgence. Lay piety is expressed in adherence to a strictly vegetarian diet and in fasts and penance emulating the monastic style at appropriate times during the year.

The relative simplicity of the ascetic yoga and clear-cut lines of patriarchal succession allowed for the maintenance of doctrinal discipline and effective integration of lay members. The only major schisms in the tradition occurred with the formation of the two primary Jain sects: the Digambaras ("space-clad"), holding to the old tradition of ascetic nudity; and the Shvetambaras ("white-clad"), allowing their adherents to wear clothes—probably as an accommodation to the preferences of adherents with middle-class sensibilities.

The worship of images of the Jain saints is common practice, but the teaching remains basically atheistic; the later incorporation of Hindu deities, however, provides possibilities for theistic worship. In its political theory Jainism was basically patrimonial, but it stressed, as did early Buddhism, the necessity of virtuous self-discipline as a moral precondition for legitimate rule.

Further Reading

Because of the difficult problems of historical reconstruction, there is no work on the life of Mahavira. Background works on Jainism include Hermann Jacobi, trans., *Gaina Sutras,* "Sacred Books of the East Series," vols. 22 and 45 (1894 and 1895; repr. Delhi, 1964); Margaret Stevenson, *The Heart of Jainism* (1915); Jagmandar Jaini, *Outlines of Jainism* (1916); and Chimanlal J. Shah, *Jainism in North India, 800 B.C.-A.D. 526* (1932). Indian sources include Herbert Warren, *Jainism in Western Garb* (Madras, 1912); Nathmal Tatia, *Studies in Jaina Philosophy* (Benares, 1951); and Mohan Lal Mehta,

Outlines of Jaina Philosophy (Bangalore, 1954). For general background consult W.H. Moreland and Atul Chandra Chatterjee, *A Short History of India* (1936; 3d ed. 1953); A.L. Basham, *The Wonder That Was India* (1937; rev. ed. 1963); J.C. Powell-Price, *A History of India* (1955); and Michael Edwardes, *A History of India* (1961). ☐

The Mahdi

Mohammed Ahmed (ca. 1844-1885) was an Islamic puritan, reformer, and military leader of the Sudan. He is better known as the Mahdi.

Mohammed Ahmed was born on an island in the Nile River near Dongola in what is now the northern Sudan. His father was a boatbuilder. Mohammed Ahmed took an early and intense interest in Islamic mysticism and asceticism, becoming a religious teacher and joining the Sammaniya order in 1861. Gathering pupils and disciples about him, he established his retreat on Aba Island in the White Nile south of Khartoum, where he earned a reputation for holiness and mystical powers.

Messianic Leader

His religious experiences and contemplations on Aba Island caused Mohammed Ahmed to feel that Allah had selected him as the true Mahdi, the right-guided one or the messianic leader called to battle against immorality and corruption and for the rejuvenation and purification of Islam. He saw himself as sent by Allah to purge Islam of its evils and to return it to the purity of the faith of Mohammed the Prophet. In addition, his theological views had eschatological overtones in that he not only viewed himself as the rightful head of the Islamic community fulfilling the role of Mohammed the Prophet but as the ultimate figure presiding over the end of time.

Mohammed Ahmed found ideal conditions in the central and northern Sudan for a mass emotional movement, not only in the religious devotion of the Moslem population of the area but especially in the resentment of the inhabitants toward the corruption and oppression of the Turkish and Egyptian rulers who had dominated the Upper Nile region since the reign of Mohammed Ali earlier in the 19th century. Mohammed Ahmed thus found support from the Sudanese for a variety of reasons and motives—from pious and religious believers who accepted his puritan and reformist views, from nomadic groups who opposed all governmental restrictions, and from others who profited from the slave trade and rejected efforts of the Egyptian khedive Ismail and Gen. Gordon to eliminate it.

Mohammed Ahmed's movement for reform and reorganization spread rapidly following his public appearance as the Mahdi in June 1881 because of its wide appeal. But the weakness and indecision of Egyptian authorities because of economic and political problems within Egypt played a key role in the success of the Mahdi's campaign. The Egyptian government declared its bankruptcy in 1876 owing to, at least in part, Khedive Ismail's efforts to build a vast Egyptian empire in the Sudan and Upper Nile area. Foreign debt supervisors secured considerable influence and power in Egypt in the late 1870s, thus popularizing the nationalist movement against this foreign presence and culminating in Col. Arabi's coup of early 1882 and the consequent British intervention and occupation later that year.

Military Victories

Successive victories over halfhearted Egyptian attempts to overcome the Mahdi vastly strengthened the new movement through the acquisition of much military equipment and the apparent proof of Allah's support. After the British occupation of Egypt in 1882, the new British authorities in Cairo ignored the Sudan, but the Egyptian government did seek to demonstrate its own power despite British overrule by ordering a new campaign to oust the Mahdi. In 1883 the Mahdists overwhelmed the Egyptian army of Gen. Hicks, and Great Britain ordered the withdrawal of all Egyptian troops and officials from the Sudan. How could Britain reestablish financial order in Egypt if the country's resources were being utilized in expensive campaigns in the Sudan?

The victorious followers of the Mahdi occupied most of the Sudan; Lord Cromer, the British consul general in Cairo, sent the famous Gen. Gordon to carry out and accelerate the Egyptian evacuation. Khartoum, the capital and center of the country, fell to the Mahdi in January 1885 following Gen. Gordon's legendary and foolhardy defense.

The Mahdi had successfully expelled foreign influences and had united most of the Sudan area in a unique religiopolitical movement. According to Mahdist theology and theocracy, the Mahdi held his superior power directly from Allah and then delegated power directly to others as he chose. The Mahdi died in 1885, probably of typhus, but his theocratic state continued for another 13 years under his follower and friend the caliph Abdullahi. The British general Kitchener reoccupied the Sudan primarily with Egyptian troops in 1898, not only because of any threat the Mahdist movement itself posed to the British position in Egypt but because of British imperial needs in the partition of Africa among the great powers of Europe.

To members of the Ansar (Helpers) movement today, a powerful religious brotherhood and an important but conservative political factor in the Republic of the Sudan, the Mahdi was a nationalist leader who liberated the people of the Sudan from alien oppression and began the modern history of the country.

Further Reading

An old and romantic view of the Mahdi is in the biography by Richard A. Bermann, *The Mahdi of Allah* (1931). The Mahdist movement is well treated in A. B. Theobald, *The Mahdiya: A History of the Anglo-Egyptian Sudan, 1881-1899* (1951), and in P. M. Holt, *The Mahdist State in the Sudan, 1881-1898* (1958). For general background on the Sudan see a work by a Sudanese, Mekki Shibeika, *The Independent Sudan* (1959), and P. M. Holt, *A Modern History of the Sudan* (1966).

Additional Sources

Farwell, Byron, *Prisoners of the Mahdi: the story of the Mahdist revolt which frustrated Queen Victoria's designs on the Sudan . . .*, New York: W.W. Norton, 1989. □

King Mahendra

King Mahendra (1920-1972) was the ninth Shah dynasty ruler of Nepal. The period of his rule (1955-1972) was marked by a wide variety of experiments in political systems and approaches to economic and social development.

King Mahendra (Bir Bikram Shah Dev), the ninth Shah (Gorkha) dynasty ruler of Nepal, was born in Kathmandu on July 11, 1920, the eldest son of King Tribhuvan and Queen Kanti. Mahendra's first three decades were a period in Nepal's history when the Shah dynasty ruled in name only and political authority was held by the Rana family. Mahendra was not allowed to participate in the political or social life in Kathmandu except under strict Rana supervision, nor did he attend a "modern" educational institution in Nepal, India, or abroad as did many of the sons of elite families prior to 1950. This sense of exclusion and deprivation, intellectually and politically, strongly influenced his political views and values even after the overthrow of the Rana "system" in 1951.

Mahendra married Indra R. L. Rana in 1940. She bore him three sons and three daughters before her death in 1950. Mahendra then married Indra's sister, Ratna R. L. Rana, in December 1952—over opposition from political party leaders and, reportedly, from his father King Tribhuvan because she came from a powerful branch of the Rana family. This was one of the first occasions on which Mahendra demonstrated the determination to make his own decisions, a characteristic evident after he came to the throne.

King Tribhuvan died on March 14, 1955, and Mahendra succeeded him on the throne. The period from the overthrow of the Ranas in 1951 until 1955 had been a transitional phase in Nepal's politics with no constitution, no elected parliament, and no responsible cabinet system. The executive, nominally acting under the authority of the monarch, was composed of various political party leaders who were, in fact, responsible to no one but lacked much political clout. King Tribhuvan was reluctant to assert a forceful role for the monarchy, but gradually felt compelled to do so. The government of India, which had "supervised" the replacement of the Rana system in 1951, found it necessary to serve as the power behind the throne in the Nepalese government whenever decisions had to be made.

King Mahendra, in contrast to his father, was not prepared to see such a tenuous political system prolonged and introduced a series of experiments shortly after ascending the gaddi (throne). His first step (1956) was a purge of the bureaucracy with the objective of making it a more efficient body in the implementation of policies—for example, Ne-

pal's first five-year plan. By 1959 he had, on his own initiative, introduced a parliamentary-type constitution that was largely modelled on India's democratic constitution, but with some protection for the institution of the monarchy. In the spring of 1959 Nepal's first free popular election based on universal franchise was held. The Nepali Congress Party swept two-thirds of the seats in the election, and the leader of the party, B. P. Koirala, was appointed prime minister. King Mahendra assumed the largely titular head of state position given the monarchy under the 1959 constitution, did not intervene with the governance of the country, and spent most of his time touring Nepal or travelling abroad.

King Mahendra noted with some apprehension, however, the ways in which the Nepali Congress was concentrating political power in its hands. Presumably because of fear about the future of the monarchy under these circumstances, Mahendra used the emergency powers given the ruler in the 1959 constitution to suspend the constitution, arrest most of the government leaders, conduct a wholesale purge of the bureaucracy, and concentrate political authority in his own hands. He then introduced in 1962 a new constitutional system based—in theory—on the traditional Hindu social/political institution, the Panchayat (Council of Five). The underlying objective of Panchayat Raj (Rule by Panchayats) was to be the decentralization of political power. As it worked out in reality, however, it constituted a centralization of power, with the final voice on almost any decision, no matter how trivial, resting with the palace and the group of high bureaucrats who served as the principal consultants to the king on policy matters.

By the time of King Mahendra's death on January 31, 1972, there were evident strains and deficiencies in the constitutional and political system he had constructed in the 1960s. In his final years Mahendra amended the 1962 constitution and made some efforts to bring talented and experienced officials into the key positions in the administrative process. But this had limited effect on the political system, which remained authoritarian, with the monarch as the fulcrum around which everything moved. It was quite evident by the time of his death that more basic political changes were required to meet the demands of an increasingly complex and developing society.

King Mahendra's reign, 1955-1972, was notable for a wide variety of experiments in political systems, ranging from the classically Western democratic parliamentary system to more authoritarian political structures based, in theory at least, on traditional Hindu concepts and institutions. There was a similar openness to different approaches to economic and social development—for example, moderate but pragmatic land reform and legal code liberalization programs. At all times, however, Mahendra maintained a special concern for the viability of the monarchical system.

Further Reading

While there is no unofficial biography on King Mahendra as yet, several studies of Nepali politics during his regnum focus on his critical role. Some of these with diverse analyses of his rule include: Pashupate S. J. B. Rana and Karmal P. Malla, *Nepal*

in Perspective (1973); Anirudra Gupta, *Politics in Nepal* (1964); and Bhuwan Lal Joshi and Leo E. Rose, *Democratic Innovations in Nepal* (1966).

Additional Sources

Shaha, Rishikesh, *Three decades and two kings (1960-1990): eclipse of Nepal's partyless monarchic rule*, New Delhi: Sterling Publishers, 1990. ☐

Samuel Maherero

Samuel Maherero (ca. 1854–1923) was the Supreme Chief of the Herero nation, who led his people in revolt against German occupation of Herero lands.

The scramble for Africa by the European powers at the close of the 19th century had tragic consequences for the Herero people of South West Africa. In its quest for a presence in southern Africa, the German imperial government claimed territory along the Atlantic Coast, north of British- and Afrikaner-settled South Africa, and south of Portuguese Angola. The Germans claimed it as German South West Africa (now the independent country of Namibia), and German interests vied for land with the cattle-herding Herero and Nama peoples of the territory. The settlers' demands for land and cattle and the ruthless policies of a German military leader resulted in the almost complete annihilation of the Herero people under the leadership of paramount chief Samuel Maherero.

In 1904, when Samuel Maherero led his people in an uprising against the Germans, the Herero population was approximately 80,000. In little more than a year, more than 64,000 had been killed in battle or died in the desert where they had been chased by German troops. Some historians consider the German policy of extermination of the Herero as a prelude to German policy of genocide against the Jews in Europe 30 years later.

Before 1884, the presence of Germans in South West Africa was limited to *Rhenish* (German) missionaries who had set up missions in the early 1800s under the auspices of the London Missionary Society. Later in the century, German and British prospectors came in search of gold and diamonds. The imperial German government raised its flag in 1884 over Angra Pequena and a stretch of coast purchased from a chief of the Nama people. At the time, the German foreign office was more interested in blocking the British from access to the interior than in settling the area; a governor-general and a small contingent of troops were sent to administer the territory.

Initially the presence of a few German civil servants made little impact. When the Germans arrived, the Herero controlled vast areas of the interior, running from the Atlantic Coast in the west to the Kalahari Desert in the east. They had the largest population and were the wealthiest of the peoples of South West Africa. Unlike most Bantu-speakers, the Herero were nomadic cattle herders whose sole basis for wealth was the size of their cattle herds.

To the south of the Hereros lived the Nama, descendants of the Khoikhoin, a nomadic pastoral people who are thought to be the earliest inhabitants of southwestern Africa. With a population in the late 1880s of about 20,000, the Namas ranged from the Orange River in the south up to a rough border along the Swakop River, separating them from the Herero.

Despite the vastness of the area (320,827 square miles) and the small population groups, the several African chiefs and their people competed for control over grazing lands. The Nama asked the Oorlams, recent newcomers from South Africa skilled in the use of rifles, to help push the Herero out of their territory and back to the north of the Swakop River. Fighting as "commando" units, the Oorlams forced the Herero beyond the Auas Mountains to Okahandja. In doing so, the Oorlams took the Herero's capital for their own and called it Windhoek. In 1850, the Oorlams attacked the Herero at Okahandja and began a long conflict between the two groups. The raiding and fighting finally ended when Oorlam chief Jonker Afrikaner died in 1861. When Herero chief Tjamuaha also died in 1861, he was succeeded by Kamaherero, the father of Samuel Maherero.

Determined to be free of the Oorlams and their Nama allies, Kamaherero crushed them in a battle at Otjimbingwe in 1863 and so became a dominant force in the territory. Fighting and raiding among the groups continued until 1870 when Rhenish missionaries, who had settled in Otjimbingwe in 1864, negotiated a peace treaty that remained in force for ten years.

Fighting resumed in August 1880. In revenge for cattle stolen by the Namas, Kamaherero ordered the death of all Namas living in his territory. About 200 Namas are reported to have been killed. With the resumption of fighting, the British—who had had a minor presence in the area and who had offered the German missionaries some protection from the warring groups—retreated hastily to the port area of Walvis Bay, leaving the territory unprotected and open to the Germans.

In 1884, the German foreign office established an official presence in South West Africa when it raised the German flag over Angra Pequena, an area claimed by Adolf Ludderitz, and a strip of land along the coast running 20 miles inland that he had purchased from Nama chief Josef Frederiks for 160 rifles and £600.

The Germans were hoping to obtain land further inland but Herero supreme chief Kamaherero steadfastly refused to sell his people's lands. Since Herero land belonged to the community at large, the *kapteins* or traditional leaders did not have the authority to sell it. Europeans were given permission to use land, and when they died or moved the land reverted back to the tribe.

Wanting to keep costs and involvement in the territory at a minimum, the German foreign office sent out a few civil servants and a high commissioner to represent its interests. Heinrich Göring, the father of Nazi leader Hermann Göring, was appointed imperial commissioner to South West Africa.

Early German policy was to offer "Protection Treaties" to the local peoples. In theory, the Germans offered protection to the chief and his clan while supporting the chief's jurisdiction over his people. In exchange, the chief promised not to cede any land or make treaties with anyone else without German approval. The Herero signed a treaty with the Germans, hoping to buy some protection from the Nama. But the Germans never intended to get involved with tribal disputes. They were more interested in playing one group against the other.

In 1888, reports of a gold strike brought in German prospectors and renewed British interest in the territory. Though reports of the find turned out to be a hoax, German foreign policy became more aggressive because of British inroads in South West Africa. Britain had recently granted Bechuanaland (Botswana) protectorate status, and the Germans wanted to block British expansion. The German foreign office sent Curt von Francois in charge of a small force of men in June 1889 under strict orders not to antagonize the Herero. From German accounts, it is evident that Francois was not able to conceal his personal animosity toward the Herero. He requested reinforcements and six months later the German military presence increased to 50 soldiers and two weeks later to 150.

In October 1890, when the Herero had temporarily withdrawn from Windhoek to move south to put pressure on the Nama, Francois took advantage of their absence and occupied the Herero capital. Later that month, on the 27th, Herero Supreme Chief Kamaherero died. Although his son Nikodemus was first in line to succeed him, the choice fell to another son, Samuel.

The fighting between the Nama and the Herero continued unabated. From the German perspective, the intertribal fighting minimized any genuine threat to the Germans, but the unstable nature of the territory frightened away prospective German settlers. In 1890, Imperial Chancellor Göring wrote to Hendrik Witbooi, an educated leader of a Nama subgroup, and asked him to stop attacking the Herero who were under German protection. Witbooi wrote to Samuel Maherero suggesting they cease fighting. He said in his letter that peace between the Nama and the Herero was always a possibility. He also said that Maherero's alliance with the Germans was unnatural and that the only reason for it was that Maherero hated the Nama so much. Two years later, in November 1892, when the Herero learned that Boer farmers from the Orange Free State in South Africa were coming north to settle, Samuel Maherero agreed to a treaty with Hendrik Witbooi. Mediated by Hermanus van Wyk, *kaptein* of the Rehobothers, the treaty brought to an end nearly 100 years of fighting.

But the peace treaty between the two rival chiefs alarmed the Germans, and they made a preemptive strike against the Witboois. In preparation, the German foreign office sent out an additional 214 men and 2 officers. The reinforcements arrived in March 1893, and in April, under Curt von Francois, German troops made a surprise attack on Hornkranz, the Witboois' capital. The Witboois were soon joined by other Nama tribesmen, and their numbers swelled from 250 to 600 men. Starting out with 100 rifles and 120 horses, they had 400 rifles and 300 horses in six months of raiding German supplies. The German foreign office recalled Von Francois for his failure and replaced him with Major Theodor Leutwein.

At first, Leutwein left the Witboois alone as he attacked and subdued smaller tribes. Maintaining divisions among the Africans was essential to continued German domination. In the latter part of 1894, Leutwein set about to alienate the Herero from their land without fighting. First, he paid Samuel Maherero a salary of 20,000 marks in exchange for his agreeing to redefine the southern boundary of Hereroland. Then he obtained Maherero's agreement to establish a so-called Crown territory (land placed at the disposal of the German governor) in the north at the White Nosob. Most affected by this treaty were Herero headmen Tjetjo, Nikodemus, and Kahimemua, who were already distressed by Samuel Maherero's dealings with the Germans.

Alarmed at the growing opposition among the Herero to his succession and his dealings with the Germans, Maherero decided to withdraw from Okahandja and move to Osona. He sought out Leutwein, and at a meeting in June 1894 Maherero said he would be "pleased to ask for a German garrison to be stationed Okahandja to protect him." Thus, without a shot being fired, German troops occupied the Herero capital.

Leutwein boasted of his successful co-option of Samuel Maherero in a letter to the foreign office: "His friendship has enabled us to remain masters of Hereroland despite our modest protective force. In order to please us, he did more harm to his people than we could ever have done by relying on our strength alone."

With the Herero neutralized, Leutwein turned back to the task of bringing the Witboois under control. When reinforcements arrived, he went after the Witboois, who had hidden out in the Noukloof Mountains. In their pursuit, the Germans suffered heavy casualties, but they finally forced the Witboois to surrender after 18 months of warfare. In September 1894, the Witboois signed a Treaty of Protection and Friendship with the Germans. Deprived of all their cattle and dependent on handouts from the Germans, the Witboois agreed to fight against any German enemy.

Leutwein's divide-and-rule policy was effective. When two subgroups, the Herero Mbandjeru and the Nama Khauas rose up against German settlers and forces, Samuel Maherero was bound to fight against his fellow Herero in support of the Germans. And Hendrik Witbooi, in honor of his treaty with the Germans, did not support the Nama forces. Leutwein confiscated the cattle belonging to the Mbandjeru for the settlers and his troops. Several years later, he confirmed that he had seized 12,000 head of cattle from Mbandjeru between 1896-97.

The Herero came under further pressure in 1897 when rinderpest killed between 90 and 95% of their remaining cattle. Germans vaccinated their own herds and cut their losses substantially. With the diminished herds, the price of cattle soared, but the Herero could not compete in the market. In a few years' time, the settlers had acquired nearly 50,000 head of cattle. From then on, the white settlers entered the cattle market and began to raise cattle for a profit. The Herero were impoverished and many were forced to work for the Germans on the railway or in the mines in South Africa.

Increasingly, the settler population rubbed against the African people. Cheating the Africans out of their cattle, they took their land and gouged them in commercial transactions. In the two years between 1901 and 1903, the settler population had swelled from 310 to 3,000. The railway from Swakopmund on the coast to Windhoek was nearing completion. Having confiscated Herero land to build the railway, the Germans wanted an additional 12-mile-wide strip on either side, plus water rights. Maherero agreed to give up the land but nothing more.

In 1903, a subclan of the Nama, the Bondelswarts, rose up against the Germans in the southern part of the country. In response, Leutwein removed almost all his troops from Hereroland and sent them south to quell the uprising. In the absence of the troops, Maherero urged his people to rise up against the Germans. The Herero uprising began on January 12, 1904. In one stroke, Supreme Chief Samuel Maherero reversed his devastating policy of collaboration with the Germans and united the Herero people. Leutwein was forced to conclude a hasty peace treaty with the Bondelswarts so he could move his troops back north.

Several days before January 12, Maherero had sent a note to Witbooi, through the trusted emissary van Wyk, to ask the Nama to join the Herero against the Germans. Van Wyk betrayed Maherero's trust and delivered the note to the German military leader. In his note, Samuel Maherero said:

> I appeal to you my brother, not to hold aloof from the uprising, but to make your voice heard so that all Africa may take up arms against the Germans. Let us die fighting rather than die as a result of maltreatment, imprisonment or some other calamity. Tell all the kapteins down there to rise and do battle.

Unaware of Maherero's appeal, the Nama contingents honored their treaty with the Germans and allowed them to concentrate solely on fighting the Herero.

For the first six months, the Herero were on the offensive. They had caught the Germans ill prepared and undermanned. In an encounter in April, when the Herero encircled the main German detachment at Oviumbo, Leutwein ordered his troops to retreat and remained on the defensive until reinforcements arrived. Toward the end of May, the Herero moved northeast to the Waterberg Plateau, away from the railway line and the German's supply lines.

Criticized by the foreign office for the retreat at Oviumbo, Leutwein submitted his resignation and awaited his replacement, Lieutenant-General Lothar von Trotha. Historian Horst Drechsler describes Von Trotha as a "veritable butcher in uniform, who embarked on a campaign of annihilation against the Herero." Arriving in June, Von Trotha issued what is referred to as his "Extermination Orders":

> The Herero people must depart from the country. If they do not, I shall force them to, with large cannons.

Within the German boundary every Herero, whether found armed or unarmed, with or without cattle, will be shot.

Von Trotha decided to engage the Herero at Waterberg. The Waterberg Plateau looms up out of the flat Namibian landscape, protected on three sides by the walls of the escarpment. On the east, it slopes into the Omaheke desert in Botswana. Von Trotha ordered six German detachments to spread out on the three sides of the plateau, with the smallest contingent in the southeast. The attack began on August 11 from the west where he had positioned the strongest detachment. With their superior weaponry, the Germans overwhelmed the Herero. The Germans had 30 artillery pieces and 12 machine-guns to the Herero's 6,000 rifles and dwindling ammunition supplies. Attacked from the west, the Herero had no alternative but to flee into the Omaheke desert to the southeast. A study of a report by the German general staff confirms that this was an intentional plan:

If, however, the Herero were to break through [in the east], such an outcome of the battle could only be even more desirable in the eyes of the German Command because the enemy would then seal his own fate, being doomed to die of thirst in the arid sandveld.

Once the Herero were beyond the waterholes, the Germans formed a line of defense along the 150-mile border, denying the Herero access to water. Those Herero who tried to go northward were repulsed by German troops. The cordon was maintained until mid-1905. Out of a population of 80,000, 64,000 Herero died, most of them from thirst and starvation in the desert.

As reports reached Witbooi of how wretchedly the Germans were treating the Herero, Witbooi and the entire Nama nation took up arms against the Germans in October 1904. A year later, in October 1905, Hendrik Witbooi was killed. Although the Namas continued the fight, engaging 14,000 German soldiers in guerrilla warfare for two more years, the Nama uprising had come too late. As Drechsler says, "It was nothing short of a tragedy that the Herero and Nama took up arms successively rather than simultaneously against the hated German yoke."

Following Witbooi's death, Von Trotha left South West Africa. With Von Trotha gone and the Germans realizing they could not win the war against the Nama, they finally negotiated an end to the war in 1907. By then half the Nama population of 20,000 had died.

Samuel Maherero and his three sons survived the desert. They made their way to British territory and eventually settled at Lake Ngami in Botswana. Samuel Maherero died in exile in 1923. His remains were returned to South West Africa, and he was buried with his grandfather and father in Okahandja. Every year, the Herero gather at the grave site to commemorate their leaders.

Further Reading

Drechsler, Horst. *Let Us Die Fighting.* Akademie-Verlag, 1966.

Jenny, Hans. *South West Africa: Land of Extremes.* Southwest Africa Scientific Society. 1976.

Lau, Brigitte. *Namibia in Jonker Afrikaner's Time.* Namibia Archives, 1987.

Soggot, David. *Namibia: The Violent Heritage.* Rex Collings, 1986. □

Najib Mahfuz

Najib Mahfuz (born 1912) was Egypt's foremost novelist and the first Arab to win the Nobel Prize in literature. He had wide influence in the Arab world and was the author from that area best known to the West in the latter half of the 20th century.

Najib Mahfuz was born in the popular quarter Hayy Al-Jamaliyya in Cairo, Egypt, on December 12, 1912, to a middle-class merchant family. During his high school years he began to read the Arabic classics as well as the Western ones that he could find in translation. He proceeded to major in philosophy at Cairo University, and after graduating in 1934 he worked his way up the bureaucracy as a civil servant. He continued to work until he retired as director of the Cinema Organization, after which he worked as a consultant to several governmental cultural organizations. He was a frequent contributor to the daily newspaper *Al-Ahram,* where most of his writings appeared in serial form before being published in book form. Mahfuz was married and the father of two daughters.

An avowed disciple of the pioneers of the literary Rennaisance of the early 20th century such as Al-Aqqad, Salama Musa, and Taha Husayn, Mahfuz—unlike his mentors and many of his peers—never studied abroad, and indeed infrequently traveled outside of Egypt. Therefore, his knowledge of the West and Western literary forms came primarily from his profuse readings. Mahfuz, who is sometimes referred to as the "Balzac of the Arabs," was an ardent admirer of the Russian classics. Tolstoy, Turgenev, and Dostoevsky were often quoted by him in interviews as the examples he would like to emulate.

Mahfuz's early writings have been categorized traditionally as historical in that he dealt with subjects inspired by ancient Egyptian history. In an interview to the literary magazine *Al-Hawadess,* Mahfuz corrected this misconception by saying that only one of the early three works—*Kifah Tiba* (The Struggle for Thebes, 1944)—was strictly a historical novel. The other two—*Abath Al-Aqdar* (The Meanderings of Fate, 1938) and *Radobis* (1943)—were fictional stories inspired by folk epics.

A new phase of realistic writings began with a series of novels that delved into more contemporary subject matter and characters. *Al-Qahira Al-Jadida* (New Cairo, 1945) ushered in the genre of novels that more specifically come to be associated with the author. Most of the novels after these bear names of the old-time quarters of Cairo, names that resonate with a continuous history of over a thousand years. *Khan Al-Khalil* (1946), *Zuqaq al-Midaq* (1947), and his trilogy, *Al-Thulathia* (comprising *Bayn al-Qasrayn, Qasr al-Shauq, Al-Sukkariyya*), recall throbbing arteries of a great city.

This epoch-making trilogy, considered his masterpiece and written between 1946 and 1952, traces the radical changes undergone by a Cairene bourgeois family dominated by the declining figure of its tyrannical patriarch, Ahmad Abd a-Jawad. In this trilogy, Mahfuz painstakingly follows the changes taking place in Egyptian society and identity through the lives of the members of this extended family. The cultural and ideological turmoil that Egypt experienced after the turn of the century came to a head by the end of World War II. It was masterfully handled by Mahfuz through his characters, who range in their ideologies from the extreme right fundamentalists of the Muslim Brothers to the extreme Leftists fighting British colonialism and seeking independence for a free Egypt. The trilogy was considered a distinctive contribution to world literature in that it was not an imitation of a Western model but a unique contribution of Egyptian genius. The trilogy was awarded Egypt's highest literary honor in 1957.

Al-Sarab (The Mirage, 1948) is generally looked upon as a turning point in Mahfuz's development. Here he probes into psychological considerations for the understanding of his characters' behavior. *Bidaya wa Nihaya* (The Beginning and the End, 1949) also belongs to this phase

In an area of the world where literacy is still not widespread, radio, cinema, and television play a crucial role in the education and entertainment of the people. Many of the writings of Mahfuz have been successfully adapted to the screen and stage. This enabled him to become widely known and admired throughout the Arab world. Mahfuz also wrote many scripts for works of other writers, which may perhaps explain the mastery of cinematic techniques that is manifest in his own writings.

Works Dealt With Philosophical Questions

Awlad Haritna (Sons of our Alley, 1967) augurs an era of neo-realism in which he questioned and probed ideas, concepts, and philosophies of the God-man relationship, good and evil, and life and death. These existential questionings are even more apparent in his short stories, which have been collected in several anthologies. His preoccupation with Sufi (Islamic mysticism) considerations and apparent discrepancies of 'ilm (knowledge) and *iman* (faith) are poignantly handled throughout his later writings, and specifically in his voluminous epic tale *Al-Harafish*. Mahfuz's later writings, such as *Alf Layla wa Layla* (A Thousand and One Nights, 1982), are modeled on its prototype. *Al'Ai'sh fi al-Hakika* (He Who Lives in Truth, 1985) was considered by him more as an historical novel than fictional writing.

Writings Encountered Controversy

His novels have often gotten him into trouble with authorities, both in his native land and elsewhere in the Arab world. *The Children of Gabalawi* (1959) was banned in Egypt because it was seen as offensive to Islam and considered blasphemous by many Muslims. In the 1960's

Mahfuz found himself in trouble with the government because several of his novels were considered allegorical attacks on the administration of President Gamal Nasser. Because of his support for Egyptian President Anwar Sadat's peace treaty with Israel in 1979, Mafuz's writings were banned in many Arab countries during the 1980's, although the prohibitions were eventually lifted. Women often play a significant role in his novels, going beyond their traditional passive role in Egyptian society.

First Arab Wins Literature Nobel

In October of 1988 Mahfuz was awarded the Nobel Prize in literature, the first Arab writer—and second from the African continent—to be so rewarded. A modest man with a dry sense of humor, Mahfuz, according to the report in the October 14th edition of the *New York Times,* took his Nobel in stride. The citation from the Swedish Academy of Letters said his work was "now clearsightedly realistic, now evocatively ambiguous," to which Mahfuz commented, "Clarity is valuable, but ambiguity has its value too." Asked about his plans for spending the $300,000 prize money, *New York Times* reported that he looked at his spouse and replied, "That is my wife's job." Perhaps more than any other Arab writer, Najib Mahfuz has been the subject of scholarly study in the West. Since the 1970s master's and doctoral dissertations have been partially or wholly dedicated to the study of the short stories and novels, characters, and techniques of this writer.

In view of his own prior conflicts with Muslim leaders, it surprised many when, in a 1992 interview with the *Paris Review* Mahfuz criticized fellow author Salmon Rushdie for the latter's novel, *The Satanic Verses.* The novel had been condemned as blasphemous by many Muslims, and Iran's religious leader, the Ayatollah Khomeini, had offered a million-dollar reward for Rushdie's death. Mahfuz had previously defended Rushie, but in an interview with Charlotte El Shabrawy, he told her he had been unaware of the contests of Rushdie's novel. After Mahfuz, who had failing eyesight, had the book read to him, he said he was "appalled" by what he felt were the insults to Muslims and the Prophet Mohammed. While standing by his prior statements that Khomeini had no right to threaten Rushdie with death, Mahfuz said Rushdie "does not have the right to insult anything, especially a prophet or anything considered holy."

Further Reading

The works of Najib Mahfuz have been widely translated into English and other Western languages. His novel *Midaq Alley,* translated in 1975 by Trevor LeGassick and published in London in paperback, is accessible work that introduces the student to his inimitable style; *God's World,* as well as *Mirrors,* translated by Roger Allen and published by Bibliotheca Islamica (1977) provide a representative selection of the works by this writer; two parts of his trilogy, *Bayn-AlQasryn* and *Qasr al-Shauq,* were translated and published by the American University Press in Cairo; *Sons of Gebalawi,* a voluminous novel translated by Philip Stewart (1981) and published by Heinemann, is a fascinating voyage into the world of Mahfuz. Other books by Mahfuz are *Adrift on the Nile* (New York, Doubleday, 1993); *Autumn Quail* (Doubleday,

1985,1990); and *Arabian Nights and Days* (Double-day,1995). In *Echoes of an Autobiography* (translated by Denys Johnson, New York, Davies/Doubleday, 1997) the author discusses his life and writings. Scholarly articles that treat the different aspects of Mahfuz's writings occur in such journals as *Journal of Arabic Literature, Al-Arabiyya, World Literature Today,* and several works wholly dedicated to his contribution; S. Sasson's *Changing Rhythms,* published by Brill, and M. Peled's *Religion, My Own* are critical analyses of the literary works of Mahfuz. Mahfouz's reaction to winning the Nobel Prize was reported by William Honan in, "From 'Balzac of Egypt,' Energy and Nuance" and "Egyptian Wins Nobel in Literature," in the October 14th edition of *New York Times;* his statements about Rushdie were quoted by Esthen Fein, "Book Notes," in the August 5th edition of *New York Times.* □

Gustav Mahler

The Austrian composer and conductor Gustav Mahler (1860-1911) introduced innovations that had a profound influence on the Viennese composers of the next generation and initiated significant trends in operatic production that set a new standard.

G ustav Mahler once said: "Composing a symphony means, to me, building a new world with every available technical means. The ever-new and changing content determines its own form." This free concept of symphonic form included such innovations as "progressive tonality," that is, beginning a symphony in one key and ending it in a quite different one. Such practices were often misunderstood and rejected by Mahler's contemporaries. However, he became resigned to this, for, as he liked to say, "My time will yet come." His prophecy proved to be right, for in the second half of the 20th century he became one of the most popular symphonic composers.

Mahler can be seen as an important transitional figure between the 19th and 20th centuries. His taste for gigantic forms, monumental instrumentation, and long lyrical themes (often derived from his own songs) is certainly related to 19th-century esthetic ideals. So, too, is his frequent inclusion of the chorus or the solo voice in his symphonies—an idea inspired by Ludwig van Beethoven's Ninth Symphony. Mahler's last works, especially the Ninth Symphony and the unfinished Tenth Symphony, show ever greater economy in the use of available means. Many sections of these works are almost like chamber music in their soloistic treatment of instruments. Such passages were well understood and used as models by Arnold Schoenberg and his disciples. This kind of instrumentation, as well as Mahler's increasing freedom in the handling of tonality, foreshadowed the new age's ideal of sound. Thus, for all his romantic, 19th-century traits, in many ways Mahler can be considered a truly "modern" composer.

Mahler was born on July 7, 1860, in Kalište, Bohemia. When he was a few months old, his family moved to the larger town of Jihlava (Iglau), where the father, Bernhard, kept a distillery and bar. Here Gustav acquired his first musical impressions. Loitering in the neighborhood of the military barracks, he learned many marches, which he would play on the accordion. At the age of 4 he could sing about 200 folk songs, which he learned from the family maid. Perhaps the great emphasis on march rhythms and folklike melodies in his works comes in part from these sources.

Mahler's musical gifts developed rapidly, and his ambitious father did all he could to advance them. At the age of 15 the boy was taken to Vienna, where he was immediately accepted at the conservatory. His career there was a successful one; he won prizes in both composition and piano playing. Most of his works from that time are lost, but two song fragments and part of a piano quartet in A minor were preserved. The first movement of the quartet is virtually complete in manuscript except for a missing passage in the piano part which is easily reconstructed. It shows the influence of Johannes Brahms and Robert Schumann but, especially in its principal theme, already foreshadows later Mahlerian ideas.

Mahler graduated in July 1878. That fall he began the composition of the cantata *Das klagende Lied* (The Song of Grief). He wrote the text himself, basing it on fairy tales by Ludwig Bechstein and the Grimm brothers. The work, finished the following year, was submitted for the Beethoven Prize, but the judges rejected it. Between 1878 and 1883 Mahler worked at three operas: *Herzog Ernst von Schwaben, Die Argonauten,* and *Rübezahl.* The music of all of them has been lost, but the manuscript of the *Rübezahl* libretto has survived.

In 1880 Mahler took a conducting position in the light-opera theater at the summer resort of Bad Hall in Upper Austria. This was the first of many opera-conducting posts he was to hold until 1897: Ljubljana, Olomouc, Kassel, Prague, Leipzig, Budapest, and Hamburg. Theatrical duties generally kept him fully occupied during these winter seasons, so that he was forced to be a "summer composer." Nevertheless, he completed important works. The *Lieder eines fahrenden Gesellen* (1883-1885; Songs of a Wayfarer), composed to his own texts, reflect his unhappy love affair with the soprano Johanne Richter in Kassel. They furnished major thematic material for the First Symphony (1884-1888). The Second Symphony (1887-1894) is often known as the *Resurrection* Symphony, after its grandiose choral setting of Friedrich Gottlieb Klopstock's resurrection hymn. The Third Symphony (1893-1896), with its six extended movements, is perhaps the longest symphony ever written.

Mahler became the director of the Vienna Court Opera in 1897. He brought new standards to that institution and initiated many reforms which are taken for granted today. He was the first in Vienna to bar latecomers from the opera house till the end of an act. He performed Richard Wagner's music dramas without cuts, following the stylistic principles established by Wagner at Bayreuth. In producing Wolfgang Amadeus Mozart's operas, too, Mahler strove for stylistic authenticity, restoring the recitatives with harpsichord accompaniment which had often been cut by his predecessors. He tried to simplify operatic staging, seeking symbolism rather than excessive realism; the painter Alfred Roller, who became his stage designer, helped him to achieve this aim.

Despite his heavy responsibilities at the opera house, Mahler was able to compose five symphonies during his Vienna years. The Fourth (1899-1900) is a cheerful work; its finale is a delightful song for soprano based on a poem from *Des Knaben Wunderhorn* (The Youth's Magic Horn), a collection of folk poetry which was one of Mahler's favorite text sources. The Fifth, Sixth, and Seventh Symphonies (1901-1905) are purely instrumental; they show his ever-increasing mastery of his chosen medium. The Eighth (1906-1907), for eight vocal soloists, double chorus, and boys' chorus, with a very large orchestra, was nicknamed the *Symphony of a Thousand* at the time of its first performance, under the composer's direction, in 1910. An innovation here was the setting of texts in two different languages: the Latin hymn *Veni Creator Spiritus* (Come, Creator Spirit) and the final scene of Goethe's *Faust*. Important songs of the Vienna period were the *Sieben Lieder aus letzter Zeit* (1899-1904; Seven Last Songs; texts from *Des Knaben Wunderhorn* and by Friedrich Rückert) and the *Kindertotenlieder* (1901-1904; Songs on the Death of Children; texts by Rückert).

The intrigues of Mahler's professional and personal enemies forced him to leave the Vienna Court Opera in 1907. His final seasons as a conductor were spent in New York City, where he was very successful at the Metropolitan Op-

era and the Philharmonic. He knew that, because of a serious heart condition, he might die soon. In this knowledge, he composed his last and greatest works. *Das Lied von der Erde* (1907-1908; The Song of the Earth) is a six-movement symphony with alto and tenor soloists; the texts are from a collection of translated Chinese poetry, *Die chinesische Flöte* (The Chinese Flute) by Hans Bethge. The dominating theme is the transitoriness of human existence in the face of eternity.

Musically and spiritually, Mahler's last two numbered symphonies are closely related to *Das Lied*. The Ninth was completed in 1910. Mahler never finished the Tenth, but in recent years several attempts have been made to bring his manuscript into performable condition. This aim was most convincingly realized by Deryck Cooke; his version, first heard in 1964, is still controversial but has been widely performed and recorded with great success.

Mahler conducted his last concert in New York on Feb. 21, 1911, and collapsed immediately thereafter from a severe streptococcal infection. Taken back to Europe, he seemed to recover briefly, but the infection could not be cured. On May 18 he died in Vienna.

Further Reading

A vivid, if often inaccurate, account of Mahler's later life is in Alma Mahler Werfel's memoir, *Gustav Mahler: Memories and Letters* (rev. ed. by Donald Mitchell, 1969). The younger Mahler is revealed in Natalie Bauer-Lechner, *Recollections of Gustav Mahler,* translated by Dika Newlin (publication pending). Bruno Walter, *Gustav Mahler* (1936; trans. 1941), is a warmly personal appreciation by one of Mahler's greatest interpreters. Dika Newlin, *Bruckner-Mahler-Schoenberg* (1947), places Mahler in historical perspective and offers analyses of the principal works. Neville Cardus, *Gustav Mahler, His Mind and His Music: The First Five Symphonies* (1966), is the first detailed study in English of Mahler's first five symphonies and is to be followed by a second volume dealing with the remaining symphonies. Mahler's early works are rather sketchily discussed in Donald Mitchell, *Gustav Mahler: The Early Years* (1958). H. F. Redlich, *Bruckner and Mahler* (1955), convincingly links the two composers. Arnold Schoenberg's essay "Gustav Mahler" in his *Style and Idea* (1950) should not be overlooked by any student of the subject. □

Mahmud II

The Ottoman sultan Mahmud II (1785-1839) attempted to hold together and rebuild the empire by administrative reforms, but interior instability and foreign wars proved obstacles too great to overcome.

Mahmud was born on July 20, 1785, son of Abdul Hamid I and cousin of the reforming ruler Selim III. Immured, as his predecessors had been, within the harem, he was removed from formal education and administrative experience. But the highly intelligent and energetic Mahmud escaped the debilitating weakness trapping other Osmanli through the instruction accorded him by Selim III between the latter's dethronement in May 1807 and his execution in July 1808 as his reform-minded supporters battered down the palace gates. The reigning sultan, Mustafa IV, even ordered the execution of Mahmud, his own brother, but the prince escaped detection by hiding in an empty furnace.

Mustafa was deposed, Mahmud was elevated to the throne, and a reform administration was returned to power. Within the year a Janissary revolt temporarily ended modernization efforts. To assure his position, Mahmud had Mustafa, his only male Ottoman relative, executed, assuring loyalty to himself as the last of the Osmanli.

Few changes were made domestically through the Napoleonic period, since Mahmud was consolidating governmental control over the provinces. Local power structures were reduced on both sides of the Bosporus, and Ottoman authority was reestablished in Mesopotamia (1810) and the Hejaz (1813). Serbian autonomy was recognized after the Turks failed to regain control, and the Russians, in a war begun in December 1806, acquired Bessarabia by the Treaty of Bucharest on May 28, 1812. Internationally, the Great Powers at the Congress of Vienna tacitly allowed Turkey to reestablish the ancient rule on Straits navigation, providing the waterway be closed to all warships in peacetime.

Wars and Revolts

The Greek War for Independence occupied nearly a decade of Mahmud's reign, from the initial weak rebellion in the Morea (Peloponnesus) in 1820 to the Russian intervention of 1828—1829. Despite Turco-Egyptian control of the situation, international pressure, including the destruction of the Turkish and Egyptian fleets by a tripartite European force at Navarino in 1827, forced recognition of full Greek independence upon the Sultan.

The purpose of the reforms for which Mahmud is noted was to strengthen the central government's powers and widen its sphere of influence. The basis for change was a modern army, not the fractious, undisciplined Janissaries, whose complaints had disrupted the state, to one degree or another, since raiding had ceased to be a profitable enterprise. On June 16, 1826, backed by 14,000 loyal artillerymen, Mahmud provoked a typical Janissary assault on the palace. The attackers were wiped out, and Janissaries throughout the empire were destroyed or dispersed.

Unfortunately, before Mahmud could fully train their replacements and so gain the power to enforce his restored authority, Russia declared war. This attack permanently stunted the growth of the new Turkish army; it also resulted in the Treaty of Adrianople (1829), which, although not seriously affecting Ottoman borders, ended most Turkish control over the Balkans by providing for the lifetime appointment of governors and reducing provincial obligations to a province's annual tribute payment.

Mahmud's Reforms

Internal changes during Mahmud's reign were largely military. Feudalism was abolished throughout the empire, eliminating the cavalry and recruits provided by local fief holders. National recruiting was less effective; yet, by 1834, a militia provided at least fundamental training at the local level. To strengthen his new army, the Sultan established military schools, sent officers to England to study, and imported Prussian military advisers.

The result of these military changes was increased control over local government. The Kurds of Iraq were subdued. Tripoli was effectively reintegrated, but Algiers was lost to France, straining relations with the Sultan. One salutary administrative change was removal of the right of provincial governors to impose the death penalty. Civil service training was improved, and better salaries created a more efficient administration, reducing the need for graft. Further improvement resulted from tax reforms which eliminated inefficient collection methods and so improved revenues.

Power Struggles

To ensure his changes, Mahmud attempted to curtail religious powers that might inspire counterreformation movements. Persecution of the various dervish orders followed the Janissary massacre. In this attempt the Sultan only partially succeeded. However, widespread distribution of Western literature through the establishment of local presses spread Europe's 19th-century liberal ideas and advanced the modernizing process. For his efforts, Mahmud was roundly hated by his Moslem subjects, a factor exacerbating his dislike of popular Mohammed Ali, his Egyptian vassal.

The Egyptians, seeking compensation for their assistance during the Greek revolt, invaded the Levant in 1831, taking city after city, even into Anatolia. In the Convention of Kütahya on April 8, 1833, Cairo gained Syria, but Egyptian troops pulled back behind the Taurus Mountains.

The Russians had landed troops in the Bosporus region during the crisis, ostensibly to aid the Sultan. This led to the Treaty of Hunkiar Iskelesi (July 4, 1833), which effected a major change in Turkey's relations with Europe. The treaty was an alliance between the signatories assigning to the Czar the right unilaterally to intervene in Turkish affairs—heretofore the prerogative of the Great Powers acting in concert. Mahmud's hatred of Mohammed Ali grew.

Toward the end of his reign, the strong-minded Mahmud was faced with rebellions in Bosnia and Albania, but the European provinces were nevertheless sufficiently stable in 1837 for the energetic sultan to make an unprecedented trip through that area. In his last days, he ill-advisedly ordered a new attack on the Egyptians in Syria. News of the Turkish defeat at Nizib on June 24, 1839, never reached the dying Mahmud. On July 1, 1839, he was succeeded by his 16-year-old son, Abdul Mejid.

Further Reading

General biographical information on Mahmud II is in Frederick Stanley Rodkey, *The Turco-Egyptian Question in the Relations of England, France and Russia, 1832-1841* (1924), and A. D. Alderson, *The Structure of the Ottoman Dynasty* (1956). □

Mahmud of Ghazni

Mahmud of Ghazni (971-1030) was the first sultan of the Ghaznavid dynasty in Afghanistan. A zealous Sunni Moslem, he plundered wealthy India and used the booty to patronize culture in Ghazni, making it the center of Perso-Islamic civilization.

Born on Nov. 2, 971, eldest son of Emir Subuktigin, Mahmud helped his father gain a kingdom from the Samanids through successful campaigns against Turkish nobles of Samarkand and Bukhara. In 997 he overthrew his younger brother, Ismail, who had been nominated by Subuktigin as his successor, and 2 years later Mahmud was confirmed as sultan of Ghazni by Caliph al-Kadir. Challenged several times by the Qarakhanid rulers, Mahmud repulsed all attempts against his territories. Elsewhere, he annexed parts of Murghab (1012) and Khwarizm (1017). In the south and the west he asserted his suzerainty over Seistan, Ghor, Qudsar, and Baluchistan.

Mahmud is chiefly remembered as the plunderer of India. Between 1000 and 1026 he mounted at least 17 raids

against India with the aim of extirpating idol-worshiping Hindu infidels and destroying Hindu temples, which were great repositories of wealth. His most important expedition was against the temple of Somanth in 1025. It is estimated that Mahmud took from India jewels, gold, and silver in excess of 3 billion dinars, in addition to hundreds of thousands of slaves. His only territorial acquisition in India was the Punjab (1021).

A patron of the arts, Mahmud attracted poets from all parts of Asia. Among these were Uzari, Asadi Tusi, Unsuri, and perhaps the most famous of them all, Firdausi. All were commissioned to write panegyrics. Firdausi's *Shahnama* has placed Mahmud among the immortals of history. Fanatical, cruel to Hindus as well as to Moslem heretics, fickle, and uncertain in temper, Mahmud was extremely greedy of wealth. He refused to pay the 60,000 goldpieces he had promised Firdausi for the *Shahnama,* making the poet so bitter that he wrote a satire about the Sultan.

When Mahmud was about to die, he ordered all his hoards to be placed before his eyes. He grieved over his impending separation from his wealth but refused to give the smallest amount to charity. Yet though he loved money passionately, he also spent it lavishly. A library, a museum, and a university were endowed at Ghazni. To his court came scholars like al-Biruni; Utbi, the historian; Farabi, the philosopher; and Baihaki, the diarist. Mahmud became the hero of many legends, many of them centering on his relationship with his favorite slave, Ayaz.

The administrative system that Mahmud established—using a predominantly Turkish elite, often of slave origin, promoted to army commands, and a Persian elite responsible for civil and revenue administration—was used in Moslem India for several centuries. He died on April 30, 1030, and his tomb at Ghazni has survived.

Further Reading

The outstanding work on Mahmud and his times is Clifford Edmund Bosworth, *The Ghaznavids: Their Empire in Afghanistan and Eastern Iran, 994-1040* (1963). A superior biography is Muhammad Nazim, *The Life and Times of Sultan Mahmud of Ghazna* (1931). Edward G. Browne, *A Literary History of Persia* (4 vols., 1906-1924), gives information on Mahmud's scholars. □

William Mahone

William Mahone (1826-1895), American political leader and Confederate Army officer, led a movement of reformers in Virginia known as the Readjustors, with whose backing he won election to the U.S. Senate.

William Mahone was born on Dec. 1, 1826, in Monroe, Va. He graduated from the Virginia Military Institute and decided to become an engineer. He succeeded so well that at the age of 26 he was chief engineer of the Norfolk and Petersburg Railroad and at 33 was elected its president. He was a tiny man, hardly 5 1/2 feet tall and weighing less than 100 pounds, but he had complete confidence in himself and a commanding manner.

During the Civil War, Mahone distinguished himself in the Army of Northern Virginia, rising to the rank of major general. After the war he returned to the presidency of the Norfolk and Petersburg Railroad and began to consolidate it with other railroads in order to build a line that would extend to the Ohio River. He encountered strong opposition from other railroad interests, including the powerful Baltimore and Ohio. In order to get state aid, he began to help Conservative party candidates who appeared sympathetic to his interests. Nevertheless, after the Panic of 1873 his railroad system failed, and he turned his attention to politics.

In 1879 Mahone emerged as the leader of a movement of reformers known as the Readjustors, who gained control of the Virginia Legislature in 1879 and of the governorship in 1881. They enacted many reforms, such as abolition of the whipping post and poll tax, tax relief for farmers, and funds for public schools. They also elected Mahone to the U.S. Senate in 1881, where the election year membership had been evenly divided between Democrats and Republicans. As an independent, Mahone could cast the vote which would decide which party would control the Senate. He voted with the Republicans, who rewarded him with all the Federal patronage in his state. This support combined with

the strict control he had established over the Readjustor organization made him briefly the political boss of Virginia.

But Mahone's arbitrary rule made many enemies and his appeal for black votes enabled his opponents to raise the question of race. In 1883 the Conservatives regained control of the legislature by endorsing the Readjustors' reforms while exciting white prejudice. Mahone and the Readjustors now officially joined the Republican party but were unable to win back political control of their state. Mahone served as chairman of the state Republican party until his death in Washington, D. C., on Oct. 8, 1895.

Further Reading

A well-written account of Mahone's life is Nelson Morehouse Blake, *William Mahone of Virginia: Soldier and Political Insurgent* (1935). See also Robert H. Smith, *General William Mahone, Frederick J. Kimball and Others: A Short History of the Norfolk and Western Railway* (1949). □

Norman Kingsley Mailer

Norman Kingsley Mailer (born 1923), American author, film producer and director, wrote one of the most noteworthy American novels about World War II. Only in his later political journalism did he reach that level of achievement again.

Norman Mailer was born in Long Branch, New Jersey, on Jan. 31, 1923. The family soon moved to Brooklyn. Mailer graduated from high school in 1939 and earned a bachelor of science degree in aeronautical engineering from Harvard University. He won a college fiction contest, wrote for the *Harvard Advocate,* worked on two ambitious (unpublished) novels, and contributed a novella to an anthology. Drafted into the Army in 1944, he served in the Philippines in an infantry regiment, as both intelligence clerk and combat reconnaissance rifleman.

In the Army, Mailer knew he was living the material for his third novel. From notes in letters to his wife, he fashioned a brilliant narrative around an Army platoon's taking of a Japanese-held Pacific island. Borrowing naturalist techniques from John Dos Passos and James Farrell, a symbolist's stance from Herman Melville, and the instinctive journalist's observations from Ernest Hemingway, he described (in language considered objectionable in its day) the ironies of war and the inner conflicts of a cross section of American fighting men. Many readers saw only the realism in *The Naked and the Dead* (1948). Mailer insisted he was writing not only of a specific war but of "death and man's creative urge, fate, man's desire to conquer the elements. . ." The work was a popular success and won him critical acclaim.

After attending the Sorbonne in Paris under the G.I. Bill, Mailer returned to the United States in the mid-1950s, and founded, along with Daniel Wolf and Edwin Fancher, the newspaper *Village Voice.*

In his next four novels, Mailer wrote from "intense political preoccupation and a voyage in political affairs which began with the Progressive Party and has ended in the *cul-de-sac* (at least so far as action is concerned) of being an anti-Stalinist Marxist who feels that war is probably inevitable." *Barbary Shore* (1951) is set in a Brooklyn rooming house. *The Deer Park* (1955), both the novel and the play Mailer adapted from it, takes place at a kind of Palm Springs of the imagination and focuses on two of Mailer's most memorable characters, Sergius O'Shaugnessy, former Air Force pilot, and Elena Esposito, broken-down dancer and actress. *An American Dream* (1965) shows Steve Rojack, trapped in an urban nightmare of sexual orgy, murder, and despair, escaping with what remains of his soul to the jungles of Yucatán. *Why Are We in Vietnam?* (1967), the low ebb of Mailer's fiction, takes its 18-year-old hero on an Alaskan hunting expedition that ends with his initiation into manhood. These books voiced Mailer's view of the frustrations and compulsions that lay beneath the surface of American life, violently portrayed through existential heroes and at times written with flamboyant crudeness.

Mailer began a second career in the mid-1950s as essayist and journalist. He became a national personality with the publication of *Advertisements for Myself* (1959), a compendium of earlier writings that included bitter polemics, personal interviews, psychocultural essays, stories, works in progress, and unabashed confessions of how Mailer reached the depths of his own existential state and found a "new consciousness."

Although the sixties were a time of personal conflict and public rebellion for Mailer, he wrote many nonfiction works during that period that helped establish him as a preeminent writer in the genre. *The Presidential Papers* (1963) presented a critique of American politics and society that introduced a revitalized Mailer, the public historian of the John Kennedy years. This work along with *Cannibals and Christians* (1966) attempted to establish him as "self-appointed master of the Now." Issues pertaining to gender and sex were the basis of *The Prisoner of Sex* (1971), a treatise on Mailer's various sexual relationships in which he responds to Kate Millett's attack on his presumed sexism in her *Sexual Politics* (1970).

The peace march on Washington (1967) and the presidential conventions (1968) gave Mailer some of his most fruitful material. A seasoned reporter, he wove his copious notes into "non-fictional novels" using the style of New Journalism, in which factual events are related from the writer's perspective and incorporate prose devices such as narrative, dialogue, and multiple points of view. The Washington experience became *The Armies of the Night: History as a Novel, the Novel as History* (1968), for which he received a National Book Award and a Pulitzer Prize. The political conventions shaped *Miami and the Siege of Chicago* (1968). In addition to reportage, these works reflect Mailer's personality and controversial opinions on historic events, creating incisive portraits of the conflict between individual and collective power.

Other works using New Journalism techniques include *Of a Fire on the Moon* (1971) about man's first landing on the moon, *The Executioner's Song* (1979), an examination of the life and death of convicted murderer Gary Gilmore, the first person executed (in 1977) in the United States under death-penalty legislation in more than a decade, and *Harlot's Ghost* (1991), in which Mailer treats factual events such as the Cuban missile crisis and the Bay of Pigs from an overtly fictional perspective to imagine the inner workings of the United States Central Intelligence Agency.

During the 1990s, the prolific and egocentric writer again turned his attention to biographical essays and novels. *Portrait of Picasso As A Young Man* (1995) and *Oswald's Tale: An American Mystery* (1995) received poor critical reviews for his reliance on what many considered dubious new sources for subjects whose lives were already well chronicled. Still, David Gelernter in the *National Review* credited Mailer's heavy use of other authors in *Picasso* saying, "*Picasso* is a collage. . .The counterpoint that results is odd but effective," and that there were occasional flourishes of brilliant writing. Among the theories he presents is that violence and death are at the heart of Picasso's Cubism.

Not one to shy away from challenging subjects, Mailer chose to write a novel about Jesus Christ in 1997. As noted in the *New York Times Book Review,* Mailer wrote not merely a life of Jesus, but a contemporary apocryphal Gospel, *The Gospel According to the Son,* in the first-person voice of Jesus Himself—a choice avoided by all surviving ancient Gospels and by virtually all modern novelists. As in many of his other works, critics pointed to spotty narrative brilliance and "rare powerful moments of invention." However, in Gospel, Mailer also was credited for his knowledge of canonical texts, as well as his surprising—and to some, disappointing—adherence to tradition.

Mailer continued analyzing and commenting on major social and political issues throughout the 1990s, often interviewing his philosophical opposites, such as the staunch right-wing politican and newscaster Patrick Buchanan. The self-styled maverick and outspoken social and political arbiter of the times was widely regarded as the most prominent writer of his generation, and praised for the diversity and scope of his works.

Further Reading

The fullest critiques of Mailer are Richard J. Foster, *Norman Mailer* (1968), and Barry H. Leeds, *The Structural Vision of Norman Mailer* (1969); see also Norman Podhoretz, *Doings and Undoings: The Fifties and After in American Writing* (1964); Ronald Berman, *America in the Sixties: An Intellectual History* (1968); Richard Gilman, *The Confusion of Realms* (1969); Laura Adams, *Norman Mailer: A Comprehensive Bibliography* (1974), Scarecrow; Laura Adams, editor, *Will the Real Norman Mailer Please Stand Up?* (1974), Kennikat Press; Laura Adams, *Existential Battles: The Growth of Norman Mailer* (1976), Ohio University Press; Robert Alter, *Motives for Fiction* (1984), Harvard University Press; Martin Amis, *The Moronic Inferno and Other Visits to America* (1986), Jonathan Cape; and Chris Anderson, *Style as Argument: Contemporary American Nonfiction* (1987), Southern Illinois University Press. □

Aristide Maillol

The sculpture of the French artist Aristide Maillol (1861-1944) is classical in form and spirit but does not imitate ancient art or the academic, Greco-Roman traditions. He was also a painter, printmaker, and tapestry designer.

Aristide Maillol was born on Dec. 8, 1861, in Banyuls-sur-Mer, the son of a ship captain who was also a fisherman and cultivator of vineyards. Maillol, second of four children, was brought up in a region once colonized by the ancient Greeks. His home looked out on the Mediterranean. After attending a local school, he was sent to Perpignan to further his education. He began to draw and to develop an interest in art early in life.

At the age of 21, Maillol became a painting student of Jean Léon Gérôme at the École des Beaux-Arts in Paris. Dissatisfied, he turned to other teachers, Alexandre Cabanel and Jean Paul Laurens, but then rejected official instruction as sterile and pointless. Maillol was not alone in his opinion: other artists of consequence throughout the second half of the 19th century reacted in a similar manner.

In 1884 Maillol saw the paintings of Paul Gauguin and Maurice Denis. "Gauguin's painting was a revelation to me!" he exclaimed. Indeed it was. Maillol's style changed, but without assuming the mannerisms of Gauguin's style,

only its breadth and innocence. Later, in 1894, Gauguin saw some of Maillol's tapestries and said they could not be "too highly praised." The two artists met once, but they never developed a close relationship.

In 1889 Maillol began to design tapestries. He was inspired by medieval examples he had seen at the Musée de Cluny in Paris. He returned to Banyuls to set up a small tapestry factory and hired some local women to assist him. He made the designs and dyed the wool to obtain colors not found in commercial wools. His drawings, paintings, and cartoons reveal the influence of the Nabis, many of whom he knew personally. Superintending his factory was such a strain that his eyesight began to fail.

About 1898 Maillol began to model in clay, and soon he confined himself exclusively to sculpture. By 1900 he had developed a style so distinctive and personally satisfying that it was to undergo no critical change thereafter. He depicted only the human figure, especially the female nude. A fine example of his early work is *The Mediterranean* (1901), a larger-than-life, seated female figure. It is a strong work and betrays no lack of experience or confidence.

In 1902 Maillol had his first one-man exhibition, which was a great success and led to a number of commissions. His earliest pieces were carved in stone and wood. After 1905 he concentrated on modeling and having the completed works cast in bronze. He was to follow this procedure throughout his life.

In 1904 Maillol had established a studio at Marly-le-Roi near Paris. He continued to spend his winters in his

hometown. He did little traveling usually, but he did go to Greece, primarily to view ancient sculptures in the original. Seeing them caused no change in his work. Rather it seemed to confirm him in his approach. In a sense, Maillol had already recreated the Greek spirit without imitating the sculpture.

In 1906 Maillol was commissioned to design a monument in memory of the socialist Louis Blanqui, who had spent half of his life in prison in defense of his principles. For it Maillol conceived his *Chained Action,* an aggressively striding female nude; this sculpture is not typical of his production. Most of his figures appear placid, self-contained, and yet earthy, almost sensuous. They closely resemble those of Auguste Renoir; like Renoir's nudes, they are refined, sensitive, innocent pagans. It is as if they were untouched by time or other external pressures—except possibly for a slight air of melancholy. Maillol's *Three Nymphs* (1936-1938) exhibits no appreciable difference over his earlier works. In fact, the figures are very close in pose and attitude to his *Pomona* (1907).

In 1912 Maillol executed woodcuts for Virgil's *Eclogues,* and in 1931 he made lithographs to illustrate Emile Verhaeren's *Belle Chair.* Maillol died on Sept. 28, 1944, in Perpignan.

Further Reading

Waldemar George, *Aristide Maillol* (1965), with a biographical sketch by D. Vierny, and John Rewald, *Maillol* (1939), have many reproductions. The texts provide the basic biographical information, but they are essentially tributes to the artist. Rewald is the editor of *The Woodcuts of Aristide Maillol: A Complete Catalog with 176 Illustrations* (1943).

Additional Sources

Lorquin, Bertrand, *Aristide Maillol,* London; New York, N.Y.: Skira in association with Thames and Hudson, 1995, 1994.
Slatkin, Wendy, *Aristide Maillol in the 1890s,* Ann Arbor, Mich.: UMI Research Press, 1982. ☐

Maimonides

Maimonides (1135-1204), or Moses ben Maimon, was the greatest Jewish philosopher of the Middle Ages. His commentaries on, and codification of, the rabbinic tradition established him as a major religious authority in Judaism.

Maimonides was born at Cordova, Spain, on March 30, 1135. From his father, Rabbi Maimon ben Joseph, he received his early education in mathematics and astronomy as well as in rabbinic literature, which interpreted the Jewish Scriptures and defined the laws and ritual of the Jewish community. Living in southern Spain, Maimonides also came into contact with Greek and Arabian philosophy, especially the thought of Avicenna.

In 1148, when Maimonides was only 13, the Almohads conquered Cordova and introduced a policy that forced conversion, exile, or death on non-Moslems. After 12 years of wandering from town to town in southern Spain, the family finally settled at Fez in Morocco. During this period of wandering, Maimonides wrote a treatise on the Jewish calendar and began his commentary on the Mishnah, a codification of the Jewish Oral Law arranged according to subjects.

Rather than abandon the Jewish faith or undergo martyrdom, Maimonides and his family left the intolerant rule of the Almohads and sailed to Palestine on April 18, 1165, arriving at Acre a month later. Much of Palestine at this time was under the control of the Christian crusaders, and under their protection Maimonides visited many of the holy places of ancient Jewish history, including Jerusalem and Hebron.

The next year the family settled at al-Fustât (Old Cairo) in Egypt, where Maimonides was to remain for the rest of his life. After the death of the father in 1166, the family was supported for a time by Maimonides's younger brother, David, who engaged in the jewel trade. David died by drowning while on a voyage to the Indies, and the accompanying loss of the family's resources as well as those of other investors forced Maimonides into a career in medicine. Maimonides soon became the personal physician of al-Qadi al-Fadil, the vizier of Saladin. Shortly thereafter, Maimonides was made the head of all the Jewish communities in Egypt, a nonsalaried position which he held until his death.

Settling at al-Fustât allowed Maimonides to complete his commentary on the Mishnah, which appeared in 1168 and soon became popular among the Jewish communities of the Mediterranean world. About 1180 Maimonides completed his code of the Jewish law, which had a similarly favorable reception.

The major work of Maimonides, *The Guide of the Perplexed,* was completed in 1190 and published in Arabic. In this work Maimonides tried to reconcile faith and reason. It was written for those who possessed a firm knowledge of the Jewish faith, mathematics, and logic but who, having little or no knowledge of physics and metaphysics, believed that religion and philosophy contradicted each other. Maimonides believed that philosophy, properly understood and used, supported rather than destroyed the faith. In order to demonstrate this, he adopted many of the arguments for the existence of God and the nature of the human soul found in such Arabian philosophers as al-Farabi and Avicenna. Where philosophical demonstration is inconclusive, as in establishing the eternity of the world or the doctrine of creation, one must rely on the surer teaching of revelation, the Bible.

Maimonides died at al-Fustât on Dec. 13, 1204, and, after a period of mourning in the Jewish communities in Egypt, his body was transported to Palestine and buried at Tiberias in Galilee. His *Guide* became the fundamental text for medieval Jewish philosophy.

Further Reading

There are two English translations of Maimonides's *Guide.* The best is *The Guide of the Perplexed,* translated with an excellent introduction by Shlomo Pines (1963). Older but still useful is the translation by M. Friedländer (1881; rev. ed. 1962). Of high quality is the work of I. Münz, *Maimonides: The Story of His Life and Genius,* translated by H. T. Schnittkind (1912; trans. 1935). Two collections of essays on Maimonides that reflect scholarship are I. Epstein, ed., *Moses Maimonides: 1135-1204* (1935), and Salo Baron, ed., *Essays on Maimonides: An Octocentennial Volume* (1941). Also useful is A. Cohen, ed., *The Teachings of Maimonides* (1927; repr. 1968). □

Sir Henry James Sumner Maine

Sir Henry James Sumner Maine (1822-1888) was an English legal historian and historical anthropologist and a leading Victorian antidemocrat.

Born on Aug. 15, 1822, Henry Maine received his schooling at Christ's Hospital and Pembroke College, Cambridge. He received his degree in 1844 and the following year was appointed junior tutor at Trinity College, Cambridge, which position he held until appointed regius professor of civil law at Cambridge in 1847. In 1850 he was called to the bar and 2 years later accepted appointment as first reader in Roman law and jurisprudence at the

Inns of Court. He steadily gained in reputation as a philosopher of law and a brilliant legal antiquary until, with the publication of his first work, *Ancient Law* (1861), he emerged on the Victorian scene as a leading scholar-intellectual.

Maine was a legal member of the Council in India (1863-1869) and served for a time as vice-chancellor of the University of Calcutta. He formulated a general scheme for the codification of Indian law and organized the legislative department of the Indian government. He was corpus professor of jurisprudence at Oxford from 1869 until 1877, when he assumed the mastership of Trinity Hall, Cambridge.

Maine continued to write extensively on the theme that the history of law illustrated a course of development which he did not entirely approve. He contended that the whole idea that material improvement was linked with political democracy was a mistaken conception of some of his contemporaries. Unlike the historical-anthropological school, which thought of liberty as having originated in primitive communes, Maine believed that the legal relationships of most primitive societies were based upon long-established historical customs deriving from the patriarchal family system. Under such a system, land and goods were held in common by all members of the family and individual private property was unknown. Gradually the family was absorbed in the larger tribal unit and then, with the passage of time and the growth of trade, evolved into an urbanized, economically sophisticated society.

Meanwhile, property holding in common gave way to property holding in severalty, so that men, in a famous Maine phrase, moved "from status to contract" in their legal relations. Common ownership in the family-organized society was thus transformed into private ownership in an individual-organized society, and, by implication, a larger measure of political freedom became possible.

Some critics have seen Maine as an antagonist of late Victorian mass democracy and a defender of laissez-faire economic individualism. Others have regarded him as a brilliant innovator in the fields of anthropology and comparative history. He has also been defined as an evolutionary determinist, although he explicitly rejected the belief that "human society went everywhere through the same series of changes." Maine was not a systematic thinker and could not always perceive some of his own intellectual contradictions. Undoubtedly his major contribution lay in the interest he stimulated and the arguments he raised among his contemporaries.

Maine's most important works (in addition to *Ancient Law*) were *Village Communities* (1871), *Early History of Institutions* (1876), *Dissertations on Early Law and Custom* (1883), *Popular Government* (1885), and *International Law* (1888). He died on Feb. 3, 1888, in Cannes, France.

Further Reading

Two accounts of Maine's life are Sir M. E. Grant Duff, *Sir Henry Maine: A Brief Memoir of His Life* (1892), and George Feaver, *From Status to Contract: A Biography of Sir Henry Maine, 1822-1888* (1969). □

Sieur de Maisoneuve

Paul de Chomedey, Sieur de Maisoneuve (1612-1676), was a French explorer and colonizer in Canada and the founder of Montreal. He also administered the settlement until it was taken over by a royal governor.

Paul de Chomedey de Maisoneuve was born in Champagne, the son of a prominent seigneur. After he had a short career in the army, his path crossed that of a group of French philanthropists and Jesuits who wanted to establish a missionary town in New France (Canada) to work for the conversion of the Native Americans. This group had founded the Société Notre-Dame de Montréal and were looking for a military-civilian leader who would direct the overseas operation. The society would recruit, finance, and buttress the proposed town in New France; Maisoneuve would lead it.

Maisoneuve arrived in Canada in the autumn of 1641, too late to do anything about a colony at Montreal that year. He used his time at Quebec to attempt to mitigate the antipathy to a colony at Montreal that prevailed in government circles there. The governor general of New France, Huault de Montmagny, offered Maisoneuve the Ile d'Orléans, a fine, rich island in the St. Lawrence within sight of Quebec. Maisoneuve, however, stuck to his guns: Montreal Island was what his group had been instructed to colonize, and Montreal was what it would be.

Thus in May 1642 Montreal was founded, deep in what can be thought of as Indian country, 150 miles upriver from Quebec, at the junction of two great rivers, the Ottawa and the St. Lawrence. Iroquois first appeared in the summer of 1643 and from then on harried the Montrealers continually by those most insidious and unnerving of techniques, stealth and ambush.

Battling the Native Americans

Maisoneuve was loath to attack the Native Americans until his forces were stronger, but his settlers were angry, and in March 1644 a sortie was made in which Maisoneuve, owing to the sudden desertion of his men, narrowly escaped death himself. He returned to France in 1645, coming back to Montreal in 1647. He was needed; the most serious problem was the threat implied in the devastating Iroquois attacks on the Jesuit missions in Huronia that began in 1648. (Huronia lay on the south side of Georgian Bay, in Lake Huron, some 400 miles west of Montreal.) Refugees drifted back to Montreal, and by 1651, with the Huron resistance almost wiped out and the French missions destroyed, Montreal was fairly in the battle line.

Maisoneuve went to France for financial and military relief, returning in 1653 with new settlers and soldiers supplied—as was much else in these years—by private energy and philanthropy. This reinforcement seems to have been the turning point in Montreal's fortunes. The settlers could now return to the fields around the village. A peace,

though temporary, was patched up with the Iroquois in 1655. In 1663 the old Company of One Hundred Associates, the group that had been largely instrumental in making a colony of New France, was handed over to the Crown, and New France became a crown colony. The arrival of a royal governor, the Marquis de Tracy, with royal regiments in June 1665 marked the beginning of a new regime in New France and also marked the end of the regime of Maisoneuve. Strong-minded governors at Quebec had always been a little uncomfortable about Maisoneuve, and Tracy asked Maisoneuve to return to France on indefinite leave. He died in Paris.

Further Reading

A useful study of Maisoneuve is Gustave Lanctot, *Montreal under Maisonneuve, 1642-1665* (trans. 1969). Maisoneuve's career is recounted more briefly in William John Eccles, *The Canadian Frontier, 1534-1760* (1969), and Leslie Roberts, *Montreal: From Mission Colony to World City* (1969). □

Joseph de Maistre

The French political philosopher Joseph de Maistre (1753-1821) is considered perhaps the leading contemporary philosophical opponent of the Enlightenment on the European continent.

Joseph de Maistre was born on April 1, 1753, at Chambéry in Savoy, which is now part of France but was then part of the kingdom of Sardinia. His family had for generations been among the leading families of this state, where they served as virtual hereditary magistrates. When the relatively progressive Savoy was invaded by Napoleon's troops, Maistre left his property and family and took refuge in Switzerland and Italy. Although he could have returned to regain his ancestral estates, out of loyalty to his sovereign he endured many lonely and impecunious years, from 1803 until 1817, as ambassador to the Russian court at St. Petersburg.

While in this virtual exile in Russia, awaiting the defeat of Napoleon, Maistre wrote at least 13 volumes of collected works, including letters and diplomatic correspondence, most of which was designed to refute the principles and programs of the philosophical Enlightenment and its concrete historical expression, the French Revolution. He died in Savoy on Feb. 26, 1821.

Maistre's first major work was *Considerations on France* (1796), in which he perceptively argues that paper constitutions never have and never will establish rights for a people. Disputing in particular the theories of J. J. Rousseau, he maintains that no people can ever give itself a body of rights through the fiat of a social contract. If the rights do not exist in the political tradition of a people, then that written document either will not be followed, or it will be interpreted in such a way that the rights become meaningless. Thus, in examining the political practices of two nations,

tion of the monarchy which would be restrained by newly instituted councils named by electors appointed by the king. If such checks on the power of the king proved inadequate, it would be necessary to submit a question to the authority of the pope, whom he believed to be divinely instituted as the ultimate judge for human affairs. It is this aspect of his thought which has led some commentators to characterize him as an ultramontanist, or theocrat. He believed also that because of original sin man was inclined to be selfish; furthermore, all human institutions are the work of God operating through secondary causes, such as the character of a people, and natural, moral, and physical laws. He attacked his opponents for being dogmatic and abstract and for deducing propositions from an arbitrarily and artificially developed ideology. In his own methods he relied on history, experience, and comparative analyses.

Further Reading

A comprehensive edition of Maistre's writings is his *Works,* translated and edited by Jack Lively (1965). Richard Allen Lebrun, *Throne and Altar: The Political and Religious Thought of Joseph de Maistre* (1965), is recommended. Elio Gianturco, *Joseph de Maistre and Giambattista Vico* (1937), includes an extensive bibliography.

Additional Sources

Lebrun, Richard, *Joseph de Maistre: an intellectual militant,* Kingston, Ont.: McGill-Queen's University Press, 1988. □

each with virtually the same bill of rights, it is often found that in the one they are effective guarantees, but in the other they are not. The reason why rights are meaningful in the one nation, then, cannot be the written document which supposedly guarantees them; it can only be the tradition of liberty in that nation, with the written constitution being at most the visible manifestation of these deeply felt ideas. In no sense can the written constitution produce rights where they had not existed in the historical habits of the people. History in turn is determined by divine providence, and thus it alone makes a government truly legitimate. The most influential agent on the world scene is the Church, which civilizes men to their social duties.

Most of Maistre's views are succinctly stated in *The Essay on the Generative Principle of Political Constitutions,* written in 1808-1809 before his much longer major works *On the Pope* (1819) and *Soirées de St. Petersbourg* (1821). In this essay may be found his critical analysis of the French Revolution, his providential view of history, and his justification of ultramontanism (the theocratic view that the pope and/or Church was meant to be not only the spiritual but the indirect temporal ruler of the world).

The true constitution of any nation, Maistre contended, was unwritten and the product of a slow organic growth, not the arbitrary consent or will of a moment. There was, in his opinion, no absolutely best form of government, but each nation has a spirit or soul of its own for which a specific form of government is best. In most cases it would be monarchy, since that form had the longest history and was the most common. For France, for example, he advocated a restora-

Frederic William Maitland

Historian, lawyer, and legal scholar Frederic William Maitland (1850-1906) was the first major English historian to break with the classic Whiggish interpretation of English legal and constitutional history.

Frederic William Maitland was born in London on May 28, 1850, the son of John Gorham and Emma Daniell Maitland. He was prepared in a number of fortuitous ways for his extraordinary scholarly career. Perhaps most important, the early deaths of both his parents placed him in the care of an aunt who provided him with a series of German governesses from whom he learned the language so well that the whole range of 19th-century German historical scholarship was opened to him at a time when that scholarly tradition was at its peak. Educated at Eton and Trinity College, Cambridge, where he took a degree in moral sciences (philosophy) in 1872, he afterward enrolled at Lincoln's Inn and was called to the bar in 1876.

The year 1879 saw the publication of Maitland's first learned article, which marked the beginning of an extraordinarily productive scholarly career. His work, although specialized, was characterized by a subtle perception and a style of writing so clear and supple that it has never ceased to awe and charm scholars, a circumstance which helps to account for his great reputation as a historian's historian. The most important works of his extensive personal bibliography are *History of English Law before the Time of Edward I*, with Sir Frederick Pollock (1895; rev. ed. 1898); *Domesday Book and Beyond* (1897); *Township and Borough* (1898); *Canon Law in England* (1898); and *English Law and the Renaissance* (1901).

Maitland's originality of outlook and his ability to comprehend the essential nature of a scholarly problem made it possible for him to break through the deeply rooted assumptions of English historiography, which had been so widely accepted by 19th-century historical scholarship. He realized that the past had to be understood in its own terms and not in the light of later developments or 19th-century scholarly presuppositions. He tried to see the world of the past through the eyes of men who had lived it. This imaginative transposition sufficed to make his scholarship both original and seminal in its influence upon others.

For Maitland, history was a product of human thoughts and actions which create uncertainties, paradoxes, and confusions that cannot always be resolved by imposing the sometimes false clarity of scholarly analysis. He raised questions and suggested hypotheses within a new context which may be said to have profoundly altered Englishmen's views of their medieval past and to have significantly influenced the whole nature of historical inquiry throughout the English-speaking world. If his specific findings in certain areas of study—parliamentary origins, for example—do not always square with the researches of a later generation, still he suggested the right lines of inquiry. His profound intelligence, his thoroughly Victorian habits of intellectual labor, and the firmness of will which kept him at work in the face of a long illness that forced him to live in a warmer climate during much of his last years all combined to make him "a man of notable goodness and nobility of character and of singularly attractive personality." He died in the Canary Islands on Dec. 19, 1906.

Further Reading

Studies of Maitland include H. A. L. Fisher, *Frederic William Maitland: Downing Professor of the Laws of England* (1910); A. L. Smith, *Frederic William Maitland: Two Lectures and a Bibliography* (1908); James R. Cameron, *Fredrick William Maitland and the History of English Law* (1961); and H. E. Bell, *Maitland: A Critical Examination and Assessment* (1965).

Additional Sources

Cameron, James Reese, *Frederick William Maitland and the history of English law,* Westport, Conn.: Greenwood Press, 1977, 1961.

Elton, G. R. (Geoffrey Rudolph), *F.W. Maitland,* New Haven: Yale University Press, 1985. ☐

John Major

The youngest British prime minister of the 20th century, John Major (born 1943) succeeded Margaret Thatcher as leader of the Conservative Party and **political head of the United Kingdom in 1990, a post he held until 1997.**

John Major had a highly unusual background for a Conservative Party leader. Born on March 29, 1943, in the middle-class London suburb of Merton, he was the son of Gwendolyn and Thomas Major. Thomas Major, 66 when his son was born, was a colorful man who had a remarkably varied career as a circus acrobat, vaudevillian, mercenary, and manufacturer of garden ornaments. When John Major was very young, the family lived in comfortable circumstances, and he attended Rutlish Grammar School, a state-run school for bright children. When Major was 11, however, the family moved to Brixton, the so-called "South Bronx of London," after Thomas Major's business suffered financial reverses.

Young Major disliked the authoritarian atmosphere of school and left at 16 to find work. His first job was a clerical position, which he soon left to pursue a more lucrative career as a construction laborer. Shortly after this change he was laid off and spent several months on the dole. These months were a formative experience for Major, who became a Conservative after deciding that socialistic paternalism only perpetuated poverty. At 18 Major found another clerical position, and this time he started a career. Through his native intelligence and hard work he rapidly made his way through the ranks of the Standard Chartered bank, eventually becoming assistant to the bank's chairman. In the mid-1960s Major went to Nigeria, where he performed

community service work and where he acquired a heart-felt hatred of racism.

Upon his return Major continued working at the bank and, after determining that he "wanted to be inside the goldfish bowl rather than outside, longingly looking in," he began to take an active role in politics, at first at the local level. He served as a member of the Lambeth Borough Council from 1968 to 1971 and was chairman of the council's housing committee from 1970 to 1971. It was during this time that he met a quiet, opera-loving, young campaign worker, Norma Johnson, a home economics teacher. They married in 1970, which was, Major later said, "the best decision of my life." Major made two unsuccessful attempts to win a parliamentary seat in 1974 and eventually succeeded in 1979, becoming the Conservative member for Huntingdonshire in east central England.

John Major in Parliament

Major's parliamentary career progressed steadily from committee work to parliamentary private secretary in the early 1980s. In 1983 he became an assistant government whip and in 1984 a full-fledged whip, a position which helped him to understand the interests and concerns of backbenchers as well as providing him with much greater visibility to all members of Parliament. It was in this capacity that he first came prominently to Margaret Thatcher's attention. At a dinner party he held his own against her in a heated argument about economic policy. Thatcher was impressed (Major later stated that Thatcher "doesn't like wimps"), and thereafter served as Major's patron.

Major was soon appointed undersecretary of social security (1985-1986) and social security secretary (1986-1987), where he was noted for his compassionate concern for the elderly. From 1987 to 1989 he served as chief secretary to the treasury, the effective deputy chancellor of the exchequer. In this position, serving under the brilliant but controversial Nigel Lawson, Major was able to emulate his father's acrobatic skills by holding a firm line on government spending without making enemies of his more senior colleagues. Like his mentor Thatcher a devotee of a strict monetary policy, he said, "Public expenditure must be restricted. People must understand that if they have jam today, they may not be able to afford butter tomorrow."

In July 1989 Major's career took a quantum leap when, during a Cabinet reshuffle, Margaret Thatcher appointed him foreign secretary. The appointment attracted a great deal of attention—and no little surprise. Major professed himself to be "totally astonished," and political observers were stunned that the young and wholly inexperienced Major had been placed in one of the top positions in the British government. Many attributed the appointment to Thatcher's desire to move Major's predecessor, Sir Geoffrey Howe, to a less visible position, and most realized that it was a great tribute to Thatcher's confidence in Major. Nonetheless, Major did not much enjoy his stay at the Foreign Office, where his informal style offended traditionalist civil servants and diplomats and where he found the work unfamiliar and uncongenial.

He had very little time to make his mark in foreign affairs because, as the result of another Cabinet reshuffle, he was appointed chancellor of the exchequer in October 1989. As a former banker and deputy chancellor, Major had strong credentials for the job, which was, said his wife Norma, "the job he's always wanted." The circumstances surrounding Major's appointment, however, were not auspicious. He replaced the confrontational Nigel Lawson, whose strong differences with Thatcher over the issue of the European Community's impending economic union had caused internal divisions in the party. Also, the economy, racked by rising inflation and unemployment, was headed towards recession. Despite these drawbacks, Major quickly established his authority in the Treasury and proved to be a very well-respected and well-liked boss known for his approachability, thoughtfulness, hard work, and careful decision-making. As chancellor Major emphasized his strict anti-inflation policy, characterized by tight controls on government spending and high interest rates.

In March 1990 Major passed his first big test as chancellor when he presented the fiscal year 1991 budget. The budget proposed no sweeping changes: high interest rates would remain to combat inflation. Calling for a return to a "culture of thrift," Major sought to stimulate savings by offering special tax-exempt savings plans. More important than the substance of the budget speech, however, was its style. Major self-confidently, skillfully, and clearly presented his budget to Parliament and a large television audience, helping restore confidence in the government and doing his own career no little good.

Like many of his Conservative colleagues, Major took a cautious view on the impending European Community's economic union. Though not as anti-Europe as his leader, Major fully understood her fears of the impact of European economic union on British sovereignty, and he had to tread a careful path between Thatcher's manifest disapproval and complying with Britain's obligations to her European partners. Utilizing all his skills as a peacemaker, he slowly eased Britain's path to Europe, entering Britain into the Exchange Rate Mechanism of the European Monetary System in October 1990.

Replaces Thatcher as Prime Minister

Following a challenge to her leadership from former Cabinet minister Michael Heseltine, Thatcher resigned as prime minister on November 22, 1990. Major quickly emerged as a strong candidate to succeed her: he had the backing of Thatcher and the "Thatcherite" wing of the party, his background in economic affairs provided him with important experience, and he was widely liked. After a brief campaign, in which he was opposed by Heseltine and Foreign Secretary Douglas Hurd, he won the leadership election on November 27, 1990, and became prime minister the next day.

As the new prime minister, Major called for party unity and took steps to achieve it by immediately appointing his electoral opponents to Cabinet positions: Heseltine as environment secretary and Hurd again as foreign secretary. His new Cabinet was substantially different from Thatcher's and served to demonstrate that Major was his own man and not, as his critics impugned, "Son of Thatcher." The former poor boy from Brixton also pledged to help build a "society of opportunity . . . in which what people fulfill will depend upon their talent, their application and their good fortune."

The first problem confronting the new prime minister occurred within the Conservative Party when a black lawyer was selected as the party's parliamentary candidate in Cheltenham. This selection caused some blatantly racist opposition from a small group of local Tories, which Major quickly squelched. But Major also had to face long-term problems whose solutions have eluded both Tory and Labor governments for the past 20 years: integration with Europe and the ailing British economy.

Major's chances for success were greater than his predecessor's, however. Although the giant shadow of Thatcher loomed over him, Major was, and, just as important, seemed to be, a "kinder, gentler" person. He had the ability to inspire both respect and liking, could be firm without being strident, could encourage discussion without dominating it, and could be polite without being condescending. He had a quiet, modest, and self-effacing manner which colleagues and opponents alike found congenial.

Major was different in other ways as well. He was, as was widely observed, the first world leader not to remember World War II, and his perceptions and expectations set him apart from his elders. In addition, he was viewed by some as a sort of symbol, living proof of Thatcher's Toryism of upward mobility through individual achievement, not through family connections. And unlike Thatcher, Major was no ideologue. Indeed, he was often described by British politics critics as a "grey man" because he was calm, efficient, and a little dull and because it was difficult to pin down his views on controversial matters. Despite his strict views on economic matters, he was not an aggressively right-wing Tory, nor was he a left winger, even though on social issues such as capital punishment and racism he was determinedly liberal. He was, in fact, a centrist, who could gain support from all factions within the party.

In mid-1995 Major resigned as the head of the Conservative Party and called for a parliamentary election to establish leadership of the party. With that move, Major became the first British Prime Minister to subject himself to a leadership role while in office. Major won the election on July 4, 1995. In 1997, however, Major lost the election to Labor Party leader Tony Blair and stepped down from the office of prime minister.

Further Reading

The first book-length biography of John Major was Edward Pearce, *The Quiet Rise of John Major* (London: 1991); an excellent introduction to Major's background, characteristics as a politician, and prospects can be found in Sheila Rule's "A Meteor in Thatcher's Political Constellation," *New York Times* (October 27, 1989); for useful information on Norma Major and the Majors' personal life, see Maurice Chittenden's "Purdah Reduces Major's Wife to Tears," *London Sunday Times* (March 18, 1990); Guy Garcia gives a balanced examination of Major's leadership victory in "A Victory of Major Proportions," *Time* (December 10, 1990); Craig R. Whitney's article in the *New York Times* on November 28, 1990, is a good overview of Major's prospects as prime minister, especially regarding the economy; more discussion of Major's prime ministerial prospects is provided by Daniel Pedersen's "The Tory of the Future," *Newsweek* (December 10, 1990), which additionally presents a thorough analysis of Major's political background; "The Surprising Mr. Major," in *The Economist* (December 1, 1990), also discusses Major's prospects as prime minister, but from a Conservative perspective; another article in the same issue of *The Economist*, "John Major: More Than a Tedious Talent," praises Major's achievements and hails his "greyness" as being uniquely suited to British politics and the British national character. □

Makarios III

His Beatitude, Makarios III (1913-1977), archbishop and ethnarch of the Orthodox Church of Cyprus and the first president of the Republic of Cyprus, 1959-1977, championed the campaign to unite the island politically with Greece for a quarter-century.

Archbishop Makarios III was born Michael Christodoulou Mouskos on August 13, 1913, the son of a goatherder in the village of Ano Panayia, near Paphos in western Cyprus. The island was then under British administration. At age 13, after a primary education in the village, he was accepted as a novice in the famed monastery of Kykko and began a brilliant career as a student. At age 20 he was sent to the Pancyprian Gymnasium in Nicosia, where he completed his secondary education in 1936. Returning to Kykko, he was ordained a deacon in the Greek Orthodox Church in August 1938, taking the name of Makarios, meaning "blessed." A month later the monastery gave him a small grant to help him continue his studies in Greece.

Makarios spent the difficult years of World War II studying theology and law at the University of Athens. In 1946 he was ordained a priest and awarded a scholarship by the World Council of Churches to do further theological study in the United States. Makarios was studying religion and sociology at the theological school at Boston University when in the spring of 1948 he was informed that he had been elected bishop of Kitium (one of the four sees of the Orthodox Church in Cyprus) and was to return home. Two years later, in October 1950, following the death of his aged superior, Makarios II, the 400,000 Greek Cypriots elected him archbishop and ethnarch (national leader) of Cyprus. At age 37 Archbishop Makarios III took charge of one of the 14 autocephalous churches of Eastern Orthodoxy.

Makarios promptly became the dedicated and acknowledged spokesman for *enosis,* the near-unanimous desire of Greek Cypriots for the end of British rule and the political union of Cyprus with Greece, a cause that had moved him personally since his late teens. During the next five years he worked tirelessly and successfully to attract the world's attention to the issue of self-determination for Cyprus—in Athens, London, Washington, and various Eu-

ropean capitals; at the United Nations General Assembly; and at the Asian-African Conference of third-world leaders in Bandung, Indonesia, in April 1955. Great Britain was hesitant. It was prepared to offer a measure of home rule to Cyprus but was concerned about the political status of the 100,000 Cypriot Turks and the security of its own extensive military installations there, the headquarters of its Middle-East Command. Turkey threatened to take Cyprus (located only 40 miles from Turkish shores but 700 miles from Greece) rather than let Greece acquire it.

In response, after 1955 Makarios became increasingly combative, accepting support not only from Greek Cypriot nationalists but also from the Communists and EOKA (the National Organization for the Liberation of Cyprus), the underground guerrilla movement led by the implacable Colonel (later General) George Grivas. He appeared to condone, even encourage, the rising tide of demonstrations and riots, acts of sabotage and violence, and open terrorism that engulfed the island and precipitated bloody disturbances in Turkey and Greece. The British replied by sending crack troops to Cyprus and making mass arrests. In March 1956, when Makarios himself was allegedly implicated in terrorism, the British authorities deported him to Mahé, one of the Seychelles Islands in the Indian Ocean. He was freed in early 1957 and, forbidden to return to Cyprus, he went to Athens. Finally, in February 1959, he met with the prime ministers of Britain, Turkey, and Greece in London to work out a compromise agreement for an independent Cypriot republic.

Makarios returned to Cyprus in triumph and was easily elected its first president in December 1959. He was re-elected twice—in 1968 and 1973—with overwhelming majorities. Gradually, however, the continuing friction between the Greek and Turkish populations and the precarious status of the new republic convinced him that enosis was inopportune and would have to be postponed. This alienated Greek Cypriot extremists who, with the backing of the military junta then ruling Greece, mounted pressure to remove Makarios from office. He managed to survive several attempts to assassinate him and a move by several Cypriot bishops to depose him as archbishop. Finally, in July 1974, he was briefly removed from the presidency and exiled by a right-wing coup. He returned in December, but not before Turkey, interpreting his removal as a prelude to *enosis,* had sent troops to invade Cyprus and occupy the northern 40 percent of the island. Three years later, when Makarios died of a heart attack in Nicosia on August 3, 1977, Cyprus was still divided. It remained so into the mid-1980s, separated practically into two hostile states, the Republic of Cyprus and the Turkish Republic of Northern Cyprus, with a United Nations peacekeeping force manning a demilitarized buffer zone between them.

Makarios was buried in a tomb he himself had designed on a mountain peak above Kykko. Without the charismatic "dark priest," with his dour intransigence, his "Byzantine" shrewdness, and his wide personal influence, the "Cyprus Question" seemed destined to remain unsolved.

Further Reading

Stanley Mayes, *Makarios: A Biography* (1981) is, like Mayes' earlier book *Cyprus & Makarios* (1960), a sympathetic but critical treatment of Makarios based on long study of the Cyprus problem and close personal contact with the prelate-statesman. Nancy Crawshaw's *The Cyprus Revolt: An Account of the Struggle for Union with Greece* (1978) deals with the broader context of enosis, primarily to about 1960, and contains a comprehensive bibliography on the subject. □

Francis Makemie

Francis Makemie (1658-1708) was the Irish-born Presbyterian missionary who organized the first American presbytery.

F rancis Makemie was born in County Donegal, Ireland. He belonged to the population of northern Ireland transplanted by Scottish colonization. His boyhood belonged to the years of turbulent political struggle between Presbyterian leaders and Anglican bishops. The bishops' victory resulted in the Scots-Irish exodus to America at the beginning of the 18th century. Makemie's missionary zeal and lifelong battle for religious freedom can be understood in the light of this earlier history.

Barred from the Irish University because he was Presbyterian, Makemie took a degree from the University of

Glasgow. In 1681 he was licensed to preach and in 1682 was ordained as a missionary to America. This was more than a generation before the great migration of Scots-Irish to America. Because New England, particularly Massachusetts, was inhospitable territory for Presbyterians, he preached in Maryland, North Carolina, and Virginia, combining his missionary work with business, as there was no provision for financial support for a missionary at that time. At some time before 1698 he had become the settled pastor at Rehoboth, one of various churches he had organized; nevertheless, he continued missionary work in Delaware and Virginia.

In 1705 Makemie visited England and interested the Presbyterian Union of London in supporting missionary work in America. Two other missionaries returned with him to take charge of several churches in Maryland. In 1706 he formed seven missionaries working in scattered churches of the Middle colonies into a voluntary association. This became the first presbytery in America, with power to license its own preachers. This was a significant act of churchmanship, making American Presbyterianism independent of external control.

In 1707 Makemie and a fellow missionary, visiting New York, preached in a private house and were discovered, arrested, and brought before Governor Cornbury for preaching without a New York license. Makemie protested that no law justified this arrest. His refusal to promise that he would not preach again resulted in a 6-week jail term.

Francis Makemie (standing, pointing)

Defended at his trial by three of the ablest lawyers of the colony, he was acquitted, although required to pay complete charges for the prosecution as well as for his defense. This case became widely known throughout America. The recall of Lord Cornbury was an immediate result. The long-range result was a victory for freedom of worship not limited to New York.

Makemie died in 1708. At the bicentennial of American Presbyterianism in 1906, a monument in his honor was erected on the Virginia farm where he is buried.

Further Reading

A biography of Makemie is I. Marshall Page, *The Life Story of Rev. Francis Makemie* (1938). Additional information can be found in the appendix, chapter 3, of C. A. Briggs, *American Presbyterianism: Its Origin and Early History* (1885), and in Guy Soulliard Klett, *Presbyterians in Colonial Pennsylvania* (1937). □

Fumihiko Maki

Architect Fumihiko Maki (born 1928) came to prominence in the 1960s, a period of growth and vibrancy in Japanese architecture.

Although still identified with the classic modernism of the International Style, he moved on to create more complicated and ambiguous buildings that relate to the contemporary movement known as Deconstruction. His high-profile designs include the Museum of Modern Art in Tokyo, the Tokyo Metropolitan Gymnasium in Kyoto, and the Nippon Convention Center. In the United States his work includes Washington University's Steinberg Hall Art Center, St. Louis, MO, and the Yerba Buena Gardens Visual Arts Center in San Francisco, CA. He has won several honors—including the 1993 Pritzker Architecture Prize and the Union Internationale des Architectes (UIA) Gold Medal Prize.

Fumihiko Maki was born in Tokyo in 1928 and was raised there. After graduating from the University of Tokyo in 1952 with a degree in architecture, Maki pursued graduate work in the United States. He studied at Michigan's Cranbrook Academy and at Harvard University, where he received a master's degree from the Graduate School of Design. After completing his formal education in the mid-1950s, Maki worked first as a designer for the large and successful commercial firm of Skidmore, Owings, and Merrill in New York, and then went on to teach at various academic institutions, including Washington University (St. Louis, MO), Harvard University, and the University of Tokyo. Upon his return to Japan he established his own architectural firm, Maki and Associates.

Never content to simply write or talk about architecture, Fumihiko Maki was an active designer throughout his professional life. About his desire to build, he remarked: "I do not want to put my thoughts only on the level of drawings and models. I am a fairly pragmatic sort of practitioner and I want to express these thoughts in real buildings.''

At the beginning of his career, Maki's designs reflected his Modernist education in the United States: his Toyota Memorial Hall at Nagoya University (1960), the Hillside Terrace House Project, Tokyo (1969), and the Kanazawa Municipal Center, Yokohama (1971), are representative of this early phase. For example, for the series of undecorated, cube-like structures of Hillside Terrace Maki initially chose to stress unity, simplicity, and harmony in a group of individual buildings. As with virtually all of his early buildings, Maki's Hillside Terrace is built of modern materials, including steel and concrete.

Maki was associated with the Japanese architectural movement of the 1960s called Metabolism. In 1960 he contributed to an early publication on that subject (much as the celebrated American architect Philip Johnson helped ''write the book'' on the International Style in the 1920s). The Metabolist idea that buildings should respond to a changing world seems to have had a profound impact on Maki's work while he matured as an architect. Further, beginning in the 1980s Fumihiko Maki took a more overtly eclectic approach to design, and his designs during this period appear more harmonious with the contemporary world, and particularly with the nature of the modern city.

This later trend is exemplified by a commercial building in Tokyo known as ''The Spiral'' (1985). A succession of complicated and fragmented spaces and forms, The Spiral pays tribute to the densely-built urban environment of Tokyo—the city Maki knew best. A remark he made about ''The Spiral''—''First I decompose the elements and then recompose''—suggests his comfort and familiarity with the contemporary movement called Deconstruction.

Maki generally avoided the approach of the Post-Modernists, however, seeking instead to affirm his Modernist roots in works that acknowledge place without evoking styles of the past. At Tokyo's Keio University he created a new library building (1981) in which he chose not to mimic the Victorian architecture of the neighboring old library. His salmon-pink, tile-covered cubic structure, with the majority of its usable space buried underground, unites in color and scale with the older structure but does not attempt to make the connection between old and new.

Maki's Modernist roots appear in another aspect of his architecture: the wedding of form and function. Speaking of his Fujisawa Gymnasium (1984) in particular, and of his work in general, he said: ''I think ambiguity in the meanings of forms is quite interesting. However, coming back to the architects' responsibility to society, you cannot just play a game either. You must satisfy certain basic requirements. I would say that architecture has to be able to accommodate these needs.'' The Fujisawa Gymnasium nevertheless houses with ease all the activities that are required of a suburban school gymnasium.

Maki also designed Maki House, at the Children's Village in Oswiecim, Poland, and Izar-Buro Park, Munich, Germany.

He has written extensively, often about his own work. His writing includes: ''Yerba Buena Gardens Visual Arts Center'' *The Japan Architect* (Aug./Sept. 1990); ''TEPIA'' *The Japan Architect* (Aug./Sept. 1990); ''Fumihiko Maki'' *GA Document No. 25* (1990); ''Driving Forces of the 1990s'' *The Japan Architect* (Spring 1991); ''Swimming and Diving Hall, Cycling Hall for Berlin Olympics 2000: Design Competition Proposal'' *The Japan Architect* (Summer 1992); ''The Tokyo Design Center'' *Domus* (Nov. 1992); ''Fumihiko Maki'' *Architectural Design* (Sept./Oct. 1992); ''New Congress Center, Salzburg, Austria'' *GA Document No. 36* (1993); ''Space, Image and Materiality'' *The Japan Architect* (Winter 1994); ''Notes on Collective Form'' *The Japan Architect* (Winter 1994); ''Public Architecture for a New Age'' *Places* (Cambridge, MA, Summer 1994); ''Fumihiko Maki'' *GA Document No. 39* (1994); ''Winners in the Shinkenchiku Residential Design Competition 1994'' *The Japan Architect* (Spring 1995); ''Fumihiko Maki'' *Casabella* (Jan./Feb. 1996); and ''Stillness and Plenitude'' *The Japan Architect* (Spring 1996).

Fumihiko Maki has been honored with a variety of national and international awards and fellowships. Among the most prestigious of these were the Japan Institute of Architects' Award (1985); the American Institute of Architects' Reynolds Award (1987); the Thomas Jefferson Medal of Architecture (1990); the Pritzker Architecture Prize (1993); and the Union Internationale des Architectes (UIA) Gold Medal Prize (1993).

Further Reading

To learn more about Japanese architecture in general, consult David Stewart's *The Making of a Modern Japanese Architecture: 1868 to the Present* (Harper & Row, 1987); and Suzuki and Banham's *Contemporary Architecture of Japan, 1958-1984* (Rizzoli, 1985). Interesting monographs covering Maki's work include Dale Casper's *Fumihiko Maki: Master Architect* (Vance, 1988); and *Maki, Isozaki: New Public Architecture* (Japan Society, 1985). *Fumihiko Maki: An Aesthetic of Fragmentation* (Rizzoli, 1988) by Serge Salat is also engaging. In *Japan Architect* (March 1987) there is a lively and revealing interview with Maki conducted by Roger Connah, and that issue is devoted almost entirely to Maki and provides a look at the architect from the perspective of the Japanese artistic community. See also Botond Bognar, *The New Japanese Architecture* (Rizzoli, 1990); and James Steele, ed., *Museum Builders* (St. Martin's Press, 1994).

The following periodicals contain discussions of Fumihiko Maki: ''Two Landmarks for Tokyo'' *Progressive Architecture* (Aug. 1990); Naomi R. Pollock, ''Children's Village Includes Maki House'' *Architectural Record* (June 1992); ''That Certain Japanese Lightness'' *The Economist* (Aug. 22, 1992); Kurt Andersen, ''From the Sublime to the Meticulous'' *Time* (May 3, 1993); Suzanne Muchnic, ''Japan's Fumihiko Maki Wins Coveted Pritzker Prize'' *Los Angeles Times* (April 26, 1993); John Morris Dixon, ''Fumihiko Maki Wins Pritzker and UIA Prizes'' *Progressive Architecture* (May 1993); Susannah Temko, ''Maki, Polshek, and Botta Buildings to Bloom at Yerba Buena Gardens'' *Architectural Record* (Aug. 1993); Eva M. Kahn, ''Sailing Along the Cutting Edge'' *The Wall Street Journal* (Nov. 3, 1993); and Naomi R. Pollock, ''Silver Palette'' *Architectural Record* (March 1994).

The following articles appear in the Winter 1994 issue of *Japan Architect*: P. Polledri, ''A Modern Building for Post-Modern

Art—Fumihiko Maki Center-for-the-Arts at Yerba-Buena Gardens''; K. Ackerman, ''Place, Scale and Transparency—Izar-Buro Park, Munich, Germany, by Fumihiko Maki''; D.B. Stewart, ''Apollo in the Age of Deconstruction, Concert Hall and Graduate Research Center by Fumihiko Maki''; J.L. Cohen, ''The Recent Work of Fumihiko Maki, Beyond the Fragment, Time Regained''; and Y. Teramatsu, ''Fumihiko Maki—Project Data, Profile and Publications.'' See also: P. Chow, ''Tokyo Evolution—Fumihiko Maki Scheme for Hillside Terrace Mixed Development'' *Architectural Review* (June 1995); Naomi R. Pollock, ''A Quiet Sanctuary by the Highway: Tokyo Church of Christ, Tokyo Japan, Fumihiko Maki and Associates—Architect'' *Architectural Record* (Oct. 1996). □

Kibi-no Makibi

Kibi-no Makibi (693-775) was a Japanese courtier who became minister of the right. He was a rare example of men of exceptional ability who rose to higher status than that to which their birth entitled them.

Kibi-no Makibi, also called Kibi-no Mabi, was born in the region of Kibi, and his father became a minor official in the central government. In 717 Makibi accompanied a Japanese embassy to China as a student and returned to Japan in 735 with the next embassy. During his stay in T'ang China he studied not only Confucianism but also astronomy, military affairs, and folk arts. He was well known in the Chinese court circles for his practical wisdom, courage, and sharp wit.

Makibi became a favorite of the Japanese emperor Shomu (reigned 724-749) and was called the Togu Gakushi, or the Scholar of the Eastern Palace. He lectured on Confucian classics and managed to introduce some aspects of the mature T'ang culture to Japan. He is credited with contributing to the formation of the so-called Taihei (great peace) culture.

When Fujiwara Nakamaro, also known as Emi-no Oshikatsu, became powerful in the court, Makibi was banished to a remote area. He was sent again to T'ang China at the imperial command and returned to Japan in 754. When Fujiwara Nakamaro fell from power, Makibi was once again in the service of the court. It is said that the empress regnant Koken had the Ido Castle erected at Chikuzen (Fukuoka Prefecture) upon his advice.

Makibi was appointed minister of the right and helped in revising the laws of the land and contributed much toward governmental reforms. He was affectionately referred to as ''Minister Kibi.'' After the death of Emperor Shotoku (Koken Tenno) in 770, there arose a succession controversy in which the Buddhist priest and favorite of Empress Koken attempted to usurp the power of the throne. After this was averted, Makibi's recommendations were rejected by the Fujiwaras, and Emperor Konin ascended the throne. Minister Kibi resigned from all official posts in 771 and died 4 years later.

Further Reading

For some relevant dates and facts on Makibi see Jean and Robert Karl Reischauer, *Early Japanese History,* part B (1967). A brief background to the modification of the Chinese system in Japan and Makibi's role in it are in Edwin O. Reischauer and John King Fairbank, *A History of East Asian Civilization,* vol. 1: *East Asia: The Great Tradition* (1960). A scroll portraying the adventures of Makibi in China is mentioned in Sir George Sansom, *A History of Japan to 1334* (1958). □

Mäkonnen Endalkačäw

Mäkonnen Endalkačäw (1892-1963) was an Ethiopian writer and public official. One of the few aristocrats to attain high government office under Haile Selassie, he was responsible for the renaissance of Amharic literature after World War II.

Mäkonnen Endalkačäw was born into a family of feudal landowners in Shoa. He was educated at the court of Menelik II and was a close friend of the future emperor Haile Selassie I, one of whose nieces he married. After the appointment of Haile Selassie as regent, Mäkonnen occupied high office as minister of commerce (1926-1931), Ethiopian representative in England and at the League of Nations (1931-1933), governor of Addis Ababa (1933-1934), and governor of Illulabor Province (1935).

When the Italian war broke out, Mäkonnen was put in command of the Ogaden front. During the period of Italian occupation, he stayed in Jerusalem, where he looked after the many Ethiopian refugees there. In 1940 Haile Selassie called him to Khartoum, where he was preparing the reconquest of the country, and in January 1941 Mäkonnen crossed into Ethiopia with the Emperor. After the liberation Mäkonnen was made minister of the interior and rose to considerable influence at court. In 1942 he was appointed to the newly created office of prime minister, and in 1957 he became president of the Senate.

Modern Amharic literature, which had been launched by Heruy Wäldä-Sellasé, had suffered a grievous lapse under the Italian regime. After World War II, side by side with his important political and administrative activities, Mäkonnen played a decisive part in the restoration and tremendous growth of creative writing in the vernacular language. No one of his generation wrote as many novels, plays, and memoirs; three of his works were translated into English and published in Asmara.

Two central themes control Mäkonnen's vast literary output. The first is the deeply religious and moralizing trend which pervades the whole of Ethiopia's literary tradition. It runs through his work, from *Aläm warätänña* (1947-1948; The Inconstant World), which proclaims the vanity of this world and urges forbearance in the face of adversity, to his last novel, *Sahay Mäsfen* (1956-1957), which extols charity and altruism and deprecates all egoistic pride based on birth, wealth, or even education. The second theme is a fiery patriotic sense which had been fanned by the humiliations of the colonial period. His first work in that nationalistic direction was *Yädämdems* (1947-1948; The Voice of Blood), a play in which he dramatized the martyrdom of Abuna Petros, the head of the Coptic Church of Ethiopia, who had been shot by the Fascists.

Mäkonnen's patriotic pride and ethical preoccupations were fused in his historical novels and plays, through which he endeavored to celebrate and popularize the greatness of the Ethiopian past. But although he was a faithful upholder of the Emperor's modernizing policies, many of his works, such as *Selasawi Dawit* (1949-1950; David III), *Yä-däm zämän* (1954-1955; The Bloody Era), and *Taitu Bitull* (1957-1958), contain unmistakable warnings against the abuses and corruption of absolute power and a reminder that political might should be used in compliance with the laws of God and of the Church for the benefit of the people.

Actually, Mäkonnen's outlook was fundamentally aristocratic. His somewhat utopian ideal—illustrated in the autobiographical works of his later years, such as *Malkanu beta saboč* (1956-1957; The Good Family)—was that of a hierarchized society led by a Christian feudal class deeply conscious of the responsibilities which material wealth and secular power have placed upon its shoulders.

Mäkonnen retired from political office in 1961. He died on Feb. 27, 1963.

Further Reading

A brief biographical sketch of Mäkonnen appears in Christopher S. Clapham, *Haile-Selassie's Government* (1969). See also Margery Perham, *The Government of Ethiopia* (1948; rev. ed. 1969); Edward Ullendorff, *The Ethiopians: An Introduction to Country and People* (1960; 2d ed. 1965); and Richard Greenfield, *Ethiopia: A New Political History* (1965). □

Bernard Malamud

Bernard Malamud (1914–1986) is considered one of the most prominent figures in Jewish-American literature, a movement that originated in the 1930s and is known for its tragicomic elements.

Malamud's stories and novels, in which reality and fantasy are frequently interlaced, have been compared to parables, myths, and allegories and often illustrate the importance of moral obligation. Although he draws upon his Jewish heritage to address the themes of sin, suffering, and redemption, Malamud emphasizes human contact and compassion over orthodox religious dogma. Malamud's characters, while often awkward and isolated from society, evoke both pity and humor through their attempts at survival and salvation. Sheldon J.

Hershinow observed: "Out of the everyday defeats and indignities of ordinary people, Malamud creates beautiful parables that capture the joy as well as the pain of life; he expresses the dignity of the human spirit searching for freedom and moral growth in the face of hardship, injustice, and the existential anguish of life."

Malamud was born April 28, 1914, in Brooklyn, New York, to Russian Jewish immigrants. His parents, whom he described as "gentle, honest, kindly people," were not highly educated and knew very little about literature or the arts: "There were no books that I remember in the house, no records, music, pictures on the wall." Malamud attended high school in Brooklyn and received his Bachelor's degree from the City College of New York in 1936. After graduation, he worked in a factory and as a clerk at the Census Bureau in Washington, D. C. Although he wrote in his spare time, Malamud did not begin writing seriously until the advent of World War II and the subsequent horrors of the Holocaust. He questioned his religious identity and started reading about Jewish tradition and history. He explained: "I was concerned with what Jews stood for, with their getting down to the bare bones of things. I was concerned with their ethnicality—how Jews felt they had to live in order to go on living." In 1949, he began teaching at Oregon State University; he left this post in 1961 to teach creative writing at Bennington College in Vermont. He remained there until shortly before his death in 1986.

Malamud's first novel, *The Natural* (1952), is considered one of his most symbolic works. While the novel ostensibly traces the life of Roy Hobbs, an American

baseball player, the work has underlying mythic elements and explores such themes as initiation and isolation. For instance, some reviewers cited evidence of the Arthurian legend of the Holy Grail; others applied T. S. Eliot's "wasteland" myth in their analyses. *The Natural* also foreshadows what would become Malamud's predominant narrative focus: a suffering protagonist struggling to reconcile moral dilemmas, to act according to what is right, and to accept the complexities and hardships of existence. Malamud's second novel, *The Assistant* (1957), portrays the life of Morris Bober, a Jewish immigrant who owns a grocery store in Brooklyn. Although he is struggling to survive financially, Bober hires a cynical anti-Semitic youth, Frank Alpine, after learning that the man is homeless and on the verge of starvation. Through this contact Frank learns to find grace and dignity in his own identity. Described as a naturalistic fable, this novel affirms the redemptive value of maintaining faith in the goodness of the human soul. Malamud's first collection of short stories, *The Magic Barrel* (1958), was awarded the National Book award in 1959. Like *The Assistant,* most of the stories in this collection depict the search for hope and meaning within the grim entrapment of poor urban settings and were influenced by Yiddish folktales and Hasidic traditions. Many of Malamud's best-known short stories, including "The Last Mohican," "Angel Levine," and "Idiots First," were republished in *The Stories of Bernard Malamud* in 1983.

A New Life (1961), considered one of Malamud's most realistic novels, is based in part on Malamud's teaching career at Oregon State University. This work focuses on an ex-alcoholic Jew from New York City who, in order to escape his reputation as a drunkard, becomes a professor at an agricultural and technical college in the Pacific Northwest. Interweaving the protagonist's quest for significance and self-respect with a satiric mockery of academia, Malamud explores the destructive nature of idealism, how love can lead to deception, and the pain of loneliness. Malamud's next novel, *The Fixer* (1966), is considered one of his most powerful works. The winner of both the Pulitzer Prize and the National Book Award, this book is derived from the historical account of Mendel Beiliss, a Russian Jew who was accused of murdering a Christian child. Drawing upon Eastern European Jewish mysticism, *The Fixer* turns this terrifying story of torture and humiliation into a parable of human triumph. With *The Tenants* (1971), Malamud returns to a New York City setting, where the theme of self-exploration is developed through the contrast between two writers, one Jewish and the other black, struggling to survive in an urban ghetto. Within the context of their confrontations about artistic standards, Malamud also explores how race informs cultural identity, the purpose of literature, and the conflict between art and life. Alvin B. Kernan commented: "[*The Tenants*] is extraordinarily powerful and compelling in its realization of the view that is central to the conception of literature as a social institution: that literature and the arts are an inescapable part of society."

Malamud further addresses the nature of literature and the role of the artist in *Dubin's Lives* (1979). In this work, the protagonist, William Dubin, attempts to create a sense of worth for himself, both as a man and as a writer. A biographer who escapes into his work to avoid the reality of his life, Dubin bumbles through comically disastrous attempts at love and passion in an effort to find self-fulfillment. Malamud's next novel, *God's Grace* (1982), differs from his earlier works in scope and presentation of subject matter. Set in the near future immediately after a nuclear disaster which leaves only one human being alive, *God's Grace* explores the darkness of human morality, the nature of God, and the vanity and destruction associated with contemporary life. Critical reception to this work varied greatly. Some critics felt that the contrast between the serious moral fable and the protagonist's penchant for alternately conversing with God and a group of apes unique and challenging; others believed the structure of the novel did not support the seriousness and ambition of its themes. However, *God's Grace,* like all of his works, reveals Malamud's motivations as a writer and expresses his profound humanistic concerns. Malamud explained: "It seems to me that the writer's most important task, no matter what the current theory of man, or his prevailing mood, is to recapture his image as human being as each of us in his secret heart knows it to be."

Further Reading

Chicago Tribune, March 20, 1986.
Detroit News, March 23, 1986.
Los Angeles Times, March 19, 1986.
New Republic, May 12, 1986.
Newsweek, March 31, 1986.
New York Times, March 20, 1986.
Times (London), March 20, 1986.
Washington Post, March 20, 1986.
Alter, Iska, *The Good Man's Dilemma: Social Criticism in the Fiction of Bernard Malamud,* AMS Press, 1981.
Astro, Richard, and Jackson J. Benson, editors, *The Fiction of Bernard Malamud,* Oregon State University Press, 1977.
Avery, Evelyn G., *Rebels and Victims: The Fiction of Richard Wright and Bernard Malamud,* Kennikat, 1979.
Baumbach, Jonathan, *The Landscape of Nightmare: Studies in the Contemporary American Novel,* New York University Press, 1965.
Bilik, Dorothy Seldman, *Immigrant-Survivors: Post-Holocaust Consciousness in Recent Jewish-American Literature,* Wesleyan University Press, 1981.
Bloom, Harold, *Bernard Malamud,* Chelsea House, 1986.
Cohen, Sandy, *Bernard Malamud and the Trial by Love,* Rodopi (Amsterdam), 1974. □

Daniel Francois Malan

The Afrikaner pastor and journalist Daniel Francois Malan (1874-1959) was the fourth prime minister of South Africa. His advocacy of segregation made him the symbol of white South Africa's defiance of world condemnation of his country's racial policies.

Daniel Malan was born near Riebeeck West on May 22, 1874. He graduated in theology from Stellenbosch and obtained a doctorate in philosophy from Utrecht. On his return home he served for a while as a minister of the Dutch Reformed Church and involved himself in work to solve the poor-white problem. A dour champion of the Afrikaner's cause, he was one of the leaders of the second movement to place Afrikaans on a footing of equality with English.

James Hertzog had founded the National party in 1914. The following year Malan was appointed editor of its daily, *Die Burger.* He campaigned vigorously in its columns for Afrikaner political unity and entered Parliament in 1918. He became leader of the Cape nationalists and was appointed to Hertzog's first Cabinet in 1924. The depression forced Hertzog and Jan Christiaan Smuts into a coalition in 1933. Malan regarded this as a betrayal of nationalist Afrikanerdom. He broke with Hertzog and formed a "purified" National party. In World War II Malan opposed South Africa's participation. His relations with the Nazis were a subject of inquiry after the war.

It is impossible to give a balanced picture of a South African political leader without referring to his views on the race question. Malan's rule was an era of transition from the paternalistic segregation of his predecessors in office to what has been described as the efficient inhumanity of the apartheid ideologues.

In 1947 the National party appointed a committee to draw up a program for the 1948 general elections. Its recommendations were published as a pamphlet in which apartheid was formally stated to be the party's policy. Its main points included the preservation of white supremacy, separation of the races, and retribalization of the Africans. It

was this policy which brought the National party to power in May 1948.

African reactions to Malan's rule were without precedent in the history of South Africa. Chief Albert Luthuli, a known moderate who was later awarded the Nobel Peace Prize for his advocacy of nonviolence, started speaking publicly of "new methods of struggle." The militants demanded "direct action." Violence, in which black and white were killed and wounded, erupted in the main industrial areas between 1948 and 1954. Laws were passed disenfranchising the Africans and tightening segregation in the ownership of land. In 1952 the Africans launched a campaign for the defiance of unjust laws, and more than 8,000 people went to jail. Luthuli was deposed for his support of the campaign.

Crises erupted in the colored, Indian, and white communities. Differences on the constitution developed in the white community, and former servicemen formed the Torch Commando to oppose Malanism. India severed diplomatic relations with South Africa in 1954.

Malan opposed what he regarded as the haste with which the colonial powers were freeing Africa. When Kwame Nkrumah took his seat in the Council of Ministers, Malan protested that this would have unfortunate consequences for the British Commonwealth. He pressed—unsuccessfully—for the incorporation of Basutoland, Bechuanaland, and Swaziland.

Malan resigned as leader of the National party toward the end of 1954 and died on Feb. 7, 1959.

Further Reading

The reports of the debates in South Africa's Parliament from 1918 to 1954 constitute the most reliable references on Malan available to the reader of English. Considerable information on Malan may be found in Edward Callan, *Albert John Luthuli and the South African Race Conflict* (1962); Brian Bunting, *The Rise of the South African Reich* (1964); and C. F. J. Muller, ed., *500 Years: A History of South Africa* (1969). Recommended for historical background is Eric A. Walker, *A History of Southern Africa* (1928; 3d ed. 1962). □

Malcolm III

Malcolm III (died 1093), the king of Scotland from 1058 to 1093, established the Canmore dynasty, which ruled Scotland for two centuries. His reign was marked by the introduction into Scotland of English influences.

Malcolm was a claimant to the Scottish kingship as the son and heir of Duncan I, who had been displaced by Macbeth in 1040. Although the principle of royal succession by right of primogeniture had not been usual in Scotland, Malcolm did have precedent in the career of Duncan, and he was influenced by his knowledge of the operation of the rule in England. For him to unseat Macbeth was either to assert a valid claim of direct inheritance or to win the throne by making war on the incumbent, the way to kingship long recognized and accepted in Scottish history. After Malcolm defeated Macbeth on the field of battle, the Celts of the north resisted him as a representative of Saxon and alien influences by installing Lulach, Macbeth's stepson, as king. Malcolm defeated Lulach four months later and secured the crown in 1058.

Malcolm married twice, and in each case there was some political advantage to be had. By marrying Ingibiorg, heiress of the Earl of Orkney, he conciliated the nativist opposition forces that had supported Lulach. Although his marriage to Margaret, a princess of the Saxon royal house and a fugitive from William the Conqueror, undid the work of the first marriage, it did offer Malcolm an excuse to launch campaigns into England.

From his first marriage Malcolm had one son, Duncan; from his second, six sons were produced. Four of the six were given English names: Alexander and David were named for heroes of the past. Not only in the names of her sons did Margaret introduce Saxon elements of life into Scotland. Devoted to religion, she was instrumental in bringing about reforms in religious observances and clerical discipline, so that the Christian life and Church in Scotland followed more closely practices in England and on the Continent. So widely beloved was Margaret that immediately upon her death she was declared a saint, and yet in one part of Scotland her anti-Celtic ecclesiastical reforms had produced a rallying point for a Celtic party that appeared when Malcolm died.

Malcolm's relations with England revolved around claims to lands that he held there in his own right or in the name of Margaret and his desire to expand his realm to the south, where the boundaries were undefined. Five times he campaigned; and five times he was defeated; in his last endeavor he lost his life. The epithet Canmore (big head) was originally descriptive of Malcolm's physical attributes; in later years it was used as a surname for his descendants.

Further Reading

A shrewd assessment of Malcolm's accomplishments is in William Croft Dickinson, *A New History of Scotland,* vol. 1: *Scotland from the Earliest Times to 1603* (1961; rev. ed. 1965). A brief but sound summary is in the paperback work of J. D. Mackie, *A History of Scotland* (1964). A simple but colorful story is available in Elise Thornton Cook, *Their Majesties of Scotland* (1928). For an analysis of the work of Margaret see Sir Robert Rait and George S. Pryde, *Scotland* (1934; 2d ed. 1955). □

Malcolm X

Malcolm X (1925-1965), African American civil rights leader, was a major 20th-century spokesman for black nationalism.

Malcolm X was born Malcolm Little on May 19, 1925, in Omaha, Nebr. His father, a Baptist minister, was an outspoken follower of Marcus Garvey, the black nationalist leader in the 1920s who advocated a "back-to-Africa" movement for African Americans. During Malcolm's early years his family moved several times because they were threatened by Ku Klux Klansmen in Omaha; their home was burned in Michigan; and when Malcolm was 6 years old, his father was murdered. For a time his mother and her eight children lived on public welfare. When his mother became mentally ill, Malcolm was sent to a foster home. His mother remained in a mental institution for about 26 years. The children were divided among several families, and Malcolm lived in various state institutions and boarding-houses. He dropped out of school at the age of 15.

Living with his sister in Boston, Malcolm worked as a shoeshine boy, soda jerk, busboy, waiter, and railroad dining car waiter. At this point he began a criminal life that included gambling, selling drugs, burglary, and hustling.

In 1946 Malcolm was sentenced to 10 years for burglary. In prison he began to transform his life. His family visited and wrote to him about the Black Muslim religious movement. (The Black Muslims' official name was the Lost-Found Nation of Islam, and the spiritual leader was Elijah Muhammad, with national headquarters in Chicago.) Malcolm began to study Muhammad's teachings and to practice the religion faithfully. In addition, he enlarged his vocabulary by copying words from the dictionary, beginning with "A" and going through to "Z." He began to assimilate the

racial teachings of his new religion; that the white man is evil, doomed by Allah to destruction, and that the best course for black people is to separate themselves from Western, white civilization—culturally, politically, physically, psychologically.

In 1952 Malcolm was released from prison and went to Chicago to meet Elijah Muhammad. Accepted into the movement and given the name of Malcolm X, he became assistant minister of the Detroit Mosque. The following year he returned to Chicago to study personally under Muhammad and shortly thereafter was sent to organize a mosque in Philadelphia. In 1954 he went to lead the mosque in Harlem.

Malcolm X became the most prominent national spokesman for the Black Muslims. He was widely sought as a speaker, and his debating talents against white and black opponents helped spread the movement's message. At this time in the United States there was a major thrust for racial integration; however, Malcolm X and the Black Muslims were calling for racial separation. He believed that the civil rights gains made in America were only tokenism. He castigated those African Americans who used the tactic of nonviolence in order to achieve integration and advocated self-defense in the face of white violence. He urged black people to give up the Christian religion, reject integration, and understand that the high crime rate in black communities was essentially a result of African Americans following the decadent mores of Western, white society. During this period Malcolm X, following Elijah Muhammad, urged black people not to participate in elections because to do so meant to sanction the immoral political system of the United States.

In 1957 Malcolm X met a young student nurse in New York; she shortly became a member of the Black Muslims, and they were married in 1958; they had six daughters.

For at least two years before 1963, some observers felt that there were elements within the Black Muslim movement that wanted to oust Malcolm X. There were rumors that he was building a personal power base to succeed Elijah Muhammad and that he wanted to make the organization political. Others felt that the personal jealousy of some Black Muslim leaders was a factor.

On Dec. 1, 1963, Malcolm X stated that he saw President John F. Kennedy's assassination as a case of ''The chickens coming home to roost.'' Soon afterward Elijah Muhammad suspended him and ordered him not to speak for the movement for 90 days. On March 8, 1964, Malcolm X publicly announced that he was leaving the Nation of Islam and starting two new organizations: the Muslim Mosque, Inc., and the Organization of Afro-American Unity. He remained a believer in the Islamic religion.

During the next months Malcolm X made several trips to Africa and Europe and one to Mecca. Based on these, he wrote that he no longer believed that all white people were evil and that he had found the true meaning of the Islamic religion. He changed his name to El-Hajj Malik El-Shabazz. He announced that he planned to internationalize the black struggle by taking black people's complaints against the United States before the United Nations. For this purpose he sought aid from several African countries through the Organization of Afro-American Unity. At the same time he stated that his organizations were willing to work with other black organizations and with progressive white groups in the United States on voter registration, on black control of community public institutions such as schools and the police, and on other civil and political rights for black people. He began holding meetings in Harlem at which he enunciated the policies and programs of his new organizations. On a Sunday afternoon, Feb. 21, 1965, as he began to address one such meeting, Malcolm X was assassinated.

Since his death Malcolm X's influence on the political and social thinking of African Americans has been enormous, and the literature about him has proliferated. Malcolm X Community College in Chicago, Malcolm X Liberation University in Durham, N.C., and the Malcolm X Society are named for him.

Further Reading

Malcolm X's own words are gathered in several publications: *Malcolm X Speaks: Selected Speeches and Statements* (1965) and *By Any Means Necessary: Speeches, Interviews and a Letter by Malcolm X* (1970), both edited by George Breitman; and *The Speeches of Malcolm X at Harvard,* edited by Archie Epps (1968). *Malcolm X on Afro-American History* (1967) is valuable for its autobiographical qualities rather than for its historical insights. Malcolm X's responses to an interview with Kenneth B. Clark are recorded in *The Negro Protest: James Baldwin, Malcolm X, Martin Luther King Talk with Kenneth B. Clark* (1963). His own account of his life, written with the assistance of Alex Haley, is *The Autobiography of Malcolm X* (1965).

Although there is no definitive biography of Malcolm X, there are a number of books on various aspects of his life and work, among them Louis Lomax, *When the Word Is Given: A Report on Elijah Muhammad, Malcolm X and the Black Muslim World* (1963); George Breitman, *The Last Year of Malcolm X: The Evolution of a Revolutionary* (1967); Louis Lomax, *To Kill a Black Man* (1968), a discussion of Malcolm X and Martin Luther King; and John Henrik Clarke, ed., *Malcolm X: The Man and His Times* (1969), which contains a good bibliography of readings on Malcolm X. A brief biographical sketch of him is in Russell L. Adams, *Great Negroes: Past and Present* (1969). *El Hajj Malik,* a play written by N. R. Davidson, Jr., based on Malcolm's life, is in Ed Bullins, ed., *New Plays from the Black Theatre* (1969). See also Dudley Randall and Margaret G. Burroughs, eds., *For Malcolm: Poems on the Life and the Death of Malcolm X* (1967).

Useful background works include Louis Lomax, *The Negro Revolt* (1962); Michael Dorman, *We Shall Overcome* (1964); Anthony Lewis, *Portrait of a Decade: The Second American Revolution* (1964); and M. H. Boulware, *The Oratory of Negro Leaders, 1900-1968* (1969). □

Nicolas Malebranche

The French philosopher and theologian Nicolas Malebranche (1638-1715) was a noted Cartesian. His analysis of the fundamental presuppositions of

Descartes's philosophy led to a set of doctrines that is known as occasionalism.

Born in Paris, Nicolas Malebranche was educated at the Collège de la Marche and at the Sorbonne. In 1660 he entered the Oratorian order, which had been founded by Cardinal Pierre de Bérulle, an early supporter of René Descartes. Sometime after his ordination in 1664, Malebranche chanced upon a copy of Descartes's *On Man*. This incomplete treatise was an attempt to explain man's physiology as part of a system of universal mechanics. On the strength of this work, Malebranche devoted the next 10 years of his life to the study of science and of Descartes's philosophy.

Occasionalism is a theory of causal interaction. Descartes's metaphysics culminates in an extreme dualism according to which matter and mind are totally independent substances. The observable connections between mind and body were a fact that Descartes bequeathed to his successors for explanation. The first recourse was to a deus ex machina: God alone accounts for the interaction. A Dutch thinker, Arnold Geulincx, offered the first coherent theory with his analogy that physical actions and mental volitions are like two clocks that are synchronized by God so that they keep time together.

The culmination of occasionalism and of Malebranche's study is found in his major work, *The Search for Truth,* the first volume in 1674 and the second in 1675.

Although occasionalism, as explained above, is positive as a possible explanation, it is even more interesting in its negative connotations, since the theory means that despite appearances there is no real interaction between spirit and matter. Spirit is understanding and will, and matter is figure and motion. Malebranche stresses not only that these parallel attributes are mutually exclusive but also that both mind and matter, in themselves, have no power or activity. Hence there is no secondary causality, and God is the only real cause of ideas and motions in the universe.

The consequences of this view are most important with regard to the theory of knowledge. The mind has a disposition to receive ideas, and on the occasion of sensory impressions or movements the appropriate idea arises in consciousness. The originals of such ideas, following the Platonic, Augustinian tradition, are archetypes of the divine mind according to which all things have been created. Thus the reason a finite mind can possess infinite, eternal truth is that it has been illuminated to "see all things in God." The full implications of such a doctrine were left by Malebranche as future problems: reality consists of ideas; our experience of objects is, at best, deceptive; what reality the material world possesses other than ideal is open to question. To underscore these contentions, Malebranche offered several criticisms and arguments to prove that neither reason nor experience can discover any necessary connections between two events that we relate as cause and effect. Ironically these arguments were taken over, practically verbatim, by the Scottish philosopher David Hume in support of his skeptical empiricism.

The success of *The Search for Truth* was considerable. Opposed by other Cartesians and theologians, Malebranche spent much of the remainder of his career defending himself in print. His other major works are *Christian Conversations* (1675), *Treatise on Nature and Grace* (1680), *Treatise of Morality* (1683), and *Dialogues on Metaphysics and on Religion* (1688). His scientific work in geometry and physics was respectable, and in 1699 he was honored by election to the French Royal Academy of Sciences.

Further Reading

A work of Malebranche available in English is *Dialogues on Metaphysics and on Religion,* translated by Morris Ginsberg (1923); it contains a long introduction to Malebranche's life and thought by the translator. The secondary material on Malebranche includes Ralph W. Church, *A Study in the Philosophy of Malebranche* (1931); A. A. Luce, *Berkeley and Malebranche: A Study in the Origins of Berkeley's Thought* (1934); and Beatrice K. Rome, *The Philosophy of Malebranche: A Study of His Integration of Faith, Reason and Experimental Observation* (1963).

Additional Sources

Nadler, Steven M., *Malebranche and ideas,* New York: Oxford University Press, 1992.

Chappell, V. C. (Vere Claiborne), *Nicholas Malebranche,* New York: Garland, 1992. ☐

Georgy Maksimilianovich Malenkov

Georgy Maksimilianovich Malenkov (1902-1988) emerged briefly after the death of Joseph Stalin in March 1953 as the head of the Soviet government and leader of its Communist Party. A quintessential *apparatchik* whose claim to power rested largely on his devoted service to Stalin, Malenkov was soon outmaneuvered by Nikita Khrushchev and forced to resign his positions. Some historians have credited him with proposing initiatives which were later adopted by Soviet leaders, including the last head of the Soviet Union, Mikhail Gorbachev.

Malenkov was born on January 8, 1902, in the town of Orenburg in the Southern Urals. Although much of his biography is obscure, it is believed he grew up in a reasonably well-off white collar family which found itself dislocated during the revolution and civil war at a time when Georgy Maksimilianovich was an impressionable teenager. In 1918, at the age of 16, he joined the Red Army. He apparently served as a political commissar of some sort in Turkestan. Like others of his generation, he was rewarded after demobilization by being sent to the Bauman Higher Technical School in Moscow, from which he graduated in 1925. His first position thereafter was as a clerk or secretary in the Communist Party's Central Committee apparatus in Moscow.

In this minor but centrally located post Malenkov soon distinguished himself as an able administrator and loyal, even slavish, Stalinist. He is reported to have imitated the increasingly powerful dictator in dress and appearance and in any event became closely identified in Central Committee bureaucracy with Stalin's policies, as opposed to those of others in the party leadership. Largely for these reasons, in all likelihood, Stalin made him his personal secretary in 1934, on the eve of the Great Purges. From this position, Malenkov himself soon amassed enormous power, directing the appointment and removal of personnel and becoming deeply involved in the purge process. Many regarded him as one of Stalin's principal "triggermen." From 1939 until 1953 he served as secretary of the Central Committee. He was also deputy chairman, under Stalin, of the Council of Ministers and made the leading speech at the 19th Party Congress in 1952, shortly before Stalin's death.

Malenkov was not unintelligent. He understood the need for reform as he came to power after Stalin's death in March 1953 and quickly promised an improvement in material conditions. He also took a leading role in arresting Lavrenti Beria, head of the dreaded secret police. The "thaw" of 1954-1955 is largely associated with his name. For all his experience in the party machinery, however, Malenkov could not prevent himself from being edged aside by Nikita Khrushchev. Within weeks of Stalin's death he "requested" to be relieved of the "heavy burden" of first secretary in favor of Khrushchev, retaining his less powerful post as Council of Ministers' chairman, but he had difficulty holding this position as well. In 1955, confessing his "insufficient experience" and his "guilt and responsibility" for administrative failures, particularly in the area of Soviet agriculture, he was demoted to the minor post of minister of hydroelectric stations.

It was Malenkov's close identification with Stalin and the purges which made him a real liability for the Khrushchev regime. After the famous "Secret Speech" in February 1956 in which Khrushchev publicly exposed the "crimes of the Stalin era" for the first time, Malenkov knew his days in office were numbered. In the summer of 1957, consequently, he joined with Molotov, Kaganovich, and others in an abortive effort to drive Khrushchev from power. Denounced as a ringleader of the "anti-Soviet bloc," he was stripped of all important positions and sent to Kazakhstan as head of the Ust-Kamenogorsk hydroelectric station. His plaintive "apologies" for "incorrect thinking" hardly earned him respect. The Soviet Union was liberalizing, and he was a relic of a past many hated or wanted to forget. His heavy-set, pudgy visage (which some regarded at the time of his leadership as the West's most effective anti-Communist propaganda) quickly faded from popular consciousness. His orders as plant director were apparently ignored, leading him to resign his post in humiliation and disgrace. In April 1964 he was ousted from the party. From then on he lived in obscurity, spending time at his Moscow apartment until his death on February 1st, 1988. Some of Malenkov's proposals—such as his statement that war between the Soviet Union and America was not inevitable and that greater emphasis should be placed on increasing production of food and consumer goods, rather than heavy industry—were accepted by Krushchev and Gorbachev

Further Reading

There is no biography of Georgy Maksimilianovich Malenkov in English. Students might consult one of several general texts, however, to follow his career in the party apparatus, including Leonard Schapiro, *History of the Communist Party of the Soviet Union* (1960); and Wolfgang Leonard, *The Kremlin Since Stalin* (1962); see also R. W. Petybridge, *A History of Postwar Russia* (London, 1966), especially chapter 4; and the excellent collection of essays edited by Stephen Cohen, Alexander Rabinowitch, and Robert Sharlet, *The Soviet Union Since Stalin* (1980). As with other Soviet leaders, the best source for Malenkov's public speeches and other writings during his years in power is the *Current Digest of the Soviet Press,* issued weekly since 1949 and with quarterly and cumulative indexes; Malenkov's obituary was in the February 2nd edition of *New York Times.* □

Kasimir Malevich

The Russian painter Kasimir Malevich (1878-1935) founded suprematism and is credited with having painted the first geometric, totally nonrepresentational picture.

The son of a foreman in a sugar factory, Kasimir Malevich was born on Feb. 11, 1878, in Kiev. He received only a rudimentary formal education, but through his own energies he was well read. Even so, his writings reveal his lack of schooling. They are often disorganized and their ideas are crudely expressed, especially when they are compared with the essays of Wassily Kandinsky, whose concepts parallel Malevich's.

In 1895 Malevich became a student at the Kiev School of Art. He settled in Moscow in 1904, and 5 years later he had his first one-man show. He had been painting in the impressionist style, but his work by 1909 suggests a strong dependence on contemporary French art for direction, notably that of the post–impressionists, the Fauves, and the Nabis, whose paintings he had seen in the remarkable collections of Ivan Morosov and Sergei Shchukin (Stchoukine). Malevich became acquainted with Michael Larionov and Nathalie Gontcharova in Moscow and assumed an active role in the exhibitions of the Jack of Diamonds group.

By 1911 Malevich was working in a cubist manner that was closer to Fernand Léger in style than to Pablo Picasso and Georges Braque. An example of Malevich's cubist period is *Morning in the Country after the Rain* (1911). In it he abstracted a landscape in which cylindrical figures of peasants are featured prominently. He had dealt with similar themes the year before, but more graphically. By 1913 he had so transformed his material that recognizable imagery had disappeared, though inferences of light, bulk, and atmosphere had not. Later that year he carried abstraction to its ultimate limit: he painted a black rectangle on a white ground. This, the first suprematist work, according to the artist, expressed "the supremacy of pure feeling in creative art."

Thereafter Malevich confined himself to arrangements of geometric shapes with the goal of suggesting such sensations to the beholder as flight, wireless telegraphy, and magnetic attraction. In 1918 he painted a series of white-on-white suprematist compositions. The following year he had a retrospective exhibition in Moscow and also took over the directorship of the School of Art in Vitebsk, which he renamed the College of New Art. He spent more and more time teaching and writing. In 1922 he moved to Leningrad, where he was provided with a studio and living quarters in the newly reorganized Museum of Artistic Culture.

In the 1920s Malevich made several sculptures which look like models of modern buildings. These he called "arkhitectonics." In the early 1920s the Soviet government began to assume a negative attitude toward abstract art, since it was ineffectual as a tool for propaganda, and started to support "socialist realism." Despite this, Malevich was permitted to go to Germany in 1927 to exhibit his work and to lecture at the Bauhaus. One of his books, *The Nonobjective World* (written in 1915), was published in German by the Bauhaus that year.

In 1929 Malevich had a retrospective exhibition at the Tretyakov Gallery in Moscow. During the last years of his life he painted fewer pictures, and those he did were portraits, mostly of his family and friends. He died of cancer in Leningrad and was buried in a coffin that he himself had decorated with suprematist motifs.

Further Reading

Malevich's writings, expertly translated, were collected in a two-volume work, *Essays on Art,* edited by Troels Anderson (trans., 2 vols., 1968). Camilla Gray, *The Great Experiment: Russian Art, 1863-1922* (1962), traces the development of Malevich's art and contains handsome plates of his work, several in color.

Additional Sources

Hilton, Alison, *Kazimir Malevich,* New York, N.Y.: Rizzoli, 1992.
Malevich, Kazimir Severinovich, *Malevich: artist and philosopher,* New York: H.N. Abrams, 1990. □

François de Malherbe

The French poet François de Malherbe (1555-1628), although not a great poet, succeeded through his works and teaching in assuring the acceptance of basic reforms in French poetry.

François de Malherbe was born at or near Caen. His education took him to Paris, Basel, and Heidelberg. In 1577 he became attached to Henri d'Angoulême, soon to be named governor of Provence. Malherbe remained his secretary until Henri was assassinated in 1586. Of the poet's compositions during this period little of note remains except the *Larmes de Saint Pierre,* a long poem inspired by the Italian Luigi Tansillo. The work is of interest because of its bombast and its exaggerated images-not uncommon practices in that day but elements that Malherbe would come to censure in others. He completely disavowed the *Larmes* in later life.

Between 1586 and 1605 Malherbe lived first in Caen and then (1595) returned to Provence. His reputation was growing. The ode written in 1600 to welcome France's new queen, Marie de Médicis, proved decisive for his future. The influential Cardinal Du Perron liked the poem; and when, in 1605, Malherbe went to Paris, it was to profit at last from the prestige he had won with his ode.

Malherbe's reform should be neither over-nor underestimated. Quite independent of Malherbe many French poets in the last quarter of the 16th century, including Pierre de Ronsard, had begun to avoid hiatus and to temper the humanists' use of neologisms, archaisms, erudition, and mythology. Malherbe himself, even in his most mature poems, was not so circumspect as he expected others to be. At the same time, these facts only point out the main source of Malherbe's influence: his dogmatism. Uncompromising in his criticism, he was determined to show that such tendencies away from the excesses of 16th-century verse had to be treated as rules. He succeeded and completed a significant step in France's evolution toward classicism.

Mannered love poems, *consolations* in the Stoic vein, translations from the Psalms, and encomiastic *pièces de circonstance* account for Malherbe's best-known works. He strived in the relatively small number of poems he wrote for a distinctive clarity through careful organization, correct syntax, and above all intelligible vocabulary and imagery.

Malherbe knew greatest favor during the regency of Marie de Médicis (1610-1617). His last years were marked by the death of his son in a duel and a decline in poetic production. He died in Paris on Oct. 16, 1628.

Further Reading

The definitive studies on Malherbe to date are in French. An excellent description of the milieu in which he wrote is in Renée Winegarten, *French Lyric Poetry in the Age of Malherbe* (1954). □

Kaspar Bronislaw Malinowski

The Austrian-born British social anthropologist Kaspar Bronislaw Malinowski (1884-1942) founded the functional school of anthropology. He stressed the pragmatic functioning of human institutions within a culture.

Bronislaw Malinowski was born on April 7, 1884, in Cracow, then in a part of Poland belonging to Austria. His father was a professor of Slavic languages. Bronislaw attended Cracow's King John Sobieski public school and the Jagellonian University, earning in 1908 the doctoral degree in physics and mathematics. While ill he read Sir James Frazer's *The Golden Bough,* which turned his interest to anthropology. Brief study at the University of Leipzig under Karl Bücher and Wilhelm Wundt was followed in 1910 by further study in anthropology at the London School of Economics under C. G. Seligman and Edward Westermarck. He first lectured at the University of London's School of Economics in 1913. There he earned the doctor of science degree in 1916, was appointed reader in anthropology in 1924, and held the university's first chair in anthropology in 1927. He also lectured in Geneva, Vienna, Rome, and Oslo. He married Elsie Rosaline Masson in 1919. She died in 1935, leaving three daughters. He later married Anna Valetta Hayman-Joyce.

During visits to the United States, Malinowski studied the Pueblo Indians in 1926 and lectured at Cornell University in 1933; at Harvard University's tercentenary in 1936 he received an honorary doctoral degree. In 1939, when World War II erupted, he was teaching at Yale University and was chairman of the board of exiled members of the Polish Academy of Arts and Sciences. Malinowski died in New Haven, Conn., on May 14, 1942.

As a commanding figure in modern anthropology, Malinowski was famous because of his skillful lectures and influential writings. His command of languages included Polish, Russian, German, French, English, Italian, and Spanish, as well as the languages of tribal groups he studied. He attracted students with various career goals, particularly colonial civil servants, and trained and directed the field research of a generation of social anthropologists. He encouraged beginning students but was often intentionally devastatingly critical as they became more advanced. The most able responded with greater effort and often with self-assertive anger mixed with admiration and devotion.

Malinowski emphasized the function of such cultural characteristics as custom, ritual, religion, sexual taboos, institutions, ceremonies, and beliefs. In focusing on these and other cultural factors as functional parts of a nicely balanced system, he founded the so-called functional school of social anthropology and helped transform speculative anthropology into a modern science of man. A *New York Times* obituary called him an "integrator of ten thousand cultural characteristics" to whom students flocked, "enthralled by his command of his material."

Further Reading

Studies of Malinowski include Max Gluckman, *An Analysis of the Sociological Theories of Bronislaw Malinowski* (1949), and Raymond Firth, ed., *Man and Culture: An Evaluation of the Work of Bronislaw Malinowski* (1957). His career is recounted in Abram Kardiner and Edward Preble, *They Studied Man* (1961). A detailed critique of his theories is in Marvin Harris, *The Rise of Anthropological Theory: A History of Theories of Culture* (1968).

Additional Sources

Malinowski, Bronislaw, *A diary in the strict sense of the term*, Stanford, Calif.: Stanford University Press, 1989.

Malinowski, Bronislaw, *Malinowski among the Magi: The natives of Mailu*, London; New York: Routledge, 1988.

Malinowski, Bronislaw, *The story of a marriage: the letters of Bronislaw Malinowski and Elsie Masson*, London; New York: Routledge, 1995.

Malinowski between two worlds: the Polish roots of an anthropological tradition, Cambridge; New York: Cambridge University Press, 1988. □

Gian Francesco Malipiero

Gian Francesco Malipiero (1882-1973) was one of Italy's most respected and prolific composers. Aside from his own symphonic, operatic, vocal and chamber music compositions, he was a musicologist and music educator who edited Monteverdi and Vivaldi—for which he was well-known. He was said to write brilliantly for the orchestra, but on the whole his works found little popular acceptance. Stylistically, he fell between Puccini and Respighi.

Gian Francesco Malipiero was born Aug. 3, 1882, in Venice, and spent much of his life there. The grandson and son of musicians, he studied the violin as a boy in Venice and in Vienna. Upon returning to his native city, he entered the Liceo Musicale Benedetto Marcello as a composition student and transferred to the conservatory in Bologna.

Stravinsky Was an Early Influence

In 1913 Malipiero went to Paris, where he met Maurice Ravel and Igor Stravinsky and heard the first performance of the latter's *Rite of Spring*. This was a turning point in Malipiero's life. He repudiated all of his earlier compositions and set about achieving an individual style of music that would be freed from the clichés of the overwhelmingly popular 19th-century opera—a problem faced by several Italian composers of his generation.

He Edited Monteverdi, Vivaldi

Malipiero found elements of his mature style in the works of 17th- and 18th-century Italian composers, such as Claudio Monteverdi, Francesco Cavalli, Giuseppe Tartini, and Antonio Vivaldi. Almost none of the music of these masters was available; when Malipiero found the manuscripts and original editions in the library of the Liceo Musicale in Venice, he started the lifelong project of transcribing and publishing them.

One of the results of these efforts was *Vivaldiana*, for which Malipiero was well-known. With his original *Inventions* (two sets, the latter titled *The Feast of the Indolents*), he combined a wide range of orchestral and operatic composi-

tions. A portion of the work was used in the Walter Ruttmann film *Steel*.

Taught and Popularized Italian Music

Malipiero was a composer but he was also an academic. In 1921 he became a professor at the Parma Conservatory, and in 1924 he cofounded (with Alfredo Casella) an association for the popularization of modern Italian music. Malipiero's *Antonio e Cleopatra* was first performed on May 4, 1938, in Florence. For this opera, he wrote his own libretto. From 1939 to 1952 Malipiero would direct music institutes at Padua and Venice.

Music Didn't Survive Initial Performances

Malipiero wrote more than 25 operas, 4 ballets, 15 symphonic poems, 9 symphonies, 4 piano concertos, a violin concerto, large works for choir and orchestra, chamber music, and piano music. Most of this music was performed at the Festival of Contemporary Music held biannually in Venice, but little of it survived the premieres. This was probably because Malipiero's style was unpopular with the general public, the critics, and his fellow professional musicians.

Malipiero's style was highly intellectual and based upon his desire to return to the foundations of Italian music. He carefully avoided spectacular or exciting effects. For his librettos he frequently chose fantastic or metaphysical tales whose elusive meaning left the general audience more bewildered than satisfied.

Gian Francesco Malipiero died Jan. 8, 1973, in Venice.

Further Reading

Malipiero's *Antonio e Cleopatra* is discussed in *Opera News* (June 1988). His work is also discussed in an article titled "La musica di Gian Francesco Malipiero" *Music and Letters* (Feb. 1992); and in Cynthia Barr, "The Musicological Legacy of Elizabeth Sprague Coolidge" *Journal of Musicology* (Spring 1993).

For biographical information on Malipiero see *G. Francesco Malipiero* (Chester, 1922); Nicolas Slonimsky, *Music since 1900* (W.W. Norton and Company, Inc., 1937, 3d rev. ed. 1949); Gerald Abraham, *A Hundred Years of Music* (Duckworth, 1938, 2d ed. 1949); David Ewen, ed., *The Book of Modern Composers* (Knopf, 1942, 3d ed. 1961); and *Malipiero, Scrittura e Critica* (Firenze, 1984).

Correspondence between Malipiero and composer/author Everett Burton Helm, and between Malipiero and stage director Max Heinrich Fisher, may be found in the Manuscripts Department at Indiana University's Lilly Library. Within the 234 items are articles Helm wrote about Malipiero, including an interview Helm conducted with him. The file also contains the manuscripts of Malipiero's "Il commitato per orchestra e una voce," dated July 23, 1934, as well as newspaper clippings and photographs of Malipiero. □

Mirza Malkam Khan

The Persian diplomat Mirza Malkam Khan (1831-1908) was a forerunner of reform and modernization in Persia and an indefatigable propagandist for modern ideas and institutions.

Malkam Khan was born of Armenian parents in Esfahan and at an early age was sent to Paris to study. It was said that his father had become a Moslem. Malkam Khan, however, did not either profess or deny his faith in Islam. He returned to Persia when he was 18 and was employed as an interpreter by the famous reformer Prime Minister Tagi Khan Amir-e Kabir.

Sometime between 1855 and 1860 Malkam did two things which not only showed his restless character but also created enemies for him. One was the introduction of a Masonic lodge in Persia. He persuaded the Shah to grant permission for this novel idea and called it *faramushkhaneh,* or house of forgetfulness. Later the Shah became very suspicious when some of the members of the court whom he had encouraged to join would not divulge the "secret" of the lodge to him. About this time Malkam prepared a pamphlet called *The Notebook of Order,* which contained all sorts of reform programs, and showed it to the Shah. The Shah was displeased with both the lodge and the pamphlet and banished the young reformer from the country.

In 1870, when his friend Moshir al-Doleh became prime minister, Malkam went to Tehran as counselor in foreign affairs and received the title of Nazem al-Molk. In 1873, when the Shah went to Europe, Malkam went along and was appointed Persian minister in London. The 16 years during which he represented Persia were uneventful, except 1878, when he was a delegate to the Congress of Berlin, which dealt with the fate of the Ottoman Empire. Malkam Khan did such an outstanding job of advancing the interests of Persia that he received the title of Nazem al-Doleh and the very unusual title of prince. Notwithstanding the titles, he is known in Persia as Mirza Malkam Khan.

Interestingly, Malkam Khan's greatest period of literary activity on behalf of modernization began with a shady financial transaction in which he was involved. In 1889 he secured the signature of the Shah for a lottery concession in Persia. Later he sold the concession in London, knowing that the Shah, owing to religious objections to gambling, had asked him to cancel it. Partly because of this, Malkam was dismissed from his post and deprived of all his titles and privileges. It was then that he lashed out against his enemies in Persia and wrote pamphlets and letters demanding reform in all aspects of Persian life.

Malkam's main vehicle was the newspaper *Qanun,* which he published for nearly 3 years. It was banned in Persia and despised by the Shah, but it was smuggled in nevertheless. Malkam called for a rule of law and believed that Persia should accept the civilization of the West and change its attitudes and institutions accordingly. He wrote on a variety of subjects such as distribution of land, freedom of women, necessity of parliament, social justice, and even simplifying the Persian alphabet. He was a devout humanist and was rather successful in propagating humanism. Humanist societies were established in Persia and became centers of progressive thought in the country.

Malkam lived to see the establishment of a constitutional government in Persia. At the turn of the century the successor of Naser al-Din Shah restored all of Malkam's titles and privileges and appointed him minister to Italy.

Further Reading

A sketch in English of the thought of Malkam can be found in Edward Granville Browne, *The Persian Revolution of 1905-1909* (1966). □

Stéphane Mallarmé

The French poet Stéphane Mallarmé (1842-1898) was the master of the symbolist writers in France. His poetic theories and difficult, allusive poems separated him from the general public but won him intense admiration within the circle of his initiates.

Stéphane Mallarmé was born in Paris on March 18, 1842. After a mediocre beginning at school, young Stéphane excelled in languages (French, Latin, Greek, and English) and obtained his baccalaureate degree in November 1860. In February 1862 he published his first poem (*Placet*) in *Le Papillon.* His liaison with Maria Gerhard led to their marriage on Aug. 10, 1863, and to the birth of a daughter, Françoise Geneviève Stéphanie (in November 1864), and a son, Anatole (1871-1879). In September 1863 Mallarmé obtained his certificate for teaching English and at the end of the year went with his wife to Tournon to teach in the lycée there. His teaching career was to last for 30 years and to take him to Besançon (1866), Avignon (1867), and finally Paris (1871). An agonizing spiritual crisis in 1866 led to Mallarmé's complete loss of religious faith and to his austere, half-mystical preoccupation with eternity and *le Néant* (Nothingness, or Annihilation).

In 1875 Mallarmé published *Le Corbeau* (his translation of Edgar Allan Poe's *The Raven*) with illustrations by Édouard Manet; and the following year appeared *L'Après-midi d'un faune, églogue . . . ,* one of his most memorable poems. *L'Après-midi d'un faune* exemplifies many characteristics of Mallarmé's exquisitely evocative poetry and many of his cherished ideas—for example, that in the "pure work" the poet disappears as speaker and gives over the initiative to the words, which "kindle each other with reciprocal reflections like a virtual trail of fires over precious stones." The faun, in his evocation by the word *lis* (lily), exemplifies also Mallarmé's claim in the essay *Crise de vers* for the ideal power of verbal creation.

In *L'Après-midi d'un faune* there emerges from Mallarmé's subtle suggestion and evocation the drama of a young faun trying to decide between dream and reality in

his confused recollection of an erotic adventure with two nymphs, who finally escaped from his embrace. In a vague Sicilian landscape we see the faun, after trying vainly to resolve the mystery of his experience, turn to a fantasy of ravishing Venus herself and then, at the last, going back to sleep under the silence of the noonday sun.

Mallarmé is cited by Jules Huret in 1891 as criticizing the Parnassians' direct presentation of objects in poetry: "To *name* an object is to suppress three-fourths of the enjoyment of the poem which is made up of gradual discovery: to *suggest* it, that is the dream. . . . There must always be an enigma in poetry. . . ." In his later writings, Mallarmé aspired to the creation of hermetic poetry.

J. K. Huysmans' *À rebours* and Paul Verlaine's *Poètes maudits* in 1884 helped make Mallarmé more generally known in France. He was known also through his famous "mardis" (Tuesday receptions from 9 to midnight in his home at 89 Rue de Rome), which flourished into the 1890s and brought together over the years many of the most significant writers, musicians, and artists of the time.

In 1887 appeared Mallarmé's *Poésies,* and the following year his prose translations of *Les Poèmes d'Edgar Poe* and of *Ten o'Clock,* James McNeill Whistler's famous lecture on art. On Jan. 27, 1896, Mallarmé was elected "prince of poets," succeeding Verlaine. Publications near the end of his life included *Vers et prose* (1893), *La Musique et les lettres* (1895), *Divagations* (1897), and *Un Coup de dés jamais n'abolira le hasard* (1897). Mallarmé died at Valvins on Sept. 9, 1898, and was buried 2 days later in the ceme-

tery of Samoreau (Seine-et-Marne). Posthumous publications included a separate edition of *Un Coup de dés* (1914), *Madrigaux* (1920), *Vers de circonstance* (1920), *Igitur ou La Folie d'Elbehnon* (1925), *Contes indiens* (1927), and *Thèmes anglais* (1937). Mallarmé's *Oeuvres complètes* was published in 1945.

Critical Assessment

The exquisite qualities of Mallarmé's art are evident both in his poetry and in such prose poems as *Plainte d'automne* and *Frisson d'hiver.* Of individual poems (aside from those named earlier) one may cite such examples as *Apparition, Les Fenêtres, L'Azur, Brise marine, Soupir, Hérodiade,* the more difficult *Prose pour des Esseintes,* the three *Tombeaux* (Poe, Baudelaire, Verlaine), and the sonnets *Le vierge, le vivace et le bel aujourd'hui, Victorieusement fui le suicide beau,* and *Ses purs ongles très haut dédiant leur onyx.*

Mallarmé liked images of snow, ice, swans, gems, mirrors, cold stars, and women's fans. There is often a burning sensuality under the austere form of his poems; but there are also numerous overt images of chastity, sterility, and artistic impotence. In *Un Coup de dés* Mallarmé used typography to dramatize his words and enhance their imaginative suggestiveness. He saw the poet's function as being, above all, "to give a purer meaning to the words of the tribe." He claimed to have come to understand "the intimate correlation of Poetry with the Universe" and hinted that he was beginning where Baudelaire left off. Finally, he carried his ideal so far that, as he admitted, his art became "a dead end." But Mallarmé was not a sterile artist; he was one of the most exquisite poets of the century.

Further Reading

For translations from Mallarmé see *Some Poems of Mallarmé* (1936), translated by Roger Fry with commentaries by Charles Mauron; the *Selected Poems* (1957), translated by C. F. MacIntyre; and Anthony Hartley, ed., *Mallarmé* (1965), with prose translations. Among useful studies in English are Hasye Cooperman, *The Aesthetics of Stéphane Mallarmé* (1933); Wallace Fowlie, *Mallarmé* (1953); Joseph Chiari, *Symbolism from Poe to Mallarmé: The Growth of a Myth* (1956), with a foreword by T. S. Eliot; Haskell M. Block, *Mallarmé and the Symbolist Drama* (1963); Guy Michaud's *Mallarmé* (trans. 1965); Robert Greer Cohn, *Toward the Poems of Mallarmé* (1965) and *Mallarmé's Masterwork: New Findings* (1966); and Thomas A. Williams, *Mallarmé and the Language of Mysticism* (1970).

Additional Sources

Millan, Gordan, *A throw of the dice: the life of Stéphane Mallarmé,* New York: Farrar, Straus, Giroux, 1994.

Sartre, Jean Paul, *Mallarmé, or, The poet of nothingness,* University Park: Pennsylvania State University Press, 1988.

Woolley, Grange, *Stéphane Mallarmé, 1842-189,* New York: AMS Press, 1981. □

Dumas Malone

American historian and editor Dumas Malone (1892-1986) is known chiefly for a multi-volume, landmark biographical study of Thomas Jefferson, which garnered the 1975 Pulitzer Prize for history. He also contributed widely to other literature about the third U.S. president. But he did not apply his scholarly versatility only to the analysis of Jefferson's life and times. Indeed, Malone added a large body of work to the study of American history in general, especially with his two-volume *Empire for Liberty*. While his work has earned mixed reviews, one reviewer conceded that Malone's level of familiarity with Jefferson was "nothing short of amazing."

D umas Malone was born in Coldwater, Mississippi on January 10, 1892. He received his bachelor's degree from Emory College (now Emory University) in 1910 and his divinity degree from Yale University in 1916. During World War I, from 1917-1919, he served in the Marine Corps, rising to the rank of second lieutenant, after which he returned to Yale, where he obtained his master's degree in 1921 and his doctorate in 1923.

Also in 1921, Malone contributed to *An Outline of United States History, for Use in the General Course in United States History, Yale College.*

Malone's first academic appointment was as a history instructor at Yale (1919-1923); he then went on to the University of Virginia as an associate professor (1923-1926) and professor (1926-1929). In 1925 he married Elisabeth Gifford. The couple had a daughter, Pamela. From 1926 to 1927 Malone was also a visiting professor of American history at Yale.

Combined Editing and Teaching

Malone was an editor of the *Dictionary of American Biography* (1929-1931) and editor-in-chief (1931-1936). He was director of Harvard University Press (1936-1943) and professor of history at Columbia University (1945-1959). He returned to the University of Virginia as a Thomas Jefferson Foundation Professor of History (1959-1962), followed by an appointment as biographer-in-residence at the University of Virginia.

Wrote Biographies, Documented History

The major works of Dumas Malone are *The Public Life of Thomas Cooper* (1926), a critically acclaimed biography which traces the career of a militant southern thinker who exerted an influence on John C. Calhoun; *Saints in Action* (1939); *Edwin A. Alderman: A Biography* (1940); *Thomas Jefferson as Political Leader* (1963); and, with Basil Rauch, *Empire for Liberty: The Genesis and Growth of the United States of America* (2 vols., 1960).

The two volumes of *Empire for Liberty* were broken down into six parts: Number I: *American Origins to 1789* (1964); Number II: *The Republic Comes of Age: 1789-1841* (1964); Number III: *Crisis of the Union: 1841-1877* (1964); Number IV: *The New Nation: 1865-1917* (1964); Number V: *War and Troubled Peace: 1917-1939* (1965); and Number VI: *America and World Leadership: 1940-1965* (1965).

In addition to co-authoring and contributing to other books, Malone edited *Correspondence Between Thomas Jefferson and P. S. du Pont de Nemours* (1930) and *The Story of the Declaration of Independence* (1963).

Jefferson Biography Was Pivotal

Malone's chief accomplishment, however, was his biographical study of Thomas Jefferson—collectively titled *Jefferson and His Time,* six volumes of which were published: *Jefferson the Virginian* (1948); *Jefferson and the Rights of Man* (1951); *Jefferson and the Ordeal of Liberty* (1962); *Jefferson the President: First Term, 1801-1805* (1970); *Jefferson the President: Second Term, 1805-1809* (1974); and *Sage of Monticello* (approximately 1981). It was originally conceived as a four-volume work. However, by 1970, with the publication of volume 4, Malone had gotten only as far as Jefferson's first term as president.

Critics Found Malone Fawning

The work was notable in its emphasis on Jefferson's pragmatism and political realism. It was characterized by lively prose. While Malone's familiarity with his subject matter has been called "nothing short of amazing," a major criticism was that Malone tended to glorify Jefferson, overlooking or de-emphasizing certain aspects of his life, character, and beliefs which would detract from the image of Jefferson as the "Great Democrat" and lover of liberty and equality. Thus, some critics have stressed that Jefferson's prodigious intellectual activities were made possible to some extent through his ownership of a large number of slaves—that Jefferson was, to say the least, blind to his own hatred of the urban proletariat and to his view of cities as the source of all moral evil. In political theory and practice what he really favored was not democracy but a rural judicial oligarchy (wherein power is concentrated in the hands of a few). That Jefferson himself was a notorious bigot toward most organized religions, particularly the Roman Catholic Church, shows that as an intellectual he was really of short stature.

Said one reviewer, "While always interesting and sometimes instructive, [the biography] is seldom exciting. [But] the fault may be Jefferson's rather than Malone's. In the end, most people will agree with Mr. Malone that 'Jefferson was a hard man to know intimately, and still is.' "

Wrote Prolifically During 1950s

Malone shared his knowledge of, and insight into, the nation's third president and related subject areas by contributing in various capacities to the following historical works: *Bibliography of Virginia History since 1865* (1930); *Interpretation of History* (1943); *The Jeffersonian Heritage* (radio program) (1954); *Guide to American Biography* (1949); *The*

Right to Work: A Series of Addresses and Papers Presented at the Semi-Annual Meeting of the Academy of Political Science (1954); *The University of Virginia Library, 1825-1950: The Story of a Jeffersonian Foundation* (1954); *The Domestic Life of Thomas Jefferson* (1958); *Thomas Jefferson and his World,* (1960); and *George Mason, Reluctant Statesman* (1961).

Other editorships included *International Economic Outlook* (1953); *The American Economy: Keystone of World Prosperity* (1954); *Europe and Asia: The Cases of Germany and Japan* (1955); *Emerging Problems: Domestic and International* (1957); and *Political Science Quarterly* (1953-58).

History Was His Avocation

Malone held memberships in the American Historical Association, American Academy of Arts and Sciences, American Antiquarian Society, Southern Historical Association, Massachusetts Historical Society, Phi Beta Kappa, Omicron Delta Kappa, Century Club in New York and the Cosmos Club in Washington, D.C. His work earned many honors, most notably the 1975 Pulitzer Prize for history (for *Jefferson and His Time*).

Malone's other honors: the John Addison Porter Prize, awarded by Yale University (1923); Thomas Jefferson Award, from the University of Virginia (1964); Wilbur Lucius Cross Medal, Yale University (1972); and the John F. Kennedy Medal, Massachusetts Historical Society (1972). He was the first recipient of the Bruce Catton Prize (1984), named for the former editor of *American Heritage* and awarded every two years for outstanding history writing. Malone also was awarded an honorary degree by the College of William and Mary (1977).

On Sept. 21, 1976, Malone participated in a Library of Congress Symposium on Jefferson's contributions to the Library of Congress.

Continued to Profile Jefferson

Other books written by Malone include: *Books in Transit: from Monticello to the Library of Congress* (1977); *Thomas Jefferson and the Library of Congress* (1978); and *Rhetoric and the Founders* (1987). He contributed the article "Monticello" to *Horizon* (June 1983).

According to Malone, Thomas Jefferson impressed upon the world the merits of reasoning as a method of solving political problems—a device far preferable to misleading with partisan politics or getting caught up in narrow nationalism.

Dumas Malone died in Charlottesville, Virginia on Dec. 27, 1986.

Further Reading

Malone's contributions to American historical writing are assessed in Michael Kraus, *The Writing of American History* (University of Oklahoma Press, 1953); Malone's work on Jefferson is appraised in Merrill D. Peterson, *The Jefferson Image in the American Mind* (Oxford University Press, 1960). Dumas Malone's study of the life of Thomas Jefferson is the subject of the film *Dumas Malone, a Journey with Mr. Jeffer-*

son, produced by the United States Information Agency (1983).
Journal articles treating Malone's work include: Merrill D. Peterson, "Dumas Malone: the Completion of a Monument" *Virginia Quarterly Review: A National Journal of Literature and Discussion* (Winter 1982); Edwin Yoder, "The Sage at Sunset" *Virginia Quarterly Review* (Winter 1982); Byron Dobell, "Monuments" *American Heritage* (August/September 1984); Burton Raffel, "Jefferson and His Time" *Michigan Quarterly Review* (book review; Winter 1984); Merrill D. Peterson, "Dumas Malone: An Appreciation" *The William and Mary Quarterly* (April 1988); *Journal of the West* (October 1995); F. Shuffelton, "Being Definitive: Jefferson Biography Under the Shadow of Dumas Malone" *Biography—An Interdisciplinary Quarterly* (Fall 1995); and *Library Journal* (September 1, 1996). □

Sir Thomas Malory

The English author Sir Thomas Malory (active 15th century) wrote *Le Morte Darthur,* one of the most popular prose romances of the medieval period. The work was the first full-length book in English about the adventures of King Arthur and the Knights of the Round Table.

Although *Le Morte Darthur* (also known as *Le Morte d'Arthur*) is universally accepted as a masterpiece of imaginative literature, so much mystery surrounds the identity of the author (that is, which one of several Sir Thomas Malorys of the 15th century actually wrote it) that any one definitive biography seems imprudent. The only direct information extant concerning the author is that a Sir Thomas Malory completed the book while he was a "knight-prisoner" in the ninth year of Edward IV's reign, from March 4, 1469, to March 3, 1470. All the rest is conjecture.

In the 16th century John Bale associated Malory with Welsh origins mainly because of a place called Mailoria in Wales and because of the subject matter of the book. There are no records, however, of a Thomas Malory in Wales in the 15th century. Although several other Thomas Malorys were suggested, the next serious candidate was identified by George L. Kittredge at the end of the 19th century as Sir Thomas Malory, Knight, of New-bold Revel, Warwickshire. This Thomas Malory, who, as the record shows, led an active and colorful life, has been accepted as the author of *Le Morte Darthur* by most scholars.

Although Malory's exact date of birth is unknown (probably around the year 1410), he succeeded to his father's estates in 1434. He served at the siege of Calais in the retinue of Richard Beauchamp, Earl of Warwick, in 1436, and he was elected as knight of the shire for Warwickshire in 1445. Most of the other records show that he was frequently in conflict with the law, spending much of his last 20 years in and out of prison. In 1443 he and another man were charged with assault and robbery. Over the years he was accused of many offenses, including rape, armed assault, conspiracy to commit murder, horse stealing, and extortion. On at least two occasions he dramatically escaped from prison, and he was excluded from two general pardons in 1468. He was committed to Newgate Prison in 1460, but he was apparently freed to fight with the forces of the Earl of Warwick in Northumberland in 1462. Although he had pleaded not guilty to all charges, he probably was in prison at the time of his death on March 14, 1471.

However, a recent study by William Matthews presents a rather convincing argument for yet another candidate, about whose life unfortunately very little is known, one Thomas Malory of Studley and Hutton, Yorkshire. Emphasizing a linguistic approach, Matthews analyzes the backgrounds and careers of four possible candidates, stating that the criteria by which they must be judged are certain facts concerning *Le Morte Darthur*. These facts are that the work was written by one Sir Thomas Malory and completed by 1470; that it exemplifies the religious and secular aspects of medieval chivalry; that its major source is a French book of several prose romances; that it draws heavily from Yorkshire and other northern romances; that its language is mainly standard English with frequent scattering of northern dialect words and forms; that the author was familiar with places, institutions, and legends of northern England; that he was a knight-prisoner while he wrote the book; and that he seems to have had Lancastrian sympathies. Matthews responds to the possible weaknesses in the case of the Yorkshire Malory (he is not actually described as a knight, and there is no record of his having been a prisoner) by pointing out that, although this Malory's family was an eminent one, in the 15th century titles were used rather loosely and often not used even when appropriate, and that it was not the custom in the 15th century to keep records of prisoners of war, as Malory may have been as a result of an ill-fated expedition to France in 1469. Matthews concludes that since the author of *Le Morte Darthur* "was so remarkably familiar with northern dialect, northern literature, and northern affairs, . . . he must have been a northerner himself . . . probably a Yorkshireman [and that] Thomas Malory of Studley and Hutton is the only Yorkshireman of appropriate name and age who has been found in documents at the appropriate time."

In any case, Malory related in vigorous prose the familiar stories of the Arthurian legend. The work was first published in 1485 by William Caxton. In this edition it is divided into books and chapters, thus making it appear to have continuity, while the version in the Winchester manuscript (see the bibliography below) is divided into a series of individually entitled tales, indicating to some scholars a lack of artistic unity. The sources for Malory's work are mainly 13th-century French prose romances, with the exception of book V, which is a prose adaptation of the alliterative *Morte Arthur*, a 14th-century English poem.

Further Reading

Le Morte d'Arthur, edited by Janet Cowen, with an introduction by John Lawlor (2 vols., 1969), is recommended as a good text based on Caxton's edition. However, in 1934, a 15th-century manuscript containing *Le Morte Darthur* was found at Winchester, England. This manuscript was edited by Eugene Vinaver in 1947 and is considered the standard edition of Malory's work to date. See Eugene Vinaver, ed., *The Works of Sir Thomas Malory* (1954; 2d ed. in 3 vols., 1967).

Because of the controversy surrounding the identity of the author of *Le Morte Darthur,* the following books are especially recommended. The most comprehensive biography of the Warwickshire Malory is Edward Hicks, *Sir Thomas Malory: His Turbulent Career: A Biography* (1928). For a detailed study of four other Thomas Malorys and as a possible candidate the Malory of Studley and Hutton, Yorkshire, see William Matthews, *The Ill-framed Knight: A Skeptical Inquiry into the Identity of Sir Thomas Malory* (1966).

For critical studies of *Le Morte Darthur* consult Eugene Vinaver, *Malory* (1929), and Robert M. Lumiansky, ed., *Malory's Originality: A Critical Study of Le Morte Darthur* (1964). □

Marcello Malpighi

The Italian microscopist Marcello Malpighi (1628-1694) was the first to see the capillaries and was a founder of histology, embryology, plant anatomy, and comparative anatomy.

On March 10, 1628, Marcello Malpighi was born at Crevalcore near Bologna. He attended the University of Bologna, where he graduated in philosophy and in medicine in 1653. Malpighi became a lecturer in logic at Bologna in 1655 but left in 1656 to be professor of theoretical medicine at Pisa. There he met Giovanni Borelli, a mathematician who had recently turned his attention to the analysis of movement in animals.

Malpighi returned to Bologna in 1659, where he was made extraordinary lecturer in theoretical medicine. Through Borelli's influence, Malpighi was elected to the first chair in medicine at Messina in 1662, but in 1666 he returned to Bologna to become professor of medicine, and he remained there for the next 25 years.

By 1667 Malpighi's work had already aroused the interest of the recently formed Royal Society in London, and one of its secretaries wrote to him suggesting that he communicate his results to the society. Malpighi responded favorably, and most of his later books were published in London. He was elected a foreign member of the Royal Society in 1668.

Malpighi was also a successful physician, and in 1691 he became the personal physician of Pope Innocent XII in Rome. Malpighi died on Nov. 29, 1694, in Rome.

Discovery of Capillaries

In September 1660 Malpighi began to study the structure of the lungs, and within nine months he had communicated the results of these studies in two letters to Borelli in Pisa, who published them under the title *De pulmonibus observationes anatomicae* (1661). Malpighi presented "a few little observations that might increase the things found out about the lungs." These observations included the first descriptions of the air sacs (pulmonary alveoli) in the lungs

of a dog and of the pulmonary capillaries in the frog and tortoise.

Having convinced himself of the presence of direct connections between the arteries and veins in the lungs of the frog and the tortoise, Malpighi was prepared to speculate that the same was so in other animals: he was unable to see such anastomoses in the dog's lung, perhaps, because these "small vessels escape the senses on account of their smallness."

Histological Studies

The science of the study of the structure of tissues was established by the classical microscopists, and Malpighi's contributions were among the most important. He published four tracts in 1665. The first one described the presence of "red globules of fat" in the blood vessels of the mesentery of the hedgehog. This is one of the earliest descriptions of the red blood cell, although Malpighi did not realize the significance of his observation. In other tracts he described the papillae of the tongue and the skin and suggested that these may have a sensory function. The layer of cells in the skin now known as the Malpighian layer was also described. The last tract of 1665 concerned the general structure of the brain. Malpighi showed that the white matter consists of bundles of fibers which connect the brain with the spinal cord. He described the gray nuclei that occur in the white matter.

Malpighi's *De viscerum structura execitatio anatomica* (1666) gives a detailed and fairly accurate account of the structure of the liver, spleen, and kidney. Malpighi dissected the tissue under the microscope, and he identified small particulate masses or "lobules," resembling bunches of grapes, in the liver. Each lobule was composed of "tiny conglobate bodies like grape seeds" connected by central vessels. Having seen these lobules in the livers of several species, he concluded that the lobule was the fundamental hepatic unit. He believed that the lobules were supplied by fine blood vessels and that their function was secretory. Malpighi realized, therefore, that one function of the liver is as a gland and that the bile duct must be the passage through which the secreted material (bile) passes: the gallbladder was, therefore, not the site of origin of bile. He was also able to prove in an animal experiment that the gallbladder is only a temporary store for bile on its way to the intestine. Malpighi speculated that bile might be useful in the process of digestion.

Although Malpighi was fond of describing many structures as "glands," he realized, from his study of the blood supply to the spleen, that this organ is not a gland but a contractile vascular organ. He was the first to describe the lymphatic bodies (Malpighian corpuscles) in the spleen.

Whereas other anatomists believed that the outermost part of the kidney was structureless, Malpighi showed that it is composed of many little wormlike vessels (the renal tubules) which he called "canaliculi." Although he could not demonstrate any continuity between the convoluted canaliculi and the straight tubules in the central mass of tissue (medulla), he predicted that such a continuity exists. Malpighi's description of how he discovered the glomeruli in the outer part of the kidney is vivid: "In all kidneys which up to this time I have been able to get, I have detected a number of very small glands [that is, Malpighian corpuscles, or glomeruli]. In order to see these glands, black fluid mixed with spirit of wine should be injected through the renal artery. And when the kidney is sectioned . . . one will see these same innumerable glands attached like apples to the blood vessels, the latter swollen with the black liquid and stretched out into the form of a beautiful tree." Malpighi realized that the "glands" were connected to the "extreme ends of the arteries" and to the veins but did not observe the true nature of the "glands," that is, that they are composed of a tuft of capillaries. He speculated that their function was to secrete the urine.

Malpighi's detailed description of the medulla of the kidney showed how the canaliculi converge on the pelvis and enter the ureter. In pathological specimens he observed the formation of kidney stones in the pelvis.

Insect Anatomy

Malpighi's memoir *De bombyce* (1669), on the silkworm moth, was the first detailed account of the structure of an invertebrate. Prior to his study, it was still believed that such small creatures were devoid of internal organs, and he himself was surprised to find that the moth was just as complex as higher animals. He not only discovered the trachae and spiracles, the system of tubes and holes through which insects breathe, but also correctly guessed their function. He was the first to describe the nerve cord and ganglia, the silk glands, the multichambered heart, and the urinary tubules, which still bear his name.

Embryological Studies

With his microscope, Malpighi was able to study much earlier stages of the embryo than had hitherto been possible. His results were communicated to the Royal Society in two memoirs: *De formatione pulli in ovo* (1672) and *De ovo incubato* (1675), which placed embryological study on a firm basis of sound observation. He saw the heart within 30 hours of incubation and noticed that it began to beat before the blood reddened. He described the development of the dorsal folds, the brain, the mesoblastic somites, and structures which were later identified as gill arches. However, Malpighi believed that he had seen the form of an embryo in an unincubated egg. A possible explanation is that the egg, being 2 days old, had been "incubated" in the hot Italian August sun. This observation was used, not by Malpighi himself as much as by his followers, to support the doctrine of preformation, that is, that the whole adult was present in the egg and had only to be "unfolded" by a suitable stimulus.

Plant Anatomy

Some of Malpighi's most extensive writing, beautifully illustrated, is on plants. Malpighi and his contemporary Nehemiah Grew became the confounders of plant anatomy by their systematic studies on the microscopic structure of plants. Malpighi's book *Anatome plantarum* was published in two parts in 1675 and in 1679. His illustrations frequently show the plant cell with its wall, first described by Robert Hooke in 1665.

Malpighi's interest in the structure of plants began when he noticed the broken branch of a chestnut tree which had fine threads projecting from the surface. Upon examining these with his lens he was struck with their resemblance to the air tubes of insects. Although he wrongly concluded that they served the function of breathing, his enthusiasm for the study of plants had been awakened. His drawings of the stems of higher plants distinguished between the annular rings of the dicotyledon and the scattered bundles of the monocotyledon (the terms dicotyledon and monocotyledon were introduced in the early 18th century). He suggested that material required for growth of the plant was formed from the sap by the leaves, but the erroneous idea that the sap circulated, as blood did, was originated by other writers.

Malpighi's work on the development of plants is just as significant as that on the development of animals. He made drawings of the embryo sac and endosperm and gave a superb account of the germination of seeds in which he differentiated between those later called monocotyledons and dicotyledons. He was the first to describe tubercles on leguminous roots, and he showed that some galls contained a grub. He traced the grub back to an egg and onward to an insect, of which he illustrated the egg-laying apparatus.

Further Reading

Some biographical information on Malpighi is in Howard B. Adelmann, *Marcello Malpighi and the Evolution of*

Embryology (1966), and in *Circulation of the Blood: Men and Ideas,* edited by Alfred P. Fishman and Dickinson W. Richards (1964). For background see Charles Singer, *A History of Biology to about the Year 1900* (1931; 3d rev. ed. 1959).

Additional Sources

Malpighi, Marcello, *The correspondence of Marcello Malpighi,* Ithaca N.Y. Cornell University Press, 1975. □

André Malraux

French writer and politician André Malraux (1901-1976) was generally regarded as one of the most distinguished novelists of the 20th century. Malraux holds the distinction of having been France's first minister of culture, serving from 1959-69. In addition, his wartime activities and adventures were legendary and well-documented. Malraux was a Communist supporter until World War II, and principal themes in his writing were revolution and its philosophical implications. He was an existentialist, believing that man determines his own fate by the choices he makes.

The novels of André Malraux depart sharply from the traditional form, with their middle-class settings, careful plot development and concentration on psychological analysis. His heroes and protagonists are adventurers determined to "leave a scar on the map," and violent action, usually in a revolutionary setting, is mixed with punctuated dialogue and passages containing philosophical reflection.

Malraux was born in Paris on Nov. 3, 1901, the son of a wealthy banker, and was educated in Paris. He attended the Lycée Condorcet and the School of Oriental Languages and would eventually develop a serious interest in China. Malraux began to move on the fringes of the surrealist movement, publishing criticism and poems. He married Clara Goldschmidt in 1921, and in 1923 the couple set off for Indochina (a former French colony consisting of Cambodia, Laos and Vietnam) to search for buried temples. (see Walter Langlois, *André Malraux: the Indochina Adventure,* 1966). After removing sculpture from the temples, Malraux and his wife were arrested by the French authorities and narrowly avoided prison (the story of Clara and André Malraux's Indochina adventures is also told in *Silk Roads: the Asian Adventures of Clara and André Malraux,* 1989).

It was during this period that Malraux, now hostile to the French colonial regime, came into contact with Vietnamese and Chinese Nationalists, many with Communist sympathies. He became a supporter of the international Communist movement, and during a stay in Saigon he organized a subversive newspaper.

Malraux's first novel, *Les Conquérants* (*The Conquerors*), was published in 1928. Set in Canton in 1925, it

deals with the attempts of Chinese Nationalists and their Communist advisers to destroy imperialist influence and economic domination. The hero of the book provides a vigorously drawn portrait of the professional revolutionary. Malraux lamented the potential influences of Western culture, using China as an example, with *The Temptation of the West* (1926). In this work, the character of Ling says that many Chinese thought they could retain their cultural identities after being exposed to European influence and technology. Instead, that influence results in the "disintegrating soul" of China, a country newly "seduced" by music and movies.

Malraux's next novel, *La Voie Royale* (*The Royal Way,* 1930), was less successful; it had an autobiographical basis in the search for buried treasures, but treated the search as a kind of metaphysical adventure.

In 1933 appeared Malraux's most celebrated novel, *La Condition humaine* (*Man's Estate, Man's Fate*). Set in Shanghai, the novel describes the 1927 Communist uprising there, its initial success and ultimate failure. The novel continues to illustrate Malraux's favorite theme: that all men will attempt to escape, or to transcend, the human condition and that revolutionary action is one way of accomplishing this. In the end there is failure, but man attains dignity in making the attempt and by his very failure achieves tragic greatness.

Malraux's next novel, *Days of Wrath* (1936), a short account of a German Communist's imprisonment by the Nazis, was poorly received, considered more propaganda than art. But after Malraux assisted the Republican forces by

organizing an air corps during the Spanish Civil War in 1936-1937, his inspiration was renewed. He then published *L'Espoir* (*Man's Hope,* 1938). In this book, the Republican forces gradually organize to meet the Fascist threat, and the novel ends at a point where the "hope" of the title might have been realized.

Following the Soviet Union's signing of a nonaggression pact with Germany, Malraux broke with the Communist cause. He was captured twice while fighting with the French army and underground resistance movement, but he escaped and would become a military leader. In 1943 he published his last novel, *Les Noyers de l'Altenburg* (*The Walnut Trees of Altenburg*).

The feel of this book is very different from that of Malraux's earlier novels. The narrator, captured by the Germans in 1940, reflects on his father's experiences before and during World War I—as an agent in central Asia, at a meeting of intellectuals in Germany, and while fighting on the Russian front. Malraux explores the fundamental problem of whether men are essentially the same in different epochs and different civilizations. Intellectually the answer seems to be negative, but emotionally it is positive, and human solidarity is maintained. Political action is seen as an illusion, and the traditional values of European humanism are affirmed.

Following the liberation of France in 1944, Malraux served in the reconstituted army as a colonel, and would later work to subvert the French Communist party. He was a supporter of General Charles de Gaulle. He and de Gaulle became friends and, as president of France, de Gaulle appointed Malraux to the position of minister of information—a job Malraux held from 1945-46. After leaving the post, he remained a de Gaulle intimate and one of the leading members of the Gaullist political movement. He contributed to *The Case for de Gaulle; a Dialogue between André Malraux and James Burnham.*

Beset by marital tensions, André and Clara Malraux divorced in January, 1946. Two years later, Malraux married his sister-in-law.

In the years that followed, Malraux wrote mainly on the subject of art. One highly philosophical volume on this subject was *The Psychology of Art* (1950), in which Malraux writes of an "imaginary museum"—a "museum without walls"—in which objects of art are important for their own intrinsic value rather than for their collective underlying meanings (see also André Malraux, *Museum Without Walls* 1967).

In *Les Voix du silence* (*The Voices of Silence,* 1951), Malraux develops the idea that in the modern world, where religion is of little importance, art has taken its place as man's triumphant response to his ultimate destiny and his means of transcending death. Also on the subject of art, Malraux penned "Saturn: an Essay on (Francisco de) Goya" (1957, translated by C.W. Chilton). Malraux also wrote *Picasso's Mask* (1976).

In 1958, after de Gaulle's return to power, Malraux became minister of cultural affairs—where he remained until de Gaulle's resignation in 1969. In 1967 he published the first volume of his *Antimémoires* (*Antimemoirs*). These were not memoirs of the usual type, failing to mention the accidental deaths of his two sons and the murder of his half-brother by the Nazis. Instead, they contained reflections on various aspects of his experiences and adventures.

Malraux paid two visits to the White House; in 1972, he conferred with President Richard Nixon prior to Nixon's visit to China. That same year he also suffered a near-fatal heart attack.

Malraux died in Paris on Nov. 23, 1976. Exactly 20 years later, his ashes were moved to the Pantheon necropolis in Paris. His namesake, the André Malraux Cultural Center, is in Chambéry (France).

Further Reading

Biographies of Malraux include: Robert Payne, *André Malraux* (Buchet/Chastel, 1973); Jean Lacouture, *André Malraux* (Pantheon Books, 1975); Martine de Courcel, ed., *Malraux: Life and Work* (Harcourt Brace Jovanovich, 1976); Axel Madsen, *Malraux: a Biography* (Morrow, 1976); James Robert Hewitt, *André Malraux* (Frederick Ungar Publishing Co., 1978); Jacques B.E.B. Bonhomme, *André Malraux, ou, Le Conformiste* (R. Deforges, 1986); and Curtis Gate, *André Malraux: a Biography* (Hutchinson, 1995; reviewed in *New York Review of Books*, May 29, 1997).

Other studies of Malraux's work include the following: Ralph Tarica, *Imagery in the Novels of André Malraux* (Fairleigh Dickinson University Press, 1980); Will Morrisey, *Reflections on Malraux: Cultural Founding in Modernity* (University Press of America, 1986); David Bevan, *André Malraux, Toward the Expression of Transcendence* (McGill-Queen's University Press, 1986); Claude Tannery, *Malraux: the Absolute Agnostic, or, Metamorphosis as Universal Law* (University of Chicago Press, 1991); John Beals Romeiser, *André Malraux: a Reference Guide* (Maxwell MacMillan International, 1994); Domnica Radulescu, *André Malraux: the "Farfelu" as Expression of the Feminine and the Erotic* (P. Lang, 1994); Gino Raymond, *André Malraux: Politics and the Temptation of Myth* (Ashgate, 1995); and Geoffrey T. Harris *André Malraux: a Reassessment* (St. Martin's Press, 1996).

Malraux is discussed in the following articles: J. Semprun, "Memoirs of the Spanish War and André Malraux" *Nouvelle Revue Francaise* (Nov. 1996); T. Fabre, "André Malraux: Portrait of the Adventurer in the Mirror" *Esprit* (Dec. 1996); Herman Lebovics, "Malraux's Mission" *The Wilson Quarterly* (Winter 1997); and G. Harris, "The Self Invention of André Malraux" *Times Literary Supplement* (May 23, 1997). □

Thomas Robert Malthus

The English economist Thomas Robert Malthus (1766-1834) was of the classical school and was the first to direct attention to the danger of overpopulation in the modern world.

Thomas Malthus was born at the Rookery near Guilford, Surrey, a small estate owned by his father, Daniel Malthus. After being privately educated, Malthus entered Jesus College, Cambridge, where he was elected to a fellowship at the age of 27. He took religious orders at the age of 31 and held a curacy for a short period.

In 1798 Malthus published his *Essay on the Principle of Population.* This pamphlet was turned into a fullscale book in 1803 with the aid of demographic data drawn from a number of European countries.

In 1805 Malthus married, and shortly thereafter he was appointed professor of modern history and political economy at the East India Company's College at Haileybury—the first appointment of its kind in England. Much to the amusement of his critics, since he advocated controlling the birthrate, he fathered five children. He died at Haileybury on Dec. 23, 1834, the year that saw the passage of a new Poor Law inspired by his writings.

Debates concerning Malthusian Theory

Few thinkers in the history of social science have aroused as much controversy as Malthus. It is not difficult to find reasons for the furor: he consistently opposed all methods of reforming society which did not act directly to reduce the birthrate, and his own remedies for bringing that about were impractical; he reduced all human suffering to the single principle of the pressure of population on the food supply, and all popular proposals for political or economic reform were exposed as irrelevant and immaterial; and he drove home his theme in one harsh passage after another, suggesting that literally every other possible social order was even worse than the existing one. Those on the left hated him because he seemed to be defending the society

they hoped to change, and those on the right disliked him for defending that society as merely a necessary evil.

Toward the end of the 19th century, the discussion died down as the rise in living standards and the decline in fertility, at least in Western countries, took the sting out of the fear of overpopulation. But after World War II the problem of the underdeveloped countries brought Malthus back in favor. Most of the emerging nations of Africa, Asia, and Latin America combine the high birthrates typical of agrarian economies with the low death rates typical of industrialized economies, and there is the danger of too many mouths to feed. It is not surprising, therefore, that Malthus's name crops up repeatedly in debates on population policy in underdeveloped countries. The arguments are very different from those employed in Malthus's own day, but the participants of the debate still line up as for or against the Malthusian theory of population.

From Malthus's writings, one receives the impression of an inflexible fanatic and possibly a misanthrope, but everyone who met Malthus found him kind and benevolent. In terms of the politics of that age, he was almost, but not quite, a "liberal," and his professions of concern over the conditions of the poor must be regarded as perfectly genuine. He had unpleasant truths to tell but he told them, as it were, "for their own good."

His Theory of Population

Malthus's theory of population is baldly stated in the first two chapters of the *Essay*. The argument begins with two postulates: "that food is necessary to the existence of man" and "that the passion between the sexes is necessary, and will remain nearly in its present state." The "principle of population" followed from these with the force of deductive logic: "Assuming, then, my postulata as granted, I say, that the power of population is indefinitely greater than the power in the earth to produce subsistence for man. Population, when unchecked, increases in a geometrical ratio. Subsistence increases only in an arithmetical ratio. A slight acquaintance with numbers will show the immensity of the first power in comparison with the second. By that law of nature which makes food necessary to the life of man, the effects of these two unequal powers must be kept equal. This implies a strong and constantly operating check on population from the difficulty of subsistence."

In 1798 Malthus described all the checks, such as infanticide, abortion, wars, plagues, and death from disease or starvation, as resolvable into "misery and vice." In 1803 he added a third pigeonhole, moral restraint, defined as "that restraint from marriage which was not followed by irregular gratification." It should be noted that he did not include birth control achieved by artificial devices. In his view, man was naturally lazy and would not work to provide a livelihood for himself and his family except under the threat of starvation. Birth control, even if it could be adopted, would only remove the incentive to work and would, therefore, amount to more "misery and vice." Moral restraint was something else: it implied postponement of marriage and strict chastity until marriage. He doubted that moral restraint would ever become a common practice, and

it is precisely this that gave his doctrine a pessimistic hue: there were remedies against the pressure of population, but they were unlikely to be adopted.

The Malthusian law of population has some resemblance to Newtonian mechanics in assuming tendencies which are never observed as such in the real world: the arithmetical ratio is simply a loose generalization about things as they are, whereas the geometrical ratio is a calculation of things as they might be but never are. The saving clause in the theory is the check of moral restraint, which permits the food supply to increase without a corresponding increase in population. But how shall we know that it is in operation, as distinct from the practice of birth control? By virtue of the fact that the food supply is outstripping the growth of numbers, Malthus would answer. In short, the Malthusian theory explains everything by explaining nothing. No wonder that Malthus's critics bitterly complained that the Malthusian theory could not be disproved, because it was always true on its own terms.

Further Reading

The standard biography of Malthus is by James Bonar, *Malthus and His Work* (1885; 2d ed. 1924). The great 19th-century debate over the Malthusian doctrine is brilliantly reviewed by Kenneth Smith, *The Malthusian Controversy* (1951), and Harold A. Boner, *Hungry Generations: The 19th-century Case against Malthusianism* (1955). Mark Blaug, in *Ricardian Economics: A Historical Study* (1958), shows how Malthus was received by his fellow economists. George F. McCleary, *The Malthusian Population Theory* (1953), contains a spirited defense of Malthus's theory as still relevant to the 20th century. □

David Alan Mamet

Playwright and screenwriter David Mamet (born 1947) is highly praised for his accurate rendering of American vernacular, through which he explores the relationship between language and behavior.

David Alan Mamet was born in Chicago, Illinois, on November 30, 1947. He studied at Goddard College in Vermont and at the Neighborhood Playhouse School of Theater in New York.

Mamet's first play to receive attention, *The Duck Variations* (1972), displays features common to much of his work: a fixed setting, few characters, a sparse plot, and dialogue that captures the rhythms and syntax of everyday speech. In this play, two elderly Jewish men sit on a park bench discussing a plethora of unrelated subjects. Mamet's next play, *Sexual Perversity in Chicago* (1974), examines confusion and misconceptions surrounding relationships between men and women. While some reviewers found this work offensive and misogynistic, Julius Novick contended that the play "is a compassionate, rueful comedy about how difficult it is . . . for men to give themselves to women, and for women to give themselves to men. It suggests that the only thing to fear, sexually, is fear itself.'' This play was adapted for film as *About Last Night . . . .*

In *American Buffalo* (1975) and *The Water Engine: An American Fable* (1977), Mamet explores contradictions and myths prevalent in the business world. *American Buffalo,* for which Mamet received the New York Drama Critics Circle Award, is set in a junk shop where three men plot to steal a valuable coin. A lack of communication and understanding causes the men to abandon their efforts. The protagonist of *The Water Engine* creates an innovative engine but is murdered when he refuses to sell his invention to corporate lawyers.

A Life in the Theatre (1977) offers a stark and wryly humorous view of the theatrical world through the performances and backstage conversations between a veteran actor and a novice. Edith Oliver remarked: ''Mamet has written—in gentle ridicule; in jokes, broad and tiny; and in comedy, high and low—a love letter to the theater.'' *The Woods* (1977) involves a young couple who discover the darker realities of their relationship while vacationing in an isolated woodland cabin. Mamet followed *The Woods* with three short domestic dramas in which he places considerable emphasis on dialogue. In *Reunion* (1977), a woman and her alcoholic father come to terms with their twenty-year separation; in *Dark Pony* (1977), a father relates a story to his young daughter as they drive home late at night; and *The Sanctity of Marriage* (1979) concerns the separation of a married couple.

Glengarry Glen Ross (1982), Mamet's most acclaimed work, is an expose of American business. In this play, four Florida real estate agents in competition to become their company's top salesperson victimize unsuspecting customers. Although Mamet portrays the agents as unethical and amoral, he shows respect for their finesse and sympathizes with their overly competitive way of life. *Glengarry Glen Ross* was awarded both the Pulitzer Prize in drama and the New York Drama Critics Circle Award. Mamet's next play, *Edmond* (1982), involves an unhappy businessman who leaves his wife and ventures into the seamier districts of New York City. After being beaten and robbed, the man turns to violence and is imprisoned for murdering a waitress. Gerald Weales viewed this play as a chilling example of how ''we become part of our destructive surroundings.'' *Prairie du chien* (1985) and *The Shawl* (1985) are companion pieces in which Mamet employs supernatural elements. The first play centers on a bizarre, unsolvable murder, while the second concerns a psychic's fraudulent efforts to obtain a client's inheritance.

In addition to his work for the theater, Mamet has written several screenplays. The first, an adaptation of James M. Cain's novel *The Postman Always Rings Twice,* is generally considered Mamet's least successful effort. In *The Verdict,* based on Barry Reed's novel *Verdict,* a downtrodden, alcoholic lawyer battles injustice within the judicial system to win a malpractice suit for a woman who suffered brain damage during childbirth. Reviewers extolled Mamet's terse dialogue, citing the lawyer's jury summation as a particularly powerful sequence of the film. In his screenplay *The Untouchables,* Mamet incorporates elements from federal agent Eliot Ness's memoirs and from the popular radio and television series. Set in Chicago, the film focuses on Ness's struggle to uphold the Prohibition law and bring mobster Al Capone to justice. Although David Denby found the script substandard for a writer of Mamet's talent, he called *The Untouchables* ''a celebration of law enforcement as American spectacle—a straightforward, broadly entertaining movie.''

Mamet has also taught at Goddard College, The Yale Drama School, and New York University. Further, he often lectures to classes at the Atlantic Theater Company and was one of the company's founding members.

Further Reading

Bigsby, C. W. E., *David Mamet,* Metheun, 1985.
Bock, Hedwig, and Albert Wertheim, editors, *Essays on Contemporary American Drama,* 1981, Max Hueber, pp. 207-23.
Carroll, Dennis, *David Mamet,* St. Martin's, 1987.
Contemporary Authors Bibliographical Series, Volume 3, Gale, 1986.
Contemporary Literary Criticism, Gale, Volume 9, 1978, pp. 360-61; Volume 15, 1980, pp. 355-58; Volume 34, 1985, pp. 217-24; Volume 46, 1988, pp. 245-56.
King, Kimball, *Ten Modern American Playwrights,* Garland, 1982.
America, May 15, 1993, p. 16. □

Abdallah al-Mamun

Abdallah al-Mamun (786-833) was the seventh caliph, or ruler of the Islamic Empire, of the Abbasid dynasty. During his reign he encouraged the study of Greek thought, and the balance of power within the caliphate shifted from the Arabs to the non-Arabs.

Al-Mamun was the son of Harun al-Rashid and a Persian slave girl, Marajil. Born about May 786, he was slightly older than his half brother Amin, son of the Arab Zubayda, but Amin was first heir to the caliphate and al-Mamun second. Al-Mamun, however, became governor of the eastern provinces, with Fadl ibn-Sahl as vizier. When Harun died in March 809, al-Mamun recognized Amin as caliph but kept his position in the eastern provinces. Tension between the half brothers led to war in 811, which ended in September 813 with the fall of Baghdad and the death of Amin.

Al-Mamun became caliph but continued to reside in the East despite disturbances in Iraq, Syria, and Egypt. In the struggle of rival interest groups, al-Mamun, hoping for wider support, in 817 designated as his successor Ali ar-Rida, head of the descendants of Ali, Mohammed's cousin. This step provoked a revolt in Baghdad, and Ibrahim, al-Mamun's uncle, was proclaimed caliph. Al-Mamun moved slowly back toward Iraq, entered Baghdad without difficulty, and ended the revolt (819). Ali ar-Rida had meanwhile died at Meshed.

For most of the rest of the reign there were disorders to be suppressed in various parts of the empire. Despite this fact, however, trade flourished, and the Abbasids were at the zenith of their prosperity. By 830 al-Mamun felt capable of mounting annual expeditions against the Byzantines. It was on one of these that he died in August 833 at Tarsus.

Development of Subject Dynasties

A significant development was the rise of a semi-independent hereditary dynasty under the caliph. A Persian general called Tahir played a large part in al-Mamun's success against his brother. After some time in the West, he was in 821 made governor of Khurasan, where there was serious trouble. Tahir gave signs of aiming at independence, and, when he died in 822, al-Mamun, who could not risk losing the province, appointed Tahir's son Talha to the governorship. One of Talha's brothers succeeded in 828. On the model of the Tahirids, independent dynasties, nominally appointed by and subordinate to the caliph, became a feature of the Islamic world, until the caliphs had no real power left.

Interest in Greek Philosophy

Al-Mamun became an enthusiast for Greek thought and is credited with the foundation of the "House of Wisdom," an institute for translating foreign, especially Greek, books into Arabic. Translations had been made of Sanskrit and Persian works in the time of his great-grand-father and of Greek books in that of his father. Many Greek books were already extant in Iraq in Syriac translations, and most of the first translations into Arabic were made by Christians from these Syriac versions. The earliest interest of the Arabs was in astronomy (with astrology) and medicine, but Greek philosophy also attracted attention.

The interest in Greek philosophy is linked with the rise of the theological school of the Mutazilites. Nineteenth-century European scholars admired their apparent rationalism and liberal views, such as a belief in freedom of the will. It is now realized that, despite their interest in Greek ideas, they remained close to their Islamic basis. Several leading Mutazilites were prominent at al-Mamun's court, notably Thumama and Ahmad ibn-AbiDuad. Al-Mamun was probably attracted not only by the philosophical but also by the political aspect of their thought, for they were attempting to reconcile contemporary tensions. The stimulation of interest in Greek works influenced the whole subsequent course of Islamic thought.

In accordance with Mutazilite teaching, al-Mamun established toward the end of his reign (perhaps in 827) the Inquisition, or Mihna. All higher officials had publicly to profess that they believed the Koran to be the created, not the uncreated, speech of God. This was not mere theological hairsplitting but the basis of a hoped-for compromise between opposing forces. Most officials made the required declaration, but a leading jurist, Ahmad ibn-Hanbal, refused and was prevented from lecturing. The Inquisition lasted until about 850.

Further Reading

There is no full-length study of al-Mamun in English, although there is a chapter on him in Philip K. Hitti, *Makers of Arab History* (1968). Walter M. Patton, *Ahmed ibn Hanbal and the Mihna* (1897), is concerned in part with the Inquisition under al-Mamun. He is mentioned briefly in general histories of the period. □

Manasseh ben Israel

The Dutch rabbi, author, publisher, and communal leader Manasseh ben Israel (1604-1657) is best known for his indefatigable efforts to effect the readmission of Jews to England.

His parents had left Portugal in 1603 because of the auto-da-fé, and Manasseh ben Israel was born in France the following year. The family eventually settled in Holland, where Manasseh was ordained a rabbi in Amsterdam at the age of 16. He soon gained a reputation as an excellent preacher, and he sought to augment his meager income by private instruction and by establishing his own press. He claimed proficiency in Hebrew, English, Latin, Spanish, and Portuguese. In 1640 he sought to improve his financial status by moving to Brazil, where he established a small academy, but 2 years later he returned to Holland.

Manasseh ben Israel was interested in Cabala, or Jewish mysticism, which predicted that the Messiah would appear as soon as Jews were dispersed to all parts of the world. He was encouraged by the prevailing Christian belief in the approaching Fifth Kingdom. The Thirty Years War was considered to mark the beginning of the Messianic Age, which had been predicted in the *Book of Zohar,* a Cabalistic work.

Manasseh ben Israel was most interested in persuading Oliver Cromwell, the English lord protector, to readmit the Jews to England. (They had been expelled in 1290.) Since Cromwell considered the English people to be the descendants of the tribes of Judah and Benjamin, Manasseh pointed out that with the readmission of Jews all Israel would be reunited. He wrote *Esperanca de Israel* (The Hope of Israel) in 1650. He translated it from Portuguese into Latin and dedicated it to the High Court of England. After addressing a historic letter to Cromwell, he went to England in 1655 to plead his cause, to which there were objections which he sought to overcome in an apologetic work called *Vindiciae Judaeorum* (Defense of the Jews). Cromwell, however, could not persuade Parliament to readmit the Jews officially. Gradually, however, the Jews did return, and their economic value to the country may have been a greater inducement than the religious appeal.

Manasseh was a prolific author, but he never gained a reputation as a great scholar. In *El consiliador* he sought to reconcile contradictions in the Bible and Talmud and thereby won the great respect of many Christian Bible scholars. He published the *Index to Midrash Rabba* as well as an edition of the Mishnah. He wrote a series of theological works in Latin on problems such as creation, the soul, resurrection of the dead, and the hereafter. Among the scholars with whom he corresponded was Hugo Grotius, and the great Rembrandt did his portrait.

Further Reading

For a biographical account, see Cecil Roth, *A Life of Menasseh ben Israel, Rabbi, Printer, and Diplomat* (1934). Meyer Kayserling wrote ''The Life and Letters of Manasseh ben Israel'' in *Miscellany of Hebrew Literature* (vol. 2, 1877), edited by Albert Löwy. *Menasseh ben Israel's Mission to Oliver Cromwell,* edited by Lucien Wolf (1901), has a biographical study of Manasseh. Details of his career and general background information can be found in Albert Hyamson, *A History of the Jews in England* (1908; 2d ed. 1928), and Cecil Roth, *A History of the Jews in England* (1941; 3d ed. 1964).

Additional Sources

Menasseh Ben Israel and his world, Leiden; New York: E.J. Brill, 1989.

Roth, Cecil, *A life of Menasseh ben Israel, rabbi, printer, and diplomat,* New York: Arno Press, 1975 c1934. □

Manco Capac

The Inca emperor Manco Capac (ca. 1500-1545), though initially used as a puppet by the Spaniards, **later took to guerrilla warfare against them but could not stem their conquests.**

Manco Capac, who carried the same name as a famed early (11th century) founder of Inca civilization, was one of the many sons of Huayna Capac, last ruler over an undivided Peruvian empire. Two of Manco's half brothers, Atahualpa and Huáscar, had divided the empire on the father's death (ca. 1528). In the civil war that ensued, Huáscar was assassinated by order of Atahualpa, who in turn was captured and executed in 1533 by the Spaniards who had just invaded Peru under the command of Francisco Pizarro.

In order to reinforce his authority over the Peruvians, Pizarro placed Manco on the throne of the Incas in the imperial city of Cuzco (1534). But the puppet emperor came to resent his role and the quickening Spanish destruction of Inca civilization. He fled from Cuzco, organized Indian forces, and returned in 1536 to lay siege to the capital, as well as to other Spanish bases in Peru.

Despite the great numbers of the besiegers, the destruction of many buildings, and the menace of starvation, the few hundred Spaniards in Cuzco managed to hold off the attackers for more than a year, until the siege was broken, in part by the return from Chile of a Spanish expedition commanded by Diego de Almagro, Pizarro's partner, and in part

Manco (seated under the canopy)

by the disaffection of the besieging natives, who returned to their homes and fields.

Manco fled with his supporters into the rugged backlands of Vilcabamba, northwest of Cuzco, where he sought to maintain the vestiges of royal power at a place called Vitcos. The Spaniards fell to quarreling among themselves over the spoils of empire, and Manco took up the cause of whichever side opposed Pizarro and his followers. Manco's sporadic forays against the Spaniards were of little significance in stemming the conquest, yet the inaccessibility of his retreat protected him from attack. Death came to the Inca when he was murdered in a quarrel over a game that he was playing with some renegade Spaniards whom he had sheltered in his camp.

Further Reading

Garcilaso de la Vega, *The Incas: The Royal Commentaries of the Inca* (trans. 1961; 2d ed., 2 vols., 1966), is an early Spanish chronicle on which all subsequent books draw heavily for knowledge of the Inca empire and its conquest by the Spaniards. John Hemming, *The Conquest of the Incas* (1970), is the best scholarly account of the conquest and of Manco Capac's role. William H. Prescott's vivid *History of the Conquest of Peru* (2 vols., 1847; many subsequent editions) is still indispensable. Also useful is Philip A. Means, *Fall of the Inca Empire and the Spanish Rule in Peru, 1530-1780* (1932). □

Nelson Rolihlahla Mandela

Nelson Rolihlahla Mandela (born 1918) was a South African resistance leader who, after years of imprisonment for opposing apartheid, emerged to become the first president of a black-majority-ruled South Africa and a winner of the Nobel Peace Prize.

The father of Nelson Mandela was a Xhosa chief in the Transkei, where Mandela was born. He studied law at Witwatersrand University and set up practice in Johannesburg in 1952. The years between 1951 and 1960 were marked by turbulence. The younger nationalists, led by Mandela and others, were coming to the view that nonviolent demonstrations against apartheid invited state violence against the Africans. There was also criticism of the type of collaboration with the non-Africans which the African National Congress (ANC) practiced. These nationalists were not unanimous on the alternative to nonviolence.

Unlike the young leaders with whom he grew up, Mandela was ready to try every possible technique to destroy apartheid peacefully, though he, too, realized the futility of nonviolence in view of the conditions which prevailed in his country. His attitude enabled him to support Albert Luthuli when some of the militants walked out of the ANC.

Mandela had joined the ANC in 1944, at a time of crisis for the movement. Its younger members had opposed African participation in World War II and had demanded the declaration of South Africa's war aims for the black people.

The Old Guard, led by Dr. Alfred Batini Xuma, was reluctant to embarrass the Jan Smuts government by pressing the African people's demands for the abolition of segregation. The militants, led by Anton M. Lembede, formed the ANC Youth League in 1943. Mandela was elected its president in 1951 and campaigned extensively for the repeal of discriminatory laws. He was appointed volunteer in chief in the resistance movement which the ANC led in 1951-1952, and he was subsequently banned for 6 months and later sentenced to 9 months for his leadership of the defiance campaign.

Mandela was one of the leaders arrested with Luthuli and charged with treason in 1956. The case against him and others collapsed in 1961. He was arrested again during the state of emergency which followed the Sharpeville shootings in 1960. Both the Pan-Africanist Congress, which had organized the demonstrations which led to the shootings, and the ANC were banned.

Sharpeville had made it clear that the days of nonviolent resistance were over. A semi-underground movement, the All-African National Action Council, came into being in 1961. Mandela was appointed its honorary secretary and later became head of Umkhonto weSizwe (the Spear of the Nation), which used sabotage in its fight against apartheid.

Mandela traveled for a while in free Africa. On his return he was arrested for leaving the country illegally and for inciting the Africans to strike in protest against the establishment of the Republic of South Africa. He was sentenced to 5 years in jail. At the trial, he told the court, "I want at once to make it clear that I am not a racialist and do not support any racialism of any kind, because to me racialism is a barbaric thing whether it comes from a black man or a white man.''

Mandela subsequently figured in the Rivonia trial with other leaders of Umkhonto weSizwe on a charge of high treason and was given a life sentence, which he began serving on Robben Island.

During the 27 years that Mandela spent in prison, hidden from the eyes of the world while he quarried limestome and harvested seaweed, his example of quiet suffering was just one of numerous pressures on the apartheid government. Public discussion of Mandela was illegal, and he was allowed few visitors. But as the years dragged on, he assumed the mantle of a martyr. In 1982 Mandela was moved to the maximum security Pollsmoor Prison outside Cape Town. This move apparently stemmed from fears by the South African authorities that Mandela was exerting too great an influence on the other prisons at Robben Island. Mandela spent much of the next six years in solitary confinement, during which he was allowed a weekly 30-minute visit by his wife, Winnie. He was offered a conditional freedom in 1984 on the condition that he settle in the officially designated black "homeland" of Transkei, an offer Mandela refused with an affirmation of his allegiance to the African National Congress. In 1988, Mandela was hospitalized with tuberculosis, and after his recovery he was returned to prison under somewhat less stringent circumstances. By this time, the situation within South Africa was becoming desperate for the ruling powers. Civil unrest had spread, and international boycotts and diplomatic pressures were increasing. More and more, South Africa was isolated as a racist state. It was against this backdrop that F.W. de Klerk, the President of South Africa and leader of the white-dominated National party, finally heeded the calls from around the world to release Mandela.

On Feb. 11, 1990, Mandela, grey and thin but standing erect and appearing in surprisingly good health, walked out of Verster Prison. He received tumultuous welcomes wherever he went. He visited the United States in July 1990 to raise funds for his cause and received overwhelming acclaim at every turn. In 1991 Mandela assumed the presidency of the African National Congress, by then restored to legal status by the government. Both Mandela and deKlerk realized that only a compromise between whites and blacks could avert a disasterous civil war in South Africa. In late 1991 a multiparty Convention for a Democratic South Africa convened to establish a Democratic government. Mandela and deKlerk led the negotiations, and their efforts later won them the Nobel Peace Prize in 1993. In September 1992 the two leaders signed a Record of Understanding that created a freely elected constitutional assembly to draft a new constitution and act as a transition government. On April 27, 1994, the first free elections open to all South African citizens were held. The ANC won over 62 percent of the popular vote and Mandela was elected president.

Mandela's agenda as president consisted of defusing the still dangerous political differences and building up the South African economy. The former he attempted to

achieve by former a coalition cabinet with representatives of different groups included. The latter he attempted to attain by inviting new investment from abroad, setting aside some government contracts for black entrepreneurs, and initiating action to return to blacks land seized in 1913. Mandela ran into some personal sorrow during this period in the downfall of his wife, Winnie. After all his years of imprisonment, the Mandelas were separated in 1993 and divorced in 1996. Mandela had appointed his then-wife to his cabinet, but she was forced to exit in 1995 after evidence of her complicity in civil violence was revealed.

However, Mandela's presidency for the most part was successful to a remarkable degree. Mandela's skill as a consensus builder, plus his enormous personal authority, helped him lead the transition to a majority democracy and what promised to be a peaceful future. He backed the establishment of a Truth and Reconciliation Commission which offered amnesty to those who had committed crimes during the apartheid era in the interests of clearing up the historical record. The elderly statesman even gave rise to a new style of dress in South Africa known as "Madiba smart." "Madiba" was Mandela's Xhosa clan title, by which he was informally known. And "smart" was local slang for nicely turned out. The style became popular after Mandela traded his business suits for brightly patterned silk shirts, carefully buttoned at the neck and wrists, worn with dress slacks and shoes.

Mandela without question was both the leading political prisoner of the late 20th century and one of Africa's most important reformers. The man who spent nearly three decades in prison out of dedication to his cause became an international symbol of human rights. That he proved to be an effective negotiator and practical politician as well only added to his reputation and proved a blessing to his nation. Indeed, the question as Mandela's term drew near its end and Mandela neared his 80th birthday was ever more pointedly, "After Mandela, who?"

Further Reading

Mandela's address to the court when he was tried for leaving the country without the necessary documents remains an important statement of his views on South Africa's race question. Marion Friedmann reproduced parts of the address in her book, *I Will Still Be Moved: Reports from South Africa* (1963); Additional statements of Mandela are in *No Easy Walk to Freedom: Articles, Speeches and Trial Addresses* (1965), edited by Ruth First; For further background see Mary Benson, *Nelson Mandela: The Man and the Movement* (1986); Ronald Harwood, *Mandela* (1988); Sheridan Johns and R. Hunt Davis, Jr., editors, *Mandela, Tambo, & the African National Congress: The Struggle Against Apartheid, 1948-1990: A Documentary Study* (1991); Nelson Mandela, *Mandela: An Illustrated Autobiography* (1996); Leo Kuper, *Passive Resistance in South Africa* (1957); and Mary Benson, *The African Patriots: The Story of the African National Congress in South Africa* (1963). □

Winnie Mandela

Winnie Mandela (born 1936), South Africa's first black professional social welfare worker, chose service to needy people and devotion of her energy and skill to the struggle for equality and justice for all people in South Africa. After her marriage to Nelson Mandela in 1958 she suffered harassment, imprisonment, and periodic banishment for her continuing involvement in that struggle. In 1992, the marriage ended, but problems for Mandela continued.

The person the world knows as Winnie Mandela began life as Nomzamo ("she who strives," "she who has to undergo trials") Winifred (Winnie) Madikizela, daughter of Columbus and Gertrude Madikizela. Members of the Madikizela extended family were Xhosa-speaking people of the Pondo nation situated in what is today the so-called homeland nation of the Transkei. Both of her parents were mission-educated, English-speaking teachers: her father taught at the local eM-bongweni Primary School and represented Eastern Pondoland in the territorial council which arbitrated Pondo law and custom; her mother, while still single, taught domestic science. She died when Mandela was nine. Their children's education was always a central concern. Through a combination of curiosity, intelligence, determination, and the financial sup-

port she received from family members and sponsors, Nomzamo Winnie Madikizela completed primary school and Shawbury High School, where she distinguished herself as a person of exceptional personal and leadership qualities.

In 1953 she was admitted to the Jan Hofmeyr School of Social Work and left the Transkei to reside at the American Board Mission's Helping Hand Hostel for women in central Johannesburg. When she completed her degree in 1955 she was the first black professional social worker in South Africa. She turned down a scholarship for further study in the United States in order to take up a challenging career in medical social welfare at the Baragwaneth Hospital in Johannesburg, where one of her boarding house roommates, Adelaide Tsukudu, worked as a staff nurse.

It was through her friendship with Adelaide Tsukudu that she met Adelaide's fiancé Oliver Tambo, and they introduced her to a prominent lawyer and member of the African National Congress (ANC) Youth League, Nelson Mandela. Mandela was then on trial along with 156 other people in the now infamous "treason trial" lasting from August 1958 to March 29, 1961. It is from this period that Winnie Madikizela's devotion to the welfare of ordinary people matured from efforts to help people cope with the extreme hardship of their lives to efforts to challenge and transform the governmental structures and social relations which created and reproduced hardship for the majority population.

The Mandelas were married in a Methodist service in the Transkei on June 19, 1958, returning after the celebrations to live in Mandela's home in the Soweto township outside Johannesburg in compliance with legal constraints imposed in connection with the "treason trial" litigation. The Mandelas, both well educated and of prominent social backgrounds, shared respect for popular society, tolerance of a broad range of religious and political views, and a firm commitment to turn their relative privilege and experience to the service of the majority population. Nelson Mandela had long devoted himself to the goal of dismantling the oppressive state structures which contributed to the dehumanization and impoverishment of South African peoples through his political involvement in the African National Congress Youth League. His family shared his commitment, and, like thousands of other South Africans, suffered pain, separation, incarceration, poverty, and daily indignities for that commitment.

Winnie Mandela's first encounters with South Africa's security police also began in 1958. The government extended "pass" legislation to African women. African men had long been required to carry a pass (an identification and employment history document) which constrained their ability to sell their labor and skills to best advantage. This forced them to labor and live on terms most favorable to the dominant white population. When pass legislation was extended to African women, who already labored in the least attractive and lowest paid jobs, the women took to the streets by the thousands to protest this additional burden. The Women's League of the African National Congress naturally embraced the issue. In October 1958 Winnie Mandela was among the more than one thousand women arrested in anti-pass demonstrations. The two weeks she spent in prison for her participation proved a mere hint of the draconian treatment the South African Nationalist government had in store for her and her comrades over the next decades. She lost her job and income as a social worker, subsequent to her arrest. In 1960, after South African Police fired on a group of people who were protesting the pass laws nationwide and international protests against apartheid prompted the government to declare a state of emergency. Thousands were arrested and detained.

After the treason trial where Nelson Mandela and his co-defendants were found not guilty ended, the Mandelas and their two young daughters were able to have a semblance of family life spent between March and December. In 1962 Nelson Mandela went into hiding to continue his leadership within the then banned ANC. He was subsequently apprehended, tried, and in 1964 sentenced to life imprisonment for his political activities. Winnie Mandela waged a determined fight to raise and educate their daughters, Zenani (Zeni) born in 1959 and Zindziswa (Zinzi) born in 1960, and to earn the family's living on her own. From day to day Winnie Mandela never knew when police would tear her away from her terrified children and jail her on some triviality. She finally made the painful decision to send her children to boarding school in Swaziland so that they could live and learn unharrassed by the South African government. Although she had visitation rights she was unable to have physical contact with her husband for the next 22 years. Her indomitable spirit kept his name in the public eye and never allowed anyone to forget the injustice being done to Nelson Mandela.

After 1962 Winnie Mandela was subjected to a virtually uninterrupted series of legal orders (so-called banning orders) which prevented her from living, working, and socializing like any other ordinary person. She was prohibited from publishing or addressing more than one person at a time, subjected to house arrest, incarcerated in solitary confinement, terrorized by police harassment and arbitrary arrest, and on May 17, 1977, she was seized from her home in the Orlando section of Soweto and forced to reside in the black township outside the rural town of Brandfort in the distant Orange Free State.

The so-called banishment order separated her from friends, family, and her livelihood. Despite her isolation in Brandfort, Mandela soon bridged the social and physical barriers meant to contain her creative energy. With the monetary and emotional support she received from international sympathizers and the trust she soon built among the Brandfort community, she initiated social welfare programs and continued to politicize the township population. She consistently exploited the limited financial support and physical protection she received as an internationally known political figure to continue to advance the political goals of South Africa's majority population. The continuous and escalating level of persecution suffered by Winnie Mandela was one side of the coin. Her unwavering commitment to justice, effectiveness as a leader in the struggle for social justice, and refusal to be bullied into submission was the flip side.

In August 1985 Winnie Mandela's "prison cell" in Brandfort was firebombed. No one was charged with the crime, but the shocking attack convinced Mandela to defy the government and return to her home in Soweto. After her return Mandela's defiance continued unabated—she ignored her banning order and spoke at public gatherings and to the international media. The government chose not to meet her defiance with the fullness of police action possible under law.

In 1988, her controversial Mandela United Football Club, a group of young men who lived in her newly built house in Soweto and acted as her bodyguards, caused many other antiapartheid groups to distance themselves from her. These young men were implicated in robberies, assaults and murders in the Soweto area, and Mandela's neighbors accused them of intimidation and extortion. Matters came to a head when two club members were charged by the police with the kidnapping and beating of three African youths, as well as the kidnapping and murder of 14-year-old Stompie Moeketsi. Moeketsi was a young leader whose 1500-member "children's army" opposed Mandela's club and its tactics. Mandela claimed that the boy died of beatings and sexual abuse incurred at the Methodist church where he had been previously hiding out. Even so, Mandela's bodyguards came under suspicion in two other murders and South Africa's largest organizations. The Congress of South African Trade Unions and the United Democratic Front both issued statements in 1989 disassociating themselves from Mandela and her entourage. Mandela finally disbanded her bodyguards and had the club dismantled after pressure from the ANC and her husband. Mandela's once unblemished image was tarnished in the eyes of her people and it wasn't until Nelson Mandela's release from prison in 1990 that she was somewhat rehabilitated.

Nelson Mandela stood by his wife when she was appointed head of the ANC's social welfare department and eventually given a cabinet post in his new government. Her legal troubles continued however. She was ordered to stand trial for the death of Moeketsi when the three surviving youths of the Soweto kidnapping testified in the trial of Jerry Richardson—who was convicted of murdering Moeketsi—that Mandela took part in the beatings. The judge assigned to Mandela's case described her testimony as "vague, evasive, equivocal, inconsistent, unconvincing and brazenly untruthful". She was convicted on the charge of accessory after-the-fact in the assaults and sentenced to six months in prison. Freed on bail, Mandela was permitted to appeal her conviction, a process that would take years.

In April 1992, Nelson and Winnie Mandela agreed to separate after 33 years of marriage. During the separation, Mandela continued to be plagued with scandal and in April 1995 resigned her cabinet post. In 1996, a judge granted Nelson Mandela a divorce, feeling that the couple would never be reconciled.

After the divorce, Mandela created a museum out of the Orlando West Soweto home where she and President Mandela lived. In 1997 she was re-elected as president of the African National Congress Women's League, much to the dismay of the ANC leadership. Mandela remained popular among the poorest of the and maintained her home in Soweto, just a few moments away from the Orlando Museum House.

Further Reading

Two current biographies of Nomzamo Winnie Mandela provide complementary coverage of her personal and political life. *Winnie Mandela, Mother of a Nation* by Nancy Harrison (London, 1985) is a narrative biography; *Part of My Soul Went with Him* is a compilation of interviews with Winnie Mandela and persons close to her, edited by Anne Benjamin and Mary Benson (1985); Current issues appear in *The Economist* May 10, 1997; For background on the political struggle within South Africa readers may also wish to consult the following: Mary Benson, *Nelson Mandela, Panaf Great Lives* (London, 1980); and Tom Lodge, *Black Politics in South Africa Since 1945* (1983). □

Benoit B. Mandelbrot

The Polish-born French-American mathematician Benoit B. Mandelbrot (born 1924) was the inventor of fractals. Fractal geometry has been described as one of the major developments of 20th-century mathematics. He called himself "a physicist also, and an economist, and an artist of sorts, and...."

Benoit Mandelbrot was born in Warsaw, Poland, on November 20, 1924. He described his father (1883-1952) as "a very scholarly person, and the descendant of long lines of scholars. In fact, it often seemed everyone in the family was—or was expected to become—a scholar of some kind, at least part- time. Unfortunately, many were starving scholars, and my father—being a practical man—saw virtues in a good steady job." So Mandelbrot manufactured and sold clothing. He helped raise his youngest (by 16 years) brother, Szolem Mandelbrot, who later became a famous mathematician. His mother was a doctor. Afraid of epidemics, she tried to keep him out of school. His uncle Loterman, unemployed, was his tutor, and from him Mandelbrot mastered chess and maps and learned to read very fast. In 1929, when he was five, his uncle Szolem became professor at the University of Clermont-Ferrand in France, and in 1938 at the Collège de France in Paris.

In 1936 Mandelbrot's family moved to Paris, where he attended the lycée, or secondary school. When World War II broke out, he moved south to Tulle, where he attended the lycée in Clermont-Ferrand. As he later recalled, "poverty and the wish to keep away from big cities to maximize the chances of survival made me skip most of what you might call college, so I am essentially self-taught in many ways."

College and Early Career

When Paris was liberated in 1944, Mandelbrot took the entrance exams of both the Ecole Normale Supérieure and Ecole Polytechnique. He started Ecole Normale (ranking first among an entering class of 15) but after a few days transferred to Polytechnique. Here his hopes "were thoroughly romantic: to be the first to find order where everyone else had only seen chaos." In 1947 Mandelbrot graduated from Polytechnique as Ingénieur diplômé. He obtained French and American scholarships to study in the United States.

Mandelbrot went for two years to Caltech, in Pasadena, California, earning the titles of Master of Science and Professional Engineer in Aeronautics in 1949. Back in France, he spent a year with the Air Force, then developed his doctoral thesis at the University of Paris (Faculté des Sciences). In December 1952 he was awarded a Doctorat d'Etat ès Sciences Mathématiques. His thesis title was *Games of Communication,* due to the influence of mathematicians John von Neumann and Norbert Wiener. From 1949 to 1957 Mandelbrot was a staff member at the Centre National de la Recherche Scientifique, Paris. From 1950 to 1953 he was ingénieur, Group de Télévision en Couleur: LEP, S.A. (Groupe Philips), Paris.

The last man whom Von Neumann sponsored at the Institute for Advanced Study in Princeton was Mandelbrot, who spent a "marvelous year" there in 1953-1954. From 1953 to 1971 he often visited the Massachusetts Institution of Technology in Cambridge as a research associate, then lecturer in electrical engineering, and then Institute Lecturer.

Mandelbrot returned to France, married Aliette in 1955 (they later had two children), and moved to Geneva. From 1955 to 1975 he was chargé de cours de mathématiques and belonged to the seminar of psychologist Jean Piaget at the University of Geneva.

French universities suddenly started expanding and were looking for applied mathematicians. Mandelbrot became maître de conférences d'analyse mathématique at the University of Lille and, at the request of his former mathematics teacher Paul Lévy, at the Ecole Polytechnique in Paris.

Career at IBM

Mandelbrot went to IBM as a faculty visitor in the summer of 1958 and "decided to take the gamble of staying a bit longer." He was a research staff member at IBM Thomas J. Watson Research Center, Yorktown Heights, New York, from 1958 to 1974. From 1974 to 1997 he was an IBM fellow. As Mandelbrot noted, "A few dozen IBM'ers are designated as IBM Fellows. ... Thus, it was stated officially that my work had become widely respected, and that I could proceed in my very own way."

As Mandelbrot put it, "My wild gamble started paying off during 1961-1962. By then, there was no question in my mind that I had identified a new phenomenon present in many aspects of nature, but all the examples were peripheral in their fields, and the phenomenon itself eluded definition." He added: "Many years were to go by before I formulated fractal geometry, and became able to say that I had long been concerned with the fractal aspects of nature, with seeking them out and with building theories around them."

In 1961 he established the new phenomenon as central to economics. Next, he established it was central to vital parts of physical science. And finally, he "was back to geometry after years of analytic wilderness."

In 1967 Mandelbrot raised the question, "How long is the coast of Britain?" The usual answer was, "It all depends." But he was able to show the wiggliness of a coastline can be measured using the notion of fractal dimension: this is a number like 1.15 or 1.21 which can be measured quite accurately. A favorite line of Mandelbrot became, he said, "an instant cliché": "Clouds are not spheres, mountains are not cones, coastlines are not circles and bark is not smooth, nor does lightning travel in a straight line."

As Mandelbrot summed up: "I conceived, developed and applied in many areas a new geometry of nature, which finds order in chaotic shapes and processes. It grew without a name until 1975, when I coined a new word to denote it, *fractal* geometry, from the Latin word for irregular and broken up, *fractus*. Today you might say that, until fractal geometry became organized, my life had followed a fractal orbit."

In the *Proceedings of the Royal Society* in 1989 Mandelbrot summarized fractal geometry as a "workable geometric middle ground between the excessive geometric order of Euclid and the geometric chaos of general mathematics." It was based on a form of symmetry that had previously been underused. It can be used in art and pure mathematics, being without practical application.

Many Honors and Awards

At Harvard University Mandelbrot was visiting professor of economics and research fellow in psychology (1962-1963), visiting professor of applied mathematics and staff member of the Joint Committee on Biomedical Computer Science (1963-1964), and visiting professor, later professor of the practice of mathematics, Mathematics Department (1979-1980; 1984-1987). Beginning in 1987 Mandelbrot was Abraham Robinson Adjunct Professor of Mathematical Sciences at Yale University.

He was a chevalier of the Légion d'Honneur, France (1989); a fellow of the American Academy of Arts and Sciences (1982); a foreign associate of the U.S. National Academy of Sciences (1987); a member of the European Academy of Arts, Sciences and Humanities (1987); and a member of the IBM Academy of Technology (1989).

He was made a doctor *honoris causa* of Syracuse University (1986), Laurentian University (1986), Boston University (1987), SUNY at Albany (1988), Universität Bremen, (then West) Germany (1988), Pace University (1988), and University of Guelph (1989).

He was a scholar, Rockefeller Foundation (1953) and a fellow, John Simon Guggenheim Memorial Foundation (1968, resigned). He received the Research Division outstanding innovation award (1983) and corporate award (1984) from IBM; the 1985 Barnard Medal for meritorious service to science, *Magna est Veritas*, U.S. National Academy of Sciences and Columbia University; the 1986 Franklin Medal for signal and eminent service in science from the Franklin Institute; the 1988 Charles Proteus Steinmetz Medal, IEEE and Union College; the 1988 alumni distinguished service award for outstanding achievement, Caltech; the 1988 senior award (Humboldt Preis), Alexander von Humboldt-Stiftung, Bonn, West Germany; the 1988 "Science for Art" prize, Fondation Moet-Hennessy-Louis Vuitton, Paris; the 1989 Harvey prize for science and technology, Technion-Israel Institute of Technology, Haifa, Israel; and the 1991 Nevada prize, University of Nevada System. He also received the 1993 Wolf Foundation Prize for Physics from the Wolf Foundation of Israel to Promote Science and Art for the Benefit of Mankind. He shared the 1994 Honda Prize with Abraham Robinson Adjunct Professor of Mathematical Sciences at Yale University. Mandelbrot was cited by the Honda Foundation "for contributing to the establishment of a harmony between mathematics and science and culture and the environment that surrounds human activities, and to a better understanding worldwide of science and for new tools to solve the problems induced by modern progress."

He has been visiting professor of engineering and applied science (Yale University, 1970) and visiting professor of physiology (Albert Einstein College of Medicine, Bronx, 1972; SUNY Downstate Medical Center, Brooklyn, 1974). Other institutions where he lectured included the Collége de France (1973, 1974, 1977) and as Hitchcock professor, University of California, Berkeley (1991-1992). He also belonged to the U.S. National Academy of Sciences, the American Academy of Arts and Sciences, and the European Academy. As of the (mid to late) 1990s, he was still an IBM Fellow at IBM T.J. Watson Research Center, Yorktown Heights, New York. Since 1987 he has been the Abraham Robinson Professor of Mathematical Sciences, Yale University, New Haven, Connecticut.

Further Reading

The most important autobiographical piece was "Benoit Mandelbrot, Interview by Anthony Barcellos," in *Mathematical People: Profiles and Interviews,* Donald J. Albers and G. L. Alexanderson (1985). See also James Gleick, "The Man Who Reshaped Geometry," *The New York Times Magazine* (December 8, 1985); John Rockwell, "Review/Music. Fractals: A Mystery Lingers," *The New York Times* (April 26, 1990); and L. R. Shannon, "Peripherals," *The New York Times* (October 2, 1990).

Mandelbrot was the author of *Logique, language et théorie de l'information* (with Leo Apostel and Albert Morf; 1957); *Les objets fractals: forme, hasard et dimension* (1975, 1984, 1989; translated into Hungarian, Italian, and Spanish); *Fractals: Form, Chance and Dimension* (1977); *The Fractal Geometry of Nature* (1982; translated into German and Japanese); *La geometria della natura* (1987, 1989); and *Noise and Multifractals, 1963-1976.*

In addition to books Mandelbrot published hundreds of research papers and less technical articles. The latter included "Exiles in Pursuit of Beauty," *The Scientist* (March 23, 1987); "Towards a Second Stage of Indeterminism in Science," *Interdisciplinary Science Reviews* (1987); "Fractals and the Rebirth of Iteration Theory," in *The Beauty of Fractals,* Heinz-Otto Peitgen and Peter H. Richter, editors (1986); "Foreword. People and events behind the 'Science of Fractal Images,'" in *The Science of Fractal Images,* Heinz-Otto Peitgen and

Dictmar Saupe, editors (1988); "Fractal geometry: what is it, and what does it do?" *Proc. R. Soc. Lond.* A 423 (1989); and "Fractals and the rebirth of experimental mathematics" in *Fractals for the Classroom,* Heinz-Otto Paetgen et al (1991). See also *Fractals in Physics. Essays in Honor of Benoit M. Mandelbrot,* Proceedings of the International Conference (Vence, France, 1-4 October, 1989), Amnon Aharong and Jens Feder, editors (1989). ☐

Osip Emilyevich Mandelstam

The Russian poet Osip Emilyevich Mandelstam (1891-1938) began as a member of the Acmeist movement and then evolved a style notable for its clarity, diction, concern for form, and classical allusions. His poetry is highly erudite and complex.

Osip Mandelstam was born on Jan. 15, 1891, in Warsaw, the son of a Jewish leather merchant. The family soon moved to St. Petersburg (Leningrad). Mandelstam finished secondary school at the age of 16 and immediately went to Paris. In 1910 he studied at Heidelberg and visited Switzerland. The next year he entered St. Petersburg University to study Old French.

Mandelstam's university years were also the years of his debut as a poet. The classical grace and erudition of his poetry made him an immediate success. His first book of poetry, *Stone* (1913), was well received. During the years prior to World War I, Mandelstam worked in the Guild of Poets, the Acmeist workshop that stressed artistic craftsmanship. In 1922 his second book of poems, *Tristia,* was published.

During the 1920s and early 1930s Mandelstam's attitude toward the Russian Revolution and the new Soviet regime was one of indifference. He had little faith in the Marxist view of history as progress. He deplored the popularization of culture at the expense of true cultural achievement. His poetry of these years is marked by a quiet diction, striving for balance and tension. Many of his poems celebrate architectural monuments that embody this balance and tension, such as Notre Dame in Paris and the Hagia Sophia in Istanbul. In his critical essays and artistic prose Mandelstam makes use of the classics of Western culture to show that the level of culture attained is not necessarily the result of societal or industrial achievements. He was saddened by the bleakness of Soviet life in comparison with the brilliance of his beloved city, St. Petersburg. He viewed the new mass audience of Soviet literature as detrimental to the creation of good literature and directed his own writings toward a future, enlightened audience.

In the 1930s Mandelstam's apolitical attitude and the outspoken quality of his writings brought him into direct conflict with Stalin. He was arrested in 1934 for writing an unflattering epigram on Stalin and exiled from the major Russian capitals for 3 years. Upon his return to Moscow from exile in 1937, Mandelstam found life extremely difficult. He was arrested again in May 1938, charged with counterrevolutionary activity, and sentenced to 5 years in a concentration camp in the Far East. This hardship soon drove him insane, and he died in the severe winter of 1938.

Further Reading

The best translations of Mandelstam's poetry are those in Olga Carlisle, ed., *Poets on Street Corners: Portraits of Fifteen Russian Poets* (1968). The preferred discussion of Mandelstam's life is in the moving account by his widow, Nadezhda Mandelstam, *Hope against Hope: A Memoir* (trans. 1970). Interesting views of his life and work are in Helen Muchnic, *Russian Writers: Notes and Essays* (1971). His life and creative method are explored in Clarence Brown's introduction to *The Prose of Osip Mandelstam* (trans. 1965). An informative book on Mandelstam and his place in modern poetry is Leonid I. Strakhovsky, *Craftsmen of the Word: Three Poets of Modern Russia* (1949).

Additional Sources

Mandelshtam, Nadezhda, *Hope abandoned,* New York: Atheneum, 1981, 1974.

Mandelshtam, Nadezhda, *Hope against hope: a memoir,* New York, N.Y.: Atheneum, 1987, 1970.

Mandelshtam, Osip, *Journey to Armenia,* San Francisco: G. F. Ritchie, 1979. ☐

Bernard Mandeville

The English satirist and moral philosopher Bernard Mandeville (ca. 1670-1733) is famous as the author of *The Fable of the Bees*.

Bernard Mandeville was probably born in Rotterdam, Holland, the son of a prominent doctor. In 1685 he entered the University of Rotterdam and in 1689 went on to study medicine at the University of Leiden, where he received his medical degree in 1691. Afterward he went to England to "learn the language" and set up practice as a physician. However, he had very few patients and after a short time virtually gave up medicine to devote himself exclusively to his writings.

Mandeville's best-known work is *The Fable of the Bees, or Private Vices, Publick Benefits* (1714), originally published as a poem, "The Grumbling Hive, or Knaves Turned Honest" (1705). This was intended at first to be a political satire on the state of England in 1705, when the Tories accused the ministry of favoring the French war for their own personal gains. In the later version, however, enlarged to two volumes, Mandeville, in agreement with T. Hobbes, declares that men act essentially in terms of egoistical interests, in contrast to the easy optimism and idealism of Shaftesbury. The material concerns of individuals are the basic force behind all social progress, while what rulers and clergymen call virtues are simply fictions that those in power employ to maintain their control. Francis Hutcheson and Bishop Berkeley wrote treatises opposing Mandeville's views. Others, including Adam Smith, as some interpreters claim, were affected in a more positive way by Mandeville's ideas.

In some of his other works Mandeville shows an intelligent and open interest in controversial and, for the time, scandalous subjects, such as whoring and the execution of criminals. On some issues, however, Mandeville seems strangely callous. In "An Essay on Charity and Charity Schools" he objects to educating the poor because the acquisition of knowledge has the effect of increasing desires and thereby making it more difficult to meet the needs of the poor. Moreover, he seems to regard even wars as valuable to the economic development of a nation since by destroying houses and property laborers are provided an opportunity to replace the destroyed goods.

On the basis of his views Mandeville is usually placed in the moral-sense school. Some interpreters insist that he is the forerunner of the doctrine of utilitarianism.

Further Reading

The most readily available edition of Mandeville's *The Fable of the Bees, or Private Vices, Publick Benefits,* with a critical, historical, and explanatory commentary, is by F. B. Kaye (2 vols., 1714; repr. 1924). See also *The Cambridge History of English Literature,* vol. 9 (1912), and Cecil A. Moore, *Backgrounds of English Literature, 1700-1760* (1953). □

Sir John Mandeville

Sir John Mandeville is the pen name used by the unidentified 14th-century English author of one of the most famous and widely read travel romances of Europe—*The Voyage and Travels of Sir John Mandeville, Knight*.

Originally written in Norman French about 1360 and translated into 10 major European languages, including English and Latin, by the end of the century, the *Travels* enjoyed undiminished popularity for over 400 years. Purporting to be a travel guide emphasizing the exotic wonders of the Near and Far East, it is generally considered one of the finest works of imaginative literature of the medieval period.

The question of authorship has met with much controversy in recent years. In the *Travels* the author claims that his name is Sir John Mandeville, born and educated at St. Albans, England, and that he began his travels in 1322, returning home in 1356 to write the account of his experiences. This is further expanded by Jean d'Outremeuse (1338-1400), the Liège chronicler, who writes that one Jean de Bourgogne, also known as John with the Beard, confessed on his deathbed in 1372 that he was the Sir John Mandeville who left England in 1322 after killing a nobleman. Although this view is accepted by Malcolm Letts, Josephine Bennett rejects it as fiction, noting that the Liège version of the *Travels,* the most corrupt of the three French versions, was made from the Paris, not the Norman French, copy. Thus she concludes that it is highly unlikely that the original Norman French version could have been written by one who lived in Liège for 30 years and yet was unknown there.

Regardless of who actually wrote the *Travels,* it is generally accepted that the author may never have traveled at all. It has been shown that practically the entire work was compiled from several earlier authors such as Vincent of Beauvais (active 1260), John of Piano Carpini (active 1245), Odoric of Pordenone (active 1330), and the German friar William of Rubruck (active 1250). However, the author of the *Travels* brilliantly organized the eclectic travel material into an artistic first-person narrative. He begins with a guide to the Holy Land, relating many anecdotes of his "experiences" and "observations." Then he describes the fabulous wealth and wonder of the court of the Great Khan and details of Prester John's kingdom. Among the marvels he describes are various types of monsters such as dog-headed cannibals, flatfaced people without noses or mouths, a race of hermaphrodites, people with ears hanging to their knees, and men whose heads grow beneath their shoulders.

Although there is no question that the author of the *Travels* plagiarized his material, he did cast it into his own highly entertaining style in what has been correctly described as a masterpiece of literary collage.

Further Reading

The best available edition for the general reader is the 1964 reprint of *The Travels of Sir John Mandeville,* edited in modern spelling by A. W. Pollard (1900). Sir John Mandeville, *Travels,* edited by Malcolm Letts (2 vols., 1953), contains a comprehensive introduction followed by the Egerton text in modern spelling, annotated, with the oldest (1371) French version and the Bodleian English translation.

A succinct analysis of Mandeville is in chapter 3, ''The Beginnings of English Prose,'' by Alice D. Greenwood, in volume 2 of *The Cambridge History of English Literature* (15 vols., 1919-1931). For an interesting analysis of the *Travels,* its author, and its sources see Malcolm Letts, *Sir John Mandeville: The Man and His Book* (1949). However, the latest and most definitive study to date, which refutes Letts's theory that Mandeville was John of Bourgogne, is Josephine Bennett, *The Rediscovery of Sir John Mandeville* (1954), in which the author thoroughly discusses the problems of authorship, the sources, and the literary quality of the *Travels.* □

Édouard Manet

The art of the French painter Édouard Manet (1832-1883) broke with 19th-century academic precepts and marks the beginning of modern painting.

Édouard Manet was born in Paris on Jan. 23, 1832, to Auguste Manet, an official at the Ministry of Justice, and Eugénie Désirée Manet. The father, who had expected Édouard to study law, vigorously opposed his wish to become a painter. The career of naval officer was decided upon as a compromise, and at the age of 16 Édouard sailed to Rio de Janeiro on a training vessel. Upon his return he failed to pass the entrance examination of the naval academy. His father relented, and in 1850 Manet entered the studio of Thomas Couture, where, in spite of many disagreements with his teacher, he remained until 1856. During this period Manet traveled abroad and made numerous copies after the Old Masters in both foreign and French public collections.

Early Works

Manet's entry for the Salon of 1859, the *Absinthe Drinker,* a thematically romantic but conceptually already daring work, was rejected. At the Salon of 1861, his *Spanish Singer,* one of a number of works of Spanish character painted in this period, not only was admitted to the Salon but won an honorable mention and the acclaim of the poet Théophile Gautier. This was to be Manet's last success for many years.

In 1863 Manet married Suzanne Leenhoff, a Dutch pianist. That year he showed 14 paintings at the Martinet Gallery; one of them, *Music in the Tuileries,* remarkable for its freshness in the handling of a contemporary scene, was greeted with considerable hostility. Also in 1863 the Salon rejected Manet's large painting *Luncheon on the Grass,* and the artist elected to have it shown at the now famous Salon des Refusés, created by the Emperor under the pressure of the exceptionally large number of painters whose work had been turned away. Here, Manet's picture attracted the most attention and brought forth a kind of abusive criticism which was to set a pattern for years to come. Although this painting is a paraphrase of Giorgione's *Concert champêtre,* the combination of clothed men and a nude woman in a modern context was found offensive.

In 1865 Manet's *Olympia* produced a still more violent reaction at the official Salon, and his reputation as a renegade became widespread. Upset by the criticism, Manet made a brief trip to Spain, where he admired many works by Diego Velázquez, to whom he referred as ''the painter of painters.''

Support of Baudelaire and Zola

Manet's close friend and supporter during the early years was Charles Baudelaire, who, in 1862, had written a quatrain to accompany one of Manet's Spanish subjects, *Lola de Valence,* and the public, largely as a result of the strange atmosphere of the *Olympia,* linked the two men readily. In 1866, after the Salon jury had rejected two of Manet's works, Émile Zola came to his defense with a series of articles filled with strongly expressed, uncompromising praise. In 1867 he published a book which contains the prediction, ''Manet's place is destined to be in the Louvre.'' This book appears on Zola's desk in Manet's portrait of the writer (1868). In May of that year the Paris World's Fair opened its doors, and Manet, at his own expense, exhibited 50 of his works in a temporary structure, not far from Gustave Courbet's private exhibition. This was in keeping with Manet's view, expressed years later to his friend Antonin Proust, that his paintings must be seen together in order to be fully understood.

Although Manet insisted that a painter be "resolutely of his own time" and that he paint what he sees, he nevertheless produced two important religious works, the *Dead Christ with Angels and Christ Mocked by the Soldiers*, which were shown at the Salons of 1864 and 1865, respectively, and ridiculed. Only Zola could defend the former work on the grounds of its vigorous realism while playing down its alleged lack of piety. It is also true that although Manet despised the academic category of "history painting" he did paint the contemporary *Naval Battle between the Kearsarge and the Alabama* (1864) and the *Execution of Maximilian* (1867). The latter is based upon a careful gathering of the facts surrounding the incident and composed, largely, after Francisco Goya's *Executions of the Third of May*, resulting in a curious amalgam of the particular and the universal. Manet's use of older works of art in elaborating his own major compositions has long been, and continues to be, a problematic subject, since the old view that this procedure was needed to compensate for the artist's own inadequate imagination is rapidly being discarded.

Late Works

Although the impressionists were influenced by Manet during the 1860s, during the next decade it appears that it was he who learned from them. His palette became lighter; his stroke, without ever achieving the analytical intensity of Claude Monet's, was shorter and more rapid. Nevertheless, Manet never cultivated pleinairism seriously, and he remained essentially a figure and studio painter. Also, despite his sympathy for most of the impressionists with whom the public associated him, he never exhibited with them at their series of private exhibitions which began in 1874.

Manet had his first resounding success since the *Spanish Singer* at the Salon of 1873 with his *Bon Bock*, which radiates a touch and joviality of expression reminiscent of Frans Hals, in contrast to Manet's usually austere figures. In spite of the popularity of this painting, his success was not to extend to the following season. About this time he met the poet Stéphane Mallarmé, with whom he remained on intimate terms for the remainder of his life. After Manet's rejection by the jury in 1876, Mallarmé took up his defense.

Toward the end of the 1870s, although Manet retained the bright palette and the touch of his impressionist works, he returned to the figure problems of the early years. The undeniable sense of mystery is found again in several bar scenes, notably the *Brasserie Reichshoffen*, in which the relationships of the figures recall those of the *Luncheon on the Grass*. Perhaps the apotheosis of his lifelong endeavors is to be found in his last major work, *A Bar at the Folies-Bergère*. Here, in the expression of the barmaid, is all the starkness of the great confrontations of the 1860s, but bathed in a profusion of colors. While we are drawn to the brilliantly painted accessories, it is the girl, placed at the center before a mirror, who dominates the composition and ultimately demands our attention. Although her reflected image, showing her to be in conversation with a man, is

absorbed into the brilliant atmosphere of the setting, she remains enigmatic and aloof. Manet produced two aspects of the same personality, combined the fleeting with the eternal, and, by "misplacing" the reflected image, took a step toward abstraction as a solution to certain lifelong philosophical and technical problems.

In 1881 Manet was finally admitted to membership in the Legion of Honor, an award he had long coveted. By then he was seriously ill. Therapy at the sanatorium at Bellevue failed to improve his health, and walking became increasingly difficult for him. In his weakened condition he found it easier to handle pastels than oils, and he produced a great many flower pieces and portraits in that medium. In the spring of 1883 his left leg was amputated, but this did not prolong his life. He died peacefully in Paris on April 30.

Manet was short, unusually handsome, and witty. His biographers stress his kindness and unaffected generosity toward his friends. The paradoxical elements in his art are an extension of the man: although a revolutionary in art, he craved official honors; while fashionably dressed, he affected a Parisian slang at odds with his appearance and impeccable manners; and although he espoused the style of life of the conservative classes, his political sentiments were those of the republican liberal.

Further Reading

Useful general works on Manet are Georges Bataille, *Manet* (trans. 1955), which has a good text and small color illustrations; and John Richardson, *Édouard Manet: Paintings and Drawings* (1958), with good, large color illustrations. Recommended catalogs are A. C. Hanson, *Manet* (1966), an excellent study but with poor color plates; Alain de Leiris, *The Drawings of Édouard Manet* (1969); and Jean C. Harris, *Édouard Manet, Graphic Works: A Definitive Catalog* (1970). For specialized studies see George Heard Hamilton, *Manet and His Critics* (1954); Nils Gösta Sandblad, *Manet: Three Studies in Artistic Conception* (1954); and George Mauner, *Manet, Peintre-Philosophe: A Study of the Painter's Themes* (1972). A great deal of useful historical information is in John Rewald, *The History of Impressionism* (1946; rev. ed. 1961). □

Mangas Coloradas

As a member of the Mimbreno Apache, Mangas Coloradas (ca. 1790-1863) was a leader in the early years of the Apache Wars of the 1860s.

Some authorities cite Mangas Coloradas as the most significant Apache war chief of the nineteenth century, although some dispute whether he was formally recognized as their chief. Americans and Hispanics of the period described Mangas as an influential statesman, diplomat, and sage, as well as a ferocious, uncompromising, and brutal butcher who laid waste huge tracts of northern Mexico, all of Arizona, and much of New Mexico. His name was synonymous with terror. Despite his apparent penchant for violence, however, he was said to be a peace-loving man whose only interest was in preventing the Hispanics and Americans from overrunning his people's lands.

A member of the Mimbreno ("Willow") band of the eastern Chihenne ("Red Paint People") Apache, Mangas Coloradas was born between 1790 and 1795, probably somewhere in what is now southern New Mexico. His nomadic band inhabited the area of the Mimbres Mountains and along the Mimbres River. At that time this territory was part of the Janos district of New Spain. The early nineteenth century was characterized by a low level of hostility between the Spanish and Apache. This would change around 1831, however, and Mangas would figure prominently in the Apaches' attempts to drive the Spanish, and later the Mexicans and Americans, from ancestral Apache lands.

Physically Mangas was described as very muscular and unusually tall for an Apache: over six feet. His most prominent feature was his large head, described by John Cremony in *Life among the Apaches* as having "a broad, bold forehead, a large aquiline nose, a most capacious mouth, and broad, heavy chin. His eyes were rather small, but exceedingly brilliant and flashing when under any excitement— although his outside demeanor was as imperturbable as brass." One legend suggested he was at least half white, his father being an Apache warrior and his mother Mexican.

Origins Are Subject of Speculation

Mangas Colorado's name initially appeared in historical documents in 1842. He was cited as a Mogollon leader, with the Mogollons being another of the eastern Apache bands. It has been suggested that prior to 1842 he was known by some other name. He may have received his Spanish name meaning "red sleeves" or "roan shirt" either because his shirt had sleeves of red fabric, or because it was covered with his victims' blood. The latter may be applicable given Mangas' revenge for the murder in 1837 of Juan Jose Compa, his predecessor.

Prior to this event he may have been known as Fuerte, who was the dominant Chihenne leader from 1815 through the 1830s. "Fuerte," Spanish for "strong," could well have been used to describe a man like Mangas. Mangas and Fuerte seemed to be about the same age, and both were called by the title "general." Fuerte, however, is on record of officially receiving this title, while Mangas is not. Besides a similarity in their physical features, they seemed to share the practice of distancing themselves from Mexicans, taking what the administrators could be made to give them but keeping personal contact to a minimum. Fuerte lived near the Mimbres River and Santa Rita del Cobre, where Mangas had his stronghold. He disappeared around 1840. It is also possible that up until 1840 Mangas was simply overshadowed by Fuerte, and assumed power as his position weakened. Mangas reportedly became chief of the Mimbrenos about 1837.

The Apache language was a difficult one to learn and speak. This was possibly one reason why Spanish names were often assigned to people and places. Thus virtually none of the original Apache names are known. The Spanish intended to create out of the nomadic Apache a population of self-sufficient farmers. Some of the regulations they imposed on the Apache to force them into farming were requiring passports for those who wished to travel in the territory and forbidding traditional hunting and gathering without a permit. They rewarded loyal Apache allies with gifts of horses or in some cases the return of incarcerated relatives. When the Mexicans gained independence from Spain in 1821, the region was opened to commerce from the outside, and raiding became more profitable than farming. Many Apache left their farms and assumed very successful and lucrative roles of middlemen; raiding and trading, especially in horses, mules, and captives. One of these captives became Mangas Colorado's principal wife.

Arranged Inter-Tribal Alliances

While on a raid in Sonora, Mangas abducted an attractive, intelligent Mexican girl. She was given the name Tu-es-seh and they had three daughters. When Dos-teh-seh, the eldest, came of age, Mangas presented her to Cochise, leader of the Chiricahua ("Mountain of the Wild Turkeys") Apache, for his wife. He gave his second daughter to Katuhala, leader of the White Mountain Apache, and the third to Cosito, chief of the Coyotero Apache. While it is well-documented that Dos-teh-seh married Cochise, the identity of the husbands of the other two daughters are disputed. Some claim Mangas gave one to the chief of the Navajo and another to the head chief of the Mescalero Apache. In any case, Mangas' intent with all the marital arrangements was to forge alliances and create stronger relationships within the tribes, including the Navajo, who were enemies of the Mexicans and the Spanish before them.

Mangas was described as a statesman, actively shaping and conducting Apache policy with respect to the whites. These marriages seemed to show that he knew the threat from the Mexicans and Americans was greater than any inter-tribal or inter-band dispute, and the only hope of overcoming that threat was to unify the bands and tribes against it. If indeed this was his strategy, he was for all practical purposes the only Indian since Tecumseh to realize the value of unification. Despite this, only his alliance with Cochise was completely successful. In addition to his daughters, he had at least three sons: Seth-mooda, Casco, and Mangas. His brothers of record were Jose Mangas, Phalis Palacio, and Chaha. He may have had additional brothers or sisters.

Attempted to Drive Whites from Apache Lands

The Spanish government and the Mexican government which succeeded it had customarily provided rations to the Apache. When the Mexican government discontinued this practice in 1831, strained relations between the Mexicans and Apaches caused the Indians to intensify their raids on towns and ranches. The state of Chihuahua declared general war on Apaches on October 16, 1831. Mangas' theater of operations in the early 1840s encompassed Chihuahua state and the Mogollon Mountains. He expanded this to include Sonora state by the 1850s. In 1856 Mexican officials offered a bounty for Mangas Colorado's head.

Raiding allowed the Apache to maintain some semblance of their traditional livelihood; it suited their nomadic nature. But atrocities against their victims were generally not part of their raids. In the case of Mangas, however, this changed radically as a result of two notable incidents which precipitated his hatred of all whites.

The first of these concerned John Johnson, an American who made his living hunting Apaches. He traded the scalps of his victims to the Mexican government in exchange for a bounty. In April of 1837, Johnson, after befriending the Mimbreno head chief Juan Jose Compa, ambushed and massacred Juan Jose and about 20 members of his band near Santa Rita in the Sierra de las Animas (modern Hidalgo County, New Mexico). Mangas was apparently related to Juan Jose, and he retaliated by killing a group of 22 American miners as well as whatever other Americans he could find in the area. In an interesting turnaround, when he met General Stephen Kearney in 1846, he pledged his friendship to the Americans and alliance if Kearney wanted to invade Mexico. Kearney refused.

The second incident, in April 1851, also occurred near Santa Rita. An influx of gold miners angered the Apaches because it drove off game and mocked their spiritual traditions. Mangas offered to lead the miners to an area richer in gold than the mines at Santa Rita, where they could pick large nuggets off the ground. Suspecting he was trying to lure them away individually and kill them, the miners bound him to a tree and whipped him to near unconsciousness. The beating was so humiliating, Mangas hid in the mountains for two weeks until his back healed.

As a result of these experiences, Mangas' assaults against the whites became increasingly brutal and murderous. His infamous trademark was leaving the hats on the scalped heads of his victims. Since whites wore hats and Apaches did not, Mangas ordered his men to shoot anyone wearing a hat. The hat would remain even when only bones were left, testifying to Mangas' killing of another enemy. In yet another turnaround, Mangas and a group of chiefs signed a treaty with the U.S. government in 1852 at Acoma Pueblo, but Congress refused to ratify it. Atrocities thus continued, and Colonel E. V. Sumner's official report for 1852 strongly recommended giving New Mexico back to the Indians and Mexicans.

Tortured and Murdered at Ft. McLean

Mangas and Cochise joined forces in 1861, when several of Cochise's relatives were executed by Lieutenant George M. Bascom's Seventh Infantry. Mangas and Cochise intended to drive all Americans from their lands. In 1862 Mangas was wounded in the chest by John Teal in the battle of Apache Pass in Arizona. He was taken to Janos, Chihuahua, where his band coerced a doctor to treat him. He made a full recovery.

In January 1863, he was captured by Captain Edmond Shirland's First California Volunteer Cavalry. Lured into Shirland's camp by a flag of truce, Mangas trusted Shirland and rode in alone. He was taken to Fort McLean in Arizona, where he was killed by guards when he protested against their torturing him with hot bayonets. An inaccurate report of his capture and death stated he was killed while attempting escape. Convinced the Americans could not be trusted, the Apaches began another campaign to eliminate the whites.

Mangas' murder in itself had a profound effect on the Apache, but the mutilation of his body by the soldiers (he was scalped and buried in a ditch) further excited their rage. Capt D. B. Sturgeon, fort surgeon, exhumed the body, had the head cut off, the meat boiled from the bones, and the skull sent to a phrenologist, Professor O. S. Fowler. Fowler pronounced it of greater capacity than Daniel Webster's.

Despite his years of savage tactics, Mangas' principal aim seemed to be obtaining a lasting peace for his people, a goal for which he continually placed himself in harm's way. A 1970s survey of Chiricahua Apaches living in New Mexico and Oklahoma revealed that while many remembered the murder of Mangas Coloradas, comparatively few recalled Pearl Harbor—despite the fact that radical changes had taken place in Chiricahua culture in the century since Mangas' death occurred.

Further Reading

Ball, Eve, Nora Henn, and Lynda Sanchez, *Indeh, an Apache Odyssey*, Provo, Utah, Brigham Young University Press, 1980.

Betzinez, Jason, and Wilbur Sturtevant Nye, *I Fought with Geronimo*, Harrisburg, Pennsylvania, Stackpole, 1959.

Brown, Dee, *Bury My Heart at Wounded Knee*, New York, Henry Holt and Company, 1970.

Clum, Woodworth, *Apache Agent*, Cambridge, Massachusetts, Riverside Press, 1936.

Cremony, John C., *Life among the Apaches*, Glorieta, New Mexico, Rio Grande Press, 1970.

Griffen, William B., *Apaches at War and Peace: The Janos Presidio, 1750-1858*, Albuquerque, University of New Mexico, 1988.

Roberts, David, *Once They Moved Like the Wind*, New York, Simon and Schuster, 1993.

Santee, Ross, *Apache Land*, Lincoln, University of Nebraska Press, 1947.

Sweeney, Edwin R., *Cochise, Chiricahua Apache Chief*, Norman, University of Oklahoma Press, 1991.

Thrapp, Dan L., *The Conquest of Apacheria*, Norman, University of Oklahoma Press, 1967.

Worcester, Donald E., *The Apaches*, Norman, University of Oklahoma Press, 1979. □

Mani

Mani (216-276) was a Persian prophet and the founder of Manichaeism, the best known and most developed of the Gnostic religions. Mani's religion spread quickly but was eventually stamped out through opposition from other religions, notably Zoroastrianism, Christianity, and Islam.

Patek, the father of Mani, was a native of Hamadan, ancient Ecbatana, and apparently belonged to the Arsacid princely family. He left Hamadan and settled in Babylonia, where Mani grew up among the Mandaeans, a Baptist sect of Gnostic tendencies. In 240-241 he felt called upon to proclaim openly his new religion and call people to the truth. His faith was a universal one. He believed that God had periodically revealed the truth through His chosen apostles, Zoroaster, Buddha, and Christ, and Mani considered himself the true prophet of his day for all humanity.

His teachings were primarily based on an old Persian dualism pushed to the extreme. He envisaged two separate and independent principles, light and darkness (or spirit and matter). The creation of the world was the outcome of an invasion on the realm of light by the forces of darkness, as a result of which elements of light were devoured by demons of darkness. Man, animals, and plants were conceived by demons in a desperate attempt to retain the particles of light they had swallowed.

The universe is a machinery set up by the deities of light to redeem the absorbed light and return it to its original abode. The light in man could be released, or his spirit saved, by a realization of his origin and of his place in the scheme of things through the teachings of an inspired leader. In practice, salvation can be achieved through abstinence, prayers, and worship. To attend to the business of the world would be to promote the scheme of the demons.

A strongly moralistic religion, with marked ascetic tendencies, Manichaeism forbids its elite (from whom the clergy is drawn) to marry, engage in trade, slaughter animals, or cut plants. The commoners (hearers), however, are reluctantly allowed to do so. Mani's cosmology reveals syncretic elements with a strong Gnostic bias. Several cycles of gods are postulated as emanating from the Father of Greatness, the supreme Lord of Light.

Mani seems to have begun his career by a journey to the easternmost provinces of Persia and Sind. He is reported to have attracted or converted Peroz and Mehrshah, two sons of Ardashir I, founder of the Sassanid dynasty. Upon Ardashir's death in 241, Mani returned to western Persia, where he found favor with Ardashir's successor, Shahpur I, to whom he dedicated one of his books, *Shapurgan*. During Shahpur's reign Mani engaged in intense missionary activities. Eventually, however, the opposition of the Zoroastrian priesthood enlisted the support of Bahram I, who ordered Mani arrested and fettered. He died in prison a martyr.

Mani left a number of books, treatises, and epistles, mostly in Syriac, among which were the *Book of the Two Principles, The Book of Secrets,* and *The Living Gospel.* Popular Persian beliefs regard him as an extraordinary painter and the author of *Artang,* a wonderfully illustrated work. Manichaean manuscripts were in fact written with calligraphic artistry and were often illustrated.

Further Reading

Selections of Manichaean writings are in A. V. Williams Jackson, *Researches in Manichaeism* (1932); Charles Allberry, *A Manichaean Psalm-book, Part II* (1938); and Mary Boyce, *The Manichaean Hymn-cycles in Parthian* (1954). The latest work on Mani in English is George Widengren, *Mani and Manichaeism,* translated by Charles Kessler, in the "History of Religion" Series (1965). See also F. C. Burkitt, *The Religion of the Manichees* (1925). ☐

Daniele Manin

The Venetian patriot Daniele Manin (1804-1857) labored for the liberation of Venice from Austria and made an important contribution to the unification of Italy.

Daniele Manin was born on May 13, 1804, the son of a converted Jew who adopted the name of the patrician family that had sponsored him. Manin studied law at the University of Padua and then took up practice in Venice. As his practice grew, his reputation as a brilliant and profound jurist grew with it.

Manin's first act in the cause of liberation was the presentation of a petition in 1847 to a body called the Venetian Congregation, a purely advisory assembly that the Austrian government permitted to gather precisely because it had no power at all. The petition, addressed to the Emperor, listed the grievances of the Venetian people. Manin hated the Austrian domination of Venice and was injudiciously frank about it.

On Jan. 18, 1848, he was arrested for treason. His arrest served only to increase his popularity. Within 2 months the revolution had broken out, and the Venetians forced the Austrian governor to release him on March 17. Nine days later the Austrians were driven from the city, and Manin guided the erection of a provisional government and became president of the short-lived Venetian Republic.

Manin cooperated, albeit reluctantly, with the efforts of the Piedmontese government to unite Italy under its own auspices. When this effort failed, and the king of Piedmont, Charles Albert, signed an armistice leaving Venetia under Austria, there was a wild scene in Venice leading to an attempt to lynch the Piedmontese representatives. Manin intervened and, through the great prestige he enjoyed, saved their lives.

Venice managed to retain its independence from Austria for almost another year. After the support of the Piedmont ended, the Austrians began gradually to reoccupy all the Venetian mainland. Hope was fading, but early in 1849 the Venetian Assembly reaffirmed Manin as president of the republic and gave him unlimited authority. They voted to resist to the end.

Austrian forces surrounded the city and began to bombard it from land and sea. Under siege conditions the supply of food dwindled, and in July cholera spread throughout the city. Defeat was inevitable, and on Aug. 24, 1849, Manin capitulated under the best terms possible: amnesty for all except himself and some other prominent citizens who had helped him.

On August 27 Manin left for Paris, where he came to believe that the only hope for Italian unity lay with the Piedmontese monarchy. He cooperated in the founding of the Società Nazionale Italiana, an organization devoted to the goal of unification under the Piedmont. On Sept. 22, 1857, Manin died, only a few years before Italy realized the goals he had spent his life to achieve.

Further Reading

For a lively and accurate account of Manin see George M. Trevelyan, *Manin and the Venetian Revolution of 1848* (1923). Not specifically about Manin but dealing thoroughly with the period is G. F. H. and J. Berkeley, *Italy in the Making* (3 vols., 1932-1940). Also useful is A. J. P. Taylor, *The Italian Problem in European Diplomacy, 1847-1849* (1934).

Additional Sources

Ginsborg, Paul, *Daniele Manin and the Venetian revolution of 1848-49,* Cambridge; New York: Cambridge University Press, 1979.

Trevelyan, George Macaulay, *Manin and the Venetian revolution of 184,* New York, H. Fertig, 1974. □

Wilma Mankiller

Wilma Mankiller (born 1945) became active in Native American causes in San Francisco in the late 1960s and early 1970s and gained skills in community organization and program development. With 56 percent of the vote, Mankiller became the first woman elected Cherokee principal chief in the historic Cherokee election of 1987.

Wilma Pearl Mankiller is both the first woman Deputy Chief and first woman Principal Chief of the Cherokee Nation of Oklahoma. She overcame many personal tragedies and returned home to Mankiller Flats, Oklahoma, to establish herself as a political power working for the betterment of all people. Mankiller was born at Tahlequah, the capitol of the Cherokee Nation, in November 1945, and was raised until she was ten years old at Mankiller Flats. Her father was Charlie Mankiller, Cherokee, and her mother was Irene Mankiller, Dutch-Irish. She had four sisters and six brothers.

Trail of Tears

Mankiller's great-grandfather was one of the over 16,000 Cherokees, Choctaws, Creeks, Chickasaws, Seminoles, and African slaves who struggled along the Trail of Tears to Oklahoma during the removal period, when Andrew Jackson was President in the 1830s. According to Carl Waldman in *Atlas of the North American Indian,* their journey was one of much pain and death: "At least a quarter of the Indians died before even reaching the Indian Territory. And many more died afterward, as they struggled to build new lives in the rugged terrain, with meager supplies and surrounded by hostile western Indians."

The Mankillers were very poor in Oklahoma, their ancestors being deposited there in 1838 and 1839, and it was difficult for Mankiller's father to maintain his family with any semblance of dignity. Although they did not want to move to California, Charlie Mankiller thought he could make a better life there for them and accepted a government offer to relocate. However, program promises faltered, money did not arrive, and there was often no employment available, so their life did not improve after their arrival in San Francisco.

The children were homesick even before they started for California. As Mankiller recalled in her autobiography, *Mankiller: A Chief and Her People,* "I experienced my own Trail of Tears when I was a young girl. No one pointed a gun at me or at members of my family. No show of force was used. It was not necessary. Nevertheless, the United States government through the Bureau of Indian Affairs, was again trying to settle the 'Indian problem' by removal. I learned through this ordeal about the fear and anguish that occur when you give up your home, your community, and everything you have ever known to move far away to a strange place. I cried for days, not unlike the children who had stumbled down the Trail of Tears so many years before. I wept tears that came from deep within the Cherokee part of me. They were tears from my history, from my tribe's past. They were Cherokee tears."

In California, cringing at the snickering that always followed the school roll call when the teacher said "Mankiller," she nevertheless finished high school and pursued higher education. In the 1960s she attended Skyline Junior College in San Bruno then San Francisco State College. At San Francisco State she met and married Hector Hugo Olaya de Bardi. In 1964 they had a daughter, Felicia, and in 1966 another, Gina. In college, Mankiller was introduced to some of the Native Americans who would soon occupy and reclaim Alcatraz Island for the Native American people.

Alcatraz Occupation Fuels Political Awakening

The "invasion" of Alcatraz by the Native Americans quickly became a focal point for many Native people, Mankiller included. Because of the bold move onto Alcatraz by San Francisco State student and Mohawk Richard Oakes, along with his "All Tribes" group, Mankiller realized that her mission in life was to serve her people. She yearned for independence, something that caused a conflict with her marriage. "Once I began to become more independent, more active with school and in the community, it became increasingly difficult to keep my marriage together. Before that, Hugo had viewed me as someone he had rescued from a very bad life," she noted in her autobiography. In 1974 she was divorced and became a single head of the household. Mankiller longed to do more for her people. Soon she was volunteering to work for attorney Aubrey Grossman of San Francisco, who was defending the Pit River people against charges from Pacific Gas and Electric Company.

There were many political and social movements across America during the 1960s. To many Native people across America, however, the defiant occupation of Alcatraz in a challenge of treaty rights, which led to the arrest of many people, ushered in a new and real feeling of self-determination. "When Alcatraz occurred, I became aware of what needed to be done to let the rest of the world know that Indians had rights, too. Alcatraz articulated my own feelings about being an Indian," Mankiller stated in her autobiography. She became involved in the movement and began a commitment to serve the Native people to the best of her ability in the area of law and legal defense.

Endures Personal Tragedies and Health Problems

In 1971, Mankiller's father died from a kidney disease in San Francisco, which she said "tore through my spirit like a blade of lightning." The family took Charlie Mankiller home to Oklahoma for burial, then Mankiller returned to California. It was not long before she too had kidney problems, inherited from her father. Her early kidney problems could be treated, though later she had to have surgery and eventually, in 1990, she had to have a transplant. Her brother Donald became her "hero" by donating one of his kidneys so that she could live.

In 1960, Mankiller's brother Bob was badly burned in a fire. Not wanting to be an added burden to the survival of the family, he had traveled north and was picking apples in Washington State. In the chill of early morning, he made a mistake by starting a fire with gasoline instead of kerosene, and his wooden shack exploded in flames. Bob survived for only six days. He was Mankiller's role model for a "care free" spirit.

In 1976, Mankiller returned to Oklahoma for good and found time to pursue higher education. She enrolled in graduate courses at the University of Arkansas, Fayetteville, which required her to drive the distance daily. She was returning home one morning when an automobile approached her on a blind curve and, from seemingly nowhere, another automobile attempted to pass it. She swerved to miss the approaching automobile, but failed. The vehicles hurtled together, almost head on.

Mankiller was seriously injured, and many thought she would not survive. The driver of the other automobile did not. It turned out to be Sherry Morris, Mankiller's best friend. It was terribly difficult, both physically and emotionally, but Mankiller recovered. Shortly after this accident, she came down with myasthenia gravis, a muscle disease. Again her life was threatened, but her will to live and her determination to mend her body with the power of her mind prevailed.

Becomes Principal Chief of the Cherokee Nation

In 1983, Ross Swimmer, then Principal Chief of the Cherokee Nation of Oklahoma, asked Mankiller to be his Deputy Chief in the election. She accepted, and they won the election and took office on August 14, 1983. On December 5, 1985, Swimmer was nominated to head the Bureau of Indian Affairs in Washington, D.C., and Mankiller was sworn in as Principal Chief.

Mankiller overcame many tragedies to become a guiding power for the Cherokee people of Oklahoma and a symbol of achievement for women everywhere. Yet through all the trying times, she worried for all people everywhere and planned for their happiness. She herself found love and strength in Charlie Soap. She gives him much credit for her successes and her will to overcome the many obstacles that threatened her political and physical life after her return to Oklahoma.

Throughout her life, Mankiller has managed to not complain about how bad things are for herself, for her people, and for Native people in general, but instead to help make life better. Fittingly, she was inducted into the Woman's Hall of Fame in New York City in 1994.

Further Reading

Mankiller, Wilma, and Michael Wallis, *Mankiller: A Chief and Her People,* New York, St. Martin's Press, 1993.
Waldman, Carl, *Atlas of the North American Indian,* New York, Facts on File, 1985. □

Michael Norman Manley

Michael Manley (1924-1997) was the leader of the People's National Party of Jamaica, prime minister (1972-1980, 1989-1992), and theoretician for a new International Economic Order. A fiery leftist and critic of the United States in his first two terms, in his third term he was a moderate with close ties to America.

Michael Norman Manley was born in St. Andrew, Jamaica, on December 10, 1924, the second son of illustrious parents. His father, Norman Washington Manley, was a Rhodes scholar, decorated World War I hero, and the most distinguished legal advocate in the history of Jamaica. In 1938 Norman Manley founded the People's National Party, and he served as premier of Jamaica between 1955 and 1962. Along with his cousin, Alexander Bustamante, the elder Manley was a dominant force in the political system of his c}ountry until his retirement in 1969. Michael Manley's mother, Edna (nee Swithenbank), was an internationally recognized sculptor and patron of the arts

Manley attended Jamaica College, his father's *alma mater,* in suburban Saint Andrew parish and in the early 1940s was a writer for the weekly newspaper *Public Opinion.* He volunteered for service in the Royal Canadian Air

Force in 1943 while at McGill University and at the end of the war studied politics, philosophy, and economics at the London School of Economics. Upon graduation he worked as a freelance journalist with the British Broadcasting Service from 1950 to December 1951, when he accepted the invitation to be associate editor of *Public Opinion.*

Jamaica in the early 1950s was an exciting place politically. The People's National Party had lost the general elections of 1949 although they gained the largest number of popular votes. More significantly, an irreparable rift had developed between the party and its labor union, culminating in a break in 1952. Manley became a member of the executive committee of the People's National Party in 1952 and helped organize the National Worker's Union, the successor to the Trade's Union Congress dominated by the expelled dissident faction

In 1953 Manley quit *Public Opinion* to work full time with the National Worker's Union. He is credited with the rapid expansion of the union not only among sugar workers, the traditional stronghold of the rival Bustamante Industrial Trades Union, but also among elite bauxite and mine workers, as well as urban industrial workers. In 1955 he was elected Island supervisor and first vice president of the National Workers Union, and in 1962, the year he was appointed a senator, he was elected president of the Caribbean Bauxite and Mineworkers Union. Before his formal entry into politics Manley had the reputation of being the foremost union organizer in the Caribbean—an energetic, fearless, dynamic, and gifted leader.

In the general elections of 1967 Manley won the seat in the House of Representatives for the constituency of Central Kingston, later reclassified as East Central Kingston. Elected leader of the People's National Party in 1969 after the resignation of his father, Manley led the party to victory in 1972.

Manley's Stormy Years in Office

Manley's first two terms as prime minister created great controversy and projected his country into international headlines. In an effort to implement his brand of "democratic socialism" he sought to drastically restructure the politics and economy of Jamaica through far-reaching legislation. On the positive side, over 40,000 new housing units were built, free education was made available for all students, new hospitals were established and the infant mortality rate was cut in half. However, the Jamaican economy took a nosedive due to several factors. The price of oil increased nearly ten-fold during Manley's term; the government's purchase of most of the sugar estates resulted in them becoming unproductive white elephants; and many business and professional people, fearing Manley's leftist rhetoric, left the country. As a result, unemployment skyrocketed to thirty percent by 1980.

In the international sphere, Manley developed closer ties between Jamaica and Fidel Castro's Cuba, and criticized America and other western countries. He sought to lead the Movement of Non-Aligned Nations into the formation of a New International Economic Order against what he considered the exploitation of the West.

Manley won reelection easily in 1976, but shortly afterwards the island's increasing economic problems forced him to turn to the International Monetary Fund (IMF). To obtain loans, the prime minister agreed to reduce the value of his country's currency. Unfortunately, this failed to help the economy, while meeting the conditions of the loans hurt the living standards of Jamaicans. By March of 1988, Manley refused to accept the conditions of the IMF for new loans.

As the economy continued to sour, violence broke out between Manley's supporters and his opponents, driving away visitors and eliminating a major source of revenue from tourism. The 1980 elections were held in an atmosphere of near-civil war, with over 750 dying and thousands being injured in the shootings and stabbings that broke out over the country. In November's elections, Manley and the People's National Party were routed by Ed Seaga and his Jamaican Labor Party, managing to retain only nine out of 60 seats in Parliament.

Manley Returns to Power

Just after his defeat, Manley expressed no regrets about his policies, saying "We lost because we challenged the power of the Western economic order. And for that I am unrepentant," quoted in "Seaga Knocks Out the Left," by John Brecher, *Newsweek*. He also indicated his desire to return to private life. The latter was shortlived, and a new Manley—more moderate than he had been previously—became leader of the opposition. Manley's decision not to contest the December 1983 elections cost him his seat in Parliament, but he continued to be highly-regarded by the Jamaican people. Seaga—never particularly popular—became even more unpopular with his austerity program, and in February of 1989 Manley and the People's National Party won a decisive victory, capturing 44 seats in Parliament. In an interview with *Newsweek*'s Eric Calonius, Manley acknowledged making mistakes in his previous tenure, and said, "The country has evolved, the world has evolved, and we must evolve with it. I think I have evolved."

In his third term as Prime Minister, Manley followed many of Seaga's policies, although he tended to put greater emphasis on small-scale businesses and increased spending on education. Also, like Seaga, he forged a close relationship with the United States, even supporting President George Bush's proposed North American Free Trade Agreement (NAFTA) to reduce tariffs between the United States, Mexico, and Canada. In 1990 Manley was diagnosed with cancer, and on March 16th he announced he was stepping down, for reasons of health, from his position as prime minister. In spite of his illness, he led the Commonwealth Observer Mission to oversee the historic 1994 elections in South Africa, which ended apartheid in that country.

Manley died of prostate cancer March 7th, 1997, in Kingston after having served his country in one form or another for over 40 years. In a letter to the Jamaican Prime Minister, Secretary General of the Commonwealth Emeka Anyaoku called Manley "a statesman of courage and conviction who extended his vision of a better and more just society beyond his island shores" who was "endeared not only to his Commonwealth colleagues but to people so many parts of the world."

Manley's life boasted many personal and political accomplishments. He was prime minister for three terms and lead the People's National Party for almost a quarter-century. Manley also founded the International Bauxite Association and spearheaded the International Seabed Authority, which both have their headquarters in Kingston, and served as vice-president of the Socialist International for Latin America and the Caribbean in 1978. He also received many awards, including a United Nations special award for his contributions to the struggle against apartheid (1978), the Joliot Curie Medal of the World Peace Council (1979), the Order of the Liberator from Venezuela (1973) and the Order of the Mexican Eagle (1975).

Further Reading

Manley is listed in the *International Who's Who* and *Personalities Caribbean;* His political career can be gleaned from his writings as well as from Rex Nettleford, *Identity, Race and Protest in Jamaica* (1971); Carl Stone, *Electoral Behaviour and Public Opinion in Jamaica* (1974); Manley's tenure as prime minister from 1972-1980 and the 1980 elections were given an overview in "Political Storm Over Jamaica," by Jo Thomas, *New York Times Magazine;* and the 1980 election results were given in "Seaga Knocks Out the Left," by John Brecher, *Newsweek,* November 10th, 1980; Interviews with Manley shortly after his 1989 victory are given to Erik Calonius in "A Comeback in Jamaica," *Newsweek,* February 20th, 1989; and with Hans Massaquoi of *Ebony,* February, 1990; Manley authored five books: *The Politics of Change* (1974), *A Voice at the Workplace* (1976), *The Search for Solutions* (1977), *Jamaica: Struggle in the Periphery* (1982), and *Up the Down Escalator: Development and the International Economy* (Washington, D.C., Howard University Press, 1987). Two biographies of him are *Michael Manley: The Making of a Leader* by Darrell Levi (Athens, University of Georgia Press, 1990); and *Michael Manley: The Great Transformation* by David Panton (Kingston Pub. Ltd., 1993). □

Heinrich Mann

The German novelist, essayist, and social critic Heinrich Mann (1871-1950) achieved his greatest success with his critiques of German society.

Heinrich Mann was born in Lübeck, northern Germany, on March 27, 1871. After completing his education in his hometown, Mann went to Dresden and a year later began working for a publishing house in Berlin while attending lectures at its university. At first a disciple of the French realists, especially Émile Zola and Guy de Maupassant, he wrote impressions, sketches, novelettes, and some poetry. His first novel, *In einer Familie* (1894), was published at his mother's expense. It was as a reviewer that he made a name for himself from 1891 to

1896. Between 1895 and 1898 he spent most of his time in Italy, much of it with his brother Thomas, later a world-famous author.

Heinrich Mann's first creative phase, 1900-1914, began with a realistic, even naturalistic novel entitled *Im Schlaraffenland* (1900; *In the Land of Cockaigne,* 1929). This was followed by two more novels, *Die Göttinnen* (1903; vol. 1 trans. as *Diana,* 1929), a glorification of estheticism, and *Die Jagd nach Liebe* (1903; *Pursuit of Love*), another novel of decadence.

In 1905 the book on which Mann's early fame rested was published, the novel *Professor Unrat, oder: Das Ende eines Tyrannen* (*The Blue Angel,* 1931), followed 2 years later by his novel *Zwischen den Rassen.* Usually recognized as one of his masterpieces, the novel *Die kleine Stadt* (1909; *The Little Town,* 1930) tells the story of a visit of a company of actors to a small Italian town.

In his next creative phase, 1914-1933, Mann played a prominent role as a social critic of his country. His first important wartime document was his famous essay on Zola, which appeared in 1915. This caused a complete breakdown of relations between the two brothers, and Thomas composed a reply in which he referred to Heinrich only as the *Zivilisationsliterat,* the man who represents French spirit and wants to Romanize Germany. This alienation between Heinrich and Thomas lasted until January 1922.

During the war years Mann started his powerful critique of German society, a trilogy entitled *Das Kaiserreich,* which was to become his greatest success. It was published in November 1918. Its continuation, *Die Armen* (*The Poor*), a novel about the proletariat and a bitter indictment of the ruling classes, appeared in 1917. The last volume, *Der Kopf* (*The Chief*), a critique of bureaucracy, diplomacy, and industry, came out in 1925.

In 1927 Mann moved to Berlin and reached the climax of his career. In the spring of 1930 he won public recognition after the successful premiere of the film *The Blue Angel.* He was also elected president of the Literary Section of the Prussian Academy of the Arts and worked vigorously for the creation of one European culture within a united Europe. Two years later, however, the Nazis, whom he had attacked and publicly warned against, came to power, and on Feb. 21, 1933, he emigrated to France. His historical studies now bore fruit, and his *magnum opus* appeared: *Die Jugend des Königs Henri IV* (1935; *Young Henry of Navarre,* 1937) and *Die Vollendung des Königs Henri IV* (1938; *Henry, King of France,* 1939).

Mann's final creative period, 1940-1950, was spent in exile in the United States. He wrote four more books in this decade. *Lidice* (1943) deals with the annihilation of an entire Czech town; another novel in dialogue form, *Die traurige Geschichte Friedrichs des Grossen* (published posthumously in 1956), remained a fragment. Partly autobiographical are his last two books, *Empfang bei der Welt* (1943) and *Ein Zeitalter wird besichtigt* (1945; *Review of an Age*). He died on March 12, 1950.

Further Reading

The best introduction for American readers is the monograph of Rolf N. Linn, *Heinrich Mann* (1967). Also helpful as a first orientation is a brief but highly informative article by W. E. Yulli in Alex Natan, ed., *German Men of Letters* (4 vols., 1961-1966).

Additional Sources

Hamilton, Nigel, *The brothers Mann: the lives of Heinrich and Thomas Mann, 1871-1950 and 1875-1955,* New Haven: Yale University Press, 1979, 1978. □

Horace Mann

The American educational reformer and humanitarian Horace Mann (1796-1859) was enormously influential in promoting and refining public education in Massachusetts and throughout the nation in the 19th century.

Horace Mann was born in Franklin, Mass., on May 4, 1796. He labored on the family farm and learned his letters at home and in the district school, supplemented by long hours in the town library. Guided by his parents, he developed an appetite for knowledge. Mann's father died in 1809. The next year, when his older brother drowned while swimming on a Sunday, the local Congregational minister elaborated on the dangers of breaking the Sabbath, instead of consoling the family. This confirmed Mann's growing alienation from the Church.

After briefly attending an academy in Wrentham and intensive tutoring by an itinerant schoolmaster, Mann entered the sophomore class of Brown University in 1816. He developed a lively interest in debating, frequently speaking in support of humanitarian causes. He graduated as valedictorian in 1819. A growing interest in public affairs led him to study law after graduation. He interrupted his legal education to serve as tutor of Latin and Greek at Brown but returned to legal study in 1821 at the famous school of Tapping Reeve in Litchfield, Conn. He was admitted to the bar in 1823.

Mann practiced in Dedham and Boston, acquired an admiration for Whig politics, and was elected to the Massachusetts Legislature in 1827. Essentially an activist, Mann came to believe that public education, which he called "the great equalizer of the conditions of men," was more likely to yield the general social improvements he desired than piecemeal efforts in behalf of prison reform, humane treatment of the insane, and temperance. A fellow legislator had studied educational conditions in Massachusetts and reported that barely a third of the school-age children were attending school; that teachers were ill-prepared, poorly paid, and unable to maintain discipline; and that public schools were avoided by those who could afford private education. As a result, in 1837 the assembly created the Massachusetts State Board of Education. The board was required to collect and disseminate information about pub-

lic schools and, through its secretary, report annually to the legislature.

First Secretary of the State Board

Mann abandoned his promising political career to become secretary of the board. For 12 years he campaigned to bring educational issues before the people. He toured the state speaking on the relationship between public education and public morality, developing the theme of education as "the balance wheel of the social machinery." He believed that social and economic distinctions, unless reduced by a common educational experience, would create communities of interest that would eventually harden into warring factions.

In publicizing his cause, Mann found arguments attractive to all segments of the community, but he sometimes irritated powerful interests. Because he admired the Prussian system of education, his loyalty to democratic institutions was questioned. Because he believed the schools should be nonsectarian, he was attacked as antireligious. His advocacy of state supervision antagonized local politicians. His criticism of corporal punishment angered the influential Boston schoolmasters.

All the reform impulses of the American 1830s and 1840s converged in Mann's devotion to the cause of the common schools. He created teachers' institutes to improve teaching methods and arranged public meetings to discuss educational theory. He established and edited the *Common School Journal*. With private benefaction and state support he established three state normal schools for teacher education, the first in the country. His annual reports were lucid examinations of educational issues. Widely distributed and discussed, they exerted a powerful influence on public opinion in Massachusetts and the nation.

In Massachusetts, Mann's leadership produced dramatic change. The school curriculum was broadened and related more closely to the social outcomes he admired. Teaching methods, especially the teaching of reading, and the professional status and salary of teachers were improved. Facilities and equipment were increased, and more than 50 new high schools were established. Mann's influence became national and international.

Later Years

In 1848 Mann resigned his secretaryship to accept election to the U.S. Congress. He now enthusiastically entered the slavery debate, opposing the extension of slavery into the territories. His stand generated such hostility that he declined to run in the 1852 election and, instead, unsuccessfully campaigned for the governorship as a Free Soil candidate.

In 1852 Mann was elected president of Antioch College in Ohio. He discharged his new duties with customary zeal, creating a curriculum, doing much of the teaching, and contending with difficult economic problems. But the work proved too much for Mann, in ill health since boyhood. He died on Aug. 2, 1859, 2 weeks after telling the graduating class to "be ashamed to die until you have won some victory for humanity."

Further Reading

The Republic and the School: The Education of Free Men (1957), edited by Lawrence A. Cremin, contains a thorough analysis of Mann's educational positions and extracts from his annual reports. E. I. F. Williams, *Horace Mann: Educational Statesman* (1937), is somewhat eulogistic but complete and well documented. Louise Hall Tharp, *Until Victory: Horace Mann and Mary Peabody* (1953), is a popular treatment, well written and rich in background but sometimes casual in documentation. Jonathan Messerli, *Horace Mann* (1972), is a perceptive and revealing biography, particularly informative on Mann's 12 years as secretary of the Massachusetts State Board of Education.

Additional Sources

Downs, Robert Bingham, *Horace Mann: champion of public schools,* New York, Twayne Publishers 1974.

Sawyer, Kem Knapp, *Horace Mann,* New York: Chelsea House Publishers, 1993.

Tharp, Louise Hall, *Until victory: Horace Mann and Mary Peabody,* Westport, Conn.: Greenwood Press, 1977. □

Thomas Mann

The German novelist and essayist Thomas Mann (1875-1955) was perhaps the most influential and representative German author of his time.

Born in the free Hanseatic city of Lübeck on the Baltic Sea, the second son of a north German patrician merchant and senator in the city government, Thomas Mann often stressed his twofold heritage: his South American mother, from Rio de Janeiro, was the daughter of a German planter who had emigrated to Brazil and married a woman of Portuguese-Creole origin.

Mann's family can be compared to that of the brothers August Wilhelm and Friedrich von Schlegel, leading poet-critics in German romanticism: his elder brother Heinrich was an outstanding novelist and essayist. A younger brother, Viktor, a civil servant in Germany, made a name for himself as author of an important family chronicle, *Wir waren fünf* (1948). Two of Mann's six children, Erika and Klaus, were talented writers in their own right, and his son Golo was a noted historian.

Early Career

As a pupil of the "Katherineum" in Lübeck, Mann hated school. Devoted to music and above all to writing, at the age of 17 he edited a school periodical, *Frühlingssturm* (Spring Storm), in which his first prose and poetry appeared under the pseudonym Paul Thomas.

After the death of her husband and the liquidation of the family's grain business, Senator Mann's widow moved to Munich. Thomas, however, remained at school in Lübeck until he passed the qualifying exam for the 1-year military service certificate. When he finally joined his mother, two sisters, and younger brother in Munich in 1894, he worked briefly as a clerk in an insurance company. There he wrote his first story, *Gefallen* (Fallen), published in the avant-garde naturalistic monthly *Die Gesellschaft.* Soon the young author gave up his job and, under the pretense of becoming a journalist, attended lectures at the university without formally enrolling as a student. For a while he was a member of the editorial staff of the satiric magazine *Simplicissimus,* in which his next story, *Der Wille zum Glück* (The Will to Happiness), appeared.

In 1895 Mann joined his brother Heinrich in Italy, and together they spent most of the next 3 years in Rome and Palestrina. Isolated from Italian society, he read voluminously, mostly Scandinavian, French, and Russian literature. It was here that he began writing the novel which climaxed this first phase of his literary career, *Buddenbrooks.* While he was living in Rome, Mann's first book, *Der kleine Herr Friedemann* (1898), a collection of naturalistic short stories, was published by S. Fischer in Berlin. These sharply drawn, youthful narratives are variations of a single theme; they deal, for the most part, with the "marked" man, the isolated individual, the artist and his relationship to life. These stories foreshadow many characteristics of Mann's later works: dualism, or the divided mind; the opposition of spirit to life; and the resulting antithesis of artist and bourgeois. Also evident here is his frequent and effective use of the leitmotiv, which calls to mind his admired masters, Theodor Fontane and Richard Wagner. In these stories of his youth the leitmotiv is handled in a more obvious, mechanical way than in his later work, where it is applied with far greater subtlety.

Buddenbrooks and Death in Venice

Most representative of the work from Mann's first stage as a writer (1896-1906) was his first novel, *Buddenbrooks*. Originally envisioned as a brief novel of some 250 pages, to be written jointly with his brother Heinrich, it was executed by Thomas alone and assumed massive proportions. It appeared in 1901 and became a best seller both at home and abroad. Again, the technique of the linguistic leitmotiv is present, but this time it is lifted from the external, mechanical basis into the musical sphere.

Written in the tradition of the Scandinavian genealogical novel, *Buddenbrooks* gives a broad account of the rise and fall, through several generations, of a fictitious Hanseatic family, patterned after that of the author, and immediately calls to mind John Galsworthy's *Forsyte Saga*, with which it has much in common. The first two generations, who created the family wealth, are sturdy and aggressive burghers, and for their bourgeois code, their rigorous ethical standards, Mann shows profound respect. Only the last two generations are marked by decadence, both physical and mental, but they, at the same time, show increased intellectual gifts and greater artistic sensibility. The fourth generation is represented by little Hanno, a pathetic, sickly, neurotic boy whose only love is his music. With his death at the age of 16, the once distinguished family comes to an end.

After *Buddenbrooks* came *Tristan* (1902), a parody of Wagner's opera, set in an Alpine sanatorium. Mann's next work, his most lyrical artist's story, *Tonio Kröger,* (1903), exceeded even *Buddenbrooks* in popularity. It deals with a gifted writer, Tonio Kröger, from north Germany, again a marked man isolated from his environment, and his unrequited love for Hans Hansen and Ingeborg Holm, who represent the blond and the beautiful, the normal and bourgeois world.

In February 1905 Mann married Katharina (Katja) Pringsheim, the daughter of a famous Munich mathematician. The first fruit of his marriage was a fairy tale, or light comedy, in the form of a novel, *Königliche Hoheit* (1909; *Royal Highness*). Marking the beginning of his second stage as a writer, this book reveals an optimism thus far unknown in Thomas Mann's work. Decadence, Mann now believed, could be overcome, and a synthesis of life and art could be attained.

A visit to the Lido in May 1911 provided the raw material for Mann's most complex novella, *Der Tod in Venedig* (*Death in Venice*). A series of sinister circumstances and strange impressions almost immediately suggested to him the basis for this story, which truly reflects Mann's preoccupation with the irrationalism of Arthur Schopenhauer, Richard Wagner, and Friedrich Nietzsche. Its hero, Gustav von Aschenbach (resembling, in some ways, the composer Gustav Mahler), is a fictitious German writer in his early 50s whose self-discipline makes him what Mann calls a *Leistungsethiker*, a man who has sacrificed everything for the sake of achievement. Having suppressed his emotions for too long, he goes on a trip to Venice, ignoring all warnings not to visit the cholera-infected city. It is not cholera, however, but Italy itself which disintegrates

his carefully calculated self-control. He is obsessed by a homoerotic love for 14-year-old Tadzio, who represents both death and Apollonian beauty, but he excuses his passion on the grounds of classical precedent and Nietzsche's conception of Dionysian Greece. Death comes to him, finally, as he sits in a deck chair on the beach, looking out to the sea and longing for the boy.

The Magic Mountain

A 3-week stay in a Davos sanatorium during the summer of 1912 gave Mann the impetus for his next book, *Der Zauberberg* (1924; *The Magic Mountain*), the highlight of the second phase of his career (1912-1933). His first major novel since *Buddenbrooks,* this work attempts to overcome the dualism that had marked Mann's youthful stories and to reconcile the enmity of life and spirit that dominated those works. It deals with the intellectual development of an ordinary young man who spends 7 years in a tuberculosis sanatorium in the mountains of Switzerland, against a broad panorama of European society in the 7 years preceding World War I.

Hans Castorp, the simpleminded hero, stands between two men engaged in an ideological battle: an Italian humanist and liberal, Settembrini, a champion of reason and life who believes in progress, and Naphta, a Polish Jew turned Jesuit, representing the nonrational forces, who combines a fervent belief in Catholicism with Marxist doctrines. A third "educator," introduced toward the end of the book, is a Dutch planter from Indonesia, Mynheer Peeperkorn, who, anything but an intellectual, impresses Hans through the power of his personality, which is patterned after dramatist Gerhart Hauptmann.

Der Zauberberg is largely a romantic book, a book about the "sympathy with death," and in the author's own words, Hans Castorp's dream, his vision of the good life, could not have appeared in any of his previous works. While lost in the mountains (in the chapter "Snow"), Hans dreams that "for the sake of goodness and love, man shall let death have no sovereignty over his thoughts." Surely, this is an impossible dream, either in the alpine sanatorium with its eccentric patients or down in the flatland of bourgeois triviality from which Hans has come. In the end he accepts life and, when the war breaks out, returns to his homeland, leaving the sheltered atmosphere of the magic mountain for military service, only to meet his death on a battlefield in Flanders.

Political Views

Until World War I Mann's tastes and cultural tradition had been those of a nationalist and a German patriot, and he was convinced of the superiority of its authoritarian constitution over the democratic institutions of France and England. During the years 1914-1918 he interrupted his work on the novel *Der Zauberberg* to embark upon "war service with the weapon of thought." In a series of highly introspective essays, examining the very foundations of his own philosophy, he presented a vigorous defense of the German Reich (*Betrachtungen eines Unpolitischen*, 1918; *Reflections of an Unpolitical Man*). But when this book appeared,

Mann was already evolving from a romantic conservative to a believer in democracy who was to become a champion of the Weimar Republic. With his speech honoring Hauptmann on his sixtieth birthday, on Nov. 15, 1922, *Von deutscher Republik,* the process of his transformation was complete, and for the next 10 years, the decisive period of his second, or middle, phase, he was the spokesman of the Weimar Republic.

Mann's first works published after the 1918 armistice are largely autobiographical: *Gesang vom Kindchen (The Song of a Child),* written in hexameter and dealing with the birth and baptism of his youngest daughter, and *Herr und Hund (Bashan and I),* an account of his life in Munich with his dog, Bashan (both published in 1919). Two of his finest novellas were written in that decade: *Unordnung und frühes Leid* (1925; *Disorder and Early Sorrow*), an affectionately ironic, melancholic treatment of the relations between the generations in a middleclass German family in Munich in the 1920s and the moral and social confusion which resulted from the chaotic inflation of values in postwar Germany, and *Mario und der Zauberer* (1930; *Mario and the Magician*), a "tragedy of travel with moral and political implications," as Mann himself called it. Again largely autobiographical, *Mario* presents a terrifying picture of the rise of fascism in Italy and clearly warns against its dangers. Cipolla, the hypnotist who is shot to death by Mario, the goodnatured waiter whose human dignity he has outraged, stands symbolically for Mussolini, and his end foreshadows that of the dictator in 1945.

In 1929 Mann was awarded the Nobel Prize in literature. As early as 1930 he warned publicly against the dangers of Hitler and his followers in his courageous philippic against the Nazis, *Appell an die Vernunft (An Appeal to Reason).*

On Feb. 10, 1933, Mann delivered a lecture in Munich on the occasion of the fiftieth anniversary of the death of Richard Wagner (*Leiden und Grösse Richard Wagners; The Sufferings and Greatness of Richard Wagner*), and the next day he left Germany with his wife to repeat his lecture in Amsterdam, Brussels, and Paris, a trip from which he was not to return for 16 years. Finding himself a voluntary exile from Nazi Germany, Mann spent the summer in southern France and settled in Küsnacht, near Zurich, where he remained until 1938. He attacked the Nazi regime in an open letter published by the *Neue Züriche Zeitung* on Feb. 3, 1936. Soon the Nazis deprived him of his German citizenship and banned his books, and the University of Bonn withdrew the honorary doctorate awarded him shortly after World War I.

Mann's reply became his best-known political tract, the famous *Letter to the Dean of the Philosophical Faculty of Bonn,* published early in 1937. As a further manifestation of his political engagement, he founded in 1937 a literary magazine devoted to the ideals of the "Third Humanism": *Mass und Wert* (Measure and Value), edited in cooperation with Konrad Falke and published in Zurich until 1940. In 1938 Mann and his family emigrated to the United States. For 2 1/2 years they lived in Princeton, N.J., where he served as a lecturer in the humanities at the university. In 1941 he

moved to southern California, built a home in Pacific Palisades outside Los Angeles, and became one of a colony of German and Austrian exiles which included, in addition to his brother Heinrich, Lion Feuchtwanger, Bruno Frank, Lotte Lehmann, Erich Maria Remarque, Arnold Schoenberg, Bruno Walter, and Franz Werfel. In 1944 he became an American citizen.

During the war years Mann's life was filled with numerous activities: he was actively engaged in helping refugees from Europe through the Emergency Rescue Committee; he served as a consultant in Germanic literature for the Library of Congress; he lectured in many American cities and appealed to the German people over the British Broadcasting Corporation. Whatever time was left, he devoted to his literary work. At Princeton, he completed a "Goethe novel," *Lotte in Weimar* (1939; *The Beloved Returns*), relating the historic visit of Charlotte Kestner to Weimar in 1816, 44 years after the love affair which had become common knowledge through the European success of Goethe's *Werther.*

Later Works

During the first 2 California years Mann completed his gigantic Joseph cycle, on which he had been working, with interruptions, since 1926. At that time he had found in the story of Joseph a theme embracing, as he called it, "the typical, the eternally human, eternally recurring, timeless— in short, the mythical." *Joseph und seine Brüder* (1933-1943; *Joseph and His Brothers*), his version of the biblical story, was to become his greatest critical success in the United States, ending on an optimistic note with its fourth volume, *Joseph der Ernährer (Joseph, the Provider).*

In California between 1943 and 1946 Mann wrote what is usually considered his most difficult and complex book, *Doktor Faustus: The Life of the German Composer Adrian Leverkühn as Told by a Friend* (1947). In contrast to the optimistic tone of the Joseph tetralogy, this is a deeply pessimistic, somber book, a bitter accusation against his former country, which, like Doktor Faustus, has made a pact with the devil. But it is also a self-accusation, for Mann does not distinguish between a good and a bad Germany. He finds some negative characteristics manifest in every German of all times. In this fictional biography Mann writes about an artist, a musician—since music, in Mann's thinking, is closely linked with decay, decadence, disease, danger, and death and since it is the one art he considers most characteristically German. In describing the life of an artist (closely patterned after that of Nietzsche), Mann shows himself as a master of the technique of montage by succeeding in combining several time levels. Of the third phase of Mann's writing career (1933-1955), this book represents the highlight, the climax.

In 1952 Mann returned to Europe to spend his remaining years in Switzerland, taking up the life he had lived there from 1933 to 1938. Mann's last major work, *Bekenntnisse des Hochstaplers Felix Krull (Confessions of Felix Krull, Confidence Man),* was published in 1954 as *Der Memoiren Erster Teil.* Having begun the book in 1911, the author had published additional fragments in 1922 and 1937. The projected second part, however, was never written. Following the tradition of the picaresque, or rogue, novel, Mann presents a humorous portrait of the artist as mountebank, or criminal, a thought that had always caught his imagination. *Felix Krull* is among his most vivid and effective books and attracted huge audiences in many countries. With its publication Thomas Mann achieved an immediate popular and critical success. His last completed work was his brilliant essay on Friedrich von Schiller.

Mann's eightieth birthday, on June 6, 1955, brought him honors from all sides, both East and West. Respected throughout the world as Germany's greatest man of letters since Goethe, Mann died 2 months later, on August 12, in Kilchberg near Zurich.

Further Reading

The most comprehensive biography of Mann in English, well documented and illustrated, is Hans Bürgin and Hans-Otto Mayer, *Thomas Mann: A Chronicle of His Life* (trans. 1969). Of the large number of books about Mann, the best introductions in English for the nonspecialist are Henry C. Hatfield, *Thomas Mann* (1951; rev. ed. 1962), and Ignace Feuerlicht, *Thomas Mann* (1968).

The more advanced student will find a selection of the best critical opinion on Mann in Henry Hatfield, ed., *Thomas Mann: A Collection of Critical Essays* (1964). Also recommended is the excellent critical analysis of Erich Heller, *The Ironic German: A Study of Thomas Mann* (1958). Erich Kahler, *The Orbit of Thomas Mann* (1969), is a collection of five excellent essays by a close friend of Mann. A critical essay on Mann's major novels is J. P. Stern, *Thomas Mann* (1967). Gunilla Bergsten, *Thomas Mann's Doctor Faustus: The Sources and Structures of the Novel,* translated by Krishna Winston (1969), deals with one of Mann's best-known works. Two studies that discuss Mann in the context of philosophy are Joseph Gerard Brennan, *Three Philosophical Novelists: James Joyce, André Gide, Thomas Mann* (1963), and Peter Heller, *Dialectics and Nihilism: Essays on Lessing, Nietzsche, Mann and Kafka* (1966).

For a treatment of the German literary background see Ronald Gray, *The German Tradition in Literature,* 1871-1945 (1965). A guide to the worldwide literature on Mann is in a two-volume bibliography of criticism by Klaus W. Jonas, *Fifty Years of Thomas Mann Studies* (1955), which covers the years 1901-1954, and its supplement, Klaus W. Jonas and Ilsedore B. Jonas, *Thomas Mann Studies: A Bibliography of Criticism* (1967), which continues the bibliographical record to 1966.

Additional Sources

Hamilton, Nigel, *The brothers Mann: the lives of Heinrich and Thomas Mann, 1871-1950 and 1875-1955,* New Haven: Yale University Press, 1979, 1978. □

Baron Carl Gustav Emil Von Mannerheim

The Finnish military leader and statesman Baron Carl Gustav Emil von Mannerheim (1867-1951) was the father of modern Finland.

Carl Gustav von Mannerheim was born on June 4, 1867, near Turku of a prominent family. He received his early military training in imperial Russia and early showed courage and adaptability to the vigorous life. He explored Central Africa, served in the Russo-Japanese War, and was commander of Russia's VI Cavalry Corps on the Romanian front in World War I. With Russia's collapse he returned to a Finland in turmoil.

On Jan. 4, 1918, the president of the Finnish Senate had received from the Soviets recognition of Finnish independence in a document signed by Stalin, Trotsky, and Lenin. On January 28, however, the Red Guards, dominated by Finnish left-wing Social Democrats, seized power in most of the major cities. Members of the government, the Whites, made up of leading members of the government and those who believed in parliamentary democracy, gathered at Vaasa, where they offered the seasoned Mannerheim command of their army.

Mannerheim's first task was to disarm the more than 40,000 Russian soldiers still on Finnish soil to prevent them from joining the rebel forces, who already outnumbered his own. His initial objective achieved, he trained his forces and struck against the overmanned and underofficered Red strongholds at Helsinki, Viipuri, and Tampere. In the interim he tried without success to prevent the Germans from entering the struggle as allies. With unneeded German aid the Reds were defeated, and by the middle of the summer the Red bloodbath had been followed by a White one. Mannerheim meanwhile labored to erect a republic of Finland free of German and Soviet ties. Although he cooperated in the Allied attack on the Soviets, his chief concerns in 1918, as later in the 1940s, were Finnish independence and national security. On May 16, 1918, he resigned as commander in chief because of the pro-German policy of the government, and on December 12 he became chief executive of Finland. On the first election under the new constitution, however, he was defeated by Professor Kaarlo J. Ståhlberg and left office in July 1919.

Mannerheim realized that Finland had to live amicably with the Soviets, but he also knew that the Russians understood strength. Consequently, as defense minister, he built a series of fortifications known as the Mannerheim Line, which stood Finland in good stead in November 1941, when the Soviet Union, after gobbling up part of Poland and the Baltic Provinces, invaded Finland by land, sea, and air without declaring war.

At the age of 72 Mannerheim was called back as commander in chief and successfully guided Finnish defenses during the Winter War, which ended in March 1940. The relatively favorable peace settlement was violated by the Soviet Union in June 1941, and Mannerheim remained as commander in chief until peace was negotiated in August 1944. In June 1942 he was named the only marshal in Finnish history and became president of the republic in 1944. He soon retired because of ill health and died in Lausanne, Switzerland, on Jan. 27, 1951. Controversial though he was, the bulk of the Finnish people sincerely mourned his passing.

Further Reading

The best account for details is Mannerheim's *Memoirs,* translated by Count Eric Lewenhaupt (1954). Perhaps the best-balanced interpretation is Anatole G. Mazour, *Finland between East and West* (1956). Also worth consulting are Tancred Borenius, *Field-Marshall Mannerheim* (1940), and John H. Wuorinen, *A History of Finland* (1965).

Additional Sources

Mannerheim, Marshal of Finland, Minneapolis: University of Minnesota Press, 1986. □

Karl Mannheim

The Hungarian-born sociologist and educator Karl Mannheim (1893-1947) explored the role of the intellectual in political and social reconstruction. He also wrote on the sociology of knowledge.

Karl Mannheim was born on March 27, 1893, in Budapest to a German mother and a Jewish middle-class Hungarian father. He attended a humanistic school in Budapest and did further study in philosophy (particularly epistemology), languages, and the social sciences at the universities of Budapest, Berlin, Paris, Freiburg,

and Heidelberg (1920). His doctoral dissertation in 1922 was *The Structural Analysis of Knowledge.* In 1921 he married Juliska Lang.

Mannheim was a lecturer in sociology at the University of Heidelberg (1926-1930) and then became professor of sociology and head of the department at the University of Frankfurt. The Nazi government forced his dismissal in 1933. He moved to England, where he became a lecturer in sociology at the London School of Economics (1933-1945). He was also lecturer in the sociology of education (1941-1944) and then professor of education and sociology (1944-1947) at the Institute of Education of the University of London. He died in London on Jan. 9, 1947.

Mannheim's early writings dealt with the leadership role of intellectual elites in maintaining freedom. This concern reflected his study of Max Weber, Max Scheler, and Karl Marx. Mannheim's most important early book, *Ideology and Utopia* (1929 in German, 1936 in English), introduced the sociology of knowledge as a new field of study in the social sciences. Antipathy to the Nazi movement in Germany deepened his interest in democratic dynamics. His writings increasingly focused on the political, social, and moral problems involved in the survival of democracy and freedom. He saw interdependence as the characteristic feature of the modern era and viewed education and planning as essential for improving society. This concern is expressed in *Man and Society in an Age of Reconstruction* (1940), in which he weighed the political strengths and weaknesses of intellectual elites. His *Diagnosis of Our Time* (1943) explored ways to reestablish rational means of social organization. In *Freedom, Power, and Democratic Planning* (1950), published after his death, he continued his concern about the intellectual as leader in a planned society.

In his last years Mannheim made the problem of planning and education his principal concern. As editor of the International Library of Sociology and Social Reconstruction, he stimulated thought and publications in sociology, education, and planning. He sought democratic ways to achieve consensus in a mass society, believing that studies in the sociology of education could help achieve this consensus.

Mannheim was a successful and inspiring teacher with a contagious passion for his subject. He was articulate and provocative, had a Socratic tolerance for opposition and a lively sense of humor, and was nonpartisan in sociological controversies. Although he did not create a sector school, he influenced many students and colleagues.

Further Reading

Jacques J. Maquet, *The Sociology of Knowledge* (1949; trans. 1951), is a critical analysis of the systems of Mannheim and Pitirim A. Sorokin. Margaret B. Fisher, *Leadership and Intelligence* (1954), discusses Mannheim's writings in this field.

Additional Sources

Kettler, David, *Karl Mannheim and the crisis of liberalism: the secret of these new times,* New Brunswick, N.J.: Transaction Publishers, 1995.

Loader, Colin, *The intellectual development of Karl Mannheim: culture, politics, and planning,* Cambridge Cambridgeshire; New York: Cambridge University Press, 1985.

Woldring, H. E. S., *Karl Mannheim: the development of his thought: philosophy, sociology, and social ethics, with a detailed biography,* New York: St. Martin's Press, 1987, 1986. □

Henry Edward Manning

The English prelate Henry Edward Manning (1808-1892) was directly responsible for the efflorescence of English Catholicism in the first half of the 20th century.

Henry Manning was born on July 5, 1808, at Totteridge, Hertfordshire, into a family that belonged to the Anglican High Church. He studied at Harrow and Balliol College, Oxford, and became president of the Oxford Union in 1829. Graduating with high honors in classics, he entered the Colonial Office in 1830 but returned to Merton College, Oxford, in 1832 to receive Anglican orders. A deacon in 1832, a priest in 1833, an archdeacon in 1840, Manning did not become a Roman Catholic until April 1851.

As a curate at Lavington, Surrey, Manning married a daughter of his rector. When she died, Manning felt profoundly disenchanted and gave himself to a thorough reading of the early Christian Fathers of the Church. At Oxford he had known John Henry Newman, whose *Development of Christian Doctrine* he found to be an unassailable thesis justifying the historical development of ecclesiastical jurisdiction in the Roman Catholic Church. During a protracted visit to Rome in 1847, he had occasion to study the governmental structure of the Roman Church. His conversion was precipitated by a single incident. An Anglican divine, G. C. Gorham, was suspected of holding unorthodox views. The bishop refused to institute proceedings against Gorham, but the Privy Council of Laymen overruled this refusal. Manning, who abhorred all lay interference in ecclesiastical affairs, was shocked. After a short period he was received into the Roman Church by Cardinal Nicholas Wiseman in April 1851, ordained a priest 2 months later, and sent to Rome to study theology.

During his stay in Rome Manning was brilliant in theology, and he successfully cultivated the friendship and the esteem of Pius IX and his cardinals. Manning grew to appreciate the Roman style of government; he liked its authoritarian character, its secretiveness, and its immunity, and he developed an almost fanatic devotion to the papal cause. On his return to England, he became provost of the Westminster Cathedral Chapter. He founded a new religious congregation, the Oblates of St. Charles (Borromeo), and became its first superior. Manning's rapid rise in power and his obvious influence with Roman offices of the Vatican provoked much opposition to him, so much so that Cardinal Wiseman had to defend Manning by letter to Rome. Wiseman's preference, Manning's obvious capabilities, and

his devotion to the papacy influenced the Pope, and he chose Manning as Wiseman's successor in 1865 to be archbishop of Westminster.

Manning's policy as archbishop was extremely ultramontanist: he wished to model the English Church as closely as possible on Rome. He was an extremely authoritarian man, was deeply liked by his priests, and brooked no opposition. He clashed with the Jesuits over jurisdictional matters and with Newman over doctrinal issues, particularly the authority of Rome. For Manning the hierarchy was all-sacred, could be overridden by no one except the pope, and deserved extreme forms of obedience. Manning participated very actively in the First Vatican Council (1869-1870), being one of the leaders of the "infallibilists" (the supporters of the definition concerning the pope's infallibility), but the final definition of papal infallibility did not live up to his extremist wishes.

Created a cardinal in 1875, Manning attained much prestige in England. He was a member of the Royal Housing Commission in 1884. In his own diocese, he had particularly cared for child education and for the welfare of the homeless, building schools, orphanages, and shelters. He mediated successfully in the great London dock strike of 1889 (a goodly number of dock workers were Irish Roman Catholics). But he aroused many bitter controversies and made personal enemies among both the hierarchy and lay people by his apparent high-handedness, his resort to backstairs influence in Rome, and his extreme devotion to Roman wishes. More than any other modern churchman of the English Roman Catholic establishment, Manning contributed to the development of the conservative character that English Catholicism showed until well into the middle of the 20th century. Manning died in London on Jan. 14, 1892.

Further Reading

Biographies of Manning include Arthur Wollaston Hutton, *Cardinal Manning* (1892); Edmund Sheridan Purcell, *Life of Cardinal Manning, Archbishop of Westminster* (2 vols., 1896); Shane Leslie, *Henry Edward Manning: His Life and Labours* (1921); and V. A. McClelland, *Cardinal Manning: His Public Life and Influence, 1865-1892* (1962). Manning is discussed in E. E. Reynolds, *Three Cardinals: Newman, Wiseman, Manning* (1958). For background see Georgiana Putman McEntee, *The Social Catholic Movement in Great Britain* (1927).

Additional Sources

Fitzsimons, John, *Manning, Anglican and Catholic,* Westport, Conn.: Greenwood Press, 1979.

Gray, Robert, *Cardinal Manning: a biography,* New York: St. Martin's Press, 1985.

Newsome, David, *The parting of friends: the Wilberforces and Henry Manning,* Grand Rapids, Mich.: Eerdmans; Leominster, U.K.: Gracewing, 1993.

Strachey, Lytton, *Eminent Victorians,* Harmondsworth, Middlesex, England; New York: Penguin Books, 1986; New York: Weidenfeld & Nicolson, 1989, 1988. □

Daniel Mannix

Daniel Mannix (1864-1963) was the Roman Catholic archbishop of Melbourne for nearly half a century and an active force in Australian politics, especially in Victoria.

D aniel Mannix was born at Charleville in County Cork, Ireland, on March 4, 1864. He was ordained in 1890 at Maynooth, where he became successively junior professor of philosophy and professor of theology. The Irish bishops selected him as president in 1903, and it was during his tenure of this office that Maynooth acquired the status of a university college.

In 1912 Mannix was appointed titular archbishop of Pharsalus and coadjutor of Melbourne, and in 1917 he succeeded to the see. He quickly became the main spokesman in Australia for the Irish nationalist movement Sinn Fein. During World War I he campaigned openly alongside the Labour party against conscription for the armed forces, and by the end of the war he and the Catholics who looked to him for leadership had become a powerful influence on the Labour party in Australia. In 1920 he visited Rome by way of the United States, where large and vocal audiences marked his tour at every stop, but he was forbidden to land in Ireland. He was a strong opponent of the Irish Free State and of the Anglo-Irish Treaty of 1922.

Australian Catholic Action originated in Mannix's Melbourne diocese in 1937 and developed into one of the most efficient and highly organized systems of Catholic Action in the world. In World War II Mannix was more prepared to accept the justice of the Allied cause than he had been in World War I, and he supported the "Food for Britain" campaign that was organized in Australia.

Mannix was a firm believer in the idea that communism was now the principal enemy and partly for this reason was a close supporter of Bartholomew Santamaria and what was termed "The Movement" in Victoria, but in his advancing years he tended to lose touch with the work of Catholic Action in the trade unions and the Labour party. Nevertheless, after the split in the Australian Labour party in 1955, Mannix supported the dissident Democratic Labour party and in the federal elections of 1958 issued a statement warning Catholics against voting for the Australian Labour party, led by Herbert Vere Evatt, on the grounds that "every Communist and Communist sympathizer in Australia wants a victory for the Evatt party."

Mannix was a man of strong enthusiasms and spent his energies in many causes. It was largely owing to him, for instance, that funds were collected for the opening of Newman College, a constituent college of the University of Melbourne. More than anything else, however, he was a political prelate, and for most of his remarkable career in Victoria there was a close link between the Catholic hierarchy and the Labour party. He died on Nov. 6, 1963.

Further Reading

A biography of Mannix is Niall Brennan, *Dr. Mannix* (1964). Mannix is discussed in James G. Murtagh, *Australia: The Catholic Chapter* (1946; rev. ed. 1959) and *Catholics and the Commonwealth* (1950), and Tom Truman, *Catholic Action and Politics* (1959; rev. ed. 1960). The various writings of Bartholomew Santamaria should also be consulted.

Additional Sources

Ebsworth, Walter A., *Archbishop Mannix,* Armadale, Vic.: H. H. Stephenson, 1977.

Gilchrist, Michael, *Daniel Mannix, priest & patriot,* Blackburn, Vic., Australia: Dove Communications, 1982.

Kiernan, Colm, *Daniel Mannix and Ireland,* Morwell, Vic., Australia: Alella Books; Dublin: Gill and Macmillan, 1984.

Santamaria, Bartholomew Augustine, *Archbishop Mannix: his contribution to the art of public leadership in Australia,* Carlton South, Vic.: Melbourne University Press, 1978.

Santamaria, Bartholomew Augustine, *Daniel Mannix, the quality of leadership,* Carlton, Vic.: Melbourne University Press; Beaverton, Or.: International Scholarly Book Services, 1984. □

Jorge Manrique

The Spanish poet and soldier Jorge Manrique (c. 1440-1478) wrote the *Coplas,* one of the great elegies of all times, and was the poetic voice of his generation.

J orge Manrique was probably born in the family fief of Paredes de Nava (Palencia). He belonged to the powerful and warlike clan of the Manriques, was a nephew of Gómez Manrique, another poet-soldier, and a grandnephew of the Marquis of Santillana, the literary arbiter of Castile. His father was Rodrigo Manrique, Count of Paredes and Grand Master of the Order of Santiago. Arms and letters against an aristocratic background define the personality of Jorge Manrique.

At this time Castile was again in the throes of civil war. King Henry IV was ineffectual to the point of being nicknamed the Impotent. The Manrique clan fought him and his presumably bastard daughter Juana. This meant that Manrique fought first for Prince Alfonso against his half brother Henry IV and then for Princess Isabella (later the Catholic Queen) against Princess Juana. He was a faithful and distinguished warrior and was rewarded with the title of knight commander of Montizón in the Order of Santiago. Manrique participated actively in the innumerable battles and skirmishes of the civil war. When Henry IV died, Portugal entered the fray on the side of Juana. At this time Manrique was put in command, by the Catholic Monarchs, of their forces in the Campo de Calatrava. When the Hermandades were created (a sort of national militia), he was made their captain in the kingdom of Toledo. He was killed in the siege of the castle of Garci-Muñoz, in La Mancha, held by the Marquis of Villena, a partisan of Juana and Portugal.

Manrique left a substantial body of amorous poetry (some 40 poems, including some satiric verse), but in none of it does he rise much above the literary level of his times. It just shows him to have been a quick-witted and facile versifier. But in the *Coplas* (40 stanzas to his father's death, which occurred in 1476), Manrique wrote the most famous elegy of the Spanish language. The strong emotion caused by death is restrained, and the tone is serene; but in trying to explain to himself the meaning of his father's death, after a life which had earned him the appellation of a second Cid, Manrique manages to give voice to his age's sentiments about the meaning of life and death. The poet's noble and Christian resignation has struck a responsive chord in every generation of readers since his death, for, in the words of Pedro Salinas, the *Coplas* is "one of the most beautiful and shining lights in universal poetry."

Further Reading

The *Coplas* of Manrique was admirably translated by Henry Wadsworth Longfellow in 1833. Pedro Salinas, the author of an excellent book in Spanish on Manrique, gives a fine analysis of the *Coplas* in *Reality and the Poet in Spanish Poetry* (1940). *The Oxford Book of Spanish Verse*, edited by J. B. Trend (1913), contains some biographical information on Manrique. □

François Mansart

François Mansart (1598-1666), one of the first French architects to embrace the ideals of classicism, was an eloquent spokesman for classical restraint, beauty of proportion, and clarity of form.

François Mansart was born in Paris on Jan. 13, 1598. A pupil of Salomon de Brosse, architect of the Luxembourg Palace, Mansart clearly derived his early style from this master. Together they worked on the château of Coulommiers, begun in 1618.

At 25, Mansart was well established and flooded with commissions, mostly from the wealthy officers of the Crown. Among his early works were the châteaux of Berny (1623) and Balleroy (begun 1626). From Gaston d'Orléans, brother of King Louis XIII, he received the important commission for rebuilding the château of Blois. The only part of the vast project executed was the principal *corps de logis* (1635-1638) with its high-pitched, broken roof of the type popularized by the architect and bearing his name (mansard roof). Of grand simplicity, the facade demonstrates Mansart's knowledgeable use of classical orders, restrained detail, and unusually harmonious proportions.

Mansart designed many town houses in Paris, among the most notable being the Hôtel de la Vrillière (1635) and the Hôtel Le Jars (1648). His best-known domestic structure is the château of Maisons (now Maisons-Lafitte; 1642-1646), built for René de Longueil. It reveals the architect's ability to deal with complex series of masses which are ingeniously related to one another so as to create a perfect visual harmony of the whole. The interior staircase, of unique design, mounts in four flights around a square chamber, and the whole space is covered by a dome. The crisp, restrained decoration of the interior is outstanding.

In 1645 Anne of Austria commissioned Mansart to design the church and convent of the Val-de-Grâce in Paris. Possibly inspired by Andrea Palladio's plan of Il Redentore in Venice, Mansart's scheme was executed only through the entablatures of the nave and the first story of the facade; Mansart kept changing his original plan and hence was dismissed from the project, which was handed over to Jacques Lemercier. Mansart's obsession for modifying his designs lost him a number of commissions, not the least of which was that for the eastern wing of the Great Court of the Louvre, for which he was asked to submit plans in 1664.

The last decade of Mansart's life saw few significant undertakings. Arrogant and obstinate, he was unwilling to bow to the whims of his potential clients and therefore was virtually ignored by the time of his death in Paris on Sept. 3, 1666. His only solace was the certain realization that he had been instrumental in establishing a pure brand of classicism in France.

Further Reading

A detailed study of Mansart's life and works is provided by Anthony Blunt, *François Mansart and the Origins of French Classical Architecture* (1941). For a more general knowledge of the architect's work and contribution, Blunt's *Art and Architecture in France, 1500-1700* (1954; 2d ed. 1970) is adequate. □

Jules Hardouin Mansart

The French architect Jules Hardouin Mansart (1646-1708) consolidated the many classical tendencies of his predecessors and produced architectural monuments of an impressive grandeur rare in the annals of art.

The talents of Jules Hardouin Mansart were perfectly suited to the principal task to which they were assigned, namely, the glorification of absolutism centering in the person of Louis XIV. Like the monarch he so enthusiastically served, the architect had dreams of considerable magnitude. His grandiose conceptions and their subsequent execution were made possible by unparalleled financial backing.

Born Jules Hardouin in April 1646 in Paris, he was the son of a painter and the grandnephew of François Mansart, with whom he studied architecture and whose family name he later adopted. His further training was under Libéral Bruant. Though J. H. Mansart did not study with Louis Le Vau, this master's style had a very formative influence on him.

Mansart's earliest royal commission appears to have been the rebuilding in 1674 of the small Château du Val at Saint-Germain-en-Laye. Here, and in the Hôtel de Noailles in the same town, he introduced a new type of domestic structure: the single-storied building with a strong horizontal emphasis-which he revived in his Grand Trianon at Versailles (1689). The Saint-Germain houses, as well as his contemporaneous Hôtel de Lorge in Paris, conveyed a new interest in convenience of plan; the rooms were often of a variety of shapes and so disposed at the Château du Val as to be heated simultaneously by a single, carefully placed heating unit.

The château of Clagny (1676-1683), built to house the natural children of Louis XIV by the Marquise de Montespan, was Mansart's first large structure commissioned by the King. The monumental scale of its simple masses and the inherent understanding of the proper use of classical motifs reveal the architect's knowledge of François Mansart's Gaston d'Orléans wing at Blois and his later château of Maisons (now Maisons-Lafitte).

J. H. Mansart's rise to fame became meteoric when, in 1678, Louis XIV charged him with the vast modifications and additions to the château of Versailles. He first reworked Le Vau's garden facade, filling in the large terrace set into the middle of the building's second story, in order to create the Galerie des Glaces. Later Mansart erected the great wings which extend symmetrically north and south of the central block, creating in the overall 1,800-foot length an unparalleled monumentality. Among his most imaginative efforts at Versailles were the splendid horseshoe-shaped stables (1679-1686), which were carefully planned to fill in the wedge-shaped areas formed by the avenues radiating out from the château's forecourt. Equally notable is his work on the second Orangery, with its magnificently scaled em-

bracing staircases. His last undertaking at Versailles was the chapel (conceived 1688; built 1697-1710).

Mansart was responsible for two significant urban projects in Paris: the Place des Victoires and the Place Vendôme. Both squares, designed to provide handsome settings for equestrian statues of Louis XIV, were surrounded by monumentally scaled architecture suggestive of pure scenography. Though the round Place des Victoires has since been so modified as to obscure its original majestic appearance, the Place Vendôme, with its noble arcades surmounted by giant orders and beautifully proportioned pediments, is one of Mansart's most impressive achievements.

The architect's crowning glory was his church of Les Invalides, the Dôme (1680-1706). The structure is Greek cross in plan with circular chapels located in the corners, following the projected arrangement of the Bourbon chapel at Saint-Denis by François Mansart. The building is surmounted by a high dome which derives from earlier domical structures, such as St. Peter's in Rome and, in Paris, the church of the Sorbonne by Jacques Lemercier and the Collège des Quatre Nations by Le Vau. J. H. Mansart carefully adjusted his building to Bruant's earlier adjacent church in order to achieve a pleasing visual and physical unity between the two structures. The great height of the dome was determined by its relation to Bruant's broad facade of the Hôtel des Invalides as it was to be viewed from a position near the Seine. From this point, the dome is perfectly proportioned to the extended facade and provides a splendid sense of visual focus toward the center of the complex.

Beginning in 1679 and continuing to the time of his death, Mansart was occupied at Marly-le-Roi, building a novel weekend retreat for Louis XIV. In the perfectly balanced layout of the entire complex, the building reserved for the King's exclusive use stood as an isolated block, bounded on its flanks by individual pavilions designed to accommodate those members of the court who were invited to spend several days at Marly. The arrangement suggests a new intimacy in French architecture and can also be regarded as symbolic, for the central building is the dwelling of the Sun king and the pavilions are his satellites.

When Mansart died at Marly on May 11, 1708, there was no other architect of his stature to take his place. He had been perfectly suited to the needs of the age, and owing to his aggressive and, it is said, often ruthless methods and his remarkable ability to command myriad teams of underlings, he was able to realize the grand schemes devoted to glorifying the absolute monarchy of Louis XIV.

Further Reading

There are no comprehensive studies of Mansart in English, but for a general treatment of his work see Anthony Blunt, *Art and Architecture in France, 1500-1700* (1954; 2d ed. 1970). □

Katherine Mansfield

Short story writer Katherine Mansfield (1888-1923) is noted for her short stories with themes relating to women's lives and social hierarchies as well as her sense of wit and characterizations.

Katherine Mansfield has played an important role in the genre of the short story. The New Zealand-born writer, who spent much of her adulthood in Europe, "is a central figure in the development of the modern short story," noted *Twentieth-Century Literary Criticism.* "An early practitioner of stream-of-consciousness narration, she applied this technique to create stories based on the illumination of character rather than the contrivances of plot." Mansfield also attempted to free herself from the domination of her bourgeois family and the expectations for women of her class. As a young woman she often heeded her own determined whims, but later settled into a period of stability and literary creativity with her 1918 marriage to a fellow writer, editor, and literary critic. Together they moved in social circles that included some of the most acclaimed English-language writers of the early twentieth century.

Mansfield was born Kathleen Mansfield Beauchamp in Wellington, New Zealand, to a family of English descent in 1888. Her father, Harold Beauchamp, was a successful merchant who eventually became one of the English colony's most prominent citizens, rising to the position of chair of the Bank of New Zealand. She once described her mother as "constantly suspicious, constantly overbearingly tyrannous," and from an early age Mansfield seemed resentful toward her middle-class provincial family. As a writer, she later explored the theme of the hierarchy of class distinctions that restricted upbringings such as hers. As a teenager she was sent away to a finishing school in London that was a more intellectually rigorous institution than most girls of her class attended. There she became active in its magazine, for which she wrote several short stories, and established a lifelong friendship with classmate Ida Baker. When her schooling came to an end, Mansfield returned to her family's increasingly prosperous household in Wellington, but was determined to take leave again permanently. Enrolling in secretarial and bookkeeping courses, her parents allowed her to live abroad on her own, and in 1908 she returned to London. There she resided in a hostel for young, unmarried women pursuing artistic careers (she herself was an accomplished cellist) paid for by a stipend she received from her father until her death at age 34.

Courting Disaster Led to First Success

A long crush on musician Garnet Trowell eventually led to an unexpected pregnancy, and Mansfield suddenly married another man whom she had been seeing casually, George Bowden. She disappeared for a time, perhaps to serve as a chorus girl in the company of the light opera troupe that Trowell performed in, but her mother soon arrived from New Zealand and took her to a spa in southern Germany. "The most widely recommended cure for girls with Kathleen's difficult complaint was a course of cold baths and wholesome exercise," noted Antony Alpers in *The Life of Katherine Mansfield.* She suffered a miscarriage later that summer, but remained in Germany for several months. Out of her sojourn came her first collection of short stories, *In a German Pension,* first published in 1911. The volume was noted for its rather unflattering portrayal of Germans, and "the early appeal of the collection, most said, was to the anti-German sentiments felt by Britons in the years preceding the First World War," noted C. A. Hankin in *Katherine Mansfield and Her Confessional Stories.* In retrospect, the content of the stories "again and again [underline] her sense that sexual love for women is fraught with physical danger," as Mansfield was attracted to both men and women.

Moving back to London, in 1912 Mansfield met John Middleton Murry, the catalyst behind an acclaimed new English literary magazine out of Oxford called *Rhythm.* "Henceforth, she had a center to work from, and her early disastrous affairs, though they continued to provide a few themes for stories, sank below the horizon," observed Ian A. Gordon in *British Writers.* Mansfield instead began to mine her New Zealand upbringing for subject matter, and many of these were published in *Rhythm* and its successor, the *Blue Review.*

World War I Brought Tragedy

By 1914 Mansfield and Murry were living together, and the literary journals had ceased publication; for a time he was a reviewer of French books for the *Times Literary Supplement*. The next year, Mansfield's younger brother stopped by London for a rare visit before joining the British Army. His death later that year in World War I resolved Katherine to further explore their childhood in colonial New Zealand for her stories. It devastated her and she produced little work for a time, and her mental anguish was compounded by her own increasingly fragile physical health. Since arriving in England as a teenager she had been plagued by illness, and by 1916 she and Murry were living in the south of France to escape its damp and chilly climate.

During these years Mansfield and Murry were becoming well-acquainted with such literary and historical figures as D.H. Lawrence, Virginia Woolf, Lytton Strachey, and Bertrand Russell. Mansfield also began writing short stories for a journal called *New Age*. It was in the south of France that she penned her first major story, "The Aloe," which in a revised form was published first in 1918 as "Prelude." It "set the standard and established the pattern for all her later work," wrote Gordon in *British Writers*. "Prelude" chronicles the doings of the fictional Burnell family of New Zealand, whose structure and members resemble the Beauchamps of Wellington quite distinctly. There is Stanley, the aggressive tycoon, the harsh mother Linda, the unmarried maiden aunt Beryl, and daughter Kezia, who in some of her youngest incarnations caused Joanne Trautman Banks to assert in *The English Short Story* that Mansfield was "one of our greatest portrayers of children in short fiction."

Entered Period of Intense Creativity

In 1917 Mansfield was diagnosed with tuberculosis, and began spending even more time in the south of France. The following year she married Murry after finally winning a divorce from her first husband. This next period saw the publication of some of her most acclaimed works, including the collections *Je ne parle pas francais* and *Bliss and Other Short Stories*. Like much of her work, many of the stories feature women prominently, and often portray the few choices available to them outside of marriage. In Mansfield's era, to forsake a husband and children was almost like a death sentence.

"The success of these volumes established Mansfield as a major talent comparable to such contemporaries as Virginia Woolf and James Joyce," noted *Twentieth-Century Literary Criticism*. Now dividing her time between Switzerland, Paris, and the south of France, Mansfield wrote at a feverish pace, sometimes one story a day. They frequently appeared in publications such as the *Athenaeum*, the *Nation*, and the *London Mercury*. Much of what Mansfield wrote during 1920 and 1921 was published in the collection *The Garden Party*. Its title story may be her most well-known, and as in much of her fiction the tale is taken from an actual incident. The wealthy Burnell family in many of her stories is here called the Sheridans, as the story opens their sensitive daughter Laura is excited by the prospect of her family's impending afternoon fete. However, the Sheridans' idyllic afternoon is marred by the death of one of the workmen in the area just outside the Sheridan manse. The family he has left behind lives at the bottom of the hill from

the lawn where the party will take place. Upset, Laura wishes to cancel the party, but the other Sheridans convince her otherwise. Later, she brings the party's leftover food to the destitute family, which Mansfield's older sister actually did when the incident happened to them in New Zealand in 1907. Grief, like the miserable fate mapped out for most women of her class, was a strong theme in much of her work. In "The Garden Party" and other stories like "The Fly" and "Six Years After," death and loss are predominant.

Mansfield also penned several pieces of literary criticism during her writing career and a final burst of short stories that appeared as *The Dove's Nest*, published the year she died. The work contains more of the fictional Burnells, and further explorations into the genre of the short story that "treat such universal concerns as family and love relationships and the everyday experiences of childhood, and are noted for their distinctive wit, psychological acuity, and perceptive characterizations," as *Twentieth-Century Literary Criticism* assessed. Mansfield spent much of the last two years of her life between Italy and France, eventually staying at a priory in Fontainebleau for a holistic-type cure for her tuberculosis. She sometimes lived apart from Murry for long stretches of time, but her longtime friend Ida Baker was often living nearby.

Some critics charge that Murry, while also serving as an editor of Mansfield's literary efforts, inhibited or excised some elements of her earlier work, most notably her preoccupation with a romantic attraction between women. Biographers assert that both Mansfield and Murry conducted affairs during their marriage, and that after her death of a lung hemorrhage in early 1923, her widower exploited her work, as "he profited from the publication of stories that Mansfield had rejected for publication, as well as notebook jottings, intermittent diaries, and letters," stated *Twentieth-Century Literary Criticism*.

Further Reading

Scott-Kilvert, Ian, editor, *British Writers: Edited under the auspices of the British Council,* Vol. Volume VII: Sean O'Casey to Poets of World War II, Scribner's, 1984, pp. 171-183.
Alpers, Antony, *The Life of Katherine Mansfield,* Viking Press, 1980.
Twentieth Century Literary Criticism, Gale Research, Vol. 39, 1991, pp. 292-331. □

Abu Jafar ibn Muhammad al-Mansur

Abu Jafar ibn Muhammad al-Mansur (712-775) was the second caliph and real founder of the Arab Abbasid dynasty.

Abu Jafar, later al-Mansur, was the son of a Berber slave girl called Sallama and a brother of the first Abbasid caliph, Abu al-Abbas al Saffah. A great-

great-grandson of Abd al-Abbas, the uncle of Mohammed, Abu Jafar and advocates of the Abbasid line considered themselves the true heirs of the Prophet as opposed to the Umayyads and the Shiite followers of Mohammed's cousin Ali. The rebellion of Abbasid forces in Khurasan in 747 led to defeat of the last Umayyad caliph, Marwan II, in 750 and the establishment of the Abbasid dynasty. During the fighting, Abu Jafar distinguished himself, particularly at the siege of Wasit.

Abu Jafar administered Armenia, Azerbaidzhan, and Mesopotamia during the short reign of Abu al-Abbas. Abu Jafar's succession as al-Mansur was announced during a pilgrimage to Mecca but was immediately challenged by an uncle, Abdallah ibn Ali, the governor of Syria. To suppress this opposition, al-Mansur called upon Abu Muslim, the original revolutionary agent his family had sent into Khurasan. This highly popular religious leader successfully eliminated Abdallah but then was summoned to court, where al-Mansur had him murdered.

Revolts against al-Mansur

This was the beginning of a series of revolts which wracked the empire during al-Mansur's reign. The Muslimiya, outraged Persian converts of Abu Muslim, marched against the Caliph. The group was destroyed by an Abbasid general who, in turn, renounced his own allegiance and had to be eliminated himself. About the same time, 756, revolt also rocked Mesopotamia. Not all the uprisings were politically motivated, however. The fanatic Rawandis, who equated the caliph with God, stormed the palace seeking the release of their imprisoned leaders. The fortuitous appearance of a former opponent routed the attackers.

A more serious affair concerned the Alids. The Shiite Hashimiya of Kufa had been allies of the Abbasids in their bid for power, even acknowledging al-Mansur's father, Muhammad, as their imam. Al-Mansur became embarrassed by the devotional attention of this heretical group. After a Shiite demonstration in 758, he suppressed it. This was followed by an outburst of the true Shiites, now united behind a grandson of Hasan ibn Ali. The Hasanite Muhammad was proclaimed caliph in Medina in 762 in opposition to al-Mansur but was defeated. Muhammad's brother Ibrahim was defeated and killed at Bakhamra in February 763, and the Alid threat was over.

Consolidation of Power

With these successes, Abbasid power was firmly established. In 762 al-Mansur began building a new capital at an old market town called Baghdad on the west bank of the Tigris near the Euphrates canal. Officially called Madinat as-Salem, "City of Peace," it was finished in 766, built in part of materials taken from the nearby old Persian capital of Ctesiphon. Although originally a circular fortified garrison structure consisting of a mosque and palace, Baghdad ultimately grew into a great metropolis, the center of the world in the days of al-Mansur's grandson Harun al-Rashid.

Al-Mansur failed in his attempts to oust the Umayyad family from its refuge in Spain, but he did succeed, with Khurasanian help, in restoring order to troubled North Af-

rica in 772. Along the Byzantine frontier, raiding was constant, and the Caliph built several fortresses to strengthen his hold on the marches. Tabaristan was added to the empire in 759; a Khazar invasion of Georgia was repelled 3 years later; and expeditions were undertaken into Transoxiana and India but to no permanent advantage.

In government, al-Mansur reorganized the administration. He created the office of vizier, under which were established several ministries (divans) such as army, finance, and posts. His best-known minister was Khalid ibn Barmak, who served as director of finance, was active in the founding of Baghdad, and inaugurated the influence of the Barmacides, or Barmakids.

Al-Mansur had an active interest in literature and was renowned as a public speaker but otherwise lived a simple life with no music or song permitted at court. He was a well-informed ruler, devoted to administration. Particularly concerned with improvement of finances, he left a sizable treasury for his heirs. So firm and thrifty was his system of government that it was over a century before the extravagances of his successors could dislocate the economy. Al-Mansur, an appellation meaning "the victorious" or, in Mahdist terms, "the divinely aided," died in October 775 while on a pilgrimage to Mecca.

Further Reading

Al-Mansur figures in histories of early Islam, among them John Joseph Saunders, *A History of Medieval Islam* (1965), and G. E. von Grunebaum, *Classical Islam: A History, 600-1258* (trans. 1970). See also Philip K. Hitti, *History of the Arabs from the Earliest Times to the Present* (1937; 10th ed. 1970); John Bagot Glubb, *The Empire of the Arabs* (1963); and Wilson B. Bishai, *Islamic History of the Middle East: Background, Development, and Fall of the Arab Empire* (1968).

Additional Sources

Tabari, *Al-Mansur and Al-Mahdi,* Albany, N.Y.: State University of New York Press, 1990. □

Andrea Mantegna

Andrea Mantegna (ca. 1430-1506), painter and engraver, was the leading artist of the school of Padua and one of the most important early Renaissance Italian masters.

A ndrea Mantegna, the son of the carpenter Biagio, was born at Isola di Carturo about halfway between Padua and Vicenza. The inscription on a lost altarpiece he executed (the inscription was preserved in written records) in 1447 states that the artist was 17. His name appeared on the painters' roll for Padua between 1441 and 1445 as an apprentice and adopted son of Francesco Squarcione. It was not unusual for childless masters to adopt promising apprentices. In 1448 Mantegna left Squarcione's household and established himself as an independent artist.

Seven years later Mantegna went to court to dissolve their relationship. He declared that he had earned more than 400 ducats for Squarcione and sued for reimbursement of the money. Squarcione contested Mantegna's suit, citing an agreement they had signed in 1448 in Venice. The court awarded Mantegna 200 ducats and denounced the 1448 agreement. These accounts suggest that Mantegna was responsible for a substantial number of paintings while serving in Squarcione's studio and, furthermore, that his efforts were generally well known.

Ovetari Chapel

In 1448 Mantegna, Giovanni d'Alemagna, Antonio Vivarini, and Niccolo Pizzolo were commissioned to fresco the Ovetari Chapel in the Church of the Eremitani, Padua, with the stories of St. James and St. Christopher. The initial contract divided the work more or less equally among the four artists, but, owing to subsequent disputes and the deaths of Giovanni d'Alemagna and Pizzolo, Mantegna painted the greater part of the frescoes. An appraisal of the work was carried out in 1454, which confirmed that the other three artists had only partially finished their assignments. Mantegna completed the project in 1455. There are numerous references to his difficult personality. It seems that he was a proud and abrasive person who did not get along well with others.

The Ovetari Chapel frescoes, Mantegna's early masterpiece, were almost totally destroyed during World War II. They showed Mantegna's concern for establishing rather crisp, sculpturesque forms in an accurately rendered perspective space which carefully took into account the beholder's viewpoint. Also, details of costume, armor, and architecture demonstrated that Mantegna had an archeological interest in classical antiquity.

In 1453 Mantegna married Niccolosa Bellini, the daughter of the Venetian painter Jacopo Bellini. The marriage brought Mantegna into an important artistic family.

Mantegna painted a number of important works during his Paduan period (1448-1460), including the *St. Luke Altarpiece* (Milan), *St. Sebastian* (Vienna), *Agony in the Garden* (London), the portraits of Cardinal Mezzarota (Berlin) and Cardinal Francesco Gonzaga (Naples), and the altarpiece for the church of S. Zeno in Verona. The *S. Zeno Altarpiece* was inspired by Donatello's high altar for the church of S. Antonio in Padua and combined real and painted elements in a unified way that anticipated Mantegna's paintings in the Camera degli Sposi in Mantua.

Camera degli Sposi

In 1459 Mantegna was appointed court painter to Ludovico Gonzaga in Mantua, and the following year the artist moved there from Padua. The Camera degli Sposi in the Ducal Palace was completed in 1474. It is not known for certain when Mantegna began the project. In 1466-1467 he visited Florence and Pisa. Stylistic aspects of the frescoes suggest that Mantegna did not begin them until he returned from Florence. It is known by a letter that the artist was working on the project in October 1471.

The Camera degli Sposi is a rectangular room with a moved barrel vault broken by three lunettes on each wall. Mantegna transformed the ceiling into a painted dome with an oculus in the center through which we catch a glimpse of a cloud-flecked sky and see the faces of people and cherubs looking down into the chamber. The walls are painted to resemble a landscape seen through openings in an airy pavilion. On one wall is the return of Cardinal Francesco Gonzaga; on another wall is a portrait of the Gonzaga family posed on a platform that seems to rest on the real mantle of the fireplace. In his decorations Mantegna unified the actual space of the room with the painted space of the frescoes to create an illusionism that foretells the work of Correggio.

Last Works

Mantegna's artistic output was of remarkably high quality. In 1484 he began the series of nine canvases of the *Triumph of Caesar* (Hampton Court) for Francesco II Gonzaga, which was not finished before 1492. Lorenzo the Magnificent, the ruler of Florence, called on Mantegna in his studio in Mantua in 1484. Between 1488 and 1490 Mantegna was in Rome working for Pope Innocent VIII. His *Madonna della Vittoria* (Paris) of 1496 commemorates the battle of Fornovo of the preceding year. Other important works of the 1490s include the *Dead Christ* (Milan) and *St. Sebastian* (Venice). In the 1500s he painted two canvases for the *studiolo* of Isabella d'Este: *Parnassus* and *Minerva Expelling the Vices from the Garden of Virtue* (both Paris).

A number of engravings are attributed to Mantegna. Whether he engraved the plates himself or—and this seems more plausible—made the designs which were then engraved by other craftsmen is not known. The so-called autograph engravings include the *Entombment, Risen Christ between Saints Andrew and Longinus, Madonna and Child, Battle of the Sea Gods, Bacchanal with Silenus,* and *Bacchanal with a Vat.* Mantegna died on Sept. 13, 1506, in Mantua.

Further Reading

A sound monograph on Mantegna is E. Tietze-Conrat, *Mantegna: Paintings, Drawings and Engravings* (1955). Paul Kristeller, *Andrea Mantegna* (1901), is still useful. See also Millard Meiss, *Andrea Mantegna as Illuminator* (1957). □

Mickey Mantle

"The Mick," switch-hitting Mickey Mantle (1932-1995) won four home-run championships, a Triple Crown, and three most valuable player awards during his 18-year career with the New York Yankees.

ickey Charles Mantle was born in Spavinaw, Oklahoma, to Elvin ("Mutt") and Lowell Mantle. A former semi-pro baseball player, Mutt Mantle was so fond of baseball he named his first child after Detroit Tigers catcher Mickey Cochrane. Mickey was barely out of diapers before he was practicing baseball with his father. Mutt believed that the only way to excel in the major leagues was as a switch-hitter, so he taught his son to swing from both sides of the plate. Mickey would use his natural right-handed swing against his left-handed father, then would turn around and bat left-handed against his right-handed grandfather.

Signed with the Yankees while in High School

Mantle played baseball and basketball at his high school in Commerce, Oklahoma and was also a star halfback on the football team. During one game, however, he was kicked in the leg and developed osteomyelitis, a bone marrow disease that would affect his future baseball career. While playing high school baseball, Mantle impressed New York Yankee scout Tom Greenwade, who signed him to a contract of $140 a week with a $1500 bonus—a bargain even in the days of low salaries in professional sports.

Mantle reported to the Yankees' minor league team in Independence, Kansas, in 1949 as a switch-hitting shortstop. After two years in the minor leagues, the Yankees invited him to their major league spring training camp. He earned a place on the roster, and the New York media soon began comparing him to Babe Ruth and other past Yankee greats. Only 19 years old and two years out of high school,

Mantle did not immediately live up to the public's high expectations. He started slowly in his new position—right field—and was sent back briefly to the minors. Mantle's first year in the majors was marred by inconsistent play and jeering from fans both in New York and around the league. His difficulties continued when, early in 1952, Mutt Mantle died of Hodgkin's disease at the age of 39. Mantle had been very close to his father, and he took the death hard.

Mantle was moved to center field when Joe DiMaggio retired from the Yankees following the 1951 season. He began to adjust to big-league play, and in 1952 batted .311 with 23 home runs and 87 runs batted in (RBIs). That season Mantle began to establish himself as one of baseball's premier power hitters. During one game against the Washington Senators, Mantle hit a ball completely out of Griffith Stadium in Washington, D.C. Measured at 565 feet, the home run is believed to be the longest ever hit. The New York Yankees won the American League pennant and World Series during each of Mantle's first three seasons, from 1951 to 1953. During the 1952 World Series against the Brooklyn Dodgers, Mantle batted .345 with two home runs. In the 1953 Series, again against the Dodgers, he batted only .208, but hit two more home runs.

Led the Yankees in the 50s

Mantle's talents led the Yankees as they dominated the American League throughout the late 1950s. They won the pennant each year from 1955 to 1958, taking the World Series in 1956 and 1958. Mantle became a genuine superstar in 1956 when he won baseball's Triple Crown, with a .353 batting average, 52 home runs, and 130 RBIs. He was also selected the American League's most valuable player (MVP). In 1957 he hit .365 and was again named the league MVP.

Mantle's success at the plate continued as the Yankees remained strong well into the 1960s. After losing the pennant to the Chicago White Sox in 1959, the Yankees came back to win it the next five seasons, joined by new stars such as Tony Kubek, Bobby Richardson, Ryne Duren, Bill Skowron, and Roger Maris. Mantle captured the home run title again in 1960 with 40 round-trippers, and he led the competition for the title again in 1961—the most dramatic home run season in the history of the game. By early August Mantle already had hit 43 home runs and Maris 42. The record for home runs in a season was held by the legendary Baby Ruth, who had blasted 60 in 1927. Although Mantle ended the year with 54 home runs (his all-time high), Maris hit 61 homers and established the new all-time record.

Mantle continued to excel even though his legs hurt most of the time from the osteomyelitis and other injuries. In 1962 he was named American League MVP for the third time. Although the Yankees continued to win pennants, their days of glory were waning. They lost the 1963 World Series to the Los Angeles Dodgers and were swept in the 1964 World Series by the St. Louis Cardinals. By 1965 the Yankees' heyday was finished. Mantle became frustrated with his pain and with his many strikeouts. During the 1965 season he said, "It isn't any fun when things are like this. I'm only 33, but I feel like 40." Mantle continued to play through the 1968 season; he announced his retirement in the spring of 1969.

Elected to Hall of Fame

Mantle left the Yankees with many great achievements. In addition to hitting 536 lifetime home runs, he led the American League in homers four times and was chosen as its most valuable player three times. He is one of only a few players to win a Triple Crown. He played on 12 pennant-winning and seven World Series-winning teams. He still holds the all-time record for home runs in World Series play (18) as well as numerous other World Series records. As much as DiMaggio before him, Mantle symbolized the Yankees and their dominance of baseball. In 1974 Mantle was elected to baseball's Hall of Fame in his first year of eligibility, an honor bestowed on few players in the history of the sport.

After retiring from baseball, Mantle pursued a business career, opening a restaurant franchise and dabbling in public relations for an Atlantic City casino. He also made appearances to sign autographs and play in celebrity golf tournaments. His experience in television commercials and small film roles led to occasional stints providing color commentary for televised Yankees games. His career and personal life had been marred by alcoholism, however.

Years of Heavy Drinking Took Their Toll

Mantle had married Merlyn, who was a bank employee, in the 1950s and had they four sons—David, Danny, Billy, and Mickey, Jr. Mantle was absent for much of their childhood, however, and had a reputation for his drinking and all-night carousing. He and his wife separated in 1988. Their son Billy died of heart failure in March of 1994 after being diagnosed with Hodgkin's disease, the same illness that had taken Mantle's father and grandfather at an early age and that Mantle thought would eventually afflict him as well. He would face a different fate, though. Earlier in 1994 Mantle had stayed at the Betty Ford clinic to treat his alcoholism, but it was too late—his liver was damaged from years of heavy drinking. He was diagnosed with cirrhosis, hepatitis, and cancer of the liver. Although he underwent a liver transplant in June of 1995, the cancer had spread to most of his internal organs and Mantle died on August 13, 1995.

Epitomizing home run power greater than any man's since Babe Ruth, Mantle's name was on the lips of every would-be slugger on the sandlots of America during the 1950s and 1960s. Mantle's outstanding abilities and courage in the face of pain made him a hero to a generation of youngsters and adults alike.

Further Reading

Gallagher, Mark, *Explosion! Mickey Mantle's Legendary Home Runs,* Arbor House, 1987.

Mantle, Mickey, *Education of a Ball Player,* Simon & Schuster, 1967.

Mantle, Mickey, and Herb Glick, *The Mick,* Doubleday, 1985.

Mantle, Mickey, and Ben Epstein, *The Mickey Mantle Story,* Holt, 1953.

Schaap, Dick, *Mickey Mantle: The Indispensable Yankee,* Bartholomew House, 1961.

Schoor, Gene, *Mickey Mantle of the Yankees,* Putnam, 1959.

Silverman, Al, *Mickey Mantle, Mister Yankee,* Putnam, 1963.

Life, July 30, 1965, pp. 47- 53.

Look, February 23, 1965, pp. 71- 75; March 18, 1969, pp. 29-32.

Newsweek, June 25, 1956, pp. 63- 67; August 14, 1961, pp. 42-46.

New York Times, August 14, 1995, p. 1A.

People, August 28, 1995, p. 76.

Washington Post, August 14, 1995, p. 1A. □

Manuel I

Manuel I Comnenus (ca. 1123-1180) was Byzantine emperor from 1143 to 1180. Although he was a talented ruler, his diplomatic and military over-extensions left his realm dangerously isolated and humiliated.

The fourth son of John II Comnenus (1118-1143), Manuel was the second one surviving at the time of his father's death in a "hunting accident" that was probably an assassination. Supposedly by the dying John's wish, Manuel was given the throne in preference to his older brother. Manuel assembled a dazzling and lavish court and presided over one of the most brilliant phases of Byzantine culture. He was also an able soldier, strategist, and commander. Nevertheless, his perception seems to have been at times superficial, and his policies, although imaginative, were often misguided.

Manuel's basic policies were to recover the lands in Asia Minor lost to the Turks, to assert control over the crusader states of the Holy Land, to maintain domination of the sub-Danubian Balkans, to recover Byzantine rights and lands in Italy, and to restore the empire's international position.

At the outset of his reign, Manuel built his diplomatic hopes on cooperation with the new Hohenstaufen dynasty of Germany, planning thereby to check the aggressive Norman king of Sicily and southern Italy, Roger II. The alliance was sealed by Manuel's marriage to Bertha of Sulzbach, sister-in-law of the German emperor Conrad III. But this entente was badly disrupted by Conrad's participation in the abortive Second Crusade (1147-1149). Freed from German pressure, Roger sent his fleets to devastate Byzantine Greece ruthlessly. Conrad renewed his alliance with Manuel, but he died soon after his return. He left the German throne to his nephew Frederick I Barbarossa, who soon ended any illusions of continued Comnenian-Hohenstaufen cooperation.

Manuel's other initial ally, and his supporter in his continuing wars with Roger, was Venice. But ill feelings developed between Manuel and Venice, so the Emperor endeavored to play off Venice and the other major Italian maritime powers, Genoa and Pisa, against each other. He also cultivated the papacy, especially under Frederick's enemy, Alexander III, in the vain hope of ending the schism of the Churches and of being recognized as emperor of both East and West. Further, he supported the north Italian cities in their struggles against Frederick. Manuel's Italian interests were not merely diplomatic, however, for he sought to restore in the peninsula the power of the Byzantines, expelled since the Norman conquest of the south a century earlier. He therefore occupied Ancona in 1151 and endeavored to annex the entire eastern coast; but reverses followed, and by 1158 these footholds were finally lost. Meanwhile, Manuel's relations with Venice deteriorated so badly that in 1171 the Emperor ordered all Venetians within the empire arrested and their properties confiscated. This led to new hostilities.

In other spheres, Manuel achieved clearer success. In the Balkans, during the 1150s and 1160s, Manuel effectively resisted the ambitions of Hungary and established the most comprehensive control of the sub-Danubian regions that the empire had enjoyed since the 6th century. Likewise successful was his domination of the Armenians of Cilicia and, especially, the Latins of the crusader states. The climax of this effort was his triumphant reception in Antioch in 1159, where both that city's prince and the king of Jerusalem acknowledged his suzerainty.

Yet, it was in the East that Manuel's ultimate humiliation came. His strategic blunders as commander delivered his army to a dreadful massacre by the Turks in 1176, at Myriokephalon, from which Manuel himself fled for his life. This disaster sealed forever the Byzantine loss of central Asia Minor. This humiliation also capped the destruction of his international image; he was reduced to insignificance beside the prestigious Frederick Barbarossa.

Likewise in his domestic regime, Manuel was imaginative but not consistently successful. His ecclesiastical policies were firm and constructive, aimed at curbing excessive monastic wealth. The empire's economy also flourished to a considerable extent, but its effects were qualified by Manuel's lavish expenditures and heavy taxation. He found it impossible to check the progress of quasi-feudal power and independence among the powerful landed aristocrats, and his efforts at cultivating or encouraging other orders of society were ill-timed. He made free and open-minded use of Westerners and other peoples, but his cosmopolitanism was out of tune with the increasingly narrow Hellenism of his people, and it antagonized them. The Emperor died on Sept. 24, 1180.

Further Reading

The basic study of the Comneni is in French. Lively sketches of Manuel's two Latin wives are in Joseph McCabe, *The Empresses of Constantinople* (1913), and Charles Diehl, *Byzantine Empresses* (1963). A general account of the reign is in *The Cambridge Medieval History,* vol. 4 (1923; 2d ed., 2 pts., 1966), and George Ostrogorsky, *History of the Byzantine State* (1956; rev. ed. 1969). Andrew B. Urbansky, *Byzantium and the Danube Frontier* (1968), is a study of the relations between Byzantium, Hungary, and the Balkan states during the period of the Comneni.

Additional Sources

Cinnamus, Joannes, *Deeds of John and Manuel Comnenus,* New York: Columbia University Press, 1976.

Magdalino, Paul, *The empire of Manuel I Komnenos, 1143-1180,* Cambridge England; New York: Cambridge University Press, 1993. □

Manuel I

Manuel I (1469-1521) was king of Portugal from 1495 to 1521. Known as "the Fortunate," he oversaw the formation of the Portuguese Empire and strengthened the position of the monarchy.

The son of the Duke of Viseu, Manuel was born on May 31, 1469, at Alcochete. He was the cousin and brother-in-law of King John II of Portugal. The heir to the throne, Prince Afonso, was killed in an accident in 1491, and thereafter the royal succession devolved upon Manuel.

Manuel married in turn two daughters of the joint rulers of Castile and Aragon, Ferdinand and Isabella; his third marriage was to their granddaughter Leonor, sister of the emperor Charles V. Manuel's Spanish marriages extracted from him a reluctant promise to Ferdinand and Isabella to expel all Portuguese Jews. Himself unmoved by anti-Semitic passions, he accepted the "technical conversion" of the Jews, granting them a 20-year period of grace before allowing inquiries to be made into the character of their actual beliefs.

In other ways Manuel's policies more closely paralleled the centralizing measures of his Spanish in-laws. He restored the powerful Braganza faction, exiled under his predecessor. But he also turned the nobility into a pensioned clientele of the monarchy, and he ordered a revision of the legal code to bolster the royal supremacy. The government now passed under the control of administrative professionals, and the Cortes (Parliament) gave up its legislative initiative. He further reduced municipal liberties and suppressed the autonomous governing functions of the Lisbon guilds.

Abroad, although there was a decisive setback in the Portuguese effort to conquer North Africa, Manuel bolstered the Portuguese presence in Morocco. Under royal control, small-scale sugar production in Madeira was expanded to reach markets all over Europe. In West Africa the slave and gold trades increased their profitability, and the Portuguese expanded their influence in the Congo.

But the greatest achievements of Manuel's reign were the completion of the oceanic link with East Africa and India begun by Prince Henry the Navigator's captains; the discovery of Brazil; and the laying of the foundations of the Portuguese commercial empire in the East. The first of these tasks was entrusted to Vasco da Gama, whose epochal voyage (1497-1499) established direct contact with an Indian center of the spice trade, Calicut. On a second voyage to India, Pedro Álvares Cabral sailed far to the southwest and landed on a strip of Brazilian coast (April 1500) before heading eastward for the Cape of Good Hope.

Under two viceregal agents, Francisco de Almeida and Afonso de Albuquerque, the Portuguese made a dramatic, if not wholly successful, attempt to drive the Moslems from the Indian Ocean and to replace them and their Venetian commercial allies as spice merchants to Europe. Albuquerque acquired a permanent base of Portuguese power in Goa; and he pursued the retreating Moslems even farther east, to the Malay spice port of Malacca.

Yet, although these accomplishments brought in an immediate flow of treasure to the royal coffers, the Portuguese found their resources insufficient to complete their strategy of gaining total military-commercial control of Eastern waters. The Venetians were later to regain an important share of the Oriental spice trade, and the costs of covering the long Portuguese voyages, combined with falling prices based on the increased influx of spices, were to greatly reduce the profitability of the Eastern commercial empire to the Crown. Manuel died on Dec. 13, 1521.

Further Reading

An account of Manuel's reign is in H. V. Livermore, *A New History of Portugal* (1966). There is a vast literature in Portuguese and a growing number of studies in English concerned with Portuguese power in the East. A brief account of the concluding voyages of exploration and the first engagements in Eastern waters is Boies Penrose, *Travel and Discovery in the Renaissance, 1420-1620* (1952). For the Portuguese Eastern Empire see any of the following works by Charles R. Boxer: "The Portuguese in the East, 1500-1800" in H. V. Livermore, ed., *Portugal and Brazil: An Introduction* (1953); *Four Centuries of Portuguese Expansion, 1415-1825: A Succinct Survey* (1961); and *The Portuguese Seaborne Empire, 1415-1825* (1969). A history of the region into which the Portuguese incursion was made is Auguste Toussaint, *History of the Indian Ocean* (1966). Extracts from firsthand accounts of the Portuguese ventures are in J. H. Parry, ed., *The European Reconnaissance: Selected Documents* (1968). □

Manuelito

Manuelito (1818-1893) was a Navajo leader during the Navajo War of 1863-66. Unlike the peaceful Navajo leader, Ganado Mucho, Manuelito carried out a number of attacks and maintained resistance against U.S. Army troops.

Manuelito was a tribal leader who led his warriors in the Navajo wars of 1863-1866. He and his followers were the last to surrender after Kit Carson's scorched earth campaign to force them to relocate to the Bosque Redondo Reservation near Fort Sumner. As their leader, Manuelito was a source of support and encouragement during their days in confinement. He pleaded with the government for the release of his people to be returned to their homeland, and lead them back from exile in 1868. There he was selected to be the head of tribal police. In his later years he advocated education for his people in the hopes that they might improve their lives.

Manuelito was born a member of the To'Tsohnii (Big Water) clan in 1818, in southeastern Utah, probably near Bears' Ear Peak. He was a powerful warrior who rose to prominence among his people during years of attacks and raids against Mexicans, U.S. army troops, and neighboring Indian tribes. In 1855, he became headman of his tribe, succeeding Zarcillas Largas (Long Earrings) who resigned because of his inability to control his warriors. Manuelito had two wives—the first was the daughter of Narbona, the great Navajo leader and the second a Mexican woman named Juana.

The Navajo Indians then lived in the southwest, in what is now the states of Utah, Colorado, Arizona, and New Mexico. Their territory was bordered by four mountains which they considered sacred. They believed they could only be happy if they stayed within the confines of those boundaries. They called themselves Dineh or Diné, which means "the people." Navajo was a name given to them by the Spanish. They made their living by raising sheep, by hunting wild game, by growing wheat, corn, melons, and peaches, and by gathering wild pinon nuts and berries.

The Navajo's territory had been claimed by many nations, including the Spanish, the Mexicans, and the Americans, for many years. The signing of the Treaty of Guadalupe Hidalgo in 1848, marked the end of the Mexican-American War. Under this treaty Mexico ceded to the United States the present-day states of Texas, New Mexico,

Arizona, Colorado, Utah, Nevada, and California. All Mexicans who were living in that region became U. S. citizens automatically, but the Indians did not. The U.S. government considered itself responsible to protect its citizens from the Indians and instructed the Navajos to stop all raids against Americans and Mexicans.

The Government Moves In

In 1855, Fort Defiance was built in the heart of Navajo country in Canyon de Chelly. The same year the Navajo signed a treaty decreasing the size of their territory to 7,000 square miles, of which only 125 square miles were suitable for cultivation. The Navajo leaders found it too difficult to keep their people from raiding neighboring Indian or American settlement, and clashes between the Indians and the settlers continued.

In 1858, the pasture land around Fort Defiance became a point of contention when the new post commander, Major William T. H. Brooks decided that he wanted to use the land as grazing ground for the army's horses. Brooks ordered Manuelito to move his livestock or they would be killed. Manuelito, whose father and grandfather before him had used the land to graze their livestock, refused to give it up. Under Brooks' orders, the army shot and killed 60 of Manuelito's horses and over 100 of his sheep. The Navajos were outraged by the slaughter of their leader's livestock and retaliated by killing a negro slave who belonged to Major Brooks. Brooks ordered the killer to be found and turned in, and the army began to harass the Indians. Manuelito attempted to settle the matter, but assaults against the Navajo continued. After several weeks of fighting, the Navajo chiefs went to the fort to sign a peace treaty promising to remain on their land.

In 1860, many of the troops began to leave the fort to join the Civil War. With the strength of the army decreased, the Indians saw an opportunity to attack the fort and run the intruders out of their country. The headman held a council to discuss their plans. Manuelito, Barboncito, and Herrero were in favor of the attack. Ganado Mucho, another headman, opposed the plan. The Navajos invited other tribes of the region, including the Utes, Apaches, and Pueblos to join them in war. On April 30, 1860, between 1000 and 2000 warriors stormed the fort. However, the army had been warned of the impending attack and was prepared with canons and guns ready when the Indians arrived. The warriors made an impressive show against the well armed troops, but were driven back. Many warriors were killed, and the rest retreated to their stronghold in the Chuska Mountain canyons. Colonel Edward R. S. Canby pursued them but the Indians eluded him in the many hiding places of Canyon de Chelly.

The government stepped up its efforts to control the hostiles. On June 23, 1863, General James H. Carleton sent a message from Fort Wingate to the Navajo headmen, demanding that they turn themselves in by July 20th and threatening war against them if they did not. Carleton wanted to convince the Indians that they could no longer resist the power of the U. S. government. He believed that they had no choice but to give up their land and relocate to a new home beyond the Rio Grande. The deadline passed but the Navajo refused to surrender. Carleton then recruited Colonel Christopher "Kit" Carson to help him to persuade the Indians to leave their homeland. Carson began a scorched earth campaign to drive the Navajos out. He and his troops confiscated as much of the crops and livestock as they could use for their own purposes and destroyed the rest. Fields of crops were burned, hogans were destroyed, and livestock was slaughtered.

With nothing left to eat but wild berries and pinon nuts, some of the Indians moved on to join other tribes. Manuelito and his band, however, went down into the Grande Canyon. Kit Carson and his men went back to Fort Defiance to wait for the winter when the Indians would be forced by starvation to surrender. The Indians who stayed begin in the Chuska Mountains struggled to survive as best they could on whatever wild foods they could gather. Many died of starvation or froze to death during the winter, yet they still refused to surrender. It was not until February of 1864 that thousands of weak, sick, and hungry Indians began to turn themselves in at Fort Defiance.

The Long Walk

On March 6, 1864, the soldiers at the fort formed the 2,500 refugees into a long line and started them on a long trek past the borders of their homeland to the reservation of Bosque Redondo near Fort Sumner. This was "The Long Walk," a part of Navajo history still remembered with great sorrow and bitterness. Many people died or were killed on that journey. The army had not supplied enough food, but the Indians were forced to continue marching onward in spite of hunger and cold. Those who were too sick, weak, or old to keep up were killed or left behind.

By the time the group reached the Rio Grande the spring melt had flooded the river, making it very treacherous to cross. The Indians tried to get across any way they could but many were swept away and drowned. At the end of their ordeal they arrived at the wasteland that was to be their new home, the Bosque Redondo reservation. This place that Carleton had promised would be a "garden of Eden" was nothing but a desolate, barren flatland with no means of support for the Indians. Carleton had not provided enough food or supplies for the large number of new inhabitants to the remote reservation, nor had he realized how difficult it would be for the Indians to become self-supporting as farmers on such a worthless piece of land.

Delgadito, Herrero Grande, Armijo, and Barboncito had all surrendered with their bands by September of 1864. However, Manuelito and his followers held out longer than any of the others. Carleton sent Herrero Grande and five other Navajo headmen to find Manuelito and give him a message. He was advised to turn himself in peaceably or be hunted down and killed. Dee Brown records Manuelito's response in his book, *Bury My Heart at Wounded Knee*. According to Brown, Manuelito replied to his fellow tribesmen, "My God and my mother live in the West, and I will not leave them. It is a tradition of my people that we must never cross the three rivers—the Grande, the San Juan, the Colorado. Nor could I leave the Chuska Mountains. I was born there. I shall remain. I have nothing to lose but my life, and that they can come and take whenever they please, but I will not move. I have never done any wrong to the Americans or the Mexicans. I have never robbed. If I am killed, innocent blood will be shed." Herrero Grande went back to Carleton alone.

In September of 1866, however, Manuelito and twenty-three of his still surviving people were forced by hunger to surrender at Fort Wingate. He then joined the others at Bosque Redondo. The conditions at the reservation continued to worsen as each year the crops failed. About 2000 Navajos died at Bosque Redondo of disease or starvation. The horrific conditions that the Indians were forced to live under, as well as their continued longing to return home, increased anger and unrest among them.

In the late 1860s Manuelito traveled to Washington, DC, to petition on behalf of his people for their return to their homeland. On May 28, 1868, General William D. Sherman and General Samuel F. Tappen called a council with the Navajo headmen Manuelito, Barboncito, Delgadito, Herrero, Armijo, Largo, and Torivo. Manuelito pleaded for his people to be allowed to return to the Chuska mountains. General Sherman offered them land in Indian territory in Oklahoma instead. After much debate it was finally decided that the Navajo would be allowed to return home. They were happy to agree to any terms just to be in their beloved lands again.

The new treaty was signed June 1, 1868, at Fort Sumner. The Navajo promised never to fight again and to remain on the 5,500 square mile reservation in their former homeland that the treaty provided for them. The U. S. government promised to provide sheep, goats, farm tools and a yearly clothing allowance, as well as schools for their children.

Home from Exile

In the early morning hours on June 18, 1868, more than 7,000 Navajo people began their six week journey home from exile. Manuelito was one of two men in charge of leading the people safely home. Once they were back in their familiar environment the Navajo began to rebuild their lives. The area of land that was allotted to them was much less than what they had been accustomed to before their forced evacuation. They were no longer free to roam between the four sacred mountains that had previously been their boundaries. The U. S. government was slow to follow through with their promises and the Indians had many setbacks with their crops.

To try to maintain some sense of order the people were divided into groups with appointed leaders. Barboncito was appointed head chief, and Manuelito and Ganado Mucho served as subchiefs. All three of them urged their people to live peacefully on the reservation and work hard to rebuild their herds and fields. Slowly the Navajo people began to recover and prosper. In 1870, Barboncito died and Ganado Mucho became head chief, while Manuelito became second in command. A Navajo police force, led by Manuelito, was established in 1872 to guard the reservation. He lived in an area the people called the "place dark with plants,"

which is now called Manuelito Springs. He was a popular leader, and his hogan was always full of his followers.

Even though Manuelito still commanded the respect of his people, the pressures of reservation made living difficult. After traders brought whiskey to the reservation, Manuelito began to drink. His last years were spent in and out of prison for drinking. Even so he continued to represent his people. In 1875, he traveled again to Washington, DC, to meet with President Ulysses S. Grant to discuss his concerns about the construction of the railroad through Navajo grazing lands. Before his death in the winter of 1893, he traveled to the World's Fair in Chicago, where he was once again impressed by the white man's accomplishments. His counsel to his people is recorded by Marie Mitchell in her book, *The Navajo Peace Treaty, 1868*. On his return home he advised his people for the last time, "The white men have many things we Navajo need but we cannot get them unless we change our ways. My children, education is the ladder to all our needs. Tell our people to take it."

Further Reading

Brown, Dee, *Bury My Heart at Wounded Knee,* Holt, 1970, pp. 11-33.
Dockstader, Frederick J., *Great North American Indians,* Van Nostrand Rheinhold, 1977, pp. 164-165.
Loh, Jules, *Lords of the Earth: A History of the Navajo Indians,* Crowell-Collier Press, 1971, pp. 9, 19, 23, 49, 87, 92, 104.
Mitchell, Marie, *The Navajo Peace Treaty, 1868,* Mason and Lipscomb, 1973, pp. 46, 73, 105, 122.
Native North American Almanac, edited by Duane Champagne, Gale, 1994, 1100.
Navajo Stories of the Long Walk Period, Navajo Community College Press, 1973.
Underhill, Ruth M., *The Navajos,* University of Oklahoma Press, 1956, pp. 119, 134, 142, 152, 206.
Waldman, Carl, *Who Was Who in Native American History,* Facts on File, 1990, pp. 219.
Wood, Leigh Hope, *The Navajo Indians,* Chelsea House, 1991, pp. 30. □

Alessandro Manzoni

Alessandro Manzoni (1785-1873) wrote *I promessi sposi*, or *The Betrothed*, Italy's most widely read novel. His works signaled the unique direction of Italian romanticism.

Alessandro Manzoni was born in Milan on March 7, 1785. His parents, elderly Count Pietro and young Giulia, separated shortly after his birth. Educated at religious schools, Manzoni subsequently joined his mother in Paris, where she was living. In that cosmopolitan atmosphere, imbued with the ideas of the Enlightenment, Manzoni came in contact with many of the great minds of Europe. His poems from this period include "On the Death of Carlo Imbonati" (1806), a contemplative elegy reflecting genuine fondness for his mother's Parisian lover.

Manzoni's Protestant marriage to Enrichetta Blondel in 1808 was reconsecrated according to Roman Catholic rites in 1810. Although many have spoken of his "conversion," it would be more appropriate to state that Manzoni outgrew his early anticlericalism and matured intellectually during the gradual return to his traditional faith. His *Inni sacri* (*Sacred Hymns*) constitutes the artistic representation of this rekindled spirit. These hymns, intended to commemorate Christian holidays, indicate Manzoni's desire to "bring those great, noble, human sentiments back to the fold of religion from which they stem." Although he had planned 12 hymns, only 5 were completed: "The Resurrection" (1812), "The Name of Mary" (1812-1813), "Christmas" (1813), "The Passion" (1814-1815), and "Pentecost" (1817), of which the last is considered artistically most successful. In all these are found Manzoni's Enlightenment views on human equality and the brotherhood of nations fused with the belief that religion and the Church have benefited mankind.

Dramatic Works

Manzoni's study of theater history, especially the works of Shakespeare in French translation, awoke in him the possibility of pursuing truth through dramatic works based on psychological realism. He sought plausible tragedies with protagonists whose sufferings would cause the viewer to meditate on life and the transcendent forces at work upon man. Insisting that such works must stem from reality and history—not from farfetched plots or actions—Manzoni wrote two important verse plays. *The Count of Carmagnola*

(1820) treats the Renaissance Italian warrior who, unfairly accused of betrayal, was condemned to death. However, in presenting this instance of extreme injustice that would emotionally move the spectator, he neglected character development in the count. Manzoni's preface to this play offered historical background and distinguished between invented and real characters in the belief that the essence of poetry lay in the reconstruction of the moral truths of history, not in the invention of detail or character.

Faulted for disregarding the traditional dramatic unities, Manzoni wrote a lengthy defense, "Letter to M. Chauvet on the Unities of Time and Place within the Tragedy" (1820), in which he held that all obstacles to the plausibility of a play (for example, obedience to classical rules) must be discarded. His next play, *Adelchi* (1822), omitted the prefatory historical clarifications, but Manzoni appended a commentary that provided the factual basis for this play on Adelchi, a Lombard prince compelled to wage war against Charlemagne. The essence of the drama concerns the inner conflict of the protagonist, torn between desires for revenge and Christian reconciliation, a dilemma posed by Charlemagne's repudiation of Princess Ermengarda, Adelchi's sister. Set in 722-774, this tragedy, lamenting political factionalism, stirred 19th-century Italians beset by similar civil strife.

Manzoni's quest for artistic truth was evidenced in numerous theoretical works, especially his letter of Sept. 23, 1823, to Cesare d'Azeglio, which clarifies Manzoni's views on what romanticism should be. Rejecting several literary clichés (among them the presence of witches and ghosts, the idolatrous use of mythology, and the servile imitation of foreign writers), Manzoni developed a romanticism that was fundamentally religious in feeling and held that a study of real things could lead to the discovery of historical and moral truths. This conception, differing greatly from that of other European romantics, brought Manzoni much closer to the realists of the following generation.

I promessi sposi

Manzoni began his masterpiece in 1823; it appeared after several revisions and title changes as *I promessi sposi* (1827). Aware of linguistic and other shortcomings, he dedicated the next 13 years almost exclusively to recasting this long novel, which achieved definitive form in 1840. This work, in which Manzoni assumes the role of editor of a discovered manuscript, affords him ample opportunity to reconstruct historically the events and circumstances of early-17th-century Italy and to give literary expression to his view of history and man.

The plot consists of the persistent attempts of Lucia and Renzo to marry despite the obstacles posed by the lustful, corrupt nobleman Don Rodrigo, whose machinations separate the young lovers and expose them to frequently melodramatic travails. Only at the end, when Manzoni has demonstrated that a firm faith in God can alleviate man's sufferings, does he eliminate the evil Rodrigo via the plague and permit Renzo and Lucia to marry in their native village, where they resume their interrupted lives 2 years later.

This mere summary cannot pay adequate tribute to Manzoni's subtle irony, satirical wit, historical knowledge, and extraordinary ability to create both major and minor characters to populate the universe that he so credibly brings to life.

Manzoni's important role in Italian letters stems from his discovery of a national prose language, his creation of the first modern Italian novel, and his giving literary expression to nascent nationalistic ideals. These triumphs overshadow the polemics surrounding the interpretations of religion and society in this work, in which Manzoni truly succeeded in capturing the spiritual essence of his nation.

Further Reading

The recommended translation of Manzoni's masterpiece, *The Betrothed,* is by Archibald Colquhoun (1951); it is complete and very readable and has the advantage of being based on Manzoni's last revised text. Joseph Francis de Simone, *Alessandro Manzoni: Esthetics and Literary Criticism* (1946), gives the most comprehensive English review of Manzoni scholarship and attempts to situate the artist in the literary environment of his time. Other studies are Archibald Colquhoun, *Manzoni and His Times* (1954), and Bernard Wall, *Alessandro Manzoni* (1954).

Additional Sources

Colquhoun, Archibald, *Manzoni and his times: a biography of the author of The Betrothed (I promessi sposi),* Westport, Conn.: Hyperion Press, 1979. □

Giacomo Manzù

The Italian sculptor Giacomo Manzù (born 1908) brought new vitality to the sculptural traditions of the past. He is best known for his relief sculptures, which give contemporary dimensions to Christian themes.

Born in Bergamo, the son of a convent sacristan, Giacomo Manzù was apprenticed to a carver and gilder at the age of 11. In 1928 he enrolled at the Institute of Art in Verona. The first period of Manzù's work (1928-1938) was one of research and experimentation, and he drew on a variety of sources: Donatello, the Romanesque high-relief doors of S. Zeno Maggiore in Verona, the archaic and Etruscan traditions, Auguste Rodin (whose work he discovered on a trip to Paris in 1936), and Medardo Rosso.

The range of materials employed also reflected the experimental nature of Manzù's early period. He used wrought iron, copper, silver, polychromed stucco, granite, and wax. The end of this early period also shows, in addition to the choice of wax, his great interest in the modeling properties of this material handled in Rosso's manner. *Red Mask* (1936) and *Susanna* (1937) are particularly representative of this trend.

Manzù's mature work dates from 1938, the year in which he turned to relief sculpture and first stated two

recurring themes: the Crucifixion and the cardinal. His eight reliefs entitled *Cristo nella nostra umanità* (1938/1939) were controversial images, criticized by both the Church and the Fascists because they depicted the crucified Christ in contemporary terms. The image of the cardinal addressed itself to a different set of sculptural problems: Manzù was concerned with modeling in the round, with large simple masses that emphasize the majesty of the churchman in his robes.

The *Crucifixion* relief Manzù executed in 1942 was restated in the 1950 commission of *Four Stations of the Cross* for the church of S. Eugenio in Rome. In 1951 he did the high reliefs for Antwerp's Middelheimpark (*Crucifixion* and *Entombment*). The most extensive elaboration of the Crucifixion motif appears in two series that are smaller in scale and shallower in relief: *Variations on the Theme of Cristo nella nostra umanità* (1947-1957) and *Variations on a Theme* (1955-1965).

The cardinal image also varied in scale and treatment, moving to life-size figures beginning in 1949. The degree of abstraction ranged from a 1948 *Cardinal* with greater attention to naturalistic details to a 1954 *Cardinal* with an angular orientation in space and obliteration of specific features.

Manzù became a professor at the Brera Academy of Fine Arts in Milan in 1940. Two years later he won the Grand Prix of the Quadriennale in Rome for *Francesca* (1941). Essentially a full-length portrait, *Francesca* represents the third set of themes Manzù handled: secular portraits and the female form. Included in this category are

Portrait of a Lady (1946), numerous studies of dancers, and the theme of the artist and his model. Manzù first portrayed the artist and model theme in 1942 in relief. Later he depicted the subject fully modeled in the round; the *Self-portrait with Model* (1946) is a representative example.

Manzù's work of the 1950s and 1960s included important public commissions, the majority being relief panels for European churches. Best known is the *Portal of Death,* the bronze doors for St. Peter's in Rome, completed in 1963. He won the international competition for the Portal in 1950. It portrays the deaths of saints and martyrs. Depicted on the inner side is the processional frieze *Inauguration of the Second Vatican Council.* Other doors executed by Manzù are the *Door of Love* for the Salzburg Cathedral, completed in 1958, and the portal reliefs for St. Laurents Church in Rotterdam, commissioned in 1966, the same year he was awarded the International Lenin Peace Prize.

Further Reading

The most complete book in English on Manzù's work is John Rewald, *Giacomo Manzù* (1967). The numerous plates, together with important biographical and bibliographic information, make this monograph extremely useful. Curtis Pepper, *An Artist and the Pope* (1968), is an informative appraisal of the St. Peter's commission based on personal recollections of the sculptor. See also Carlo Ludovico Ragghianti, *Giacomo Manzù, Sculptor* (1957). □

Mao Zedong

Mao Zedong (1893-1976) was a Chinese statesman whose status as a revolutionary in world history is probably next only to that of Lenin.

More than anyone else in recent times, Mao Zedong, with his supple mind and astute judgment, helped to reshape the social and political structures of his ancient and populous country. In doing so, Mao is likely to influence the destiny of the "third world" as well. Highly literate and sensitive, he was dedicated to a relentless struggle against inequality and injustice; thus at times he was capable of utter ruthlessness. He lived through reform and revolution in the early years of China's awakening nationalism, accepting at first the philosophies behind both movements. With the onset of the warlords' reaction after the revolution of 1911, disillusionment drove him to radicalism. This occurred at a time when Wilsonian self-determination was being ignored at the Paris Peace Conference and the messianic messages of the Russian October Revolution had attracted the attention of Chinese intellectuals, as China itself was passing through a period of traumatic cultural changes. Skeptical of Western sincerity and iconoclastic toward Confucianism, Mao sought inspiration from Marx's class struggle and Lenin's anti-imperialism to become a Communist.

Born in Hunan on Dec. 26, 1893, Mao Zedong did not venture outside his home province until he was 25. Up to

then, his formal education was limited to 6 years at a junior normal school where he acquired a meager knowledge of science, learned almost no foreign language, but developed a lucid written style and a considerable understanding of social problems, Chinese history, and current affairs. He was, however, still parochial in the sense that he had inherited the pragmatic and utilitarian tradition of Hunan scholarship with the hope that somehow it would help him in his groping for ways and means to strengthen and enrich his country.

Mao's visit to Peking in 1918 broadened his view. Although his life there was miserable, he was working under the chief librarian of Peking University, who was one of the pioneer Marxists of China. On his return to Hunan in the following year, Mao was already committed to communism. While making a living as a primary schoolteacher, he edited radical magazines, organized trade unions, and set up politically oriented schools of his own in the orthodox manner of Communist agitation among city workers and students. With the inauguration of the Chinese Communist party (CCP) in 1921, of which Mao was one of the 50 founder-members, these activities were pursued with added energy and to a greater depth.

Meanwhile, the major political party, the Kuomintang (KMT), was reorganized, and a coalition was formed between the KMT and CCP on antiwarlord and anti-imperialist principles. Mao's principal task was to coordinate the policies of both parties, an ill-suited role on account of his lack of academic and social standing. In 1925, when the coali-

tion ran into heavy weather, Mao was sent back to Hunan to "convalesce."

Champion of the Peasants

An unfortunate result of this rebuff was that he was completely left out of the nationwide strikes against Japan and Britain in the summer of that year, during which many of his comrades made their mark as leaders of the trade union movement or party politics. A by-product of his "convalescence" was that he discovered the revolutionary potential of the peasants, who had in such great numbers been displaced and pauperized by the misrule of the warlords. From then on Mao switched his attention to this vast underprivileged class of people. He studied them, tried to understand their grievances, and agitated among them.

Mao's newly acquired knowledge and experience enabled him to play a leading role in the peasant movement led by both the KMT and CCP. By 1927 he was in a position to advocate a class substitution in the Chinese Revolution. Instead of the traditional proletarian hegemony, Mao proposed that the poor peasants fill the role of revolutionary vanguard. Shortly after the publication of his *Report on the Peasant Movement in Hunan,* the KMT-CCP coalition broke up and the Communists were persecuted everywhere in the country.

Establishment of Soviets

Some survivors of the party went underground in the cities, to continue their struggle as a working-class party; the rest took up arms to defy the government and eventually to set up rural soviets in central and northern China. One of these soviets was Mao's Ching-kang Mountain base area between Kiangsi and Hunan, where he had to rely chiefly on the support of the poor peasants.

Under conditions of siege, the autonomy of these soviets threatened to disrupt the unity of the revolutionary movement, breaking it up into small pockets of resistance like premodern peasant wars. Doctrinally, this development was anything but orthodox Marxism. The center of the CCP, located underground in Shanghai, therefore assigned to itself the task of strengthening its leadership and party discipline. A successful revolution, in its view, had to take the course of a series of urban uprisings under proletarian leadership.

In its effort to achieve this, the center had to curb the growing powers of the soviet leaders like Mao, and it had the authority of the Comintern behind it. Its effort gradually produced results: Mao first lost his control over the army he had organized and trained, then his position in the soviet party, and finally even much of his power in the soviet government.

The Long March

The years of this intraparty struggle coincided with Chiang Kai-shek's successes in his anti-Communist campaigns. Eventually Chiang was able to drive the Communists out of their base areas on the Long March. The loss of nearly all the soviets in central China and crippling casualties and desertions suffered by the Communists in the first stages of the march were sufficient evidence of the ineptitude of the central party leadership. At the historic Tsunyi Conference of the party's Politburo in January 1935, Mao turned the tables against the pro-Russian leaders. On that occasion Mao was elected, thanks mainly to his support from the military, to the chairmanship of the Politburo.

During the low ebb of the revolutionary tide and the hardships of the Long March, those who might have challenged Mao fell by the wayside, largely through their own fault. By the time the Communists arrived at Yenan, the party had attained a measure of unity, to be further consolidated after the outbreak of the Sino-Japanese War in 1937. This was the first truly nationalist war China had ever fought, in which the nation as a whole united to face the common foe. However, from 1939 onward, as the war entered a long period of stalemate, clashes began to occur between KMT and Communist troops.

By early 1941 the united front between the KMT and CCP had come to exist in name only. This new situation called for the emergence of a Communist leader who could rival Chiang in his claim to national leadership in the event of a resumption of the civil war. But this could not be done so long as the CCP remained under the Russian wing.

Events in the early 1940s helped the CCP, in its search for independence, to become nationalistic. Russia, preoccupied with its war against Hitler, was unable to influence the CCP effectively, and soon the Comintern was dissolved. Mao seized this opportunity to sinicize the Chinese Communist movement in the famous rectification campaign of 1942-1944.

Leader of the Chinese Communists

The personality cult of Mao grew until his thought was written into the party's constitution of 1945 as a guiding principle of the party, side by side with Marxism-Leninism. Under Mao's brilliant leadership the party fought from one victory to another, till it took power in 1949.

Mao's thought now guided the Communists in their way of thinking, their organization, and their action. In giving their faith to Mao's thought, they found unity and strength, an understanding of the nature, strategy, and tactics of the revolution, a set of values and attitudes which made them welcome to the peasant masses, and a style of work and life which differentiated them from the bureaucrats and the romantic, culturally alienated intellectuals.

But Mao's thought had very little to say on the modernization and industrialization of China, on its socialist construction. Therefore, after 1949 the CCP was left to follow the example of Russia, with Russian aid in the years of the cold war. The importance, and relevance, of Mao therefore declined steadily while China introduced its first Five-Year Plan and socialist constitution. Once more the pro-Russian wing of the CCP was on the ascendancy, though still unable to challenge Mao's ideological authority. This authority enabled Mao to fight back by launching the Socialist Upsurge in the Countryside of 1955 and the Great Leap Forward in 1958. The essential feature of these movements was to rely upon the voluntary zeal of the people motivated by a new moral discipline, rather than upon monetary incentives, price mechanism, professionalism, and the legalism of gradual progress. The failure of the Great Leap Forward impaired Mao's power and prestige even further. His critics within the CCP attributed the failure to the impracticability of his mass line of socialist construction; in his own view, the failure was due to inadequate ideological preparation and, perhaps, abortive implementation by the pro-Russian wing of the CCP.

Cultural Revolution

At this juncture, the worsening Sino-Soviet dispute made its fatal impact. The condemnation of Russian ''revisionism'' cut the pro-Russian wing from its ideological source, and the withdrawal of Russian material aid practically sounded the death knell of China's attempt to emulate the Russian model. In the midst of this, Mao began his comeback.

The groundwork had been laid through the socialist education movement early in the 1960s, which started with the remolding of the People's Liberation Army under the command of Lin Piao. When this had been accomplished, Mao, with the help of the army and young students organized into the Red Guards, waged a fierce struggle against what he called the revisionists in power in his own party. This was the famous cultural revolution of 1966-1969. In this struggle it was revealed how elitist, bureaucratic, and brittle the CCP had become since 1949.

With Mao's victory in the cultural revolution, China became the most politicized nation of the world. No Chinese thought beyond the premises of Mao's thought—a state of affairs reminiscent of the Christianization of Europe in the Middle Ages. By this Mao hoped to whip up the unbound enthusiasm and altruistic spirit of the Chinese masses to work harder while enduring a frugal life. This may be the only way for a poor and populous country like China to accumulate enough capital for its rapid industrialization.

By the time Mao was in his late 70s, his lifework was essentially done, although he retained power until the end. Physically debilitated, suffering from a lifetime of effort and Parkinson's Disease, Mao's ability to rule in new and innovative ways to meet the demands of China's modernization grew increasingly enfeebled. To what degree his radical actions in his later years were due to his illness and age is a matter of debate among historians. His final years were marked by bitter maneuvering among his clique to succeed him upon his death. One of his final major acts was to reopen contact with the United States. In September of 1976, Mao died. Mao was undoubtedly the key figure in China in the 20th century and one of the century's most important movers and reformers. He had devoted his life to the advancement of a peasant class terrorized for centuries by those in power. However, in pursuit of his own goals, Mao himself could be violent and dictatorial. To Mao must go the credit for developing a revolutionary strategy of encircling the cities from the countryside, a mass line of political thought and application to bridge the chasm between the leaders and the led, and, finally, a strategy of permanent violent and nonviolent revolution to guard against the recurrence of that kind of bureaucratism which so far in history

has always emerged once a revolution is over and revolutionaries have turned into reformers.

Further Reading

Mao's own writings, *Selected Works* (4 vols., 1961-1965), *Selected Readings from the Works of Mao Tse-tung* (1967), and *Quotations from Chairman Mao* (1966; 2d ed. 1967), have all been published in English in Peking. For Mao's own writings also consult Anne Freemantle, *Mao Tse-tung: An Anthology of His Writings* (1954), and Jerome Ch'en, *Mao Papers: Anthology and Bibliography* (1970).

An understanding of the historical background of Mao's revolutionary activities is provided by Jerome Ch'en, *Mao and the Chinese Revolution* (1965). Another biography is Stuart Schram, *Mao Tse-tung* (1966; rev. ed. 1969). Edgar Snow's books *Red Star over China* (rev. ed. 1968), which contains Mao's autobiography, and *The Other Side of the River* (1962) are both excellent works on Mao and the Chinese Communist movement. A brief guide to Mao, his views, and other people's views of him is provided in Jerome Ch'en, *Mao* (1969). See also Harrison Salisbury's *The Long March* (1987); Dic, Wilson's *Mao Tse-tung in the Scales of History;* and Brantly Womack's *The Foundations of Mao Zedong's Political Thought 1917-1935* (1982).

Benjamin Schwartz, *Chinese Communism and the Rise of Mao* (1951), and Stuart Schram, *The Political Thought of Mao Tse-tung* (1963; rev. ed. 1969), are also outstanding works as is Siao-Yu, *Mao Tse-tung and I Were Beggars* (1961). Biographies of 500 leaders of the Communist movement in China, including Mao, are in Donald W. Klein and Anne B. Clark, *Biographic Dictionary of Chinese Communism, 1921-1965* (2 vols., 1971). □

Robert Mapplethorpe

Robert Mapplethorpe (1946-1989) was a controversial American photographer whose work centered on still lifes (mainly flower images), portraiture, and figurative work which was sexually explicit and sensual. A retrospective of his work in 1989 led to a reexamination of government support of the arts.

Robert Mapplethorpe was born in Floral Park, New York, in 1946. Although he found his middle-class upbringing and neighborhood somewhat confining, he responded with fascination to the Catholic ritual and mystery which were a part of his early years. This aspect of the Church influenced his entire life. It informed the haunted, mysterious quality of much of his art even though in later years he did not consider himself a religious person.

During the 1960s Mapplethorpe attended Pratt Institute in Brooklyn where he studied painting, drawing, and sculpture. His earliest recognition came from mixed media collages, done in the late 1960s and early 1970s, which incorporated magazine pictures of nudes.

Mapplethorpe soon began his own experiments with photography, first using a Polaroid. By the mid 1970s he considered himself a photographer. He had his first one-person show in 1976 at New York's Light Gallery, an exhibit which included Polaroid photos of flowers, portraits, and erotic images.

Mapplethorpe's notoriety came from a series of sexually explicit photographs of Manhattan's gay community which he made during the 1970s. The implied violence and sadomasochism of some of these images have caused some critics to label them pornography. Others feel that because Mapplethorpe was a part of the community which he recorded, he helped New York gays to define themselves in a positive way. The reaction to these photographs is very much the viewer's own, as Mapplethorpe included no moralizing commentary in his pictures.

From his earliest work in Polaroid, he went on to produce silver and platinum prints on both paper and canvas. He also worked with color photography and continued to produce photocollages and work in three dimensions, allowing his art to cross the line from photography into the realms of painting and sculpture.

There are three major themes in Robert Mapplethorpe's photographic work: still life, portraiture, and the figure. These themes remained constant from his earliest experiments in the medium to the end of his career.

Mapplethorpe's still lifes are mainly flower images— lilies, orchids, tulips, irises, birds of paradise— photographed in both color and black and white. The images are pristine and perfect, with a single blossom or a grouping of flowers isolated against a dark background. Both the structure and the texture of these subjects appealed to Mapplethorpe's sensibilities, and the sensuality of the images is arresting. Mapplethorpe spoke of a "black edge" to his flowers, rather than of their softness.

In the realm of portraiture, Mapplethorpe photographed many prominent contemporary figures, mainly artists and celebrities, including artist Andy Warhol, artist/ musician Laurie Anderson, singer Patti Smith, artist Louise Bourgeois, actress Kathleen Turner, actor Donald Sutherland, and fellow photographer Lord Snowdon. These cool, detached images reveal Mapplethorpe's careful way of working. Some have criticized them for being "slick," while others feel they are among the finest portrait photographs ever made. Mapplethorpe also created a series of self-portraits. Often sexually ambiguous or androgynous, these images chronicle the artist's maturation process.

Most controversial, of course, is Mapplethorpe's figurative work, which is also the most sexually explicit and sensual. Once again, an interest in gender ambiguity and androgyny is evident. In addition to the period of interest in specifically homoerotic subject matter, Mapplethorpe also pushed the limits of gender definition and identity in a photo essay made between 1980 and 1982 of the female body builder Lisa Lyon, in which he explored various "types" of representation of woman—goddess, temptress, bride, etc. Also noteworthy in his figurative work are his studies of African American males.

Mapplethorpe's work became increasingly respectable in the 1980s as it became less sexual and more classical. Always a formalist, his emphasis throughout his career was on clear, geometric composition and skillful manipulation

of studio lighting in order to bring out the subtle nuances of surface textures. Working in a controlled studio setting, he managed to freeze a moment in time.

Mapplethorpe drew inspiration from late 19th-and early 20th-century photography. He particularly liked the work of Julia Margaret Cameron, Nadar, Edward Weston, Man Ray, Cecil Beaton, and F. Holland Day.

Although his work deals with sex, violence, and race, three extremely sensitive and often confrontational themes, its pristine quality enables his photography to bridge the gap between provocative subject matter and artistic respectability. Today his photographs are in the permanent collections of most major art museums.

Robert Mapplethorpe died of AIDS on March 9, 1989. Soon after, his name came to be linked with controversies surrounding government support of the arts. In the summer of 1989 some members of Congress vocally opposed the use of National Endowment for the Arts funding in support of *Robert Mapplethorpe: The Perfect Moment* a retrospective exhibition which included some of Mapplethorpe's sexually explicit images. This spurred an ongoing debate not only about the use of government funds to support the arts, but also about censorship in general. The issue in question is whether the government should place restrictions on its arts funding based on the content of the work. In Washington, DC *The Perfect Moment* was canceled by the Corcoran Gallery of Art in 1989. The following year the Contemporary Arts Center in Cincinnati mounted an exhibit of Mapplethorpe's photographs that was challenged by local police. As controversial after death as he was during his lifetime, Mapplethorpe has become something of a symbol for artistic freedom in the late 20th century.

Further Reading

Janet Kardon's exhibition catalog, *Robert Mapplethorpe: The Perfect Moment* (1989), is a recent and well-documented source of information on Mapplethorpe's photography. It includes an exhaustive bibliography and an exhibition history as well as essays by Kardon, Kay Larson, and David Joselit and a dedication by Patti Smith. An earlier catalog, *Robert Mapplethorpe*, by Richard Marshall, was created for the photographer's first major retrospective at the Whitney Museum (1988). Among Mapplethorpe's own books are a monograph, *Robert Mapplethorpe* (1987), *Some Women* (1989), and *Black Book* (1986), as well as several collaborative efforts, the most noteworthy being *Certain People: A Book of Portraits* done with Susan Sontag (1985). □

Mustafā al-Marāghī

Shaykh (Sheik) Mustafā al-Marāghī (1881-1945) was an Egyptian jurist and educator who served twice as rector of al-Azhar University and was responsible for modernizing reforms in that institution.

Al-Marāghī was born in Marāghah, the village after which he is called; the village is headquarters of one of the administrative districts of Egypt. His father, Mustafā, was a shaykh (learned doctor) of al-Azhar and a qādī (judge of a religious court); the family is famous in Egypt for the pursuit of the qādī's profession. Because of his father's position the boy grew up in reasonably comfortable circumstances.

Al-Marāghī began his education in the village school, and he had memorized the Koran by age ten; his father then sent him to a shaykh in a neighboring village to learn the art of Koran recitation (tilāwah). Shortly after, he was sent to Cairo to study in al-Azhar, where he excelled in his work. By age 12 he was studying some of the most difficult books then being taught by the shaykhs of al-Azhar. As a student al-Marāghī was dissatisfied with the method of study used in al-Azhar; he felt that it would not lead students to an independent understanding of the subjects nor to proper comprehension of them. He banded together with a group of companions for self study of the classics of the Islamic tradition, which they felt would enlarge their knowledge and strengthen their general culture.

Al-Marāghī completed the 12-year course leading to the highest degree of al-Azhar in ten years, impressing his examining committee with his grasp of the subject matter and his comprehension of the problems involved. The chairman of the committee was the famous reformer Muhammad 'Abduh, whose ideas deeply influenced al-Marāghī's mental outlook. 'Abduh was also of much assistance to al-Marāghī in the latter's subsequent career.

In October 1904 al-Marāghī was appointed qādī in Dongola in the Sudan, but after only two years he was transferred to Khartoum where he occupied the second highest judicial post in the country. In September 1907 he returned to Egypt to take up service as an inspector of religious endowments in the Ministry of Religious Endowments. His responsibilities there included administration of mosques, and he was responsible for such reforms as improvement of the mosque baths and the formulation of a set of regulations for mosques.

He had done this work for less than one year when the government of Sudan requested that he be made Qādī alQudāt (chief qādī) of the country. He returned to Sudan in August 1908 and remained there until 1919. Al-Marāghī's greatest gift lay in the area of organization, and he effected important reforms in the system of religious courts in Sudan that made them function more smoothly. During this period he learned English and had close contacts with English administrators, some of whom spoke warmly of his abilities and personal qualities.

While in Sudan al-Marāghī had often requested to be allowed to return to Egypt, but the authorities had refused. When he did go home he went as chief inspector of the religious courts. Shortly after, in 1920, he became a judge in a religious court. In 1921 he became a member of the High Religious Court and finally in 1923 became its chief justice. In the latter position he was a leader in legal reform in Egypt, especially in the area of Muslim personal law.

In 1928 when the rectorship of al-Azhar fell vacant, the Egyptian prime minister chose al-Marāghī to fill the post. He was 48 years old, the youngest person ever to hold the office, and was not one of the select group of learned doctors known as the "high 'ulamā'." Al-Marāghī, it seems, actively sought the post, but the Azharīs considered him an outsider, and he had little support within the institution. His most significant accomplishment was the submission of a memo that resulted in reorganization of the institution. A distinction was made between pre-college and college level education, and three divisions were established at the college level: one for law, one for religion, and one for the Arabic language. Al-Marāghī's proposed reforms, however, went much beyond this reorganization, and he had to resign in 1929 because of opposition from the Khedive and conservative Azharī shaykhs who found his support for the ideas of Muhammad 'Abduh too radical. Of all that he had attempted, only the reorganization remained, but the era of real reform in al-Azhar may be considered to have begun with his efforts.

Al-Marāghī was appointed rector of al-Azhar for a second time in April 1935 after an interregnum of six years; he held the post until his death. Little had changed during the interval, and he began once more his work of reform. He created a section that specialized in the preparation of teachers to carry out instruction in the Amīrīyah Madrasah (palace school) and in the religious institutes of al-Azhar and a section that specialized in the preparation of teaching materials. The work in these sections extended over a five year period, and at the end the students received the doctorate of al-Azhar. He was also responsible for sending students abroad for higher studies to Britain, France, and Germany. Upon their return these individuals exerted great influence for the further reform of the university.

Al-Marāghī died in a hospital in Alexandria on August 22, 1948, and was buried in a special tomb near the shrine of Sayyidnā Nafīsah.

Al-Marāghī wrote extensively on a variety of subjects in the fields of politics, administration, and jurisprudence. His writings, however, are scattered, and there is no one comprehensive work that gives the gist of his thought.

Further Reading

Source materials for the life of al-Marāghī are available only in Arabic. There is a discussion of the reformist ideas that al-Marāghī shared with Muhammad 'Abduh in Albert Hourani, *Arabic Thought in the Liberal Age* (London, 1962). A detailed history of al-Azhar in the modern period and of al-Marāghī's role in its reform is available in Chris Eccel, *al-Azhar in Conflict and Accommodation* (Berlin, 1984). The laws enacted for the reform of al-Azhar may be studied in the various issues of *Revue des Études Islamiques* beginning with an article by Achille Sékaly in vol. 1, 1927. □

Jean Paul Marat

The French journalist and political leader Jean Paul Marat (1743-1793) was an influential advocate of extreme revolutionary views and measures.

Jean Paul Marat was born in Boudry, Neuchâtel, Switzerland, on May 24, 1743, the son of lower-middle-class parents. Of his early years very little is known. He acquired a medical education and for some years was a successful physician in both England and France. He also conducted scientific experiments in the fields of optics and electricity. But failure to achieve what he considered to be proper recognition for this work left him with a feeling of persecution.

Marat also published several books on philosophical and political themes, the most important of which was *The Chains of Slavery,* in which he voiced an uncompromising denunciation of royal despotism, a defense of the sovereignty of the people, and a sympathy for the poor and downtrodden which he never abandoned. The coming of the French Revolution in 1789 gave him his opportunity to pursue these themes, and before the year was out, he had begun to publish his journal, *Ami du peuple (Friend of the People).* In his opinion the moderate Revolution of 1789, although it had ended royal despotism, had left a new aristocracy of the rich in control, with the grievances of the poor still unsatisfied. Thus a radical revolutionary uprising

was necessary, in his opinion, and he bluntly called time and again for popular executions and a temporary dictatorship to save the Revolution and bring about a regime of social justice.

Marat's radical views and the ferocity with which he voiced them won him great popularity among the lower classes in Paris and the provinces. But he was the object of particular fear and hatred to those who supported the moderate revolution that had produced the limited monarchy. The authorities frequently tried to silence him, but he avoided arrest by hiding with the aid of his supporters and published his journal at least intermittently.

When the moderate experiment with limited monarchy failed in the midst of disastrous military reverses, the King was deposed in August 1792, and less than a month later the September massacres, an outbreak of popular executions such as Marat had been urging, took place in Paris. These events inaugurated the radical phase of the French Revolution. The Paris voters elected Marat to the Convention, which was to serve France as a legislature for the next 3 years, and he sat and voted with the "Mountain," the left-wing Jacobin faction. But he was blamed by many for the September massacres, and his continued incitement to direct action and purges, plus his advocacy of an extensive program of social legislation, kept all but the most radical aloof from him. His extreme ideas and language were matched by his informality of dress and unkempt appearance, which was heightened by the evidence of a chronic skin disease.

Marat concentrated his invective during the early months of 1793 against the moderate Girondin party, and they responded in kind. They tried to silence him and persuaded the Convention to decree his arrest and trial. But he emerged from hiding and by a brilliant speech won a triumphant acquittal in April 1793. His Girondin opponents now came under attack from the Jacobin Mountain, and Marat reached the height of his influence as he led the attack in his journal. With the decisive aid of the Paris masses, the Convention was forced to unseat and then order the arrest of the Girondin leaders (June 2, 1793).

Marat's triumph led ironically to his own death. Charlotte Corday, an idealistic young girl of Girondin sympathies from the provinces, came to Paris to seek revenge and to rid her country of the monster Marat. By this time his health had so deteriorated that he was living and working in seclusion in his apartment under a regimen of medicinal baths. On July 13, 1793, she managed to gain admittance to his apartment, under the pretense of bringing information to aid him in his continued campaign against the Girondins, and stabbed him to death in his bath.

Further Reading

The best biography of Marat in English is Louis Gottschalk, *Jean Paul Marat: A Study in Radicalism* (1927). The author emphasizes the ideas of Marat rather than the detailed facts of his career. There has not been a more recent scholarly biography in English. A much older and very laudatory biography is Ernest Belfort Bax, *Jean Paul Marat: The People's Friend* (1900).

Additional Sources

Germani, Ian, *Jean-Paul Marat: hero and anti-hero of the French Revolution,* Lewiston: F. Mellen Press, 1992. □

Franz Marc

The German painter Franz Marc (1880-1916) was a cofounder of the Blaue Reiter, or Blue Rider, an influential avant-garde art group.

Franz Marc was born on Feb. 8, 1880, in Munich, the son of a painter. At the age of 20 Franz entered the Munich Academy, which had a strong academic tradition. His earliest works show the influence of the decorative, linear Jugendstil that flourished in his youth.

In 1903 Marc made his first trip to Paris, where he came into contact with impressionism. He had originally intended to become a theologian, and he now carried his religious inclinations into his pictorial investigations, treating the shapes of nature as images filled with secret meaning. He used certain cubist formal elements to imbue his art with a kind of mystical constructivism. The animal images for which he is best known are the expression of his deep union with all creation. In 1907, fleeing from an undesirable marriage, Marc revisited Paris, where the paintings of Vincent Van Gogh made a deep impression on him.

In 1909, together with Wassily Kandinsky, Marc prepared the almanac *Der blaue Reiter.* He discovered the great possibilities of color as a means of expression in 1910 through August Macke, who was fascinated by the Fauves. In the same year Marc moved to Sindelsdorf, where he had his first exhibition. When, in 1911, Kandinsky's Neue Künstlervereinigung (New Artists' Federation) broke up, Marc, Kandinsky, Alfred Kubin, and Gabriele Münter exhibited on December 18 in the Galerie Tannhauser as the Blaue Reiter group. This show marks one of the most important dates of the German modern movement.

From then on Marc went his own way, deepening his vision into a kind of nature symbolism. Even his colors were conceived in a symbolic manner. In the series of animal paintings of 1911, of which *Red Horses* is the best known, Marc detached color from nature and gave it a radiant independent life. In 1912 he met Robert Delaunay, whose Orphism was an important source of inspiration to Marc. His large animal compositions of 1912-1913, such as *Tower of the Blue Horses* and *Animal Destinies,* radiate great power. *Tirol* (1913-1914) offers a complex dynamics in which landscape and light, planes and lines interact. In 1914 Marc took a step toward emotional abstractionism in paintings with titles such as *Serene, Playful,* and *Struggling.*

Marc entered the army when World War I broke out. He stopped painting, but he kept a sketchbook in which he depicted problems of growth, such as *Plant Life Coming into Being* and *Arsenal for Creation.* On March 4, 1916, he was killed at Verdun.

Further Reading

Most of the literature on Marc is in German. Klaus Lankheit, *Franz Marc: Watercolours, Drawings, Writings* (1950; trans. 1960), is a useful work. Background studies include Werner Haftmann and others, *German Art of the Twentieth Century,* edited by Andrew C. Ritchie (1957), and Haftmann's *Painting in the Twentieth Century,* vol. 1 (trans. 1960; 2d ed. 1965); Bernard S. Myers, *The German Expressionists: A Generation in Revolt* (1957); Peter Selz, *German Expressionist Painting* (1957); and Franz Roh, *German Art in the 20th Century* (1958; trans. 1968).

Additional Sources

Marc, Franz, *Letters from the war,* New York: P. Lang, 1992.
Levine, Frederick S., *The apocalyptic vision: the art of Franz Marc as German expressionism,* New York: Harper & Row, 1979. □

Marcel Marceau

Marcel Marceau (born 1923) has been acknowledged as the world's greatest practitioner of pantomime. He revived this ancient form of acting and created a new school to train young people who aspired to follow his style.

Marcel Marceau was born in Strasbourg, France, on March 22, 1923. His father, Charles, was a butcher and his mother, Ann, née Werzberg, was a native Alsatian. Later the family moved to Lille where his father also raised pigeons on the roof. Marcel remembered in his mature years that he was raised hearing the sound of wing beats. The sound enchanted him; so did silent films. Marceau once commented, "When I was five years old my mother took me to see Charlie Chaplin's moving pictures. . . . I sat entranced. . . . It was then that I decided to become a mime." Borrowing his father's pants and using ink to paint on a moustache, he tried to imitate the famous comedian of the silent screen. Soon he began imitating birds, plants, trees, and eventually people. Encouraged by his parents, he turned to a career in the theater. Much later—in 1967—he met Chaplin for the first time, only briefly between planes at Paris' Orly Airport, where they expressed their mutual admiration. He was deeply touched. When parting he brought the old man's hands to his lips and kissed them.

Marceau returned to Alsace, where he entered the Lycée Fustel de Coulanges. But he was unable to complete his training. In 1940, just ahead of the German invaders, he sought refuge in Limoges. There he studied ceramics, and at the age of 17 he won the Masson prize for his enamel work. He also studied oratory with Dorsanne. The war, however, brought personal tragedy. His father was seized by the Germans and died in Auschwitz. Marcel joined his brother in the resistance movement; his activities consisted of mak-

ing fake ration cards and smuggling children into Switzerland.

When the police began to close in, Marceau fled to Paris where a cousin saved him by placing him in the Maison d'Enfants de Sèvres, an orphanage. There Marceau taught dramatics. In his spare time he also began studying with Charles Dullin in the Sarah Bernhardt Theatre. He also came under the tutelage of the master of mime, Etienne Decroux, of whom he said, "He was a kind of Christ. . . . In his class we dedicated our bodies to the discipline of silence." The art of pantomime did not attract many students, and even fewer spectators; in fact, the children of the Maison de Sèvres were his first audience. Small wonder that he came to believe that chiefly the young understood his art. Decroux was his most critical admirer and told him, "Marceau, you are a born mime." He interrupted his studies in December, 1944, to join the French army. In Germany he played in a military theater before troops until he was demobilized in 1946. Immediately he returned to playing minor roles at the Sarah Bernhardt Theater. As a member of the Decroux Company he put on his first mimodrama, "Praxitele and the Golden Fish," which won enough praise to launch his career.

In 1947 Marceau set up his own company at the Theatre de Poche (Pocket Theatre), a tiny hall with only 80 seats. Here he created his own whitefaced clown, Bip, a name he derived from the youngster Pip in Charles Dickens' novel *Great Expectations*. Bip's costume consisted of a broken top hat with a red flower and striped pull-over middy to symbolize the gaiety of Paris streets and white pants. Bip first appeared on Marceau's 24th birthday in "Bip and the Street Girl." Pantomime did not attract large audiences at first, and he had to perform in cabarets to earn enough to live on until he won success in 1952 with "Pierrot of Montmartre" in the 1,200 seat Sarah Bernhardt Theatre. By this time Marceau had attained fame beyond the confines of Paris and France. In 1949 his company toured Israel and Holland, in 1951 it played in Berlin, in 1955 the United States and Canada. Beginning in New York, the tour—originally scheduled for two weeks—lasted three months. This enabled him to become famous not just in Europe, but throughout the world. "When I went back to Paris after being a hit on Broadway in 1955, everything changed for me. It was a new, almost frightening experience," he recalled in the *New York Times*.

Marceau also found himself involved in other media. Television offered him vast audiences; he even won two Emmy Awards from the Academy of Television Arts and Sciences, and showed himself to be articulate when he was interviewed. Through his work, Marceau obtained a knighthood in the French Legion of Honor, an officer's rank in the National Order of Merit, and a comedy rank in the National Order of Arts and Letters of France. He appeared in six feature films, among them *Barbarella* (1968), *Shanks* (1974), in which he played the leading role, and *Silent Movie*. He also wrote a novel, *Pimparello*.

Marceau truly became a worldwide figure, eventually giving 18,000 performances in over a hundred countries. Marceau's original mime company disbanded in 1964, but in the 1980s a subsidy from the French government enabled him to form a new company, with graduates from his Paris mime school. The latter was founded in 1978, and instructed students in the art of mime. Among the often-sophisticated plots Marceau used in his performances were adaptations of Gogol's *The Overcoat* and Kafka's *The Trial*. He acknowledged owing a great deal to the silent comics, including Chaplin, Buster Keaton, and Harold Lloyd. Marceau summed up his career in the *New York Times* by commenting, "The art of mime is an art of metamorphosis. . . . [Y]ou cannot say in mime what you can say better in words. You have to make a choice. It is the art of the essential. And you cannot lie. You have to show the truth."

Further Reading

Biographies of Marceau in English include Ben Martin's *Marcel Marceau: Master of Mime* (1979); and in French Guy and Jeanne Verrient-Lefert's *Marcel Marceau ou l'aventure du silence* (Desclé and De Brouwer, 1974) which consists of a very long interview with Marceau; There is also information in Pierre Ricky's *Jeu Silencieux* (edition de l'Amicole, 1970), a study of pantomime. Critical evaluations of him can be found in the *New York Times* (September 18th, 1955); *New Yorker* (October 15th, 1955); *Horizon* (April, 1978); *People* (February 12th, 1979); and *New York Times* (December 2nd, 1993). □

Gabriel Marcel

French philosopher Gabriel Marcel (1889-1973) described man's place in the world in terms of such fundamental human experiences as relationships, love, fidelity, hope, and faith. His brand of existentialism was said to be largely unknown in the English-speaking world, where it was mistakenly associated with that of Jean-Paul Sartre. Marcel's view of the human condition was that "beings" are beset by tension, contradiction and ambiguity. He was also interested in life's religious dimension and was considered the first French existentialist philosopher.

Gabriel Marcel was born in Paris on Dec. 7, 1889, the only child of a distinguished diplomat. His mother died when he was 4, and he was raised by an aunt whom his father married. Although he had little visual memory of his mother, Marcel described her continued "spiritual presence" during his youth as an important influence on his thoughts—giving rise to an awareness of the "hidden polarity between the seen and the unseen." At the age of 8 he began writing plays, and as an adult he would achieve a reputation as a playwright as well as a philosopher. Marcel's plays, which flesh out the basic issues of his philosophy, were performed in the early 1920s. Starting in his youth he also displayed a keen ability to play music—an avocation which would also influence his thinking.

Moved Away From Traditional Philosophy

Marcel received his degree in philosophy from the Sorbonne in 1910 and married professor Jacqueline Boegner in 1919. Together they adopted a son, Jean. Marcel lived and taught for a time in Switzerland, where he began writing his *Metaphysical Journal* (1927). The journal reflects a movement away from traditional academic philosophy and was influenced by Sören Kirkegaard, in whom Marcel was deeply interested. In some ways, the book is overlooked in serious examinations of Marcel. Another publication from Marcel's diaries was *Being and Having* (1935).

Developed "Spirit of Abstraction"

During World War I Marcel was a Red Cross official whose job was obtaining news of wounded and missing soldiers and contacting their relatives. These intensely demanding encounters with people were a living source of Marcel's highly concrete and personalistic philosophy, and of his lifelong suspicion of what he called the "spirit of abstraction."

During the war Marcel wrote his thorough study of the American philosopher Josiah Royce, *Royce's Metaphysics* (1956), and taught at the Lycée Condorcet in Paris. He taught philosophy at the University of Sens (1919-1923) and then returned to Paris, where he continued his philosophy research, wrote plays, and contributed to leading periodicals as both a philosopher and a theater critic.

Converted to Catholicism

Marcel's philosophy was always preoccupied with the religious dimension of life, but his upbringing had been religiously agnostic (uncertain as to whether one can really know that God exists), and he was not formally a believer. In 1929, however, an open letter from the distinguished French Catholic writer François Mauriac challenged Marcel to admit that his views suggested a belief in God. His subsequent conversion to Catholicism gave a new dimension to certain aspects of his philosophy. But he remained a strikingly independent thinker whose ideas were formed before his conversion—and as such could be regarded as important indicators of certain Godly aspects of the human experience. Marcel became a leader in French Catholic intellectual circles, and his Paris home was the locale for stimulating discussion among leading European intellectuals of all persuasions.

Was Compared to Sartre

During World War II Marcel lived in Lyons. After the war he lectured in France and other countries. Following the war his "Christian existentialism" aroused sharp contrasts between his work and the atheistic existentialism of Jean-Paul Sartre. Marcel was fond of improvising at the piano throughout his adult life, but it wasn't until 1945 that—with his wife's encouragement—he undertook to write formal compositions. His wife died in 1947. Marcel continued his creative endeavors, however, as well as teaching and traveling.

Late in life Marcel became associated with Moral Re-Armament, which he discussed in *Fresh Hope for the World: Moral Re-Armament in Action* (1960). Among his chief philosophical works are *The Mystery of Being* (1951); the Gifford Lectures for 1949-1950 at the University of Aberdeen; *Homo Viator* (1951); *Man Against Mass Society* (1951); *Being and Having* (1957); *The Existential Background of Human Dignity* (1963); and the William James Lectures at Harvard for 1961-1962.

At the Frankfort Book Fair in 1964, Marcel received major international recognition in the form of the German Peace Prize. He died in Paris on Oct. 8, 1973.

Marcel's essential dramatic and philosophical insights can be summarized in the difference between a problem and a mystery. He believed that once a problem is solved it is dismissed from consciousness, whereas a mystery always remains alive and interesting. Problems, Marcel believed, are resolved using "primary reflection"—which is abstract, analytical and objective. Mysteries, on the other hand, are approached with "secondary reflection," which concerns itself with deeper personal insights.

Along with Martin Buber, Marcel is one of the founders of 20th-century dialogue-oriented I-Thou philosophy.

Other philosophical writings of Gabriel Marcel include: *The Philosophy of Existence* (1948); *The Decline of Wisdom* (1955); *Philosophical Fragments* (1965); *The Funeral Pyre* (1965); *Searchings* (1967); *Problematic Man* (1967); *Presence and Immortality* (1967); *Tragic Wisdom and Beyond; Including Conversations Between Paul Ricoeur and Gabriel Marcel* (1973); and *The Participant Perspective: A Gabriel Marcel Reader* (published 1987).

Dramatizations include: *Three Plays: (A Man of God, Ariadne,. The Votive Candle)* (1965); *Double Expertise* (translated to English, 1985); and *Fanal: Two Plays by Gabriel Marcel* (translated to English, 1988).

Further Reading

Further information on Marcel is in Vincent Miceli, *Ascent to Being: Gabriel Marcel's Philosophy of Communion* (Desclee, 1965); Seymour Cain, *Gabriel Marcel* (Hillary House, 1963); Sam Keen, *Gabriel Marcel* (John Knox Press, 1967); Kenneth T. Gallagher, *The Philosophy of Gabriel Marcel* (Fordham University Press, 1962); Clyde Pax, *An Existential Approach to God: A Study of Gabriel Marcel* (Martinus Nijhoff, 1972); François Lapointe, *Gabriel Marcel and His Critics* (Garland Pub., 1977); Hilda Lazaron, *Gabriel Marcel the Dramatist* (Smythe, 1978); Joe McCown, *Availability: Gabriel Marcel and the Phenomenology of Human Openness* (Scholars Press for the American Academy of Religion, 1978); Neil Gillman, *Gabriel Marcel on Religious Knowledge* (University Press of America, 1980); Pietro Prini, *Gabriel Marcel* (Economica, 1984); Paul Arthur Schlipp and Lewis Edwin Hahn, eds., *The Philosophy of Gabriel Marcel* (essays) (Open Court Publishing Co., 1984); A.J.L. Busst, ed., *French Literature and the Philosophy of Consciousness: Phenomenological Essays by Ian W. Alexander* (University of Wales Press, 1984); Ved Prakash Gaur, *Indian Thought and Existentialism: With Special Reference to the Concept of Being in Gabriel Marcel and the Upanisads* (Eastern Book Linkers, 1985); Katharine Rose Hanley, *Dramatic Approaches to Creative Fidelity: A Study in the Theater and Philosophy of Gabriel Marcel* (University Press of America, 1987); David Applebaum, *Contact and Attention: The Anatomy of Gabriel Marcel's Metaphysical Method* (Center for Advanced Research in Phenomenology, 1987); Donald Traub, *Toward a Fraternal Society A Study of Gabriel Marcel's Approach to Being, Technology and Intersubjectivity* (P. Lang, 1988); Mary D. Howland, *The Gift of the Other: Gabriel Marcel's Concept of Intersubjectivity in Walker Percy's Novels* (Duquesne University Press, 1990); Denis P. Moran, *Gabriel Marcel: Existentialist Philosopher, Dramatist, Educator* (University Press of America, 1992); and Gerald Hanratty, *Studies in Gnosticism in the Philosophy of Religion* (Four Courts Press, 1997).

The Harry Ransom Humanities Research Center, University of Texas-Austin, maintains seven boxes of archival documentation related to Marcel. They are available to researchers.

The following are scholarly articles on Gabriel Marcel: Thomas C. Anderson, "The Nature of the Human Self According to Gabriel Marcel" *Philosophy Today* (Winter 1985); Joseph Godfrey, "Appraising Marcel on Hope" *Philosophy Today* (Fall 1987); Preston Browning, "Walker Percy and Gabriel Marcel: The Dialectical Self in The Moviegoer" *Renascence* (Summer 1988); Thomas Michaud, "Secondary Reflection and Marcelian Anthropology" *Philosophy Today* (Fall 1990); and Danne W. Polk, "Gabriel Marcel's Kinship to Ecophilosophy" *Environmental Ethics* (Summer 1984). □

Jean-Baptiste Marchand

Jean-Baptiste Marchand (1863-1934) was a French soldier who led an expedition from the Atlantic coast

of Africa to the Nile River in order to expand French territory. He was confronted by the British at the Sudanese town of Fashoda and forced to retreat.

Jean-Baptiste Marchand was born in the little French town of Thoissey in eastern France north of the city of Lyons. His family was poor, and he was forced to quit school after the first year of high school (lycée). He was apprenticed to a notary at the age of 13 and worked there until the death of his mother when he was 20. He enlisted in the French Army on October 1, 1883. He was promoted to corporal on April 1, 1884 and then progressed to sergeant. His superiors thought so highly of him that he was sent to officer training school in 1886 and returned to his former regiment as a second lieutenant in March 1887.

In January 1888 Marchand was sent to serve in France's colony of Senegal in west Africa. At that time France was engaged in a colonial war to expand its empire throughout west Africa. In what is now Mali, there was a war going on with the Tukulors. Marchand distinguished himself in his first combat, helping to capture the Tukulor stronghold of Koundian in early 1889. In April 1890 he took part in the capture of the fortress of Segu, was promoted to lieutenant and awarded the Legion of Honor. On February 21, 1891 he was wounded in the assault on the Tukulor capital of Jenné.

Following the defeat of the Tukulor, Marchand joined the campaign against another foe of French imperialism, Samori Turé, in Guinea. He fought in battles against Turé

from April 1891 to the end of 1894. He was wounded in the Battle of Bonua in November 1894 in which Turé's forces defeated the French in spite of the notable bravery of Marchand. Marchand returned to France on June 14, 1895.

On Marchand's return to France, he almost immediately began agitating for a plan that he had conceived with his French colleagues in Africa. He proposed to lead an expedition from France's settlement of Brazzaville on the Congo River across Africa to the Nile, thereby winning for France control of the upper Nile and eventually linking it with France's outpost on the Red Sea at Djibouti by forming an alliance with Ethiopia.

The upper Nile had been originally explored by British explorers such as John Hanning Speke and Samuel Baker. An Anglo-Egyptian government had been imposed on the Sudan that reached as far south as the sources of the Nile in what is now Uganda. That government had been led by Charles "Chinese" Gordon and had used such agents as Charles Chaillé-Long and Emin Pasha to control the upper Nile. But all of that had been wiped out by the Muslim forces of "El-Mahdi" in 1885. Marchand now proposed to step into the confused situation along the Nile by replacing British power with French. In effect, it was a French imperialist design to control the sources of the Nile by taking over a band stretching from the Atlantic on the west to the Red Sea on the east. This would counter, and derail, British attempts to control Africa from north to south: from "the Cape to Cairo."

Marchand presented his ideas at a meeting with the French Foreign Minister on July 18, 1895. He then submitted a detailed proposal to the Ministry of Colonies on September 11, 1895. During this period, governments in France changed frequently. One of the main political divisions was between the colonialist faction that thought that France should make itself stronger following its defeat by Germany in the Franco-Prussian War of 1870 by expanding outside of Europe—in Africa and Asia. The other side thought that France should not weaken itself by using its forces overseas while the main struggle was in Europe. Marchand happened to make his proposals at a time when the imperialists were in control and when they were not too worried about offending the British, who they knew were trying to defeat the Mahdi and return to the upper Nile. On February 24, 1896, therefore, Marchand's proposal was tentatively agreed to, and this was approved by the Prime Minister on April 7.

In the meantime, Marchand had been making preparations, and the first of four detachments of officers and supplies left France on April 24, 1896. Marchand himself sailed on June 25. They traveled to the small port of Loango in the French Congo, where Marchand arrived in August. The governor of the French Congo at the time was Pierre Savorgnan de Brazza, a native Italian who had explored the Congo and had founded France's colony along the great river.

When Marchand reached Loango, he found that it was impossible to move his supplies inland to the Congo River port of Brazzaville because there was a revolt by the Basundi and Bakongo tribes against the French. Marchand was in a hurry, and on August 18, 1896 he convinced Brazza to declare martial law in the Congo with Marchand in control. He then organized his French officers and Senegalese soldiers into a campaign against the rebels. Some of the rebel leaders were captured and executed on October 17. The last resistance to Marchand ended on December 12, by which time he was in Brazzaville. The rest of his men and supplies caught up with him by the end of February 1897.

Marchand was now faced with a problem. The French had no transport adequate to carry the supplies up the Congo. They requested help from the Belgians who ruled the other side of the river from Léopoldville (now Kinshasa). The Belgians initially refused, but new orders came from Brussels and the use of the steamship *Ville de Bruges* was approved. It made two trips with Frenchmen and supplies up the Congo as far as it was possible to navigate. The first one left Brazzaville on January 13, 1897, and the second followed with Marchand, sick with malaria, on board on March 10, 1897. They were deposited in the village of Zinga and then had to proceed up the Ubangi River to Bangui (now the capital of the Central African Republic) in 72 dugout canoes. They reached Bangui in early April.

From Bangui the expedition traveled 450 miles to Ouango, the last outpost before the Mbomu Rapids. At this point, Marchand seized a small riverboat, the 50-foot long *Faidherbe* to take with him to the Nile with the plan of floating it down the Nile with the French flag flying. Since they had reached the limit of navigation, the *Faidherbe* had to be totally disassembled and hauled overland by the African porters, each carrying a 55-pound load. This considerably slowed down the progress of the expedition. Fortunately, along the way the French discovered two other streams, the Mboku and the Méré, by which the *Faidherbe* could be sailed 160 miles farther. At that point, Marchand had a road 100 miles long built to carry the pieces of the boat from Méré to Khojali. Once they reached Khojali in November, they realized they would have to wait until the spring rains before they would be able to proceed any farther. In the meantime Marchand sent part of the force ahead to build a French post near the present Sudanese city of Wau.

While they were waiting for the rains to come, Marchand and other members of his force went exploring in different directions throughout the southern Sudan. It was not until June 4 that the boat reached the new French outpost, and it was possible to continue on the Sué River, a tributary of the Nile. After sailing for seven days they reached a vast swamp, the Sudd, and it took them until June 25 before they could fight their way out onto the Bahr-el-Ghazal, a bigger river flowing into the White Nile. They reached the little village of Fashoda on the Nile on July 10, 1898. Later that day the French force took possession of a fort a little ways outside of the town that had been abandoned by Egyptian troops years before.

The next day, Marchand had a formal ceremony raising the French flag over the fort of Fashoda and thereby claimed that part of the Nile valley for France. Significantly, on their first attempt to raise the flag, the flagpole broke. They were then able to celebrate Bastille Day, July 14, in their new outpost. On August 25 they were surprised by an attack of Mahdist forces, but the French easily drove them away with no loss of life. They were soon faced, however, with a much more serious challenge. The British arrived on September 19.

A joint Anglo-Egyptian force under the command of Lord Kitchener had been fighting the Mahdists since 1896. At the Battle of Omdurman on September 2, 1898, they had destroyed the power of the Sudanese in their capital and restored the country to Anglo-Egyptian control. Kitchener had immediately headed up the Nile after his victory to oust the French from Fashoda. At a famous meeting on September 19, 1898, Kitchener demanded that Marchand withdraw. Marchand refused. The matter was then referred to the two governments in London and Paris.

The news of the confrontation at Fashoda drove the newspapers of both countries into a nationalistic frenzy. The British began threatening the French with recriminations. In the midst of this, the French government sent a message to Marchand by way of a British Nile steamer that reached him on October 9. It announced his promotion to major and ordered him to send an officer to Paris to report on the expedition. When that officer reached Paris on October 27, he found the French government in the midst of backtracking. It realized that it did not have the wherewithal to confront the British government nor the means of supplying Marchand by his impractical overland route. Marchand himself took a British steamer down the Nile to Cairo, where he arrived on November 3 to communicate with his government by telegram. The next day, he received instructions from Paris to evacuate.

A furious Marchand spent the next several days arguing with his superiors in Paris. He was then ordered to return to Fashoda and carry out his instructions. The only concession granted was that he was not required to accept the humiliating offer of the British to evacuate the French soldiers on British steamships down the Nile. They were allowed to continue their march eastward through Ethiopia to the French port of Djibouti. Marchand arrived back in Fashoda on December 4, 1898. The French troops played the "Marseillaise" and struck the tricolor flag on the morning of December 12 and marched out of the fort of Fashoda.

They reached Addis Ababa on March 9, 1899. They arrived in Djibouti on May 16 and embarked for France on a steamship sent to pick them up. On their return to Paris at the end of May, they were met by enormous crowds who cheered the French heroes. The popular sentiment was used by French nationalists to try to bring down the government. This attempt failed, and Marchand and his force marched together for the last time on the parade to celebrate Bastille Day, 1899. Marchand then was reintegrated into the French Army where he continued to make a name for himself. He was promoted to general and fought with notable success in World War I. He died in Paris in 1934.

The "Fashoda Incident" was one of the major turning points in modern European history. The failure at Fashoda taught the French that they would never be able to achieve their goals without the support of Great Britain. The country's leaders therefore started a conscious policy of befriending the government in London and quickly settled all the major problems it had with the British. The two countries signed a treaty of friendship, the "Entente Cordiale" in 1904. This eventually led to a military alliance that pitted France and Britain against Germany in World War I.

Further Reading

There is a very good summary in English of the Marchand expedition and the Fashoda crisis, based largely on secondary sources: David Levering Lewis, *The Race to Fashoda: European Colonialism and African Resistance in the Scramble for Africa* (New York: Weidenfield & Nicolson, 1988; also available in paperback.) A very detailed study in French, based on primary sources is Marc Michel, *La Mission Marchand, 1895-1899* (Paris: Mouton, 1972). For the diplomatic repercussions of the Fashoda Incident, see William L. Langer, *Diplomacy of Imperialism, 1890-1902*, 2nd edition (New York: Alfred A. Knopf, 1965) and Charles Andres, *Théophile Delcassé and the Making of the Entente Cordiale* (London: Macmillan, 1968). □

Rocky Marciano

Boxer Rocky Marciano (1923-1969), who held the heavyweight boxing title for four years during the 1950s, is the only boxing champion to ever retire undefeated.

Certain names always come up, and always will come up, when boxing fans discuss the question of who was the greatest heavyweight boxing champion of all time. Muhammad Ali, Joe Louis, Jack Dempsey are all names which have their supporters. So is Rocky Marciano, who held the title for four years in the 1950s and who has one accomplishment no other heavyweight champ can claim: He is the only one ever to retire undefeated.

Boxing Not First Choice

Marciano was born Rocco Francis Marchegiano on September 1, 1923 in Brockton, Massachusetts. His father, Pierino, worked at a shoe factory. His mother's name was Pasqualena, and Rocky would spend much of his life making sure she didn't have to live in the poverty Rocky knew growing up. Rocky was a typical American kid growing up, playing baseball and football and dreaming of a professional career in one of those sports. He didn't take up boxing until after 1943, when he was drafted into the army. He took the sport up mainly as a way to avoid KP (assisting the cooks) and other less desirable activities, but he showed a natural ability and fought as an amateur following his discharge in 1946.

Tries Baseball

In 1947 Marciano had a tryout with the Chicago Cubs as a catcher, but was let go because he couldn't make the throw from home plate to second base with accuracy. It was

the end of his baseball dreams, and the following year he turned professional in the ring. By the spring of 1949 his boxing skills had garnered some attention, as he knocked out his first 16 opponents. The quality of his opponents improved over the latter half of 1949 and 1950, but Marciano continued to beat all comers, knocking out most of them.

Proved Doubters Wrong

There were those who thought not much would become of the 190-pound heavyweight from Brockton in the early days, however. Goody Petronelli, noted fight trainer, caught one of his early fights and recalled for *Sports Illustrated*, "I never thought he'd make it. He was too old, almost 25. He was too short, he was too light. He had no reach. Rough and tough, but no finesse." The hometown folks became believers, though, traveling in groups to Marciano's fights in nearby Providence, Rhode Island and yelling "Timmmmberrr" when Rocky had an opponent ready to go down.

Boxing Technique

The trainer Charley Goldman taught Marciano his trademark technique, which would serve him well as champion. Legendary trainer Angelo Dundee remembered for *Sports Illustrated* Goldman telling him for the first time about his new young fighter: "So Charley told me, 'Ange, I gotta guy who's short, stoop-shouldered, balding, got two left feet and God, how he can punch!'" He went on, "Charley taught the technique that if you're tall, stand taller. If you are shorter, make yourself smaller. Charley let him bend his knees completely in a deep knee squat. He was able to punch from that position, come straight up from the bag and hit a heck of a shot. . . . It was just *bang-bang-bang-bang-BANG* and get him outta there. And he was the best-conditioned athlete out there.''

Marciano Defeats Joe Louis

On October 26, 1951, with 37 wins and 32 knockouts under his belt, Marciano faced his most formidable opponent in former heavyweight champion Joe Louis. Louis was past his prime and when Marciano knocked him out in the eighth round, he had such mixed feelings at beating his hero that he cried in Louis's dressing room after the fight. Sentiment aside, however, the fight established Marciano as one of the marquee fighters in the heavyweight division, and assured him of a title shot before too long.

Takes the Belt from Jersey Joe

Five fights later, on September 23, 1952, he got that chance. Jersey Joe Walcott was the defending champion and Marciano the challenger when the pair met in Philadelphia. Marciano pulled out a victory which would be remembered as typical of his tough-guy, never-say-die style: Way behind on points and struggling offensively all night, he caught Walcott with a short, overhand right on the jaw in the 13th round which knocked him unconscious, giving Marciano the championship belt.

Marciano only defended the title six times, but some of those fights are considered classics by boxing fans. He knocked out Walcott in the first round of their rematch in 1953, then knocked out Roland La Starza later that year. He won a decision against Ezzard Charles in 1954, and almost lost his title in their rematch later that year. In the sixth round Charles cut Marciano's nose so badly his cornerman couldn't stop the bleeding. With the ring doctor watching the cut closely and considering stopping the fight, Marciano erupted against Charles in the eighth round and knocked him out.

Marciano defended his title against Don Cockell in 1955, knocking him out despite organized crime enticements for him to throw the fight. His last fight was September 21, 1955, his third Yankee Stadium defense. He knocked out Archie Moore in the ninth round. The unofficial attendance through closed-circuit television across the great cities of North America was over 400,000.

Retired from Boxing

On April 27, 1956 Marciano retired from boxing at the age of 31. "I thought it was a mistake when Joe Louis tried a comeback," *The New York Times* quoted him as saying. "No man can say what he will do in the future, but barring poverty, the ring has seen the last of me. I am comfortably fixed, and I am not afraid of the future." He said he wanted to spend more time with his family; it has been said since that he resented having to pay 50 percent of his earnings to his manager.

The Last Years

Marciano spent the years following his retirement making money from personal appearances. Notoriously frugal, Marciano insisted on bumming rides from friends with private planes, even though he could usually be given paid transportation to and from any of his personal appearances. On August 31, 1969, the day before his 46th birthday, he died in a private-plane crash near Des Moines, Iowa. He was survived by his wife of 19 years, Barbara, and two children, Rocco Kevin and Mary Anne.

Remembered for his Grit

Although he may not rank in the top five boxers of all time in terms of skill, speed, or power, Rocky Marciano was tough enough to compensate, and his fans recognized his grit. A sports writer commented that if all the heavyweight champions of all time were locked together in a room, Marciano would be the one to walk out.

Further Reading

Everett M. Skehan, *Rocky Marciano: The Biography of a First Son* (Boston: Houghton Mifflin, 1977). □

Marcion

The Christian theologian and leader Marcion (active mid-2nd century) promulgated views that were condemned as heterodoxy.

Marcion came from the Black Sea seaport town of Sinope on what is now the northern shore of Turkey. According to the writer Hippolytus, his father was the bishop of Sinope, so Marcion may well have been raised as a Christian. Once grown, Marcion entered the ministry and, toward the middle of the 2nd century, moved to Rome. There he gathered followers and in time began publically promulgating his theological views to the Roman Church at large. To his surprise, these views were not received sympathetically, and at the first known Roman synod, Marcion was excommunicated (144). Subsequently he became the founder of the rival Marcionite Church, which, in its ecclesiastical life, liturgy, and sacraments, paralleled the Christian Church. Marcion's rival church grew with considerable success, and Marcionite communities were found throughout the Mediterranean area well into the 4th century.

That the Marcionite Church, and more particularly, its heterodox doctrines, posed a threat to the early Christian Church is well attested to by the number of, as well as the vehemence of, treatises written against it in the 2nd and 3rd centuries. The longest and most important of these is by Tertullian. In spite of his severe opposition to Marcion's doctrinal views, that Tertullian could at the same time commend Marcion and his numerous followers for the purity and austerity of their moral life probably gives lie to the story, circulated later (4th century) by Epiphanius, that

Marcion was forced to leave Sinope for Rome because he had been caught in an act of gross sexual immorality and excommunicated by his father.

The view for which Marcion was most soundly criticized was not only that he denied any connection between the Old and New Testaments but that he also rejected the Old Testament in its entirety. The God of the Old Testament, his studies led him to assert, was a God of Law and Judgment, completely different from the God of Love and Mercy, the Father of Jesus Christ, as revealed in the New Testament. The former, "Creator God," held mankind in a deceitful grasp from which the "Redeemer God" sought, through the mission of Jesus, to save him.

These views, expounded in Marcion's "Antitheses," led the Marcionite Church to develop its own canon of Scripture, a fact that played no small part in forcing the Christian Church to regularize its own canon. The Marcionite "Bible" consisted of major portions of the Pauline Epistles (especially where law and spirit were opposed) and an expurgated version of the Gospel of Luke in which the passion and death of Jesus appear as the vengeful work of the Old Testament God.

Further Reading

The best study of Marcion is in German. Of great value in English is Edwin Cyril Blackman, *Marcion and His Influence* (1948).

□

Guglielmo Marconi

The Italian inventor Guglielmo Marconi (1874-1937) designed and constructed the first wireless telegraph. For this work he received a Nobel Prize.

The son of a wealthy Italian father and an Irish mother, Guglielmo Marconi was born April 25, 1874, in Bologna. He was educated by private tutors and attended the Livorno (Leghorn) technical institute for a short time.

In 1894 Marconi began experiments on electromagnetics near Bologna. Leaving aside the fundamental nature of electromagnetic waves, he directed his attention to the distance over which they could be detected with the possibility in mind that they might be used in a telegraph. He repeated Heinrich Hertz's experiments and rapidly extended the range of detection. Moving out of doors in 1895, he introduced a transmitter sparking between an elevated aerial and earth. For detection he used a "coherer" (a glass tube containing metal filings which becomes, and remains, conducting when an electrical discharge passes through it but which loses its conductivity following mechanical shock), similarly connected between an aerial and earth. By the end of 1895 he was able to detect wireless signals at ranges greater than a mile and out of the line of sight. By interrupting the spark signal, he was able to transmit Morse code. Marconi patented his invention in 1896.

Marconi was unable to interest the Italian government in wireless, so in 1896 he went to England, where he aroused official interest and received support from the British Post Office. Ranges attained by his instrument rose quickly, to 8 miles and then 25 miles and more. In 1899 signals across the English Channel, between Boulogne and Dover, caused a sensation, though the distance was less than that covered by other transmissions. In 1900 Marconi determined to try sending wireless signals across the Atlantic, despite the theoretical conflict between rectilinear propagation of Hertz radiation and the curvature of the earth. He had, however, already received signals at 250-mile range. Using the Poldhu transmitter, an established station in southwestern England, and a temporary aerial supported by a kite on Signal Hill, St. John's, Newfoundland, nearly 1,800 miles away, he received the first transatlantic wireless signals on Dec. 12, 1901.

Also in 1901 Marconi patented his "four-circuit" tuning system. Thus multiplex wireless telegraphy became possible, and the interference of one signal with another was minimized. In 1902 Marconi patented a sensitive magnetic radiodetector to replace the coherer and, in 1905, the horizontal directional aerial, which at once brought improvements in signal strengths and allowed the development of long-distance commercial wireless.

After 1905 Marconi spent much of his time as an entrepreneur, surrounded by a talented staff of engineers and administrators, developing wireless telegraphy. Attempts to introduce a transatlantic wireless press service in 1903 had been premature, but in 1907 commercial communication

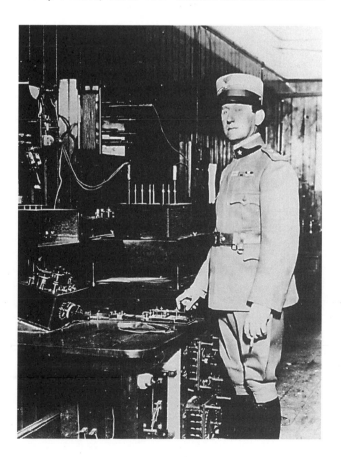

was established between Marconi stations at Clifden in western Ireland and Glace Bay, Nova Scotia.

During World War I Marconi began experiments on shortwave radio and on aerials designed to transmit along narrow beams to minimize detection by an enemy. The year 1917 saw him as a member of the Italian mission to the United States on its entry into the war, and in 1919 he was a signatory to the Paris Treaty for Italy. He spent much of the next decade continuing the shortwave investigations begun in wartime, making useful discoveries, but none to compete with the great postwar expansion of the radio networks consequent on the development of radiotelephony and voice radio. He was hailed as the father of radio, but, especially in the United States, the real progress was made by a new generation.

Marconi died on July 20, 1937, in Rome of a heart attack. He was a modest man of great scientific integrity, and his uncorroborated word was perhaps more readily accepted than that of any other inventor. He shared the 1909 Nobel Prize for physics with K. F. Braun.

Further Reading

Marconi has attracted many biographers, though only two thorough works can be recommended. It should be noted that both were published in his lifetime and both received his imprimatur: B. L. Jacot de Boinod and D. M. B. Collier, *Marconi: Master of Space* (1935), and Orrin E. Dunlap, Jr., *Marconi: The Man and His Wireless* (1937). □

Friar Marcos de Niza

Friar Marcos de Niza (ca. 1500-1558), Franciscan missionary in Spanish America, set the route to the fabled "Seven Cities of Cibola" for the expedition of Coronado.

The birthplace of Marcos de Niza is unknown, but he was either French or Italian, probably the former. In his youth he lived at Nice in the duchy of Savoy. He became a Franciscan and went to Santo Domingo as a missionary in 1531, later going to Guatemala, Peru, and Mexico City.

The reports of Álvar Núñez Cabeza de Vaca and three companions, who walked from the Texas coast to Culiacán in 1536, raised hopes in Mexico of fabulous riches to the north. Viceroy Antonio de Mendoza prepared the expedition of Francisco Vásquez de Coronado to investigate. However, in 1539 he dispatched Marcos de Niza with Estabanico (who had been with Cabeza de Vaca) to explore in advance. The friar sent his companion ahead. Estabanico reached the Zuni pueblo of Hawikuh in western New Mexico and was killed by Indians. Marcos learned of his companion's death but pressed on, escorted by friendly Mexican Indians, until he saw Hawikuh from a neighboring hillside. He gained an "incredibly distorted impression of

Hawikuh," and it has been suggested that the sun shining on the dwellings made them look like gold and silver.

Marcos believed he had seen one of the "Seven Cities," originally located by legend on an Atlantic island but now thought to be westward. Returning to Mexico, he described the place as larger than Mexico City, with houses 10 stories high whose doors and fronts were made of turquoise.

Mendoza needed no more convincing. The Coronado expedition, with the friar as guide, departed early in 1540. They reached Hawikuh on July 7 and captured it. But the soldiers were enraged on finding nothing but a poor Indian village. They cursed the friar so vehemently that Coronado, not wishing to have the blood of a churchman on his hands, sent him back to Mexico City. The accompanying message stated, "Friar Marcos has not told the truth in a single thing that he said."

The rest of the friar's career proved uneventful. He apparently became stricken with paralysis and lived first at Jalapa and then in a monastery at Xochimilco. Bishop Juan de Zumárraga gave him aid until his own death in 1548. Nothing more is known other than that the friar died on March 25, 1558.

Further Reading

Mendoza's instructions to Marcos de Niza and the friar's report of Hawikuh were edited and translated by George P. Hammond and Agapito Rey, *Narratives of the Coronado Expedition, 1540-1542* (1940). All that is known of Marcos is discussed in Herbert Eugene Bolton, *Coronado: Knight of Pueblos and Plains* (1949). Also useful is A. Grove Day, *Coronado's Quest: The Discovery of the Southwestern States* (1940). A brief account which contains the essential information is George P. Hammond, *Coronado's Seven Cities* (1940).

Additional Sources

Hallenbeck, Cleve, *The journey of Fray Marcos de Niz,* Westport, Conn., Greenwood Press 1973, 1949; Dallas, Tex.: Southern Methodist University Press, 1987. □

Ferdinand Marcos

Philippine president Ferdinand Edralin Marcos (1917-1989) began his career in politics with the murder of Julio Nalundasan in 1935, and ended it with the murder of Benigno Aquino, Jr., in 1983. Some believe his entire life was based on fraud, deceit, and plunder, and his two decades as president have come to epitomize the worst excesses of autocratic rule.

Ferdinand Marcos was born in Sarrat, Ilocos North, on September 11, 1917, to Josefa Edralin and Mariano Marcos, both teachers. Mariano was later a two-term congressman and during World War II, a collaborator with the Japanese. Subsequently he was tied to four water buffalo by Filipino guerrillas and pulled apart. Marcos' *real* father, a man Marcos claimed was his "godfather," was a wealthy Chinese named Ferdinand Chua. He was a well-connected municipal judge who was responsible for much of Marcos' unusually good luck. Among other things, Chua paid for young Marcos' schooling and managed to influence the Philippine Supreme Court to throw out the solid testimony which in 1939 had convicted Marcos of murder.

Marcos did well in school, as he had an extraordinary memory which allowed him to quickly memorize complicated texts and recite them forwards or backwards. In college, Marcos' principal interest was the .22-caliber college pistol team. On September 20, 1935, Julio Nalundasan was at home celebrating that day's Congressional election victory over Mariano Marcos when he was shot and killed with a .22-caliber bullet fired by the 18-year-old Marcos. Three years later, the honors student who was in his senior year of law school, was arrested for Nalundasan's murder. A year later, now a law school graduate, he was found guilty "beyond any reasonable doubt." Jailed, Marcos spent six months writing his own 830-page appeal. He also took the Philippine bar exam and passed with scores so high he was accused of cheating. Upon an oral re-examination by the Supreme Court, Marcos scored even higher with his remarkable memory. When the Supreme Court finally took up Marcos's appeal in 1940, the judge in charge (allegedly influenced by Judge Chua) was disposed to simply throw the case out. Marcos was a free man. The next day, he returned

to the Supreme Court where he was administered his oath as a lawyer.

Marcos emerged from World War II with the reputation of being the greatest Filipino resistance leader of the war and the most decorated soldier in the U.S. Armed forces. (Marcos served in the U.S. Army at the beginning and the end of the war as a "third lieutenant" on clerical duty, for a time in 1944 he was a U.S. prisoner of war under a death sentence) The Army investigated these claims after the war and found them to be false and "criminal." In fact, Marcos seems to have spent the war on both sides, and at various times, was in hospitals with fevers and stomach pains, possibly from the onset of lupus, the degenerative disease that ultimately ruined his health. In early 1943 in Manila, Marcos concocted a "secret" resistance organization called *Ang Mga Maharlika* ("Noble Studs") which he claimed consisted of spies, saboteurs and assassins, but in fact consisted of many forgers, pickpockets, gunmen and racketeers, united by an interest in black market operations.

At the war's end, as a deputy to the U.S. Army judge advocate general in northern Luzon, Marcos was involved in choosing friends and relatives to fill minor civil service jobs, passing out favors to be redeemed later. After, he resumed his law practice, often filing false claims in Washington on behalf of Filipino veterans seeking back pay and benefits. Emboldened by his success, he filed a $595,000 claim on his own behalf, stating that the U.S. Army had commandeered over 2,000 head of brahmin cattle from Mariano Marcos's wholly imaginary ranch in Mindinao. Washington concluded that the cattle had never existed. Marcos also tried to get recognition and benefits for his resistance force, the *Ang Mga Maharlika;* army investigators concluded that Marcos's unit was fraudulent.

In December, 1948, after a luncheon meeting with Marcos, a magazine editor published four articles on Marcos's extraordinary war exploits, including the history of the Maharlika just after the army's findings of fraud. Marcos' reputation grew. In 1949, campaigning on promises to get veterans' benefits for 2 million more "unrecognized" Filipinos, Marcos ran on the Liberal Party ticket for a seat in the Philippine House of Representatives and won astonishingly, with 70 percent of the vote. In less than a year he was worth a million dollars and owned a Cadillac convertible, mostly because of his American tobacco subsidies, a colossal cigarette smuggling operation, and his practice of extorting commissions from Chinese businesses. In 1954 he formally met Imelda Romualdez and married her.

Marcos was reelected twice, and in 1959 was elected to the Philippine Senate. He was also the Liberal Party's vice-president from 1954-1961, when he successfully managed Diosdado Macapagal's campaign for the Philippine presidency. As part of the deal, Macapagal was supposed to step aside after one term to allow Marcos to run for the presidency, but when Macapagal reneged, Marcos joined the opposition Nationalist Party and became their candidate in the 1965 election against Macapagal, which Marcos won handily strongly helped by Hartzell Spence's biography, called *For Every Tear A Victory.*

In 1969, Marcos became the first Philippine president to win a second term; the month following produced the most violent and bloody public demonstrations so far in the history of the country. Three years later, facing growing student unrest and a crumbling economy, Marcos declared martial law, using as his excuse the growing rebel presence of the Communist New People's Army. During the nine years of martial law, he tripled the armed forces to some 200,000 troops, guaranteeing his grip on government, and when martial law was lifted in 1981, he kept all the power he had been granted by himself. Bled to death, the economy continued to crumble as Ferdinand and Imelda became "arguably the richest couple on the planet." Marcos's health began to fail, the United States cooled off, and political opposition took hold in the Philippine middle class.

The Marcos regime began its accelerated collapse after the August 1983 assassination of Benigno S. Aquino, Jr., gunned down at the Manila airport upon his return after a self-imposed three-year exile. The killing enraged Filipinos, as did the official story that the murder was the work of a single assassin. A year later, a civilian investigation brought indictments against a number of soldiers and government officials, but by 1985 they all had been acquitted. In a surprising blunder, Marcos, thinking to regain control of the situation, called for a "snap election" to be held early in 1986. The election was marred by violence and charges of fraud; his opponent was the martyred Aquino's widow, Corazon. When the Philippine National Assembly announced that Marcos was the winner, a military rebellion, supported by hundreds of thousands of Filipinos marching in the streets, forced the Marcos to flee the country. Marcos' plea to the Americans for help produced nothing more than a U.S. Air Force jet, which flew him and Imelda to Hawaii. He remained there until his death in 1989. They took with them some 300 crates of prized possessions and more than 28 million cash, in Philippine currency. President Aquino's administration said this was only a small part of the Marcos's five to ten billion of illegally acquired wealth; Ferdinand's frozen bank accounts in Switzerland were said to have $475 million. In 1995, the government was able to auction off three jewelry collections worth $13 million.

Further Reading

The official biography of Marcos is Hartzell Spence, *For Every Tear a Victory: The Story of Ferdinand E. Marcos* (1964), expanded and reissued as *Marcos of the Philippines: A Biography* (1969), an interesting but uncritical journalistic work which created and perpetuated many of the myths about Marcos. This article is based on Sterling Seagrave, *The Marcos Dynasty* (1988). Other works readers should consult are Herie Rotea, *Marcos' Lovey Dovie* (1984); Raymond Bonner, *Waltzing With A Dictator: The Marcoses and The Making of American Policy* (1988); Lewis E, Gleek, Jr., *President Marcos and the Philippine Political Culture* (1988); Beth Day Romulo, *Inside the Palace: The Rise and Fall of Ferdinand and Imelda Marcos* (1987); William C. Rempel, *Delusions of a Dictator: The Mind of Marcos As Revealed in His Secret Diaries* (1993); Mark R. Thompson, *The Anti-Marcos Struggle: Personalistic Rule and Democratic Transition in the Philippines* (1996); Albert F. Cerloza, *Ferdinand Marcos and The Philippines: The Political Economy of Authoritarianism* (1997). □

Imelda Romualdez Marcos

Imelda Romualdez Marcos (born 1930) was one of the most influential leaders of the Philippines in the 1970s and early 1980s. She was the wife of President Ferdinand Marcos and a political power in her own right. She served as governor of Metro Manila and controlled considerable government spending. She fled with her husband to Hawaii early in 1986 and after his death, ran into legal problems concerning money she and her husband had allegedly stolen from their country

Imelda Romualdez Marcos was born in 1930 to a prominent family in the Central Visayas in Leyte Province in the Philippine Islands. After winning a nation-wide beauty contest she married Ferdinand Marcos, a rising political leader who later became president of the Philippines.

Imelda Romualdez Marcos became one of the most influential leaders of the Philippines. Much of her power came from her position as First Lady. On her own, however, she cultivated an influential entourage who were loyal to her personally. This entourage included important economic, military, and political leaders of the country.

Years as First Lady

After becoming First Lady, Marcos was appointed to a number of significant positions. In 1975 she became the governor of Metro Manila, giving her far-reaching power to determine the policies affecting ten percent of the Filipinos. As governor, Marcos became famous for spending hundreds of millions of dollars to build luxury hotels and a cultural center. These buildings were erected for tourists and the upper classes of the capital city and later lost a great deal of money.

The president used his wife as a traveling diplomat to nations throughout the world. She was named roving ambassador to the Peoples Republic of China, and she took part in negotiations in Libya over proposed self-government for Mindanao, a southern island in the Philippines where a civil war existed between Muslim and Christian inhabitants.

In 1978 she was elected to the Interim National Assembly of the Philippines, although her election (from Manila) was tainted by accusations of massive voting fraud. In the same year she was named to the cabinet as minister of human settlements, a post which gave her access to virtually unlimited resources. In that position she was able to allocate funds for countless projects, all of which gave her increased political clout throughout the country.

Marcos Leaves Power

Following the assassination of Senator Benigno Aquino in August 1983 and the deterioration of the president's health during the same period, Imelda Marcos emerged as a major spokeswoman for the government. Her prominence led many analysts to assume t hat she was preparing to

succeed her husband in the event of his death or resignation. Early in 1986, however, a "snap" election called by President Marcos backfired. Vote fraud and pro-Marcos violence on election day inflamed the general public, which refused to believe the Marcos' claim of victory. When the people rallied behind the "defeated" candidate Corazon Aquino, Imelda Marcos fled with her husband and about a hundred family and friends, settling in Hawaii. She left behind evidence of being a compulsive shopper for several items of apparel including a thousand pairs of shoes. Thus in the matter of a few weeks the image of Imelda Marcos changed from a haughty, imperial first lady of the Philippines to that of an almost ludicrous figure obsessed with material possessions

Life for Imelda After the Fall

Imelda Marcos lived in exile with her husband in Hawaii until his death in 1989, with the Philippine government demanding compensation for money the Marcos' allegedly stole from the country. In 1990 she went to trial on racketeering charges in New York City, with the government alleging she and her husband had stolen some $200 million from the Philippines National Bank and invested it in America; she was eventually acquitted. Marcos returned to the Philippines in 1991 and the next year ran for president on the New Society Movement. She ultimately came in fifth in a field of seven, receiving only eight percent of the vote. In 1993 Marcos went on trial in that country for graft and was found guilty in September as reported in the *New York Times.* She was sentenced to 18 to 24 years in jail, but was

released pending appeal. A comeback of sorts was in store for Marcos when she was elected to the country's house of representative by a large majority in November of 1995. According to Emily Mitchell and Andrea Pawlyna in *People,* Imelda Marcos was still battling the government over the Marcos fortune, estimated to be as much as ten billion dollars, and could not sell her family's real estate holdings or get the estimated $500 million she and her husband had placed in Swiss Banks. According to Marcus Broucher of the *Wall Street Journal,* Marcos was planning to establish a page on the World Wide Web (http://www.imelda.com) to tell her and her husband's side to interested parties.

Further Reading

Imelda Marcos's speeches have been published in *Identity and Consciousness: The Philippine Experience* (1974); Primitivo Mijores has written a critical book on Marcos and her husband entitled *The Conjugal Dictatorship of Ferdinand and Imelda Marcos* (1976). Another interesting view of Imelda Marcos is *Two Terrorists Meet* (1981) by Stephen Psinakis, an anti-Marcos dissident. See also *The Steel Butterfly of the Phillipines* by Katherine Ellison (New York, McGraw Hill, 1988); and *Imelda Marcos* by Carmen Pedroso (New York, St. Martin's Press, 1987). "Judge Wapner, Where Are You?" by B. Angelo in *Time,* reports on her acquittal on the American changes of racketeering; Marcos's graft conviction in the Philippines was mentioned in the *New York Times,* September 24th, 1993; Marcos' life after her trial and her election to congress were detailed in "Forever Imelda," by Emily Mitchell and Andrea Pawlyn, in the July 29th, 1996 edition of *People;* and by Seth Mydoz, "Quirky Imelda Marcos Holds Court," in the March 4th, 1996 edition of the *New York Times.* The plan for a Web page (http://www.imelda.com) was mentioned in "Imelda.com Anyone," by Marcus Broucher, in the February 13th, 1997 edition of the *Wall Street Journal.* □

Marcus Aurelius Antoninus

The Roman emperor Marcus Aurelius Antoninus (121-180) was a convinced Stoic philosopher, and at his accession there was widespread rejoicing that at last Plato's dream of a philosopher-king had become reality.

Born Marcus Annius Verus on April 26, 121, of a noble family originally Spanish, Marcus Aurelius grew up close to the center of power. When he was a child, the emperor Hadrian noticed him and punned on his name, Verus ("True"), calling him Verissimus ("Truest") for his uprightness. In his final arrangement Hadrian, who had difficulty in choosing a successor, destined Marcus for ultimate rule, for when he adopted Marcus's uncle by marriage, Antoninus (soon to be known as Antoninus Pius), he had Antoninus adopt Marcus Aurelius along with the young Lucius Ceionius Commodus, later called Lucius Verus.

Youth and Accession

Marcus Aurelius had an excellent education, numbering among his tutors M. Cornelius Fronto, the rhetorician; the very wealthy Herodes Atticus, whose Odeon still stands in Athens; Plutarch's grandson Sextus of Chaeronea; and Diognetus, the painter and Stoic philosopher. Under Diognetus's influence young Marcus became a precocious Stoic at the age of 11 and remained a devoted follower of stoicism for the rest of his life.

Antoninus Pius was that rarity among emperors, one who had his acknowledged heir beside him throughout his reign. He had the title Caesar conferred on Marcus in 139, only a year after his own accession, and betrothed him to his own daughter Faustina; Marcus and Faustina were married probably in 140. Through the reign of Antoninus (138-161) Marcus worked most closely with him.

Though Antoninus at his death seems to have designated Marcus as sole heir, Marcus insisted that his adoptive brother Verus also be given full power. Thus for the first time Rome had two exactly equal emperors, colleagues like the consuls of old. That this arrangement, which had sometimes caused trouble even with merely annual magistrates, did not produce friction between lifetime equals was due in large measure to the good nature of Verus and his deference to Marcus's seniority in years and judgment.

Foreign Wars

The reign opened with floods on the Tiber and a variety of other natural disasters, but the overshadowing problem

was the Eastern question. Parthia, the only large, organized power that Rome faced, was always a rival for dominance in Armenia, and now, in 162, Parthia attacked, defeated the Romans in Cappadocia, and overran the rich province of Syria. Marcus Aurelius, for reasons which still are not entirely clear, remained at Rome and sent Verus to take charge of the war in the East. Verus was no soldier, but Marcus supplied him with able subordinates, and the war went well though slowly; the Roman counteroffensive did not get under way until 163, but then Armenia was occupied and a vassal king installed.

In 164 three Roman armies, one headed by the able Avidius Cassius, cleared northern Mesopotamia; in 165 southern Mesopotamia and the chief Parthian capitals were taken; finally, in 166, Media was overrun. But in late 165 a terrible plague broke out among the Roman troops, a plague which they were to carry back with them and which would carry off a quarter or more of the population of the empire. Rome recalled its armies with Parthia defeated but not conquered. Nevertheless, Marcus and Verus celebrated a magnificent triumph.

The Parthian War had ended none too soon, for the German War, which was to run with only the briefest of intervals for the rest of the reign, had already begun. Another of those great waves of unrest which occasionally troubled the barbarians beyond the frontier was setting the Germans in motion, and in 167 a group of tribes crossed the Danube, destroyed a Roman army, and actually besieged Aquileia in Italy. The danger was critical, for the plague was raging, particularly in the army camps, and the imperial treasury, always short of money, was worse off than usual.

Marcus raised new legions, even accepting slaves and gladiators, auctioned off furnishings from the imperial palaces to raise funds, and in 168 went with Verus to the front. Verus died in early 169, and Marcus was left to face the war alone. The barbarians were driven back, but still the war dragged on in a mixture of victories and defeats, with Marcus living mainly at the front, sometimes on the Danube, sometimes on the Rhine as the focus of crisis shifted. Gradually the Romans gained the upper hand, and by 175 we are told that Marcus was intending to annex the lands of the tribes nearest the frontier when he was suddenly forced to call off the war because of the revolt of Avidius Cassius in the East.

Revolt of Avidius Cassius

After distinguished service in the Parthian War, Avidius Cassius, himself a Syrian, had been made governor of Syria and, with the deepening of the German crisis, had gradually been raised to the position almost of viceroy for the entire East. In 175 Marcus grew sick, and rumor went round that he was dying or dead; partly for this reason Avidius was hailed emperor and accepted by most of the East, including Egypt—Rome's granary—thus threatening Rome itself with famine. Marcus had to break off the war in Germany with less than total victory and hurry eastward.

Cassius was murdered after only 3 months, and the immediate danger passed; but Marcus could not avoid showing himself in the East and making a fairly extended sojourn there. He exhibited his customary leniency in dealing with Cassius's supporters and returned to Rome in late 176, where he celebrated a splendid triumph with his son Commodus, who was soon given the title Augustus and made an equal sharer of power. Thus through his own act Marcus Aurelius ended his reign as he had begun it, with a partner his equal in power but not in virtue.

In 177 began a serious persecution of the Christians. Much ink has been spilled trying to reconcile Marcus's kindness and high principles with his evident hostility toward the Christians; but the fact remains that he considered the Christians to be dangerous fanatics, subversive alike of society and the state—and on the evidence available to him, how should he not? Then, too, if his persecution was more severe than those that went before, this was partly because the Christians were more numerous and more visible than before.

Renewed German War and Death

The German War erupted again in 177, and Marcus shortly returned to the front. Once again he had the war almost won; but his death, which occurred on March 17, 180, precluded final victory over the Germans. He was given a grand funeral and deified, and memorials of him are yet visible in Rome—the column celebrating his German victories in the Piazza Colonna and his equestrian statue where Michelangelo placed it on the Capitoline.

Marcus Aurelius's reign was marked by near, rather than complete, success and marred both by his fondness for sharing power with unworthy partners and by a willingness to forgive carried at times beyond the point of prudence in one responsible for the well-being of millions; but there can be no question of his personal goodness or of the greatness of his soul.

The *Meditations*

The reason for which Marcus Aurelius deservedly is most remembered is the collection of his thoughts or reflections, usually entitled the *Meditations*. Apparently jotted down from time to time as inclination or opportunity offered, the thoughts form no organized system of philosophy; rather, they are the record of a spirit whose principles were elevated above the somewhat grim rectitude of stoicism by a warm love of mankind and a philosophy closely akin to religion.

To Marcus, happiness was to be achieved by living "according to nature," in harmony with the principle which ordered the universe; the serenity of one who so lived could not be really affected by the buffetings of fate. Since the *Meditations* were composed in bits, they are best read so; they are to be savored rather than downed at a gulp.

Further Reading

There is no good surviving ancient treatment of Marcus Aurelius. His life is included in the collection known as *The Scriptores Historiae Augustae* (trans., 3 vols., 1921-1932), and his reign in the fragments of books 70-71 in the general history of Cassius Dio. Otherwise there are his own *Meditations* and the surviving letters he exchanged with his old tutor Fronto.

Among modern works are Henry Dwight Sedgwick, *Marcus Aurelius: A Biography* (1921); C. Clayton Dove, *Marcus Aurelius Antoninus: His Life and Times* (1930); Arthur Spencer Loat Farquharson, *Marcus Aurelius: His Life and His World* (1951), a posthumous work dealing with Marcus's youth up to his accession; and Anthony Birley's full and interesting *Marcus Aurelius* (1966). □

Herbert Marcuse

Herbert Marcuse (1898-1979) was a leading 20th-century New Left philosopher in the United States and a follower of Karl Marx. Marcuse's writing reflected a discontent with modern society and technology and their "destructive" influences, as well as the necessity of revolution. His application of the theories of Sigmund Freud to the character of contemporary society and politics was the subject of much research, scholarly and otherwise. He was considered by some to be a philosopher of the sexual revolution.

Herbert Marcuse was born in Berlin on July 19, 1898. In 1922 he received his doctorate of philosophy from the universities of Berlin and Freiburg. Marcuse's distinctive intellectual heritage was based on the democratic and socialist philosophy originated by G. W. F. Hegel and developed by Karl Marx—combined with the psychoanalytic theories of Sigmund Freud. On this basis he took a stand against fascism, as it appeared in Europe from the 1920s until the end of World War II and as it appeared later in the allegedly fascist elements of advanced industrial society.

In 1934 Marcuse emigrated to the United States and joined the Institute of Social Research in New York City. In 1941 he became a U.S. citizen. Also in 1941 Marcuse published *Reason and Revolution,* a study of Hegel and the rise of social theory. Marcuse's intention was to draw a distinction between Hegel and the contemporary fascist interpretations of Hegel's theories.

Worked for U.S. Government

During World War II Marcuse served in the OSS (Office of Strategic Services, which later became the Central Intelligence Agency [CIA]). He worked for the U.S. Department of State until 1950. For several years thereafter he was a member of the Russian Institutes of Columbia University and Harvard University. From 1954 to 1965 he was a professor at Brandeis University. He married Inge S. Werner in 1955.

Advocated Sexual Openness

Marcuse's *Eros and Civilization* (1955) presents a Neo-Freudian view of man. It argues for a greater tolerance of eroticism than that permitted by the status quo. The book argues that a tolerant attitude toward sexuality would lead to a more satisfactory life in a society devoid of aggression.

Because of this book Marcuse is considered one of the philosophers of the "sexual revolution."

Attacked Industrial Advancement

Marcuse criticized the advanced industrial societies of the United States and the Soviet Union for constructing a civilization that requires ceaseless production and consumption of unnecessary goods and for perpetuating themselves at the expense not only of other nations but also of their own populations. In *Soviet Marxism* (1958) Marcuse views the Soviet Union as actually worse but potentially better than the United States.

One-Dimensional Man (1964) continues Marcuse's attack on advanced industrial society—especially that found in the United States. He writes that America's affluence is facilitated by self-serving technology—such as military defense—in which the only reason products are consumed is that they are available. As a result, humanity's authenticity is undermined, and its potential for aggression is elevated to the point at which nuclear holocaust is probable. *One-Dimensional Man* is a pessimistic work in which the United States emerges as the most dangerous nation on Earth. It was, however, an important work during the following decade of radical political change.

Advocated Revolution

In 1965 Marcuse joined the faculty of the University of California in San Diego. That year his controversial essay "Repressive Tolerance" appeared. It states that the United States is repressive, since dissent goes unheard and no alternative to the view of the Establishment is considered. Accordingly, in defense of tolerance it is correct to disrupt and obstruct Establishment spokesmen. At this time Marcuse collaborated on *A Critique of Pure Tolerance* (1965).

College campus uprisings, culminating in the revolt of French students in May 1968, rendered Marcuse open to attack. In July 1968 he disappeared from his home in California after reportedly receiving a threatening letter from the Ku Klux Klan. In October 1968 a campaign was launched to dislodge him from his teaching position. And in 1969 Pope Paul criticized his views on sex.

An Essay on Liberation (1969), written before the French student rebellion, is dedicated to the student militants. Clearly, Marcuse hoped that they might effect the revolution he deemed justifiable against the oppressiveness and aggressiveness of contemporary industrial society. He published *Five Lectures: Psychoanalysis, Politics, and Utopia* in 1970.

In 1972 Marcuse published *Studies in Critical Philosophy,* a study of authority; *From Luther to Popper;* and *Counterrevolution and Revolt.* Then, in 1978, he focused again on Marx in *The Aesthetic Dimension: Toward a Critique of Marxist Aesthetics.*

Other articles and essays Marcuse wrote include: "Remarks on a Redefinition of Culture" *Daedalus: Journal of the American Academy of Arts and Sciences* (1965); *Negations: Essays in Critical Theory"* (1968); "Art and Revolution," *Partisan Review* (1972); "Marxism and Feminism," *Women's Studies: An Interdisciplinary Journal* (1974); "The Obsolescence of the Freudian Concept of Man" (published 1989); and "Philosophy and Critical Theory," *Critical Theory and Society: A Reader* (1989).

Shortly before his death in 1979, Marcuse reflected upon the inseparability of human beings and nature in "Ecology and the Critique of Modern Society," in which he stated that the natural environment must be shielded from capitalist—and Communist—destruction.

Further Reading

Sound recordings based on Marcuse's writings include: "Art as a Revolutionary Weapon," "The New Sensibility," "One Dimensional Man," and "Reason and Revolution Today" (all published by Pacifica Tape Library).

Marcuse is discussed in: Kurt H. Wolff and Barrington Moore, Jr., eds., *The Critical Spirit: Essays in Honor of Herbert Marcuse* (Beacon Press, 1967); Paul A. Robinson, *The Freudian Left* (Harper & Row, 1969); Paul Breines, ed., *Critical Interruptions: New Left Perspectives on Herbert Marcuse* (Herder and Herder, 1970); Alasdair MacIntyre, *Herbert Marcuse: An Exposition and a Polemic* (Viking Press, 1970); Robert W. Marks, *The Meaning of Marcuse* (Ballantine Books, 1970); Maurice Cranston, ed., *The New Left: Six Critical Essays* (Library Press, 1970); Michael A. Weinstein, compiler, *Identity, Power, and Change: Selected Readings in Political Theory* (Scott, Foresman, 1971); Eliseo Vivas, *Contra Marcuse* (Arlington House, 1971); Maurice Cranston, *Prophetic Politics: Critical Interpretations of the Revolutionary Impulse: Che Guevara, Jean-Paul Sartre, Herbert Marcuse, Frantz Fanon, Black Power, R.D. Lang* (Simon and Schuster, 1972); Jack Woddis, *New Theories of Revolution: A Commentary on the*

Views of Frantz Fanon, Regis Debray and Herbert Marcuse (International Publishers, 1972); Paul Mattick, *Critique of Marcuse* (Herder and Herder, 1972); John Fry, *Marcuse, Dilemma and Liberation: A Critical Analysis* (Harvester Press, 1974); Sidney Lipshires, *Herbert Marcuse: From Marx to Freud and Beyond* (Schenkman Publishing Co., 1974); Gad Horowitz, *Repression: Basic and Surplus Repression in Psychoanalytic Theory: Freud, Reich, and Marcuse* (University of Toronto Press, 1977); Harold Bleich, *The Philosophy of Herbert Marcuse* (University Press of America, 1977); Gertrude A. Steuernagel, *Political Philosophy as Therapy: Marcuse Recommended* (Greenwood Press, 1979); Morton Schoolman, *The Imaginary Witness: The Critical Theory of Herbert Marcuse* (Collier MacMillan, 1980); Richard A. Brosio, *The Frankfurt School: An Analysis of the Contradictions and Crises of Liberal Capitalist Societies* (Ball State University, 1980); Raya Dunayevskaya, *Marxism and Freedom from 1776 Until Today* (Harvester Press, 1982); Barry Katz, *Herbert Marcuse and the Art of Liberation* (Schocken Books, 1982); Peter Lind, *Marcuse and Freedom: the Genesis and Development of a Theory of Human Liberation* (Croom Helm, 1984); Douglas Kellner, *Herbert Marcuse and the Crisis of Marxism* (University of California Press, 1984); Richard Kearney, *Dialogues with Contemporary Thinkers: the Phenomenological Heritage: Paul Ricoeur, Emmanuel Levinas, Herbert Marcuse, Stanislas Breton, Jacques Derrida* (Manchester University Press, 1986); Fred C. Alford, *Science and the Revenge of Nature* (University Presses of Florida, 1985); Timothy J. Lukes, *The Flight Into Inwardness: An Exposition and Critique of Herbert Marcuse's Theory of Liberative Aesthetics* (Associated University Presses, 1985); Mark Thomas, *Ethics and Technoculture* (University Press of America, 1987); Robert B. Pippin, *Marcuse: Critical Theory & the Promise of Utopia* (Bergin & Garvey, 1988); Ben Agger, *The Discourse of Domination: From the Frankfurt School to Post-Modernism* (Northwestern University Press, 1992); John Bokina and Timothy J. Lukes, eds., *Marcuse: From the New Left to the Next Left* (University Press of Kansas, 1994); Marsha Hewitt, *Critical Theory of Religion: A Feminist Analysis* (Fortress Press, 1995); and Joan Alwy, *Critical Theory and Political Possibilities: Conceptions of Emancipatory Politics in the Works of Horkheimer, Adorno, Marcuse, and Habermas* (Greenwood Press, 1995). □

William Learned Marcy

American statesman William Learned Marcy (1786-1857), a leader of the Democratic party from its origin in the 1820s, served as secretary of war and as secretary of state.

William Marcy was born in Sturbridge, Mass., on Dec. 12, 1786. After graduating from Brown University, he studied law in New York and became a resident of the state. In the confused politics of the "Era of Good Feelings" (1815-1824) in New York State, Marcy was associated with the faction headed by Martin Van Buren in opposition to the group headed by DeWitt Clinton. Van Buren, Marcy's early patron in politics, was responsible for his rapid advancement, and Marcy followed the "Little Magician" into the Democratic party.

After holding several state offices, Marcy was elected to the U.S. Senate in 1831 and became governor of New York State in 1833. As governor, Marcy broke with Van Buren (now president) over the latter's financial policies, especially his proposal for an independent treasury system. This split was to dominate New York State politics for about 15 years. Marcy's appointment as secretary of war by President James K. Polk alienated Van Buren from the administration.

As secretary of war, Marcy supported Polk's ambitions in Mexico and took the responsibility for properly supplying the army during the Mexican War. He also had the odious task of trying to arbitrate the various disputes between Polk and his generals in Mexico—Winfield Scott and Zachary Taylor. Polk assumed the major burden for the actual battlefield tactics.

A leading contender for the Democratic presidential nomination in 1852, Marcy was appointed secretary of state by the victorious candidate, Franklin Pierce. Marcy was the administration's foreign policy adviser and its chief dispenser of patronage. He reorganized the State Department, bringing in many able men. Two major foreign policy problems occupied him: an Anglo-American negotiations involved American opposition to British expansion in Central America, and all efforts at reaching an agreement failed.

To satisfy the more expansionist-minded Democrats, Marcy sought the acquisition of Cuba through negotiations with Spain. But the Ostend Manifesto of 1854, circulated by the American ministers to France, Spain, and England, which maintained that "by every law, human and Divine,

we shall be justified in wresting it (Cuba) from Spain . . . ,'' caused such a reaction in Spain that all hope of peaceful acquisition of the island ended. Marcy died shortly after leaving office, on July 4, 1857.

Further Reading

Ivon Debeham Spencer wrote a full-scale biography of Marcy, *The Victor and the Spoils: A Life of William L. Marcy* (1959). As no study of Marcy is complete without reference to Martin Van Buren see Holmes Alexander, *The American Talleyrand: The Career and Contemporaries of Martin Van Buren* (1935). □

Luca Marenzio

The Italian composer Luca Marenzio (c. 1553-1599) was the greatest master of the Italian madrigal. His works spread throughout the Low Countries and Germany, and he was the main foreign influence in the development of the English madrigal school.

Luca Marenzio was born in Coccaglio and may have been a chorister in the nearby Cathedral of Brescia under G. Contini. In 1577 Marenzio contributed some madrigals to a minor Venetian anthology. Two years later he entered the employ of Cardinal Luigi d'Este in Rome. The cardinal spent a good deal of time at Ferrara, the home of the Este family, and it is likely that Marenzio accompanied him on most of these visits and met the court poets Torquato Tasso and G. B. Guarini, much of whose verse he set to music. During his 7 years with the cardinal, Marenzio published his first four books of madrigals for five voices, the first three volumes of madrigals for six voices, the *madrigali spirituali,* and the first three books of villanelle, in addition to a number of pieces for anthologies and the first of his five volumes of motets.

Marenzio served the Medici family in Florence from 1588 to 1589. He contributed music for the wedding festivities of Ferdinand de' Medici in May 1589 and published his fifth book of madrigals for five voices and the fourth for six voices, the volume of madrigals for four, five, and six voices, and the fourth and fifth books of villanelle. Marenzio was now at the height of his fame, and when he left the Medicean court he found no dearth of patrons. He spent most of his remaining years in Rome, where he died on Aug. 22, 1599.

Seventeen volumes of madrigals containing over 200 pieces were published during Marenzio's lifetime; of these more than half were reprinted at least once before his death and continued to be reprinted for a decade after. His villanelle were almost as popular as his madrigals.

Marenzio represents the summation of the madrigal. He utilized the entire range of style and expression (except polychoral writing) bequeathed by earlier composers to the development of the type. His most remarkable characteristic, however, in which he outstrips all his predecessors and

contemporaries, is his ''word painting,'' a technique that was not new but which Marenzio raised to a new significance. This technique is a much more integral and important aspect of his style in his earlier and most popular madrigals, for from 1588 on he became more concerned with expression of mood as well as more serious in his choice of texts, both features reflecting the impact of the religious emotion engendered by the Counter Reformation.

Further Reading

A biography of Marenzio is Denis Arnold, *Marenzio* (1965). Information on Marenzio and historical background are in Gustave Reese, *Music in the Renaissance* (1954; rev. ed. 1959), and *The New Oxford History of Music,* vol. 4 (1968). See also Alfred Einstein, *The Italian Madrigal* (1949). □

Sir Milton Augustus Striery Margai

Sir Milton Augustus Striery Margai (1895-1964) was a Sierra Leonean physician and political leader who became his country's first prime minister.

Milton Margai was born on Dec. 7, 1895, at Gbangbatoke in the southern protectorate. The son of a wealthy Mende merchant, Margai was educated at the Evangelical United Brethren School in Bonthe and at the Albert Academy and Fourah Bay College in Freetown, where he received a bachelor's degree in history.

The first protectorate student to graduate from the college and to become a doctor, Margai earned several additional degrees from King's College Medical School, University of Durham. He also attended the Liverpool School of Tropical Medicine.

After practicing a few months, Margai entered government service, rising, between 1928 and 1950, to senior medical officer. He served in 11 of 12 districts in the protectorate, working with women's groups on pre-and postnatal care and child welfare. Margai also trained midwives for the Native Administration and wrote Mende instructions on midwifery.

Margai's political activity began in 1930 with election to the Bonthe District Council, a local governmental unit of representatives from the chiefdoms. Later he represented the council in the Protectorate Assembly, a governmental advisory body on economic, social, and political matters. Both groups reportedly developed from suggestions Margai had made earlier to tribal leaders. In 1946 he joined the Sierra Leone Organization Society (SLOS), formed to promote the cooperative movement. He also organized and helped manage the first protectorate newspaper, the politically influential *Sierra Leone Observer.*

Five years later, with the help of his lawyer brother Albert, Margai founded the Sierra Leone People's party

(SLPP), the first significant indication of a nationalistic movement in the country. An outgrowth of the SLOS, the SLPP aimed to promote colony-protectorate cooperation. Basically conservative, it stood for political unification and self-government within the British Commonwealth.

In November 1951 the SLPP became the majority party in the Legislative Council, and the British appointed Margai to the Executive Council. He became minister of health, agriculture, and forestry in 1953. When Sierra Leone gained self-government a year later, Margai became chief minister as well. In 1957 he was reappointed, assuming also the Ministry of Internal Affairs and Development.

At this time, the more active nationalist Albert Margai contested the leadership of the SLPP, opposing the mild nature of his brother's policy. Although winning 22 to 21, the rebel faction withdrew and formed a new party. In 1959 Milton Margai was named premier and knighted; in anticipation of independence, his title was changed the following year to prime minister.

A man of considerable energy, slight and wiry, Sir Milton was able, direct of speech, conservative, and pro-British in outlook and temperament—in short, one of the mildest nationalists in Africa. He enjoyed music and played piano, violin, and organ. He died on April 28, 1964, after several months' illness.

Further Reading

Material on Margai appears in several recent works on Sierra Leone: Christopher Fyfe, *A Short History of Sierra Leone* (1965); Martin Kilson, *Political Change in a West African State: A Study of the Modernization Process in Sierra Leone* (1966); Gershon Collier, *Sierra Leone's Experiment in Democracy in an African Nation* (1970); and John R. Cartwright, *Politics in Sierra Leone, 1947-67* (1970). □

Margaret of Anjou

Margaret of Anjou (1430-1482) was queen consort of Henry VI, Lancastrian king of England. She was a niece of Charles VII of France and a cousin of Louis XI.

On March 23, 1430, Margaret was born in Lorraine to Isabel of Lorraine and René I, then Count of Guise. Margaret's betrothal to Henry VI on May 24, 1444, and marriage in March 1445 were negotiated by the Duke of Suffolk, protected by a Council indemnity, as a truce sanctioned by Henry for want of a better policy. Without his father's military skill and with little artillery and no money, Henry clung to the title of king of France while marrying a penniless niece of his rival for that throne. Charles lent ceremony to the marriage and prepared for the reconquest of western France from the disorganized and bankrupt government of Henry VI.

The "bride of peace" charade thrust upon Margaret was a disadvantageous introduction to English politics.

From 1449 to 1453 Henry lost claims to holdings in Anjou, Maine, Normandy, and Guienne, as well as the alliance of Brittany, to Margaret's uncle. These defeats made the Suffolk faction of the Council unpopular, but Margaret regarded this faction and their adherents as her only friends. She treated Humphrey of Gloucester, Richard of York, and the "war party" as enemies on all questions of policy and place. Thus Margaret united her opponents and also lost any prospect of support by the London populace. To the absence of improvement in Henry's muddled finances and policy must be added Margaret's inability to forgo foreign sources of support or to win adherence from more than a faction of feudal favorites. Her language of asperity, reproof, and moral instruction was not well calculated to win English approval for a French queen.

In 1450 defeats in France provoked a clamor against the Duke of Suffolk, whom Henry saved from the action of Parliament but not from murder, and a popular rising called Jack Cade's Rebellion temporarily drove the King and Queen from London. Henry's first attack of insanity, from August of 1453 to December of 1454, spanned the end of the Hundred Years War; the birth of Edward, Margaret's only child, on Oct. 13, 1453; and York's 1454 regency by act of Parliament.

In 1455 York's ambition and Margaret's lack of moderation led to a parliamentary and military conflict later misnamed the War of the Roses. Margaret organized the army that surprised and slew York at Wakefield (Dec. 30, 1460), but York's sons and the Earl of Warwick profited by London's support, and their victory at Towton (March 29,

1461) made the Lancastrian royalty fugitives from the first Yorkist king, Edward IV.

Henry VI was captured, imprisoned in the Tower of London, and lost his sanity, while Margaret and her son, with some help from Louis XI, made picturesque attempts to regain power. The defection of Warwick and the Duke of Clarence from Edward IV in 1469 provided an opportunity for an anti-Yorkist combination, with Warwick's daughter, Anne Neville, betrothed to Prince Edward and Warwick leading a 1470 expedition that swiftly drove Edward IV to refuge in Burgundy. Henry VI was restored to his throne if not to his wits, and Edward IV prepared to return to the struggle with help from Charles the Bold of Burgundy.

Margaret was prudent enough to wait 6 months before bringing her son to England and unlucky enough to land on the day Warwick was defeated and slain at Barnet (April 14, 1471). Prince Edward's defeat and death at Tewkesbury (May 4, 1471) left Margaret a captive and Edward IV with no further motive for keeping Henry VI alive. Margaret's imprisonment in the Tower was coincident with Henry's death (May 21, 1471). In 1475 Louis XI agreed to ransom Margaret and gave her a small pension in return for the surrender of all her inheritance claims. Margaret died on April 25, 1482.

Further Reading

Margaret's *Letters,* edited by Cecil Monro (1863), sheds no light on major political issues but illustrates her interference in the local disputes of her favorites. J. J. Bagley, *Margaret of Anjou, Queen of England* (1948), provides a concise modern account. Mrs. Mary Ann Hookham, *Life and Times of Margaret of Anjou* (2 vols., 1872), is comprehensive but uncritical of its many sources. Useful background information is in Sir James H. Ramsay, *Lancaster and York: A Century of English History* (2 vols., 1892), and Ernest Fraser Jacob, *The Fifteenth Century* (1961).

Additional Sources

Haswell, Jock, *The ardent queen: Margaret of Anjou and the Lancastrian heritage,* London: Peter Davies, 1976. □

Margaret of Denmark

Margaret of Denmark (1353–1412) was a fourteenth-century Danish queen and first medieval queen to rule in Europe, who united three powerful Scandinavian kingdoms.

I n the 11th century, the kingdoms of Scandinavia were a relatively new feature of medieval Europe. During the earliest phase of Viking attacks on Europe, the area was characterized by disunity; bands of Vikings from various Scandinavian areas looted Western Europe for personal or regional gain. But from the late ninth through the 11th centuries, the Scandinavian rulers had consolidated the area; by 1100 three distinct kingdoms—Norway, Sweden, and Denmark—had been created. By this time, there were significant regional differences in language and in rules of

royal succession which ensured the separate development of the kingdoms. Of these northern realms, only Iceland existed without a king; by the mid-13th century, however, the king of Norway claimed jurisdiction there. Notwithstanding the 11th-century achievements of King Canute of Norway, Denmark, and England, the Scandinavian kingdoms remained separate realms with separate monarchs until the 14th century. The individual who succeeded in uniting the three was a woman—Margaret Valdemarsdottir.

A glance at the years immediately preceding her reign reveals the enormity of her accomplishment. Early in the 14th century, Norway and Sweden were joined into one kingdom under Magnus Eriksson. Magnus was three years old, and the only available heir, when his grandfather, Norway's King Haakon V, died in 1319. The boy's father, Swedish prince Erik Magnusson, had died in prison at the hands of his uncle King Birger of Sweden. Thus, when Birger was forced out of his kingdom by dissident nobles, three-year-old Magnus became king of both Norway and Sweden. His mother Ingebjorg exerted great influence over the affairs of her son, and her plans to enlarge the combined kingdom included designs on Denmark. But the war she provoked with the Danes proved to be so costly to Norway that a popular noble, Erling Vidkunnsson, was made viceroy and ruled Norway until Magnus Eriksson came of age in 1332.

Four years later, in 1336, King Magnus married Blanca of Namur, and by 1340, they had two sons. Erik, the elder, was elected king of Sweden in 1344; the younger son, Haakon (VI), became king of Norway. As the brothers grew to manhood and ascended their thrones, relations between

Magnus Eriksson and his sons were marked by turbulence, jealousy, and aggression. In 1362, when Erik died, Haakon was named as his brother's successor in Sweden; he was to rule jointly with his father. The two kings then entered into a war with their powerful neighbor, Waldemar IV of Denmark, over rights to Skaane. During this war, Magnus and Haakon enlisted the aid of the Hanseatic League, a powerful alliance of German cities with trading interests in northern Europe. The League's presence in Scandinavia would prove a significantly disruptive influence in the political and economic life of later medieval Scandinavia. Shortly thereafter, in 1363, Magnus and Haakon arrived at an agreement with Waldemar. Their friendship was cemented by the marriage of the 23-year-old Haakon with Waldemar's 10-year-old daughter Margaret.

Soon after the marriage, Waldemar's son Christopher died, and it became apparent that Margaret would succeed her father—not only as queen in Denmark, but as queen of Norway and heir to the throne of Sweden as well. This alarming prospect stiffened the determination of the German Hanseatic League to extend its control over Denmark by military might, and the 1360s witnessed great strife between the two parties.

By 1370, the great power of the united German cities prevailed, forcing Waldemar to sign the humiliating Peace of Stralsund, which awarded enormous commercial concessions to the Hanse (German merchant guild) and placed the fate of the Danish king under German control. According to the terms of this treaty:

> If it should be that our lord and king, Valdemar, desires to abdicate his land of Denmark during his lifetime, we will and shall not suffer it, unless it be that the [Hanse] cities have given their consent, and that he has sealed to them their privileges with his great seal. Thus, too, it shall be if our lord and king Valdemar, be carried off by death. . . . Then, too, we will accept no ruler but in council with the cities.

Strained relations between German commercial interests and Scandinavian monarchs would continue in the reign of Waldemar's daughter Margaret; indeed, the tension would persist for the rest of the medieval period.

Margaret was one of several children born to Waldemar and his wife Helvig, who was the sister of the Duke of Schleswig. Although little is known of Margaret's childhood, the normal expectation for noble girls of her period was that they would serve as participants in diplomatic marriages. This was an expectation Margaret clearly fulfilled. As Haakon's 10-year-old bride, Margaret lived in Oslo's Akerhus castle, and her guardian, Marta Ulfsdottir, was a daughter of St. Birgitta of Sweden. By the time Margaret was 18, she had borne her only child, Olaf.

When Waldemar died in 1375, Margaret advanced the candidacy of her young son for the throne of Denmark. There was at the time one other possible heir: Albrecht, the son of Margaret's deceased older sister. Though Waldemar IV had arranged for Albrecht to succeed him, two factors helped Margaret's determination to establish Olaf as king: (1) Albrecht offended the Danish nobility by assuming the title of king, thereby violating the elective nature of that office; and (2) in exchange for commercial privileges in Norway and Denmark, Margaret convinced the Hanse towns not to intervene on Albrecht's behalf. Margaret at age 22 demonstrated great charm, according to contemporary chroniclers, and her political maneuvering resulted in the election of her son Olaf (now Olaf V) to Denmark's kingship in May of 1376.

When Margaret's husband King Haakon VI died in 1380, Margaret immediately went to Norway to ensure Olaf's succession to the throne. Thus began a union between Norway and Denmark that was to last for over four centuries until 1814. Although Margaret was given the power of regency, she was to allow a Norwegian council to rule on her son's behalf when she was in Denmark. With the Hanseatic League controlling important areas of Denmark, the situation there required her energetic attention. Contemporary chronicles attest to her ability to provide effective leadership. "It is quite astonishing," said one source, "that a woman . . . became so powerful in a quarter of a year that she lacked nothing in the whole kingdom."

When Olaf reached the age of 15 in 1385, he declared his intention to rule without a regent. Nevertheless, Margaret remained his chief advisor and convinced him to press for the title of king of Sweden, despite the fact that Albrecht of Mecklenburg (uncle of the Albrecht who claimed the Danish throne in 1375) had ruled there since Magnus Eriksson's death in 1374. As Olaf's father had continually agitated to obtain the Swedish throne right up to his death in 1380, Margaret encouraged her son to carry on Haakon's policy.

Olaf's sudden death in 1387 did not dissuade Margaret from her determination to acquire the Swedish throne. Swedish nobles, resentful of the favors their King Albrecht granted to Germans, worked with her in their attempt to depose him. Margaret's position in Denmark and Norway was strengthened in 1387 and 1388 when both countries declared her to be Olaf's rightful heir; the Norwegian council declared her their "mighty lady and rightful ruler." Soon after, a council of Swedish nobles followed their example, vowing not only to overthrow Albrecht, but to accept Margaret and anyone she designated as her successor. In 1389, Albrecht was defeated, and most of Sweden was in Margaret's control.

Stockholm, however, presented a problem for the new queen of Sweden. German Hanse merchants controlled the town and were supplied by a notorious gang of pirates known as the Victuals Brothers. Their illegal activities had been encouraged by the Hanseatic League during its frequent altercations with Denmark. The lawless Brothers were responsible for various atrocities throughout Scandinavia, including the brutal sack of Bergen, Norway. By 1398, Margaret was able to subdue Stockholm, although she was forced to confirm privileges to the Hanse towns.

As Margaret's desire to maintain a united Scandinavian kingdom required her to find an acceptable heir, she chose her great-nephew Erik of Pomerania as her successor. In 1389, the Norwegians proclaimed eight-year-old Erik as king; it required several more years, until 1396, for Margaret to see her adopted son proclaimed king in Denmark and Sweden as well. Despite their shared king, each Scandinavian country retained its own separate government.

In 1397, a meeting was held at Kalmar with hopes of firmly establishing a hereditary state. At this gathering, Erik was officially crowned as king of all the Scandinavian countries. While plans for an even more thorough union were drawn up at Kalmar, they appear not to have been adopted officially by the participants. The first provision of the Kalmar document holds that: "The three kingdoms shall henceforth have one king and shall never be parted." But Danish and Norwegian seals were not attached to this document, indicating that the dynastic choice of Erik was intended to be a singular event. The Kingdoms preferred to make case-by-case decisions regarding future rulers.

Though King Erik was recognized as old enough to rule in 1400, Margaret—whose concerns remained both dynastic and political—managed affairs until her death in 1412. To maintain close ties with England and thus ensure protection against the Hanseatic naval power, she arranged for the marriage of King Henry IV's daughter Philippa to her adopted son Erik. Margaret's administrative policy was to increase the centralizing power of the crown, effected by appointing Danish nobles to oversee her interests in Sweden and Norway.

Critics have said that Margaret strengthened Denmark at the expense of Swedish and Norwegian national aspirations; if so, the more strategic location of Denmark and the vastly greater population perhaps provide the rationale for such a policy. By the end of her reign, she came under significant criticism. According to a Swedish monk: "Albrecht levied heavy taxes, but Margaret made them still heavier. What he left, she took; the peasant's horse, ox, and cow; in short, all his possessions."

In creating a Scandinavian union, Margaret changed the nature of government throughout her realms. Before 1389, each separate Scandinavian country had a system that entailed the sovereign's actual presence in the realm, making rule intensely personal. Margaret, however, ruled Norway and Sweden from Denmark; thus, she could not provide the important personal element that characterized earlier royal practice. Upon her death, probably from plague in 1412, Margaret left her successor a strong, united Scandinavia, but discontent in Norway and Sweden was to be the legacy of the united kingdoms of the North.

Further Reading

Gjerset, Knut. *History of the Norwegian People.* Macmillan, 1932.

Larsen, Karen. *A History of Norway.* Princeton University Press, 1948.

Zimmern, Helen. *The Hansa Towns.* London: T. Fisher Unwin, 1889. □

St. Margaret of Scotland

St. Margaret of Scotland (1045-1093), wife of the Scottish king Malcolm III, introduced important religious reforms into Scotland and was a civilizing agent in the social life of that country.

I nformation about the early life of Margaret is based on tradition; for her later years there is a dependable *Life of St. Margaret,* written by her confessor, Turgot. After some years spent in exile in Hungary, Margaret and her family returned to their homeland, England, in 1057. With the seizure of the English crown by William the Conqueror in 1066, Margaret's brother, Edgar Atheling, was clearly unable to realize his own claim to kingship, and soon the family was forced to flee the land. They sailed for the Continent, but contrary winds carried them to Scotland, where Malcolm offered first hospitality and then a marriage that in time produced eight children. Of the six sons, three became kings of Scotland, and one daughter, Maud, was married to Henry I of England. That none of her sons was given a traditional Scottish name is evidence of Margaret's influence.

Margaret set about to reshape the religious life and social patterns of Scotland. In public religion Margaret concerned herself with practices rather than with doctrine or

Margaret on her tomb

administration. Because certain Scottish religious customs differed from the usages of Rome and England, she caused a council to meet to deal with five points: the establishment of the initial date of Lent, the reception of Communion by the clergy at Easter, the mode of observance of the Sabbath, the manner of celebration of the Mass, and the legality of marriage between a man and his stepmother or the widow of his brother. Through persuasion and persistence Margaret caused the Scottish traditions to be abandoned, and the cultural isolation of Scotland was ended. In her private life Margaret won fame and affection for her piety, humility, and generosity to the poor.

Margaret reformed the manners of the Scottish court and further diversified the cultural life of the land. Under her leadership, ceremonies were made more elaborate; tapestries were hung on the walls; gold and silver dishes came into use; and court costumes were marked by the appearance of fur, velvet, and jewelry.

Only 3 days after her husband was killed in battle, Margaret died. So widely beloved was she that the people of Scotland immediately hailed her as a true saint. Her official canonization, however, did not come until 1250.

Further Reading

A recent scholarly appraisal of Margaret's place in Scottish history is in William Croft Dickinson, *A New History of Scotland,* vol. 1: *Scotland from the Earliest Times to 1603* (1961; rev. ed. 1965). Janet R. Glover, *The Story of Scotland* (1960), gives an adequate summary of Margaret's career within a straightforward narrative history of Scotland. T. Ratcliffe Barnett, *Margaret of Scotland, Queen and Saint* (1926), is chiefly concerned with the religious character and work of Margaret. Jane Oliver, *Sing, Morning Star* (1956), is a fictionalized biography that is informative, colorful, and pleasing to read.

Additional Sources

Wilson, Alan, J., *St Margaret, Queen of Scotland,* Edinburgh: J. Donald, 1993. □

Lynn Margulis

Lynn Margulis (born 1938) is a renowned theoretical biologist and professor of botany at the University of Massachusetts at Amherst. Her research on the evolutionary links between cells containing nuclei (eukaryotes) and cells without nuclei (prokaryotes) led her to formulate a symbiotic theory of evolution that was initially spurned in the scientific community but has become more widely accepted.

Margulis, the eldest of four daughters, was born in Chicago on March 5, 1938. Her father, Morris Alexander, was a lawyer who owned a company that developed and marketed a long-lasting thermoplastic material used to mark streets and highways. He also served as an assistant state's attorney for the state of Illinois. Her mother, Leone, operated a travel agency. When Margulis was fifteen, she completed her second year at Hyde Park High School and was accepted into an early entrant program at the University of Chicago.

Margulis was particularly inspired by her science courses, in large part because reading assignments consisted not of textbooks but of the original works of the world's great scientists. A course in natural science made an immediate impression and would influence her life, raising questions that she has pursued throughout her career: What is heredity? How do genetic components influence the development of offspring? What are the common bonds between generations? While at the University of Chicago she met Carl Sagan, then a graduate student in physics. At the age of nineteen, she married Sagan, received a B.A. in liberal arts, and moved to Madison, Wisconsin, to pursue a joint master's degree in zoology and genetics at the University of Wisconsin under the guidance of noted cell biologist Hans Ris. In 1960 she and Sagan moved to the University of California at Berkeley, where she conducted genetic research for her doctoral dissertation.

The marriage to Sagan ended before she received her doctorate. She moved to Waltham, Massachusetts, with her two sons, Dorion and Jeremy, to accept a position as lecturer in the department of biology at Brandeis University. She was awarded her Ph.D. in 1965. The following year, she became an adjunct assistant of biology at Boston University, leaving twenty-two years later as full professor. During her tenure at Boston University she taught two or three courses per semester and directed a $100,000-a-year research lab. In 1967 she married crystallographer Thomas N. Margulis. The couple had two children before they divorced in 1980. Since 1988, Margulis has been a distinguished university professor with the Department of Botany at the University of Massachusetts at Amherst.

Her interest in genetics and the development of cells can be traced to her earliest days as a University of Chicago undergraduate. She always questioned the commonly accepted theories of genetics, however, challenging the traditionalists by presenting hypotheses that contradicted current beliefs. She has been called the most gifted theoretical biologist of her generation by numerous colleagues. A profile of Margulis by Jeanne McDermott in the *Smithsonian* quotes Peter Raven, director of the Missouri Botanical Garden and a MacArthur fellow: "Her mind keeps shooting off sparks. Some critics say she's off in left field. To me she's one of the most exciting, original thinkers in the whole field of biology." Although few know more about cellular biology, Margulis considers herself a "microbial evolutionist," mapping out a field of study that doesn't in fact exist.

As a graduate student, Margulis became interested in cases of non-Mendelian inheritance, occurring when the genetic make-up of a cell's descendants cannot be traced solely to the genes in a cell's nucleus. For several years, she concentrated her research on a search for genes in the cytoplasm of cells, the area outside of the cell's nucleus. In the early 1960s, Margulis presented evidence for the existence of extranuclear genes. She and other researchers had found DNA in the cytoplasm of plant cells, indicating that heredity in higher organisms is not solely determined by genetic information carried in the cell nucleus. Her continued work in this field led her to formulate the serial endosymbiotic theory, or SET, which offered a new approach to evolution as well as an account of the origin of cells with nuclei.

Prokaryotes—bacteria and blue-green algae, now commonly referred to as cyanobacteria—are single-celled organisms that carry genetic material in the cytoplasm. Margulis proposes that eukaryotes (cells with nuclei) evolved when different kinds of prokaryotes formed symbiotic systems to enhance their chances for survival. The first such symbiotic fusion would have taken place between fermenting bacteria and oxygen-using bacteria. All cells with nuclei, Margulis contends, are derived from bacteria that formed symbiotic relationships with other primordial bacteria some two billion years ago. It has now become widely accepted that mitochondria—those components of eukaryotic cells that process oxygen—are remnants of oxygen-using bacteria. Margulis' hypothesis that cell hairs, found in a vast array of eukaryotic cells, descend from another group of primordial bacteria much like the modern spirochaete still encounters resistance, however.

The resistance to Margulis' work in microbiology may perhaps be explained by its implications for the more theoretical aspects of evolutionary theory. Evolutionary theorists, particularly in the English-speaking countries, have always put a particular emphasis on the notion that competition for scarce resources leads to the survival of the most well-adapted representatives of a species by natural selection, favoring adaptive genetic mutations. According to Margulis, natural selection as traditionally defined cannot account for the "creative novelty" to be found in evolutionary history. She argues instead that the primary mechanism driving biological change is symbiosis, while competition plays a secondary role.

Margulis doesn't limit her concept of symbiosis to the origin of plant and animal cells. She subscribes to the "Gaia" hypothesis first formulated by James E. Lovelock, British inventor and chemist. The "Gaia theory" (named for the Greek goddess of the earth) essentially states that all life, as well as the oceans, the atmosphere, and the earth itself are parts of a single, all-encompassing symbiosis and may fruitfully be considered as elements of a single organism.

Margulis has authored more than one hundred and thirty scientific articles and ten books, several of which are written with her son Dorion. She has also served on more than two dozen committees, including the American Association for the Advancement of Science, the MacArthur Foundation Fellowship Nominating Committee, and the editorial boards of several scientific journals. Margulis is co-director of NASA's Planetary Biology Internship Program and, in 1983, was elected to the National Academy of Sciences.

Further Reading

"The Creativity of Symbiosis," in *Scientific American*, Volume 266, Number 1, 1992, p. 131.

McCoy, Dan, "The Wizard of Ooze," in *Omni*, Volume 7, Number 49, 1985, pp. 49–78.

McDermott, Jeanne, "A Biologist Whose Heresy Redraws Earth's Tree of Life," in *Smithsonian*, Volume 20, Number 72, 1989, pp. 72–80.

"The Microbes' Mardi Gras," in *Economist*, Volume 314, Number 7643, 1990, pp. 85–86. □

Juan de Mariana

The Spanish Jesuit Juan de Mariana (1536-1624), a man of critical insight, accuracy, and courage, is well known as a historian and political thinker.

Juan de Mariana was born in Talavera de la Reina in the old kingdom of Toledo. He joined the Jesuits in 1554 and studied at the University of Alcalá de Henares. In 1561 he went to Rome, where he taught theology to, among other pupils, Robert Bellarmine, who was to become the most famous cardinal of his time. From there he went to Sicily, and in 1569 he was sent to Paris. His lectures on St. Thomas Aquinas were a great success, but in 1574, pleading ill health, he obtained permission to return to Spain. He retired to the Jesuit house in Toledo, where his literary activity was occasionally, and rudely, interrupted by the outside world. He died there on Feb. 16, 1624.

In Mariana's lifetime his writings had brought him into conflict with the Spanish monarchy, the French monarchy, and his own order. His first published work was *Historiae de rebus Hispaniae* (Toledo, 1592), in two different printings, one containing 20 and the other one 25 books. It reached to the conquest of Granada (1492). He then added 5 more books, making a total of 30 (Mainz, 1605) and bringing the history of Spain to the death of Ferdinand V and the accession of Charles V (1516). In a later abstract he brought events to the accession of Philip IV (1621). The success of the work was such that Mariana himself translated it into Spanish (the first edition was published in Madrid in 1601; J. Stevens translated it into English in 1699). Although uncritical about the legendary past, Mariana does try to bring the history of his country to the best standards of historiography and research of his times; the documentary part, however, is sadly lacking. Stylistically, it is a classic of Spanish prose.

In Toledo in 1599 Mariana published *De rege et regis institutione*, which was soon to become notorious. When Henry IV of France was murdered in 1610, it was quickly remembered that Mariana had advocated tyrannicide (book I, chapter 6); the book was burned in France, and it attracted considerable odium upon the Jesuits. His *Tractatus septem* (Cologne, 1609) again brought the author into the limelight of scandal, for two of the treatises (*De morte et immortalitate* and *De monetae mutatione*) were placed on the Index Expurgatorius, and the author came to grief with state and Inquisition alike. His tract criticizing his order (*De los grandes defectos que hay en la forma del govierno de los Jesuitas*, Bordeaux, 1625) came out posthumously, and it did not improve his standing with his own order.

Further Reading

John Laures, *The Political Economy of Juan de Mariana* (1928), has valuable pages on Mariana's economics, but it has been largely superseded by Guenter Lewy, *Constitutionalism and Statecraft during the Golden Age of Spain: A Study of the Political Philosophy of Juan de Mariana S. J.* (1960). Indispensable background information is contained in Bernice Hamilton, *Political Thought in Sixteenth-century Spain* (1963).

Additional Sources

Soons, Alan, *Juan de Mariana*, Boston: Twayne, 1982. □

José Carlos Mariátegui

The Peruvian writer José Carlos Mariátegui (1895-1930) was one of the most influential political and social theorists of his country in his time. He exposed in intense, probing essays many of the problematic aspects of Peru's cultural, social, and economic life.

José Carlos Mariátegui was born on June 14, 1895, in Lima. As a child, he was introverted and meditative, owing in part to having been invalided for years by an injury which eventually resulted in the loss of a leg. During his young manhood he wavered between accepting life passively and aggressively imposing his nonconformist will on the world about him. This conflict was decided when Mariátegui, an avid reader of all types of writing, came across the work of the Spanish socialist Luis Araquistán.

Mariátegui was now stirred to witness socialism in action. He made a lengthy and significant visit to Europe, where, particularly in Italy, he was exposed to socialist theories and practice. On his return to Peru, he found the country seething with proposals for nationalist reform. Along with other young idealists—all followers of the programs laid down by fellow countryman Manuel González Prada—Mariátegui gave vociferous support to such issues as the defense of the Indian and wide-sweeping reform in political as well as social spheres.

In 1924 the APRA (Alianza Popular Revolucionaria Americana) movement was instituted, and in 1926 Mariátegui founded the magazine *Amauta,* which came to be the principal voice of the leftist APRA rebels. Striking out on his own in 1928, Mariátegui was instrumental in the founding of the Socialist party of Peru, supported mainly by middle-class adherents and characterized by a specifically Marxist-Leninist line.

His Writings

In 1925 Mariátegui published his first book, *The Contemporary Scene,* a group of essays written on a wide variety of issues, such as the crisis of democracy, anti-Semitism, fascism, and the Indian problem. Much more influential, however, was his second work, *Seven Essays on the Interpretation of Peruvian Reality,* published in 1928. Professor Solomon Lipp stated that the *Seven Essays* "did much to channelize leftist thought in Peru," adding that these essays "constituted an incisive, penetrating analysis of the nation's cultural and economic life."

The topics treated by Mariátegui in this treatise are varied and far-reaching: the role of religion in Peru's history; the effect of colonial feudalism on the country; economic development; the problem of the enormous imbalance between the nation's urban and rural areas; the place of the Indian in Latin American society; and the questions of education and the need for university reform constitute the subjects of six of the essays.

The seventh essay deals with the manner in which the country's social structure has influenced the literature produced by Peruvian writers. Largely as a consequence of this fresh examination of the sources of literary expression, Mariátegui was able to contribute significantly to a critical evaluation and reorientation of his country's literature.

Though Mariátegui lived only two years longer, his message had been heard. His death on April 16, 1930, in Lima, did not still the urgings of his socially aware conscience. He remains today one of the most important voices of reform to have been raised in Latin America.

An edition of his complete works has been undertaken by his son. In addition to the two titles mentioned above, the following collections of Mariátegui's essays have appeared: *The Morning Soul and Other Seasons of Today's Man* (1950) and *Novel and Life* (1955).

Further Reading

Major sources on Mariátegui are in Spanish. A biographical sketch and other information on him are in William Rex Crawford, *A Century of Latin-American Thought* (1944; rev. ed. 1961), and Earl M. Aldrich, Jr., *The Modern Short Story in Peru* (1966).

Additional Sources

Chavarria, Jesus, *José Carlos Mariátegui and the rise of modern Peru, 1890-1930,* Albuquerque: University of New Mexico Press, 1979. □

Maria Theresa

Maria Theresa (1717-1780) was Holy Roman empress from 1740 to 1780. Ruling in the most difficult period of Austrian history, she modernized her dominions and saved them from dissolution.

The eldest daughter of the emperor Charles VI, Maria Theresa was born in Vienna on May 13, 1717. Her education did not differ in the main from that given any imperial princess, being both clerical and superficial, even though by the time she was an adolescent it was becoming increasingly probable that Charles would produce no male heir and that one day Maria Theresa would succeed to all his dominions. Charles did not act upon the insistent advice of his most capable adviser, Prince Eugene of Savoy, and marry his daughter off to a prince powerful and influential enough himself to protect her dominions in time of need. Instead he chose to rely upon the fanciful diplomatic guarantees offered by the Pragmatic Sanction. Thus, in 1736 Maria Theresa was permitted to marry for love. Her choice was Duke Francis Stephen of Lorraine. So that France might not object to the prospect of an eventual incorporation of Lorraine into the empire, Francis Stephen was forced to exchange his beloved province for the rather less valuable Tuscany.

In spite of this, and even though the marriage in its first 3 years produced three daughters, Maria Theresa was boundlessly happy. Then suddenly, in October 1740, her father died. At the age of 23, without anything in the way of formal preparation, without the least acquaintance with affairs of state, Maria Theresa had supreme responsibility thrust upon her.

War of the Austrian Succession

Francis Stephen was designated coregent and put in charge of restoring the finances of the empire, a task to which he brought considerable ability but for which he was not to have the requisite time. The treasury was empty, the army had been badly neglected, and as Prince Eugene had warned, Austria's neighbors now engaged in a contest to establish which of them could repudiate most completely the obligations they had subscribed to in the Pragmatic Sanction. Bavaria advanced claims to a considerable portion of the Hapsburg lands and was supported in this venture by France. Spain demanded the empire's Italian territories. Frederick II of Prussia, himself very recently come to the throne of his country, now offered to support Maria Theresa against these importunities if Austria would pay for this service by turning over to Prussia the province of Silesia. When this cynical offer was indignantly rejected in Vienna, Frederick sent his troops into Silesia in December 1740. Bavaria and France soon joined in this attack, thus launching the 8-year War of the Austrian Succession.

At first it seemed as if the young Maria Theresa could quickly be overwhelmed. The elector Charles of Bavaria secured his election as Emperor Charles VII and with German and French troops captured Prague. If his army had achieved a juncture with the Prussians, the Austrians would no longer have been in a position to defend themselves. But Frederick II had not launched his attack on Silesia to introduce a French hegemony in central Europe. He now concluded an armistice with the Austrians, who were, in 1742, able to concentrate their forces against the French and Bavarians, whom they threw out of Bohemia. Frederick came back into the war in 1744, withdrew again the next year, in which, the Bavarian Charles VII having died, Francis Stephen was elected emperor. The war was ended at last in 1748, Austria being forced to acquiesce in the Prussian retention of Silesia and losing also the Italian districts of Parma, Piacenza, and Guastalla to France. The loss of Silesia was very painful indeed, as it was perhaps the richest of all the Hapsburg provinces.

Domestic Reform

Maria Theresa had learned her job under the most difficult conditions during the war. But she had soon found that, among the members of the high court aristocracy, the only class from which, traditionally, important servants of the Crown could be drawn, there was no dearth of able men willing to unite their fate with that of the house of Hapsburg. Although she had never, in the course of the war, found a really satisfactory general, she had recognized the talents of, and placed in responsible positions, a number of able administrators, men such as counts Sinzendorf, Sylva-Tarouca, and Kaunitz. Thus, at the end of the war, the basis for a reform of the governmental apparatus already existed.

The actual work of reform, with the explicit end of strengthening Austria so that one day in the not too distant future Silesia might be recovered, was turned over to a Silesian exile, Count Frederick William Haugwitz. The key to Haugwitz's reform program was centralization. Bohemia and Austria were placed under a combined ministry, and the Provincial Estates were, insofar as possible, deprived of their authority or at least circumvented. At the same time industry was encouraged as a producer of wealth that could most readily be tapped by the state. In the provinces to which it was applied, the system produced dramatic results: on the average, the military contributions of the districts in question rose by 150 percent. Unfortunately, the concerted opposition of the nobility in Hungary prevented it from being applied there. Moreover, Haugwitz's position was being continually undermined by his colleague Kaunitz, who himself wished to play the role of Austria's savior.

Foreign Policy

In 1753 Kaunitz was given the title of state chancellor with unrestricted powers in the realm of foreign policy. While serving as Austrian ambassador to France, he had convinced himself that Austria's defeat in the recent war had been due largely to an unfortunate choice of allies. In particular, he thought, the empire had been badly let down by England. He now set about forging a new alliance whose chief aim was to surround Prussia with an insurmountable coalition. Saxony, Sweden, and Russia became Austria's allies. In 1755 Kaunitz's diplomatic efforts were crowned with the conclusion of an alliance with Austria's old enemy France, a circumstance that led to the conclusion of an alliance between Prussia and England. This diplomatic revolution seemed to leave the Prussians at a hopeless disadvantage, but Frederick II was not the man to await his own funeral, and in 1756 he opened hostilities, thus launching what was to become the Seven Years War.

Maria Theresa, although no lover of warfare for its own sake, welcomed the war as the only practical means of at last recovering Silesia. It was not to be. In spite of a much more energetic conduct of the war on the part of Austria, Frederick was for the most part able to fight his enemies one at a time. And when, in 1762, his situation at last appeared desperate, the death of Empress Elisabeth brought about a Russian withdrawal from the war, which now could no longer be won by the allies. In 1763 peace was concluded, and Silesia remained firmly in Prussian hands.

In the course of this second war, Maria Theresa developed the habit of governing autocratically, excluding Francis Stephen from all participation in the affairs of state. In spite of this the marriage was a happy one. From the dynastic point of view, the birth of Archduke Joseph in 1741 had assured the male succession. His birth was followed by numerous others, the imperial couple producing 16 children in all. Then suddenly, in 1765, the Emperor died of a stroke. Maria Theresa was inconsolable. For a time she thought of withdrawing to a cloister and turning the government over to Joseph, who was then 24. It was only with great difficulty that her ministers, with Kaunitz in the lead, managed to dissuade her from this course. And when she did return to public life, it was as a different woman. For the rest of her days she wore only black; she never again appeared at the gay divertisements of what had been a very lighthearted court; and if she had all her life been a pious Catholic, her devotion to religion now came to border on both fanaticism and bigotry.

Later Reign

At his father's death Joseph had been appointed coregent. Unlike his father, the archduke meant in fact to share in the governance of the realm. But this Maria Theresa was unwilling to let him do. After many recriminations, a compromise was arrived at: Joseph was to take charge of army reform and to share with Kaunitz the responsibility of making foreign policy. This arrangement was unfortunate

not only because it deprived Joseph of any real influence on the internal affairs of Austria, the sector in which his ideas were most promising, but also because he had no talent whatever either for diplomacy or for warfare.

The 15 years of the coregency were a time of continual struggle between mother and son, but it would be a mistake to construe them as an unrelenting struggle between the forces of progress, as represented by Joseph, and those of reaction, led by Maria Theresa. Although the archduke vigorously defended the principle of religious toleration, anathema to his mother, and once threatened to resign when she proposed to expel some Protestants from Bohemia, on the equally important question of peasant emancipation, Maria Theresa took a stand distinctly more favorable to the peasants than Joseph. In foreign affairs, she opposed Joseph's adventurous attempt to acquire Bavaria, which, as she had feared, led to war with Prussia in 1778; and when Joseph lost his nerve in the midst of the struggle, she took matters into her own hands and negotiated a by no means disadvantageous peace that resulted in the acquisition of the Innviertel.

These last events, incidentally, confirm that after the unsatisfactory conclusion of the Seven Years War the main Austrian objective was no longer a redress of balance against Prussia. If political and social reforms continued, it was in part because reform had become a way of life, in part because Maria Theresa recognized that a more centralized and effective government was an end worth pursuing for itself. Although it is true that throughout the coregency Joseph kept up a clamor for various changes, some of the major reforms of the period can nevertheless be attributed chiefly to the desires of the Empress. This is particularly true of the new penal code of 1768 and of the abolition of judicial torture in 1776. The penal code, although objected to as still unduly harsh, nevertheless had the virtue of standardizing both judicial proceedings and punishments. In spite of her devotion to the Catholic Church, Maria Theresa insisted on defending with great vigor the rights of the state vis-à-vis the Church.

In her reign, neither papal bulls nor the pastoral letters of bishops could circulate in her dominions without her prior permission, and in 1777 Maria Theresa joined a number of other European monarchs in banishing the Society of Jesus from her lands. In the course of 1780 Maria Theresa's health deteriorated rapidly. She died on November 29 of that year, probably of a heart condition.

Further Reading

The standard work on Maria Theresa is in German. The best biography in English is Robert Pick, *Empress Maria Theresa: The Earlier Years, 1717-1757* (1966). Other biographies are J. Alexander Mahan, *Maria Theresa of Austria* (1932); Constance Lily Morris, *Maria Theresa: The Last Conservative* (1937); and Edward Crankshaw, *Maria Theresa* (1970). George P. Gooch's excellent *Maria Theresa and Other Studies* (1951; repr. 1965) is part biography and part historiography, ending with a survey of European historical novels. For historical background and further information on Maria Theresa see Edith M. Link, *The Emancipation of the Austrian Peasant, 1740-1798* (1949).

Additional Sources

Crankshaw, Edward, *Maria Theresa*, New York: Atheneum, 1986. □

Marie Antoinette

Marie Antoinette (1755-1793) was queen of France at the outbreak of the Revolution. Her activities and reputation contributed to the decline of the prestige of the French monarchy.

Marie Antoinette was the daughter of the Holy Roman emperor Francis I and the empress Maria Theresa. In 1770 she was married to the French Dauphin, who 4 years later ascended the throne as Louis XVI. The personalities of the two rulers were very different: while Louis XVI was phlegmatic and withdrawn, Marie Antoinette was gay, frivolous, and imprudent in her actions and choice of friends. She soon became unpopular in the court and the country, antagonizing many of the nobles, including the King's brothers and those Frenchmen who regretted the recently concluded alliance with Austria, long regarded as the traditional enemy; for the population as a whole she became the symbol for the extravagance of the court.

Although Marie Antoinette did not intervene in foreign affairs as frequently as has been asserted, she soon forgot her statement on first entering France, when she interrupted an official greeting in German, "Speak French, Monsieur. From now on I hear no language other than French." She sometimes sought, usually without great success, to obtain French support for Austrian objectives, for example, against Prussia and the Low Countries.

The Queen's influence on domestic policy before 1789 has also been exaggerated. Her interventions in politics were usually in order to obtain positions and subsidies for her friends. It is true, however, that she usually opposed the efforts of reforming ministers such as A. R. J. Turgot and became involved in court intrigues against them. Such activities, as well as her associates and personal life, particularly the "diamond necklace affair," when it appeared that the Queen had yielded herself to a wealthy cardinal for an expensive diamond necklace, increased her unpopularity and led to a stream of pamphlets and satires against her. The fact that after the birth of her children Marie Antoinette's way of life became more restrained did not alter the popular image of an immoral and extravagant woman.

In the summer of 1788, when Louis XVI yielded to pressure and convoked the Estates General to deal with the fiscal crisis, Marie Antoinette agreed, or appeared to agree, to the return of Jacques Necker as chief minister and to granting the Third Estate as many representatives as the other two combined. However, after the meeting of the Estates General in May 1789 and such events as the taking of the Bastille (July 14, 1789), Marie Antoinette supported the conservative court faction most insistent upon maintaining the Old Regime.

On Oct. 1, 1789, the Queen was received enthusiastically at a royalist banquet at Versailles during which the Revolution was denounced and its symbols insulted. A few days later (October 4-5) a Parisian crowd forced the court to move to Paris, where it could be controlled more readily. Marie Antoinette's role in the efforts of the monarchy to work with such moderates as the Comte de Mirabeau and later with the constitutional monarchist A. P. Barnave is unclear, but it appears that she lacked confidence in them. After the attempt of the royal couple to escape was thwarted at Varennes (June 21, 1791), the Queen, convinced that only foreign intervention could save the monarchy, sought the aid of her brother, the Holy Roman emperor Leopold II. Convinced that France, in its weakened condition, with many officers already émigrés, would be easily defeated, she favored the declaration of war on Austria in April 1792. On Aug. 10, 1792, the Paris crowd stormed the Tuileries Palace and ended the monarchy (the following month the National Convention established the First French Republic).

On August 13 Marie Antoinette began a captivity that was to end only with her death. She was first imprisoned in the Temple with her family and, after Aug. 1, 1793, in the Conciergerie. After a number of unsuccessful attempts to obtain her escape failed, Marie Antoinette appeared before the Revolutionary Tribunal, charged with aiding the enemy and inciting civil war within France. The Tribunal found her guilty and condemned her to death. On Oct. 16, 1793, she went to the guillotine. As did Louis XVI, Marie Antoinette aroused sympathy by her dignity and courage in prison and before the executioner.

Further Reading

Most biographers of Marie Antoinette have been popularizers or men of letters rather than professional historians. In English, recommended are Hilaire Belloc, *Marie Antoinette* (1909; 2d ed. 1924), generally objective despite Belloc's sympathy for the monarchy; and Stefan Zweig, *Marie Antoinette: The Portrait of an Average Woman* (trans. 1933), the subtitle of which suggests the interpretation. A more recent and good introductory account of the Queen is Dorothy Moulton Mayer, *Marie Antoinette: The Tragic Queen* (1969). See also André Castelot, *Queen of France: A Biography of Marie Antoinette* (1957). □

Marie de France

The French poet Marie de France (active late 12th century) was an accomplished writer of lais and was probably the originator of that form.

Marie de France is one of those authors whose work is well known but whose life is largely conjectural. Her status as a *trouvère,* her education in both Latin and French, and her vocabulary and style identify her as a member of an aristocratic circle, possibly of noble birth. Her assumption of "de France" indicates no title but merely her connection with the Île-de-France. The themes of her lais reveal her close association with the *amour courtois* movement and strongly suggest that if, as a number of literary historians claim, she is the illegitimate half sister of Henry II, she was one of the young women who came under the direct influence of Marie de Champagne at the Poitevin court of Queen Eleanor of Aquitaine. This would account for her romantic inspiration.

Marie wrote in a dialect that indicates Normandy on the border of the Île-de-France. This would explain her use of Breton contes and fabliaux as the source of her stories, stories she said she had heard, not read. Breton entertainers were ubiquitous in Normandy and in Poitiers during the period Eleanor was in residence. They had to be bilingual, for otherwise their patrons and audiences would have been very small. The strange tales were seized upon and synthesized with the love code of Poitou to create the lais which Marie dedicated to Henry II.

The lais are done skillfully in octosyllabic rhymed couplets extending to 100 lines or less. This is a most satisfying length for a reading with a circle of ladies, and a handsome little page could hold their attention with his clear young voice. Also, in beautiful manuscripts the lais were entertaining private reading. They never were intended for public gatherings; they were too tenuous and dreamy. Of the dozen or so lais acknowledged as Marie's, only one, *Sir Lanval,* belongs specifically to the Arthurian legend.

Later work (ca. 1180) includes the didactic *Ysopet,* based on the fables of shrewd Reynart the Fox. Though the title refers her fables to Aesop, Marie claims that the collection she used was produced by "Alfred," presumably Alfred the Great. This has strengthened the contention that Marie de France lived many years in England, where she was at her death the abbess of Shaftesbury.

Marie's last known work is her *La Espurgatoire de Saint Patrice.* Basically this is a translation of a Latin source which proved so popular that several French poets produced "purgatories" at about the same time.

Further Reading

Urban Tigner Holmes, *A History of Old French Literature, from the Origins to 1300* (1937; rev. ed. 1962), is a satisfactory substitute for the many fine surveys written in French. Holmes's treatment of Marie de France sets her in relationship to the poets of her time. A remarkably complete look into the lives of the courts in various parts of France and England where Eleanor, Henry II, and their sons presided is in Amy R. Kelly, *Eleanor of Aquitaine and the Four Kings* (1950), which provides a brilliant introduction to the workings of the Poitevin courts of love. E.K. Chambers, *Arthur of Britain* (1927), gives careful attention to Marie's place in the Arthurian legend. □

John Marin III

Remembered primarily as a watercolorist, the American painter John Marin III (1870-1953) emphasized the rhythmic structure of natural forms through abstraction.

John Marin was born on Dec. 23, 1870, in Rutherford, N. J. His mother died 9 days later. His father was forced to travel, so John grew up with his mother's relations in Delaware and New Jersey. Marin began to draw when he was 8. He attended public schools and spent a year at the Stevens Institute of Technology. His early works in watercolor, though able, do not anticipate later accomplishments. In 1889 he went to New York City, receiving a haphazard training in architecture as an apprentice in various offices. Despite this, in 1893 Marin opened his own office. He designed his own house in Union City as well as six others.

During this time Marin continued painting. When he was 28, he began classes at the Pennsylvania Academy of Fine Arts in Philadelphia and won a prize for drawings. Even so, he found the prevailing academic approach unproductive and left. Marin did not know what he wanted as much as he knew what he did not. "I was a kid until I was thirty," he said of himself. He admired James McNeill Whistler and imitated him in several of the small oils he did between 1900 and 1905. In 1904 he studied briefly at the Art Students League in New York City.

The following year Marin settled in Paris. His father provided the necessary funds. He made several excursions throughout Europe, to Amsterdam, Belgium, Italy, and London, and was abroad for nearly 5 years. While in Paris he tried etching and continued to paint and had some success.

The *Mills of Meaux* (1906), an oil, was purchased by the French government. Marin was represented at the Salon d'Automne. One of his etchings was included in an issue of the *Gazette des beaux-arts* and another in *L'Art décoratif*. His etchings began to sell in 1907.

In 1908 Marin met Alfred Stieglitz, the famous photographer whose New York City art gallery, called "291," was among the first to support modern art in America. Stieglitz may have introduced the art of Georges Seurat and Paul Cézanne to Marin. In 1909 Stieglitz exhibited paintings by Alfred Maurer and Marin and the next year gave Marin his first one-man show. Marin, who was then 40, went home briefly for the show but returned to paint in Switzerland. In 1912 he married. He was represented in the celebrated 1913 Armory Show in New York.

Marin's style matured at this time. In his Tirol series, he contrasts the frozen energies of rising mountains with the neat rectilinear ordering of the Swiss village below. He employs a shorthand method to define the dynamic properties of forms. His brush rides lightly on the surface of the coarse paper to suggest light and atmosphere. The white of the paper plays a critical role; forms appear to emerge from it as if coalescing from a flux. The paintings sparkle. The execution suggests spontaneous improvisation held in check by masterful control. In 1912 he interpreted the Woolworth Building, Brooklyn Bridge, and downtown Manhattan in such a fragmented, staccato manner as to threaten structure and stability. Skyscrapers appear futuristically disjointed and twisted, as do the sky and surrounding elements, in a manner suggesting pervasive syncopation and rapid tempo.

Marin's later work advanced little. He and his wife settled in America, and the locale of his painting changed. Now he explored the Maine seacoast and the New England states. In 1929 and 1930 he went to Taos and Santa Fe, N. Mex., making such excursions to paint during the summers. The Museum of Modern Art in New York City gave him a retrospective show in 1936. In 1950 he had a large one-man exhibition at the Venice Biennale, and there were several others later. In the final decade of his life he worked more and more in oil. He died at Cape Split, Maine, on Oct. 1, 1953.

Further Reading

Marin's letters, poetry, and essays were collected in Dorothy Norman, ed., *The Selected Writings of John Marin* (1949). E. M. Benson, *John Marin: The Man and His Work* (1935), was the first extended study on Marin. MacKinley Helm, *John Marin* (1948), offers a more extended picture. The selection of plates is comprehensive, although the quality is generally not satisfying. A recent work, Sheldon Reich, *John Marin: A Stylistic Analysis and Catalogue Raisonné* (2 vols., 1969), is a scholarly, well-written study.

Additional Sources

John Marin, Chicago: International Film Bureau, 1976. □

Marino Marini

Marino Marini (1901-1980) infused new life into Italian sculpture by invoking both antique and Renaissance traditions in his horse-and-rider images. He dwelt upon the equestrian theme throughout his career. Considered a highly original artist, his talents were not limited to sculpture. He was also a prolific painter, as well as a draftsman and graphic artist, whose work is today exhibited worldwide—and in the Marino Marini museum, located in one of the oldest churches in Florence.

Marino Marini was born in Pistoia, Tuscany, on February 27, 1901. His artistic endeavors began early and were intense; in 1917 he enrolled at the Academy of Fine Arts (Accademia di Belle Arti) in Florence and studied painting and sculpture. Marini's early teachers were Galileo Chini (painting) and Domenico Trentacoste (sculpture).

His first significant sculpture dates from the late 1920s, and from this period *Popola* (People) (terra cotta, 1929) is the most mature piece; it is essentially a double portrait in the manner of early Roman busts.

In 1929 Marini, at the invitation of Arturo Martini, became the chair of sculpture at the Art School of the Villa Reale in Monza, Milan. Also in 1929, Marini exhibited in Nice, during his first visit to Paris. During the 1930s his style and imagery developed, and he began to explore the textural and coloristic possibilities of terra cotta, plaster, and bronze. His subjects included wrestlers and acrobats—some conventional, some more skillfully composed— and occasionally he depicted mythological figures such as Icarus, Bacchus, and Pomona. His fame derives in part from some of these works.

Marini's first solo exhibition took place in Milan in 1932, and in 1935 he won his first prize at the Rome Quadriennale.

He married Mercedes "Marina" Pedrazzini, who would eventually help to draw Marini out artistically.

Sought Meaning Through His Work

Marini became a professor at Brera Academy of Fine Arts in Milan in 1940, a career move which afforded him the time to travel widely, meet some of the most important artists of the era, such as Pablo Picasso, and further his quest for artistic meaning. It was during this time that Marini's paintings took on a near-abstract style. Some of his trips brought him to the United States. His first loyalty, however, was to his native Tuscany. Marini is quoted as saying: "One must return to Tuscany often, for it is the architecture of ourselves. One always discovers a new and absolute perfection, which is of the soul."

Relocated to Switzerland

He remained at Villa Reale until 1943, when his studio was destroyed amidst the fighting of World War II. It was at this time that he visited his wife's birthplace, the Swiss Canton of Ticino, and reunited with old friends like Wotruba, Germaine Richier, Giacometti, Haller and Banninger. Marini produced several bronze and plaster portraits during this time, and in 1945 he exhibited at the Kunstmuseum in Basle.

Marini's portraits maintained an unusual degree of distance and coolness, in part a result of the rather abstract rendering of his subjects and the independent life which he gave to them. One typical example is his portrait of composer Igor Stravinsky (2 versions: 1950, 1951).

In his depictions of the female form, such as *Pomona* (1941) and *Dancer* (1949), the artist took on a different set of problems. These freestanding figures have heavy, squat proportions and an archaic demeanor, yet they retain their grace and poise in spite of their apparent weight.

Equestrian Theme Develops

The horse-and-rider theme, embodied early in *The Pilgrim* (1939), most clearly reveals Marini's prowess and introspection as a sculptor. Another early example appeared in 1936—*Horseman,* a somewhat conventional updating of the traditional equestrian portrait. But the following year Marini altered the situation between horse and rider considerably, with the seated figure thrown back at a radical angle, as in *Horse and Rider* (1937). That image recurred often, from the frontally-composed terra cotta relief *Quadriga* (1941) to the geometrically abstract *The Miracle, Horse and Rider* (1959-1960).

Interpretation of the horse-and-rider theme, and its historical significance, varied considerably. After World War

II, the theme evoked for Marini a symbol of mankind's twilight—the human figure representing ecstasy and at the same time tragedy, the horse representing nature's unrestrained forces. Before World War II, however, Marini's equestrian was intended to appear timelessly serene and symbolic of man's universal search. Yet no one interpretation exhausts the image, just as Marini seemingly did not exhaust the variety of materials and textures used to create it.

Returned to Italy Following WWII

Following the war, Marini returned to Milan and Brera. A room was dedicated to his work during the 24th Venice Biennale in 1948. He formed lifelong friendships with Henry Moore and Curt Valentin, an American merchant who helped to organize a 1950 New York exhibition for him. Marini was awarded the Feltrinelli prize in 1952, and in 1957 he received a commission for more equestrian sculpture from The Hague city council (a copy of which remains on display at San Pancrazio).

Marini continued to exhibit throughout northern Europe and turned out many more paintings (he actually painted continually throughout his life) in the mid-1960s. The Marino Marini Museum exhibition was opened in Milan in 1973 and contained a significant portrait collection. A permanent showing was dedicated to Marini in 1976 in Munich, and in 1978 Japan received an exhibition of Marini sculptures and paintings. An archive of significant Marini documentation was installed at the former convent of Tau in Pistoia in 1979.

Marino Museum Opened

Marino Marini died in Viareggio in 1980, but his artistic legacy has been preserved at the Marino Marini Museum in Florence. The museum is formerly the church of San Pancrazio, one of Florence's oldest. After serving briefly as a military depot, it became home to a collection of works first donated by Marini and then by his wife Marina. The Marino Marini Museum opened in 1988 and houses close to 200 pieces, arranged by subject matter.

Further Reading

Umbro Apollonio, *Marino Marini* (Edizioni del Milione, 1953; 3d ed. 1958), is an appreciation and interpretation rather than a critical examination of the sculptor's work; See also: Carli Enzo, *Marino Marini* (Hoepli, 1950); Marino Marini and Émile Langui, *Marino Marini* (Universe Books, 1959); Douglas Cooper, *Marino Marini* (New York Graphic Society, 1959); Eduard Trier, *The Sculpture of Marino Marini* (Praeger, 1961); A.M. Hammacher, *Marino Marini: Sculpture, Painting, Drawing* (H.N. Abrams, 1970); Marino Marini, *Marino Marini: Complete Works* (Tudor Publishing Co., 1970); Alberto Busignami, *Marini* (Hamlynm, 1971); and Sam Hunter, *Marino Marini—The Sculpture* (Abrams, 1993), with an introduction by Marina Marini.

Marini's work is also treated in the following journal articles, some of which were written by Marini himself and published posthumously: Marino Marini, "Man on Horse" *Apollo* (Nov. 1984); Marino Marini, "Miracle" *Art News* (Feb. 1985); Marino Marini, "Cavallo" *Artforum* (Summer 1985); Marino Marini, "Henry Miller" *Arts Review* (Feb. 14, 1986); Marino

Marini, ''Henry Moore'' *The Burlington Magazine* (Oct. 1986); Marino Marini, ''Angel of the Citadel'' *Architectural Digest* (Dec. 1986); Marino Marini, ''Horse and Rider'' *Art News* (Dec. 1987); Marino Marini, ''Jean Arp'' *The Magazine Antiques* (Nov. 1991); Bonnie Barrett Stretch, ''Kent Gallery, Inc., New York, Exhibit'' *Art News* (Jan. 1992); Megan Mueller, ''A Selection of Modern Italian Art'' *Art News* (Feb. 1992); Marino Marini, ''Gentleman on a Horse'' *Art in America''* (April 1992); Stanley Bleifield, ''Marino Marini—The Sculpture'' *Sculpture Review* (book review) (1993); Massimo Carboni, ''Museo Marino Marini, Florence Exhibit'' *Artforum* (Sept. 1994); and Marino Marini, ''Rider and Horse'' *Art & Antiques* (Jan. 1996). □

Francis Marion

Francis Marion (1732-1795), one of the great partisan leaders of the American Revolutionary War, was known as the ''Swamp Fox'' because of his craftiness in eluding pursuers in the Carolina swamps and his brilliant guerrilla operations.

Francis Marion was born in Berkeley County, S.C. He had little education and remained semiliterate to the end of his life. As a boy of 15, he went to sea for a year. After that, he turned to farming on the family land. In 1761 he took part in the war against the Cherokee Indians as a lieutenant of militia. He made something of a reputation by leading a successful attack against a strong Indian position. More importantly, he became familiar with the very special tactics of guerrilla warfare—using small forces, hitting and running, dispersing troops in one place and reforming them in another, and employing the element of surprise. When the campaign ended, he returned to farming, at first on leased land and then, in 1773, on a plantation of his own, Pond Bluff, near Eutaw Springs, S.C. Two years later he was elected to the provincial legislature and also accepted appointment as a captain in the second of two infantry regiments South Carolina raised at the outbreak of the Revolutionary War.

In the first several years of the war, Marion saw service in and around Charleston, S.C. In September 1775 he led his company in capturing the forts in Charleston harbor from the British. In the summer of the next year he joined in repulsing the English attempt to retake Charleston. Meanwhile he had been promoted to major in February 1776 and to lieutenant colonel in November. He spent the next two years skirmishing in the Charleston area and drilling militia troops. In November 1778 he took command of the 2nd Regiment; in November 1779 he led the regiment in an unsuccessful attack on Savannah. The following year was a disastrous one for the colonial cause. In May 1780 British forces retook Charleston, and in August they shattered the American army under Gen. Horatio Gates at the battle of Camden. This ended organized resistance by the Americans in South Carolina.

Marion now took to the swamps and to guerrilla warfare. With a small mobile force of 20 to 70 men, he embarked upon harassing operations, hitting British supply lines and cutting communications between their posts. ''Fertile of stratagems and expedients'' and moving like a phantom, he roamed the area between Charleston and Camden and along the Santee and Peedee rivers. In August 1780 he rescued 150 American prisoners being transported by the British; in September he scattered a force of Tories; in December he shot up a column of British replacements. Every effort to capture him failed. In the fall of 1780 Lt. Col. Banastre Tarleton, one of England's ablest cavalrymen, pursued Marion relentlessly but could not catch him. After a 7-hour chase through 26 miles of swamp he said, ''But as for this damn old fox, the devil himself could not catch him.'' Another pursuer, Lt. Col. John W. T. Watson, who searched for Marion in March 1781, explained his failure by concluding that Marion ''would not fight like a gentleman or a Christian.''

In December 1780 Marion, having been made a brigadier general of militia by the governor of South Carolina, began recruiting a brigade and establishing a base at Snow's Island at the confluence of the Peedee and Lynches rivers not far from the North Carolina border. From this place he operated in support of Gen. Nathanael Greene, who had come south to replace Gates in October and to restore American supremacy in the Carolinas. Marion took part in several operations in the summer of 1781 while continuing his guerrilla action. That September he reached the peak of his career at the battle of Eutaw Springs. In this fight, which ended with the British forces in retreat to North Carolina, Marion commanded the American right wing; this was the largest number of troops he ever commanded. His men, whom he had trained, fought superbly, and he led them with courage and coolness. To Congress, Greene reported, "the militia gained much honor by their firmness."

After Eutaw Springs, Marion went to the South Carolina Legislature as an elected representative in the session of 1781. He was reelected in 1782 and 1784. Between times, he returned to his brigade, leading it in several engagements. At the end of the war he married a wealthy cousin, Mary Videau, and settled down at Pond Bluff, where he died on Feb. 26, 1795.

Further Reading

The only reliable account of Marion is Robert Duncan Bass, *Swamp Fox: The Life and Campaigns of General Francis Marion* (1959).

Additional Sources

The life of Gen. Francis Marion, a celebrated partisan officer in the Revolutionary War, against the British and Tories in South Carolina and Georgia, Charleston, S.C.: Tradd Street Press, 1976. □

Jacques Maritain

The French Roman Catholic philosopher Jacques Maritain (1882-1973) was the leading figure in the 20th-century renascence of Thomism.

Jacques Maritain was born in Paris on Nov. 18, 1882. Under the auspices of his mother, Mauritain's religious training was Protestant and his education rationalistic and humanitarian; his Catholic father played little part in these aspects of his upbringing. Maritain attended the Lycée Henri IV and the Sorbonne, where he devoted himself to studying modern thought in philosophy, literature, biology, and social questions. At the Sorbonne he met Raïssa Oumansoff, a Jewish Russian émigré, whom he married in 1904. A highly creative person who later established a career and a reputation in her own right, working closely with her husband on several of his books and publishing a number of her own, she attended with Maritain the lectures of the famous philosopher Henri Bergson while both were university students, and for a time they were influenced by his thought.

Shortly after their marriage the Maritains came under the influence of Léon Bloy, a tempestuous intellectual and ardent Roman Catholic. Disillusioned in their intense quest for knowledge by the alternatives offered by modern thought, they were converted to Catholicism and baptized in 1906. Their conversion became the vanguard of a return to Catholicism among some leading French intellectuals.

After completing his work at the Sorbonne, Maritain studied biology for 2 years at the University of Heidelberg (1907-1908) under the distinguished biologist Hans Driesch. Upon his return to France he studied the philoso-phy of St. Thomas Aquinas, fulfilling an interest which had begun while he was in Heidelberg. Maritain found the fullest satisfaction of both the intellect and the soul in the thought of St. Thomas, with its harmonizing of revelation and reason and its holistic and realistic description of reality. At this time Maritain decided to dedicate his career to the communication of Thomistic ideas and their application to modern problems. While he was studying, he supported himself by editing a lexicon for a French publisher.

From 1912 to 1914 Maritain taught philosophy at the Collège Stanislas. In 1914 he was appointed to the chair of the history of modern philosophy at the Institut Catholique, continuing also his teaching at the Collège. For his *Introduction to Philosophy* (1921) he was awarded the title *doctor ad honorem* by the Congregation of Studies in Rome.

In the years that followed, Maritain was enormously productive as a teacher, lecturer, writer, reviewer, editor, and organizer of Thomistic study, as well as a political philosopher and champion of social justice. During World War II Maritain lived in the United States, his "second home," where he taught at Princeton, Columbia, and the University of Chicago. From 1945 to 1948 Maritain was French ambassador to the Vatican. He spent the remainder of his active career teaching at Princeton. After his retirement in 1953 he returned to Paris to live. He died on April 28, 1973, at the age of 90. He received many honors both from universities and from the Church.

Of Maritain's many books perhaps the best-known and most significant are *Art and Scholasticism* (1920), the first of several works on art which constitute one of his major contributions; *The Angelic Doctor* (1929), a study of the life and thought of St. Thomas; *The Degrees of Knowledge* (1932), probably his single most important writing and the fullest statement of his philosophical position; *Scholasticism and Politics* (1940); *Existence and the Existent* (1947); *The Person and the Common Good* (1947); *Man and the State* (1951); and *Moral Philosophy* (1960). *The Peasant of the Garonne* (1968) is a sharply critical look at a number of trends in the Catholic Church since the Second Vatican Council.

Maritain's work continued to be published by academic and scholarly presses even two decades after his death. Recent works include *Integral Humanism, Freedom in the Modern World, and a Letter on Independence* (1996) and *The Degrees of Knowledge* (1995)

Further Reading

The best biography of Jacques Maritain is his wife's memoirs, Raïssa Maritain, *We Have Been Friends Together* (trans. 1942) and *Adventures in Grace* (trans. 1945); A short but very useful biographical account appears in Donald and Idella Gallagher, *The Achievement of Jacques and Raïssa Maritain: A Bibliography, 1906-1961* (1962); DiJoseph, John *Jacques Maritain and the Moral Foundation of Democracy*, Rowman 1996. □

Gaius Marius

Gaius Marius (ca. 157-86 B.C.) was a Roman general and popular politician. His military reforms and great commands led to the growing involvement of the army in politics and the eventual collapse of the republican system.

B orn near Arpinum in central Italy, Marius was of country stock. However, his family was well enough situated that Marius could enter a public career in Rome. He saw his first military service in 134-133 B.C. with Scipio Aemilianus (Scipio Africanus Minor) at Numantia, where Marius was decorated for bravery. Ten years later, as military tribune, he may have served under Q. Caecilius Metellus Balearicus against the Balearic pirates. In 122 Marius returned to Rome to be elected to the quaestorship and may have accompanied Q. Fabius Maximus, son of Scipio Aemilianus, to Gaul.

Marius thus earned powerful backing among the Roman nobility. In consequence, under the patronage of the Metelli, he won election to the plebeian tribunate for 119. But in an unexpected show of independence as tribune, he carried a bill limiting the influence of the powerful families at elections and so lost the support of the Metelli. In 118 he ran for the curule and plebeian aedileship and lost both elections. Undaunted, he applied for the praetorship for 116 and won, but he escaped a bribery charge only because of a

tie vote by the jury. His praetorship was undistinguished, but he may have placated the nobility and so was made governor of Father Spain. At this point his political career might well have ended.

Jugurthine War

When Q. Caecilius Metellus Numidicus was sent to Africa in 109 to deal with Jugurtha, he chose Marius as a member of his staff, perhaps to placate equestrian and Italian interests. From the outset Marius intended to use the appointment for his political advancement. Cooperating with equestrians in Africa and popular agitators in Rome, he openly criticized Metellus's conduct of the war. Over Metellus's objections he returned to Rome to run for the consulship for 107. Marius was the first "new man" in 35 years to win the office.

After Marius's election the people voted to transfer the command in Africa to him. When the Senate tried to embarrass him by authorizing the recruitment of additional troops for the unpopular war, Marius took the unprecedented step of enrolling men from the propertyless class, who in the past had been excluded from legionary service. As the people's consul, he intended to win the war with a people's army. Within 2 years Marius beat Jugurtha from the field, but part of the glory of the victory was stolen by his quaestor, L. Cornelius Sulla, who negotiated the surrender of Jugurtha. As a result, bitter enmity developed between Marius and Sulla.

Consular Career

Meanwhile, senatorial leaders had failed to meet a threat to northern Italy from migrating Cimbri and Teutons. In reaction the people turned to Marius, whom they elected in absentia against all constitutional practice to the consulship for 104 and to four successive consulships from 103 to 100. For the northern war, Marius recruited another popular army. He also introduced major reforms in the training and organization of the Roman legions, making the cohort, instead of the smaller maniple, the chief tactical unit. His reorganization continued in effect through the early empire. Again Marius was victorious. He slaughtered the Teutons and Ambrones at Aquae Sextiae in 102 and the Cimbri at Vercellae in 101 to save Italy.

But Marius had won his six consulships not without a price. In 103 the demagogue L. Appuleius Saturninus had attached himself to Marius's cause by passing legislation benefiting Marius's African veterans. In 101 Marius used his veterans to secure the consulship for himself and a second tribunate for Saturninus. As tribune in 100, Saturninus then rammed through an agrarian-colonial bill with the help of the veterans. The bill provided for allotments to veterans in Gaul and called for the establishment of colonies in Sicily and Greece open to Italians as well as veterans and city poor.

When Metellus Numidicus refused to swear the oath attached to the measure, Marius and Saturninus forced him into exile and so got rid of a mutual enemy. But when Saturninus tried for a third tribunate and attempted to install C. Servilius Glaucia in the consulship for 99 by murdering his competitor, Marius abandoned him and cooperated with the Senate in restoring public order.

Marius failed, however, to prevent the lynching of Saturninus and Glaucia and so lost political credit among the city crowd. When Metellus Numidicus was recalled from exile in 98, Marius left for a tour of the East. He returned in 97, but although he still commanded a large following among his veterans and the Italians, he found himself outmaneuvered in Rome by the senatorial leaders whom he had antagonized.

Social War

In the Social War, Marius came out of semiretirement to serve as legate to the consul P. Rutilius Lupus in 90. After the death of the consul and another legate, Marius defeated the Marsi and Marrucini and saved the situation in the north. But he refused reappointment in 89 ostensibly for reasons of health but perhaps because he sympathized with the Italians and hoped for the command against Mithridates in the East. To his disappointment the Senate awarded the Eastern command to Sulla, who was elected consul for 88.

But to get Marian support for his proposal to distribute the new Italian citizens in all the tribes, the tribune P. Sulpicius Rufus introduced a bill to transfer the command to Marius and pushed his measures through with the help of Marius's veterans. When Sulla marched on Rome to reclaim the command, he had Marius and Sulpicius declared public enemies. Marius fled to Africa after barely escaping execution at Minturnae.

In Africa, Marius watched for an opportunity to return to Rome. It came when Gnaeus Octavius deposed his colleague L. Cornelius Cinna for again trying to support Italian claims for full franchise. Marius joined Cinna in his march on the city, collecting an army in Etruria and taking charge of Cinna's military operations. When Octavius surrendered and Cinna was again recognized as consul, Marius grimly refused to enter the city until the sentence of exile had been formally repealed by the people. For the murders and executions which followed his entry into the city, Marius was only partly responsible. Cinna deliberately planned some, and others were committed by the victorious troops, who got out of hand, or by lesser men seeking private revenge. There is no evidence that Marius was mentally unbalanced when he returned to Italy.

To reward Marius for his services, Cinna reassigned to him the Eastern command and chose him as his colleague in the consulship for 86. But, 70 years old and worn out by the rigors of his exile and return, Marius took sick shortly after entering that office for the seventh time. He died of pneumonia on Jan. 13, 86.

Further Reading

The chief ancient sources for Marius are Plutarch, *Life of Marius;* Sallust, *Jugurthine War;* and Appian, *Bellum Civile.* For a sympathetic view of Marius and a full discussion of the major problems see T. F. Carney, *A Biography of C. Marius* (1961; 2d ed. 1970). *The Cambridge Ancient History,* vol. 9 (1932), and H. H. Scullard, *From the Gracchi to Nero* (1959; 2d ed.

1963), give valuable accounts of Marius's career. See also Phillip A. Kildahl, *Caius Marius* (1968). ☐

Pierre Carlet de Chamblain de Marivaux

The French novelist and dramatist Pierre Carlet de Chamblain de Marivaux (1688-1763) created a complex and eminently personal style, indicating the gradual transition in France from 17th-century neoclassic art to an introspective art of individual sentiment and experience.

Born in Paris, the son of a royal mint official whose bourgeois origins fringed on those of the lesser nobility, Pierre Carlet de Marivaux spent his childhood in the provinces and returned to the capital in 1710. While ostensibly though rather fitfully studying law, he was already immersed in literary efforts, composing first satires and then serious imitations of extravagant adventure novels. Little is known about his private life, except that he married in 1717, fathered a daughter 2 years later, and never remarried after his wife's death in 1723.

The year 1720 was doubly significant for Marivaux: he was financially ruined in the collapse of the Law Bank, and he saw his first dramatic work produced, *L'Amour et la vérité,* a dismal failure in its own right. Undaunted, he struggled to earn a living writing for newspapers, even launching the ephemeral *Spectateur français* (1722). Meanwhile, an unsuccessful stage encounter with the heroism and classical verse required by the Théâtre Français (*Annibal,* a tragedy in five acts, 1720) convinced him that his fantasy *Arlequin poli par l'amour* (*Robin, Bachelor of Love*), well handled by the Théâtre Italien that same year, and marked the real domain of his dramatic talent. This "minor" genre of irregular prose comedy, although it earned him the disdain of contemporary arbiters such as Voltaire, was to promise survival and eventual glory to a talent ranked second in France only to that of Molière.

Among 30 pieces written for the stage, Marivaux's most important comedies remain *La Surprise de l'amour* (1722), *La Double inconstance* (1722; *Double Infidelity*), *Le Jeu de l'amour et du hasard* (1730; *The Game of Love and Chance*), and *Les Fausses confidences* (1737; *Sylvia Hears a Secret*). Departing from the farcical inspiration of Molière but holding to the conventional figures provided by his best interpreters, the Italian players, Marivaux sought to mingle fantasy with a graceful portrayal of amorous sentiment. His eternal subject is the nascent sentiment of love, its arduous avowal, the blind simplicity of its disguises, and the drastic involvements required by this world for the pursuit of happiness. Love, in Marivaux's sometimes precious dialogue analyses, is forever that "surprise" generously assured to youthful pride and purity of heart.

Although scarcely a year passed at the height of Marivaux's career without at least one successful comedy in production, he was never able to attain real celebrity in his own time, a fact due largely to current prejudice in favor of the neoclassic heroic genre, tragedy. Destined to announce preferred genres of the future, Marivaux was important in the evolution of narrative as well as dramatic art: his two unfinished novels, *La Vie de Marianne* (1731-1741; *The Life of Marianne*) and *Le paysan parvenu* (1735-1736), remain signal efforts in the long fight of that other ''minor'' genre to attain recognition. Although admitted to the French Academy in 1742, Marivaux outlived the uncertain literary renown he had won. Producing little over the final 20 years of his life, he died in relative poverty.

Further Reading

Critical works in English include the general study by Edward Joseph Hollingsworth Greene, *Marivaux* (1965), as well as Ruth Kirby Jamieson, *Marivaux: A Study in Sensibility* (1941), and Kenneth Newton McKee, *The Theater of Marivaux* (1958). For additional material on Marivaux, Geoffroy Atkinson, *The Sentimental Revolution: French Writers of 1690-1740* (1966), and John Cruickshank, ed., *French Literature and its Background* (1968), vol. 3, are recommended. □

St. Mark

St. Mark (first century A.D.), one of the 12 Apostles chosen by Jesus, is traditionally considered the author of the Second Gospel.

Little is known of Mark as a person. He is called ''John'' in three of the texts of the New Testament (Acts 12:12,25; 13:5,13; 15:37). The early Christians gathered at his family's house in Jerusalem (Acts 13:13). He accompanied Paul and Barnabas on Paul's first missionary journey as far as Perga in Pamphylia. The last mention of Mark is in the Acts when it is noted that he journeyed to Cyprus with Barnabas.

Mark's closest relationship seems to have been with Peter. Peter sends Mark greetings in his first letter (5:13), and Papias, a 2nd-century Christian writer, states that Mark copied down the words of Peter and thus composed the Gospel that carries his name. As far as can be judged from the testimony of Christian writers in the 2d and 3d centuries, Mark composed his Gospel in Greek some time between A.D. 63 and 70. If, as has been surmised, Peter was one important source for Mark's Gospel, and if the assigned date of composition is correct, it is possible that Mark accompanied Peter to Rome, going on from there after Peter's death.

Scholars who have studied the text of Mark's Gospel agree in general that he used some basic literary source related to the present Gospels of Matthew and Luke. Mark's Gospel presents the least amount of historical or geographical information of all four Gospels. Mark is the first author to use the term Gospel, which originally seems to have referred to the sufferings, death, and resurrection of Jesus. To this basic core of early Christian teaching Mark added other elements of Jesus' early life, thereby creating the Gospel format we find in the other Gospels.

Mark presents the life of Jesus within a framework which is made up of certain themes: the Messiahship of Jesus; his preaching of the Kingdom of God; the miracles of Jesus; the sufferings, death, and resurrection of Jesus; and the last instructions of Jesus to his followers. Internal examination of his Gospel supports the view that Peter was a direct source for much of Mark's material. Mark's Gospel in one sense represents the most simple form of the early Christian message, or kerygma. As the Messiah, Jesus spends some time in the desert. He then assembles his disciples, preaches the new message, works miracles to prove its authenticity, and is finally overtaken by his God-appointed destiny to die on a cross and thus achieve the salvation of all men. He shows himself after death to prove that he is alive and is the source of life.

It is not known how or where Mark finished his life. The Egyptian Church claimed Mark as its founder and patron saint. Another tradition associates Mark with Aquileia in northern Italy. It was a group of refugees from Aquileia who founded Venice on the Adriatic in the 6th century and designated Mark, under the symbol of the winged lion, as the patron saint and defender of the future, prestigious Republic of Venice.

Further Reading

Relevant studies on St. Mark include Frederick C. Grant, *The Earliest Gospel* (1943); Alfred E.J. Rawlinson, *The Gospel of St. Mark* (6th ed. 1947); Vincent Taylor, ed., *The Gospel of St. Mark* (1952); Harold A. Guy, *The Origin of the Gospel of Mark* (1955); and Curtis Beach, *The Gospel of Mark* (1959). ☐

Edwin Markham

Edwin Markham (1852-1940), American poet, leapt to fame with one poem, "The Man with the Hoe."

Edwin Markham was born Charles Edward Anson Markham in Oregon City, Ore., on April 23, 1852, the youngest of 10 children. When he was 4, his mother took him to a small farm north of San Francisco; shortly thereafter she remarried. Markham attended rural schools, worked as a cowboy and ranch hand, ran away from home at least once, and at the age of 16 entered California College in Vacaville. Two years later he transferred to San Jose State Normal School, from which he graduated in 1872.

Markham's first teaching jobs were in the mountains of San Luis Obispo County, Calif., then at Christian College in Santa Rosa, and finally at Coloma. In 1875 he married Annie Cox and became county superintendent of schools. In 1884 he divorced his wife and became a school headmaster in Hayward. In 1887 he remarried and became a school principal in Oakland. During the next 10 years, under the adopted name of Edwin Markham, he built up a small reputation as a poet in the pages of the *Century Magazine,* the *Overland Monthly,* and *Scribner's Magazine.* On his first trip east, in 1893, he met William Dean Howells and Edmund Clarence Stedman; both had admired his work. He married his third wife, Anna Murphy, in 1897.

On Jan. 15, 1899, the *San Francisco Examiner* published "The Man with the Hoe," 49 lines of traditional blank verse inspired by Jean François Millet's painting. This protest against exploited labor "flew eastward across the continent like a contagion" and on around the world. Its popularity cannot be overestimated. Before the year was out, Markham's first collection, *The Man with the Hoe and Other Poems,* appeared. He followed it with *Lincoln and Other Poems* (1901).

For the next 40 years Markham's reputation slowly deflated as newer poetic styles came into fashion. His later volumes—*The Shoes of Happiness* (1915), *The Gates of Paradise* (1920), and *New Poems* (1932)—reveal a continuing concern for the underdog but also, in the love lyrics and the flights of rhetoric, a thin reedy voice coupled with a pedestrian vocabulary. As a lecturer and literary journalist, however, Markham traveled the familiar circuits, delighting women's clubs. Most notable was the invitation of former president William Howard Taft in 1922 to read "Lincoln, the Man of the People" at the dedication of the Lincoln Memorial in Washington, D.C.

The Markhams had moved to Brooklyn in 1900. The East, thereafter, was their home, particularly Staten Island. Before his death, on March 7, 1940, Markham received innumerable honors as the "Dean of American Poetry." But, with the exception of his now legendary poem, lasting fame was not his.

Further Reading

The Markham papers are at Wagner College, Staten Island, N.Y. The best book on Markham is William L. Stidger, *Edwin Markham* (1933). See also David G. Downey, *Modern Poets and Christian Teaching: Richard Watson Gilder, Edwin Markham, Edgar Rowland Sill* (1906). Sophie K. Shields compiled *Edwin Markham: A Bibliography* (3 pts. in 1 vol., 1952-1955). ☐

Constance Markievicz

Constance Markievicz (1868–1927) was an Irish nationalist, labor activist, and feminist, who fought against the British in the 1916 Easter Rising but, as a diehard republican, later refused to compromise in the creation of the Irish Free State.

The Irish Rebellion of 1916-22 was inspired chiefly by Catholic revolutionaries seeking to throw off the yoke of a centuries-old British domination, but the idea of Irish independence attracted a wide variety of enthusiasts and idealists. None was a stranger, or a more unlikely candidate for the role of Irish freedom-fighter than Constance Markievicz, a rich, privileged Protestant woman, who had once dabbled in art, theater, and feminism but who spent the later years of her life as a guerrilla fighter, parliamentarian, prisoner, and fugitive.

Constance was born in 1868 to the Gore-Booth family, one of the largest landowning families in County Sligo on the Irish west coast. Her wealthy Protestant family was part of the Anglo-Irish ''Ascendancy,'' whose control of nearly all Irish farmland was a source of long-standing resentment to the Catholic Irish majority. From his estate at Lissadell, her father supervised his estates and acted the part of a paternalistic despot to his farm tenants, some of them desperately poor. Whereas many Irish landowners did not even live on their estates, treating them solely as sources of income, the Gore-Booths were at least physically present for part of every year. Her father's hobby was Arctic exploration and Constance, the eldest daughter, grew up like him to be adventurous, high spirited, and daring. She loved hunting and shooting and rode well. At 18, she became a debutante and enjoyed several London ''seasons'' but was unable to attract a husband, possibly because of her abrasive mockery and an inclination toward practical jokes.

By the age of 25, she had become an annoyance to her parents, and she in turn found living with them hard to

endure. After months of persuasion, she won their consent to become an art student in the Slade School, London. From that time on, she and her sister Eva began to move in artistic and literary circles, the best known of their literary friends being the poet W.B. Yeats, who knew them well and admired both. After two years in London, Constance moved on to an art school for women in Paris, and there she met Count Casimir Markievicz. He was six years younger than she, a more talented artist who had won several portrait commissions and held the prospect of a distinguished future. The son of Ukrainian landowners, he too had come to Paris to make his career as an artist. He was already married, but his first wife died in 1899 in the Ukraine, just as Markievicz and Constance were beginning an intense relationship—he even fought a duel with swords to defend Constance's honor when a Frenchman insulted her at a ball. They wed the following year, and spent the early years of their marriage moving between Paris, Lissadell, and his family estates at Zywotowka. When Constance gave birth to a daughter, Maeve, she paid her child scant attention, leaving her to be brought up almost entirely by her grandmother. And when the Markieviczs settled in Dublin in 1903, it was his son Stanislas by his first marriage who moved in with them, while Maeve paid occasional visits before returning to her grandmother.

Dublin was then experiencing a cultural awakening, a widespread revival of the Irish language, and a burst of artistic creativity from Yeats, George Bernard Shaw, James Joyce, Oscar Wilde, J.M. Synge, Padraic Colum, and dozens of other writers, artists, and poets. The Markieviczs joined Yeats and George ''AE'' Russell in an arts society, wrote and performed plays, painted, and began to show an interest in nationalist politics, to the dismay of Constance's Ascendancy relatives. At first Arthur Griffith, a moderate Irish nationalist and leader of the nationalist group Sinn Fein, assumed she was a spy sent from Dublin Castle to keep watch on potential troublemakers, but gradually both he and the women's branch of the revolutionary movement ''Daughters of Ireland'' (founded by Yeats's unrequited love Maud Gonne) , recognized that Constance was sincere and was abandoning her old way of life for the more alien and arduous life of politics. Moreover, Constance Markievicz quickly gravitated to the radical side of the Irish nationalist movement and came to regard Griffith's Sinn Fein, with its policy of parliamentary moderation, irritatingly slow. A member of its council from 1909, she constantly urged Sinn Fein to more direct action and provocation against the British.

Before her marriage, she and her sister Eva had organized a votes for women movement in their home parish; now Markievicz took up the issue of feminism more seriously and began to write for (and illustrate) the Daughters of Ireland journal *Bean na hEirean*. Eva was living in the north of England, agitating for improved working conditions for women and for women's suffrage, cooperating with the famous Pankhurst family in the Women's Social and Political Union. From Eva and from her new acquaintances and experiences in Dublin, Markievicz too began to develop a sympathy for socialism. These three convictions—Irish nationalism, feminism, and socialism—were to guide her through the rest of her life. She began to make speeches on these issues, especially women's rights, and as biographer Diana Norman notes, "she was always in demand as a speaker because she could rouse uneducated or apathetic audiences in a way more sophisticated orators could not."

Unconventional and increasingly impatient with upper-class family life, she and Casimir spent less time together as the years passed, and their marriage appears to have virtually dissolved by 1912. He was a colorful fixture in the life of the Dublin theater between 1907 and 1913 and still spent part of each year with Constance but rarely joined his wife in her political obsessions. He left Ireland for the last time in 1913.

In 1909, she founded the *Na Fianna Eireann,* an Irish nationalist version of the Boy Scouts. Just as Baden-Powell's scouts (founded during the Boer War) cultivated patriotic militarism in English boys, so she aimed to raise Irish patriot soldiers in the *Fianna.* At times, *Fianna* lads from the poor quarters of Dublin would attack Anglo-Irish Boy Scouts from the wealthier areas and fight pitched battles in the streets of Dublin, with her implicit approval. Thinking that a taste of rural life might also benefit boys from the slums, she hired a large country house and for two years ran it as a *Fianna* commune, at a steady financial loss and to the growing irritation of Casimir. One of her assistants, Liam Mellowes, spread the movement to other parts of Ireland and later helped organize the Irish Volunteers during the Easter Rising of 1916; Constance's coaching of the boys in marksmanship prepared some of them for roles in the coming revolution.

When Constance Markievicz and other Irish suffragists realized that John Redmond's Irish Party in the British Parliament intended to exclude women from the vote if they achieved their goal of Home Rule, these women went into open opposition and began to imitate the violent demonstrations of their English sisters, smashing the windows of public buildings and hunger striking in prison. Moderate Irish nationalists, supporters of Redmond, detested the suffragists for threatening their movement in this way, but Markievicz won steady support from the Irish Trade Unions and their mercurial leader Jim Larkin.

She repaid them by supporting the unions and unemployed workers during the massive lockout of summer 1913 in which Dublin employers tried to break the growing unions' power once and for all. Larkin stayed at the Markievicz house on the night before "Bloody Sunday," August 31, 1913, when a huge police contingent, possibly drunk, attacked a large crowd of trade unionists in O'Connell Street, killing two and injuring more than 450. Markievicz herself was severely beaten by the police:

> One hit me a back hand blow across the left side of my face with his baton. I fell back against the corner of a shop, when another policeman started to seize me by the throat, but I was pulled out of the crowd by some men, who took me down Sackville Place and into a house to stop the blood flowing from my nose and mouth.

Despite the shocked public response to this outrage, the lockout continued into the winter and at last the men,

hungry and defeated, were forced back to work, their unions in disarray.

Experiences like this made Markievicz implacable; hating industrial exploitation and male domination, she yet believed that British power lay at the root of all Irish evils. The year 1914 witnessed a general arming for battle in Ireland as the prospect of Home Rule increased. Protestant Ulstermen in northern Ireland took up arms to resist the nationalists and fight *against* independence. Republicans in Dublin countered by forming volunteer armies of their own and publishing strident manifestos. Markievicz helped organize the Irish Citizen Army and cooperated as gunrunners brought weapons ashore to arm it. The mounting crisis was interrupted, however, when the First World War began that summer. Redmond, leader of the Home Rule Members of Parliament, pledged the support of Ireland for the British war effort; he felt certain that Home Rule would be its quid pro quo (something received for something given), and thousands of young Irishmen responded to his call by enlisting for service in the trenches. Markievicz and the radical Irish Citizen Army, on the other hand, disdained Redmond's call; they saw themselves fighting *against* Britain, not for it, and did all they could to obstruct the British recruitment drive in Dublin, while carrying on their own drilling and marksmanship practice. She made shrill speeches, expressing the hope that Germany would win the war, and now seemed, to British eyes, a traitor.

Thousands of English and Irish men died in the trench warfare of the following years, and as British resources became thinly stretched to meet the crisis, the Irish militants realized that the perfect moment had come for them to strike a blow for independence. The secret military council of the Irish Republican Brotherhood (IRB), led by Tom Clark and Sean MacDermott, planned the rising for Easter 1916, and gradually drew into their confidence the leaders of the Irish Citizen Army, including Markievicz; the leaders of the Volunteers; and key figures from the trade unions and universities. It was obvious to the British administration in Dublin, led by Augustine Birrell, that some Irish militants were planning revolt—the Volunteers marched in the streets quite openly with their rifles and bayonets. But Birrell, a mild Liberal, maintained a policy of salutary neglect and thought the drilling was more a matter of bluster than serious intent. He was wrong.

Despite a mix-up over timing and deployment, the IRB went into action on Easter Monday, seizing the General Post Office (GPO), the College of Surgeons, the Law Courts, and other prominently placed public buildings, with about a thousand men and women in arms. They raided Dublin Castle, seat of the British administration, and could have taken it since it was then badly understaffed, but decided it was too sprawling to be defensible. They declared themselves the provisional government of the Irish Republic and raised a tricolor flag—orange, green, and white—over the GPO, along with a flag bearing a gold harp on a green background designed and made by Constance Markievicz herself. The poet and activist Padraic Pearse read out the Irish Declaration of Independence from the steps of the GPO to bemused passers-by and Easter strollers.

After their initial amazement, the British retaliated powerfully, moving first troops, then artillery and a gunboat into action. Constance Markievicz, acting as a liaison officer, hurried between the different republican strongholds until the gunfire became too heavy; she spent the latter half of the week pinned down with a small group in the College of Surgeons. She was a crack shot with years of experience and acted as a sniper against British soldiers in the nearby Shelbourne Hotel. Soon she and all the rebels were desperately hungry; food supplies into the city were disrupted by the rising, and the rebels had been forced to retreat from St. Stephen's Green where they had stockpiled several days' supplies.

The rebels knew that much of the Irish population was indifferent to their action, and that some, whose relatives were fighting in the British army, were actively opposed to them. Nevertheless they believed that even if they failed, as seemed almost certain from the start, they would light the spark of revolution for others to follow. Within a week, British bombardment had battered them into submission and the survivors, including Constance Markievicz, surrendered and were marched off to prison. She felt exhilarated that they had held out for as much as a week, longer than any earlier Irish rising against the British, and now awaited her anticipated execution with equanimity. Sure enough, she was found guilty of sedition and sentenced to death, but the military judges, in view of her sex, commuted her sentence to life imprisonment with hard labor. She then had to sit in a lonely prison cell and listen each morning as volleys of shots announced the death by firing squad of nearly all her remaining comrades, some of whom she had known for 15 or 20 years.

As Clark, MacDermott, James Connally and the other leaders had anticipated, what the rebellion failed to achieve, its aftermath created. Public opinion swung around in favor of the rebels, each of whom, by his death, became a martyr to Irish freedom. News that Connally had been so badly wounded that he had to be tied to a chair to be kept upright at his execution and that the British army had killed such innocent bystanders as Constance's friend Francis Sheehy Skeffington (a radical pacifist who deplored the resort to arms) intensified the shift in Irish public opinion. The British retribution, far from ending the Irish Revolution, in effect brought it to life.

Because the British feared she would become the center of a cult if left in a Dublin prison, Constance was moved to a prison in Aylesbury, England. Treated as a regular criminal rather than a political prisoner, she was placed with prostitutes, thieves, and infanticides, and suffered the squalid miseries and perpetual hunger of the prison regimen for the next year and a half. While in prison, however, she converted to Catholicism, the religion of most of her fellow rebels. Meanwhile Irish friends were working to have her status changed to that of a political prisoner. Others were making propaganda tours of the United States, addressing its large Irish population and urging their support for Irish freedom. When the United States entered the First World War in the spring of 1917, the British government conciliated Irish opinion in America by releasing most of the remaining Irish internees from the rising, and in July of that year, Markievicz emerged from jail and returned to a hero's welcome in Ireland.

She was elected to the Sinn Fein executive council, but now the organization was a mass revolutionary movement with nearly 100,000 members, rather than a tiny cluster of Dublin moderates. It acted as though the Declaration of Independence, and the Irish Republic, were already political facts of life and gained a surge of new members when the British tried to impose military conscription on Irish men in early 1918. In response to Sinn Fein's anticonscription actions, the British arrested the party's leaders, including Constance Markievicz, and she was once more sent to prison in England, but this time granted political status and the company of other Sinn Feiners; one of them was Maud Gonne. Markievicz was still in prison when the First World War ended in November 1918, and Prime Minister Lloyd George called a general election. Sinn Fein ran her as its candidate in the St. Patrick division of Dublin and she won, thus becoming the first woman ever elected to the British Parliament.

Markievicz was one of 73 Sinn Fein candidates to win seats. Rather than go to Westminster, however, those who were at liberty met in Dublin and constituted themselves as the *Dail Eireann* (Irish Parliament). Eamon de Valera, who had fought in the Easter rising and added luster to his name by a daring prison escape (he had avoided execution because he was an American citizen and not technically guilty of treason), became the first president of the Republic and appointed Markievicz as his Minister of Labor. In March 1919, she was released from jail by a British government which was anxious lest she die in the influenza epidemic; she again received a hero's welcome on her return to Dublin. Throwing herself into political activity once more and trying to make sure that the nascent (budding) government held fast to its pro-Labor pledges, she urged Irish people to boycott everything British and to carry on their guerrilla war against the Royal Irish Constabulary and the notorious ''Black and Tans.''

She was rearrested for seditious speeches and jailed a third time in County Cork. Released in October 1919, she found that Sinn Fein was now an illegal organization and spent the following months on the run to avoid further imprisonment, moving constantly from place to place. The Dail had to meet covertly, but it made a point of taking over every aspect of administration it could handle, to give itself an image of effectiveness and plausibility in the eyes of the anxious, war-torn population. Meanwhile a fourth arrest led to another long stay at Mountjoy Prison, Dublin, for Markievicz, during which she learned to speak the Irish language.

When she emerged from this term in prison, momentous negotiations were under way in London between Dail representatives and the British government on the status of a self-governing Ireland. Markievicz and Eamon de Valera insisted on a completely self-governing republic, but the British would only grant Ireland ''Free State'' dominion status within the British Empire. Fearing renewed British hostilities throughout Ireland which they were ill prepared to repel, the Irish negotiators, led by the guerrilla captain Michael Collins, miserably accepted the Free State compromise, and then tried to defend it in the Dail debate which followed. Markievicz spoke passionately against the compromise and joined de Valera and the large antitreaty minority by walking out of the assembly. She toured the United States later that year, speaking on behalf of the Republic and against the Free State, but found on her return in 1922 that civil war had broken out between the two factions. Although she was now 54, she once more took to the barricades as a sniper, lived on the run, and was again arrested while speaking from a cart in Dublin. This fifth term of imprisonment was at the hands of some of the men she had fought beside in 1916, a bitterly ironic outcome of her work.

For the last years of her life, Constance Markievicz was a member of the Free State parliament but could not take her seat because she, like all the antitreaty diehards, refused to take the oath to the king of England which it required. She remained personally popular and helped de Valera, in 1926, to found the *Fianna Fail,* a party aimed at gaining entry to Parliament without taking the oath. But although she held her seat in another election, she never again spoke in Parliament. Constance Markievicz died disappointed at the outcome of her life's labors, dismayed that the Irish Free State was such a prosaic, compromised affair rather than the radical workers' democracy she had dreamed of and worked for throughout her adult life. Truckloads of flowers and thousands of mourners attended her funeral, though the Free State government refused to grant this hero of 1916 official funeral honors.

Further Reading

Haverty, Anne. *Constance Markievicz: An Independent Life.* London: Pandora, 1988.

Norman, Diana. *Terrible Beauty: A Life of Constance Markievicz, 1868-1927.* London: Hodder & Stoughton, 1987.

O'Connor, Ulick. *The Troubles: Ireland, 1912-1922.* Bobbs-Merrill, 1975.

Sebestyen, Amanda, ed. *Prison Letters of Countess Markievicz.* London: Virago, 1986. □

1st Duke of Marlborough

The English general and statesman John Churchill, 1st Duke of Marlborough (1650-1722), was responsible for the British victory at Blenheim in 1704, which is second only to the triumph of Waterloo in British military annals.

Though the Duke of Marlborough was active during three earlier reigns, it was under Queen Anne that he became famous. In the century-long (1689-1783) struggle with France, no war was longer or bloodier than that of the Spanish Succession (1702-1713), and Marlborough's role in that war was decisive. The son of an obscure squire, through his ability as soldier and diplomat Marlborough rose to the highest rank in the army and in the peerage, was given the palace of Blenheim by a grateful nation, and founded a distinguished family represented in the 20th century by Sir Winston Churchill.

John Churchill was born about June 1, 1650, at Ashe in Devonshire, was educated at St. Paul's School in London, and as early as 1667 had a position with the Duke of York and a commission in the guards. Strikingly handsome and charming, Churchill was also ambitious and acquisitive. He might have married for wealth and position, but he married for love, choosing the beautiful and imperious Sarah Jennings, already (1678) a favorite with Princess Anne. When the Duke of York became king, Churchill continued to enjoy his favor. He became Baron Churchill in 1685 and held military commands but took no active part in politics beyond consolidating his position with Princess Anne.

The Revolution of 1688 saw Marlborough desert James II at a critical point, and his wife helped persuade Anne to desert the King, her father. Churchill's assistance to the new king was rewarded. William III made him Earl of Marlborough and gave him commands in Ireland and on the Continent. A rift soon developed between the King and his sister-in-law Anne, and the Churchills were involved. When Marlborough was discovered writing to the exiled James, he was dismissed from his posts on suspicion of treason. Only in 1701, with war against France (over dividing up the Spanish Empire) about to break out, did William relent, appointing Marlborough commander in chief. Marlborough was then in his fiftysecond year; had he died at this point, his name would be practically unknown.

With William III's death (1702) Anne became queen, and she put Marlborough in charge of military and diplomatic affairs, with his friend Sidney Godolphin in charge of finances and Robert Harley manager of the Commons. It was this three-man team which successfully carried on the first 6 years of the war. These were also the years of Marlborough's great victories. Campaigns in 1702 and 1703 were uneventful largely because Marlborough was engaged in strenuous efforts to keep together the Grand Alliance against Louis XIV of France.

Military Victories

In the third year of the War of the Spanish Succession, Marlborough learned of the French plan to send an army through Germany to attack the Austrian capital, Vienna. Fearing that the cautious Dutch would recall their troops if they suspected his true design, Marlborough feinted an attack at France and then marched his troops clear across central Europe to the upper Danube. At Blenheim (near Augsburg) a decisive engagement took place on Aug. 15, 1704. The French forces were about equal to the Allied army under Marlborough—roughly 50,000. A cavalry charge across marshy land against the French center turned the tide. The cavalry broke through, and the enemy forces were disorganized and, by the end of the day, completely routed.

Marlborough had saved Vienna and had kept the empire in the war. At a single stroke he had also raised the prestige of British arms higher than at any time since Agincourt (1415). A hero and high in favor with the Queen, Marlborough was given a dukedom. Anne presented him with the royal manor of Woodstock and ordered a palace built for him there, named Blenheim after his victory.

No succeeding triumph was as splendid as Blenheim. At Ramillies (1706), Oudenaarde (1708), and Malplaquet (1709) the duke was successful, but each of these battles was costlier and less decisive than the one before. By 1709 France was ready to negotiate a peace, and the English people were becoming tired of the war. The breakdown of negotiations between France and England weakened Marlborough's position at home. His friend Godolphin had been forced into too close an alliance with the Whigs for either the Queen or Harley. In preaching favor to the Whigs, Lady Marlborough acted more as political tutor to Anne than as friend, and gradually the duchess lost the Queen's affection. With Anne's support Harley tried to take over the government. He failed in 1708 and was driven into opposition. Two years later he was able to realize his ambition. Anne dismissed Godolphin in August 1710 and made Harley lord treasurer.

Marlborough did not lose his post of commander in chief until late December 1711. Meanwhile, the new government negotiated a secret peace with France behind his back and accused him of corruption. The charges were dropped, but the duke was glad to see the last of the Harley administration on the death of Queen Anne. Marlborough was active in welcoming her German successor, George I, in 1714. He was given back his military offices; but by 1716, already broken in health, he suffered a paralytic stroke from which he never recovered. He died of a second stroke on June 16, 1722.

Further Reading

Marlborough's military dispatches are printed in Sir George Murray, ed., Letters and Dispatches of John Churchill, First Duke of Marlborough (5 vols., 1845; repr. 1968). Much of his correspondence with Godolphin and others, from the manuscripts at Blenheim, is in William Coxe, Memoirs of John, Duke of Marlborough (3 vols., 1818-1819; 2d ed., 6 vols., 1820). Of the many biographies of Marlborough, two deserve special mention: Sir Winston Churchill, in Marlborough: His Life and Times (4 vols., 1933-1938; abridged in one volume, by Henry Steele Commager, 1970), is intent on vindicating his ancestor from Thomas Babington Macaulay's aspersions, and the work is full of special pleading; it prints little not already found in Coxe, but it has some splendid battle pieces. More accurate and professional, and much more modest in length, is Ivor F. Burton, The Captain General: The Career of John Churchill, Duke of Marlborough (1968).

Additional Sources

Barnett, Correlli, The first Churchill: Marlborough, soldier and statesman, New York: Putnam, 1974.
Bevan, Bryan, Marlborough the man: a biography of John Churchill first Duke of Marlborough, London: R. Hale, 1975.
Cowles, Virginia, The great Marlborough and his duchess, New York: Macmillan, 1983.
Defoe, Daniel, A short narrative of the life and actions of His Grace John, D. of Marlborough, New York: AMS Press, 1992.
Jones, J. R. (James Rees), Marlborough, Cambridge; New York: Cambridge University Press, 1993.
Saintsbury, George, Marlborough, Philadelphia: R. West, 1978.
Thomson, George Malcolm, The first Churchill: the life of John, 1st Duke of Marlborough, New York: Morrow, 1980, 1979. □

Christopher Marlowe

The English dramatist Christopher Marlowe (1564-1593) was the first English playwright to reveal the full potential of dramatic blank verse and the first to exploit the tragic implications of Renaissance humanism.

Although a number of English dramatists before Christopher Marlowe had achieved some notable successes in the field of comedy, none had produced a first-rate tragedy. It was Marlowe who made the first significant advances in tragedy. In each of his major plays he focuses on a single character who dominates the action by virtue of his extraordinary strength of will. Marlowe's thundering blank verse, although for the most part lacking the subtlety of Shakespeare's mature poetry, proved a remarkably effective medium for this kind of drama.

Marlowe was born in February 1564, about 2 months before Shakespeare. His father was a prosperous middle-class merchant of Canterbury. Christopher received his early education at King's School in Canterbury and at the age of 17 went to Cambridge, where he held a scholarship requiring him to study for the ministry. He received a bachelor of arts degree in 1584 and a master of arts degree in 1587. Toward the end of his stay at Cambridge he evidently aroused the suspicions of the university authorities, who threatened to withhold his degree. The Queen's Privy Council intervened, however, and assured the authorities that Marlowe "had done Her Majesty good service." The nature of this service is still a mystery, but it is likely that Marlowe was involved in a secret espionage mission abroad.

Shortly after receiving his master's degree, Marlowe went to London. He soon became known for his wild, bohemian ways and his unorthodox thinking. In 1589, for example, he was imprisoned for a time in connection with the death of a certain William Bradley, who had been killed in a violent quarrel in which Marlowe played an important part. He was several times accused of being an "atheist" and a "blasphemer," most notably by his fellow playwright Thomas Kyd. These charges led to Marlowe's arrest in 1593, but he died before his case was decided.

Literary Career

Marlowe's career as a poet and dramatist spanned a mere 6 years. Between his graduation from Cambridge in 1587 and his death in 1593 he wrote only one major poem (*Hero and Leander,* unfinished at his death) and six or seven plays (one play, *Dido Queen of Carthage,* may have been written while he was still a student). Since the dating of several plays is uncertain, it is impossible to construct a reliable history of Marlowe's intellectual and artistic development.

Tamburlaine the Great, a two-part play, was first printed in 1590 but was probably composed several years earlier. The famous prologue to the first part announces a new poetic and dramatic style: "From jigging veins of rhyming mother wits,/ And such conceits as clownage keeps in pay/ We'll lead you to the stately tent of war,/ Where you shall hear the Scythian Tamburlaine/ Threat'ning the world with high astounding terms/ And scourging kingdoms with his conquering sword./ View but his picture in this tragic glass,/ And then applaud his fortunes as you please." The play itself is a bold demonstration of Tamburlaine's rise to power and his singleminded, often inhumanly cruel exercise of that power. The hero provokes awe and wonder but little sympathy.

Although written sometime between 1588 and 1592, *The Jew of Malta* was not printed until 1633. The chief figure, the phenomenally wealthy merchant-prince Barabas, is one of the most powerful Machiavellian figures of the Elizabethan drama. Unlike Tamburlaine, who asserts his will openly and without guile, Barabas is shrewd, devious, and secretive.

Doctor Faustus, which is generally considered Marlowe's greatest work, was probably also his last. Its central figure, a scholar who feels he has exhausted all the conventional areas of human learning, attempts to gain the ultimate in knowledge and power by selling his soul to the devil. The high point comes in the portrayal of the hero's final moments, as he awaits the powers of darkness who demand his soul.

His Death

The circumstances of Marlowe's death first came to light in the 20th century. On May 30, 1593, Marlowe dined at Deptford with a certain Ingram Frizer and two others. In the course of an argument over the tavern bill, Marlowe wounded Frizer with a dagger, whereupon Frizer seized the same dagger and stabbed Marlowe over the right eye. According to the coroner's inquest, from which this information is drawn, Marlowe died instantly.

Despite the unusual wealth of detail surrounding this fatal episode, there has been much speculation about the affair. It has been suggested, for example, that the deed was politically motivated and that Frizer (who was subsequently judged to have acted in self-defense) was simply acting as an agent for a more prominent person. In any case, within 3 or 4 years of his death, Marlowe's career was being cited by contemporary moralists as a classic illustration of the workings of divine retribution against a blasphemous atheist. But he was also recognized as a remarkable dramatic genius who, if he had lived longer, would certainly have rivaled Shakespeare and Ben Jonson.

Further Reading

Among the best of the many full-length studies of Marlowe's life are Frederick S. Boas, *Christopher Marlowe: A Biographical and Critical Study* (1940); John E. Bakeless, *The Tragicall History of Christopher Marlowe* (2 vols., 1942); and Paul H. Kocher, *Christopher Marlowe: A Study of His Thought, Learning, and Character* (1946). The facts of Marlowe's death were discovered by Leslie Hotson and set forth in his *The Death of Christopher Marlowe* (1925; repr. 1967).

Among the critical studies that take in all of Marlowe's works are Harry Levin, *The Overreacher: A Study of Christopher Marlowe* (1952), and J. B. Steane, *Marlowe: A Critical Study* (1964). An important critical study is Roy W. Battenhouse, *Marlowe's Tamburlaine: A Study in Renaissance Moral Philosophy* (1941). For an interesting aspect of Renaissance drama see Eugene M. Waith, *The Herculean Hero in Marlowe, Chapman, Shakespeare and Dryden* (1962).

Additional Sources

Bakeless, John Edwin, *Christopher Marlowe,* New York: Haskell House Publishers, 1975.

Henderson, Philip, *Christopher Marlowe,* New York: Barnes & Noble Books, 1974.

Hilton, Della, *Christopher Marlowe and the new London theatre,* Edinburgh: Pentland Press, 1993.

Hilton, Della, *Who was Kit Marlowe?: The story of the poet and playwright,* London: Weidenfeld and Nicolson, 1977.

Ingram, John Henry, *Marlowe & his poetry,* Philadelphia: R. West, 1977.

Lewis, J. G., *Christopher Marlowe: outlines of his life and works,* Philadelphia: R. West, 1977.

Pinciss, G. M., *Christopher Marlowe,* New York: Ungar, 1975.

Urry, William, *Christopher Marlowe and Canterbury,* London; Boston: Faber and Faber, 1988. □

José Mármol

José Mármol (1817-1871) was one of the celebrated Argentine exiled writers and intellectuals. He gained his greatest recognition as the author of "Amalia," a long, melodramatic novel of intrigue about the secret resistance against the dictator Rosas.

José Mármol was born on Dec. 2, 1817, in Buenos Aires. He was an erratic student but eventually determined to be a lawyer and enrolled in the faculty of law of the University of Buenos Aires in 1836. He was destined not to finish his studies, however, for this was a period of great agitation in the country, and the university was one of the hotbeds of conspiracy against the dictatorship of Juan Manuel de Rosas.

On April 1, 1839, Mármol was briefly jailed for having in his possession newspapers published in Montevideo, Uruguay, by the principal Argentine intellectuals in exile, the *proscriptos.* Mármol claimed to have written his first poem (against Rosas) on the wall of his cell. In 1840 he joined his friends in Montevideo and began a long and active association with the liberal press, devoting his energies to an unswerving attack on the Argentine dictator. A year later, his first romantic poems were attracting the attention of his fellow writers in exile.

In 1842 two undistinguished plays by Mármol, *The Poet* and *The Crusader,* were presented in Montevideo. However, on the occasion of the 1843 anniversary of the Argentine independence day, Mármol composed his celebrated poem "To Rosas," which converted him into the lyrical spokesman of the social romanticism of his time. Shortly thereafter, with Montevideo under siege by Rosas' forces, the poet left for Rio de Janeiro and the company of other exiles, among them Juan Bautista Alberdi, who had just written a long poem about the high seas after the fashion of Byron's *Childe Harold's Pilgrimage.*

In early 1844 Mármol embarked from Rio with several other Argentines for Valparaiso, Chile. The 3-month journey was tempestuous, hazardous, and, in the end, unsuccessful, for stormy seas at Cape Horn eventually forced the ship back to Brazil. But Mármol, inspired by the fearful spectacle of raging nature, by his isolation, and by his own romantic inclination (as well as Alberdi's example, no doubt), composed a long poem sequence entitled *Songs of the Pilgrim,* which stands as his most celebrated poetic work.

Mármol was back in Montevideo in 1846, continuing his attack on Rosas in the press, and in 1851 he published in installments his long novel, *Amalia,* a thoroughly romantic and colorful narrative that related the adventures of two young lovers involved in the antiRosas movement in Buenos Aires. In 1852 Rosas was overthrown, and Mármol returned to his homeland, his literary career now ended, as if the removal of the object of his hatred had suddenly deprived him of his source of creative energy. The final 2 decades of his life were given to various political and diplomatic posts, and from 1858 until his death he was the director of the Public Library (today the National Library) of Buenos Aires. Mármol died in Buenos Aires on Aug. 9, 1871.

Further Reading

A detailed study in English of Mármol's writings is Stuart Cuthbertson, *The Poetry of José Mármol* (1935). He is also discussed in Myron Lichtblau, *The Argentine Novel of the Nineteenth Century* (1959). □

Jacques Marquette

Jacques Marquette (1637-1675) was a French Jesuit, missionary, and explorer who followed the Illinois and Mississippi rivers on a journey of discovery.

Jacques Marquette was the son of a seigneur of Laon. In 1654 he entered the Jesuit novitiate at Nancy, went on to teaching, and began theological studies in 1665. He pleaded to be allowed to become a missionary, feeling that he was not suited to theology. He was accordingly sent to New France, arriving in Quebec in September 1666.

For about 2 years Marquette studied the Montagnais language at Trois-Rivières. Then, in May 1668, he left by canoe from Montreal to join a mission at Sault Sainte Marie. In 1669 he founded a mission at the far western end of Lake Superior. Here he met for the first time the Illinois Indians, whom he came to enjoy and to admire. When they were forced to shift eastward owing to pressure from the Sioux, Marquette went too and in 1671 founded the mission of St-

Ignace (named after Ignatius of Loyola) on the north shore of the Straits of Michilimackinac (Mackinac).

In December 1672 Louis Jolliet arrived at St-Ignace, carrying with him a commission from Quebec to explore the western rivers. The French had already acquired some knowledge of the Illinois country from the Indians and were anxious to explore it further. The winter of 1672/1673 was spent discussing and arranging the expedition for the spring, and in mid-May 1673 Marquette and Jolliet left together on their epic exploration of the Illinois and Mississippi.

They got a long way south, beyond the present city of Memphis, and probably to about the northern border of Louisiana at 33°N, in other words, nearly 800 miles south of St-Ignace. There they had to stop. Jolliet, although he spoke six Indian languages, could no longer make himself understood, and increasing Indian hostility made it seem undesirable to proceed further, although they believed—erroneously—that they were only 150 miles from the sea. They turned north about mid-July, and using the Illinois River and the Chicago portage they were back at Lake Michigan in September.

Jolliet went on to Sault Sainte Marie, where he wintered (1673-1674), going on to Quebec in the spring. But Marquette was unwell; he stayed at a mission at Baie des Puants (Green Bay) for a whole year, returning south to the Illinois country in October 1674. Bad weather and Marquette's recurring dysentery forced them to winter not far from present-day Chicago. They were helped by visits from Marquette's old friends, the Illinois, and in Easter week of 1675

he was sufficiently well to visit a magnificent gathering of Indian braves and chiefs on the Illinois River. Marquette headed northward to St-Ignace but died in May, near present-day Ludington, Mich.

Further Reading

The Jesuit Relations and Allied Documents, edited by Reuben Gold Thwaites (73 vols., 1896-1901), contains in volume 59 what is reputed to be Marquette's account of his expedition. A good deal of controversy has arisen in recent years over the authenticity of this account. The opposition to Marquette's reputed role is led mainly by Francis Borgia Steck in his *Marquette Legends* (1960). The older and probably still standard account is Louise Phelps Kellogg, *The French Régime in Wisconsin and the Northwest* (1925). Joseph P. Donnelly, *Jacques Marquette, S. I.* (1968), defends the traditional view of Marquette. The work by Jesuit scholar Raphael N. Hamilton, *Marquette's Explorations: The Narrative Reexamined* (1970), is a critical analysis. Marquette figures in a reissue of an old work whose original edition is a collector's item because of its maps and sketches, Justin Winsor, *Cartier to Frontenac: Geographical Discovery in the Interior of North America in its Historical Relations, 1534-1700* (1894; repr. 1970). □

Othniel Charles Marsh

The American paleontologist Othniel Charles Marsh (1831-1899) discovered extinct birds with teeth, the Dinocerata, a kind of missing link between the reptiles and the birds, and traced the development of the modern horse.

On Oct. 29, 1831, O. C. Marsh was born in Lockport, N. Y. He graduated from Yale College in 1860. In 1860-1861 he pursued graduate studies in the Yale Scientific School and then spent 3 years in study at Berlin, Breslau, and Heidelberg. In 1866 he was appointed to the chair of paleontology at Yale, the first such chair to be established in America. Marsh held this position, which carried no teaching duties and no salary until 1896, for the rest of his life. He was aided financially by an inheritance from his uncle George Peabody, whom he induced to establish the Peabody Museum at Yale, which Marsh headed.

In 1870 Marsh organized the first of his Yale scientific expeditions, to the fossil-rich West. The first year they explored the Pliocene deposits of Nebraska and the Miocene of northern Colorado, crossed over the Bridger Basin in Wyoming, and then went southward into California. A succession of such expeditions followed throughout the 1870s. Marsh published his findings in a series of volumes on toothed birds and North American dinosaurs.

In 1882, following a major reorganization of the Federal surveys, Marsh was appointed vertebrate paleontologist to the U. S. Geological Survey. This position gave him first choice of the wealth of specimens being brought in by government surveying parties. Thereafter the fossils came

Schuchert, Charles, *O. C. Marsh: pioneer in paleontology,* New York: Arno Press, 1978, 1940. □

into his museum faster than he could study them, and an immense pile remained unclassified at his death.

Marsh is given credit for putting the collection and preparation of vertebrate fossils upon a truly scientific basis. Always a careful worker, he was responsible for the complete reconstruction of a great many extinct animals, including a large number of dinosaurs found near Laramie, Wyo., the greatest dinosaur boneyard in the world.

Despite his nasty temperament and his often unscrupulous means of dealing with rivals and subordinates, Marsh was widely honored in the scientific world. He was president of the prestigious National Academy of Sciences (1883-1895), and he received the Bigsby Medal from the Geological Society of London (1877) and the Cuvier Prize from the French Academy. He died on March 18, 1899.

Further Reading

The only biography of Marsh is Charles Schuchert and Clara Mae LeVene, *O. C. Marsh, Pioneer in Paleontology* (1940). The authors, Marsh's successor as director of the Peabody Museum and the museum librarian, deal admirably with his career and scientific work.

Additional Sources

Lanham, Url, *The bone hunters: the heroic age of paleontology in the American West,* New York: Dover Publications, 1991.
McCarren, Mark J., *The scientific contributions of Othniel Charles Marsh: birds, bones, and brontotheres,* New Haven, Conn.: Peabody Museum of Natural History, Yale University, c1993.

Reginald Marsh

The genre scenes of the American painter and print-maker Reginald Marsh (1898-1954), often showing the seamy side of city life, reflected his acute powers of observation.

Both of Reginald Marsh's parents were painters. His father was one of America's first painters of industrial scenes. Reginald was born in Paris; the Marshes returned to America when he was 2, settling in Nutley, N. J. He attended Yale, then settled in New York in 1920 and began working as a free-lance artist. Eventually he became a staff artist for the *Daily News* and the *New Yorker*. He thought of himself as an illustrator, not a painter, until, in 1925, he went abroad for several months and copied paintings by Rubens and Delacroix. Back home, Marsh dabbled in radicalism, contributing to the *New Masses* during the 1930s.

Marsh worked in a variety of media. His first paintings were watercolors. In 1929 he worked in the egg-yolk medium, getting his lights from the gesso ground. Print-making went along with his painting. In the late 1920s he tried lithography, then changed to etching; in the 1940s he took up copper engraving. During the 1930s he did mural paintings and in 1935 decorated in fresco the Post Office Building in Washington, D. C., and the Custom House in New York City. In the 1940s he used oils frequently. Also during that period he used Chinese ink on paper, sometimes combined with egg tempera.

A part of Marsh's reportage art touches on social commentary. His scenes of the Bowery focus on homeless and beaten people. *Tattoo and Haircut* (1932) features a hunched cripple. Vagrants huddle in doorways beneath the tracks of the elevated train, against a sign advertising a shave-haircut for 10 cents and 20 cents. *The Bowery* shows crowds of vagrants standing forlornly beneath rows of hotel signs, their arms crossed or their hands in their pockets.

Marsh was attracted to the noise and movement of New York City. He liked to depict crowds pursuing public pleasures at theaters, burlesque houses, dance halls, and beaches. His figures are imbued with a bawdiness, a sensuousness, and often a sleaziness. His attraction to crowds went with his love of spectacles. In 1937 he defended public burlesque, and when it was banned in New York, he followed it to New Jersey. Among his burlesque subjects is *Minsky's Chorus* (1935). His beach scenes usually show healthy young people sunning, wrestling, embracing—unabashed in their exuberance, as in *Negroes of Rockaway Beach* (1934). Anatomical drawing was a lifelong interest. His work also reveals a knowledge of Renaissance compositions.

Reginald Marsh (at easel)

Further Reading

A catalog of the *Whitney Museum of American Art, Reginald Marsh* (1955), is informative and well done. It is based on an exhibition of 160 works, about one-third of them illustrated in the catalog. See also Norman Sasowsky, *Reginald Marsh: Etchings, Engravings, Lithographs* (1956). □

Alfred Marshall

The English economist Alfred Marshall (1842-1924) was the founder of the "new economics." He rejected the traditional definition of economics as the "science of wealth" to establish a discipline concerned with social welfare.

Alfred Marshall was born in London on July 26, 1842, the son of a cashier at the Bank of England. At Cambridge he abandoned plans to enter the Anglican clergy and graduated in mathematics. Elected to a Cambridge fellowship, Marshall planned then to pursue molecular physics. Instead, he was drawn first to metaphysics, particularly ethics, which he studied in Germany for a year, then to psychology, and finally to economics as a practical means for implementing ethics.

In 1868 Marshall's college, St. John's, established a special lectureship for him in moral science. In 1875 he returned from a study of trade protection in the United States to attempt to make political economy a serious subject at Cambridge. When, in 1877, he married Mary Paley, a former student then lecturing in economics at Newnham, the women's college at Cambridge, he became ineligible to continue his fellowship. University College, Bristol, had just been founded, and Marshall, a firm believer in extending adult educational opportunities, agreed to become first principal and professor of political economy. In 1883 Marshall became a fellow of Balliol and lecturer in political economy to students preparing for the Indian civil service. Two years later he took the chair in political economy at Cambridge. Until his retirement in 1908, Marshall dominated a singularly influential school of economics, with separate and tripos status after 1903. From 1890 until his death on July 13, 1924, Marshall was the patriarch of the new economics.

In 1890 Marshall's *Principles of Economics* was welcomed enthusiastically by economists and a popular audience as a revolutionary work in economics. His other major works were *The Economics of Industry* (1879), written with his wife; *Elements of Economics of Industry* (1892); and *Industry and Trade* (1919). Besides his writing and dedicated teaching, Marshall created the British Economics Association in 1890 (Royal Economics Society after 1902), and he directly influenced government policy on currency, prices, gold and silver, fiscal affairs, poor relief, local taxes, and international trade.

The content and method of Marshall's economics were largely original, but his basic assumptions were derived from the 19th-century belief that social reform depended initially upon the reform of character. He never doubted that every man sought his own, or at least his children's, best interest; that "work" purified human nature, stimulating personal and social progress; or that capitalism would be inherently progressive if it was made more efficient.

Marshall's economic analysis began with the quasistatic, evolutionary institutions of free enterprise and developed as a search for measurable regularities in economic phenomena. Since money could be measured regularly, Marshall studied prices. His most important technical contributions were in price and value analysis. The value of things, which he recognized as necessarily relative and subjective, was expressed as money prices, reached through an elastic play of forces behind demand and supply. "Utility," the power of goods and services to satisfy consumers' wants, and demand fluctuated in relation to price. Price, in turn, was determined both by the cost of production and by judgments about utility, the two inseparable blades of the economic scissors. Utility, being subjective, was not measurable, but it did reflect a psychological attitude critical in any economic activity. This was typical of the "marginal disutility of labor," that point at which the worker decided that he had nothing further to gain from additional work.

Nineteenth-century political economy ended and the new economics began with Marshall's pioneering use of econometrics; his creation of economics as a rigorous discipline with its own content and method; his attempt to unify competitive economic theories and practices; and his belief in the evolutionary nature of economic knowledge. Marshall's overweening influence led two generations of economists in Britain and America to spend their professional lives discussing, restating, developing, interpreting, altering, and questioning his doctrines and tools of analysis.

Further Reading

The Memorials of Alfred Marshall (1925), edited by A. C. Pigou, is an indispensable collection, including John Maynard Keynes's classic essay "Alfred Marshall, 1842-1924." Marshall's testimony before Parliamentary commissions was published for the Royal Economic Society as *Official Papers* (1926). Marshall's wife, Mary Paley Marshall, wrote *What I Remember* (1947). There is a great deal of interpretation and commentary on Marshall. Two of the most objective accounts, written within a proper historical context, are in Terence Wilmot Hutchison, *A Review of Economic Doctrines, 1870-1929* (1953), and Robert Lekachman, *A History of Economic Ideas* (1959).

Additional Sources

Coase, R. H. (Ronald Henry), *Essays on economics and economists,* Chicago: University of Chicago Press, 1994.
Groenewegen, Peter D., *A soaring eagle: Alfred Marshall, 1842-1924,* Aldershot; Brookfield, Vt.: E. Elgar, 1995. □

George Catlett Marshall

George Catlett Marshall (1880-1959), American soldier and statesman, was one of the most important military leaders during World War II.

George C. Marshall was born at Uniontown, Pa., on Dec. 31, 1880. He early chose a military career and graduated from the Virginia Military Institute in 1902. His first assignment was in the Philippines (1902-1903). In World War I he served as chief of operations of the 1st Army and chief of staff of the 1st Army Corps. In these capacities he directed operations in France at Saint-Mihiel in September 1918 and then transferred a military force of almost 250,000 men to the front in the Argonne. At the end of the war he was assigned to the staff of Gen. John Pershing (1919-1924) and served in China (1924-1927). From 1927 to 1932 Marshall was in charge of instruction at the military school at Fort Benning, Ga., where he left an important mark on American military doctrine and made contact with many of the military figures who were to play important roles in World War II.

In 1939 President Franklin D. Roosevelt appointed Marshall chief of staff of the army, and during the next 2 years he had a central role in preparing for United States entrance into World War II. Austere in person, Marshall was an administrator of the first order. He was a strong advocate of universal military training and played an important role in the passage of the draft law of 1941.

The Japanese attack on Pearl Harbor came in December 1941. This surprise attack has been the subject of much controversy. Marshall has been criticized for his failure to give more specific warning to the commanders on the spot, for the War Department, when informed of the increasing diplomatic tension, never alerted the Hawaiian base except against sabotage. Much of the responsibility must lie, however, with the local commanders.

Marshall directed the war operations from 1941 to 1945. He would have dearly liked to be in command of the operations in Europe, but he accepted with his customary coolness, detachment, and patriotism the nomination of Dwight Eisenhower to that important post. Marshall had, however, a highly positive influence on the general strategy of the war. His belief that the primary task was the defeat of Germany's Adolf Hitler brought him into conflict with Gen. Douglas MacArthur and with powerful elements in the Navy, but his view prevailed.

Marshall not only organized the immense armed forces of the United States but served as an adviser to President Roosevelt at the wartime conferences at Casablanca, Teheran, and Yalta. On the President's death in 1945, he retained his post and enjoyed the entire confidence of the new president, Harry Truman. Marshall was present at Potsdam in July 1945 and shared in the decision to drop the atomic bomb on Japan.

Resigning in November 1945, Marshall undertook, with reluctance but in obedience to his strong sense of duty, a mission to China. His purpose was to bring about an

understanding between the Nationalist government of Gen. Chiang Kai-shek and the growing Communist forces under Mao Tse-tung. He failed in this effort because of the intransigence of both sides.

On Jan. 21, 1947, Marshall was named secretary of state. He had a principal part in negotiations with the Soviet Union. More important, at Harvard on June 5, 1947, he propounded the plan for the rehabilitation of Europe (the Marshall Plan). The credit for this plan must go in no small part to the men Marshall had placed around him, notably William Clayton, Dean Acheson, and George Kennan, but Marshall lent it the immense prestige of his name. (In 1953 he received the Nobel Peace Prize for his work on this plan.) He was also central in the formation of the North Atlantic Treaty Organization (NATO).

Marshall resigned in January 1949 but was called back by President Truman to serve as secretary of defense in the period of the Korean War. His voice was important during the crisis created by Gen. Douglas MacArthur's defiance of the civil authority, when MacArthur took the war across the 38th parallel into North Korea. Marshall favored removal of the general.

There has rarely been a more disinterested public servant than Marshall. His judgments were sound rather than brilliant, but his record of achievement stands almost unequaled. Primarily a military man, he served with immense distinction in other fields, and he had much to do with bringing out many of the distinguished soldiers of the war period. Marshall died in Washington Oct. 16, 1959, and was buried in Arlington National Cemetery.

Further Reading

An authoritative biography of Marshall in three volumes is in preparation by Forrest C. Pogue, *George C. Marshall* (2 vols., 1963, 1967). The first two volumes carry his career to 1943. Pogue also wrote *George C. Marshall: Global Commander* (1968). A specialized study of Marshall is John Robinson Beal, *Marshall in China* (1970). See also Rose Page Wilson, *General Marshall Remembered* (1968). Marshall's career as secretary of state is covered in Robert H. Ferrell, ed., *The American Secretaries of State and Their Diplomacy*, vol. 15 (1966), and in George F. Kennan, *Memoirs, 1925-1950* (1967). □

John Marshall

As the fourth chief justice of the United States, John Marshall (1755-1835) was the principal architect in consolidating and defining the powers of the Supreme Court. Perhaps more than any other man he set the prevailing tone of American constitutional law.

The eldest of Thomas and Mary Marshall's 15 children, John Marshall was born on Sept. 24, 1755, near Germantown, Va. Frontier and family were the shap-

ing forces of his youth. His mother came from the aristocratic Randolphs of "Turkey Island." His father—"the foundation of all my own success in life," recalled John Marshall—was a man of humble origin who, through native ability and strength of character, rose to relative prominence. Marshall's spare formal education consisted mainly of tutored lessons in the classics and Latin. His father saw to it, however, that John was solidly grounded in English literature and history; he also brought home practical lessons in politics from his service in the Virginia House of Burgesses during the years preceding the American Revolution.

Family unity, a tradition of learning, and a concern for affairs of the world shielded young Marshall from the barbarity of the frontier. But the West also left its mark—in a gaiety of heart, an open democratic demeanor, and a manliness of character that were no small part of Marshall's gift of leadership.

American Revolution

A dedicated patriot from the outset, Marshall saw action with the Culpepper Minutemen in 1775. As an officer in the Continental Line, he took part in several important battles and endured the hardships of Valley Forge. His experience, fortified by his association with George Washington and other nationalist leaders, left him with the passionate love of union and chronic distrust of state particularism that later became the twin pillars of his constitutional law.

Before Capt. Marshall was mustered out of the Army in 1781, he had decided on law as a profession. He heard

George Wythe's law lectures at the College of William and Mary in 1780, and during that summer he was licensed to practice and that August was admitted to the county bar. During this same period Marshall fell in love with Mary Ambler. They were married in January 1783 and took up residence in Richmond, Va.

Early Political Career

Marshall's natural eloquence, charismatic personality, and rare gift for logical analysis overcame the deficiencies in his legal education. He rose quickly to the head of the Richmond bar. He also distinguished himself in state politics. He sat in the House of Burgesses (1782-1784, 1787-1791, and 1795-1797), where he consistently supported nationalist measures. He served on the important Committee on the Courts of Justice and when only 27 was elected by the legislature to the governor's Council of State.

Marshall's legislative experience confirmed his belief that the Articles of Confederation needed to be strengthened against the irresponsible and selfish forces of state power. As a delegate to the Virginia convention for the ratification of the Federal Constitution (1788), he put his nationalist ideas to use. Though somewhat overshadowed by established statesmen, he spoke influentially for ratification. And on the hotly debated subject of the Federal judiciary, he led the nationalist offensive.

Federalist orthodoxy and demonstrated ability soon won Marshall national prominence. During the crisis over the Jay Treaty in 1795, when party lines began to crystallize, Marshall supported Washington and Alexander Hamilton against the Jeffersonian Republicans. As a lawyer in the Supreme Court case of *Ware v. Hylton* (1796), he adhered to Federalist principles by arguing the supremacy of national law.

Marshall had turned down offers from President Washington to be attorney general and minister to France. In 1797 he agreed to serve on the "XYZ mission" to France. Shortly after his return, President John Adams offered him an appointment to the Supreme Court, but he declined. Elected to Congress in 1798, he soon became a leader of the Federalists in the House. Declining to serve as secretary of war, he accepted appointment in 1800 as secretary of state. Eight months later Adams appointed him chief justice of the Supreme Court, hoping to hold back the forces of states'-rights democracy, which in the form of the Jeffersonian Republicans had gained control of the Federal government.

Chief Justice

Marshall took his seat on the Court on March 5, 1801, and from that time until his death was absorbed in judicial duties. He did find time, however, to write a five-volume biography of George Washington (1804-1807) and to serve in the Virginia constitutional convention (1829-1830). But it was as chief justice that Marshall made his mark on American history. The pressing problem in 1801 was to unify and strengthen the Court. Accordingly he persuaded his colleagues to abandon the practice of delivering separate opinions and to permit him to write the opinion of the Court, which he did in the great majority of cases from 1801 to

1811. In addition, Marshall gave the Court a needed victory. His opinion in *Marbury v. Madison* (1803) for the first time declared an act of Congress unconstitutional, thus consolidating the Court's power of judicial review and providing future Courts with an elaborate defense of judicial power.

In *United States v. Peters* (1809) Marshall struck another blow for judicial power, this time against the claims of a state, by establishing the Court's right to be the final interpreter of Federal law. His opinion in *Fletcher v. Peck* held that the contract clause of the Constitution prevented state legislatures from repealing grants of land to private-interest groups. This was the first in a series of contract decisions that encouraged the growth of corporate capitalism. Few of Marshall's opinions touched civil rights; but in the Aaron Burr treason case, he struck a powerful blow for political freedom by defining treason narrowly and requiring strict proof for conviction.

Precedent-setting Cases

From the end of the War of 1812 through 1824 the Marshall Court was most creative. Marshall's position on the Court was less dominant than it had been before because able, new justices appeared. But he was unquestionably the guiding spirit and personally wrote opinions in the most important constitutional cases. Two such were *McCulloch v. Maryland* (1819) and *Gibbons v. Ogden* (1824). In the first case, Marshall upheld the congressional act chartering the Second Bank of the United States, thereby securing a national currency and credit structure for interstate capitalism. Also, by authorizing Congress to go beyond enumerated powers through a broad interpretation of the "necessary and proper" clause, he created a body of implied national powers.

Marshall's *Gibbons* opinion gave Congress supreme and comprehensive authority within the enumerated powers of Article I, Section 8, of the Constitution. The definition of commerce in the *Gibbons* case was sufficiently broad to bring the revolutionary developments in transportation and communication of the 20th century within the scope of congressional authority. These two cases created a reservoir of national power and guaranteed a flexible Constitution that could meet the nation's changing needs. That the Court should be the final interpreter of that flexible Constitution was the message of Marshall's compelling opinion in *Cohens v. Virginia* (1821).

Marshall's Concept of the Nation

Nationalist though he was, Marshall did not intend to destroy the states or establish the nation as an end in itself. He envisaged the national good as the sum of the productive individuals who constituted it, each pursuing his self-interest. Accordingly Marshall's opinions worked to release the creative energies of private enterprise and create a national arena for their operation. In *Dartmouth College v. Woodward* (1819) Marshall ruled that a corporation charter was a contract within the meaning of the Constitution which the states could not impair. As a result, private educational institutions, along with hundreds of business corporations chartered by the states, were secured against state interference. The unleashed forces of commerce, Marshall believed, would transcend selfish provincialism and create a powerful, self-sufficient nation.

Aroused states'-rights pressures in the 1820s forced the Marshall Court to curtail its nationalism. In addition, new appointments to the Court allowed division and dissent to burst into the open. The chief justice did not surrender national principles—as evidenced in *Brown v. Maryland* (1827) and *Worcester v. Georgia* (1832)—and he continued to lead the Court, but the age of judicial creativity was temporarily over. With the election of President Andrew Jackson in 1828, Marshall became increasingly pessimistic.

Meanwhile the death of Marshall's wife left him disconsolate. And his own health began to fail, though he remained intellectually alert and continued performing his duties until his death on July 6, 1835.

Marshall died believing that the Constitution and the republic for which he had labored were gone, but history proved him wrong. The nation continued along the course of nationalism and capitalism that he had done so much to establish; the Court and the law continued to follow the lines he projected. His reputation as the "great chief justice" seems secure.

Further Reading

Albert J. Beveridge, *The Life of John Marshall* (4 vols., 1916-1919; rev. ed., 2 vols., 1947), despite its nationalist bias, remains the standard biography. Edward S. Corwin, *John Marshall and the Constitution: A Chronicle of the Supreme Court* (1919), concentrates on his judicial career.
James Bradley Thayer and others, *John Marshall* (1967), is a collection of classic essays. William M. Jones, ed., *Chief Justice John Marshall: A Reappraisal* (1956), is another collection of distinguished essays. The most exhaustive analysis of Marshall's judicial philosophy is Robert K. Faulkner, *The Jurisprudence of John Marshall* (1968). The relationship between the two giants of American constitutional development is examined in Samuel J. Konefsky, *John Marshall and Alexander Hamilton: Architects of the American Constitution* (1964). Standard constitutional histories, such as Charles Warren, *The Supreme Court in United States History* (3 vols., 1923; rev. ed., 2 vols., 1926), and Charles G. Haines, *The Role of the Supreme Court in American Government and Politics*, 1789-1835 (1944), also contain material on Marshall's career. For further material the reader should consult James A. Servies, *A Bibliography of John Marshall* (1956), and numerous essays on him in historical and legal periodicals. □

Paule Burke Marshall

Paule Burke Marshall (born 1929) was an American author whose works reflected her Bajan background and twin themes of the need to confront the past and the need to change the present.

Paule Marshall was born April 9, 1929, in Brooklyn, New York, to Samuel and Ada Burke, who had immigrated separately from Barbados after World War I. At 18 her mother paid her passage with money inherited from an older brother. This money, called "Panama money," was the legacy of a man who had died, like thousands of other West Indian migrant laborers, digging the Panama Canal.

Marshall grew up in a bicultural environment rich with the language and folklore of Barbados. Her parents admired Franklin Roosevelt but were far more enthusiastic about Marcus Garvey. Marshall did not visit Barbados until she was nine years old, but island culture was made real to her by the lively conversations of her mother's friends around the kitchen table. Their metaphoric, often ironic language inspired her own attempts to find a narrative voice and to seek a literary career.

Marshall attended Brooklyn College and graduated *cum laude* in 1953. She pursued a job in the publishing world of New York but was unable to find a job with a major company. She began working for *Our World,* a small African-American magazine, as the food and fashion editor. While working there between 1953 and 1956, she began writing her first and best known work, *Brown Girl, Brownstones.* She married Kenneth E. Marshall in 1957 and soon afterwards completed her novel (1959).

The novel *Brown Girl, Brownstones* chronicled the coming of age of Selina Boyce, a first generation American whose Bajan parents fight each other for her allegiance and

love. The mother, Silla, was a hard-working, cruelly honest woman who singlemindedly pursued her vision of the American Dream but feels thwarted by her husband, Deighton, whose Walter Mitty fantasies of instant success alternate with dreams of returning home. Selina rejected her mother's seemingly heartless materialism even as she subconsciously admired her strength. She was very much her father's daughter but had regrets about his passive and delusional approach to life. Although much of the drama of the novel was fueled by the struggle between Silla and Deighton, Selina's personality and identity were shaped by other feminine forces. One such was Miss Thompson, a hairdresser from the South, who educated her about love, sacrifice, and the history of African people in America. In *Brown Girl, Brownstones* Selina also experienced her first love affair and confronted American racism. A gem of a novel which explored the intersections of race, class, and culture, *Brown Girl, Brownstones* has been rediscovered by scholars in African-American, Caribbean, and feminist criticisms.

Marshall's second book-length publication was *Soul Clap Hands and Sing* (1961), a collection of four short stories entitled "Barbados," "Brooklyn," "British Guiana," and "Brazil." This collection was completed after the birth of her only child, Eran-Keith, and without the approval of her husband, who doubted she could fulfill the duties of wife, mother and creative writer. Each story focused on an elderly man—a Bajan who returns home after years in America, a radical Jewish professor, a middle-class Guyanese, and a retired comedian in Brazil—who recognized his life has been spent in the pursuit of goals which leave him empty and unloved as death approaches. Marshall contended the confrontation with "the past, both in personal and historical terms," was a key theme in all of her works. An equally important idea was "the necessity of reversing the present order."

These two themes served as key elements in Marshall's subsequent works. *The Chosen Place, the Timeless People* (1969) explored the attempts of Merle Kinbona to come to grips with the many contradictions of her own life after she returns to Bournehills, a fictional West Indian island. In the plot Western values confronted the African peasant past, white meets black, and Africans of the Western Hemisphere meet Africans of the homeland. In *Praisesong for the Widow* (1983) Avey Johnson, a widow whose middle-class existence has been disrupted by the death of her husband and reoccurring dreams about her childhood, discovered the significance of her African past and the need for self-identification on a cruise in the Caribbean. In the novel Marshall made use of the famous folk story "Iboes' Landing," which told of a group of African slaves who walk into the ocean to return to Africa. Marshall's childhood identification with Africa through the Marcus Garvey movement was intensified after visits in 1977 and 1980 to Africa. Here she was welcomed by the people of Nigeria, Kenya, and Uganda as a long-lost daughter returning home. In 1983 Marshall's published short stories were collected in a book entitled *Reena and Other Stories*. Her novel *Daughters,* published in 1991, was a story of an African-American female executive.

Marshall supplemented her income from writing and grants with teaching positions. She served as a writer-in-residence at Oxford University, Columbia, Cornell, Washington State, Lake Forest University, and Iowa. Divorced from her first husband in 1963, she married Nourry Menard in 1970 and spent time living in both New York and the West Indies. Marshall was the recipient of a Guggenheim award (1960), a Rosenthal award from the National Institute for Arts and Letters (1962), a Ford Foundation grant (1964-1965), and a grant from the National Endowment for the Arts (1967-1968). In 1984 *Praisesong for the Widow* was awarded the Before Columbus American Book Award. Other works included *Early Short Fiction of Paule Marshall*, Callaloo, Spring 1984, and *The Fiction of Paule Marshall: Reconstructing History, Culture and Gender*, University of Tennessee Press, October 1995.

Since 1991, besides writing, Marshall has held several conferences and become a well-known keynote speaker. The Institute for African American Affairs at New York University was the host for Marshall's keynote address at NYU in March, 1996. She read passages for The North Country American Conversation: A Community Alliance, a series based at St. Lawrence University which aimed to further discussions of how Americans feel about their ethnic identities and about being Americans.

In 1990, she was an honoree of the PEN/Faulkner Foundation, and in 1992, she was the recipient of a MacArthur Fellowship. Marshall has taught at several universities, and in 1997 was a Distinguished Professor of English and Creative Writing at New York University.

Further Reading

For more biographical information on Paule Marshall see Marshall, "Black Immigrant Women in *Brown Girl, Brownstones*" in *Female Immigrants to the United States* (1981). For critical analysis, see Leela Kapai, "Dominant Themes and Techniques in Paule Marshall's Fiction," in *CLA Journal* (September 1972); Mari Evans, *Black Women Writers (1950-1980)* (1984); Hortense Spillers, "Chosen Place, Timeless People. . ." in *Conjuring: Black Women, Fiction and Literary Tradition* (1985). □

Thurgood Marshall

Thurgood Marshall (1908-1993) was an American civil rights lawyer, solicitor general, and associate justice of the U.S. Supreme Court.

Thurgood Marshall was born on July 2, 1908, in Baltimore, Maryland, where his mother was a teacher and his father a headwaiter and country club steward. Parental qualities of thoroughness, excellence, justice, and equality, along with humility, pride, and aggressiveness, early impressed him. Marshall attended Lincoln University, where he received his bachelor's degree *cum laude,* and then enrolled in the law school at Howard University in 1930, from which he graduated *magna cum laude* in 1933.

While at Howard he came under the influence of Charles Houston and the group of legal scholars who developed and perfected techniques and procedures for civil rights litigation.

Passing the Maryland bar in 1933, Marshall practiced in Baltimore until 1938, serving also as counsel for the Baltimore branch of the National Association for the Advancement of Colored People (NAACP). In 1935 he successfully attacked segregation and discrimination in education when he participated in the desegregation of the University of Maryland Law School (where he had been denied admission because of race). Marshall became director of the NAACP's Legal Defense and Education Fund in 1939. A year earlier he had been admitted to practice before the U.S. Supreme Court, the U.S. Circuit Court of Appeals for the fourth, fifth, and eighth circuits, and the U.S. District Court for the Eastern District of Louisiana.

Winning 29 of the 32 civil rights cases which he and his aides argued before the Supreme Court (and sometimes threatened with death as he argued cases in the lower courts of some southern states), Marshall earned the reputation of "America's outstanding civil rights lawyer." Some of the important cases he argued, which became landmarks in the destruction of segregation, as well as constitutional precedents with their decisions, include *Smith v. Allwright* (1944), establishing the rights of African-Americans to vote in Democratic primary elections; *Morgan v. Virginia* (1946), outlawing the state's segregation policy as applied to interstate bus transportation; *Shelley v. Kramer* (1948), outlawing restrictive covenants in housing; and *Sweatt v. Painter*

(1950), requiring admission of an African-American student to the University of Texas Law School. The most famous was *Brown vs. Board of Education* (1954), which outlawed segregation in public schools and for all practical purposes "sounded the death knell for all forms of legally sanctioned segregation."

The NAACP sent Marshall to Japan and Korea in 1951 to investigate complaints that African-American soldiers convicted by U. S. Army courts-martial had not received fair trials. His appeal arguments got the sentences of 22 of the 40 men reduced.

President John Kennedy nominated Marshall on Sept. 23, 1961, for judge of the Second Court of Appeals; he was confirmed by the Senate a year later after undergoing strenuous hearings. Three years later Marshall accepted President Lyndon Johnson's appointment as solicitor general. In this post Marshall successfully defended the United States in a number of important cases concerning industry. Of no little interest was the fact that through his office he now defended civil rights actions as advocate for the American people instead of (as in his NAACP days) as counsel strictly for African-Americans; however, he personally did not argue cases in which he had previously been involved.

In 1967 President Johnson nominated Marshall as associate justice to the U. S. Supreme Court. Marshall's nomination was strenuously opposed by several Southern senators on the Judiciary Committee but nevertheless he was confirmed by a vote of 69 to 11. He took his seat on October 2, 1967, and was the first African-American justice to sit on the U.S. Supreme Court.

During his nearly quarter-century on the Supreme Court, he remained a strong advocate of individual rights and never wavered in his devotion to ending discrimination. He formed a key part of the Court's progressive majority which voted to uphold a woman's right to abortion. His majority opinions covered such areas as ecology, the right of appeal of persons convicted of narcotic charges, failure to report for and submit to induction into the U. S. Armed Forces, obscenity, and the rights of Native Americans.

The Reagan-Bush years in the White House and the slow dwindling of the liberal influence on the Court was a time of sadness for Marshall. Always tart tongued, in 1987 Marshall dismissed President Reagan in an interview with *Ebony* as "the bottom" in terms of his commitment to black Americans. He later told the magazine: "I wouldn't do the job of dogcatcher for Ronald Reagan." There is no question that Marshall viewed the actions of the conservative Republican presidents as a throwback to the days when "we (African-Americans) didn't really have a chance." Marshall was keenly disappointed when his friend and liberal colleague, Justice William J. Brennan Jr., retired from the Court due to ill heath. Marshall vowed to serve until he was 110 and then die "shot by a jealous husband." However, suffering heart attacks, pneumonia, blood clots, and glaucoma, Marshall himself was forced by illness to give up his seat in 1991. He died in 1993 at the age of 84.

Justice Marshall had been born during Theodore Roosevelt's administration but lived to see African-Americans rise to positions of power and influence in America. To no small degree, the progress of black Americans toward equal opportunity turned upon the legal victories won by him. By his death, even in retirement, he had risen to the stature of mythic hero. His numerous honors included more than 20 honorary degrees from educational institutions in America and abroad. The University of Maryland Law School was named in his honor, as were a variety of elementary and secondary schools around the nation. During his life he received the NAACP's Spingarn Medal (1946), the Negro Newspaper Publisher Association's Russwurm Medal (1948), and the Living Makers of Negro History Award of the Iota Phi Lambda Sorority (1950), and his name was inscribed on the honor roll of the Schomburg History Collection of New York for the advancement of race relations. He enjoyed the family life of his second wife and their two sons, Thurgood Jr. and John, who themselves pursued careers in public life. Marshall's first wife died in 1955. A little over 6 feet tall and dignified and solemn in manner, but endowed with a sense of humor, Marshall portrayed homely virtues and a deep reverence for God. Unique as his career was, it epitomized the potential of American democracy.

Further Reading

For periodical articles dealing with Marshall's life and career, see *Newsweek* (Sept. 21, 1987 and Aug. 6, 1990). Of the numerous books on Marshall's life and career, a well-received analysis was contained in the twin volumes *Making Civil Rights Law: Thurgood Marshall and the Supreme Court 1936-1961* (1994) and *Making Constitutional Law: Thurgood Marshall and the Supreme Court 1961-1991* (1997) by Mark V. Thusnet. An early biography of Marshall is Lewis H. Fenderson, ed., *Thurgood Marshall* (1969). □

Marsilius of Padua

The Italian political philosopher Marsilius of Padua (c. 1275-1342) wrote *Defensor pacis,* the most important political treatise written in the late Middle Ages.

Marsilio dei Mainardini, who is known as Marsilius of Padua, was born at Padua. He was the son of a notary, and he received his early education in Padua, probably completing his arts degree and, perhaps, even a degree in medicine at the university there. Marsilius soon moved north to the leading university of his day, the University of Paris, where he became rector in 1313.

The years at Paris, first as a student, then as a teacher, were formative for Marsilius. He must have come into contact with the two most important theologians at Paris during that period, Durand of Saint-Pourçain and Peter Aureol. He certainly met the two leading Averroists, Peter of Abano and John of Jandun. Marsilius's teaching career culminated with the publication in 1324 of his extensive treatise on political power, the *Defensor pacis.* In this work Marsilius attacked many of the arguments used to support the political and temporal authority of the papacy. Going beyond this, Marsilius further attacked the absolute authority of the papacy within the administrative structure of the Church.

The principal idea upon which Marsilius established his political theory was the idea of popular sovereignty. All power is ultimately vested in the people. The secular monarch exercises his political authority not because he receives it as a divine right but because he derives it from the citizens of the state. The Roman pontiff derives his authority not from God, as Christ's vicar, but from the members of the Church. Desiring to counter the claims of the papal propagandists, Marsilius placed greater stress on "democratic" institutions in the Church than he did for secular society.

Political authority in the state, which Marsilius treats in the first book of his treatise, is derived from the citizens. Only they, acting as a whole or through a delegated authority, have the right to prescribe laws for the state. In order to ensure peace in the state, it is necessary to have one governing agency, which may be, but does not need to be, a hereditary monarchy. Such a head of state should be elected by the entire community. If the monarch acts against the welfare of the community or its laws, he can be deposed.

Stronger limits are placed on the authority of the papacy, a subject treated in the second book of *Defensor pacis.* According to Marsilius, the papacy has no authority in temporal affairs. Even in the Church, authority was to be shared with the bishops. Ultimately pope and bishops were to be answerable to the members of the Church.

When the work and his authorship became widely known in 1326, Marsilius decided to move outside the area of influence of Pope John XXII, who resided at Avignon in southern France. Marsilius sought protection and patronage from the German monarch Louis IV of Bavaria, who was already in conflict with John XXII. In 1327 Marsilius took part in Louis's expedition into Italy and was with him at Rome in 1328, when he was proclaimed emperor by the people of Rome. Marsilius was appointed vicar of Rome, a position in which he persecuted those members of the Roman clergy who remained faithful to John XXII.

When Louis was forced to return to Germany, Marsilius accompanied him. He remained at the imperial court for the rest of his life. In 1342 he wrote a short work entitled *Defensor minor,* a restatement of his earlier and better-known work. A few months later he died.

Further Reading

The *Defensor pacis* was translated into English by Alan Gewirth in *Marsilius of Padua: The Defender of Peace* (2 vols., 1951-1956), which includes an excellent introduction. Volume 1 was first printed alone as *Marsilius of Padua and Medieval Political Philosophy* (1951). Still useful is R. W. and A. J. Carlyle, *A History of Mediaeval Political Theory in the West* (6 vols., 1903-1936). A briefer summary of Marsilius's thought is in John B. Morrall, *Political Thought in Medieval Times* (1958). □

Charles Martel

The Frankish ruler Charles Martel (ca. 690-741) re-established central authority in Francia and constructed a power base on which the Carolingian monarchs founded their empire.

To understand the historical importance of Charles Martel ("the Hammer"), it is necessary to appreciate the situation of the last Merovingian kings of Francia and to understand what historians generally refer to as the crisis of the mid-8th century, namely, the expansion of Islam and the sealing off of the Mediterranean. After the reign of Dagobert I (629-639) the Merovingian royal house was weakened by the fact that none of the later kings survived until manhood. Therefore in the 7th century the real power of government was exercised by the mayors of the palace. These officials controlled the royal treasury, dispersed patronage, and granted land and privileges in the name of the king.

The Merovingian kingdom in Gaul comprised two major subkingdoms, Neustria (the northwestern portion) and Austrasia (northeastern Gaul and the Rhineland), each of which was ruled by a mayor of the palace. The respective rulers of the two kingdoms fought bitterly for supremacy, and in 687 at the battle of Tetry, the Austrasian mayor, Pepin of Heristal, defeated the Neustrian mayor and united the two kingdoms. It was thus the task of Pepin and his son Charles Martel to restore centralized government in the Frankish kingdom and to combat the expanding power of Islam.

Charles Martel was the illegitimate son of Pepin of Heristal and a noblewoman named Alpaide. When Pepin died in 714, Charles successfully asserted his claims to power over the resistance of Pepin's widow, Plectrude, and became mayor of the palace. Charles attracted and maintained a group of personal retainers who formed the core of the royal army. Most of his reign as mayor of the palace was spent in checking the expansion of the Saracens in southern France and in the Rhone-Saône Valley.

In October 732 Charles won a major victory against the Saracens outside Poitiers despite the fact that the invaders were mounted and the Franks were on foot. The battle, aside from temporarily checking the expansion of the Moslems, was of long-range significance because it was here that Charles became convinced of the necessity of cavalry. After Poitiers, Charles developed the cavalry as his primary offensive fighting force. This change, however, proved highly expensive, and the cost of supporting and training men on horseback led to the adoption of a means of support that had far-reaching consequences. Charles found it necessary to "borrow" considerable lands from the Church; he then dispersed these properties among his lay retainers. The old army of Frankish freemen became less important, and gradually a considerable social distinction developed between the mounted knight and the ordinary foot soldier. Thus the elite class of mounted warriors who dominated medieval France owed their origins to the military policy of Charles Martel.

In his effort to maintain unity in the Frankish realm and to combat the Saracens, Charles relied heavily on the support of the Church and particularly on that of Boniface, the great missionary to the Germans. Charles encouraged the missionary efforts of Boniface and in return received new territories and considerable ecclesiastical revenues to support his fighting force. His role as protector of Christendom lay primarily in his wars against the Saracens. In 739 Pope Gregory III asked him to defend the Holy See against the Lombards; Charles, however, did not intervene because of an earlier treaty with the Lombards.

Charles Martel died at the royal palace at Quierzy on Oct. 22, 741, and was buried at the abbey of St. Denis.

Further Reading

A brief survey of the historical contribution of Charles Martel is in Heinrich Fichtenau, *The Carolingian Empire,* translated by Peter Munz (1957). See also Ferdinand Lot, *The End of the Ancient World and the Beginnings of the Middle Ages* (1927; trans. 1931). ☐

José Martí

José Martí (1853-1895) was a Cuban revolutionary, poet, and journalist. The principal organizer of Cuba's war against Spain, he was the apostle of Cuban independence.

José Martí was born in Havana on Jan. 28, 1853, of Spanish parents. In school, where he was an eager student, his teachers aroused in him a devotion to the cause of freedom, and he also achieved early recognition as a writer. At the age of 15 he composed several poems; at 16 he published a Havana newspaper, *La Patria Libre,* and wrote a dramatic poem, *Abdala.* Arrested for political reasons, Martí served several months at hard labor before he was deported to Spain in January 1871.

In Exile

There Martí published a political essay, *El presidio político en Cuba,* an indictment of Spanish oppression and conditions in Cuban jails. The young revolutionary also resumed his studies, and in 1874 he received a degree in philosophy and law from the University of Saragossa. Martí then traveled through Europe and in 1875 went to Mexico, where he worked as a journalist. After a short visit to Cuba in 1877, he settled in Guatemala, where he taught literature and philosophy. That same year he married Carmen Zayas Bazán, daughter of a Cuban exile, and shortly afterward published his first book, *Guatemala.*

Unhappy with Guatemala's political conditions, Martí returned to Cuba in December 1878. The Peace of Zanjón, which ended the Ten Years War (1868-1878) against Spain, had just been signed, and Martí felt that conditions on the

island would be propitious for his return. Spanish authorities, however, soon discovered his continued revolutionary activities and again deported him to Spain. He escaped to France and from there moved to the United States and Venezuela.

Journalist and Poet

In 1881 Martí made New York the center of his activities, although he continued to travel and to write about the many problems of Latin American nations. Through regular newspaper columns for *La Opinión Nacional* of Caracas and for *La Nación* of Buenos Aires, he gained recognition throughout Latin America.

Martí was noted not only for his journalistic abilities but also for his poetry and prose. He was a precursor of the modernistic movement in poetry. In 1882 his most significant poems, composed for his son, were published in a book called *Ismaelillo.* Martí's best-known poems appear in *Versos sencillos* (1891) and emphasize the themes of friendship, sincerity, love, justice, and freedom. Martí also won the hearts of Latin American youngsters with his *Edad de oro* (1889), a magazine especially devoted to children. His greatest contribution to Spanish American letters was his essays. Written in a highly personal style, they brought about an innovation in prose writing.

Revolutionary Activities

Martí realized very early that independence from Spain was the only solution for Cuba and that this could be

achieved only through a war that was sudden and that would at the same time prevent United States Intervention in Cuba. His fear of a military dictatorship after independence led in 1884 to a break with Máximo Gómez and Antonio Maceo, two generals who at the time were engaged in a conspiracy against Spain. Martí withdrew from the movement temporarily, but by 1887 the three men were working together again, with Martí assuming political leadership. In 1892 he formed the Cuban Revolutionary party in the United States and directed his efforts toward organizing the war against Spain.

In 1895 Martí gave the order for the resumption of hostilities against Spain and landed in Cuba to lead the war. He was killed in a skirmish with Spanish troops at Dos Rios, Oriente Province, on May 19, 1895.

What distinguished Martí was his ability to organize and harmonize. His oratory inspired his listeners, his honesty and sincerity inspired faith, and his conviction in the ideas he was pursuing gained him the respect and loyalty of his followers. His writings were not mere rhetorical exercises but moral teachings aimed at making man better, and their impact was felt not only in Cuba but throughout Latin America. Like Simón Bolívar, he thought in terms of a continent and advocated the unity of Latin America.

Further Reading

Martí has generated an extensive body of literature. Four good studies are Jorge Mañach, *Martí: Apostle of Freedom* (1933; trans. 1950); Felix Lizaso, *Martí: Martyr of Cuban Independence* (1940; trans. 1953); Juan de Onis, ed., *The America of José Martí: Selected Writings* (1953); and Richard B. Gray, *José Martí: Cuban Patriot* (1962). □ 　·

Marcus Valerius Martialis

Martial (ca. 38-ca. 104), whose full name was Marcus Valerius Martialis, was a Roman epigrammatist. The development of the epigram as we know it was largely due to Martial's influence. His works give one of the best pictures of life in ancient Rome.

Martial was born at Bilbilis in Spain on March 1 (his cognomen was derived from the date) of a year probably between 38 and 41. He was a Roman citizen, although of Celtic and Iberian stock, and was given a good literary education by his parents, Fronto and Flaccilla. He left Spain for Rome in 64, "a fellow citizen of the Tagus, with bristling Spanish hair," determined to make his fortune as a verse writer, and soon placed himself under the powerful patronage of his fellow Spaniards Seneca and Lucan and was received with friendship by Calpurnius Piso. In 65 Piso's conspiracy against Nero was discovered, and Seneca and Lucan were implicated and met their deaths.

For the next 33 years Martial lived in Rome solely as a writer. An author could sell his original manuscript to a bookseller-publisher, although the sums involved were usually quite small, but he then had no claim to royalties whatever, and unless he had a private fortune (and Martial seems to have had little if any), or a separate career, he was dependent for his livelihood on the patronage of the rich and powerful. This could be a happy relationship, with a generous and tactful patron, but it usually, as in Martial's case, led to servility. It is painful to read some of Martial's begging epigrams, whining, impudent, and ungrateful as they seem (his adulation of the tyrant Domitian, who apparently paid little attention, is especially sickening), but the distress must have been real, and he must have been genuinely dependent on the daily visits at dawn to the houses of the great, to pay attendance and in return to receive a basket containing a little food or a few coins, according to the customs of ancient Rome.

Those years were not, however, without success. Martial had a small and barren farm near Nomentum in the Sabine country, that may have been a bequest from Seneca, and after years of living in a backroom of a fourthfloor tenement he had acquired a small house in Rome by 94. He received from Titus, with a later confirmation from Domitian, the rights (of inheritance and so forth) accorded to parents of three children, although he was apparently never married. He was also made an honorary military tribune, thereby being admitted to the equestrian order, although he did not have the necessary financial qualifications. He was thus in the curious situation of being on good terms with the Emperor, many great nobles, and the great literary figures of his day, including Frontinus, Juvenal, Pliny the Younger, Quintilian, and Silius Italicus (but not Statius, whose *Silvae* are on many of the same subjects covered by Martial's epigrams and who was probably a rival), and of also being acquainted on a day-to-day basis with the lowest level of Roman life. After the death of Domitian in 96 and the succession of the moral and benevolent Nerva, Martial realized that the climate of opinion in Rome would no longer tolerate indecency and servility in verse, and in 98, helped by Pliny the Younger, he returned to Spain, where he settled on a farm given him by his patroness, Marcella. A letter of Pliny's, of about 104, speaks of his recent death with real regret.

His Works

Martial's first extant work was a book of epigrams on the shows presented at the opening of the Colosseum in 80. In 84 and 85 he issued the *Xenia* and *Apophoreta* (now books 13 and 14, respectively), mottoes for gifts given to guests at banquets and for gifts in general. From 86 to 98 he issued about a book (averaging 100 epigrams a book) a year (books 1 to 11). Book 12 was completed about 3 years after his departure from Rome.

The over 1,500 epigrams of Martial are of the most bewildering variety. Romans of every sort and condition appear in his pages, engaged in every conceivable activity. He was the ideal spectator, amiable, witty, at times tender and sentimental. His flattery of great persons can be forgiven; his scurrilous abuse (never, however, directed at persons under their own names), sometimes marked by the

most graphic and imaginative obscenity, is usually amusing; and at his best Martial is unsurpassed for wit, elegance, and point. It is this last which has proved his most lasting contribution: the epigram before Martial was characterized by a high lapidary polish but seldom by the wit and satirical point which he gave it.

Further Reading

A comprehensive survey of Martial as poet and satirist is still lacking. Works on Martial include Kirby Flower Smith, *Martial the Epigrammatist and Other Essays* (1920); T. K. Whipple, *Martial and the English Epigram from Sir Thomas Wyatt to Ben Jonson* (1925); Paul Nixon, *Martial and the Modern Epigram* (1927); and A. G. Carrington, *Aspects of Martial's Epigrams* (1960). Martial figures prominently in H. E. Butler, *Post-Augustan Poetry from Seneca to Juvenal* (1909), and in two works by J. Wight Duff, *A Literary History of Rome in the Silver Age from Tiberius to Hadrian* (1927; 3d ed. 1963) and *Roman Satire* (1936). □

Martin V

Martin V (1368-1431) was pope from 1417 to 1431. He was elected by the Council of Constance, which thus terminated the Great Schism of the West.

The man who was to become Pope Martin V was born in Genazzano, Italy, on Feb. 20, 1368. His name was Oddone Colonna, and he was the only member of that illustrious Roman family ever to be elected to the throne of Peter. He was made a cardinal by Innocent VII in 1405 and three years later, at the height of the quarrel between the Avignonese and the Roman claimants to the papal chair, withdrew his obedience from Gregory XII. Thereupon, in 1409, he participated in the Council of Pisa, which had been convoked in a desperate effort to end the schism. He voted in the election of Alexander V in 1409 and of John XXIII in 1410, hoping in each case, as did all men of goodwill, that the choice of the council would prevail and that the two reigning popes, Benedict XIII and Gregory XII, would accept the conciliar decision that they be deposed. They did not, and another council was convoked, this time at Constance (1414-1418).

After a long debate on electoral procedure, 22 cardinals and 30 delegates from the five nations represented chose Oddone Colonna as Pope Martin V. The election took place on Nov. 11, 1417. With the temporary exception of Aragon, all Western Christendom now recognized Martin V as the true and only vicar of Christ.

Before leaving for Rome, Martin made known his hostile feeling toward the possibility of future supremacy of councils over popes, implied during several sessions at Constance. On May 10, 1418, he ordered read in consistory the constitution which prohibited all appeals from the judgment of the pope in matters of faith.

Six days later, on May 16, Martin left Constance. His ultimate destination was Rome, but he could not go there at once because the roads were under the control of Braccio da Montone, a mercenary general. He spent some time in Mantua and Florence and arrived at Rome only on Sept. 28, 1420. He found the city in a shocking condition of decay. Rome and the entire states of the Church had fallen under petty despots in the long absence of firm papal control.

Martin V was not the man to permit such conditions to persist. Though the papal treasury was almost empty, he set about the task of restoring the Vatican and Lateran basilicas and of widening the streets. He commissioned Masaccio and Pisanello to paint frescoes in S. Maria Maggiore. He codified the laws of Rome and reorganized the Curia, incorporating it with the now leaderless Curia of Avignon. Poggio Bracciolini, a leading humanist, was put to work as papal secretary. To finance all this and the papal army, with which he successfully restored the papal territories to order, Martin was constrained to continue the vicious practice of selling Church offices.

With these projects under way, the Pope summoned a council to Pavia in April 1423 in obedience to the decree *Frequens* promulgated at Constance. One of the principal tasks of the Council of Pavia was an undertaking dear to the heart of the Pope: reunion of the Roman and Greek Churches, for which hope had been quickened by some of the sessions of Constance. All efforts failed, however; and when the delegates moved to establish the principle of conciliar superiority to popes, Martin quickly dissolved the council. It is fair to say that without Martin V's unswerving support of papal supremacy at a time when either road could have been taken, the Roman Church might well have changed from an authoritarian to a democratic institution. In a bull of 1425, the Pope proposed changes in the financing of the Curia, but this effort at reform found little support and died quickly.

It has been said that Martin V was a gentle man, and this judgment seems to be borne out by his many attempts, through correspondence and emissaries, to bring about peace between England and France, engaged at that time in the Hundred Years War. Obedient to the letter if not always to the spirit of Constance, Martin summoned another council, to meet in 1431 at Basel. On Feb. 20, 1431, shortly before the council was to meet, he died.

Further Reading

A thorough treatment of Martin V's struggle to restore papal control over Rome is Peter Partner, *The Papal State under Martin V* (1958). Volume 1 of Ludwig von Pastor's classic work on the papacy, *History of the Popes from the Close of the Middle Ages* (40 vols., 1891-1953), discusses the period of Martin V. For an understanding of the schism see Walter Ullmann, *The Origins of the Great Schism* (1948). □

Agnes Martin

Agnes Martin (born 1912) was a Canadian-born American painter who became well known in the **mid-1970s for her spare canvases of geometric lines and grids.**

Agnes Martin was born in Saskatchewan, Canada, where her father was a wheat farmer, in 1912. After his early death, she spent her youth in Vancouver, where her mother renovated and sold old houses. She studied in Washington State, the University of New Mexico, and Columbia University in New York City, after which she taught in public schools and universities in the West, Southwest, and East Coast of the United States. She became an American citizen in 1950, and took several sojourns in New York between 1941 and 1954. In the 1950s she settled in Taos, New Mexico, only to come back to New York in 1957 at the urging of art dealer Betty Parsons. She returned again to the Southwest, where she remained.

Prior to her move to New York in 1957 Martin's work consisted of conventional still-lifes and portraits, followed by more abstracted and biomorphic canvases reminiscent of surrealists such as Jean Arp, Joan Miro, and Archile Gorky who used the exploration of the unconscious as subject matter and process in their work. In New York Martin lived in Coenties Slip in lower Manhattan where she was close to a group of younger American artists who became associated with a kind of abstraction characterized by large, simple, geometric forms painted or sculpted with a hard-edged precision. Among her colleagues there were Ellsworth Kelly, Jack Youngerman, and Robert Indiana, as well as James Rosenquist and artist-performer Ann Wilson.

From about 1958 on she adopted a more geometric style using the motifs of squares, rectangles, and finally grids lightly drawn over areas of pale color. These works, large in scale, projected a sense of pure abstraction, a "classicism" softened by the delicate tension of the stroke of a human hand. It is this work for which she is best known, coinciding with a general tendency in American art towards reductivism, or the reducing of a work of art to a few well-chosen elements which, together, project a wholeness and unity and reject representation and illusion. This was a kind of outgrowth of Abstract Expressionism that can be traced through the more stark canvases of Barnett Newman and Ad Reinhardt. Other artists connected with this movement, labeled "Minimalism" by critics but often renounced by the artists themselves, were Donald Judd, Frank Stella, Richard Serra, and Dorothea Rockburne, as well as Martin's friend Ellsworth Kelly. This purist sensibility had earlier origins in the 20th century in the work of Russian Constructivists such as Vladimir Malevich and El Lissitzky and the Dutch De Stijl artists Piet Mondrian and Theo Van Doesburg.

What distinguishes Martin's work from the other Minimalists is her light touch. Her use of delicate, barely discernable color, along with an insistent horizontal line, leaves an evocative sense of landscape, specifically the desert in which she spent so much of her life. While many of the artists around Martin deny that their work is "referential"—that is, refers to anything in the real world—Martin's paintings, while not descriptions of specific times or places, allude to general states of mind and to the "spirit" or "essence" that Oriental artists seek to capture in traditional Japanese and Chinese painting and calligraphy. In fact, Martin was interested in Chinese theories and practices of art and she wrote a number of long statements and poems based loosely on an Oriental manner of inquiry. Especially interested in the power of absences, an excerpt from one states: "Two late Tang dishes, one with a flower image one empty. The empty form goes all the way to heaven."

In 1967 Martin left New York, resettled in New Mexico, and did not paint again until 1974. Her refusal to paint for seven years at the height of her professional success added to her enigma, as though she were choosing spirit over matter. Prior to this departure she showed her work with the legendary Ms. Parsons, an early champion of American artists, but in 1975 she had an exhibition at the Pace Gallery in New York where she showed thereafter. Major exhibitions of her work were held at the Institute of Contemporary Art in Philadelphia in 1973 and at the Hayward Gallery in London in 1977. She was included in numerous group exhibitions in the United States and Europe.

Most of the critical attention given to Agnes Martin focused on her work from the mid-1960s through the mid-1970s when it, along with the work of her colleagues, formed a dialogue central to issues of new art at that time. After the mid-1970s she remained a private person by distancing herself from New York. She became an object of fascination and respect for many younger artists. In 1976 she produced a film called *Gabriel*, which features no dialogue and shows Martin following a boy along a western

Canadian landscape. She continued painting and holding exhibitions, and in 1989 was inducted into the American Academy and Institute of Arts and Letters. A major retrospective of her work was held from 1992 to 1994 by the Whitney Museum of American Art in New York, and in 1995 she participated in the Biennial Exhibition at the Whitney.

In an interview with Holland Cotter in the *New York Times* Martin expressed the philosophy guiding her in painting, saying, "I say to my mind, 'what am I going to paint next?' Then I wait for the inspiration. You have to wait if you're going to be inspired. You have to clear out your mind, to have a quiet and empty mind."

Further Reading

There is little written about Agnes Martin or her work prior to her arrival in New York at the age of 45, but much was written in art journals and magazines after that. A catalogue was published for her exhibition at the Hayward Gallery with an essay by art critic Dore Ashton (1973) and another catalogue was published in 1977 for her exhibition in Philadelphia with an essay by Lawrence Alloway. The latter catalogue also contains oral and written statements by the artist titled "The Untroubled Mind," "Willie Stories," and "Parable of the Equal Hearts." Another catalogue published in Germany in 1973 included notes by Agnes Martin "On the Perfection Underlying Life." A single issue of the magazine *Artforum* in April 1973 had two articles on the artist, one about her work at that time and another by art critic Lizzie Borden about earlier work and its relationship to what followed. A profile of her by Holland Cotter, "Like Her Paintings, Quiet, Unchanging and Revered," was in the *New York Times*, and an interview with her, "Agnes Martin Attention!" by Peter Schjeldahl, was in *Interview* magazine. A biography of Agnes Martin with a list of her exhibitions and articles about her is available from the Pace Wildenstein Art Museum in New York City. □

Luther Martin

Luther Martin (1748-1826) was an American lawyer, Revolutionary War patriot, and member of the Constitutional Convention.

Luther Martin was born in Metuchen, N. J., on Feb. 9, 1748. He attended the grammar school of the College of New Jersey (Princeton) and the college itself, graduating in 1766. Moving to Maryland, he taught school and studied law. Admitted to the Virginia bar in 1771 and to the Maryland bar the next year, he practiced in both colonies. Despite his land ownership and lucrative law practice, Martin mismanaged his financial affairs, and was sued for debt as early as 1770.

Martin's personal life was a succession of tragedies. The deaths of two wives left him with three daughters. One daughter became insane and died. Another married against her father's wishes and died a few years later; her son died in early manhood. Martin himself became infatuated with Aaron Burr's daughter, who was already married.

Martin lent his legal talent to the Revolutionary cause. He published defenses of the patriot position and, as Maryland's attorney general during the war, vigorously prosecuted Tories. As a Maryland delegate to the Constitutional Convention, he made prolix, ungrammatical, and often disorganized speeches, that commanded attention and made him a leading spokesman of the states'-rights interests. He insisted on equal representation of the states in Congress, sought to limit the powers of both Congress and the president, and insisted that the Constitution be submitted to the state legislatures for ratification. He refused to sign the finished document and led opposition to its ratification in Maryland.

Martin's political career became a peculiar combination of adherence to the Federalist party and continued defense of states' rights. His federalism stemmed in part from his intense, personal anti-Jeffersonianism, which exploded in public attacks. His hostility to Jefferson was exacerbated by the 1805 impeachment trial of Supreme Court Justice Samuel Chase, Martin's lifelong friend. Martin's arguments helped bring about Chase's acquittal. In 1807 Martin again opposed Jefferson in the famous treason trial of Aaron Burr; Martin's skillful defense aided in getting Burr acquitted.

In two other important cases, *Fletcher v. Peck* (1810) and *McCulloch v. Maryland* (1819), Martin argued for states' rights. However, Chief Justice John Marshall's nationalism proved to be more compelling in both instances and, in the process, produced historic Supreme Court decisions enlarging the scope of national jurisdiction.

Though Martin became increasingly intemperate in later years, his popular reputation was attested by the extraordinary action of the Maryland Legislature in levying a license tax on attorneys to create a trust fund for its now destitute former attorney general. Martin died in New York City on July 10, 1826. Universally acknowledged as a distinguished orator and a legal genius in his day, Martin contributed to the nation's legal development.

Further Reading

The only full-length biography is Paul Clarkson and R. Samuel Jett, *Luther Martin of Maryland* (1970). It is as definitive as the absence of any significant body of Martin papers allows. Martin's legal career is treated briefly in Charles Warren, *History of the American Bar* (1911; repr. 1966), and his participation in the Chase and Burr trials more fully in Albert J. Beveridge, *Life of John Marshall* (4 vols., 1916-1919). Martin's role in the Constitution struggle may be traced in Max Farrand, ed., *The Records of the Federal Convention of 1787* (4 vols., 1911-1937; rev. ed. 1966). □

Lynn Morley Martin

As a 10-year member of Congress, Lynn (Morley) Martin (born 1939) sat on the powerful House Rules, Armed Services and Budget committees. She was also vice chair of the House Republican Conference—the first woman ever elected to a congressional leadership post. As secretary of Labor in the Bush Administration, Martin was outspoken on workplace reform—a subject about which she continues to lecture and write extensively while serving on the boards of several large corporations.

Lynn Martin was born Lynn Morley in Evanston, Illinois, on Dec. 26, 1939, the second of two daughters of Lawrence William Morley, an accountant, and Helen Catherine (Hall) Morley. She grew up on Chicago's North Side and graduated in 1957 with honors from William Howard Taft High School in Chicago.

An English major, Morley graduated Phi Beta Kappa in 1960 from the University of Illinois at Champaign-Urbana with a teaching certificate. During college she switched from the Democratic to the Republican Party, expressing the sentiment that the Democrats had abandoned individual rights in favor of the rights of groups.

Started Career as a Teacher

In the spring of 1960 she married engineering student John Martin. After the birth of their daughter Julia, she taught English, economics, and government at Wheaton Central and Saint Francis high schools in Du Page County, Illinois. The Martins' second daughter, Caroline, was born in 1969.

Starting her political career in 1972, Martin served four years on the Winnebago County Board, sitting on the Finance and Public Works committees. She unseated a

Democratic incumbent to win a seat in the Illinois House of Representatives, serving from 1977-79. With the support of the House Republican leader, she was assigned to the Appropriations Committee, where she became known as a fiscal conservative. Martin moved from the Illinois House to the Senate, winning a seat on that body's Appropriations Committee and continuing to press for reduced government spending.

Set Sights on Washington

Her marriage to John Martin ended in divorce in 1978, and in 1980 she left state government to run for Congress. During her campaign to represent Illinois' 16th Congressional District in the U.S. House of Representatives, Martin presented a platform that pleased conservatives by backing business deregulation, a smaller central government, and lower taxes. At the same time she appealed to liberals by supporting the Equal Rights Amendment and the pro-choice position on abortion.

Congressional Career Included "Firsts"

Lynn Martin was the first freshman in Congress to be assigned to the powerful House Budget Committee. In 1982, she became the first woman to be elected to a congressional leadership post—vice chair of the House Republican Conference. Although Martin supported and helped shape the Reagan administration's budget policy, which included a military buildup, she maintained her commitment to what she called "underfunded domestic needs programs." She sided with the administration on a number

of defense issues, voting for the MX missile and the space-based missile defense system known as "Star Wars," but also supported a nuclear freeze and federal funding of abortions for poor women. Over President Ronald Reagan's veto, she voted to impose economic sanctions against South Africa in retaliation for that government's policies of apartheid. Her congressional tenure would run from 1981 to 1991.

Rose to National Prominence

Martin was chosen to stand in for Geraldine Ferraro during mock debates with Vice President George Bush prior to the 1984 election. Martin's sharp wit and quick thinking so impressed the vice president that he selected her to deliver the vice presidential nominating speech at the Republican convention in Dallas. As the national co-chairperson of Bush's 1988 presidential campaign (the only woman so honored), Martin again gained national exposure when she gave one of the speeches nominating Bush for president.

In 1987 she married Judge Harry Leinenweber of the United States Court of the Northern District of Illinois—making her the mother of two and stepmother of five. In 1990 she lost her bid for the U.S. Senate seat held by Democrat Paul Simon. But President Bush appointed her to succeed Elizabeth H. Dole as secretary of labor, and she was sworn in February 22, 1991. As head of the labor department, Martin pushed for greater representation of women and minorities in America's executive suites, attacked the "glass ceiling" as a discriminatory practice that prevents women from rising to positions of corporate power, and fought against corporate sexual harassment and drug use. She led by example, putting many of her ideas into practice at the department.

Martin criticized the North American Free Trade Agreement (NAFTA, a pact intended to loosen restrictions on trade between the U.S., Canada and Mexico), warning that it would cost 150,000 jobs, and questioned the effectiveness of state Occupational Health and Safety Administration (OSHA) programs. On Nov. 12, 1991, Martin appeared (with future Secretary of Labor Robert Reich) in the nationally broadcast teleconference *Educating to Compete,* a discussion of the impact of the quality of schools on the nation's ability to compete on the world stage.

Under Martin's leadership, the labor department also researched legislation that would allow workers to transfer pensions when they switch jobs.

Continued Political Life

Following Bush's 1992 defeat by Bill Clinton, Martin continued to be outspoken upon her return to private life—lecturing and writing extensively on contemporary politics and labor policy. In a 1993 *New York Times* article, she proposed a welfare system that places pregnant girls under the age of 16 into group homes. That year, she became a professor in the J.J. Kellogg Graduate School of Management at Northwestern University's business school, teaching public policy. She has also been a fellow at Harvard University's Kennedy School of Government and consulted for the international accounting firm Deloitte & Touche. She serves on the boards of several large corporations, including Ameritech. In 1993 she was named to the short list of candidates for commissioner of Major League Baseball. In 1996, Mitsubishi Motors asked her to lead a panel investigating allegations of sexual harassment within the company.

Opening the way, observers believed, for a possible Republican Party presidential run in 1996, Martin established her own political action committee as a source of funding and expressed her desire to contribute to the debate on the Republican Party's future. ABC-TV news anchor Ted Koppel called Martin "one of the most skilled politicians in the Republican party."

Further Reading

Martin's interest in more business opportunities for women was reflected in "Can the Feds Bust Through the 'Glass Ceiling'?" *Business Week* (April 29, 1991).

Martin explained the U.S. Department of Labor's anti-sexual harassment policies in "A Model Program Against Sexual Harassment at the Department of Labor," *Employment Relations Today* (Winter 1991).

Martin elaborated on her small business anti-drug stance in "Drug-Free Policy: Key to Success for Small Businesses," *HR Focus* (Sept. 1992).

Martin discussed the social aspects of the legislative process, and the role women play, in "The Senate is a Bastion of Stubborn Men," *Los Angeles Daily Journal* (Feb. 8, 1993).

Details of Martin's proposal for placing pregnant girls age 16 and under into group homes can be found in "For Children Who Have Children," *New York Times* (Sept. 8, 1983).

For a broad array of her positions on issues see Lynn Martin, "We Who Have Dared to Dream," a speech delivered at the Republican National Convention, Houston, Texas, Aug. 19, 1992, in *Vital Speeches* (Sept. 15, 1992). See also Judy Mann, "Martin in '96?" *Washington Post* (July 14, 1993); and "Out in Right Field," *Washington Post* (Oct. 29, 1993). □

Mary Martin

Mary Martin (1913-1990) was a popular stage actress, singer, dancer, television and movie star.

Mary Martin was born in Weatherford, Texas, on December 1, 1913. As a child she was encouraged by her parents, Juanita and Judge Preston Martin, to study violin and voice. Her love of the theater was obvious at an early age. She sang in almost every church choir in town, wrote and performed plays for family and friends, and was an avid movie-goer.

At the age of 15 Martin left school to marry Benjamin Hagman. After the birth of her son, Larry, she opened the Mary Hagman School of Dance in Weatherford. During a trip to Hollywood to further her dancing studies, Martin's childhood desire to perform was rekindled. Subsequently she moved to Hollywood, divorced her husband, and spent two years auditioning for the movies.

Nightclub Performance Launched Broadway Career

It was not in the movies, but rather at the Trocadero nightclub, where Martin's career was finally launched. She sang a swing version of "Il Bacio," and the audience, including Broadway producer Lawrence Schwab, went wild. If "Il Bacio" took Martin to Broadway (by way of Schwab), it was "My Heart Belongs to Daddy" which kept her there. In 1938 she landed the part of Dolly in *Leave It to Me* at the Imperial Theatre. Her rendition of "Daddy" was a spectacular hit and led to star billing and a contract with Paramount Pictures.

Although Martin's first love was the stage, she accepted the Hollywood contract to star in a series of films including *The Great Victor Herbert, Rhythm on the River, Love Thy Neighbor, Kiss the Boys Goodbye, New York Town, The Birth of Blues, Star Spangled Rhythm,* and *Happy Go Lucky.*

It was during this period that Mary Martin met and married the love of her life, producer Richard Halliday. Mary's yearning to work on the stage led them to return to New York, where Halliday assumed his new vocation as her manager. From 1943 through the remainder of her career Martin worked almost exclusively on the stage, for she loved most to work directly with people rather than with a camera. It was her ability to share her exuberance with the people who watched her that made her so loved by musical comedy audiences.

Found Niche on Stage

The roles that she played on film and stage were the standard female images of the time—the sophisticated or exotic woman or the dumb blond. Before she found her true niche she played in *Dancing on the Streets* (1943), Venus in *One Touch of Venus* (1945), and Tchao-Ou-Niag in *Lute Song* (1945-1946). She also made her London debut as Elena Salvador in Noel Coward's *Pacific 1860.*

Although she had been successful in these parts, her career zoomed when she was finally able to express her true self—a warm, feisty, exciting, down-home girl—on stage. She played Annie Oakley in the touring production of *Annie Get Your Gun* (1947-1948) and catapulted to stardom. Martin's next big success, and perhaps the role for which she is most well known, was as Ensign Nellie Forbush in Richard Rodgers and Oscar Hammerstein's *South Pacific.* She created this role and starred in it at the Majestic Theatre from 1949 to 1951 and later performed the same role at Drury Lane in London.

Mary Martin's own favorite part was Peter in *Peter Pan,* with music by Comden and Green. The production, staged by Jerome Robbins, originated at the San Francisco Civic Light Opera (1954), later went to Broadway (1954-1955), and eventually toured the entire country. Martin's exuberant spirit went into this production—she recalled her youthful dreams and her desire to fly. As a child she had, in fact, even broken her collarbone while attempting to fly off the roof of her garage. The accident didn't deter Mary Martin, and as Peter she finally got her chance to fly, albeit on wires, to the delight of adults and children everywhere. Martin's talents were recorded for future generations to enjoy in the 1955 and 1956 television versions of *Peter Pan.*

Another role for which Mary Martin will be remembered is that of Maria in *The Sound of Music,* another successful collaboration between writers Hammerstein and Rodgers and the actress. Martin found the spirit of the determined, energetic, dedicated singer and former nun Maria through her work with the real Maria, Baroness Von Trapp, and her longtime friend Sister Gregory. She received the Theatre Wing's coveted Tony Award and the New York Drama Critics Award for this performance in 1959.

Two other roles which Martin played to great acclaim were Dolly Levi in *Hello Dolly,* which toured to Vietnam, Tokyo, and London (1965), and Agnes in *I Do! I Do!* with co-star Robert Preston. The latter musical was based on a play, *The Fourposter,* about the lives of two people from their wedding day until 50 years later. Martin felt that the subject matter of this play—marriage—would represent the essence of her life. In fact, the production (1966-1969) was the last musical that Martin appeared in before her semi-retirement.

Retired to Brazil

In 1969 the Hallidays moved to Anapolis, Brazil, and bought a farm. For several years Martin operated a boutique featuring her fashion designs and her needlepoint, about which she and her husband published a book in 1969. While in Brazil she was also the subject of the television show *This Is Your Life.* After her husband's death, Martin returned to the United States where she was co-host of the PBS television show *Over Easy,* which focused on issues of the elderly. Martin enjoyed the successes of her children—Larry Hagman and Heller Halligan DeMeritt—and her six grandchildren.

In 1987 Martin toured with Carol Channing in a non-musical production called *Legends!* about a pair of bitchy Hollywood battle-axes. To Martin, the world was her theater. Contemplating her own end, she said in, *People* "It's been a fabulous life and a wonderful career. I'll keep on living until it's time. Then I'll just go on to another stage."

Martin died on November 3, 1990, at the age of 76. Her long-time friend, Carol Channing, had been at her bedside at Martin's Rancho Mirage, California, home less than an hour before she died of liver cancer. "She was heaven," said Channing.

Further Reading

Martin is listed in *Who's Who in the Theatre,* edited by Freda Gaye (14th ed., 1967); Her autobiography, *My Heart Belongs* (1984), includes information on her entire theatrical career as well as her personal life; For background information on musical comedy and Martin's role in its development, see Cecil Smith and Glenn Litton, *Musical Comedy in America* (1981). Also see *People,* November 19, 1990. □

William McChesney Martin Jr.

American business executive and federal government official William McChesney Martin, Jr. (born 1906) directed major financial institutions and had a prominent role in shaping national economic policy in the 1950s and 1960s.

William McChesney Martin Jr., the elder of two sons of Rebecca Woods Martin and William McChesney Martin, was born December 17, 1906, in St. Louis, Missouri. His father, a lawyer and banker, was chief executive officer of the St. Louis Federal Reserve Bank, one of 12 regional banks in the Federal Reserve System, from 1914 to 1941.

Bill Martin was influenced by his father and by his family's strict Presbyterian tenets. Discipline, study, and athletics were stressed. He was interested in economics and finance, but his father advised him to study liberal arts in college. After graduating from private and public schools in St. Louis, he attended Yale University and received a B.A. in English in 1928.

Martin first worked in the bank examination department of the St. Louis Federal Reserve Bank. In 1929 he joined A. G. Edwards & Sons, a brokerage and investment banking firm. In 1931 he became head of their statistical department while a part-time student at Benton College of

Law. That year he became a partner and moved to New York City to operate the firm's membership on the floor of the New York Stock Exchange.

The Great Depression, however, had severely damaged the stock exchange's reputation. The Securities and Exchange Commission (SEC), established by Congress in 1934, was investigating its activities when Martin was elected by fellow brokers to the stock exchange's governing board in 1935. He served on several committees and worked for internal reforms.

Martin also studied economics at Columbia University and belonged to an association that met at the New School for Social Research. From 1932 to 1934 he was treasurer of The Economic Forum and associate editor of its quarterly publication of the same name.

The aims of this "civic organization" give insight to Martin's career. Members believed in "promoting sound improvements in our economic life," and agreed "the times demand the realization of economic theory in action, and the burden of this application rests on practical economists, the Men of the Marketplace."

In December 1937 Martin became secretary of the "Conway Committee," created by the stock exchange's governing board to advise on reorganization. Its report, written by Martin and issued in January 1938, contained recommendations designed to satisfy SEC Chairman William O. Douglas and to reassure the public. After the Whitney scandal surfaced in March 1938, the reform group assumed power and Martin was elected chairman of the new board of

governors. In May he was elected president pro tem, and on July 1, 1938, he became the first salaried president of the New York Stock Exchange.

Only 31, Martin was called the "Boy Wonder of Wall Street." His reputation as a teetotaler, non-smoker, nongambler, and studious bachelor helped the stock exchange regain its prestige. Martin worked to end its private club atmosphere and to improve efficiency. He saw the stock exchange as a "national institution that exists to serve the needs of the American public."

He resigned in April 1941 after being drafted as a private into the U.S. Army. Martin served on the Munitions Assignments Board and the President's Soviet Protocol Committee. In October 1945 he was discharged as a full colonel and received the Legion of Merit.

President Truman appointed him chairman of the board of directors of the Export-Import Bank in November 1945, and from February 1946 to February 1949 Martin was its president and chairman. He next became assistant secretary of the treasury in charge of international finance, and in December 1949 he was also named United States executive director of the World Bank.

In early 1951 he mediated a serious policy dispute between the Federal Reserve System and the Treasury over "pegging" or supporting of prices of government securities sold by the Treasury. The "accord" of March 1951 freed the Federal Reserve from this policy and clearly established the agency as coequal with the Treasury in the area of their overlapping responsibilities. Martin's successful role provided his next opportunity.

In mid-March Truman appointed, and the U.S. Senate approved, Martin to complete the term of resigning Federal Reserve Board Chairman Thomas B. McCabe. He also became chairman, a four-year position. On April 2, 1951, Martin entered this position, which made him what many have called "the second most powerful man in America." Decisions by the seven-member board of governors and 12-member Federal Open Market Committee, both headed by the chairman, have a powerful impact on the economy and can cause heated controversy.

The Federal Reserve System, the central bank, controls the nation's supply of money and credit. The independent agency, created by Congress in December 1913, is responsible to but not funded by Congress. The Federal Reserve's objective, Martin stated in 1955, is "to contribute to sustainable economic growth and to maintenance of a stable value for the dollar."

Speeches delivered over almost 19 years and an unprecedented five presidential administrations reveal Martin's basic principles. In 1951 he said, "Our economic strength is founded on preserving the integrity of the dollar, symbolizing as it does the good faith and credit of our country." In 1968 he warned against the "wage-cost-price push" and about avoiding responsibilities to tax ourselves and cut expenditures. He said he would fight to keep the dollar from being devalued.

Martin, a Democrat, was not considered a doctrinaire economist, however. Overall, he pursued flexible, nonpartisan policies and believed in a degree of accommodation while maintaining the Federal Reserve's independent status within government. His cooperation at congressional hearings, skill in conciliation and negotiation, thorough knowledge of central banking, and total integrity won him respect, even from such critics as Representative Wright Patman (Democrat) of Texas, a constant foe of "tight money."

Martin earned the confidence of presidents and financiers. Eisenhower, with Senate approval, renamed him chairman in 1955 and to a full four year term in 1956. He was again named chairman in 1959, 1963, and 1967. In December 1965, concerned over inflation from the booming economy and domestic and Vietnam War expenditures, Martin increased the discount (interest) rate and tightened the money supply against President Johnson's wishes. Despite their differences, Johnson reappointed him chairman because Martin was a symbol of sound public finance. His leadership reassured the financial community here and abroad.

Martin liked to use analogies to explain complex monetary policy. He often said, "Our purpose is to lean against the winds of deflation or inflation, whichever way they are blowing, but we do not make those winds," and "We are the people who take away the punch bowl just when the party is getting good."

When his term ended in January 1970, Martin left government service but continued working for improvements in economic life and reentered private business. "The Martin Report," a study commissioned by the New York Stock Exchange and issued in August 1971, recommended internal reforms and modernization.

On April 3, 1942, Martin married Cynthia Davis, the daughter of General Dwight F. Davis, who donated the Davis Cup in tennis. They had three children. Martin, who served on several corporate boards, received 23 honorary Doctor of Laws degrees and the new Federal Reserve Board building in Washington, D.C. is named for him.

Further Reading

Numerous primary and secondary sources document Martin's career, but his biography has yet to be written. He has been in *Who's Who in America* since 1938-1939; Noteworthy articles include Richard A. Smith, "Bill Martin: A Talent for Timing," *Fortune* (October 1955); "The Banker's Banker," *TIME* (September 10, 1956); and "Reserve Board Raises Bank Rate," *New York Times* (December 6, 1965); "Replacing a Monetary Legend," *The Economist* (October 25, 1969) gives an international viewpoint; Significant references to Martin are in Robert Sobel, *N.Y.S.E. A History of The New York Stock Exchange 1935-1975* (1975); Herbert Stein, *The Fiscal Revolution in America* (1969); Martin Mayer, *The Bankers* (1974); Milton Friedman and Anna J. Schwartz, *A Monetary History of the United States 1867-1960* (1963); and James L. Knipe, *The Federal Reserve and the American Dollar. Problems and Policies 1946-1964* (1965). □

Roger Martin du Gard

The French author Roger Martin du Gard (1881-1958) portrayed the conflicts in man's consciousness between religion and science against the backdrop of the social upheaval in France during the early 20th century.

Roger Martin du Gard was born at Neuilly-sur-Seine on March 23, 1881, the son of a lawyer. In 1892 he began studying at the Catholic École Fénelon and met a leader of the Catholic modernist movement, the Abbé Marcel Hébert; their friendship lasted until the priest's death in 1916. After studying literature at the Sorbonne, Martin du Gard enrolled in the École des Chartes to prepare himself as an archivist and paleographer. In 1905 he successfully defended his thesis *Les Ruines de l'Abbaye de Jumièges* and was awarded the *diplôme d'archivistepaléographe*.

In 1906 Martin du Gard married Hélène Foucault. During their honeymoon in North Africa he drew up a plan of his first novel, *Une Vie de Saint*. Inspired by the Abbé Hébert, the novel was to be a detailed biography of a country priest. Realizing that his ambitions outdistanced his capacities, he abandoned his work in 1907. But his experience provided him with familiar material for his next venture. He decided, he says in his memoirs, to tell the life of a young and presumptuous writer, André Mazerelles, lacking talent but not illusions concerning his ability. In *Devenir!* (1908) he relied upon the traditional third-person narrative, which allowed ironic observation on character and situation.

Martin du Gard immediately began work on a long novel (*Marise*) based on the life of a woman and developing the themes of solitude and death. Again he realized that his experience was too limited; he abandoned *Marise,* publishing only a fragment as a short story, *L'Une de nous* (1910). That same year he began work on "a long masculine monograph, the destiny of a man and the history of a conscience." This novel, *Jean Barois* (1913), traces the evolution of a scientist and journalist from the religion of his youth to his espousal of science as the only source of truth and certainty and, finally, to his return in weakness and old age to Catholicism. The novel strives to be a symbolic concentration not only of a man's life but also of a spiritual crisis in pre-World War I France.

After World War I Martin du Gard began work on his long saga novel, *Les Thibault*. Six volumes were published: *Le Cahier gris* and *Le Pénitencier* (1922), *La Belle saison* (1923), *La Consultation* (1928), *La Sorellina* (1928), and *La Mort du Père* (1929); they represented only a third of the projected work. Realizing that his original plan for *Les Thibault* was much too cumbersome, he decided to abandon it and graft a new conclusion onto the old stock. *L'Été 1914,* in three volumes, appeared in 1936, and *Épilogue* in 1940.

In *Les Thibault,* Jacques Thibault, a revolutionary, and his brother Antoine, a doctor and man of science, attempt to fashion a meaningful life in a world without God. Into this double pattern, Martin du Gard introduces a third alternative, that of art and passion, in the person of the Thibault's childhood friend Daniel de Fontanin. Neither alternative can permanently fill the void left by God's absence, but only Antoine's adaptability and moderation enable him emotionally to survive the disaster of World War I. Although he, too, is a victim of the war, his diary, kept as he approaches death, is intended as a model of will and reason for the edification of his nephew Jean-Paul.

In 1937 Martin du Gard won the Nobel Prize for literature. After 1940 he published little. He died on Aug 22, 1958, at Bellême.

Further Reading

There are several useful biographies and critical studies of Martin du Gard: Robert Gibson, *Roger Martin du Gard* (1961); Denis Boak, *Roger Martin du Gard* (1963); and David L. Schalk, *Roger Martin du Gard: the Novelist and History* (1967). Recommended for general historical background are Guy Chapman, *The Dreyfus Case: A Reassessment* (1955); Alfred Cobban, *A History of Modern France* (2 vols., 1957-1961; rev. ed., 3 vols., 1962-1965); and Barbara W. Tuchman, *The Proud Tower: A Portrait of the World before the War, 1890-1914* (1966). □

Harriet Martineau

Harriet Martineau (1802-1876), an English writer and an adherent of positivist philosophy, was one of the most widely admired writers of her day.

Harriet Martineau was born in Norwich on June 12, 1802. Her life is the story of adversity overcome. Armed with an excellent childhood education, she had to overcome deafness, the loss of her senses of smell and taste, extensive nervous disorder, and finally, heart disease. Her father died when she was in her early 20s, leaving the family destitute, and Martineau had to work for pennies by hack writing and doing needlework. With the publication in 1832-1834 of a series of short stories interpreting political economy for the layman, she gained a wide reading public. Her work in magazines and pamphlets, as well as her books, began to bring very adequate, if not rich, returns, and she quickly became one of the literary lions of London. England in the 1830s was a world in which politicians courted popular writers for political support, and Harriet Martineau became one of the most courted.

Attempting to improve her health, Martineau spent 1834 to 1836 in the United States. During this time she adopted the cause of abolitionism, the first of several relatively radical political causes which she would champion. Her impressions of America were recorded in *Society in America* (1837) and *A Retrospect of Western Travel* (1838).

Investing her time heavily in journalism, Martineau nevertheless brought out a new volume almost every year, speaking for a variety of forms of "philosophical radi-

calism." Though she began as a deeply religious person, she finally became a spokesman for the antitheological views of the philosopher Auguste Comte, popularizing him in a two-volume work (1853).

After her heart disease was diagnosed as fatal, Martineau began her autobiography in 1855 (it was published posthumously in 1877). But she lived another 21 years, produced at least eight more volumes of serious work, and became England's leading woman of letters, holding a kind of court at her tiny estate in Westmoreland, where she died on June 27, 1876. Historically she is remembered as a tough-minded writer who fought great odds to achieve a distinguished literary career.

Further Reading

Works on Martineau which subsume most earlier efforts are Vera Wheatley, *The Life and Work of Harriet Martineau* (1957), and Robert Kiefer Webb, *Harriet Martineau: A Radical Victorian* (1960). Also interesting are Theodora Bosanquat, *Harriet Martineau: An Essay in Comprehension* (1927), and John Cranstoun Nevill, *Harriet Martineau* (1943). Her life as a cultural commentator is placed in the context of the time by Una Pope-Hennessy, *Three English Women in America* (1929). See also Maria Weston Chapman, ed., *Harriet Martineau's Autobiography* (2 vols., 1877).

Additional Sources

Bosanquet, Theodora, *Harriet Martineau; an essay in comprehensio,* Folcroft, Pa. Folcroft Library Editions, 1974; Norwood, Pa.: Norwood Editions, 1976; Philadelphia: R. West, 1977; St. Clair Shores, Mich., Scholarly Press, 1971.

David, Deirdre, *Intellectual women and Victorian patriarchy: Harriet Martineau, Elizabeth Barrett Browning, George Eliot,* Ithaca, N.Y.: Cornell University Press, 1987.

Hoecker-Drysdale, Susan, *Harriet Martineau, first woman sociologist,* Oxford England; New York: Berg; New York: Distributed exclusively in the U.S. and Canada by St. Martin's Press, 1992.

Martineau, Harriet, *Harriet Martineau's Autobiography,* London: Virago, 1983.

Nevill, John Cranstoun, *Harriet Martinea,* Folcroft, Pa. Folcroft Library Editions, 1973 i.e. 1974; Norwood, Pa.: Norwood Editions, 1976; Philadelphia: R. West, 1978.

Pichanick, Valerie Kossew, *Harriet Martineau, the woman and her work, 1802-76,* Ann Arbor: University of Michigan Press, 1980.

Webb, R. K. (Robert Kiefer), *Harriet Martineau: a radical Victorian,* New York: Octagon Books, 1983, 1960. ☐

Maximiliano Hernández Martínez

General Maximiliano Hernández Martínez (1882-1966) served as president of El Salvador from 1931 to 1944. His regime was a strict dictatorship which suppressed a Communist-led uprising during its initial days in office. He promoted economic growth based on the expansion of the large coffee estates, thereby benefiting the landowners and initiating links between the military and the oligarchy.

Maximiliano Hernández Martínez, who was born October 29, 1882, entered El Salvador's army at an early age. He gained combat experience in the 1906 war with Guatemala, establishing a solid record and rising to brigadier general by 1919. During much of his career he served as a professor at the Salvadoran Military Academy.

Martínez rose to power in 1931 during a tumultuous year of political maneuvering. The only military officer considered a leading candidate for the presidency in the election of 1931, Martínez emerged as the vice president on a ticket headed by Arturo Araujo, a wealthy landowner with aspirations for reform. However, after winning the election Araujo proved to be a weak ruler, unable to deal with the severe problems resulting from the global depression, especially the depressed price of coffee, the nation's principal export. In December 1931 a group of young army officers ousted Araujo in a military coup. Martínez was arrested, though the young officers later installed him as president since under the constitution he was next in line as vice president. The United States vigorously opposed the coup, invoking the 1923 Washington Treaty, by which the governments of Central America had pledged not to grant diplomatic recognition to any regime installed by an armed revolt. While the United States had not signed the treaty, it had sponsored the idea. However, since this revolt occurred at a moment when the United States had pledged not to

intervene militarily in Latin America, the Salvadoran military felt that it could resist pressure from Washington.

In the midst of the maneuvering the situation was changed by the outbreak of an agrarian revolt in which discontented peasants sought to seize land. Fighting erupted throughout the interior of the nation, and several landowners were killed by peasant mobs. While the revolt reflected the conditions of the peasants, it was led by avowed Communists, including Agustín Farabundo Martí. The uprising alarmed the landowners and forced them to seek military support. In the process they turned to General Martínez, who was largely Native American Mestizo of poor origin with little in common with the elite. Martínez perceived his opportunity and ruthlessly put down the revolt. The death toll in the uprising and the subsequent repression was very high.

Martínez was able to consolidate his position with his new found support from the oligarchy and carefully orchestrated his own election. In later years Martínez twice extended his term of office through constitutional conventions.

A recluse who seldom appeared in public, Martínez was a vegetarian, a nondrinker, and a theosophist who believed in reincarnation and engaged in occult practices. The general held seances at his home and was fond of recommending colored water to cure all ills. Because of his beliefs, he was quoted as stating that "It is a greater crime to kill an ant than a man, for when a man dies he becomes reincarnated, while an ant dies forever."

El Salvador was essentially bankrupt during the 1930s, and as this left little money for government projects, Martínez's efforts were based on minimal expenditures and were more modest than those of neighboring countries. Martínez refused to contract new loans abroad, instead insisting that his nation live on its resources. In 1937 he had a plaque installed in the National Congress Building over his signature saying: "I propose before the Nation that it never consent to the incurrance of new debts." The Martínez government did construct a modest network of dirt roads, several governmental buildings, and a few schools and hospitals. Martínez also launched a land distribution effort by which the government divided the lands it owned into small parcels to be deeded to landless peasants. His regime purchased several estates for division, though, since the government had little money, the program proceeded slowly and its effect was limited.

The general maintained tight personal control of the nation through an extensive system of repression and spies. His regime became more oppressive in its later years, especially after 1938. Police methods were harsh. Among his "reforms" were laws reinstituting the death penalty for such crimes as rebellion. A revolt on May 8, 1944, led to his resignation. After that he lived in obscurity in exile in Honduras for many years and died there in 1966.

The Martínez regime constituted an important watershed in the politics of El Salvador, marking the initial control of the nation by the military and the origin of the alliance between the military and the landowners which dominated politics in that nation for many decades. The unsuccessful peasant uprising that enabled him to consolidate power also polarized his nation between upper and lower classes. These legacies were to continue to affect the politics of El Salvador for decades after Martínez abandoned power.

Further Reading

For details of the early days of the Martínez regime see Thomas P. Anderson, *Matanza: El Salvador's Communist Revolt of 1932* (1971) and Kenneth J. Grieb, "The United States and the Rise of General Maximiliano Hernández Martínez," in the *Journal of Latin American Studies* (London, November 1971). There are no detailed histories covering the entire regime. □

Simone Martini

The Italian painter Simone Martini (active 1315-1344) created a perfect synthesis of the ideals of the Gothic age: courtly elegance, chivalric pageantry, civic pride, poetic fantasy, and vivid description.

Giotto in Florence and Ambrogio and Pietro Lorenzetti and Simone Martini in Siena were the principal figures in the transformation of Italian painting from a traditional Byzantine mode into a vehicle for the depiction of the varieties of visual and psychological experience. Their impact on Italian art is thus analogous with the roles of Dante and Petrarch in the history of Italian language and literature.

The earliest evidence of Simone's activity is the *Maestà* fresco in the Palazzo Pubblico (Town Hall) in Siena, signed and dated 1315 (restored and perhaps revised by Simone's himself in 1321). The relationship between Simone's fresco and Duccio di Buoninsegna's *Maestà* altarpiece of 1311 for the Cathedral of Siena, in the theme of the Madonna in Majesty and in the figure types, suggests that Simone may have received his training in the shop of that earlier Sienese master. If Giorgio Vasari's statement that Simone died at the age of 60 is correct, then the painter was born about 1284 and the *Maestà* is a mature work by a man of 30, for whom there is no trace of formative years.

The divergence from Duccio's primarily Italo-Byzantine form and expression indicates that Simone's art was rooted in the French Gothic tradition, although there is still no answer to the question of whether he actually worked in France in his earlier years. In the courtly treatment of the subject, the emphasis on richly decorative detail, and the naturalness of space and scale, Simone's fresco announces a new Sienese style. The Virgin's specific role as protector of Siena is conveyed by the location of the fresco in the Council Room of the Town Hall, by a moralizing inscription on justice and oppression, and by the presence of the patron saints of the town.

About 1317 King Robert of Anjou called Simone to Naples and knighted the painter during his stay. The French accent in Simone's art was welcome at the Angevin court. *St. Louis of Toulouse Crowning Robert of Anjou* (Naples)

depicts the saint, canonized in 1317, receiving the heavenly crown and bestowing on his brother the secular crown of the Angevins, thereby renouncing his right to the throne. The altarpiece thus served as both votive icon and testimony to the right of kingship. Simone reveals in this work his consummate skill in the use of the tempera medium and ornamented gold leaf. A series of small scenes (predella) beneath the main panel, depicting episodes from the life of St. Louis, heralds the painter's subsequent works in the varieties of spatial construction and the dramatic force of figure groupings, facial expressions, and gestures. The Renaissance preoccupation of a century later with methods of space depiction had its origins in such early Sienese works.

Following the sojourn in Naples, Simone worked in Pisa (*Madonna and Saints,* 1319) and Orvieto (*Madonna and Saints,* 1320). There are no documents or works to affirm Vasari's mention of Simone's activity in Florence, nor is there certainty as to the period of his stay in Assisi, where he frescoed the Chapel of St. Martin in the Lower Church of S. Francesco. These frescoes, along with the fresco *Condottiere Guidoriccio da Fogliano* (1328) in the Town Hall in Siena, demonstrate Simone's superb talent as a mural decorator and as a recorder of the world of Gothic chivalry and elegance.

In the St. Martin frescoes the entire range of the artist's vision and method unfolds: the sophisticated rendering of interior space and details of architectural setting; a rich interplay of linear rhythms, subtly variegated and luminous colors, and elaborately ornamented costumes and trappings; the close observation of facial expression and a clear division of the personages of a narrative into a social hierarchy through the differentiation of types. The fresco of *Guidoriccio* faces Simone's earlier *Maestà* so that in the same official room the religious and secular protectors of the city are confronted. The *condottiere* had liberated the Tuscan fortress-towns of Montemassi and Sassoforte in 1328. He rides his handsomely bedecked horse proudly in the foreground, both master and steed displaying the armorial device of diamond and vine. At the crest of the barren landscape the besieged towns rise in stark silhouette against the deep-blue background, while the general's encampment holds the far-right hill and valley. This fresco stands as the first in a series of equestrian portraits of heroes in Italian medieval and Renaissance art.

In contrast to the concern for time and place in the frescoes, the *Annunciation* altarpiece, painted in 1333 for the Cathedral of Siena (now in Florence), emits an atmosphere of sublime unreality. The inscription on the panel records that Lippo Memmi, whose sister Simone had married in 1324, collaborated on the altarpiece. In its elegance of line and rhythm, the exquisitely rendered details of costume, setting, and flower symbols, and the fragile sentiment of the participants in the sacred event, the *Annunciation* is a supreme masterpiece in the history of lyrical art.

Simone spent his last years at the papal court in Avignon, where he arrived in 1340 accompanied by his brother and collaborator, Donato. They came to Avignon as artists and as official representatives of the Church in Siena. Only one signed and dated work is known from this period in France, the *Holy Family* (1342; Liverpool). Frescoes in the Cathedral are in a ruined state. A group of four small panels with scenes of the Passion and an *Annunciation* diptych (now in various museums) project a fervent emotionalism and dramatic tension matched only by the late sculpture of Giovanni Pisano. At Avignon, Simone and the poet-humanist Petrarch formed a close friendship. The painter executed a frontispiece for Petrarch's copy of *Commentaries on Virgil* (now in Milan), and the poet records in one of his sonnets that Simone painted a portrait, now lost, of his beloved Laura.

Subsequent generations of lesser Sienese painters of the 14th century relied heavily on Simone's model, but a more crucial inheritance is found in that late Gothic mode of European art about 1400—the International Style. It was Simone Martini who brought Sienese painting into the mainstream of European art.

Further Reading

Giovanni Paccagnini, *Simone Martini* (1955; trans. 1957), is the most complete and dependable monograph on Martini's work. John White, *Art and Architecture in Italy, 1250-1400* (1966), is a masterful survey of late medieval Italian art with penetrating critical essays on individual artists. Evelyn Sandberg Vavalà's two works, *Uffizi Studies* (1948) and *Sienese Studies* (1953), provide a history of Florentine and Sienese painting based on a close formal analysis of paintings in the principal galleries of the two cities. An old but still useful study is Ferdinand Schevill, *Siena: The History of a Mediaeval Commune* (1909). □

Bohuslav Martinu

The Czech composer Bohuslav Martinu (1890-1959) was the most important composer of his generation in the former Czechoslovakia.

Bohuslav Martinu was the son of a small-town shoemaker who was also the custodian of a church tower used as a fire-lookout station. Bohuslav was born in the tower and spent his childhood there. The composer suggested that this physical detachment from the usual childhood experiences helped to form his introspective and reflective nature. Violin lessons from a village teacher revealed his strong musical aptitude, and when he was 16 he went to Prague to attend the conservatory. He did not respond well to the rigid training and was soon expelled.

In spite of his failure at the conservatory, Martinu became a violinist in the Czech Philharmonic Orchestra, a post he held from 1913 to 1923, except for the war years (1914-1918), when he returned to his native village. His early works include the *Czech Rhapsody* (1920) and the ballet *Istar* (1922). Realizing that he needed more formal training in composition, he returned to the conservatory to study with Josef Suk.

With the aid of a government grant Martinu went to Paris in 1923, where he lived for the next 17 years. He became a pupil of Albert Roussel, whose economical but vigorous scores he admired. Martinu lived in the simplest manner, making his living by teaching a few private pupils and from the commissions he received from time to time. Important compositions of this era are *Half-time* (1925), inspired by a soccer game, and *La Bagarre* (1926; Tumult), dedicated to Charles Lindbergh, who had just made his flight to Paris. Serge Koussevitsky, the conductor of the Boston Symphony Orchestra, introduced Martinu's music to the United States. In 1932 his String Sextet won the Coolidge Prize for chamber music.

During the Paris years Martinu did not lose contact with Czechoslovakia. He wrote a folk ballet called *Spalicek* (1931), a kind of variety show of sketches from Czech life; *The Miracle of Our Lady* (1933), a medievalstyle miracle play; and the opera *Juliette* (1938). The major work of this period is his Double Concerto (1938), a powerful work expressing his feelings just before World War II and the imminent downfall of his country.

With the outbreak of war Martinu went to the United States, where he remained until 1953. He taught at the Berkshire Summer School and at Princeton University. Works of the American period include a Symphony (1942), a Violin Concerto (1943), and a Concerto for Two Pianos and Orchestra (1943). An accidental fall in 1946 resulted in a period of amnesia and partial deafness.

Martinu lived in Rome from 1953 to 1955, where he wrote *Fresques de Piero della Francesca* for orchestra, the opera *Mirandolina,* and his Sixth Symphony. He completed his twelfth and last opera, based on Nikos Kazantzakis's *Greek Passion Play,* shortly before his death in Switzerland.

Martinu's music was in no sense reactionary, but at the same time it was never blatantly "modern" or "experimental." It is characterized by the freedom of its melodies, perhaps influenced by Czech inflections, the vigor of its rhythms, and the transparency of its textures. He favored concerto grosso-like structures, contrapuntal and continuous, over sonata forms, and he avoided sentimentality and dramatic effects.

Further Reading

Miloš Šafránek, *Bohuslav Martinu: The Man and His Music* (1944; rev. ed. 1946), was written by a friend of the composer and contains a thorough discussion of Martinu's personality and style. More recent studies of Martinu are in Arthur Cohn, *Twentieth-century Music in Western Europe: The Compositions and the Recordings* (1965), and David Ewen, *The World of Twentieth-century Music* (1968).

Additional Sources

Martinu, Charlotta, *My life with Bohuslav Martinu,* Prague: Orbis Press Agency, 1978. □

Martin E. Marty

Martin E. Marty (born 1928), a Lutheran pastor, historian of American religion, and commentator on contemporary religious life, wrote prolifically on American religion and culture. His work was noted for blending solid scholarship and popular, readable style.

Martin E. Marty was born on February 5, 1928, at West Point, Nebraska, into a family descended from Swiss immigrants. After graduating from Concordia High School in Milwaukee he earned undergraduate and graduate degrees from Concordia Seminary in St. Louis, Luther School of Theology in Chicago, and the University of Chicago, receiving a Ph.D. from the latter institution in 1956.

Contributed to Religious Field in Diverse Ways

His pastoral career began with ordination to the Lutheran Church-Missouri Synod ministry in 1952. In 1957 he took up duties as founding pastor of the Church of the Holy Spirit in Elk Grove Village, Illinois, a position he held for six years. His founding of that church was innovative at the time; in those days few churches had moved out of downtown locations to serve the booming suburbs. During those years he also was a contributor to the Protestant weekly magazine *The Christian Century,* becoming associate editor in 1958. He resigned his pastorate in 1963 to join the faculty of the University of Chicago Divinity School, where he taught American religious history.

Explored Ecumenical Movement

Marty's wide-ranging interests within the field of American religion were exemplified by the subject matter of his books, which emerged at a rate of more than one per year after 1959. He probed specific religious beliefs and practices, such as baptism; he examined unbelief and infidelity in America; he explored and analyzed the ecumenical movement and its quest for church union; he charted emerging trends for American churches, and especially for Protestants; and he undertook major historical studies, especially of Protestantism. The most influential of his books was *Righteous Empire: The Protestant Experience in America,* a conceptual survey of Protestantism and its interactions with the larger culture since the American Revolution. That work received the National Book Award in 1972. A later major book, *Pilgrims in Their Own Land: 500 Years of Religion in America* (1984), was an even more comprehensive compendium of facts and interpretations.

Through all of his work in teaching and the writing of books, Marty kept heavily occupied with other activities. His associate editorship of *The Christian Century* continued over the years; he wrote many major articles, editorials, book reviews, and a weekly column (called M.E.M.O.) for that journal, all the while performing the gamut of other editorial functions. He also founded a newsletter on religion and society, called *Context,* which he wrote and edited entirely. He served as co-editor for the scholarly journal *Church History.* His articles were published in many places, ranging from tiny specialized publications to the largest national magazines. Marty's casual and witty personal style made him a much sought after public speaker who travelled extensively. He also found time for other service, such as the presidency of the Park Ridge Center, an institute for the study of health, faith, and ethics located in suburban Chicago.

Pluralism Recurred as a Theme in Writings

Perhaps the most pervasive theme in Marty's writing was that of his commitment to pluralism and, therefore, to civility. He argued that the only basis for a moral, just, and humane society is a respect for the beliefs and practices of others who are unlike ourselves; yet the fact of respect for the ways of others does not mean that one should not have passion about his or her own ways. Our own roots and convictions define us, and individuals with strong—although differing—commitments make for a strong society. Outwardly, Marty argued, a key to maintaining the American social fabric is civility—the respect that one must have for others, the fair treatment that one must give others, which leads to a wholesome, fulfilling society.

In his observations concerning American religion, Marty clung to a belief in the parish, the local community of believers. He argued that the lessons of all of society can be learned in interaction with individuals and small groups gathered for worship and religious service. While other commentators were dismissing the parish as an outmoded organizational unit (and Marty himself certainly contributed some criticism of its shortcomings), Marty kept arguing that its faults were simply the faults of human beings and that in the community of the faithful was the promising hope for the future of religion.

Marty was also a leading ecumenist, committed to the belief that a divided Christendom has been not only a disappointment to those who believe that all of Christianity should work toward common goals, but a source (and a symptom) of destructive conflict over relatively trivial issues and a source of inefficient use of religious bodies' resources. His work at *The Christian Century* began in the headiest, most optimistic days of ecumenical thinking in the 1950s; later many of his colleagues became discouraged at the impediments to Christian unity which appeared insurmountable, but Marty persevered in seeing the real possibility of a unified Christianity at some future time.

Joined Civil Rights Movement

He was not only an observer of situations, but a promoter of causes and ideals in which he believed. He was an active propagandist for the civil rights movement in the 1950s and 1960s, and at the invitation of Martin Luther King, Jr., joined many other religious leaders in journeying to Selma, Alabama, for the movement's most historic march, from Selma to Montgomery, in 1965. Later he became an active spokesperson for those opposed to the American role in the war in Vietnam, helping to found the influential Christian antiwar group Clergy and Laity Concerned about Vietnam and lending his influential name to other antiwar protests.

Was Co-Director of the Fundamentalist Project

Marty was also a co-director of the Fundamentalist Project for the American Academy of Arts and Sciences. From 1988 to 1994, he and R. Scott Appleby explored current questions in fundamentalism with scholars from around the world. The culmination of this project was edited by Marty and Appleby in *Fundamentalisms Comprehended.* Other titles in this encyclopedia of fundamentalism include *Accounting for Fundamentalisms,* (1994), *Fundamentalisms and the State,* (1993), *Fundamentalisms and Society,* (1992), and *Fundamentalisms Observed,* (1991). The series was based upon the interdisciplinary program directed by the American Academy of Arts and Sciences. The purpose was to explore the nature and impact of fundamentalist movements in the twentieth century.

Life, be it religious or secular, isn't so much about achieving goals as it is about getting there, Marty wrote; he thus had a sense of his work as a journey, one in which he could change and grow and learn. That kind of openness to new experiences and the sense that he had much yet to learn, even while he shared the many insights he had had, pervaded his work.

Further Reading

Marty's most influential book was probably *Righteous Empire: The Protestant Experience in America* (1970); Another important historical work was *Pilgrims in Their Own Land: 500 Years of Religion in America* (1984); *By Way of Response* (1981) was Marty's closest work to an autobiography, dealing as much with his ideas as with his life; *The Public Church* (1981) dealt with Marty's ideas about religious pluralism; His numerous contributions to *The Christian Century* since the 1950s and his newsletter, *Context,* provided ongoing outlets for his thought; Marty was the subject of a few master's theses, but no major biography has yet appeared. Also see *Christian Century* February 2-9, 1994. □

Andrew Marvell

The English poet and politician Andrew Marvell (1621-1678), one of the writers of the 17th century most admired by the 20th, composed lyric poetry which is sensuous, witty, elegant, and sometimes passionate.

Were Andrew Marvell not a major poet in his own right, he might be regarded primarily as a fascinating transitional figure. His work is deeply under the influence of John Donne and the metaphysical school, yet it shares its formal elegance and smoothness with the "tribe of Ben," the poets who clustered about the influential Ben Jonson and came to form the Cavalier school. Furthermore he was a protégé and disciple of John Milton, whose intense and broad-ranging participation in Renaissance philosophical, poetic, and theological traditions finds its counterpart in his own work. Like Milton, he wrote considerable poetry devoted to contemporary political questions, and he wrote verse satire akin to that of John Dryden, who is generally seen as the leading spirit of a new age.

Marvell was born on March 31, 1621, at Winestead-in-Holderness, Yorkshire. His father, a Calvinistic Anglican clergyman, became master of the Charterhouse, an almshouse, and preacher at Holy Trinity Church in Hull, where the family moved in 1624; the poet's mother was to die in 1638, his father in 1641. In 1633 Marvell began his studies at Trinity College, Cambridge, where he remained until 1641, receiving a bachelor of arts degree in 1639. Late in his Trinity years, a plausible tradition holds, Marvell was converted to Roman Catholicism by persuasive Jesuits but was promptly brought back to the Anglican faith by his father. By the outbreak of the civil war in 1642 Marvell's academic career had ended short of his completing a master of arts degree, perhaps as a result of his father's accidental death, and he began a 4-year sojourn in Europe, probably tutoring the son of a well-to-do family.

First Works

Though in poems written between 1645 and 1649 he had evinced royalist sympathies, Marvell seems to have been attracted by the strong personality of Oliver Cromwell, and in 1650 he wrote "An Horatian Ode upon Cromwell's Return from Ireland." Commonly acknowledged a masterful piece of political poetry, this ode has occasioned some controversy as to the degree of unqualified admiration with

which the poet regards the military harshness of the Puritan general.

For 2 or 3 years beginning in 1651, Marvell was tutor to Mary Fairfax, daughter of Lord General Fairfax, a retired Commonwealth general who lived at Nun Appleton, and here he wrote some memorable poems. Among them are the lovely "Music's Empire" and "Upon Appleton House, to My Lord Fairfax," a complex and sophisticated compliment to Mary Fairfax consisting of almost 400 octosyllabic couplets in which landscape description serves emblematically to convey political and philosophical ideals.

Political Career

In 1653 Milton attempted unsuccessfully to have Marvell made his assistant as Latin secretary (a position like that of secretary of state) to Cromwell; instead Marvell became tutor to a young ward of Cromwell named William Dutton. He tutored first at Eton, in the house of a man who had been to Bermuda and may possibly have provided the inspiration for the charming "Bermudas," in which a tropical island is presented as a Puritan paradise. Later, his tutoring duties took him to France.

In 1657 Marvell was appointed Latin secretary himself and remained in office until the restoration of the Stuart monarchy in 1660. He continued to write political poetry, much of it celebrating his admiration for Cromwell, such as "The First Anniversary of the Government under Oliver Cromwell" in 1655 and "Upon the Death of O.C." in 1658. In 1659 he was elected member of Parliament for Hull and served in the House of Commons for the rest of his life. Unlike the tempestuous Milton, however, Marvell was not an embattled and passionately committed politician but rather a quiet civil servant. In 1662 he served with the British minister in Holland; in 1663 he embarked on 2 years of diplomatic missions to Russia, Denmark, and Sweden. The latter years of his life were devoted to his service to the government, to the composition of political satire in verse, and to the writing of prose dealing with contemporary issues. He is said to have protected Milton from the vindictiveness of the new royal government after the Restoration—not the least of his contributions to poetry. He died on Aug. 16, 1678, of a fever compounded by medical treatment, still a bachelor. In 1681 his housekeeper published *Miscellaneous Poems by Andrew Marvell, Esq.,* the basis of his reputation as a poet.

Assessment of His Poetry

To the student of cultural history, Marvell's poetry is a fascinating amalgam of intellectual currents of his age—stoicism, Christian Platonism, antischolastic mysticism—and an Anglican sense of the order and harmony of nature. To the historian of poetry, his achievement is remarkable for its balance between a never-abandoned wit and dramatic atmosphere reminiscent of Donne, a precision and verbal elegance modeled on Horace and other classical poets, a detachment and metrical sophistication shared with the Cavaliers, and a sensuous evocation of landscape shared with the classical pastoral tradition.

Most of the finest poems seem to have been composed in the 1650s; few of them are without central images of gardens. Perhaps the most famous of Marvell's lyrics is "To His Coy Mistress": "Had we but world enough and time,/ This coyness, Lady, were no crime. . . . / But at my back I always hear/ Time's winged chariot hurrying near:/ And yonder all before us lie/ Deserts of vast eternity." Like many of Marvell's best poems, it masks extraordinary subtlety and complexity beneath a surface of smooth and deceptively simple octosyllabic couplets. It is, in fact, as perfect an example of the metaphysical mode as anything by Donne and, for all its cool and witty tone, a passionate lyric. Similarly powerful is "The Garden," whose sensuous images constitute a complex blending of Renaissance traditions that bear on the rival virtues of the active and the contemplative life; one of the most famous images in the poem is that of the mind, "that ocean where each kind/ Does straight its own resemblance find," withdrawn into itself and detached from the world, "Annihilating all that's made/ To a green thought in a green shade."

Further Reading

The most authoritative biography of Marvell is in French. In English, briefer and less reliable biographies are Augustine Birrell, *Andrew Marvell* (1905), and V. Sackville-West, *Andrew Marvell* (1929). Some of the most influential modern essays on Marvell—by Frank Kermode, Leo Spitzer, Douglas Bush, and Cleanth Brooks—are conveniently assembled in William R. Keast, ed., *Seventeenth Century English Poetry: Modern Essays in Criticism* (1962). The seminal essay by T. S. Eliot (1921) is reprinted in his *Selected Essays* (1932; subsequent editions), and the essay by William Empson, "Marvell's Garden," in his *Some Versions of Pastoral* (1935). Most of Ruth C. Wallerstein's *Studies in Seventeenth-century Poetic* (1950) is devoted to Marvell. John M. Wallace, *Destiny His Choice: The Loyalism of Andrew Marvell* (1968), relates the poet's work to its political context, and Donald M. Friedman, *Marvell's Pastoral Art* (1970), relates the poems to literary and intellectual traditions. The literary background is best provided by Douglas Bush, *English Literature in the Earlier Seventeenth Century, 1600-1660* (1945; 2d ed. 1962). Also recommended is Basil Willey, *The Seventeenth Century Background: Studies in the Thought of the Age in Relation to Poetry and Religion* (1934).

Additional Sources

Birrell, Augustine, *Andrew Marvell*, Folcroft, Pa.: Folcroft Library Editions, 1978 c1905.

Craze, Michael, *The life and lyrics of Andrew Marvell,* New York: Barnes & Noble Books, 1979.

Griffin, Patsy, *The modest ambition of Andrew Marvell: a study of Marvell and his relation to Lovelace, Fairfax, Cromwell, and Milton,* Newark: University of Delaware Press; London: Associated University Presses, 1995.

Hunt, John Dixon, *Andrew Marvell: his life and writings,* Ithaca, N.Y.: Cornell University Press, 1978; London: P. Elek, 1978.

Sackville-West, V. (Victoria), *Andrew Marvell*, Folcroft, Pa.: Folcroft Library Editions, 1974; Philadelphia: R. West, 1977. □

Harpo, Groucho, Chico (left to right)

The Marx brothers

The Marx brothers were American stage and film comedians whose lunatic antics dominated comedy during the 1930s.

Samuel Marx, an immigrant tailor, and Minna Schoenberg, a German vaudevillian turned factory worker, met and married in New York and raised five sons: Leonard (Chico), born in 1891; Adolph (Harpo), 1893; Milton (Gummo), 1894; Julius (Groucho), 1895; and Herbert (Zeppo), 1901.

A true stage mother, Minnie Marx tirelessly arranged interviews and created skits and revues for her boys. In Chico's vaudeville debut he wrestled, clowned, and played piano. Harpo began his career performing in two nightclubs; since he used identical routines, he was fired for presenting "used" material. Unable to find a job, he discovered his grandmother's "broken-down harp" and by his own unorthodox methods became a virtuoso. Possessor of a delightful soprano voice, adolescent Groucho won a part in *The Messenger Boys,* a benefit revue for San Francisco earthquake victims. But his tour with a troupe impersonating female singers ended when his voice suddenly changed.

Although all were living in New York, the three experienced Marx brothers—Chico, Harpo, and Groucho—worked separately. Finally they teamed together, touring the vaudeville circuit. Harpo, extremely nervous onstage, could not be trusted to deliver his lines; he himself imposed muteness on his public image. Harpo and Gummo disbanded the group when they enlisted in World War I, and Chico and Groucho entertained soldiers in army camps.

After the war Gummo left show business for manufacturing, and Zeppo gained his initiation into comedy in revues. During the early 1920s the Marx brothers achieved their final stage identities: Groucho, the almost schizophrenic, mustached punster with the stooped glide, ever-arching eyebrows, and the fat cigar; Harpo, the mute but expressive curly-headed imp, with one hand on somebody's silver service and the other playing his harp; Chico, almost as voluble as Groucho, dressed in an organ-grinder's costume, speaking a number of tortured dialects while performing at the piano; and Zeppo, the straight man. Their "spontaneous idiocy" and frenzied burlesque of their own revues captivated audiences.

A successful New York musical, *I'll Say She Is,* was followed by *Coconuts* (1926), a spoof of the Florida land-development boom, and *Animal Crackers* (1928), perhaps the most representative of the Marx brothers' insane antics; the last two were effectively adapted as movies. Their first talkie, *Monkey Business* (1929), enabled Groucho to pour forth a cascade of puns and quick wit. *Horsefeathers* (1932) mocks cultural restrictions and is irreverent toward the "sacred" institution, the university. After *Duck Soup* (1933), a spoof on political intrigue, Zeppo left to operate his own talent agency, joined later by Gummo.

Chico, Harpo, and Groucho clowned through six more movies. *A Night at the Opera* (1935), considered by many critics to be their masterpiece, takes a playful swipe at "highbrow" musicians. Crammed full of familiar gags and hackneyed jokes, the slew of films that followed had one saving grace: the three talented brothers, whose very presence induced laughter. *A Day at the Races* (1939) and *Go West* (1940) exhibit the nonstop clowning but lack the refined twists. After their eleventh production, *The Big Store* (1941), with Groucho as a bungling department store detective, the brothers separated for 5 years. Harpo and Chico returned to the stage, and Groucho began a long tenure in radio. American entry into World War II brought the three brothers together again, tirelessly touring army camps and selling millions of war bonds.

The Marx brothers' *A Night in Casablanca* (1946) was only moderately successful, and the trio once again disbanded. Groucho became the witty, sarcastic host of an otherwise inane television quiz show; Harpo and Chico returned to nightclubs, playing the London Palladium in 1949. During the 1950s the brothers went into semiretirement, appearing only as television and stage guests. All five had married and desired to spend time with their families. Popular demand brought them back in *The Incredible Jewel Robbery* (1959), their last film, a testament to comic talents able to provoke laughter from Depression and Cold War

audiences alike. In 1961 Chico died of a heart condition; Harpo died three years later; both Groucho and Gummo passed away in 1977; and the last living Marx brother, Zeppo, died in 1979. One reviewer remarked of their brand of comedy, "They were exactly like ordinary people and act just as we should act if social regulations did not prevent us from behaving in that way." A biographical musical about the brothers, *Minnie's Boys,* enjoyed moderate success on Broadway in 1969 but provided only a hint of their lifestyles; the brothers themselves, and the essence of their humor, are inimitable.

Further Reading

Two competent studies of the Marx brothers are Allen Eyles, *The Marx Brothers: Their World of Comedy* (1966; 2d ed. 1969), and Burt Goldblatt and Paul D. Zimmerman, *The Marx Brothers at the Movies* (1968). See also Kyle Crichton, *The Marx Brothers* (1950). □

Karl Marx

The German philosopher, radical economist, and revolutionary leader Karl Marx (1818-1883) founded modern "scientific" socialism. His basic ideas—known as Marxism—form the foundation of socialist and communist movements throughout the world.

Karl Marx spent most of his life in exile. He was exiled from his native Prussia in 1849 and went to Paris, from which he was expelled a few months later. He then settled in London, where he spent the rest of his life in dire poverty and relative obscurity. He was hardly known to the English public in his lifetime. His reputation as a radical thinker began to spread only after the emergence of the socialist parties in Europe, especially in Germany and France, in the 1870s and 1880s. From then on, Marx's theories continued to be hotly debated in the growing labor and socialist movements everywhere, including Czarist Russia.

By the end of the 19th and beginning of the 20th century, socialist parties everywhere had by and large accepted a considerable measure of Marxism, even though with modifications. This was especially true of the idea of the class struggle and the establishment of a socialist society, in which economic exploitation and social inequality would be abolished. Marxism achieved its first great triumph in the Russian Revolution of 1917, when its successful leader, V. I. Lenin, a lifelong disciple of Marx, organized the Soviet Union as a proletarian dictatorship based on Marx's philosophy, as Lenin interpreted it. Henceforth, Marx became a world figure and his theories a subject of universal attention and controversy.

Early Life

Marx was born in Trier, Rhenish Prussia, on May 5, 1818, the son of Heinrich Marx, a lawyer, and Henriette Presburg Marx, a Dutchwoman. Both Heinrich and Henriette were descendants of a long line of rabbis. Barred from the practice of law as a Jew, Heinrich Marx became converted to Lutheranism about 1817, and Karl was baptized in the same church in 1824, at the age of 6. Karl attended a Lutheran elementary school but later became an atheist and materialist, rejecting both the Christian and Jewish religions. It was he who coined the aphorism "Religion is the opium of the people," a cardinal principle in modern communism.

Karl attended the Friedrich Wilhelm Gymnasium in Trier for 5 years, graduating in 1835, at the age of 17. The gymnasium curriculum was the usual classical one—history, mathematics, literature, and languages, particularly Greek and Latin. Karl became proficient in French and Latin, both of which he learned to read and write fluently. In later years he taught himself other languages, so that as a mature scholar he could also read Spanish, Italian, Dutch, Scandinavian, Russian, and English. As his articles in the New York Daily Tribune show, he came to handle the English language masterfully (he loved Shakespeare, whose works he knew by heart), although he never lost his heavy Teutonic accent in speaking.

In October 1835 Marx matriculated in Bonn University, where he attended courses primarily in jurisprudence, as it was his father's ardent wish that he become a lawyer.

Marx, however, was more interested in philosophy and literature than in law. He wanted to be a poet and dramatist, and in his student days he wrote a great deal of poetry—most of it preserved—which in his mature years he rightly recognized as imitative and mediocre. He spent a year at Bonn, studying little but roistering and drinking. He spent a day in jail for disturbing the peace and fought one duel, in which he was wounded in the right eye. He also piled up heavy debts.

Marx's dismayed father took him out of Bonn and had him enter the University of Berlin, then a hub of intellectual ferment. In Berlin a galaxy of brilliant thinkers was challenging existing institutions and ideas, including religion, philosophy, ethics, and politics. The spirit of the great philosopher G. W. F. Hegel was still palpable there. A group known as the Young Hegelians, which included teachers such as Bruno Bauer and bright, philosophically oriented students, met frequently to debate and interpret the subtle ideas of the master. Young Marx soon became a member of the Young Hegelian circle and was deeply influenced by its prevailing ideas.

Marx spent more than 4 years in Berlin, completing his studies there in March 1841. He had given up jurisprudence and devoted himself primarily to philosophy. On April 15, 1841, the University of Jena awarded "Carolo Henrico Marx" the degree of doctor of philosophy on the strength of his abstruse and learned dissertation, *Difference between Democritean and Epicurean Natural Philosophy,* which was based on Greek-language sources.

His Exile

Marx's hopes of teaching philosophy at Bonn University were frustrated by the reactionary policy of the Prussian government. He then turned to writing and journalism for his livelihood. In 1842 he became editor of the liberal Cologne newspaper *Rheinische Zeitung,* but it was suppressed by the Berlin government the following year. Marx then moved to Paris. There he first came in contact with the working class, gave up philosophy as a life goal, and undertook his serious study of economics.

In January 1845 Marx was expelled from France "at the instigation of the Prussian government," as he said. He moved to Brussels, where he lived until 1848 and where he founded the German Workers' party and was active in the Communist League. It was for the latter that he, with his friend and collaborator Friedrich Engels, published, in 1848, the famous Manifesto of the Communist Party (known as the Communist Manifesto). Expelled by the Belgian government for his radicalism, Marx moved back to Cologne, where he became editor of the *Neue Rheinische Zeitung* in June 1848. Less than a year later, in May 1849, the paper was suppressed by the Prussian government, and Marx himself was exiled. He returned to Paris, but in September the French government expelled him again. Hounded from the Continent, Marx finally settled in London, where he lived as a stateless exile (Britain denied him citizenship and Prussia refused to renaturalize him) for the rest of his life.

In London, Marx's sole means of support was journalism. He wrote for both German- and English-language publications. From August 1852 to March 1862 he was correspondent for the *New York Daily Tribune,* contributing a total of about 355 articles, many of which were used by that paper as leading (unsigned) editorials. Journalism, however, paid wretchedly (£2 per article); Marx was literally saved from starvation by the continuous financial support of Engels. In 1864 Marx helped to found in London the International Workingmen's Association (known as the First International), for which he wrote the inaugural address. In 1872 he dissolved the International, to prevent it from falling into the hands of the anarchists under the leadership of Mikhail Bakunin. Thereafter, Marx's political activities were confined mainly to correspondence with radicals in Europe and America, offering advice and helping to shape the socialist and labor movements.

Appearance and Personal Life

Marx was short and stocky, with a bushy head of hair and flashing eyes. His skin was swarthy, so that his family and friends called him *Mohr* in German, or Moor in English. He himself adopted the nickname and used it with intimates. His physique gave an impression of vigor, despite the fact that he was a latent tubercular (four of his younger siblings died of tuberculosis). A man of immense learning and sharp intellectual power, Marx, often impatient and irascible, antagonized people by his sardonic wit, bluntness, and dogmatism, which bordered on arrogance. His enemies were legion. Yet, despite his deserved reputation as a hard and disagreeable person, he had a soft spot for children; he deeply loved his own daughters, who, in turn, adored him.

Marx was married to his childhood sweetheart, Jenny von Westphalen, who was known as the "most beautiful girl in Trier," on June 19, 1843. She was totally devoted to him. She died of cancer on Dec. 2, 1881, at the age of 67. For Marx it was a blow from which he never recovered.

The Marxes had seven children, four of whom died in infancy or childhood. Of the three surviving daughters—Jenny (1844-1883), Laura (1845-1911), and Eleanor (1855-1898)—two married Frenchmen: Jenny, Charles Longuet; Laura, Paul Lafargue. Both of Marx's sons-in-law became prominent French socialists and members of Parliament. Eleanor lived with Edward Aveling and was active as a British labor organizer. Both Laura and Eleanor committed suicide.

Marx spent most of his working time in the British Museum, doing research both for his newspaper articles and his books. He was a most conscientious scholar, never satisfied with secondhand information but tracing facts and figures to their original sources. In preparation for *Das Kapital,* he read virtually every available work in economic and financial theory and practice in the major languages of Europe.

At home, Marx often stayed up till four in the morning, reading and making voluminous notes in his tight handwriting, which was so crabbed as to be almost unreadable. He was a heavy smoker of pipes and cigars, using up quantities of matches in the process. His workroom was densely smoke-filled. "*Das Kapital,*" he told his son-in-law Paul

Lafargue, "will not even pay for the cigars I smoked writing it."

Marx's excessive smoking, wine drinking, and consumption of heavily spiced foods may have been contributory causes to his illnesses, most of which would appear to be, in the light of modern knowledge, allergic and psychosomatic. In the last two decades of his life he was tormented by a mounting succession of ailments that would have tried the patience of Job. He suffered from hereditary liver derangement (of which, he claimed, his father died); frequent outbreaks of carbuncles and furuncles on his neck, chest, back, and buttocks (often he could not sit); toothaches; eye inflammations; lung abscesses; hemorrhoids; pleurisy; and persistent headaches and coughs that made sleep impossible without drugs. In the final dozen or so years of his life, he could no longer do any sustained intellectual work. He died in his armchair in London on March 14, 1883, about two months before his sixty-fifth birthday. He lies buried in London's Highgate Cemetery, where the grave is marked by a bust of him.

His Works

Marx's writings fall into two general categories, the polemical-philosophical and the economic-political. The first reflected his Hegelian-idealistic period; the second, his revolutionary-political interests.

Marx wrote hundreds of articles, brochures, and reports but few books as such. He published only five books during his lifetime. Two of them were polemical, and three were political-economic. The first, *The Holy Family* (1845), written in collaboration with Engels, was a polemic against Marx's former teacher and Young Hegelian philosopher Bruno Bauer. The second was *Misère de la philosophie* (The Poverty of Philosophy), written by Marx himself in French and published in Paris and Brussels in 1847. As its subtitle indicates, this polemical work was "An Answer to the *Philosophy of Poverty* by M. Proudhon."

Marx's third book, *The Eighteenth Brumaire of Louis Bonaparte,* published serially in a German publication in New York City in 1852, is a brilliant historical-political analysis of the rise and intrigues of the Bonaparte who became Napoleon III. The remaining two books, both on economics, are the ones on which Marx's worldwide reputation rests: *Critique of Political Economy* and, more particularly, *Das Kapital* (Capital).

Critique was published in 1859, after about 14 years of intermittent research. Marx considered it merely a first installment, expecting to bring out additional volumes, but he scrapped his plan in favor of another approach. The result was *Das Kapital,* subtitled *Critique of Political Economy,* of which only the first volume appeared, in 1867, in Marx's lifetime. After his death, two other volumes were brought out by Engels on the basis of the materials Marx left behind. Volumes 2 (1885) and 3 (1894) can be properly regarded as works by Marx and Engels, rather than by Marx himself. Indeed, without Engels, as Marx admitted, the whole monumental enterprise might not have been produced at all. On the night of Aug. 16, 1867, when Marx completed correcting the proof sheets of volume 1, he wrote to Engels in

Manchester: "I have YOU alone to thank that this has been made possible. Without your sacrifices for me I could never possibly have done the enormous work for the three volumes. I embrace you, full of thanks!"

A fourth volume of *Das Kapital* was brought together by Karl Kautsky after Engels's death. It was based on Marx's notes and materials from *Critique of Political Economy* and was published in three parts, under the title *Theories of Surplus Value,* between 1905 and 1910. A Russian edition, also in three parts, came out between 1954 and 1961, and an English translation in 1968.

Two of Marx's books were published posthumously. *The Class Struggles in France, 1848-1850,* written in 1871, appeared in 1895. It was, Engels wrote in his introduction, "Marx's first attempt, with the aid of his materialist conception, to explain a section of contemporary history from the given economic situation." The second posthumous work, *The German Ideology,* which Marx wrote in collaboration with Engels in 1845-1846, was not published in full until 1932. The book is an attack on the philosophers Ludwig Andreas Feuerbach and Max Stirner and on the so-called true socialists.

The rest of Marx's publications, mostly printed posthumously, consist of brochures. *Herr Vogt* (1860) is a furious polemic against a man named Karl Vogt, whom Marx accused of being a police spy. *Wage-Labor and Capital* (1884) is a reprint of newspaper articles. *Critique of the Gotha Programme* (1891) consists of notes which Marx sent to the German Socialist party congress in 1875. *Wages, Price and Profit* (1898) is an address that Marx delivered at the General Council of the International in 1865.

His Ideas

Marx's world importance does not lie in his economic system, which, as critics point out, was not original but was derived from the classical economists Adam Smith and David Ricardo. *Das Kapital,* indeed, is not primarily a technical work on economics but one that uses economic materials to establish a moral-philosophical-sociological structure. Marx's universal appeal lies in his moral approach to social-economic problems, in his insights into the relationships between institutions and values, and in his conception of the salvation of mankind. Hence Marx is best understood if one studies, not his economics, but his theory of history and politics.

The central idea in Marx's thought is the materialistic conception of history. This involves two basic notions: that the economic system at any given time determines the prevailing ideas; and that history is an ongoing process regulated—predetermined—by the economic institutions which evolve in regular stages.

The first notion turned Hegel upside down. In Hegel's view, history is determined by the universal idea (God), which shapes worldly institutions. Marx formulated the reverse: that institutions shape ideas. This is known as the materialistic interpretation of history. Marx's second notion, that of historical evolution, is connected with his concept of dialectics. He saw in history a continuing dialectical pro-

cess, each stage of development being the product of thesis, antithesis, and synthesis.

Thus thesis corresponds to the ancient, precapitalist period, when there were no classes or exploitation. Antithesis corresponds to the era of capitalism and labor exploitation. Synthesis is the final product—communism, under which capital would be owned in common and there would be no exploitation.

To Marx, capitalism is the last stage of historical development before communism. The proletariat, produced by capitalism, is the last historical class. The two are fated to be in conflict—the class struggle, which Marx proclaimed so eloquently in the Communist Manifesto—until the proletariat is inevitably victorious and establishes a transitional order, the proletarian dictatorship, a political system which Marx did not elaborate or explain. The proletarian dictatorship, in turn, evolves into communism, or the classless society, the final stage of historical development, when there are no classes, no exploitation, and no inequalities. The logical implication is that with the final establishment of communism, history comes to a sudden end. The dialectical process then presumably ceases, and there are no more historical evolutions or social struggles. This Marxist interpretation of history, with its final utopian-apocalyptic vision, has been criticized in the noncommunist world as historically inaccurate, scientifically untenable, and logically absurd.

Nevertheless, Marx's message of an earthly paradise has provided millions with hope and new meaning of life. From this point of view, one may agree with the Austrian economist Joseph A. Schumpeter that "Marxism is a religion" and Marx is its "prophet."

Further Reading

The first volumes in the 13-volume Karl Marx Library, edited and translated by Saul K. Padover, have been published: *Karl Marx on Revolution,* vol. 1 (1971) and *Karl Marx on the First International,* vol. 2 (1972).

There are no scholarly, comprehensive, or objective biographies of Marx. The best is Franz Mehring, *Karl Marx: The Story of His Life* (1935), but it is now outdated. Also outdated are Otto Rühle, *Karl Marx: His Life and Work* (1929), and Karl Korsch, *Karl Marx* (1938). A more recent book, Robert Payne, *Marx* (1968), lacks analysis, and John Lewis, *The Life and Teaching of Karl Marx* (1965), is slanted. Sir Isaiah Berlin, *Karl Marx: His Life and Environment* (1939), is recommended as an acute interpretation of Marx's life, although it is not a biography. A political and intellectual biography of Marx and Engels is Oscar J. Hammen, *The Red '48ers: Karl Marx and Friedrich Engels* (1969). See also Edward Hallett Carr, *Karl Marx: A Study in Fanaticism* (1934), and Leopold Schwarzschild, *The Red Prussian: The Life and Legend of Karl Marx* (1947).

Recommended for the treatment of various aspects of Marxism are Sidney Hook, *Towards the Understanding of Karl Marx* (1933); Joseph A. Schumpeter, *Capitalism, Socialism, and Democracy* (1942); Henry B. Mayo, *Democracy and Marxism* (1955; published in 1960 as *Introduction to Marxist Theory*); Erich From, ed., *Marx's Concept of Man* (1961); Henry Collins and Chimen Abramsky, *Karl Marx and the British Labour Movement: Years of the First International* (1965); Bertram D. Wolfe, *Marxism: One Hundred Years in the Life of a Doctrine* (1965); Shlomo Avineri, *The Social and Political Thought of*

Karl Marx (1968); Henry Lefebvre, *The Sociology of Marx* (1968); Raymond Aron, *Marxism and the Existentialists* (1969); and Louis Althusser, *For Marx* (1969). □

Mary

Mary, mother of Jesus of Nazareth, occupies a preeminent position in the theology and piety of the traditional Eastern and Western Churches.

Information about the life of Mary is extremely sparse (Matthew 1 and 2; Luke 1 and 2). It is clear that for Matthew and Luke in their Gospels, Mary's conception of Jesus was miraculous, involving no human paternity, and that her son was the Messiah expected by Israel. Mary belonged to the house of David (Luke 1:26), was engaged to a man called Joseph (Matthew 1:18), and lived in Nazareth in lower Galilee (Luke 1:26). The Gospel relates how an angel of God announced that she, though a virgin, would conceive the son of the "Most High," to be named Jesus, and that he would found a new Davidic kingdom (Luke 1:31-33). Mary consented. Joseph discovered that Mary was with child and wished to dissolve the engagement quietly. In a dream, however, God's angel admonished him to marry Mary because the son she would bear was the result of a divine intervention (Matthew 1:19-21).

Before her marriage, Mary visited her cousin Elizabeth, the mother of John the Baptist, and on that occasion more prophetic utterances made quite clear that Mary's future son would be the fulfillment of Israel's hopes. No further personal details are given of Mary. Her silent presence at the birth of Jesus (Matthew 1:12-21; Luke 2:1-7) is recorded. When the child was presented at the Temple to be redeemed according to Jewish law, the aging Simeon told Mary that she would suffer much (Luke 2:21-35). Later, when Jesus at the age of 12 was lost for 3 days, his parents found him among the doctors of the law, and the first of Mary's two recorded statements appears: "My son, why have you acted so with us? Your father and I have looked for you in sorrow" (Luke 2:41-48). Luke adds: Mary kept all these happenings in her memory.

Mary appears again (John 2:1 ff) at a marriage in the town of Cana when her second recorded statement occurs: "They have no wine," she told Jesus. Jesus thereupon turned water into wine. She appears with the relatives of Jesus in an attempt to see him during his public life (Mark 3:3 ff) and at the foot of Jesus' cross when he entrusts her to the care of John the Apostle (John 19:26 ff). She is also mentioned briefly in the Acts of the Apostles (1:14).

The dates of Mary's life can only be surmised. Present researches place the birth of Jesus between 7 and 4 B.C. Granting Mary a minimal age of 16 to 18 years at the time of Jesus' birth, this would place her birth at sometime about 22-20 B.C. There is no precise information as to her death. In the later development of the Eastern and Western Churches, Mary was proclaimed the mother of God. Her position was further defined in the Roman Catholic Church,

which in 1854 stated as an article of faith that she had been conceived without the original sin which affects all men. In 1950 Pius XII declared that at her death Mary's body had not corrupted in a grave but that God had taken her body and soul into heaven.

Further Reading

Most of the books written on this subject are either Roman Catholic devotional books, such as Juniper B. Carol, *Mariology* (1955), or Roman Catholic studies of theology. Nothing has been published concerning the archaeological excavations at Nazareth. For a view of Mary by a Protestant Church historian consult Giovanni Miegge, *The Virgin Mary: The Roman Catholic Marian Doctrine* (1950; trans. 1955). □

Mary I

Mary I (1516-1558) was queen of England from 1553 to 1558. Her reign marked a reversal of Edward VI's Protestant policies and a return to Catholicism.

Born on Feb. 18, 1516, at Greenwich Palace, Mary was the daughter of Henry VIII and Catherine of Aragon. The birth of the little Spanish Tudor bitterly disappointed Henry VIII, who hoped for a son and heir. Nonetheless, he took courage and expressed the forlorn hope at her christening that "If it was a daughter this time, by the grace of God the sons will follow." Mary became a good student and an accomplished linguist. She learned Latin, French, Spanish, Italian, and Greek. She studied astronomy, natural science, and mathematics and became familiar with the works of Erasmus, More, and Vives. Like all Tudors, she was musically inclined; she played the lute, virginal, regal, and spinet. She also danced and embroidered.

In 1528 Henry VIII requested Pope Clement VII's dispensation for the marriage of Mary to her half brother, the illegitimate Henry (1519-1536), Duke of Richmond and Somerset, the natural child of Henry and his mistress Elizabeth Blount. When the Pope agreed on condition that Henry give up his plan for nullifying his marriage to Catherine, Henry balked and the project was dropped.

Mary did not like her father's new wife, Anne Boleyn, who reciprocated in kind. Mary was forced to leave her own household and become a member of that of her half sister Elizabeth. She lost her title of princess and was declared illegitimate via the Act of Succession (1534). During Catherine's last days Henry refused to let mother and daughter see one another. With the appearance of Henry's third wife, Jane Seymour, Mary's life altered. She took the oath of supremacy, revisited the palace, and entered into amicable relations with Henry. She was god-mother to Edward, Jane's son, and chief mourner at Jane's funeral.

Mary got along well with Henry's fourth wife, Anne of Cleves (1540) but not with his fifth, Catherine Howard. She attended Henry's marriage to Catherine Parr (July 1543). By the parliamentary Act of Succession of 1544 she was re-

took Calais, the last English possession on the Continent. Mary, disappointed at her husband's absence, her failure to produce an heir, and the loss of Calais, died on Nov. 25, 1558. Stubborn, temperamental, and soured in spirit by the opposition of her people and bodily ills, she was nonetheless true to her faith and to those faithful to her. Her uncompromising attitude toward Protestantism, and Elizabeth's triumphs have ensured that she be remembered as the least successful Tudor sovereign.

Further Reading

The best biography of Mary is H.F.M. Prescott, *A Spanish Tudor: The Life of "Bloody Mary"* (1940; rev. ed. titled *Mary Tudor,* 1953), which is a soundly researched, fascinating work. See also the older, Catholic study of J. M. Stone, *The History of Mary I, Queen of England* (1901), and Beatrice White, *Mary Tudor* (1935). □

Mary II

Mary II (1662-1694) was queen of England, Scotland, and Ireland from 1689 to 1694. The Glorious Revolution of 1688 deposed her father and made Mary and her husband, William III, the only joint rulers in English history.

Of a gentle and retiring nature, Mary always deferred to her husband's wishes in politics. Her independent reputation rests on her solicitude for the Anglican Church and her charitable and educational works. She encouraged Latitudinarian appointments among the bishops—Henry Compton, John Tillotson, and Gilbert Burnet being among the liberal theologians she favored. Among her missionary acts, she supported the Society for the Promotion of Christian Knowledge, endowed the College of William and Mary in Virginia, and founded Greenwich Hospital for disabled seamen.

Their Catholic father, James II, reluctantly allowed Mary and Anne to be reared as Anglicans for "fear of their being taken away from him altogether." At 15 Mary was betrothed to William of Orange. Initially both James and her uncle, Charles II, disapproved since there was some indication that the Dauphin of France might become her suitor, but they yielded since a Dutch alliance was largely favored. The marriage was solemnized in November 1677. Mary's lonely residence in Holland was heightened by the loss of two children in childbirth and by William's preoccupation with politics. He was not only inattentive but publicly established Elizabeth Villiers as his mistress. The relationship was further impaired by William's jealousy of Mary's position as heiress presumptive to the English throne. Yet, prior to his invasion of England, when William spoke to her of remarriage should he fall in battle, Mary replied that if she lost him she should not care for an angel.

Relations between Mary and her father were increasingly strained by his pro-Catholic religious policies after

stored to the royal succession. During the reign of her half brother Edward VI she refused to subscribe to the new Protestant service; resolutely she declared in council that "her soul was God's and her faith she would not change." On Edward's death on July 6, 1553, she became queen but not without disposing of the Duke of Northumberland's plot to place Lady Jane Grey on the throne.

Mary was 37 on her accession. She was an attractive woman, delicately featured, thin, short, well-complexioned, nearsighted, and deep-voiced with a grave demeanor. Her pro-Catholic and pro-Spanish policies immediately became apparent. She restored the Catholic Church but did not restore the monasteries to it and married Philip (later King Philip II of Spain) on July 25, 1554. Announcement of her marriage precipitated three insurrections, including Wyatt's Rebellion, which was not extinguished until the rebels were at the gates of London (February 1554).

Statutes against heretics were reinstituted. Prominent Protestants such as Thomas Cranmer, Nicholas Ridley, and Hugh Latimer, as well as lesser folk, suffered the heretics' death: burning at the stake. About 300 died. Many Protestants fled to such places as Geneva, John Calvin's home. Calvin's protégé John Knox, the Scottish reformer, called Mary "that wicked Jezebel of England." Later writers called her "Bloody Mary."

Philip left England in 1555 after a 10-month stay; he did not return until March 1557 for a sojourn of 3 1/2 months. He convinced Mary to join Spain's war against France. The war went badly for the English. Early in 1558 the French

James attained the throne. She interceded in behalf of Bishop Compton, who had been arraigned before the Court of High Commission, and continued a closeness with her cousin, the insurrectionary Duke of Monmouth. Her rejection of her father's plea that she convert to Catholicism, and her refusal to recognize James's son, born in 1688, precipitated a permanent breach. On William's successful invasion of England in 1688, overtures were made to enthrone her as sole ruler, which, in loyalty to her husband, she refused. On Feb. 13, 1689, William accepted the crown in both their names. The coronation was held on April 11.

In 1690 Mary was empowered by Parliament to exercise rule during William's many absences abroad. This uncomfortable role demanded such unpleasant duties as signing the arrest for her uncle (Clarendon). Yet her policies generally earned the thanks of her husband and both houses of parliament.

On Dec. 28, 1694, Mary died of smallpox at the age of 32. William, deeply mourning her loss, converted to Anglicanism. Still his regime lost much of its popularity.

Further Reading

Mary's letters are unusually revealing of the times and of her own views: *Memoirs, 1689-1693,* edited by R. P. Doebner (1886), and *Letters of Two Queens,* edited by Benjamin Bathurst (1924). The most complete biography of Mary II is Hester W. Chapman, *Mary II: Queen of England* (1953). Elizabeth Hamilton, *William's Mary: A Biography of Mary II* (1971), emphasizes Mary's family relationships and devotion to Protestantism.

Additional Sources

Chapman, Hester W., *Mary II, Queen of England,* Westport, Conn.: Greenwood Press, 1976.
Miller, John, *The life and times of William and Mary,* London, Weidenfeld and Nicolson 1974. □

Mary Queen of Scots

Mary, Queen of Scots (1542-1587), was queen of France and Scotland and claimant to the throne of England. As the rival of Elizabeth I, she was perhaps the last real hope of a restored Catholicism in England.

The relations of England, Scotland, and France in the mid-16th century were dictated more by considerations of religion than they were by any emergent nationalism. Both France and Scotland were rocked by internal struggles over religion, but in international relations France emerged as the champion of the Scottish Catholics. King James V of Scotland had cemented this relationship by marrying Mary of Guise, the daughter of one of the most powerful Catholics in France. The Scottish-French alliance posed a considerable threat to England in its own struggles with France, but the English were able to silence the threat momentarily by defeating the Scots at Solway Moss (November 1542).

Mary Stuart was the third child and only daughter of James V and Mary of Guise. Both of her brothers had died before she was born at Linlithgow Palace on Dec. 7/8, 1542. Her father, already dejected by the disgrace of Solway Moss, thought the birth of a female heir a portent of disaster. A week after her birth he died, and the infant princess became queen of Scots. The period following the death of James V was an unhappy one for Scotland. In 1547 an English invasion led to the military occupation of the country. One of the chief results of this action was to drive Scotland more firmly than ever into alliance with France. On July 7, 1548, the Estates of Scotland ratified an agreement for the marriage of Queen Mary to the Dauphin of France, the future Francis II, and ordered that she go to France immediately.

For the following decade Scotland was under heavy French influence; the queen mother, Mary of Guise, was appointed regent, and many high offices went to Frenchmen. As a result, a feeling of reaction against the French began to be noticeable in Scotland, and it was fanned for religious purposes by the Protestant party in the country.

Queen of France

Mary meanwhile was educated with the French royal children. She appears to have been a quick and able student whose charming personality had a great impact on all around her. In April 1558 her marriage to the Dauphin was celebrated. In November of the same year, Mary Tudor, Queen of England, died. Mary Stuart laid a claim to the

English throne as great-granddaughter of Henry VII on the grounds that Elizabeth had been declared illegitimate. Elizabeth I ascended the throne without opposition in England, but Mary and the Dauphin assumed the royal titles of England and Ireland. They continued to use them when they ascended to the French throne in July 1559, and though the Treaty of Edinburgh of July 1560 required them to abandon their claims to the English throne, they refused to ratify it.

Mary's husband, Francis II, ruled in France only a little more than a year, dying on Dec. 5, 1560. His death meant an end to Guise dominance in France, and as Catherine de Médicis asserted power there, the cause of Mary Stuart ceased to be a major concern of French politics. After a year of semiretirement in France, Mary resolved, on the advice of her friends, to return to Scotland to see whether she could reassert her power there. On April 19, 1561, the young queen landed at Leith, arriving in a dense fog which John Knox, the Protestant leader, saw as an omen of the "sorrow, dolour, darkness, and all impiety" which her coming was to bring. Her arrival was conceived of as a threat by Queen Elizabeth. In Mary's absence the Protestant party had gained power in Scotland, and this was to England's advantage; her return raised the possibility of a reassertion of Catholic influence, since few doubted that Mary, a devout Catholic herself, meant to reestablish the old religion and realign Scotland with the Continental Catholic powers.

Rule in Scotland

Elizabeth's policy toward Mary was confusing. She recognized the threat, but she was emotionally and perhaps politically unwilling to question the authority of another legitimate sovereign. Her policy thus vacillated between attacking Mary when she was strong and aiding her when she was weak. For some 7 years Mary precariously held her position as sovereign of Scotland. There was little likelihood of permanent success, for Mary was clearly out of sympathy with important elements in Scotland.

Various negotiations for Mary's marriage took place; it appears that Mary herself had the highest hopes of an alliance with Spain through marriage to Don Carlos, the son of Philip II. In July 1565, she married Henry, Lord Darnley. It was a political, not a love, match, for through this marriage Mary strengthened her claims to be heir presumptive to the throne of England, Darnley being the next lineal heir after herself to the English throne. The marriage had somewhat different political results from those Mary hoped for; the Protestant lords, led by the Earl of Moray with support from Queen Elizabeth, rebelled. Mary was able to counter this threat by military force, but she could not compensate for the arrogance and stupidity of Darnley himself. She refused the grant to him of the crown matrimonial and increasingly turned for comfort to her Italian secretary, David Riccio. Darnley in turn, wounded by the widespread rumors that Riccio was her lover, closed with the Protestant lords, who promised to make him king consort if he would destroy Riccio and restore them to power. On March 9, 1566, Darnley and the nobles dragged Riccio from Mary's room and murdered him. Within a short period, Moray and the other exiled rebel leaders had returned.

Murder of Darnley

Though Mary gave birth to a son (the later James VI of Scotland and James I of England) in June 1566, she was never reconciled to Darnley. Hiding her true feelings well, she made an outward show of reconciliation to Darnley while she actually drew close to one of the Protestant lords, the Earl of Bothwell. In February 1567 Darnley was murdered under curious circumstances; the house in which he was convalescing, Kirk o'Field, was destroyed by a violent explosion, and he was found dead in the grounds. Evidence, including the controversial Casket Letters, suggested that Mary had plotted with Bothwell the death of her second husband. The suspicions were strengthened when Mary did little to investigate the murder, allowed herself to be abducted by Bothwell, and in May 1567 she married him. The result was an almost total loss of public support for Mary. Civil war in Scotland ensued; Mary was captured and forced to abdicate in favor of her son, James (July 24, 1567). After somewhat less than a year of confinement, she escaped and once again raised a party on her behalf with the aid of the house of Hamilton. Her new-found supporters were routed at the battle of Langside (May 13, 1568), and after a futile effort to sail for France, Mary crossed the border into England on May 16, 1568, a refugee from the Scotland she had tried to rule.

Exile in England

It was a daring move and placed Elizabeth of England in an awkward position. Elizabeth was not in favor of having the Catholic claimant to the throne so close, where she could and did become the focus of Spanish intrigue. On the other hand, she did not want to use English force against the Scottish Protestants to restore Mary, nor did she wish Mary to take refuge in some Catholic court. Moreover, Elizabeth was troubled by her own conception of the divine nature of a monarch and upset by the implications of a forcible removal of a legitimate ruler. To resolve the dilemma, Elizabeth decided, in effect, to sit in judgment on the case. A commission met at York in the summer of 1568 and terminated its proceedings at Hampton Court early the following year. Elizabeth did not allow the commission to make a definite judgment on the issue of Mary's complicity in the murder of Darnley, but two results emerged from the hearing: the rebel government of Moray in Scotland was for the present to remain undisturbed, and Mary was to remain in England.

Catholic Plots

Mary had arrived in England as a refugee seeking aid; she was to remain there the rest of her life as a virtual prisoner. Early in 1569 she was moved to Tutbury in Staffordshire to begin her captivity. Quickly she became the center of Catholic plots. Complicated plotting involving the proposed marriage of Mary to the Duke of Norfolk established her connection with the discontented English Catholics. The northern earls rebelled in 1569 but were quickly put down, Mary being moved south out of harm's way. In March 1571 Mary was involved in the Ridolphi plot, by which the Catholics were to rise in revolt and place Mary on the throne at the same time as a Spanish expeditionary force landed. The details of the plot were discovered by the government; Norfolk was arrested, tried, and executed. The implication of Mary in the plot was undoubted; she and her agent, the bishop of Ross, had been at the center of it. There were petitions from both houses of Parliament that action be taken against her, but Elizabeth opposed such measures. Such was the pattern of the remaining 14 years of her life.

Mary was closely watched by the authorities, but she continued to conspire with her Catholic friends to escape and take the English throne. Plot after plot followed in the main the course of the Ridolphi scheme. In some Mary played a direct part; in others she was simply the cause for which the rebels gathered. In 1586 Secretary Walsingham uncovered the details of the Babington plot; in July he secured a letter from Mary, giving her assent to the assassination of Elizabeth. Elizabeth could not reject this evidence, and orders were given for Mary's trial. She was formally condemned on October 14-15.

Parliament petitioned for Mary's execution; after much delay and uncertainty, Elizabeth signed the death warrant. The Council, acting on its own initiative because the Queen still hesitated, sent the warrant to Fotheringhay Castle, Northamptonshire, where Mary was executed on Feb. 8, 1587. Elizabeth displayed great public displeasure at the action and even sent the bearer of the warrant, William Davison, to the Tower. But realistically she knew that the action was necessary; by the death of Mary, the center of dangerous Catholic plotting was removed, and since the

new Catholic claimant was the Infanta of Spain, fears of a popular rising on behalf of the Catholic cause were sharply diminished.

Further Reading

The bibliography on Mary, Queen of Scots, is vast. A recent major study is Antonia Fraser, *Mary Queen of Scots* (1969), which has an excellent bibliography. Other biographies are David Hay Fleming, *Mary Queen of Scots* (2d ed. 1898); Thomas F. Henderson, *Mary Queen of Scots* (2 vols., 1905; repr. 1969); Stefan Zweig, *The Queen of Scots* (trans. 1935), less scholarly but a good interpretive study; and Eric Linklater, *Mary, Queen of Scots* (1952).

Mortimer Levine, *The Early Elizabethan Succession Question* (1966), is a useful discussion of the claims to the English throne. Leo Hicks, *An Elizabeth Problem* (1964), sheds much light on Catholic plotting, as does Francis Edwards, *The Dangerous Queen* (1966). George M. Thomson, *The Crime of Mary Stuart* (1967), explores in detail the murder of Darnley; and Gordon Donaldson, *The First Trial of Mary, Queen of Scots* (1970), is a scholarly account of that trial.

Recommended for historical background are John Bennett Black, *The Reign of Elizabeth, 1558-1603* (1936; 2d ed. 1959); Agnes Mure MacKenzie, *The Scotland of Queen Mary* (1936); Stanley Thomas Bindoff, *Tudor England* (1950); Geoffrey Rudolf Elton, *England under the Tudors* (1955); William Croft Dickinson and George S. Pryde, *A New History of Scotland*, vol. 1 (1961); and Gordon Donaldson, *Scotland: James V-James VII* (1965). □

Masaccio

The Italian painter Masaccio (1401-1428) was the first great exponent of Renaissance painting. In his brief life he produced four major works utilizing the new discipline of space defined in perspective.

Tommaso di Giovanni, called Masaccio, was born in San Giovanni Valdarno on the day of St. Thomas, for whom he was named. His father, Giovanni Cassai, died when Masaccio was 5; his mother remarried, and a stepsister's husband, the only local painter, Mariotto di Cristofano, in all likelihood took Masaccio on as an apprentice. He probably received the nickname Masaccio (Terrible Tom) to distinguish him from his collaborator Masolino (Little Tom).

Masaccio went to Florence when he was about 20 and very soon joined the most modern and prominent artist group there, headed by the sculptor-architect Filippo Brunelleschi and the sculptor Donatello. Claiming as their own the heritage of Roman antiquity and of Giotto, the great Florentine master of the 14th century, they developed a new art of space and form. It utilized exact perspective invented by Brunelleschi and anatomical realism and applied these skills to narratives depicting critical moments in human relationships. Brunelleschi and Donatello found in the young Masaccio someone who could transfer these concerns into the medium of painting, using as well realistic contrasts of light and shade and the startling novelty of continuous luminous color areas that built forms and almost eliminated drawn edges. All of these innovations were recorded in the handbook on painting written in 1435 by Leon Battista Alberti, which was dedicated to Brunelleschi and alluded to Masaccio.

The *Sagra del Carmine,* a fresco that was in the cloister of S. Maria del Carmine in Florence, Masaccio's only major lost work, was apparently also his first large project. The *Sagra* represents the consecration of the church, which took place in 1422, and the painting was executed by 1425. Such a monumental representation of a local current event was apparently an innovation. Some 16th-century drawings have been called copies of it, but this is an error. In 1425 Masolino, a leading painter of the late Gothic style, left for Hungary, and he seems to have bequeathed some work in progress to Masaccio, who came from the same region. This may account for their collaboration on the small altarpiece *Madonna and Child with St. Anne.* Most of the figures are by Masolino, but the Madonna appears to have been painted by Masaccio over Masolino's outline drawing, and the Christ Child is entirely Masaccio's creation. It reveals a powerful vitality evoked by glowing light and a convincing solidity of forms.

Probably also of 1425 is Masaccio's first fresco, usually called the *Trinity,* in S. Maria Novella, Florence. A new approach to its remarkable use of perspective, often cited as typical of the time but actually more complex by far than any other cases, has been stimulated by recent study of the circumstances of its commission, involving the learned prior of the Dominican convent of S. Maria Novella. Proba-

bly much helped by Brunelleschi in rendering the perspective, Masaccio used it to support the theological theme, the relation of the Trinity and Crucifixion, where one figure, Christ, participates in both themes and thus illustrates the dual nature of Christ as immortal God and suffering man, a doctrine, "Corpus Domini," of special concern to Dominicans. The realistic perspective spaces are cut into compartments that underline this presentation.

In 1426, as an unusually full set of documents reveals, Masaccio painted a polyptych for S. Maria del Carmine in Pisa, Donatello apparently being his sponsor. It was later disassembled, and only some parts survive: the *Madonna and Child Enthroned,* the central panel; two small saints, *St. Paul* and *St. Andrew;* the pinnacle with the *Crucifixion;* and the predella and framing columns. While the central panel recalls the thickset bodies and glowing vigor of the earlier *Madonna and Child with St. Anne,* the tiny scenes of the predella introduce Masaccio's narrative art, with strong, sometimes ugly people bathed in warm color and situated in tightly orchestrated spaces.

Brancacci Chapel

That is the style of Masaccio's last and greatest work, the frescoes of the Brancacci Chapel in S. Maria del Carmine, Florence. The work, begun by Masolino for the merchant Felice Brancacci, was probably resumed by him in 1427, when he returned from Hungary, but now in collaboration with Masaccio, who did half of it, six scenes. Five are stories from the life of St. Peter, and the sixth is the *Expulsion from the Garden of Eden,* a "preface" painted in the narrow thickness of the entrance archway.

In the first scene, *St. Peter Baptizing,* a jostling crowd is arranged in a semicircle, much as in the predella of the Pisa polyptych. In the famous *Tribute Money* (the rare subject was probably chosen to propagandize for an income tax reform in Florence of the same year) Masaccio simplified the grouping, making a more skeletal geometry but also giving each figure a massive grandeur. The Expulsion takes this geometry of spatial siting of each figure to an extreme, and the figures of Adam and Eve have powerful emotional expressiveness.

The three remaining scenes, on a lower tier, are spatially more complex and sketchier in brushwork-advanced work not reached by other artists for some generations. In the *Miracle of the Shadow,* St. Peter and St. John walk forward, and three cripples are shown in recession in stages of being cured; where the two groups pass each other, the miracle happens, and theme and geometry coincide. In *St. Peter and St. John Distributing Alms,* another reference to Florentine fiscal policy, Masaccio employs a complex W-shaped space. The *Raising of the Pagan King's Son* was partly repainted 50 years later; for unknown reasons Masaccio went to Rome, where he died at the age of 26.

Further Reading

Ugo Procacci, *All the Paintings of Masaccio* (1962), is brief but authoritative. A full and up-to-date account is Luciano Berti, *Masaccio* (1967). □

Tomáš Garrigue Masaryk

The Czech philosopher Tomáš Garrigue Masaryk (1850-1937) was the founding father and first president of the former Czechoslovakia. A proponent of realism in both philosophy and politics, he first became known to the world through his championship of unpopular causes.

The age of Tomáš Masaryk was an age of liberalism and nationalism, ideologies which called for political freedom and national independence. Being a true son of his age, and a member of one of Austria-Hungary's unrepresented nationalities, Masaryk picked up this challenge and brought his ideas to their logical conclusion in the foundation of Czechoslovakia.

Education and Early Career

The son of a Slovak father and Germanized Czech mother, Masaryk was born on March 7, 1850, near Hodonin (Göding), Moravia, on the imperial estate where his father, a coachman, was employed. Given the low social position of his parents, his education got off to a rather rocky start, and for a while it seemed that he would become a blacksmith. But after studying at several local village schools and at Brno (Brünn), Masaryk completed his secondary education in Vienna in 1872, where he then entered the university. Receiving his doctorate in philosophy 4 years later, he spent a year at Leipzig (1876-1877), took a brief excursion to America to get married (1877-1878), and then returned to Vienna to become a lecturer at the university.

The Vienna and Leipzig years were of considerable influence on young Masaryk's mind. He had already developed a rebellious disposition and independent mind at Brno, but only in Vienna and Leipzig did these characteristics become part of his personality. (These character traits went well with his erect and vigorous physique, topped by a high-domed head that sculptors later liked to model). In Vienna he fell under Plato's influence (his thesis was entitled *The Essence of Plato's Soul*); and in Leipzig he embraced Protestantism, whose teachings appeared to him to be more in accord with the revered Hussite traditions, and his own quest for freedom, than the "authoritarian" thought of the Catholic Church. It was also in Leipzig that he had met his future wife and life companion, the American Charlotte Garrigue (1850-1923), who brought her own Huguenot-Unitarian traditions to bear upon Masaryk's mind.

After his return to Vienna, Masaryk supported himself and his growing family partly on his university lectures and partly on subsidies from his father-in-law. His first important work, *Suicide as a Mass Phenomenon of Modern Civilization,* appeared in 1881, and it was on the strength of this work that in the following year he received a professorship in the Czech University of Prague. His decision to accept this offer proved to be one of the most important milestones in Czech history. It was in Prague that his nascent national

consciousness turned into a living force, and he became the most articulate and level-headed spokesman of his nation.

Philosopher and Politician

When making this important move, Masaryk was only 32 but already enjoying a reputation as a philosopher. His philosophy had been inspired chiefly by Plato, whose logic and language taught him to acquire the habit of accuracy necessary for the attainment of his selfdeclared goal of "search for truth" through "realism." For this same reason, and also "to overcome the Slavanarchy in myself," he became interested in such Western thinkers as the British empiricists John Locke and David Hume, whose philosophy he tried to emulate and live by, teaching others to do likewise. Simultaneously, however, he was also fascinated by the Slavic models of social and religious thought (particularly Russian mysticism) and produced his epoch-making *The Spirit of Russia* (1913).

During the 1880s, in addition to writing a number of works on philosophy, Masaryk involved himself in the affairs of the day, propagating his views in the *Athenaeum* and the *Naše Doba* (Our Epoch). It was in the former that he exposed the *Königinhof* (Karlovy Dvur) and *Grünberg* (Zelena Hora) manuscripts, forged 6 decades earlier to prove the alleged preeminence of medieval Czech literary culture over its German counterpart. With this exposure Masaryk earned the hate and abuse of his countrymen but also the respect of the whole scholarly world. This also holds true for his brave denunciation of anti-Semitism in the notorious ritual murder case of Leopold Hilsner (1899), whose trial revived the hoary medieval myth of Jewish ritual sacrifice. It is correct to say, therefore, that Masaryk achieved fame by his unpopularity.

Masaryk's unpopularity did not prevent him from lecturing his countrymen on the form in which life should present itself to the Czech mind. Thus, in a series of essays in the *Naše Doba* (published as *The Czech Question* in 1895), he advocated a return to the humanitarian ideals of the Czech Brethren. Simultaneously, he also dealt with the question of Marxism (*The Philosophical and Sociological Foundation of Marxism, The Social Question,* both 1898). Although he criticized historical materialism, he spoke up for progressive social reform.

Since Masaryk could not dissociate thought from action, he became active in politics and served in the Austrian Reichsrat (1891-1893, 1907-1914) as the representative of his own Realist (later, Progressive) party. Generally, he tried to dissociate himself from the squabbles of the Young and Old Czechs and advocated a human, liberal, and realistic approach to the solution of political questions. Meanwhile he retained his custom of championing unpopular causes, as attested to by the famed Zagreb treason (1908) and Friedjung (1909) trials, where he proved that the government's case against a number of South Slavs rested on forged documents. With this, his worldwide reputation was further enhanced.

Founding Father

Prior to 1914, Masaryk worked for reform within the Hapsburg Empire. The empire's involvement in World War I, however, altered his views diametrically, and he became an advocate of Czech independence. He left Austria in December 1914. Then, relying on his great European fame, and on the aid of such well-known Western critics of the empire as E. Denis, W. Steed, and R. W. Seton-Watson, he launched a campaign of propaganda to convince the Allies of the desirability of carving up Austria-Hungary. Making good use of the propaganda effects of the activities of the "Czechoslovak Legion" in Russia (1917-1918), and coming to terms with the leaders of the Slovak emigration (Pittsburgh Pact, May 30, 1918), he managed to get Allied support for his independence movement (May-June), largely on the basis of his ideas elaborated in his *The New Europe* (1918). On the strength of this support, on Oct. 14, 1918, he declared the independence of Czechoslovakia and a month later (Nov. 14) was elected the new state's first president. *The Making of a State* (1927) is Masaryk's own version of his struggle for the creation of Czechoslovakia.

Masaryk served as president for 17 years, and during this relatively long period he tried to implement his ideas on progress and democracy. Like many others, he was only partially successful. He retired at the age of 85 in December 1935 and died on Sept. 14, 1937, at Lány near Prague.

Further Reading

President Masaryk Tells His Story, recounted by Karel Čapek (trans. 1934), and Čapek's *Masaryk on Thought and Life: Conversations with Karel Čapek* (trans. 1938) are valuable sources. Although there is no definitive study of Masaryk,

there are many popular biographies by British and American authors. The best of these is Paul Selver, *Masaryk: A Biography* (1940); the most recent, Edward W. P. Newman, *Masaryk* (1960). See also Donald A. Lowrie, *Masaryk of Czechoslovakia* (1930; new enlarged ed. 1937); Emil Ludwig, *Defender of Democracy: Masaryk of Czechoslovakia* (1936); Robert Joseph Kerner, *Masaryk* (1938); Victor Cohen, *The Life and Times of Masaryk, the President-Liberator* (1941); R. W. Seton-Watson, *Masaryk in England* (1943); and Robert Birley, *Thomas Masaryk* (1951).

There are no adequate works about Masaryk's philosophy and teachings; W. Preston Warren, *Masaryk's Democracy: A Philosophy of Scientific and Moral Culture* (1941), is the best available treatment. For general historical background C. A. Macartney's monumental *The Habsburg Empire, 1790-1918* (1968) supersedes all previous works. One may also consult with profit Arthur J. May's two works, *The Hapsburg Monarchy, 1867-1914* (1951) and *The Passing of the Hapsburg Monarchy, 1914-1918* (2 vols., 1966), and A. J. P. Taylor, *The Habsburg Monarchy* (1941; new ed. 1948). Robert A. Kann, *The Multinational Empire* (2 vols., 1950), is still the best source covering the nationality problems of the empire. □

Masinissa

Masinissa (240 B.C.-148 B.C.) was Prince of the Massylians, who consolidated the fragmented Numidian tribes, creating a kingdom in North Africa which expanded and thrived in the context of the Punic Wars.

Carthage, a port city on the north coast of Africa in the area of present-day Tunisia and Algeria, was established in 814 b.c. by Phoenician settlers who eventually dominated the local North African farmers and nomads. Phoenician merchants along the Mediterranean coast, settled farmers of the watered plains, and the migrating shepherds of the steppe land bordering the Sahara Desert coexisted with the exchange of both trade and culture. The increasing economic and military power of the unified city-state of Carthage resulted in its domination of the fragmented tribes of the Numidians.

Masinissa was born around 240 b.c. at a time of conflict in the long-standing relationship between the Carthaginians and the local African people. The Numidian tribesmen had provided the Carthaginians with swift, skilled cavalry auxiliaries, sharpened through generations of intertribal conflict; but, following the defeat of Carthage in war against Rome, they were not paid for their services. Rebelling against Carthage, the fragmented Numidian tribes were not able to form a united front against the Carthaginians and soon were dominated once more by their powerful neighbor.

Masinissa's father Gala was the chief of the Massylians—a traditionally nomadic tribe that lived southwest of Carthage—who apparently had established treaties of friendship with Carthage and may have sealed those treaties by his marriage to a Carthaginian woman from a prominent family. Egyptian historian Appian reports that

Masinissa was brought up and educated in the city of Carthage, making him familiar with the combined Phoenician and Greek ideas that formed Carthage's Punic culture. He also learned the traditional skills and wisdom of the nomadic Massylians, such as horsemanship and survival in the desert, and this combined education would later serve him well.

According to the account of Diodorus Siculus, Masinissa, as the heir of an important ally of Carthage, was engaged to marry Sophoniba, the lovely daughter of Hasdrubal Gisgo, a leading Carthaginian general. Following the outbreak of the Second Punic War in 218 b.c., Masinissa led a contingent of Numidian cavalrymen in supporting Hasdrubal against the Romans in Spain. Livy in his famous history reports that the young Masinissa and his Numidian cavalry played a key role in the 212 b.c. defeat of the Roman legions led by Gnaeus and Publius Scipio. After his first campaign, Masinissa returned to Africa in 210 b.c., where he raised an additional force of 5,000 Numidians to support Hasdrubal in Spain.

In 209 b.c., Publius Scipio drove Hasdrubal's Carthaginian forces, which included Masinissa, to flight. Among those captured was the impetuous Massiva, a young nephew of Masinissa who had joined with the cavalry against his uncle's orders. This boy was allowed to return unharmed to his uncle, an action which caused Masinissa to be grateful to Scipio. While the Carthaginian forces were in retreat, Masinissa and a force of 3,000 Numidian horsemen were assigned the task of harrying the Romans throughout Spain, destroying farms and towns that supported their enemy; in 207 b.c., a new Carthaginian offensive was mounted. One Carthaginian force reached into Italy before it was defeated, while another offensive, led by Hasdrubal and supported by Masinissa, was undertaken in Spain. Confronted in 206 b.c. by Scipio's newly reinforced Roman army, Hasdrubal's and Masinissa's forces were defeated and driven to flight, thus diminishing the Carthaginian threat from Spain. Seeing the Carthaginians' change in fortune, Masinissa opened negotiations with the Romans; he then returned to Africa and conferred with tribal leaders on his decision to switch his allegiance to Rome.

With the Romans eager to subvert Carthaginian allies among the Numidians, Scipio courted and won the support of Syphax, the chief of the Masaesylians away from the Carthaginians. Meanwhile, after his conference, Masinissa returned to Gades in Spain and entered into an alliance with Scipio, promising to support him in Africa against Carthage. But Roman senators like Quintus Fabius Maximus were not supportive of Scipio's strategy, wanting him instead to force Hannibal out of Italy before leading an African campaign; such senators assessed Syphax and Masinissa as selfishly desiring supremacy in Africa with the fall of Carthage. The next two years proved frustrating for Masinissa, who was forced to endure the subsequent delay in Scipio's African invasion.

In Masinissa's absence, the leadership of his tribe was usurped by Mazaetullus, leaving Masinissa struggling from 205-203 b.c. to regain his position. Syphax proved an obstacle as well when—entreated by Hasdrubal—he became an ally of Carthage once more, sealing the treaty by marriage to Hasdrubal's daughter Sophoniba to whom Masinissa had been engaged. With limited resources, Masinissa then had to struggle against the combined opposition of Mazaetullus and his ally Syphax. Some loyal veterans of Gala supported Masinissa, and early successes led to an increase of popular support among the Massylians against the superior forces of his opponent. Masinissa defeated Mazaetullus, only to be threatened by Syphax's forces in 204 b.c. and driven into the desert; many of his subjects then submitted to Syphax. Continuing to lead raids from mountain strongholds, Masinissa plundered the territories of Syphax and the Carthaginians until Syphax's forces retaliated, driving Masinissa from his stronghold and wounding him. Masinissa and a handful of survivors charged into a flood-swollen river; swept downstream, they escaped.

After healing from his wounds, Masinissa recruited a new army from among his tribesmen who were amazed at his survival. He established a new base in the mountains between Syphax's fortress capital at Cirta and the coastal city Hippo Regis. Once again, however, his base of operations was seized and Masinissa narrowly escaped. With his surviving horsemen, he fled eastward to Scipio's beachhead in the Lesser Syrtis, collecting local supporters along the way.

Masinissa's fortune changed as he joined Scipio. His Numidian horsemen contributed to the string of victories won by the Roman forces, especially as they acted as the bait to lure opposing forces out of fortified cities into Roman traps.

Though Scipio courted Syphax's defection from the Carthaginians and failed, he successfully devised a plan to disrupt the camps of the huge armies led by their opponents, Hasdrubal and Syphax. Masinissa and his Numidian supporters initiated the subsequent attack, sneaking at night into the camp and starting fires in the huts. In the smoke and confusion, Masinissa's forces created havoc, distracting the sentries of the nearby Carthaginian camp, making it vulnerable to Scipio's attack. While Syphax and Hasdrubal escaped, Livy reports that 40,000 soldiers were killed, 5,000 captured, and large quantities of supplies were secured. This defeat led Carthage's leaders to recall Hannibal from Italy, as they feared an attack on Carthage. Masinissa, supporting Scipio, defeated the briefly reassembled forces of Hasdrubal and Syphax. The survivors of the battle were pursued by a combined Roman and Numidian force west into Masaesylian territory, while Scipio tightened his hold over the southern part of Carthaginian territory.

With his victories, Masinissa consolidated his position among his own people while his opponent Syphax took the brief respite to raise yet another army from his tribal stronghold around the capital at Cirta, an army defeated by the Roman and Allied forces who captured Syphax. Pressing on to Cirta ahead of the Roman legions, Masinissa exhibited Syphax in chains and convinced the city's leading citizens to surrender. Entering the city, he was met by Sophoniba who begged not to be turned over to the Romans. Though Masinissa easily gave his word, it was a promise he would have trouble keeping. According to Livy, he married

Sophoniba that day before the Roman leaders arrived in Cirta. The Roman officers were outraged and disputed Masinissa's decision. Judgment in the case was left to Scipio who was away in the east. Masinissa and the Romans in the west continued to subdue Numidian towns and the forces led by Vermina, a son of Syphax who continued to support Carthage.

Scipio eventually confronted the traitorous Syphax, who blamed his betrayal on the manipulations of Sophoniba and warned that she would likely persuade Masinissa to go over to the Carthaginians. As a result, Scipio later took Masinissa aside, commending his achievements but proclaiming that, charged with subverting an ally, Sophoniba should be sent for trial in Rome. Distraught, Masinissa pleaded unsuccessfully. After agonizing over what to do, he sent a faithful servant with poison to his new wife, with hopes of keeping the promise he had made, that he would not turn her over to the Romans. Sophoniba chose to commit suicide. While upset by Masinissa's action, Scipio was eager to keep Masinissa as a Roman ally and personal friend. In a public ceremony, Scipio proclaimed Masinissa as "King of the Numidians" and gave him gifts symbolic of his new rank.

The Roman Senate's affirmation cemented the relationship and Masinissa loyally threw his efforts behind the Romans. A shrewd politician among his own people, Masinissa requested and secured the release of many Numidians who had been captured. The new king then led a contingent of 6,000 cavalry and 4,000 infantry east to Zama where Scipio faced Hannibal and the forces which Carthage had recalled to Africa. In the ensuing battle, Masinissa led the allied Numidian horsemen on the right side of the battle formation and succeeded in disbursing the opposing cavalry. The collapse of Hannibal's formidable forces led Carthage to seek an armistice. In mopping-up operations, Masinissa defeated Vermina and others who challenged his authority.

Following the battle at Zama, Scipio—nearing the end of his term in office—was eager to complete a treaty with the Carthaginians. The terms of the treaty were nonetheless very demanding, and included provision for Scipio's protégé Masinissa. After the provisions for war reparations and arms limitations came an absolute restriction on the Carthaginian's right to wage war without the consent of Rome, and a demand that they live at peace with Masinissa and the Numidians. In his settlement, Scipio gave Masinissa the city of Cirta and the whole realm of Syphax as well as rule over the Massylians.

Now master of all Numidia and free of Carthaginian interference, Masinissa took advantage of his status as an ally of Rome in the postwar situation. He consolidated his position by promoting the economic well-being of his subjects, which won their loyalty. Over time, he promoted the growth of settled farms whose produce supplied Rome with food and brought money into Numidia, while economic growth was also facilitated by coinage minted bearing Masinissa's image. Numidia's prosperity was benefited by the long peaceful rule of their king.

Increasing his territory and power while gaining a reputation as a consummate ally of Rome, he encroached on the fertile land of the Badradus river valley and prosperous towns of the Carthaginians along the border, claiming them as ancestral lands. Under the provisions of the peace treaty, Carthage was unable to retaliate and so appealed to Rome. In 193 b.c., a Roman commission examined the case of the Carthaginians, but found in favor of Masinissa. Further appeals were made in 182, 174, and 162 b.c. as Masinissa seized more land, territory he was never forced to return. Some have since shown Masinissa as a clever politician making his incursions in times of Roman displeasure with Carthage, which led them to ignore his offenses.

Frustrated by the Roman decisions, the Carthaginians eventually violated the treaty of 201 b.c. and attacked Numidia in 149. Masinissa, though quite aged, directed a successful counteroffensive in a dispute recognized by classical authors as the immediate cause of the Third Punic War. Charging a breach in the peace treaty of 201 b.c., the Romans declared war and Appian reports that the elderly Masinissa was offended that he was not consulted or asked to participate in the formulation of Roman war plans. In 148 b.c., during the early stages of the war, Masinissa died, leaving his successors to support the Roman effort which would destroy Carthage two years later in 146 b.c.

As a client-king, Masinissa achieved a great deal in the shadow of Rome. While our accounts of his life come from sources that focus on the Romans, it is clear that he created a nation in a large geographic region inhabited by nomadic tribesmen and settled farmers. An inspiring general, always willing to ride into battle, and a shrewd politician, who could manipulate diplomatic situations for his nation's benefit, Masinissa was given the title of king by the Romans. Among the Numidians, he had earned it.

Further Reading

Appian. *Appian's Roman History*. Translated by Horace White (Loeb Classical Library). 4 vols. Harvard University Press, 1964.

Siculus, Diodorus. *Diodorus of Sicily*. Translated by C. H. Oldfather (Loeb Classical Library). 10 vols. Harvard University Press, 1966.

Livy. *Livy*. Translated by Frank Gardner Moore (Loeb Classical Library). 14 vols. Harvard University Press, 1971.

Polybius. *The Histories*. Translated by W. R. Paton (Loeb Classical Library). 6 vols. William Heinemann, 1922.

Law, R. C. C. "North Africa in the Hellenistic and Roman Periods, 325 b.c. to a.d. 305," in *The Cambridge History of Africa*. Vol. II. Cambridge University Press, 1984.

Mackendrick, Paul. *North African Stones Speak*. University of North Carolina Press, 1980.

Raven, Susan. *Rome in Africa*. Routledge, 1992.

Saumagne, Charles. *La Numidie et Rome: Masinissa et Jugurtha*. Presses Universitaires de France, 1966.

Walsh, P. "Masinissa," in *Journal of Roman Studies*. Vol. 55. 1965.

Warmington, J. "The Carthaginian Period," in *UNESCO: General History of Africa*. Vol. II. Edited by G. Mokhtar, University of California Press, 1981. □

Quett Ketumile Masire

Quett Ketumile Masire (born 1925) was a leading nationalist politician during Botswana's transition to independence. As the nation's first vice-president he played a key role in making his country a model of economic development in Africa. From 1980-1997 he served as Botswana's president.

Quett Masire was born on July 23, 1925, at Kanye, the capital of the Bangwaketse Reserve, Bechuanaland Protectorate (now Botswana). Son of a minor headman, he grew up in a community where male commoners, such as himself, were expected to become low-paid migrant laborers in the mines of South Africa. From an early age Masire set himself apart through academic achievement. After graduating at the top of his class at the Kanye school, he received a scholarship to further his education at the Tiger Kloof Institute in South Africa. During school breaks he supported himself by selling refreshments at local football matches. Despite continued good grades, his ambition to attend university was frustrated by financial and health constraints.

In 1950, after graduating from Tiger Kloof, Masire helped found the Seepapitso II Secondary School, the first institution of higher learning in the Bangwaketse Reserve. He served as the school's headmaster for five years. During this period he clashed with Bathoen II, the autocratic Bangwaketse ruler. Resenting Bathoen's many petty interferences in school affairs, Masire, working through the revived Bechuanaland African Teachers Association, became an advocate for the autonomy of protectorate schools from chiefly authority.

In 1957 Masire earned a Master Farmers Certificate and established himself as one of the territory's leading agriculturalists. His success led to renewed conflict with the jealous Bathoen, who seized his farms as a penalty for the supposed infraction of fencing communal land. When Masire challenged this decision, the chief went further by threatening his banishment. By now the public, as well as leading members of the colonial administration, looked upon Masire as an articulate critic of the dominant role of chiefs over local politics.

In 1958 Masire was appointed as the protectorate reporter for the *African Echo/Naledi ya Botswana* newspaper. He was also elected to the newly reformed Bangwaketse Tribal Council and, after 1960, the protectorate-wide African and Legislative Councils. Although he attended the first Kanye meeting of the People's Party, the earliest nationalist grouping to enjoy a mass following in the territory, he declined to join the movement. Instead, in 1961 and 1962, he helped organize the rival Democratic Party, serving as its secretary-general.

From the beginning the Democratic Party was dominated by Seretse Khama, its popular leader, and Masire, its chief organizer. One of the principal reasons for the party's early electoral success was Masire's energy; in one two-week period in 1964, for example, while campaigning in remote areas of the Kalahari desert, he traveled across some 3,000 miles of sandy tracks to address 24 meetings. Besides spreading his party's message, he used such junkets to build up a strong network of local party organizers, many of whom were teachers and/or master farmers. He also was the editor of the party's newspaper, *Therisanyo*, which was the protectorate's first independent newspaper.

In 1965 the Democratic Party won 28 of the 31 contested seats in the new Legislative Assembly, giving it a clear mandate to lead Botswana to independence. The following year Masire became the new nation's vice-president, serving under Seretse. Until 1980 he also occupied the significant portfolios of finance (from 1966) and development planning (from 1967), which were formally merged in 1971.

As a principal architect of Botswana's steady economic and infastructural growth between 1966 and 1980, Masire earned a reputation as a highly competent technocrat. However, his local Bangwaketse political base was eroded by his old nemesis Bathoen. During the initial years of independence the Democratic Party government moved decisively to undercut many of the residual powers of the chiefs. As a result, in 1969 Bathoen abdicated, only to reemerge as the leader of the opposition National Front. This set the stage for Bathoen's local electoral victory over Masire during the same year. However, the ruling party won decisively at the national level, thus allowing Masire to maintain his position as one of the four "specially elected" members of Parliament.

With the death of Seretse in July of 1980, Masire became Botswana's second president. His leadership was subsequently confirmed by Democratic Party landslides in the 1984 and 1989 general elections. Under his leadership Botswana continued to enjoy its remarkable post-independence economic growth rate of some 10 percent per annum, one of the highest in the world. Most of this growth came from diamonds, the nation's leading export earner. Expanded revenues allowed Masire's administration to expand social services considerably, particularly in the areas of education, health, and communications. Perhaps the greatest tribute to Masire's leadership was the award he received in 1989 from the Hunger Project in recognition of the improvement in nutritional levels throughout the country between 1981 and 1988, despite the onset of severe drought.

Despite Botswana's enviable record of development during the decade of the 1980s, many problems remained. Although most citizens benefited from the nation's prosperity, the gap between the small but growing middle class and the much larger number of unemployed or underemployed poor posed a significant challenge. Throughout his career Masire sought to create jobs and wealth through the promotion of a strong private sector, but heretofore the economy has been dominated by a handful of capital-intensive parastatal companies.

Another continuing challenge was relations with South Africa. Botswana consistently championed the cause of majority rule there but, while granting asylum to refugees from apartheid, refused to allow its territory to be used as a base for guerrilla attacks against its powerful neighbor. Despite this stand, the 1980s witnessed an upsurge in South African acts of aggression against Botswana. Contacts between Afrikaners and anti-apartheid groups within the country in the early 1990s, however, underscored the potential of Masire's efforts to help mediate a negotiated end to white minority rule there.

Yet this was not the only problem he faced during the turbulent 1990s; he had his people's hunger, education and welfare problems. In 1996, the United States agreed to give $203 million in aid over three decades. In September, 1995 AID (Agency for International Development) had shuttered its bilateral mission in Botswana, asserting the nation had "graduated" from foreign assistance. According to Masire, it was a rite of passage the nation had been preparing for all along. "We used to say to our donors, 'Help us to help ourselves, and the more you help us, the sooner you will get rid of us,'" he recalled.

The U.S. funds paid for more than 300 business owners to bone up on finance, marketing and other subjects. For the smallest and neediest, AID helped set up the Women's Finance House, offering training, savings accounts and loans of up to $1,700 to poor female entrepreneurs. For an example, a seamstress turned to it when she received an order for 101 outfits for a large wedding. The fabric alone cost three times what she made in most months. With a $400 loan, however, she completed the order.

Masire was the 1989 Laureate of the Africa Prize for Leadership for the Sustainable End of Hunger, and was cited for his sustaining efforts to develop nutrition, health, education and housing.

Further Reading

There are no biographies of Quett Masire. Fred Morton, Andrew Murray, and Jeff Ramsay, *Historical Dictionary of Botswana* (1989) is a useful reference and provides an up-to-date bibliography. Fred Morton and Jeff Ramsay, editors, *Birth of Botswana, A History of the Bechuanaland Protectorate, 1910-1930* (Botswana: 1987) traces modern political history but is not found in many American libraries. Somewhat dated but useful is Christopher Colclough and Stephen McCarthy, *The Political Economy of Botswana* (Oxford University Press: 1980). □

George Mason

The American statesman George Mason (1725-1792) wrote the Virginia Declaration of Rights and persistently advocated safeguarding the rights of individuals during the formative years of the republic.

George Mason was born in Virginia, son of a wealthy planter. He inherited several large estates along the Potomac River and became a friend and neighbor of George Washington. He married Ann Eilbeck in 1750 and soon was performing the tasks incumbent on a gentleman planter—justice of the peace, vestryman, and county delegate in the House of Burgesses. He speculated in land and became expert in colonial land law. In 1773 he became a widower with nine children. Despondent for months, he turned his attention to the growing Revolutionary crisis. A year later his Fairfax Resolves set the tone for Virginia's resistance to British domination.

Mason preferred to advise statesmen rather than be one. He served in the 1775 Virginia convention and so impressed fellow delegates that he was selected to the Continental Congress delegation. He declined to serve, as he steadfastly avoided higher offices in his reluctant role as a Revolutionary statesman.

At the 1776 Virginia convention Mason's drafts of the Declaration of Rights and the constitution emerged as models for other colonies turned states. Though ill, Mason was hardworking and helped write key legislation in the state assembly. Between 1776 and 1780 his bills for western land sales were designed to erase the public debt. In 1780 he outlined a plan which evolved into the western land cession act that eventually created the Northwest Territory.

Mason remarried and after the Revolution turned to his family and his fields. At the urging of friends he served at the Mount Vernon Convention of 1785 but avoided the Annapolis Convention. He went to the Federal Constitutional Convention of 1787, convinced that the Revolution and "the Formations of our new Governments at that time, were nothing compared to the great Business now before us". Though some of his suggestions in the Federal Constitutional Convention seemed to favor southern interests, his

James Murray Mason

James Murray Mason (1798-1871), U.S. Senator and Confederate diplomat, is best known for his authorship of the 1850 Fugitive Slave Law and his Confederate mission to England.

James M. Mason was born on Nov. 3, 1798, at Georgetown, D.C. After an excellent elementary education, he graduated from the University of Pennsylvania in 1818. He studied law at the College of William and Mary and established his law practice at Winchester, Va., in 1820.

During the 1820s Mason served in the Virginia Legislature. In 1837 he served one term in the U.S. Congress as a Jacksonian Democrat. The Virginia Legislature selected him for the Senate in 1847.

In Washington, Mason associated with the most prominent Southern Rights Democrats, especially John C. Calhoun. It is not surprising that Mason drafted the famous Fugitive Slave Law of 1850 or that he read Calhoun's speech to the Senate on the proposed compromise measures. When Abraham Lincoln was elected president in 1860, Mason argued for Southern secession. For Mason, the "irrepressible conflict" was between two social and economic civilizations, one agrarian and the other industrial. Slavery, advocated by Mason, was only one part of the Southern civilization.

attack on slave importation showed that he could place humanitarianism beyond local concerns.

Many details in the approved Constitution, such as the mandatory origin of tax bills in the House, bore testimony to Mason's persistence. He refused to sign the Constitution, however, and worked indefatigably for its revision prior to a final ratification. He and Patrick Henry almost brought the ratification process to a standstill in Virginia, but after the Federal Bill of Rights was adopted, Mason conceded that with a few more alterations "I could chearfully put my hand & heart to the new government." He died at his plantation home, Gunston Hall, on Oct. 7, 1792.

Further Reading

The Papers of George Mason, 1725-1796 was edited by Robert A. Rutland (3 vols., 1970). There is no thorough study of Mason's life. The standard work is Kate Mason Rowland, *The Life of George Mason* (1892). Interpretive studies are Helen Hill [Miller], *George Mason: Constitutionalist* (1938), and Robert A. Rutland, *George Mason: Reluctant Statesman* (1961).

Additional Sources

Rutland, Robert Allen, *George Mason and the War for Independence,* Williamsburg, Va.: Virginia Independence Bicentennial Commission, 1976.

Rutland, Robert Allen, *George Mason, reluctant statesman,* Baton Rouge: Louisiana State University Press, 1980 1961. □

Confederate president Jefferson Davis appointed Mason diplomatic commissioner to England in 1861. Mason had great personal charm, despite his critics' charge that he was untidy and chewed tobacco and spat on the floor of Parliament. He possessed impressive qualifications: a clear position on the issue of Southern rights, a conciliatory demeanor, high social connections, and 10 years as chairman of the Senate Foreign Relations Committee. The U.S. Navy's seizure of Mason and John Slidell, Confederate commissioner to France, while they were aboard the British ship *Trent* caused a serious diplomatic crisis between the United States and England. In January 1862 Mason and Slidell were released and resumed their mission.

Mason was never received officially by the British government, and he obtained only three interviews with British officials, all as a private citizen. He cultivated friendships with powerful political and economic figures, acted as a central purchasing agent for the Confederacy, cooperated with propagandists, and promoted the sale of Confederate bonds. Yet his primary mission, to persuade the British to recognize and aid the Confederacy, was singularly unsuccessful.

After the Civil War, Mason fled to Canada. In 1868 he returned to Virginia and settled near Alexandria, where he died on April 28, 1871.

Further Reading

The only attempt to treat Mason's life is Virginia Mason, *The Public Life and Diplomatic Correspondence of James M. Mason with Some Personal History* (1903). Charles Francis Adams, *The Trent Affair* (1912), is useful for this aspect of his life. □

Lowell Mason

Lowell Mason (1792-1872), American music educator, tune-book compiler, and composer, was called the "father of singing among the children." He was the outstanding American music educator for over half a century and was the leading reformer of American church music.

Lowell Mason, born in Medfield, Mass., on Jan. 8, 1792, was basically self-taught in music. At the age of 13 he learned the rudiments from a local schoolmaster, and he directed singing schools in the area while still a teen-ager. Moving to Savannah, Ga., in 1812, he served as organist-choirmaster of the Independent Presbyterian Church while earning his living as a bank clerk. He also began to study harmony and composition.

By 1820 Mason had compiled a collection of psalm and hymn tunes in which he utilized many melodies then popular in England, some snippets from such masters as Handel, Haydn, and Mozart, and a few of his own compositions. The collection was published anonymously as *The Boston Handel and Haydn Society Collection of Church Music* (1822), and its success (it went through 22 editions and sold more than 50,000 copies) led Mason to Boston in 1827.

Influenced by the theories of Johann Pestalozzi, Mason began teaching children's music classes in 1829, and in 1833 he founded the Boston Academy of Music. Music was introduced into the Boston public school system in 1838 as a direct result. Mason served as Boston's superintendent of music until 1845.

Teacher training was also a matter of concern to Mason. Out of his experiences in the academy grew the idea of a "musical convention," a crash course in musical pedagogics. By 1850 some 1,500 teachers from all over the country were flocking to Boston for 5 days of lectures and music making under Mason's direction, and musical conventions in other cities were almost as popular. Out of the musical convention grew the idea, in 1853, of the "normal musical institute," which was to provide still more comprehensive training.

In 1853, after a 15-month visit to Europe, Mason moved to New York City. He devoted his later years primarily to compiling collections of music for religious and educational purposes and to writing and teaching. He died in Orange, N.J., on Aug. 11, 1872.

More than a hundred compilations bear Mason's name. Among the most popular are *The Boston Academy's Collection of Church Music* (1835), *The Boston School Song Book* (1840), and *Carmina Sacra* (1841). Mason's most important writings are the *Address on Church Music* (1826),

Manual of the Boston Academy of Music (1843), and *Musical Letters from Abroad* (1853).

Further Reading

The best biography of Mason is Arthur Lowndes Rich, *Lowell Mason* (1946), which also contains a comprehensive catalog of his works. A complete listing of Mason's original hymn tunes and hymn-tune arrangements is in Henry L. Mason, *Hymn Tunes of Lowell Mason* (1944). Mason's career in sacred music is discussed in Frank J. Metcalf, *American Writers and Compilers of Sacred Music* (1925), and Robert Stevenson, *Protestant Church Music in America* (1966).

Additional Sources

Pemberton, Carol A. (Carol Ann), *Lowell Mason: his life and work,* Ann Arbor, Mich.: UMI Research Press, 1985. □

Massasoit

Massasoit (died 1661) was a principal leader of the Wampanoag people in the early 1600s who encouraged friendship with English settlers. As leader of the Wampanoag, Massasoit exercised control over a number of Indian groups that occupied lands from Narragansett Bay to Cape Cod in present-day Massachusetts.

I n concluding his article on Massasoit for the *Dictionary of American Biography,* James Truslow Adams sums up the standard view of this influential New England chief: "Always inclined to peace, even among his own race, Massassoit remained a faithful friend to the English throughout his entire life." Though there is a large measure of truth to this opinion, along with generations of schoolbooks presenting a eupeptic and rather bland portrait of Massasoit, it also misses many of the likely conflicts both within this powerful Indian leader and swirling about him.

Massasoit and the Pilgrims

As to the bare facts of the matter, from his home village in Pokanoket, near present-day Bristol, Rhode Island, Massasoit held sway over a number of related tribes in southeastern New England. Some months after the Pilgrims arrived in Plymouth in 1620, the Indian leader appeared in the new colony and offered friendship. After some negotiations, the chief signed a peace treaty with the English, one vowing nonaggression and mutual defense in case either were attacked. It was a treaty and a friendship that Massasoit would keep for the next 40 years of his life.

Over the decades, the two groups exchanged amiable visits. When Massasoit took ill, Plymouth sent emissaries on the two-day trek through the forest to Pokanoket to help cure their ally. On several occasions, Massasoit or his fellow Wampanoags probably saved the colonists from slaughter by warning them of mischief brewing in warring tribes. When Roger Williams, a renegade religious thinker forced

out of the rigid theocracy of the English towns, appeared cold and starving at Massasoit's door, the chief took the desperate man in and made him welcome.

Little is known personally of Massasoit except that he was physically vigorous and when treating with the whites "grave of countenance and spare of speech." Still, as might be expected, when in March of 1621 the great chief first appeared at the head of 60 warriors, face painted red and wearing a thick necklace of white beads, the sign of his authority, on a hill overlooking the hovels of tiny Plymouth, striking fear into the little band of Europeans huddled below, much more was going on than the beginning of friendship between a good-souled Anglophile holding out the olive branch and the English settlers eager to return the gesture to their new Indian brothers.

For his part, despite his authority, Massasoit was in a threatened state. Disease had recently swept through the tribe, ravaging his people. And he had enemies eager to take advantage of the sharp reduction in the number of his warriors. To the west, across Rhode Island's Narragansett Bay roved the powerful Narragansett tribe, eager to slaughter both Massasoit and the Wampanoags. To the east, the English, whatever their troubles, were rumored to have valuable trade goods and strange, new, fire-breathing weapons. Caught in the middle, then, between his traditional enemies to the west and the English on the coast to the east, Massasoit may well have thought he had little choice than to throw in his lot with the potentially helpful newcomers.

As to the situation of the English, when the Mayflower sailed back to England in the winter of 1620, it left behind a group of men, women, and children almost totally unprepared to deal with the realities of their new situation in a wild land. Around them as they shivered in their brush huts against the New England cold was the ''howling wilderness,'' an endless, impenetrable forest full of, so they had heard, bloodthirsty savages, wolves, and, some thought, devils. The new settlers knew neither how to hunt, fish, plant, or build adequate shelters. They had few supplies to carry them through to spring. In their grinding circumstances, staying alive itself became the foremost issue. One by one they started dying of malnutrition, disease, and gnawing hunger. Only half of them survived that first winter, and those who remained, weakened, confused, had little hope for the future. It seemed they would soon all be gone, dying thousands of miles from home on this wild, foreign shore, their bones dragged into the forest by the fierce beasts who would consume their dead flesh.

Thus, when Massasoit and his 60 warriors stepped out of the wilderness and stood on the hilltop fearsomely looking down on Plymouth, and the few able-bodied colonists left scrambled for their guns, then slowly realized they were confronting not enemies capable of killing off the remainder of the weakened settlers but friendly human beings who would give them food in exchange for baubles and, on top of that, help protect them against marauding tribes, Massasoit seemed a Godsend, a blessing sent by Providence.

Massasoit and Squanto

What we have, then, in this meeting is not so much two human groups coming together in mutual benignity but in pledged cooperation, each for its own, self-serving advantages. Actually, the situation was far more convoluted than the immediate interactions of these two, small groups, and to catch the complexities requires some comment on the historical background behind the meeting of Massasoit and the colonists. Insights into this can be seen in the related story of Squanto, famous to schoolchildren for helping the Plymouth settlers even before the friendship with Massasoit began.

Years before, in 1614, an English sea captain had kidnapped a number of Indians in the area where the Plymouth colonists would later land and sold them as slaves in Spain. Through a fantastic turn of events, monks ransomed Squanto, who made his way to England and from there gained passage to his homeland. To his dismay, however, upon his arrival Squanto found his home village abandoned, ravaged by disease. Tribeless, he became a subject of Massasoit. When a year later the Pilgrims arrived, Squanto stepped out of the forest to greet them in English, and through his woodcraft he helped them survive their harsh conditions. Squanto's earlier friendship, then, helped ease the way for the friendship of the far more powerful Massasoit. Whatever the twists and turns of Squanto's story, it illustrates a larger set of negative circumstances. European contact with the Indians in the New England area had gone on for decades before the colonists set foot on Plymouth

Rock, and it often was not kindly. Not only kidnappings and other violence took place between the sea captains and fishermen touching the New England shore and the Indians they met, but the Europeans unwittingly introduced diseases, among them smallpox, typhus, and measles. Lacking immunity to the new maladies, whole Indian villages fell before wave on wave of virulent epidemics sweeping up and down the coast. Understandably, most of the Indians, even those who had not yet seen white men, considered the newcomers to be both ruthless deprecators and bearers of deadly illnesses. In short, Indian societies already were in an unfriendly turmoil upon the colonist's arrival, and in light of this Massasoit's friendship was the decided exception.

Given the problems, despite some earnest efforts at good will, such as Massasoit's, the situation almost inevitably became worse. New colonists starting other settlements cared nothing about an old, carefully nurtured friendship. Land-poor in Europe, they had not pulled up stakes and risked the dangerous, months-long voyage across the stormy Atlantic Ocean to be restrained upon their arrival. What they wanted was land of their own, land that seemed theirs for the taking, except for the obstacles the native peoples, waxing ever fiercer in their resistance as the pressures of the invasion increased, represented. Further complicating the situation was the diversity of the settlers and the consequent rivalry among them. Originally conceived as a religious community with central and, hence, consistent authority, Plymouth soon found itself assailed by Englishmen with a variety of often conflicting sacred and secular notions. In light of the turmoil within the white community itself, it was impossible to carry out a humane and consistent policy toward the Indians. Massive, bloody conflict was all but inevitable.

In the face of these building pressures and loss of land to the new colonists, Massasoit kept mending his good relations with the whites. In hindsight, depending on the perspective one wishes to take, the chief of the Wampanoags might be seen as exchanging his people's birthright for the trade goods, renown, and personal power he gained against the enemy Narragansetts through his associations with the whites. Whatever one's view, however, in Massasoit's friendship lies one of the grand ironies of New England history. Massasoit had taken a minority position by casting his fortunes with the English. As pressures against the Indians mounted, many of them resolved to unite and either drive out the invaders or die in the attempt. In this the peacemaker Massasoit became an unwilling instrument. Fourteen years after his death, his son Philip angrily burst into patriotic fervor and flew to the opposite extreme of his father by becoming the leader of what is known as King Philip's War, the bloodiest Indian-white conflict to rake New England.

Further Reading

Adams, James Truslow, ''Massasoit,'' in *Dictionary of American Biography*, Volume 6, Part 2, New York, Scribner's, 1933; 380-381.
Biographical Dictionary of Indians of the Americas, Volume 1, Newport Beach, American Indian Publishers, 1991; 400-401.

Peirce, Ebenezer W., *Indian History, Biography, and Genealogy: Pertaining to the Good Sachem Massasoit,* North Abington, Zerviah Gould Mitchell, 1878.

Weeks, Alvin Gardner, *Massasoit of the Wampanoags,* Fall River, privately printed, 1919.

Wood, Norman B., *Lives of Famous Indian Chiefs,* Aurora, American Indian Historical Publishing Company, 1906; 65-84. ☐

William Ferguson Massey

William Ferguson Massey (1856-1925) was a New Zealand political leader and prime minister. His talent for administration saw his country through World War I and led New Zealand to economic recovery.

Williiam Ferguson Massey was born in the village of Limavady a few miles from Londonderry, Ireland, on March 26, 1856. In 1870 he followed his father to New Zealand, where he gained farming experience and by 1890 had set himself up near Auckland as a small farmer. He took to politics as a spokesman for the small farmers and was elected to Parliament in 1894. For 18 years he sat on the opposition benches with the independent Conservatives and was elected opposition leader in September 1903. In February 1909 he announced that his party would thenceforth be known as the Reform party, and in 1912 he emerged from the political confusion to form a government, though lacking a clear majority of seats, and remained in office until his death 13 years later.

During World War I Massey showed his ability in organizing the country for the crisis. In August 1915 he led the Reform party into a coalition with the Liberal party under Sir Joseph Ward, leaving a small Labour minority as the opposition. Both Ward and Massey went to England twice to attend meetings of the imperial War Cabinet, and after the war Massey represented New Zealand at the peace conference.

Massey did not work easily with Ward, who was minister of finance and not inclined to accept a subordinate role, and in 1919 the coalition was dissolved. At the election in December the Reform party won a substantial majority, and Massey was able for the first time to govern without maneuvering among the other parties. He retained his majority in the election of 1922. In 1923 he was able to effect large reductions in income tax and a return to penny postage, but his health was failing, and he died at Wellington on May 10, 1925, just before an election in which his party was to triumph yet again.

Massey was a large man with a homespun appearance and was an effective, if harsh and verbose, speaker. He was devoted to politics and was in some ways stubborn and narrow in outlook, but he gave the impression of sincerity, was respected by his opponents, and was admired for his courage, tenacity, and political acumen.

Further Reading

For information on Massey's career see L. C. Webb, *Rise of the Reform Party* (1928), and W. D. Bell, *Sir Francis Bell* (1937). See also J. C. Beaglehole, *New Zealand: A Short History* (1936); A. H. Reed, *The Story of New Zealand* (1955); and Keith Sinclair, *A History of New Zealand* (1959; rev. ed. 1969). Information on New Zealand politics can be found in R. S. Milne, *Political Parties in New Zealand* (1966). ☐

Philip Massinger

The English playwright Philip Massinger (1583-1640) was a productive dramatist, although much of his energy was devoted to collaboration and revision. His most distinctive work reflects a religious and moral earnestness but somewhat limited powers of characterization.

Philip Massinger was born in Salisbury, southern England. He was the son of Arthur Massinger, a trusted and responsible servant to the prominent Herbert family and at one time a fellow of Merton College, Oxford. Philip attended Oxford for 2 or 3 years but apparently left without a degree. Nothing else is known of his activities before 1613, when he began his association with the London stage.

During the first phase of his career as a dramatic writer, from about 1613 to 1625, Massinger worked for the most part in collaboration with other dramatists, particularly John Fletcher. Fletcher was one of the most popular dramatists of the Jacobean period, and after Shakespeare's death in 1616 he became the leading playwright of the King's Men. At his own death in 1625, he was succeeded by Massinger, who continued to write regularly for the same company for the next 15 years, occasionally rewriting or revising earlier plays of Fletcher.

Massinger's best-known plays are *A New Way to Pay Old Debts,* a comedy written in 1621 or 1622, and *The Roman Actor,* a tragedy written in 1626.

A New Way to Pay Old Debts relies heavily on Thomas Middleton's *A Trick to Catch the Old One* (1608). Its chief character, however, is closely modeled on the notorious Sir Giles Mompesson, an extortioner convicted in 1621. Massinger's character, called Sir Giles Overreach, is driven to insanity when he is outsmarted by his nephew Frank Wellborn, whose property he has acquired by devious means.

The Roman Actor, which Massinger considered his finest work, is based on the life of the Roman emperor Domitian, who was murdered in A.D. 96. Although Massinger makes much of the Emperor's inhuman cruelty and insatiable lust, the play is remarkably modest and restrained, at least by Jacobean standards. The title character, the noble and talented actor Paris, defends his profession—as well as the drama generally—as a force for social and

moral good. This was evidently a doctrine which Massinger shared with other literary artists of the period, who found themselves under increasing attack from Puritan moralists.

Details about Massinger's personal life are lacking, but he seems to have led a quieter and more comfortable existence than most of his fellow playwrights. Although never as popular as Fletcher or Jonson, he was patronized by several persons of distinction. He died in London, where he had spent most of his adult life, early in 1640.

Further Reading

The best biography of Massinger is Thomas A. Dunn, *Philip Massinger: The Man and the Playwright* (1957). □

Quentin Massys

The paintings of the Flemish artist Quentin Massys (c. 1465-1530) hark back to the works of his great predecessors but at the same time show an awareness of the Italian art of his own period.

Quentin Massys, also spelled Matsys or Metsys, was born in Louvain, the son of a blacksmith. He is traditionally thought to have been trained in that craft by his father. Art in Louvain while Massys was growing up was dominated by Dirk Bouts. Massys became a member of the painters' guild in Antwerp in 1491 and died there in 1530. He represented a current of painting that flourished in Antwerp at this time of its sudden new prosperity. Erwin Panofsky (1953) described this trend, "archaism of around 1500," as "a prelude to, in fact a fact of, the Renaissance in Netherlandish painting," which prevailed in the southern Netherlands.

The monumental *Enthroned Madonna* (Brussels), an early work by Massys, has features recalling both Robert Campin and Jan van Eyck. The central panel of Massys' imposing *St. Anne Altarpiece,* or the *Holy Kinship* (Brussels), which was commissioned for the church of St-Pierre in Louvain in 1507 and signed and dated 1509, has a prototype in the *Holy Kinship* of Geertgen tot Sint Jans. Even the physical types and costumes in Massys' version refer to Geertgen's. But Massys placed his rhythmically balanced figure groups in a domed, arcaded loggia that in architectural style appears to be reaching for a Renaissance vocabulary it cannot quite attain; certainly the architecture evokes a later period than that represented by the Gothic throne of the *Enthroned Madonna.*

The calm and restraint of the *St. Anne Altarpiece* are replaced by heightened emotional expression in the next important painting by Massys that can be firmly dated, the *Deposition* triptych (Antwerp). This was commissioned in 1508 by the guild of joiners in Antwerp for their chapel in the Cathedral; Massys completed the composition in 1511. It was inspired by Rogier van der Weyden's great *Deposition,* which was in the church of St-Pierre in Louvain in Massys' time, and also quotes from Rogier's *Entombment.*

River Anthology," a collection of free verse about small-town American life.

Massys painted genre subjects, possibly with emblematic meaning, such as *A Money Changer and His Wife,* which belonged to a Netherlandish tradition that maintained its popularity right through the 17th century. In portraiture he made significant contributions. His pair of portraits of Erasmus and Petrus Aegidius, painted in 1517 for Sir Thomas More, set the pattern for representations of the scholar in his study.

The physiognomic types and soft modeling in some of Massy's late paintings, particularly Madonnas, as well as the grotesque quality of some of his portraits, have led to the supposition that he was familiar with works by Leonardo da Vinci. The Renaissance types of architecture and ornament with which Massys embellished his later works give proof of his interest in the new developments in Italian art, which, however, always remained foreign to him.

Further Reading

Massys is dealt with in Max J. Friedlaender, *From Van Eyck to Bruegel: Early Netherlandish Painting* (1921; trans. 1956; rev. ed. 1965), and Erwin Panofsky, *Early Netherlandish Painting, Its Origins and Character* (2 vols., 1953). □

Edgar Lee Masters

Edgar Lee Masters (1869-1950), American author and lawyer, is mainly remembered for his "Spoon

E dgar Lee Masters was born on Aug. 23, 1869, in Garnett, Kans. A year later his father's law practice failed and the family moved to the grandfather's Illinois farm. Edgar's father won appointment as state's attorney in Petersburg, and there the young boy started school. In 1880 the family moved to Lewistown near the Spoon River. Masters continued his schooling, worked in a printer's office, and reported for local newspapers. He read James Cullen Bryant, Edgar Allan Poe, Robert Burns, and Percy Bysshe Shelley, wrote poetry, and read law in his father's office. In 1889 he entered Knox College, but his father refused help, so he returned to law in Lewistown. Admitted to the bar in 1891, in 1892 he left for Chicago.

Masters entered a law partnership in 1893 and succeeded professionally, socially, and financially. He married Helen Jenkins in 1898 and published *A Book of Verse.* He was active in Democratic party politics, traveled west in 1904, and in 1906 toured Europe. He contributed to *Reedy's Mirror* and met novelist Theodore Dreiser. Masters's next two volumes—*The Blood of the Prophets* (1905) and *Songs and Sonnets* (1910)—were published under pseudonyms. Between 1907 and 1911 he wrote four plays. When his second law partner defaulted in 1910, Masters set up his own office. When *Poetry* magazine started publication in Chicago in 1912, he joined its coterie, meeting Carl Sandburg and others.

Masters's *Spoon River Anthology* (1915) drew on the values and frustrations of his youth in Lewistown, the style of the *Greek Anthology,* and contemporary experiments in free verse or rhythmical prose. In it, Masters reveals the spiritual impoverishment of the small midwestern town as its dead speak of their repressed, frightened, hypocritical, stoical, and occasionally fulfilled lives and sometimes contrast hardy pioneer days with the decadent present. The book was immediately controversial.

Masters's next volume of poems, *Domesday Book,* appeared in 1920, as did the first of seven novels, *Mitch Miller.* Meanwhile his two careers, law and literature, the breakup of the Chicago literary movement, and his wife's refusal to grant a divorce were bringing his life to a crisis. Finding no relief in a 1921 Mediterranean vacation, he abandoned both family and the law and moved to New York to concentrate on literature. Divorced in 1923, in 1924 he brought out *The New Spoon River,* an unsuccessful treatment of American urban life.

Masters married again in 1926 and published the first of a series of historical verse plays. In the 1930s he turned to biography and history, writing of Lincoln, Walt Whitman, Mark Twain, and his friend Vachel Lindsay and of Chicago. His autobiography, *Across Spoon River,* appeared in 1936. He died on March 6, 1950.

Further Reading

A short study of Masters is in Lois Teal Hartley, *Spoon River Revisited* (1963). He is also discussed in *Poets and Their Art* (1926; rev. ed. 1967) by Harriet Monroe; in Horace Gregory and Marya Zaturenska, *A History of American Poetry* (1946); and in *Literary History of the United States,* edited by Robert E. Spiller and others (1948; rev. ed. 1964).

Additional Sources

Masters, Edgar Lee, *Across Spoon River: an autobiography,* Urbana: University of Illinois Press, 1991, 1936.

Masters, Hardin Wallace, *Edgar Lee Masters: a biographical sketchbook about a famous American author,* Rutherford N.J.: Fairleigh Dickinson University Press, 1978.

Masters, Hilary, *Last stands: notes from memory,* Boston: D.R. Godine, 1982; New York: McGraw-Hill, 1984, 1982. □

William Howell Masters

William Howell Masters (born 1915) was the first to study the anatomy and physiology of human sexuality in the laboratory, and the publication of the reports on his findings created much interest and criticism. Since then, he and his colleague, Virginia Johnson, have become well-known as researchers and therapists in the field of human sexuality, and together they have established the Reproduction Biology Center and later the Masters and Johnson Institute in St. Louis, Missouri.

William Howell Masters was born on December 27, 1915, in Cleveland, Ohio, to Francis Wynne and Estabrooks (Taylor) Masters. He attended public school in Kansas City through the eighth grade and then went to the Lawrenceville School in Lawrenceville, New Jersey. In 1938 he received a B.S. degree from Hamilton College, where he divided his time between science courses and sports such as baseball, football, and basketball. He was also active in campus debate. He entered the University of Rochester School of Medicine and started working in the laboratory of Dr. George Corner, who was comparing and studying the reproductive tracts of animals and humans.

During his junior year in medical school, Masters became interested in sexuality because it was the last scientifically unexplored physiological function. After briefly serving in the navy, he received his M.D. degree in 1943. Masters became interested in the work of Dr. Alfred Kinsey, a University of Indiana zoology professor who had interviewed thousands of men and women about their sexual experiences. Choosing a field that would help him prepare himself for human sexuality research, Masters became an intern and later a resident in obstetrics and gynecology at St. Louis Hospital and Barnes Hospital in St. Louis. He also did an internship in pathology at the Washington University School of Medicine. In 1947 he joined the faculty at Washington and advanced from instructor to associate professor of clinical obstetrics and gynecology. Masters conducted research in the field and contributed dozens of papers to

scientific journals. One of his areas of interest was hormone treatment and replacement in post-menopausal women.

By 1954 Masters decided that he was ready to undertake research on the physiology of sex. He was concerned that the medical profession had too little information on sexuality to understand clients' problems. Kinsey had depended on case histories, interviews, and secondhand data. Masters took the next step, which was to study human sexual stimulation using measuring technology in a laboratory situation.

Masters launched his project at Washington University, assisted by a grant from the United States Institute of Health. At first he recruited prostitutes for study, but found them unsuitable for his studies of "normal" sexuality. In 1956 he hired Virginia Eshelman Johnson, a sociology student, to help in the interviewing and screening of volunteers. The study was conducted over an eleven-year period with 382 women and 312 men participating. Subjects ranged in age from eighteen to eighty-nine and were paid for their time. Masters found a four-phased cycle relating to male and female sexual responses. To measure physiological changes, he used electroencephalographs, electrocardiographs, color cinematography, and biochemical studies.

Masters was very cautious and meticulous about protecting the identity of his volunteers. In 1959 he sent some results to medical journals, but continued to work in relative secrecy. After the content of the studies leaked out, the team had difficulty procuring grant money, so in 1964 Masters became director of the Reproductive Biology Foundation, a nonprofit group, to obtain private funds. In November of that same year, Dr. Leslie H. Farber, a respected Washington D.C. psychiatrist, wrote an article in *Commentary* entitled "I'm sorry, Dear," in which he attacked the "scientizing" of sex. This attack was only the beginning of the criticism the research would receive.

In 1966 Masters and Johnson published *Human Sexual Response.* In this book, the researchers used highly technical terminology and had their publisher, Little, Brown and Co., promote the book only to medical professionals and journals. Nevertheless, the book became a popular sensation and the team embarked on a speaking and lecture tour, winning immediate fame. As early as 1959 Masters and Johnson had begun counseling couples as a dual-sex team. Believing that partners would be more comfortable talking with a same-sex therapist, the team began working with couples' sexual problems. In their second book, *Human Sexual Inadequacy* (1970), they discuss problems such as impotence.

Masters divorced his first wife, Elisabeth Ellis, not long after the publication of *Human Sexual Inadequacy* and married Johnson on January 1, 1971, in Fayetteville, Arkansas. In 1973 they became codirectors of the Masters and Johnson Institute. In 1979 Masters and Johnson studied and described the sexual responses of homosexuals and lesbians in *Homosexuality in Perspective.* They also claimed to be able to change the sexual preferences of homosexuals who wanted it. Masters also maintained a biochemistry lab and continued to receive fees from a gynecology practice. He retired from practice in 1975 at the age of sixty. In 1981

Masters and Johnson sold their lab and moved to another location in St. Louis. At this time they had a staff of twenty-five and a long list of therapy clients.

Further controversy over their work developed when in 1988 Masters and Johnson coauthored a book with an associate, Dr. Robert Kolodny. The book, *Crisis: Heterosexual Behavior in the Age of AIDS* predicted an epidemic of AIDS among the heterosexual population. Some members of the medical community severely condemned the study, and C. Everett Koop, then surgeon general of the United States, called Masters and Johnson irresponsible. Perhaps as a result of the negative publicity, the number of clients seeking sex therapy at the institute decreased. In early 1992, Bill Walters, acting director of the institute, announced that Masters and Johnson were divorcing after twenty-one years of marriage—conflict in their ideas about retirement was cited as the reason for the breakup. Masters vowed he would never retire and continued speaking and lecturing at the institute, in addition to working on another book. The divorce ended their work together at the clinic.

For his pioneering efforts in making human sexuality a subject of scientific study, Masters received the Paul H. Hoch Award from the American Psychopathic Association in 1971, the Sex Information and Education Council of the United States (SIECUS) award in 1972, and three other prestigious awards. He belongs to the American Association for the Advancement of Science (AAAS), the American Fertility Society, and several other medical associations.

Further Reading

Robinson, Paul A., *The Modernization of Sex: Havelock Ellis, Albert Kinsey, William Masters, and Virginia Johnson,* Harper, 1976.
Fried, Stephen, "The New Sexperts," in *Vanity Fair,* December 1992, p. 132.
"Repairing the Conjugal Bed," in *Time,* March 25, 1970. □

Ali ibn al-Husayn al-Masudi

Ali ibn al-Husayn al-Masudi (died 956) was an Arab historian and one of the most versatile and original authors in the age of efflorescence of Moslem civilization.

Al-Masudi was born in Baghdad, a descendant of Abd Allah ibn Masud, a prominent companion of Mohammed. Numerous notices in al-Masudi's extant works indicate that he traveled extensively, but they do not suffice to establish his itineraries. In 915/916 he visited Basra and Istakhr (Persepolis) and then traveled in India, where he saw the area of Bombay, the Gulf of Cambay, and the Moslem towns of Multan and Mansura in Sind. That he also saw Ceylon and the China Sea, as he claims, has been doubted.

Still, in 916/917 al-Masudi reached Zanzibar and sailed from there to Oman. In 921/922 he visited Aleppo. Probably after this trip he visited the area south of the Caspian Sea. He mentions visiting other provinces of Persia without specifying dates. Also unknown are the dates of his journeys on the Red Sea, in Yemen, and in Hadhramaut. In 925 he mentions his presence in Baghdad and Tikrit; in 926 he was in Tiberias in Palestine; and at the beginning of 928 he was back in Hit in Iraq on the way to Baghdad.

During the last period of his life al-Masudi lived mostly in al-Fustât (Old Cairo), Egypt, where his first recorded visit was in 942. He visited Antioch in 943 and Damascus in 946. He traveled to Upper Egypt as far as Nubia.

Nothing is known about the purpose of his voyages and his means of financing them. It has been suggested that he was active as a missionary for the Ismailite movement, but this appears unlikely. Though his works reflect definite Shiite leanings, they lack the purposeful engagement to be expected in an active propagandist. His religious sentiments are, moreover, closer to the Imamite than the Ismailite branch of Shiism.

Whatever the immediate motive for his travels, al-Masudi satisfied his immense curiosity and supplemented and corrected the information he had gained from his wide reading through personal observation, conversations with people of all walks of life, and reports of other travelers. He was equally competent in the religious and the rational fields of learning, though his restless life and manifold interests prevented him from pursuing any science in depth. His keen interest and open-mindedness in respect to foreign peoples and religions reflect the cosmopolitan spirit of the age.

His Writings

Although the titles of over 30 works of al-Masudi are known, only two of certain authenticity are extant. Al-Masudi wrote a universal history in 30 volumes. This work and an abridged version of it are lost. His most famous book, the *Meadows of Gold*, is a further abridgment with later additions. The first volume, on pre-Islamic history, deals with the story of creation, biblical history, description of the world, history and ethnography of the non-Arab nations and the pagan Arabs, archeological remains, and calendars.

The second volume, on Islamic history, is also replete with observations outside the scope of conventional works of history. His *Book of Notification and Review* was written shortly before his death as a summary of his literary activity. Though shorter than the *Meadows of Gold* and similar in subject matter, it contains much independent information. The authenticity of a book about the imams from the time of Adam to the 12 imams of Imamite Shiism ascribed to him is uncertain.

Al-Masudi died at al-Fustât in September/October 956.

Further Reading

The first part of al-Masudi's *Meadows of Gold* was translated into English by Aloys Sprenger, *El-Masudi's Historical Encyclopaedia Entitled "Meadows of Gold and Mines of Gems"*

(1841). For background see Reynold A. Nicholson, *A Literary History of the Arabs* (1914; 2d ed. 1930).

Additional Sources

Shboul, Ahmad M. H., *Al-Masudi & his world: a Muslim humanist and his interest in non-Muslims,* London: Ithaca Press, 1979. ☐

Mariano Matamoros

The Mexican priest and independence hero Mariano Matamoros (1770-1814) gained the admiration of his contemporaries for his military exploits. He became second in command to independence leader José María Morelos.

Mariano Matamoros was born in Mexico City and attended schools there. In October 1789 he received a degree in theology and was soon appointed priest at Jantetelco in the present state of Morelos.

A sympathizer of Mexican independence, Matamoros soon clashed with Spanish authorities. In 1811 he was arrested briefly but was able to escape and join the revolutionary movement being led by another priest, Father José María Morelos. He supported Morelos's program to break up the large haciendas, abolish slavery, and curtail the power and wealth of the Church. Matamoros soon achieved the rank of colonel and was entrusted by Morelos to organize several cavalry and artillery regiments. On Jan. 23, 1812, Matamoros's troops successfully engaged the Spanish forces in the battle of Tenancingo.

This victory was followed by a major encounter with Spanish forces in the town of Cuautla in March 1812. Cuautla had become the stronghold of Morelos's army, which numbered about 3,000 men, including a well-trained division under Matamoros's command. The royalist forces began a siege which lasted for 72 days. Despite a courageous and brave resistance against an overpowering foe, the insurgents could not hold their positions. Spanish military superiority as well as lack of food forced the insurgents to evacuate the town. The defeat was very costly, but Morelos escaped, thus preventing the Spaniards from crushing completely the independence movement.

Fall of Oaxaca

Following the defeat at Cuautla, the insurgents accomplished little. In desperate need of a military victory, Morelos chose the provincial capital of Oaxaca as a possible target for an attack. He named Matamoros second in command of his army, and with a force of about 5,000 men the two leaders marched on Oaxaca. The rebels took the city on November 25. Insurgent prisoners were freed and paraded through the streets to impress the people with royalist abuses. Morelos was unable, however, to restrain his own troops from sacking the city. Many royalist officers were executed, but pro-Spanish ecclesiastics were spared.

Matamoros's bravery and military ability gained him the rank of lieutenant general. In battle after battle he now defeated the Spanish forces, expanding the territory under his control. At the time of the insurgent Congress of Chilpancingo in late 1813, Morelos appointed him commander in chief for Tecpán, Oaxaca, Mexico, Puebla, and Veracruz.

Morelos called upon Matamoros for support in the capture of the royalist town of Valladolid in December 1813. Morelos and Matamoros had assembled the largest and best-equipped army they had ever commanded. But what looked like an easy victory turned into a costly defeat. The well-trained royalist troops, now supported by fresh reinforcements from Spain, repelled the insurgent attack, countercharging with determination and courage. The insurgents were scattered and cut down by the hundreds.

Capture and Death

The insurgents suffered overwhelming human and material losses. But perhaps the heaviest blow dealt to the revolutionary movement was Matamoros's capture. The rebel leader was taken to Valladolid and placed on exhibition in the plaza, where he suffered countless indignities. He was soon tried and sentenced to death. Although Morelos made a desperate effort to save him by offering the royalists 200 Spanish prisoners in exchange for Matamoros's life, the sentence was carried out on Feb. 3, 1814, two days before Morelos's proposal reached Spanish authorities.

Further Reading

There is very little in English on Matamoros. Some information on his life is in Wilbert H. Timmons, *Morelos: Priest, Soldier, Statesman of Mexico* (rev. ed. 1970). □

Cotton Mather

Cotton Mather (1663-1728), Puritan clergyman, historian, and pioneering student of science, was an indefatigable man of letters. Of the third generation of a New England founding family, he is popularly associated with the Salem witchcraft trials.

Cotton Mather recorded the passing of an era. The Massachusetts Bay Colony had been a radical, Bible-based community of "saints," whose existence as an example to the rest of the world was to be safeguarded till Christ's second coming by the strictest tutelage of educated clergymen in all civil as well as ecclesiastical matters. In Mather's lifetime the separation of church and state and the development of the frontier and of a society absorbed in business and profits greatly increased popular apathy toward the church. The rise of democracy within the Colonies is seen in the disintegration of orthodox creeds and practices. American-born colonists felt estranged from Europe and its culture and turned to nature and to reason for the sources of their new identity. Rationalism and evangelism vied to replace orthodoxy.

Mather was both behind and ahead of his times. As an internationally known scholar and innovative scientist, he was ahead of his New England contemporaries. In his theories of child rearing his emphasis on indirection, persuasion, and rewards considerably anticipated the future. But on questions of ecclesiastical organization and in all matters relating to Harvard College, he adhered passionately to past example. He deplored New England's decline and eagerly anticipated a future day when all people would be brought to judgment and Christ's kingdom come.

Born in Boston on March 19, 1663, Cotton was the eldest son of Increase and Maria Mather and grandson of Richard Mather, the first minister of Dorchester, and of John Cotton, probably the most learned of first-generation American theologians. Increase Mather was minister to the Second Church in Boston, agent of the colony to England, and nonresident president of Harvard College from 1685 to 1701. He was the most productive man of letters of his generation. Cotton was a partner in all his father's endeavors.

Having made remarkable progress in Latin and Greek, Cotton was admitted to Harvard at the age of 12. He had begun studying Hebrew and showed great interest in philosophy and science. He read avidly. His father conferred Cotton's first degree at the age of 16. Cotton soon took up the study of medicine and, as a young man, attended meetings organized by Increase for scientific experimentation

and discussion. At 19 he received his master's degree. He was made a fellow of Harvard College in 1690 and was involved in the affairs of the college throughout his life. One of his bitterest disappointments was that he was never asked to be its president.

Disappointment and bereavement marked Cotton Mather's life. In 1686 he married Abigail Philips; they had nine children. She died in 1702. In 1703 he married the widow Mrs. Elizabeth Hubbard; they had six children. She died in 1713. His last wife, Mrs. Lydia George, whom he married in 1715, went insane. Of his fifteen children, only six lived to maturity and only two survived him. Three widowed sisters depended largely on him, and he was burdened by severe financial problems.

Overly jealous where family pride was concerned, Mather dealt rancorously with opposition. Anxiety and depression, no doubt, contributed to an already impulsive and dictatorial nature. But his was a complex temperament. He was deeply introspective. When very young he began to read Scripture daily and to develop habits of prayer. His efforts to do good works and to perfect Christian attitudes lasted a lifetime. Tireless on behalf of any worthwhile project, he was both pragmatic and susceptible to change. His early bitter denunciations of other sects later gave way to a spirit of tolerance. His will to overcome reversals can be seen in his triumph over stammering—a childhood affliction so severe that he doubted his fitness for the pulpit. By his own efforts he corrected his stammering and in 1685 was ordained at the Second Church. He served as assistant minister until his father's death in 1723, when Cotton became minister.

A Many-faceted Career

For a time the Mathers dominated the life of Massachusetts colony. When Increase went secretly to England in 1688 to plead for the restoration of the Massachusetts charter, Cotton was left not only with the spiritual leadership of the Second Church but with responsibility for heading the opposition at home to James II, specifically to his representative, Governor Edmund Andros. Cotton was a ringleader in the "Happy Revolution," as he called it, of 1689, which fortunately for the insurgents coincided with the deposition in England of James II. In 1692, after a period of provisional government by magistrates who had served under the old charter, Increase, unable to regain that charter, returned to Boston with a new charter and a new governor, Sir William Phips. Both the new charter and Governor Phips's policies proved unpopular, and from this time on the Mathers' power declined.

Witchcraft Trials at Salem

One of Sir William's first acts in office was the establishment of a court to try the suspected witches recently arrested at Salem. Mather had attempted to demonstrate the reality of spirits, particularly of the demonic, in his study *Memorable Providences, Relating to Witchcrafts and Possessions . . .* (1689). Although he had urged vigorous prosecution of the devil's work, he suggested punishment milder than execution for convicted witches. Mather's approach

was both theological and scientific. He separated himself from the trials per se and in fact warned the judges against "spectral evidences," but his advice went unheeded. In his *Magnalia Christi Americana* (1702) Mather declared his disapproval of the methods used in the trials. But while they were going on, he had registered no public protest.

Clearly, politics, as well as theology and science, determined the Mathers' role in the witchcraft controversy. At the judges' request, Cotton, apparently unwillingly, agreed to write an apologetical account of a few of the trials. Phips, after all, had been baptized by Cotton and was Increase's appointment. *The Wonders of the Invisible World* (1693) was followed in 1700 by a work sponsored by the Mathers' opponents, entitled *More Wonders of the Invisible World*. Compiled by Robert Calef, a man skeptical of and outraged by the witchcraft accusations, it contained, without Cotton's permission, his account, written in 1693, of his investigations of a girl he believed bewitched. Mather again had focused on supernatural phenomena; he had made no attempt to start a prosecution. But by 1700 popular feeling had risen against the Salem trials, and the Mathers were firmly identified both with the causes of the hysteria and with the political appointees who made the tragic judgments. Most 19th-century historians place full responsibility for the trials with Cotton Mather; Brooks Adams called the trials themselves the central moral issue of the 17th century. To modern scholars, however, both allegations seem to overstate the case.

Other Ecclesiastical Controversies

A combination of forces effected the wane of the Mathers' influence. A new breed of more liberal and catholic men gathered in the recently established Brattle Church, under the leadership of Benjamin Coleman. These, with others, secured the removal of Increase from the presidency of Harvard in 1701. The House of Representatives appointed Cotton president, but the electors of the college overruled their action and passed him by. Cotton then directed his attention to Yale. But when Yale's president, Timothy Cutler, resigned to join the Anglican Church in 1722, Cotton, apparently, refused the invitation to replace him. This was Cotton's last opportunity for high office.

During this period the Mathers saw the collapse of their scheme to bring more centralized control to individual congregations and to effect closer cooperation between Congregational and Presbyterian churches. Meanwhile in western Massachusetts age-old standards governing admission to membership in the Congregational Church were being eased by the powerful Northampton minister Solomon Stoddard. The Mathers directly challenged Stoddard but were unable to curb him. A series of revivals under Stoddard prepared the soil in the Connecticut valley for Stoddard's grandson, Jonathan Edwards, and for the coming of the Great Awakening.

Pioneer Scientist and Intellectual

Although the Mathers maintained standfast attitudes toward many cultural and ecclesiastical changes, they were in the intellectual vanguard of the Colonies. Cotton corresponded with men of learning around the world. In 1710 he was awarded a doctorate of divinity by the University of Glasgow. In 1713 he had the great honor of being elected to the Royal Society of London. He and Increase were among the first in the Colonies to advocate inoculation against smallpox and were threatened and maligned for so doing. Undismayed (even by a bomb thrown through the window of Cotton's house), the Mathers succeeded, with Dr. Zabdiel Boylston, in putting the project into effect.

Career as a Writer

Despite disfavor, Cotton's activities continued. He wrote in seven languages and also mastered the Iroquois Indian language. In his lifetime 382 of his works were published. These took many forms: history, sermons, biography, fables, books of practical piety, theological and scientific treatises, and verse. Often pedantic and heavily embellished with simile, metaphor, and learned reference, his writing could also achieve simplicity, straight-forwardness, and practicality. Mather saw instruction as the chief function of good writing and made sophisticated adaptations of style and mode to that end. He might instruct explicitly, as in the medical manual *The Angel of Bethesda* (1722), or by humorous indirection, as in his *Political Fables* (1692), written in the manner of 18th-century essayists.

In the *Psalterium Americanum* (1718) the versatile Mather turned his talents to translating the Psalms and adapting them to music. The unpublished *Biblia Americana* is an exhaustively annotated scholarly interpretation of the Bible. His *Bonifacius, or Essays To Do Good* (1718) makes practical prescriptions for personal piety. An immensely popular book, Benjamin Franklin called it the work that most influenced his youth. Suggestive of Franklin too is the popular science mode in such works as Mather's *Essay for the Recording of Illustrious Providences* (1684).

Probably Mather's greatest work was his *Magnalia Christi Americana* (1702). Primarily a history of New England, it is composed from many of Mather's other writings. The seven sections tell of the settlement of New England, the lives of its governors and ministers, and the story of Harvard College and of the Congregational Church and conclude with a treatment of "remarkable providences" and "various disturbances." The *Magnalia* provides a detailed and eloquent statement of the Puritan mind as it addressed itself to its historical mission in an hour of darkness, perhaps even of eclipse.

Strategies for keeping alive the reality of Christ's Judgment and of His future kingdom permeated all Mather's works. His biographies, one of Phips (1697) and another of Increase, *Parentator* (1724), were designed as exemplary lives of eminent men. The late work *The Christian Philosopher* (1721) attempts to wed the observations of the 18th-century naturalist with Christian faith in the order and purpose of the created world. Cotton was working with "modern" ideas, seeking to express them within the basic framework of Christian eschatology.

Cotton Mather outlived his father by only 5 years. Later American writers, Ralph Waldo Emerson, Henry Thoreau, Harriet Beecher Stowe, James Russell Lowell, Nathaniel Hawthorne, and Henry Wadsworth Longfellow all acknowledged their debt to him.

Further Reading

A valuable introduction to Mather and representative selections from his work are in Kenneth B. Murdock, ed., *Selections from Cotton Mather* (1926). The best biography is Barrett Wendell, *Cotton Mather: The Puritan Priest* (1891; rev. ed. 1963). Ralph and Louise Boas, *Cotton Mather: Keeper of the Puritan Conscience* (1928), is more popular. The New England background may be found in Perry Miller, *The New England Mind: From Colony to Province* (1953). Robert Middlekauff, *The Mathers: Three Generations of Puritan Intellectuals, 1596-1728* (1971), is a study in biography and intellectual history that seeks to revise the affirmative view of Puritan history taken by Miller. Recommended for its general analysis of the literature of the colonial period is Kenneth B. Murdock, *Literature and Theology in Colonial New England* (1949). □

Increase Mather

Increase Mather (1639-1723), American colonial representative, president of Harvard College, and author, was the most prominent member of the second generation in Massachusetts colony.

Born in Dorchester, Mass., where his father was first minister, Increase Mather was educated at home and at Boston's free school. Taking his bachelor of arts degree from Harvard (1656), he studied and preached in England and Ireland. He received his master of arts in 1658 from Trinity College, Dublin. Returning to Boston, he married Maria Cotton, daughter of John Cotton, in 1662. They had 10 children; the eldest, Cotton, was his lifetime aid. In 1664 Increase became teacher of the Second Church, which he served until his death.

Increase Mather went to England in 1688 to negotiate restoration of the colonial charter, revoked by James II. Failing in this, he returned with a charter that nullified the colonists' right to elect their governors but preserved the power of the representative assembly elected by voters. Disappointed colonists felt that he had conceded too much.

Mather believed that New England was a nation in covenant with God, preparing to witness the day when Christ comes to judge the world and establish His kingdom. He preached that only a chaste and obedient people would enter the kingdom. This sense of New England's mission determined his stand on many questions. The voice of orthodoxy, Mather finally accepted the Halfway Covenant, a compromise admitting children of unconverted second-generation Puritans to a kind of partial membership in the Congregational Church. However, a proposal architected by Mather and others in England for the cooperation of Presbyterian and Congregational churches and the tightening of centralized control over individual congregations failed.

Although Mather took no part in the Salem witchcraft trials, he had chosen the governor, Sir William Phips, who was responsible for them. In *Cases of Conscience concerning Evil Spirits* (1693), Mather's opposition to some of the trial procedures led Phips to close the trials. Yet Increase and Cotton Mather were implicated by their researches into demonology and their association with Phips. The Mathers' enemies used the trials to discredit them.

The worst defeat, at least for Cotton, was Increase's removal from the Harvard College presidency in 1701. Gradually Increase Mather turned more of his energy to writing. He published 130 books. Direct and simple in style, his theological work is often, in its way, scientific. He pioneered in science, organizing a society for scientific discussions and successfully introducing smallpox inoculation into the colony.

Further Reading

Cotton Mather's *Parentator* (1724; rev. ed. 1970) is a life of his father. The definitive work on Increase Mather is Kenneth B. Murdock, *Increase Mather: The Foremost American Puritan* (1925). He is discussed in Robert Middlekauff, *The Mathers: Three Generations of Puritan Intellectuals, 1596-1728* (1971). A thorough account of the New England background and the issues surrounding the Mathers is in Perry Miller, *The New England Mind: From Colony to Province* (1953). □

Albert Mathiez

The French historian Albert Mathiez (1874-1932) was one of the major 20th-century historians of the French Revolution.

Albert Mathiez was born to an innkeeper's family at La Bruyère in eastern France on Jan. 10, 1874. He graduated from the École Normale in 1897. After teaching for a short time in the provinces, he returned to Paris to prepare a doctoral thesis under the direction of Alphonse Aulard. The thesis, on Revolutionary religious cults (1904), marked him as a historian of independent mind. Mathiez argued that these cults were profoundly related to the Revolutionaries' views of the role of religion in society. Though the thesis derived much of its argument from the work of the sociologist Émile Durkheim, Mathiez later became dubious about the use of sociology in historical writing.

Three years after presenting his thesis Mathiez broke with Aulard, beginning a feud that continued for the rest of his life. Whether the feud was caused by personal pique, psychological conflict, or scholarly ambition, it took public form as a dispute over the characters and historical roles of Georges Jacques Danton and Maximilien de Robespierre. Danton, whom Aulard admired as a patriot, was to Mathiez a corrupt demagogue; Robespierre, a tyrant to Aulard, became for Mathiez the champion of social democracy. To prove his point Mathiez, in 1908, founded a new journal, the *Annales revolutionnaires,* and the Society for Robespierre Studies. In a series of articles and books— *Robespierre Studies* (2 vols., 1917-1918); *Danton and the Peace* (1919); and *The India Company* (1920)—he exposed Danton's graft and his "defeatist" attempts to negotiate with the enemies of the Revolution. In *Danton* (1926) he covered his subject's entire career. At the same time he explored Robespierre's career and promoted an edition of his writings. In these articles and books Mathiez demonstrated his mastery of critical history, illuminating with his forceful imagination the new evidence he had found in the archives.

Strongly influenced by Jean Jaurès, Mathiez also wrote on the economic history of the Revolution. He had early come to see the Revolution as a class conflict, and the Russian Revolution confirmed his view that political events had to be related to economic and social movements.

Mathiez wrote one narrative of the Revolution (3 vols., 1922-1927). Writing for the general public, and confined to a short text by the publisher, Mathiez here showed his mastery of French style and his ability to convince his readers. He continued this narrative in a much more detailed manner in *The Thermidorian Reaction* (1929) and *The Directorate* (1934).

Mathiez's dispute with Aulard, his brusque manner toward those who were not his friends, his criticism of the government during World War I, and his defense of bolshevism left him few supporters in the Parisian academic world. Professor at Dijon (1919-1926), he was finally called to

Paris in 1926 as a substitute and then as a lecturer. On Feb. 25, 1932, while delivering a lecture, he suffered a stroke and died.

Further Reading

Profiles of Mathiez are in Paul Farmer, *France Reviews Its Revolutionary Origins: Social Politics and Historical Opinion in the Third Republic* (1944), and Pieter Geyl, *Napoleon: For and Against* (trans. 1949). See also Arthur Marwick, *The Nature of History* (1970). □

Matilda of Tuscany

Matilda of Tuscany (1046–1115) was a strong supporter of the papacy during the Investiture Controversy, who mediated at the famous meeting between Pope Gregory VII and Emperor Henry IV at her ancestral castle of Canossa in 1077.

With independence and conviction, Matilda, countess of Tuscany, led an unusual life for a woman of medieval days. Her military, financial, cultural, and, above all, spiritual support were instrumental in strengthening the power of the Church, especially the papacy, at a crucial time of conflict between the Church and the state known as the Investiture Controversy.

Matilda was born probably in 1046 in northern Italy, possibly in or near Lucca. Her father was Boniface II of Canossa; her mother was Boniface's second wife Beatrice. Matilda's heritage was illustrative of the political relationships that then connected Germany and Italy. When the Lombard kingdom of northern and central Italy became part of the Carolingian Empire under Emperor Charlemagne in the late eighth century, German rulers sought to impose their control over Italian lands. The Canossa were a family of the Lombard nobility whose territorial holdings were built, in part, through patronage and grants from German emperors.

Matilda's father controlled large amounts of land in northern Italy, including counties of Reggio, Modena, Mantua, Ferrara, and Brescia. In addition, around 1027, Conrad II, the German emperor, made Boniface margrave (marquis) of Tuscany. Matilda's mother was a niece of Emperor Conrad II which made Matilda directly related to German rulers Henry III and Henry IV, with whom she would eventually struggle.

Although Matilda had an older brother and perhaps another sibling, the six-year-old became sole heir to the family's extensive lands and power base in northern Italy upon the death of her father and brother in 1052. Because female inheritance was difficult to uphold during the Middle Ages, two years after her father's death, Matilda's mother Beatrice married Godfrey, duke of Upper Lorraine, to afford some protection for her daughter's claims. Godfrey, however, was in conflict with German emperor Henry III who took Beatrice and Matilda and held them captive in Ger-

many from 1055 to 1056. Upon their release shortly before Henry III's death, they returned to their Italian homeland.

Matilda's upbringing was somewhat unconventional for a young woman of the 11th century. Greatly influenced by her strong, intelligent, cultured, and pious mother, Matilda's development included not only traditionally feminine pursuits, such as needlework and religious training, but also literate studies including knowledge of Latin as well as vernacular languages of Italian, German, and French. Matilda's later acquisition of manuscripts, her donations of books, and her patronage of arts connected with religious institutions are evidence of her educated background. In addition, it is believed that she had some skill in the military arts. Her later presence at several armed conflicts between imperial forces and papal supporters lends credence to the suggestion.

Her mother's greatest influence on Matilda was probably in her religious beliefs and support for the Church. Matilda's youth coincided with a strong movement of Church reform headed by the papacy. On the one hand, medieval rulers, especially the German emperors, believed in theocratic kingship which included exercising control over appointments of Church officials; the imperial position was symbolized by the investiture of Church leaders with both sacred and secular insignia. On the other hand, Church reform in the 11th century advocated the separation of affairs of the Church from those of the state; Church reformers, especially the popes, asserted that the spiritual powers of the Church were superior to secular powers. This conflict, known as the Investiture Controversy, would reach its greatest intensity in the second half of the 11th century during Matilda's maturity.

Through her teens, Matilda became an active supporter of the papacy as she defended, along with her mother and stepfather, the canonically elected pope Alexander II against an imperially backed antipope Caladus of Parma, who took the name Honorius II. It is likely that she was also present at several important battles, such as the battle of Aquino in 1066 where her stepfather's forces defeated the antipope's Roman and Norman supporters. She was present as well at several Church councils, beginning with the Council of Sutri in 1059 which she attended at age 13.

Probably in 1069, after the death of her stepfather Duke Godfrey, Matilda married his son, Godfrey the Hunchback, duke of Upper Lorraine, in what appears to have been primarily a political union. After the death of her infant son in 1071, she returned to Italy while her husband remained in Lorraine. Their political views parted ways as well; Godfrey became more closely aligned with the German emperor Henry IV while Matilda continued her strong backing of the reforming papacy. Godfrey died in 1076.

During the decade of the 1070s when Matilda reached maturity, the Investiture Controversy became a dramatic struggle between its two major protagonists: Pope Gregory VII and Emperor Henry IV. Matilda and her mother had long been associated with the archdeacon Hildebrand who became Pope Gregory VII in 1073 and with his strong advocacy of Church reform. At the same time, Matilda's familial and feudal relationship to Henry IV brought her into close association with the German imperial cause. After her mother's death in 1076, Matilda became a leading figure in the heated controversy between Church and state.

As a cornerstone of his reform policy, in 1075 Pope Gregory prohibited lay investiture, a practice central to German imperial policy and ideals of kingship. Henry IV countered in 1076 with a declaration renouncing and deposing the pope. In return, Gregory excommunicated Henry. During one of the most famous and pivotal episodes in the Investiture Controversy, Henry, in order to maintain his rule, traveled across the Alps in a bitter winter of 1077 to do penance before the pope. Pope Gregory received him at Matilda's fortress at Canossa only after Henry waited three days in the snow before being admitted. Then Matilda acted as intermediary between her spiritual father Pope Gregory and her relative Henry.

Henry, however, continued to pursue his policies and his opposition to the papacy. After the 1080 death of Rudolf of Swabia, elected king in place of Henry by the German princes, Henry invaded Italy. Although her forces were no match for Henry's, Matilda remained a steadfast supporter of the papacy. Her one major victory was a surprise attack on Henry's army at Sobara, near Modena, in 1084. During this year, however, Henry was able to crown an antipope in Rome while the Normans rescued Gregory VII and took him to south Italy where he died in 1085.

Matilda supported the legitimately elected popes, first Pope Victor III (1086-87) and then Pope Urban II (1088-89). In 1089, probably to add military strength to her cause, 43-year-old Matilda agreed to another political marriage to 17-year-old Welf V of Bavaria. The marriage did little to assist her position since Henry continued to take over cities and territory that had been in Matilda's possession. This marriage ended six years later.

Though neither side abandoned its ideological positions, the intensity of the Investiture Controversy diminished after Pope Gregory's death. During her later years, Matilda therefore turned her attention to governing and administering her territories, to patronage of religious institutions, and to her spiritual life. As a result of Henry's inroads into her holdings and a general movement for independence among northern Italian cities, many of Matilda's estates were less directly under her control. She made numerous donations of land to churches and monasteries within her dominions while supporting building projects and provision of church furnishings for many of these religious foundations. She also was a patron of the developing school of canon law at Bologna under canonists such as Irnerius.

The last years of her life were increasingly spent in quiet and periods of withdrawal to the Benedictine monastery of San Benedetto Polirone which her grandfather had founded. After the death of her nemesis Henry, she became reconciled with his son and heir Emperor Henry V. Matilda died in 1115 and was buried at Polirone. Her remains were later removed for burial at St. Peter's in Rome in 1635 where her tomb in the crossing of the church is marked by a monument by the great Baroque sculptor, Bernini.

Because Matilda died without heirs or successors, the fate of the Canossa holdings remained a point of contention well after her death. Henry V effectively claimed all her territories when she died, leaving the popes to dispute with the emperors about the disposition of Matilda's grant of her alodial lands to the Church.

Matilda's life and accomplishments were chronicled and praised in a long heroic poem composed by Donizo, her chaplain at Canossa. With allowances for its laudatory aim and literary stylistics, this poem and other contemporary references reveal her to have been a complex woman of exceptional abilities. She had great strength, displayed in physical terms as a Christian warrior, and steadfast character, witnessed by her unwavering support of the papal cause. At the same time, her compassion was evident: she tended the wounded on the battlefield and was especially generous in the patronage she bestowed on the Church. She was also educated and cultured, with some understanding of the subtleties of the political and theological positions that inspired the controversy between Church and state. During this critical episode in medieval history, her multifaceted support was instrumental in advancing the position of the Church.

Further Reading

Bellochi, Ugo, and Giovanni Marzi. *Matilde e Canossa. Il Poema di Donizone.* Aedes Muratoriana, 1984.

Duff, Nora. *Matilda of Tuscany.* Methuen, 1909.

Fraser, Antonio. *Boadicea's Chariot: The Warrior Queens.* Weidenfeld & Nicolson, 1988.

Grimaldi, Natale. *La Contessa Matilde e la su stirpe feudale.* Vallechi Editore, 1928.

Huddy, Mary E. *Matilda, Countess of Tuscany.* John Long, 1906.

Blumenthal, Uta-Renate. *The Investiture Controversy.* University of Pennsylvania Press, 1988.

Fuhrmann, Horst. *Germany in the High Middle Ages c. 1050-1200.* Cambridge University Press, 1986.

Rough, Robert H. *The Reformist Illuminations in the Gospels of Matilda, Countess of Tuscany.* Martinus Nijhoff, 1973. □

Henri Matisse

The French painter and sculptor Henri Matisse (1869-1954) was one of the great initiators of the modern art movement and the most outstanding personality of the first revolution in 20th-century art—Fauvism.

About the turn of the 20th century there were several artists who simultaneously and independently of each other developed a taste for strong color. This liking was derived from the work of Vincent Van Gogh, that of the divisionists (or pointillists), and Paul Gauguin's experience of primitivism in Tahiti. The combination of a primary color scheme with the primitive approach to visual experience, in which simplification and distortion enhance expressiveness, resulted in Fauvism, which initiated the modern movement.

The greatest master of modern sophistication, Henri Matisse, learned from the manner in which children draw how to see natural objects in an innocent way, as if perceiving them for the first time. Matisse was the artist who fulfilled the national tradition of French painting in the modern movement. When cubism entered the arena as a new alternative to the art of the past, what entered with it was the analytical, cerebral quality in modern art. Fauvism, on the other hand, represented in its first stage the victory of sensualism, which particularly through color transmitted its message with a strong direct impact. Fauvism developed in the oeuvre of Matisse into a classical art. A balance was achieved between color, expressing light, and form, presenting objects as pure forms in a two-dimensional manner without any illusionism.

Henri Matisse was born on Dec. 31, 1869, at Le Cateau-Cambrésis. After the war of 1870-71 his family returned to Bohain-en-Vermandois. Matisse's father was a corn merchant, his mother an amateur painter. He studied law from 1887 to 1891 and then decided to go to Paris and become a painter. He worked under Adolphe William Bouguereau at the Académie Julian in Paris, but he left in 1892 to enter the studio of Gustave Moreau at the École des Beaux-Arts, where he studied until 1897. Moreau was a liberal teacher who did not interfere with the individuality of his pupils, among whom were Georges Rouault, Albert Marquet, Henri Manguin, Charles Camoin, and Jean Puy. Moreau encouraged his students to look at nature and to paint outdoors, as well as to frequent the museums. Matisse copied pictures by Philippe de Champaigne, Nicolas Poussin, and Jean Baptiste Chardin in the Louvre and painted outdoors in Paris.

About 1898, under the influence of impressionism, Matisse's palette became lighter, as in his seascapes of Belle-Île and landscapes of Corsica and the Côte d'Azur. Although impressionist in character, these early works of Matisse already show a noticeable emphasis on color and simplified forms. Matisse married in 1898 and visited London in the same year to study the works of J. M. W. Turner on Camille Pissarro's advice. On his return to Paris he attended classes at the Académie Carrière, where he met André Derain. Matisse created his first sculptures in 1899.

From 1900 Matisse suffered great material hardship for years. In 1902 the artist, his wife, and their three children were forced to return to Bohain. In 1903 the Salon d'Automne was founded, and Matisse exhibited there. From 1900 to 1903, under the influence of Paul Cézanne, Matisse produced still lifes and nudes which excel in clarity and harmony. In 1904 he had his first one-man show at the gallery of Ambroise Vollard in Paris and spent the summer in Saint-Tropez, where Paul Signac lived. Signac bought Matisse's famous picture *Luxe, calme et volupté* (1904-1905), which was exhibited at the Salon des Indépendants. In 1905 Matisse painted with Derain at Collioure; the works Matisse executed there are the very essence of Fauvism in their vivid colors and flat patterning.

Fauve Period

Matisse's Fauve period extended from 1905 to 1908, during which time he executed a magnificent series of masterpieces. Three groups of artists made up the Fauvist movement, centered on Matisse. The first group was that of the Atelier Moreau and the Académie Carrière: Marquet, Manguin, Camoin, and Puy. The second group consisted of the two artists who painted at Châtou: Maurice Vlaminck and Derain. The third was the Le Havre group: Othon Friesz, Raoul Dufy, and Georges Braque. The Dutch painter Kees van Dongen also belonged to the Fauves. At the 1905 Salon d'Automne the Fauves made their first public appearance. In 1906 Matisse's *Joie de vivre* was exhibited at the Indépendants; the painting, which is arranged in a series of unbroken surfaces related by color harmonies and embodies his new ideas, gained him the title of the King of the Fauves. The American collector Leo Stein began to buy his work.

Matisse made his first trip to North Africa in 1906. His *Blue Nude,* or *Souvenir de Biskra* (1907), is a memento of the journey. In this painting he experimented with *contrapposto* (an undulating S-curve pose), and he used the same form in the sculpture *Reclining Nude I* (1907). He had established a studio in the former Convent des Oiseaux in 1905; this became a meeting place for foreign artists. He developed into the leader of an international art school with mainly German and Scandinavian pupils who spread his ideas. His ''Notes of a Painter,'' published in *La Grande revue* in 1908, became the artistic credo of a whole generation. Matisse was an amiable man and looked more like a shy government official than an artist. He never accepted any fees for his tuition so that he might remain free to take his leave at any time, should this commitment interfere with his creative activity.

Change in Style

Between 1908 and 1913 Matisse made journeys to Spain, Germany, Russia, and Africa. In Munich he saw the exhibition of Islamic art (1910), and in Moscow he studied Russian icons (1911). Russian collectors began to buy his pictures. He produced five sculptures—heads of Jeannette—during 1910 and 1911, which show affinities with African masks and sculptures. His Moroccan journey of 1911-12 had a decisive influence on his development, exemplified in *Dance, Music, the Red Fishes,* and the series of interiors recording his studio and its contents. They show a stern and compact style with blacks and grays, mauves, greens, and ochers. Great Matisse exhibitions were held in 1910, 1913, and 1919.

By 1919 Matisse had become an internationally known master. His style at that time was characterized by the use of pure colors and their sophisticated interplay (harmonies and contrasts); the two-dimensionality of the picture surface enriched by decorative patterns taken from wallpapers, Oriental carpets, and fabrics; and the musicality of outlines and arabesques, the human figures being treated in the same manner as the decorative elements. The goal of Matisse's art was the portrayal of the joy of living in contrast to the stresses of our technological age. Between 1920 and 1925 he executed a series of odalisques, such as the *Odalisque with Raised Arms;* this period has been called an oasis of lightness.

Last Years

In 1925 Matisse was made chevalier of the Legion of Honor, and in 1927 he received the first prize at the Carnegie International Exhibition at Pittsburgh. After a visit to Tahiti, Matisse was a guest at the Barnes Foundation at Merion, Pa., and accepted Dr. Barnes's commission to paint a mural, *The Dance* (1932-1933), for the hall of the foundation. A crescendo of work distinguished his life. He produced paintings, drawings, book illustrations (etchings and lithographs), sculptures (he made 54 bronzes altogether), ballet sets, and designs for tapestry and glass. He spent the war years in the south of France. In 1944 Pablo Picasso arranged for him to be represented in the Salon d'Automne to celebrate the Liberation.

Matisse considered the culmination of his lifework to be his design and decoration of the Chapel of the Rosary for the Dominican nuns at Vence (1948-1951). He designed the black-and-white tile pictures, stained glass, altar crucifix, and vestments. At the time of the consecration of the Vence chapel Matisse held a large retrospective exhibition in the Museum of Modern Art in New York.

The ultimate step in the art of Matisse was taken in his *papiers découpés,* abstract cutouts in colored paper, executed in the mid-1940s, for example, the *Negro Boxer, Tristesse du roi,* and *Jazz.* The master died on Nov. 3, 1954, in Cimiez near Nice.

Further Reading

The most comprehensive study of Matisse to date is Alfred H. Barr, Jr., *Matisse, His Art and His Public* (1951), which includes biography, a full bibliography, and documentation. Older studies of interest are Roger Fry, *Henri Matisse* (1935), and Henry McBride, *Matisse* (1930). Of the more recent works, University of California at Los Angeles, Art Council, *Henri Matisse,* with text by Jean Leymarie and others (1966), provides commentary and representative selections from all of Matisse's work. Georges Duthuit, *The Fauvist Painters* (1950), and Jean Leymarie, *Fauvism: Biographical and Critical Study* (1959), contain detailed information on Matisse and his work. □

Enrico Mattei

Enrico Mattei (1906-1962) was the most acclaimed entrepreneur in Italy after World War II. A small industrialist before the war and a leading anti-fascist partisan during the war, Mattei in the 1950s created one of the largest public industrial conglomerates in Italy.

Mattei was born in Acqualagna (Pesaro), a small, non-descript village in which a leather processing plant was the main employer and the only manufacturing activity. As a young man he was a high school dropout but did well as a blue collar worker. By the age of 20 he became the director of the only plant in the village. When the plant had to be liquidated, he moved to the big city—Milan—where at first he acted as a sales representative for German chemical firms. Eventually, he opened his own small chemical plant, which in spite of the 1930s depression had a tremendous financial success. By 1936, at the age of 30, Mattei, a prosperous Italian small industrialist, married an Austrian actress with whom he lived despite his frequent infidelities.

The first two years of World War II confounded Mattei, and he seemed incapable of any action. Mattei studied accounting and learned social philosophy from Boldrini, a professor living in the same housing complex and a native of the same village.

By 1943, when the Allies invaded Italy, Mattei became an active anti-fascist partisan. At the time, the partisan movement was controlled by Communists and Socialists. Mattei believed in a Christian socialist philosophy and felt that it was necessary that the non-Marxists take part in the anti-fascist struggle in order to have a voice after the war. He therefore initiated a mobilization of the clergy and that part of the middle class that were anti-fascist but afraid of a Socialist and Communist takeover. This was a difficult task, but Mattei succeeded by leading and organizing anti-government and anti-Nazi activities on the part of the "Christian Democrats." Eventually he became the financial coordinator and spokesman for a large group of partisans. He succeeded in gaining respect for his integrity and organizational skills.

At the end of the war, as a payoff for his contribution to the Christian Democrat Party, the new coalition government appointed Mattei as a special commissary for AGIP, the Italian Petroleum Agency, a public company created in the 1930s for the research and development of petroleum. The charge was to liquidate the agency by closing drilling sites and selling the assets to private interests.

Enrico Mattei did not believe in defeat and had strong nationalist feelings. Instead of liquidation, he began secretly to expand AGIP's activities. By perseverance and luck he found important reserves of natural gas in northern Italy. He distributed the gas to industrial plants by building a large pipeline network. This, among other things, contributed to the expansion of the steel industry, which had been stagnating at that time.

The multinational oil companies did not appreciate Mattei's activities and through the United States government put pressure on the Italian government to cease and desist oil and gas operations. But Mattei, by subterfuge, even when removed from the leadership of AGIP, continued expansion. When a little oil was found in the Po Valley, the government tacitly went along with Mattei's ventures and in 1953 created the ENI, the Natural Hydrocarbons Agency, a financial body meant to incorporate all government operations in the field. Inevitably, Mattei took charge. In Italy within ten years ENI expanded in oil and gas related fields such as exploration, refining, oil and gas pipes, distribution networks, oil drilling equipment, and petrochemicals. It also entered such fields as motels, textiles, and even newspapers.

To the dismay and displeasure of the Seven Sisters (the principal oil multinationals), Mattei expanded his operations also into the Middle East and Africa. The diplomatic pressure brought on the Italian government was to no avail because Mattei through his intrigues and control of the 50 or so companies under the ENI umbrella could not be stopped without grave political repercussions.

When Mattei died in a plane accident in 1962, at the age of 56, he left a legacy in Italy never matched by private or public entrepreneurs. As a political man—he was a deputy in parliament between 1948 and 1953—he used his position to enhance the economic goals of the mammoth enterprise. In his private life, he was easily persuaded by women; he tried to be a caring husband but spent little time at home. Enrico Mattei was always on the move, in search of new horizons. While some attribute his death to foul play by those he had antagonized, this theory was never proven.

Further Reading

The chief account of Mattei's active life is Cyrus Sulzberger, *The Last of the Giants* (London, 1979). A prime Italian source is Luigi Bazzoli and Ricardo Renzi, *Il Miracolo Mattei* (The Mattei Miracle) (Milan, 1984). A kind of "house written" biography (by ENI) is *Mattei idea di liberta* (Mattei: The Idea of Liberty) (Milan, 1982). Other Italian sources include Marcello Colitti, *Energia e sviluppo in Italia. La vicenda di Enrico Mattei* (Bari, 1979); Mario Ferrari Aggradi, *Mattei e Mentasti nella lotta di liberazione* (Rome, 1965); Paul Frankel, *Petrolio e potere: Enrico Mattei. Storia politica dal 1945 al 1966* (Florence, 1970); Giorgio Galli, *La sfida perduta. Biografia politica di Enrico Mattei* (Milan, 1962); and Dow Votaw, *Il cane a sei zampe* (Milan, 1975). ☐

Giacomo Matteotti

Giacomo Matteoti (1885–1924) was leader of the Italian Socialist Party and bitter and effective critic of Mussolini's dictatorship, whose murder by Fascist thugs led to a crisis that nearly overthrew Mussolini.

Giacomo Matteotti, one of the foremost leaders of Italian socialism following World War I, contested the rise of fascism with courage and eloquence. With his death in 1924, Fascist Italy was soon transformed into a full-fledged dictatorship. On the other hand, the murder of the prominent Socialist stimulated the growth of an anti-Fascist movement that lasted until the overthrow of Mussolini in 1945.

Italy at the start of the 20th century was a recently created country suffering from severe social, economic, and political problems. Unified only in 1861, there remained vast economic and cultural differences between the relatively prosperous northern regions and the poor areas south of Rome. With the unrest in the country's cities, a Socialist Party emerged to help Italy's factory workers. There was even more unrest in the countryside as movements of agricultural workers formed to improve wages and working conditions, but they faced harsh resistance by landowners.

While Socialist leaders promoted a program of reform in the name of the workers, prior to 1914 Italian nationalist leaders like Enrico Corradini spoke of the need to link all Italians together and to carry out a plan of imperial expansion. Universal suffrage was established in 1912, creating a large number of new voters whose future political loyalties were uncertain.

After bitter debate and violent public demonstrations, the Italian government of Giovanni Giolitti entered World War I in the spring of 1915. Both sides in the war bid to attract Italy. Britain and France won over the Italians by promising large postwar territorial gains at the expense of Austria-Hungary. But the war brought massive Italian casualties, disrupted the Italian economy, and resulted in only disappointing territorial gains at the 1919 peace conference. Italian Socialists, inspired by the success of Communist revolution in Russia, were speaking about revolution in their own country.

At the same time, a movement on the political right—a movement called fascism—emerged under the leadership of Benito Mussolini. A former Socialist who had abandoned the Socialist Party in 1914 to lead a movement to bring Italy into World War I, Mussolini now gathered a variety of followers: embittered war veterans, nationalists, opponents of Socialist revolution. The Fascist program mixed calls for radical economic change with a strong devotion to Italian nationalism and opposition to socialism.

Over the years from 1919 to 1922, its program lost some of its radical character. Fascism became dominated by nationalism and opposition to the political left. The party was also distinguished by its use of violence against its political opponents: Socialist meetings were broken up by armed Fascist bands; rival political leaders were beaten; leaders of rural workers' groups were assaulted.

By 1922, fascism gained support from even moderate conservatives who hoped it would be a barrier against Socialist revolution. In the face of bitter opposition from the Socialists, Mussolini came to power as prime minister. His rise to power was technically legal, but the threat of violence stood in the background. He had threatened to lead his movement in a "March on Rome" to force his appointment. In the end, the authorities decided to give in to his wishes without armed resistance, and he headed a coalition cabinet starting on October 31, 1922. But Mussolini was openly contemptuous of parliamentary government. He intended to tighten his control over the country pushing aside opponents of fascism and abolishing the parliamentary system he hated. Matteotti emerged as one of his most effective critics.

Giacomo Matteotti was the son of a prosperous hardware merchant and property owner in the Po Valley. Born in the town of Fratta Polesine in Rovigno province on May 22, 1885, he was attracted to the Socialist movement while he was still in secondary school. He studied law at the University of Bologna and traveled widely inside and outside Italy during his school vacations.

The young man was an enthusiastic scholar of criminal law, and in 1910 he wrote his first book on this subject. Even in this work his Socialist convictions were evident, and he stressed the role of social and economic conditions in producing criminal behavior. Abandoning his plans for a career in teaching, he was elected to posts in municipal and then provincial government.

During the war years, Matteotti, an outspoken opponent of Italy's participation in World War I, rose rapidly as an official of the Italian Socialist Party. He made a national reputation for himself in speeches at the 1916 Party Conference on city government, which dealt with the problems of postwar planning. He was also one of the Party's leading figures in dealing with the problems of rural laborers. In 1922, the Italian Socialist Party split, some of its members moving toward the militancy and authoritarian organization of the Russian Communist Party. Matteotti became the leader of the moderate, democratic Socialist faction, the PSU.

The young Socialist leader was horrified to see fascism emerging as a political force in his home region of the Po Valley. As one friend put it, he saw fascism as "agricultural slavery." When Mussolini took over as prime minister, Matteotti quickly challenged the future dictator. In 1922, he interrupted a speech by the new prime minister with the call, "Long Live Parliament."

Mussolini's control over Italian politics remained a shaky one for years after 1922. His most serious weakness was the lack of a Fascist majority in Parliament. To remove this barrier, Mussolini had a new election law passed. The

Acerbo Law of 1923 permitted the Fascists to get an overwhelming majority of the seats in Parliament merely by getting the largest number of votes cast for any party. Thus the elections of April 1924 were crucial to the future of fascism.

The Fascists obtained their majority, but Matteotti immediately challenged the election results when Parliament met on May 30, 1924. In a dramatic speech lasting more than an hour, Matteotti accused the government of committing election fraud. The balloting, especially in northern Italy, had been marred by violence and intimidation, he claimed. With Fascist bullies overseeing the voting, the results were predetermined and they were corrupt. Matteotti maintained his long-standing reputation for precision and accuracy by citing numerous instances of wrongdoing. Interrupted by a storm of protest from Fascist deputies, he called for the election to be declared invalid.

The speech cost Matteotti his life. Aware of the danger, he had remarked to a colleague at the conclusion of his speech: "Now you can prepare my funeral oration."

In early June, Matteotti disappeared. Witnesses in Rome reported seeing a group of men drag someone into a car on June 10; the bloodstained car was quickly found and traced to officials of the Fascist Party. Although Matteotti's body was not discovered until weeks later, the shock of his kidnapping and probable murder had an immediate effect.

The killers acted without direct orders from Mussolini, and it is possible they intended only to kidnap Matteotti. In trying to fight off his attackers, Matteotti may have led them to kill him. Nonetheless, Mussolini's movement had made a practice of using violence against political opponents, and Mussolini himself had responded to Matteotti's speech by saying that it deserved more than just words in reply.

Outside Italy, protests developed, notably in Britain and France. Inside Italy, it seemed that Mussolini's Fascist government would fall. When many political leaders called for his resignation as prime minister, Mussolini was forced to give up his cabinet position as minister of the interior (an office charged with maintaining domestic order), and several other Fascist leaders gave up high-ranking positions in the police. Five Fascist thugs with long records for attacks on opposition political figures were arrested for assaulting and kidnapping Matteotti.

Gradually, however, Mussolini regained his footing, and anti-Fascist groups in Italy let the opportunity to remove him slip away. The most vigorous protest against the crime came when more than 100 deputies boycotted all sessions of the Italian Parliament beginning in late June. Opponents of Mussolini hoped that King Victor Emmanuel III would demand the resignation of the Fascist leader, but the king never took this decisive step. Matteotti's killers went unpunished. During 1925, Mussolini moved to consolidate his dictatorship. Socialist leaders were arrested, censorship was tightened, and Mussolini ended parliamentary control over his government.

The significance of Matteotti's life and death continued to reverberate for more than two decades. Matteotti's Socialist colleague Filippo Turati helped to found a coalition of anti-Fascist exile groups. A symbol of Matteotti's memory was a statue of the murdered leader erected in Brussels, Belgium, in 1927. In 1943 in the midst of World War II, Italian Socialist partisan units formed themselves into "Matteotti brigades" to fight the Fascists.

A remarkable sequel to the Matteotti case came in the aftermath of World War II. In 1945, four of the individuals implicated in the murder of the Socialist leader were arrested. Two of them, including Amerigo Dumini, the leader of the group that killed Matteotti, were convicted and sentenced to 30 years in prison.

Further Reading

Delzell, Charles F. *Mussolini's Enemies: The Italian Anti-Fascist Resistance.* Princeton University Press, 1961.
Lyttelton, Adrian. *The Seizure of Power: Fascism in Italy, 1919-1929.* Scribner, 1973.
Seton-Watson, Christopher. *Italy from Liberalism to Fascism, 1870-1925.* Methuen, 1967.
De Grand, Alexander. *Italian Fascism: Its Origins & Development.* University of Nebraska Press, 1982.
————. *The Italian Left in the Twentieth Century: A History of the Socialist and Communist Parties,* Indiana University Press, 1989.
Tannenbaum, Edward R. *The Fascist Experience: Italian Society and Culture, 1922-1945.* Basic Books, 1972. □

St. Matthew

St. Matthew (active 1st century), one of the Apostles chosen by Jesus, is traditionally considered the author of the First Gospel.

The first recorded information of Matthew tells of a meeting between him and Jesus. At that time Matthew's name was Levi; he was the son of Alphaeus. He was sitting at his tax collector's desk near the Sea of Galilee when Jesus told him to follow him (Matthew 9:9; Mark 2:14). Levi did this promptly. It is supposed that Jesus, as he did in other cases, gave Levi another name, Matthew, meaning "gift of Yahweh." After this event Matthew Levi threw a feast for Jesus and his companions in his own house (Luke 5:9). Apart from some other passing references to him, there are no further precise details concerning Matthew's life, except that he seems to have been associated closely with the Apostle Thomas in the ministry of preaching the Gospel (Matthew 9:3; Mark 3:13-19; Luke 6:13-16). The Apostles of Jesus generally worked in pairs, and the above texts seem to associate Thomas and Matthew. It is not known how or where Matthew ended his life. Traditions and legends differ as to whether he died a martyr's death or of natural causes.

Outside the New Testament, the most ancient and authoritative reference to Matthew is found in fragments of a work by Papias (born ca. A.D. 70), who apparently knew some of the early Apostles, including Matthew. Papias tells us that "Matthew wrote down the sayings in the Hebrew language." The "sayings" refer to the oral traditions con-

cerning Jesus which circulated after his death. Scholars generally agree that the term "Hebrew" in Papias's mouth refers to the Aramaic language and not to Hebrew. This testimony of Papias, in addition to extensive examination of the Gospel text, has led most modern critics to conclude that the First Gospel is a Greek text modeled on an Aramaic original which has been lost. Modern research has not been able to decide definitively whether Matthew was the author of the First Gospel in its present Greek form or in the Aramaic original.

The framework of the present Greek Gospel of Matthew seems to have been taken from the Gospel of Mark, but the author of the First Gospel filled in the gaps between units of the Marcan text with material drawn from another source. This source, it has been surmised, may have been the original Aramaic text. Matthew also introduced collections of sayings which Mark apparently did not possess.

According to Matthew, also, the content of the Gospel message is not the life and personality of Jesus but the doctrine and the preaching of Jesus, by which he gave a new and final interpretation to the Law of Moses. Matthew's Gospel is also the one which makes abundant use of Old Testament texts and a rabbinic method of exegesis in order to establish the authenticity of Jesus as the expected Messiah of Israel. Finally, Matthew stresses the ecclesiastical aspect of Jesus' preaching and his new movement. The composition of the First Gospel in its present Greek form is generally assigned to the years 75-80.

Further Reading

For information on Matthew consult George D. Kilpatrick, *The Origins of the Gospel according to St. Matthew* (1946), and Krister Stendahl, *The School of St. Matthew and Its Use of the Old Testament* (1954). □

Matthew Paris

The English Benedictine monk Matthew Paris (ca. 1200-1259) was the most important chronicler of the 13th century. He was also an accomplished manuscript illustrator, biographer, and cartographer.

Matthew Paris, sometimes referred to as Matthew of Paris, probably had no connection with France by birth or education. Although no information exists concerning his parentage or his early life, he became a monk at St. Albans, a monastery on a main road about 15 miles northwest of London, on Jan. 21, 1217. There he received his training as a scribe and artist and, under Roger Wendover, as the abbey's historiographer. In 1248-1249 Matthew was called upon by Norway's King Haakon IV and by Pope Innocent IV to adjust the financial and spiritual affairs of the Benedictine abbey of St. Benet Holm on the island of Niderholm in Norway. Except for this successful journey, Matthew, for the most part, remained at St. Albans until his death in 1259.

After Roger Wendover's death in 1235, Matthew incorporated Roger's *Flores historiarum* into his own chief work, the *Chronica majora,* revising Roger's text and extending it from 1235 to 1259. A prolific and indefatigable writer, Matthew wrote some 300,000 words in his section alone. In it he narrated events with his personal commentary that often demonstrates his strong prejudices against King Henry III, the Pope, friars, foreigners, civil servants, theologians, and almost any person or group who, in Matthew's eyes, was guilty of either abuse of power or interference with the home rule of his monastic movement. He wrote in Latin, the lingua franca of the Middle Ages, and his style is vivid and colorful.

As a respected intimate of such important figures as Henry III and his brother Richard, Earl of Cornwall, among many others, Matthew's fame as a chronicler was so widespread that distinguished guests at St. Albans freely shared their adventures with him, supplying him with details for his chronicle.

Although Matthew is considered by modern scholars more a chronicler than a historian, he assiduously collected, albeit not always accurately, about 350 documents in an appendix to his *Chronica,* the *Liber additamentorum.* His abridgments of the *Chronica majora*—the *Historia Anglorum,* devoted primarily to English affairs, and the *Abbreviatio chronicorum* (or *Historia minor*), concentrating on the period 1067—1253—contain differing versions of the same events. In his *Gesta abbatum,* Matthew recorded the lives of the first 23 abbots of St. Albans and sketched a miniature portrait of each.

In addition to his Latin biographies of Edmund Rich and Stephen Langton, Matthew wrote in Anglo-Norman verse the lives of Saints Alban, Edward the Confessor, Thomas Becket, and Edmund Rich, each work amply illustrated.

As an artist, Matthew enjoyed high esteem. His manuscript illustrations, both drawings and paintings, demonstrate his skill and talent in illuminating his narrative. Further, his valuable contributions to cartography include the earliest known detail maps of England and Scotland, listing as many as 280 place names. His itineraries, or road maps, from London to Italy and several maps of Palestine admirably executed in color attest to his talents as an artist and cartographer. He also ranks high as a pioneer in the history of heraldry because he depicted quite accurately about 130 coats of arms of the period.

Although Matthew is not always reliable because of his frequent exaggerations, prejudices, and carelessness, he nevertheless left a readable account and, more important, one with a feeling of his time.

Further Reading

The best book on Matthew is Richard Vaughan, *Matthew Paris* (1958), a scholarly yet readable study with an excellent bibliography. Vivian Hunter Galbraith's monograph, *Roger Wendover and Matthew Paris* (1944), discusses the roles of both men as chroniclers of St. Albans. For background on Matthew and his time see Claude Jenkins, *The Monastic Chronicler and the Early School of St. Albans* (1922), and David Knowles, *The Religious Orders in England* (1948). □

Garrett Mattingly

The historian and professor Garrett Mattingly (1900-1962) was a student of 16th-century Europe who wrote the novel-like histories *Catherine of Aragon* and *The Armada*.

Born on May 6, 1900, in Washington, D.C., Garrett Mattingly was the son of Ida Garrett and Leonard Mattingly, a civil servant and industrialist. Young Mattingly attended elementary school in Washington until 1913, when his family moved to Kalamazoo, Michigan. Here he enrolled as a student at the local public high school and graduated in 1918.

After graduation he enlisted in the Army and served with the 43d Infantry Division until 1919. In that year he entered Harvard University, where he majored in 16th-century literature and history and from which he received all three of his degrees: a B.A. in 1923, an M.A. in 1926, and a Ph.D. in 1935. At Harvard he studied European diplomatic history under the direction of the distinguished historian of 16th- and 17th-century Spain, Roger Bigelow Merriman, who, Mattingly once said, "taught me whatever I know of my craft." Mattingly was an outstanding student

who published an article on Shakespeare, was elected to Phi Beta Kappa, and, in 1922, while still an undergraduate, received a Sheldon Travelling Fellowship which enabled him to spend a year studying in France and Italy. Even at this stage of his life Mattingly's interests were eclectic—in addition to his historical studies he wrote poetry, began a novel, and served as a stringer for several French and Italian newspapers.

Mattingly's professional career began at Northwestern University in Evanston, Illinois, where he was appointed an instructor in English in 1926. At Northwestern he met writer and historian (chiefly of the American West) Bernard DeVoto, who became one of his closest friends and who had a significant and enduring influence on his career. DeVoto, a fellow Harvard graduate, was a brilliant and iconoclastic writer whose wide knowledge, ability to synthesize, and evocative historical narratives Mattingly greatly admired.

A Study of the Celebrated Catherine

In 1928 Mattingly married former teacher Gertrude McCollum. He also became an instructor in English and history at Long Island University, where he remained for some 14 years, rising through the academic ranks to become an assistant professor and finally associate professor. It was while he was at Long Island University that Mattingly began his lifelong affair with New York, a city he loved because it was, in his view, both civilized and cosmopolitan. It was also while he was at Long Island University that Mattingly published his first important professional articles on 16th-century Western European diplomatic history. In 1936 Mattingly received the first of what eventually would be three Guggenheim Foundation fellowships, which enabled him to study Catherine of Aragon in the context of Anglo-Spanish diplomacy in the 16th century; this study resulted in the publication of *Catherine of Aragon* in 1941.

Catherine of Aragon was an immediate critical and popular success and was a 1942 Literary Guild selection. It examines the personalities, the motivations, and the quite extraordinary complexities involved in Catherine's life, her marriages, and her divorce and the parts they played on the wider—and often seamy and always shifting—stage of Western European politics and diplomacy. The book is based on an immense amount of research into varied primary sources in many languages. This scholarship, however, is never obtrusive in the book, which is written novel-fashion without footnotes and in a seamless, compelling, and often witty narrative.

Mattingly was able to paint, in a few lines, unforgettable portraits of remote figures. Pope Clement VII, for example, was described as a "sensitive, delicate, nervous man, with a talent for log-rolling and devious, personal intrigue, and the soul, if not of an artist, at least of a good, second-rate art critic; he was temperamentally unfitted for the dangerous decisions called for by these iron times." Mattingly sympathetically dealt with most of the characters, though one senses that he tired quickly of Henry VIII and his flexible conscience. It is clear that he greatly admired Catherine, her intelligence, her patience, her integrity, and her ability to view Western Europe as an organic whole, Christendom. It is also clear that Mattingly saw in Henry VIII's ruthless consolidation of power an implicit lesson for his own time: "Henry wielded the twin weapons of his future despotism, the appropriate weapons, for that matter, of any despotism, which seeks to break the pattern of a people's life—cant and terror."

From 1942 to 1945 Mattingly served on active duty in the U.S. Naval Reserve as a lieutenant commander. In July 1946 he joined the faculty at Cooper Union in New York City as professor of history and chairman of the Division of Social Philosophy. In the latter capacity he scheduled and hosted a series of lectures on topics of general interest, an activity which allowed him to perfect his own lecturing skills. He received his second Guggenheim fellowship in 1946. In 1946 he also became professor of history at Columbia University, where he remained for the rest of his life. He was a popular teacher whose dramatic and unconventional lectures were always well-attended and a stimulating mentor to a whole generation of graduate students.

He received a Fulbright scholarship for research in Italy for the 1953-1954 school year, the fruits of which were published in *Renaissance Diplomacy* (1954). Dedicated to Bernard DeVoto, *Renaissance Diplomacy,* a more conventionally academic though no less interesting and critically successful work than its predecessor, is, as Mattingly indicated, "a general account of the development of Western diplomacy in its formative period."

A Study of a Great Naval Disaster

Five years later Mattingly's best-known book, *The Armada,* was published. Like *Catherine of Aragon, The Armada* was a great popular as well as critical success. It was a Book Society choice in England and a History Book Club and Book-of-the-Month Club selection in the United States and received a Pulitzer special citation in 1960. Mattingly recognized that the Armada's story had been frequently told. His purpose was to look at the vast array of primary sources with a "fresh eye" and to place the "narrative of the naval campaign in the broader European context," emphasizing the important political and diplomatic features of what he called the "first international crisis of modern history."

By employing his talents as a writer and a scholar, Mattingly was able to describe such intricate matters as 16th-century naval and military tactics, economic problems, and political and diplomatic intrigues. He also was able to evoke luminous images of the individuals involved. Unlike most other historians writing in English, Mattingly did not make the Spanish into cartoon villains. Elizabeth I's archenemy, Philip II, emerges as a sad, consciencious, and "terribly industrious" monarch, and the often maligned commander of the Armada, the Duke of Medina Sidonia, is presented as an honorable man who was the unhappy victim of circumstance. Despite his attention to the details concerning the Armada's defeat, Mattingly emphasized that the actual outcome of the battle was far less significant than the impact it had on Spanish and English prestige throughout Europe and on the growth of the myth of the Armada

defeat, a "victory of freedom over tyranny, of David over Goliath."

An Author Who Loved History

By 1960 Mattingly had reached the pinnacle of a distinguished academic career. In January of that year he was named as the first incumbent of the William R. Shepherd Chair of European History at Columbia. Several months later he was awarded his third Guggenheim for research on the Italian Renaissance. Wesleyan University made him an honorary D.Litt. in 1961. He was named George Eastman Visiting Professor at Oxford University for the 1962-1963 school year, and it was at Oxford that he died of emphysema on December 18, 1962.

Although he died relatively young, Mattingly left a three-fold and far from insignificant legacy. First, he left a large number of students who revered him and were influenced by him and who themselves became historians. Second, he left friends and colleagues who respected him for his scholarship; envied his wide interest in and knowledge of art, music, literature, food, and wine; admired him for his skill and talents; and cherished the memory of one who was in their minds a 20th-century Renaissance man. Finally, he left three important books which provide not only a wealth of information about the subject matters themselves but also much insight into Garrett Mattingly. They reflect his distaste for despotism and dogmatic opinion of any flavor and his concern with the idea of Western civilization (including the United States) as a cultural and historical unity. In addition, they indicate his regard for factual accuracy: "History," he once remarked, "is the most difficult of the *belles lettres,* for it must be true." He based his work on a technical mastery of the material in his field, which was no easy task, for he was required to read a mind-boggling variety of formal and informal documents in 16th-century handwriting in several 16th-century languages and local variations thereof ranging from Latin to Spanish to French to German to Flemish to English. His work further shows his concern for literary craftsmanship—for carefully constructed and polished prose—and a keen interest in individual personality and situational nuance. These books, especially *Catherine of Aragon* and *The Armada,* are important in that they have been read and applauded not merely by a scholarly few but by a large audience and have presented to several decades of readers and history students a fascinating and far too often neglected glimpse of 16th-century losers.

Mattingly made distinct contributions to the modern historical profession. As he was well aware, his type of "literary," political, narrative history with a potentially wide appeal was rather out of fashion even in the early 1960s. It has been replaced in the vanguard of the profession by the less personal—and often less readable—and more analytical *annales* type of history, which may cover the same era and area but treat them very differently. It is as yet impossible to judge what Mattingly's long range place in the pantheon of American historians may be. But students who attended his lectures and those who have read his books have retained a vivid and indelible picture of the people and the world he depicted. As an historian and as a teacher, he could not have hoped for more.

Further Reading

Robert M. Kingdon's "Garrett Mattingly" in *The American Scholar* (Summer 1982) is a thoughtful, analytical, and sympathetic appraisal of Mattingly's importance as a teacher and writer by one of his former students at Columbia. *From the Renaissance to the Counter-Reformation: Essays in Honor of Garrett Mattingly,* edited by Charles H. Carter (1965), contains two essays which specifically address themselves to Mattingly. Leo Gershoy's "Garrett Mattingly: A Personal Appreciation" describes Mattingly's multi-faceted personality and gives readers an idea of why Mattingly was such a fascinating and admired figure. J. H. Hexter's "Garrett Mattingly, Historian" discusses the seeming paradox of Mattingly's painstakingly researched books' wide popularity, which Hexter attributes both to Mattingly's literary talents and to his hatred of pedantry and of both "new wave" and "old wave" theoretical type history. For an appreciative essay on Mattingly's academic career and its successes, as well as an interesting account of his extra-curricular pursuits and tastes, see "Garrett Mattingly," *Political Science Quarterly* (September 1963). □

William Somerset Maugham

The British novelist William Somerset Maugham (1874-1965), one of the most popular writers in English in the 20th century, is noted for his clarity of style and skill in storytelling.

Born in Paris, on Jan. 25, 1874, where his father was solicitor to the British embassy, Somerset Maugham was orphaned by the time he was 8 years old. He was reared by a paternal uncle, a clergyman, and at 13 was sent to king's School, Cambridge, intended for Oxford and preparation for the Church. Wanting to write, he obtained his uncle's permission to go to Heidelberg for a time. He chose the profession of medicine and spent 6 years in training at a London hospital. A year as an intern in the Lambeth slums followed, but he never practiced. For 10 years he wrote and lived in poverty in Paris.

In 1907 Maugham's first play, *Lady Frederick,* was successfully produced, and he became known as an author. In the early 1930s he settled in the Villa Mauresque in the south of France, though he continued to travel widely. He was forced to flee the Nazis in 1940 but returned after the war. In 1954, on his eightieth birthday, he was made a Companion of Honour. In 1961 he was named honorary senator of Heidelberg University. Maugham died in Nice on Dec. 16, 1965. Maugham archives were established in the Yale University Library.

The titles of some of Maugham's early novels were familiar to a whole generation of readers: *Of Human Bondage* (1915), *The Moon and Sixpence* (1919), *Ashenden: or, The British Agent* (1938), and *Cakes and Ale: or, The Skeleton in the Cupboard* (1930). A later novel that had some-

thing of the same success was *The Razor's Edge* (1944). Among his plays, perhaps best known and much produced was *Rain* (1922). An early autobiography is *The Summing Up* (1938). Praised by some critics for his craftsmanship and professionalism, he wrote much on the subject of fiction: *Essays—Great Novelists and Their Novels* (1948); *A Writer's Notebook* (1949); and *The Art of Fiction* (1955). *His Travel Books* appeared in 1955; *The Magician, A Novel, Together with a Fragment of Autobiography* in 1956; and essays titled *Points of View* in 1958. In his last years he worked on an autobiography to be published posthumously.

Productive throughout a long life, Maugham is still regarded as having done his great work in the early, largely autobiographical novel *Of Human Bondage*. Though his work was popular, he had a great many enemies because of his apparently malicious portraits of living people (for example, the characters based on Thomas Hardy and Hugh Walpole in *Cakes and Ale*) and because his view of humanity seemed to be one of contempt or of patronizing tolerance. He replied to the latter charge that humanity was like that; he also said that his sympathies were limited and that he had never felt some of the fundamental emotions.

Further Reading

A good introduction to Maugham's works is *The Maugham Reader* (1952). Biographical and critical studies include Cyril Connolly, *The Condemned Playground* (1946); John Brophy, *Somerset Maugham* (1952); Karl G. Pfeiffer, *W. Somerset Maugham: A Candid Portrait* (1959); and Richard A. Cordell,

Somerset Maugham: A Biographical and Critical Study (1961). □

Franz Anton Maulbertsch

The frescoes of Franz Anton Maulbertsch (1724-1796) are the culminating achievement of 18th-century Austrian fresco painting. His highly personal interpretation of the rococo gradually gave way to a more rational, classicizing approach.

Franz Anton Maulbertsch was born in Langenargen on Lake Constance on June 8, 1724, the son of a painter. He studied in Vienna with Peter van Roy and in 1741 enrolled at the academy, where he received the painting prize in 1750. Maulbertsch became a member of the academy in 1759 and a professor there in 1770, for which occasion he produced his *Allegory of the Destiny of Art.*

Although Maulbertsch produced easel paintings of great beauty (*Holy Kindred, St. Narcissus, Self-portrait*), he is chiefly and justly famous for his frescoes. In Vienna and other cities of Austria, Bohemia, Moravia, and Hungary he created scores of vibrantly dramatic and brilliantly colored frescoes filled with an intense and highly personal religious feeling, beginning with the dome (1752) of the Church of Maria Treu in Vienna. Only the most outstanding can be mentioned here: the frescoes in the churches at Heiligenkreuz-Gutenbrunn (1757) and Sümeg in Hungary (1758), in the archepiscopal palace (1758-1760) at Kremsier (Kroměříž) in Moravia, and in the church (1765; destroyed in World War II) at Schwechat near Vienna. These examples of his early period are characterized by agitated compositions, shifting, fragmented color, and elongated ecstatic figures.

From about 1770 a change in Maulbertsch's style can be discerned, with a calmer, more static composition, cooler color, and clearer contours, all the result of his attempts to adjust to the new classicizing ideas becoming popular at the time. In the paintings in the church at Korneuburg (1773) and the frescoes in the Riesensaal (1775) of the Hofburg in Innsbruck and in Mühlfrauen (Dyje) in Bohemia, he shows the influence of these ideas. In his later works, as in the church at Pápa (1782-1783), the archbishop's palace (1783) at Steinamanger (Szombathely) in Hungary, and the library (1794) at Strahov near Prague, his attempts to vitalize the new rationalistic style with reminiscences of his earlier style do not succeed and result in works of high intellectual complexity and great accomplishment but which lack the emotional and visual appeal of those of his youth.

For all of his frescoes Maulbertsch produced oil sketches, which are among the most prized and popular of his works, filled with the expressionistic qualities associated with his name. The most famous is the *Victory of St. James at Clavigo,* made for the Schwechat frescoes. His etchings, such as the *Allegory of Tolerance* (1785), glorifying the edict of toleration of Emperor Joseph II (1781) and the *Charlatan* and the *Peep-show Man* (1785), mirrored the new interests in social reform and folklore of the late 18th century. In his *Self-portrait* (between 1767 and 1794) Maulbertsch created one of the most intriguing, searching Self-portraits in the history of art.

Little is known of the artist's personality, though he was apparently a man of simple, good-natured character, strangely at odds with his very dramatic painting. He lived the life of a quietly successful but not phenomenally wealthy citizen of Vienna. His wife of 34 years died in 1779; they were childless. The next year he married Katherina Schmutzer, the 24-year-old daughter of Jakob Schmutzer, head of the Engravers' Academy in Vienna and his old friend. Two sons were born of this marriage.

Maulbertsch was active in the artistic life of Vienna, participating in academic affairs and helping to found and direct the Pensionsgesellschaft bildender Künstler in 1788, a society created by artists to ensure financial security. He was elected an honorary member of the Academy of Fine Arts of Berlin the same year. While preparing to continue his work at Steinamanger in the decoration of its Cathedral, he died on Aug. 8, 1796, in Vienna, the last of the great Austrian painters of the 18th century, a relic of the rococo in a new epoch in history.

Further Reading

The standard monograph on Maulbertsch is in German. The only work in English to deal with the artist at any length is Eberhard Hempel, *Baroque Art and Architecture in Central Europe* (1965). □

Bill Mauldin

The incomparable cartoon biographer of the ordinary GI in World War II, Bill Mauldin (born 1921) earned two Pulitzer prizes and syndication in over 250 newspapers for his mordant drawings.

The son of Sidney Albert and Edith Katrina (Bemis), Bill Mauldin was born on October 29, 1921, in Mountain Park, New Mexico. He attended public schools in New Mexico and Arizona, depending upon where his father happened to be unemployed. A scrawny boy, often confined to bed by rickets, he expressed his daydreams in drawings of himself as a cowboy or other heroic figure. While in high school, Mauldin took a correspondence course in cartooning. In 1939 he studied cartooning at the Chicago Academy of Fine Arts. Mauldin then worked in Phoenix, drawing gag cartoons for *Arizona Highways.*

Awarded Purple Heart in WWII

In September 1940 he enlisted in the Arizona National Guard, which five days later was federalized. A member of the U.S. Army's 45th Division, Mauldin went overseas in

1943 to Sicily, where he joined the Mediterranean edition of *Stars and Stripes,* the Army's wartime newspaper. Mauldin covered the fighting in Sicily, Salerno, Monte Cassino, and Anzio and then in France and Germany. He was wounded at Salerno and received the Purple Heart.

Mauldin's cartoons for *Stars and Stripes* pictured the ordinary, unheroic GIs, wearily slogging on, getting a job done, and wanting to go home. Like Ernie Pyle's prose, they vividly portrayed what GI life was really like and intimately expressed the GI's hopes and dreams, fears and hardships. For many Americans, Mauldin's combat-weary team of Willie and Joe became the archetypical GIs of the war in Europe. Disenchanted yet dignified, dirty and bearded, the battle-hardened Willie and Joe were more interested in dry socks than in the lofty rhetoric of war aims, and they hated officers almost as much as they hated the war.

Cartoons Portrayed Real Army Life

While most of the Army hierarchy approved of Mauldin's cartoons as a healthy outlet for the average conscript's emotions, some officers—particularly Gen. George S. Patton—objected to the grimy, realistic public image Willie and Joe were projecting of the U.S. Army. Nevertheless, Mauldin's melancholy pen-and-ink commentaries on GI life were brought together in several published collections, including *Star Spangled Banter* (1941 and 1944), *Mud, Mules and Mountains* (1944), and *Up Front* (1945), which earned Mauldin a 1945 Pulitzer Prize.

Released from the army in June 1945, Mauldin went to work for United Features Syndicate, which distributed his cartoon strips to more than 180 newspapers in the United States under the evolving titles "Sweating It Out," "Back Home," and "Willie and Joe." Although his first postwar collection, *Back Home,* won critical acclaim, the angry, bitter tone of Mauldin's liberal cartoons soon led him to be dropped by one newspaper after another.

In 1950 he went to Hollywood to try his hand as an actor and technical advisor in several films, and early in 1952 he went to the war front in Korea. His report of the experience was published as *Bill Mauldin in Korea* (1952). In 1956 he ran as a Democrat for Congress in New York's heavily Republican 28th Congressional District and was easily trounced by the incumbent, Katherine St. George.

Cartoons Syndicated to Newspapers

Mauldin joined the staff of the St. Louis *Post-Dispatch* as editorial cartoonist in 1958 and won another Pulitzer Prize for his cartoons the next year. His wry satires on the politics of Eisenhower's last years in the presidency were collected in *What's Got Your Back Up?* (1961). *I've Decided I Want My Seat Back* (1965) summed up his liberal commentaries on the desegregation struggles of the early 1960s. In June 1962 Mauldin moved to the Chicago *Sun-Times,* where his editorial cartoons were syndicated to more than 200 newspapers. Continuing "to buck power," as he put it, to satirize the high and mighty, Mauldin earned the reputation as a worthy successor to Herblock, the editorial cartoonist for the *Washington Post.* His books included *The Brass Ring* (1971) and *Mud and Guts* (1978). An avid flying buff, Mauldin described his air experiences in articles for *Sports Illustrated.* His honors included the 1962 Cartoonist of the Year award of the National Cartoonists Society and the Sigma Delta Chi journalism fraternity's 1963, 1969, and 1972 awards for editorial cartooning.

Mauldin's work was part of an exhibit at the National Archives in Washington, D.C. in 1992. The exhibit, called "Draw! Political Cartoons From Left to Right," featured Mauldin and five other prominent political cartoonists. A fiftieth-anniversary edition of his classic *Up Front* was published in 1995.

Further Reading

Bill Mauldin's best known books are *Up Front* (1945); *Back Home* (1947); *What's Got Your Back Up?* (1961); and *I've Decided I Want My Seat Back* (1965); His wartime cartoons are analyzed in John Morton Blum, *V Was For Victory, Politics and American Culture During World War II* (1976); Biographical data appears in *Who's Who in America* (1964-1965). Also see *American History Illustrated* (March/April 1992); and *The Atlantic Monthly* (June 1995). □

ceeding years his stories were in great demand, for newspaper publication in the first instance. Collected, they eventually provided material for 16 volumes.

For the subjects of his stories Maupassant drew on his experiences as a boy among the farming folk and fishermen of Normandy and also on the observations he made of his colleagues and superiors when he was working as a government official in Paris; though it was Balzac who first introduced the lowly clerks into literature, it was Maupassant who explored every aspect of the lives of these underpaid bureaucrats. Maupassant's humor is sometimes racy but more often bitter; the famous "whiplash ending," which he invented, can be cruel in the extreme. His work as a whole is permeated by irony and pessimism; humanity is shown motivated more by greed and snobbery than by any finer passions. Some of his later stories, dealing with eerie hallucinations, reflect the breakdown in Maupassant's mental health, attributable to syphilis. In the last 18 months of his life he was confined to a sanatorium for the insane, where he died on July 6, 1893.

Apart from the short stories, Maupassant published six novels, including *Bel-Ami* (1885), the saga of a handsome scoundrel who makes good, and *Pierre et Jean* (1888), which tells how a young man's image of his mother is shattered when he discovers that she had conceived his younger brother out of wedlock. Henry James described Maupassant as a "lion in the path"—meaning that he represented a formidable barrier to the development of a morally significant literature.

Henri René Albert Guy de Maupassant

Henri René Albert Guy de Maupassant (1850-1893) is the most celebrated of French short-story writers. The brilliance of his technique is combined with an ethical nihilism.

G uy de Maupassant was born on Aug. 5, 1850, in Normandy; his exact birthplace has never been established. His father, a libertine with a roving disposition, and his mother were legally separated when Guy was still a boy, and he spent a carefree adolescence under the indulgent surveillance of his cultivated mother. When he reached man's estate, the place of his father was to some extent taken by the novelist Gustave Flaubert, who had been a close friend of Madame de Maupassant for many years.

Under Flaubert's tutelage, the young Maupassant underwent a strict course of training in the craft of literature, at the same time as he was earning his living in the civil service. He became known to members of the naturalist school and collaborated with Zola and four of his disciples in producing in 1880 a volume of short stories about the Franco-Prussian War entitled *Soirées de Médan*. Maupassant's contribution, *Boule de suif*, was so superior to the others that his reputation was made on the spot. In suc-

Further Reading

The best study in English of Maupassant's life is Francis Steegmuller, *Maupassant: A Lion in the Path* (1949). Two scholarly literary studies were written by Edward D. Sullivan, *Maupassant the Novelist* (1954) and *Maupassant: The Short Stories* (1962).

Additional Sources

Jackson, Stanley, *Guy de Maupassant,* Folcroft, Pa. Folcroft Library Editions, 1974; Norwood, Pa.: Norwood Editions, 1977.
Lerner, Michael G., *Maupassant,* London: Allen & Unwin, 1975.
Sherard, Robert Harborough, *The life, work, and evil fate of Guy de Maupassant (gentilhomme de lettres),* Folcroft, Pa.: Folcroft Library Editions, 1976.
Troyat, Henri, *Maupassant,* Paris: Flammarion, 1989. □

François Mauriac

The French author François Mauriac (1885-1970), a fervent Catholic, is best known for his novels, usually set in Bordeaux or the Landes district of southwestern France, with their central themes of faith, sin, and divine grace.

François Mauriac was born in Bordeaux on Nov. 11, 1885, of a prosperous middle-class family. He lost his father in infancy, but the influence of his mother, a stern and puritanical Catholic, pervades his literary works. Educated at a Catholic school and at Bordeaux University, Mauriac moved to Paris in 1906, determined to become a writer. He published his first volume of poems in 1909; more poetry and two novels followed before he was mobilized as an army medical orderly in 1914. He was invalided out 3 years later. From 1920 date Mauriac's most productive years as a novelist, his novels including *Le Baiser au lépreux* (1922; *A Kiss for the Leper*), *Genitrix* (1923; *Genitrix*), *Le Désert de l'amour* (1925; *The Desert of Love*), and *Thérèse Desqueyroux* (1927; *Thérèse*).

About 1928 came a religious crisis in Mauriac's life, with a corresponding change of emphasis in his works. Earlier he had been criticized for portraying sinners more attractively than believers in the narrow, provincial, middle-class families of his novels, where, as all sexuality implies sin, love and happiness become impossible. Now he began to stress the possibility of divine grace, even for the hardened atheist and family tyrant who is the hero of *Le Noeud de vipères* (1932; *Vipers' Tangle*), the most successful of the later novels. In 1933 Mauriac was elected to the French Academy. Other works of this period include biographies, more poetry, and religious essays.

In the late 1930s Mauriac found politics coming to the forefront of his attention: he denounced Gen. Franco's insurrection in Spain and later, after the German defeat of France in 1940, helped the cause of the French Resistance with his pen. After the Liberation he continued to write hard-hitting political articles in several newspapers. More novels, stage plays, volumes of criticism, memoirs, and diaries brought Mauriac's total number of books to over 60. Awarded the Nobel Prize for literature in 1952, Mauriac became, after De Gaulle's return to power in 1958, one of the President's most passionate supporters. Mauriac died on Sept. 1, 1970.

Mauriac's fictional world is that of his childhood and adolescence in the Landes region in the period about 1900, which he evokes with poetic intensity; his primary theme, the clash between sin and the desire for religious salvation. "I try to make the Catholic universe of evil palpable, tangible, odorous." This powerful creation of atmosphere and shrewd psychological insight—if perhaps in a somewhat narrow field—have brought Mauriac an extremely high reputation as a novelist.

Further Reading

Books devoted to Mauriac include Martin Jarrett-Kerr, *François Mauriac* (1954); M. F. Moloney, *François Mauriac: A Critical Study* (1958); Cecil Jenkins, *Mauriac* (1965); and J. E. Flower, *Intention and Achievement: The Novels of François Mauriac* (1969). There are discussions of Mauriac in Martin Turnell, *The Art of French Fiction* (1959); Conor Cruise O'Brien, *Maria Cross* (1963); and Philip Stratford, *Faith and Fiction* (1964).

Additional Sources

Simon, Pierre Henri, *Mauriac,* Paris: Seuil, 1974 1953.
Speaight, Robert, *François Mauriac: a study of the writer and the man,* London: Chatto and Windus, 1976. □

Maurice of Nassau

The Dutch general and statesman Maurice of Nassau, Prince of Orange (1567-1625), was the founder with Oldenbarnevelt of the Dutch Republic, or United Provinces of the Netherlands.

Maurice of Nassau was the second son of William I, "the Silent," and the only child of his second marriage, to Anna of Saxony. Born at the Nassaus' ancestral castle of Dillenburg, Germany, on Nov. 14, 1567, he spent the first decade of his life in Germany and then went to the Netherlands, where his father was leading the revolt against Spain. Only 16 years of age when his father was murdered, he was called at once to preside over the Council of State, then the principal organ of central government in the north, the United Provinces. His career was aided by the sponsorship of Johan van Oldenbarnevelt, the advocate of the States of Holland and the political leader of the province.

As soon as he reached the age of 18, in 1585, Maurice was named *stadholder* (governor) of Holland and Zeeland at Oldenbarnevelt's initiative, as well as provincial captain and admiral general, in order to provide a Dutch political and military authority to set against the Earl of Leicester, who was coming to the United Provinces as governor general on behalf of Elizabeth I of England. Maurice was later elected stadholder of Utrecht and Overijssel (1590), Gelderland (1591), and Groningen and Drenthe (1620).

After Leicester's recall in 1587, Maurice became in effect the commander in chief of the army of the United Provinces, although legally he was in command only in the provinces where he was *stadholder* and in the lands under the direct authority of the States General. Maurice undertook reorganization of the Dutch military forces on the basis of the principles and methods which he drew from study of the warfare and the military writings of the Romans of antiquity. He paid special attention to *siegecraft,* employing the great mathematician Simon Stevin as a military engineer and introducing the use of regular soldiers in trench digging and similar operations. His success in creating the most modern army of his time was demonstrated in a series of victories beginning with the capture of Breda in 1590, followed the next year by the conquest of Zutphen and Deventer in Overijssel and Delfzijl in the north, the defense of Arnhem against Allessandro Farnese, and then the capture of Hulst in Zeeland and Nijmegen far to the east. The successful siege of Geertruidenberg in 1593 was the supreme achievement of his military science.

A period of reversals followed until 1597, when Maurice defeated the Spaniards at Turnhout and then captured a chain of towns in the eastern Netherlands which deprived the Spaniards of their last foothold north of the Rhine River: the Dutch proclaimed that he had completed fencing-in their "garden," and the United Provinces became in reality the independent republic they already claimed to be in law. Although Maurice was able to win a brilliant victory over the Spaniards at Nieuwpoort in 1600, the southern Netherlands remained under Spanish control, especially after Ambrogio de Spinola took over command of the Spanish armies in 1603.

The close political collaboration between Oldenbarnevelt and Maurice broke up, especially after peace negotiations began with the Spaniards in 1607 over the prince's objections. Maurice, himself indifferent to theological questions, aligned himself with the Contraremonstrants against Oldenbarnevelt, because, as strict Calvinists, they were adamant against peace with the papist foe. However, the Twelve Years Truce was concluded in 1609. It was not until expiration of the truce began to approach that the question of its extension or renewal of the war brought Maurice and Oldenbarnevelt into mortal enmity. When the States of Holland, led by Oldenbarnevelt, began to raise its own troops in an effort to enforce its authority upon the Contraremonstrants, Maurice saw his own powers put in jeopardy, and he arranged the arrest and trial of Oldenbarnevelt and three collaborators (among them Hugo Grotius) and the former's execution as a traitor in 1619. Meanwhile, in 1618, he had inherited the title of Prince of Orange when his elder brother, Philip William, who had remained a Catholic and loyal to Spain, died.

The war was resumed in 1621, but Maurice was now a worn old man and unable to recapture his battlefield gifts. He was the victim of an unsuccessful assassination attempt in 1623 in which two sons of Oldenbarnevelt were implicated, but he lived until 1625, dying at The Hague on April 23, only 2 months before Spinola recaptured Breda. However, he had trained his younger brother, Frederick Henry, to be a military leader after his own best principles, and the United Provinces remained intact and free.

Further Reading

Although there is no adequate biographical study of Maurice in English, he is discussed in several useful background works: Pieter Geyl, *Netherlands in the Seventeenth Century* (2 vols., 1936; rev. ed. 1961-1964); Charles Wilson, *Dutch Republic and the Civilization of the Seventeenth Century* (1968); and Edward Grierson, *The Fatal Inheritance* (1969). ☐

John Frederick Denison Maurice

The English theologian and cleric John Frederick Denison Maurice (1805-1872) was a founder of Christian socialism.

Frederick Denison Maurice was born in Suffolk on Aug. 29, 1805, the son of a deeply pious, politically radical Unitarian minister-teacher. When he went to Trinity College, Cambridge, he was much influenced by the Platonically derived, idealist philosophy then coming from

Germany, especially through the works of S. T. Coleridge. He studied law but became an editor in London. However, about 1828, convinced that he had wasted his Cambridge years, he entered Oxford.

In 1831 Maurice was baptized an Anglican; in 1834 he was ordained. At this time he made a considerable stir with a long novel, *Eustace Conway,* and a tract in defense of the Oxford requirement of subscription to the Thirty-nine Articles, the Anglican creed, on entrance. He was professor of literature and history, and later of divinity, at King's College, until he was forced to resign in 1853, charged with unorthodox principles. He was professor of theology at Cambridge from 1866 until his death on April 1, 1872.

Maurice's greatest prominence, by the standard of public activity, came in the late 1840s and early 1850s: Christian socialism was a product of these politically disturbed years. In 1848 he helped to found and became principal of Queen's College, the first serious institution of higher learning for women. Maurice and his friends had been meeting with groups of radical, free-thinking workingmen, and in 1849-1850 they sponsored producers' cooperatives among tailors and seamstresses. These survived only briefly, but in 1854 Maurice extended his work in this direction when he organized and became first principal of a "Working Man's College" in London, which soon added classes for women.

Maurice was not primarily a social reformer, although, as he early said, he felt a "mighty impulse" toward politics in service to his spiritual objectives. He called himself a theologian (a "digger"), meaning that he worked to instate his simple but subtle religion at the basis of British society, especially in its Church, education, and economy. Christian socialism—Maurice invented the phrase in 1850—was a logical outgrowth of this steady purpose. (In a tactical sense, it was frankly meant to Christianize socialism and avert revolution.) Yet his religion, though liberal, was so idiosyncratic as to set him at odds with all the contending mid-Victorian sects, from Evangelicals to Anglo-Catholics. Further, he refused to sponsor any party or static, narrow creed or to give formulaic responses to his correspondents. He was tagged a "muddy mystic," and John Stuart Mill concluded that "there was more intellectual power wasted in Maurice than in any other of my contemporaries." But, he added, "few of them . . . have had so much to waste."

Further Reading

The earliest and most important biography of Maurice is by his son, Frederick Maurice, *The Life of Frederick Denison Maurice* (2 vols., 1884). A modern study, topically organized, is Herbert George Wood, *Frederick Denison Maurice* (1950). The most authoritative work on Maurice's theological and ecclesiastical thought is A. R. Vidler, *Witness to the Light: F. D. Maurice's Message for Today* (1948). Two modern studies of Maurice's legacy of Christian social concern are Charles E. Raven, *Christian Socialism, 1848-1854* (1920; repr. 1968), and Torbey Christensen, *Origin and History of Christian Socialism, 1848-54* (1962). ☐

Charles Marie Photius Maurras

Charles Marie Photius Maurras (1868-1952) was a French political writer and reactionary. Moving spirit and principal spokesman of Action Française, he was an antidemocrat, racist, monarchist, and worshiper of tradition and of the organic nation-state.

Charles Maurras was born in Martigues near Marseilles. He studied philosophy in Paris, where he was influenced by Auguste Comte, George Sorel, Henri Bergson, Maurice Barrès, and the racist journalist Édouard Drumont.

With Jean Moreas, in 1891 Maurras helped found the École Romane, and in 1892, with Frederico Amouretti, successfully took over the *Felibrige de Paris*—both movements dedicated to the purification of the French language and culture.

In both literature and politics Maurras sought to identify in history, especially in 17th-century classical traditions, all these concepts, ideals, institutions, and attributes of character which seemingly had succeeded. He considered his historical approach empirical and from this data sought to distill or induce a method for correcting evils and solving problems. He was committed to rescuing France from supposed literary and political degradation and corruption brought on by the Revolution, individualistic materialism, and predisposition toward relativism, eclecticism, and nihilism.

Believing the liberal individualism of the Revolution had opened the floodgates to degrading foreign forces—especially Jews—Maurras was clearly racist. Though nominally a man of letters, by 1899 his interests inclined toward politics, and he carried both his ideas and energies into the Ligue d'Action Française, which he and Barrès quickly appropriated and converted into the stillexisting Action Française. Maurras's reverence for the past remained, and applying his literary methods to political analysis, he coined in 1900 the term ''integral nationalism''—''the exclusive pursuit of national policies, the absolute maintenance of national integrity, and the steady increase of national power''—a concept remarkably paralleling Barrès's ''collective egotism.'' Then, combining the classical ideals of order, hierarchy, and discipline with attitudes of authoritarianism and the spirit of romantic patriotism, he sought to lay the foundations of an effective political movement.

Having conceived the principle, Maurras then developed his method—''organizing empiricism''—the use of historical experience as a model and guide for programs of action. Application of the method, in his hands, indicated that a return to monarchy alone could save France. This movement, too, was perhaps as much literary as political, despite Maurras's fanatic insistence upon the latter orientation. His insistence brought him imprisonment. In 1926 five of his works were put on the Index, and the Action Française was banned by the Church.

Though against collaboration, following the German invasion, Maurras strongly supported Marshal Pétain. His efforts were in vain. His anachronistic ideas could not effectively be written into Vichy legislation. In 1945, for his part in the Vichy regime, he was sentenced to life imprisonment and deprived of his civil rights by Liberation leaders. Simultaneously, he was condemned and dismissed from the French Academy, to which he had been elected in 1938. Because of illness, in 1952 he was released to a clinic in Tours, where he died a few months later. Throughout these years, except for reconciliation with the Church, he remained intransigent and wrote prodigiously, both literary works (reminiscences) and political polemics. Maurras provided footnotes for French rightists—so long as such remain. The Action Française still exists, is admired by some, and lists a few members in the French Academy.

Further Reading

Most of the writing about Maurras is published in French. The best and most extensive treatments of his life and work, in English, are William Curt Buthman, *The Rise of Integral Nationalism in France* (1939), and Michael Curtis, *Three against the Third Republic: Sorel, Barrès, and Maurras* (1959). Useful bibliographies are included in both of these works. For the story of Action Française, in which Maurras played a most important role, see the books by this title of Edward R. Tannenbaum (1962) and Eugen Weber (1962). See also Samuel M. Osgood, *French Royalism under the Third and Fourth Republics* (1960). □

Matthew Fontaine Maury

The American naval officer and oceanographer Matthew Fontaine Maury (1806-1873) is remembered chiefly for his *The Physical Geography of the Sea* of 1855, now recognized as the first textbook of modern oceanography.

On Jan. 14, 1806, Matthew Fontaine Maury was born near Fredericksburg, Va. When he was 5, his family emigrated to a farm near the frontier village of Franklin, Tenn., where he attended country schools and then entered Harpeth Academy. In 1825 he secured a midshipman's warrant and in the following 9 years made three extensive cruises, including one around the world. In 1836 he published *A New Theoretical and Practical Treatise on Navigation,* which the Navy immediately adopted as a textbook.

Maury first came into wide public notice through a series of articles dealing with naval reform written between 1838 and 1841. During this period he sustained a severe knee injury in a stagecoach accident, which resulted in permanent lameness and made him unfit for sea duty. He was appointed superintendent of the Depot of Charts and Instruments of the Navy Department at Washington, a post which included the superintendency of the new Naval Observatory. Soon afterward he began his researches on winds and currents and, in 1847, issued his *Wind and Current Chart of the North Atlantic,* which was followed by supplementary sailing directions in subsequent years. The savings in time that ships were able to make by following his directions attracted so much notice that at an international congress held in Brussels in 1853 the uniform system of recording oceanographic data he advocated was adopted for the naval vessels and merchant marine of most European nations. Within a few years nations owning three-fourths of the world's shipping were sending their oceanographic observations to Maury, who evaluated the information and distributed the results throughout the world.

So extensive was Maury's knowledge of the sea that he was called upon for help in selecting the most advantageous time and place for laying the Atlantic cable. He prepared a chart representing in profile the bottom of the Atlantic between Europe and America, calling attention to the existence of what he termed the telegraphic plateau. He also helped persuade the public that such a cable was practical.

Despite Maury's pioneering efforts in oceanography, his de-emphasis of astronomy and preference for what he conceived as more practical work brought him into continuing conflict with leaders of American science, so much so that they met with genuine relief his defection to the Confederacy at the outbreak of the Civil War. He was commissioned in the Confederate Navy, assigned to harbor defense, and began experimenting with electric mines. In 1862 the Confederate government sent him to England as a special agent.

After the collapse of the Confederacy, Maury went to Mexico to promote a scheme for the colonization of former Confederates, lived in England for a while, and finally returned to Virginia, where he spent the last 4 years of his life as a professor of meteorology in the Virginia Military Institute at Lexington. He died on Feb. 1, 1873.

Further Reading

Frances Leigh Williams, *Matthew Fontaine Maury: Scientist of the Sea* (1963), has good accounts of Maury's relations with other scientists and supersedes all earlier accounts of his career. For an assessment of his scientific work see John Leighly, ed., *The Physical Geography of the Sea and Its Meteorology* (1963). Earlier works are Charles Lee Lewis, *Matthew Fontaine Maury: The Pathfinder of the Seas* (1927), and John W. Wayland, *The Pathfinder of the Seas' The Life of Matthew Fontaine Maury* (1930). □

Marcel Mauss

The French sociologist and anthropologist Marcel Mauss (1872-1950) is best known as an ethnologist and historian of religion.

Marcel Mauss was born in Épinal on May 10, 1872, to a pious Jewish family against whose traditions he rebelled as a young man. He attended the University of Bordeaux, where he studied philosophy; one of his professors was his uncle, the sociologist Émile Durkheim. Although Mauss did not receive a degree, he placed high in the national *Agrégation* competition in 1895. He then studied history, philology, and religion at the University of Paris and, in 1897-1898, took a study tour including Oxford, where he met Edward Tylor, who was considered to be the founder of anthropology.

Mauss taught Hindu and Buddhist philosophy at the University of Paris from 1900 to 1902, when he succeeded to a chair in the history of religion of primitive peoples. He taught there until 1930 and then at the Collège de France until 1939. He also taught ethnography from 1927 to 1939 at the Institute of Ethnography, which he helped to found in 1927. These lectures were compiled in the *Manual of Ethnography* (1947). Although Mauss was not himself a fieldworker, he trained French anthropologists who were, and he stressed ethnography more than other Durkheimians.

Mauss is best known for his contributions to *L'Année sociologique,* the journal founded by Durkheim and his students, appearing in 12 volumes between 1898 and 1913. The journal was intended primarily as an outlet for specialized researches. Mauss edited the sections on religion and classification of the science of sociology. He took seriously Durkheim's dictum that science progressed through collective effort and neglected his own researches. In 1908, as a result, Durkheim decided to publish the journal only every third year.

Most of Mauss's early published work was in collaboration with other scholars and was published in *L'Année*. With Henry Hubert, he wrote *The Nature and Function of Sacrifice* (1899), *Prolegomena to a General Theory of Magic* (1904; a work which influenced Durkheim's classic *Elementary Forms of the Religious Life* in 1912), and *Introduction to Religious Phenomena* (1908). With Durkheim, he wrote *Primitive Classification* (1903) and collaborated on numerous articles and reviews. Mauss never knowingly violated Durkheim's sociological teachings, although the division of labor between them had left examples (both classical and ethnographic) to Mauss and theory to Durkheim.

When Durkheim died in 1917, Mauss became director of *L'Année*. His own work became more ethnographic after World War I as he tried to maintain the old scope of *L'Année*. His *The Gift* (1925) built on Bronislaw Malinowski's ethnographic studies of exchange and social structure in Melanesia. Mauss defined exchange patterns cross-culturally, using Roman, Hindu, and Germanic as well as primitive examples to demonstrate that exchange was a "total social fact" in which economic and social motives were inseparable.

Mauss wrote extensively for the *Journal of Normal and Pathological Psychology* and served as president of the Society of Psychology from 1923 to 1926. He believed that data about primitive cultures were necessary to the science of psychology, and he wanted to facilitate exchange of information between it and sociology. He died on Feb. 10, 1950.

Further Reading

There has been no biographical treatment of Mauss. Some background on his life and work is in Rodney Needham's "Introduction" in Émile Durkheim and Marcel Mauss, *Primitive Classification* (1903; trans. 1963); Robert H. Lowie, *The History of Ethnological Theory* (1937); Claude Lévi-Strauss's "French Sociology" in George Gurvitch and Wilbert E. Moore, eds., *Twentieth Century Sociology* (1945); Kurt H. Wolff, ed., *Emile Durkheim, 1858-1917* (1960); and Marvin Harris, *The Rise of Anthropological Theory* (1968). □

Abu-l A'la Mawdūdī

Abū-l A'lā Mawdūdī (1903-1979) was a Muslim writer and religious and political leader in the Indian sub-continent. He was the founder and head of the fundamentalist religio-political party, the Jamā'at-i Islāmī.

Mawdūdī, usually referred to as Mawlānā Mawdūdī because of his religious learning, was born in Awrangabad in the present Hyderabad state of India into a family with a strong religious and traditional Muslim culture. His father, Ahmad Hasan Mawdūdī, was an advocate who for several years during Mawdūdī's childhood renounced his profession and gave himself over to mystical exercises. Mawdūdī received his formal education in the schools of Hyderabad, but at age 15 he was forced to leave school never to return upon the death of his father; much of his earliest instruction was conducted in the home. He never attended a traditional Muslim religious school, a fact that later brought him much criticism when he began to publish his religious views.

Mawdūdī's earliest profession was journalism. At the age of 17 he became a correspondent and then editor of the newspaper *Tāj* in Jabalpur. In 1920 he assumed the editorship of *Muslim,* the publication of the Jam'īyat-i 'Ulamā,' the organization of India's learned Muslim divines. He continued in that position until the newspaper closed in 1923 and, after an interregnum of 18 months, became editor of its replacement, the prestigious *al-Jam'īyah.* Mawdūdī left journalism in 1927 to engage in scholarly writing. During this period he wrote a history of the Asafīyah dynasty of Hyderabad and a history of the Seljuk Turks, as well as a slim volume called *Toward Understanding Islam* which established him in India as a serious religious writer.

Mawdūdī along with one of his elder brothers, Abū-l Khayr, was an ardent supporter of the Khilāfat and *satyagrāhā* movements of 1919-1921. He continued his support for the former until its collapse after the establishment of the Turkish Republic, and he was bitterly disappointed when Gandhi called off the *satyagrāhā* effort in 1921 in response to the events at Chauri Chaura. From that point onwards Mawdūdī came increasingly to feel that the interests of India's two major communities, the Hindus and the Muslims, were divergent and irreconcilable.

The years of journalism also marked his first significant venture into writing on Islamic subjects in the volume *The Holy War in Islam* (1926), composed as a series of essays in *al-Jam'īyah* to refute Hindu charges that Islam was a militant and bloodthirsty religion. The principles espoused in Mawdūdī's later writing may all be found in this initial work.

In 1932 Mawdūdī became associated with the Hyderabadi journal *Tarjumān al-Qur'ān,* and in the following year he assumed sole responsibility for it. It was—and remains—the principal vehicle of his views and those of the organization he later founded. At first Mawdūdī used the journal to advocate reform among Muslims, but in the late 1930s he turned to Indian politics. He opposed both the all-India nationalism of the Indian National Congress and the Muslim nationalism of the Muslim League. His own solution to India's political problem lay in urging Muslims to recognize Islam as their sole identity and to become better Muslims. His views during this period are collected in the three volumes of *Muslims and the Present Day Political Struggle.*

In 1941 Mawdūdī convoked a meeting in Lahore to found a body that would put his views into practice. The organization was called Jamā'at-i Islāmī (The Islamic Society), and Mawdūdī was elected its head or *amīr.* The purpose of the Jamā'at was to propagate true Islam and to train a cadre of devoted men capable of establishing an Islamic system of government and society. It was thus a religiously-based political party of fundamentalist persuasion. The organization became a major factor in Pakistani national politics.

When the Indian sub-continent was partitioned in 1947, Mawdūdī moved with some of his followers to Pakistan, where he quickly assumed an important political role as the principal advocate of the Islamic state. He evoked the displeasure of the government and in 1948 was put in jail, where he remained for more than a year. Upon his release he resumed the agitation for an Islamic state with renewed vigor. The peak of his political influence was achieved in 1951 in connection with the controversy over the *Basic Principles Report* of the Pakistani Constituent Assembly. Mawdūdī acted as leader and spokesman of the Pakistani 'ulamā' in their response to the report.

Mawdūdī was again arrested in 1953 for his alleged part in the agitation against the Ahmadīyah sect. He was sentenced to death by a military court, but the sentence was never carried out. In 1958 Pakistan came under military rule, and political parties, including the Jamā'at-i Islāmī, were banned. From that time Mawdūdī's interest turned from the Islamic state to the achievement of true democracy in Pakistan. Mawdūdī was again arrested for his bitter opposition to the Ayyūb Khān government in 1964, and in the 1965 elections he supported the presidential candidacy of Fātimah Jinnāh against Ayyūb Khān—though it was counter to his Islamic beliefs that a woman should hold high office. Mawdūdī joined with other right wing and religious parties in 1970 to oppose the socialism of Zūlfiqār Alī Bhutto and the demands of Shaykh (Sheik) Mujīb al-Rahmān's Awami League. During the 1971 civil war that led to the emergence of Bangladesh Mawdūdī supported the military action of the government against the Bengalis. In 1972 he resigned as amir of the Jamā'at-i Islāmī, having held the post, though not without challenge, since the inception of the organization. He died in September 1979 in Rochester, New York, where he had gone to visit a son and to receive medical treatment for a long standing ailment.

Mawdūdī was a prolific writer and speaker whose works have been translated into many languages and widely distributed. He was one of the foundation stones of the 20th-century Islamic resurgence and one of the most read Muslim writers of his time; he exerted great influence, for example, on Sayyid Qutb, the Egyptian Islamic radical. Especially important were his emphases that Islam is a total way of life, that it requires control of the state for its full realization, and that Islamic objectives are not attainable without a disciplined and effective organization.

Further Reading

There are articles on Mawdūdī by Charles J. Adams in Donald Smith, editor, *South Asian Politics and Religion* (1966) and in John Esposito, editor, *Voices of Resurgent Islam* (1983). A full history of the Jamā'at-i Islāmī is available in Kalim Bahadur, *The Jama'at-i Islami of Pakistan* (Lahore, 1978); further discussion of the early period may be found in Leonard Binder, *Religion and Politics in Pakistan* (1961). A biography and a list of Mawdūdī's writings is found in Khurshid Ahmad and Zafar Ishaq Ansari, editors, *Islamic Perspectives*. □

Sir Douglas Mawson

Sir Douglas Mawson (1882-1958) was an Australian scientist and explorer of the Antarctic. His intellectual boldness and skill were matched by a practical initiative and courage which confirms his place among the world's greatest explorers.

Douglas Mawson was born in Yorkshire on May 5, 1882. His parents took him to Sydney, New South Wales, when he was 4 years old, and he was educated at Fort Street High School and the University of Sydney. A student of the famous geologist Sir Edgeworth David, Mawson early showed high forensic capability in the field as well as a meticulous scholarly talent. In 1902 he graduated in mining engineering and taught briefly at the University of Sydney.

In 1903 Mawson was invited to accompany the team which made the first intensive geological survey of the New Hebrides Islands in the Pacific. From 1905 he held the lectureship and later the professorship of mineralogy and petrology (geology) at the University of Adelaide. He quickly gained the reputation of an outstanding teacher as well as that of a fine scientist and man of action.

Antarctic Explorations

By 1907 Mawson had turned his mind and energies toward Antarctica. Hitherto Britain, Sweden, and Germany had been engaged in surveying the land mass of the continent. Ernest Shackleton, a member of Robert F. Scott's team, had determined that year to reach the South Pole. Mawson accompanied the expedition as physicist and surveyor, and Edgeworth David joined the party. During 1908, together with Dr. A. F. MacKay, Mawson and David conquered the summit of Mt. Erebus—an ice-covered volcanic cone 11,400 feet high—for the first time. Among other notable achievements they observed, also for the first time, the shifting position of the magnetic pole. It was a thorough and successful introduction to the life and labor demanded of Antarctic scientists and explorers. Mawson had earned an invitation to join Scott in his forthcoming voyage of discovery.

In January 1911 the Australian and New Zealand Association for the Advancement of Science initiated a government-aided expedition under Mawson's leadership to survey the unknown and unmapped ice plateau west of the magnetic pole. When the expedition sailed from Hobart, Tasmania, in December, Mawson had already earned the utmost affection and respect of his crew.

During the course of the survey Mawson found himself, after the death of two companions, alone, without supplies, on foot, and a hundred miles from safety. His courage and ingenuity enabled him to survive a most terrible journey through blizzards and across frightening crevasses. At one stage the soles of his feet separated from the flesh. Yet by 1914 the objects of the scientific research had been triumphantly achieved.

In 1929 Mawson was asked to lead a combined British, Australian, and New Zealand expedition to Antarctica and to explore that huge part of the continent which lay to the south of Australia. Scott's old ship, the *Discovery*, was fitted out for them, and on the voyage from Cape Town Mawson carried out research on the unexplored islands of the Crozets and also on Kerguelen and Heard islands. The phenomenon of the shallowing of the ocean depths toward the Antarctic was observed carefully.

Mawson named Mac-Robertson Land and, in the 1930 season, Princess Elizabeth Land. Notable was his use of an airplane for scientific purposes. As an outcome of this expedition and of Mawson's work, Britain made over to Australia its claims in Antarctica, and in 1936 the present Australian sector of the continent was annexed. The chief Australian Antarctic base was named after Mawson, and he firmly established his country's status as an Antarctic power.

In addition to many scientific papers and reports, Mawson wrote a remarkable two-volume book on his experiences, *The Land of the Blizzard* (1915).

Though Mawson is chiefly remembered for his Antarctic exploration, his geological work at the University of Adelaide was outstanding. He was a pioneer in research on uranium and other minerals connected with radioactivity. In 1914 he was knighted for his services and later filled many high official positions in the scientific world. He died on Oct. 14, 1958.

Further Reading

Books that deal with Mawson's life and work include Sir Ernest Henry Shackleton, *The Heart of the Antarctic* (2 vols., 1909); Charles F. Laseron, *South with Mawson* (2d ed. 1958); Sir A. Grenfell Price, *The Winning of Australian Antarctica* (1962); and Lady Paquita Mawson, *Mawson of the Antarctic* (1964).

Additional Sources

Bickel, Lennard, *This accursed land,* London: Macmillan, 1977.
□

Sir Hiram Stevens Maxim

The American-born British inventor Sir Hiram Stevens Maxim (1840-1916) is chiefly known for the automatic rifle, or machine gun, that bears his name.

Hiram Stevens Maxim was born near Sangerville, Maine, on Feb. 5, 1840. He received only a common-school education while working on his father's farm, but he spent his spare time studying science. At the age of 14 he was apprenticed to a carriage builder and later worked in his uncle's engineering firm in Fitchburg, Mass.

Moving to Boston, Maxim was employed in a scientific instrument shop, during which time (1866) he received his first patent, for an improved curling iron. Soon he became a draftsman with a New York shipbuilding firm where he invented many items, including a locomotive headlight. In 1878 he was appointed chief engineer of the first electric lighting company in the United States, and he soon produced a new type of filament for an incandescent light (the Maxim lamp). Maxim represented the electric lighting company at the Paris Exposition of 1881, where he was honored for still another invention, his electric pressure regulator.

In 1881 Maxim took up residence in England. He began to experiment on ways to improve weapons and in 1883 developed an automatic gun based on an entirely new principle. It used the recoil of the gun to advance the cartridge belt automatically. The Maxim gun could fire 666 rounds a minute and wold not jam from hasty operation by its handler. At first Maxim produced the gun himself, but his company merged with the Nordenfeldt company in 1888 and with Vickers in 1896. The Maxim gun was adopted for use by armies all over the world. For this and other inventions, Maxim was knighted by Queen Victoria in 1901.

A gifted and versatile inventor, Maxim received 122 United States patents and 149 British patents. He devoted much time and money near the turn of the century to aeronautical experiments. An airship he built in 1894 to study the lift and thrust of various wing shapes and propellers actually rose from the ground, but he had not developed methods for controlling his machine in the air and did not achieve manned flight. He had, however, using an incredibly heavy, steam-propelled machine, proved that mechanical flight in heavier-than-air machines was possible.

power of the Hapsburgs. His intense interest in the arts and in public display earned him a place in legend as well as history.

Although he was never crowned by the Pope, Maximilian became king of Germany in 1486 and emperor-elect in 1493, and he won papal approval as emperor in 1508. His talent, however, lay less in his success as emperor than in his securing the imperial title for the Hapsburg house and ensuring Hapsburg predominance in European diplomacy for the next 4 centuries. The empire had become by the end of the 15th century rather an aid to dynastic ambition than an effective form of government for Germany. Maximilian I's career was more an example of manipulating the advantages afforded by the imperial title than an actual rule of the fragmented empire. He was a better knight than he was a general, and he appears to have been far more a storybook king than a hardworking 15th-century monarch. He spent a great deal of time and money perpetuating his own memory, both in works and pictures about himself and in several romantic versions of his own life which he wrote.

Maximilian's marriage to Mary of Burgundy in 1477 plunged him into a conflict with the king of France, Louis XI, over the Burgundian territories. Holding his own against Louis, Maximilian also had to put down revolts in Flanders. His son and heir, Philip of Burgundy, was born in 1478, and his wife died in 1482. Maximilian held his Burgundian dominions, and in 1496 married Philip to Juana, daughter of

Maxim was a brilliant, artistic, and accomplished man, although it was difficult for others to get along with him. He was opinionated and self-centered, and even his younger brother Hudson, also an inventor, found him impossible as a colleague. Twice married, Maxim had two children; his son, Hiram Percy Maxim, became well known as an inventor in his own right. Maxim died in Streatham, London, on Nov. 24, 1916.

Further Reading

The sources on Maxim's life are limited. The only relatively complete account is by Maxim himself, *My Life* (1915). But see also his brother's reminiscences in Clifton Johnson, ed., *The Rise of an American Inventor: Hudson Maxim's Life Story* (1927), and Hiram P. Maxim, *A Genius in the Family: Sir Hiram Stevens Maxim through a Small Son's Eyes* (1936). There is a critical account of the machine gun and its inventor in H. C. Engelbrecht and F. C. Hanighen, *Merchants of Death* (1934). For Maxim's aeronautical work see his own *Artificial and Natural Flight* (1908); R. P. Hearne, *Airships in Peace and War* (1910), which has an introduction by Maxim; and various histories of flight, such as Archibald Black, *The Story of Flying* (1940), and the illustrated *American Heritage History of Flight* (1962), by the editors of American Heritage. □

Maximilian I

Maximilian I (1459-1519), Holy Roman emperor from 1493 to 1519, began the restoration of the

Ferdinand and Isabella of Spain, thus linking the Hapsburg house to the most vigorous dynasty of Europe. In 1500 the future emperor Charles V was born to Juana and Philip, and by a series of dynastic accidents Charles became the heir not only of Maximilian's Hapsburg territories and claim to the imperial title but to Burgundy and Spain as well, thus laying the foundations for the power of the Spanish monarchy for the next century.

Maximilian's success in the dynastic marriage market was greater than his military and diplomatic success. He failed to defeat France on an abortive expedition to Italy in 1496 and was himself defeated by the Swiss in 1499 and outmaneuvered in Italy by Louis XII of France in 1500. Between 1500 and 1504 Maximilian was busy putting down rebellions in Germany, and after the death of his son Philip in 1506 the problems of the Netherlands regency were added to those of Germany and Italy. In 1508 Maximilian's expedition to Italy was stopped by Venetian resistance, and the Emperor retaliated by entering into the League of Cambrai with France and the papacy against Venice. In 1510, however, Pope Julius II reversed his policy and rejected the league, and from 1510 until his death Maximilian was faced with the rising power of France in Italy.

Besides external political threats, Maximilian faced the perennial administrative chaos of Germany and accomplished a number of governmental and judicial reforms, including the establishment of the Imperial Court in 1495, in which Roman law was to be used. Maximilian also urged reform of the Church, particularly in Germany. At his death in 1519 the crises which would trouble the 16th century were already evident: the rivalry between Spain and France, the use of Italy and the papacy as a battleground for the conflict, and the stirrings of anticlericalism and the questioning of ecclesiastical dogma which would usher in the Reformation. Maximilian's reputation as the "last knight" was a fitting one.

Further Reading

The most thorough work in English on Maximilian is the somewhat romanticized biography by Christopher Hare (pseudonym for Mrs. Marian Andrews), *Maximilian the Dreamer* (1913). An older biography is by Robert W. Seton-Watson, *Maximilian I* (1901). Since Maximilian's reputation is so varied, the reader should also consult Glenn E. Waas, *The Legendary Character of Kaiser Maximilian* (1941), which provides both a good bibliography and a survey of Maximilian's legend. Useful background works are *The Cambridge Medieval History*, edited by J. B. Bury and others (8 vols., 1913-1936), and *The New Cambridge Modern History* (14 vols., 1957-1970).

Additional Sources

Benecke, Gerhard, *Maximilian I (1459-1519): an analytical biography,* London; Boston: Routledge & Kegan Paul, 1982. □

Maximilian II

Maximilian II (1527-1576) was Holy Roman emperor from 1564 to 1576. Although Protestant, he was not successful in uniting Protestants in the empire.

Maximilian was the son of Ferdinand I, who succeeded as Holy Roman emperor after the abdication of Charles V. In 1548 Maximilian married his cousin Maria, daughter of Charles V. Although Charles V had to give the imperial succession of Ferdinand I, he had tried to reserve the succession of Ferdinand for his own son Philip II of Spain rather than Maximilian. This created a deep division between the two main branches of the Hapsburg family; in 1551 Ferdinand and Maximilian had to yield to Charles V's wishes, although they did not plan to keep the agreement. A complicating factor was that Maximilian's Catholicism was suspect; he was on very good terms with the German princes who had defeated Charles V in 1552.

After Ferdinand succeeded Charles V in 1555, he tried to bring Maximilian back to the Catholic Church. In spite of his insistence and threats from Pope Paul IV, Maximilian kept his Lutheran chaplain. In 1560 relations with his father were near a rupture, and he canvassed the Protestant princes for their support against his father. When he found this support lacking, Maximilian gave in and nominally returned to Catholicism. Maximilian's behavior remained ambiguous, and it was anticipated that he would favor Protestantism if he ever became emperor. In 1562 Ferdinand had Maximilian elected king of the Romans, thus securing his succession and overriding the earlier settlement in favor of Philip II.

In 1564 Maximilian succeeded his father as emperor. He was now in a unique position to help Protestantism win in the empire. But his was a peaceful and vacillating character, and he was not up to the historical role he might have played. All he did was to work for a piecemeal reform of the Church, favoring the lay cup and priestly marriage; in his own Austrian lands he introduced a large measure of religious freedom in 1568.

Maximilian II's dealings with the German Protestants were made more difficult by the ferocious dogmatic hostilities between the several Lutheran sects and between the Lutherans and Calvinists. His continued wavering was certainly influenced by political interests as well; as emperor, he did not want to include in the Augsburg Peace of Religion ecclesiastical princes turned Lutheran, as he had promised the princes before. He also attended vigilantly to dynastic interests. In order to placate the Spanish family, and with an eye on the Spanish succession, he sent his oldest son, Rudolph, to Spain for a solid Catholic education.

As was the case with all the emperors of the period, the Turkish threat in Hungary determined much of Maximilian's policy toward the German princes and foreign powers. He tried to remain at peace with the Sultan and abandoned all attempts to roll back the Turkish inroads. In 1575 Maximilian became involved in intrigues to win the Polish crown for his house, but he died before he could prepare the military campaign to unseat another pretender. The year before, however, he had yielded to Spanish demands and had obtained the designation of his Catholic son Rudolph II as his successor, thus securing the Catholic future of the Hapsburg lands and of the imperial office.

Further Reading

For material on Maximilian see Adam Wandruszka, *The House of Habsburg: Six Hundred Years of a European Dynasty* (trans. 1964), and Friedrich Heer, *The Holy Roman Empire* (1967; trans. 1968). □

Maximilian of Hapsburg

Maximilian of Hapsburg (1832-1867) was an Austrian archduke and emperor of Mexico. His short rule was characterized by financial disaster, political weakness, and betrayal. His final defeat and execution clearly showed that Mexico would not accept a foreign prince.

In 1860 the Mexican Liberal party emerged victorious over the Conservative party after a bloody 3-year war. Benito Juárez, the Liberal leader whose aim was the end of chaos and the beginning of constructive reforms, faced an empty treasury and a stagnant economy. He placed a 2-year moratorium on the national external debt, which his government could not hope to pay.

Simultaneously, the remnants of the defeated forces of the large landowners and great merchants, as well as clerical and professional military interests toured Europe trying to gain converts and support for a restoration of the old order. They claimed that Mexico, a potentially wealthy nation, was being desiccated by corrupt Liberal politicians. They painted a picture of a restive Indian proletariat waiting for the opportunity to strike a blow at the hated anticlerical Liberals.

The Mexican debt cancellation of 1862 played into their hands; Louis Napoleon seized upon the opportunity to found a Latin empire based upon Mexico's proverbial wealth and a religiously fanatic indigenous army. The results showed that Mexico was neither prodigiously wealthy nor fanatically Catholic.

Early Career

Maximilian of Hapsburg was born at the castle of Schoenbrun outside Vienna on July 6, 1832. He was the second son of Archduke Francis Charles, the brother of the Austrian emperor, Franz Joseph. Maximilian was reared in splendor and wealth, but he received a liberal cosmopolitan education. By an early age he traveled widely and spoke German, English, Hungarian, Slavic, and Spanish fluently. The young archduke capably served his uncle, the Emperor, as commander of the imperial fleet and as the imperial envoy in Paris. While in the latter post he visited Belgium, where he met and married the attractive Princess Carlotta, the daughter of King Leopold I, in 1857.

That same year the Austrian court sent Maximilian as viceroy to the Italian province of Lombardy-Venetia. In Italy he attempted to promulgate liberal reforms and soften the harsh policy followed by Austria after the Italian 1848 Revolution. Displeased by his liberality, the court assigned him back to the Adriatic fleet. In 1854 he retired to private life. He then visited Brazil and returned home to build the idyllic castle of Miramar on his Austrian estates.

Maximilian was described at the time as being 6 feet 2 inches in height, handsome, diplomatic, and gracious, or the ideal monarch for the age of enlightened despotism. Unaware of approaching storms, Maximilian and Carlotta lived happily in their beautiful home, seemingly content to escape the difficulties of public life. Their respite was to be short.

French Intervention in Mexico

The French court of Louis Napoleon had become the mecca of conservative Mexican exiles. A faction composed of Empress Eugénie, the Emperor's brother, the Duc de Morny, and unscrupulous bankers hoping to milk Mexico's wealth pressed the cause of intervention on the far from unwilling French emperor. French agents in Mexico reinforced the exiles' pleas by describing widespread dissatisfaction and hope for a strong government. The Mexican debt cancellation gave Napoleon the excuse to intervene in 1862. He sent a large French contingent to Mexico to cooperate with the English and Spanish to force Juárez to retract.

Both England and Spain, realizing Napoleon's intent to remain in Mexico, soon withdrew, leaving the French alone. Having first secured Veracruz, the French sent a 6,000-man army toward Mexico City. On May 5, 1862, the Mexicans defeated this French force at Puebla with the loss of over a thousand French troops. Too far extended to withdraw, Napoleon next sent a larger force of 40,000 under Gen. Forey. The new French commander reorganized his forces and took Puebla in May 1863. On June 10 he entered Mexico City, applauded by the clergy and Conservative survivors.

After a thorough search through Europe the clerical Conservatives and their French allies focused upon Maximilian as the perfect foil to institutionalize their victory. A Conservative junta in Mexico City adopted a monarchy and offered him the crown. Maximilian's natural prudence made him hesitate, but the politically ambitious Carlotta urged him to accept. The Mexicans assured them that their nation impatiently awaited their arrival; the French occupation forces held a plebiscite and announced that the people had voted in his favor. On April 10, 1864, Maximilian accepted the crown and declared the Conservative general Juan Almonte his regent until he arrived.

Before leaving for Mexico, Maximilian renounced all claims on the Austrian crown and made a fatal deal with the French by the Treaty of Miramar. In this treaty Napoleon promised to keep French troops in Mexico until the end of 1867. Maximilian, in turn, promised to pay the entire cost of intervention, the costs of French supporting troops, and all prior debts due England, France, and Spain, including the exorbitant Jecker loan (bonds extorted by a greedy Swiss banker from the Mexican Conservatives in the 1850s).

A proponent of intervention, Jecker had a partnership with the Duc de Morny. French bankers then floated Mexican government bonds, most of whose proceeds were discounted in advance. By this very first act Maximilian had tripled Mexico's already exorbitant external debt. He then visited the Pope but did not promise to return expropriated Church lands. In May 1864 the royal couple set sail for their tropical kingdom expecting to be greeted joyously by the Mexican people. On the voyage Maximilian passed his time by composing a 600-page book on court etiquette.

Emperor of Mexico

Maximilian reached Veracruz on May 28. The city, a Liberal stronghold, greeted the royal couple with coldness. They had to dine on board ship as there was no reception committee. Juárez and Juan Álvarez, the old Liberal general, immediately declared their intention to do battle. The journey to Mexico City was also largely a disappointment, until they arrived at the capital, where Conservatives and clergy displayed a convincing show of enthusiasm. Most foreign governments immediately recognized Maximilian's govern-

ment with the notable exception of the United States. Maximilian and Carlotta, enamored of their adopted country, had great hopes of success. In reality they had no chance.

From June 1864 to February 1866 the French army dominated the new Mexican Empire. Napoleon's proconsul, Gen. Bazaine, took orders directly from Paris and recklessly spent imperial funds. French officials took over the treasury and customs revenues. Mexican dignitaries were treated with contempt, and to make matters worse, Maximilian immediately angered his clerical allies by refusing to restore Church lands and the clerical courts. The Emperor tried to win over Liberals and even talked of establishing religious freedom. Clerical support fell away, and the new Mexican archbishop, Labastida (formerly exiled by Juárez and later made archbishop by Maximilian), openly denounced the imperial government.

Despite their obstacles, the royal couple did their best. They set up a lavish court and gave banquets and large receptions. Enormous sums went into refurbishing the ancient castle of Chapultepec, all of which increased the monarchy's indebtedness. Many excellent new laws were legislated, but unfortunately few were ever enacted. Maximilian often worked from early morning to late night, trying to make his policies work. He and Carlotta praised everything Mexican, ate local food, and affected Mexican dress. He decreed freedom of the press and showed great courage in going freely and unarmed among the Mexican people. He even attempted unsuccessfully to win over leading Liberals. A rumored 100,000 Mexicans applied for jobs under his empire but Juárez, Profirio Diaz, Mariano Escobedo, and other leading Liberals resisted his conciliatory overtures.

French Desertion

French guns and loans kept the empire working. In 1865 French aid began to wane. The American Civil War ended, and the U.S government began to mobilize troops on the Rio Grande. French opposition to the war's cost in men and materials mounted in France. These protests coupled with Prussia's victory over Austria caused Louis Napoleon to reconsider. The French government assured the United States that it would leave Mexico. Still hoping for a speedy victory, Bazaine convinced Maximilian to decree that as of October 1865 all Liberal officers would be executed. Aided by United States funds, the Liberal armies began to grow larger and bolder. By March 1866 Bazaine was in full retreat with the Mexican armies taking over areas abandoned by the French.

At last convinced that the French would pull out in 1867, Maximilian tried to keep his government in power with the aid of Mexican Conservative forces and some European volunteers. In July 1866 the worried Carlotta set sail for Europe to request help from the Pope and the French. Rebuffed everywhere, she lost her sanity. Preparing to withdraw from Mexico, the French urged Maximilian to depart with them and fully expected that he would heed their advice. Once again Maximilian hesitated but yielded finally to the advice of his ambitious clerical adviser, Father Fischer, who urged him to remain. On Feb. 5, 1867, Bazaine led the French troops out of Mexico despite his royal protégé's decision to remain. Maximilian had hoped that the French withdrawal would lessen the opposition to him as a foreign puppet.

Defeat and Execution

Maximilian and his Conservative followers held out only until May 1867. He tried bravely to rally his followers under capable generals like Mejía, Miramón, and Márquez, but the Liberal tide was overwhelming. The Emperor led his imperial army of 9,000 men to Querétaro, hoping for a decisive victory. He was soon confronted by 40,000 Liberals under Escobedo; the Emperor behaved courageously, taking the role of a common soldier, but the situation was hopeless. Querétaro fell on May 15, 1867, and Maximilian was taken prisoner. In June a military court-martial condemned him to death by a vote of 4 to 3. Juárez refused clemency. Maximilian retained his dignity to the end. On July 19 a firing squad executed him with his generals Mejia and Miramón. He died as bravely as he had lived.

Further Reading

Maximilian's own account is *Recollections of My Life* (1865; trans. 1868). A contemporary view of Maximilian is in José Luis Blasio, *Maximilian, Emperor of Mexico: Memoirs of His Private Secretary, José Luis Blasio,* translated and edited by R. H. Murray (1934). No period of Mexican history has been as fully examined in English as the short reign of Maximilian and Carlotta. The most thorough studies are E. C. Corti, *Maximilian and Charlotte of Mexico* (1924; trans., 2 vols., 1928), and Ralph Roeder, *Juarez and His Mexico: A Biographical History* (2 vols., 1947). Other full accounts are Percy F. Martin, *Maximilian in Mexico: The Story of the French Intervention* (1914); Daniel Dawson, *The Mexican Adventure* (1935); and H. Montgomery Hyde, *Mexican Empire* (1946). See also John Musser, *The Establishment of Maximilian's Empire in Mexico* (1918). □

Ian Robert Maxwell

A refugee from eastern Czechoslovakia, Ian Robert Maxwell (Ludvik Hoch; 1923-1991) eventually became one of the richest men in Great Britain and the head of a powerful publishing empire.

Robert Maxwell promised his wife Betty, "I shall win an MC. I shall recreate a family. I shall make my fortune. I shall be Prime Minister of England. And I shall make you happy until the end of my days." Joe Haines, in his book *Maxwell* (1988), suggests that only one of those promises—prime minister—remained unfilled in the early 1990s. That the promises could have been made at all in December of 1944 by a penniless, recently created officer of the British Army who was a refugee from the Carpathian mountains says a great deal about the character and career of Robert Maxwell.

Maxwell was born on June 10, 1923, in the small village of Solotvino in the Carpathian mountains of what was then eastern Czechoslovakia. This was in an area some-

times known as Ruthenia that was variously held by Austria, Hungary, Ukraine, and, most recently, the Soviet Union. His birth name was Ludvik Hoch, and his parents were part of the Orthodox Jewish community of Solotvino. Maxwell maintained that his early memories of the grinding poverty of Solotvino, an area dominated by forests and salt mines, influenced his socialist sympathies. He had limited early education, possibly only three years at a national school. By 1939 he joined the Czech resistance to fight Nazi Germany, and after Czechoslovakia fell he made his way to France to join the French Foreign Legion and then be transferred to the 1st Czech Division of the French Army. When France fell to the Nazis in 1940, Maxwell was among 4,000 Czechs who made it to England. He joined the British Army and eventually changed his name to Ian Robert Maxwell. He rose from private to the rank of captain, eventually winning the Military Cross for heroism.

At the conclusion of World War II in 1945, Captain Robert Maxwell, by this time an accomplished linguist, was assigned to Berlin. By 1946 he was involved in the publishing of *Der Berliner* and in the process of re-establishing the postwar German economy. As a result of these experiences, he gained an understanding of international business, publishing enterprises, and the new importance of scientific research and publishing. By 1947 Maxwell had returned to England and became instrumental in disseminating scientific and technical information in journals and magazines. By 1951 Maxwell held the controlling interest in Pergamon Press, a publishing concern dedicated to scientific journals, textbooks, and papers.

Pergamon Press became the basis for Maxwell's fortune. He gained a virtual monopoly on scientific publication, especially Soviet scientific publications, at that point when such publication became of critical importance. During the 1950s he was concerned with other business ventures and was particularly involved with the trading concerns of Dr. Kurt Waller. Maxwell also purchased Simpkin Marshall, an almost defunct wholesale book selling company. The eventual failure of this company added to the controversy surrounding Maxwell, since many of his critics blamed the failure of the concern on his aggressiveness.

In 1958 Maxwell entered British politics. He joined the Labour Party, and in 1959 stood as candidate for Parliament from Buckingham, finally winning in 1964. Maxwell presented an anomaly as a parliamentary member of the Labour Party. He was an enormously wealthy man in the party of the working class. He was an employer who was sometimes at odds with the trade unions seeking to represent the party of trade unionism. No one could doubt his history of poverty and hard work, nor could his efforts on the battlefield fighting for Britain be diminished. But the idea of a rich foreigner representing working-class Britain provided severe paradoxes.

Despite Maxwell's pledge to become prime minister, his political career lacked the spectacular success of his business career. He never achieved distinction in Parliament, his main achievements coming from clean air legislation and a reform of the parliamentary food services. While he fully participated in his party's arguments and questions, adding to vigorous parliamentary debate, he never became a cabinet minister. He lost his seat in the election of 1970 and did not return to Parliament, even though his continued career in publishing and journalism kept him at the center of British political life.

By 1969 Maxwell was mired in a bitter dispute over the resale of Pergamon Press. This was ultimately resolved through a series of civil suits, but it tarnished Maxwell's reputation and held back the advancement of his publishing interests. Despite these setbacks, in 1981 Maxwell acquired the British Printing Corporation, at the time the largest printer in Britain but a company that had serious personnel and equipment problems. In 1984 Maxwell purchased his first newspapers, the Mirror Group, including the *Daily Mirror.* This launched his involvement in journalism.

Throughout the 1980s Maxwell's interest in and influence on journalism increased. His efforts clearly revitalized the Mirror Group, and he sought to update the technological side of British journalism. He also invested heavily in British cable television, had a controlling interest in European MTV (Music TeleVision), and invested well over $500 million in publishing and journalism interests in the United States, chiefly the Macmillan book company and Official Airline Guides. The Maxwell Communication Corporation was the second largest printing concern in the United States. The chief executive serving under his chairman father was son Kevin (born 1959).

In 1990 Maxwell added three U.S. tabloids to his holdings—the *Globe, Sun,* and *National Enquirer,* copies of all three sold exclusively in supermarkets. Then in March 1991

he bought the zesty New York City tabloid the *Daily News.* Meanwhile he launched the *European,* an English-language weekly designed to cover all of Europe, despite a mounting debt in his media corporation.

Robert Maxwell was also devoted to his family. He and his French-born wife Elisabeth had seven children, most of whom worked for his companies. He expected his children to make their own way without benefit of inheritance. On November 11, 1991, Maxwell died at sea off the Canary Islands, falling overboard from his yacht, Lady Ghislaine. He was buried on the Mount of Olives in Israel.

Further Reading

The best work on Robert Maxwell is *Maxwell* (1988) by Joseph Haines. The only significant additional information comes from lengthy articles in *Economist* (November 1986); *Forbes* (October 1987); *New York Times Magazine* (May 1, 1988) and *Business Week* (July 29, 1991). □

James Clerk Maxwell

The Scottish physicist James Clerk Maxwell (1831-1879) formulated important mathematical expressions describing electric and magnetic phenomena and postulated the identity of light as an electromagnetic action.

James Clerk Maxwell was born in Edinburgh on June 13, 1831. His father, who was a lawyer, was first named John Clerk but adopted the surname of Maxwell upon his succession to an estate, Glenlair, situated near Dalbeattie. James was a quiet child "much given to reading, drawing pictures, chiefly of animals, and constructing geometric models." A favorite pastime was reflecting the sun about his room with a highly polished tinplate, an activity which seemed to presage his adult preoccupation with optical phenomena.

Education and Early Researches

James's strange mode of dress helped earn him the nickname "Dafty" at Edinburgh Academy, where he was enrolled in 1841. His father, aware of his son's scholarly aptitude, began taking James to meetings of the Edinburgh Society of Arts and of the Royal Society. Through his school studies James had become interested in a problem in applied mathematics, the construction of a perfect oval. At the age of 15 he communicated a paper to the Edinburgh Royal Society, "On the Description of Oval Curves and Those Having a Plurality of Foci." He remained at Edinburgh Academy until 1847.

Optical studies occupied much of Maxwell's time in 1847. At Glenlair he experimented with Newton's rings, a chromatic effect produced by pressing lenses together, and studied the color variations of soap bubbles. In the spring of that year his uncle took him to see a demonstration of a "polarizing prism," and he engaged in observing the effects

of polarized light by means of specimens of Iceland spar. A paper read to the Edinburgh Royal Society in 1850, "On the Equilibrium of Elastic Solids," was the outcome of these studies. There Maxwell described strains set up in elastic substances such as gelatin and compared his experimental results which had been optically obtained with his newly derived theory of such equilibrium. This work was written in Maxwell's third, and last, year at the University of Edinburgh; he had enrolled in 1847.

In 1850 Maxwell went to Cambridge University as an undergraduate. He enrolled at Peterhouse but in December moved to Trinity College. In due course he became a scholar of the college and a member of the select Essay Club, familiarly known as the "apostles" since its membership was limited to 12. He took the bachelor's degree in 1854. Following graduation Maxwell was elected a fellow of Trinity College and joined its staff of lecturers, with responsibility for the subjects of hydrostatics and optics. He also carried out optical investigations with tops which were proportionally colored and rapidly revolved to determine the true mixture of colors.

Aberdeen and King's College Professorships

Maxwell left Cambridge in 1856 to accept an appointment as professor of natural philosophy in Marischal College, Aberdeen. There he met Katherine Mary Dewar, daughter of the principal of the college. They were married in 1858. During the years of his Aberdeen professorship

Maxwell continued his study of the theory of colors. However, a problem regarding the stability of the rings of Saturn also occupied much of his attention.

The French mathematician Pierre Simon de Laplace had shown that if Saturn's ring were a solid it could not be stable. Maxwell decided to study a hypothetical mathematical model of the planet in which the ring was "loaded" at one or more points. In this manner he found a solution which accounted for the motion of the ring on Newtonian laws of physics but which predicted that the loads would be visible as satellites. Eventually, however, he discovered an alternative solution which entailed a fluid ring or one constructed of a colloidal arrangement of separate small solid particles. For this work Maxwell received the Adam Prize offered by St. John's College in 1857, in honor of the discovery of Neptune by John Couch Adams.

The following year Maxwell's professorship was dissolved when Marischal College was amalgamated with King's College to form the University of Aberdeen. He obtained, however, the professorship of natural philosophy and astronomy in King's College, London. There his formal responsibilities to the college were quite demanding, involving regular evening classes for working men and artisans in addition to 9 months of lecturing for the regular students. Nevertheless he continued his scientific researches.

At the British Association meeting in Oxford in 1860, Maxwell exhibited a device for mixing colors of the spectrum. He also presented an important paper on Daniel Bernoulli's theory of gases. The theory depicted gas as consisting of a number of independent particles moving without mutual interference except upon collision. Maxwell demonstrated mathematically that the apparent viscosity of gases, their low heat conductivity, and the known laws of gas diffusion could be satisfactorily explained by this theory.

Maxwell resigned his professorship at King's College in 1865 and retired to Glenlair, where he produced some of his most important scientific writing. He presented his dynamic theory of gases to the Royal Society of London in 1866. His treatise on heat appeared in 1870, and the great work on electricity and magnetism was published in 1873.

Organization of the Cavendish Laboratory

In 1870 the Duke of Devonshire, who was chancellor of Cambridge, indicated his desire to build and outfit a physical laboratory for the university. In accepting the offer, university officials established a chair of experimental physics for the laboratory directorship. Maxwell became the first director of the Cavendish Laboratory in 1871.

Two important investigations undertaken at the Cavendish Laboratory when it opened in 1874, and supervised personally by Maxwell, concerned the accurate measurement of electrical resistance. The first was the testing of Ohm's law, a mathematical statement of the linear proportionality between electrical potential and the product of electrical resistance and current. Prior to the Cavendish researches there was no evidence that the law was more than a good approximation of the behavior of nature, nor was there any theoretical reason why the law should hold accurately over extended ranges of current or potential. The Cavendish investigations demonstrated the adequacy of Ohm's statement to within 1 part in 200,000 over large variations of these variables. Paralleling this work was an investigation of electrical standards and the determination of the ohm in absolute units of measure.

Influence on American Physics

In the early 1870s Maxwell not only played an important role in the scientific renaissance at Cambridge, but he was also instrumental in encouraging the development of high-level experimental physics in America. Original researchers who could understand the sophisticated mathematical formalism of European physicists such as Maxwell were rare at that time in the United States. The most eminent American scientific publication, *American Journal of Science,* was largely devoted to geological, botanical, and zoological topics; its editors simply did not understand exact science and its methods.

This was the situation faced by Henry Augustus Rowland, a young civil engineer from Rensselaer Institute, when he attempted to publish some magnetic researches. The *American Journal* editors repeatedly rejected Rowland's papers, forcing him in desperation to write directly to Maxwell. Maxwell received Rowland's work "with great interest" and saw to its immediate publication in the English *Philosophical Magazine.*

When Daniel Coit Gilman set out to find a faculty for a newly endowed university in Baltimore in 1875, he heard of Maxwell's interest in Rowland's work. For Gilman this endorsement was worth more than a "whole stack of recommendations." Thus Rowland became the first chairman of the physics department at Johns Hopkins University and until his death in 1901 led the way in establishing high-quality experimental physics in America.

Other Researches

Maxwell's work in optics, kinetic theory of gases, and electromagnetism forms some of his most important contributions to science. His paper "On the Theory of Compound Colours" of 1860 summarized numerous experiments with the colored tops mentioned above. By means of another device of his own invention, the "Colour-box," he investigated the effect of mixing given proportions of light taken from the spectrum. He showed that any given color sensation may be produced by combinations in due proportion of rays taken from three parts of the spectrum; that is, from three so-called primary colors. These experiments also tended to confirm the hypothesis that color blindness was due to the viewer's insensitivity to one of the three primary colors. For this work Maxwell received the Rumford Medal of the Royal Society of London.

The concept of discrete particles in his solution of the Saturn's rings problem may have led Maxwell to the study of gases; his first papers on this subject appeared in 1860. He pointed out that the velocities of different molecules of a gas, even if equal to start with, would become different in consequence of collisions with their neighbors. He therefore employed a statistical method of treating the problem in which the total number of molecules was divided into a series of groups. The velocities of all of the molecules constituting a group were the same within narrow limits. By taking the average velocity of each group into account, he was able to determine an important relationship between this velocity and the number of molecules in the group. He published papers on gas theory almost continuously until his death.

However, Maxwell is best remembered for his work on electricity and magnetism, which began with the important study of 1856 on lines of force as conceived by the English physicist Michael Faraday. Maxwell took Faraday's view that electrical and magnetic effects did not arise from attractions at a distance of electric or magnetic matter. Rather these effects were the means by which changes of some unknown description in an "ether" which filled all space became known to the experimenter.

Maxwell studied attractions of magnetic lines of force by means of a model based on the vortices or whirlpools of a fluid or mobile medium. This model was used as a mechanical illustration "to assist the imagination, but not to account for the phenomena." The centrifugal force of the vortices was accompanied by a tension directed parallel to the lines of force issuing from a magnetic pole. He found great difficulty, however, in conceiving of vortices revolving side by side in the same direction about parallel axes. The difficulty lay in understanding how contiguous portions of consecutive vortices could move in opposite directions.

Maxwell's well-known solution was to imagine that a layer of "particles, acting as idle wheels" was interposed between each vortex and its neighbor. Contiguous sides of the vortices then acted on the idle wheels to produce a direction of rotation opposite to that of the vortices themselves. The remarkable feature of this model discovered by Maxwell was that the action of the "idle wheels" could be used to analyze electric currents. His discovery yielded a mathematical relationship between electricity and magnetism.

Maxwell also studied dynamical changes in the lines of force and introduced the concept of energy storage and distribution in the ether. These ideas were developed in a great paper, "On a Dynamical Theory of the Electromagnetic Field," read to the Royal Society of London in 1864. He portrayed electromagnetic action as traveling through space at a definite rate in waves which were transverse to the direction of propagation. The paper was expanded into his classic *Treatise on Electricity and Magnetism* (1873), in which he postulated the identity of light as an electromagnetic phenomenon. The test of this theory in various experimental forms occupied the time of a large number of physicists throughout the world for the remainder of the century.

During the last years of his life Maxwell devoted much time to editing the *Electrical Researches of Henry Cavendish* (1879). He also wrote a textbook on heat and a small treatise on dynamics called "Matter and Motion." Among his other papers are some on geometric optics and several, published mostly in the *Transactions of the Royal Edinburgh Society,* on reciprocal figures and diagrams of force.

Maxwell died at Cambridge on Nov. 5, 1879. A memorial edition of his scientific papers was organized and published by the Cambridge University Press in 1890. Several lines from one of his essays written at Cambridge in 1856 serve as a fitting memorial to this great electrical theorist: "They know the laws by heart, and do the calculations by fingers. . . . When will they begin to think? Then comes active life: What do they do that by? Precedent, wheeltracks, and finger-posts."

Further Reading

An authoritative and well-documented biography of Maxwell is Lewis Campbell and William Garnett, *The Life of James Clerk Maxwell* (1882; rev. ed. 1884); the authors, who were personally acquainted with Maxwell, made use of a family diary as well as numerous papers and correspondence collected from members of the British scientific community. A highly readable account is R. T. Glazebrook, *James Clerk Maxwell and Modern Physics* (1901). Other studies are in J. G. Crowther, *British Scientists of the Nineteenth Century* (1935) and *Men of Science* (1936). A recent study is David K. C. MacDonald, *Faraday, Maxwell and Kelvin* (1964). C. Domb, ed., *Clerk Maxwell and Modern Science: Six Commemorative Lectures by Sir Edward V. Appleton and Others* (1964), provides extensive discussion of Maxwell's work by a number of highly competent British scientists. □

Vladimir Vladimirovich Mayakovsky

The Russian poet Vladimir Vladimirovich Mayakovsky (1893-1930) is best known for his colorful, declamatory style and his use of the language of the streets as poetic material. His artistic innovations strongly influenced the development of Soviet poetry.

Vladimir Mayakovsky was born on July 19, 1893, in Russian Georgia. When his father, a forester, died in 1906, the family moved to Moscow. This was to be Mayakovsky's city until his death. Between 1906 and 1911 Mayakovsky was arrested several times for his political activities. He joined the Bolshevik party in 1908. In 1909, during one of his terms in prison, he wrote his first verses.

Mayakovsky studied at the Moscow Institute of Painting, Sculpture, and Architecture from 1911 until he was expelled in 1914. During this period he published his first book of poetry, *I!* (1913), and became the leading figure in the avant-garde futurist movement in Russian poetry.

Russian futurism was as much a way of life as it was a poetic doctrine. It arose as a reaction to the extreme estheticism of Russian poetry at the turn of the century and to the prevailing mysticism in Russian intellectual life.

Mayakovsky and his companions advocated the abandonment of the Russian tradition and the creation of a new art, one free of the past. They took their cause to the streets, declaiming their verses to chance audiences and going to any lengths to shock a tradition-bound public. Their shocking behavior and mode of dress gained them an instant reputation. Mayakovsky's poetry of these prerevolutionary years is polemical but not devoid of poetic content. It is an exceptionally personal poetry. Often it takes the form of a monologue addressed to the poet's mother and sister. The poet bares his self to the public in a style which is by turns ironic and sad. The title of his long verse drama is *Vladimir Mayakovsky* (1913), and it is subtitled "A Tragedy." In his most successful book, *A Cloud in Trousers* (1915), he acclaims the poet as the thirteenth apostle. Increasingly after 1915 Mayakovsky appears to have been trapped between his public role of apostle and his private suffering, the wellspring of his poetry.

Mayakovsky welcomed revolution in 1917 and put himself wholeheartedly at the service of the new Soviet state. He wrote popular verse, created propaganda posters, and lent his name to numerous public causes. In his own poetry, Mayakovsky continued his attack on the classical Russian tradition and proclaimed a poetry of the masses. He sought to write only for the masses, excluding any reference to the poetic self. Thus, his epic poem *150,000,000* (1921) was published anonymously. Mayakovsky described his postrevolutionary poetry as "tendentious realism," and there is no doubt that he achieved this realism at the expense of his true poetic talent.

Mayakovsky traveled widely in the 1920s. He went several times to western Europe and in 1925 to America. During a trip to Paris, he fell in love with a Russian émigré. Toward the end of the 1920s it became more and more difficult for Mayakovsky to get permission to travel abroad. He felt increasingly the burden of his public posture and the pain of having abandoned his private poetic self. This alienation from the woman he loved and from his very self led him to commit suicide on April 14, 1930, in Moscow. He could no longer maintain the dual role of public apostle and private poet.

Further Reading

A good selection of Mayakovsky's writings is available as *The Bedbug and Selected Poetry* (1964), which has a good introductory essay by the editor, Patricia Blake. A full-length biography of Mayakovsky is Wiktor Woroszylski, *The Life of Mayakovsky* (trans. 1971). The account of Mayakovsky's life in ''Safe Conduct'' in Boris Pasternak, *Selected Writings* (1949; new ed. 1958), is an interesting interpretive biography. The best treatment of Mayakovsky's artistic innovations and his role in the futurist movement is Cecil Maurice Bowra, *The Creative Experiment* (1949).

Additional Sources

Terras, Victor, *Vladimir Mayakovsky,* Boston: Twayne, 1983. □

Jean Mayer

Recognized as one of the world's foremost nutritionists, Jean Mayer (1920-1993) was a researcher, university professor, presidential adviser, consultant to government and international organizations, and president and subsequently chancellor of Tufts University.

A naturalized citizen, Mayer was born in Paris, France, on February 19, 1920. The older of two children, he was the son of André and Jeanne Eugenie Mayer, both physiologists. His father, a president of the French Academy of Medicine and member of the League of Nations Commission on Hunger, later played an important role in founding the United Nations Food and Agricultural Organization (FAO). During Jean's youth conversations at home often centered on hunger and malnutrition, as well as on the subject of physiology.

After completing his secondary education, Jean enrolled in the University of Paris, where he was awarded a B.Litt. degree (1937), B.S. (1938), and M.Sc. (1939). A visit to the United States and Harvard University in the summer of 1939 impressed Mayer greatly and ultimately influenced him to leave his homeland.

Taken Prisoner During WWII

The outbreak of World War II forced postponement of his plans, for he was commissioned a second lieutenant in

the French army. Although captured by German troops in 1940 and taken to a prison camp, Mayer escaped by shooting a guard. He served in the French underground and later fought with the Free French and Allied forces in France, Italy, and North Africa. He was the recipient of 14 military decorations, including the Croix de Guerre with gold star, bronze star, and two palms and the Resistance Medal.

During the war Mayer travelled with forged papers to the United States and there married Bostonian Elizabeth Van Huysen on March 16, 1942. He was the father of five children—André, Laura, John-Paul, Theodore, and Pierre.

Advocated Use of Exercise in Weight Control

After the war he studied at Yale University, wrote a dissertation on vitamin A, and obtained his Ph.D. in physiological chemistry in 1948. He also attended the Sorbonne, where he was awarded a D.Sc. in physiology *summa cum laude* in 1950. Thereafter began a long association with Harvard University which commenced in 1950 as an assistant professor of nutrition and which saw him promoted through the ranks to full professor in 1965. As a researcher who studied obesity, the physiological controls on hunger, and the relationship to disease, Mayer also became a strong advocate of physical exercise and promoted its benefits in weight control and the maintenance of good health.

Crusaded Against World Hunger

Of equal concern to Mayer was the problem of a lack of food and its companions—hunger, malnutrition, and poverty. He studied ways to alleviate famine and its consequences on Harvard missions to India in 1955 and to Ghana in 1961; was a member of United Nations FAOWHO (World Health Organization) advisory missions to Ghana in 1959 and to the Ivory Coast and West Africa in 1960; and in 1969 he went to Biafra, Nigeria.

In 1967 Mayer joined the U.S. Citizen's Crusade Against Poverty and later helped to found the National Council on Hunger and Malnutrition in the United States, becoming its first chairman in 1969. He played a role in calling the nation's attention to the nutritional problems of the poor in America and testified on these problems before congressional committees.

During the 1960s the problems of poverty and hunger received wide public attention which resulted in President Richard Nixon appointing Mayer as his special consultant on nutrition in 1969. His task was to plan and direct the first White House Conference on Food, Nutrition, and Health. Opening on December 2, 1969, the three-day conference was addressed by Nixon, who pledged to eliminate hunger in the United States. Among the 3,000 invited guests were scientists, food processors, government representatives, civil rights leaders, medical personnel, consumer representatives, and spokespersons for the poor. Disgruntled representatives of the poor, whose priorities differed from those of other guests, held separate sessions of their own. But Mayer claimed the conference was a success in dramatizing hunger and poverty to the press and all segments of society. He is credited with persuading Nixon to include a food stamp program for the poor in his plans for welfare reform and an expanded school lunch program for needy children.

Became President of Tufts University

In 1970 Mayer returned to Harvard's Center for Population Studies, and in July 1976 he became the tenth president of Tufts University. During the 1970s he received presidential and congressional appointments, including appointments to the President's Consumer Advisory Council, 1970-1977; as chairman of the Nutrition Division of the White House Conference on Aging, 1971; as general coordinator of the U.S. Senate National Nutrition Policy Study, 1974; and on the Presidential Commission on World Hunger, 1978-1980. At the United Nations he was a member of the Protein Advisory Group, 1973-1975, and director of the Project on Priorities in Child Nutrition, United Nations International Children's and Educational Fund (UNICEF), 1973-1975.

In 1989, then President Bush bestowed Mayer with the Presidential End Hunger Award. In presenting the award to Mayer, President Bush said, "The goal of ending hunger requires involvement, and Jean Mayer is an example of the rare breed on individual who has never hesitated to get involved when he saw a need." Mayer later was also given another Presidential award by Bush for his environmental and conservation work.

On September 1, 1992, Mayer became the Chancellor of Tufts University. During his 16 years of tenure as President of Tufts, he was credited with the creation of a graduate school of nutrition and building the only veterinary medicine school in New England. A center for environmental management was also established during his tenure as president. Mayer died of a heart attack in Sarasota, Florida on January 1, 1993 while vacationing.

Researched Mechanisms of Obesity

Mayer was known for his research on mechanisms regulating food intake and the development of experimental and human obesities. He published approximately 750 scientific papers, as well as numerous articles for the public in popular magazines. His books include *Overweight: Causes, Cost, and Control* (1968), *Human Nutrition* (1972), *A Nutrition Glossary* (1973), *U.S. Nutrition Policies in the Seventies* (1973), *Health* (1974), *A Diet for Living* (1975), *Food and Nutrition in Health and Disease* (1977), *World Nutrition: A U.S. View* (1978), and *Food and Nutrition Policy in a Changing World* (1979). A syndicated newspaper column on nutrition was published weekly in 150 papers.

Further Reading

Biographies appear in *American Men & Women of Science* (1982) and *World Who's Who in Science* (1968). Articles appear in *LIFE,* November 28, 1969; *TIME,* December 12, 1969; *Forbes,* October 1969; and *New York Times,* December 1, 1969. See also the *New York Times* January 2, 1993. □

Robert Clyve Maynard

Robert Maynard (1937–1993) was the first black owner of a major daily newspaper.

When Robert Maynard bought the *Oakland Tribune* in 1983, he became the first black in the United States to own a major daily newspaper. But Maynard had a career full of firsts, from being the first black national newspaper correspondent to being the first black newspaper editor in chief.

The son of immigrants from Barbados, Maynard grew up in the Bedford-Stuyvesant section of Brooklyn, New York. Interested in writing from an early age, Maynard frequently cut classes at Boys High School in Brooklyn to hang around the editorial offices of the black weekly newspaper the *New York Age.* By the age of sixteen he had dropped out of school to work full-time as a reporter for the *New York Age.* In 1956 he moved to Greenwich Village, where he wrote freelance articles and met writers such as James Baldwin and Langston Hughes.

Niemann Fellowship

Applying for jobs on white-owned newspapers brought no results, and it was 1961 before he found a job on a mainstream paper. Maynard began as a police and urban-affairs reporter for the *York* (Pa.) *Gazette and Daily.* In 1965

Maynard applied for a Niemann Fellowship and won, spending 1966 at Harvard University studying economics, art, and music history. After Harvard, he returned to the *York Gazette and Daily* as night city editor.

Washington Post

In 1967 Maynard was hired by the *Washington Post* as national correspondent, the first black to hold that position on any major newspaper. He was widely praised for his 1967 series on urban blacks. In 1972 he was appointed as ombudsman and associate editor for the *Washington Post* and also began working as senior editor for the new black monthly magazine *Encore.* In 1976 he was chosen to be one of three questioners for the final debate between Jimmy Carter and President Gerald Ford.

California

In 1977 Maynard left the *Washington Post* and moved to the University of California, Berkeley, to found the Institute for Journalism Education, a program for the training of minority journalists. In 1979 he was hired by the mammoth newspaper publisher Gannett as editor of its newly acquired but struggling *Oakland Tribune.* When he became editor of the paper, which was renamed simply the *Tribune,* circulation was at 170,000. By 1982 circulation had plummeted to 110,000, and the paper lost $5 million in 1981.

Owner

In response to the declining readership, Maynard started a morning edition, which was named *Eastbay Today.* Although the morning edition drew only 90,000 readers, in the fall of 1982 Maynard announced the end of the afternoon *Tribune.* The afternoon paper was merged with *Eastbay Today* into a morning *Tribune,* a move that was a prelude to Maynard's purchase of the paper in 1983 from the Gannett Company for $22 million.

Leadership and Illness

By 1985 the paper's circulation had increased to more than 150,000, but expenses still outpaced revenues. Maynard was forced to sell real estate holdings to meet expenses. Despite the losses the *Tribune* and Maynard's leadership garnered much praise and many awards for editorial excellence. In 1992 Maynard was diagnosed with prostate cancer and was forced to sell the *Tribune.* He died on 17 August 1993, an important figure in American journalism and a pathfinder for black journalists.

Further Reading

Black Enterprise, December 1993, p. 26.
Christian Science Monitor, June 16, 1983, p. 1; August 22, 1986, p. 3.
Ebony, June 1985, p. 105.
Fresno Bee, November 30, 1992, p. A-3.
Los Angeles Times, June 29, 1990, p. D-1; August 19, 1993, p. A-1.
Newsweek, September 24, 1979, p. 89; May 16, 1983, p. 93; August 30, 1993.
Sacramento Bee, October 18, 1992, p. J-1; August 19, 1993, p. A-3; August 21, 1993, p. B-5; December 13, 1993, p. E-1.
San Francisco Chronicle, August 19, 1993, p. A-1; August 21, 1993, p. B-5; August 27, 1993, p. A-23.
San Francisco Examiner, November 3, 1991, p. I-8; October 16, 1992, p. A-1, B-1; August 18, 1993, p. A-1. □

William J. and Charles H. Mayo

The American physicians William J. Mayo (1861-1939) and Charles H. Mayo (1865-1939) were brothers who led the development of the Mayo Clinic into a world-renowned center of medical treatment and research. Outstanding surgeons in their own right, the Mayos encouraged an atmosphere of cooperation and information sharing both within their institution and with other medical practitioners throughout the world. Their facility has drawn top physicians to practice and research there and also serves as a training center in medical specialties.

William J. Mayo and Charles H. Mayo were the leading figures in the founding and development of the Mayo Clinic, a world-class medical treatment, research, and training facility in Rochester, Minnesota. Beginning as St. Mary's Hospital in 1889, an institution run under the auspices of the Roman Catholic Sisters of St. Francis of Rochester, the facility became known for the surgical expertise of the Mayo brothers and their staff. As the clinic grew in size, it drew leading medical practitioners in a number of specialty areas. The success of the Mayo Clinic is based not only on the high caliber of its physicians, but also on the ideals of cooperation, collaboration, and information sharing that the Mayo brothers promoted there. By 1915, the institution had also incorporated an educational branch, the Mayo Foundation for Education and Research, which was designed to train new generations of physicians in a variety of medical specialties.

Natives of Minnesota, the Mayos were two of the five children of the English-born doctor William Worall Mayo and his wife, Louise Abigail (Wright) Mayo. William James Mayo was born in Le Sueur, Minnesota, on June 29, 1861. His younger brother, Charles Horace Mayo, was born on July 19, 1865, in Rochester, Minnesota. Although their father was a very successful physician, the boys' childhood was not very different from that of other children in the area. They attended local schools and assisted with chores on the family farm in Rochester. In addition to their regular coursework, however, the Mayo brothers were also

Charles Mayo

instructed in a wide range of scientific topics by their parents at home. Their mother taught them botany by identifying the plants and trees that they found while walking on the farm. She also encouraged their interest in astronomy by installing a telescope on the roof of their house. Their father would instruct them in chemistry, physics, anatomy, and other topics applying to medical science as the boys did chores around the home.

Social Values Shaped Career

William and Charles were also exposed to ideas in the arts and literature. They were sent to the Rochester Training School for lessons in Latin, art, and the classics. They also indulged in reading classic works of literature from the family library, including novels by the authors Charles Dickens and James Fenimore Cooper. These readings, as well as their parents' stories about their experiences during the Civil War and the 1862 Sioux Outbreak, helped the brothers to develop the social values that would distinguish their careers. Under the guidance of their parents, they gained a strong sense of humanitarianism, the benefits of cooperative work, and respect for individual achievement. Both of the young men set their sights on a medical career, no doubt due to their lifelong training in the subject. William completed his medical studies at the University of Michigan in 1883. Charles studied medicine at the Chicago Medical School, later known as Northwestern University Medical School, and graduated in 1888.

In 1883, a tornado struck Rochester, devastating a large part of the town and injuring many of its residents. The city had no hospital at that time, so temporary facilities to care for the victims were set up under the leadership of William Worall Mayo. He was assisted in his work by the Catholic nuns of the Sisters of St. Francis order in Rochester. The experience inspired the Sisters to create a permanent hospital, and they hired William Worall Mayo to direct the project. St. Mary's Hospital opened on October 1, 1889, with a small staff consisting of the elder Dr. Mayo and his two sons and a handful of the Sisters. The Mayos' father, then in his seventies, retired shortly after the founding of the hospital, leaving the operation in the hands of the young doctors William and Charles in 1892.

Specialized in Surgical Techniques

The hospital had been created with the mission of providing humane care to anyone who was in need, and patients were charged based on their ability to pay. This system brought in a huge number of poor patients, and for the first few years, the limited staff struggled to meet the overwhelming demand. To eliminate the huge numbers of hopeless patients being sent to them from other doctors, a rule was instituted that only patients who had been seen by one of the Mayo doctors could be admitted. This allowed the hospital to take on the atmosphere of a more limited clinic where the Mayos specialized in surgical techniques. Both of the brothers became talented and respected surgeons with distinctive areas of expertise. William specialized in surgery of the abdomen, pelvis, and kidneys, while Charles had an even wider range of surgical ability—he pioneered important procedures in a variety of areas, including thyroid, neurologic, cataract, and orthopedic surgery. As the reputation of the Mayo Clinic grew, more paying patients were drawn to the institution and the brothers were able to improve and expand their facilities.

The Mayo Clinic became known as a unique medical facility not only for the talented physicians that came to work there, but also because of its liberal social and professional ideals. Its mission included not only treating patients on the premises, but providing information that could be of use to doctors and patients everywhere. It featured a comprehensive library of clinical records that were available to any doctor that needed them and a tradition of professional cooperation balanced with recognition of individual contributions. Throughout the years, the clinic developed specialized divisions in surgery as well as other areas, including anesthesia, physiotherapy, social services, dietetics, and nursing education. It also included excellent laboratory and diagnostic facilities and was the site of leading efforts in medical research. In 1915, the clinic's role in educating medical professionals was formalized with the creation of the Mayo Foundation for Medical Education and Research, a joint venture with the University of Minnesota.

Recognized for Medical Talents

William and Charles Mayo also earned individual recognition for their medical talents. Charles was named president of the American Medical Association in 1906 and beginning in 1915 he served as a professor of surgery for the University of Minnesota. William was named to the University's Board of Regents in 1907, a position he held for the rest of his life. During World War I, the brothers divided the duty of serving as chief consultant in surgery for the United States Army; for their service they were both awarded the rank of colonel. While William retired from surgery in 1928, and Charles followed in 1930, they both remained active on the board of the Mayo Clinic until their deaths. By 1930, they had seen the clinic grow from a 45-bed hospital with one operating room to a multi-building complex with more than 1,000 beds that treated tens of thousands of patients a year.

After their retirements, the brothers purchased neighboring houses in Tucson, Arizona, where they spent much of their time in the winters. Upon a visit to the Mayo Clinic in the spring of 1939, however, William was diagnosed with stomach cancer and underwent surgery. Charles traveled to Rochester to be with his brother during his recuperation, and when it appeared that William was recovering rapidly, he took a short trip to see his tailor in Chicago. While there, he developed pneumonia and died on May 26, 1939. William's surgery proved to be unsuccessful in removing the cancer, and he retired to his home in Rochester, where he died only two months later on July 28, 1939. They left behind a thriving institution, which they had incorporated in 1919 under the Mayo Properties Association in order to ensure the ongoing success of the clinic after their departure. The Mayo Clinic, the first institution of its kind in the United States, remains a respected facility that balances the needs of patients for humane and effective treatment with the needs of doctors to share professional experience and information in research and education.

Further Reading

For more information, see Clapesattle, Helen B., *The Doctors Mayo,* University of Minnesota Press, 1941; Mayo, Charles H., "Early Days of the Mayo Clinic," *Proceedings of the Mayo Clinic,* October, 1932, pp. 584-87; Mayo, Charles H., *Mayo: The Story of My Family and My Career,* Doubleday, 1968; and *Sketch of the History of the Mayo Clinic and the Mayo Foundation,* W. B. Saunders, 1926. □

Federico Mayor Zaragosa

The Spanish biochemist Federico Mayor Zaragosa (born 1934) served on various medical and scientific advisory committees and in the Spanish government before beginning his association with UNESCO (United Nations Educational, Scientific, and Cultural Organization). He became director-general of UNESCO in 1987.

Federico Mayor Zaragosa was born in Barcelona, Spain, the capital of Catalonia province, on January 27, 1934. He studied pharmacy at the University of Madrid, where he obtained his degree in 1956 and his Doctorate in pharmacy in 1958. He received both degrees with special distinction (*Premio Extraordinario*). Mayor lectured and took part in scientific congresses held throughout the world.

In June 1963 Mayor was appointed to the Chair of Biochemistry at the University of Granada and in 1967 he headed the interdisciplinary Department of Pharmacy and Natural Sciences at the university. He was credited with helping to popularize the studies of molecular biology at the university level in Spanish universities and contributed to the establishment of the "Specialization in Biochemistry," equivalent to a Master's degree in biochemistry, in the Faculties of Biology, Chemistry, and Pharmacy. He introduced the teaching of molecular pathology and perinatal biochemistry.

Research and Administration

Mayor then went to do some research in England under Hans A. Krebs in the Department of Biochemistry at the University of Oxford. He was visiting professor and senior research fellow of Trinity College during 1966-1967. As a result of his research at Oxford, Mayor was able to develop imaginative work on perinatal neurobiochemistry. In 1997, there were several groups in Spain related to the etiology at the molecular level of palsy due to lack of oxygen at the moment of birth, pathology of neuroreceptors, biochemical basis of phenylketonuria, alterations arising from changes in the fluidity of the synaptosomal membrane, etc. However, the massive screening of fetal abnormalities and the appropriate treatment of the identified patients (Plan Nacional de

Prevencion de la Subnormalidad) has been, from the social point of view, the most relevant activity of Mayor's research. The improvement of medical care during gestation and delivery, with the postnatal biochemical and genetic analysis, led to a consistent decrease of mentally disabled children in Spain.

Upon his return to the University of Granada Mayor became rector, serving in that capacity from 1968 to 1972. As rector of the University of Granada, he designed and developed a completely new campus and introduced an efficient and democratic management of the university's affairs. Federico Mayor was also the founder and first director of the Center of Molecular Biology, "Severo Ochoa," of the Spanish Higher Council for Scientific Research (1975-1978), the most important national institution of research in this field.

Mayor was a professor of biochemistry in the Faculty of Sciences of the Universidad Autonoma of Madrid, and from 1973 to 1978 he was director of the Department of Biochemistry and Molecular Biology of that same university. Among the department's outstanding activities were those devoted to the biochemistry of the brain and to perinatal molecular biology. He was responsible for supervising 23 doctoral theses and published 75 scientific papers.

Federico Mayor served as Spain's under-secretary for education and science from 1974 to 1975. He was elected to the Spanish Parliament in June 1977 and became chairman of the Education and Science Commission of the Chamber of Deputies, as well as being the promoter and member of the special commission responsible for studying the problems affecting the mentally and physically handicapped. The national plans for scientific research and for the early detection of children with mental disabilities were drawn up under his direction.

He was an adviser to the prime minister (1977-1978); chairman of the Spanish Advisory Commission on Scientific and Technical Research (1974-1978); member of the Royal Foundation for Special Education (1976-1978); and a member of the advisory committee of the United Nations Educational, Scientific and Cultural Organization (UNESCO) on "Research and Human Needs" beginning in 1974.

Up the UNESCO Ladder

From 1974 to 1978, Federico Mayor was a member of the advisory committee of the Center of Higher Education of UNESCO, in Bucharest. After having served as deputy director-general of UNESCO from 1978 to 1981, Mayor served as Spain's education and science minister (1981-1982). In 1983 he became director of the Institute of the Sciences of Man, Madrid. He was also special adviser to the director general of UNESCO (1983-1984). Member of the advisory board of the International Federation of Institutes of Advanced Studies (IFIAS) and member of the Club of Rome since 1981, and member of the policy board of the Interaction Council beginning in 1984, Mayor is also a member of the European Academy of Sciences and Arts, and beginning in 1987, a member of the European Parliament.

Mayor's Challenge: Reforming UNESCO

During the period 1978 to 1981 Mayor had an active role in the United Nations University, Tokyo, on behalf of the director-general of UNESCO. When he assumed the director-general position at UNESCO in November 1987, his main task was to undo the mess created by his predecessor, Amadou-Mahtar M'Bow, whose 13-year term was marred by nepotism, inefficient administration, and political bias. Mayor also wanted to lure the United States back into the UNESCO agency.

Soon after Federico Mayor was elected he made a special request to the Headquarters Committee of the General Conference of member states: He wanted a new apartment. The previous director-general had been living in the converted sixth- and seventh-floor wings of the agency's Fontenoy headquarters in Paris. The lodgings were comfortable, but Mayor asked for a special arrangement so UNESCO would pay for the rent, maintenance and services of an apartment overlooking the Esplanade des Invalides in the pricey 7th arrondissement in Paris.

In 1984, the United States withdrew from UNESCO, charging mismanagement of "personnel, programs and financial activities." A perceived anti-Western bias by UNESCO members and management also contributed to the U.S. departure. In 1996, however, the Clinton administration expressed interest in rejoining. During 50th-anniversary celebrations of the United Nations (1995), Clinton wrote to Mayor, citing the "great strides" he had made in reforming UNESCO.

While progress was made, in 1996, U.S. news groups found numerous instances of mismanagement and unusual expenditures. For example, while the number of UNESCO professionals assigned to combat illiteracy dropped from 20 to just five at headquarters last year, Mayor approved payments of some $1.9 million to hire outside consultants, many of whose duties were unknown to even UNESCO's deputy director-general and director of personnel. Among the consultants are five senior special advisers "for regions" who were paid about $280,000 a year—despite the fact UNESCO already had assigned to its Bureau of External Relations regional advisers who could perform the same function.

Mayor also directed thousands of dollars in UNESCO payments to organizations led by individuals with whom he had personal ties, according to sources in the inspector general's office. One of the firms in question received $100,000 in UNESCO funds and then vanished. Another received $25,000 to help arrange a UNESCO-sponsored concert by Stevie Wonder; $14,750 of that went to pay for a $4,000-a-month New York apartment the organization's executives claim as their current residence.

UNESCO critics said the appearance was just that. Instead of putting UNESCO in the forefront on issues like education or science, the critics said, Mayor simply did a makeover—one resulting in funding for projects which seem to have little relevance to the UNESCO mandate to promote peace through education, science and culture.

Under the UNESCO charter, Mayor had broad discretionary authority over the use of agency funds. He withheld 20 percent of the UNESCO budget after some states failed to pay the full amount of their annual contributions. Mayor said the money withheld from regular UNESCO programs would be used to fund "priorities" like programs for Africa, women, and developing countries. That may be so, but Mayor also created a new office at UNESCO headquarters to deal with "cultural events." The responsibilities of the new office included coordinating exhibits, concerts and the cocktail parties which preceded them at UNESCO's Paris headquarters.

Supporters of the organization say such incidents should not overshadow the good work UNESCO does. It was instrumental in coordinating worldwide research on oceans and works on preservation of historical sites. Many current and former UNESCO employees acknowledged the good works, but described an organization which appears to have lost its way—one whose expenditures on glittery cultural affairs and lavish consulting contracts came increasingly at the expense of the hard work of increasing literacy and improving education in developing countries.

Federico Mayor Zaragosa was a full member of the Royal Academy of Pharmacy beginning in 1975; an honorary member of the Royal Academy of Medicine of Sevilla beginning in 1977; a corresponding member of the Royal Academy of Sciences and Arts of Barcelona beginning in 1976 and of the Académie de Pharmacie Française, Paris, beginning in 1984. He was at one time president of the Spanish Federation of Experimental Biology Societies.

Mayor was a member of many other scientific bodies, including the Biochemical Society, the Société de Chimie Biologique, and the American Association for the Advancement of Science. He was also a member of the Instituto de Ciencas del Hombre.

Mayor lived in Paris with his wife, Maria Angeles. They had three children.

Further Reading

For Mayor's six-year plan for UNESCO see "UNESCO Chief Vows Major Reforms," *The Washington Post* (February 25, 1989). "Time for a New Look at UNESCO," by Robert Mauthmer, *Financial Times* (March 27, 1990), focuses on Mayor's accomplishments during his first few years at UNESCO. □

Richmond Mayo-Smith

The American statistician and sociologist Richmond Mayo-Smith (1854-1901) pioneered in teaching statistics and applying it to the social sciences. He was one of the founders of the American Economic Association.

Born in Troy, Ohio, the third son of Preserved and Lucy Smith, Richmond Mayo-Smith was the direct descendant of a famous Puritan family of clergymen. He did his undergraduate work at Amherst College. There he came under the influence of John W. Burgess, who interested him in economics and allied subjects. After receiving his bachelor's degree, he spent 2 years in graduate study at the universities of Heidelberg and Berlin at the suggestion of Burgess, who offered him the chair in economics and statistics in the soon to be established faculty of political science at Columbia College if he would complete his studies abroad. In 1877 he received his appointment at Columbia as an instructor in history and political science, beginning an association with that institution which terminated only with his death.

From 1878 to 1883 Mayo-Smith was assistant and adjunct professor of political economy and social science, becoming a full professor in 1883. In 1880 he became one of the five original members of the graduate faculty of political science, although he continued to teach undergraduates. In the same year he developed and gave the first course on statistics in an American college. This course, which he continued to give for 20 years, and his textbooks in statistics, prototypes in the field, were the chief reasons for his extraordinary influence in the United States on the development and use of the quantitative approach in the social sciences and on the teaching of statistics in American universities.

With newly developed and more highly sophisticated methods of gathering statistics on social phenomena, statistics was now seen as a quantitative instrument to solve social problems. Mayo-Smith believed that earlier sociologists had overemphasized the complexity of social phenomena as compared to natural phenomena. They had also, he felt, added to the problem by gathering useless data, by collecting it without any rational scheme or method of investigation, and by using a terminology which was artificial in that it was based on biological categories. He proposed instead a more simplified method of collecting data, based on cause and effect, and of coexistence and sequence, in social phenomena. To propagate these views he published many influential papers in learned journals. In 1889 he helped revive the American Statistical Association, becoming one of its vice presidents, a position he held until his death. In 1890 he became a member of the National Academy of Sciences, which prior to this had usually selected only scholars in the pure and natural sciences. He was also an active member of the International Statistical Institute and was elected an honorary fellow of the Royal Statistical Society.

Mayo-Smith's most definitive work on statistics is the two-volume *Science of Statistics,* with volume 1 appearing in 1895 as *Statistics and Sociology,* and volume 2 in 1899 as *Statistics and Economics.* Basically, the first volume was intended to demonstrate that social problems could be solved by statistics, and the second volume to show that economic problems could also be thus solved.

Although his writings on economics were also quite extensive, Mayo-Smith published only one book in this field, *Emigration and Immigration* (1890). It dealt mainly with the effects of population movements on ethnic and ethical standards of communities. The work had a great influence. He advocated strict control of immigration to exclude defectives, delinquents, and others who possessed traits incompatible with the American standard of civilization. He believed that the enormous number of immigrants with disparate sociocultural habits then entering America threatened to overwhelm the political institutions of the United States and would generate economic disturbances.

With the beginning of the *Political Science Quarterly* at Columbia in 1886, Mayo-Smith became a member of the editorial board and was a frequent contributor. In 1895 he read a paper, "The Desirability of a Permanent Census Bureau," to the American Economic Association. With its and the Statistical Association's joint sponsorship, a book was ultimately published, in 1899, under Mayo-Smith's chairmanship, *The Federal Census: Critical Essays by Members of the American Economic Association.*

Following a crippling boating accident, Mayo-Smith sustained a nervous breakdown and committed suicide a few months later in New York City.

Further Reading

No definitive biography of Mayo-Smith has yet been published. There is a biographical memoir by E. R. Seligman in National Academy of Sciences, *Biographical Memoirs,* vol. 17 (1924).
□

Ernst Mayr

The German-born American evolutionary biologist Ernst Mayr (born 1904) helped lead the modern synthesis of evolutionary theory. Mayr made major contributions to ornithology, evolutionary theory and the history and philosophy of biology. He is best known for his work on speciation—how one species arises from another.

Ernst Mayr was born in Kepten Germany, near the borders of Austria and Switzerland on July 5, 1904. He was one of three sons of Helene Pusinelli Mayr and Otto Mayr, who was a judge. The Mayr family valued education and Mayr and his brothers were provided with a broad education that included the study of Latin and Greek. All three sons became professionals. As a boy, Mayr developed a keen interest in birdwatching—an interest that remained with him for life. Mayr began to study medicine in 1923 at the University of Greifswald, but within two years he became so enthralled with the evolutionary works and studies of Charles Darwin that he switched his studies from medicine to zoology. His interest in birds had led him to the German ornithologist Erwin Stresemann, who induced him to make the switch to zoology. As his mentor, Stresemann had a great influence on Mayr's thinking as well as his career. Starting with his earliest work, Mayr saw the value of asking evolutionary questions in biogeographical studies,

and he consistently argued for an evolutionary basis to species concepts. Conversely, he used biogeography and taxonomy in the effort to explain evolution where in 1926 he received his Ph.D. in zoology. Soon afterward he became the zoological museum's assistant curator.

Following his doctoral degree in zoology from the University of Berlin in 1926, Mayr became an assistant curator in the university's museum. His chance to explore was provided by the wealthy zoologist and collector Lord Walter Rothschild the next year when Mayr agreed to lead his expedition for ornithological exploration and collection in the mountains of Dutch New Guinea. Although the trip was not easy, his success gave him experience and fame in the ornithological world; invitations for expeditions immediately followed, including one to New Guinea for the University of Berlin and the Whitney South Sea expedition to the Solomon Islands for the American Museum of Natural History, New York. This led to his appointment to work on the collected material at the museum in New York. When the museum bought Rothschild's enormous bird collection in 1931, Mayr was an obvious choice for curator, and he became a permanent staff member—and a naturalized U.S. citizen. He married Margarete Simon in 1935; they had two daughters.

The experiences and insights crowded into these years in the South Pacific were to stimulate Mayr's thinking about biology and the development of species for decades to come. In a number of monographs during the 1930s, as he worked on the taxonomy of South Pacific birds, Mayr turned to the theoretical problems of distinguishing species. More

complex than its modest title implies *List of New Guinea Birds* (1941) explores the ways closely related species can be distinguished from one another and variations can arise within a species. This work and two field guides for South Pacific birds included bio-geographical work that led him to the idea that natural population groups might provide the proper basis for differentiations. Stephen Jay Gould wrote that Mayr "sharpened his notion of species as fundamental units in nature and deepened his understanding of evolution." Also, he had worked with Rothschild's curators Ernst Hartert and Karl Jordan, pioneers of both a biological species concept and the use of subspecific names reflecting geography.

During the 1930's and 1940's biologists accepted the broad premise of Darwin's theory about evolution—that species change and evolve through a process called natural selection. Mayr realized, along with many taxonomists and other biologists, that reform was needed in the concept of species, for the traditional dependence on morphological difference was misleading. Mayr argued brilliantly for a new synthesis, to wed species concepts more firmly to genetics and to the updated Darwinian theory being produced by population geneticists and evolutionary theorists in many subdisciplines. Neo-Darwinism stresses natural selection of genetic differences within populations as the fundamental cause of evolution, and Mayr's biological species concept reflects the reality of populations in the history of life. His "new systematics" thus defines a species as a genetically interacting group, isolated in reproduction from others.

Biologists embraced the revised concept, for it also made species into a real entity, and not merely an arbitrary grouping. Moreover, the variation seen within species became a biologically important phenomenon. Mayr, more than anyone else, led the promotion of the biological species concept and introduced evolutionary genetics to taxonomists with his highly influential *Systematics and the Origin of Species* (1942).

This book also argued that in the evolving of new species the crucial step is reproductive (genetical) isolation, by whatever means. Rejecting current alternative theories of rapid speciation by mutation or Lamarckism, Mayr's geographical speciation process depends on the gradual accumulation of small changes under natural selection; the usual causes would be environmental change or geographical barriers establishing local, isolated populations.

The decline of Darwinism within biology that had persisted since the late 1800s was reversed after the 1930s, with natural selection again regarded as a fundamental cause of evolution. By answering the speciation question with ideas from genetics and from ecological studies, Mayr became an important architect and spokesman for the modern synthesis of evolutionary theory. He also was instrumental in the founding of the Society for the Study of Evolution and its journal *Evolution,* serving as its first editor from 1947 to 1949. His theories about speciation not only found general acceptance but won Mayr great respect as well. E.O. Wilson commented that "He gave taxonomy an evolutionary perspective. He got the show on the road."

Mayr resigned his curatorship in 1953 and moved to Harvard University's Museum of Comparative Zoology; he was director of that museum from 1961 to 1970. In further work on speciation theory he emphasized the founder effect, in which changes start with isolation of a small subpopulation, carrying a limited gene pool and perhaps living in changed environmental circumstances. Mayr's field experience led him to conclude that selection would operate in this way often on the periphery of a species' range, allowing what he termed peripatetic speciation. Presented as a staunchly neo-Darwinian position, especially in his landmark *Animal Species and Evolution* (1963), this speciation theory does allow rapid change in founder populations and has led some evolutionists, such as Stephen Jay Gould, to argue for a less gradual mode of evolution. Mayr maintained the adequacy of the Modern Synthesis position, as so ably expounded in his 1963 book.

Always interested in a wide range of subjects, Mayr also wrote influentially on the philosophy and history of biology. Summing up and expanding upon his many papers is *The Growth of Biological Thought* (1982), which presents his historical analysis of ideas about the organization and evolution of life.

Already honored with numerous degrees and medals, Mayr was the recipient in 1984 of the Balzan prize, considered to be the equivalent of the Nobel Prize for the biological sciences. He also holds ten honorary degrees, was elected to the National Academy of Sciences, received the Darwin-Wallace Medal in 1958, the Linnean Medal in 1977, the Gregor Mendel medal in 1980 and the Darwin Medal of the Royal Society in 1987. In 1994, at the age of 90, Mayr was awarded the prestigious Japan Prize by the Committee on the International prize for biology.

In an 1983 interview in Omni, Mayr discussed many of the concerns that he expressed throughout his career "Man must realize that he is part of the ecosystem and that his own survival depends on not destroying that ecosystem". He remained pessimistic about the future of the human race. When Mayr retired from Harvard as professor emeritus of zoology in 1975, Stephen Jay Gould observed that he really only changed careers—from a scientist he became a historian of science. In 1991, at age 87, he published another carefully wrought discussion of evolution *One Long Argument* in which he stated "the basic theory of evolution has been confirmed so completely that modern biologists consider evolution simply a fact . . . Where evolutionists today differ from Darwin is almost entirely on matters of emphasis. While Darwin was fully aware of the probabalistic nature of selection, the modern evolutionist emphasizes this even more. The modern evolutionist realizes how great a role chance plays in evolution."

In 1997, *The Science of the Living World* was released to great acclaim by the scientific community. In it Mayr managed to condense the complicated history of biological thought. He tried to promote a view of knowledge acquisition called evolutionary epistemology which suggests that human understanding evolves like life itself.

Further Reading

Mayr anthologized his most influential articles, with an autobiographical and explanatory section, in his *Evolution and the Diversity of Life* (1976). He is also included in the McGraw-Hill *Modern Men of Science*, vol. II (1968). His own works include *List of New Guinea Birds* (1941); *Systematics and the Origin of the Species* (1942); *Animal Species and Evolution* (1963); *The Growth of Biological Thought* (1982); *One Long Argument* (1991); *The Science of the Living World* (1997). □

Benjamin E. Mays

In addition to occupying the president's office at Morehouse, Benjamin Mays (1894-1984) wrote, taught mathematics, worked for the Office of Education, served as chairman of the Atlanta Board of Education, preached in a Baptist church, acted as an advisor to the Southern Christian Leadership Council, and was a church historian.

African American scholar Benjamin E. Mays was among the first generation of people of color to be born into freedom in the southern United States. Still, he was forced to battle racial discrimination and economic hardship in the drive to obtain an education. Later, during his 27 years as president of Atlanta's Morehouse College, one of the country's leading black educational institutions, he worked to provide African American students with the academic and social opportunities for which he had fought so hard. Among the many distinguished Morehouse graduates he inspired were former mayor of Atlanta, Andrew Young; Georgia state senator Julian Bond; and civil rights legend Dr. Martin Luther King, Jr. According to Frank J. Prial of the *New York Times*, King once described Mays as his "spiritual mentor and . . . intellectual father."

During the early 1960s, having entered the third decade of his presidency of Morehouse College, Mays played an important role in the integration of Atlanta by helping students organize sit-ins at lunch counters and other segregated facilities. He later held a prominent position on the Atlanta Board of Education.

Throughout his life, Mays maintained that education, personal pride, and peaceful protest were the most effective weapons in the war against racial bigotry. "To me black power must mean hard work, trained minds, and perfected skills to perform in a competitive society," he wrote in his critically acclaimed autobiography *Born to Rebel*, published in 1971. "The injustices imposed upon the black man for centuries make it all the more obligatory that he develop himself. . . . There must be no dichotomy between the development of one's mind and a deep sense of appreciation of one's heritage. An unjust penalty has been imposed upon the Negro because he is black. The dice are loaded against him. Knowing this, as the Jew knows about anti-Semitism, the black man must never forget the necessity that he perfect his talents and potentials to the ultimate."

Found Fulfillment in Academic Achievement

The youngest of eight children, Benjamin Mays was born in Epworth, South Carolina, in 1894, and raised on an isolated cotton farm. At that time, the maximum school term for black children was only four months—November through February—so he and his brothers and sisters spent most of the year helping with the planting and picking. Mays was an avid student, however; thanks to early lessons from his elder sister, Susie, by the time he arrived at the one-room Brickhouse School at the age of six, he already knew how to count, read, and write. He quickly became the star pupil there and wept whenever bad weather kept him at home.

Church provided another outlet for his talents. At the age of nine he received a standing ovation from the Mount Zion Baptist congregation for his recitation of the Sermon on the Mount. "The people in the church did not contribute one dime to help me with my education," he recalled in *Born to Rebel*. "But they gave me something far more valuable. They gave me the thing I most needed. They expressed such confidence in me that I always felt that I could never betray their trust, never let them down."

Mays needed all the encouragement he could get. During his childhood, mob violence against blacks was rampant, and brutal lynchings were a common occurrence. Among his earliest memories was that of a group of white men with rifles riding up to his home on horseback and demanding that his father remove his cap and bow down to them. "As a child my life was one of frustration and doubt," he recalled in *Born to Rebel*. "Nor did the situation improve as I grew older. Long before I could visualize them, I knew within my body, my mind, and my spirit that I faced galling restrictions, seemingly insurmountable barriers, dangers and pitfalls."

When Mays expressed a desire to continue his education beyond the elementary level, his father responded with anger and disdain. At that time, it was believed that the only honest occupations for black men were farming and preaching. Education, his father maintained, made men both liars and fools. Eventually Mays overcame his father's objections, however, and enrolled at the high school of South Carolina State College at Orangeburg. He graduated in 1916 as valedictorian.

Determined to prove his worth in the white man's world, Mays resolved to leave his native South Carolina and continue his education in New England. "How could I know I was not inferior to the white man, having never had a chance to compete with him?" he wrote in *Born to Rebel*. Mays spent a year at Virginia Union University and obtained letters of recommendation from two of his professors before gaining admission to Bates College in Maine. He began his studies there as a sophomore in September 1917. Summer work as a Pullman porter—as well as scholarships and loans from the college—helped him pay his way.

At Bates, where he was one of only a handful of black students, Mays was surprised and heartened to find himself treated as an equal for the very first time. Both his academic gifts and his enthusiastic participation in extracurricular activities quickly made him a campus leader. After graduating with honors in 1920, Mays completed several semesters of graduate work at the University of Chicago. He then accepted an invitation from Morehouse College president John Hope (whom he happened to meet in the University of Chicago library) to teach higher mathematics in Atlanta. He arrived at Morehouse in 1921, and remained there for the next three years, teaching math, psychology, and religious education. In 1922 he was ordained a Baptist minister and assumed the pastorate of nearby Shiloh Baptist Church. He returned to the University of Chicago in 1924 to complete work on his master's degree, and ten years later received his doctorate in ethics and Christian theology.

Encountered Anger and Racism in Atlanta

Mays's positive experiences as a student at Bates College had filled him with a new sense of pride and optimism. But the Atlanta he encountered in the early 1920s was a tense and angry place, where streetcars, elevators, parks, waiting rooms, and even ambulances were segregated; where Ku Klux Klan rallies and lynchings were everyday facts of life; where people of color were prohibited from voting; and where the only high school education available for African Americans was provided by private academies connected to the all-black colleges. The return of black soldiers from Europe at the end of World War I had only served to heighten racial tensions in the city. "It was in Atlanta, Georgia, that I was to see the race problem in greater depth, and observe and experience it in larger dimensions," Mays wrote in *Born to Rebel*. "It was in Atlanta

that I was to find that the cruel tentacles of race prejudice reached out to invade and distort every aspect of Southern life."

After completing his master's degree at the University of Chicago in 1925, Mays spent a year teaching English at the State College of South Carolina at Orangeburg. The following year, he and his wife, Sadie Grey, a teacher and social worker whom he had met in Chicago, moved to Florida, where Mays took over the position of executive secretary for the Tampa Urban League. Two years later, he was named national student secretary of the Young Men's Christian Association (YMCA), based in Atlanta.

In 1930 Mays left this post to direct a study of black churches in the United States for the Institute of Social and Religious Research in New York City. He and a fellow minister, Joseph W. Nicholson, spent 14 months collecting data from some 800 rural and urban churches throughout the country in an effort to identify the church's influence in the black community. Among the subjects addressed were the education and training of ministers, the churches' financial resources, and the kinds of religious and social programs offered. The results of the study were published in 1933 under the title *The Negro's Church*. In a review for the periodical *Books*, NAACP executive secretary Walter White described the report as "one of the few examinations of this sort" and "an important achievement in its understanding of all the social, economic and other forces which have made [the black church] what it is."

Mays would focus on the vital importance of the black church in American society in a host of other writings published in the 1930s and 1940s. In an article appearing in the summer 1940 issue of *Christendom*, he maintained that the black church was largely responsible for "keeping one-tenth of America's population sanely religious in the midst of an environment that is, for the most part, hostile to it."

Worked to Strengthen Black Colleges

In 1934 Mays became dean of the School of Religion at Howard University. During his six-year tenure, he succeeded in strengthening the faculty and facilities to such an extent that the school achieved a Class A rating from the American Association of Theological Schools. This made it only the second all-black seminary in the nation to receive such accreditation. During this period, Mays traveled widely, attending church and YMCA conferences around the world and earning an international reputation for academic excellence. His wife, Sadie, accompanied him on most of his trips.

Mays was named president of Morehouse College in July of 1940, exactly 19 years after he had begun his teaching career there. In *Born to Rebel*, published some 30 years later, he reflected upon the ineffable energy and spirit of the place. "I found a special, intangible something at Morehouse in 1921 which sent men out into life with a sense of mission, believing that they could accomplish whatever they set out to do," he wrote. "This priceless quality was still alive when I returned in 1940, and for twenty-seven years I built on what I found, instilling in Morehouse students the idea that despite crippling circumscriptions the sky was their limit.''

While president of Morehouse, Mays fought for the integration of all-white colleges but remained an outspoken advocate of predominantly black institutions, such as Morehouse and Howard. ''If white America really wants to improve Negro higher education, it would do well to recognize the fact that it will not be adequately done by allowing black colleges to die the slow death of starvation,'' he wrote in *Born to Rebel.* His steadfast devotion to academic excellence helped Morehouse become one of only four Georgia colleges to be approved for a chapter of the Phi Beta Kappa honor society.

Inspired Civil Rights Activists

Perhaps Mays's greatest influence was on the individual students he encountered both in the classroom and through the college chapel. His greatest honor, he later said, was having taught and inspired Martin Luther King, Jr., the college's most celebrated alumnus. During Morehouse commencement ceremonies in June of 1957, Mays honored Dr. King for his leadership in the 1956 Montgomery Bus Boycott by conferring upon him the honorary degree of Doctor of Humane Letters. King later became a member of the Morehouse College board of trustees. Mays also convinced two of Georgia's brightest African American politicians, Andrew Young and Julian Bond, to seek public office.

Mays became even more directly involved in the civil rights movement in 1960 when he agreed to help students from Morehouse and other Atlanta colleges organize peaceful protests throughout the city—an action which, after 18 months, resulted in the integration of the Atlanta public school system. Prial remembered Mays in a *New York Times* obituary as ''a voice of moderation in the critical years of the civil rights movement. He attacked white liberals who paid only lip service to racial equality, but he [also] criticized . . . black extremists'' for undermining attempts at unity between races.

After his retirement from Morehouse College in 1967, Mays served as a consultant for a variety of governmental, educational, civic, and religious organizations, and in 1969 he became a member of the Atlanta Board of Education. He remained on the board until 1981. During this time he also produced his powerful autobiography, *Born to Rebel.* In his preface, Mays described the book as ''the story of the lifelong quest of a man who desired to be looked upon first as a human being and incidentally as a Negro, to be accepted first as an American and secondarily as a black man.'' J. B. Cullen of *Books* called it a ''condemnation of the white treatment of the blacks in the United States'' and ''a story that should be read by everyone.'' Prior to his death in 1984 at the age of 89, Mays wrote dozens of scholarly articles on racial, educational, and religious issues, spoke at more than 200 universities and colleges, and received some 45 honorary degrees.

Further Reading

Mays, Benjamin, *Born to Rebel: An Autobiography,* Scribner, 1971.

Salley, Columbus, *The Black 100,* Citadel Press, 1993.
Best Sellers, April 15, 1971.
Black Enterprise, May 1977, pp. 26-29.
Books, March 26, 1933.
Christendom, Summer 1940.
Christian Science Monitor, April 17, 1971.
Ebony, July 1954, p. 27; January 1961, p. 48; June 1965, pp. 165-72; July 1971, pp. 88-94; August 1971, p. 52; December 1977, pp. 72-80.
Jet, August 3, 1992, p. 24.
New York Times, March 29, 1984, p. D23.
New York Times Book Review, April 25, 1971, pp. 47-48.
Washington Post, March 29, 1984.
Benjamin E. Mays, History on Video (30-minute biographical tape), first televised on Black Entertainment Television, 1992. □

Willie Mays

During his 21 seasons with the San Francisco Giants, Willie Mays (born 1931) hit more than 600 home runs. Besides being a solid hitter, Mays also has been called the game's finest defensive outfielder and perhaps its best baserunner as well.

Willie Mays has often been described as the finest all-around baseball player ever to pick up a bat. During his 22-year-long professional ballplaying career, most of it with the Giants of New York and San Francisco, Mays displayed superlative skill in every aspect of the game. He hit for average, hit for power, stole bases, played center field with almost magical grace, and set several records for durability. Throughout the 1950s and 1960s, the name ''Willie Mays'' was a synonym for baseball excellence, and he remains the standard against which young players measure their versatility on the ballfield.

From the time he could first walk, Mays was either throwing, catching, or hitting a baseball. Mays was born on May 6, 1931, in Westfield, Alabama, the son of a steelworker who also played a good center field for the local Birmingham Industrial League semi-pro team. Mays' mother, Ann, had been a high school track star, and it was clear from a very early age that Willie had inherited his parents' athletic gifts. According to his father, William Howard Mays, Sr., young Willie learned to walk at the age of six months, and soon thereafter the two center fielders were playing catch with each other, father instructing son in the rudiments of the game that would one day make him famous.

High School Pro

The parents of Willie Mays were divorced when he was only three, but Willie continued to live with his father, which meant that he continued to play baseball. It was not long before Mays realized that baseball offered him a way out of the steel mills, and he later frankly admitted that when given the choice he always preferred playing ball to doing schoolwork. Not only did Mays play ball constantly, he

The manager of the Black Barons, Piper Davis, became an important tutor to the outstanding young ballplayer. Davis recognized and helped perfect Mays's innate abilities while also serving as something of a father figure for the teenaged member of his Black Baron team. The Black Barons traveled as far as Chicago and New York, often riding all night in a secondhand bus to make the next day's game and lodging in mediocre hotels in the "colored part" of each town; yet the irrepressible Mays thrived on the routine of constant competition and challenge.

By the time Mays had secured for himself the center fielder's spot on the Black Barons, legendary ballplayer Jackie Robinson had broken the color barrier in major league baseball, and the Negro Leagues were being scouted heavily by the newly integrated professional teams. One such scout for the New York Giants came to a Black Barons game to watch a teammate of Mays, but it was Willie Mays who captured his attention; the scout raved to his supervisors in the Giants' organization about him. The Giants had already signed a number of black baseball players, and it was not long before they offered Mays $4,000 bonus and $250 a month salary to play for their Sioux City, Iowa, Class A team. He was nineteen years old.

The Talk of New York

Racial problems in Sioux City prevented Mays from joining the team in 1950, however, and he went instead to Trenton in the Class B Interstate League, becoming the first black ever to play in that league. His .353 average led the league in hitting. Mays then began the 1951 season playing for the Minneapolis Millers in AAA ball. The young center fielder was nothing less than a sensation in Minneapolis, where, after the season's first sixteen games he was batting .608 and routinely making amazing plays in the outfield.

Such initial success was highly unusual at the AAA level, and Mays's name quickly became familiar to Leo Durocher, the manager of the New York Giants. The Giants were suffering through a mediocre season in 1951, and Durocher saw no reason to delay the elevation of Mays to the major league level. On May 25, 1951, Mays became the starting center fielder and number-three hitter in the New York Giants' lineup. Durocher's confidence in Mays was unbounded, and even after Mays's slow start (only one hit in his first twenty-five at bats) Durocher never doubted that Mays would remain his center fielder for the next ten years. Like Davis, manager of the Black Barons, Durocher took an almost fatherly interest in enabling the young star to realize his enormous potential.

By mid-August of the 1951 season, neither the Giants nor their young prodigy appeared to be going anywhere fast. Mays showed flashes of brilliance but he was still only a rookie, and the Giants remained thirteen and one-half games back of the Brooklyn Dodgers in the National League pennant race. The Giants went on to sweep a three game series with the Dodgers, however, and after winning sixteen games in a row they managed to catch their rivals on the last day of the regular season and force a play-off for the pennant. In one of the most famous episodes in baseball history, Mays's teammate Bobby Thompson won the third and de-

would sit in the dugout with his father's Industrial League teammates and listen to baseball strategy and technique, absorbing the game's finer points and learning to be at his ease in a competitive environment. Mays literally grew up on a ballfield and for that reason developed the habits and skills of a big league ballplayer at an astonishingly early age. By the age of thirteen, he was playing on a semi-professional team called the Gray Sox.

At one point, father and son played in the same outfield in the Birmingham Industrial League, the younger Mays in center and the elder in left. So gifted was Mays as a teenager that his friends urged him to try out for the Birmingham Black Barons, the local entry in the Negro Leagues, which was then the black equivalent of the major leagues. Blacks and whites did not yet play baseball together at this point in America's history; Negro League teams played throughout the South and in some northern cities, often to large crowds and with some financial rewards, but black Americans could not play in the so-called "big leagues."

Therefore, when the fifteen-year-old Mays was asked by the manager of the Birmingham Black Barons to join his squad, he immediately accepted the offer and took over center field on a team comprised of men ten years his senior. Mays was initially paid a salary of $250 a month to play with the Black Barons, far more money than he could have earned at part-time jobs as a high-school student. He eventually finished high school, but he did so as a professional baseball player.

ciding game of the ensuing play-off with a three-run home run in the bottom of the ninth inning. In the World Series, the Giants faced their crosstown rivals, the New York Yankees, and after a fine series lost in seven games to the perennial champions. Mays hit only .182 in the series, but in recognition of his 20 home runs and .274 batting average he was named the National League's Rookie of the Year for 1951.

Although Mays was not the star of that 1951 pennant-winning Giants team, his obvious talent and superlative grace on the ballfield made him one of the most talked about players in the major leagues. Still only 20 years old, Mays was certain to develop into one of the game's leading players, but he and his fans would first have to endure a two-year hiatus while Mays served in the U.S. Army. The army did not waste Mays's talents, employing him primarily as an instructor on its baseball teams, but many observers wondered how the lay-off would affect Mays's still-maturing abilities.

Mays answered that question with an extraordinary return in 1954, when he led the Giants to a world championship while hitting .345, 41 home runs, and winning the Most Valuable Player Award. Mays led the league in batting average, and in the first game of the World Series he made a catch of such remarkable skill that it has ever since been known simply as "The Catch." Mays appeared on the *Ed Sullivan Show* and the *Colgate Comedy Hour* and was then hustled off to play winter ball in Puerto Rico for the Giants. The apparently tireless center fielder could have used some rest, but as a favor to the Giants he played all winter in Puerto Rico, also leading that league in hitting and slugging percentage. Giants' management rewarded Mays with a fat new contract, and he entered the 1955 season as an indisputable superstar.

Doing It All

It should not be forgotten that 1954 was Mays's first full season in the big leagues. What is especially remarkable is that the promise shown by his 1954 season would later be confirmed in season after season of excellence, beginning with the 51 homers he clubbed in 1955. Not only was Mays the seventh player in the history of the game to hit 50 or more home runs in one season, he also led the National League in triples and slugging percentage, was second in stolen bases, and led all outfielders with 23 assists.

Mays's combination of speed and power had never been seen before: sluggers do not often steal bases, and they are often maladroit in the outfield. While Mays was not a particularly big man, he was so gifted an athlete and he hit the baseball squarely and hard with such regularity that he could reportedly alter the number of home runs he hit depending on the needs of his team. In 1955, for example, Durocher asked Mays to supply the Giants with power, so he hit 51 homers; the year before, Durocher had been worried that Mays was thinking too much about the fences, so he limited himself to five homers in the last third of the season and won the batting title. When left to follow his own inclinations, Mays would generally hit about 30 home runs while batting somewhere above .300, a pattern he maintained for nearly the whole of his long career.

The 1955 season saw the departure of Durocher as manager of the Giants. He was replaced by Bill Rigney, but under neither man were the Giants considered contenders for another title. Mays would never be as close to a manager as he had been to Durocher, but by this point in his career, he could play for anyone: in 1956, he hit "only" 36 home runs but led the league with 40 stolen bases, the first of four consecutive years in which he stole more bases than anyone else in the National League. Mays also married for the first time in 1956, wedding Marguerite Wendell just before his 25th birthday. The couple remained together for about seven years, adopting a baby boy, Michael, in 1958 before divorcing at the close of the 1962 season.

After the 1957 season the Giants left New York for the West Coast, moving the franchise to San Francisco, while the Dodgers shifted from Brooklyn to Los Angeles. Mays was a much-loved figure in New York, and the transition to the West Coast was perhaps harder on him than on his teammates. Californians did not idolize Mays the way New Yorkers had, and he was justifiably disappointed by the reception he received from the San Francisco press, which adopted a somewhat skeptical attitude to the phenomenon of the East. As a center fielder, Mays also had to cope with the wildly shifting winds common at Candlestick Park, the home of the Giants from 1960 onward. Mays eventually learned the tricks of life out west, however, winning over the fans with his routine brilliance on the field and with the bat. In 1961 Mays became the fifth player ever to hit four home runs in a single game; in 1962 he led the Giants back to the World Series with a career-high 141 runs batted in; and in the following year he joined an exclusive club by smashing his 400th career homer. It was at least possible that Mays could one day catch Babe Ruth as the all-time leader in home runs.

660 Home Runs

Several times in his long career Willie Mays literally drove himself into the ground, once collapsing from exhaustion while at bat, and he was periodically hospitalized for tests. It appeared that Mays's extraordinary play in all aspects of the game simply required more energy than he could muster, leaving him vulnerable to the occasional fainting spell. In spite of these sporadic problems, the Giants again rose to excellence in the 1965 season under manager Herman Franks, chasing the Dodgers for the pennant all year only to fall two games short at the end. Franks used Mays as team captain and unofficial coach, often consulting with him on player personnel and strategy, and the 33-year-old Mays responded with the last of his truly great seasons. He finished with 52 home runs, including the 500th of his career, and won his second Most Valuable Player award. His performance was especially impressive because the other great stars of the 1950s—including Yankees slugger Mickey Mantle, Dodger outfielder Duke Snider, and Braves southpaw pitcher Warren Spahn—had for the most part ceased to play at their peak levels of performance. Eleven years after his first MVP award, Mays continued to play baseball as well as he ever had.

The only question remaining for Mays was Babe Ruth's record of 714 career home runs. Mays passed the records of many of the game's all-time greats—immortal Yankees first baseman Lou Gehrig's 493, New York Giants outfielder Mel Ott's 511, and four-time American League home run champ Jimmie Foxx's 54—until at last Mays was alone with the Babe, still 170 homers distant. Mays's many years of continuous effort had taken its toll, however, and after the 1966 season his home runs and batting average both began to taper off. But by the time he wound up his career with the New York Mets in 1973, he had made a strong case for himself as the greatest all-around player in baseball history.

The record of his accomplishments is long—the combination of his 24 straight All Star Game appearances, his more than three thousand career basehits, and his first-year election to the baseball Hall of Fame with 94.6% of the possible votes was unparalleled—but Mays will be remembered as much for the wonderful effortlessness of his play as for the numbers he racked up. In the field, at bat, and on the bases, he remained for more than twenty years the epitome of athletic grace.

Further Reading

Mays, Willie, and Lou Sahadi, *Say Hey: The Autobiography of Willie Mays,* Simon and Schuster, 1988.
Smith, Robert, *Baseball,* Simon and Schuster, 1947, reprinted, 1970.
Atlanta Constitution, May 20, 1986; June 10, 1988.
Ebony, October 1966.
Jet, March 27, 1980; March 3, 1986; April 10, 1989.
Los Angeles Times, June 3, 1988; March 13, 1989.
Newsweek, September 10, 1951; July 19, 1954.
New York Times, February 12, 1966; April 26, 1966.
New York Times Book Review, June 5, 1988.
New York Times Magazine, July 11, 1954.
Sporting News, September 1, 1986.
Sports Illustrated, October 6, 1986.
Time, July 26, 1954; April 1, 1985. □

Ma Yüan

Ma Yüan (active ca. 1190-ca. 1229) was a Chinese painter. With Hsia Kuei, he was one of the creators of the Ma-Hsia school of landscape painting and one of the great masters of the Southern Sung period.

M a Yüan, also called Ch'in-shan, was born around the middle of the 12th century in Ch'ien-t'ang (modern Hangzhou), Chekiang Province. He represented the fourth generation in a tradition of painters spanning five generations, beginning with his great-grandfather, Ma Fen, and ending with his son, Ma Lin, all of whom served the Sung emperors as court painters-in-attendance. The family seat was in Ho-chung, Shansi Province, but the occupation of North China in 1126 by the Chin Tatars forced the family, and the government, to flee to the south.

Although the family tradition doubtless had strong influence on Ma Yüan's development as a painter, he was also indebted to the great northern landscape and figure master Li T'ang (died after 1130), whose style bridged the transition from the monumental art of Northern Sung to the more intimate, lyrical taste of Southern Sung.

Ma Yüan's art at its best is a masterpiece of understatement and evocative suggestion. His typical compositions, featuring the extensive use of swirling mist and empty spaces, with only a few sharply etched forms dramatically silhouetted against the whiteness, lent him the nickname "One-corner Ma." One of his finest works, however, the *Landscape in Rain,* in the Iwasaki Collection, is a monumental vision of wind-and-rain-swept mountains and towering pines, recalling the heroic vision of the 10th and 11th centuries.

The style that has made such a favorable impression on Ma Yüan's admirers in Japan and the West is better suggested in the small fan painting in the Museum of Fine Arts, Boston, representing two willow trees rising against the faint shadow of distant mountains. The time is early spring, and the first stirring of life rustles in the dry branches. Mood is all-important, the poetry of an instant captured in a few brush strokes. Often crystallizing the lyrical essence of such paintings are a few well-chosen words, or a poetic couplet written on the work by an imperial patron.

One small hanging scroll in the Palace Museum, Taipei, Taiwan, comes near to achieving a monumental vision in this same lyrical mode. It represents a few egrets hurdled in the frozen snow of a mountain pass, above them the crackling branches of a gnarled pine and the icy infinity of the sky. To convey so much with such sparing means— black ink on plain silk—is an artistic achievement of the first rank and places Ma Yüan among the leading artists of the Sung period.

The Ma-Hsia style was sometimes dismissed by later critics as consisting of "leftover mountains and broken trees," largely because of the weakness of the dynasty itself, which lost China to the Mongols. Nonetheless, the style was vigorously revived in the late 14th century under the early Ming emperors, as a symbol of the restored Chinese Empire, and had a formative influence on Japanese professional painters.

Further Reading

Ma Yüan is extensively discussed in Oswald Siren, *Chinese Painting: Leading Masters and Principles,* vol. 1 (1956). The art of the Southern Sung period as a whole is treated by James Cahill, *The Art of Southern Sung China* (1962). □

Jules Mazarin

The French statesman Jules Mazarin (1602-1661) was the chosen successor of Richelieu. He governed France from 1643 until his death and laid the foundations for the monarchy of Louis XIV.

Jules Mazarin was born Giulio Mazarin on July 14, 1602, at Pescina, a village in the Abruzzi, Italy. He began his career as a soldier and diplomat in the service of the Pope. In this capacity he met Cardinal Richelieu in 1629 and decided to transfer his allegiance to him. He earned Richelieu's regard by acting in the French interest rather than the Pope's in certain treaty negotiations. He went to France as papal nuncio in 1636 and was naturalized as a French subject in 1639. In 1641 Richelieu persuaded the Pope to make Mazarin a cardinal, though he was not a priest.

Before Richelieu died in December 1642, he recommended Mazarin to Louis XIII as his successor, and the king accepted. Louis XIII died in May 1643, and the regent for the 5-year-old Louis XIV was his widow, Anne of Austria. The nobility welcomed the change. Anne was known to have been Richelieu's enemy, and Mazarin, though acknowledged as his nominee, was universally regarded as soft, ingratiating, and harmless. To everyone's utter astonishment, Anne confirmed Mazarin as first minister, and it soon became clear that she was in love with him. It is possible, though there is no proof, that later they were secretly married. They remained intimate friends and allies to the end of Mazarin's life.

Mazarin's task was to maintain the royal authority established by Richelieu and to win the war against France and Spain that he had started. Austria was humbled at the Peace of Westphalia in 1648; the war with Spain dragged on until 1659. The maintenance of royal authority was the most difficult task. Nobles who had reluctantly given way to

Richelieu would not accept his successor, who was despised as a lowborn foreigner and thought to be weak-willed. The country was bitter at the taxes imposed by Richelieu to support the war, and its mounting resentment found dangerous expression in the Parliament of Paris, whose opposition was supported by all classes in the city.

To suppress the defiance that immediately arose in Paris, Mazarin had to call on the Prince de Condé, a cousin of the King and a very successful general. Finding himself indispensable, Condé became intolerably greedy and arrogant, and Mazarin finally had him and his friends arrested. The result was that the civil war that had already broken out became much worse, and several times it appeared as if Mazarin could not survive.

This war was called the Fronde, a name used to this day in France to denote irresponsible opposition. Paris, led by its Parliament, had rebelled in 1648. When this revolt was settled a year later, it was soon followed by the break with Condé. More humane than Richelieu, Mazarin imprisoned his enemies but did not put them to death, and as a result he could not make himself feared. The Fronde dragged on until 1653, but in the end, thanks to his own cleverness, the Queen's loyalty, and the mistakes of his enemies, Mazarin was completely victorious.

For the rest of his life Mazarin was the unchallenged master of France. His final triumph came with the Peace of the Pyrenees in November 1659. France had finally defeated Spain and was rewarded with territorial acquisitions and the fateful marriage of Louis XIV to a Spanish princess. When Mazarin died on March 9, 1661, he had accomplished his task as he saw it. He had also accumulated a colossal fortune for himself.

In some ways Mazarin was a worthy successor to Richelieu. Behind a mask of affability, he was equally resolved to tolerate no opposition; his method of eliminating it was more devious and much less bloody but equally effective. As far as any man could have done, he fulfilled Richelieu's declared purpose of making "the king supreme in France, and France supreme in Europe." But, unlike Richelieu, he took no interest in the economic or cultural development of France. Once the Fronde was over, the country simply stagnated. The recovery that came in the 1660s was essentially the work of Jean Baptiste Colbert, whom Mazarin had picked out and recommended to the King.

Further Reading

There is no adequate biography of Mazarin. James Breck Perkins, *France under Mazarin, with a Review of the Administration of Richelieu* (1886), and Arthur Hassell, *Mazarin* (1903), contain biographical information, but both are dated. For an excellent general history of the period see John Laugh, *An Introduction to Seventeenth Century France* (1954).

Additional Sources

Treasure, G. R. R. (Geoffrey Russell Richards), *Mazarin: the crisis of absolutism in France,* London; New York: Routledge, 1995.
□

Ivan Stepanovich Mazepa

The Ukrainian Cossack leader Ivan Stepanovich Mazepa (ca. 1644-1709) is considered a traitor by Russian historians, a great patriot by Ukrainian historians.

Neither the place nor the date of the birth of Ivan Mazepa can be given with certainty, but there is evidence that he was born a Polish subject in what is now the Ukraine and that his parents were landed gentry of the Eastern Orthodox faith. He received an excellent education and then went into the service of the Polish king John Casimir as a courtier. Soon, however, he became involved in a scandal, was dismissed from the royal court, and was forced to return to his home. There, his amorous misconduct provoked a jealous husband into having him bound naked to the back of an unreined horse and exposed to the uncertainty of rescue. When extricated from that misadventure, he left for the eastern Ukraine and entered the military service of the newly organized Ukrainian Cossack state, which had received Russian aid in shaking off Polish rule and accepted autonomous status under Russia.

On the strength of his ability and cleverness, Mazepa advanced rapidly, reaching the rank of inspector general while still in his early 30s. He also succeeded in winning favor among influential men in Moscow and, when Peter I became czar, in gaining his complete confidence. With the aid of his Russian friends, he was elected hetman (chief) of the Ukrainian Cossack state in 1687.

As hetman, Mazepa found it necessary to devote much of his time to coping with turbulent and rebellious groups under his jurisdiction. But he managed to build new schools and churches in the area and to bring a measure of justice to the peasants and the rank-and-file Cossacks. His chief goal became the freeing of his people from Russian domination and the formation, under his rule, of an independent state including all of the Ukraine. Yet he was careful to continue cultivating the Czar's trust, even at the cost of sending Cossack contingents to fight for Russia, in order to gain time for finding the outside assistance he would need to achieve his ultimate goal.

The war between Russia and Sweden which began in 1700 fed the discontent among the hetman's people as it dragged on, disrupting their commerce and giving the Czar reason to call an increased number of them into combat. Hoping to capitalize on this discontent as well as to take advantage of Sweden's hostility to Russia, Mazepa began secret negotiations in 1705 with Sweden and Poland, then under a pro-Swedish ruler. The outcome was an understanding that a united Ukraine ruled by Mazepa would be federated with Poland in return for Mazepa's provision of aid to Sweden. Rumors of these traitorous dealings reached Czar Peter, but he retained his faith in the hetman; and Mazepa, while waiting for a favorable opportunity to join the Swedes, continued to maintain the appearance of loyalty to the Czar.

When Sweden's Charles XII invaded Russia in the fall of 1708, Mazepa believed that his opportunity had come. He expected to be able to summon not only the Ukrainian Cossacks but also other Cossacks and the Crimean Tatars to follow him to the Swedish side. When ordered by Peter to bring his Cossacks to join the Russians, he pleaded illness as an excuse for delay, hoping to gain time in which to organize a large-scale defection. However, he soon learned that he was not to have that time, for one of the Czar's most trusted generals, accompanied by a military contingent, was on the way to Baturin, the Cossack headquarters, to investigate.

With no choice but to flee before he had completed preparations for an open break, Mazepa hastily left Baturin with about 1,500 Cossacks late in October and, calling all other Cossacks to join him, made his way to the chief Swedish camp in the northern part of the Ukraine. The consequences of that flight were inauspicious for his cause: few Cossacks answered his call, the Russian troops ravaged Baturin, and the Czar tightened his hold over the Ukrainian Cossacks by having a docile hetman elected to replace Mazepa.

The only hope remaining for Mazepa lay in Swedish military strength; and when the Swedes were decisively defeated by the Russians at Poltava on June 27, 1709, even that hope was dissipated. He had to join Charles XII in hazardous flight to Turkey, the nearest place of safety. Despite Peter's efforts to extradite Mazepa, the aged and ailing hetman was given sanctuary in Turkey. He died there, of natural causes, a few months later.

Further Reading

There is very little material in English on Mazepa. A brief and interesting account of his life is given in Clarence Manning, *The Story of the Ukraine* (1947). □

Giuseppe Mazzini

The Italian patriot Giuseppe Mazzini (1805-1872) devoted his life to achieving liberty and unity for Italy. He placed the skill of his pen at the service of a vigorous republicanism.

Giuseppe Mazzini was born on June 22, 1805, at Genoa. He was a sickly but brilliant child, sufficiently precocious to take a law degree from the university of his native city at the age of 21. He began very early to write reviews, but after joining the Carbonari during the flurry of revolutionary activity of 1830, he turned his writing to more exclusively political ends. As a result, he was imprisoned and kept in the fortress of Savona for 6 months, after which he was released for lack of evidence.

Revolutionary Organizations

In the solitude of his prison cell Mazzini developed a clear idea of the direction he wanted his life to take and conceived plans for a new organization which was formed shortly after his release. La Giovine Italia (Young Italy) would devote itself to liberation, unity, and republicanism. It would seek these goals through elaborate educational programs and, if need be, guerrilla warfare. During the formation of Young Italy, Mazzini was in Marseilles, where he had gone into exile after his release from prison. In the summer of 1832 he withdrew into Switzerland under pressure from the French government. From there in 1833 he played an incidental part in an attempt to cause mutiny in the Sardinian army. The effort was a failure, and Mazzini was sentenced to death in absentia. This did not cause him to flinch or slacken his efforts, and in the same year he founded *Central Europe,* a journal devoted to the liberation of Savoy.

In 1834 a second and a third association were formed under Mazzini's influence, Young Europe and Young Switzerland, respectively. These groups were devoted to the principles of liberty and equality for all. There followed upon these activities a period of some restlessness and uncertainty for Mazzini. Trouble with the Swiss government caused him to be exiled, and in early 1837 he moved to London, where he scratched a meager living from some desultory writing of reviews. He increased his revolutionary contacts during the next few years and in 1840 established a workingmen's association.

Roman Republic

Suspicions grew in London over Mazzini's clandestine relationships, and the dubious practice of opening his mail

was undertaken by the home secretary, Sir James Graham. It was certainly true that the uncomfortable Italian guest was corresponding secretly with revolutionaries in his homeland. In 1848, when revolts broke out in Milan and Messina, he returned to Italy in the knowledge that the leaders of the rising were men of his acquaintance. That he had already achieved a considerable reputation is attested to by the fact that he was named in 1849, almost simultaneously, to the provisional government of Tuscany and the constituent assembly of the Roman Republic, both ill-fated outgrowths of the insurrections taking place throughout Europe.

On March 23, 1849, with defeat hovering over the revolution, Mazzini was made one of the Roman Triumvirate. His strong hand kept some order in the city until its surrender on June 30 forced him first into seclusion and then once again into exile. He kept his revolutionary fervor and in the next decade became involved, from London, in several more abortive Italian uprisings. His new journal, *Pensiero e azione* (Thought and Action), published in London, urged violence in the cause of liberty and unity.

Later Years

Mazzini came to believe, as the fateful years of 1859 and 1860 approached, that the only force capable of leading a successful insurrection against the repressive regimes of Italy was the kingdom of the Piedmont. Accordingly, he wrote to King Victor Emmanuel II, urging him in powerful language to take up the cause of Italian unity. He did this without surrendering to the monarchical principle. Inwardly at least he had not lost hope of a republican form of government for his countrymen, and when practical necessity made of the new Italian state a kingdom rather than a republic, he was disappointed. He demonstrated this continuing antipathy to monarchy as a governmental form when, in 1865, he rejected a seat in the Italian Parliament to which he had been elected by Messina. He did this because, as he put it, he felt that he could not take an oath of allegiance to the monarchy.

At that time Mazzini was still technically under sentence of death, and it was only in the following year, in a general amnesty granted when Venice was ceded to Italy, that the sentence was reversed. This was not the end of his troubles. In 1869 the Swiss government, at the request of the Italian one, forced him to leave Switzerland, where he had taken up residence. It was known that he was in touch with Giuseppe Garibaldi, who had run afoul of the Italian government over the status of Rome.

In 1870 on his way to Sicily, Mazzini was arrested and imprisoned. He was soon released but the confinement further embittered him, and he turned the energies of his last years to social questions. He tried his hand at guiding a working-class movement and even became involved, uncharacteristically, with theoreticians like Karl Marx and the nihilist Mikhail Bakunin. These relationships lasted only briefly, and Mazzini, no socialist, parted company with the working classes.

Mazzini's death at Pisa on March 10, 1872, brought forth a national public display of grief, voted unanimously by the Italian Parliament. Italy was already grateful to Mazzini, although the magnitude of his contribution to its emergence as a modern state would be fully understood only later.

Further Reading

The best source for Mazzini is his own writings, many of which are given in *Life and Writings of Joseph Mazzini* (6 vols., 1890-1891). Valuable works in English are Bolton King's *Mazzini* (1903) and his more general *A History of Italian Unity: Being a Political History of Italy from 1814 to 1871* (2 vols., 1899; rev. ed. 1924). Other studies of Mazzini include Edyth Hinkley, *Mazzini: The Story of a Great Italian* (1924); G. O. Griffith, *Mazzini: Prophet of Modern Europe* (1932); Stringfellow Barr, *Mazzini: Portrait of an Exile* (1935); Edward Elton Young Hales, *Mazzini and the Secret Societies* (1956); and Gaetano Salvemini, *Mazzini* (trans. 1956). Mazzini is discussed in several works on the struggle for Italy's unification: George Martin, *The Red Shirt and the Cross of Savoy: The Story of Italy's Risorgimento, 1748-1871* (1969), and Edgar Holt, *The Making of Italy, 1815-1870* (1971).

Additional Sources

Barr, Stringfellow, *Mazzini: portrait of an exile,* New York: Octagon Books, 1975, 1935.
Mazzini, Budapest: Gondolat, 1977.
Mack Smith, Denis, *Mazzini,* New Haven: Yale University Press, 1994.
Srivastava, Gita, *Mazzini and his impact on the Indian national movement,* Allahabad: Chugh Publications, 1982. ☐

and a majority of Senegalese favored continued affiliation with the French community.

In 1966 M'Bow became a member of UNESCO's executive board and twice—in 1966 and 1968—he served as head delegate of the Senegalese mission to UNESCO. In 1970 M'Bow became assistant director general for education of UNESCO.

Four years later, at age 53, M'Bow became UNESCO's director general, succeeding Réné Maheu. M'Bow was the first Black African to head a United Nations support organization. He won unanimous reelection to a second term of seven years in September of 1980.

M'Bow's leadership triggered strong Western criticism, and a number of nations withdrew from UNESCO. M'Bow emphasized such politically-charged topics as disarmament, Israel, and South Africa, rather than such less controversial subjects as scientific cooperation, literacy programs, and cultural preservation and exchanges. M'Bow explained his emphasis by describing UNESCO's major function as intellectual collaboration rather than international development and preservation. Supporters of M'Bow, largely from the developing or Soviet-bloc countries, believed that political issues are basic to education, science, and culture. The United States and some other nations perceive UNESCO's politically-inclined resolutions often as ''anti-Western'' and as deviating from UNESCO's original functions and mission.

Amadou-Mahtar M'Bow

In his two terms as director general of UNESCO, Amadou-Mahtar M'Bow (born 1921) implemented goals and procedures which proved highly controversial, prompting the withdrawal of the United States and other countries from the organization

Amadou-Mahtar M'Bow, a man who was to become the sixth director general of the United Nations Education, Scientific and Cultural Organization (UNESCO), had humble beginnings. Born in Dakar, Senegal, in 1921, M'Bow grew up in a small town where he learned traditional farming and animal tending skills.

M'Bow volunteered for the French army and served in France and North Africa during World War II. In 1947 he passed the Baccalaureat and entered the Sorbonne University in Paris. He graduated in 1951 with a License ès Lettres degree in geography.

M'Bow began working for UNESCO in 1953 with the literacy program "Le Service de l'Education de Base." Back home in 1957, M'Bow assumed the post of minister of national education and culture in the first indigenous Senegalese government to handle internal affairs. In 1958 M'Bow clashed with Léopold Senghor, another nationalist leader and Senegal's future president, over the issue of transition to independence. M'Bow supported immediate and complete independence for Senegal, while Senghor

Media Proposal Drew Fire

Western nations especially criticized the proposed New World Information and Communications Order (NWIOCO). While there was general agreement on the goal of giving underdeveloped countries greater access to media technology, controversy developed over sections of the resolution that proposed licensing journalists and requiring the news media to allow rebuttals by governments to stories they find unfair. Western governments—and most media representatives throughout the world—strongly opposed this proposal on the grounds that it would mean censorship. In the words of Cushrow Irani, Chairman of the International Press Institute and publisher of the *Calcutta Statesman* the licensing proposal would "transform the press into an instrument of governments." While the provision for licensing was deleted from the NWIOCO program at the 1983 UNESCO general convention, other problems had already cropped for M'Bow and UNESCO.

M'Bow Alienated America

M'Bow also faced criticism for administrative and budgetary practices. He centralized operations at UNESCO's Paris headquarters: UNESCO spent 80 percent of its budget on Paris operations, and its Paris bureaucracy grew while its field staff declined. The U.S. General Accounting Office in 1984 concluded that M'Bow made "all substantive and most routine decisions." Western states, especially the United States, objected to an imbalance between their budgetary contributions and their organizational influence. While they contributed the bulk of UNESCO's budget, they were often outvoted on resolutions. Finally, some opponents of M'Bow claimed that UNESCO suffered from substantial nepotism and fiscal irregularities. A report by the US General Accounting Office found that a conference in Latin America originally budgeted at $54,000 actually cost $600,000. According to an article in *US News & World Report,* M'Bow also remodeled the two top floors of the organization's headquarters into a rent-free penthouse for his family.

Concerned at what it considered the mismanagement and anti-Western bias of UNESCO, the Reagan administration demanded major reforms, but these were not forthcoming. M'Bow further angered the United States by characterizing the American representative at UNESCO, Jean Gerard, as "that woman [who has] no idea how UNESCO works," and that she treated him "like an American black who has no rights," at which point Gerard walked out. Shortly thereafter, in July 1983, President Reagan announced there would be a "thorough review" of continued participation in UNESCO, and in December, he announced withdrawal from the organization by December of 1984.

M'Bow labeled the criticisms as a "veritable smear campaign" which could have far-reaching international consequences. After the United States left UNESCO M'Bow spoke of "certain circles [which] wish to put into doubt the foundations of the international system." Defenders of M'Bow claimed that his tenure at UNESCO gave an important voice to the developing nations, that many of UNESCO's activities—notably its environmental "Man and

the Biosphere" program—were valuable, and that under M'Bow's leadership UNESCO's membership grew from 135 to 158 nations.

Criticism of M'Bow—and how he was running UNESCO—continued with both Great Britain and Singapore also leaving the organization and several other nations expressing reservations about continued membership. In an interview with John O'Leary in the *London Times Higher Education Supplement,* M'Bow dismissed the threatened exodus and declared, "If one, two, three, or even ten (countries) leave, as long as the others have the will to continue to cooperate internationally, that will not affect the organization."

M'Bow Defeated for Reelection

As dissatisfaction continued to mount, 26 nations announced their decision in February of 1986 to oppose M'Bow's reelection for a third term as director-general. In October, M'Bow suddenly announced to a UNESCO executive board he would not run for a third term the next year, stating, "It is necessary, whatever the cost, to get UNESCO out of the hurricane zone while remaining faithful to its democratic principals," as quoted in the *New York Times.* However, M'Bow quickly changed his mind and campaigned for a third term. He was able to receive a plurality over his opponents when the fifty-member executive board met in September of 1987, but could not muster the necessary majority. On October 17th, just before the fifth ballot, M'Bow withdrew his name, reportedly at the urging of delegates from the Soviet bloc who were concerned about a mass exodus of nations from UNESCO if M'Bow was reelected. The next day Federico Mayor Zaragosa, a Spanish biochemist and former Minister of Education, was chosen to be the new director-general of UNESCO. However, 20 members of the executive board—mostly from African and Arab countries—still voted for M'Bow.

Further Reading

No biography of M'Bow has been written. He has written at least six books, all published by UNESCO in Paris: *Suicide or Survival? The Challenge of the Year 2000* (1978); *Consensus and Peace* (1980); *Building the Future: UNESCO and the Solidarity of Nations* (1981); *Legacy for All: The World's Major Natural, Cultural and Historical Sites* (1982); *Where the Future Begins* (1982); and *Hope for the Future* (1984); Details of M'Bow's stormy tenure can be found in "The Man Who Pulls the Strings at UNESCO," *US News & World Report* (December 25th,1984); "M'Bow: An Interview," by John O'Leary, *London Times Higher Education* (January 11th, 1985). M'Bow's unsuccessful bid for a third term as Unesco chief is discussed in "Unesco Board Votes to Support Spaniard in Post," by Steven Greenhouse, *New York Times,* October 19th, 1987. □

Thomas Joseph Mboya

The Kenyan political leader Thomas Joseph Mboya (1930-1969) was one of the principal leaders of

Kenya's independence movement. His tragic death undoubtedly prevented him from fulfilling a career as one of the great East Africans of the 20th century.

Tom Mboya was born about Aug. 15, 1930, at Kilima Mbogu, near Nairobi, where his father, a Luo tribesman from Rusinga Island in Lake Victoria, was employed on a European sisal estate. Since his parents were Roman Catholics, he attended a series of mission schools, completing this phase of education at Holy Ghost College, a secondary school located near his birthplace. Mboya then left school so that the family's limited funds could be used to educate his siblings. He next enrolled in a program of the Kenya Medical Department for training as a sanitary inspector (1948-1950).

Here Mboya's first political inclinations became apparent when he was elected president of the student council. On successfully completing the course he accepted employment in Nairobi (1951-1953), devoting his abundant energies to union work. He helped to found the Kenya Local Government Workers Union, comprising employees of the Nairobi City Council, and became its general secretary (1953-1957).

Mboya's increasing involvement in union affairs led to difficulties with his employers, and he soon resigned his position as sanitary inspector to participate fully in union work; by 1954 he had developed his organization into one of Africa's most successful unions. The European-domi-

nated society of Kenya had been struck by the Mau Mau resistance movement in 1952, and Mboya, already much impressed by the leadership qualities of Jomo Kenyatta, whom the British had sent into detention, gradually moved into politics. He was one of the few African leaders not to be detained during the years of the Mau Mau.

Mboya joined Kenyatta's party, the Kenya Africa Union, and served as its acting treasurer until the organization was banned by the British in 1953. With open political action made virtually impossible, Mboya worked for the same ends through the labor movement, especially through the Kenya Federation of Labour; he was its secretary general from 1953 to 1963. This work brought him into the orbit of the International Confederation of Free Trade Unions. In 1958 Mboya was elected to its board, and he became an increasingly well-known member to the European and American supporters of the confederation. Within Kenya he gained his first general fame for his role in the Mombasa dock strike of 1955, where his involvement helped the workers to gain a 33 percent pay raise. Realizing his need for more education, Mboya attended Ruskin College, Oxford, in 1955 for a year's study.

On returning to Kenya, Mboya entered directly into politics; he was elected to the Legislative Council in 1957. He rose in importance as Kenya went on to independence. When it was achieved in 1963, he gained Cabinet rank as minister of economic planning and development, continuing to exercise a predominant role in the affairs of his country until his assassination in July 1969.

Further Reading

Alan Rake, *Tom Mboya* (1962), offers a very personal biography. B. A. Ogot and J. A. Kieran, eds., *Zamani* (1968), places his career in historical perspective.

Additional Sources

Goldsworthy, David, *Tom Mboya, the man Kenya wanted to forget,* Nairobi: Heinemann; New York: Africana Pub. Co., 1982. □

William Gibbs McAdoo

One of the ablest Democratic politicians of his time, William Gibbs McAdoo (1863-1941) was a superb administrator and organizer who served as a U.S. senator and a Cabinet officer in Wilson's administration.

The son of a southern jurist, William Gibbs McAdoo was born near Marietta, Ga., and educated at the University of Tennessee. After practicing law in Chattanooga, Tenn., for several years, he opened a law office in New York City in 1892. Ten years later he organized and directed the company that completed construction of the railroad tubes under the Hudson River. After service as vice-chairman of the Democratic National Committee in 1912, McAdoo became President Woodrow Wilson's secretary of the Treasury. In addition to his duties as secretary, he served as chairman of the Federal Reserve Board, the Federal Farm Loan Board, the War Finance Corporation, and the United States section of the International High Commission. He also floated four Liberty Loans and was responsible for extending credit to the Allied Powers in World War I. In January 1918, with the railroads on the verge of collapse, he became director general of railways and instituted operational reforms. A widower, he married the President's daughter, Eleanor Randolph Wilson. (They were divorced 20 years later.)

McAdoo's superior abilities won him a strong following within the administration. If President Wilson had withdrawn himself categorically from contention for a third nomination in 1920, McAdoo would undoubtedly have been selected, although he could not, as the President's son-in-law, make an open bid. McAdoo would probably have won the nomination in 1924, also, but he was linked indirectly to the Teapot Dome scandal (though not involved in the scandal itself) and had committed certain professional improprieties. As it was, he and Al Smith deadlocked the Democratic nominating convention for dozens of ballots, and only after both men reluctantly withdrew was John W. Davis named on the 103rd ballot.

McAdoo had support from the agrarian progressives, the railroad brotherhoods, the temperance forces, and the Ku Klux Klan. A jaunty man of great personal charm, McAdoo also had a strong strain of opportunism. As Walter

Lippmann wrote in 1920, he was not "fundamentally moved by the simple moralities" and his "honest" liberalism catered largely to popular feeling.

Embittered by his failure to win the nomination, McAdoo practiced law in California until he was elected to the U.S. Senate in 1932. He was a staunch supporter, but not truly a leader, of the New Deal. He was defeated for renomination in 1938 and died three years later.

Further Reading

McAdoo lacks a biography. *Crowded Years,* an autobiography (1931), ends with his resignation from the Cabinet. It should be supplemented with the many books on the Wilson administration. The best coverage of McAdoo's part in the presidential nominations of 1920 and 1924 is in David Burner, *The Policies of Provincialism: The Democratic Party in Transition, 1918-1932* (1968). □

Eugene Joseph McCarthy

Eugene Joseph McCarthy (born 1916) had a long and influential career in American politics. As a member of the U.S. House of Representatives he stood up to the Communist-hunting Sen. Joseph McCarthy. In the late 1950s he chaired the Senate Special Committee on Unemployment, part of an effort to investigate the causes of and solutions to unemployment. He also opposed incumbent President Lyndon Johnson for the Democratic presidential nomination in 1967 in an effort to force debate on Vietnam. Since leaving politics, McCarthy has enjoyed a second career as a prolific writer.

Eugene McCarthy was born March 29, 1916, in Watkins, Minnesota. He received his bachelor of arts degree from St. John's University, Collegeville, Minnesota (1935), and his master of arts at the University of Minnesota (1939). From 1935 to 1940 he taught in the Minnesota Public Schools, returning to St. John's University in 1940 as an instructor in economics. From 1946 until 1949 he taught economics and sociology at St. Thomas College in St. Paul, Minnesota. In 1945 McCarthy married Abigail Quigley. They had four children: Margaret, Michael, Mary and Ellen.

Organized New Party

McCarthy entered politics in St. Paul in 1947 as an organizer of the newly fused Democratic-Farmer-Labor Party. The following year he ran for Congress in Minnesota's traditionally Republican Fourth Congressional District and won by 25,000 votes. During his 10 years in the House of Representatives, McCarthy built a solid liberal-internationalist record. In 1952 he showed great courage by debating the Communist-hunting Sen. Joseph McCarthy on national television. On numerous occasions in the House,

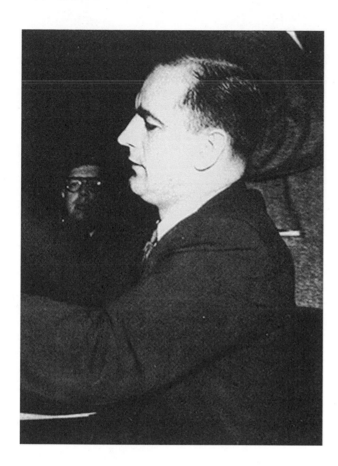

he attempted to curtail the activities of the Central Intelligence Agency (CIA). His chief goal was to reorganize the House to facilitate the passage of liberal legislation. But by 1958 McCarthy had grown tired of the House. "The House," he remarked, "is not a home."

Chaired Committee on Unemployment

McCarthy won a Senate seat in 1958 following another of his low-budget campaigns. While a senator, he chaired the Special Committee on Unemployment. The committee dedicated itself to studying the causes of unemployment—and ways to alleviate them—holding hearings in McCarthy's native Minnesota, as well as in Michigan and Pennsylvania.

"Unemployment," he said in 1959, "is first of all a human and social problem, affecting the welfare and happiness of individual workers and of their families." He was critical of the government's lack of urgency about maintaining full employment. He said, "there has been no real recognition of the basic fact that to be strong and healthy and secure an economy must expand and grow dynamically" (from committee archives, Walter Reuther Library, Wayne State University, Detroit, MI).

McCarthy supported Hubert Humphrey in the 1960 Democratic primaries, nominated Adlai Stevenson at the Democratic National Convention, and traveled cross-country in support of John F. Kennedy's run for the presidency. In the Senate, McCarthy was more concerned about the general quality and direction of policy than with the detailed work of committees or the drafting of legislation. This aloofness made him an intellectually effective, yet totally unconventional, member of the Senate. Until the selection of Humphrey as the vice presidential nominee in 1964, many Democratic leaders had considered McCarthy the logical choice for the nomination. President Lyndon Johnson himself had led McCarthy to expect it.

Tried to Force Vietnam Talks

During his second Senate term McCarthy emerged as one of the country's leading foreign policy critics. He first broke with the Johnson administration in 1965 over American intervention in the Dominican Republic. Possessing no special knowledge or interest in Vietnam, McCarthy at first accepted administration rationalizations regarding American participation in that conflict—even after other senators had begun to condemn United States involvement. In 1966, however, McCarthy became convinced that peace in Vietnam required a political settlement with the Vietcong. He began to oppose American participation in the war at every turn.

Unable to affect policy, McCarthy entered the presidential race on Nov. 30, 1967, in order to force a debate over Vietnam within his party. Supported by students and suburban volunteers, McCarthy ran a close race against Johnson in the New Hampshire primary, took the Wisconsin primary easily, and defeated Robert Kennedy in Oregon. He lost to Kennedy in California. McCarthy's low-key, polished style, and his frequent insistence on a coalition government in South Vietnam, made him a symbol of the nation's widespread dissatisfaction with the war. As a way of attempting to force Humphrey to adopt his positions, McCarthy withheld his support until late in the 1968 campaign. Shortly after the presidential election McCarthy announced that he would not seek reelection to the Senate.

McCarthy has written numerous books on American politics and foreign policy: *Frontiers in American Democracy* (1960); *Dictionary of American Politics* (1962); *A Liberal Answer to the Conservative Challenge* (1964); *The Limits of Power: America's Role in the World* (1967); *The Year of the People* (1969): *The Hard Years: A Look at Contemporary America and American Institutions* (1975); *A Political Bestiary: Viable Alternatives, Impressive Mandates and Other Fables* (1978); *America Revisited: 150 Years after Tocqueville* (1978); *The Ultimate Tyranny: the Majority Over the Majority* (1980); *Gene McCarthy's Minnesota: Memories of a Native Son* (1982); *The View from Rappahannock* (1984); *Up Until Now: A Memoir* (1987); *Required Reading: A Decade of Political Wit and Wisdom* (1988); *Nonfinancial Economics: The Case for Shorter Hours of Work* (1989); and *A Colony of the World: the United States Today: America's Senior Statesman Warns His Countrymen* (1992).

McCarthy's writings have not been limited to politics. In 1977 he published *Mr. Raccoon and His Friends,* a collection of stories he originally shared with his children. The book includes a brief introduction by Ellen McCarthy. His published poetry includes the books *Ground Fog and Night* (1979); *Other Things and the Aardvark* (1970); "Older

Sisters" *McCall's* (March 1985); and "Fawn Hall Among the Antinomians *New Republic* (Sept. 14-21, 1987). He also wrote the foreword to Alban Boultwood's *Into His Splendid Light* (1968), a collection of spiritual meditations.

McCarthy has published the following articles: "Dimpled Neos" *New Republic* (June 13, 1980); "Bad Calls" *New Republic* (Aug. 29, 1983); "Going Spare" *New Republic* (April 23, 1984); "Tips for Veeps" *New Republic* (July 16-23, 1984); "Big Benny" *New Republic* (Aug. 4, 1986); "Capital Takes Advantage" *Commonweal* (Jan. 30, 1987); "The 15 Commandments" *New Republic* (Feb. 22, 1988); "Pollution Absolution" *New Republic* (Oct. 29, 1990); "The Enclosure Movement" *America* (June 4-11, 1994); "The Vindicator" *New Republic* (May 15, 1995); and "Elegy for the Evening News" *Commonweal* (Nov. 3, 1995).

Further Reading

Eugene McCarthy is a subject of the 90-minute motion picture *American is Hard to See* (1970), a documentary of the 1968 American presidential campaign beginning with McCarthy's entry into the race.

Books on aspects of McCarthy's life include Joseph Frank, ed., *The New Look in Politics: McCarthy's Campaign* (University of New Mexico Press, 1968); David Frost, *The Presidential Debate, 1968; David Frost Talks With Vice President Hubert H. Humphrey* (Stein and Day, 1968); Arthur Herzog, *McCarthy for President* (Viking Press, 1969); Ben Stavis, *We Were the Campaign: New Hampshire to Chicago for McCarthy* (Beacon Press, 1969); Jeremy Larner, *Nobody Knows: Reflections on the McCarthy Campaign of 1968* (MacMillan, 1970). □

Joseph Raymond McCarthy

Joseph Raymond McCarthy (1908-1957), U.S. senator, in a highly publicized pursuit of a Communist "conspiracy" became a national figure. The term "McCarthyism" became a synonym for reckless smear tactics intended to destroy the victim's political standing and public character.

Joseph McCarthy was born on Nov. 14, 1908, on a farm at Grand Chute, Wis. The family was part of the "Irish Settlement," an enclave surrounded by farmers mainly of German and Dutch descent. His parents were devout Catholics, literate but uneducated. The fifth of nine children, Joseph seems to have grown up shy and awkward, often rejected by his peers but favored by a protective mother. At the age of 14, after finishing grade school, he took up chicken farming; his venture prospered briefly.

McCarthy moved to the nearby town of Manawa, managed a grocery store for a while, and then—when he was almost 20—enrolled in high school, completing the course in a single year. After two years as an engineering student at Marquette University, he went to law school and was president of his class on graduation.

McCarthy tried practicing as a lawyer in several county seats, supplementing his scanty legal fees by winnings at poker but also playing at the game of politics. After an unsuccessful bid as Democratic candidate for district attorney, he shifted his field and became the Republican candidate for a circuit court judgeship. He won, and this victory foreshadowed his later methods: his campaign literature had falsified his opponent's age (adding 7 years to it) and his own (moving his birth date back). At 30, his basic personality was pretty well shaped—fluid, resourceful, ambitious, amoral.

During World War II, McCarthy served with the U.S. Marines. In 1944, while still in the Marines, he ran unsuccessfully for the Senate. Two years later he ran for senator against Robert M. La Follette and won. McCarthy had been a poor judge, involved in at least one shady case; he had falsified his war record to make it look more heroic; and he had cut moral corners in his campaigning. But he was a popular candidate for the particular mood and ethnic mix of Wisconsin at the time and appealed both to patriotism and to end-of-war disillusionment.

McCarthy's first years in the Senate were thoroughly mediocre and at least slightly shady. As a number of his past adventures, including some questionable tax returns, began catching up with him, he needed an issue that would obscure all this. On Jan. 7, 1950, he asked three dinner companions to suggest an issue; they suggested Communist power and subversion.

In a speech at Wheeling, W. Va., on February 9 McCarthy claimed to have in hand a list of 205 people in the State Department known to be members of the Communist party. In subsequent speeches and interviews he kept shifting the figures, depending on his forum and his mood. On February 20 he held forth for six hours on the Senate floor, in a tumultuous session punctuated by the efforts of administration senators to pin him down factually.

In the 1950 elections McCarthy secured the defeat of several Democratic senators who had dared question and oppose him. Thus he spread terror even among his peers. His Republican colleagues were torn between fear of his prowess and willingness to use his attacks on President Harry Truman, Secretary of State Dean Acheson, and former Secretary of State George Marshall. In 1952 McCarthy was reelected. He then used his investigative subcommittee as his fulcrum and the press and television as his playing field. He even tried to develop a counterintelligence unit of his own inside the administration's agencies. He finally turned his guns against the Army in the Ft. Monmouth hearings.

The Army-McCarthy televised hearings from April 22 to June 17, 1954, turned the tables on McCarthy and his committee counsel, Roy Cohn, with evidence that they had sought special favors for G. David Schine (a subcommittee staff member) as an Army inductee. It is hard to guess why McCarthy tangled with the Army so wantonly, when he must have known that his anti-Communist rhetoric could not prevail against the array of Army medals facing him on the television screen. The impassioned response of the Army counsel, Joseph Welch, to McCarthy's attack on a member of Welch's firm marked the end. In December the

Senate passed a vote of censure on McCarthy. He died three years later, on May 2, 1957, a broken man whose end had really come at the Army hearing, when the nation recoiled from him and his power to inspire terror was halted.

"McCarthyism" came into the nation's history at a moment when Americans felt an anxiety and dread about the future; McCarthy gave this apprehension the name of "communism." He used the fear of internal subversion by an external enemy, and by giving it the concrete form of conspiracy and a spy network he provided Americans with a simple target for their hostility. He also came at a time when the cold war and the nuclear arms race had brought on a need for secrecy that led to a paranoid feeling of being surrounded by enemies within.

Scholars have debated whether McCarthy expressed a basic Populist appeal, with his attacks on the eastern intellectuals and the establishment, but this Populist theory is oversubtle for a man who gave no thought to mass welfare or to the release from any oppressive bonds. He was often called a "fascist" by liberals and the left, but this was as loose an epithet as his own accusations of "Communist." His support came mainly from a desperate segment on the right who saw their world threatened by an elusive conspiracy and were willing to see extreme methods used against it.

Further Reading

McCarthy's books about his crusade are *McCarthyism: The Fight for America* and *The Story of General George C. Marshall* (both 1952). The best biography is Richard H. Rovere, *Senator Joe McCarthy* (1959). An earlier one, written in the heat of battle, is Jack Anderson and Ronald W. May, *McCarthy: The Man, the Senator, the Ism* (1952). Two books that tend to offset each other are William F. Buckley and L. Brent Bozell, *McCarthy and His Enemies* (1954; new ed. 1961), and James Rorty and Moshe Decter, *McCarthy and the Communists* (1954). An important book is Robert Griffith, *The Politics of Fear: Joseph R. McCarthy and the Senate* (1970). On the issue of McCarthy's "populism" see Daniel Bell, ed., *The Radical Right* (1964), and for an answer to it see Michael P. Rogin, *The Intellectuals and McCarthy* (1967).

Other books wrestling with the meaning of McCarthyism are Edward A. Shils, *The Torment of Secrecy* (1956); Max Lerner, *The Unfinished Country* (1959), which reprints a cluster of articles entitled "McCarthy: The Life and Death of a Nightmare"; John P. Roche, *The Quest for the Dream* (1963); and Richard Hofstadter, *The Paranoid Style in American Politics* (1965). Especially good for its historical-sociological perspective is Seymour M. Lipset and Earl Raab, *Politics of Unreason*, vol. 5: *Rightwing Movements in America, 1790-1970* (1970). □

Mary T. McCarthy

The American writer Mary T. McCarthy (1912-1989) wrote novels and short stories as well as reportage, autobiographical essays, theater criticism, political essays, and art history.

Mary Therese McCarthy was born on June 21, 1912, in Seattle, Washington, to Roy and Therese Preston McCarthy. Her father was a lawyer. Kevin McCarthy, the actor, was her brother. Her parents died of the 1918 flu epidemic when she was six years old. For awhile she was raised by an abusive uncle; later she escaped into the care of her grandfather who sent her to school in a convent. Subsequently he provided for her education at Vassar College, where she graduated in 1933 with an A.B. While there, she helped found a literary magazine with three classmates, all of whom went on to become important persons in American writing: Elizabeth Bishop, Muriel Rukeyser, and Eleanor Clark. After graduation she taught briefly at Bard and Sarah Lawrence colleges.

Wrote on Political Topics

She began her career in New York holding various jobs: as an editor for magazines and publishing houses; as a writer for the radio commentator H. V. Kaltenborn; as an assistant to the political analyst Benjamin Stolberg; and writing promotion for an art gallery. Most significant, however, were her reviews for *The Nation* and *The New Republic,* at that time both leftist journals. She came to prominence with an article charging that the major New York critics and reviewers, including Joseph Wood Krutch, who was on the board of editors of *The Nation,* were in the habit of writing shallow appraisals that merely provided publicity to encourage business. She was later to exempt Krutch from this charge and still later to remark that her early opinions were "insufferably patronizing."

She soon joined *Partisan Review,* the leftist political and intellectual journal, as an editor whose main assignment was to write drama reviews. "Had she been an active figure in the magazine," wrote William Barrett in his book about the publication, *The Truants,* "her presence might very well have overshadowed everyone else's and this memoir would accordingly have had to take a different shape. I am rather glad that she was not, for it would require three volumes at least to begin to do justice to this extraordinary woman—one of the most extraordinary, I believe, of our time."

McCarthy is equally famous for her fiction—novels and short stories—and for her non-fiction, which includes reportage, autobiographical essays, theater criticism, political essays, and art history.

Novel Made into Movie

She is generally supposed to have begun writing her fiction under the encouragement of Edmund Wilson, her second husband. *The Groves of Academe;* a novel published in 1952, recounts how an incompetent professor on a small, elite campus keeps from being fired by claiming, falsely, to be a member of the Communist Party. He thus makes it impossible for the liberal president to dismiss him lest he be charged with being reactionary. *The Group* (1963), a novel about eight classmates from Vassar who make their way after graduation in the business and intellectual world of New York, was made into a popular movie which starred Candice Bergen and Hal Holbrook, among others. Her other novels included *The Company She Keeps* (1942); *The Oasis* (1949); *A Charmed Life* (1955); *Birds of America* (1971); and *Cannibals and Missionaries* (1979). *Cast a Cold Eye* (1950) was the title of her first collection of short stories, although some critics regard her first novel, *The Company She Keeps,* as really being a gathering of separate stories with the same characters.

Published Essays and Collections of Theater Reviews

McCarthy's theater reviews were first collected under the title *Sights and Spectacles* (1956) and later, somewhat expanded, as *Mary McCarthy's Theatre Chronicles: 1937-1962* (1963). One of her memorable essays, a review of Oscar Wilde's *The Importance of Being Earnest,* was entitled "The Unimportance of Being Oscar." "As a writer," she said in her introduction to *Sights and Spectacles,* "I am troubled by the fact that most American plays are so badly written."

Wrote in a Variety of Forms

The *New Yorker* magazine, which had first published her short stories, including the classic "The Man in the Brooks Brothers Shirt," also published her autobiographical essays, which were later collected under the title *Memories of a Catholic Girlhood* (1957). Her collections of literary and occasional essays include: *On the Contrary* (1961); *The Writing on the Wall and Other Literary Essays* (1970); *Ideas and the Novel* (1980); and *Occasional Prose* (1985). All of her books continued to be reprinted, in whole or in part, sometimes under other titles, sometimes with several titles combined under a new one, both in the United States and in England through the 1980s. They were also widely translated.

Among McCarthy's most striking efforts were her reports of public events in the tradition of such other great women writers of the late 20th century as Hannah Arendt and Rebecca West. Her reports from Vietnam, many first published in the *New York Review of Books,* appeared in three books (*Vietnam, Hanoi,* and *Medina*) that were subsequently collected under the title *The Seventeenth Degree* (1974). Her other book of reportage is *The Mask of State: Watergate Portraits* (1974).

She also published monumental studies of Italian Renaissance art, *Venice Observed* (1956) and *The Stones of Florence* (1959). These were combined in a Penguin paperback in 1979.

Pursuit for Clarity Brings Lawsuit Upon Her

The prolific McCarthy may have been the most important and widely-ranging woman writer of the latter half of the 20th century, and certainly was one of the period's most important political writers without regard to gender, to be ranked in the company of George Orwell and Albert Camus. McCarthy's work is noted for its sharpness of observation and expression, its wit, its independence of mind, and its unflagging intellectual excitement. From her comments about characters in her fiction, her candid recollections of her childhood, and her unsparing reports of news events it is plain that she abhorred distortion, shallowness, and sentimentality. These tastes and convictions, no doubt, inspired her attacks on Lillian Hellman as writer and polemicist, which, in turn, prompted Hellman's famous libel suit against McCarthy. On Hellman's death, her estate dropped the suit.

McCarthy was generally so insistent on seeing her subjects with absolute clarity that she was often charged with lacking the fiction writer's capacity to blur and shade his or her raw material in the cause of the mystery inherent in all reality. She was, for example, called an "essayist" in all of her writing, both in admiration and to suggest her limitations. "She lacks the essential gift: She cannot imagine others," wrote Hilton Kramer, the critic and editor.

Her honorary degrees included doctorates in letters from Syracuse University, 1973; the University of Hull, in England, 1974; and Bard College, 1976. She had doctorates in literature from Bowdoin College, 1981, and from the University of Maine, 1982. The University of Aberdeen, Scotland, awarded her a Doctor of Laws in 1979. She held two Guggenheim fellowships, in 1949-1950 and in 1959-1960; received the National Medal for Literature; and was a member of Phi Beta Kappa and the National Institute of Arts and Letters.

Personal Life

She was married four times, to Harold Johnsrud, playwright and actor, from 1933 to 1936; to Edmund Wilson, novelist and critic, from 1938 to 1946; to Bowden Broadwater, a sometimes writer and publisher's person, from 1946 to 1961; and to James Raymond West, a U.S. State Department official, in 1961. She had a son, Reuel Kimball Wilson, born in 1938. She lived half the year in Paris, France, and half in the United States, in Maine.

McCarthy died of cancer in October, 1989, in New York. She was 77.

Further Reading

An extended though still compact survey of McCarthy's work may be found in Vol. 16 of *Contemporary Authors,* New Revision Series; Books about her life and work include Doris Grumbach, *The Company She Kept: A Revealing Portrait of Mary McCarthy* (1976); Irvin Stock, *Mary McCarthy* (1968); and Barbara McKenzie, *Mary McCarthy* (1966); The best sources for insight to McCarthy's life and work remain McCarthy's own works, especially the frankly autobiographical ones.

Also see *Newsweek,* November 6, 1989; *National Review,* November 24, 1989; *Conversations with Mary McCarthy,* University Press of Mississippi, 1991; Hardy, Willene Schaefer, *Mary McCarthy/Willene Schaefer Hardy,* F. Ungar Pub. Co., 1981. □

George Brinton McClellan

A Union Army commander in the American Civil War, George Brinton McClellan (1826-1885) repelled Gen. Robert E. Lee's first invasion of the North. He was later a governor of New Jersey.

George B. McClellan was born in Philadelphia, Pa., on Dec. 3, 1826, the son of a prominent physician. He attended the University of Pennsylvania Preparatory School and, by special action, was permitted to enter West Point two years before attaining the minimum age. He graduated second in the 1846 class of 59 cadets.

McClellan won two brevets in the Mexican War in 1847 "for gallant and meritorious conduct." He was named to the American military commission which observed the siege of Sevastopol in the Crimean War (1853-1856). McClellan then studied military organizations, weapons, and systems in several European countries and wrote an excellent, comprehensive report on his observations (1857). Resigning his commission in the army Jan. 16, 1857, he became an executive with the Illinois Central Railroad. He was president of the Ohio and Mississippi Railroad when the Civil War erupted in 1861.

Early Civil War Services

McClellan immediately volunteered his services on behalf of the Union and was commissioned a major general in command of the Department of the Ohio in May 1861. In this capacity he led the Federal forces into the pro-Union northwestern area of Virginia to confront Confederate troops ordered there by Robert E. Lee. McClellan soundly trounced the enemy at the battles of Philippi (June 3, 1861), Rich Mountain (July 11), and Carrick's Ford (July 13), paving the way for the creation of the new state of West Virginia (admitted to the Union in 1863). Called to Washington, D.C., to assume command of the army that had been routed at First Bull Run, McClellan was named head of the Department of the Potomac. On Nov. 1, 1861, he became general in chief. He delayed an advance until 1862 in order to train, equip, and perfect his army but, as a result, he clashed with President Abraham Lincoln and the difficult secretary of war, Edwin M. Stanton.

Finally permitted to advance into Virginia via the peninsula between the York and James rivers, McClellan overcautiously laid siege to Yorktown in April 1862 and fought a drawn battle at Williamsburg on May 5. With his army of some 95,000 men—smaller by one-third than that which had been assured him—he inched to within 4 miles of Richmond through unusually heavy rains. When attacked by Confederate general Joseph E. Johnston in the Battle of Fair Oaks (Seven Pines), May 31-June 1, he essentially repulsed the enemy assaults and maintained his position. Endless bickering with the Lincoln administration continued. In the sprawling Seven Days Battle initiated by Lee (June 25-July 1) McClellan lost only one engagement—at Gaines's Mill—and succeeded, in a brilliant change-of-base operation, in checking Lee's continued attacks. At Malvern Hill on July 1 McClellan administered one of the bloodiest repulses the Confederate commander ever suffered. Though the Army of the Potomac was safe at Harrison's Landing, Lincoln nonetheless withdrew it to

Washington, against McClellan's protests, and gave it to another commander.

Later Civil War Actions

After the severe defeat of John Pope's Union army at Second Bull Run in August 1862, McClellan was renamed to command the army. Meanwhile Lee was pressing his advantage by invading Maryland. Plagued by contradictory orders from his superiors and obliged to reorganize his army on the march, McClellan pursued Lee into western Maryland, winning the important Battle of South Mountain (September 14) and wresting the initiative from him. Finally, at Antietam (Sharpsburg), McClellan attacked the Confederates in the bloodiest single-day battle of the war, gaining a strategic victory that forced Lee to retreat into Virginia. However, when he failed to follow up his success to the satisfaction of Lincoln, McClellan was fired on Nov. 5, 1862. He never held another Civil War command and resigned his commission on Nov. 8, 1864, to run unsuccessfully as the Democratic candidate for president against Lincoln.

Postwar Services

After Appomattox, McClellan pursued his varied literary and cultural tastes in America and abroad. He was fond of mountain climbing, and he moved in high-society circles. Service in several large engineering enterprises was followed by his election as governor of New Jersey—a position he held with distinction from 1878 to 1881. He died of coronary trouble on Oct. 29, 1885, at Orange, N.J.

McClellan was powerfully built, handsome, and graceful. On May 22, 1860, he married the vivacious Ellen Mary Marcy, and his personal life was without blemish. Despite a tendency to magnify difficulties, his achievements during the Civil War were substantial, and some were masterful.

Further Reading

A scholarly, fully documented study is Warren W. Hassler, Jr., *General George B. McClellan: Shield of the Union* (1957). A strongly pro-McClellan treatment is H. J. Eckenrode and Bryan Conrad, *George B. McClellan: The Man Who Saved the Union* (1941), while the leading anti-McClellan biography is Peter S. Michie, *General McClellan* (1901). Clarence E. Macartney, *Little Mac: The Life of General George B. McClellan* (1940), is popularly written. More sophisticated is William Starr Myers, *A Study in Personality: General George Brinton McClellan* (1934). No student of the Civil War should neglect the general's memoirs, *McClellan's Own Story* (1887), which, while persuasive and containing the invaluable letters written by McClellan to his wife, is painfully defensive in tone. □

John Little McClellan

John Little McClellan (1896-1977) served for 35 years as a U.S. senator from Arkansas. He was one of the old-time Southern senators, born at the turn of the century, who opposed all civil rights legislation and rose to power because of seniority.

John Little McClellan was born on a farm in southcentral Arkansas near Sheridan on February 25, 1896, the son of Issac Scott and Belle (Suddeth) McClellan. His mother died while he was a youth. Educated in the local schools, he graduated from the Sheridan High School. At age 12 he began five years of legal studies in his father's office and under a special Arkansas statute was admitted to the bar at age 17. He practiced law in Sheridan until he joined the army during World War I and rose to the rank of first lieutenant in the aviation section of the Signal Corps.

After the war he settled in Malvern, Arkansas, where he served as city attorney from 1920 to 1926, when he was elected prosecuting attorney for Hot Spring County. Active in local Democratic politics, he sought and won election to the U.S. House of Representatives in 1934 and again in 1936. Generally supporting the New Deal legislative program of Franklin D. Roosevelt when not inimical to Arkansas interests, he began his life long opposition to civil rights legislation when he voted against the anti-lynching bill. He also commenced his long term interest in flood control and soil reclamation.

In 1938 he abandoned his House seat and was one of three Democratic Senate candidates in the primaries seeking the seat held by Sen. Hattie Caraway, who eventually won renomination. Following his defeat McClellan resettled in Camden and helped form the law firm of Gaughan, McClellan and Gaughan. In 1942 he entered the Senate primary among a field of several candidates and won the nomination by 50,000 votes in a runoff election which assured his seat in the U.S. Senate. In January 1943 his initial committee assignments included banking and currency, expenditures in executive departments, manufactures, and post offices and post roads; in 1945 he joined the commerce and naval affairs committees.

During his first two terms in the Senate McClellan generally supported wartime legislation—except for the soldier's vote bill, which he opposed because it failed to require state registration or payment of state poll tax. Agricultural and slightly left of center liberal legislation received his approval. He similarly endorsed the move towards international cooperation by voting for the Connally Resolution favoring an international peace-keeping organization. He supported the Bretton Woods Agreements, the United Nations Charter, and extension of the lend-lease program; he joined those in the Senate, however, who opposed the British loan following the war. Thus his stance was that of a moderate in both domestic legislation and international cooperation.

When the Republicans gained control of the Senate in 1947, McClellan's committee assignments were reduced under the terms of the legislative reorganization plan which he had voted against in 1946. Except for unsuccessfully proposing amendments—such as one which would have prevented giving any aid to countries under Russian domination—McClellan went along with the bipartisan foreign policy of 1947-1948, which included aid to Greece and Turkey, the Marshall Plan, and the Vandenberg Resolution which led to the negotiation of the North Atlantic Treaty Organization.

By the time of the 1948 elections, however, McClellan had become so disenchanted with the liberal program of the Harry S. Truman administration and by the civil rights plank of the Democratic Party that he declared himself an Independent Democrat and handily won reelection to the Senate. When the Democrats regained control of the Senate in 1949, McClellan became chairman of the expenditures of the executive departments committee, where he helped expedite the recommendations of the Hoover Commission on government reorganization, on which he had served as a member. He was also assigned to the public works committee, reflecting his expertise on flood control, and, most important, he joined the powerful Senate Appropriations Committee, where he consistently supported measures designed to cut federal expenditures.

In 1953 McClellan came to national attention when he led a boycott by Democratic Senate members of the permanent investigations subcommittee chaired by Wisconsin's Joseph R. McCarthy, whom McClellan charged with dictatorial one-man control of the committee. McClellan became chairman of the committee in 1955 and began a decade of highly visible committee hearings which drew much attention. Under McClellan the committee conducted investigations of organized crime, labor union racketeering, student revolts, urban riots, the TFX aircraft, and service clubs located abroad. During these highly publicized hearings, McClellan exhibited a stern, judge-like manner. These investigations led to the imprisonment of Dave Beck and James R. Hoffa of the Teamsters Union. Another witness was Joseph Valachi, who thrilled the public with an insider's account of the Mafia.

A quiet unassuming senator widely respected by his colleagues, McClellan's personal life was marked by tragedy. His first marriage ended in divorce, his second wife died, and he married a third time. He lost two of his five children. He was active in bar association activities and as a life-long member of the Baptist Church.

In 1973 McClellan became chairman of the influential Senate Appropriations Committee, but his greatest contribution was in working on the Judiciary Committee, where he and Sen. Edward M. Kennedy completely overhauled the federal criminal code, which Attorney General Griffin Bell and others praised. After 35 years in the upper chamber, on November 27, 1977, a week after he had announced that at age 81 he would retire, McClellan died of cancer in Little Rock.

Further Reading

McClellan is listed in *Political Profiles* for Presidents Truman, Eisenhower, Kennedy, Johnson, Nixon, Ford, and Carter, whose biographies also provide much valuable information. McClellan's speeches are in the *Congressional Record,* and articles about him are cited in the *New York Times Index* and the *Reader's Guide to Periodical Literature.* There is no adequate biography of McClellan, but essential background information can be found in Arthur S. Link and William B. Catton, *American Epoch* (1980) and Lawrence S. Wittner, *Cold War America* (1974). McClellan is listed in the *Biographical Directory of Congress.* His obituary appeared in the *New York Times.* □

Barbara McClintock

Geneticist Barbara McClintock (1902-1992) received the Nobel Prize in Physiology for her discovery that genes could move from place to place on a chromosome.

Barbara McClintock was born in Hartford, Connecticut, on June 16, 1902. She had two older sisters and gained a brother when she was two. Her father, Thomas Henry McClintock, was a physician. Upon the birth of their son, the McClintocks sent Barbara off to live with relatives in the country, where she lived on and off until she was of school age. It was here that she developed the deep love of nature that lasted her lifetime. In 1908, the family moved to the Flatbush section of Brooklyn where her father had taken a job with Standard Oil. McClintock rejoined the family and attended the local school. Her love of nature, however, persisted.

After graduating from Erasmus High School in 1918, she took a job rather than go on to college, in part because of lack of parental support. She did so well at private studies, however, that the following year she was allowed to enter Cornell University as a biology major in the College of Agriculture. During her freshman and sophomore years, she had a normal college life, including dating and playing tenor banjo in a jazz band. She was elected president of the freshman class and was asked to join a sorority. Upon discovering that the sorority would not accept Jews, McClintock refused the invitation. She never hesitated to snub the social conventions of her time. Upon receiving her B.A. in 1923 she pressed on to take her M.A. in 1925 and her Ph.D. in 1927, studying cytology. She was appointed an instructor in Cornell's botany department.

The faculty at Cornell's agricultural school during those years was pioneering the development of hybrid corn, and McClintock soon discovered a way to identify individual chromosomes of maize. Between 1929 and 1931 she published, with others, nine papers describing her work. Then, in August 1931, the National Academy of Sciences published a paper on the subject, done jointly with Harriet Creighton, which has been described as "the cornerstone of experimental genetics."

Despite the world wide recognition for her work and temporary teaching positions as well as grants from such major foundations as the Guggenheim Fellowship and the Rockefeller Foundation, Cornell University refused her a tenured faculty position. She accepted one from 1939 to 1941 at the University of Missouri but it turned out badly. It was clear that while she might have gotten a regular appointment at a women's college, other doors were closed to her because of her gender. In 1941 her friend fellow geneticist Marcus Rhoades obtained an invitation for her to spend the summer at the Cold Spring Harbor Laboratory, run by the Carnegie Foundation of Washington on Long Island. The laboratory was a self contained facility that had its own summer houses for researchers. She was offered a one-year position December 1, 1941 and she remained there for the

Prize in Medicine for her work, as well as the Lasker Award. The MacArthur Foundation appointed her its first Prize Fellow Laureate; then in 1983 she received the Nobel Prize for Physiology or Medicine.

A deeply private person, McClintock continued to pursue her work alone and with the same holistic perspective she used throughout her career. Although the basics of her experimental work were not only accepted but honored, some of her larger hypotheses were yet to find an audience.

McClintock spent the remainder of her life studying transposition at Cold Spring Harbor. She died on September 2, 1992 shortly after her friends had celebrated her ninetieth birthday. In her obituary, Gerald R. Finks notes that her "burning curiosity, enthusiasm and uncompromising honesty serve as a constant reminder of what drew us all to science in the first place." In 1996 Cold Spring Harbor's DNA Learning Center held an exhibit in her honor featuring a replica of her original 1942 laboratory.

Further Reading

A good short sketch of McClintock's life and work may be found in *Science, 222* (October 28, 1983). A full-length biography is Evelyn Fox Keller, *A Feeling for the Organism: The Life and Work of Barbara McClintock* (1983). Also see *Long Island Business News,* October 21, 1996. □

Sir Francis Leopold McClintock

Sir Francis Leopold McClintock (1819-1907) was a British admiral and Arctic explorer. He mapped a great deal of hitherto-uncharted territory and made a number of geographical discoveries.

Leopold McClintock was born on July 8, 1819, in Dundalk, Ireland. At the age of 12 he went to sea as a first-class volunteer on a ship sailing in American coastal waters. Following 12 years of experience on various ships he was commissioned as acting lieutenant and soon started studies at the Royal Naval College.

One year later, in 1848, McClintock became second lieutenant under Sir James Clark Ross on the *Enterprise*. Their task was to make an Arctic voyage to look for Sir John Franklin and his lost party, who had gone north in search of a Northwest Passage. McClintock first learned about the Eskimo skill of hauling men and supplies by sledges while on his 500-mile land trip, and subsequently he experimented with sledge designing. On Arctic expeditions in 1850-1851 and 1852-1853 he made geographical discoveries on the coast of Prince Patrick Island and Melville Island.

In 1857 Lady Franklin selected McClintock to lead a private search expedition in the *Fox* for her husband's party. The ship held a total of 26 persons, including two Eskimos. Between 1857 and 1859 the *Fox* explored various coasts

rest of her career well into the mid-1980s. During her first decade at the laboratory she won many honors, including presidency of the Genetics Society of America and election to the National Academy of Sciences, only the third woman to be admitted to that body.

It was during the decade of the 1940s that she began the work which was later to result in the Nobel Prize. Essentially, it was her discovery that genes "jumped" from place to place in a chromosome, what she called transposable genetic elements. Since accepted opinion had it that genes were static, rather like beads on a string, her theory was generally received with either hostility or a lack of understanding. Soon after she presented these findings at a symposium in 1951, she stopped publishing her work, so disappointed was she at its reception. Furthermore, the discovery of the double helix structure of DNA in 1953 turned many geneticists away from the "old-fashioned" technique of McClintock (careful experiment, observation, and recording) to the more mechanistic models of James Watson, Francis Crick, and their associates. Partly because of her solitary nature, but also partly because she wanted to stay in close touch with her experiments, McClintock chose to work alone rather than as part of a large research team. As a result, she was in physical and intellectual control of all aspects of her work. As one colleague put it, "she has a feeling for the organism."

The rediscovery of McClintock's work began in the mid-1960s with the study of aspects of bacteria and became unavoidable in the 1980s with the growth of genetic engineering. In 1981 she was awarded the prestigious Wolfe

south of the areas covered by other search expeditions. Finally they discovered relics of the Franklin party with some Eskimos; and skeletons, a wrecked boat, and written notes were located on King William Island. In the papers McClintock found evidence that Franklin had, in fact, found the passage he was looking for. The fate of Franklin was thus resolved. During the 2-year voyage McClintock discovered the channel that bears his name.

Returning to England, McClintock was knighted and received the Gold Medal of the Royal Geographical Society and several honorary degrees. His book *Voyage of the Fox in the Arctic Seas* was published in London in 1859 and reprinted many times. McClintock's later ship commands involved deep-sea soundings near Iceland, Greenland, and Labrador and sailing in the Mediterranean and Caribbean. In 1865 he stood for Parliament and lost. Five years later he married Annette Elizabeth Dunlop and subsequently served in various Admiralty posts in England and the West Indies, attaining the rank of admiral. He died on Nov. 17, 1907, at the age of 88, a respected naval officer and renowned Arctic explorer.

Further Reading

A full-length biography of McClintock is Sir Clements Markham, *Life of Admiral Sir Leopold McClintock ... By an Old Messmate* (1909), which includes illustrations and maps. □

John McCloskey

John McCloskey (1810-1885) was the second archbishop of New York and the first American to be elevated to the Roman Catholic College of Cardinals.

John McCloskey was born in Brooklyn, N.Y., on March 10, 1810, the son of Patrick and Elizabeth Harron McCloskey, recent immigrants from Ireland. His father, a clerk, died when John was 15 years old, at which time the young man became the ward of Cornelius Heeney, a wealthy merchant. He graduated from Mount Saint Mary's College in Emmitsburg, Md., in 1828 and returned to the school a year later to study for the priesthood.

Ordained in 1834, McCloskey served as a parish assistant and seminary instructor until he was given an opportunity to study in Rome. He was in Italy from 1835 to 1837. When he returned he was appointed rector of St. Joseph's Church in Greenwich, Conn. He served also as president of St. John's College, Fordham, N. Y. (now Fordham University), and rector of St. John's Seminary.

In 1844 McCloskey was appointed coadjutor bishop of New York's vigorous archbishop John Hughes. Because he was cosmopolitan, fluent in several languages, and at ease with members of the city's upper classes, McCloskey's personality complemented that of the archbishop. In 1847 he was named first bishop of Albany, N. Y. In 1864 he was chosen to succeed Hughes as archbishop of New York.

McCloskey continued the diocesan work begun by Hughes, although he conducted affairs in a more subdued manner. He settled disputes with religious orders and condemned Fenian (Irish nationalist) extremists, who hoped to liberate Ireland from Great Britain by invading Canada. In 1869-1870 McCloskey attended the First Vatican Council, where he reluctantly voted for the declaration of the dogma of papal infallibility, a step he regarded as inexpedient. In 1875 he was made the first American member of the College of Cardinals, an event which brought him wide attention in the United States.

At home McCloskey carried forward the building of St. Patrick's Cathedral in New York City and raised large amounts of money for charitable work. Although his most significant tangible work was the raising of St. Patrick's, he was also responsible for the establishment of seminaries, missions, and churches within the diocese. In 1880 his work was lightened by the appointment of a coadjutor, Michael Augustine Corrigan. After his golden jubilee as a priest in 1884, McCloskey withdrew from active management of the diocese. He died on Oct. 10, 1885, in New York City.

Further Reading

A biography of McCloskey was written by an archbishop of New York, John Cardinal Farley, *The Life of John Cardinal McCloskey: First Prince of the Church in America* (1918). The early years of his career to his appointment as archbishop can be followed in John R. G. Hassard, *Life of Most Reverend John Hughes* (1866), and the later years in John Talbot Smith, *The Catholic Church in New York* (2 vols., 1908). □

Nellie Letitia McClung

Nellie Letitia McClung (1873-1951) was a Canadian suffragist, social reformer, legislator, and author. She is probably the most frequently quoted feminist writer in Canada.

Nellie Letitia (Mooney) McClung was born on October 20, 1873, near Chatsworth, Ontario. In 1880 the Mooneys, lured by reports of fertile soil and free land, left their marginally profitable farm to homestead in southern Manitoba. Nellie was ten before this pioneer district had a school, but at 16 she received a teaching certificate. She was an innovative teacher in Hazel, Manitou, and Treherne before marrying Robert Wesley McClung in 1896. In Manitou, where Wesley was a druggist, Nellie became active in the Women's Christian Temperance Union, a progressive organization which in western Canada supported votes for women as well as prohibition. In 1908 Doubleday published the first of her five novels, *Sowing Seeds in Danny,* a witty portrayal of a small western town also serialized in the *Woman's Home Companion.* In Canada it quickly became a best seller. McClung was soon well known as an author of short stories and articles in Canadian and American magazines and was a popular speaker in demand throughout the West.

In 1911 the McClungs moved to Winnipeg, the booming provincial capital. Here a vigorous women's rights and reform movement appreciated Nellie's capacity to win audiences with humorous arguments and to debate effectively with hecklers. The Conservative government of Manitoba under Premier Sir Rodmond Roblin repeatedly refused to consider women's suffrage or prohibition; therefore, McClung took a leading role in the 1914 political campaign in which the Liberal Party advocated these and many other reforms. In a hilarious stage presentation of a women's parliament approached by a delegation of men seeking the vote, McClung's devastating mimicry of the pompous Roblin was credited with opening the eyes of many to the absurdity of the arguments against women's suffrage. During the campaign her much-quoted speeches made her the target of bitter attack in the Conservative press.

With their five children the McClungs moved, in 1914, to Edmonton, Alberta, where Nellie also fought for prohibition and suffrage—achieved in western Canada during World War I. Subsequently she continued to fight for factory safety legislation, better rural health care, minimum wage laws, dower rights, equality under the Divorce Act, and equal opportunities for women in education and the work force. McClung was one of five Alberta women who, under the leadership of Judge Emily Murphy, won "The Persons' Case": the judicial decision that women as "persons" had the right to be appointed to the non-elected Canadian Senate.

By this time McClung's speaking tours had covered most of Canada, and in 1917 and 1918 she had also toured extensively in the United States for the National American Woman Suffrage Association. Her popular appeal was as strong in the United States as it was at home. In 1921 she was a delegate and challenging speaker to the Methodist Ecumenical Conference in London, England, and made a speaking tour through England and Scotland. The same year McClung won election as a Liberal member of the Provincial Legislature of Alberta. Although sitting as an opposition (minority party) member, she staunchly supported any reform legislation introduced by the government. Defeated in 1926, she did not run again for political office.

In 1933 the McClungs moved to Lantern Lane, a country home near Victoria, British Columbia. Here Nellie completed a two-volume autobiography: *Clearing in the West* (1935), a graphic portrayal of Manitoba pioneer life, and *The Stream Runs Fast* (1945), a less effective account of her political activities and writing career. She continued to write short stories and a popular syndicated column. Many of her shorter works were published as collections. In all she published 16 books. In addition to her writing she continued an active life in the Canadian Authors' Association, as the only woman on the first board of governors of the Canadian Broadcasting Corporation, as a delegate to the League of Nations in 1938, and as a public lecturer. During the last ten years of her life poor health severely limited her activities, but she still welcomed many visitors and kept in close touch with world affairs through radio, books, and magazines. She died on September 1, 1951.

Forgotten for a decade, McClung was re-discovered by feminists of the 1960s. Some criticized her support of the traditional family structure, but most credited her advancement of the feminist cause in her day and her recognition of the need for further progress: particularly economic independence of women. She is still a frequently quoted feminist writer because her pithy and witty comments on the role of women are as timely today as when they were written. Women still share her hope that "we may yet live to see the day when women will no longer be news! . . . I want to be a peaceful, happy, normal, human being, pursuing my unimpeded way through life, never having to explain, defend, or apologize for my sex."

Further Reading

McClung's *In Times Like These* (1915, reprinted 1972) is a book of essays on her feminist ideas, and *Painted Fires* (1925) is a novel about a Finnish immigrant girl. Candace Savage, *Our Nell: A Scrapbook Biography* (1979) combines quotations by and about McClung with connecting narrative-analysis.

Additional Sources

Benham, Mary Lile, *Nellie McClung,* Don Mills, Ont.: Fitzhenry & Whiteside, 1975.

Hancock, Carol L. (Carol Lula), *No small legacy: a study guide,* Winfield, BC: Wood Lake Books, 1986.

McClung, Mark, *Text of talk entitled "Portrait of my mother,"* Canada: M. McClung, 1975.

McClung, Nellie, *Tea with the Queen,* Vancouver: Intermedia Press, 1980.

Warne, R. R. (Randi Ruth), *Literature as pulpit: the Christian social activism of Nellie L. McClung,* Waterloo, Ont.: Published for the Canadian Corporation for Studies in Religion, 1993.

Wright, Helen K., *Nellie McClung and women's rights,* Agincourt, Ont.: Book Society of Canada, 1980. □

Sir Robert McClure

Sir Robert McClure (1807-1873) was a British naval officer who, while searching for the lost expedition of Sir John Franklin, discovered the Northwest Passage.

Robert McClure was born in Wexford, Ireland and educated at Eton (an English private school) and Sandhurst (the British military academy). He entered the Royal Navy in 1824. He first traveled to the Arctic in 1836-1837 as mate on the *Terror* under the command of Sir George Back on an expedition that went to Hudson Bay and explored the Melville Peninsula. He was promoted to lieutenant on his return to England in September 1837. He then served on British ships in the Great Lakes and in the Caribbean.

In 1848 McClure was chosen to be an officer on the first ship sent out to look for the missing expedition of Sir John Franklin, serving under James Clark Ross. They returned to England in the fall of 1849 without finding any trace of Franklin. McClure was then appointed to command the *Investigator* under the general command of Captain Richard Collinson in the *Enterprise* on a second attempt to find Franklin. This time they proposed to solve the mystery of Franklin's disappearance by attacking the problem from the opposite side—from the Pacific and Alaska.

They sailed together from England on January 10, 1850 but were separated by a storm in the Pacific Ocean soon after they had passed through the Straits of Magellan. As McClure's ship headed through the Pacific, it was hit by a sudden storm that knocked down all three masts. The *Investigator* arrived in Honolulu on July 1, 1850, only to find that Collinson had sailed the day before.

By cutting through the Aleutian Islands rather than following his instructions and sailing west of them, McClure reached Bering Strait between Alaska and Siberia before Collinson. For unknown reasons that have since caused much speculation, he did not wait for his superior but set out on his own. McClure's goal was to reach Melville Island in the northwestern Arctic, which had been visited by William Edward Parry as long ago as 1819. He rammed the ship through one patch of pack ice and then had to use five rowboats to tow the *Investigator* past Point Barrow. Forced by the pack ice of the Beaufort Sea to travel eastward along the coast of Alaska to the Mackenzie delta, McClure turned northwards east of the Mackenzie and reached the south shore of Banks Island, which had been spotted from the north by Parry, who named it in honor of Sir Joseph Banks.

Off the east coast of Banks Island, McClure saw a channel, later named Prince of Wales Strait, with a clear stretch of water leading to the northeast. As he sailed up it, he realized that if this body of water connected with Mel-

ville Sound, already sailed by Parry, he would have found the long-sought-after Northwest Passage.

By then, however, it was getting late in the year. On September 17, 1850, at a point about 30 miles from Melville Sound, McClure was forced to stop by increasing ice and rising winds. Wind pushed the *Investigator* 30 miles farther back down the channel. The growing ice toppled the ship on its side and threatened to crush it against some rocks. The men on the ship were convinced they were doomed and broke out the store of alcohol. On September 28, however, the storm died, the ship righted itself and was iced in for the winter.

On October 21, 1850, McClure took seven companions and headed north over the ice in sledges. On the fifth day, they reached the north end of Banks Island. On October 27, 1850, they climbed a small mountain and looked out on Melville Sound—McClure and his men had found the Northwest Passage. On the return trip, McClure ran ahead of the rest of his crew, got lost, and arrived barely alive after a sleepless night fighting his way through a storm.

The *Investigator* stayed locked in the ice during the winter of 1850-1851. During that time, McClure sent out three land parties to try to find traces of the Franklin expedition, without any success. In the summer of 1851 he tried to sail through Prince of Wales Strait into Melville Sound once again. This time he was stopped by ice 25 miles short of his goal. He then decided to sail south and try to get around Banks Island from the west side. Initially, he made very good time—300 miles in three days. Then, on August 20, 1851, the ship got caught in the ice once again. It was wedged in a small channel of open water too narrow to turn around in—so McClure continued north for another week. Once he had sailed around the northern end of Banks Island into Melville Sound he was once again stopped by ice.

McClure found a small harbor on the north coast of Banks Island, which he named Mercy Bay, and spent the winter of 1851-1852 there. While his men spent their time hunting, McClure took a small party north to Melville Island, hoping to find another one of the ships sent out to search for Franklin. He did find a note from Francis McClintock who had been there the previous June but who had long since left.

During the summer of 1852, McClure tried to get the *Investigator* free from the ice that blocked Mercy Bay but to no avail. By September when it became obvious that they were going to have to spend another winter in the Arctic, food supplies were dangerously low. Two of the junior officers showed signs of insanity, and 20 men were ill with scurvy. The following spring, McClure proposed to split up his crew into three different groups to try to get help overland.

In the meantime, the British government had sent out ships to look for McClure and Collinson, who had also disappeared. In September 1852 Captain Henry Kellett found a note on Melville Island that McClure had left five months previously indicating his location. Also iced in by the winter, Kellett could not go look for McClure until the following year. On April 6, 1853, shortly before he was to send out his land parties, McClure and his first officer were walking on the beach discussing the burial of a crew member who had died of scurvy. They looked up to see a strange man running down the beach towards them. It was Lieutenant Bedford Pim, an officer from Kellett's ship sent to fetch them.

At first, McClure refused to abandon the *Investigator,* and three more men died while waiting for supplies. When only four men volunteered to stay with him, McClure was forced to give up and leave the *Investigator* in Mercy Bay. Once his men reached Kellett's ship and crowded on board, it was too late in the year to depart. The following year, on the orders of Sir Edward Belcher, they abandoned Kellett's two ships and used supply ships to sail back to England via Baffin Bay, arriving home in September 1854.

McClure was given credit for discovering the Northwest Passage, even though he had not been able to navigate it. He was promoted to captain, knighted, and given a reward of £10,000. The journal of his voyage was edited and published in 1856. He then served in the Pacific Ocean from 1856 to 1861. After that, he returned to the Admiralty Office in London. He was promoted to rear admiral in 1857 and vice admiral in 1873 shortly before his death.

Further Reading

There are three original accounts of the *Investigator* expedition by participants in it. There is also an account by the ship's doctor, Alexander Armstrong: *A Personal Narrative of the Discovery of the North-West Passage* (London: Hurst & Blackett, 1857) and by a Moravian missionary, Johann August Miertsching, who served as interpreter with the Inuit: Leslie H. Neatby, editor, *Frozen Ships: The Arctic Diary of Johann Miertsching, 1850-54* 20(Toronto: Macmillan of Canada, 1967).
There are two fairly recent studies of the expedition: J.H. Nelson, "The Last Voyage of H.M.S. *Investigator,* 1850-53 and the Discovery of the North West Passage," *Polar Record,* vol. 13 (1967), no. 87 and Leslie H. Neatby, *The Search for Franklin* (London: Arthur Barker, 1970).
Other histories of Arctic exploration have good summaries of McClure's voyage: Jeannette Mirsky, *To the Arctic! The Story of Northern Exploration from Earliest Times to the Present* (New York: Alfred A. Knopf, 1948); George Malcolm Thomson, *The Search for the North-West Passage* (New York: Macmillan, 1975); and Pierre Berton, *The Arctic Grail: The Quest for the North West Passage and the North Pole, 1818-1909* (New York: Viking, 1988; paperback edition, New York: Penguin, 1989). □

Samuel Sidney McClure

Samuel Sidney McClure (1857-1949) created the first literary syndicate and developed "muckraking," which established him as one of America's notable editors.

Born in County Antrim, Ireland, on Feb. 17, 1857, S. S. McClure was taken to the United States as a boy. Raised in poverty, he worked his way through Knox College, Galesburg, Ill., where he was an outstanding student. In 1882, by good fortune, he became editor of the *Wheelman;* then he was associated with the De Vinne Press in New York. Dissatisfied, McClure turned to the *Century Magazine,* which despite its high status he found constrictive in opportunities.

The idea of a syndicate, capable of circulating a story or article to numerous publications at a small fee, rather than to one at a large fee, became an obsession with McClure. He left regular employment to sell his idea to writers and editors. Although difficult years followed, McClure's syndicate introduced a wider audience than ever before to such authors as Rudyard Kipling and George Meredith and inspired imitators who helped create a more popular journalism and literature.

In 1893 McClure expanded his still insecure operations by issuing *McClure's Magazine.* It aspired to sell more widely than such elite publications as *Century,* yet to match it in quality. In time *McClure's* offered opportunities to new writers, including Jack London and O. Henry. McClure effectively encouraged writers to display their thoroughly researched topics in clear, arresting prose.

In his January 1903 issue, McClure published his milestone editorial remarking the coincidence of the magazine's articles by Lincoln Steffens on municipal corruption, Ida Tarbell on the Standard Oil Company, and Ray Standard Baker on problems of labor—an issue which inaugurated "muckraking." Other publications took up what mounted into a sensational scrutiny of American society, but *McClure's* continued distinguished among them.

In 1906 Steffens, Tarbell, and others of *McClure's* staff grew dissatisfied, partly because of McClure's own irresponsible business policies and plans. In addition they were disturbed by what they considered his conservative social perspective. They seceded from *McClure's* and began to issue the notable *American Magazine.* McClure reorganized and continued with outstanding editors and writers, including George Kibbe Turner and Willa Cather.

Yet his former associates were correct in thinking that McClure was skeptical of democracy's potential. He sought a government for, rather than of, the people. Tired and temperamental, McClure abandoned editorial work in 1914 and absorbed himself in theoretical speculations regarding democracy's workings: *Obstacles to Peace* (1917), *The Achievements of Liberty* (1935), and *What Freedom Means to Man* (1938). These books made little impression, and McClure himself receded into obscurity. He died on March 21, 1949, in New York.

Further Reading

Peter Lyon, *Success Story: The Life and Times of S. S. McClure* (1963), makes use of McClure's private papers and is vividly written. Louis Filler, *Crusaders for American Liberalism* (1939), treats McClure in the context of his times. See also McClure's *My Autobiography* (1914; new ed. 1963), which owes much of its distinction to Willa Cather. Harold S. Wilson, *McClure's Magazine and the Muckrakers* (1970), is an interesting study. □

John William McCormack

U.S. Congressman John William McCormack (1891-1980) served in the House of Representatives for 42 years, including eight as Speaker of the House. During those four decades McCormack helped enact much of the major legislation of the 20th century, including the Social Security Act, the G. I. Bill, the Marshall Plan, and the 1964 Civil Rights Act.

John W. McCormack, the very model of the cigar chewing big-city Irish politician, rose slowly but steadily to the highest circles of power in Washington. McCormack was born in South Boston, Massachusetts, on December 21, 1891, to Joseph H. McCormack, a bricklayer, and Ellen (O'Brien) McCormack. Both Joseph McCormack and Ellen O'Brien were children of Irish immigrants who arrived in the United States during the Irish potato famine in 1848. John McCormack was born into a family of 12 children, but only three survived to be adults. When young McCormack was in the eighth grade at John Andrew Grammar School his father died, and the 13-year-old left school to support the family. After a series of low paying jobs McCormack became an office boy in a Boston law firm. He studied the firm's law books, attended law school at night, and at the age of 21 passed the Massachusetts Bar exam even though he had not completed high school.

McCormack became a successful trial lawyer, but soon was attracted to politics. He joined the Democratic Party and won his first elective office at 25 as a delegate to the Massachusetts Constitutional Convention in 1917. Three years later he married Harriet Joyce, a former singer.

In 1920 McCormack was elected to the Massachusetts House of Representatives and two years later to the State Senate. In 1926 McCormack experienced the only election defeat of his career when he unsuccessfully challenged 12th District Congressman James A. Gallivan in the Democratic primary. Following that defeat he resumed his law practice, but when Gallivan died in office in 1928 McCormack won a special election for the vacant seat and was later reelected 21 times.

McCormack's repeated victories were attributed to his style of personal politics. He knew every ward of the district—its fish piers, tenements, and modest working class homes. Before the social welfare legislation of the 1930s was enacted the young congressman trudged through the 12th District each Thanksgiving and Christmas passing out canned goods and turkeys. Although the district changed from predominantly Irish to an ethnically and racially mixed area of Italians, Eastern Europeans, and African Americans, McCormack remained popular. The congressman's Washington office was once described as "chummy chaos," as constituents often dropped in for unscheduled meetings.

Although often considered one of the last practitioners of old-style machine politics, much of McCormack's popularity stemmed from his 40-year advocacy of social legislation designed to assist the working class voters of his district. As one of the earliest supporters of the New Deal he helped win passage of key measures such as the National Housing Act (1934), Social Security (1936), and the National Minimum Wage Act (1938). In 1944 he supported the G. I. Bill, and while Speaker of the House of Representatives between 1962 and 1970 he presided over the massive outpouring of domestic legislation in one of the most productive eras of Congress including the Civil Rights Act (1964), Medicare (1965), and Model Cities (1966). In 1970 McCormack helped enact the law lowering the voting age to 18, and in one of his last speeches before the House in August of that year he urged passage of the Equal Rights Amendment.

McCormack's fervent anti-Communism dominated his foreign policy views. However, he argued that economic aid was often more effective than military aid in combating communist aggression. Consequently, he supported the Marshall Plan to reconstruct Europe after World War II. He urged economic aid for Korea, Formosa, and the Middle East in the 1950s, and in 1961 he helped pass the Peace Corps Act. Recognizing the importance of the space race with the Soviet Union, McCormack in 1958 sponsored the bill creating the National Aeronautics and Space Administration (NASA). McCormack's staunch anti-Communism also led him to support American involvement in the Vietnam War, prompting criticism by other liberal Democrats.

John W. McCormack's long climb to Speaker of the House of Representatives began in 1936 when he backed Texas Congressman Sam Rayburn's successful bid to become House majority leader. Four years later when Rayburn became Speaker he chose McCormack as the new majority leader. McCormack served as Rayburn's political confidant and deputy for 21 years, and in January 1962 at the age of 70 he was elected Speaker after Rayburn's death.

McCormack's handling of the Speakership position evoked much criticism. Some in Congress felt he lacked the strong leadership qualities of his predecessor and that he too readily compromised on major legislative issues. Young, liberal House Democrats were concerned with his unwavering support of the Vietnam War and his close friendship with Southern conservatives. In January 1969 McCormack faced the first of two challenges to his authority as House Speaker. Arizona Representative Morris Udall, claiming there was "an overriding need for new directions and new leadership" in the House, became the first congressman to attempt to unseat as Speaker a member of his own party. McCormack defeated the challenge, but his prestige and authority were weakened. In 1970 California Democratic Congressman Jerome Waldie placed a resolution of no confidence in McCormack before the House Democratic Caucus. The Speaker's supporters defeated the resolution, but they nevertheless made concessions to disgruntled House Democrats.

While facing these political challenges McCormack's long career was for the first time tainted by scandal. In October 1969 columnist Jack Anderson and *LIFE* magazine independently revealed that Martin Sweig, McCormack's administrative assistant and protege of 24 years, and Martin Voloshen, a professional lobbyist and close friend of the Speaker, had taken payments in exchange for interceding in various criminal cases and arranging government contracts. Voloshen pleaded guilty to influence peddling in the subsequent trial, and Sweig was convicted. Although McCormack was not implicated in any wrong doing, the scandal, the challenges to his authority as Speaker, and his wife's prolonged illness prompted the 78-year-old congressman to announce his retirement in May 1970. Following his wife's death in Washington in 1971 McCormack returned to Boston, where he lived on the income from his congressional pension. He died in a nursing home on November 22, 1980.

Further Reading

No book length biographies currently exist on McCormack. However, brief discussions of his life and political accomplishments can be found in Robert Sobel, editor, *U.S. Congress, House, Biographical Directory of the American Congress, 1774-1971* (1971); Eleanora W. Schoenebaum, editor, *Political Profiles: The Nixon/Ford Years* (1979); and the *New York Times Biographical Service* (1980).

Additional Sources

Memorial addresses and other tributes in the Congress of the United States on the life and contributions of John W. McCormack, Washington: U.S. G.P.O., 1981. □

Cyrus Hall McCormick

The American inventor, manufacturer, and philanthropist Cyrus Hall McCormick (1809-1884) was the first to successfully mechanize grain harvesting.

Cyrus McCormick was born in rural Virginia and received a limited formal education. His interest in mechanical problems led him to seek improvements in various farm implements, and in 1831 he got a patent for a hillside plow.

During the early years of the 19th century, farming was still largely a hand operation. Animals, used exclusively for transportation, plowing, and harrowing, provided the only other power. During the first half of the century, inventors concentrated on trying to bring power to bear on harvesting, which was not only exhausting but highly seasonal. In 1831 McCormick, living in a grain-producing region, turned his attention to this problem, which had also long intrigued his father.

In approaching the problem of harvesting by machine, McCormick made progress almost immediately, and the initial seven principal parts of his reaper have remained standard down to the present time. He was not satisfied with his success, however, and continued to improve his machine while working on other problems. In 1832, for example, he took out a patent for a self-sharpening horizontal plow. In 1834 he was spurred on to more work on his reaper by the news that Obed Hussey had announced a reaper of his own. He immediately warned Hussey that he had had a working reaper previous to 1833 and proceeded at long last to take out a patent on June 21, 1834.

The announcement of two new reapers was met with some skepticism. McCormick was cautious too. For the next several years, while operating an iron furnace in Virginia, he continued to make improvements on his reaper. When the Panic of 1837 wiped out his iron venture, he began selling his reapers to the public. Beginning in 1844, he issued licenses to individuals in different parts of the country to manufacture the machines. This proved to be a mistake because he was unable to control the quality of the reapers made under these agreements, and poorly constructed machines were giving his invention an undeserved bad name. In 1847 he erected his own reaper factory in Chicago. He was so successful that by 1850 he had virtually cornered the national market for reapers, despite the fact that his patent had run out in 1848 and he already had as many as 30 rivals in the field—a figure that was to rise to at least 100 ten years later. Obed Hussey was still his major competitor.

The two rivals had a well-publicized contest in 1851 at the London Crystal Palace Exhibition. On a wet July day in a field of green wheat, the McCormick Virginia Reaper (as it was called) handily beat the Hussey machine. There were then no other reapers in the British Isles, and the effect of this demonstration was dramatic. The generally anti-American *London Times* wrote that "the reaping machine from the United States is the most valuable contribution from

Further Reading

The standard biography of McCormick is William T. Hutchinson, *Cyrus Hall McCormick* (2 vols., 1930-1935). A more popular, but biased, account is Cyrus McCormick, *The Century of the Reaper* (1931). The claim that Robert McCormick, not his son Cyrus Hall, deserves credit for the reaper is made in Norbert Lyons, *The McCormick Reaper Legend: The True Story of a Great Invention* (1955). The case for Hussey is made in Follett L. Greeno, ed., *Obed Hussey, Who, of All Inventors, Made Bread Cheap* (1912). □

Robert Rutherford McCormick

Robert Rutherford McCormick (1880-1955), American publisher, was the head of the multimillion-dollar Tribune Company and an "America First" patriot.

Robert R. McCormick was born on July 30, 1880, in Chicago, the scion of two illustrious families. His father was the first American ambassador to Austria-Hungary; his mother was the daughter of Joseph Medill, a founder of the Republican party.

Young McCormick went to school in England while his father was an attaché in London. He graduated from Yale University in 1903. He studied law at Northwestern University. In 1904 he was elected alderman and served on the Chicago City Council for 2 years. When he was 25, McCormick was elected head of the Chicago Sanitary District Board. He was admitted to the bar in 1907. His political career came to an end in 1910 when he took over the *Chicago Tribune,* which his maternal grandfather had controlled. McCormick became a colonel during World War I. In 1918 he commanded the 61st Artillery Regiment in France.

The Tribune Company was a tribute to McCormick's powers of organization. His newspaper empire at one time contained three major papers: *Chicago Tribune, New York Daily News,* and *Washington Times-Herald.* An expert estimated that in 1953 the Tribune enterprises earned $10 million. McCormick, in his 1953 annual report, said assets of the company and its 14 subsidiaries in the United States and Canada totaled almost $250 million.

A self-appointed guardian of orthodox Republicanism, McCormick championed individualism and fought for free enterprise and freedom of the press. President Franklin D. Roosevelt was his chief political target, and Ohio senator Robert A. Taft and Gen. Douglas MacArthur were his principal heroes. An isolationist, McCormick opposed the League of Nations, the World Court, and the United Nations. His guns were constantly trained on British imperialism, socialism, and communism.

McCormick was referred to as the "greatest mind of the 14th century." Although his paper was sneered at as a

abroad, to the stock of our previous knowledge, that we have yet discovered."

McCormick continued to expand his factory, and the reaper itself was constantly improved, though the actual inventive work after about 1860 was left to mechanics hired by the firm. McCormick himself was embroiled in many court fights but was successful on that front as well. The machine was most widely used in the Middle West, as McCormick knew it would be when he built his factory in Chicago. The South remained unmechanized for many years after the Civil War; and as late as the beginning of the 20th century, harvesting in New England was still primarily a hand operation. By that time in the Far West, however, the machine had been transformed into a steam-powered, self-propelled combine that both cut and threshed the grain in one pass across the field. The basic unit was still, of course, McCormick's original reaper.

The last quarter century of McCormick's life was devoted to good works and to building his industrial empire. His innovations of this period were largely managerial rather than mechanical. He invested heavily in western mines, was a supporter of the idea for a canal across Nicaragua, and was a director of such enterprises as the Union Pacific Railroad. As a philanthropist, he patronized religion extensively. In 1878 he was honored by election to the prestigious French Academy of Sciences for "having done more for the cause of agriculture than any other living man."

"ceaseless drip of poison," he was perhaps the last of the personalized journalists; he allowed his opinions to flow into news columns. He so sharply criticized Roosevelt during World War II that many people suspected him of being "unpatriotic"; this was a crowning heresy for the man who published the American flag on his front page each day. In 1943 McCormick was boomed briefly for president by the Republican Nationalist Revival Committee. In 1954 he helped found "For America," an organization to combat "supernationalism."

In 1915 McCormick had married Amie Irwin Adams, who died in 1939. He married Maryland Matheson Hooper in 1944. He had no children. McCormick died at his estate in Wheaton on April 1, 1955.

Further Reading

McCormick arouses controversy among his biographers. Frank C. Waldrop, *McCormick of Chicago: An Unconventional Portrait of a Controversial Figure* (1966), strives remarkably well for impartiality. Frank Luther Mott, *American Journalism* (1941; 3d ed. 1962), puts McCormick in focus with the rest of America.

Additional Sources

Morgan, Gwen, *Poor little rich boy (and how he made good)*, Carpentersville, Ill.: Crossroad Communications, 1985.
Waldrop, Frank C., *McCormick of Chicago: an unconventional portrait of a controversial figure*, Westport, Conn.: Greenwood Press, 1975, 1966. □

James McCosh

James McCosh (1811-1894), Scottish-American minister, philosopher, and college president, summarized the achievements of the Scottish philosophy and prepared Princeton for its transition from a small college to a modern university.

James McCosh was born on April 1, 1811, in Ayrshire, Scotland. He studied at the University of Glasgow and then at the University of Edinburgh, from which he received his master's degree in 1833. The following year he became a minister of the Established Church of Scotland. He later considered the greatest event in his life to have been his participation in the Free Church of Scotland movement; the Free Church seceded from the establishment in 1843.

While a student McCosh had developed a serious interest in natural theology and philosophy which culminated in his first book, *The Method of the Divine Government, Physical and Moral* (1850). This defense of supernaturalism and Christianity against materialism won him the chair of logic and metaphysics at Queen's College, Belfast. During his Belfast years (1852-1868) he published four books; the most important was *The Intuitions of the Mind Inductively Investigated* (1860).

In opposition to skepticism and Kantian idealism, McCosh's version of the Scottish philosophy argued that there existed intuitions of the mind (sometimes called the principles of common sense). These intuitions were self-evident, necessary, and universal principles of the human mind; they were immediate perceptions of the real objective order. Man could generalize from these individual, intuitive truths to formulate general principles. In all areas of inquiry, including ethics, certitude rested firmly on immediate, self-evident knowledge. McCosh, constantly concerned with the relations between philosophy and religion, believed that this form of philosophical realism was both true and most favorable to religion. He was not an innovator, but a synthesizer of a philosophical tradition that was becoming outmoded even as he wrote.

McCosh's books were popular in the United States because he was the leading philosophical writer within the Presbyterian family of churches. It was, then, appropriate that the Presbyterian-founded College of New Jersey (now Princeton University) chose McCosh as its president in 1868. He undertook the presidency of the small school with his accustomed earnestness, energy, and force. He expanded the faculty, the program, and the physical plant and increased enrollment and financial support. He continued to write on philosophy and religion during his 20 vigorous years as president. He distinguished himself by his courageous public insistence that Darwinian evolution did not conflict with Christianity. Thus he was instrumental in accommodating theology and 19th-century science.

In 1888 McCosh retired from the presidency because of age. He died on Nov. 16, 1894, in Princeton.

Kickapoo Indians in the Wabash Valley, and later he served in the same capacity among the Potawatomi and Ottawa Indians in Michigan.

In 1828 McCoy was appointed a member of the Federal commission assigned to move the Ottawa and Miami Indians westward as part of a government policy to remove all Indians to the Great Plains region. He became an ardent supporter of this policy, for he believed that thereby the Indians would be removed from the evil influences of frontiersmen. He began advocating a separate Indian state in the West. On a trip to Washington, D.C., he persuaded Secretary of War John C. Calhoun to endorse his idea and then went to survey a capital city for his proposed state (near the Ottawa mission in Kansas).

In 1830 McCoy was appointed an agent to assist the Indians in their westward movement and surveyor to draw the boundaries of their new reservations. His next few years were spent thus. In fact, with the help of his two sons, he surveyed most Indian reservations in Nebraska and Kansas and the Cherokee Outlet in Oklahoma.

To promote his concept of a state in the West entirely for Indians, McCoy wrote extensively, publishing one book on the subject in 1827 and authoring many pamphlets. However, his dream never became reality, for technological advances and changes in pioneering techniques brought so many white settlers to the trans-Mississippi country that the Indians were eventually confined to smaller and smaller reservations.

In 1842 McCoy moved to Louisville, Ky., to become first corresponding secretary and general agent for the American Indian Mission Association. He died there on June 21, 1846. McCoy had only the best intentions—to Christianize the Indians and to remove them westward to escape the influence of the whites—but in the process he helped deprive the natives of much of their original lands.

Further Reading

Helpful in understanding McCoy are his own *Remarks on the Practicability of Indian Reform* (1827) and *History of Baptist Indian Missions.* The only biography is W. N. Wyeth, *Isaac McCoy* (1895). Also helpful are general histories of Kansas and Oklahoma. □

Further Reading

The Life of James McCosh: A Record Chiefly Autobiographical, edited by William M. Sloane (1897), intersperses biography and autobiography.

Additional Sources

Hoeveler, J. David, *James McCosh and the Scottish intellectual tradition: from Glasgow to Princeton,* Princeton, N.J.: Princeton University Press, 1981. □

Isaac McCoy

Isaac McCoy (1784-1846), American Indian agent and missionary, worked with several tribes in the Midwest, urging them to move to reservations. He advocated a separate state solely for Indians.

Born near Uniontown, Pa., on June 13, 1784, Isaac McCoy moved with his family to Kentucky in 1790. There his father pastored a church, and young McCoy experienced a religious conversion at the age of 17. Two years later he married Christiana Polke, who eventually would bear 13 children.

In 1804 McCoy moved to Indiana, where he settled in Clark County as the minister at Maria Creek Baptist Church. In 1817 he was appointed missionary to the Miami and

Joseph Geiting McCoy

Joseph Geiting McCoy (1837-1915), American cattleman, built the first livestock shipping center on the Great Plains.

Joseph G. McCoy was born on a farm in Sangamon County, Ill., on Dec. 21, 1837. He was educated in local schools and spent a year in the academy of Knox College in Galesburg. After his marriage to Sarah Epler in 1861, he entered the mule and cattle raising business. At the close of the Civil War, McCoy expanded his enterprise by buying animals in large quantities and shipping them to major livestock centers. In 1867 he joined a firm that shipped as many as a thousand cattle a week.

McCoy viewed the livestock industry from a national perspective and recognized the need for better contacts between southwestern ranchers, midwestern feeders, and meat-packers. He resolved to build a stock depot west of farming sections on the Great Plains to which cowboys from Texas could drive Longhorn herds. Although the railroad builders considered his plans impractical, he finally succeeded in obtaining cooperation from the Kansas Pacific Railway provided he assumed all the financial risks. The cattle would be shipped from his proposed stockyards to Kansas City. He then made an agreement with the Hannibal and St. Joseph line, which provided a route to Quincy, Ill.; from there the cattle could be sent to Chicago.

Abilene, Kans., was chosen as the site for McCoy's cattle pens. He purchased a 250-acre tract at the edge of this frontier village and built a pen to handle a thousand head of cattle, a hotel known as the Drover's Cottage, a bank, office, and livery stable. He sent agents south to acquaint Texas cowmen with his plan to receive the fall drives.

The first herds arrived in August 1867; an initial shipment to Chicago left Abilene in September. By the end of the year 35,000 head had been driven over the Chisholm Trail to Abilene, and in 1868 the number rose to 75,000 head; by 1870 the number doubled. As Abilene's leading citizen, McCoy was elected mayor.

Rival railroad terminal towns, farther west and south, soon diverted trade from Abilene, and McCoy moved to the new cow towns. In 1872 he went to Wichita, Kans., where he became a promotion agent for American and Texas Refrigerator Car. By 1880 he was a commission dealer in livestock in Kansas City and had been employed by the U.S. Census Bureau to report on the livestock industry for the eleventh census. For a time he lived in Oklahoma and served as agent for the Cherokee Nation in collecting land revenues. In 1890 he was an unsuccessful Democratic candidate for the U.S. Congress. He died in Kansas City on Oct. 19, 1915.

Further Reading

The chief source on the life of McCoy is his own *Historic Sketches of the Cattle Trade of the West and Southwest* (1874; repr. 1966). Additional evidence can be obtained from Wayne Gard's well-written *The Chisholm Trail* (1954). McCoy's significance in the development of the cattle industry is noted in most books on the subject, such as Walter Prescott Webb's *The Great Plains* (1931). □

Hugh McCulloch

Hugh McCulloch (1808-1895), American banker who helped launch the national banking system, was secretary of the Treasury during the Civil War and Reconstruction.

Hugh McCulloch was born on Dec. 7, 1808, in Kennebunk, Maine. He attended Bowdoin College, leaving in his sophomore year to study law in Boston. A year after his admission to the bar in 1832 he moved to Fort Wayne, Ind., where he practiced law for 2 years. In 1835 he became cashier and manager of the Fort Wayne branch of the State Bank of Indiana. Though he had no banking experience, McCulloch learned fast and was soon one of the soundest bankers in the country. His bank was one of the few that did not suspend specie payments in the Panic of 1857.

In 1862 McCulloch went to Washington, D.C., as a lobbyist for state banks against the proposed legislation creating a national banking system. Despite his efforts the law was passed in 1863. It was intended to help finance the Civil War and provide a uniform, stable national currency. Secretary of the Treasury Salmon P. Chase, impressed by McCulloch's abilities, asked him to help put the new system into effect as comptroller of the currency. Deciding that the new system was better than the old, McCulloch accepted the job. He persuaded existing state banks to apply for Federal charters, and more than any other single person he was responsible for the successful inauguration of the national banking network.

In March 1865 President Abraham Lincoln appointed McCulloch secretary of the Treasury. After the Civil War, McCulloch urged that greenbacks issued as emergency currency during the conflict, with no specie backing, be gradually retired in order to reduce war-inflated prices and end speculation in gold. From 1866 to 1868 some $82 million of

the greenbacks was gradually retired. In 1868, however, Congress heeded anticontractionist pressures and suspended retirement. The rest of the greenbacks remained in circulation, though in 1879 they were brought to a par with gold, thus achieving McCulloch's objective.

In 1869 McCulloch returned to banking. He served again briefly (1884-1885) as secretary of the Treasury under President Chester A. Arthur. In 1888 his autobiography, *Men and Measures of Half a Century,* appeared. He died at his Maryland estate on May 24, 1895.

Further Reading

The main source for McCulloch's career is his autobiography. Information on his work as comptroller of the currency, secretary of the Treasury, and, later, banking partner of Jay Cooke is in Ellis P. Oberholtzer, *Jay Cooke: Financier of the Civil War* (2 vols., 1907); Robert Sharkey, *Money, Class, and Party: An Economic Study of the Civil War and Reconstruction* (1959); and Irwin Unger, *The Greenback Era: A Social and Political History of American Finance, 1865-1879* (1964). The last two are critical of aspects of McCulloch's activities as secretary of the Treasury. □

Hattie McDaniel

Hattie McDaniel's portrayal of a "mammy" figure in *Gone with the Wind,* a role for which she received an Oscar award in 1940 as best supporting actress, is still regarded as a definitive interpretation. McDaniel (1895-1952) was the first African American to receive an Oscar award.

Hattie McDaniel's 1939 portrayal of Mammy in *Gone with the Wind* set the screen image of the loyal black maid serving a household of well-to-do white people. Known for her broad smile, ample proportions, and ebullient manner, the actress appeared in over 300 films during the 1930s and 1940s, almost without exception in the character of maid or cook, a role with which she became so identified after the success of *Gone with the Wind* that many of her fans and friends took to calling her Mammy.

McDaniel enjoyed a long and prosperous career in film and radio drama and in 1940 became the first African American to win an Academy Award; but because she was used exclusively in the role of a domestic, she became the object of intense criticism from progressive blacks in the 1940s. By the time she appeared in *Gone with the Wind,* McDaniel had broadened her portrait of the Mammy role, endowing the character with an earthy, all-knowing sensibility and delivering her lines with saucy self-assurance. But, caught between the demands of two cultures, McDaniel became embittered by the attacks on her integrity made by the black intelligentsia, and when she died in 1952 the role of Mammy pretty well died with her.

Hattie McDaniel was born in 1895, in Wichita, Kansas, the thirteenth child in a family of performers. Her father, Henry McDaniel, led a varied life as a Baptist minister, carpenter, banjo player, and minstrel showman, eventually organizing his own family into a minstrel troupe. Henry married a gospel singer named Susan Holbert in 1875 and moved their growing family to Denver, Colorado, in 1901.

McDaniel was one of only two black children in her elementary school class in Denver. Racial prejudice was less virulent in the West than elsewhere in the United States, and she became something of a favorite at the 24th Street Elementary School for her talents as a singer and reciter of poetry. Even as a child, according to a letter written to Hattie years later by her teacher, "you had an outstanding dramatic ability, an ability to project to your listeners your strong personality and your ever present sense of humor." McDaniel sang at church, at school, and at home; she sang so continuously that her mother reportedly bribed her into silence with spare change. Before long she was also singing in professional minstrel shows, as well as dancing, performing humorous skits, and later writing her own songs.

In 1910 McDaniel left school in her sophomore year and became a full-time minstrel performer, traveling the western states with her father's Henry McDaniel Minstrel Show and several other troupes. The minstrel shows, usually performed by blacks but sometimes by whites in blackface, presented a variety of entertainments based on caricatures of black cultural life for the enjoyment of mostly white audiences. With her father's troupe, which also featured a number of her brothers and sisters, she visited most of the major cities in the western United States while honing the skills that would later make her famous.

When her father retired around 1920, McDaniel joined Professor George Morrison's famous "Melody Hounds" on longer and more publicized tours. As recounted by Carlton Jackson in *Hattie: The Life of Hattie McDaniel,* she was unquestionably one of the stars of Morrison's troupe; of one concert, the *Portland Telegram* wrote that "the biggest show stopper of them all was Morrison's orchestra and its Hattie McDaniel." She also wrote dozens of show tunes such as "Sam Henry Blues," "Poor Wandering Boy Blues," and "Quittin' My Man Today."

Broke into Radio and Film

In the 1920s McDaniel toured constantly with Morrison's troupe and other well-known vaudeville companies. A first marriage ended abruptly in 1922 when her husband of three months, George Langford, was reportedly killed by gunfire. Little is known of this or any of McDaniel's three subsequent marriages, except that they were all relatively short and unhappy. More heartening was the progress of her career, which included a first radio performance in 1925 on Denver's KOA station. McDaniel was one of the first black women to be heard on American radio, the medium in which she would always remain most comfortable.

In 1929, the booking organization for whom she was working went bankrupt at the onset of the Great Depression, stranding McDaniel in Chicago with little money and no job. On a tip from a friend, she went north to Milwaukee and found work at Sam Pick's Club Madrid—as a bathroom attendant. At that time, the Club Madrid engaged only white nightclub performers and had no use for a black minstrel/vaudeville entertainer such as Hattie McDaniel. True to her nature, however, McDaniel could not refrain from singing while she worked, and she became well known among the club's patrons for her unfailing good humor and obvious talent. After repeated promptings from McDaniel's fans, the club's owner gave her a shot at performing on his main stage, where her rendition of "St. Louis Blues" was a smash hit. She remained as a performer at the Club Madrid for about a year, until she was lured to Hollywood by the enthusiastic reports of her brother Sam and sister Etta, who had been living in Los Angeles for several years.

Sam and Etta McDaniel already had small roles in a number of motion pictures, but Hattie was forced to take menial jobs in order to support herself in Los Angeles. Opportunities for blacks in Hollywood were severely limited to a handful of stereotypic roles, and even these parts were hard to come by. Sam McDaniel had a regular part on LA's KNX radio show "The Optimistic Do-Nuts" and was able to get Hattie a small part, which she promptly turned into a big opportunity. McDaniel earned the nickname "Hi-Hat Hattie" after showing up for the first radio broadcast in formal evening wear. According to Jackson, "she instantly became a hit with black West Coast listeners," and eventually stole the show.

McDaniel landed her first movie role in 1931 as an extra in the chorus scenes of a routine Hollywood musical. The next year, she played in her first major motion picture—

the Twentieth Century Fox film *The Golden West*—as a house servant. She continued to appear in a number of similar bit parts, receiving screen credit for none of them, until famed director John Ford cast her in the 1934 Fox production of *Judge Priest.* In this picture, McDaniel was given the opportunity to sing a duet with Will Rogers, the well-known American humorist, and her performance was well received by the press and her fellow actors alike.

In 1935 McDaniel played "Mom Beck" in *The Little Colonel,* which starred Shirley Temple and Lionel Barrymore, faithfully reflected the image then held by many white Americans of the happy black servant in the Old South. A number of black journalists objected to Hattie's performance in the film, charging that the character of Mom Beck implied that blacks might have been happier as slaves than they were as free individuals. This movie marked the beginning of McDaniel's long feud with the more progressive elements of the black community.

Won Oscar for *Gone with the Wind*

Once established in Hollywood, McDaniel found no shortage of work. In 1936 alone she appeared in twelve films, including the Universal release *Show Boat,* starring Paul Robeson. For the decade as a whole, her performances numbered about forty—nearly all of them in the role of maid or cook to a household of whites. As such, she was a leading candidate for the role of Mammy in David O. Selznick's 1939 production of *Gone with the Wind,* adapted from Margaret Mitchell's bestselling novel of the same name.

Gone with the Wind was dead certain to be a hugely successful film, and competition for parts was intense in Hollywood. McDaniel won the role of Mammy over several rivals, signing a contract with Selznick that gave him exclusive rights to her work for a number of years. Her salary for *Gone with the Wind* was to be $450 a week, which—while not in the same league as the pay of stars like Clark Gable and Vivien Leigh—was nevertheless a long way from what her real-life counterparts could hope to earn. Responding to a friend who objected to the limited scope of her film roles, McDaniel is often quoted as having said: "Hell, I'd rather play a maid than be one."

Gone with the Wind rewarded McDaniel with far more than a weekly salary, however. As the loving but occasionally sharp-tongued Mammy, Hattie McDaniel became known and loved by the millions of people who would eventually see the movie, one of Hollywood's all-time hits. Her performance as Mammy was more than a bit part, and it so impressed the Academy of Motion Picture Arts and Sciences that she was awarded the 1940 Oscar for best supporting actress, the first ever won by an African American. In contrast to the widespread criticism she had received for some of her earlier roles, McDaniel's award-winning performance was *generally* seen by the black press as a symbol of progress for African Americans, although some members of the NAACP were still displeased with her work. At the least, her Oscar was a symbol of possible conciliation between the races, especially potent at a time when the country was preparing to do battle with fascist enemies such as German leader Adolf Hitler.

Feuds with NAACP

Gone with the Wind lifted McDaniel to the ranks of known film personalities and was unquestionably the high point of her career. In the wake of the film's great success, she spent much of 1940 touring the country as Mammy, and in the following year she appeared in three substantial film roles, earning no less than $31,000 for her efforts. She was married, for a third time, to James L. Crawford in 1941, and once released from her contract with Selznick in 1943, she became a free agent in the Hollywood markets.

During World War II, McDaniel worked with the Hollywood Victory Committee, entertaining black troops and encouraging Americans to buy war bonds. But the mid-1940s brought trying times for McDaniel, who experienced a heart-wrenching false pregnancy in 1944 and soon after became the victim of racist-inspired legal problems. At about the time the war ended, the actress found herself embroiled in a legal battle over a restrictive covenant system in Los Angeles, which limited black land and home ownership rights. Having purchased a thirty-room house in the city back in 1942, McDaniel faced the possibility of eviction if the discriminatory restrictive covenant were enforced. She was one of several black entertainers who challenged the racist system in court, however, and won.

Still, throughout the 1940s, a growing number of activists viewed McDaniel and all she represented as a detriment to the budding fight for civil rights. By the end of the war, the United States had entered a new phase in the struggle for equality between the races. Minstrel shows and the stereotyped roles heretofore allowed blacks were no longer acceptable to a growing community of intellectuals and activists, who demanded that films represent people of color as capable of greater accomplishments than those of cook, servant, and shoe shine boy. NAACP president Walter White pressed both actors and studios to stop making films which tended to degrade blacks, and he singled out the roles of Hattie McDaniel as particularly offensive. According to Jackson in *Hattie,* McDaniel was referred to as "that Twentieth Century Fox specialist in the bug-eye" by a reporter for the *New York Post,* and she appeared in all three of the films White described as excessively "anti-Negro" (*Gone with the Wind, The Little Colonel,* and *Maryland*).

In response, McDaniel defended her right to choose whichever roles she saw fit, adding that many of her screen personae, like Mammy in *Gone with the Wind,* had shown themselves to be more than the equals of their white employers. Jackson suggested that McDaniel "was a gradualist, 'inadvertent,' reformer, and she accomplished more in this capacity than many of those who had set out specifically to change the system. . . . Hattie's fight against restrictive covenants, and her straight playing of [black roles] influenced the [civil rights] revolution more than she or anyone around her realized. She . . . [proved] to listeners that a black person could have a comedic role without degradation. . . . She was able to instill a mood of rising expectations in young blacks on their way up in the entertainment and business worlds."

Renewed Success in Radio

By the late 1940s McDaniel found herself in a difficult position. She was nationally famous and loved as the personification of the hard-working, humble black servant yet was under attack for playing that character by many members of the black community; and, perhaps most difficult of all, such roles were disappearing in the changing racial climate of post-World War II America. Inevitably, McDaniel found her screen opportunities drying up even as she suffered insults from progressive blacks, and after her third marriage ended in divorce in 1945, she became increasingly depressed and confused as to her proper path.

Although her screen image was permanently linked to a now outdated stereotype, McDaniel could still use her vocal talent on radio. In 1947 she won the starring role of Beulah on *The Beulah Show,* a CBS radio show about a black maid and the white family for whom she worked. *The Beulah Show* had been on the air for some years, but always with white males taking the role of Beulah; when Hattie McDaniel took over the role, she became the first black to star in a radio program intended for a general audience. Beulah was an ideal role for the actress, allowing her to make use of her considerable comedic gifts while not being limited to a crude racial cliche. Moreover, the program was generally praised by the NAACP and the Urban League, along with the twenty million other Americans who listened to it every evening at the height of its popularity in 1950.

McDaniel's last marriage, to an interior decorator named Larry Williams, lasted only a few months. In 1951 she suffered a heart attack while filming the first few segments of a projected television version of *The Beulah Show.* Although she recovered enough to tape more than an dozen episodes of the *Beulah* radio show in the spring of 1952, by summer she was diagnosed with breast cancer. McDaniel died on October 26, 1952. She will always be remembered as Mammy of *Gone with the Wind,* a role that many critics find offensive, many others prize as the movie's finest performance, and all agree could have been played by no one but Hattie McDaniel.

Further Reading

Bogle, Donald, *Toms, Coons, Mulattoes, Mammies and Bucks: An Interpretive History of Blacks in American Films,* Viking Press, 1973.

Bogle, Donald, *Brown Sugar: Eighty Years of America's Black Female Superstars,* Harmony Books, 1980.

Jackson, Carlton, *Hattie: The Life of Hattie McDaniel,* Madison Books, 1990.

Noble, Peter, *The Negro in Films: Literature of the Cinema,* Arno Press, 1970.

Amsterdam News (New York), November 19, 1949; November 1, 1952; April 28, 1979, p. 37.

Collier's, December 1939, pp. 20-21, 32.

Crisis, October 1937, p. 297.

Ebony, August 1948, p. 57; December 1949, p. 92.

Hollywood Studio Magazine, April 1977, pp. 19-20.

Journal of Popular Film, Fall 1973, pp. 366-71.

New York Times, March 7, 1948; October 27, 1952.

New York Times Magazine, December 10, 1939.
Our World Magazine, February 1952.
Village Voice, May 5, 1975. □

George McDuffie

George McDuffie (1790-1851), U.S. senator, was a leading exponent of states' rights in the period before the Civil War.

George McDuffie was born near Augusta, Ga., on Aug. 10, 1790, the son of a poor farmer. At the age of 12, while working as a clerk, he attracted the attention of William Calhoun (the brother of John C. Calhoun), who helped him attend South Carolina College. Upon admission to the bar in 1815, McDuffie settled in Edgefield, S.C., developing such a lucrative practice that he was able to buy a cotton plantation (Cherry Hill) in 1829. That same year he married Mary Rebecca Singleton.

In 1821 McDuffie was elected a member of the House of Representatives from South Carolina, serving until 1834, when he was elected governor of the state. Like John C. Calhoun, he began his career as a nationalist but soon joined the ranks of the states' righters. As a delegate to the state nullification convention in 1832, he preferred to secede from the Union rather than to submit to Federal authority. After the adoption of the compromise tariff, he reluctantly agreed to Calhoun's desire that South Carolina follow a moderate course. In later years McDuffie frequently intervened in state affairs to prevent adoption of extreme states' rights measures opposed by Calhoun.

In Congress, McDuffie proved a sensational speaker whose appearances filled the galleries with spectators. His speeches did not conform to the popular florid mold but were frenzied affairs, extravagant in language and furious in tone. In private he was a reserved and unsmiling figure whom many, like John Quincy Adams, found grim and repellent. As he grew older, chronic illness (he had received a spinal injury in a duel shortly after entering Congress) made him subject to fits of depression and irritability. Throughout his congressional career he was one of the most radical opponents of the protective tariff, which he condemned as an unfair, direct levy on the Southern cotton grower for the profit of the North.

Originally a supporter of Andrew Jackson, McDuffie had followed Calhoun in his break with the President in 1832. Following his two terms as governor, he was elected to the U.S. Senate in 1842, where he was a leading advocate of the annexation of Texas. However, failing health compelled him to resign from the Senate in 1846. He died on March 11, 1851.

Further Reading

Material on McDuffie is scant. He is discussed or referred to in John Quincy Adams, *Memoirs,* edited by Charles Francis Adams (12 vols., 1874-1877); Chauncey Samuel Boucher, *The Nullification Controversy in South Carolina* (1916); and

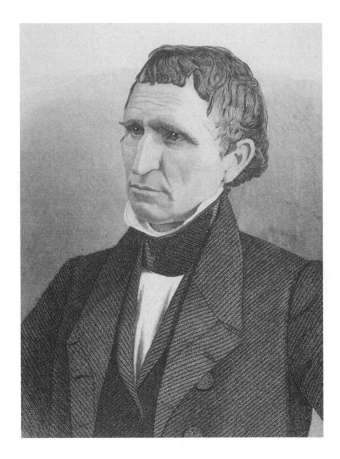

Charles Maurice Wiltse, *John C. Calhoun* (3 vols., 1944-1951). □

John Patrick McEnroe Jr.

John McEnroe (born 1959) was one of the most successful and high-profile players in the history of tennis. Throughout his career, McEnroe won 17 Grand Slam titles, 77 career single titles, and 77 doubles titles.

In addition to John McEnroe's skill on the tennis court and championship career, he is best known for his aggressive and intense playing style as well as his rivalry with Swedish tennis player Bjorn Borg. "If you play John, you must play your best. He doesn't have any weaknesses," said Borg of McEnroe in the *Lincoln Library of Sports Champions.* In the 1980 Wimbledon final, which Mike Lupica of *Esquire* called the most famous match ever, Borg found out just how tenacious the talented and controversial southpaw from Queens, New York, really was. Unfortunately, mention of McEnroe is just as likely to call to mind images of abused racquets and berated linesmen as it is the devastating serves and volleys that led to 17 Grand Slam titles.

John Patrick McEnroe was born on February 16, 1959, in Wiesbaden, Germany, where his father, John McEnroe, Sr., was serving in the United States Air Force and his mother, Kay McEnroe, was a surgical nurse. He was the oldest of three sons. In 1963, his family moved to Douglaston, Queens, New York, where he was raised. At an early age, he exhibited unusually developed eye-hand coordination and athletic ability. According to his father, when John, Jr. was only two years of age, he could strike a ball with a plastic bat, and at age four he could hit it a considerable distance.

Early Education and Training

While McEnroe exhibited qualities of a tennis prodigy, he enthusiastically played many other sports. However, it soon became obvious that he possessed a great deal of natural ability on the tennis court. Oddly, although he won several Junior tournaments, and moved steadily upward in rank, he was never rated number one on the National Junior circuit. In 1970, McEnroe was placed under the tutelage of Tony Palafox, a former Davis Cup player for Mexico and Harry "Hop" Hopman, a former Australian Davis Cup coach, at the Port Washington (Long Island) Tennis Academy.

McEnroe attended Trinity School, a prestigious and expensive Ivy League preparatory school in Manhattan, where he was known to be funny, witty, and rowdy. He did above average scholastically—although by his own admission, he could have done better if it weren't for his many sports activities: four years of soccer and tennis; two years of basketball. At the age of 16, McEnroe received a six month suspension from the Port Washington Tennis Academy for an adolescent prank. As a result, his parents switched the

young talent to the Cove Racquet Club, where Palafox had also moved.

Youngest Man in Wimbeldon Finals

A pivotal series of events in McEnroe's career took place in 1977, after he graduated from high school. He was given the opportunity to play in Europe, where he won the French Juniors Tournament. Aiming for the Junior's title at Wimbledon, he had to pull out of the event when he qualified for the men's competition. Not only did he qualify for this important tournament, but he advanced to the semi-finals, where he was beaten by the more experienced Jimmy Connors, who won in four sets. At that time, McEnroe became the youngest man ever to reach the Wimbledon semi-finals. He also solidified his reputation as one of tennis' "bad boys" along with Jimmy Connors and Ilie Nastase. His disturbing and emotional outbursts were directed at linesman, opponents, and himself. Pete Axthelm from *Newsweek* noted later, "He is a young man who raised perfectly placed strokes to a high art form, only to resort to tantrums that smear his masterpieces like graffiti." Although McEnroe played somewhat inconsistently for the remainder of the year, he was voted *Tennis* magazine's Rookie of the Year for 1977.

McEnroe Turned Pro

That fall, McEnroe attended Stanford University in Palo Alto, California, on a tennis scholarship. He led the school's tennis team to the NCAA Championship in 1978. After his freshman year he decided to turn pro. In the summer of 1978, McEnroe was eliminated in the first round at Wimbledon but reached the semi-finals of the U.S. Open. By the end of that year, he was ranked sixth in the world in singles and fifth in doubles. It was during this time that McEnroe began his long commitment to Davis Cup play (earlier seeds may have been planted by Palafox and Hop's involvement in the Davis Cup). Tony Trabert, then Davis Cup coach, took a risk with the 19-year-old McEnroe, who handled the pressure well, winning his matches against England to help clinch the first U.S. Davis Cup victory in six years. In the next four months, McEnroe won four singles championships, including an important (and portentous) victory over Bjorn Borg on his home turf in Stockholm, Sweden. In 1978, the Association of Tennis Professionals (ATP) recognized him with a Newcomer of the Year Award and ranked him number four in the world, behind Borg, Connors and Vilas. In his first six months as a pro, he earned nearly half a million dollars.

After decisive victories over both Connors and Borg in 1979, McEnroe's playing style matured. It was an interesting contrast to the machine-gun like attacks of Connors and Borg. Like his idol, Rod Laver, McEnroe used finesse to keep his opponents off guard. His serve did not overpower, but he had extremely quick reflexes and an uncanny court sense—he seemed to know instinctively where to place his shots. Arthur Ashe, the late tennis champion, summed up his style in an interview with *Sports Illustrated*'s Curry Kirkpatrick, "Against Connors and Borg, you feel like your being hit with a sledge hammer, but McEnroe is a stiletto."

Temper Tantrums and Superstardom

As his talent came to public attention, so did his "superstar" personality. At no tournament did his comments and disruptive actions stand out more than they did at Wimbledon, which was run by the traditional All England Club. Whether there was any truth to his claims or not, McEnroe believed that the Wimbledon umpires were out to get him. "I get screwed by the umpires in this place," he was quoted as saying. There is a theory that these disruptions were beneficial to McEnroe. "He's the only player in the history of the game to go berserk and play better tennis," said George Plimpton in *Esquire*. Needless to say, the All England Club and the British fans were happy to see McEnroe lose in the fourth round at the 1979 Wimbledon tournament. Later that year McEnroe bounced back and won his first United States Open Championship, defeating fellow New Yorker Vitas Gerulaitis. McEnroe became the youngest player to win the U.S. Open since 1948. Shortly after his U.S. Open triumph, he led the U.S. Davis Cup team to victory over Argentina, Australia, and Italy to allow the team to retain the cup.

Rivalry with Bjorn Borg

In 1980, one of tennis' most notorious rivalries between McEnroe and the unflappable Swede, Bjorn Borg, took shape. It began in July of that year at the Wimbledon finals. Although Borg started the first set erratically, the remaining four sets saw both players in top form. The highlight of the match took place in the fourth set which went into a tie breaker. It took 22 minutes and 34 points for McEnroe to finally win the set. But Borg emerged victorious (1-6, 7-5, 6-3, 6-7, 8-6). It was Borg's fifth consecutive Wimbledon title, but it also showed the world that McEnroe had the stamina and mental toughness to be a top player. The rivals met again at the U.S., Open where McEnroe found himself defending the title against a determined Borg as he had yet to win at Flushing Meadow. In a match with as many games as their famous Wimbledon final, McEnroe emerged the winner (7-6, 6-1, 6-7, 5-7, 6-4). McEnroe then set his sights on Wimbeldon.

The 1981 Wimbledon tournament saw McEnroe and Borg once again in the final. This time McEnroe ended Borg's five year reign as he won in four sets (4-6, 7-6, 7-6, 6-4). That same year, in September, McEnroe defended his U.S. Open title once again against Borg (4-6, 6-2, 6-4, 6-3). Borg, perhaps feeling that his reign was over, retired after this defeat. McEnroe became the only man since Bill Tilden to win three consecutive U.S. Open titles.

Last Grand Slam Title

1982 was not a good year for McEnroe as he failed to win any major tournaments. He was back in form in 1983, winning his second Wimbledon by crushing Chris Lewis (6-2, 6-2, 6-2). He also captured his 28th singles victory in Davis Cup play—a record.

In 1984, McEnroe won 82 of 84 matches, including his fourth WCT final, his third U.S. Pro Indoor Championship and his second Grand Prix Masters title. He captured his third Wimbledon title, soundly defeating Connors (6-1, 6-1,

6-2), and his fourth U.S. Open title (beating Ivan Lendl 6-3, 6-4, 6-1). This victory was to mark the last Grand Slam title of his career.

McEnroe's Decline and Comeback

After having won a total of seven Grand Slam titles in singles and seven in doubles, and being number one in ATP year-end rankings from 1981 to 1984, McEnroe began to decline in 1985. Although he won eight singles titles that year, none of them were Grand Slam events. Several factors may have contributed to McEnroe's decline. First, McEnroe was notoriously negligent in his training. Second, it was, perhaps ironically, his tantrums, thought to pump him up while he was champion, that contributed to his fall. His 1990 default from the Australian Open for bouncing his racquet and yelling numerous obscenities happened at a time when he seemed to have his game together. Sally Jenkins summed it up in an article for *Sports Illustrated*, "McEnroe's seven Grand Slam titles amount to about half of what he could have won had he bothered to train properly and gain control of his temper."

In 1986, McEnroe took a sabbatical, married actress Tatum O'Neil, his girlfriend of two years (after the birth of their first child, Kevin) and retreated to his Malibu, California, home. His break from tennis did not last long as he came back in August to face Boris Becker in a tournament in Stratton Mountain, Vermont. The match invited comparisons to the earlier Borg-McEnroe rivalries. Unfortunately, his comeback never fully took shape. He continued as a Davis Cup player and his successes in Cup play earned him more press than his occasional singles titles. McEnroe, who has four children, divorced O'Neil in 1992.

Sports Broadcasting and Charity Work

In 1995, McEnroe began to call matches with the U.S.A. coverage of the French Open. This began his present broadcasting career. He is a network television commentator for both NBC and CBS at Wimbledon, the French Open and the U.S. Open. He currently competes in a select number of tournaments and special events, largely for charity. Most of his charity work targets children's causes and he devotes a good deal of time to the Arthur Ashe foundation for the defeat of AIDS.

Unlike many top tennis players, tennis was not the end-all-be-all for McEnroe. He has always enjoyed a wide range of activities. An avid rock fan and guitar player, he occasionally plays at charity events. His interest in art led him to open an art gallery in New York City which features up-and-coming young artists. Although his lack of single-minded devotion may have brought his tennis career to a halt, his charitable activities have brought to the public eye a side of McEnroe that was unseen during his reign as champion.

Further Reading

Axthelm, Pete, "McEnroe: The Champ You Love to Hate," in *Newsweek*, Vol. 98, September 7, 1981, pp. 50-55.
Evans, Richard, *McEnroe: Taming the Talent*, 2nd ed., Penguin Books, 1990.

Sports Illustrated, January 27, 1986, pp. 70-71; June 8, 1992, p. 92; December 14, 1992, pp. 28-29.

Lincoln Library of Sports Champions, Vol. 11, Frontier Press, 1989, pp. 60-67.

Esquire, July 1987, pp. 84-88.

Phillips, B. J., "Fire and Ice at Wimbledon," in *Time,* Vol. 118, July 13, 1981, p. 65.

Sandomir, Richard, "You're Kidding, McEnroe Is Blunt?," in *New York Times,* Vol. 144, June 6, 1995.

Additional information provided by press material from International Management Group. □

Ralph Emerson McGill

The American journalist Ralph Emerson McGill (1898-1969) was the 1959 Pulitzer prize winner for his editorials on race, desegregation, and Southern politics—views that made him and the *Atlanta Constitution* major symbols of Southern liberalism.

Ralph McGill was born on February 3, 1898, on a farm in eastern Tennessee. When he was six the family moved to Chattanooga and lived on a farm bequeathed by his grandfather. McGill's father, who influenced his son with a passion for learning and who had changed his own name from Benjamin Wallace to Benjamin Franklin McGill, took a job as a salesman for a small heating and roofing company. The son's middle name came in honor of a friend who was a devotee of Ralph Waldo Emerson. McGill always had happy memories of his childhood and of his family, including his mother, Mary Lou Skillern McGill.

The region of his boyhood undoubtedly influenced McGill's later views. McGill recalled that "I lived in history," surrounded by monuments and memorabilia of the Civil War and its nearby battlefields. But Chattanooga was never a die-hard Southern city, and eastern Tennessee, a non-slaveholding area, had dominant Republican Party and Union sympathies. McGill's grandfathers had taken opposite sides in the war, and his parents had opposing party loyalties.

McGill, who customarily as a boy walked the two miles to the nearest library, pursued his education at McCallie Preparatory School, where he also played football. In 1917 he entered Vanderbilt University in Nashville, although he did not complete his undergraduate studies. At the university McGill befriended several people who forged the literary group known as the "Fugitives," although McGill did not join the group. He was especially close to Allen Tate and lived next door to Robert Penn Warren. Here also McGill found his enthusiasm for journalism with work on the campus paper the *Hustler* and part-time work with the city paper the *Banner.* In 1929 he joined the staff of the *Atlanta Constitution* as a sports writer, but he also covered other subjects, such as his stories on the Ku Klux Klan that he derived from personal interviews. In 1938 McGill became executive editor of the paper and in 1942 publisher.

At the *Atlanta Constitution* McGill was an appropriate distant successor to Henry W. Grady who in the 1880s had made the paper the vehicle of his "New South" philosophy, for McGill also championed a new South. He saw the region dominated by a series of local baronial autocrats who exploited the people they controlled and thrived from the corrupt political systems they nourished. McGill saw education and economic growth as the key to the South's progressive future but despaired that these forces of change could be generated from the inside. He consequently hailed migration into the South from outside and looked to new businessmen in the region to form a countervailing political voice to the regressive demagogues in the state capitals. McGill often breathed contempt for the Old South myths and remarked that the Confederate flag, worn on the black jackets of long-haired motorcyclists, had become a symbol of the social outcast. McGill constantly assailed Southern political leadership for its yielding to mob emotions and its failure to foster rational public dialogue on the day's critical issues.

McGill particularly recoiled from the outmoded recourse to "state's rights" by Southern politicians. This ancient shibboleth, he believed, had kept the South, from the antebellum years, through the Confederacy, and into the 20th century, in a backward and isolationist condition with respect to the rest of the nation. The dogma was essentially a cover for racism, he added, and he depicted Alabama Governor George Wallace as one who exploited the anachronism in inflammatory fashion. In the school integration crisis that struck the South in the late 1950s and the early

1960s McGill spoke out courageously for racial integration and won national attention for his efforts. He tried painstakingly to defuse the racial aspects of the issue by joining desegregation to the cause of children's education and the hope of lifting both black and white children of the South from the region's shameful record in public education.

Although some people found that McGill's views became tiresomely predictable, he was not a simple person. He wrote with a sense of irony about Southern life and appreciated the complexity of its history. He had a love of poetry that made his essays impassioned, sometimes lyrical, and always readable. He could be bitingly caustic, and his confrontational style was answered with the mean and degrading harrassment and intimidation that he and his family suffered from militant segregationists. McGill immersed himself in Southern history and could cite dates, statistics, and events for his editorial commentaries. He did some of his best and most interesting writing on Southern personalities past and present. His essays on Tom Watson, for example, show McGill's sense of the terrible irony of Southern history. In the story of this populist turned racist, McGill saw the liberal and progressive forces of the South succumb to the darker and more powerful hatred that ultimately consumed Watson and left a bitter legacy in Southern politics.

McGill, raised a Presbyterian, became an Episcopalian. He was married three times, his first two wives preceding him in death, and he had three children. McGill died February 5, 1969.

Further Reading

Much has been written about McGill, but one may best begin with his own partly autobiographical account, *The South and the Southerner* (1969), a prize-winning book that contains many reflections on Southern life and history. *Southern Encounters: Southerners of Note in Ralph McGill's South* (1983), edited by Calvin M. Logue, has McGill essays on a variety of people from Martin Luther King, Jr. to Lester Maddox. Some of the best of McGill's essays appeared in *Saturday Review*, including "The Case for the Southern Progressive" (June 13, 1964), "The Decade of Slow, Painful Progress" (May 16, 1964), and "Race: Results Instead of Reasons" (January 9, 1965). A comprehensive biography, with details of McGill's professional and private life, is Harold H. Martin's *Ralph McGill, Reporter* (1973). Also useful is Logue, *Ralph McGill: Editor and Publisher* (1969). □

Alexander McGillivray

Alexander McGillivray (ca. 1759-1793) was the American Indian chief of the Creek nation during the period of Spanish and American rivalries for Florida.

Alexander McGillivray lived until the age of 14 at his father's trading post on the Tallapoosa River. His mother belonged to a clan of the Creek Indians and was half French; his father, a Scot, was a trader with political influence among the Creeks. In 1773 McGillivray went to Charleston, S.C., and then to Savannah, Ga., where he received a good education. He then worked in a mercantile firm and continued to study history.

During the American Revolution, McGillivray's father served the British. Because he was a loyalist, his property was confiscated, and he fled to Scotland; McGillivray returned to his mother's people. After the war, McGillivray's alliance with British traders in Spanish Florida against the Americans was of great importance, for, at his mother's death, the council chose him as their tribal leader. Soon he was called Emperor of the Creek Nation, a title he fancied.

McGillivray's goal was to form an alliance of southern Indians and use aid from England and Spain to force the United States to withdraw from Georgia, Kentucky, and Tennessee. In 1784 he signed a treaty with Spain making him a colonel on a salary of $50 per month. In return Spain would monopolize trade with the Creeks, and McGillivray was to expel the Americans.

Hating the Americans for confiscating his family's property, McGillivray began a war on the United States; battles soon were being fought from Georgia to Cumberland, Tenn. This war was so successful that in 1787 a congressional agent visited McGillivray. Possibly the Creek chief suggested that the Creeks be organized and admitted as a state. That same year the Spaniards stopped supplying munitions to McGillivray. This supplying resumed in 1789, but the Spaniards never fully trusted him again.

With the organization of a stronger U.S. government, President George Washington sent agents to negotiate with the Creeks. The first attempt failed. But in 1790 McGillivray was persuaded to journey to New York City; there he repudiated his treaty with Spain and signed an agreement with the United States ceding some Creek lands and making him a brigadier general with pay of $1,200 per year. With his income McGillivray became owner of three plantations and 60 slaves.

Soon after his return from New York, McGillivray made a new agreement with Spain repudiating the Treaty of New York; he received $2,000 per year from the Spaniards (raised later to $3,500 annually). On Feb. 17, 1793, while negotiating with the Spaniards to raise another Indian confederation to oppose the United States, he died of a fever.

Further Reading

The best work on McGillivray is John Walton Caughey, *McGillivray of the Creeks* (1938). Other details may be secured from John Pope, *A Tour through the Southern and Western Territories of the United States* (1792), and David H. Corkran, *The Creek Frontier, 1540-1783* (1967). □

George Stanley McGovern

George Stanley McGovern (born 1922), a U.S. senator since 1962 and an early opponent of the war in Vietnam, was the unsuccessful Democratic candidate for president in 1972.

George McGovern was born on July 19, 1922, in Avon, South Dakota, a son of the Middle Border—the great prairie region steeped in agrarian, small-town, churchgoing ways and in populist liberalism and hope. His father, Joseph McGovern, a Wesleyan Methodist preacher, was stern about faith and morals and regarded drinking, smoking, and dancing as temptations to be fled. Joseph McGovern's last pastorate was at Mitchell, South Dakota, where George attended school.

George's formative years were shaped by the Puritan ethos of work, self-restraint, abstinence, sacrifice, and inner discipline. He was a shy, bookish boy, but he discovered himself in high school debating and was so good at it that he got a scholarship to attend Dakota Wesleyan University in 1940.

At college McGovern wooed a girl he had met in his high school debating, Eleanor Stegeberg, whom he later married. In 1942 he enlisted in the U.S. Army Air Force; he flew 35 missions in Europe as a bomber pilot, although he hated flying and did it only because of his sense of duty, and he was decorated for valor.

Political Interest Grows

After his discharge in 1945 McGovern was torn between history study and the ministry. Feeling drawn to the Social Gospel movement of Walter Rauschenbusch, with its emphasis on applying Christian ethics to practical life, McGovern entered a theological seminary in 1946 and became a student minister. He left after a year to do graduate

work in history at Northwestern University, receiving his master's degree in 1950, and then taught at Dakota Wesleyan until 1953. That year he received his doctorate from Northwestern with a socially conscious dissertation on the Colorado coal strikes and the "Ludlow massacre" of 1914. The Northwestern years were the watershed for McGovern, turning him into a strong believer in the Democratic left. But in 1948 he supported the Progressive party candidacy of Henry A. Wallace and was a delegate to their convention—where he encountered a "fanaticism" that troubled him, and in the end did not vote. But his anti-cold war liberalism continued, his national and world horizons broadened.

McGovern became executive secretary of the South Dakota Democratic party in 1953, a year of low Democratic morale, in a state where the party scarcely existed; he served until 1956, when he was elected to Congress. He was reelected in 1958. After he lost a senatorial race in 1960, McGovern was director of the Food for Peace program (1961-1962) and then ran again for the Senate and won. In January 1965 he made a major speech in the Senate against the war in Vietnam and thereafter was a leading dove. When Allard Lowenstein, the organizer of the movement to dump President Lyndon Johnson, asked McGovern to challenge Johnson in the 1968 primaries, McGovern refused, preferring to focus on reelection to the Senate. After Robert Kennedy's assassination in 1968 McGovern entered the convention struggle belatedly against Hubert Humphrey and Eugene McCarthy, and while he made little delegate impact he grew certain of his future course.

A Bid for the Presidency

On Jan. 18, 1971, McGovern announced his candidacy for the presidential nomination with a pledge to remove all American troops from Southeast Asia if elected. In the 1972 primaries, despite all the polls, McGovern came up from behind—using a populist appeal on taxes and other reforms as well as a sharp antiwar stand—and captured the Democratic nomination for president at the Miami convention in July. In the election he and his running mate, Sargent Shriver, were defeated by Republicans Richard Nixon and Spiro Agnew; McGovern received 38 percent of the popular vote and carried only Massachusetts and the District of Columbia, with 17 electoral votes. After this crushing defeat, McGovern was reelected to the Senate in 1974. He lost the seat to James Abdnor in the 1980 election.

McGovern again tossed his hat into the presidential ring in 1983, when he announced his candidacy for the 1984 Democratic nomination. His main campaign issues would be promoting a national health care system and decreasing the military's budget. He ended his bid after trailing in early primary elections.

Although McGovern considered running for president again in 1992, he never did again. In 1991, he took over as head of the Middle East Policy Council, an organization dedicated to better public understanding of the region. He made several trips to the Middle East in conjunction with this responsibility. In 1993, he submitted a proposition to President Clinton calling the United States to protect access to Arabian oil by cracking down on Israel for its failure to end conflict with Arab countries.

Innkeeper

In 1988, McGovern fulfilled a lifelong dream by purchasing the Stratford Hotel in Connecticut. He owned the hotel for two and half years. The hotel went out of business in part because of two lawsuits brought against McGovern by guests that were injured on his property. As a result, he began to believe that the existing law made it too easy to bring lawsuits against business owners. In several magazine articles and newspaper editorials, he called for tort reform. It was very unusual position for a lifelong liberal to take and McGovern was criticized for this by consumer advocate Ralph Nader.

Writing Career

McGovern wrote about political subjects throughout his career, publishing numerous articles, and the books *War Against Want* in 1964, and *A Time of War, a Time of Peace* in 1968. In 1996, he published *Terry: My Daughter's Life and Death Struggle With Alcoholism,* a frank discussion of the circumstances that led his daughter to freeze to death after a night of heavy drinking. The book was a moving portrait of his daughter, and the impact of his career on her life. It was widely reviewed and received excellent notices.

Further Reading

A good biography is Robert S. Anson, *McGovern* (1972). □

William Holmes McGuffey

Through his enormously popular series of elementary school readers, William Holmes McGuffey (1800-1873) educated several generations of Americans.

Williliam McGuffey was born on Sept. 28, 1800, in Washington County, Pa. He learned his letters at home, was tutored in Latin by a nearby minister, and attended the Old Stone Academy in Darlington, Pa. He graduated from Washington College in 1826 and became professor of ancient languages at Miami University in Oxford, Ohio. In 1829 he was licensed to preach in the Presbyterian Church.

In 1836 McGuffey was elected president of Cincinnati College, where he became prominently associated with a citizens' group seeking to promote public education. This group, which evolved into the Western Literary Institute, sponsored educational meetings and successfully lobbied for the organization of Ohio's common schools.

McGuffey's interest in public education led to a publishing agreement to produce a series of elementary readers to serve student needs on the western frontier, which was divided by ethnic differences and denominational factions. In 1836 the first and second *Eclectic Readers* were pub-

lished, initiating a series that ended in 1857 with the sixth *Eclectic Reader,* compiled by McGuffey's brother.

Each *Reader,* carefully graduated in difficulty, was a compilation of classical selections, homely aphorisms, and patriotic messages that set a dour tone of piety, thrift, and industry. The righteous wisdom of the *Readers,* deriving as much from Benjamin Franklin's *Poor Richard's Almanac* as from John Calvin's writings, dictated the moral position and literary taste of emerging America, influencing the courts, statehouses, and home-steads alike. The growth of free common schools, the stringent nonsectarian Protestantism of the books, and a choice of readings that appealed to all walks of life in all sections of the nation gave the *Readers* great popularity. It is estimated that over 120 million copies were sold in English and various translations, primarily during the 19th century. Although they no longer reflect the dominant mood of America, the *Readers* still command a nostalgic following in some areas.

McGuffey became president of Ohio University in 1839 and professor of natural and moral philosophy at the University of Virginia in 1845. With characteristic energy, he continued revising and enlarging the *Readers,* substituting American for English selections as they became available but never tampering with his successful formula. Although his celebrity rested on his texts, McGuffey achieved local eminence as a teacher at Virginia rather than as a scholar. His sole scholarly effort, a book on mental philosophy, was a derivative and outmoded defense of Protestant orthodoxy published posthumously. He died in Charlottesville on May 4, 1873.

Further Reading

The essentials of McGuffey's life and a detailed analysis of the various editions of the *Readers* are in Harvey C. Minnich, *William Holmes McGuffey and His Readers* (1936). Ruth M. Elson, in *Guardians of Tradition: American Schoolbooks of the Nineteenth Century* (1964), contrasts the McGuffey series with other texts. See also Richard D. Mosier, *Making the American Mind: Social and Moral Ideas in the McGuffey Readers* (1947), and Alice M. Ruggles, *The Story of the McGuffeys* (1950).

Additional Sources

Crawford, Benjamin Franklin, *The life of William Holmes McGuffey,* Delaware, Ohio, Carnegie Church Press 1974.

Sullivan, Dolores P., *William Holmes McGuffey: schoolmaster to the nation,* Rutherford, N.J.: Fairleigh Dickinson University Press; London: Associated University Presses, 1994.

Westerhoff, John H., *McGuffey and his readers: piety, morality, and education in nineteenth-century America,* Nashville: Abingdon, 1978. □

Samuel McIntire

Samuel McIntire (1757-1811), American builder and furniture maker, was the most representative craftsman in New England in the late 18th century.

Samuel McIntire was born in Salem, Mass., and his career was summarized in his obituary in the *Salem Gazette* on Feb. 12, 1811: "Mr. McIntire was originally bred to the occupation of a housewright (his father's trade), but his vigorous mind soon passed the ordinary limits of his profession, and aspired to the highest departments of the interesting and admirable science of architecture. . . . To a delicate native taste in this art, he had united a high degree of that polish which can only be acquired by an assiduous study of the great classical masters; with whose works, notwithstanding their rarity in this country, Mr. M. had a very intimate acquaintance."

McIntire's evolution from artisan-carpenter through master craftsman and professional sculptor to the position of head architect of an "office" (consisting in this case mainly of his son and his brothers) can be traced by stylistic analysis of works attributable to him. The earlier (1782) parts of the Pierce-Nichols House in Salem, which McIntire designed from the half-century-old *Builder's Treasury* of Batty Langley, are relatively naive in conception. However, growing refinement is visible in the later (1801) woodwork in the hall, east parlor, and chamber of the house. The Pingree House (1804) in Salem reveals decorative and spatial subtleties suggesting the influence of Charles Bulfinch.

McIntire stamped Salem with his personality; the stylistic standards and character of the town's architecture were established in his shop. In Sidney Fiske Kimball's words (1940): "Salem at the end of his life presented a very different aspect from its appearance when he began his work. The churches and public buildings had been rebuilt or re-

modelled from his designs . . . rows of tall stately mansions, a great number from McIntire's hand, lined Essex Street, Federal Street, and Washington Square. That was no idle phrase when the town clerk called Samuel McIntire . . . 'the architect of Salem.'"

In 1792 McIntire, who had never left his native town, submitted a design for the national capitol. Though unsuccessful, it was an indication of how times were changing, so that a man thoroughly in the tradition of anonymous artisanship could now assert individuality and make his art a means of personal expression, fame, and fortune as never before.

McIntire's achievement was recognized by his contemporaries. "This day," wrote Salem diarist William Bentley on hearing of McIntire's death, "Salem is deprived of one of the most ingenious men it had in it." And on his tombstone McIntire was recorded as "distinguished for Genius in Architecture, Sculpture and Musick."

Further Reading

Sidney Fiske Kimball rediscovered McIntire in his *American Architecture* (1928) and later devoted a special monograph to him, *Samuel McIntire, Carver: The Architect of Salem* (1940). Decades of research were summarized in Benjamin W. Labaree, ed., *Samuel McIntire: A Bicentennial Symposium 1757-1957* (1957). □

Claude McKay

Claude McKay (1890-1948), Jamaican-born poet and novelist, is often called "the first voice of the Harlem renaissance." His verse and fiction are best known for protesting the social evils that plagued blacks.

Claude McKay was born in Jamaica, British West Indies, on Sept. 15, 1890. He began writing poetry, principally in Jamaican dialect, while a schoolboy. After a brief apprenticeship to a cabinetmaker and a short time as a policeman, he went to the United States and enrolled at Tuskegee Institute; later he went to Kansas State University. Neither school suited him, so he moved to New York, where a little interest in his first two volumes of poems—*Constab Ballads* and *Songs from Jamaica* (published in England, 1912)—preceded him.

Under the name Eli Edwards, McKay published a number of poems in American magazines; under his own name he published (in England) *Spring in New Hampshire* (1920). He was listed as associate editor of the *Liberator,* a "radical" magazine, which was the first to print "If We Must Die." This poem has come to be thought of as the birth cry of the "new Negro." It set the tone of protest that marks his fourth and best-known volume of verse, *Harlem Shadows* (1922), which also contains poems on conventional romantic themes.

In 1922 McKay represented the American Workers party at the Third Internationale in Moscow. He stayed in Europe for several years, settling in southern France, where he wrote most of his fiction. *Home to Harlem* (1928), a sensational revelation of black ghetto life, is his best-known novel. *Banjo* (1929) does for the French seaport city of Marseilles what the first novel did for New York's Harlem: it portrays life in the lower depths. *Gingertown* (1932) is a volume of unexceptional short stories, and *Banana Bottom* (1933), set in the West Indies, returns to his earlier subject matter. His fiction tended to be sensationally "realistic" and to emphasize those sordid elements in Negro life that attracted the prurient interest of the public.

Back in America in 1936 McKay wrote his autobiography, *A Long Way from Home* (1937). The fluent ease that characterized his best prose style is missing in this book. In 1940 he published *Harlem: Negro Metropolis,* a kind of sociohistorical narrative that is interesting but without much substance.

All but forgotten, McKay died in Chicago on May 22, 1948. *Selected Poems of Claude McKay* appeared in 1953.

Further Reading

There is no full-length work, either critical or biographical, on McKay. For critical comments see J. Saunders Redding, *To Make a Poet Black* (1939); Sterling A. Brown, Arthur P. Davis, and Ulysses Lee, eds., *Negro Caravan: Writings by American Negroes* (1940); Rebecca C. Barton, *Witnesses for Freedom: Negro Americans in Autobiography* (1948); Hugh M. Gloster,

Negro Voices in American Fiction (1948); and Stephen H. Bronz, *Roots of Negro Racial Consciousness, the 1920s: Three Harlem Renaissance Authors* (1964). □

Donald McKay

Donald McKay (1810-1880), American ship builder, designed and constructed many of the world's great clipper ships that set numerous transoceanic speed records.

Donald McKay was born on a farm in Shelburne County, Nova Scotia. He was educated in the common schools there and was apprenticed as a ship carpenter in New York City after emigrating in 1827. After mastering his trade, he was commissioned in 1839 to finish a ship in Wiscasset, Maine. He soon formed a partnership in Newburyport, Mass., where he built a number of packet ships. As his reputation spread, he received other assignments for design and construction. In 1844 he was chosen to build a ship for the transatlantic traffic by Enoch Train, who also induced him to set up a shipyard in East Boston.

This was the dawn of the clipper ship era. There was great demand for ships that could guarantee fast delivery of cargo from China, as well as rapid passage to the goldfields of California and Australia. Great emphasis was placed on the design of these clipper ships so that they could successfully travel long distances at high speed. McKay applied the most advanced theories of design and construction in his yard, personally supervising every step, from the laying of the keel to the final outfitting. He turned out the greatest tonnage of successful clippers in the world.

McKay's name became synonymous with excellence from the first clipper, the *Stag Hound* in 1850, to the last, the *Glory of the Seas,* launched in 1869. Among his most famous vessels were the *Flying Cloud, Sovereign of the Seas, Lightning,* and the *Great Republic.* His vessels set marks, some of which are still unsurpassed.

The Panic of 1857 adversely affected McKay, but he survived the lean years that followed by building less spectacular ships. Travel and study in Britain convinced him that the day of the armored steamship was at hand, and he made serious efforts to persuade the U.S. government to replace outmoded naval sailing vessels.

During the Civil War, McKay built ships for the U.S. Navy, and in the postwar years, after retooling his yard, he devoted himself to building steamships. His merely moderate success in these endeavors led him to dispose of his yard in 1869. Ill health forced him to retire in 1877. He died at his country estate in Hamilton, Mass.

Further Reading

Richard Cornelius McKay, *Some Famous Sailing Ships and Their Builder, Donald McKay* (1928), has a good biography. John Robinson, *The Sailing Ships of New England* (1924), includes a long section on McKay. Alexander Kinnan Laing, *Clipper Ship Men* (1944), deals with McKay and his contemporaries. William Armstrong Fairburn, *Merchant Sail* (6 vols., 1945-1955), has extensive material on McKay and his ships.

Additional Sources

McKay, Richard C. (Richard Cornelius), *Donald McKay and his famous sailing ships,* New York: Dover Publications, 1995.

McKay, Richard C. (Richard Cornelius), *Some famous sailing ships and their builder, Donald McKay: a study of the American sailing packet and clipper eras, with biographical sketches of America's foremost designer and master-builder of ships, and a comprehensive history of his many famous ships,* Norwalk, Conn.: Easton Press, 1988. □

Charles Follen McKim

Charles Follen McKim (1847-1909), American architect, was the founding partner in the firm of McKim, Mead & White, which set the standard for architectural taste in the United States between 1879 and 1909.

Charles Follen McKim was born at Isabella Furnace, Pa., on Aug. 24, 1847. His father was a fervent abolitionist and his mother was a Quaker. After attending the Weld School in New Jersey and Philadelphia public schools for 3 years, McKim entered Harvard's Scientific School in 1866. Finding his studies difficult and disagreeable, he tried instead the architectural course in Paris at the École des Beaux-Arts and spent 3 happy years there (1867-1870).

On his return to America, McKim began working in the architectural office of Gambrill and Richardson in New York City. Here McKim learned from Henry Hobson Richardson that architecture was a "fine art" and should be practiced as such. In 1872 McKim opened his own office in New York. His friend William Rutherford Mead soon joined him, and then a partnership was formed in 1878 with William B. Bigelow. Bigelow resigned and was replaced by the flamboyant Stanford White in 1879.

In 1874 McKim had married Annie Bigelow, William's sister; they were divorced in 1878. They had one daughter. In 1885 he married Julia Amory Appleton, who had commissioned him to build her summer home at Stockbridge, Mass. She died in 1887.

For McKim the first realization that classical architectural forms and ornament were finer than any other came during a sketching trip through New England in 1877 with Bigelow and White. They visited Salem, Marblehead, and Newburyport and made measured drawings of the best colonial houses.

As a summer resident of Newport, R. I., McKim was well acquainted with wealthy socialites, and many commissions came from these friends. The Newport Casino (1881) was one of his earliest buildings in the resort community. The design was appropriately informal, gay, and picturesque; its broad verandas easily coped with the crowds.

McKim and his partners designed the Villard houses (1882), which were attached to form a three-sided court, on Madison Avenue in New York City, in a style adapted from the Italian Renaissance. This veritable palace favorably impressed his client's friends and led them to choose McKim's firm to design many other buildings.

The complicated Boston Public Library (1887-1898), though generally Italianate, derives in part from Henri Labrouste's Bibliothèque Ste-Geneviève in Paris—particularly the high, arched windows that light the reading room. Many of McKim's artist friends, such as Augustus Saint-Gaudens, John LaFarge, and James McNeill Whistler, contributed their work to make the library a splendid museum of contemporary art.

McKim's guiding influence is visible in the correctly proportioned Johnson Gate (1889) at Harvard University; the Algonquin Club (1889) and Symphony Hall (1892) in Boston; the important Columbia University Library (1893-1896); the American Academy (1895-1904) in Rome; and the University Club (1896-1899), the Pierpont Morgan Library (1902), and the vast Pennsylvania Station (1902-1910; demolished) in New York City. McKim also represented the firm on the building commission for the Chicago World's Columbian Exposition (1890-1893) and designed the classical Agricultural Building.

McKim was a highly persuasive personality. He knew with confidence what was esthetically right; he knew how to please wealthy clients; and he designed with dignity and sobriety, never giving way to frills and picturesqueness for their own sake. He received many honors, including the coveted Royal Institute of British Architects King's Medal (1903), and honorary degrees from Harvard University, Bowdoin College, Columbia University, and the University of Pennsylvania. He was elected academician of the National Academy of Design in 1907 and was presented the Gold Medal of the American Institute of Architects in 1909. He died in St. James, Long Island, N. Y., on Sept. 14, 1909.

Further Reading

There is no definitive book on the firm of McKim, Mead & White, although four large volumes of plans and photographs were published. The best work on McKim is Charles Moore, *The Life and Times of Charles Follen McKim* (1929). Another work worth consulting is Alfred Hoyt Granger, *Charles Follen McKim: A Study of His Life and Work* (1913). □

William McKinley

William McKinley (1843-1901) was the twenty-fifth president of the United States. During his administration the Spanish-American War of 1898 overshadowed the two important issues of tariff and currency, presenting the United States with new problems of world power and territorial expansion.

With the growth of post-Civil War industrialism, serious social and economic problems developed in the United States. Agricultural depression brought severe hardship and farm unrest; relations between laborers and employers deteriorated; and Americans argued over what monetary policies the U.S. government should adopt to maintain a healthy economy.

As congressman, governor, and president, William McKinley emphasized obtaining prosperity by stimulating American business via a favorable tariff structure. Although early in his career he directed his energies toward protective tariffs on finished materials, he later favored tariffs modified by reciprocity treaties. Under these, he hoped that raw materials would enter the United States at low tariff rates, making possible low prices on finished goods, which could then compete on the world market. By agreeing to admit raw materials with low tariffs, the United States would gain low tariff entry to other nations for finished products.

Second in McKinley's thinking was the currency problem. Much of the political debate in the late 19th century focused on the currency question—whether the amount of currency in circulation should be increased and, if so, by what means. For 30 years McKinley advocated limited silver coinage. Yet, by the time he became president, he had been converted to international bimetallism: an agreement by several countries to base currency on both gold and silver, set at a fixed ratio. If international bimetallism was unobtainable, he favored maintaining currency soundness by using the gold standard. Devoted to business interests and a healthy economy, McKinley supported a foreign policy creating new markets for United States products. This was particularly manifest in his handling of the Spanish-American War and in the open-door policy with China.

Background and Early Career

William McKinley was born in Niles, Ohio, on Jan. 29, 1843. He was educated and later taught school in Ohio. In the Civil War he fought with the Union Army. Discharged with the brevet rank of major, he studied law briefly at the Albany Law School and opened an office in Canton, Ohio, in 1867, simultaneously plunging into Republican politics.

First elected to public office as Stark County prosecuting attorney in 1869, McKinley became a congressman in 1876. In and out of the House of Representatives until 1890 (depending on the gerrymandering of his district) he rose steadily in influence within Ohio Republican politics as well as in national circles. During this period, many prominent politicians came from Ohio. Although this made competition for leadership in the state very keen, it also assisted ambitious young men. For example, having served under Rutherford B. Hayes in the Civil War, McKinley continued to benefit from his counsel and prominence.

The Ohio Republican party, mirroring the diversity of the state, was held together through compromises, by middle-of-the-roaders. Moreover, Ohio was a two-party state, with Democrats effectively vying for all offices. A successful politician had to be sensitive to the wishes of farmers, steel mill owners, emerging labor unions, urban ethnic enclaves, city machines, soft-currency men, and powerful figures in commerce and finance. Aware of this, McKinley tried to balance between extreme positions on tariffs and on fiscal policy. This moderation was a key to his handling of men and his approach to problems.

McKinley made some concessions to the Ohio forces demanding bimetallism, cloaking his restrained advocacy of silver coinage with exhortations that currency must be stable and safe. On one side, gold proponents argued that every dollar should be backed by gold and the government should purchase no other metals. On the other side, silver forces argued for widespread silver purchasing and distribution of paper based on silver. Greenback forces advocated increasing the volume of paper money, without attempting to maintain deposits of metal sufficient for redemption. Finally, some argued that the best system would be an international agreement for currency based on both gold and silver. McKinley accepted something of each argument, emerging with views that were palatable rather than consistent or rational.

Not innovative in approaching issues, McKinley responded to others' suggestions without becoming a captive of their ideas. To some extent, his interest in tariff problems exceeded the sophistication of his economic analysis: in this, he shared the view widespread in the Republican party that tariff legislation was critical to the nation's economy.

Skilled in organization and administration, McKinley was effective with other politicians and convincing to constituents. He was considered sincere and amiable. Identified first with the Ohio gubernatorial campaign of Rutherford B. Hayes, he later supported Joseph Foraker for governor, Hayes for president, and, still later, John Sherman and then James G. Blaine for the presidency. At several national Republican conventions, he played a prominent role, primarily because he was able to compromise party disharmony and to defend the tariff policy.

Congressman and Governor

McKinley's forte in Congress was the tariff, which he believed was the key to economic vitality. He defended the tariff as a means of producing higher wages by expanding home markets; expanding home markets would be possible only if low-cost foreign products were kept off United States markets. Initially he supported high protective tariffs, but later he advocated a scheme of selective tariffs tied to reciprocity provisions.

After serving on the House Judiciary Committee and the Ways and Means Committee, McKinley became chairman of the latter in 1889, charged with bringing forth a new tariff bill. The McKinley Tariff of 1890, including limited reciprocity provisions, was oriented toward protection and included many compromise provisions favorable to special-interest groups. His tariff posture helped spread his fame outside the halls of Congress, even though he was defeated in the election of 1890.

Mark Hanna, a wealthy Cleveland industrialist, lent assistance to McKinley after 1890, helping him win the Ohio gubernatorial race in 1891 and secure reelection in 1893. Hanna, a skillful organizer and generous donor, encouraged McKinley to travel and to speak on public issues, especially the tariff. McKinley's views on fiscal policy had not been consistent, and he viewed the passion of the silver issue as misdirected.

As governor, McKinley won labor sympathy by contributing to relief funds for strikers, as well as by passing laws favorable to labor. Labor leaders, normally suspicious of a politician so sympathetic to industry, gave him lukewarm backing.

By the opening of the 1896 Republican convention in St. Louis, McKinley was the logical choice for the presidential nomination. Hanna's planning, McKinley's identification with tariffs as the protectors of prosperity, plus his ability to blur issues and to hold together a party split over both tariffs and currency gave him important advantages. As nominee, McKinley campaigned from Canton, Ohio, in a restrained manner, stressing that a Republican victory would mean prosperity for the nation. His opponent, William Jennings Bryan, traveled extensively, emphasizing the merits of free silver and seeming to challenge the familiar patterns of American politics. To many, Bryan seemed a threat to the whole system of government, if not to the social order. After a bitter campaign, McKinley, benefiting from the anti-Democratic voting pattern visible since 1893, swept handily into the White House.

The President

For his Cabinet, McKinley chose politicians and businessmen, including John Sherman as secretary of state. Later, he added several other men of considerable stature and ability. Though he had enjoyed cordial relations with colleagues in Congress, he settled for a cautious domestic program, central to which was tariff reform. The Dingley Tariff, incorporating additional reciprocity features, raised tariffs to new heights. Administration efforts to promote international bimetallism came to naught, opening the way to the passage of the Gold Standard Act of 1900 (legalizing the gold standard and setting aside special funds for currency redemption). The battle between gold and silver was for all practical purposes at an end, as world production of gold increased simultaneously with the return of prosperity.

Benefiting from better times, McKinley skillfully manipulated both politicians and the public, welding a more united Republican party with tours and personal charm. His domestic program and achievements as party leader were overwhelmed, however, by the diplomatic imbroglio that led to the Spanish-American War and annexation of overseas territories.

The Cuban revolution of 1895 against Spain inflamed United States citizens for various reasons: the press reported in detail the savage repressive techniques used by the Spanish army; American sugar companies decried the interruption of their trade and profit by protracted war; and some business and financial leaders saw declaration of war against Spain as necessary for the growth of American trade and the stability of the stock market. Meanwhile, proponents of world power and leadership for the United States spread the opinion that Spanish tyranny had to be curtailed in the Western Hemisphere. The fever pitch of interest in the

1896 election and the agrarian resentment of the 1890s were replaced by widespread calls for war.

To these pressures McKinley responded reluctantly, resisting congressional insistence on war in favor of negotiation with Spain. He preferred an autonomous Cuba, perhaps loosely linked to Spain—a suggestion that Spain at first resisted strongly and then accepted. But events moved too fast: domestic pressure for war was very strong, and McKinley hardened his policy, going to Congress with a war message in April 1898. By that time Spain had met most of McKinley's earlier demands, but it was too late to avert a military clash.

The Spanish-American War was brief, with United States forces triumphant over the Spanish fleet in the Philippines and later over both land and naval forces in Cuba. In establishing peace terms, the United States faced the vexatious problem of how to dispose of former Spanish colonies. The President, admitting to indecision and lack of knowledge, was urged by anti-imperialists to renounce permanent sovereignty or protectorate arrangements as hostile to American traditions of freedom of choice for peoples. However, the proannexation forces carried the day, arguing that national interest lay with expansion, that it was America's duty to uplift the people of the Spanish possessions, and that relinquishing the Philippines would invite a power scramble among other nations. Confused and uncertain, McKinley finally opted for annexation of the Philippines, which was accomplished by the Treaty of Paris (ratified in 1899). Cuba was set free of Spain; Puerto Rico and Guam were ceded to the United States. In choosing territorial expansion, McKinley was enhancing the prospects for development of United States trade, an end to which he had long been devoted.

One of the key pins of American diplomacy was securing trade rights, preferably without political or military intervention. To safeguard trading rights in the Far East, McKinley sent to the Great Powers the open-door notes of 1899 and 1900. Basically, these stipulated that the United States expected nations with spheres of influence in China not to interfere with American rights and privileges nor to discriminate against other nations in setting port and railroad rates.

The major issue of the 1900 campaign, in which McKinley was again opposed by Bryan, was imperialism, though for all practical purposes the decisions had already been taken. McKinley was reelected by a large margin. Of great concern during his second administration were problems of governing the new dependencies. But before McKinley could turn to another round of tariff reform, he was shot by Leon F. Czolgosz, an anarchist, in Buffalo, N.Y., on Sept. 6, 1901. McKinley died eight days later.

Further Reading

The best biographies of McKinley are Margaret Leech, *In the Days of McKinley* (1959), and Howard W. Morgan, *William McKinley and His America* (1963). George H. Mayer, *The Republican Party, 1854-1966* (2d ed. 1967), describes Republican politics on the national level; and Joseph R. Hollingsworth, *The Whirligig of Politics: The Democracy of*

Cleveland and Bryan (1963), emphasizes the contest between the Republican and Democratic parties at the turn of the century. The excitement of the 1896 election is captured in Paul W. Glad, *McKinley, Bryan and the People* (1964). For an overview Harold U. Faulkner, *Politics, Reform, and Expansion, 1890-1900* (1959), is helpful. A broader view of the problems in the United States faced after Reconstruction is offered by Robert H. Wiebe, *The Search for Order, 1877-1920* (1967). □

Floyd B. McKissick

Under the direction of Floyd B. McKissick (1922-1991), the Congress of Racial Equality (CORE) moved more firmly into the Black Power movement, refusing to support Martin Luther King's call for massive nonviolent civil disobedience in northern cities, concentrating instead on programs aimed at increasing the political power and improving the economic position of African Americans. In 1967 the organization moved to eliminate the word "multiracial" from its constitution.

As head of the Congress of Racial Equality (CORE), Floyd B. McKissick helped to determine the direction of the Black Power movement during the turbulent 1960s. McKissick, who was national chairman of CORE from 1963 to 1966, and national director from 1966 to 1968, incited members of his organization into spearheading a nonviolent "revolution" that would widen civic, political, and economic opportunities for blacks; he also helped to popularize the "Black Power" slogan.

McKissick was the first black student admitted to the University of North Carolina at Chapel Hill Law School. Having earned the right to practice law in his home state of North Carolina, he dedicated his legal talents and expertise to the cause of integrating the South. Ironically, later in his life he was accused of harboring separatist sentiments when he used federal aid to fund Soul City, a North Carolina community dedicated to black business opportunity. That very vision drew praise from the Reverend Ben Chavis, who proclaimed in the *Atlanta Journal:* "The [civil rights] struggle was never about individuals, but about lifting up a race of people. We need to exemplify what Floyd was about."

No More Uncle Toms

Floyd Bixler McKissick was born in the affluent community of Asheville, North Carolina, in 1922. A summer vacation spot for the wealthy near the Smokey Mountains, Asheville boasted several large hotels and estates. McKissick's father worked at the Vanderbilt Hotel as head bellhop, a position that provided the family financial comfort at the cost of individual dignity. According to the *New York Post,* McKissick's father told him: "There isn't going to be but one [Uncle] Tom in this family, and that's going to be me. So you go out and get yourself an education, so you

don't have to be an Uncle Tom." The same message was repeated to McKissick's three sisters, who also attended college and took white collar jobs.

McKissick's later talents as a speaker and a leader may have been honed by watching his grandfathers, both of whom were ministers—his paternal grandfather in the Baptist faith and his maternal grandfather in the Methodist faith. Up until his death in 1991, McKissick was an active member of the Baptist denomination, serving as a deacon and a youth leader.

Even though he was an excellent student and a model citizen, McKissick had his share of unfair experiences as a black youngster in the South. One pivotal incident occurred when he was 12 years old. A member of the Boy Scouts of America, he was assigned by his scoutmaster to direct traffic during an all-black, street roller skating tournament. A policeman who spotted him performing the task knocked him down and then arrested him. "I knew then that God's word wasn't reaching folks the way it ought to," McKissick disclosed in the New York Post years later.

McKissick worked his way through high school by delivering groceries and newspapers and by shining shoes. He graduated from high school at the outset of World War II and was drafted into the Army, where he climbed the ranks to sergeant. Seeing action in Europe, he was awarded a Purple Heart for an injury sustained during battle. After the war, McKissick used funds from the GI bill to help him attend college. He entered the all-black Morehouse College

in Atlanta, but returned to North Carolina College in Durham to complete his degree.

An Activist and Groundbreaker

Aware of the odds against his career development in the segregated South, McKissick became a member and firm supporter of the National Association for the Advancement of Colored People (NAACP); while still in college he was named youth chairman of the North Carolina NAACP. McKissick was also an early member of the Congress of Racial Equality, an interracial organization that sought to publicize the plight of blacks through nonviolent demonstrations. In 1947 McKissick joined CORE founder James Farmer on the Journey of Reconciliation—an integrated bus ride through parts of the South. All along the way, the CORE bus riders—black and white—were subjected to hostility and even physical violence by some Southern whites. The members of CORE eventually triumphed, however. The Freedom Rides resulted in the desegregation of 120 interstate bus terminals in the South.

Having determined that he wanted to become a lawyer, McKissick applied to the University of North Carolina at Chapel Hill Law School in the early the 1950s. The school was not integrated, hence McKissick was denied admission. With the help of NAACP lawyer Thurgood Marshall—who would one day distinguish himself as a Supreme Court justice—McKissick sued the college and won. He became the first black law student at the university, and the first to earn an LL.B. degree there.

That experience, and his work with CORE, filled McKissick with a sense of righteous indignation over the lack of opportunities for blacks. He saw injustice everywhere, not just in the South, and—like Marshall before him—was determined to use his legal talents to change the prevailing norms. McKissick informed the New York Post that he realized education was not the sole solution for oppressed American blacks. "I was as educated as any white lawyer in my area," he commented. "Do you think I had the opportunity to be a judge? . . . You can educate the black man [but] you've got to overcome the racism to get him the job. There's got to be some counterpart in education of that portion of the white community that is bigoted."

Using his own children as test cases, McKissick successfully challenged several all-white schools in Durham, North Carolina. He also quickly became an *ad hoc* lawyer for CORE, defending demonstrators who were brought to trial on charges of sitting at lunch counters and in theaters marked "for whites only." At one point in the early 1960s, McKissick's law firm was handling 5,600 cases simultaneously, and the zealous lawyer was traveling throughout the United States.

Work With CORE

Founded in 1942, CORE was an integrated group, well attended by liberal whites. The group became famous for sit-ins and demonstrations, lawsuits against segregated public accommodations, and active support for black economic advancement and opportunity. As a high-ranking official in CORE, McKissick was concerned with the segment of the black population that suffered under, but could not change, the status quo. While others pointed to the progress the civil rights movement was making in the areas of school and public facility integration, McKissick complained that those changes were cosmetic and that the economic gulf was only widening for blacks in the South and for those in northern cities.

McKissick was not alone in this assessment. As the 1960s progressed, more and more blacks became impatient with the rate of social change. The words revolution and power began to surface as rallying cries. CORE responded by replacing national chairman Charles R. Oldham, a white man, with McKissick in 1963. In his acceptance speech for the unpaid position, McKissick suggested that if blacks could not obtain their rights through the courts, they must resort to direct action. He warned that if the white majority ignored nonviolent black protests, a violence born of intense frustration would follow. His dire predictions would came true in 1965 and the summers following, when race riots broke out in a number of U.S. cities.

In January 1966, McKissick succeeded James Farmer as national director of CORE. He took over the office in March and quickly made a name for himself as an impassioned advocate of federal aid to inner cities and as an avid protester of American involvement in the Vietnam War. Echoing Muhammad Ali's famous refusal to fight because no North Vietnamese person had ever called him "nigger," McKissick asserted in the *Washington Post* that black men were "going over to Vietnam and dying for something that they don't have a right for here."

Under McKissick's direction, CORE moved more firmly into the Black Power movement. "Black power is no mere slogan," McKissick iterated in the *New York Times* in 1966. "It is a movement dedicated to the exercise of American democracy in its highest tradition; it is a drive to mobilize the black communities of this country in a monumental effort to remove the basic causes of alienation, frustration, despair, low self-esteem, and hopelessness." McKissick added that under his supervision, CORE would seek to bring political economic power to blacks, especially those in the ghetto.

Founded Soul City

McKissick resigned from his position with CORE in 1968. He was criticized in some quarters for becoming a Republican and supporting Richard Nixon's candidacy for president. That support yielded monetary rewards, however. In 1970 McKissick won federal funds from the New Communities Act to build a whole new town, Soul City, in rural North Carolina. Fired by visions of a black-run metropolis with business and industrial opportunities for minority enterprises, McKissick and his family became pioneer residents of Soul City. McKissick predicted that the community would have more than 40,000 residents by the turn of the century.

His plans never materialized; additional government grants did not arrive, and by the end of the 1970s the U.S. Department of Housing and Urban Development foreclosed on its multimillion dollar loan to the city. In 1991

it was estimated that Soul City had a population of about 200, all living in homes built by the federal government. Although the community has a health clinic and several small industries, retail shopping facilities are lacking. The nearest grocery store is 15 miles away, and the children must travel long distances to school by bus.

Atlanta Constitution correspondent Pete Scott suggested in 1991, though, that the Soul City experiment was far from a total failure. "Soul City . . . is a curious mix of the planned and unimagined," he noted. "It has never come close to the size or self-sufficiency that . . . McKissick had hoped for. But for the people who live there, it has become a closely knit community."

One year prior to his death, McKissick finally received a judicial appointment in North Carolina. The governor named him to the state's ninth district court in the autumn of 1990. By then McKissick was already suffering from lung cancer, which would claim his life in the spring of 1991. Up until his death he and his wife lived in Soul City at 2 Liberation Road. McKissick is buried in Soul City, several blocks from the house he shared with his family.

More than 700 mourners attended McKissick's funeral at the Union Baptist Church in Durham. One of the speakers at the service, the Reverend Jesse Jackson, recalled working with CORE as a young student and admiring the outspoken, idealistic McKissick. In his eulogy, quoted in the *Atlanta Journal,* Jackson concluded that Judge McKissick "had a big streak of crazy in him. He was permanently maladjusted. He would not adjust to segregation. He would not adjust to little ways of thinking."

Further Reading

Atlanta Constitution, May 5, 1991.
Atlanta Journal, May 3, 1991.
Los Angeles Times, April 30, 1991.
New York Post, April 25, 1966; June 20, 1967.
New York Times, June 30, 1963; July 8, 1966.
Washington Post, April 30, 1991. □

John McLean

The American politician and judge John McLean (1785-1861) was perhaps the most politically conscious justice in the history of the U.S. Supreme Court.

John McLean was born in Morris County, N.J., on March 11, 1785, to Fergus McLean, a Scotch-Irish Presbyterian weaver turned farmer, and Sophia Blackford McLean. The family moved several times with stops in western Virginia and Kentucky before settling in Warren County, Ohio, about 40 miles from Cincinnati, in 1797. In this frontier atmosphere McLean managed to get an irregular but sound education. His legal education was gained, starting in 1804, by simultaneously serving as apprentice to the clerk of the

Hamilton County Court of Common Pleas and reading law with Arthur St. Clair, Jr., for a 2-year period. In 1807 he founded a Jeffersonian weekly, *Western Star,* at Lebanon and married Rebecca Edwards. They had four daughters and three sons.

McLean became an enthusiastic Methodist through conversion by a circuit rider in 1811 and remained active in the faith throughout his life. Republican activities led in 1812 to his nomination and election to the U.S. House of Representatives, where he supported the administration in the fight with England. In 1816 the Ohio Legislature elected him to the state supreme court. A preview of his work on the U.S. Supreme Court was his opinion in the case of the slave Thomas Lunsford, in which he engaged in obiter dicta, maintaining that slavery was contrary to natural justice, but that "as judge I am sworn to support the Constitution of the United States." In Congress, McLean had effectively supported James Monroe's nomination.

In 1822 McLean was appointed commissioner of the Public Land Office. The following year he was appointed postmaster general and through energy and ability brought expansion and efficiency to the office, where he remained until 1829. Through his example the postmastership was raised to Cabinet status in 1829. In the bitter Adams-Jackson campaign of 1828 McLean displayed enough political adroitness to be both retained by Adams and ultimately appointed to the Supreme Court by Jackson.

But if McLean's appointment was due to political acumen, he was also considered one of the two best lawyers in the West. There has been no thorough examination of all his opinions delivered in more than 30 years on the Federal bench, and thus his reputation as a judicial craftsman has suffered. With emphasis placed on his opinions in great cases in which his reasoning was based largely on nonlegal factors, McLean emerges as a nationalist who was well aware of the needs of the business community. He was, however, able to adjust his nationalism as circumstances provided. He also usually practiced judicial activism—considering questions that were not essential to the decision at hand, just as he had done on the state bench. The slavery questions illustrate well his values. In *Groves v. Slaughter* (1841), he upheld the right of Mississippi to restrict the introduction of slaves from other states. But even though it was "not necessary" to the decision, McLean restated his nationalism by holding that the power to regulate commerce rested exclusively with Congress. The following year in *Prigg v. Pa.,* he continued his reasoning that slavery was subject only to state regulations by asserting that in the North "every person is presumed to be free regardless of color." Thus the personal liberty laws of northern states were constitutional. Finally, his insistence on discussing Congress's authority to prohibit slavery in the territories provided five proslavery justices with the excuse to respond and made the Dred Scott case a *cause célèbre.* In a long dissent he held that Scott should be free. McLean was the most pronounced opponent of slavery to sit in antebellum days.

A large, impressive man in appearance, McLean is known for the presidential aspirations which governed his last 30 years on the bench. Virtually every election saw him as an active contender, and virtually every party at one time or another received his attention; at the age of 75 he sought the Republican nomination. McLean was widowed in 1840 and he married again in 1843, to Sarah Bella Garrard. He died of pneumonia on April 4, 1861.

Further Reading

Francis P. Weisenburger, *The Life of John McLean: A Politician on the United States Supreme Court* (1937), effectively treats McLean's political life but is less thorough on his judicial career.

Additional Sources

McLean, John, *The wind at my back: memoirs of an Irish immigrant,* Riverdale, N.Y.: Malcolm Publications, 1995. □

John McLoughlin

More than any other man, John McLoughlin (1784-1857), Canadian pioneer and trader, opened Oregon to permanent settlement by proving its agricultural potential.

John McLoughlin was born in Quebec of Irish and Scottish parents. He studied medicine in Quebec and Scotland, returning to Canada as a licensed physician. In 1814 he became a partner in the North West Company, a fur-trading firm, and was assigned to the Rainy Lake District in Ontario.

In 1821, when the North West Company merged with the Hudson's Bay Company, McLoughlin was sent as factor of the Columbia District. At this time Oregon was subject by treaty to joint occupation by England and the United States, although when McLoughlin arrived no Americans were there. His duty to monopolize the fur trade and to make maximum profits coincided with British interests in Oregon, but McLoughlin never allowed duty to override his humanitarian impulses.

In 1825 he established Ft. Vancouver (present Vancouver, Wash.) as the capital of his empire. He established farms, orchards, mills, a shipyard, and a dairy to supply the needs of his fur-trapping brigades. Also, he brought peace among the Indians and induced them to gather furs. Ships from England arrived annually with merchandise, departing with furs estimated in value as high as $150,000 per year.

McLoughlin tried to persuade the Indians not to trade with Americans, but he also tried to prevent Indian murders of whites and entertained all travelers. The Indians called him ''White Eagle'' because of his long white hair, and American travelers described the 6-foot 4-inch ''Father of Oregon'' as dignified and imposing.

In the mid-1830s, when Americans began arriving in Oregon to farm, McLoughlin extended them credit until their crops could be harvested. Hudson's Bay Company officials complained of his losses from failures to repay these loans, but he replied that on humanitarian grounds he could not refuse to help the newcomers.

In 1846, when the present international boundary was drawn, McLoughlin resigned. He filed a claim for land embracing the falls of the Willamette River, built a mill, and laid out Oregon City. Although he signed a declaration of intent to become an American citizen, in 1850 Congress nullified his claim because of many American protests and gave the land to the territory for a future state university.

McLoughlin never moved from Oregon City, however; he died there on Sept. 3, 1857. Five years later the state recognized his contribution by deeding the land to McLoughlin's heirs.

Further Reading

Standard biographies of McLoughlin include Eva Emery Dye, *McLoughlin and Old Oregon: A Chronicle* (1900; 4th ed. 1936), out of date but quite good; Frederick V. Holman, *Dr. John McLoughlin: The Father of Oregon* (1907), which is eulogistic; and Robert C. Johnson, *John McLoughlin* (1935), a balanced view. Another useful biography is Richard G. Montgomery, *The White-headed Eagle: John McLoughlin, Builder of an Empire* (1934). Herbert Beaver, *Reports and Letters of Herbert Beaver, 1836-1838,* edited by Thomas E. Jessett (1959), gives a contemporary view of McLoughlin.

Additional Sources

Fogdall, Alberta Brooks, *Royal family of the Columbia: Dr. John McLoughlin and his family,* Fairfield, Wash.: Ye Galleon Press, 1978.

Morrison, Dorothy Nafus, *The eagle & the fort: the story of John McLoughlin,* New York: Atheneum, 1979.

Wilson, Nancy, *Dr. John McLoughlin: master of Fort Vancouver, father of Oregon,* Medford, Or.: Webb Research Group, 1994. □

Marshall McLuhan

Marshall McLuhan (1911-1980), Canadian professor of literature and culture, developed a theory of media and human development claiming that ''the medium is the message.''

Herbert Marshall McLuhan was born in Edmonton, Alberta, Canada, on July 21, 1911. His father was a real estate and insurance salesman, his mother an actress. McLuhan studied first engineering and then literature at the University of Manitoba, earning his B.A. degree in 1933 and M.A. in 1934. He then continued his studies in medieval education and Renaissance literature at Cambridge University, which granted him the M.A. degree in 1940 and the Ph.D. in 1942. After several years of teaching in American universities, McLuhan returned to Canada and became a full professor at the University of Toronto in 1952.

In a series of books written while he was at Toronto, McLuhan set forth his "probes" and "explorations" about the way communication influences society. He frankly declined to follow the rules of systematic social scientific empiricism or the rigorous logic of theory building, preferring instead to draw upon his wide erudition and his flair for popularizing his ideas. His books became influential and were highly controversial.

McLuhan's theories consisted of a core of related propositions. He argued that human communication media are extensions of one or more of the senses and that use of these media re-arranges the sensory balance by stressing one sense over another. The self-definition of a culture (or a person) can thus be traced, says McLuhan, to the media that the culture relies on. To emphasize the importance of the sensory reorganization imposed by a medium, McLuhan claimed that "the medium is the message," which he later extended to the metaphor that "the medium is the massage."

In *The Mechanical Bride: Folklore of Industrial Man* (1951), written before McLuhan's theories had reached their full development, one can see the brilliant attempt of a professor of literature to demonstrate to his students the ideologies that are invisibly (and therefore influentially) built into the content and structure of popular culture. Drawing mainly upon newspaper and magazine advertising, McLuhan argued that images of mechanical technology had come to dominate popular consciousness, so that human beings reduced themselves to mechanical and instrumental objects.

The Gutenberg Galaxy: The Making of Typographic Man (1962), which won the 1963 Governor-General's Award for critical writing, is a study of the results of introducing movable type into the culture of 15th-century Western Europe. McLuhan argued that the invention of print culture made possible the creation of the public and the organization of the public into a nation. Movable type also changed the culture by altering people's sensory balance, emphasizing a visual fragmentation and linearity consistent with mechanical print.

McLuhan became famous with the publication of *Understanding Media: The Extensions of Man* (1964). In this book McLuhan made his most comprehensive statement of his theory. He argued that "the medium is the message," in the sense that

the 'message' of any medium or technology is the change of scale or pace or pattern that it introduces into human affairs. The railway did not introduce movement or transportation or wheel or road into human society, but it accelerated and enlarged the scale of previous human functions, creating totally new kinds of cities and new kinds of work or leisure. This happened whether the railway functioned in a tropical or a northern environment, and is quite independent of the freight or content of the railway medium. The airplane, on the other hand, by accelerating the rate of transportation, tends to dissolve the railway form of city, politics, and association, quite independently of what the airplane is used for.

Understanding Media also advanced McLuhan's notions of the narcotizing effects of media and of the distinction between hot and cool media. McLuhan claimed that when one of our senses is "extended" through a new medium, our sensory balance is altered in such a way that the other senses become dimmed or "narcotized." The hot versus cool distinction claims that hot media deliver information in high definition, and hence require little effort from the receiver. Cool media, on the other hand, provide little information, forcing the receiver to fill in what is missing to make sense out of the message, thus demanding a high degree of participation by the receiver. McLuhan wrote that, just as the change from oral and manuscript cultures to print culture had altered history, so, too, the change from print to electronic culture (television, computers) would, apart from whatever messages might be sent on television or computers, bring about a fundamental alteration in human consciousness.

McLuhan became a sensation in the popular press and among academics from many different disciplines. His ideas and methods were widely debated. Some critics pointed out that McLuhan was not as original as he seemed, having borrowed and perhaps distorted his fundamental premises about technological determinism from Toronto economist and historian Harold Innis. Others derided his views as utopian or mythical, or pointed out that, though it might be true that a medium has some structural influence as a medium, McLuhan was wrong to ignore the content, purpose, and context of particular messages, such as books, films, television shows, poems, songs, and paintings. McLuhan's refusal to respond to his academic critics with systematic proof, his grandly historical scope, his utopian tone, and the difficulty of translating his ideas into theory and research led to a decline of his enormous influence on academic and popular discussions of media. But, as one of his critics pointed out, ''if he is wrong, it matters.''

Further Reading

The following works of McLuhan are important to understanding the development of his theories: *The Mechanical Bride: Folklore of Industrial Man* (1951); *The Gutenberg Galaxy: The Making of Typographic Man* (1962); *Understanding Media: The Extensions of Man* (1964); and *The Medium Is the Massage* (1967). For the essential works of Harold Innis, which exerted a strong influence on McLuhan, see Innis, *The Bias of Communication* (1951) and *Empire and Communications* (1950, 1972). Good examples of the debate about McLuhan can be found in Raymond Rosenthal (editor), *McLuhan: Pro and Con* (1968) and in Gerald Emanuel Stearn (editor), *McLuhan: Hot & Cool* (1967). On McLuhan's place in communication theory, see Richard L. Johannesen (editor), *Contemporary Theories of Rhetoric: Selected Readings* (1971) and Stephen W. Littlejohn, *Theories of Human Communication* (1978).

Additional Sources

Marchand, Philip, *Marshall McLuhan: the medium and the messenger,* New York: Ticknor & Fields, 1989; Toronto: Random House, 1989.

Marshall McLuhan: the man and his message, Golden, Colo.: Fulcrum, 1989. □

John Bach McMaster

American historian John Bach McMaster (1852-1932) pioneered in the study of social history in the United States.

John Bach McMaster was born on June 29, 1852, in Brooklyn, N.Y. His father's varied business interests kept the family in comfortable circumstances until McMaster was studying at the College of the City of New York, when financial reverses forced him to take a part-time job. He graduated in 1872, showing more aptitude for the sciences than for history. After brief periods as a surveyor and private tutor, he was hired to teach engineering at Princeton in 1877.

By this time McMaster had become interested in history, apparently through his reading of Thomas Babington Macaulay's *History of England.* McMaster determined to do for the United States what Macaulay had done for England. Working furiously, part time and in secret, he finished the first volume of his *History of the People of the United States* in 1881 and finally succeeded in publishing it 1883. It was an immediate success and resulted in the University of Pennsylvania's invitation to McMaster to accept a newly

established chair in American history. McMaster remained at Pennsylvania until his retirement in 1920. The subsequent volumes of his history were published at intervals, the eighth, and last, appearing in 1913.

As a historian, McMaster was distinguished by his emphasis on social history, that is the conditions under which ordinary Americans lived. His technique was cross-sectional in that he strove to portray America and the American people at certain points in the past. In doing this he considered topics which usually escaped the notice of contemporary historians. He was among the first American historians to appreciate the importance to history of economic developments, to understand the importance of the West, to use newspapers as important sources of historical information, and to break away from the narrative form in writing history.

McMaster's work also had defects. It tended to be weak in research in original sources, to ignore important social groups such as farmers, to give too much attention to the passing and ephemeral and too little to long-range historical forces, and to be insufficiently balanced and impartial in its judgments of individuals. Yet with all these defects, his work opened new doors for American historians by using new approaches, new perspectives, and new materials on the American past. McMaster died of pneumonia in Darien, Conn., on May 24, 1932.

Further Reading

The standard account is Eric Goldman, *John Bach McMaster, American Historian* (1943), although it lays perhaps too much emphasis on McMaster's defects. William T. Hutchinson's essay on McMaster in *The Marcus W. Jernegan Essays in American Historiography,* edited by Hutchinson (1937), offers another perspective, although, like Goldman's account it is highly critical.

Additional Sources

Goldman, Eric Frederick, *John Bach McMaster, American historia, New York, Octagon Books, 1971 c1943. □*

Terry McMillan

Terry McMillan (born 1951), an African American novelist and short story writer, profiled in her works the urban experiences of African American women and men.

The oldest of five children, Terry McMillan was born on October 18, 1951, in Port Huron, Michigan, a predominately white, working-class, factory city. Her father, who suffered from tuberculosis and was confined to a sanitarium during most of McMillan's childhood, was a blue-collar worker. He also suffered from alcoholism and was physically abusive to his wife. They divorced when McMillan was 13. Her mother, in order to support the family, held various jobs as a domestic, an auto worker, and a pickle factory employee.

To assist her mother with family finances, McMillan, at age 16, got a job as a page reshelving books in a local library. There, she discovered the world of the imagination. She became an avid reader, and enjoyed the works of Nathaniel Hawthorne, Henry David Thoreau, Ralph Waldo Emerson, and Thomas Mann. Reading the works of these great writers led McMillan to believe that the literary world was a white one. Upon seeing a book by James Baldwin, she was astonished to learn that black people also wrote books.

When she was 17, McMillan left Port Huron and moved to Los Angeles, where she worked as a secretary and took a class in African American literature at Los Angeles City College. This course introduced her to the works of such writers as Richard Wright, Zora Neale Hurston, Jean Toomer, and especially to Ann Petry, whose novel *The Street,* with its frank and naturalistic documentation of a black woman living in a brutal urban environment, would greatly influence McMillan's early fiction.

A Writer Is Born

It was during this period of her life while she was in California that McMillan started to write. A love poem—the result of a failed relationship—was her first attempt at writing. As she stated in an interview: "That is how it started. It kept going and it started turning into this other stuff, started turning into sentences."

McMillan continued her interest in writing and her education by moving to northern California, where she studied journalism at the University of California at Berkeley. While at Berkeley she took a workshop with novelist and critic Ishmael Reed. Reed was excited by McMillan's writing and encouraged her. He published "The End" (1976), her first short story, in *Yardbird Reader.*

After she graduated with a B.S. degree from Berkeley, McMillan left California and moved to New York City. She joined the Harlem Writers Guild and went to artists' colonies such as Yaddo, in upstate New York, and MacDowell, in New Hampshire. At MacDowell she finished the first draft of what would become *Mama,* her first novel.

Art Based on Life Experienes

Highly autobiographical in tone, *Mama* (1987) explores the grim and humorous realities of an urban African American family. Set in Point Haven, Michigan, and in Los Angeles, the novel revolves around the lives of Mildred Peacock and her five children. As *Mama* unfolds, two of Mildred's children endure violent and gruesome experiences. Her oldest daughter, Freda, is sexually abused at 14 and her only son, Money, becomes a drug addict who is eventually incarcerated. Despite the harrowing state of affairs that assault the Peacock household, Mildred tenaciously and comically fights the forces in her orbit that would prevent her from raising her family.

In its harsh examination of the urban landscape, the novel echoes Petry's *The Street.* However, *Mama* is no mere imitation of Petry's work but an original work of fiction in its own right. Although critics felt the text lacked the lyrical and metaphorical narrative focus of the novels written by other contemporary African American women writers, and some objected to McMillan's sociological commentary and uneven narrative, McMillan's work was generally greeted with praise. The reviewers hailed the novel as unique. As the critic Michael Awkward remarked: "*Mama* stands boldly outside of the mainstream of contemporary African American women's fiction. Unlike the tradition's most representative texts, *Mama* offers no journeys back to blackness, no empowering black female communities, no sustained condemnation of American materialism or male hegemony. What it does provide, in its largely episodic depictions of the travails of Mildred and her family, is a moving, often hilarious and insightful exploration of a slice of urban life that is rarely seen in contemporary African American women's fiction."

Bold, Realistic Characters Emerged

Disappearing Acts (1989), her next novel, charts the volatile love affair between Zora Banks, a junior high school music teacher and aspiring singer, and Franklin Swift, a high school dropout and frequently unemployed carpenter and construction worker. Told in the alternating first person narrative voices of Zora and Franklin and set in the urban milieu of Brooklyn, the novel paints a compelling and realistic portrait of their relationship, as well as the complexities of class and gender that obstruct their happiness together. Although McMillan anchors her story and her characters in a contemporary world, *Disappearing Acts* resonates, as Thulani Davis observed, with "classic folklore characters," Zora being "the wily black woman of yore, [a] smart-talking Eve" and Franklin being "a savvy urban John Henry."

While some reviewers applauded McMillan's deft creation of the psychologically complex character of Franklin and extolled her for not letting her narrative collapse into another contemporary Black discourse of victim and victimizer, many critics cited the novel's earthy vernacular as a major distraction. "The language that I use is accurate," McMillan later defended in an interview. "That's the way we talk. And I want to know why I've never read a review where they complain about the language that male writers use!"

Waiting To Exhale (1992), McMillan's third novel, chronicles the lives of Robin, Bernadine, Gloria, and Savannah, four educated African American women living in Phoenix, Arizona who have an ongoing discussion about their problems in finding and keeping lovers. Structurally, the text is filtered through the lenses of shifting first and third person narrative voices and, as the heroines voyage through a highly materialistic world in search of love, the novel shows McMillan's sharp eye for social criticism.

Attained Fame, Fortune, and Critical Acclaim

Waiting To Exhale was greeted with tremendous critical and commercial success. By the end of 1996, more than 700,000 copies of the hard cover and three million copies of the paperback had been sold. The film version, which grossed $67 million in its first year, also proved there was a largely untapped African American female audience eager for pop movies and novels. Critics acclaimed the work as yet further evidence of McMillan's bold and provocative writing talent. Like her two previous novels, this text essentially eschews ideological concerns of race—a dominant thread found throughout traditional African American literature—and posits the intricate nuances of African American relationships as its primary focus.

In an anthology that she edited, *Breaking Ice: An Anthology of Contemporary African American Fiction* (1990), McMillan wrote:

> There is indeed a new generation of African American writers emerging . . . We are capturing and making permanent and indelible, reactions to, and impressions of, our most intimate observations, dreams, and nightmares, experiences and feelings about what it felt like for 'us' to be African Americans from the seventies until now—the nineties.

The popularity of *Exhale* was a prelude to even greater commercial success with her next novel, *How Stella Got Her Groove Back*, which was selected by Book-of-the-Month Club as one of its main selections. The novel had a first printing of 800,000 copies, an unprecedented number for an African American female author, and film rights were sold immediately for an undisclosed seven-figure amount. Again, Mcmillan based the storyline on her own experience, this time focusing on a middle-aged woman who falls for a 20-year-old while vacationing in Jamaica. As Evette Porter pointed out in an interview with McMillan that appeared in the *Village Voice*, there are many similarities between the novel and its author, including a young Jamaican boyfriend she met on the island. Some critics regarded Stella as largely autobiographical light weight fluff without McMillan's customary satirical bite. Others warned against letting real-life similarities blur the novel's larger message about exercising personal freedom in the way one chooses to live.

There was no question in the late 1990s that the former writing professor at Stanford and the University of Wyoming had established herself as a major novelist and pioneer in a new genre of fiction—the African American urban romance novel.

Further Reading

Critical commentary of McMillan's works is provided in *Contemporary Literary Criticism,* Volume 50 (1988) and Volume 61 (1990). Also worth reading are articles in *Callaloo* (Summer 1988); *Esquire* (July 1988); *Village Voice* (May 8, 1990 and May 21, 1996); *Essence* (February 1990, October 1992, and June 1996); *Time* (May 6, 1996); and *Ebony* (July 1996). □

Bette Clair McMurray

Betty Clair McMurray (1924–1980) was a typist who invented Liquid Paper.

Bette Clair McMurray dropped out of school when she was seventeen because of disciplinary difficulties. In the 1940s there were very few jobs open to young women. She could not type, but she got a job as a secretary for a law firm because of her personality. The attorneys sent her to night school for her high-school diploma and secretarial training. She married Warren Nesmith in 1942, and their son (Michael) was born in 1943. After she and her husband divorced in 1946, she had to provide for her son and herself, and she attempted to do so, relying on her shaky secretarial skills.

Tempera Solution

In 1951 McMurray was an executive secretary at Texas Bank and Trust in Dallas. The typewriters used there had ribbons made with carbon film. Erasing errors made on these typewriters looked messy. As an amateur painter, McMurray knew that artists made corrections by painting over mistakes rather than erasing them. So, she began using a white tempera paint to paint over her mistakes.

Mistake Out

It did not take long for the secretaries at the Texas Bank and Trust to catch on to McMurray's idea. By 1956 she was bottling "Mistake Out" in her garage for their use. She started learning about how paints are made and experimented with changing the formula. She developed a quick-drying modification that was nearly undetectable after use. By 1957 she had patented her product with the new name "Liquid Paper." She had her son fill little bottles with Liquid Paper in a work space at her home. After she was fired for accidentally typing "The Liquid Paper Company" on a letter instead of her employer's company name, she devoted herself full-time to selling Liquid Paper.

Gillette

It was not until the late 1960s that McMurray's efforts began to pay off, and then it became very successful. Gillette bought Liquid Paper in 1979 for $47.5 million and agreed to pay royalties to McMurray on every bottle sold until the year 2000. Her son Michael Nesmith, meanwhile, had become a rock 'n' roll star in the 1960s with the Monkees.

Further Reading

Ethlie Ann Vare and G. Ptacek, *Mothers of Invention: From the Bra to the Bomb, Forgotten Women and Their Unforgettable Ideas* (New York: Morrow, 1988). ☐

Robert S. McNamara

Robert S. McNamara (born 1916) was a business executive, U.S. secretary of defense, and president of the World Bank.

Robert Strange McNamara was born in San Francisco on June 9, 1916, the son of Robert James McNamara, sales manager for a wholesale shoe company, and the former Clara Nell Strange. Educated in the public schools of Piedmont, California, McNamara proved an excellent student, achieving a straight "A" average at Piedmont High School. He continued his education at the University of California, Berkeley, where he majored in philosophy and economics and earned the unusual distinction of being elected to Phi Beta Kappa at the end of his sophomore year. Following graduation in 1937, he was admitted to Harvard University's Graduate School of Business Administration. Two years later, after compiling a superb academic record, he was awarded the M.B.A. degree.

Military Career

In 1939 McNamara accepted a position in the San Francisco office of the accounting firm Price Waterhouse & Company. He returned to Harvard the following year as an assistant professor of business administration. With U.S. entry into World War II, McNamara volunteered for the Navy; his poor eyesight, however, prevented him from entering into active duty. Instead, McNamara remained in Cambridge and in 1942, as part of a special arrangement between the Harvard Business School and the U.S. Army, taught a course for Army Air Force officers. He also served as a special consultant to the Army Air Forces on the establishment of a statistical system to help monitor and control wartime logistical problems.

In 1943 he took a leave of absence from Harvard to serve with the Army Air Forces in England. While there he applied his accounting and statistical expertise to the B-17 bomber program, in the process earning a commission as a temporary captain in the Army Air Forces. He also worked on the development of the B-29, the long range bomber that was to play a critical role in the final years of the war. His role included working on the problem of flying the b-29 bombers from India to their forward bases in China and their targets in Japan without running out of fuel. Subsequently McNamara served with the Army Air Forces in India, China, and the Pacific and was released from active service in April 1946 with the rank of lieutenant colonel. For his wartime service McNamara was awarded the Legion of Merit.

Success as Business Executive

Upon release from the military, McNamara initially intended to return to Harvard University. However, Col. Charles B. Thornton, who had worked with McNamara during the war, presented him with a more intriguing possibility. Thornton induced McNamara to join a group of statistical control specialists who were planning to apply the skills developed during their wartime service to the corporate world. Late in 1946 the financially plagued Ford Motor Company hired these nine so-called "Whiz Kids" as a unit. McNamara soon proved himself the most adept of the group; he rose rapidly through Ford's corporate hierarchy.

Initially named manager of the company's planning and financial offices, by 1949 McNamara had become comptroller. In August 1953 he was promoted to assistant general manager of the Ford division. Two years later he was elected manager of the Ford division, and in 1957 he advanced to vice-president in charge of all car and truck divisions, was elected to the board of directors, and was named to the company's powerful executive and administration committees. On November 9, 1960, McNamara succeeded Henry Ford 2nd as president of the Ford Motor Company, becoming the first non-family member to occupy that position. Ironically, he was to serve as Ford's president only for about one month before being offered the position of secretary of defense by President-elect John F. Kennedy.

During his years with Ford McNamara established a reputation as a brilliantly innovative manager. He helped modernize the company by setting up a comprehensive corporate accounting system. In addition, he helped increase sales; introduced the popular Falcon, one of the first compacts; and pioneered in the installation of seat belts and other safety features. By 1960 Ford ranked as the third largest industrial concern in the United States.

Secretary of Defense

McNamara was sworn in as secretary of defense on January 21, 1961. At considerable personal loss he had previously disposed of all his Ford Motor Company stock and stock options in order to avoid any possible conflict of interest. Kennedy wanted someone to manage the world largest bureaucracy and his choice of McNamara seemed logical. He continued to serve as secretary of defense until his resignation in 1968. During those years he solidified his reputation as a financial and managerial wizard while also emerging as one of the top national security and foreign policy advisers to Presidents John F. Kennedy and Lyndon B. Johnson.

His main task, McNamara explained to a *New York Times* correspondent the day after taking the oath of office, was "to bring efficiency to a $40 billion enterprise beset by jealousies and political pressures while maintaining American military superiority." He was assisted in reorganizing the Pentagon by many of the "whiz kids" who accompanied him from Ford. McNamara and his "whiz kids" established elaborate controls over department resource use, closed down uneconomical military based and refused to spend funds for weapon systems of which he did not approve. He consolidated seven of the Defense Department's assistant secretaryships under five aides, while creating a new Office of Management Planning and Organization Studies.

Applying the techniques of systems analysis to the Pentagon's huge bureaucracy, McNamara inaugurated a planning-programming-budgeting system. This innovation enabled him to project the first five-year budget in the history of the Defense Department, a plan that he unveiled to Congress in January 1963. Much of his energy during his first few years at Defense was devoted to revitalizing America's conventional forces and moving away from what he viewed as an excessive reliance on nuclear deterrence during the administration of Dwight D. Eisenhower. He accepted the doctrine of "flexible response," which called for the development of a broad choice of deterrent forces, ranging from the nuclear to the anti-guerrilla.

Under Presidents Kennedy and Johnson U.S. military involvement in Vietnam increased steadily, and Vietnam ultimately became McNamara's principal preoccupation. Unquestionably, that divisive war was the most difficult—and controversial—episode in his career. The secretary of defense fully supported President Johnson's decisions for escalation, including the dispatch of American combat troops in 1965 and the inauguration of a massive bombing campaign that same year. Publicly, he continued to support the U.S. war effort until his resignation, and his public projections were almost unfailingly optimistic. Privately, however, McNamara began to express doubts about the war as early as November 1965, following a disappointing trip to Saigon. As his disillusionment grew, in 1967 the Defense secretary commissioned a study of American involvement in Vietnam, a project that eventually became known as the *Pentagon Papers* following its unauthorized release in 1971. Increasingly dissatisfied with the direction of American policy in Vietnam and at odds with Johnson, in early 1968

McNamara resigned to accept a position with the World Bank.

President of the World Bank

McNamara served as president of the World Bank for 13 years, from 1968 to 1981. Under his direction the bank became the world's largest and most important single source of international development assistance. When Mc-Namara took office the bank was lending about $1 billion a day; by 1980 that figure had grown to $12 billion. During his last year with the institution it was supervising over 1,600 projects with a total value of approximately $100 billion in more than 100 developing countries. In his final address to the World Bank's board of governors, McNamara said that the most fundamental problem facing the world was the persistence of widespread poverty. "This World Bank—born out of the ruins of World War II—has grown into one of the world's most constructive instruments of human aspiration and progress," McNamara exclaimed. "And yet, it has only barely begun to develop its full potential."

Following his retirement from the World Bank in 1981, McNamara continued to write and speak on a broad range of public issues, including world poverty, development strategies, nuclear policy, and South Africa. He also served on a number of corporate and other boards, including Royal Dutch Petroleum, the *Washington Post,* Trans World Airlines, Corning Glass Works, Bank of America, the Ford Foundation, the Brookings Institution, and the California Institute of Technology.

After leaving the World Bank, McNamara became a strong critic of nuclear arms. He argued that the U.S. and Soviet officials should each maintain "a nuclear arsenal powerful enough to discourage anyone else from using nuclear weapons" and that "nuclear weapons have no military purpose whatsoever other than to deter one's opponent from their use."

During the 1980s McNamara devoted much of his time to writing books and articles delineating his position on nuclear arms proliferation, arms control, comprehensive test bans, restriction of antiballistic missiles. He also proposed the establishment of "new rules" of conduct that could provide each side the chance to pursue their own agenda through diplomacy rather than threat or use of force. He suggested that each side's military forces be restructured to be defensive and reduced in number; that they refrain from becoming involved in regional conflicts; and that they work together to solve regional and global problems peacefully.

In 1995, McNamara released a new book *In Retrospect: The Tragedy and Lessons of Vietnam,* in which he reveals that he lied to Congress and the American people about the causes for U.S. involvement in the Vietnam War. McNamara, while not entirely blaming himself, admits that his misunderstanding of Vietnam and Asian politics cost nearly 60,000 American lives. Many critics feel that the book is a self-serving way for McNamara to assuage his own guilt over his mishandling of the facts during the early years of the war. David Halberstam, author of *The Best and the Brightest* doesn't believe that McNamara understands what he did at all and stated, "the book is shallow and deeply disingenuous. For him to say 'we couldn't get information' borders on a felony, because he was creator of the lying machine that gave him that information. The point was to make a flawed policy look better."

Further Reading

A full-length biography is Deborah Shapley, *Robert McNamara: Soldier of the American Century;* A brief sketch of his career up to 1968 can be found in David Halberstam, *The Best and the Brightest* (1972); Two studies of his tenure as Defense secretary are: William W. Kaufmann, *The McNamara Strategy* (1964) and Robert M. Roherty, *Decisions of Robert S. McNamara: A Study of the Role of the Secretary of Defense* (1970); His involvement with the war in Vietnam has been treated in a large number of secondary works on that conflict, including George C. Herring, *America's Longest War* (1979) and Stanley Karnow, *Vietnam: A History* (1983); McNamara is the author of *The Essence of Security: Reflections in Office* (1968) and *One Hundred Countries, Two Billion People: The Dimensions of Development* (1973); A compilation of his speeches has also been published as *The McNamara Years at the World Bank: Major Policy Addresses of Robert S. McNamara, 1968-1981* (1981). Also see a review of *In Retrospect: The Tragedy and Lessons of Vietnam,* in *National Review,* July 10, 1995. □

Andrew McNaughton

Andrew McNaughton (1887-1966) was Canada's most prominent soldier in the 20th century. After World War II McNaughton served in a variety of political and diplomatic capacities.

Andrew George Latta McNaughton was born February 25, 1887, at Moosomin, North West Territories (now Saskatchewan), Canada. He enlisted in the army reserve in 1909 and by 1914 commanded the 3rd Field Battery in Montreal while doing academic research and lecturing in electrical engineering at McGill University.

He fought as a gunner with the Canadian Corps on the Western Front throughout World War I. In a war in which artillery became the dominant arm, McNaughton attracted attention and won steady advancement largely on the basis of his organizational skills and application of scientific principles to techniques such as sound ranging and barrage fire. Twice wounded, three times mentioned in despatches, by war's end he had been awarded the Distinguished Service Order (DSO) and was a brigadier general.

There McNaughton's military career might have ended, but his old Canadian Corps commander, Gen. Sir Arthur Currie, convinced him to join the permanent army. He was soon deputy army chief, bringing his science skills to bear on a northern radio signals system using improved survey techniques based on aerial photography and the cathode ray detection finder, an essential component of what would become radar. He became chief of the general

staff on the first day of 1929, dominating his colleagues in the military establishment, as one author puts it, "as a great oak dominates a scrub forest."

In 1930 a Conservative government came to power under an admiring R. B. Bennett, and McNaughton extended his influence throughout official Ottawa. During the worst days of the Depression he held sway over numerous committees, ran the government's unemployment relief program, and made inquiries into a St. Lawrence seaway system. As the chief military adviser of a hard-pressed government, however, he was unable to push through major reforms or strengthen Canada's armed forces. His valedictory in 1935 was a memorandum on the low state of the country's defenses. The presidency of the National Research Council was next, McNaughton immersing himself in the problems of preparation for a scientific war which it seemed must come before long.

When war did come again, McNaughton was chosen as commander of the Canadian division which was sent to England in December 1939. He looked the part. McNaughton, one journalist wrote, "was the answer to a propagandist's prayer. His iron-grey head, miraculously photogenic, was the epitome of last-ditch fight. He played himself and his hand uniformly—to the full." He was a fine trainer and motivator, building his force to army strength by 1942 while launching a wide variety of technological innovations. McNaughton felt passionately about his army and its men, and they reciprocated his affection. He spoke often and eloquently about the need for national control of Can-

ada's armed forces. That, especially for a young country, was the acid test of sovereignty.

McNaughton had weaknesses, and his sheer visibility made them more apparent. His judgment, a leading historian has said, was never the equal of his intellect. Compromise did not come easily. His nationalism made enemies among Canadian politicians and military bureaucrats. He over-worked and, with his health in question, British reservations about his qualities as a commander became impossible to ignore. He resigned in December 1943. "Whether McNaughton would have proved an effective commander in the field may be questionable," wrote the British military theorist Sir Basil Liddell Hart, "but he was certainly a soldier of outstanding visions and ability who grasped the conditions of modern war earlier and more fully than most."

McNaughton's prestige, not least with wartime Prime Minister Mackenzie King, was undiminished. A member of his staff in England captured the widespread feeling: "with his force of character and electricity of personality, McNaughton had come to symbolize Canada and its place both in the war and in the world." It was thus no surprise that he was King's choice as the next governor general of Canada. He would have become the first native-born head of state—all the rest had been British—but for the government's wish to avoid introducing overseas conscription, which brought him into the cabinet as minister of national defense in late 1944. His political career was brief, unhappy, and accident-prone. He failed utterly to ward off conscription and was twice defeated by nonentities in a bid for a parliamentary seat.

McNaughton was not done yet. Just a week after he left politics in the summer of 1945 he was named chairman of the Canadian section of the Canada-United States Permanent Joint Board on Defense. He held that post until 1959, and a similar one from 1950 to 1962 on another Canadian-American body, the International Joint Commission; he combined these roles to good effect in helping to secure final agreement on the St. Lawrence Seaway. In the late 1940s he spent a period as president of the Atomic Energy Control Board of Canada and as the country's permanent delegate to the United Nations. With his knowledge of and zeal for science at the ready, he was a tough bargainer and a staunch defender of Canadian independence. He proved a skillful diplomat as well.

After 53 continuous years in the public service of Canada, McNaughton spent the last period of his life in an all-out fight for the safeguarding of Canadian natural resources and against the Columbia River treaty. His patriotism, as his biographer wrote, burned as brightly as ever.

Further Reading

Additional information on McNaughton may be found in John Swettenham, *McNaughton*, 3 vols. (Toronto, 1968-1969); James Eayrs, *In Defense of Canada*, Vols. I-III (Toronto, 1965-1972); John Holmes, *The Shaping of Peace* (Toronto, 1979-1982); Douglas LePan, *Bright Glass of Memory* (Toronto, 1979); and C. P. Stacey, *A Date with History* (Ottawa, 1983). □

D'Arcy McNickle

D'Arcy McNickle (1904-1977) was an advocate for Native American rights and is considered to be among the founders of modern Native American literature.

As a writer, historian, activist, government project manager, community organizer, and university professor, McNickle's career was as diverse as his accomplishments. His voice was heard in the halls of Congress and the halls of universities, in homes on the reservation and homes in urban America. He was an advocate for Native rights both when Indian causes were championed and when Indian rights were being eliminated. Not only was he able to speak to non-Natives about the Native world, but he talked to the Natives about the changes coming from the non-Native world. Throughout it all, he was a cultural mediator, thoroughly at home in both worlds.

He was born William D'Arcy McNickle on January 18, 1904, in St. Ignatius, Montana. His mother, Philomena Parenteau married Irish rancher William McNickle and lived with him on the Flathead reservation. The Parenteaus, of Cree descent, had fled to Montana after the failure of the Métis uprising in 1885 and were formally adopted into the Flathead tribe.

In his early years, McNickle attended school on the reservation. Then over his own and mother's objections, he was sent to the Bureau of Indian Affairs boarding school at Chemawa for three years. He was shocked by the harsh, culturally insensitive attitude that permeated the school, preferring the schooling in Washington state and Montana. When he entered the University of Montana at the age of 17, he was drawn to the world of literature and the study of languages, including Greek and Latin. He was encouraged by one of his professors to attend Oxford. In 1925, he sold his tribal allotment and traveled to England. Difficulty with the transferability of his college credits kept him from matriculating, and, with money running out, he moved to Paris with uncertain thoughts of being a writer or a musician.

Returning to New York, McNickle took a series of jobs, including positions as editor for the *Encyclopaedia Britannica* and the *National Cyclopaedia of American Biography*. In November 1926 he married Joran Birkeland and they had a daughter, Antoinette. During his years in New York, he periodically attended courses at the New School for Social Research and at Columbia. However, he was continually working on his writing. He finished a number of short stories and revised his novel, which was published in 1936 as *The Surrounded*.

Joins Collier Administration

When the Collier administration took over the Bureau of Indian Affairs (BIA), McNickle joined the staff as an administrative assistant. During his 16 years with the BIA, he held a number of positions, including field representative and director of tribal relations. He was a tireless advocate of Indian rights, believing in change, but change with respect and Native initiative. By 1944 he was aware of the necessity of unified political action on the part of tribal groups. He cofounded the National Congress of American Indians to create an effective Indian political voice.

In 1949 he published *They Came Here First: The Epic of the American Indian,* which drew on anthropological sources to chronicle Indian history and the interaction of Indians and settlers. This work initiated a series of publications that included his juvenile novel, *Runner in the Sun: A Story of Indian Maize* (1954), *Indians and Other Americans: Two Ways of Life Meet* (1959) with Harold Fey, and *Indian Tribes of North America* (1962). These last two books reviewed Federal Indian policy and the history of white/Indian interaction so as to explain the clash of values and cultural misunderstanding that have resulted in so much tragedy.

In the early 1950s the federal government increasingly strove for the termination of tribal groups and their relocation to urban centers. McNickle did not agree with the federal goals and resigned from BIA to pursue community development work with the American Indian Development Corporation. He worked extensively in Crownpoint, New Mexico, for a number of years before he moved on to other work with students and Indian communities. He sat on the United States Civil Rights Commission and worked on leadership workshops for Native students.

In 1966 he was awarded an honorary doctorate from the University of Colorado. Moving from community work to academia, McNickle accepted a professorship at the new Regina campus of the University of Saskatchewan. He was given the position of chairman and asked to set up a small anthropology department.

In 1971, he published a biography of Oliver La Farge, *Indian Man: A Life of Oliver La Farge,* which was nominated for a National Book Award; and retired to Albuquerque to work on his writing. He remained on the editorial board of the Smithsonian Institution's revision of the *Handbook of North American Indians.* He also agreed to serve as founding director of the Newberry Library's Center for the History of the American Indian. During his retirement, he revised two of his books and wrote numerous book reviews and entries, but most importantly he worked on his novel, *Wind from an Enemy Sky.* In October of 1977, he died in Albuquerque of a massive heart attack.

Further Reading

Owens, Louis, *Other Destinies: Understanding the American Indian Novel,* Norman, University of Oklahoma Press, 1992.
Parker, Dorothy, *Singing an Indian Song: A Biography of D'Arcy McNickle,* Lincoln, University of Nebraska Press, 1992.
Purdy, John Lloyd, *WordWays: The Novels of D'Arcy McNickle,* Tucson, University of Arizona Press, 1990.
Ruppert, James, *D'Arcy McNickle,* Boise, Boise State University, 1988. □

Aimee Semple McPherson

Aimee Semple McPherson (1890-1944), American evangelist, symbolized important attributes of American popular religion in the 1920s and 1930s.

Aimee Kennedy was born on Oct. 9, 1890, near Ingersoll, Ontario, Canada. Her father was a struggling farmer, her mother a former member of the Salvation Army. Aimee remained a nonbeliever until, at the age of 17, she experienced conversion under the guidance of Scottish evangelist Robert Semple. In 1908 she married him and followed him to China as a missionary. He died soon after arriving in China, leaving her penniless and with a month-old daughter. Returning home, Semple married a grocery clerk, Harold S. McPherson, in 1913; this marriage ended in divorce five years later. Thereafter she set out as an untrained lay evangelist to preach a Pentecostal-type of revivalism to the people of Ontario.

Physically attractive and possessed of a dynamic personality and instinctive ability to sway crowds, Aimee Semple McPherson gradually perfected her skills. By this time professional revivalism had achieved a distinctive style and organization; McPherson illustrated the newer tendencies. Though she initially lived an almost hand-to-mouth existence following the route of itinerant evangelists from Maine to Florida, success meant a move into larger cities in America, England, and Australia. In the cities audiences were often immense, with 10,000 to 15,000 partisans deliriously applauding her. McPherson's preaching also identified her with the "fringe" sects of American Protestantism that were especially influential among the masses in America's newly emerging urban centers. "Speaking with tongues" and successful efforts at faith healing—both practiced by the Pentecostal churches—were a part of her performance.

By 1920 McPherson was permanently established in Los Angeles. In 1923 she and her followers dedicated Angelus Temple. Seating over 5,000 people, this served as her center of activity. Backed by a shrewd business manager (her mother), the evangelist organized a private cult of devoted followers. She also became a public figure in tune with the garish, publicity-oriented life of the film capital of the world.

As a popular evangelist, Aimee Semple McPherson symbolized the vulgarization that occurred when grassroots religion fused uncritically with secular mass culture. Popular evangelists always ran the risk of identifying their personal concerns too much with the nonreligious aspects of culture. This tendency was strikingly illustrated by McPherson. She thrived on publicity and sensationalism. The most astounding incident occurred in 1926, when McPherson, believed to have drowned in the Pacific Ocean, "miraculously" reappeared in the Mexican desert. Her tale of kidnaping and mistreatment was challenged by some who claimed she had been in hiding with one of her male followers. The ensuing court battle attracted national attention.

McPherson continued her unconventional ways until her death in Oakland, Calif., on Sept. 27, 1944. She engaged in a slander suit with her daughter, publicly quarreled with her mother, and carried on well-publicized vendettas with other religious groups.

Further Reading

Aimee Semple McPherson's own reminiscence, *The Story of My Life* (1951), is too romanticized and sketchy to be of much value. A biographical study is Lately Thomas, *Storming Heaven: The Lives and Turmoils of Minnie Kennedy and Aimee Semple McPherson* (1970). One account dealing principally with the celebrated "kidnaping incident" of 1926 is Thomas's *The Vanishing Evangelist* (1959). An older though valuable study is Nancy Mavity, *Sister Aimee* (1931). □

Butterfly McQueen

Butterfly (1911-1995) McQueen's portrayal of Prissy in *Gone With the Wind* (1939) rivals Hattie McDaniel's Oscar-winning role as the "mammy," and is certainly as popular with audiences as Vivien Leigh's Scarlett O'Hara or Clark Gable's Rhett Butler.

Known to generations of movie viewers as Prissy, the frantic, squeaky-voiced servant who is harshly upbraided by Scarlett O'Hara in the 1939 Civil War epic *Gone With the Wind*, actress Butterfly McQueen was actually a successful Broadway dancer who went on to win critical acclaim for her quirky portrayal of seemingly scatterbrained maids in a handful of popular films in the 1940s. Offscreen, however, she rebelled against Hollywood's rigid system of racial stereotyping and often insisted on altering scenes and dialogue that demeaned people of color. McQueen's announcement in 1947 that she would no longer accept so-called "handkerchief head" parts nearly cost the actress her career. Except for the part of a secretary in the all-black film *Killer Diller* in 1948, she had no movie offers for the next 20 years. "I didn't mind playing a maid the first time, because I thought that was how you got into the business," she explained in an interview with *People*. "But after I did the same thing over and over I resented it. I didn't mind being funny but I didn't like being stupid." Returning to New York, she worked as a sales clerk, a waitress, a dishwasher, and an old ladies' companion in order to make ends meet.

Yet McQueen's objection to stereotyped roles was only one of the things that hindered her career. She also had a unique, ethereal quality which made her difficult to cast. "Her comedic gifts were too special and delicate, too unique a blending of the comic and the pathetic, to be effective" in the limited roles available to African Americans throughout the first half of the twentieth century, commented Donald Bogle in *Toms, Coons, Mulattoes,*

Mammies and Bucks: An Interpretive History of Blacks in American Films. "With her large, expressive eyes, her bewildered and perplexed stare, and her quivering tremor of a voice, she seemed almost otherworldly." In the late 1960s McQueen returned to the New York stage, where she had launched her theatrical career more than 30 years before. Soon afterwards a variety of small film and television roles came her way, but none earned her the fame of her early work in *Gone With the Wind*.

Stage, screen, and radio actress Thelma "Butterfly" McQueen was born in Tampa, Florida, in 1911. Her father was a stevedore and her mother worked as a domestic. When McQueen was five years old, her father deserted the family. In order to support herself and her daughter, Mrs. McQueen sought full-time employment in a number of cities up and down the East Coast, sending Thelma to live with an aunt in Augusta, Georgia, until she had settled on a job as a cook in Harlem. Young Thelma completed her high school education in Babylon, Long Island, after yet another move and went on to study nursing at the Lincoln Training School in the Bronx. In 1934, however, she joined Venezuela Jones's Harlem-based Youth Theatre Group, and her career took a different turn. She began to study dance, music, and drama on a professional level, and in 1935 made her stage debut as part of the Butterfly Ballet in Jones's off-Broadway production of *A Midsummer Night's Dream*. Upon seeing her dance, a friend nicknamed her "Butterfly." She immediately adopted the name as her own, and it remained with her throughout her career.

Two years later McQueen made her Broadway debut as the maid, Lucille, in George Abbott's all-black production, *Brown Sugar*. Although she played only a minor part and the show closed after only four performances, Brooks Atkinson of the *New York Times* remarked upon "the extraordinary artistry of a high-stepping, little dusky creature who describes herself as Butterfly McQueen." Following her success in *Brown Sugar*, McQueen was cast in two more George Abbott productions, *Brother Rat* (1937) and *What A Life* (1938). She was still working for Abbott when she auditioned for the part of Prissy in *Gone With the Wind*.

The Role of a Lifetime

Although McQueen, then 28, was dismissed as too overweight, too old, and too dignified to play a young slave girl, *Gone With the Wind* producer David O. Selznick ultimately decided that experienced actors with unusual presence—such as film veteran Hattie McDaniel, who portrayed the O'Hara family's faithful Mammy, and McQueen, who had won critical praise as a member of the Abbott Acting Company—would be more effective than lesser-known players. On the surface, *Gone With the Wind*, which took more than two years to film and cost close to $4 million, was little more than an elaborate romance between two strong-willed, temperamental characters set against the backdrop of the Civil War-torn South. But in fact, it was much, much more than that.

According to Bogle, Selznick's epic was the first of the Civil War spectacles to provide a realistic picture of black-white relationships in antebellum America. It was also the first in which black actors were given the freedom to transform pasteboard slave characters into complex, three-dimensional human beings. Hattie McDaniel's towering, domineering Mammy contrasted sharply with McQueen's fragile and hysterical Prissy, yet both were equally powerful. "McDaniel was tough and resilient and could take a small incident and magnify it into a mountain," wrote Bogle. "Butterfly, however, could take a big scene and condense it into the tiniest of lyrical poems."

As Prissy, slave girl to the O'Hara family, Butterfly McQueen uttered one of the most memorable lines in cinema history. When the townspeople are fleeing Atlanta in the face of Union Army commander William Sherman's onslaught, Prissy assures Scarlett that she will stay on and help deliver Melanie's baby, claiming, "I'se knows all 'bout birthin' babies." On the day of the baby's arrival, however, Prissy is nowhere to be found. When Scarlett finally locates her and orders her to take over, Prissy stares fearfully into Scarlett's eyes and squeals, "Lawdy, Miss Scarlett, I'se don't know nothin' 'bout birthin' babies!" Her ill-timed admission earns her an angry slap from Scarlett. In another scene Prissy is shown packing chinaware and other essential items in preparation for the flight from Atlanta. As cannons roar in the background, she screams in terror and rushes frantically from place to place, dropping the dishes as she goes. Later, when she accompanies Rhett Butler, Melanie, and the newborn baby on the journey from Atlanta, she cowers on the floor of the wagon, popping her head up every moment or so to scream hysterically at the sight of the burning city.

According to Bogle, Prissy offered a unique combination of comedy and pathos which, like a tasteless joke told during a time of tragedy, provided "an outlet for the repressed fears of the audience." Because of her "artistic mayhem, her controlled fright, and her heightened awareness and articulation of the emotions of the audience," he wrote, "Butterfly McQueen seemed to flow wonderfully with the rest of the film."

Objected to Racial Stereotyping

Although she had accepted her role in *Gone With the Wind* with enthusiasm, upon studying the novel more closely, McQueen was distressed by its portrayal of African Americans. "The part of Prissy was so backward," she recalled in an interview with *People* nearly five decades later. "I was always whining and complaining." In one scene she was asked to appear before the camera in the stereotypical pose of eating watermelon and spitting out the seeds. She refused. In another scene Rhett Butler was instructed to refer to Prissy as a "simple-minded darkie"—a term she found insulting and unnecessary. And while the script called for her to wear her hair wrapped in a head scarf in the traditional "slave girl" style, she insisted on substituting colorful bows. In the end, however, her objections were overruled, and she was obliged to submit to the old-fashioned "wrapped head" look.

Once during an early take of the famous birthing scene, actress Vivien Leigh, who played Scarlett, apparently slapped McQueen too hard, prompting the latter to cry out, "I can't do it, she's hurting me," and insist on a proper apology

from Leigh before shooting could resume. McQueen later asked that the slap be mimed rather than risk another painful incident. "I told them, if you really slap me, I won't scream," she recalled in an article in the *Columbus Ledger Inquirer,* "but if you pretend to slap me, I'll make the best scream you ever heard." She proved equally assertive off the set, voicing her objections when all the black actors were forced to travel in one car, while the white actors rode in limousines. She also joined a group of black castmates in protesting restroom segregation.

After appearing in another servant role—that of Lulu, a perfume saleslady-turned-maid—opposite Joan Crawford in the George Cukor film *The Women,* Butterfly McQueen returned to the New York stage to play Puck in *Swingin' the Dream,* a reinterpretation of *A Midsummer Night's Dream.* Her performance earned her the praise of a *New York Times* critic, who described her as a "piping-voiced Puck whose travesty is genuinely comic . . . representing her peculiar artistry in finest fettle." Two years later, however, she was back in Hollywood playing maids. Some critics described her performance in *Affectionately Yours* (1941) as the best in the film, but she was humiliated by the role she played. At one point her character is forced to deliver what has been considered the most demeaning line ever uttered by a black performer in the movies. Turning to Hattie McDaniel, she croons, "Who dat say who dat when you say dat." The "Uncle-Remus-style" dialect coaching she had received in preparation for her role in *Gone With the Wind* had been bad enough—she later explained in a *New York Times* interview that she had not been allowed to speak that way as a child—but in *Affectionately Yours,* Hollywood had reached a new low in its portrayal of black characters. "I never thought I would have to say a line like that," Bogle quoted her as saying. "I had imagined that since I am an intelligent woman, I could play any kind of role."

Resisted Hollywood Stereotypes

During the early 1940s McQueen appeared in a handful of other films, including Vincente Minnelli's *Cabin in the Sky,* featuring Duke Ellington's Orchestra and an all-black, all-star cast, and the musical comedy *I Dood It.* Minor roles followed in *Mildred Pierce*—here she still played a servant, but a more dignified one—*Flame of Barbary Coast,* and *Duel in the Sun.* By 1947, however, she'd had her fill of servant roles, and since Hollywood had little else to offer black actors, she returned to New York in hopes of finding work in the musical theater. In 1951 McQueen mounted her own one-woman show at Carnegie Hall, during the process of which she lost most of her Hollywood earnings. Five years later she played the part of Queen Elizabeth Victoria in the all-black production, *The World's My Oyster.* This was followed by an appearance in a mediocre adaptation of Molière's *School for Wives* and, in the mid-1960s, a tedious production called *The Athenian Touch,* in which she again played a maid and cook. In between she accepted a series of casual jobs, ranging from taxi dispatcher to sales clerk to factory worker, in order to survive. At one point she moved back to Augusta, Georgia, where she gave music lessons, appeared on her own radio show, opened a restaurant, and served as a hostess at the Stone Mountain Memorial Museum of Confederate Times.

In 1968 McQueen returned to the spotlight as Hattie in the off-Broadway musical *Curley McDimple* and one year later starred in her own musical revue entitled *Butterfly McQueen and Friends*. This was followed by a powerful performance as elevator operator Dora Lee in George Abbott's play *Three Men on a Horse*. Over the years she has also appeared in a number of dramatic television productions, including *The Green Pastures* (1957) and *Our World* (1987), and in the TV series *The Beulah Show*. Her role in the 1979 children's special *The Seven Wishes of Joanna Peabody* earned her an Emmy Award. And in 1986 McQueen returned to the large screen as Ma Kennywick in *Mosquito Coast*. Three years later she appeared in the movies *Polly* and *Stiff*. Then, in 1989, she played Prissy yet again, signing autographs and quoting her most famous line at the widely publicized celebrations commemorating the fiftieth anniversary of *Gone With the Wind*.

Although the role of Prissy brought her instant fame in 1939, it did little to help her one night some 40 years later when she was passing through the Greyhound Bus Terminal in Washington, D.C., en route to Tampa. Stopping to eat some peanuts in the ladies' lounge, she was instantly accosted by a security guard who mistook her for a pickpocket. During the scuffle that ensued, she was wrestled to the ground and thrown against a metal bench, injuring several ribs. "It was absolutely the most embarrassing thing that ever happened to me," she told *People*. "I was shocked." It was some time before a Washington police officer recognized her and arranged for her release. In 1980 she filed a $300,000 suit against the bus line, and four years later was awarded $60,000.

Emphasized Education and Community Service

Throughout her life, Butterfly McQueen has made education a top priority. As early as 1946 she began taking courses in political science, Spanish, drama, dance, and music, first at the City College of Los Angeles and then at the University of California at Los Angeles, Southern Illinois University, Queen's College, and New York University. In June of 1975, at the age of 64, she was one of 3,500 students to receive a bachelor's degree during commencement ceremonies at New York's City College. She has also devoted much of her time and energy to community service work, helping out in the offices of city politicians and serving as a playground supervisor at an elementary school in Harlem. "Show business is only my hobby," she said in an interview with *People*. "My main job is community work." And McQueen maintains a philosophical attitude about the racism she continues to encounter. "I don't think you should strip people of their prejudice—that's all they have, some of them," she was quoted as saying in *People*. "We should just leave them alone until they mature."

McQueen died on December 22, 1995, at the age of 84. She died as a result of being burned in her Augusta, Georgia, cottage. According to *Jet*, McQueen was trying to light a kerosene heater in her cottage. Her clothes caught on fire and she was taken to Augusta Regional Medical Center where she was pronounced dead. She suffered second- and third-degree burns on over 70 percent of her body.

Further Reading

Bogle, Donald, *Blacks in American Film and Television*, Garland, 1988, pp. 94-95; 420-22.
Bogle, Donald, *Toms, Coons, Mulattoes, Mammies and Bucks: An Interpretive History of Blacks in American Films.*, Viking Press, 1973, pp. 86-94.
Cripps, Thomas, *Slow Fade to Black: The Negro in American Film, 1900-1942*, Oxford University Press, 1977, pp. 360-63.
Landay, Eileen, *Black Film Stars*, Drake Publishers, 1973, pp. 79-80.
Null, Gary, *Black Hollywood: The Negro in Motion Pictures*, 1975.
Sampson, Henry T., *Blacks in Black and White: A Source Book on Black Films*, Scarecrow Press, 1977.
Columbus Ledger Inquirer (Georgia), November 5, 1989.
New York Times, December 3, 1937; November 30, 1939; August 10, 1956; June 3, 1975, p. 29.
People, January 28, 1980, p. 36; December 1, 1986, pp. 69-70; January 8, 1996, p. 103. □

George Herbert Mead

The American philosopher and social psychologist George Herbert Mead (1863-1931) offered a naturalistic account of the origin of the self and explained language, conception, perception, and thinking in terms of social behavior.

George Herbert Mead was born on Feb. 27, 1863, in South Hadley, Mass. He graduated from Oberlin College in 1883 and attended Harvard University in 1887 and 1888. While studying in Leipzig and Berlin (1888-1891), he was influenced by the physiological psychologist Wilhelm Wundt. Mead taught at the University of Michigan (1891-1893) and the University of Chicago (1894-1931). He died in Chicago on April 26, 1931.

The notion of "gesture," which Mead took from Wundt, is basic to Mead's behavioristic psychology and to all of his philosophic thinking. If the behavior of one animal evokes a response in another that is useful in completing a more inclusive act, it is called a gesture, and the behavior of the participants of the act is social.

In *Mind, Self and Society*, Mead shows that human beings are distinguished from all other animals in that an individual can by his gestures (words, that is, language gestures) evoke in himself the same response that he evokes in another and can respond to his own behavior (words) as do other members of the community. This means that the human individual can look at his own behavior from the point of view of the other; or he can take the role of the other and, thus, be an object to himself. When the child can view its own behavior from the perspective of another, it is a self, or it has a self. Selves emerge in children out of social behavior with other members of the group who, with the

child, are participants in social action. The meaning of a gesture is the response it evokes; a language gesture has the same meaning to the speaker as it does to the one to whom it is addressed. When a gesture (or significant symbol) has common meaning, it is universal in that the response it evokes is the same for each member of the community. One perceives an object, such as a tree, only in relation to behavior or to responses evoked by what is seen, heard, or smelled. The lumberman "sees" the tree in terms of lumber, and his responses are organized accordingly.

It is only because of symbols having common meaning that men can think or reason. Thinking is a conversation of the self, the individual, with the other, or with what Mead calls the generalized other. Individuals have minds, therefore, because they can take the attitude of others (take the role of, or enter into the perspective of, others) and can thus anticipate the response that others will make to their gestures. The individual member of society, through thinking, can propose new ways of acting which are shareable and testable by other members of the community.

The physiological basis for thinking and for basic distinctions between man and lower animals is the hand. Not only can men move physical objects from place to place, but they can also dissect objects and reassemble them in various ways. Thinking has to do with the manipulatory phase of social action.

In Mead's last work, *The Philosophy of the Present*, he shows that the same basic principle used in creative, or reflective, thinking, resulting in acts of adjustment between the individual and its environment, applies also to every kind of adjustment in the process of evolution. The adjustments that new planets make to the system from which they emerged (and vice versa), as well as adjustments made by lower animals to their respective environments (and the environments to them), take place in accordance with the same principle applied in reflective thinking. This is the principle of sociality, and it requires that the newly arisen entity, the emergent, be in two or more different systems at once, even as reflective thinking requires that the individual be in both his own perspective and in the perspective of the other.

Through the principle of sociality Mead not only accounts for the process of adjustment, and thus strengthens his position as a process philosopher, but he also develops a system of philosophy based on the act of adjustment as a unit of existence. His system explains how emergence, novelty, creativity, thinking, communication, and continuous adjustment are interrelated and why each is a phase of the natural process of adjustment.

Further Reading

A selection of Mead's writings is in *George Herbert Mead: Essays on His Social Philosophy,* edited with an introduction by John W. Petras (1969). An exposition of Mead's philosophy is Maurice Natanson, *The Social Dynamics of George H. Mead* (1956), and Horace S. Thayer, *Meaning and Action* (1968). Mead is also discussed in Charles Morris, *The Pragmatic Movement in American Philosophy* (1970).

Additional Sources

Cook, Gary A., *George Herbert Mead: the making of a social pragmatist,* Urbana: University of Illinois Press, 1993. □

Margaret Mead

The American anthropologist Margaret Mead (1901-1978) developed the field of culture and personality research and was a dominant influence in introducing the concept of culture into education, medicine, and public policy.

Margaret Mead was born in Philadelphia, Pa., on Dec. 16, 1901. She grew up there in a liberal intellectual atmosphere. Her father, Edward Sherwood Mead, was a professor in the Wharton School of Finance and Commerce and the founder of the University of Pennsylvania's evening school and extension program. Her mother, Emily Fogg Mead, was a sociologist and an early advocate of woman's rights.

In 1919 Mead entered DePauw University but transferred after a year to Barnard College, where she majored in psychology. In her senior year she had a course in anthropology with Franz Boas which she later described as the most influential event in her life, since it was then that she decided to become an anthropologist. She graduated from

Barnard in 1923. In the same year she married Luther Cressman and entered the anthropology department of Columbia University.

The Columbia department at this time consisted of Boas, who taught everything, and Ruth Benedict, his only assistant. The catastrophe of World War I and the dislocations that followed it had had their impact on the developing discipline of anthropology. Anthropologists began to ask how their knowledge of the nature of humankind might be used to illuminate contemporary problems. At the same time the influence of Sigmund Freud was beginning to be felt in all the behavioral sciences. The atmosphere in the Columbia department was charged with intellectual excitement, and whole new perspectives for anthropology were opening up.

Early Fieldwork

Mead completed her studies in 1925 and set off for a year's fieldwork in Samoa in the face of opposition from older colleagues worried about sending a young woman alone to a Pacific island. Her problem was to study the life of adolescent girls. She learned the native language (one of seven she eventually mastered) and lived in a Samoan household as "one of the girls." She found that young Samoan girls experience none of the tensions American and European adolescents suffer from, and she demonstrated the kind of social arrangements that make this easy transition to adulthood possible.

On returning from the field Mead became assistant curator of ethnology at the American Museum of Natural History, where she remained, eventually becoming curator and, in 1969, curator emeritus. Her mandate in going to the museum was "to make Americans understand cultural anthropology as well as they understood archaeology."

When Mead wrote *Coming of Age in Samoa* (1928), her publisher, concerned that the book fell into no conventional category, asked for a chapter on what the work's significance would be for Americans. The result was the final chapter, "Education for Choice," which set the basic theme for much of her lifework.

In 1928, after completing a technical monograph, *The Social Organization of Manuá,* Mead left for New Guinea, this time with Reo Fortune, an anthropologist from New Zealand whom she had married that year. Her project was the study of the thought of young children, testing some of the then current theories. Her study of children's thought in its sociocultural context is described in *Growing Up in New Guinea* (1930). She later returned to the village of Peri, where this study was made, after 25 years, when the children she had known in 1929 were leaders of a community going through the difficulties of transition to modern life. She described this transition, with flashbacks to the earlier days, in *New Lives for Old* (1956).

New Field Methods

Mead's interest in psychiatry had turned her attention to the problem of the cultural context of schizophrenia, and with this in mind she went to Bali, a society where trance and other forms of dissociation are culturally sanctioned. She was now married to Gregory Bateson, a British anthropologist whom she had met in New Guinea. The Balinese study was especially noteworthy for development of new field techniques. The extensive use of film made it possible to record and analyze significant minutiae of behavior that escape the pencil-and-paper ethnographer. Of the 38,000 photographs which Mead and Bateson brought back, 759 were selected for *Balinese Character* (1942), a joint study with Bateson. This publication marks a major innovation in the recording and presentation of ethnological data and may prove in the long run to be one of her most significant contributions to the science of anthropology.

Studies Relevant to the "Public Good"

Largely through the work of Ruth Benedict and Margaret Mead, the relevance of anthropology to problems of public policy was recognized to a degree, though somewhat belatedly. When World War II brought the United States into contact with allies, enemies, and peoples just emerging from colonialism, the need to understand many lifestyles became apparent. Mead conducted a nationwide study of American food habits prior to the introduction of rationing. Later she was sent to England to try to explain to the British the habits of the American soldiers who were suddenly thrust among them. After the war she worked as director of Research in Contemporary Cultures, a cross-cultural, transdisciplinary project applying the insights and some of the methods of anthropology to the study of complex modern cultures. An overall view of the methods and some of the insights gained is contained in *The Study of Cultures at a Distance* (1953).

For the theoretical basis of her work in the field of culture and personality Margaret Mead drew heavily on psychology, especially learning theory and psychoanalysis. In return she contributed significantly to the development of psychoanalytic theory by emphasizing the importance of culture in personality development. She served on many national and international committees for mental health and was instrumental in introducing the study of culture into training programs for physicians and social workers.

In the 1960s Mead became deeply concerned with the unrest among the young. Her close contact with students gave her special insight into the unmet needs of youth—for better education, for autonomy, for an effective voice in decisions that affect their lives in a world which adults seem no longer able to control. Some of her views on these problems are set forth in *Culture and Commitment* (1970). Her thoughts on human survival under the threats of war, overpopulation, and degradation of the environment are contained in *A Way of Seeing* (1970).

Ever since Margaret Mead taught a class of young working women in 1926, she became deeply involved in education, both in the universities and in interpreting the lessons of anthropology to the general public. She joined the anthropology department at Columbia University in 1947 and also taught at Fordham University and the universities of Cincinnati and Topeka. She also lectured to people all over America and Europe. Mead died in 1978 and was posthumously awarded the Presidential Medal of Freedom.

Margaret Mead was a dominant force in developing the field of culture and personality and the related field of national character research. Stated briefly, her theoretical position is based on the assumption that an individual matures within a cultural context which includes an ideological system, the expectations of others, and techniques of socialization which condition not only outward responses but also inner psychic structure. Mead was criticized by certain other social scientists on methodological and conceptual grounds. She was criticized for neglecting quantitative methods in favor of depth analysis and for what has been called "anecdotal" handling of data. On the theoretical side she was accused of applying concepts of individual psychology to the analysis of social process while ignoring historical and economic factors. But since her concern lay with predicting the behavior of individuals within a given social context and not with the origin of institutions, the criticism is irrelevant.

There is no question that Mead was one of the leading American intellectuals of the 20th century. Through her best-selling books, her public lecturing, and her popular column in *Redbook* magazine, Mead popularized anthropology in the United States. She also provided American women with a role model, encouraging them to pursue professional careers previously closed to women while at the same time championing their roles as mothers.

Further Reading

Of the many studies of Margaret Mead's life and career, see *With a Daughter's Eye: A Memoir of Margaret Mead and Gregory Bateson* (1984) by Mary Catherine Bateson; *Margaret Mead: A Voice for the Century* (1982) by Robert Cassidy; and *Margaret Mead's Contradictory Legacy* (1992), edited by Leonard Foerstel and Angela Gilliam. See also *Anthropologists and What They Do* (1965), which was written for high school students and contains accounts of her life in the university and in the field. Her essay "Field Work in the Pacific Islands, 1925-1967" appears in Peggy Golde, ed., *Women in the Field: Anthropological Experiences* (1970). A full-length study of Mead is Allyn Moss, *Margaret Mead: Shaping a New World* (1963). Hoffman R. Hays, *From Ape to Angel: An Informal History of Social Anthropology* (1958), has an essay appraising her career. There are essays on Mead's life in Eleanor Clymer and Lillian Erlich, *Modern American Career Women* (1959), and Eve Parshalle, *The Kashmir Bridge-women* (1965). □

George Gordon Meade

George Gordon Meade (1815-1872), American Civil War general, is best remembered as the victor of the Battle of Gettysburg and as the last commander of the Army of the Potomac.

The son of an American merchant, George Gordon Meade was born on Dec. 31, 1815, in Cadiz, Spain. His early education was at Mount Hope Institution in Baltimore. At the age of 15 he received appointment to West Point; he graduated in 1835. After serving for a year in Florida and Massachusetts he became disillusioned with Army life and resigned to pursue a civil engineering career. In 1842 Meade returned to the Army and won a brevet promotion for gallantry in the Mexican War. Until the outbreak of the Civil War, he served in the topographical engineers.

In August 1861 Meade was appointed brigadier general and given command of a Pennsylvania brigade. He served throughout the Peninsular Campaign. On June 30, 1862, in the Battle of Glendale, he was seriously wounded in the arm, side, and back. Nevertheless, he led divisions in the Second Manassas, South Mountain, Antietam, and Fredericksburg campaigns and commanded a corps during the Battle of Chancellorsville.

Meade was genuinely surprised when, on June 28, 1863, he was named to head the Army of the Potomac. Only 3 days later Robert E. Lee's army struck Meade's forces at Gettysburg, Pa. In spite of his newness to Army command, Meade demonstrated admirable skill in the bloody 3-day battle. However, when Lee's Confederates were allowed to retire virtually unmolested to Virginia, a storm of criticism descended on Meade. He tendered his resignation from the Army, but it was refused, and he continued commanding the Army for the remainder of the war. He is overshadowed in the climactic campaigns of 1864-1865 because General-in-Chief Ulysses S. Grant traveled with the

Army of the Potomac and supervised its principal operations. Meade's promotion to major general came embarrassingly late in the conflict.

After the war Meade commanded military departments in the South and East. He died of pneumonia on Nov. 6, 1872, in Philadelphia.

Gaunt and stern, Meade suffered from fits of nervousness. Although he was routinely competent, he lacked boldness and brilliance in action. His hot temper led the soldiers to nickname him "the old snapping turtle."

Further Reading

Much of Meade's own correspondence is in *The Life and Letters of George Gordon Meade* (2 vols., 1913), edited by his son, George Gordon Meade. The best study of Meade is Freeman Cleaves, *Meade of Gettysburg* (1960), which concentrates heavily on the famous battle. More sympathetic biographies are Richard Meade Bache, *Life of General George Gordon Meade* (1897), and Isaac R. Pennypacker, *General Meade* (1901). □

Russell Means

Russell Means (born 1939) led the American Indian Movement (AIM) in a 1973 armed seizure of Wounded Knee, South Dakota, site of the previous massacre of Sioux by Seventh U.S. Cavalry troops on

December 29, 1890. With co-leaders Dennis Banks and Leonard Peltier, Means and AIM held off hundreds of federal agents on the Pine Ridge Reservation for seventy-one days before their surrender.

Russell C. Means has been an outspoken Indian rights activist for more than two decades. The organizer of numerous protests against the U.S. government's treatment of Native Americans and a major figure in the American Indian Movement (AIM), Means is perhaps best known for leading a 71-day siege at Wounded Knee, South Dakota, which drew national attention to Indian-rights issues in the early 1970s. The head of the American Indian Anti-Defamation League since 1988, Means continues to fight for the unique identity and independence of Native Americans.

Russell Charles Means, who would use the traditional term "Lakota" rather than the term "Sioux", which he views as a derogatory white word, was born November 10, 1939, on the Pine Ridge Reservation in South Dakota, the oldest son of Harold ("Hank") Means, a mixed-blood Oglala Sioux and Theodora (Feather) Means, a full-blood Yankton Sioux. He attended the Bureau of Indian Affairs (BIA) school on the reservation and later public schools in Vallejo, California. During his high school years, he transferred from the racially mixed Vallejo school to the almost all-white San Leandro High School where he experienced daily ethnic taunting. Not knowing how else to respond, Means at first

fought back and then retreated into drugs and delinquency. After barely graduating from high school, he worked through various jobs and attended five colleges without graduating. He spent much of the 1960s drifting throughout the west, working as a cowboy, day laborer, and at an advertising firm. In 1969 he moved from a position on the Rosebud Sioux tribal council on the Rosebud Reservation in South Dakota to the directorship of the government-funded American Indian Center in Cleveland, Ohio.

In Cleveland Means met Dennis Banks, one of the cofounders of the newly organized American Indian Movement, a militant Indian civil rights group. Inspired by Banks and his movement, he set up AIM's second chapter in Cleveland. Means became a national media figure representing dissident Indians on Thanksgiving Day in 1970 when he and a small group of other Indians confronted costumed "Pilgrims" on the Mayflower II in Plymouth, Massachusetts. Dressed in combination western and Indian style, he became an effective symbol for AIM. Eloquent and charismatic, he inspired support from local Indian people while his inflammatory statements riled non-Indians.

That same year, Means participated in a prayer vigil on Mount Rushmore, a symbolic demonstration of Lakota claims to Black Hills land. His next protest was to file a $9 million dollar lawsuit against the Cleveland Indians baseball club for use of Chief Wahoo as a mascot, asserting in the suit that the symbol demeaned Native Americans. This latter action provoked Cleveland ball club fans, and led to Means's decision to resign his position at the Cleveland Center in 1972. He returned to South Dakota and participated in further activities intended to bring attention to Indian rights.

In February, 1972, Means led 1,300 angry Indians into the small town of Gordon, Nebraska, to protest the suspicious death of Raymond Yellow Thunder. The demonstration convinced town authorities to conduct a second autopsy, which eventually led to the indictment of two white townsmen for manslaughter. The Indian protest gained further success when the city council suspended a police officer accused of molesting jailed Indian women and then organized a multiracial human rights council. Violence against Indians increased all over the country that summer, leading to further defensiveness among local Indian people who felt they needed to arm themselves if they were to be the targets of murderous attacks.

At the annual Rosebud Sun Dance celebration, Means helped plan a mass demonstration to occur in Washington D.C. during election week of 1972. He urged a march to demand a federal law that would make it a crime to kill an Indian, even if it had to be added as an amendment to the Endangered Species Act. A series of cross-country caravans called "The Trail of Broken Treaties" arrived in Washington November 2 only to find that the adequate housing promised by the Department of the Interior was in fact crowded and rodent-infested. Feeling that the government officials sent out to investigate were officious and patronizing, Means then led the group to the Bureau of Indian Affairs where they successfully seized the offices and renamed the building the Native American Embassy. On November 6 a

U.S. District Court Judge ordered the group's forcible eviction. Angry and frustrated, the Indians destroyed furniture and equipment and removed files they felt exploited Indian people. The next day the group agreed to leave the building peaceably after government officials promised to investigate federal programs affecting Indians and to consider the issue of Indian self-government. The government also offered $66,000 to cover travel expenses.

Occupies Town of Historic Massacre

When Means returned to South Dakota, he learned that the president of the Oglala Tribal Council, Dick Wilson, had obtained a court order prohibiting members of AIM from attending public meetings on the reservation. Wilson, a conservative opposed to the extreme activities of AIM, received government support to increase his police force, and had Means arrested twice for challenging the court order. When a white man was charged for second degree manslaughter instead of murder for the stabbing death of an Indian man, Means was among the leaders of a protest through the town of Custer where court was held. He and nearly 80 others were arrested for rioting and arson. The internal tribal governance conflict escalated as traditional leaders requested AIM's help in getting rid of council president Wilson, whom some viewed as representative of Washington bureaucracy. On February 27, 1973, Means and a group of nearly 200 armed supporters occupied the community of Wounded Knee, the site of the 1890 massacre of some 350 Sioux men, women, and children by the U.S. military. Tensions mounted as heavily armed FBI agents and federal marshals surrounded the area. More than a month later, Means agreed to fly to Washington to negotiate an agreement to end the siege, but the government refused to negotiate until all arms were laid down. Means refused to the unconditional surrender and left the meeting. He was arrested and detained for the remainder of the siege when he announced his intention to return to Wounded Knee. On May 8, 1973, the remaining Indians surrendered when the government agreed to meet with tribal elders to begin an investigation into tribal government, which had been accused, under Wilson, of ignoring the tribal constitution, among other things. Highly publicized in the national media, the ten-week siege became known as "Wounded Knee II" and garnered the support of many white Americans, including several Hollywood personalities.

Means ran against Wilson in the 1974 election of tribal council president while under federal indictment for actions during the Wounded Knee occupation. He lost the election, receiving 1530 votes to Wilson's 1709, but claimed that his election results indicated strong support for AIM causes on the reservation. His trial opened on February 12, 1974, and continued until September 16, when U.S. District Court Judge Fred Nichol dismissed the charges against Means and Banks and denounced the prosecution's handling of the case, which had included the use of information obtained from a member Means's defense team by a paid FBI informant. When asked years later about the beneficial results of the Wounded Knee occupation, Means related a story of watching three little Indian boys playing, one pretending to be Banks, one pretending to be Means, and the third refusing to be Wilson. Means felt that the protests influenced the development of a different sense of Indian identity: that "government" Indians were considered traitors.

During the Wounded Knee occupation, Means was shot by a BIA officer. In the following six years, he survived four other shootings and was stabbed while serving a term in South Dakota's prison. These attempts on his life sent a message to other Indian people that they were not safe from violent attacks. In 1975 Means was indicted for a murder in a barroom brawl, but his attorney, William Kunstler, who had been one of the defense attorneys during the Wounded Knee trial, argued that the government had created such a climate of fear that Indians were armed in self-defense. The jury acquitted Means of the murder charge on August 6, 1976. He was convicted of riot charges relating to the 1973 Custer demonstration and served one month in jail. In November 1977, he served a term for rioting in a South Dakota state penitentiary.

Reclaims Indian Land at Yellow Thunder Camp

Russell Means was also among the group who occupied federal land at Yellow Thunder Camp. In April 1981, a group of Dakota AIM and traditional Lakota people established a camp on federal land in Victoria Creek Canyon, about twelve miles southwest of Rapid City, South Dakota. Named in honor of Raymond Yellow Thunder, the man murdered in Gordon, Nebraska, in 1972, the camp was established as the first step in reclaiming the Black Hills land for Lakota use. When the U.S. Forest Service denied a use permit for the camp, Means acted as a lay attorney in the complaint against the Forest Service for violating the American Indian Freedom of Religion Act of 1978. In 1985, Judge Donald O'Brien ruled in favor of the Indian camp, but a higher court overturned the decision.

After the Yellow Thunder trial, Means became involved in native rights issues in other countries, including supporting the cause of the Miskito Indians of Nicaragua. He has been associated politically with the Libertarian Party. In 1992, he turned actor, playing the role of Chingachgook in the movie *The Last of the Mohicans*. While on the set, Means served as liaison between Indian extras and the movie producers during a labor dispute. He claimed that he had not abandoned his role as activist. In an article in *Entertainment Weekly,* Means commented, "I have been asked whether my decision to act in *The Last of the Mohicans* means that I've abandoned my role as an activist. On the contrary, I see film as an extension of the path I've been on for the past 25 years—another avenue to eliminating racism."

In the spring of 1994, AIM cofounder Clyde Bellecourt accused Means of selling out the AIM cause by accepting a $35,000 settlement from the 1972 suit against the Cleveland Indians baseball organization. Means, who left the American Indian Movement in 1988, responded that his current organization, the American Indian Anti-Defamation League, would be filing another lawsuit against the ball club he never received any of the money.

Although Means generally detests writing as a European concept, he agreed to have his words published as a chapter in *Marxism and Native Americans* in order to communicate with a wider audience. He urged each American Indian to avoid becoming Europeanized, using traditional values to resist. He criticized the European intellectual traditions, including Christianity and capitalism, and accused the Europeans of despiritualizing the universe. He also warned that Marxism, as a European tradition, is also no solution for American Indians' problems. He concluded:"I am not a 'leader.' I am an Oglala Lakota patriot. That's all I want or need to be. And I am very comfortable with who I am."

In late 1995 Means published his auto*biography Where White Men Fear to Tread: The Autobiography of Russell Means* coincidentally with Native American Heritage Month. Not surprisingly the strident Means used the occasion to show his disdain for the notion of heritage month, which he finds "abhorrent," as he does the term "Native American." Means told *Library Journal* in a telephone interview that the term "Native American" is used to " . . . describe all the prisoners of the U.S. government" and that the idea of a Native American Heritage Month is a " . . . subterfuge to hide the ongoing daily genocide being practiced against my people by this United States of America." Since being recognized nationally for his reform movements and AIM activities Means had been approached numerous times to write an autobiography. At first he regarded such a proposals as "arrogant" but after undergoing treatment for alcoholism and his anger towards white America Means relented and came to believe that an autobiography would prove helpful and relevant to his cause by shedding light on the social reform movements of the turbulent Sixties and Seventies and helping to correct prevailing stereotypes of the American Indian.

The Washington Post has called Means the " . . . biggest, baddest, meanest, angriest, most famous American Indian activist of the late 20th century." And Means was angry, angry at the White Man's "fascist government," the White Man's "economic exploitation," and the White Man's "despoiling of nature." Means was also angry at his own people, especially the women who would pull at his braids and tell him how "cute" they were. Means feeling his person had been violated by their actions would retaliate by pawing at their breasts while saying "Oh how cute!" By coming to grip with his emotions and anger however Means has worked through his "defects" and has come to find " . . . peace of mind, the exhilaration of freedom, the bursting of bonds."

Means has also continued to be active on the Hollywood scene. His acclaimed role of Chingachgook in Last of the Mohicans was followed with his doing the voice of Chief Powhatan in Walt Disney's hit *Pocahontas*. He also has credits in *Natural Born Killers, Wagons East,* and *Wind Runner.* Means is also planning a school at Pine Ridge to be called the University of the Universe and will teach Lakota culture as does his Yellow Thunder Camp in the Black Hills. Means hopes that through these spiritual youth camps he will leave a legacy of "self-dignity and self-pride" amongst his people.

Further Reading

Means, Russell, *Where White Men Fear to Tread: The Autobiography of Russell Means*, St. Martin's Press, 1995. □

George Meany

George Meany (1894 -1980) was one of America's most powerful labor leaders during the 20th century. He was president of the American Federation of Labor and Congress of Industrial Organizations (AFL-CIO) from 1955 to 1979.

George Meany was born on Aug. 16, 1894, in New York City. He inherited his dedication to the trade union movement from his father, who was president of a local plumbers' union. When George had to leave high school because of difficult family circumstances, he chose his father's trade. After a 5-year apprenticeship, he received his journeyman plumber's certificate in 1915.

In 1922 Meany was elected business agent of his union local. Although unionism did not thrive during the 1920s, Meany steadily broadened his activities within the building trades. President of the New York State Federation of Labor (1934-1939), he took advantage of the progressive mood of Franklin D. Roosevelt's New Deal by helping enact more pro-labor bills and social reform measures than had previously been passed in the entire history of the New York Legislature. In 1939 Meany was elected secretary treasurer of the American Federation of Labor (AFL).

During World War II Meany served on the War Labor Board and represented the AFL on Roosevelt's committee to draw up wartime labor policy. He also served on a special committee that the president regularly consulted on labor-management problems. After the war Meany helped establish the International Confederation of Free Trade Unions, which contributed to the success of the Marshall Plan for the rehabilitation of war-torn Europe.

In November 1952 Meany was chosen president of the AFL. Three years later he was unanimously elected president of the newly combined AFL-CIO at its first convention. He was consistently reelected without opposition.

Throughout his career Meany was interested in reform, both within the labor movement and society at large. He initiated the first major attacks on corruption in the unions and was responsible for establishing a code of ethical practices for all union affiliates. He also took important steps toward eliminating racial discrimination in the labor movement. Under Meany's leadership, the AFL-CIO vigorously supported the Occupational Safety and Health Act, designed to protect employees from dangerous work conditions. The act became law in 1970.

Meany put the full political force of the labor movement behind efforts to enact civil rights legislation. Without the trade union movement's support, none of the civil rights bills passed during the 1960s would have gone through Congress. The results of these bills testify to the persisting relevance of the labor movement and to Meany's social vision.

President Dwight D. Eisenhower twice appointed Meany a U.S. delegate to the United Nations General Assembly, and Meany received numerous awards, including the Presidential Medal of Freedom (1963). George Meany died on January 10, 1980, at the age of 86.

Further Reading

A chapter on Meany is included in Jack Barbash, ed., *Unions and Union Leadership* (1959), and some biographical information is in Thomas R. Brooks, *Toil and Trouble: A History of American Labor* (1964; rev. ed. 1971). See also Philip Taft, *Organized Labor in American History* (1964). Finke, Blythe F. *George Meany: Modern Leader of the American Federation of Labor* (1972) □

Peter Brian Medawar

The British zoologist Peter Brian Medawar (1915-1987) made important contributions to the knowledge of growth, aging, and especially the biology of tissue transplantation.

Peter Medawar was born on Feb. 28, 1915, in Petropolis, Rio de Janeiro, Brazil of a British mother and Lebanese father. He was educated at Marlborough College and subsequently at Magdalen College, Oxford, where he studied zoology and comparative anatomy in the Goodrichian tradition. His early research was concerned with the factors controlling growth in tissue culture. He was greatly influenced in this work by Darcy Thompson, author of *Growth and Form*. From an early stage in his career Medawar distinguished himself by his competence in both the experimental and the theoretical aspects of biology. He won several prizes at Oxford, where he became a university demonstrator and fellow of Magdalen College.

During World War II Medawar investigated the repair of peripheral nerve injuries. In one of these investigations he devised the first biological "glue," which he used to reunite severed nerves and to fix grafts. This work stimulated his interest in the techniques for transplantation. In 1942 Medawar turned his attention to skin grafts as a result of the need to replace skin after severe burns. He demonstrated that grafts from unrelated donors (homografts) are normally destroyed as a consequence of an immunological response—the homograft reaction—on the part of the host. He was determined then to break down this homograft barrier.

In 1948, when only 32, Medawar was appointed Mason professor of zoology at Birmingham University. A year later he was elected a fellow of the Royal Society. At Birmingham he became interested in problems of cellular heredity and transformation and renewed his attack on the homograft problem. While attempting to devise a method to distinguish between identical and fraternal cattle twins by exchanging skin grafts between twin pairs, he discovered that even fraternal twins of unlike sex would accept each other's grafts. From this he hypothesized that an exchange of cells between the cattle before birth brought about graft tolerance after birth.

In 1951, when Medawar moved to the Jodrell chair of zoology at University College, London, he followed the lead afforded by the cattle work and demonstrated that inoculation of very young mice with cells from unrelated donors created a tolerance to homografts from their donors later in life. Apart from establishing that the homograft problem was in principle soluble and providing a great impetus to research to this area, this finding introduced a new concept into immunology, that of acquired immunological tolerance. For this work Medawar received a Nobel Prize in 1960. He also succeeded in extracting from cells the antigens capable of eliciting transplantation immunity, thus setting the stage for further biochemical studies. He also demonstrated that homograft reactivity is a form of delayed allergy.

In 1962 Medawar was appointed director of the National Institute for Medical Research at Mill Hill. Undaunted by administrative responsibilities, he continued to work energetically in his laboratory. Wherever he worked Medawar attracted a dedicated group of students and research fellows. With characteristic generosity he treated them as colleagues and collaborators, and from the beginning he gave them unstinting help and encouragement. Many former members of his "school" went on to occupy distinguished positions around the world. His many recognitions and awards included a knighthood and numerous honorary degrees. Throughout the 1970s and 1980s, Medawar produced several books, some with his wife as co-author, in addition to his many essays on growth, aging, immunity, and cellular transformations. In one of his most popular books, *Advice to a Young Scientist,* Medawar wrote that scientists are not geniuses, merely people with common sense and curiosity. He died on Oct. 2, 1987, at the age of 72.

Further Reading

For sketches of Medawar's life and work see *Sir Peter Medawar (1915-1987)* by N.A. Mitchison in *Nature* (Nov. 12, 1987); J.S. Medawar's *A Very Decided Preference: Life with Peter Medawar* (1990); the Nobel Foundation, *Physiology or Medicine: Nobel Lectures, Including Presentation Speeches and Laureates' Biographies* (3 vols., 1964-1967), and Theodore L. Sourkes, *Nobel Prize Winners in Medicine and Physiology, 1901-1965* (rev. ed. 1967). □

Catherine de' Medici

Catherine de' Medici (1519–1589) was a Machiavellian politician, wife of Henry II of France, and later regent for her three feeble sons at the twilight of the Valois dynasty, who authorized the killing of French Protestants in the notorious Massacre of St. Bartholomew's Day in 1572.

Catherine de' Medici was never able to rule France as its monarch because the Salic Law restricted the succession solely to men. But this Machiavellian—whose father was Machiavelli's patron—ruled it as regent for nearly 30 years, and did everything she could to strengthen the position of her three weak sons on its throne. She presided over, and was partly responsible for, many of the horrors of the French Wars of Religion in the 1560s and 1570s, of which the worst was the massacre of Protestants gathered in Paris to witness the marriage of her daughter Marguerite Valois to Duke Henry of Navarre in 1572. Her calculating policies yielded short-term victories, but when she died in 1589 her hopes for her family's long-term future lay in ruins.

Catherine was born in 1519, daughter of a powerful Italian prince from the Medici family. Her mother died within a few days from puerperal fever and her father succumbed to consumption a week later at the age of 27, leaving her an orphan after less than one month of life. Her

father's relatives, among them popes Leo X and Clement VII, took over her care, and she grew up in the midst of the stormy Italian Wars in which they were central actors. When a German army of the Holy Roman Emperor Charles V sacked Rome in 1527, the citizens of Florence took advantage of this eclipse of Medici power to restore their republic, and took the eight-year-old Catherine hostage. Escaping from Rome and hiring a group of mercenaries to recapture Florence, her uncle Clement VII was able to rescue her from her refuge in a nunnery.

In pursuit of Pope Clement's dynastic ambitions, 14-year-old Catherine was married in 1533 to 14-year-old Henry, duke of Orleans, younger son of King Francis I of France. The elaborate ceremony at Marseilles Cathedral was conducted by the pope himself, but her childlessness for the first ten years of marriage made her unpopular in the French court. With the help, as she believed, of astrologers—she was patroness of the seer Nostradamus and a lifelong dabbler in necromancy, astronomy, and astrology—she overcame this early infertility and gave birth to ten children, beginning in 1543. Few of them were healthy, however, and she, enjoying an iron constitution and great powers of recovery, would outlive all but one, Henry III, who would follow her to the grave in a matter of months. The death of her husband's older brother in 1536 made Henry and Catherine heirs to the throne, but the circumstances of his death increased Catherine's unpopularity. One of her retinue, Count Sebastian Montecuculi, was suspected of poisoning him to promote the interests of Catherine and, possibly, of France's enemy Charles V.

Catherine's husband, now Henry II, had spent several childhood years as a hostage at the Spanish court in Madrid. On his return, at the age of 11, he had been cared for by Diane de Poitiers, who was 20 years his senior. Despite this age difference, they became lovers, and throughout most of Henry's reign, which began in 1547, Diane completely eclipsed Catherine in influence over the king, though her age and her lack of beauty made Henry's attraction and loyalty to her something of a mystery at court. Diane was even given responsibility for raising Catherine's children, and she and Henry arranged the betrothal of the oldest son, Francis, to Mary, Queen of Scots in 1548. But in 1557, Catherine's coolness in an emergency won her new respect from Henry. He had lost the battle of St. Quentin to Philip II of Spain; when Paris itself was jeopardized, Catherine made a patriotic speech to the Parlement, persuaded it to raise more troops and money to continue the fight, and put to rest the old suspicion that she was more an Italian schemer than a true queen of France.

At the time of Catherine's birth in 1519 the Reformation was beginning with Martin Luther's criticism of the Catholic Church. The challenge to Rome's religious hegemony (dominance) began in Germany but soon spread throughout Europe. The French lawyer and theologian John Calvin, living and writing in Geneva, Switzerland, was particularly inspiring to many French men and women, who saw in his version of Christianity a truer form of their faith than that offered by a politicized and often corrupt Catholic Church. In France, for example, appointments and promotions in the

Catholic Church were all at the king's disposal; political cronyism rather than piety and administrative skill led to advancement. French Protestants were known as Huguenots, and the rapid growth of their numbers among the nobility and upper classes as well as among ordinary folk soon made them a politically significant force; the Huguenots held their first general French assembly in 1559.

This was an era in which monarchs assumed that the integrity of their kingdoms depended on the religious uniformity of their peoples; religious schism of the kind which beset France by mid-century was unprecedented. The Catholic monarchs of France and Spain made peace at Cateau-Cambrésis in 1559 partly because they were bankrupt but also so that they could unite their forces against Protestantism. The treaty was sealed by the marriage of Philip II of Spain to Elisabeth, the teenaged daughter of Catherine and King Henry. At the joust held to mark the wedding celebrations, however, King Henry was fatally injured by a lance wielded by a Calvinist nobleman, the Comte de Montgomery. It shattered his helmet, pierced his eye, and entered his brain. Henry's death a few days later brought their oldest son, 16-year-old Francis II, to the throne.

France was full of demobilized soldiers, many of them unpaid for months. Tax burdens on the peasants were heavy, and Calvinist preachers with their message of an uncorrupted faith found a receptive audience. Huguenot noblemen took action almost at once, organizing a conspiracy to overthrow or at least dominate the court of Francis II, and winning the active support of England's new Protestant queen, Elizabeth I. Then, at the city of Amboise, their military uprising failed, and the royal army arrested the leaders. In the presence of Catherine, her children, and Mary, Queen of Scots, 57 of the Huguenot leaders were hanged or beheaded. This retribution did not end the religious-political conflicts besetting France, however; from this time forward, the Huguenot Navarre family and the Catholic Guises led rival religious and court factions. The death of 16-year-old Francis II the following year made Catherine regent for her second son Charles, who now became King Charles IX at the age of ten.

Herself a lifelong Catholic but always with a degree of religious cynicism, Catherine appears never to have understood the passion with which many of her contemporaries lived their religious lives. For her, religious differences seemed at first to be bargaining chips in court intrigues, which might be smoothed away by tactful diplomacy. She permitted Admiral Gaspard de Coligny, an influential Huguenot, to act as Charles's chief advisor for awhile, provoking three powerful noblemen, the duke of Guise, the cardinal of Lorraine, and the constable of France, to sink their own differences and make a three-way alliance, a triumvirate, for the defense of Catholicism against Coligny.

Catherine's miscalculation of the Reformation's impact on France was evident at the Colloquy of Poissy, 1561, when she tried to conciliate the Catholic faction, under the cardinal of Lorraine, with the Huguenots, under the reform theologian and friend of Calvin, Theodore Beza. Far from coming to an understanding with one another, the two parties hardened their differences. In the poisoned atmosphere of broken negotiation, open hostilities began, marking the first of a succession of religious wars. Interrupted by truces, but marked by fierce vendettas, the conflict raged for a decade.

Charles IX was an unstable character, and as he matured he came to dislike his mother and her favorite, younger son Henry. Charles, says the lively historian Henri Nogueres:

> had the figure of a sickly adolescent, too thin for its size, hollow-chested and with drooping shoulders . . . his sallow complexion and bilious eyes betrayed liver trouble; he had a bitter twist at the corners of his mouth and feverish eyes. . . . He hunted in order to kill, for he soon acquired a taste for blood, and almost every day he needed the bitter sensation, the uneasy satisfaction of seeing the pulsating entrails and the hounds on the quarry.

Catherine found it relatively easy to dominate Charles, despite his growing resentment, and in the face of constant warfare she also tried to carve some order out of the fiscal and administrative chaos of the kingdom, to strengthen it for her sons' reigns. She took Charles on a long royal journey through his kingdom. She incorporated in 1565 a meeting with her son-in-law, Philip II of Spain, to discuss the continuing religious crisis. Philip disliked her apparent willingness to play off Catholics and Protestants against one another; in his view, she should have been doing more to advance the Counter-Reformation. But he also knew that France's weakness was a strategic benefit for Spain. It made French intervention to aid troublesome Dutch rebels against Spain far less likely. When Philip's wife and Catherine's favorite daughter Elisabeth died in childbirth in 1568, Catherine hoped he might marry her younger daughter Marguerite, but Philip was determined to take his French connection no further. Another blow to Catherine's politicking came the same year when her daughter-in-law, Mary, Queen of Scots, was captured by her English enemies and imprisoned, leaving Scotland open to Protestant domination and effectively ending a Franco-Scottish Catholic encirclement of Elizabethan England.

Through much of the 1560s, the two religious factions were at war while Catherine and Charles tried to avoid falling too heavily into either camp. The religious warfare was complicated further by English incursions into France itself, ostensibly in alliance with the Huguenots, but largely in pursuit of traditional English designs on northern France. The war was also complicated by a blood feud among the major families, brought on when the Huguenot leader Admiral Gaspard de Coligny ordered the assassination of the duke of Guise in 1563. As the fighting continued, especially in the third religious war, from 1568 to 1570, Huguenot armies attacked convents and monasteries, torturing and massacring their inhabitants, while Catholic forces, equally merciless, slew the Huguenots of several districts indiscriminately.

After a decade of war, the Peace of St. Germain in 1570 reconciled the two sides temporarily and led to Admiral Coligny's return to court. Among the treaty's provisions was the specification that Catherine's daughter Marguerite should marry Henry of Navarre, the Huguenot leader, that the Huguenots should be given several strongholds throughout France, and that Coligny could resume his position as a royal councillor. Catherine hoped that, as a moderate Huguenot, he might act to mollify his fellow Huguenots while she played the same role among Catholics. But Coligny quickly and tactlessly reasserted himself at court, becoming a friend and confidante of King Charles IX but arousing suspicions among Catholic courtiers that he was planning another coup. When Coligny discovered that Charles and his mother were at odds, he miscalculated and chose the king's side rather than Catherine's, provoking her furious resentment.

The city of Paris had remained friendly to the ultra-Catholic Guise party throughout these years of war, and most Parisians resented the concessions to Huguenots made at the Treaty of St. Germain. The population was, accordingly, restless and angry when a large Huguenot assembly entered their city in the summer of 1572 to celebrate the wedding. Marguerite Valois, the bride, was herself a stormy personality and an inveterate intriguer. When Catherine had discovered earlier that Marguerite was having an affair with the duke of Guise, she and Charles IX had beaten her senseless. The motive for this marriage alliance was that Henry of Navarre, though a Huguenot, would have a strong claim to the French throne if neither Charles IX nor Catherine's younger son Henry had a living heir. A connection to the Valois family would strengthen Navarre's claim as well as Catherine's prospects of continued influence. Marguerite, still in love with Guise, resisted the planned marriage, says historian Hugh Williamson:

> she and Henry of Navarre had known each other during their growing up at least well enough to be aware that they had no glimmer of sexual attraction for each other and even domestic accommodation was imperilled by such differences as her liking for at least one bath a day and his aversion to more than one a year. Also he always stank of garlic.

She refused to give up her Catholic faith for this marriage, which was in any case imperiled when Henry's mother Jeanne of Navarre died suddenly during the negotiations which preceded it. In the fevered atmosphere of the time, many Huguenots were ready to believe that Catherine de' Medici had poisoned Jeanne, although that seems unlikely.

Catherine decided to dispose of Gaspard de Coligny once and for all. She accepted an offer from the Guise party to assassinate him, hoping that the outcome would be revived power for her own party. The assassin shot Coligny but failed to kill him, and Charles IX rushed to his side, promising a full inquiry and retribution against the assassins. But under interrogation from Catherine and his younger brother Henry, Charles finally accepted their claim that Coligny was manipulating him, that Coligny planned to overthrow the whole Catholic court, and that he and the other Huguenot leaders should now be finished off in a preemptive strike. According to his brother Henry's diary, Charles at last shouted; "Kill the Admiral if you wish; but you must also kill all the Huguenots, so that not one is left alive to reproach me. Kill them all!"

By careful prearrangement, church bells began to ring at two in the morning of August 24, Saint Bartholomew's Day, 1572. The bells signaled Catholic troops to begin, and at once they moved to kill the injured Coligny and other Huguenot leaders. The attacks became indiscriminate; all sense of order broke down. As widespread looting and fighting broke out across Paris, over 2,000 men, women, and children (including many people uninvolved in political and religious controversy) were shot or hacked to death. Similar massacres followed in the provinces, as Catholics seized the initiative against their local Huguenot rivals. King Charles feared that he had unleashed a revolution, but Catherine, according to one onlooker, "looks a younger woman by ten years and gives the impression of one who has recovered from a serious illness or escaped a great danger." A fourth civil war at once began, but by a strange turn of circumstances, leadership of the Huguenot party now fell to Catherine's youngest and most unscrupulous son Francis, duke of Alençon. Placing himself at the head of the Protestant forces and dreaming of a crown, he declared that his older brother Henry, who had just been elected to the throne of Poland, was no longer available as heir of France.

Henry, this third son of Catherine, was less easily dominated and manipulated than Charles. He was homosexual and had had a long succession of lovers. His mother tried to "correct" this propensity by ordering a banquet at which the food was served by naked women, but she could not succeed. Henry had spent the 1560s garnering the laurels of a successful general in the wars against the Huguenots. His victories won him the envy of King Charles IX, whose physical frailty forbade campaigning. Catherine tried to marry Henry to Elizabeth I of England, but the "Virgin Queen" tactfully declined the offer and was equally obdurate against the wooing of the pathetic fourth brother, Alençon, whom she called her "frog." The only woman to excite Henry's interest, and to whom he sent ardent love letters signed in his own blood, was already married to the prince of Conde. Henry did not relish the prospect of going to Poland, even though his mother's judicious distribution of bribes to the electors there had secured the throne for him, but at last he set out. His departure prompted another Huguenot uprising, in which Alençon, Henry of Navarre, and Marguerite Valois were all implicated as conspirators. With her usual energy, Catherine coordinated forces to quell it, and with her usual decisiveness, she witnessed the executions of the ringleaders Montgomery, La Mole, and Coconnas. She also witnessed the death of her son King Charles, aged 24. She now recalled her favorite, Henry, to his hereditary kingdom.

Henry III was crowned in 1575 and married in the same year to Louise of Lorraine, but they had no children to carry on the Valois line. From this time on, Catherine entrusted family fortunes more wholeheartedly to the Catholic Guise family, and approved the formation of the Catholic League in 1576 which marched to triumph against the Huguenots. Henry's homosexual favorites predominated at court. When

the Guise provoked a duel and killed two of them, Quelus and Saint-Megrim, Henry conceived an implacable hatred against them. Another round of blood feuding began despite Catherine's continued urging that Henry must settle his differences with the Guise for the sake of national and Catholic security.

Catherine remained politically active until the end of her life, touring France on Henry's behalf and trying to assure the loyalty of its many fractured and war-torn provinces. She also amassed a huge collection of books and paintings, built or enlarged some of Paris's finest buildings, including the Tuileries Palace, and carried on to the end her fascination with astrology. She was fat and gouty by 1589 and was taken ill that year from the exertion of dancing at the marriage of one of her granddaughters. She lived just long enough to hear that Henry's bodyguards had murdered Guise; this news, writes Williamson, "destroyed her will to live, for it epitomized her failure. Her idolized son, for whom she had spent her whole life, had destroyed all that she had built and rejected everything she had taught him." Later that year, Henry III in turn died, assassinated by a Dominican friar, Jacques Clement, who regarded him a traitor to the faith for joining Henry of Navarre against the Catholic League. In this way, the Valois dynasty came to an end. Ironically it was the Huguenot prince Henry of Navarre who succeeded to the throne, though he was unable to sit upon it until 1593 when he cynically adopted the Catholic faith with the famous remark, "Paris is worth a Mass."

Further Reading

The most satisfactory study of Catherine de' Médici is Paul Van Dyke, *Catherine de' Médici* (2 vols., 1992). The short pamphlet by N. M. Sutherland, *Catherine de' Médici and the Ancien Régime* (1966), provides an excellent introduction to the major problems in interpreting the political role of the queen mother. Sutherland also wrote *The French Secretaries of State in the Age of Catherine de Medici* (1962), a study of Catherine's closest administrative assistants. On Catherine's religious policy see H. Outram Evennett, *The Cardinal of Lorraine and the Council of Trent: A Study in the Counter Reformation* (1930), and the relevant portion of Joseph Lecler, *Toleration and the Reformation* (trans., 2 vols., 1960). An example of Catherine's use of art in support of her political program is described by Francis A. Yates, *The Valois Tapestries* (1959).

There is considerable historical literature on the wars of religion in France. Recommended are James Westfall Thompson, *The Wars of Religion in France, 1559-1576* (1909); Franklin Charles Palm, *Politics and Religion in Sixteenth-Century France* (1927); J. E. Neale, *The Age of Catherine de Medici* (1943; new ed. 1957); Robert M. Kingdom, *Geneva and the Coming of the Wars of Religion in France, 1555-1563* (1956); and Philippe Erlanger, *St. Bartholomew's Night: The Massacre of Saint Bartholomew* (trans. 1962). The French wars of religion are placed in the context of European politics in J. H. Elliot, *Europe Divided: 1559-1598* (1968).

Additional Sources

Heritier, Jean, *Catherine de Medici*. St. Martin's Press, 1963.
Mahoney, Irene, *Madame Catherine*, New York: Coward, McCann, & Geoghegan, 1975.

Nogueres, Henri, *The Massacre of Saint Bartholomew.* Macmillan, 1962.

Soman, Alfred, *The Massacre of Saint Bartholomew: Reappraisals and Documents.* Hague: Martinus Nijhoff, 1974.

Strage, Mark, *Women of Power: The, Life and Times of Catherine de Medici.* New York: Harcourt Brace Jovanovich, 1976.

Williamson, Hugh Ros, *Catherine de Medici.* Viking, 1973. □

Cosimo de' Medici

The Italian merchant prince Cosimo de' Medici (1389-1464) was the unofficial and benevolent despot of Florence, contributing much to making it the intellectual and cultural jewel of 15th-century Europe. The dynasty he founded ruled Florence until 1494.

Cosimo de' Medici was born on Sept. 27, 1389, the son of Giovanni de' Medici, who founded the family's legendary fortune, amassing enormous sums in trade and banking. After his father died in 1429, Cosimo continued the family's commercial and financial practices with great success. He brought goods of little weight and high value from the East and lent money to the princely houses of Europe.

Cosimo also adopted the policy, already traditional in his family, of supporting the lesser guilds and the poor against the wealthy aristocracy which ruled the city. These oligarchs became jealous of Cosimo's popularity and fearful of his democratic tendencies. Consequently they sought to destroy him and his family. In 1433, spurred on by Rinaldo degli Albizzi, the most influential of their number, they had Cosimo arrested with the intention of putting him to death. He was exiled instead when, from his place of imprisonment, he succeeded in buying the favor of Bernardo Guadagni, the gonfalonier of justice, for 1,000 ducats (about $25,000).

One year later, in October 1434, the sentence of exile was overturned by a new government favorable to Cosimo, and he returned to the city in triumph. From that time until his death he controlled both the foreign and domestic affairs of Florence, using his prestige and his money to keep his adherents in the government. Cosimo himself took public office only briefly. He believed it prudent to keep the institutions of government intact and to rule quietly, so as not to injure the republican sensibilities of the people.

His despotism established, Cosimo promptly reformed the system of taxation, changing from a fixed income tax to a graduated one. This placed a heavier burden on the wealthy, who grumbled that the Medici tyrant was using the tax as a weapon against them. The middle class and the poorer citizens, who were Cosimo's strength, were delighted and became even more ardent in their support, particularly when they saw that the funds gained through taxation, amplified by substantial contributions from Cosimo's own pocket, were put to use in public projects.

Cosimo employed the architectural skills of Michelozzo to build his palace and, in 1437, the Dominican convent of S. Marco. He commissioned Filippo Brunelleschi to restore the church of S. Lorenzo, which was in dire need of repair. The cloisters of Fiesole owe their erection to Cosimo, who added to these monuments of his munificence country villas of contemporary style at both Fiesole and Careggi.

Along with the physical adornment of Florence and its environs, Cosimo provided for its cultural life. He sent his ships to the East to gather the precious manuscripts of ancient writers, and he hired scribes to copy what he could not buy. He added to this growing collection the private library of Niccolò Niccoli, an enthusiastic bibliophile who left his books to Cosimo in gratitude for generous loans which had saved him from financial ruin. These valuable manuscripts were distributed to the monastery of S. Marco in Florence and the abbey at Fiesole, except for some which Cosimo kept in his own home. These collections were open to the public.

The growing accessibility of the materials of scholarship and the persuasion of Greek scholars, to whom he was always a gracious host, inspired Cosimo to found the Platonic Academy, an institution for the translation of Plato's works and the propagation of his ideas. Marsilio Ficino, a humanist of great skill, was made president of the academy in 1458. The patronage of the tyrant did not stop here. His largesse was enjoyed not only by architects and scholars but also by some of the greatest sculptors and painters of the quattrocento, among them Donatello and Fra Filippo Lippi.

In spite of his riches and the lavish entertainments he provided for his guests, Cosimo lived modestly. He ate and drank moderately and simply and worked long, regular hours. He dressed without ostentation and was accessible to the humblest Florentine. His generosity, mildness, and wit were legendary. Upon his death on Aug. 1, 1464, a grateful city decreed that on his tomb should be inscribed the words *Pater Patriae* (father of his country).

Further Reading

The best biography of Cosimo is still K. Dorothea Ewart Vernon, *Cosimo de' Medici* (1899). A scholarly treatment of Cosimo is in George Frederick Young, *The Medici* (1930). A recent history of the Medici which includes a portrait of Cosimo is Marcel Brion, *The Medici: A Great Florentine Family* (1969), a large-format book rich in color plates. Also very useful on all the Medici is Ferdinand Schevill, *History of Florence* (1936), also available in a paperback edition (2 vols., 1963).

Additional Sources

Cosimo 'il Vecchio' de' Medici, 1389-1464: essays in commemoration of the 600th anniversary of Cosimo de' Medici's birth: including papers delivered at the Society for Renaissance Studies Sexcentenary Symposium at the Warburg Institute, London, 19 May 1989, Oxford England: Clarendon Press, 1992. □

Lorenzo de' Medici

The Italian merchant prince Lorenzo de' Medici (1449-1492), called "il Magnifico," ruled both the Florentine state and a vast commercial empire. As a poet and a patron of poets, he stimulated the revival and splendor of Italian literature.

At a time when the major city-states of Italy were engaged in a fierce political and economic rivalry with one another, Lorenzo de' Medici managed to preserve the independence and territorial integrity of Florence. If he was the inferior of his Medici ancestors in financial acumen, he was their superior in artistic sensitivity and understanding, so that, during the latter half of the 15th century, when the despots of Italy strove consciously through lavish patronage of artists to enhance the prestige and stability of their houses, Lorenzo was acknowledged as the greatest Maecenas of his age.

Lorenzo de' Medici was born in Florence on Jan. 1, 1449. He was the son of Piero the Gouty and the grandson of Cosimo, *Pater Patriae*. Cosimo, aware of his son Piero's physical weakness and fearful that Piero would not long survive him, prudently groomed his grandson for the exercise of authority. Lorenzo enjoyed the best education available, learning Greek, Latin, and philosophy, both formally, in rigorous sessions with teachers, and informally, in the company of humanists and statesmen. While still a youth, he began to write sonnets and other poems, usually about love. In 1469, on the advice of his father, Piero, he married

Clarice Orsini, thereby establishing a bond with one of the oldest, most powerful noble families of Rome.

Ruler of Florence

Piero died on Dec. 5, 1469, and 2 days later the 20-year-old Lorenzo was asked by a delegation of eminent citizens to take control of the state. This he did, ruling as his father and grandfather had done, from behind the scenes and without holding any public office.

Lorenzo enhanced the prestige and stability of his house when he came to an agreement with Pope Sixtus IV in 1471 by which the Medici would continue to handle the papal finances. And in 1472 he won the hearts of all Florentines by saving the city from an imminent famine. When the bad harvest of that year threatened the population with disaster, it was Lorenzo who imported large amounts of grain.

Pazzi Conspiracy and Aftermath

Although it was a maxim of Medici policy to retain close ties with the Holy See, relations between Lorenzo and Pope Sixtus were not always cordial. The Pontiff was very displeased when Lorenzo's diplomacy achieved an alliance between Florence, Venice, and Milan, for such a combination was more than a match for the armies of the Church. Sixtus felt thwarted in his ambitions to expand the papal territory and uneasy about the safety of what the Church already held. His hostility grew when he learned that Lorenzo was trying to buy the town of Imola, which was strategically important. Consequently the Pope agreed to a plot designed to rid Florence of both Lorenzo and his brother Giuliano. The chief conspirators were the Pazzi family, a rival banking house and bitter enemies of the Medici. The plan was to assassinate the two brothers at a moment when their guard would be down, during the celebration of Mass on Easter Sunday, April 26, 1478. Giuliano was slain, but Lorenzo escaped with wounds. The people of Florence rallied to the Medici standard and visited a terrible retribution on the hapless conspirators, most of whom did not survive the day. Among those killed was Francesco Salviato, Archbishop of Pisa.

The Pope, enraged, excommunicated Lorenzo and placed an interdict on the city. In 1479, in the midst of unbearable tension, Sixtus and King Ferrante (Ferdinand) of Naples declared war on Florence. Lorenzo, knowing that the safety of his city and his dynasty were at stake, undertook the most hazardous adventure of his colorful career. He went by sea to Naples, virtually placing his life in the hands of the King. Ferrante was won over by Lorenzo's charm and his persuasive argument that it would not do for Italy to be divided or Florence destroyed. Lorenzo returned to Florence with the gift of peace and was received with great joy. Sixtus was bitter but grudgingly bowed to necessity and in 1480 made peace. Lorenzo's control over Florence and its possessions would not be challenged again.

A new constitution in 1480 simplified the structure of Florentine government. The Signory, or executive branch, chose 30 citizens, who in turn selected 40 more, all to serve for life in a new council. Hence forward all other branches, including the Signory, were responsible to this permanent Council of Seventy. Since the council was filled with Lorenzo's adherents, the effect of the constitutional change was to make his tyranny more obvious. Under this rule the prosperity of Florence grew, primarily through banking and commerce. Not the least of Lorenzo's contributions to this prosperity was the peace which his diplomacy, from 1480 until his death, maintained between Florence and the rest of Italy.

Cultural Life

The private fortune of the Medici did not fare so well under Lorenzo's management as did the economy of Florence. This is attributable to the fact that he tended to neglect business, so preoccupied was he with diplomatic and cultural concerns. It is not accidental that the last decade of his life coincided with the period of Florence's greatest artistic contributions to the Renaissance. He paid with a lavish hand the painters Sandro Botticelli, Domenico Ghirlandaio, and Fra Filippo Lippi to add beauty to the city. The humanist John Lascaris and the poet Angelo Poliziano traveled great distances at the behest and the expense of Lorenzo in search of manuscripts to enlarge the Medici libraries. What could not be bought was copied, and Lorenzo permitted the scribes of other eager book collectors to copy from his stores. When Poliziano and others scorned the new invention of printing from movable type, Lorenzo had the foresight to recognize its value and encourage its use. The famous Platonic Academy frequently met at Lorenzo's pal-

ace, where in lively philosophic discussions the ruler was quite the equal of Giovanni Pico della Mirandola, Michelangelo, and Marsilio Ficino. The University of Pisa owes it revival to Lorenzo.

The prodigious feats of patronage touched upon here, as valuable as they are, are secondary in the scale of Lorenzo's accomplishments. It is not too much to say that Lorenzo, with his verses in the vernacular, elevated Tuscan Italian to the dignity and respect it had known in Dante's time, before the humanists buried it under mounds of classical Latin. Although his friend Poliziano still favored Latin, Lorenzo composed Italian poetry not inferior to anything written in his time. His *canti carnascialeschi* (carnival songs) are still read with pleasure.

Lorenzo was not an attractive man physically. He had a heavy face with a large flat nose and a swarthy complexion. He was tall and robust and given to athletic exertions. His dignity, charm, and wit lay in his manner rather than his appearance. Physical shortcomings and a reputation for personal and commercial immorality, however, did not prevent him from being loved and admired. He died on April 9, 1492, still a despot, but one whose hand had lain lightly on his subjects.

Further Reading

An old but elegantly written biography of Lorenzo is William Roscoe, *Life of Lorenzo de' Medici* (1851). See also Cecilia Ady, *Lorenzo dei Medici and Renaissance Italy* (1955), and the two penetrating studies by Ferdinand Schevill, *The Medici* (1949) and *History of Florence* (1936), also published in paperback (2 vols., 1963); the last is the best short history of Florence in English. A recent history of the Medici which includes a portrait of Lorenzo is Marcel Brion, *The Medici: A Great Florentine Family* (1969), a large-format book that is rich in color plates. □

Joseph Medill

American editor and publisher Joseph Medill (1823-1899), a staunch abolitionist and an early advocate of the Republican party, was influential in Abraham Lincoln's presidential drive.

Joseph Medill was born near the village of St. John, New Brunswick, Canada, on April 6, 1823. His father, who had emigrated from Ireland, moved the family to Ohio in 1832. Except for brief schooling, young Medill educated himself. He studied law with attorneys and was admitted to the bar in 1846. But law practice was uncertain, so he turned to journalism, purchasing the *Coshocton Whig* in 1849 and renaming it the *Republican*. In 1851 he established the *Daily Forest City in Cleveland,* which he consolidated the following year with the *Free Democrat;* he called the new paper the *Cleveland Leader.* In 1852 Medill married Katherine Patrick.

Medill did not found the *Chicago Tribune.* He bought an interest in it in 1855, the year he became managing editor, and he bought controlling interest in 1874. Many people were involved in establishing the *Tribune,* but Medill gave the paper its impetus and direction.

Most authorities credit Medill with popularizing the name "Republican" for the rising new political party. He tried to get Abraham Lincoln to issue the Emancipation Proclamation many months before Lincoln thought reasonable. He personally reported many of Lincoln's speeches, and Lincoln often visited the *Tribune* offices before he became president. Medill was opposed to a compromise of any type with the South and joined the Radical Republicans after the Civil War.

The Chicago fire of 1871 destroyed the *Tribune* building, but the *Tribune* was back on the streets in 2 days. The first, revitalized issue carried Medill's famous editorial "Cheer Up." He ran for mayor as a Republican on the "Fireproof Ticket" and was elected.

One of the *Tribune*'s greatest achievements was the publication in May 1881 of a 16-page special supplement that gave the complete, newly revised version of the New Testament. Medill also promoted his city, and largely through his efforts Chicago became the site of the World's Columbian Exposition of 1893. He was strongly nationalistic; after the sinking of the U.S. battleship *Maine* in 1898, he beat the drums for the Spanish-American War.

Medill died on March 16, 1899, in his winter home at San Antonio, Tex. He had brought the *Tribune* from a circulation of 1,200 to 200,000. His paper cited an appropriate epitaph: "His monument is *The Chicago Tribune.*"

Further Reading

Philip Kinsley's three-volume work, *The Chicago Tribune: Its First Hundred Years* (1943-1946), is illuminating but diffuse. *The Chicago Tribune's Joseph Medill: A Brief Biography and an Appreciation* (1947), by the *Chicago Tribune* editors, gives a favorable view of Medill; and Frank C. Waldrop, *McCormick of Chicago: An Unconventional Portrait of a Controversial Figure* (1966), gives a balanced, if limited, appraisal of him. Also useful is John Tebbel, *An American Dynasty* (1947). □

Mehmed the Conqueror

Mehmed II, the Conqueror (ca. 1432–1481) was a Turkish sultan who conquered Constantinople and ruthlessly consolidated and enlarged the Ottoman Empire with a military crusade into Asia and Europe.

Mehmed Celebi, the third son of the Ottoman sultan Murad II, was born on March 30, 1432 (or 1430, as cited in some sources). Though much is known of his father, very little is known of his mother. According to some traditions she was a French princess, while others refer to her simply as an Italian woman named Estella. In later custom, she is referred to as Huma Hatan, after the bird of paradise of Persian legend. Yet most likely, Mehmed's mother was a slave, and there is evidence to suggest that she was a recent convert from Judaism.

The first years of the prince were spent in the harem of the palace at Erdine (in the European territories of the Empire), although in 1434 he was sent to Amaysa, in eastern Anatolia. According to custom, at five years of age he was given the governorship of the city, with a number of carefully chosen councillors, for his first taste of authority. In 1439, he was brought back to Erdine for his circumcision ceremonies whereupon he was given a different governorship.

Mehmed had not been his father's favorite son. The impetuous and headstrong prince had been difficult to control and to educate. Yet when his brother was strangled one night in bed, the 11-year-old Mehmed became the heir to his father's throne and was summoned to Erdine to learn of the workings of government.

Although Murad had made numerous military excursions himself, he hoped generally to secure peace to the east and to the west of the Empire. Yet in 1444, Christian forces advanced into Ottoman territory on the second crusade in two years. Leaving his son in charge at court, Murad prepared to meet this threat to his state. That summer, while his father was away, Mehmed briefly enjoyed the authority of the sultanate for the first time.

On November 10, in a major battle at Varna on the Black Sea, the Turkish army defeated the Crusaders, and the Christian prospect of pushing Islam off the European continent no longer seemed likely. Yet in the wake of this victory, Murad somewhat surprisingly abdicated the throne to his son, who had not won great respect during his recent regency. The young Mehmed already entertained the bold notion of attacking Constantinople, the capital of the waning Byzantine Empire that sat in the midst of Ottoman territories on the straits between the Mediterranean and Black seas. At the behest of his former councillors, however, Murad returned to the throne on May 5, 1446, to replace the unpopular, and unready, Mehmed and to turn his military attention toward a renewed threat from the West.

In a successful battle against Hungarian forces in October 1448, Mehmed was given his first experience of battle. In January of that same year, his first son was born to a slave girl, Gulbahar, a Christian of Albanian origin. Quickly thereafter, according to his father's wishes, he was properly married to a more suitable noblewoman, Sitt Hatun. The wedding was magnificently celebrated over a three-month period, but unfortunately for the two, their marriage was unhappy and remained childless.

In February 1451, Murad II died leaving the ambitious Mehmed II as sultan. Since the laws of succession were not entirely clear during this period, Mehmed typically had his brother drowned to eliminate potential opposition to his claim. Later, he was to formalize fratricide in law claiming, "whichever of my sons inherits the sultan's throne, it behooves him to kill his brothers in the interest of the world order." The Ottoman state had been growing in strength and organization since early in the century, but it was far from unified and stable. Mehmed was to spend his entire reign trying to consolidate his authority and to invigorate his state. Thus, his initial efforts were to the elimination of all resistance to his rule within the Empire.

With the news of Mehmed's accession to the throne, many European powers felt that affairs had changed to their advantage. Indeed, he was preoccupied with various rebellions along the eastern frontier of the Empire. Moreover, he had to face a revolt among the Janissaries, an elite military corps which he was able later to reorganize under his direct authority to enforce his will within the Empire and in newly conquered territories. Soon Mehmed no longer felt it necessary to maintain good relations with his neighbors to the west.

Throughout his life, Mehmed had declared his hatred of Christianity and his desire to destroy it. Thus, when his attentions turned toward the West his first major act was the construction of a fortress on the European side of the Bosporus straits with which to police all shipping to the Black Sea. This was a virtual declaration of war on nearby Constantinople which was thereby further isolated from its Western allies. According to Mehmed, "The *ghaza* (Holy War) is our basic duty, as it was in the case of our fathers." Specifically, he felt, "The conquest of (Constantinople) is . . . essential to the future and the safety of the Ottoman state." The remaining inhabitants of this once vibrant and important city were justifiably frightened by Mehmed's intentions. From April 6, 1453, Mehmed, with the help of huge cannon, laid siege to the final remnant of Christian greatness in the East. Venetian and Hungarian forces were mobilized for the city's defense, but Mehmed acted quickly. By May 29, when his terms were refused by the last Byzantine emperor Constantine XI Paleologus, Muslim forces

were ordered to storm the city which was quickly overrun and looted.

For many, the fall of Byzantium and the foundation of a unified Islamic Empire straddling Europe and Asia marks the division between the Middle Ages and the modern era. For Mehmed, who immediately became the most important sultan in the Muslim world, it marked the beginning of a dream to create a universal empire based on his new capital, henceforth to be called Istanbul. In an attempt to rebuild the city to its former glory, he repaired the ancient walls and built many public buildings. Among the most prominent of these were his palaces and the great Mosque of the Conqueror, with its hospitals, colleges, and public baths. His city was to be the center of the world—politically, culturally, and spiritually. To this end, he forced resettlement from all parts of the Empire of people of all religions.

As the heir to the Byzantine Empire, Mehmed was forced to modify slightly the system of government that he had inherited and to incorporate some foreign administrative and cultural institutions. All of this he codified in his Book of Laws which thereafter defined the unique character of the Ottoman Empire with its Islamic, Ottoman-Turk, Byzantine, and other influences. Under Mehmed II, now known as The Conqueror, some significant measure of local tradition and religious practice could remain under the new administration of conquered territory (if necessary), though effective and direct control remained in his hands. Clearly, Mehmed's predominant concern was with his own authority. After the fall of Constantinople, for example, he dismissed his powerful chief councillor whom he had inherited from the reign of his father. Henceforth, he would make all of his own appointments to important positions (usually from among his personal slaves). Determined to rule firmly and effectively, Mehmed was often brutal and cruel. It has been said that he delighted in killing people as someone else might kill fleas.

Further conquest was the most passionate pursuit of Mehmed II. For him, the non-Muslim world was "war territory" ordained by the Koran to be subjected. Thus, the glory of the sultan's authority and the Ottoman state was to be based primarily on the pursuit of Holy War inspired by the duty to spread Islam and the benefits of Ottoman rule.

From 1454, Mehmed turned actively against the islands in the Aegean Sea and against the Balkan Peninsula at the expense of both Serbia and Hungary. He met with much success in the Aegean, and to the north he forced an annual tribute from Moldavia. Initial expeditions into Serbia brought it more closely under Ottoman control, but the first large-scale military operation after the fall of Constantinople was directed against Hungary. Arriving at Belgrade, considered essential for further expansion into the European continent, Mehmed began his ill-fated siege in June 1456. After heavily bombarding the city over an extended period, the Turks were compelled to retreat, and Mehmed, wounded in the thigh, was forced to spend the next year at court.

Later, in April 1458, he set forth again at the head of an army toward Greece, and in August he entered Athens, which was to remain under Ottoman control for over 300 years. In 1459, the Serbian city of Smederevo capitulated without a struggle, and by the end of the year all of Serbia was occupied. In 1460, he subjugated Morea, the southern peninsula of the Greek mainland. Efforts to unite Western resistance to the powerful Ottoman threat in another crusade were largely unsuccessful, as were similar attempts by threatened princes to the east of the Empire. Indeed, the next year, Mehmed quickly became master of Trebizond which lay along the northern coast of Asia Minor on the Black Sea.

In 1462, he subdued Walachian resistance to Ottoman suzerainty, and later turned easily against the island of Lesbos with the navy that he was building up. Meanwhile, it was obvious to most observers that Mehmed was preparing another major campaign against the West, particularly against the possessions of Venice. By March 1463, his forces were afoot, and the immediate target of hostilities was Bosnia. Soon the greater part of the region was overrun. This advance terrified the Venetians. Clearly, Venice would have to give up all its possessions in Greece and the East or fight the Turk. When Ottoman forces attacked the Venetian holding of Argos in Greece that same year, Venice, with the support of Hungary, declared war against Mehmed II.

Yet Mehmed had a powerful rival to the east in Prince Uzan Hasan of the House of Karaman in southeastern Anatolia. He also had conquered many territories and now held the title of king of Persia. Karaman was annexed to the Ottoman Empire in 1468, though Hasan and his Eastern allies still presented one of Mehmed's greatest challenges. In 1472, Hasan's forces raided the city of Tokat and marched well into western Anatolia. Mehmed spent that year preparing to meet this renewed challenge. Finally, in July of 1473, the two armies met on the plain of Erzincan by the Euphrates River, and on August 11 Mehmed won another great victory extending his authority well into Asia Minor.

Though he was greatly distracted by these events in the East, the West was not spared. Ottoman raiders had long been making excursions to the eastern shore of the Adriatic sea, and in 1469 earnest preparations were undertaken for the transport of troops to Negropont in Greece, the Aegean naval base of Venice. Soon, a massive military expedition set out and the siege of Negropont began. After a long, brutal, and bloody siege that almost exhausted both parties, Negropont capitulated on July 12. This was a terrible blow to Venice and a grave portent of danger to the rest of Europe.

In the area of the Black Sea, Mehmed was also successful. Since early in his reign, he had forced tribute from the various Genoese colonies, later occupying them outright. By 1475, he had made the Crimea a vassal state of the Empire, making the entire sea virtually an Ottoman lake.

Despite recent successes, 1474 was a relatively quiet year for Mehmed, perhaps because of the greatly distressing death of his favorite son, Mustapha, or perhaps because of his own illness. Nevertheless Ottoman forces continued to raid Albania, Walachia, and even Hungary with some Ottoman raiders appearing within sight of Venice itself. By 1476, well enough again to lead his armies, Mehmed almost completely overran Albania.

Peace was concluded with Venice in 1479, ending what had become a long, troublesome struggle. Although the Italian city-state maintained many of its former trading privileges, it was forced to pay tribute to the sultan. Mehmed now looked beyond Venice. On August 11, 1480, Otranto in the south of Italy was overrun, and all the male inhabitants were killed by the invading forces. From this base, the Turks laid waste to the countryside for miles around, threatening the entire Italian peninsula.

Ottoman forces were concurrently involved in many other areas. They were storming the Aegean Islands and laid siege to the fortress on Rhodes. There were continuing raids into the Balkans, but most significantly, the Empire was involved in another struggle in southeastern Anatolia with the sultan of Syria and Egypt.

Despite the military success of the Empire, Mehmed himself was not well. Throughout his life, the sultan increasingly suffered from gout and rheumatism. An abscess had recently grossly disfigured his leg, a divine affliction (it seemed to some) for a life of gluttony. This pushed the moody Mehmed further into seclusion from the public eye. Now, on May 1, 1481, as he prepared for further conflict against the Egyptian sultan, he was struck with severe abdominal pains and died two days later. Since Mehmed had always feared being poisoned and dined alone, there was immediate suspicion that he had been murdered, perhaps even by his son and heir Bayezid, who was eager to secure his position quickly.

Although Mehmed II died unsatisfied in his goal to build a universal empire, he had established the primacy of the Ottoman Turks within the Muslim world. In his dedication to conquest, he extended Ottoman influence east as far as the Euphrates and west throughout the Balkans and even onto the Italian peninsula. Whether reviled for his brutality and his fervor or saluted for these successes, Mehmed II, the Conqueror, affirmed the authority of the sultanate and secured the character of the Ottoman Empire. From the remains of Byzantium, he built a vibrant capital of a growing Turkish Empire which would be a major world power over the next four centuries.

Further Reading

Babinger, Franz. *Mehmed the Conqueror and His Time.* Translated by Ralph Manheim, Princeton University Press, 1978.

Parry, V. J., H. Inalcik, A. N. Kurat, and J. S. Bromley. *A History of the Ottoman Empire to 1730.* Edited by Michael Cook. Cambridge University Press, 1976.

Pears, Sir Edwin. "The Ottoman Turks to the Fall of Constantinople," in *The Cambridge Medieval History.* Macmillan, 1923.

Creasy, E. S. *History of the Ottoman Turks.* Richard Bentley and Son, 1877.

Eversley, Lord. *The Turkish Empire from 1288 to 1914.* T. Fisher and Unwin, 1923.

Kinross, Lord. *The Ottoman Centuries: The Rise and Fall of the Turkish Empire.* Jonathan Cape, 1977. □

Sir Pherozeshah Mehta

Sir Pherozeshah Mehta (1845-1915) was one of the founders of the Indian National Congress, a member of the Imperial Legislative Council of India, and an outstanding leader of the Bombay municipality.

Pherozeshah Mehta was probably born in Bombay, of respectable middleclass Parsi parents. He was one of the first Indians to secure Western higher education and the first Parsi to take the master's degree. He also became a barrister-at-law in London, where he absorbed the ideals of Gladstonian liberalism, which thereafter guided his political life.

By 1872 Mehta was prominent in the Bombay municipality, and it was to his leadership that the city owed its Magna Charta, the Act of 1888. The Duke of Connaught stated that the municipal constitution of Bombay was the product of Mehta's genius. Mehta was also the founder of the Bombay Presidency Association, which, under his tutelage from 1885 to 1915, was the organizational arm of the National Congress in Bombay. In 1886 he was appointed to the Bombay Legislative Council, where he was noted for his upright and independent character and his willingness to fight for a just cause. He also came to be noted as a splendid orator.

In 1911 Mehta was chosen president of the Bombay municipality, in which he had played so prominent a role for so many years. In 1898 he was named to the Imperial Legislative Council and served with distinction until poor health forced his resignation.

Mehta was active in the founding of the Indian National Congress in 1885. He continued to play a prominent role in the affairs of the Congress until his death. In 1890, and again in 1909, he was chosen president of the Congress. For undisclosed reasons he resigned the presidency a few days before the sessions began. On two other occasions he served as chairman of the important Reception Committee, which, in those days, dominated the proceedings.

A man of broad interests, Mehta was also an elected member of the senate of Bombay University and served on the board of several pioneer Indian business concerns. His career was summarized by a leading British journalist who said that Mehta "had stood alone against the bureaucracy, had displayed a courage equal to Gokhale's, an eloquence hardly second to Surendranath Banerjea's, and power of sarcasm hardly rivaled by Motilal Ghoses's." He continued to exert great influence in the last years of his life. In 1914, when Gopal Krishna Gokhale was on the verge of arranging a harmonious resolution of the serious rift in the ranks of the Congress, it was Pherozeshah Mehta who sent an emissary to advise Gokhale against the move. Gokhale bowed to Mehta's opinion, and the rupture was not healed.

When Mehta died, the viceroy described him as "a great Parsi, a great citizen, great patriot, and a great Indian."

Further Reading

Probably the best book in English on Mehta is Hormasji P. Mody, *Sir Pherozeshah Mehta: A Political Biography* (1921). See also V. S. S. Shastri, *Life and Times of Sir Pherozeshah Mehta* (1945).

Additional Sources

Srinivasa Sastri, V. S. (Valangiman Sankaranarayana), *Life and times of Sir Pherozeshah Mehta,* Bombay: Bharatiya Vidya Bhavan, 1975. □

Zubin Mehta

A native of India, Zubin Mehta (born 1936) was the conductor and director of both the New York and the Los Angeles Philharmonic Orchestras. He made his Metropolitan Opera debut on December 29, 1965, with a highly acclaimed performance of *Aida*.

"Born to the baton" aptly describes the extraordinary career of Zubin Mehta. Maestro Mehta has served as music director of the New York Philharmonic, the Los Angeles Philharmonic, the Montreal Symphony, and the Israel Philharmonic, to name a few.

Born April 29, 1936 in Bombay, India, Zubin Mehta grew up in a home filled with music. His father was a co-founder of the Bombay Symphony, and the young Mehta heard chamber music and Beethoven quartets before he heard a symphony. He learned to sing what he heard before he could read music. At the age of sixteen, Mehta began conducting concerto accompaniments, leading the orchestra when his father was away on concert tours. At eighteen, Mehta abandoned his medical studies to pursue a career in music at the Academy of Music in Vienna. "I always had the intention of becoming a conductor, not just because I wanted to wave a stick, but because orchestral music appeals to me most," he said.

By the time he was twenty-five, Mehta had conducted both the Vienna and the Berlin Philharmonics and was the music director of the Montreal Symphony. In 1962, at age twenty-six, he became the youngest conductor of a major American orchestra when the Los Angeles Philharmonic appointed him music director. In 1978, he accepted the music directorship of the New York Philharmonic. Mehta's powerful stage presence translates into a strong, provocative management style. "In Los Angeles [as compared to New York] I'm the absolute boss. It's my orchestra," he said.

During Mehta's thirteen-year tenure with the New York Philharmonic, he conducted more that one thousand concerts, and he held the post of music director longer than anyone else in the orchestra's modern history. However, his relationship with the orchestra was a stormy one.

An intriguing question is the role that being Indian has played in the success of his career. "Mehta's career in this internationally minded age has possibly profited from the

His religious background and his membership in a minority community contribute to Mehta's strong identification with the state of Israel. "We are the Jews of India, the Persians who didn't mix," explained Mehta to Rockwell. "We enjoy the same minority complexes as the Israelis except we were not persecuted." In 1969 the Israel Philharmonic Orchestra appointed Mehta its music adviser, in 1977 its music director, and in 1981 its music director for life. Altogether he has conducted more than fifteen hundred concerts with the Israel Philharmonic.

Mehta had a mentor in his father, and he clearly has an extraordinary talent, but he also credits his success to taking opportunities when they were offered. "I made half my career by jumping in for others at the last moment. I sometimes think my success was due almost entirely to the misfortunes of my elderly colleagues," he told Goldberg.

Numerous honors have been bestowed on Mehta, including the Nikisch Ring, the Vienna Philharmonic Ring of Honor, and the Hans von Bulow medal bestowed by the Berlin Philharmonic Orchestra. Mehta has been awarded the Padma Bhushan (Order of the Lotus) by the Republic of India, has received the Defender of Jerusalem Award, and is an honorary citizen of the city of Tel Aviv. He is also the only non-Israeli ever to receive the Israel Prize.

Mehta looks forward to continuing his participation on the international music scene. On June 20, 1994, from the burned out shell of the National Library in Sarajevo, Mehta conducted Sarajevo's orchestra and chorus in a benefit that was broadcast around the globe. In August 1994, he conducted a concert at Dodger Stadium in Los Angeles at the close of the World Cup Soccer Tournament, a concert that brought together a trio of popular tenors Jose Carreras, Placido Domingo, and Luciano Pavarotti. He is a leader in the classical music world, staging events to bring performance of great musical works to the largest possible audience.

Further Reading

Bookspan, Martin, and Ross Yockey, *Zubin: The Zubin Mehta Story,* Harper & Row, 1978. □

exotic value attached to being the only India-born conductor to attain prominence," speculated Albert Goldberg, music critic of the *Los Angeles Times.* "But [Mehta] does not trade on such externals. . . . His musical abilities alone have been sufficient," concluded Goldberg. "Zubin has one of the best techniques around," agreed Los Angeles Philharmonic tympanist William Kraft. "Even the way he holds the baton makes it easier for the orchestra to follow him." In addition to his unquestioned talent, audiences respond to Mehta's impassioned, almost spiritual, performances and to his personal magnetism. Mehta, whose name means "powerful sword," understands the importance of showmanship on stage.

Mehta retains strong ties to his native country and still retains his Indian citizenship. He has taken the New York Philharmonic to Bombay, and when the Festival of India came to the United States, its gala opening on September 11, 1985, was led by Mehta conducting the New York Philharmonic. Mehta's religious roots are also quite deep. He belongs to the Zoroastrian religion, a group commonly known in India as "Parsis" because they emigrated from Persia in the sixth through eighth centuries. There are currently about ninety thousand Zoroastrians in India, twenty-five thousand in Iran, and fifteen thousand in Pakistan. Mehta has participated in a feature-length docudrama entitled *A Quest for Zarathustra* on the life of Zoroaster and his religion. "It is based on my quest for knowledge of my religion," explained Mehta to John Rockwell of the *New York Times.*

Richard Meier

Beginning in the mid-1960s, the New York architect Richard Meier (born 1934) consistently explored the potential of a white, pristine, and spatially rich modern architecture. By the mid-1980s Meier had earned himself a place with the major architects of his day.

Born in Newark, New Jersey, on October 12, 1934, Richard Meier studied architecture at Cornell University, where he graduated in 1957. During a trip to Europe in 1959 he sought to join the office of his early idol, the Swiss-French architect Le Corbusier. Although Meier was able to meet Le Corbusier in Paris, the master would not hire Meier, or any other American, at that time, since Le Corbusier believed that several major commissions throughout his career had been lost because of Americans. Meier returned to New York where he worked briefly for Skidmore, Owings & Merrill and then for about three years with Marcel Breuer, a product of the German Bauhaus and former partner of Walter Gropius.

Painted Abstract Expressionism at Night

During his early career in New York Meier was an architect by day and Abstract Expressionist painter at night. For a period of time he shared a studio with his close friend Frank Stella. Meier eventually gave up painting to devote himself more fully to architecture, although he continued to work on collages occasionally.

Established Own Firm

In 1963 Meier left Breuer to establish his own practice in New York. From 1963 to 1973 he taught at Cooper Union in New York and was a visiting critic at a number of other institutions. He began to meet with a group called CASE (Conference of Architects for the Study of the Environment), whose discussions of each other's buildings and projects resulted in the 1972 book *Five Architects,* featuring the work of Peter Eisenman, Michael Graves, Charles Gwathmey, John Hejduk, and Richard Meier. Despite Meier's assertion that this was never a unified group, the "New York Five" were identified with a return to the heroic early period of the European International Style, particularly the buildings of Le Corbusier during the 1920s and 1930s.

Some writers attempted to recognize the "white," revitalized modern architecture of the "New York Five" as the opposite pole from the "gray" architecture of such postmodern architects as Robert Venturi, Charles Moore, and Robert A. M. Stern. However, by the early 1980s such a distinction seemed less clear-cut.

Gained Recognition as Architect

Meier first gained attention with his white and immaculate neo-Corbusian villas set in nature, such as his Smith House (1965-1967) at Darien, Connecticut. With its exterior walls of vertical wooden siding, this crisply composed, compact house is a modern New England house, following a genre established earlier by Gropius and Breuer. A central theme of Meier's is seen in the clear separation between the enclosed, private rooms of the entrance front and the much more open main living area at the back, which is here organized into a tall vertical space, glazed on three sides, allowing a panoramic view of Long Island Sound. Meier stated that his "fundamental concerns are space, form, light, and how to make them."

One of Meier's most striking residences is the Douglas House (1971-1973) at Harbor Springs, Michigan. Perched on a steep bluff overlooking Lake Michigan, this tall, vertically organized, white and machine-like villa is dramatically juxtaposed with the unspoiled greenery of its idyllic site. Meier preferred the purity of white, his favorite color, for most of his buildings. White boldly contrasts with nature, yet it constantly responds, through reflection, to surrounding colors and the changing quality of light.

One of Meier's first major non-residential commissions was the Bronx Development Center (1970-1977) in New York for mentally and physically challenged children. Built on an unpromising site of wasteland between a parkway and railroad tracks, Meier chose to turn inward to a spatially rich courtyard. His approach to such an institution was to create "a city in microcosm." This was the first of Meier's buildings to be built with walls of metal panels. The silver tonality of these aluminum panels represented a temporary break for Meier away from his dominant white.

The tour de force of Meier's work of the 1970s was the Atheneum (1975-1979) at New Harmony, Indiana. This visitors' and community center serves a village which was an early 19th-century utopian community, first for George Rapp and his Harmony Society, and later for Robert Owen and his Owenites. The building stands at the entrance to the town on a miniature, Acropolis-like, knoll near the Wabash River. Responding to both the grid of the town and the edge of the river, Meier designed his building on two overlapping grids skewed five degrees from one another. This resulted in an impression of spatial contraction and expansion by means of ramps and stairs in dramatic vertical spaces lit by abundant natural light. Meier reached a new level of complexity in his neo-Corbusian language, which went well beyond the more static and Classical sensibility of Le Corbusier himself. This Baroque manipulation of space and light through complex form was partially inspired by Meier's studies in 1973 as resident architect at the American

Academy in Rome, where he was especially intrigued by the Baroque architecture of Italy and southern Germany.

The Atheneum's walls are of porcelain-enameled panels of glistening white which will not weather and age like the temporarily clean walls of the original International Style. Despite the unrelenting modernity of such buildings as this, Meier's vocabulary was, in a sense, historicist. The ocean liner aesthetic of ramps, decks, nautical railings, and scrubbed white surfaces could no longer be associated with the latest in transportation, but only regarded as a nostalgic backward glance to the now grand dinosaurs of ocean travel of the early 20th century. Although the motifs of the International Style architectural revolution are revived, they no longer kindle the spirit of their corollary, a revolution to reform society. What Meier concentrated on was an intensification and enrichment of the forms of modern architecture in search of a moving use of light and space, as seen in such examples as the spiritually uplifting interior spaces of his Hartford Seminary (1978-1981) at Hartford, Connecticut.

Emerged as Major Architect of Museums

By the early 1980s, Meier had emerged as a major architect of museums. His High Museum of Art (1980-1983) in Atlanta, Georgia, contains the drama of a four-story atrium with a ramp ascending back and forth along a quadrant curve. He also built a major addition to the Museum for the Decorative Arts (1979-1984) at Frankfurt am Main, Germany, where the early 19th-century villa of the original museum serves as one quadrant block in Meier's expansion and the source for the dimensions of the additions. For the Des Moines Art Center in Iowa, Meier skillfully appended three small additions (1982-1984) to a 1948 Eliel Saarinen building which had been added to in 1965 by I. M. Pei.

Designed Getty Complex in Los Angeles

In 1984, the year in which Richard Meier turned 50, he received the prestigious Pritzker Prize and was selected to be the architect for a new Getty complex in Los Angeles, which included the Getty Center for the History of Art and the Humanities, the Getty Conservation Institute, and a new museum building. By the mid-1980s, it was clear that this exceedingly consistent architect, who had shown that modern architecture is very much alive, had become one of the major architects of his day.

Los Angeles' Getty Center is an immense project and a high point in Meier's career. After ten years of construction, the six-building complex on 110 acres inspires awe in visitors to the site. "The rest of Los Angeles may fall," says Richard Meier in *Harper's Bazaar* while surveying the site, "but the Getty will stand." The focal point of the complex was designed to be the art museum, containing a collection of paintings, drawings, photographs, decorative arts, and manuscripts from around the world. Other elements include a bookstore, cafes, auditorium, library, and reading room.

Meier chose Italian travertine marble for the project. The tawny colored marble suited the landscape better than his signature white. Meier had the slabs of marble pried apart like giant fork-split English muffins to give the surface of the blocks a rough appearance. It is also admired for its

elegant gardens and luxurious views of the mountains and ocean.

Further Reading

The most complete book on Meier to date is Richard Meier, *Richard Meier, Architect,* introduction by Joseph Rykwert, postscript by John Hejduk (1984). An earlier book is Richard Meier, *Richard Meier, Architect: Buildings and Projects 1966-1976,* introduction by Kenneth Frampton, postscript by John Hejduk (1976). The book which established the "New York Five" is *Five Architects: Eisenman, Graves, Gwathmey, Hejduk, Meier,* introductions by Colin Rowe and Kenneth Frampton (1972). For an interview with Meier, see Barbaralee Diamonstein et al., *American Architecture Now* (1980). Robert A. M. Stern's *New Directions in American Architecture* (1977) provides a background to this period. See also *Harper's Bazaar* November 1995, and Meier, Richard, *Richard Meier sculpture,* Rizzoli International Publications, 1994. □

Henry Meiggs

Henry Meiggs (1811-1877), an American pioneer railroad builder in Chile and Peru, was a characteristic example of the "robber baron" type of entrepreneur.

H enry Meiggs was born in Catskill, N.Y., on July 7, 1811. He was drawn to California by the gold rush of 1849 but, like many others who made fortunes from this experience, did not himself look for gold. He went into the business of providing transport for the gold miners and quickly succeeded in accumulating a fortune which he lost even more quickly than he had acquired it. In 1855 he fled from California one step ahead of his angry creditors.

Meiggs next turned up in Chile. A man of great organizational and entrepreneurial talents, as well as having a profound lack of scruples, he was soon active in planning and executing projects for building bridges and establishing the first extensive railroad lines in his new homeland. He worked very closely with the governments of the time and earned a new fortune from these activities. His crowning achievement in Chile was the completion in 1863 of the railroad linking the capital city of Santiago with its port on the Pacific Ocean, Valparaiso.

In 1868 Meiggs moved to Peru. The country was in the grip of a railroad-building fever, and President José Balta was extremely interested both in having railroads constructed and in accumulating a fortune out of the process for himself. Meiggs entered into a "partnership" with the willing president.

Meiggs contructed two railroads. The first connected the southern port of Mollendo with Arequipa, Peru's second largest city, and extended to the town of Puno on Lake Titicaca and from there to Juliaca. This line ultimately was completed to the city of Cuzco, the old Inca capital of Peru. The second was a line from Callao, the port of Lima, to what

was then the silver-mining region of Huancayo, high in the Andes Mountains. This line was subsequently of major importance in opening up the exploitation of copper and base metals in the mountainous region.

Meiggs's railroad-building activity in Peru was one of the major factors in bringing about the settlement of sizable numbers of Chinese immigrants in the country. When he found it hard to recruit Peruvian laborers for his railway construction gangs, he brought in Chileans and Chinese coolies. Many of the latter settled in the Lima-Callao region once the railroad jobs were completed, and to this day their descendants make up an appreciable part of the population of that area.

While Meiggs was busy in Peru, he was approached by President Tomás Guardia of Costa Rica, who proposed construction of a railroad from the Caribbean port of Limón to the national capital, San José, in the Central Plateau. Although Meiggs received a contract for the construction of this road, the enterprise was actually carried out by one of his nephews, Minor Cooper Keith, and it was completed 14 years after Meiggs's death.

In spite of the highly favorable terms which the Chilean, Peruvian, and Costa Rican governments had signed with Meiggs, his fortune had largely disappeared by the time of his death in Lima on Sept. 29, 1877. This was due to the murder of President Balta in 1872 and the serious undermining of the financial stability of Peru in the middle 1870s, resulting in the unwillingness and inability of the Peruvian government to complete its payments to the American plunger and railroad man.

Further Reading

A full-length study of Meiggs is Watt Stewart, *Henry Meiggs: Yankee Pizarro* (1946). There are brief discussions of him in Charles R. Flint, *Memories of an Active Life* (1923), and Isaac Wistar, *Autobiography* (1937).

Additional Sources

Myers, Elisabeth P., *South America's Yankee genius, Henry Meigg*, New York, Messner 1969. □

Arthur Meighen

Arthur Meighen (1874-1960) was a Canadian lawyer and prime minister. He was one of the most respected Conservative leaders of government despite his espousal of several unpopular laws.

Arthur Meighen was born on June 16, 1874, near St. Mary's, Ontario, to parents of Ulster stock. He graduated from the University of Toronto in 1896, and after a brief period as a high school teacher he went west to Winnipeg. He was called to the Manitoba bar in 1902 and took up the practice of law in the growing town of Portage la Prairie, Manitoba, where his ability and unrelenting hard work soon made him a leading citizen. In 1904 he married Isabel Cox, a schoolteacher recently arrived from Quebec.

Meighen was elected to Parliament as Conservative member for Portage la Prairie in 1908 and reelected in 1911, when the new Conservative ministry of Robert Borden was formed. In 1913 Meighen became solicitor general of Canada and in 1917 was appointed secretary of state. Among Canadian political leaders of the day, he was without superior as a parliamentary debater and public speaker; his oratorical skills were frequently employed in defense of the protective tariff and the maintenance of close ties with Britain.

During World War I Meighen assumed an increasing role in the government and was a key figure in formulating and defending several controversial measures, including the act imposing conscription for overseas military service and the Wartime Election Act, which took the franchise away from citizens of enemy-alien origin naturalized since 1902 while giving it to the female relatives of members of the armed forces. When the Conservatives joined with a sector of the Liberal party in October 1917 to form a union government organized under Borden's leadership and committed to the enforcement of conscription, Meighen became minister of the interior. He was primarily responsible for the legislation which nationalized several railways to form the Canadian National Railways system.

On Borden's retirement on July 10, 1920, Meighen became prime minister and held office until the government was defeated in the general election of December 1921. At

the conference of Dominion prime ministers in 1921 his pro-British sentiments did not inhibit him in opposing British policy and preventing the renewal of the Anglo-Japanese alliance.

At the end of five years as leader of the opposition, Meighen faced the electors again in the election of 1925 but failed to win a clear majority, largely because of the hostility of French-Canadian voters, who continued to resent conscription. When Mackenzie King resigned in 1926, Meighen formed a minority government which was shortly defeated in Parliament and subsequently lost a general election. Thereupon Meighen retired from public life to pursue business interests and the study of Shakespeare in Toronto.

Meighen returned in 1932 as government leader in the Senate and held that position until the defeat of Richard Bedford Bennett's Conservative ministry in 1935. During World War II Meighen again accepted the leadership of the Conservative party, espousing conscription and national government once more, but he resigned after his defeat in a by-election in 1942. He died in Toronto on Aug. 5, 1960.

Further Reading

Some of Meighen's public addresses are in *Unrevised and Unrepented* (1949). An excellent three-volume biography is Roger Graham, *Arthur Meighen* (1960-1966). The last phase of Meighen's political career is discussed in J. L. Granatstein, *The Politics of Survival: The Conservative Party of Canada, 1939-1945* (1967). □

Friedrich Meinecke

Friedrich Meinecke (1862-1954), Germany's greatest historian in the period from 1890 to 1950, founded a school of the history of ideas and trained many scholars.

Friedrich Meinecke was born in Salzwedel and educated in Berlin. His family belonged to the solid middle class which formed the backbone of imperial Germany. Early in life he decided to become a historian and was trained at the universities of Bonn and Berlin. Hampered by a speech defect, he did not feel he should enter the teaching profession and chose instead the career of archivist. In "this dusty trade" he felt himself quite at home. However, his intellectual qualities were soon recognized, and he was appointed editor of the country's most distinguished review, *Die historische Zeitschrift,* an office he held until he was ousted by the Nazis in 1935.

Meinecke's first work, a two-volume biography of the Prussian general Hermann von Boyen, was immediately recognized as proof of brilliant and searching scholarship, and he was appointed professor of history at the University of Strassburg in 1901. Until then his outlook had partaken of a somewhat parochial and conservative Prussianism; the move into Alsace opened new horizons for him. In 1908 he published *Cosmopolitanism and Nation State* (*Weltbürgertum und Nationalstaat*), which established the history of political ideas as an important and new discipline and evidenced Meinecke's propensity to think in dialectic and even dualistic terms. Throughout his life he pursued the evolution of opposing and even antagonistic ideas, such as cosmopolitanism and nationalism, ethic and power, uniqueness and recurrence. In 1913 he took the chair of modern history at the University of Berlin, which he occupied until his retirement in 1932. At the outbreak of World War I, in 1914, Meinecke was as nationalistic as most Germans, but contacts with leading politicians soon altered his outlook; he began to speak out for domestic reforms and for a peace without annexation. His voice was heard but not heeded. Resignation rather than conviction converted him into a republican when Germany met defeat in 1918, and he began to work for a democratic Germany in earnest. In 1924 he published what may be considered his most important work, *Machiavellism* (*Die Idee der Staatsräson in der neuren Geschichte*), a study in intellectual history, but this time devoted to the conflict between ethics and the imperatives of political necessity.

Meinecke continued his close contacts with the leading statesmen of the Weimar Republic and wrote articles remonstrating against the rising tide of fascism. Again his warning was disregarded; Hitler became chancellor in 1933. Many of Meinecke's students fled from Germany or were ousted from their positions, but since he was already past 70, the Nazis did not attack him personally. In 1936 he published a history of the origins of historicism (*Die Ursprünge des Historismus*).

The outbreak of World War II, which Meinecke had feared and predicted, found him writing his memoirs. The Allied bombings drove him out of Berlin; he found refuge in Franconia and witnessed the American offensive in southern Germany. Surrounded by the cacophony of war, he began an inquiry into the causes of the German disaster, *The German Catastrophe* (*Die deutsche Katastrophe*). When the old University of Berlin split and the young veterans refused to commit themselves to the Communist propaganda of East Germany, Meinecke, although 86 years of age and nearly blind, offered his services and became the first rector of the Free University of Berlin.

Further Reading

A full-length study of Meinecke is Richard W. Sterling, *Ethics in a World of Power: The Political Ideas of Friedrich Meinecke* (1958). Extensive material on Meinecke can also be found in John Higham and others, *History* (1965); Georg G. Iggers, *The German Conception of History* (1968); and Fritz K. Ringer, *The Decline of the German Mandarins: The German Academic Community, 1890-1933* (1969). □

Felix Andries Vening Meinesz

The Dutch geodesist and geophysicist Felix Andries Vening Meinesz (1887-1966) pioneered in the field of gravity measurements.

On July 30, 1887, F. A. Vening Meinesz was born in Scheveningen. He attended the public schools in Amsterdam, the city in which his father was the *burgemeester,* and in 1910 obtained his diploma in civil engineering from the Technical University in Delft. He was first employed with the Geodetic Commission of the Netherlands, his task being to continue the gravimetric survey of the country with the aid of the contemporary pendulum instruments. The unstable soil of the Netherlands proved a serious handicap, and it was impossible to attain the desired accuracy. Vening Meinesz tried to eliminate the disturbing movements of the soil by using two pendulums swinging from the same support. His experiments, combined with a mathematical analysis of the sway of the entire system, proved very successful. Further experiments, carried out aboard submarines, resulted in the construction of the improved Vening Meinesz pendulum apparatus, which, for the first time in the history of geodesy, made possible the precise measurements of gravity on the oceans.

During the years 1923-1939 Vening Meinesz made 11 long journeys in submarines with his apparatus, cruising all oceans and especially in the East Indian Archipelago. At the same time, he expanded the mathematical theory which was used to convert the physical information about the gravity field to geometric information about the shape of the earth. In this way, the solution of the fundamental problem of scientific geodesy, that is, the mapping of the entire earth

in one comprehensive system, was made possible both theoretically and practically. Only the use of artificial satellites can rival, to some extent, the gravimetric method initiated by the efforts of Vening Meinesz.

Meanwhile, Vening Meinesz's scientific interest was directed into deeper things. From his gravity maps of East India he found a long narrow strip of negative anomalies which he interpreted to be the first visible sign of a future mountain range. His investigations of this dealt with the internal structure and currents of the earth, the isostatic compensation of topographic formations, and the upheaval of the mountain ranges. Other, later discoveries in the field of geophysics gave plenty of support to his theories.

Vening Meinesz taught geodesy, cartography, and geophysics at the State University in Utrecht and at the Technical University in Delft. He was also the director of the Institute of Meteorology (1945-1951) and the president of the International Union of Geodesy and Geophysics (1948-1951). On Aug. 12, 1966, he died in Amersfoort, Netherlands.

Further Reading

The *Gedenkboek F. A. Vening Meinesz* (1957), honoring Vening Meinesz on his seventieth birthday, contains, mainly in English, a description and evaluation of his achievements and a complete bibliography of his publications, together with articles by his colleagues. His contributions to geodesy are discussed in general books such as Guy Bomford, *Geodesy* (1952; 2d ed. 1962), and Weikko A. Heiskanen and Helmut Moritz, *Physical Geodesy* (1966). □

Alexius Ritter von Handschuchsheim Meinong

The Austrian philosopher Alexius Meinong, Ritter von Handschuchsheim (1853-1920), made important contributions to the general theory of reference and to the understanding of values.

Alexius Meinong was born in Lemburg, Poland, but his family soon returned to Austria. All his formal education was in Vienna, first at the Academic Gymnasium and then at the university, where in 1874 he took his degree in history and philosophy. Like the other important figures in Austrian philosophy, he then came under the influence of Franz Brentano. Brentano encouraged him to study David Hume, and in due course Meinong produced two books on the English philosopher. His philosophical apprenticeship was thus in the tradition of British empiricism, and his subsequent work owes more to this tradition than to any German philosopher.

Meinong taught at Vienna as a lecturer for four years (1878-1882) and then moved to Graz, where he taught for the remainder of his life. The major event of his long tenure at Graz was his founding of the Institute of Experimental Psychology, the first such institution in Austria.

Meinong's most original contribution to philosophy is his theory of objects. His starting point is that the theory of objects is too narrowly construed. There is a general tendency in philosophy to deal only with those objects which exist and, moreover, a tendency in commonsense thinking to equate the existent object with material entities. Against these two tendencies Meinong argues that there is an important distinction between talking about nonexistent objects and talking about nothing. It is, for example, possible to sort out true and false statements about Santa Claus, and this could not be the case if the name denoted nothing at all. What it denotes is an object with quite definite properties ("lives at the North Pole," "drives reindeer") which does not happen to exist. In general, says Meinong, it is always possible to distinguish the characteristics of an object (*sosein*) from its being (*sein*). This principle allows him to introduce highly imaginative discussions of impossible objects, incomplete objects, defective objects, inclusive objects, and the like.

In a posthumously published book, *On the Foundations of the General Theory of Values* (1924), Meinong extends his theory to ethics and esthetics. Here he tries to show that values are objects which we apprehend through various modes of feeling. He then attempts to provide criteria for situations in which these feelings could be said to be correct or incorrect, appropriate or inappropriate.

Even though Meinong's work is still largely unread, it has had considerable influence on English philosophy through the interpretations of Bertrand Russell and G. E. Moore. More recent work indicates that these early interpretations were defective and that Meinong may yet receive a more adequate hearing.

Further Reading

J. N. Findlay, *Meinong's Theory of Objects and Values* (1933; 2d ed., 1963), is a largely sympathetic exposition, but some criticisms are added together with a brief biographical sketch and an overall assessment of Meinong's significance. Gustav Bergmann, *Realism: A Critique of Brentano and Meinong* (1967), offers a full-length appraisal.

Additional Sources

Lindenfeld, David F., *The transformation of positivism: Alexius Meinong and European thought, 1880-1920,* Berkeley: University of California Press, 1980. □

Golda Meir

The Zionist Labor leader Golda Meir (1898-1978) served as Israel's foreign minister from 1956 to 1966. In 1969 she became Israel's fourth prime minister.

Golda Meir was born the daughter of Moshe and Bluma Mabovitch in Kiev, Ukraine, on May 3, 1898. She emigrated in 1906 with her family to Milwaukee, Wis. After she attended grammar and high school, she went to the Teachers' Training College in Milwaukee in 1917. In the same year she married Morris Myerson (later she modified her name to Meir). For several years she taught in the local schools and was active in the Labor Zionist party. In 1921 she left for Palestine and joined Kibbutz Merchavia, where after some training she was put in charge of the chicken farm. Because of illness in her family, she moved to Tel Aviv and started to work as treasurer of the Histadruth's Office of Public Works.

From 1928 Golda Meir was the secretary of the Working Women's Council in Palestine, and as such, she was its representative on the executive of the Histadruth. She also represented the council at a number of international labor congresses and was a delegate to its sister organization, the Pioneer Women, in the United States. After 1929 she was elected a delegate to most congresses of the World Zionist Organization. This was the beginning of her Zionist political activity. She was a member of the executive of the Jewish National Council in Palestine and served on the board of directors of a number of the Histadruth mutual aid programs, as well as a number of its industrial affiliates. In 1940 she was appointed head of the political department of the Histadruth. As such, she fought against the British White Paper of 1939 and organized illegal Jewish immigration to Palestine.

When the Palestine Administration interned the leaders of the Jewish Agency on June 29, 1946, Golda Meir was appointed acting head of the Jewish Agency's political department to replace the detained Moshe Shertok-Sharett. She continued in this position until the proclamation of the

independence of Israel on May 14, 1948, since, after his release by the British, Shertok-Sharett spent most of his time in the United States. Early in 1948 she visited the United States to organize an emergency fund campaign for Palestine, with very successful results. On May 14 she was, as a member of Israel's Provisional Council of State, among the signers of its declaration of independence.

Golda Meir started her political career in Israel as its minister plenipotentiary to Moscow. During her 6 months' tenure Russian Jewry expressed its pro-Israeli leanings in every possible way and especially during the Jewish high holidays, in spite of the restrictions of 40 years of Russian communism. With her election to the first Israeli Parliament, she returned to Israel and was appointed minister of labor and social insurance. While in this office, she worked to solve the most important internal problems of Israel: housing and employment for the new mass immigration. Still known by her married name, she engineered what became known as the "Myerson Plan," which allowed for the construction of more than 30,000 units of one-room housing. She also oversaw the construction of some 200,000 low-income apartments to house Israel's newly immigrated families.

In 1956, Prime Minister David Ben-Gurion proclaimed Meir "the best man" in his cabinet and named her to replace Shertok-Sharett as foreign minister, among the most important government jobs in the nation. It was now, under Ben-Gurion's prodding to have all Israelis bear Hebrew names, that she reluctantly altered her name while keeping it as close as possible to Myerson. In 10 years in this office she established political and economic relations with the majority of the African states. Golda Meir, tired and ill, stepped down as minister of foreign affairs in 1966, but soon after, under pressure of her political party, she agreed to take over the leadership of Israel's Labor party. She succeeded in the next 2 years in reuniting the three main Labor elements: Mapai, Achdut Ha'Avodah, and Rafi. The merger took place on Jan. 2, 1968, and in August she retired from political activity. After the death of Levi Eshkol, to avoid a confrontation between the main rival candidates, Moshe Dayan and Yigal Allon, Golda Meir again came out of retirement to assume the post of Israel's prime minister on March 17, 1969.

Though elderly and in faltering health, Meir proved her abilities to the country during her initial nine-month term such that her Labor Party won the 1969 elections. Meir thus gained her own four-year term as prime minister. This period was marked by Meir's efforts to gain United States aid in the form of military and economy assistance. The assurances she won from President Richard Nixon on this helped her and Dayan persuade the Israeli cabinet to agree to a United States proposition for a cease-fire and the opening of peace talks with the United Arab Republic. She sided with Dayan's more radical position that the occupied territories captured during the 1967 war be settled by Israelis, yet she retained the support of moderates who favored trading land for peace. However, in 1973 and 1974, Israel's unpreparedness for the Yom Kippur War brought demands for new leadership. After the 1973 elections, Meir was still able

to form a new government, but divisions only increased and on April 10, 1974, she resigned as prime minister.

Even in retirement, Meir remained an important political presence in Israel. She also achieved folk-hero status as one of the first women to head a nation in the modern era. Her autobiography *My Life* helped cement her place in the public's imagination as the doting grandmother who had risen to greatness in her nation's hour of need. Meir died in Jerusalem on Dec. 8, 1978.

Further Reading

See Golda Meir's *My Life* (1975); Menachem Meir's *My Mother: Golda Meir* (1983); and Ralph Martin's *Golda: The Romantic Years* (1988). Marie Syrkin, *Golda Meir: Israel's Leader* (1969), is a sympathetic biography based on the author's experiences with Zionism and contacts with its leaders. Other biographies are Eliyahu Agress, *Golda Meir: Portrait of a Prime Minister* (trans. 1969), and Israel and Mary Shenker, eds., *As Good as Golda: The Warmth and Wisdom of Israel's Prime Minister* (1970). □

Lise Meitner

Lise Meitner (1878-1968) helped to develop the theory behind nuclear fission, and became the first woman professor in Germany.

The prototypical female scientist of the early twentieth century was a woman devoted to her work, sacrificing family and personal relationships in favor of science; modestly brilliant; generous; and underrecognized. In many ways Austrian-born physicist Lise Meitner embodies that image. In 1938, along with her nephew Otto Robert Frisch, Meitner developed the theory behind nuclear fission that would eventually make possible the creation of the atomic bomb. She and lifelong collaborator Otto Hahn made several other key contributions to the field of nuclear physics. Although Hahn received the Nobel Prize in 1944, Meitner did not share the honor—one of the more frequently cited examples of the sexism rife in the scientific community in the first half of this century.

Elise Meitner was born November 7, 1878 to an affluent Vienna family. Her father Philipp was a lawyer and her mother Hedwig travelled in the same Vienna intellectual circles as Sigmund Freud. From the early years of her life, Meitner gained experience that would later be invaluable in combatting—or overlooking—the slights she received as a woman in a field dominated by men. The third of eight children, she expressed interest in pursuing a scientific career, but her practical father made her attend the Elevated High School for Girls in Vienna to earn a diploma that would enable her to teach French—a much more sensible career for a woman. After completing this program, Meitner's desire to become a scientist was greater than ever. In 1899, she began studying with a local tutor who prepped students for the difficult university entrance exam. She worked so hard that she successfully prepared for the test in

two years rather than the average four. Shortly before she turned twenty three, Meitner became one of the few women students at the University of Vienna.

At the beginning of her university career in 1901, Meitner could not decide between physics or mathematics; later, inspired by her physics teacher Ludwig Boltzmann, she opted for the latter. In 1906, after becoming the second woman ever to earn a Ph.D. in physics from the University of Vienna, she decided to stay on in Boltzmann's laboratory as an assistant to his assistant. This was hardly a typical career path for a recent doctorate, but Meitner had no other offers, as universities at the time did not hire women faculty. Less than a year after Meitner entered the professor's lab, Boltzmann committed suicide, leaving the future of the research team uncertain. In an effort to recruit the noted physicist Max Planck to take Boltzmann's place, the university invited him to come visit the lab. Although Planck refused the offer, he met Meitner during the visit and talked with her about quantum physics and radiation research. Inspired by this conversation, Meitner left Vienna in the winter of 1907 to go to the Institute for Experimental Physics in Berlin to study with Planck.

Soon after her arrival in Berlin, Meitner met a young chemist named Otto Hahn at one of the weekly symposia. Hahn worked at Berlin's Chemical Institute under the supervision of Emil Fischer, surrounded by organic chemists—none of whom shared his research interests in radiochemistry. Four months older than Hahn, Meitner was not only intrigued by the same research problems but had the training in physics that Hahn lacked. Unfortunately,

Hahn's supervisor balked at the idea of allowing a woman researcher to enter the all-male Chemical Institute. Finally, Fischer allowed Meitner and Hahn to set up a laboratory in a converted woodworking shop in the Institute's basement, as long as Meitner agreed never to enter the higher floors of the building.

This incident was neither the first nor the last experience of sexism that Meitner encountered in her career. According to one famous anecdote, she was solicited to write an article by an encyclopedia editor who had read an article she wrote on the physical aspects of radioactivity. When she answered the letter addressed to Herr Meitner and explained she was a woman, the editor wrote back to retract his request, saying he would never publish the work of a woman. Even in her collaboration with Hahn, Meitner at times conformed to gender roles. When British physicist Sir Ernest Rutherford visited their Berlin laboratory on his way back from the Nobel ceremonies in 1908, Meitner spent the day shopping with his wife Mary while the two men talked about their work.

Within her first year at the Institute, the school opened its classes to women, and Meitner was allowed to roam the building. For the most part, however, the early days of the collaboration between Hahn and Meitner were filled with their investigations into the behavior of beta rays as they passed through aluminum. By today's standards, the laboratory in which they worked would be appalling. Hahn and Meitner frequently suffered from headaches brought on by their adverse working conditions. In 1912 when the Kaiser-Wilhelm Institute was built in the nearby suburb of Dahlem, Hahn received an appointment in the small radioactivity department there and invited Meitner to join him in his laboratory. Soon thereafter, Planck asked Meitner to lecture as an assistant professor at the Institute for Theoretical Physics. The first woman in Germany to hold such a position, Meitner drew several members of the news media to her opening lecture.

When World War I started in 1914, Meitner interrupted her laboratory work to volunteer as an X-ray technician in the Austrian army. Hahn entered the German military. The two scientists arranged their leaves to coincide and throughout the war returned periodically to Dahlem where they continued trying to discover the precursor of the element actinium. By the end of the war, they announced that they had found this elusive element and named it protactinium, the missing link on the periodic table between thorium (previously number 90) and uranium (number 91). A few years later Meitner received the Leibniz Medal from the Berlin Academic of Science and the Leibniz Prize from the Austrian Academy of Science for this work. Shortly after she helped discover protactinium in 1917, Meitner accepted the job of establishing a radioactive physics department at the Kaiser Wilhelm Institute. Hahn remained in the chemistry department, and the two ceased working together to concentrate on research more suited to their individual training. For Meitner, this constituted a return to beta radiation studies.

Throughout the 1920s, Meitner continued her work in beta radiation, winning several prizes. In 1928, the Association to Aid Women in Science upgraded its Ellen Richards Prize—billing it as a Nobel Prize for women—and named Meitner and chemist Pauline Ramart-Lucas of the University of Paris its first recipients. In addition to the awards she received, Meitner acquired a reputation in physics circles for some of her personal quirks as well. Years later, her nephew Otto Frisch, also a physicist, would recall that she drank large quantities of strong coffee, embarked on ten mile walks whenever she had free time, and would sometimes indulge in piano duets with him. By middle age, Meitner had also adopted some of the mannerisms stereotypically associated with her male colleagues. Not the least of these, Hahn later recalled, was absent-mindedness. On one occasion, a student approached her at a lecture, saying they had met earlier. Knowing she had never met the student, Meitner responded earnestly, "You probably mistake me for Professor Hahn."

Meitner and Hahn resumed their collaboration in 1934, after Enrico Fermi published his seminal article on "transuranic" uranium. The Italian physicist announced that when he bombarded uranium with neutrons, he produced two new elements—number 93 and 94, in a mixture of lighter elements. Meitner and Hahn joined with a young German chemist named Fritz Strassmann to draw up a list of all the substances the heaviest natural elements produced when bombarded with neutrons. In three years, the three confirmed Fermi's result and expanded the list to include about ten additional substances that resulted from bombarding these elements with neutrons. Meanwhile, physicists Irène Joliot-Curie and Pavle Savitch announced that they had created a new radioactive substance by bombarding uranium by neutrons. The French team speculated that this new mysterious substance might be thorium, but Meitner, Hahn, and Strassmann could not confirm this finding. No matter how many times they bombarded uranium with neutrons, no thorium resulted. Hahn and Meitner sent a private letter to the French physicists suggesting that perhaps they had erred. Although Joliot-Curie did not reply directly, a few months later she published a paper retracting her earlier assertions and said the substance she had noted was not thorium.

Current events soon took Meitner's mind off these professional squabbles. Although her father, a proponent of cultural assimilation, had all his children baptized, Meitner was Jewish by birth. Because she continued to maintain her Austrian citizenship, she was at first relatively impervious to the political turmoil in Weimar Germany. In the mid–1930s she had been asked to stop lecturing at the university but she continued her research. When Germany annexed Austria in 1938, Meitner became a German citizen and began to look for a research position in an environment hospitable to Jews. Her tentative plans grew urgent in the spring of 1938, when Germany announced that academics could no longer leave the country. Colleagues devised an elaborate scheme to smuggle her out of Germany to Stockholm where she had made temporary arrangements to work at the Institute of the Academy of Sciences under the sponsorship of a Nobel grant. By late fall, however, Meitner's position in Sweden looked dubious: her grant provided no money for equipment and assistance, and the administration at the Stock-

holm Institute would offer her no help. Christmas found her depressed and vacationing in a town in the west of Sweden.

Back in Germany, Hahn and Strassmann had not let their colleague's departure slow their research efforts. The two read and reread the paper Joliot-Curie had published detailing her research techniques. Looking it over, they thought they had found an explanation for Joliot-Curie's confusion: perhaps instead of finding one new substance after bombarding uranium, as she had thought, she had actually found two new substances! They repeated her experiments and indeed found two substances in the final mixture, one of which was barium. This result seemed to suggest that bombarding uranium with neutrons led it to split up into a number of smaller elements. Hahn immediately wrote to Meitner to share this perplexing development with her. Meitner received his letter on her vacation in the village of Kungalv, as she awaited the arrival of her nephew, Frisch, who was currently working in Copenhagen under the direction of physicist Niels Bohr. Frisch hoped to discuss a problem in his own work with Meitner, but it was clear soon after they met that the only thing on her mind was Hahn and Strassmann's observation. Meitner and Frisch set off for a walk in the snowy woods—Frisch on skis, with his aunt trotting along—continuing to puzzle out how uranium could possibly yield barium. When they paused for a rest on a log, Meitner began to posit a theory, sketching diagrams in the snow.

If, as Bohr had previously suggested, the nucleus behaved like a liquid drop, Meitner reasoned that when this drop of a nucleus was bombarded by neutrons, it might elongate and divide itself into two smaller droplets. The forces of electrical repulsion would act to prevent it from maintaining its circular shape by forming the nucleus into a dumbbell shape that would—as the bombarding forces grew stronger—sever at the middle to yield two droplets—two completely different nuclei. But one problem still remained. When Meitner added together the weights of the resultant products, she found that the sum did not equal the weight of the original uranium. The only place the missing mass could be lost was in energy expended during the reaction.

Frisch rushed back to Copenhagen, eager to test the revelations from their walk in the woods on his mentor and boss, Bohr. He caught Bohr just as the scientist was leaving for an American tour, but as Bohr listened to what Frisch was urgently telling him, he responded: "Oh, what idiots we have been. We could have foreseen it all! This is just as it must be!" Buoyed by Bohr's obvious admiration, Frisch and Meitner spent hours on a long-distance telephone writing the paper that would publicize their theory. At the suggestion of a biologist friend, Frisch coined the word "fission" to describe the splitting of the nucleus in a process that seemed to him analogous to cell division.

The paper "On the Products of the Fission of Uranium and Thorium" appeared in *Nature* on February 11, 1939. Although it would be another five and a half years before the American military would successfully explode an atom bomb over Hiroshima, many physicists consider Meitner and Frisch's paper akin to opening a Pandora's box of atomic weapons. Physicists were not the only ones to view Meitner as an important participant in the harnessing of nuclear energy. After the bomb was dropped in 1944, a radio station asked First Lady Eleanor Roosevelt to conduct a transatlantic interview with Meitner. In this interview, the two women talked extensively about the implications and future of nuclear energy. After the war, Hahn found himself in one of the more enviable positions for a scientist—the winner of the 1944 Nobel prize in chemistry—although, because of the war, Hahn did not accept his prize until two years later. Although she attended the ceremony, Meitner did not share in the honor.

But Meitner's life after the war was not without its plaudits and pleasures. In the early part of 1946, she travelled to America to visit her sister—working in the U.S. as a chemist—for the first time in decades. While there, Meitner delivered a lecture series at Catholic University in Washington, D.C. In the following years, she won the Max Planck Medal and was awarded numerous honorary degrees from both American and European universities. In 1966 she, Hahn, and Strassmann split the $50,000 Enrico Fermi Award given by the Atomic Energy Commission. Unfortunately, by this time Meitner had become too ill to travel, so the chairman of the A. E. C. delivered it to her in Cambridge, England, where she had retired a few years earlier. Meitner died just a few weeks before her 90th birthday on October 27, 1968.

Further Reading

Crawford, Deborah, *Lise Meitner, Atomic Pioneer,* Crown, 1969.
Irving, David, *The German Atomic Bomb: The History of Nuclear Research in Nazi Germany,* Simon & Schuster, 1967.
Rhodes, Richard, *The Making of the Atom Bomb,* Simon & Schuster, 1988.
Watkins, Sallie, "Lise Meitner and the Beta-ray Energy Controversy: An Historical Perspective," in *American Journal of Physics,* Volume 51, 1983, pp. 551–553.
Watkins, Sallie, "Lise Meitner: The Making of a Physicist," in *Physics Teacher,* January, 1984, pp. 12–15. □

Philip Melancthon

The German scholar and humanist Philip Melancthon (1497-1560) was the chief systematic theologian of the early Reformation and principal author of the famous Augsburg Confession of 1530.

Philip Melancthon was born Philip Schwartzerd at Bretten in Swabia, the son of George and Barbara Schwartzerd. His earliest education was supervised by his father and grandfather and, after their deaths in 1508, was directed by his grandmother's brother, the famous jurist and Hebrew scholar Johann Reuchlin. Schwartzerd means "black earth," and Reuchlin is said to have been so impressed with his grandnephew's scholarly talents that he insisted that Philip use the Greek form of "black earth," hence the name Melancthon. The young Melancthon stud-

ied at Pforzheim and Heidelberg, receiving a bachelor of arts degree from the latter in 1511. He took his master's degree at Tübingen in 1514 and began to lecture there on Latin and Greek literature. Like many young humanists, Melancthon had considerable doubts about a number of ecclesiastical practices, and he helped to edit the scathing satire against his granduncle's ecclesiastical enemies, *The Letters of Obscure Men,* in 1514-1515.

Melancthon's academic reputation began to grow, and in 1518, at the age of 21, he was appointed professor of Greek at the University of Wittenberg, against the early objections of Martin Luther and Georg Spalatin, court chaplain to the elector Frederick the Wise. Melancthon's inaugural address on the ideal program of education for young people won over Luther completely, thus commencing a friendship which was to last until Luther's death.

In 1518-1519 Melancthon drew closer to Luther's criticisms of scholastic theology and ecclesiastical abuses, supporting Luther at the Leipzig debates with Johann Eck in 1519. In the same year he received his bachelor of theology degree, his thesis supporting many of the critical points of Luther's reform: justification by faith, and opposition to papal authority. Luther characterized their relationship with the following accurate observation: "I am rough, boisterous, stormy, and altogether warlike. I must remove stumps and stones, cut away thistles and thorns, and clear the wild forests; but Master Philip comes along softly and gently sowing and watering with joy, according to the gifts which God has abundantly bestowed upon him."

During Luther's seclusion in the Wartburg in 1521-1522, Melancthon defended his friend against the condemnations of the University of Paris and attempted to preserve Luther's moderate reforms in Wittenberg against the enthusiastic and radical take-over by Karlstadt.

In 1521 Melancthon began a new phase of his career—that of chief systematic theologian of the Reformation. He published in that year (and would spend the rest of his life revising) his *Loci communes,* a system of Christian doctrine based chiefly upon the writings of St. Paul. The work has remained to this day one of the foundations of Protestant thought. Melancthon was not merely a writer but a teacher and educational theorist as well. Like Luther, he lectured all his life at Wittenberg, for a time overworking himself by teaching theology in addition to his regularly assigned classical teaching.

In 1530 Melancthon took on the task of answering the growing Catholic criticism of the increasingly fragmented Protestant sects. Keeping before him the idea of eventually reconciling all Christians, Melancthon presented a statement of Protestant doctrine to the emperor Charles V at Augsburg in 1530 (hence the title the Augsburg Confession) in which he attempted to unite all Christians in a series of fundamental beliefs. Melancthon was bitterly answered by Eck, and his later efforts to reconcile Catholics and Protestants were rendered futile by Protestant sectarianism and Catholic intransigence. In 1529, however, he mediated between Luther and Huldreich Zwingli at the Marburg Colloquy and, in 1536, between Luther and Martin Bucer in formulating the Wittenberg Concord. "If I could purchase union by my own death," Melancthon said, "I would gladly sacrifice my life."

The death of Luther in 1546 and of Melancthon's daughter Anna in 1547 weakened the theologian, who now turned to composing prayers, some of them the most moving in all Christian liturgy. Melancthon died on April 19, 1560, his hopes for reconciliation of the Christian Churches not fulfilled to this day.

Further Reading

Melancthon's *Loci communes* has been translated into English and edited by Clyde Manschreck in his *Melanchthon on Christian Doctrine* (1965). The best life of Melancthon is also by Manschreck, *Melanchthon: The Quiet Reformer* (1958). A shorter study, particularly useful as an introduction to Melancthon's life and thought, is Robert Stupperich, *Melanchthon,* translated by R. H. Fischer (1965). For Melancthon and the Reformation in general see *The New Cambridge Modern History* (12 vols., 1957-1970). ☐

Bernard Eugene Meland

Historian of liberal theology in the modern period and professor at the Chicago School of Theology, Bernard Eugene Meland (1899-1993) articulated a postmodern and postliberal theological vision in a constructive mode. A theologian of culture, his radi-

cal empiricism incorporated aesthetic dimensions of experience both in construing the meaning of "God" and in interpreting theological method.

Bernard E. Meland was born June 28, 1899, in Chicago, Illinois. His parents were Erick Bernhard and Elizabeth Hansen Meland. He acquired skills as a carpenter and a spirit sensitive to the ambiguity of life and appreciative of what he called its problematic good. After a period of military service in 1918, he received a bachelor's degree at Park College (Missouri) in 1923. Study at the University of Illinois at Champaign (1923-1924) and at McCormick Theological Seminary in Chicago (1924-1925) followed.

He transferred to the Divinity School of the University of Chicago and took a Bachelor of Divinity degree there in 1928. He was ordained to the ministry of the Presbyterian Church in the United States in that year and honorably retired from its ministry at the time of his retirement from teaching in 1964. He married Margaret Evans McClusky on August 6, 1926. She died as he was entering retirement. Their son, Richard Dennis, lived with Meland in the 1990s. Meland died in 1993.

During his student days his mentors were his teachers at the Chicago School—Shirley Jackson Case, Shailer Mathews, and especially Gerald Birney Smith, who died while Meland was studying at the University of Marburg. Upon his return he obtained a doctorate from the University of Chicago in 1929 and began to publish prolifically in liberal religious journals.

Meland taught at Central College, Fayette, Missouri, from 1929 to 1936, and at Pomona College, Claremont, California, from 1936 to 1945. While at Pomona College he brought the arts to chapel worship with the help of his student assistant, Robert Shaw. He was professor of theology in the Divinity School of the University of Chicago from 1945 to 1964. During this time he gave the Barrows Lectures in India on two occasions. In retirement he continued active writing, teaching, lecturing, and responding at conferences on his theology until 1988, when his health confined him to his home.

Attentive to work in cultural anthropology, philosophy of science, history of religions, and phenomenology, Meland identified in experience converging streams of meaning under what he called the powers of the *mythos* and the *logos*. These meanings find form and are lived out in three interrelated "vortices": the self, the cultus, and the culture. His work focused on the embodied self and the "appreciative consciousness" shaped by culturally-mediated symbols in tension with critical consciousness shaped by science and theory. Life and faith shared an elemental organic ground in what Meland called a "stream of experience." But this was not without a pluralism of "structures of experience" that made elusive the quest for demonstrable knowledge in religion. Theology, he wrote, was a discipline midway between art and philosophy.

His constructive theology and method were most fully worked out in *Faith and Culture* (1953), *The Realities of*

Faith: The Revolution in Cultural Forms (1962), and *Fallible Forms and Symbols: Discourses on Method in a Theology of Culture* (1976). His critique of modern culture was developed in *The Secularization of Modern Cultures* (1966). Meland's appropriation of James' radical empiricism and his treatment of the appreciative consciousness was clear in *Higher Education and the Human Spirit* (1953). His indebtedness to Gerald Birney Smith was acknowledged in the book he wrote with Henry Nelson Wieman, *American Philosophies of Religion* (1936), and in *The Future of Empirical Theology* (1969). His aesthetic, mystical naturalism and early influences can be seen in *Modern Man's Worships: A Search for Reality in Religion* (1934) and in a compilation of early and later essays also informative about his method, *Essays in Constructive Theology: A Process Perspective* (1988). *Seeds of Redemption* (1947) and *The Reawakening of Christian Faith* (1949) were important brief statements of his theological vision.

Further Reading

A bibliography of Bernard E. Meland's work appeared in *Process Studies,* 5 (1975). Meland's work was receiving critical and appreciative attention from American scholars interested in postmodernism and the empirical tradition in theology. Their work has appeared in the *American Journal of Theology and Philosophy,* edited by Larry E. Axel and W. Crighton Peden. See the Meland items in the ten-year index in Volume 11 (January 1990), the essays in Lori Krafte-Jacobs, editor, "Bernard Meland and the Future of Theology," *American Journal of Theology and Philosophy,* 5 (1984), and the special issue of *The Journal of Religion,* 60 (1980). Meland's thoughts are discussed in volumes published by The Highlands Institute for American Religious Thought (1989).

Important books that discussed Meland's work are William Dean, *American Religious Empiricism* (1986); *History Making History: The New Historicism in American Religious Thought* (1988); Nancy Frankenberry, *Religion and Radical Empiricism* (1987); and Dolores Jean Rogers, *The American Empirical Movement in Theology* (1990). A short account of Meland's theology was found in Edgar A. Towne, "God and the Chicago School in the Theology of Bernard E. Meland," *American Journal of Theology and Philosophy,* 10 (1989). □

2nd Viscount Melbourne

The English statesman William Lamb, 2nd Viscount Melbourne (1779-1848), served as prime minister in 1834 and from 1835 to 1841. He was the stern suppressor of early trade unionism and the political mentor of the young Queen Victoria.

Lord Melbourne was a member of the small aristocratic oligarchy which dominated English society and politics in the 18th and early 19th centuries. By taking a leading part in reforming the oligarchical system in 1832 and afterward, the great aristocrats preserved much of their power and influence for most of the century.

William Lamb was born on March 15, 1779, at Brocket Hall, the family's Hertfordshire seat. He was generally believed to be the son of the Earl of Egremont. The Lambs were relative newcomers to aristocratic society, but their great wealth and Lady Melbourne's beauty and charm gave them a place in the highest circles. William grew up among the flower of the Whig aristocracy. The Prince of Wales, the Duchess of Devonshire, and Charles James Fox were some of his mother's close friends.

William was educated at Eton, Trinity College, Cambridge, and the University of Glasgow. Like most young men of the period, he profited little from his formal education; but he read widely in history and literature. An extraordinarily good-looking and brilliant young man, William was eagerly welcomed by society. Early on he displayed that good-natured cynicism which was to mark the rest of his career. He liked people, but he never expected much good to come from human endeavor. For a couple of years after completing his education in 1801, he did little but enjoy himself. However, as a younger son, William had to have a career. He finally settled on the law and in 1804 was admitted to the bar.

Early Career and Marriage

Lamb's legal career did not last long. His elder brother died in 1805, and Lamb became the future Lord Melbourne. As a prospective peer, he was expected to pursue a career in politics. He soon found himself a seat and entered Parliament in 1806. Just before this, in 1805, he had married Lady Caroline Ponsonby.

For the next 20 years Lamb was not to make a great success of his new career. He entered politics as Fox's devoted follower, but Fox died after a brief period in office, and the Whigs went out of power in 1807. Lamb soon found himself uncomfortable with Whiggery. He agreed with the Whigs on Catholic emancipation, but he found them too critical of the war against Napoleonic France. He also thought them soft toward parliamentary reform and popular radicalism. Lamb's closest sympathies were with a parliamentary group led by George Canning. But the Whigs were his friends, and he firmly rejected opportunities to advance his own career at their expense. This was not very satisfying, and in 1812 he retired from politics for a time.

Lamb's marriage was not a happy one. Lady Caroline was romantic to the point of mental imbalance, as she showed in her notorious affair with Lord Byron. The whole drama of the stormy romance was played in public from 1812 to 1816. Then, rejected by both Byron and society, she sank deeper into mental disorder until her death in 1828. Lamb remained loyal to his wife to the end.

Political Career

Lamb returned to Parliament in 1816. But it was not until 1827 that his career began to prosper. Then Canning finally came to power, and some of the Whigs joined his government. Lamb became chief secretary for Ireland. Canning soon died, but Lamb remained with the Canningites in two successive governments until 1828.

In 1829 Lamb succeeded to the Melbourne peerage, and in the following year he joined Lord Grey's great reform ministry. Melbourne still did not really believe in parliamentary reform. But now the great popular agitation for change seemed to make the choice one between reform and national convulsion. With such a choice, Melbourne chose reform.

But Melbourne believed that riotousness must be suppressed and, as home secretary, he was responsible for maintaining order. It was generally assumed that any kind of working-class organization was aimed at political revolution. Melbourne revived some old legislation against trade unions and encouraged its strict enforcement. The most famous sufferers were the "Tolpuddle Martyrs," agricultural laborers in Dorset who seem to have been innocent of any object other than the improvement of their miserable working conditions.

Prime Minister

Melbourne's reputation for firmness did him no harm among the upper classes. When Lord Grey resigned in 1834, Melbourne seemed the man most likely to be able to hold a Whig government together, and the King asked him to take Grey's place. Melbourne's reaction was typical. "I think it's a damned bore," he said. But he accepted.

With the exception of the brief Tory government of 1834-1835, Melbourne was to remain in office until 1841. He had a difficult task. His government, Parliament, and the country were deeply divided on the necessity for further reform and on its nature. Melbourne always greeted change without enthusiasm, but he was a realist and had a great talent for conciliation. Somehow he kept the government together and did what seemed necessary and practicable.

It was not until 1837, with the accession of Queen Victoria, that Melbourne began to enjoy office. Her innocent, straightforward character deeply appealed to him, and she responded with hero worship. It became the main object of Melbourne's life to educate the young queen for her role, and of hers to learn from "dear Lord M." On occasion, Melbourne's devotion may have got the better of his judgment, but his role as mentor was generally applauded. When he finally left office, he left a confident queen, with a competent new adviser in Prince Albert. For Melbourne his parting from the Queen was the beginning of the end. He died at Brocket Hall on Nov. 24, 1848.

Further Reading

A superb biography of Melbourne is the two volumes by Lord David Cecil: *The Young Melbourne* (1939) and *Lord M.* (1954). An interesting supplement to Cecil's books is Elizabeth Jenkins, *Lady Caroline Lamb* (1932), a biography of Melbourne's wife, who became known less for the novels she wrote than for her love affair with Lord Byron. Asa Briggs, *The Age of Improvement* (1959; 2d rev. ed. 1960), is recommended for general historical background.

Additional Sources

Cecil, David, Lord, *Melbourne,* New York: Harmony Books, 1979, 1954.

Marshall, Dorothy, *Lord Melbourne,* London: Weidenfeld and Nicolson, 1975?.

Ziegler, Philip, *Melbourne: a biography of William Lamb, 2nd Viscount Melbourne,* New York: Knopf, 1976. □

Andrew William Mellon

American businessman Andrew William Mellon (1855-1937) crowned a highly successful entrepreneurial career with over a decade of service as U.S. secretary of the Treasury.

Andrew Mellon was born on March 24, 1855, in Pittsburgh, Pa. Unlike most members of the industrial elite of his generation, Mellon attended college, although he withdrew shortly before graduation.

In 1882 Mellon became the owner and manager of the family banking firm, T. Mellon & Sons. A few years later he provided financial assistance for the enterprise which would become the Aluminum Company of America, and this concern was controlled by the Mellon family. He began to invest in the oil industry in the 1890s and was one of those who organized the Gulf Oil Corporation in 1901. Mellon invested in a variety of other industrial firms and became a director of many of them. In 1902, when the family private banking house was converted into a commercial bank, the Mellon National Bank of Pittsburgh, he was designated president. As a result of these endeavors, Mellon (gifted with an extraordinary ability to pick winners) achieved great wealth and was "one of the richest men in America."

Mellon dabbled in Republican politics in Pennsylvania, was acquainted with such political notables as Matthew S. Quay, Boies Penrose, and Philander C. Knox, and was a major financial contributor to his party. As a result of these associations plus behind-the-scenes activities, Mellon was appointed secretary of the Treasury by President Warren G. Harding. Partly because of his talent and partly because of the primacy of economic matters during the 1920s, Mellon became the most influential member of the Cabinet under both Harding and his successor, Calvin Coolidge. He was popularly referred to as the "greatest secretary of the Treasury since Alexander Hamilton."

Mellon was a political conservative, and his policies, particularly his opposition to progressive taxation, reflected this. Despite criticism by a minority of citizens, under Mellon's guidance the burden of taxation on those of above-average income was drastically reduced but that on the bulk of the taxpayers was lowered to a much lesser extent. Some of his tax policies benefited Mellon personally and his companies as well; this was true of both the law and the administrative rulings. As one critic said, "The Mellon tax policy, placing its emphasis on relief for millionaires rather than for consumers, made the maldistribution of income and oversaving even worse."

Mellon continued as secretary of the Treasury under President Herbert Hoover. Mellon interpreted the Great Depression of 1929 as a natural phenomenon and favored

deflation; he was critical of public works and pursued a traditional policy of economy. In early 1930 Mellon observed, "I see nothing in the present situation that is either menacing or warrants pessimism." However, a combination of criticism of his tax policy and the Depression itself eventuated in his resignation. Hoover persuaded him to accept an appointment as ambassador to Great Britain in 1932.

Mellon returned to private life with the end of the Republican era in the White House and devoted himself to philanthropy. His superlative art collection was donated to the Federal government in 1937 and constituted the foundation of the National Gallery of Art in Washington, D.C.

By getting in on the ground floor of what later became highly profitable enterprises, Mellon had succeeded in becoming rich. His public life, although but a dozen years in duration, was of sufficient prominence so that the history of the 1920s is incomprehensible without reference to him. The Depression resulted in a reversal of public sentiment, so that those of his policies which had once been applauded by the majority were later cited as illustrations of favoritism and special interest and perhaps even as causal factors in the magnitude of the Depression. Mellon died in Southampton, N.Y., on Aug. 26, 1937.

Further Reading

Mellon spoke for himself in *Taxation: The People's Business* (1924). There is no entirely acceptable biography of Mellon. Philip H. Love, *Andrew W. Mellon* (1929), is quite favorable, whereas Harvey O'Connor, *Mellon's Millions: The Biography of a Fortune* (1933), is very critical. See also William L. Mellon and Boyden Sparkes, *Judge Mellon's Sons* (1948), and Frank R. Denton, *The Mellons of Pittsburgh* (1948). □

Konstantin Stepanovich Melnikov

Konstantin Stepanovich Melnikov (1890-1974) was one of the Russian avant-garde's most prolific and internationally celebrated architects during the 1920s. By 1937 the individualism of his architecture no longer had a place in Stalin's U.S.S.R.

Konstantin Melnikov was born a peasant on the outskirts of Moscow in 1890. Young Melnikov showed an early proclivity for drawing and began to attend the Moscow School of Painting, Sculpture, and Architecture. After completing the general education program, he studied painting, and then resolved to be an architect. He stayed on at the Moscow School, completing the architecture program in 1917. As seen in his surviving student projects, Melnikov's education in architecture was conservative, emphasizing the classical architectural tradition. Although he would quickly move away from historical revivalism, the monumental forms of some of his later modern works occasionally suggested the undercurrent of his classical training.

Melnikov entered the profession of architecture during the year of the Bolshevik Revolution. The political, social, and economic demands upon architecture in the emerging Soviet Union were to be very different from those of Melnikov's youth and training in tsarist Russia. The economic desperation of Russia due to World War I, revolution, and the subsequent civil war resulted in few opportunities for real construction for a young architect. Like many of his architectural colleagues, Melnikov spent his first years after the communist revolution working primarily on paper architecture: unbuilt projects, often for competitions, with an emphasis upon defining a modern architecture appropriate for building a new socialist society.

During the early 1920s Melnikov taught architecture at VKhUTEMAS, a Moscow school popular with avant-garde artists and architects. With the coming of Lenin's New Economic Policy, modest opportunities to build were being presented to Melnikov. One of his important early works was the Makhorka Pavilion, built in Moscow to promote a native tobacco at the All-Russian Agricultural and Cottage Industry Exhibition of 1923. Jutting diagonals, factory-like windows, large graphics, and a spiral staircase animated the bold geometric forms of this small wooden structure. Melnikov's classical training was now distant as he worked through the dynamic and abstract aesthetic language of modernism.

Melnikov was beginning to emerge as a favored architect in the new Soviet Union. In 1924 he designed Lenin's glass-topped sarcophagus that was placed inside the Lenin Mausoleum on Red Square. Melnikov then found himself on the international architectural stage when he won a closed competition to be the architect of the Soviet Pavilion at the 1925 Exposition des Arts Décoratifs in Paris. Melnikov's pavilion announced to the West the startling modern accomplishments of the avant-garde in the U.S.S.R. The building's austere geometric planes and walls of glass were brought into dynamic tension through a dramatic outdoor stairway that sliced diagonally through the heart of the building. Despite the modernity of the forms, the structure was framed in wood, as were several of his early buildings. Melnikov was defining a new architecture while transforming the wooden structures of his own peasant origins.

After his success in Paris, Melnikov built a number of structures in the Moscow area, including an impressive series of six workers' clubs. Workers' clubs in the Soviet Union were intended to be new centers of community life, providing cultural and recreational activities for the workers. Melnikov designed each club with a unique landmark image, as most dramatically seen in his Rusakov Club in Moscow (1927-1929), an expressive wedge-shaped building. The functional considerations of acoustics and flexibility in the interior of this workers' club generated the building's powerful forms. The dynamism of this building and others by Melnikov was particularly captured in the contemporary photographs of Alexander Rodchenko.

Melnikov was not the typical Russian avant-garde architect; he was constructing many buildings, not just drawing them. Melnikov even built his own private house with studio in Moscow (1927-1929). This highly original design consists of two interlocking upright cylinders with numerous elongated hexagonal windows and a large front wall of glass. The house was built with traditional Russian materials (stuccoed brick for exterior walls and wood for floors) used structurally in inventive ways. Such buildings by Melnikov asserted a strong individualism in a country where Stalin was consolidating his growing powers into a dictatorship.

In comparison to the 1920s, Melnikov would build very little during the 1930s. He unsuccessfully entered architectural competitions with increasingly fantastic and theatrical designs, such as his grandiose projects for the Palace of Soviets (1931-1932) and the headquarters of the People's Commissariat of Heavy Industry (1934). The scale of these two unbuilt structures by Melnikov would have dwarfed Moscow's Kremlin in attempts to monumentally symbolize the triumphs of the Soviet Union.

In the 1920s, during the heyday of avant-garde architecture in the Soviet Union, the formalism of the Rationalists contrasted with the functional and structural preoccupations of the Constructivists. By the 1930s neither side of this Modernist debate was fully answering the Stalinist call for socialist realism in architecture. The avant-garde withered as Soviet architects turned upon each other in attempts to define what was wrong in contemporary architecture. Although the individualist Melnikov preferred to remain above the fray of factional divisions among Soviet architects, the categorization of Melnikov by some as a formalist most concerned with novel aesthetics would be his professional undoing. At the First All-Union Congress of Soviet Architects in 1937, Melnikov was strongly denounced, and his career as an active architect essentially came to an end.

Melnikov lived until 1974—painting, drawing, and writing in his unique Moscow house. He occasionally designed buildings that were never built, such as his 1962 Soviet Pavilion project proposed for the 1964 New York World's Fair. Finally, during the last decade of his life, Konstantin Melnikov began to receive growing attention for his earlier achievements from the Soviet and international scholarly communities.

Further Reading

An important monograph on Melnikov is S. Frederick Starr, *Melnikov: Solo Architect in a Mass Society* (1978). Starr interviewed Melnikov and had access to the family's archive of Melnikov's works. Concise discussions of Melnikov can be found in the following: William Craft Brumfield, *A History of Russian Architecture* (1993); Alexander Ryabushin and Nadia Smolina, *Landmarks of Soviet Architecture 1917-1991* (1992); Catherine Cooke and Justin Ageros, eds., *The Avant-Garde: Russian Architecture in the Twenties* (1991); Catherine Cooke, *Architectural Drawings of the Russian Avant-Garde* (1990); Selim O. Khan-Magomedov, *Pioneers of Soviet Architecture: The Search for New Solutions in the 1920s and 1930s* (1987); O.A. Shvidkovsky, ed., *Building in the USSR 1917-1932* (1971); and Anatole Kopp, *Town and Revolution: Soviet Architecture and City Planning 1917-1935* (1970). □

George Wallace Melville

The American naval officer and polar adventurer George Wallace Melville (1841-1912) is known for his Arctic explorations and his mechanical and engineering talents.

George Melville was born in New York City on Jan. 10, 1841. He graduated from the Brooklyn Collegiate and Polytechnic Institute and entered engineering work, but in 1861 he enlisted in the U.S. Navy and served throughout the Civil War. Remaining in the service after the war, Melville exhibited more than ordinary talent, devotion, and ambition. He volunteered in 1873 as chief engineer of the *Tigress* during its Arctic search for the missing *Polaris* and its crew.

In 1879 Melville was chief engineer aboard the *Jeannette,* commanded by Lt. George W. De Long, on its famous but disastrous polar voyage. Reaching the Arctic Ocean by way of Bering Strait, De Long attempted to make a deep penetration of the polar sea; instead his vessel was almost immediately enveloped by solid ice. The *Jeannette* drifted in its ice pack for two years and eventually was crushed and sank. The De Long party of 33 then attempted to reach land in Siberia, several hundred miles away, undergoing an incredibly arduous journey by sledge and boat. As they finally neared land, a storm separated the three boats, but Melville's boat and crew reached land safely. One crew per-

ished at sea, while De Long's crew landed but starved before they were located. Only the two men sent on to bring help to the others survived. When Melville learned of De Long's landing from these two men, the still feeble engineer led a desperate search for De Long. After several months Melville found the last campsite and the bodies of his former shipmates. His book, *In the Lena Delta* (1884), is a modest, straightforward account of this exploit.

In 1887 Melville became chief of the Bureau of Steam Engineering, where he participated in the construction of a new and modern navy. He supervised the machine design for 120 ships, introducing the triple screw, the watertube boiler, the vertical engine, and the repair ship. Two of the vessels whose machinery he designed, the *Columbia* and the *Minneapolis,* held the speed record for warships for almost a decade. He also instigated a general reform of the entire naval engineering department. Designated a rear admiral in 1899, Melville retired in that grade in 1903.

Among Melville's many honors was election in 1899 as president of the American Society of Mechanical Engineers. A large, balding, full-bearded man, he presented a gruff exterior that masked an indomitable and innovative spirit. He died in Philadelphia on March 17, 1912.

Further Reading

There are few secondary accounts of Melville's life. In addition to his own story of the De Long expedition see De Long's *The Voyage of the Jeannette,* edited by his wife, Emma De Long (2 vols., 1884). See also Jeannette Mirsky, *To the Arctic* (1934; rev. ed. 1948), a history of polar exploration. □

Herman Melville

American author Herman Melville (1819-1891) is best known for his novel *Moby-Dick*. His work was a response, though often in a negative or ambivalent way, to the romantic movement that dominated American literature in the mid-19th century.

Herman Melville's early autobiographical novels of adventure in the South Seas earned him a popularity that diminished as his writing turned to metaphysical themes and allegorical techniques, moving in directions that later generations would recognize as existentialism, Freudian psychologizing, and blackly comic satire. He had some success with his magazine sketches and short stories, but his poetry, a main concern during the latter part of his life, was ignored. Largely forgotten at the time of his death, he was rediscovered with the shift in taste that followed World War I. His reputation continues to grow, and *Moby-Dick* has become a world classic.

Melville was born in New York City on Aug. 1, 1819. His father, a merchant and importer, belonged to a well-connected Boston family; he died bankrupt in 1832, survived by his wife and eight children. Melville's mother was of New York Dutch ancestry. Melville's family background included Revolutionary War heroes, Dutch patricians, Calvinists, and upper-middle-class New Englanders, but his boyhood was spent in genteel poverty.

Melville's studies at the Albany Academy terminated with his father's death. Thereafter, he was largely self-educated and for a while something of a drifter (like Ishmael in *Moby-Dick,* who asserted that "a whale-ship was my Yale College and my Harvard"). He tried various occupations—bank clerk, clerk in the family business, country schoolmaster—and he studied surveying before becoming a sailor.

At 18 Melville made his first voyage as a crew member on a New York-Liverpool packet ship. At 22 he shipped on the whaler *Acushnet.* Returning four years later, he almost immediately began writing novels derived from his adventures. At this time Polynesia was a romantic and little-known region. Furthermore, maritime affairs were a matter of public interest. Also, there was a market for authentic personal narratives as opposed to fictional "romances."

Three Novels of the South Seas

Typee (1846) grew out of Melville's accidental sojourn with the presumably cannibalistic natives of the Marquesas Islands. It found a receptive audience and admitted Melville into the New York literary circles. A successful sequel, *Omoo* (1847), which paralleled Melville's experiences as a beachcomber in Tahiti, encouraged his belief that he could support himself through his writing. He married Elizabeth

Shaw, daughter of Lemuel Shaw, chief justice of Massachusetts and a family friend, in 1847.

Melville's final novel of the South Seas, *Mardi* (1849), marks a transition. It begins realistically aboard a whaler but ends in the realm of fantasy, rhapsody, and allegory. Critics have found in it reflections of his courtship and marriage and of his first reading of Shakespeare, Montaigne, Rabelais, Sir Thomas Browne, and other authors of "old books."

Melville's novels of the South Seas progress from realism toward romance, from simplicity toward complexity, and from relatively modest ambitions toward serious pretensions. *Typee* follows the outline of actual events closely. In July 1842, with a shipmate, Toby Greene, Melville had deserted the *Acushnet* in the Marquesas Islands. They planned to seek refuge among the hospitable natives of the Happar Valley but by mistake entered the Valley of the Typees, who were reputed to be cannibals. Here they lived almost idyllically. Melville, however, had injured his leg, and the Typees permitted Greene to leave to obtain medical assistance. Alone, Melville became bored by his vegetative existence and grew increasingly fearful that the friendly Typees might be cannibals after all. Greene did not return, but an Australian whaling bark effected Melville's rescue.

The narrative of *Typee* is straightforward, though Melville capitalizes on suspenseful elements in the experience. A careful observer and colorful reporter, he fleshed out his account (or jogged his memory) by using other works in the field, and he introduced some fictional material. There are elements of satire and social criticism in *Typee,* as well as symbolism and a preliminary grappling with philosophical questions that would become primary in his later writings. In addition to being an exotic travel yarn about a tropical Eden, *Typee* can be read as a study in false appearances and misguided quests.

Omoo, which takes its name from the Marquesan word for vagabond, is a loose, episodic description of Melville's wanderings in Tahiti and further experiences aboard whalers. It is in a lighthearted vein, though it hits hard at missionary despoilers of the Pacific paradise and other civilizing forces that Melville saw as superficial, exploitative, and destructive. Starting where *Typee* leaves off, it repeats the pattern of dissatisfaction on shipboard, of a desertion that represents a symbolic attempt to escape civilization, of picaresque adventures, and of rejection of Rousseauistic primitivism suggested by shipping on yet another whaler.

At this point *Mardi,* the transitional novel in the South Seas trilogy, begins. The established progression of disaffection on shipboard, desertion with a congenial companion, and adventure on the high seas recurs. But this time the realistic narrative, which is implicitly a quest, shifts overtly to an extravagant search for an elusive, symbolic maiden on allegorical islands beyond the horizon of Polynesia.

The maiden is never found, though she is pursued with a monomaniacal, self-destructive relentlessness. Sandwiched into this account are undigested philosophical speculations, dreamy poetizing, and keen satiric thrusts aimed at such topical targets as slavery, the revolutions of 1848, and popular theological and scientific theories. Melville, whose veracity was doubted in his realistic narratives, was deliberately, almost defiantly, writing fiction, embarking on adventures of the mind that were the counterparts of his actual exploits. The book did not succeed, and Melville returned to less farfetched subject matter in *Redburn* (1849) and *White-Jacket* (1850), which had modest financial rewards.

Other Early Works

Melville disparaged *Redburn* as a "little nursery tale." Its source was his Liverpool voyage in 1839. It is an initiation story—the tale of a green youth of genteel pretensions transformed by raw experience into a competent sailor and a self-reliant man with a sense of his own (and mankind's) limitations. *Redburn* has a social dimension: the descriptions of the hideous poverty of Liverpool slums and the crowded conditions of emigrants in steerage that led to epidemics.

Melville regarded *White-Jacket,* subtitled *The World in a Man-of-War,* more highly. The fictional frigate *Neversink,* naval slang for any hypothetical ship, is a microcosm of Melville's native land in particular and the world in general. He methodically described the naval hierarchy from commodore and captain down to the lowest sailor, emphasizing the irony of an authoritarian system as an instrument of American democracy.

The narrative line follows Melville's own homeward-bound cruise on the frigate *United States* in 1843-1844, but he included events not recorded in the log of this ship. For example, the narrator is issued a white duck jacket unlike the uniform jackets of the other sailors. He is pleased to be distinguished from the rest of the crew until he discovers that such distinction has severe drawbacks. He tries to divest himself of the jacket, but succeeds only when he falls into the sea and has to cut his way out of it to keep from drowning.

White-Jacket is a reform novel, advocating the abolition of flogging in the U.S. Navy and other measures to improve the lot of American seamen. Although it is more simply constructed, is generally optimistic in tone, and contains a considerable amount of direct narrative, description, and reform polemics, it foreshadows Melville's complex masterpiece, *Moby-Dick* (1851), which it immediately precedes.

Moby-Dick

In 1851 Melville wrote that he was well along with "a strange sort of book" on whaling, adding "I mean to give the truth of the thing. . . ." The narrator of *Moby-Dick,* Ishmael, is another drifter. Ishmael ships on the *Pequod,* commanded by the demon-ridden Captain Ahab, whose overweening purpose is to capture the albino whale Moby-Dick, which had severed his leg. Ahab bends his polyglot crew to this purpose. Ishmael is caught up in "fiery pursuit," until, through his fraternal relationship with a Polynesian harpooner, he achieves a balanced view. He alone escapes when Moby-Dick attacks and destroys the *Pequod.*

The book's rich texture lends itself to various interpretations. It can be read superficially as a melodramatic adventure or for the precise descriptions of the technology of whaling and the natural history of whales interspersed in the narrative. Yet virtually every detail of the book—plot line, accounts of the capture of whales and the processing of blubber, seamen's legends and lore, natural history, characterization, and descriptions of nautical gear—is a vehicle for a deliberately inconclusive, many-sided debate on the nature of the human condition.

One of Melville's favorite devices is to argue a point effectively in one chapter, undercut it with an equally effective and opposite argument in the next, then to present other arguments at various points between. A related technique is his use of traditional systems for ordering knowledge—ostensibly to clarify, present information, or advance an argument—but actually as a means of demonstrating the limitations of the system and, by extension, the impossibility of mere earthly beings coming up with categorical answers to any question whatsoever. Ishmael's ability to exist within this limitation makes possible his salvation. Ahab's inability to do so destroys him.

The writings that follow *Moby-Dick* are rich in nautical themes and allusions and also contain autobiographical matter, but Melville moved on to other forms and settings. In *Pierre* (1852) the American countryside and the American city are placed in opposition. Pierre, scion of rural gentry, is an idealistic young man whose efforts to apply Christian solutions to the problems of an imperfect world result in death and disaster. In this dark, uneven book, the subtle examination of ethical questions and deep probing into the human psyche are compelling.

Moby-Dick was not popular, though Melville had the satisfaction of knowing that it was understood and appreciated by a few discerning readers. *Pierre* did not yield even this satisfaction. So once more Melville made a special effort to recoup. He turned to the magazines, producing tales, sketches, and short novels, many of great distinction.

Magazine Writings

The best of the magazine writing includes *Israel Potter* (1855), which first appeared serially in *Putnam's Magazine,* and *The Piazza Tales* (1856). *Israel Potter* is the story of a young New Englander who fought at the Battle of Bunker Hill, served under John Paul Jones, was a courier for Benjamin Franklin in Europe, and then, as a result of a series of mishaps, lived in exile in the London slums until he could make his way home 50 years later. Melville's source, he wrote, was "Israel Potter's autobiographical story," published in a crude pamphlet. Melville made it into a book of modest dimensions compared with *Moby-Dick* or *Pierre,* and it records human hardihood in the face of high risks and wearing, undramatic misfortunes.

The Piazza Tales is introduced by an essay, "The Piazza," which delicately examines the view from the piazza of Melville's Pittsfield, Mass., farmhouse, his home from 1850 to 1863. The vista across a valley and beyond to the Berkshire Mountains is enchanting, but its charm fades upon close scrutiny. The narrator admits the need to dispel illusion but makes an exception of a lonely country girl who needs illusion in order to survive.

Two other tales, "Benito Cereno" and "The Encantadas," are also concerned with appearances and realities. "Benito Cereno," the undisguised retelling of autobiography, is a Gothic suspense story. A cargo of slaves seizes a Spanish ship and forces the captain to serve them in their attempt to return to Africa. The obvious distress of the ship attracts the attention of an American vessel whose commander tries to help, to discover the real nature of the situation, and to seek out and then draw back from the underlying complexities of the events that unfold around him.

"The Encantadas" is a series of sketches about the Galapagos, or "Enchanted," Islands—barren, volcanic inversions of the paradisiacal isles described in *Typee* and *Omoo*. They, too, are under a spell that clouds their true nature. A third notable story is "Bartleby," an existentialist parable about a lawyer's scribe who "prefers not to" act in a world where even worthy action seems fruitless and pointless and where suffering in ignorance is the common bond of humanity.

The Confidence-Man

The grimly comic underside of Melville dominates *The Confidence-Man* (1857), the last work of prose he published in his lifetime. Set on a riverboat going down the Mississippi on April Fool's Day, it consists of a series of encounters between confidence men (or perhaps a single confidence man in various disguises) and their marks. The encounters are almost ritualistic variations on a theme. The Christian watchwords of faith, hope, and charity become part of the spiel of the con men, who victimize fools, rogues, and virtuous weaklings alike.

The Confidence-Man draws heavily on American "types" and is packed with topical allusions that are now often obscure. Its ambience is the expansive, optimistic, materialistic America of the 1850s, to which Melville voiced corrosive dissent. An early, successful essay in black comedy, it was a commercial failure.

Last Years

At this point Melville withdrew from the literary marketplace. With half of his life still before him, he chose to write for his own satisfaction and that of the few kindred spirits. He had published 10 books in 11 years and additional uncollected tales and reviews, including an important review of *Mosses from an Old Manse* by his friend Nathaniel Hawthorne (1846), and he had strained himself physically and emotionally. In 1856, fearing a serious breakdown, his family arranged for him to tour Europe and the Holy Land.

Melville's pilgrimage to sacred places did little to settle the religious questions that continued to rack him, but he was exhilarated by the symmetry of Greek architecture and sculpture and by the paintings he saw in Italy and England. He returned renewed in spirit, though his financial affairs were not in good order. Efforts to improve this situation by obtaining a government position came to nothing.

Meanwhile, for two seasons Melville lectured on his travels and art theories, and with more success, on his

adventures among the South Sea islands. He also began writing the verse that was his literary focus for the next 30 years. Attempts to publish his poetry failed until, "in an impulse imparted by the fall of Richmond," he wrote *Battle-Pieces* (1866), a verse cycle that depicts many aspects and both sides of the Civil War, beginning with a prologue on the hanging of John Brown and concluding with an essay that pleads for magnanimity and patience. It was not well received.

That same year Melville was appointed an inspector in the New York Customhouse. Thereafter he lived quietly, absorbed in the routine of his employment, poetry, and family life. *Clarel* (1876), a long narrative poem, is about a group of pilgrims visiting shrines and historical sites in the Holy Land. In general, Melville was more at peace with himself, though he suffered personal tragedies in the suicide of his 18-year-old son and the premature death of his other son. Legacies eased his living situation; he could afford to buy books and prints and to publish his poetry privately.

Melville retired from the customhouse in 1885. Sometime in 1888 he began work on *Billy Budd,* a short novel about an innocent sailor who is sacrificed for the sake of maintaining order and efficiency aboard his warship. Like most of his writing, it raises more questions than it settles, but it ends on a note of relaxation if not serenity. Melville marked the manuscript "End of Book April 19th 1891," an indication that the story was nearing completion but still unfinished. Yet Melville never felt that any of his work was truly finished. He had written in *Moby-Dick:* "God keep me from ever completing anything. This whole book is but a draught—nay, but a draught of a draught."

Melville died in New York City on Sept. 28, 1891. The manuscript of *Billy Budd* was not published until 1924.

Further Reading

Melville's fiction is available in numerous editions. He has attracted so much critical attention, it is almost impossible to describe all of the available writings about him. Moreover, his works lend themselves to the application of analytic systems that have appeared since his death; thus there are provocative interpretations deriving from later psychological, historical, and sociological theories.

Stanley T. Williams surveys Melville scholarship with balance and concision in *Eight American Authors,* edited by Floyd Stovall (1956; rev. 1972). Annual surveys began with the publication of *American Literary Scholarship* (1965) for 1963, issued each year thereafter under the auspices of the Modern Language Association.

A most useful biography is Leon Howard, *Herman Melville: A Biography* (1951). Jay Leyda, *The Melville Log: A Documentary Life of Herman Melville* (2 vols., 1951; repr. with additional material, 1969), provides the raw material arranged in chronological order and constitutes a biographical record. Newton Arvin, *Herman Melville* (1950), has critical and psychological insights. Charles Roberts Anderson, *Melville and the South Seas* (1939), first established the facts behind Melville's early fiction and is still basic.

A pioneer monograph that remains important is Howard Vincent, *The Trying-out of Moby-Dick* (1949). Important commentaries include William Ellery Sedgwick, *Herman Melville: The Tragedy of Mind* (1944); Ronald Mason, *The Spirit above the Dust* (1951); Merlin Bowen, *The Long Encounter: Self and*

Experience in the Writings of Herman Melville (1960); and Warner Berthoff, *The Example of Melville* (1962). F. O. Matthiessen, *American Renaissance: Art and Expression in the Age of Emerson and Whitman* (1941), is a matchless examination of the cultural milieu, with four chapters on Melville's art and thought. □

Hans Memling

Hans Memling (ca. 1440-1494), a German-born painter active in Flanders, was one of the most graceful, charming, and technically brilliant of the early Netherlandish masters.

Hans Memling was born in Seligenstadt, a hamlet near Frankfurt. His early training probably took place in Cologne, though by 1465 "Jan van Memmelynghe" was recorded as a citizen of Bruges in the Lowlands. It is conjectured that, previous to entering the painters' guild at Bruges, Memling spent time as an apprentice in the workshop of Rogier van der Weyden in Brussels. The evidence for this association, however, is far from conclusive and does not prove a master-pupil relationship. Nothing further is known concerning the artist's early professional training.

From the first Memling displayed the highest standards of technical proficiency and pictorial sophistication in his work. The full corpus of his paintings, in fact, represents a single standard of perfection in which one can discover little stylistic change or development. His earliest known painting, for example, the *Chatsworth Triptych,* commissioned by the English lord Sir John Donne of Kidwelly in 1468, displays a surprising maturity of style. Blending a figure style derived from Rogier van der Weyden with compositional motifs and other details from Jan van Eyck, Memling created the prototype of the rational and balanced design upon which he so often relied throughout his long and active career.

Memling's search for rational order and compositional equilibrium, however, often obscures his truly progressive outlook and the many innovations found in his work. In such early paintings as the *Scenes of the Passion* he combined a bold, panoramic vista with unprecedented narrative detail. In his most famous work, the *Shrine of St. Ursula,* he further developed this closely observed anecdotal genre.

The *Triptych of the Mystic Marriage of St. Catherine* (1479) represents Memling's highest achievement as a painter. In this work he skillfully combined compositional stability with great pictorial variety. Sparkling colors and luminous surfaces interact with solid, plastic forms and broad spatial recessions to create one of the great masterpieces of 15th-century Netherlandish painting.

As a portraitist, Memling further revealed his originality. The *Diptych of Martin van Nieuwenhove* contains a unique elaboration of the interior setting, and the famous portrait *Man with a Medal* is the first northern figure posed entirely against a landscape background.

When he died, Memling was one of the hundred wealthiest citizens of Bruges. He was also, in the words of a contemporary, "the most accomplished and excellent painter of the whole Christian world."

Further Reading

The major books on Memling are in German. Short accounts of his life and work are in two works in English: Erwin Panofsky, *Early Netherlandish Painting: Its Origins and Character* (2 vols., 1953), and Margaret Dickens Whinney, *Early Flemish Painting* (1968). A brief monograph on Memling is Maur Guillaume-Linephty, *The Shrine of St. Ursula* (1939). □

Christopher Gustavus Memminger

Christopher Gustavus Memminger (1803-1888), American politician, was a South Carolina legislator and secretary of the Treasury in the Confederate government.

Christopher G. Memminger was born in Würtemberg, Germany, on Jan. 9, 1803. After the death of his father, Memminger and his mother emigrated to Charleston, S.C. When his mother died, he was taken into the home of Thomas Bennett, later governor of the state. After graduating from South Carolina College in 1819, Memminger studied law and then established a successful practice in Charleston.

Memminger wrote a satirical pamphlet attacking the leaders of the nullification movement (to nullify recent Federal tariff acts) of the 1830s. He became a member of South Carolina's House of Representatives in 1836 and, as chairman of the finance committee, began a lengthy struggle to reform state finances and the practices of the banking community. His advocacy of such reforms earned him a reputation as a sound adviser in matters of public finance.

In 1855 Memminger became Charleston's commissioner of schools (a position he held for more than 30 years) and began efforts to create a city public school system. He also served on the board of South Carolina College for 32 years.

Although fully convinced of the righteousness of slavery and apprehensive of the designs of antislavery propagandists, Memminger generally acted with the conservative Democrats of South Carolina. By December 1859, however, he had taken the position that, by seceding by itself from the Union, South Carolina could "break things up" and "drag" others with it. Memminger was an active member of the state secession convention and a delegate to the Southern convention at Montgomery, Ala. He served as chairman of the committee that drafted the provisional constitution of the Confederate States.

Confederate president Jefferson Davis named Memminger secretary of the Treasury in 1861, not so much in recognition of his reputed financial abilities as to give his state a Cabinet position. Although hesitant to employ financial means against currency inflation, Memminger was forced to issue great quantities of treasury notes. Throughout the war he promoted the sale of Confederate bonds in vain, and his attempts at direct taxation, "produce loans," and other funding schemes were mismanaged by the Confederate Congress. Rapid depreciation of the currency was inevitable, and when Confederate credit collapsed completely, Memminger was generally held responsible.

Public clamor forced Memminger to resign in June 1864, and he retired to Flat Rock, N.C. In 1867 he resumed his law practice in Charleston. His chief public service in the postwar years was on behalf of public schools for both races in Charleston. He died in Charleston on March 7, 1888.

Further Reading

Henry D. Capers, *The Life and Times of C. G. Memminger* (1893), contains excellent quotations from many useful documents. □

Menander

Menander (342-291 B.C.) was an Athenian comic playwright. He was the acknowledged master of the so-called **New Comedy in Greece. Famed for his realistic portrayal of situations and characters, he greatly influenced later comic dramatists.**

New Comedy was the term for the comedy of manners popular in Greece after 320 B.C., in strong contrast to the Old Comedy, whose most famous practitioner was the Athenian Aristophanes (ca. 450-385 B.C.). Whereas the Old Comedy was characterized by broad burlesque, fantasy, coarseness, and biting political and social satire and the Middle Comedy (ca. 400-320 B.C.) by stock "characters" like the courtesan, the parasite, and the braggart soldier, the New Comedy portrayed ordinary people and their private domestic problems. The absurdity and fantasy of the Old and Middle Comedy were abandoned in favor of realistic situations and characters who speak and act as they would in real life. The chorus virtually disappears except as an interlude between the acts.

As with most of the figures of antiquity, there are few facts on the life and career of Menander. He was born in Athens in 342 B.C.; his father, Diopeithes, was a man of wealth and distinction; his mother was Hegistrate. According to ancient sources, he was a boyhood friend of the philosopher Epicurus and a pupil of Theophrastus, Aristotle's successor as the head of the Peripatetic school. He is said to have been the nephew of the comic playwright Alexis, who instructed him in the art of writing comedies.

Menander was said to have been exceptionally handsome, as surviving portraits attest. He was elegant in manner and in dress, easy-tempered, and a lover of luxury and comfort. Tradition relates that he refused an invitation from Ptolemy I of Egypt, an admirer of his work, to visit there because this would disturb his ease. From his association with Athens's oligarchic governor, Demetrius of Phalerum, it is surmised that Menander was antidemocratic in politics, although in his surviving works there is scarcely a mention of political matters. Intellectually, Menander was very much a man of his times, and the influence of Theophrastus's *Characters* and the teachings of Epicurus and other philosophers is evident in the manner and outlook of his plays. According to the ancient account, Menander died in 291 B.C., drowning in the harbor of Piraeus.

His Plays

Menander's writing career spanned the 30 years from his first play, *Orge* (*Anger*), in 321, to his death. He wrote perhaps as many as 108 comedies, but the fact that he was awarded first prize in the competitions only eight times indicates that his popularity during his lifetime did not equal his later fame. Of his output only one play, the *Dyskolos* (*The Bad-tempered Man*), which won the prize in 316, survives in its entirety; large portions of several other plays exist. Numerous smaller fragments and titles to over 90 plays also survive.

Until the end of the 19th century Menander was known only through short quotations from his plays, many of which had survived as maxims collected in anthologies. Among them were "Whom the gods love die young" and "Bad associates spoil a good character." The only other source was Latin adaptations of his plays by the Roman dramatists Plautus and Terence. Since 1900, however, a number of substantial fragments have been recovered from papyri preserved in the dry sands of Egypt, and new discoveries are still being made.

In 1958 the *Dyskolos* was published from a papyrus manuscript. This play plus large portions of *Epitrepontes* (*Arbitrants*), *Perikeiromene* (*The Girl Who Had Her Hair Cut Off*), *Samia* (*The Girl from Samos*), and *Sikyonios* (*The Man from Sicyon*) and other fragments represent less than 10 percent of the works of Menander but give us a good idea of his style.

The plots of Menander's plays are extremely complicated, usually revolving around the obstacles which prevent a pair of young lovers from achieving happiness. The plays open on a problem which becomes increasingly more involved until, finally, all the difficulties are removed, the lovers are united, and the other characters have achieved their goals. Much of Menander's fame rested on his ability in plot construction, and his variations on the love theme are almost infinite.

One typical problem involves the foundling child who is reared as a slave or courtesan and thus is prevented from honorable marriage. Ultimately, however, the slave girl turns out to be the daughter of a rich man, and so, not only are the lovers able to marry, but also the fathers are pleased by the prosperous match.

The *Dyskolos*

The *Dyskolos* was produced in 316, when Menander was 25 years old. Sostratos, a rich young Athenian, has fallen in love with Myrrhine, the daughter of Knemon, a mean-tempered old farmer (the *dyskolos*). Because of Knemon's surly nature, his wife has left him and lives with her son by a previous marriage, Gorgias.

Sostratos's slave, Pyrrhias, is sent to ask Knemon about his daughter and is attacked by the old misanthrope. Gorgias learns of Sostratos's interest in his sister and concludes that the rich young man has dishonorable intentions. Sostratos assures him that he wants to marry Myrrhine. After a series of comic episodes, which include Knemon's fall into a well from which he is rescued by Gorgias and Sostratos, the old man "retires" and relinquishes his farm to Gorgias, who gives his consent for Sostratos to marry Myrrhine; then Callipides, Sostratos's father, impressed by the poor but honest and ambitious Gorgias, gives him his daughter to marry.

Style and Influence

The attitude of the ancients toward Menander is summed up in the famous remark of Aristophanes of Byzantium, the Alexandrian critic: "O Menander and life, which of you has imitated the other?" Modern critics are less unanimous in their praise of Menander. Some find his plots contrived, his characters mere types without depth, and his dialogue dull and insipid. An impartial assessment must consider the times in which Menander lived. His New Comedy is concerned with a small world of ordinary people and daily problems. The political climate of an Athens dominated by Macedonia precluded topical political satire. The vibrant democracy which nurtured the wit of Aristophanes had ended, and men turned inward, concentrating their creative energies on the problems of personal relationships and moral concerns.

Menander reflects this world in his quiet moralizing, gentle skepticism, and keen scrutiny of the human situation, not entirely unmixed with social criticism. In Menander's plays, goodness always conquers, and often even the villains have redeeming human qualities. Menander's speech is clear and simple; he employed the ordinary Attic dialect of his own time; his chief meter was the iambic trimeter.

Further Reading

The Dyskolos of Menander, edited by E. W. Handley (1965), is a text with an introduction and commentary. A text of the other fragments, with an English translation, is *Menander: The Principal Fragments,* translated by Francis G. Allinson for the Loeb Classical Library (1921; rev. ed., 1951). An excellent translation of the *Dyskolos* and other fragments is *The Characters by Theophrastus; Plays and Fragments by Menander,* translated by Philip Vellacott (1957). Accounts of Menander's life and works, including background material for Old, Middle, and New Comedy, are Gilbert Norwood, *Greek Comedy* (1931); Gilbert Murray, *Aristophanes: A Study* (1933); and T. B. L. Webster, *Studies in Later Greek Comedy* (1953; 2d ed., 1970). A more technical discussion of Menander's works is T. B. L. Webster, *Studies in Menander* (1950; 2d ed. 1960). □

Rigoberta Menchú

Rigoberta Menchú (born 1959) was a Guatemalan human rights activist who won the Nobel Peace Prize in 1992. Despite her youth she became an eloquent spokesperson for the rights of the indigenous peoples of the entire Western Hemisphere.

Rigoberta Menchú was born on January 9, 1959, in Chimel, a village in the Quiché province in the northwest highlands of Guatemala. Her mother, whose surname was Tum, was a midwife and traditional healer, and her father, Vicente, was a day laborer, catechist, and community leader. Both her parents belonged to one of the many indigenous groups of Guatemala, the Quiché Maya, and spoke little Spanish. Young Menchú herself spoke only Quiché (one of over twenty different languages spoken in her country) until she was 19.

Her difficult childhood is an example of how hundreds of thousands of Indian children grow up in Guatemala. Every year she followed her parents to the southern coastal plantations, *fincas*, where they spent months picking cotton and coffee. During the rest of the year the family, back in the highlands, collected wicker in the mountains and grew maize, beans, and potatoes to supplement their diet. Menchú started working when she was only eight; two of her brothers died on the plantations, one was poisoned by insecticides and the other—only two years old—from mal-

nutrition. At age 13 she had her first prolonged direct experience with people of Spanish culture (and with discrimination), when she worked as a maid for a wealthy family in Guatemala City. Soon thereafter, her father was imprisoned for his efforts to save land from seizure by large landowners.

Social and Political Unrest

Menchú's political awakening was shaped by Guatemala's turbulent history. After a coup d'état backed by the United States Central Intelligence Agency toppled a left-wing president in 1954, a series of military governments ruled the country with an iron hand. A guerrilla movement that began in 1962 triggered a violent government response directed not only at the guerrillas, but also at their supporters, real and alleged, often located in the countryside. Political violence was renewed in the 1970s, when government repression was applied in such an indiscriminate fashion that U.S. President Jimmy Carter, after repeated warnings against human rights violations, suspended economic aid in 1977. Guatemala's Indians, composing 60 percent of the population, suffered the indignities of forced relocation and military service. In this environment of political turmoil, indigenous vindication movements were considered by the government to be part of a communist conspiracy.

An Activist is Born

Menchú became politically active, inspired by her family's involvement and by her religious beliefs. Like many others in Central America, she was influenced by Liberation Theology, a movement that believes that the Bible should be read through the eyes of the poor and that Jesus Christ had a special message of liberation for poor people. In an interview she described how peasants "felt everything the Bible said was coming to pass, with Christ crucified, Christ attacked with stones, Christ dragged along the ground. One felt the pain of that Christ, and identified with it."

Another important influence was her father, Vicente, who was active in the Peasant Unity Committee, a group that fought for peasant land rights. She joined the committee in 1979, and was asked to organize the country's 22 Indian groups, each with its own culture and language, against exploitation. A few months later her 16-year-old brother, Petrocinio, was tortured and then killed by the army. The following year she lost her father in an event that received widespread coverage in the international press. Vicente Menchú, along with other representatives of indigenous groups, occupied the Spanish embassy in Guatemala City to press their demands. The army attacked the embassy and burned it, killing 39 people, including Menchú's father, who burned to death.

International Campaign Begins in Exile

The next year her mother was kidnapped, tortured, and killed by the army, and two of her sisters joined the guerrillas. Life in Guatemala was too dangerous for her, and Menchú fled to Mexico in 1981. In exile, she began an international crusade to explain the plight of the Guatemalan Indians, and joined the United Nations Working Group on Indigenous Populations.

In 1983, during a trip to Paris to promote her cause, she dictated her autobiography to a Venezuelan anthropologist, Elizabeth Burgos. The result of their collaboration was the widely read book, *I, Rigoberta Menchú: An Indian Woman in Guatemala,* which was translated into more than a dozen languages. It brought her to the attention of the rest of the world and helped her to become the foremost spokesperson for indigenous peoples.

Efforts Bring Acclaim

Although her first attempt to return to Guatemala in 1988 ended badly (she was threatened and put in jail), she later visited her country for short periods of time. It was during one such visit in October of 1992 that she learned the Nobel Peace Prize would be given to her "in recognition of her work for social justice and ethno-cultural reconciliation based on respect for the rights of indigenous peoples." She was only 33.

With the $1.2 million from the prize she set up a foundation named after her father. She was active in the continent's Five Hundred Years of Resistance Campaign and in the United Nations International Indian Treaty Council. In June of 1993, during a political crisis in Guatemala, Menchú played an instrumental role in the events that brought to power a new president, Ramiro de León Carpio, a human rights advocate. Growing international pressure also helped force the government to ease up on military repression, and in 1995 many refugees who fled to Mexico to escape torture began to return.

Menchú remained an advocate for indigenous peoples, and in June, 1996 was named a UNESCO Goodwill Ambassador for a Culture of Peace by the Director-General of UNESCO. Later the same year she went to Norway to watch Guatemalan government and rebel leaders sign a cease-fire agreement for the 42-year conflict—Latin America's longest civil war—that she and her family fought so hard to end.

Her activism was controversial. Conservative commentators accused her of being associated with communist guerrillas, but she defended herself by saying that if she were a revolutionary she would be fighting in the mountains. She summarized her views in an interview published in 1993: "I believe that in Guatemala the solution is not confrontation between indigenous people and latinos [people of Spanish culture]. Rather, we need a country where we can live together with mutual respect."

Further Reading

Rigoberta Menchú's autobiography, written in collaboration with Elizabeth Burgos, was translated into English with the title *I Rigoberta Menchú* (1984). More information appears in interviews published in *World Press Review* (December 1992), in the *Progressive* (January 1993 and December 1995), various issues of the UNESCO *Courier* (1996). and articles in the *Los Angeles Times* (October 17, 1992; May 7, 1993), the *New York Times* (October 17, 1992; October 19, 1992; December 11, 1992; June 10, 1993; September 15, 1993; May 8, 1994; November 17, 1995), and in *Time* (October 26, 1992). □

Mencius

Mencius (ca. 371-ca. 289 B.C.) was a Chinese philosopher and one of the most important early Confucian thinkers. His philosophy is characterized by its idealism and the assertion that man's nature is basically good.

Confucius, the great Chinese teacher and thinker, died in 479 B.C., and on the eastern seaboard of China his disciples established schools which carried on the teachings of the master. By the end of the 4th century a number of important Confucian philosophers emerged, and the most brilliant of these philosophers was Mencius. Mencius elaborated on and refined many of the ideas of Confucius, and his interpretations became as influential in the Chinese tradition as the ideas of the master himself.

Mencius, which is the Latinized form of Meng-tzu (Master Meng), was born in Tsou, a small state south of Lu, the home state of Confucius. Lu lay in what is now the southern part of Shantung Province and had been an important political and cultural center for much of the Chou dynasty (1122-256 B.C.). Mencius's full name was Meng K'o, and he was the descendant of the Meng, or Meng-sun, clan, one of the three ruling families in Lu.

Almost nothing is known about his early life. Like Confucius, Mencius apparently lost his father at an early age, and he was raised by his mother, who did not remarry. There are several amusing but apocryphal stories about his mother and Mencius's childhood, and these are the only pieces of information about his early life.

Mencius may have studied in one of the Confucian schools established in the Lu area, perhaps the school created by Confucius's grandson Tzu-ssu. Mencius was trained as a scholar and teacher and received instruction in the standard Confucian texts such as the *Book of Odes* (*Shih ching*) and the *Book of Documents* (*Shu ching*).

Political Career

Mencius seems to have established a reputation in Tsou as a teacher, but nothing is recorded of his activities until his arrival in Ch'i, north of Lu, and one of the most powerful states of that period. Mencius must have arrived in Ch'i during the reign of King Wei (357-320 B.C.), perhaps as early as 335. We do not know if Mencius held any position in the Ch'i government at this time or even how long he remained in Ch'i.

Mencius left Ch'i about 324 and traveled south through the states of Sung and Hsüeh, where he received travel funds from the rulers of these states, finally arriving in his home state of Tsou. At once he was invited to serve as an adviser at the court of Duke Wen of T'eng, a small state south of Tsou. Mencius went to T'eng, where he advised the duke on mourning ritual for his recently deceased father. He also held several long discussions on statecraft with Duke Wen, who was greatly impressed by Mencius's learning.

Mencius did not remain long in T'eng and most likely was forced to leave because he had incurred the animosity of some of the duke's advisers, who resented the stranger's influence. Mencius then went to Liang, the capital of Wei, a state to the west of Ch'i and Sung. He was well received by the aged King Hui, with whom he had several satisfying interviews. Mencius had a less amiable relationship with Hui's successor, Hsiang, who became king in 319, and Mencius decided to return to Ch'i.

The previous year King Wei of Ch'i had died and was succeeded by his son, King Hsüan (reigned 319-310 B.C.). King Hsüan was an extremely ambitious and energetic ruler who hoped to make Ch'i the leader of the entire Chinese state system. In order to enhance Ch'i's prestige the Ch'i rulers had built in the Ch'i capital an academy called Chi-hsia, where scholars from all parts of China were invited to study and exchange ideas. Members of the academy included some of the most important thinkers of the time. It is not certain whether Mencius was an actual participant at the Chi-hsia discussions, although he certainly must have been acquainted with many of the scholars who were there. Mencius was given an honorary position in the Ch'i government but does not seem to have held a policy-making post.

Mencius was rather stuffy, terribly serious, and somewhat of a prude. To him principle was of paramount importance. Unlike King Hsüan, who was primarily interested in practical matters of government, Mencius was willing to discuss only theoretical matters. On one occasion King Hsüan asked Mencius about early Chinese rulers who had established hegemony over other Chinese states, expressing

a wish to emulate them. Mencius arrogantly answered that the Confucian school had never professed interest in the hegemons, and thus he had nothing to say on the matter. He then proceeded to give a long, abstract discourse on what he termed true kingship, citing examples from remote antiquity to illustrate his argument.

Mencius's career in Ch'i was temporarily interrupted by the death of his mother. He returned to Lu, where he conducted an elaborate funeral for her and observed mourning for the prescribed period of 3 years.

In 315 Ch'i attacked the state of Yen in the northeast. Before sending out his expedition King Hsüan asked Mencius for advice. Mencius, not wishing to commit himself, gave an evasive answer which the King construed as approval. Actually, Mencius had reservations about this course of action and was disturbed that the King failed to understand his advice. In 312 Yen expelled the Ch'i army. Out of disgust with Ch'i's policies and irritated that King Hsüan so seldom consulted him, Mencius resolved to leave for his home.

Mencius remained in Tsou for the rest of his life. He was joined by a few loyal disciples, and they continued their study of the Confucian texts. The date of his death is uncertain, but it is traditionally given as 289 B.C. Some scholars think that he died as early as 305.

Mencius's Teachings

Mencius's teachings have been preserved in a book titled *Meng-tzu*, a seven-chapter work of anecdotes most likely collected by his disciples. Most of the anecdotes consist of conversations between Mencius and his disciples or, occasionally, a ruler. His basic philosophy, if it can be called that, is an extreme idealism which views human nature as basically good and evil as only an obfuscation of one's innate goodness. He placed great emphasis on the necessity for one to try to recover his original goodness and, through learning, to seek what he called the "lost mind" of benevolence. Mencius also believed that if the government fails to maintain benevolent rule and abuses the people, they have a right to revolt.

Further Reading

There are two acceptable English translations of the *Meng-tzu*: one by James Legge in his *The Chinese Classics* (5 vols. in 8, 1861-1872; 2d ed. rev. 1865-1895) and the other by W. A. Dobson in *Mencius* (1963). Both of these works contain valuable biographical information on Mencius. Also worth reading is I. A. Richards, *Mencius on the Mind* (1932). □

Henry Louis Mencken

Henry Louis Mencken (1880-1956) was an American journalist, editor, critic, and philologist. Though he was not a distinguished stylist, the extraordinary vigor of his expression was memorable.

The first American to be widely read as a critic was H. L. Mencken. Though, earlier, James Russell Lowell and Edgar Allan Poe had been better endowed than Mencken with critical intelligence, their proficiency in other literary forms had obscured to some degree their skills as critics.

Mencken was born in Baltimore, Md., on Sept. 12, 1880, and privately educated there. After graduating from Baltimore Polytechnic Institute at the age of 16, he became a reporter on the *Baltimore Herald*. He rose rapidly; soon he was the *Herald*'s city editor and then editor.

In 1906 Mencken joined the organization known as the Sunpapers, which he served in a variety of ways until his retirement. His outstanding piece of journalism, widely syndicated, concerned the Scopes trial of 1925 in Tennessee, in which a high school science instructor was prosecuted for teaching evolution, contrary to a state law. The *Smart Set* and the *American Mercury,* both of which Mencken shared in editing (1908-1923; 1924-1933) with George Jean Nathan, were additional vehicles for his opinions.

Mencken's journalistic skills became his chief handicap as a critic, for he sacrificed discrimination for immediate attention, esthetic and philosophical distinctions for the reductions of easy reading, and subtleties of statement for buffoonery and bombast. Yet, though one may deplore his methods, they gained a wide audience and opened the way for the development of criticism. In this sense, he was the progenitor of modern American criticism, though he himself has no disciples.

Despite what was just short of pandering to popular taste by one who derided popular taste, Mencken derived certain critical principles from his study of German philosopher Friedrich Nietzsche and French critic Rémy de Gourmont. Nietzsche's contempt for the leveling tendencies of democracy and Christianity influenced Mencken's heavily ironic *Notes on Democracy* (1926), *A Treatise on the Gods* (1930), and *A Treatise on Right and Wrong* (1934). His thorough knowledge of Nietzsche was established in his pioneering American study *The Philosophy of Friedrich Nietzsche* (1908). However, unlike Nietzsche (who was at heart an idealist and a visionary, and who, if he despised contemporary morality and mankind, nevertheless hoped to induce a master morality and to breed a race of supermen), Mencken scoffed at this "messianic delusion," adopting only the negative aspects of Nietzscheanism for his castigation of things American and "bourgeois."

After establishing himself as a misogynist with *In Defense of Women* (1918), Mencken startled his followers by marrying Sara Haardt in 1930. Their union was short, however, for his wife died in 1935.

From Rémy de Gourmont's declaration that to "erect into laws one's personal impressions" is the purpose of the "sincere" critic, Mencken derived the impetus that resulted in the six series of *Prejudices* (1919-1927), which, together with *A Book of Prefaces* (1917), constitute his strongest claim as a critic. His crusades for Theodore Dreiser, Willa Cather, and Sinclair Lewis helped establish those novelists; he was ambivalent toward William Dean Howells and George Bernard Shaw; and he greatly overestimated a class of poor writers. Lumping together certain mild practitioners of his own craft whom he suspected of timidity and prudishness—the "Mores, Brownells, Phelpses, Mabies, Brander Matthewses, and other such grave and glittering fish"—helped to clear the field for fresher talents. Unfortunately, even when Mencken was vehemently right, his reader had the uneasy suspicion that this was fortuitous.

Mencken's appreciation of the juicy phrase interested him in its informal aspects. Behind this interest was a distrust of Englishmen—a philo-Teutonism—that deluded him into holding that American speech was the unique product of a new environment. Genuine industry and the liveliest curiosity produced in 1919 *The American Language* and in the following years its supplements (1945, 1948) and revisions (1921, 1923, 1936). In a field where one finds such great names as those of Ben Jonson, the brothers Grimm, and Otto Jespersen, Mencken meets his peers. But none, not even that of Dr. Jonson, stands for livelier discourse and happier illustrations of its points than Mencken's. By the time of his death on Jan. 29, 1956, in his beloved Baltimore, recognition of his service to the language was everywhere admitted.

H. L. Mencken's other works include *Ventures into Verse* (1903), *Bernard Shaw: The Plays* (1905), *The Artist* (a play, 1912), *A Book of Burlesques* (1916), *A Little Book in C Major* (1916), *Damn: A Book of Calumny* (1918), *Heliogablus* (1920), *Making a President* (1932), *New Dictionary of Quotations* (1942), *Christmas Story* (1946), and *Mencken Chrestomathy* (1949). Mencken gathered the more outrageous attacks upon him in *Menckeniana: A Schimplexion* (1927).

Further Reading

In addition to the three volumes of autobiography, *Happy Days, 1880-1892* (1940), *Newspaper Days, 1899-1906* (1941), and *Heathen Days, 1890-1936* (1943), information on Mencken's life is in William R. Manchester, *Disturber of the Peace: The Life of H. L. Mencken* (1951), written in consultation with Mencken. An irreverent treatment is found in Charles Angoff, *H. L. Mencken: A Portrait from Memory* (1956). Douglas C. Stenerson, *Mencken: Iconoclast from Baltimore* (1971), is a sound appraisal. Sara Mayfield, in *The Constant Circle: H. L. Mencken and His Friends* (1968), tells the story of Mencken's marriage to Sara Haardt. William Nolte, *H. L. Mencken: Literary Critic* (1966), tries to evaluate Mencken's contribution to his craft. Joseph W. Beach, *The Outlook for American Prose* (1926), is a fair appraisal of Mencken's style by a contemporary. □

Álvaro de Mendaña de Neyra

The Spanish explorer Álvaro de Mendaña de Neyra (1541-1595) discovered the Solomon and Marquesas islands. The voyages of Mendaña and his associates in search of new conquests to the south ended the Spanish phase of the Age of Discovery.

Born in Saragossa, Álvaro de Mendaña de Neyra was the nephew of an appointee to the viceroyalty of Peru. Mendaña was put in charge of an expedition to the South Pacific which sailed from Callao, Peru, late in 1567. With him went Pedro Sarmiento de Gamboa, an adventurer whose campaign for the conquest of the mythical Southern Continent (also called Terra Australis, although it had no precise relationship to present-day Australia) produced this expedition.

Behind the mission lay generations of European speculation and dreaming. Ptolemy's *Geography,* rediscovered by Europeans in the 15th century, had pointed to the existence of a vast southern land mass. Luring explorers across the Atlantic was the vision of the Lost Continent, or island of Atlantis. And once they had reached the New World, they continued to be drawn by the story of the Golden One, El Dorado. Now these visions were given a new lease on life by native Peruvian legends. Sarmiento, author of the *Historía de los Incas,* drew on his Indian sources for information about Pacific exploration. Among the myths was the tale of the Inca navigator Paullu Tupac Yupanqui, whose 9-month journey to the south had brought him untold riches. Their lust for these same rewards underlay the journey of Mendaña and Sarmiento.

With their two ships the explorers passed, but did not land on, the Ellice Islands; but in 1568 they discovered Santa Isabel in the Solomons. From there, they proceeded to Guadalcanal, Malaita, and San Cristobal, where an attempt to found a settlement came to nothing. Spanish slaughters of islanders provoked bloody reprisals; the Spanish hunger for gold went unsatisfied. In the summer of 1568 Mendaña began his year-long return voyage to Peru.

Mendaña hoped to return to the Solomons. But Spain, now diverted by its long naval war with England, was concerned with holding on to existing conquests rather than acquiring new possessions for sea dogs like Sir Francis Drake to plunder. Thus it was not until April 1595 that Mendaña was able to set out again, this time with four ships and a complement including women intended as wives for future colonists.

The little fleet reached Magdalena in the Marquesas (named after the Marqués de Cañete, then Peruvian viceroy) in July 1595. Polynesian residents were admired and murdered. The voyage then proceeded to its furthest limit, Santa Cruz Island, which still fell far short of Mendaña's goal. There the expedition, riven with internal dissension and reduced by disease and war with the islanders, began to fall apart. Mendaña himself died in mid-November. The survivors were led on to the Philippines by the Portuguese pilot Pedro Fernandés de Quirós (who himself later discovered the New Hebrides). Mendaña's failure to reconfirm his original discovery meant that the Solomons were permanently lost to Spain. They were rediscovered only in the 18th century by the English explorer Capt. James Cook.

Further Reading

For information on Mendaña, Pacific exploration, and the Spanish Pacific see J. C. Beaglehole, *The Exploration of the Pacific* (1934; 3d ed. 1966); William Lytle Schurz, *The Manila Galleon* (1939); and Boies Penrose, *Travel and Discovery in the Renaissance: 1420-1620* (1952). □

Johann Gregor Mendel

The Moravian natural scientist and Augustinian abbot Johann Gregor Mendel (1822-1884) laid the foundations of modern genetics with his paper dealing with the hybridization of peas.

Gregor Mendel was born on July 22, 1822, at Hynčice, Czechoslovakia (then Heinzendorf, Austrian Silesia). His ancestors were farmers, and his father still had to work three days a week as a serf. Mendel displayed a great love for nature all his life.

Years of Preparation and Education

In 1831 Mendel was sent to the Piarist school in Lipník (Leipnik) and at the age of 12 to the grammar school in Opava (Troppau). In 1840 he enrolled at the Institute of Philosophy in Olomouc (Olmütz).

Mendel was admitted to the Augustinian order in Brno (Brünn) in 1843. The Augustinians taught philosophy, foreign languages, mathematics, and natural sciences at secondary schools and universities. Abbot Napp, the head of the monastery, devoted all his energy to the economic development of the monastery and to the scientific education of the members of the order. Surrounded by an atmosphere of dynamic activity, Mendel found optimum conditions for his studies and later for his research work. Along with his theological studies Mendel took courses in agriculture, pomiculture, and vine growing at the Institute of Philosophy in Brno. In 1847 he was ordained a priest and served for a short time as vicar at the Old Brno Monastery.

In 1849 Mendel became a teacher of mathematics and Greek at the grammar school in Znojmo (Znaim). After a year the headmaster recommended him for the university examination. Together with his application for admission to the examination Mendel enclosed his autobiography, which is the only authentic preserved document. Mendel failed the examination, probably because he lacked a complete university education. Only his written test on meteorology satisfied his examiner, and, on the latter's recommendation, Abbot Napp sent Mendel to study natural sciences at the University of Vienna (1851-1853). He heard F. Unger lecture on plant anatomy and physiology, the use of the microscope, and the practical organization of experiments. Unger was known for his views on evolution and had investigated the problem of the origin of plant variability by means of transplanting experiments. Mendel later performed these experiments also. It is now assumed that Unger's views deeply influenced Mendel in the formation of his ideas before he performed his experiments with edible peas (*Pisum*).

On his return to Brno in 1854 Mendel was appointed a teacher of physics and natural history in the Technical School. In 1856 he prepared himself for the university examination again, but he became seriously ill and did not take it. By this time, however, Mendel was fully occupied with his hybridizing experiments with *Pisum*. He remained a teacher till 1868, when he was elected abbot of the monastery.

Hybridizing Experiments

Mendel started his extensive program of hybridizing experiments in 1854. He focused his energy on the problem of the origin of plant variability. For two years he tested the purity of selected varieties of *Pisum* and then began experimenting with artificial fertilization. A new reconstruction of Mendel's experimental data illustrates that he must have tested about 28,000 *Pisum* plants during the years 1856-1863.

Mendel summarized the experimental results in a paper, "Experiments on Plant Hybrids," which he read at two meetings of the Natural Science Society in Brno in 1865; the paper was published in the proceedings of the society's journal. Though prominent natural scientists were present at the meeting, no one understood Mendel's ideas or the significance of his work. The proceedings were distributed to 134 scientific institutions in Europe and the United States, but the published paper failed to arouse interest.

Mendel's original idea, that heredity is particulate, was contrary to the theory of "blending heredity" that was generally accepted at that time. In the plants that Mendel tested (and in biparental-reproducing organisms generally), the hereditary particles (called elements by Mendel) from each parent are members of pairs. In forming the reproductive cells, the pair members segregate in different pollen or sperm nuclei and in different eggs or ovules to transmit the hereditary determinants. From one parent comes one particle determining, for example, the round shape of the seed (A), and from the other parent that representing the wrinkled shape (a). Mendel called the trait passing entirely unchanged into hybrid (derived from unlike parents) association "dominant," and the trait becoming latent in hybrids "recessive." The particles meet (recombine) in the offspring (Aa) but do not influence each other.

Suppose the pair members of these hybrid offspring now segregate in forming reproductive cells, producing two types of sperm or egg, namely A or a, and that these particles meet at random in fertilization. The resulting combination series of relevant particles is: 1/4 AA, 1/4 Aa, 1/4 aA, 1/4 aa, or $AA + 2Aa + aa$. That is, there are four genetic types of offspring from the hybrids, each type represented by 25 percent of the total. In this way, in the hybrid progeny the parental forms appear again; after 1900 this segregation of the hereditary units (in 1909 termed genes) was called Mendel's law of segregation.

Mendel found that hereditary particles belonging to different trait pairs, for example, A,a for the seed shape and B,b for the seed coloration, formed the combination series in recombining without influencing each other. The combination series could be predicted by combining the simple series *AA* + *2Aa* + *aa; BB* + *2Bb* + *bb,* resulting in the combination series *AABB* + *AAbb* + *aaBB* + *aabb* + *2AABb* + *2aaBb* + *2AaBB* + *2Aabb* + *4AaBb*. In his paper Mendel actually illustrated such a recombination in crossing peas differing in two and three trait pairs. Expected particle recombinations were realized in actual counts of the offspring. The recombination of the hereditary particles was called Mendel's law of independent assortment.

Mendel gave the impulse for his experiments in the first sentence of his paper: "Artificial fertilization undertaken on ornamental plants to obtain new color variants initiated the experiments to be discussed." His task was to find "the generally applicable law of the formation and development of hybrids as a way of finally reaching the solution to a question whose significance for the evolutionary history of organic forms must not be underestimated." In his paper he expressed the opinion that "the distinguishing traits of two plants can, after all, be caused only by differences in the composition among grouping of the elements existing in dynamic interaction in the primordial cells." He assumed the general validity of his theory because, according to him, "unity in the plan of development of organic life is beyond doubt."

Being interested in the development of hybrid forms, Mendel also explained that the population descending from hybrids tends to revert to the pure parental forms, resulting in diminishing the hybrid's form. Thus, as a consequence of Mendelian segregation, Mendel also laid the basis for the interpretation of the effect of inbreeding.

Mendel continued his hybridizing experiments, crossing various forms of 22 other genera of plants, to prove the general validity of his theory in the plant kingdom. He also cultivated wild plants in the garden with the aim of investigating Lamarck's views concerning the influence of environment upon plant variability; he could not agree with Lamarck. He was convinced, like Darwin, that it was impossible to draw a hard-and-fast line between species and varieties, and in the conclusion of his *Pisum* paper he expressed the conviction that the variability of cultivated plants could be explained by his theory.

After 1871 Mendel also tried to carry out hybridizing experiments with bees. He bred about 50 bee races which he tried crossing to obtain new cultural breeds. His crossing experiments could not be successful, however, because of the complex problem of the controlled mating of queens. For this reason Mendel focused his activity on research of the technological aspects of apiculture, such as the hibernation of bees.

As a member of the Natural Science Section of the Agricultural Society in Brno and as a respected meteorologist, Mendel summarized the results of meteorological observations in 1856 and published them in six reports (1862-1869). He also published three papers on extraordinary storms (1870-1872). He was a member of the Central Board of the Agricultural Society from 1870, and he supported the first weather forecasts for farmers in 1878. In 1861 he helped found the Natural Science Society of Brno.

Taxation and the Monastery

After Mendel was elected abbot of the monastery in 1868, he had little time for his experimental activities, although they never came to a total stop. In 1874 the government proclaimed a new law relating to the contribution of the cloisters to the religious fund. Mendel refused to pay the high assessed taxes and thus, from the end of 1875, got himself into trouble with the provincial government and with the Ministry of Education in Vienna. The result of this conflict was the lasting sequestration of the landed monasterial property. In an attempt to win Mendel over and stop his opposition to the taxation law, the government appointed him to the Board of Directors of the Moravian Mortgage Bank. In 1876 he became the vice-governor of the bank and in 1881 the governor. Nevertheless, Mendel never agreed to the taxation law.

The long struggle over taxation had a serious effect on Mendel's health. He died on Jan. 6, 1884, without any public recognition of his outstanding scientific achievements.

Contributions to Genetics

Mendel's paper of 1865 went unnoticed except for an occasional reference in scientific literature. In 1900 it was rediscovered by scientists, when his theory was generalized as Mendel's laws of heredity. That date also marked the beginning of the science of heredity, which in 1906 was named genetics. Not even after 1900 was Mendel's theory acknowledged as being generally valid, and the Darwinian selection theory was often considered to oppose the Mendelian theory.

Later, it was demonstrated that Mendel had also observed such phenomena as intermediate inheritance, complete linkage, additive gene action, and gene interaction, and that he himself appreciated the Darwinian selection theory and refused to accept the hypothesis of pangenesis. The synthesis of the Darwinian and Mendelian theories was first proved by S. S. Tchetverikoff in 1926 and finally by R. A. Fisher in 1930, Sewall Wright in 1931, and J. B. S. Haldane in 1932.

Since that time Mendel's work has been reappraised. His hypothesis of hereditary particles turned out to be quite general and provided the elementary principle of heredity in all forms of life from viruses to man. From this viewpoint his laws of heredity appear to be only the subordinate principles of Mendel's main discovery, which furnishes proof of the existence of genes as determining the whole character of each organism.

Further Reading

The best biography of Mendel is Hugo Iltis, *Life of Mendel* (1924; trans. 1932). Mendel's papers on hybridization are published in English in J. H. Bennett, ed., *Experiments in Plant Hybridization* (1965). Curt Stern and Eva R. Sherwood, eds., *The Origin of Genetics: A Mendel Source Book* (1966), is a translation of Mendel's papers. It also contains 11 letters that Mendel wrote to Karl Nägeli, which give basic information on Mendel's experiments with different plant species. Information on Mendel and on the early development of genetics is published in the series "Folia Mendeliana Musei Moraviae." The historical development of Mendelism is treated in Robert C. Olby, *Origins of Mendelism* (1966). The historical development of modern genetics is outlined in L. C. Dunn, ed., *Genetics in the 20th Century: Essays on the Progress of Genetics during its First Fifty Years* (1951). □

Dmitrii Ivanovich Mendeleev

The Russian chemist Dmitrii Ivanovich Mendeleev (1834-1907) is best known for the formulation of the periodic law of the chemical elements.

D mitrii Mendeleev was born on Feb. 8, 1834, in the Siberian town of Tobolsk. He was the seventeenth and last child of Ivan Pavlovich and Maria Dmitrievna Mendeleev. At the age of 7 Dmitrii entered the gymnasium in Tobolsk and completed his studies in 1849. He displayed brilliant intellectual ability, a sharp memory, and a fascination for mathematics, physics, and geography. The following year he enrolled in the division of mathematical and natural sciences of the Main Pedagogical Institute of St. Petersburg, his father's alma mater.

Chemistry in Russia

The universities of Kazan and St. Petersburg were the principal centers of chemical activities in Russia during the first half of the 19th century. Mendeleev worked under Aleksandr A. Voskresenskii, whom the Russians call the grandfather of Russian chemistry. Mendeleev's first scientific paper was "The Analysis of Finnish Allanite and Pyroxene," and his diploma thesis was *On Isomorphism in Connection with Other Relations between Crystalline Forms and Chemical Compositions* (published in 1856 in *Gorny zhurnal*). His studies of the phenomenon of isomorphism led him to observe the similarity of the crystalline structures of related elements, which aided him in constructing the periodic table. When he graduated in 1855, he won the gold medal for being first in his class.

Mendeleev returned to the University of St. Petersburg in May 1856 to defend his thesis, *On Specific Volumes*. The degrees of master of physics and of chemistry were conferred on Mendeleev, and soon thereafter he presented a second thesis, *The Structure of Siliceous Combinations*. This resulted in his being appointed dozent, enabling him to teach theoretical and organic chemistry at the University of St. Petersburg. Toward the end of the 1850s Mendeleev reluctantly came to the conclusion that he would have to study abroad if he desired a professional chair because the research facilities at his university were inadequate.

Mendeleev Abroad

After a brief stay at the Sorbonne, Mendeleev journeyed to Heidelberg University, where he organized his own laboratory. He concentrated on the problem of molecular cohesion as displayed in the phenomena of capillarity and surface tension. The results of his experiments were published in three papers: "The Capillary Properties of Liquids," "The Expansion of Liquids," and "The Temperature of the Absolute Boiling Points of the Same Liquids." The significant conclusion reached by Mendeleev was that the molecular cohesion of a liquid in a capillary tube disappears at a specific temperature and that no gas can be liquefied above its unique "absolute temperature," commonly designated as the "critical temperature." During his stay in Heidelberg he designed the Mendeleev pyknometer for determining the specific gravity of liquids.

In 1860 Mendeleev and several other Russian chemists participated in the work of the First International Congress of Chemistry at Karlsruhe. Its purpose was, according to Mendeleev's letter dated Sept. 7, 1860, "to clarify and, if possible, agree on the basic differences which exist between the followers of different chemical schools."

Periodic Law

In 1861 Mendeleev resumed teaching chemistry at the University of St. Petersburg, the College of Engineering, and the Transport Institute. That year he wrote *Organic Chemistry*, Russia's first university manual on the subject. Two years later Mendeleev contracted an unhappy marriage with Feozva Nikitichna Leshcheva which lasted until 1876, when he met the young art student Anna Ivanovna Popov, whom he married illegally. When the charge of bigamy was raised against Mendeleev, Czar Alexander responded,

"Mendeleev has two wives, yes, but I have only one Mendeleev."

Mendeleev accepted in 1864 the chair of technology (industrial chemistry) at the Technological Institute of St. Petersburg; received his doctorate in chemistry in 1865; filled in 1867 the chair of inorganic chemistry at the University of St. Petersburg, which he retained for the next 23 years; and helped found in 1868 the Russian Chemical Society.

It is difficult to determine precisely when Mendeleev first hit upon the periodic table. The problem of inaccurate atomic weights was solved by Stanislao Cannizzaro. Attempts to organize the chemical elements by increasing atomic weights had already been made by Alexandre Émile Béguyer de Chancourtois and by John Alexander Reina Newlands. It is known that Mendeleev also was impressed with certain regularities of the chemical properties of elements when preparing, in 1868, his highly successful text *Principles of Chemistry*. On March 18, 1869, Mendeleev's paper "An Outline of the System of the Elements, Based on Their Atomic Weights and Chemical Similarities," which contained the periodic table, was presented at the Russian Chemical Society and was subsequently published in Russian and German. In his table Mendeleev left six gaps for the yet-undiscovered elements having the atomic weights of 8, 22, 45, 68, 70, and 180.

Mendeleev had confidence in the existence of the law of periodicity of elements. He devoted considerable effort to predicting the chemical and physical properties of three elements vacant in the table. He named these hypothetical elements eka-boron, eka-aluminum, and eka-silicon (in Sanskrit the prefix *eka* means one). He was able to derive their valences and atomic weights and the formulas of compounds they are likely to form. Mendeleev's table hardly attracted attention until his predictions were fulfilled by the discoveries of gallium (1874), scandium (1879), and germanium (1885). The major drawbacks of his table were that it had difficulty in accommodating the rare-earth group and that no provision was made for the chemically inert elements, helium, neon, argon, krypton, xenon, and radon.

In recognition for his formulation of the periodic law and the systematization of organic chemistry by means of his periodic table, academicians proposed Mendeleev's candidacy to the vacant chair of chemical technology of the Imperial Academy of Sciences. On Nov. 11, 1880, a shocked academic world learned of the rejection of Mendeleev's candidacy. Contributing to his defeat were Court Tolstoy, the minister of public education and later president of the Imperial Academy, who sought to limit the teaching of science in Russian schools and found Mendeleev a formidable opponent, and the members of the "German party" at the academy, who attempted to discourage native Russian scientists from becoming academicians. In expressing displeasure with the academy's rejection of Mendeleev and recognizing his achievements, five Russian universities elected Mendeleev as an honorary member, Cambridge and Oxford designated him an honored scholar, and numerous academies and societies elected him member. Few Russians since have been able to match Mendeleev's worldwide recognition.

Technical Activities

Mendeleev also showed a great interest in technology. In 1863 he was immersed in the problems of the Baku petroleum industry. He suggested a pipeline should be built to carry the oil from Baku to the Black Sea. He noted that the system of leasing oil-rich government-owned lands for a 4-year period tended to prevent large-scale investments in needed equipment to modernize operations, and he fought the government tax on petroleum products. In 1876 Mendeleev visited the Pennsylvania oil fields, brought back some technical ideas, and presented an unflattering view of America in his book *The Oil Industry in the North American State of Pennsylvania and the Caucasus*. He developed a theory that petroleum originated from the action of water on metallic carbides inside the earth.

In 1886 Mendeleev turned his attention to agricultural productivity, earning him the reputation of being the founder of Russian agrochemistry. At the request of the Ministry of State Property, Mendeleev examined in 1888 the possibilities of organizing a coal-mining industry in the Donets Basin (Donbas). And in 1899, despite age and infirmity, he traveled to the Urals to investigate the stagnation of the iron industry. In his *The Urals Iron Industry in 1899* he concluded the problem lay with the monopolistic practices of the owners.

While looking into the properties of rarefied gases under varying pressures, Mendeleev designed a differential barometer that could determine precisely the height above sea level. He became fascinated with the problem of studying the upper strata of the atmosphere, and he even went so far as to plan a hermetically sealed gondola that could carry a human observer or automatic recording equipment. On Aug. 7, 1887, Mendeleev had the opportunity to make an ascent in a government balloon for the purpose of observing a solar eclipse. Inasmuch as the balloon lacked the power to lift Mendeleev and his experienced balloonist, Mendeleev bodily ejected the balloonist and carried out a solo flight, rising to an altitude of 11,000 feet and landing two hours later after covering 150 miles. Just before his death, Mendeleev was contemplating a journey to the North Pole by balloon.

In 1890 Mendeleev resigned from the University of St. Petersburg. Soon thereafter he worked for the Admiralty and Ministry of War. In 1892 he was appointed treasurer of the Chamber of Standard Weights and Measures, later becoming its chief. In 1899 he introduced the metric system into Russia.

Philosophy and Outlook

Mendeleev saw in science a valuable tool for remaking and modernizing Russia. He saw Russia gaining respectability in the community of nations through scientific activity benefiting mankind. And he saw in science the essential ingredient of the educated mind. However, he rejected science as a panacea for society's ills, believing that science must be complemented by religious and artistic sources of knowledge.

During his last years, Mendeleev defended his atomistic view of matter to the point of denouncing the modern ideas of physics of the divisibility of the atom and the transmutability of the chemical elements. One of these transmuted elements, the 101st in the periodic table, is named mendelevium. Mendeleev died on Jan. 20, 1907.

Further Reading

Although not a definitive study, Daniel Q. Posin, *Mendeleyev: The Story of a Great Scientist* (1948), is valuable for its broad treatment of Mendeleev's life and for its bibliography of his publications. There are many biographical sketches, but the one by Henry Leicester in Eduard Farber, ed., *Great Chemists* (1961), is most accurate and is based on Russian sources. A translation of a brief Russian study of Mendeleev is O. N. Pisarzhevsky, *Dmitry Ivanovich Mendeleyev: His Life and Work* (1954). The 19th-century history of the periodic table is described in great detail by Francis P. Venable in *The Development of the Periodic Law* (1896), and by A. E. Garrett in *The Periodic Law* (1909). □

Erich Mendelsohn

The German architect Erich Mendelsohn (1887-1953) was a leading pioneer of modern architecture. Beginning with a sculptural and emotional approach, he later became more closely allied with the International Style.

E rich Mendelsohn was born in Allenstein, East Prussia, on March 21, 1887. He received his architectural training in Berlin and Munich, and he set up in private practice in Munich at the age of 25. In Munich he was friendly with leaders of the German expressionist movement in painting. Following military service in World War I, Mendelsohn returned to his practice and prepared an exhibition of his architectural sketches. His designs showed the strong influence of expressionism in their dynamic and dramatic use of line.

Mendelsohn's first major commission was the Einstein Tower (1919-1921), an observatory in Potsdam, Germany. Although he had originally intended the building to be executed in poured concrete (to emphasize the expressive forms of the tower), for technical reasons it was constructed of brick rendered with cement. The building attracted considerable attention, particularly because of the plastic treatment of form, which made the seven-story tower seem to flow upward from its rounded base to its domed observatory. This structure typifies his interest in an architecture of abstract, sculptural expressionism.

Shortly after this Mendelsohn began to turn away from free-flowing designs. An example of this new direction is his Steinberg Hat Factory (1920-1923) in Luckenwalde, Germany. During the late 1920s he became more and more attracted to the formal lines of the International Style. At this

time he was commissioned to design several branches of the Shocken Department Store. In the one at Stuttgart (1926) he emphasized the horizontal by using continuous-ribbon windows separated with bands of brick. The rounded staircase at the corner of the asymmetrical structure was cantilevered over the entrance. Mendelsohn refined this approach in the design for the Shocken store at Chemnitz (1927-1928). Here, in an imposing curved facade, the windows alternated with opaque white bands, creating a feeling of clarity and lightness.

The rise of Nazism in Germany and its accompanying religious persecution forced Mendelsohn to flee in March 1933. In London he entered into partnership with Serge Chermayeff. Mendelsohn divided his practice between England and Palestine. His most important British design was the De la Warr Pavilion (1934) at Boxhill. In Palestine he executed a number of buildings, including a hospital at Haifa and the University Medical Center (1937-1939) on Mt. Scopus, Jerusalem.

Mendelsohn emigrated to the United States in 1941 but did not practice until after the war. His American work included many hospitals, synagogues, and community centers. Among the most important was the 14-story Maimonides Hospital in San Francisco (1946); here he emphasized the horizontal with conspicuously cantilevered balconies with small, curved projections.

Mendelsohn designed a number of synagogues and community centers in the Midwest, including those in St. Louis, Mo. (1946-1950), Cleveland, Ohio (1946-1952), Grand Rapids, Mich. (1948-1952), and St. Paul, Minn. (1950-1954). The Cleveland design was the most ambitious, successfully harmonizing the central dome of the synagogue with the building's undulating site. Mendelsohn died in San Francisco on Sept. 15, 1953.

Further Reading

A primary source is *Erich Mendelsohn: Letters of an Architect*, edited by Oskar Beyer and translated by Geoffrey Strachan (1968). An excellent discussion of Mendelsohn's early European career is Arnold Whittick, *Eric Mendelsohn* (1940). A more recent treatment, including his American projects, is Wolf von Eckardt, *Eric Mendelsohn* (1960). □

Moses Mendelssohn

The German philosopher Moses Mendelssohn (1729-1786) was a major figure of the German Enlightenment. An intellectually emancipated and cultured German as well as a faithful Jew, he was referred to as the "German Socrates" and as the "Jewish Socrates."

M oses Mendelssohn was born on Sept. 6, 1729, in Dessau. He suffered from curvature of the spine. His father was a Torah scribe. The young man followed traditional Talmudic studies under Rabbi David

Frankel, who introduced him to the thought of the medieval Jewish thinker Maimonides. In 1743 Mendelssohn's teacher received an appointment to Berlin, and the young student accompanied him. During the next years Mendelssohn's intellectual training expanded to include Latin, French, and English as well as mathematics and science.

At 21, Mendelssohn began a chain of fortunate associations. He became a tutor to the family of Isaac Bernhard, and he rose successively to bookkeeper and partner in a silk manufacturing firm. This position made him financially independent and left him free to follow his studies. Bernhard also introduced him to Gotthold Ephraim Lessing, the writer and dramatist. Lessing and Mendelssohn began a lifelong friendship and active collaboration. The noble and enlightened Jew in Lessing's famous comedy *Nathan the Wise* is modeled after the philosopher. Lessing encouraged Mendelssohn in his writing and arranged for the publication of his first essays and his translation of Jean Jacques Rousseau's *Discourse on Unequality* (1756). With Friedrich Nicolai, Mendelssohn edited a radical and popular magazine, *Letters on Literature,* which made Mendelssohn well known. In 1762 Mendelssohn married, and he and his wife eventually became the parents of six children. Two of his sons established a famous banking house, and the world-renowned composer Felix Mendelssohn was the philosopher's grandson.

In 1764 Mendelssohn competed against Immanuel Kant and won the Berlin Academy prize with an essay, "Evidence of Metaphysical Science." His main philosophic reputation stemmed from his influential treatises on es-

thetics and on the philosophy of religion. In 1776 he published a work on immortality. The *Phaedo* was modeled on Plato's dialogue of the same name. This book became the most popular work in German philosophy. Mendelssohn's writing skill was also reflected in his translation of the Pentateuch from Hebrew into German (1778-1783) as well as in *Morning Hours* (1785), a volume dealing with the existence of God.

The remainder of Mendelssohn's important work stemmed from two specific controversies. He was challenged by Christian writers either to convert or to explain the compatibility of his philosophy with Judaism. In a response to the Swiss theologian J. K. Lavater (1769) and in *Jerusalem* (1783) Mendelssohn attempted to interpret Judaism as a religion of reason available to all enlightened humanitarians. After Lessing's death, Lessing was attacked as an atheist, and Mendelssohn produced a series of writings in defense of his friend. Mendelssohn died in Berlin on Jan. 4, 1786.

Further Reading

The only work of Mendelssohn to appear recently in English translation is *Jerusalem and Other Jewish Writings* (1969). Secondary literature includes Hermann Walter, *Moses Mendelssohn: Critic and Philosopher* (1930), and a chapter on his philosophy in Jacob B. Agus, *The Evolution of Jewish Thought: From Biblical Times to the Opening of the Modern Era* (1959). □

Felix Jakob Ludwig Mendelssohn-Bartholdy

Felix Jakob Ludwig Mendelssohn-Bartholdy (1809-1847) was a German composer, conductor, pianist, and organist. He infused a basic classical approach to musical composition with fresh romantic harmonies and expressiveness.

Felix Mendelssohn was born in Hamburg on Feb. 3, 1809, the son of Abraham and Leah Mendelssohn and the grandson of the famous Jewish philosopher Moses Mendelssohn. In later years Felix's father humorously referred to himself as "formerly the son of my father and now the father of my son." In 1812 the family moved to Berlin, where Abraham established himself as a banker, converted to Protestantism, and changed the family name to Mendelssohn-Bartholdy.

Felix and his elder sister, Fanny, received their initial piano instruction from their mother. In 1816, on a visit to Paris, he studied with the pianist Marie Bigot. The next year he began formal composition studies with Carl Friedrich Zelter, a composer greatly admired by the poet Johann Wolfgang von Goethe.

Mendelssohn's first public appearance occurred at the age of 9. Famous musicians gave concerts every Sunday at his father's house; in addition to broadening the musical horizons of the gifted boy, they enabled him, as a budding composer, to test many of his works as he wrote them. In 1819 he entered the Singakademie, and from that time on compositions flowed steadily from his pen. In 1820, for example, he produced two piano sonatas, a violin sonata, songs, a quartet for men's voices, a cantata, and a short opera.

In 1821 Mendelssohn became acquainted with Carl Maria von Weber, whose compositions served as a romantic model for his own. Later that year Zelter took him to Weimar to meet Goethe, who described the lad of 12 as having "the smallest modicum of the phlegmatic and the maximum of the opposite quality."

The first public presentation of Mendelssohn's works took place in 1822. That year he also wrote his official Opus 1, a Piano Quartet in C Minor. All these works were well received. He had a private orchestra, for which he wrote the work now known as Symphony No. 1 in C Minor. He also continued with work in other genres, such as the Piano Quartet in F Minor (1823).

In 1824 the famous pianist Ignaz Moscheles arrived in Berlin from London, and for a time Mendelssohn studied piano with him. The following year Mendelssohn visited Paris, where he met many eminent composers and performed his Piano Quartet in B Minor, dedicated to Goethe. Luigi Cherubini, who was present at the performance, offered to take Mendelssohn as a pupil, but he decided to return to Berlin, greatly elated with his French successes.

There he wrote with mature craftsmanship the celebrated *Midsummer Night's Dream* Overture. The remainder of the incidental music to Shakespeare's play did not appear until 1842.

In 1827 Mendelssohn's only opera, *Die Hochzeit des Camacho* (The Marriage of Camacho), based on Cervantes' *Don Quixote*, was presented in Berlin. It was not successful, owing in part to the machinations of Gasparo Spontini, who had earlier tried to prevent its production. More successful was the Octet for Strings, one of Mendelssohn's freshest and most original works. The same year he became acquainted with Anton Thibaut, a professor of law and a gifted amateur writer on music who was concerned with revitalizing interest in old church music. Through him, Mendelssohn came to know the masterpieces of Renaissance and early baroque choral music. For some years he also attended the University of Berlin but kept on with his flow of compositions. In 1828 appeared the Goethe-inspired overture *Calm Sea and Prosperous Voyage*.

On March 11, 1829, a great musical event occurred: Mendelssohn conducted the Singakademie in the first complete performance of Johann Sebastian Bach's *St. Matthew Passion* since the composer's death. The work was a huge success, and the performance was of decisive importance to all subsequent German composers for it marked the beginning of the revival of Bach's works.

Later that year Mendelssohn visited England, where he conducted a concert of the Philharmonic Society. He took a long trip through Scotland, where he sketched the now famous *Hebrides*, or *Fingal's Cave*, Overture. On his return to Berlin he was offered the post of professor of music at the university but turned it down.

After writing the *Reformation* Symphony (1830) Mendelssohn began a series of visits to various European cities that lasted for almost 3 years. After a short stay with Goethe at Weimar, Mendelssohn went to Rome. Both the *Scottish* and the *Italian* Symphonies were begun in Italy. In the autumn he returned to Germany and played his newly composed Piano Concerto in G Minor in Munich. In 1832 he left for London, where he conducted the *Hebrides* Overture and the Piano Concerto in G Minor with great acclaim. That same year his first book of *Songs without Words* (*Lieder ohne Worte*) was published.

On Mendelssohn's return to Berlin he tried to succeed Zelter at the Singakademie but was passed over. In 1833 he was made conductor of the Lower Rhine Music Festival in Düsseldorf, where he annually presented both new and old works otherwise rarely heard. As a result of his success with the festival, he was appointed general musical director in Düsseldorf later that year. He also produced the *Schöne Melusine* Overture and the beginning of his oratorio *St. Paul*.

In 1835 Mendelssohn became director of the Gewandhaus concerts in Leipzig. He made Leipzig into a musical center of European significance because of his gifts as conductor, his creativity, and his all-encompassing musical erudition. He featured many contemporary compositions, such works as the C Major Symphony of Franz Schubert, newly discovered by Robert Schumann, whom

Mendelssohn had met shortly before, and selected compositions of J.S. Bach. The only sadness he experienced was the death of his father in 1835.

In 1836 Mendelssohn received an honorary doctorate from the University of Leipzig. He finished the oratorio *St. Paul* in the spring, and it was performed in May at the Lower Rhine Festival in Düsseldorf. Later that year he met Cécile Jeanrenaud, the daughter of a Huguenot minister, whom he married in 1837. Five children were born of this marriage.

The next few years witnessed a literal outpouring of new compositions, including the overture *Ruy Blas,* the *Lobgesang* (Hymn of Praise), and the *Variations sérieuses.* In 1837 Mendelssohn visited London, conducted his *St. Paul* at the Birmingham Festival, and conceived the idea for a new oratorio on the subject of Elijah.

Upon the urging of the king of Prussia, Mendelssohn was appointed music director of the Academy of Arts in Berlin. Until 1845 he worked intermittently in Berlin without relinquishing his post at Leipzig. Interspersed were trips to London, with performances of his works in London and Birmingham.

In 1843 Mendelssohn founded the Leipzig Conservatory of Music, the first of its kind in Germany. He completed the *Scottish* Symphony, the Violin Concerto, and other major works of his maturity in Leipzig. In 1844 he conducted five Philharmonic concerts in London, and in 1846 he gave the first performance of his *Elijah,* written for the Birmingham Festival of that year. His chief occupation was still as conductor of the Gewandhaus concerts, but he also functioned as director of the Leipzig Conservatory, teaching piano and composition as part of his duties.

Mendelssohn's health began to fail in 1844. Three years later he was literally devastated by the death of his beloved sister, Fanny, on May 14. From then on his health deteriorated markedly, and although he ventured a short summer trip to Switzerland to recuperate, finishing the String Quartet in F Minor, he returned exhausted to Leipzig, where he died on Nov. 4, 1847, at the age of 38.

Further Reading

The best all-around work in English on Mendelssohn is Eric Werner, *Mendelssohn: A New Image of the Composer and His Age* (trans. 1963). Also useful are Percy M. Young, *Introduction to the Music of Mendelssohn* (1949), and Philip Radcliffe, *Mendelssohn* (1954). For a detailed approach to one of Mendelssohn's major works, which is much broader in its approach than the title suggests, Jack Werner, *Mendelssohn's "Elijah": A Historical and Analytical Guide to the Oratorio* (1965), is strongly recommended. For general historical background see Donald Jay Grout, *A History of Western Music* (1960). □

Dorothy Reed Mendenhall

Dorothy Reed Mendenhall (1874-1964) was a well-respected researcher, obstetrician, and pioneer in methods of childbirth. She was the first to discover that Hodgkin's disease was actually not a form of tuberculosis, a finding that received international acclaim.

As a result of her work, the cell type characteristic of Hodgkin's disease bears Mendenhall's name. The loss of her first child due to poor obstetrics changed her research career to a lifelong effort to reduce infant mortality rates. Mendenhall's efforts paid off with standards being set for weight and height for children ages birth to six, and also in programs that stressed the health of both the mother and child in the birthing process.

Dorothy Reed Mendenhall, the last of three children, was born September 22, 1874, in Columbus, Ohio, to William Pratt Reed, a shoe manufacturer, and Grace Kimball Reed, both of whom had descended from English settlers who came to America in the seventeenth century. Mendenhall attended Smith College and obtained a baccalaureate degree. Although she initially contemplated a career in journalism, Mendenhall's interest in medicine was inspired by a biology course she attended.

When they opened the school up to women, Mendenhall applied to Johns Hopkins Medical School in Baltimore, Maryland. In 1900, she was one of the first women to graduate from this school with a doctorate of medicine degree. The next year she received a fellowship in pathology at Johns Hopkins. While there, she taught bacteriology and performed research on Hodgkin's disease, which physicians then believed was a form of tuberculosis. She disproved this theory when she discovered a common link between diagnosed patients. She found that the blood of these patients carried a specific type of cell. The presence of these giant cells, now known as the Reed cell, distinctly identifies the disease. Mendenhall's work produced the first thorough descriptions, both verbal and illustrated, of the tissue changes that occur with Hodgkin's. She was the first to describe the disease's growth through several progressive states. Mendenhall determined that a patient's prognosis worsened with each successive stage. She incorrectly speculated, however, that the disease was a chronic inflammatory process. Her finding of the distinctive cell had worldwide importance and was a significant step forward in the understanding and treatment of Hodgkin's disease. Today, researchers know that Hodgkin's is a type of cancer characterized by a progressive enlargement of the lymph nodes.

Because she felt that there were few opportunities for advancement at Johns Hopkins, Mendenhall transferred her work to Babies Hospital of New York, becoming the first resident physician there. In 1906, she married Charles Elwood Mendenhall and began to raise a family. She had four children, one who died a few hours after birth. This loss was to shape the rest of her career. Mendenhall undertook a study of infant mortality, that, when released, brought government attention to the problems of maternal and child health. To determine the extent of infant mortality in the United States, she obtained epidemiological data for the Wisconsin State Board of Health. A major problem she identified was the prevalence of malnutrition among children. In her efforts to remedy the problems of childbearing and childrearing, Mendenhall developed correspondence courses for new and prospective mothers. She also lectured to groups across Wisconsin and wrote bulletins on nutrition for the United States Department of Agriculture. Mendenhall's efforts helped create some of Wisconsin's first infant welfare clinics, particularly in Madison. In 1937, she was gratified when Madison had the lowest infant mortality rate in the United States.

While employed as a field lecturer for the Department of Home Economics at the University of Wisconsin, in 1918, Mendenhall initiated a nationwide effort in which all children under six years of age were weighed and measured. This project helped establish standards for that normal, healthy children of these ages should weigh and how tall they should be. In 1926, Mendenhall undertook a study of birthing methods in Denmark, which had one of the lowest rates of childbirth complications. She later travelled to the country to gain firsthand information on their techniques, which included the utilization of specialized midwives and a reduced role of medical procedures. Through this, Mendenhall determined that there was too much medical intervention in normal childbirth, and that this intervention is often the source of health problems for the mother and child. She helped institute natural childbirth in the U.S. and also suggested that obstetrics become a specialty profession. From 1917 to 1936, Mendenhall also worked intermittently as a medical officer for the United States Children's Bureau. After her husband's death, she withdrew from public life. In her spare time she loved to read Marcus Aurelius. As a tribute to her dedication as a researcher, teacher, and physician, Smith College dedicated Sabin-Reed Hall in 1965. The hall honors Mendenhall and Florence Sabin, a fellow student at both Smith and Johns Hopkins. Mendenhall died July 31, 1964, in Chester, Connecticut, from heart disease.

Further Reading

Sicherman, Barbara, Carol Hurd Green, Ilene Kantrov, and Harriette Walker, editors, *Notable American Women: The Modern Period,* Belknap Press of Harvard University Press, 1980, pp. 468–70. □

Pierre Mendès France

Although Pierre Mendès France (1907-1982) only held the prime ministry for seven months and spent most of his political career criticizing rather than participating in governments, he was one of the most influential and important figures in 20th-century French politics.

Pierre Mendès France was born in Paris on January 11, 1907. His was a fully assimilated Jewish family that had first come to France from Spain during the Inquisition. By the 19th century the Mendès France family had

firmly entered the bourgeoisie; Pierre's father, in fact, was a highly successful merchant who was also a staunch supporter of the Third Republic.

Mendès (he was frequently referred to simply as Mendès) was a brilliant student who was the youngest lawyer in France when he passed the bar. His doctoral thesis on Poincaré's economic policies immediately propelled him into the public eye as one of the first people in France to argue that the state had to coordinate market forces to modernize the woefully backward French economy.

Not surprisingly, the young lawyer soon turned to politics. As a student he had joined the Radical-Socialist Party and headed its youth organization. In 1934 party leaders suggested he run for mayor of Louviers in Normandy, and, much to the surprise of local political observers, he won. In 1936 he was elected to Parliament from Louviers, becoming the youngest member of the Chamber of Deputies. His meteoric rise continued. He was immediately elected chairman of the Customs Committee of the Chamber and was named under secretary of state in the Treasury Department the following year.

Even that early in his career, Mendès France was known for two things—his commitment to modern Keynesian economic policy and his desire for a better blend of effective decision making and popular control over government. Thus he both supported the Popular Front's social reforms and advocated more government intervention in basic macro- and micro-economic policy making.

Mendès France's career was interrupted by World War II. At the outbreak of the war he took a regular army air corps commission and served in the Middle East. France's defeat found him in Paris, and he was one of but 80 members of Parliament to vote against surrender in June 1940. Instead, he and his family left for Morocco to try to continue the war and free France from its German occupiers and the new collaborationist Vichy government. However, he was soon arrested, sent back to France, and put on trial as a traitor. He was quickly convicted and sentenced to six years in jail on August 31, 1940. The following June he escaped from a prison hospital and, upon escaping France, joined General de Gaulle's resistance movement in London. De Gaulle named Mendès to a series of ministerial positions in the government-in-exile and in the provisional governments once France was liberated. In 1946 de Gaulle and Mendès parted ways over the general's failure to endorse Mendès' economic and political view regarding the reconstruction of France.

During the late 1940s and early 1950s the Fourth Republic reverted to the ineffectual politics of "immobilism" that had paralyzed the country before World War II. Mendès grew more critical of the system and found himself further and further from the center of power. As the domestic and international situations worsened, men such as Mendès became more viable candidates for the prime ministry as alternatives to those who seemed incapable of helping France solve its many problems.

Pierre Mendès France finally got his chance after the French army in Vietnam was defeated in 1954. In his investiture speech as prime minister he promised to end French involvement in Indo-China within 60 days and then proceed to major economic and political changes. He succeeded in ending French involvement in Indochina, but that was all. Once that crisis ended, politics returned to normal. His innovative policy proposals were blocked by politicians on the left and on the right, including many members of his own Radical Party. Finally, after less than seven months in office, his government lost a vote of confidence on February 5, 1955, and resigned. Pierre Mendès France never held a major office again.

His first 20 years in politics did convince Mendès France that the system needed a fundamental overhaul. By the end of the 1950s he had left the Radical Party and had helped form the new Unified Socialist Party (PSU). Like many others, he hoped the PSU would reinvigorate the left and help move the country toward what he called a "modern Republic" capable of making humane and efficient economic policy while giving people more control over the decisions shaping their lives.

In 1967 Mendès France was reelected to Parliament, this time from the booming, modern city of Grenoble. In May 1968 he joined the PSU in supporting student and worker demonstrations, but, unlike the young radicals, Mendès could not endorse a revolutionary solution to the crisis. Instead, he and François Mitterrand proposed themselves as prime minister and president respectively in a provisional government to replace the teetering Gaullist regime. That proposal proved a political catastrophe as the

right, not the left, won the elections held that June. Mendès even lost his seat in Parliament in the Gaullist landslide.

He then broke with the PSU, which had veered sharply to the left in the aftermath of the "events of May." He joined the new Socialist Party, headed by François Mitterrand, shortly thereafter and was elected to Parliament again in 1973, 1978, and 1981.

By the time the Socialist Party finally won in 1981 Mendès France was too old and too ill to serve in President Mitterrand's cabinet. But, in many respects, the goals of the new government were his—hopes for more coordinated economic policy, government control over growth sectors of the economy, decentralization, and expansion of respect for human rights. By the time he died on October 18, 1982, everyone from left to right realized that a man whose great gifts had never fully been utilized had passed from the scene.

Further Reading

Unlike most French politicians, there is quite a bit of material on Pierre Mendès France in English. The definitive biography is Jean Lacouture, *Pierre Mendès France* (1984). For Mendès' own views, the best source is Pierre Mendès France, *A Modern French Republic* (1962). □

Fernao Mendes Pinto

The first European to visit Japan was Portuguese adventurer Fernao Mendes Pinto, unjustly called the "Prince of Liars" because his book about his travels was so widely disbelieved by his contemporaries.

Fernao Mendes Pinto was born in the Portuguese town of Montemor-o-Velho not far from the ancient university city of Coimbra. At the age of ten or twelve he was taken to Lisbon by an uncle and placed in the household of a rich noblewoman. He stayed there a year and a half until "something happened that placed me in such great jeopardy that I was forced to leave the house at a moment's notice and flee for my life." We do not know what had happened. Mendes Pinto fled to the Alfama section of Lisbon where he caught a ship bound for southern Portugal. Fifteen miles from their destination it was captured by French pirates. Mendes Pinto was eventually put ashore on the coast of Spain and made his way to the Portuguese city of Setubal. He entered the employ of a nobleman there and stayed for a year and a half.

Determined to seek his fortune elsewhere, Mendes Pinto sailed from Portugal on March 11, 1537 bound for India. He sailed around the Cape of Good Hope, stopped in Mozambique, and arrived at the Portuguese fortress of Diu on the northwestern coast of India on September 5, 1537. He then joined an expedition to the Red Sea and delivered a message to the Portuguese soldiers who were fighting on the side of the Christian king of Ethiopia. Leaving Ethiopia, his ship was captured by the Turks and the crew was taken to the port of Mocha in Yemen and sold into slavery. Eventually being bought by a Jewish merchant, Mendes Pinto was taken to the port of Ormuz on the south coast of Persia, where he joined a Portuguese trading ship.

Reaching the Portuguese headquarters of Goa, Mendes Pinto entered the service of the newly appointed captain of Malacca on the coast of Malay. He arrived in Malacca in 1539 and worked for the captain of the fortress there as an emissary to the kingdoms of Sumatra and Malaya. He then went to Patani on the east side of the Malay Peninsula and started a thriving business trading with the Thais in Bangkok. Robbed by pirates, he and his partners got revenge by becoming pirates themselves. He then traded along the coast of Indochina. He was shipwrecked on the coast of China and sold as a slave to work on the Great Wall of China. (Mendes Pinto claimed to have been shipwrecked, captured, and sold into slavery 16 or 17 times.)

Helping Tartar invaders penetrate into China, Mendes Pinto was freed and returned overland to Indochina. Hoping to travel back to India, Mendes Pinto took passage on a Chinese pirate junk that was driven off course during a storm and ended up on the Japanese island of Tanegashima, south of Kyushu in 1542 or 1543, the first European to reach that country. He then returned to Canton in south China and told Portuguese merchants there of the wealth to be gained by trading with Japan. He accompanied a group of them, and they were shipwrecked in the Ryukyu Islands where they were saved by the pleas of the women of the island. He then went back to Malacca.

From Malacca he was sent on a mission to the Burmese who had just captured the Kingdom of Pegu. He was taken prisoner by the Burmese and traveled as far as Luang Prabang in what is now Laos. He escaped and returned to Goa. He then undertook a trading mission to Java where he got involved in a local war and left just in the nick of time. Trying to travel on to China, his ship was attacked by Japanese pirates and was shipwrecked on the coast of Thailand. He and his men built a raft that ended up once again in Java, where they were reduced to cannibalism in order to survive and sold themselves into slavery. Freed again, Mendes Pinto borrowed money to start a trading operation with Thailand. He became involved in Burmese-Thai wars and wrote the first European account of Burmese politics and history.

From Thailand Mendes Pinto made his second trip to Japan where he landed in the port of Kagoshima. On his departure, he brought back a Japanese stowaway whom he handed over to St. Francis Xavier in Malacca and thus inspired Xavier's effort to travel to Japan and Christianize the inhabitants. Sometime during these years in Asia, Mendes Pinto had accumulated a large fortune. He was a wealthy merchant when he made his third voyage to Japan in 1551, where Francis Xavier was installed at the court of one of the feudal lords of southern Japan. He gave Xavier the money to build the first Christian church in Japan.

In 1554 Mendes Pinto decided to return with his fortune to Portugal. While waiting in Goa for a ship back to Europe, he underwent a sudden conversion and turned over half of his fortune to the Jesuit missionaries and was ac-

cepted by them as a lay brother. He then traveled back to Japan in the company of a group of these missionaries. He was charged by the Portuguese governor in Goa with opening up diplomatic relations between Portugal and Japan, and Mendes Pinto was largely responsible for paying for this mission. At some point following his final departure from Japan in 1557, he voluntarily separated himself from the Jesuits, although he remained on good terms with the Church.

Mendes Pinto returned to Portugal on September 22, 1558. He stayed at court for four years hoping for some reward or recognition for his years of service in the Far East. When this was not forthcoming, he retired to a small estate on the Tagus River opposite Lisbon where he got married and raised a family. Sometime between the years 1569 and 1578 he wrote the book called the *Travels,* which was not published until 1614. It was then translated into most Western languages and became a best-seller throughout Europe. However, it contained so many fantastic stories that it was considered to be a work of fiction. It was only as more information about the exotic lands he visited became available that the book was recognized to be largely (but not totally) factual. Mendes Pinto died on his estate on July 8, 1583, shortly after being awarded a small pension by the Portuguese government.

Further Reading

Mendes Pinto's *Peregrinação* was first published in 1614. Since then, there have been many versions in many languages. All previous versions in English have now been superseded by a new translation: Rebecca D. Catz, trans. and ed. *The Travels of Mendes Pinto* (Chicago: University of Chicago Press, 1989). Catz includes a long introductory essay that discusses Mendes Pinto's life and the question of the accuracy of his reports. Excerpts from an earlier edition of the book can be found in Charles David Ley, *Portuguese Voyages, 1498-1663* (London: Everyman's Library, 1947; reprinted, 1965).
A previous book, Maurice Collis, *The Grand Peregrination: Life and Adventures of F.M. Pinto* (London: 1949), is also full of exciting tales and makes an interesting contrast to Catz. □

Antonio de Mendoza

Antonio de Mendoza (1490-1552) was a Spanish viceroy in Mexico and Peru who inaugurated the system of viceregal administration, which lasted nearly 3 centuries.

Antonio de Mendoza was born near Granada into one of the country's oldest and most famous families. He entered the service of Emperor Charles V, for whom he performed a number of successful diplomatic missions in Italy. He was then selected to become the first Spanish viceroy of New Spain in the New World, where he arrived in 1535.

Mendoza proved a prudent, firm, and hardworking viceroy. He had the difficult task of consolidating the royal authority, correcting the abuses of tyrannical officials, completing the pacification and conversion of the conquered Indians, and promoting the economic prosperity of the new colony to the maximum advantage of the royal treasury.

Conservative Regent

Mendoza showed a patriarchal concern for the natives and did much to secure improved treatment and legal status for them. Any sign of rebellion, however, he ruthlessly repressed. Nor did he subscribe to the views of liberal advocates of Indian rights such as Bartolomé de Las Casas, who persuaded the Crown to enact the New Laws of the Indies (1542), exempting the Indians from forced labor in the mines and on the lands of their Spanish masters. Convinced that this would only lead to economic chaos and drive the Spaniards to rebel, Mendoza suspended the New Laws until they were rescinded.

While suppressing an Indian rising, Mendoza's men had the good fortune to come upon the rich silver deposits of Zacatecas, which were to provide the Crown with one of its greatest sources of revenue from the New World. In addition to mining, the viceroy also encouraged the production of wheat, olives, silk, cloth, and cattle, and other such activities. His keen interest in exploration aroused the envy of Hernán Cortés, who had conquered Mexico and been rewarded with great estates there. Mendoza sent ships to explore the Pacific and in 1542 dispatched an expedition to the north under the command of Francisco Vásquez de Coronado in a vain attempt to discover the fabled Seven Cities of Cíbola, which he believed to be a mightier empire than that of the Aztecs.

Viceroy of Peru

Worn out after 15 years of conscientiously discharging his varied duties, Mendoza requested permission to end his days in Spain. This was refused, and he was sent instead to Peru to consolidate the royal authority after a civil war among the conquistadores. One of his first acts there was to send his son to inspect and report on the conditions under which the Indians were working in the mines. Mendoza fell ill and died before he could introduce the reforms which he saw to be necessary but which needed to be tactfully implemented if the unruly Spaniards were not to be provoked to fresh unrest. He was remembered as a stern but humane and just administrator, genuinely concerned with the welfare of the people under his jurisdiction but loyally dedicated to the service of the Crown.

Further Reading

A full-length study of the viceroy's career and achievements is Arthur S. Aiton, *Antonio de Mendoza, First Viceroy of New Spain* (1927). For background see J. H. Parry, *The Spanish Seaborne Empire* (1966), and John Hemming, *The Conquest of the Incas* (1970). □

Menelik II

Menelik (Menilik) II (1844-1913) was an Ethiopian emperor, who preserved the independence of his people by defeating a major Italian military expedition and who strengthened his kingdom through expansion and political and economic modernization.

Menelik II was born Sahle Mariam on August 19, 1844, in Ankober, one of the capitals of the autonomous central Ethiopian province of Shoa. The infant boy was formally named by his paternal grandfather, Sahle Sellasie, who was the first Shoan leader to rise to become a *negus*, or king. The name, Menelik, recalls the legendary son of Solomon and the queen of Sheba who, according to Ethiopian tradition, was the first ruler of Ethiopia, and the one to whom the family traced its ancestry. The story is told that the old Shoan king foretold that the boy would one day be a great man who would rebuild the Ethiopian empire. That such a day would come, however, was anything but certain since Ethiopia was then beset by wars and rebellions and lacked any strong, centralized authority.

Shoan independence came to an end following the brief and undistinguished reign of Menelik's father Haile Malakot (1847-55). The Shoan army was defeated by the forces of the Ethiopian emperor Tewodros II (1855-68), and

Menelik's father died while on campaign. Along with his mother, a woman of humble origins, and leading Shoan nobles, Menelik was sent into exile at Tewodros's court, and Shoa was incorporated into the renascent Ethiopian empire. The boy was tutored by his guardian, Ato Nedaw, and, beyond receiving a clerical and martial education, learned much about politics from living at the court. Not only was Menelik well treated by Tewodros, but the emperor took a personal interest in the youth's education. Menelik rose to become a *dejazmach,* or earl, and married Altash, Tewodros's daughter.

By 1865, Menelik was faced with a difficult personal decision. Shoa had broken away from Tewodros's fledgling empire and a usurper claimed the Shoan throne. Deciding to flee the imperial court to reclaim his patrimony, Menelik quickly defeated the Shoan usurper and proclaimed himself *negus.* The young king built his power base from the Shoan army and conservative nobles. At the same time, he pursued enlightened policies such as extending religious toleration to Muslims and animists in his Christian kingdom. Fortunately for the young monarch, Shoa was relatively insulated from the civil wars which ravaged northern Ethiopia during the last years of Tewodros's reign. When Tewodros became involved in a diplomatic imbroglio with Great Britain over the taking of British hostages, Menelik remained neutral. Unable or unwilling to move against his former benefactor, Menelik's failure to join forces with the Europeans resulted in a major setback for the Shoan's ambitions after a British expeditionary force defeated Tewodros at Magdala in 1868. With Tewodros dead, power now passed to a rival named Kasa who used British arms to advance his claim to the imperial title. Although Menelik had also proclaimed himself emperor, he could only watch and wait when Kasa assumed the crown as Yohannes IV (1872-89).

Menelik had made a serious strategic blunder, as his biographer Harold Marcus points out, but he had also learned the value of using European power and technology for furthering his aspirations. He turned to the Italians and French for weapons as well as to other European countries for Western technology. It was roughly at this time that Alfred Ilg arrived from Zurich and began a long sojourn in Ethiopia, serving as an engineer, architect, and eventually as a trusted advisor to his royal patron. Likewise, Menelik also permitted foreign missionaries to enter his kingdom to convert the Oromo peoples who constituted a significant proportion of the population.

Beyond the importation of technology from Europe, Menelik recognized the importance of establishing diplomatic ties with foreign powers. Although he was forced to renounce his claim to the imperial throne and to do fealty to Yohannes in March 1878, in reality he continued to act as an independent sovereign. The Shoan *negus* had earlier cultivated the friendship of Egypt in its short-lived attempt at imperialistic expansion into the Horn of Africa. Menelik next went behind Yohannes's back and negotiated with the Mahdists, a group of fundamentalist Muslims who had taken power in neighboring Sudan. Furthermore, Menelik had long maintained friendly relations with Victorian England

and had, in 1883, entered into a treaty of amity and commerce with the Italians.

The other significant development during this part of Menelik's life was the expansion of the Shoan kingdom. Imperialist adventures were made necessary by the need for increased revenues to pay tribute to Yohannes. Blocked toward the north by Yohannes, Shoan armies marched south into Oromo-speaking areas and to the east where they conquered the Muslim emirate of Harar. Using arms purchased from the West, these expeditions not only plundered these prosperous regions, but also gave Menelik access to important trade routes and new sources of ivory and slaves. Moreover, the Shoans established fortified villages throughout the newly conquered territories from which they maintained control and into which settlers and missionaries came from the north. Such colonization led to the diffusion of Shoa's Amharic culture into these newly aggrandized lands. This Amharization was a significant development because it contributed to the integration of diverse societies into Menelik's burgeoning empire. It is important to note that by forcing Menelik to pay tribute, Yohannes's policies had the paradoxical effect of strengthening his rival. Indeed, these decades were a turning point in Ethiopian history as there was a strategic shift in the locus of wealth and power in Ethiopia from the north to the south.

Menelik's growing might put him on a collision course with Yohannes. At a time when Yohannes was preparing to fight the Italians, Menelik concluded a secret agreement with Italy (1887), whereby he exchanged Shoan neutrality for European weapons. Although nominally a subject to Yohannes, Menelik even proposed that he act as a mediator between the Ethiopian emperor and Italy. However, the seemingly inevitable confrontation between the Ethiopian rivals was not to be. At the battle of Metemma in March 1889, Yohannes died fighting, not Menelik or the Italian colonialists, but a Mahdist army. Henceforward, no force could stand in the way of Menelik's ambitions.

Acting quickly, Menelik was crowned *negus negast* (king of kings), or emperor, on November 3, 1889. By May the following year, he had concluded the famous Treaty of Wichale with the Italian representative Pietro Antonelli. As the historian G.N. Sanderson has observed, the treaty was important because it insured that Italy would not recognize any other claim to Menelik's imperial title. For the Italians, the treaty confirmed their special relationship with Ethiopia.

From this point forward, however, relations between Italy and Ethiopia progressively degenerated. It soon was revealed that there was a difference in the Amharic and Italian translations of Article XVII of the Treaty of Wichale. Basing their assertion on the Italian text of the treaty, Italy claimed protectorate status over Ethiopia even though the Amharic version recognized Menelik's sovereignty. Beyond this diplomatic deception, Menelik became more and more suspicious of Italian ambitions in the northern Ethiopian province of Tigre. He renounced the treaty in 1893 and, even while famine raged in his kingdom, imposed new taxes to pay off the huge debts he owed to Italy. The failure of Italian attempts to divide and conquer Ethiopia through an alliance with rebellious Tigre ultimately led Italy to take more forceful measures. Italian forces moved into Tigre in December 1894, and Italy publicly proclaimed Ethiopia as its protectorate. In September of the following year, Menelik called for the mobilization of Ethiopia. Able to amass an army of 120,000 men, the emperor moved north and at Adwa, on March 1, 1896, met an overconfident Italian expeditionary force composed of 20,000 troops. By inflicting a crushing defeat on the Italians (70% of whom were either killed, wounded, or taken prisoner), Menelik won Ethiopia another 40 years of independence.

The battle at Adwa also put an end to centuries of Ethiopian isolation. Menelik had demonstrated to the world that an African kingdom could defeat a European army and diplomats flocked to his new capital, Addis Ababa. The Ethiopian emperor proved himself an astute statesman and beat the Europeans at their own diplomatic game. Pragmatic in victory, Menelik did not seek to expel the Italians from their colony of Eritrea; instead, he settled for Italy's recognition of Ethiopian independence. Moreover he used the Europeans' concept of "effective occupation" to wring territorial concessions from neighboring French and British colonies. Finally, Menelik's policy of detente with Mahdist Sudan saved Ethiopia from continued warfare with his Muslim neighbors.

With the threat of foreign intervention removed, Menelik spent the last active decade of his rule strengthening centralized power and modernizing Ethiopia's political system. In the provinces, he replaced hereditary rulers with appointed officials and garrisoned troops in some of the empire's potentially rebellious districts. Changes were also made in the judicial system whereby appellate judges were placed over the provinces. As the emperor sought to enhance the national power of Ethiopia, he increasingly took a direct hand in administration and, like the great French monarch, Louis XIV, he identified himself with the state. Only when he recognized the nature of his declining health, did Menelik create Ethiopia's first cabinet in 1907. In addition, he sought to regularize taxation and end a system whereby soldiers in effect looted the peasantry.

In his last years, Menelik promoted a host of notable reforms in Ethiopia. Bridges and modern roads were built, a postal system was organized, and telegraph lines were erected. More important still, a railroad was begun which eventually linked Addis Ababa with the French-controlled Red Sea port of Djibouti. The creation of this transportation and communications infrastructure opened new markets as well as contributing to the national integrity of the empire. Among many other changes which occurred in this period were the introduction of a national currency and mint, as well as the establishment of the Bank of Abyssinia. The capital had its first hotel, Western-style school, and hospital, and a state printing press began operations in 1911.

Menelik at the height of his power was often compared with the great German nation-builder, Otto von Bismarck. Along with his diplomatic and military accomplishments, there was near unanimity among foreign visitors as to his intelligence and ability. Fascinated by Western machinery and technology, Menelik took a personal interest in photography, medicine, and mechanical devices.

Perhaps the greatest failure of his reign was his inability to provide for a stable succession. Beginning in 1906, he suffered a series of apoplectic seizures and gradually began to lose his faculties. The emperor designated his grandson, Lij Iyasu, as heir in 1908, and a regency was created since Iyasu was still a youth. By Octoer 1909, Menelik lay paralyzed and totally incapacitated. With the emperor supine, his wife, the empress Taitu, ruled in all but name until she was deposed by a palace coup in 1910. The untimely death of the regent and the impetuosity of young Lij Iyasu further contributed to the breakdown of centralized authority in Ethiopia. While the emperor lingered on, much of the work which he had done to build a strong national monarchy came undone. The merciful denouement came on the night of December 12-13, 1913, when Menelik breathed his last. The great task of modernizing Ethiopia lay unfinished and would be left to another great emperor—Haile Selassie.

Further Reading

A good analysis of Menelek is in Harold Marcus's chapter in Lewis Gann, ed., *Colonialism in Africa*, vol. 1 (1969). Richard Greenfield, *Ethiopia: A New Political History* (1965), is a good general history of the country, and Edward Ullendorff, *The Ethiopians* (1960; 2d ed. 1965), is a fine treatment of the people and their culture.

Additional Sources

Akpan, M. B. "Liberia and Ethiopia, 1880-1914: the Survival of Two African States," in *General History of Africa, VII.* Edited by A. Adu Boahen, University of California Press, 1985.

Berkeley, G.F-H. *The Campaign of Adowa and the Rise of Menelik.* 1902, reprinted, Negro Universities Press, 1969.

Lipschutz, Mark R., and R. Kent Rasmussen. *Dictionary of African Historical Biography.* Aldine, 1978.

Marcus, Harold G. "Imperialism and expansionism in Ethiopia from 1865 to 1900," in *Colonialism in Africa 1870-1960.* Vol. 1. Edited by L. H. Gann and Peter Duignan. Cambridge University Press, 1969.

———. *The Life and Times of Menelik II: Ethiopia 1844-1913,* Clarendon Press, 1975; Lawrenceville, N.J.: Red Sea Press, 1995.

Prather, Ray, *The King of Kings of Ethiopia, Menelik II,* Nairobi: Kenya Literature Bureau, 1981.

Prouty, Chris, and Eugene Rosenfeld. *Historical Dictionary of Ethiopia.* Scarecrow Press, 1981.

Pankhurst, Richard. *History of Ethiopia.* Addis Ababa: Ministry of Education and Fine Arts, 1970.

Prouty, Chris. *Empress Taytu and Menilek II: Ethiopia 1883-1910.* Trenton, N.J.: Red Sea Press, 1986. □

Carlos Sául Menem

Carlos Sául Menem (born 1930) was the first Peronist president to come to power in Argentina after the overthrow of Isabel Perón by the military in 1976 and the first legally elected civilian president to succeed another civilian government since 1928. He was also one of the few to serve two terms in succession.

Born on July 2, 1930, Carlos Sául Menem was the son of Syrian immigrants who settled in the interior province of La Rioja, Argentina, and eventually built up a prosperous wine business. After receiving a degree in law in 1955, he practiced law in his native province and became a popular Peronist politician, heading the party's provincial council. He ran for office several times during the 1960s and in 1973 easily won the election for governor. However, his term was curtailed by the military's overthrow of Isabel Perón in 1976, and he was arrested along with the other Peronist leaders. He spent the next five years in prison or in internal exile.

In the elections of 1983, which witnessed the triumph of Rául Alfonsín and the Radical Party, Menem was again elected governor of La Rioja province. He was reelected for a third term in 1987 and served until July 1989 when, as the result of his victory in the presidential election, he took over the presidency of Argentina. He would then win each election through 1996. The last was only allowed though constitutional reforms allowing him to run for re-election.

Menem had been one of the leaders of the Renovator, or social democratic wing, of the Peronist Party which emerged with a new national plan in 1985. He was above all, however, a pragmatic politician who, because of his political ambitions, had converted from the Sunni Muslim faith to Roman Catholicism, since in Argentina only Roman Catholics are constitutionally eligible to hold public office. He was, therefore, willing to compromise in his pursuit of the presidency. In the party's first ever presidential primary, held in mid-1988, he sought the support of various Peronist politicians, including a number of the old-line party bosses who were opposed by the Renovators. Promising to represent the workers and the neglected people of the interior, Menem won the primary in July, defeating his main rival and the front-running candidate, Antonio Cafiero, a long-time Peronist politician and governor of Buenos Aires province.

In the presidential campaign Menem promised a production revolution to solve Argentina's economic crisis. He also called for wage increases and jobs for the workers, as well as a corporatist social pact among business, labor, and the state on the economy. In the area of foreign policy he favored a five-year moratorium on Argentina's international debt and implied that he would attempt to regain militarily the British-ruled Malvinas (or Falkland) Islands. He did not, however, promise the armed forces the amnesty which they had been seeking for the violation of human rights in the so-called Dirty War under the military regime, in which thousands of Argentines were tortured, murdered, and/or disappeared—by varying estimates, anywhere from about 10,000 to 30,000 people.

The principal issue in the presidential campaign was the economic performance of the government of President Rául Alfonsín, which failed to provide continued economic stability or halt Argentina's rapidly accelerating inflation despite a series of anti-inflation austerity plans. Vying with the economy as a major issue was the personality of Menem, who cultivated a playboy image and was well known to enjoy racing sports cars, playing soccer, and spending time with glamorous show people.

Menem won a decisive victory in the election held on May 14, 1989, sweeping the Peronists back into power for the first time since 1976 when Isabel Perón was ousted by the military. Winning 47.3 percent of the vote, he clearly defeated his seven opponents, including Eduardo Angeloz, the candidate of the governing Radical Party, who ran second with 37 percent of the votes. Besides winning the presidency, the Peronists gained control of both houses of Congress and most of the provincial legislatures. The election, which left the Radical Party the strongest party in the opposition, was the first time since 1928 in which one democratically elected civilian president succeeded another.

According to the constitution Alfonsín was to hand over the presidency to Menem on December 1, 1989, six months after the election. But public confidence in Alfonsín had sunk to such a low level, primarily because of the failure of his economic plan, he finally decided to give in to the general demand he depart early in order to give Menem a head start with his program to restore Argentina's economy. On July 8, 1989, some five months ahead of schedule, Alfonsín turned over the presidency to Menem.

The Peronist victory occurred at the time when Argentina was facing one of its most serious economic crises. Economically, the primary task of the new Menem government was to solve the problem of Argentina's hyperinflation, which was running at an annual rate of 6000 percent and devastating the economy. In conjunction with his plan of economic restructuring, Menem initiated a pro-

gram to trim payrolls of the public sector, eliminate government subsidies for the private sector, privatize a number of state-run companies, and increase tax revenues. Although his austerity measures faced substantial resistance from the opposition parties, the business community, and organized labor, by the early part of 1990 Argentina's rampant inflation had subsided considerably and there were signs that the economy was improving.

By pardoning a number of military officers found guilty of human rights violations in the 1970s and by supporting the military high command, Menem managed to ease civil-military relations, which had plagued the administration of Alfonsín. President Menem also exonerated the officers responsible for the Malvinas Islands war and the military personnel involved in the barracks revolts during the last two years of the Alfonsín regime. In addition to pardoning several military men awaiting trial for crimes during the dirty war, he pardoned some of the guerrilla leaders accused of leftist terrorist activities during the 1970s.

On the question of the Malvinas Islands, Menem temporarily put aside the issue of sovereignty and, in what amounted to a major foreign policy coup, renewed full diplomatic relations with the United Kingdom. Regarding the problem of Argentina's international debt, Menem was quick to visit the United States and the various European capitals in order to assure Argentina's creditors that his government was eager to negotiate a solution to Argentina's indebtedness. Menem suggested negotiating debt relief measures, including a grace period on interest payments to Argentina's creditors. To deal with the international drug traffic, Menem advocated a multilateral approach and created a drug secretariat which represented Argentina in various regional and international organizations. Favoring Latin American economic integration, in August 1989 the government of Menem signed a series of economic cooperation protocols with Argentina's traditional South American rival, Brazil.

But the violence continued. Two terrorist attacks in Buenos Aires, one on the Israeli embassy in 1992, a second on a Jewish centre in 1994, were not solved. The bombing of the embassy killed between 32 and 40 people, and at least 86 died in the community-centre bombing. Yet, though alleged accomplices were arrested, no one was charged or even credibly named as directly responsible for the bombings.

This was just one of many examples of mishandled Argentine criminal investigations. In July 1996, Menem tried to help the situation by firing his justice minister, who was revealed to have belonged, as a youth, to a Nazi-leaning group. Menem made fresh efforts to track down known ex-Nazis and stolen Jewish assets, but with little success.

Menem was married to Zulema FatimaYoma, who was highly visible throughout the presidential campaigns. Menem's brother Eduardo was a senator and one of his chief advisers, while another brother, Munir, was ambassador to Syria.

Further Reading

For autobiographical information and a summary of Menem's ideas see in Spanish his *Menem* (1986); *Yo Carlos Menem* (1989); *Renovacíon a fondo* (1986); and *Argentina, ahoca o nunca* (1988). Additional information on Menem and the program of the Renovators is provided in Alfredo Leuco and José Antonio Díaz, *El heredor del Peron* (1989), and Antonio Francisco Cafiero, *Hablan los renovadores* (1986). For an excellent discussion of the Peronist movement since the fall of Isabel Perón in 1976 see Donald C. Hodges, in English, *Argentina 1943-1987; The National Revolution and Resistance. Revised and Enlarged Edition* (1988). See also the *Economist,* (April 26, 1997) and *Los Angeles Times,* (October 25, 1996). ☐

Pedro Menéndez de Avilés

Pedro Menéndez de Avilés (1519-1574) was a Spanish seaman and colonizer. Among the most renowned seamen of his time, he founded St. Augustine, the first permanent white settlement in what is now the United States.

Pedro Menéndez was born on Feb. 15, 1519, at Avilés, a seaport in Asturias. Being one of 20 brothers and sisters, he knew his inheritance would be small and decided to earn his livelihood as a seaman. At the age of 14 he ran away to sea, embarking on a ship which sailed from Santander to engage French corsairs. Upon his return he sold a portion of his patrimony and purchased a vessel of his own. One of his most celebrated feats occurred in 1549, when he encountered Jean Alphonse, the most feared of the corsairs. After boarding the pirate's ship he fought a single-handed duel with Alphonse, mortally wounding him.

Menéndez's daring exploits and naval prowess won him fame, fortune, and increasingly important missions to command. In 1554 Emperor Charles V named Menéndez captain general of the Fleet of the Indies, a position which offered great opportunities for personal gain by irregular methods. But, unlike many of his predecessors, Menéndez was a man of integrity and refused to take bribes. In 1555 he made the first of six transatlantic voyages to America.

Philip II selected Menéndez to outfit and command a colonizing expedition to Florida. The first objective of the mission was to eradicate a French Huguenot settlement at Ft. Caroline at the mouth of the St. Johns River. The second objective was to plant fortified settlements along the coastline to provide refuge, from hurricanes and pirates, for the treasure fleets returning to Spain by way of the Bahama Channel.

Sailing from Spain on July 29, 1565, Menéndez first sighted Florida off Cape Canaveral on August 28. While sailing northward he discovered a harbor on September 6 where he established a settlement and fort, naming it St. Augustine. Meanwhile, the French had divided their forces, some remaining at Ft. Caroline but most boarding ships and sailing southward in search of the Spaniards. A hurricane

Menéndez: Captain General of the Ocean Sea (1965). Other useful accounts of his career are included in Edward G. Bourne, *Spain in America, 1450-1580* (1904), and Herbert E. Bolten, *The Spanish Borderlands* (1921).

Additional Sources

Manucy, Albert C., *Florida's Menéndez: captain general of the ocean sea,* St. Augustine, Fla.: St. Augustine Historical Society, 1983.
Manucy, Albert C., *Menéndez: Pedro Menéndez de Avilés, Captain General of the Ocean Sea,* Sarasota, Fla.: Pineapple Press, 1992.
Pedro Menéndez de Avilés, New York: Garland Pub., 1995. □

King Menes

Menes's reign of Egypt from 3407 to 3346 B.C. was treated as the dawn of Egyptian civilization in many classical histories. In earlier Egyptian lore he was called Ohe and Mena, "The Fighter," and then was referred to as "The Established." He is remembered as the conqueror who first united Egypt under one rule and established the famous capital of Memphis, the seat of Egypt's unparalleled cultural achievements during the time of the Pharaohs.

I n the fourth century B.C., Ptolemy II Philadelphus ordered the priest Manetho to compile a complete history of Egypt for his great library at Alexandria. Menes was the earliest man that he mentioned by name, as the first king of the First Dynasty of Upper and Lower Egypt. Modern archaeological findings have since displaced Menes as the first name in Egyptian history, and though experts today agree that Mena is the correct name for one of the first kings of Upper and Lower Egypt, there is some doubt that Menes was the military "Unifier of the Two Lands." Discerning the role of Menes in the "hazy outline of the general drift of events" in predynastic Egypt has been a major topic of discussion for J. H. Breasted and other twentieth century Egyptologists, and the reader of modern histories of Egypt will find that Menes is still a favorite subject for creative hypothesis and scholarly debate. He is still regarded by some scholars as the legendary military conqueror who unified Egypt through war, but others now hypothesize that Lower Egypt had already been conquered at least a generation before Menes, and that Menes was actually a savvy politician who consolidated the legal claim to the throne of the southern "Hawk-kings" by assuming the gods and rituals of the north, and by marrying into their most prominent royal family.

The Unification of Upper and Lower Egypt

Manetho's treatment of the generations before Menes as "prehistoric" or "predynastic" has fostered the misconception that Menes was the first king *in* Egypt. Today it is

struck, sinking or dismasting all of the ships. By October, Menéndez had captured Ft. Caroline and dispassionately massacred most of the shipwrecked French Huguenots. The site of the massacres is still known by its Spanish name of Matanzas (massacres).

In 1568 Menéndez was appointed governor of Cuba. Drawing upon his experiences as captain general of the Fleet of the Indies, he perfected the convoy-escort fleet, which helped protect the treasure fleets from the depredations of pirates.

In 1572 Menéndez returned to Spain, where Philip II appointed him captain general of the Armada that was to invade England. Menéndez unexpected death on Sept. 17, 1574, may have altered the course of history. The "invincible" Armada, which sailed on its disastrous mission in 1588, was subsequently entrusted to the Duke of Medina-Sidonia, a courageous man but an inept seaman.

Further Reading

Two biographies written by contemporaries of Menéndez have been translated: Gonzalo Solis, *Pedro de Menéndez de Aviles: Memorial,* translated by Jeanette Thurber Conner (1923), was written by Menéndez's brother-in-law, who participated in the expedition of 1565; and *Pedro Menéndez de Aviles, Founder of Florida,* translated by Anthony Kerrigan (1965), was written by a professor of Latin at the University of Salamanca. The most extensive and balanced narrative history of Menéndez's career is Woodbury Lowery, *The Spanish Settlements within the Present Limits of the United States: Florida, 1562-1574* (1905). See also Albert Manucy, *Florida's*

known that Egypt contained a number of advanced and organized societies as early as the sixth millennium B.C. The ancestors of Menes, named "Horus-people" or "Hawk-people" after an early king who became one of their chief gods, consolidated the disparate southern districts around the First Cataract of Aswan in the Nile Valley into the Upper Kingdom, named for its location upstream on the north-ward-flowing Nile. The Hawk-people established their center at Theni during the reigns of as many as 50 kings while they gradually fought their way northward (down the Nile) against the "Set-people," presumably a wealthier and more advanced civilization who controlled the enviable farmland in the Fertile Crescent. Besides ideal farmland that never required irrigation, the Delta region also had the advantage of proximity to the Mediterranean Sea, the ancient highway of commerce, for trading with the ancient Syrians and Libyans. In roughly 3400 B.C. after a very long period of war, the Horus-worshipers defeated the north in a battle near Anu (Heliopolis), and established their rule over the Delta region and the entrance to the sea.

By the account of Manetho, recorded three millennia later, the victorious Hawk-king was Menes. Egyptologists in the twentieth century, however, try to give Manetho as little credence as the availability of more reliable evidence allows. J. H. Breasted, the premier Egyptian scholar of the early 20th century, even called Manetho's writings "the compilation of puerile folk-tales . . . hardly worthy of the name history." In the case of Menes, however, the most informative artifacts have actually confused his identity by providing the descriptions of two other kings that correspond in name or in deed with his legend: Narmer and Aha.

The most famous piece of evidence concerning the "Unifier of the Two Lands" is a predynastic slate palette found among the ruins of Nekhen (Hierakonpolis) and entitled 'Narmer.' The slate depicts a king wearing the signature White Crown of the south with a mace held over his head, preparing to club a kneeling figure wearing the Red Crown of the north. Scholars all agree that Narmer was the king who took control of the north, but because it was traditional for Egyptian kings to be known by as many as five names, some Egyptologists are comfortable with the simple explanation that Menes and Narmer were two names used by the same man. The complications with the archaeological record arose when a piece of ivory label was found near Thebes, bearing the first and only contemporary mention of the fabled Menes.

The Horus-king inscription was that of Aha, previously known as a king who reigned shortly before or shortly after Narmer. Along with the Horus-inscription was a so-called Nebti title, which referred to the two great goddesses of the north and south, indicating that the label referred to a time after the unification of the two lands. This sign bore the name of Mena, and many scholars now argue that Aha is the Upper Kingdom or Horus-name, and Mena the combined kingdom or Nebti-name for the same king. In 1961 Sir Alan Gardiner gave a scenario in which Ohe Meni (Aha-Menes) was actually the son of Narmer, born a Horus-king, who took several important political steps in consolidating the kingdom after the military conquest that later earned him

the title of Meni "The Established" in the north and in the south.

Gardiner posited that Menes followed Narmer as the Hawk-king at Theni when he was not much older than 15, at which time he was known as Ohe or Aha. Some time after he was recognized in the south he married Princess Neihotpe, the heiress to the throne of the Set-people of Fayum, just south of the Delta region and then took on the title of Meni. This strategic marriage could explain why Menes could become tradition's first king of the Upper and Lower Kingdoms even if Narmer had gained the surrender of the northern armies before Menes acceded the throne. According to Gardiner, "The Egyptians were ever sticklers for legal form," and the northern people would not be apt to recognize the power of a man who had no legal ties to their ruling family. Menes's name could easily have eclipsed Narmer's as the story was passed down through generations if his kingship was more widely recognized.

Menes's Architectural and Cultural Legacy

Menes left the temples and festivals of Set in place, and assumed the other gods of the north as well. His wise actions make it clear that the worshipers of Horus had no intention of wiping out the advancements of the Set-people, but attacked in order to establish a premise for the civilizations to merge, albeit under Horus's control. It was not until the fifth king of the unified kingdom, King Semti, that the combined hieroglyph meaning "King of the South, King of the North" was put into use, indicating that the First Dynasty kings did establish their power in the north gradually, and not in a single, decisive, imperialistic step.

The city of Memphis, a Greek rendering of the Egyptian Men-nofre, meaning "The Well-Established," was built on the site of an earlier stronghold of the Upper or "White" Kingdom known as White Wall. It was strategically located in the center of the unified kingdom, a few miles south of modern Cairo on the west side of the Nile. In order to capture "the sweet northern breeze" that blew south along the Nile from the Mediterranean, Menes built the city right in the Nile's flood plain, and constructed a great dam to divert the river during the annual inundation. Memphis was a nearly unassailable city, because the temperate valley of the Nile turned immediately into hot, barren desert on the East and West.

Diodorus recorded that Menes established the rituals of divine worship in the new city, and that he taught the citizens "how to adorn their couches and tables with rich cloths and coverings, and was the first that brought in an elegant and sumptuous way of living." The tradition continued that Menes founded the temple of Ptah, the divine Craftsman and Potter of the gods, and we can see from later events that Ptah was lavishly worshiped at Memphis. Some 600 years later the Third Dynasty vizier Imhotep, who became the divine son of Ptah, was said to have appeased the god by instructing his King Zoser to make an offering of 70 miles on either side of the Nile along with its full harvest, in addition to the temple's usual endowment of food and precious metals.

With the Upper and Lower Kingdoms continuing to stabilize as a single culture, the Memphites took advantage of the security of the capital and the superb farming conditions there to amass an unprecedentedly large surplus of food, a luxury which historians believe was the key to the rapid advancement of government institutions and the phenomenal leaps in technology that occurred at Memphis over the next thousand years. With easy access to the Mediterranean, the surplus food could be dearly traded with the Syria-Palestinians, Libyans, and Mesopotamians, and the Memphites quickly progressed from the elegant, sumptuous way of living introduced by Menes to the opulent displays of wealth and achievement that they are known for today.

Duplicate Tombs Present Questions

The ancient Egyptians had a custom of honoring their kings by taking their bodies to the site of their rule for burial. For the kings who ruled exclusively at Memphis, the burial site was nearby Sakkara. Menes and the other kings of the First Dynasty who ruled during the construction of Memphis, however, were also recognized at Theni, posing a dilemma for those who had to decide where they should be enshrined. The First Dynasty kings, including King Aha, solved this problem by constructing tombs at both Sakkara and Abydos—a real tomb which would house the mummy, and a cenotaph, an empty tomb to serve as a shrine rather than an actual grave. Since no bones were found in either location, Egyptologists will never know which was the real grave and which was the empty marker, and the scant evidence that can be gleaned from Menes's burial is as duplicitous as the record of his life. Instead of providing new answers, the evidence of Aha's tombs has provided only another heated topic for discussion in the attempt to discover the identity of Menes.

Further Reading

Mertz, Barbara, *Temples, Tombs and Hieroglyphs,* Coward-McCann, Inc., 1964.
Breasted, James Henry, *A History of the Ancient Egyptians,* John Murray, 1928.
Budge, E. A. Wallace, *A Short History of the Egyptian People,* E. P. Dutton & Co., 1914.
Gardiner, Sir Alan, *Egypt of the Pharaohs:,* Oxford University Press, 1961. □

Josef Mengele

During the last two years of World War II Josef Mengele (1911-1979), a German physician, conducted atrocious medical experiments and sent tens of thousands of Jews to the gas chambers at Auschwitz/Birkenau, a concentration camp in southwestern Poland. In 1949 he fled Germany for Latin America where, 30 years later, he died by drowning. He was never apprehended and thus was never prosecuted as a war criminal.

The son of an agricultural machinery manufacturer in Günzburg, Bavaria, Josef Mengele was born on March 16, 1911. Brought up as a Catholic, the popular and talented boy grew into a promising, ambitious student. He received his doctorate in medicine under Otmar Freiherr von Verschuer in 1938 with a dissertation on hereditary deformities. Von Verschuer, director of the Frankfurt University Institute for Hereditary Biology and Racial Hygiene—established in 1934 to pursue research in a field strongly supported by the fanatically racist National Socialist regime—made Mengele his assistant. Since twins were especially suited for genetics research, Mengele focussed his work on them.

His academic career was interrupted by World War II, during which he served in the military, first with the army mountain troops, then with the 5th SS Panzer "Viking" Division. He became a battalion surgeon with the rank of SS-captain and was repeatedly decorated for valor. Severely wounded in fighting on the Donets River in Russia during the spring of 1943, Mengele was declared unfit for combat duty, and in May he was assigned to Auschwitz (Oswiecim), where some two million people, most of them Jews, were murdered—largely by poison gas. Until January 20, 1945, he conducted experiments on inmates, concentrating on twins and dwarfs. His victims were Jews and Gypsies, females as well as males, children as well as grown-ups.

In his position as "health director" Mengele, according to an inmate-physician's postwar testimony, "was the first one to rid the entire women's camp of lice. He simply had an entire block gassed." Disposing of 750 women in this manner, and thereby reducing the danger of typhus, was for Mengele a morally and scientifically rational option.

Mengele was interested in eyes. He sent pairs of different colors to Verschuer, who after the war said he had not known that they had come from persons killed for their sake. Also, in order to see if it were possible to change the color of the iris, Mengele gave dozens of children eye injections, causing agony, at least one case of partial blindness, and the death of a newborn baby.

His primary interest remained twins. Mengele studied their similarities and differences under conditions unprecedented in his field: the circumstance, for example, of both twins dying at the same time from the same cause—such as an injection, according to the postwar testimony of his autopsist, of chloroform into the heart.

Aside from conducting experiments on humans and screening new arrivals at Auschwitz for slave labor, laboratory exploitation, or the gas chamber, Mengele organized Bach concerts, wrote skits, and created a lilliputian circus for the dwarfs he collected for his lethal research—to which, in the end, they also were sacrificed.

As World War II drew to a close and the SS destroyed the gas chamber and crematoria in Auschwitz, Mengele reluctantly gathered up his extensive research notes and disappeared. The notes never resurfaced, but Mengele did a number of times. He was reportedly arrested in 1947 by two American servicemen in Vienna, Austria, but released by the U.S. Army's C.I.C. (Counter-intelligence Corps) because the British wanted to use him as an agent. In 1949, before going to Latin America, he lived in his home town of Günzburg in the U.S. Zone of Occupation; the Cold War had begun, West Germany was being brought into the Western alliance, and Washington had no interest in harassing old Nazis who, if nothing else, were known to be anti-communist.

After about ten years in Argentina Mengele moved on to Paraguay, ruled by a pro-German, right-wing military dictatorship. Repeated requests were made to extradite Mengele to West Germany, where he was wanted for the murder of 2,000 human beings and for rendering assistance in the killing of another 200,000, but a concerted international effort to apprehend him, supported by a reward of some $2 million, was made only in the mid-1980s. By then he was (supposedly) dead, having drowned in 1979 at a Brazilian beach resort and having been buried under an assumed name. His remains were identified in 1985 by Brazilian, German, and American forensic specialists, and his death was confirmed by his family in Germany. By that time, the five-year statute of limitations in the Federal Republic of Germany precluded anyone being prosecuted for having aided and abetted Mengele's flight from justice. During the second half of his life he evidently was treated as a political refugee rather than as one of the cruelest tormentors of his fellow man in recorded history.

Further Reading

The "Last" Nazi! The Life and Times of Dr. Josef Mengele (1985) by Gerald Astor argues that he was the product of his time and environment. An article by Robert Jay Lifton, "What Made This Man? Mengele," published on July 21, 1985, in the New York Times Magazine, was adapted from a book on Nazi doctors published in 1986. A graphic picture of Mengele's activity emerges from a report on a West German trial of Auschwitz personnel in the mid-1960s by Bernd Naumann in Auschwitz, translated by Jean Steinberg, with an introduction by Hannah Arendt (1966). The Holocaust, vol. 9, Medical Experiments on Jewish Inmates of Concentration Camps, edited and with an introduction by John Mendelsohn (1982), provides authentic archival material in facsimile (in English or in German with English translation) on the kind of work in which Mengele and his colleagues were engaged. In The Destruction of the European Jews (1961) Raul Hilberg describes the medical experiments in the context of his comprehensive history of the Holocaust. In German, there is a probing, analytical, yet humane account of what went on in Auschwitz by a former Austrian inmate, Menschen in Auschwitz (Vienna, 1972) by Hermann Langbein, who also carefully edited and annotated a two-volume account of the West German trial mentioned above, Der Auschwitz-Prozess. Eine Dokumentation (Frankfurt, 1965). In Mengele: The Complete Story (1986) authors Gerald L. Posner and John Ware discuss how he escaped from Germany after World War II and survived for more than 30 years in South America.

Additional Sources

Abraham, Ben, The Angel of Death: the Mengele dossier, Sao Paulo, Brazil: Sherit Hapleita, Brazilian Association of the Survivors of Nazism, 1986. □

Mengistu Haile Mariam

Lt. Col. Mengistu Haile Mariam (born 1937) became the head of state of Ethiopia and chairman of the ruling military government (the *Derg*) after a 1974 revolution deposed Emperor Haile Selassie. He was also the head of the central committee of Ethiopia's Socialist Workers Party. Mengistu resigned as head of state in 1991 and fled into exile.

There are few details available on the early life of Mengistu. He was born in 1937 in the southern Ethiopian district of Walayta. His father was a soldier and his mother a servant. Some accounts of his youth maintain that at a young age he moved to Addis Ababa with his mother and grew up in the household of a prominent nobleman Ras Kebbede Tesemma.

Rose to Position of Power

As a young man Mengistu joined the army and served as a private before attending Ethiopia's Holeta Military Academy. He graduated in 1966 with the rank of second lieutenant and was assigned to the logistical and ordnance section of the Ethiopian army's Third Division in Harar, a strategically important southwestern market town. By 1974 Mengistu had risen to the rank of major and had developed effective leadership skills which made him popular among his fellow junior officers and the rank and file of the Third Division. These talents proved important in his rise to the top of Ethiopia's military government in the political vacuum during the revolution.

Mengistu rose to prominence as a result of the military's key role in the Ethiopian revolution that in September 1974 deposed Emperor Haile Selassie, who had ruled Ethiopia since 1916. The revolution began in the wake of the 1973 oil crisis, revelations that the Haile Selassie government had covered up a major famine in the north, and general dissatisfaction in the modern sector with the rule of Ethiopia's elite classes. In the rural south and west absentee landlords from the north imposed heavy taxes and tributes on peasant farmers whose lands had been conquered by northern armies a generation earlier. In the political vacuum which followed the fall of the imperial government Ethiopia's military gradually took control, a process which culminated in the massacre of 60 members of the Haile Selassie government in November 1974.

Emerged as Leader

In the summer of 1974 the new 126-member Provisional Military Advisory Council (PMAC), or Derg, had nationalized many key foreign investments and declared a policy of *Ethiopia Tikdem* (Ethiopia First). In July 1974 the PMAC elected Mengistu as its chairman. When the PMAC was formally organized in September he was named first vice-chairman, a position he held until he took complete control in February 1977.

the problem of Eritrea, a former Italian colony and province of Ethiopia in which rebels had been fighting for independence since 1962.

Formed New Governing Body

In mid-1980 Mengistu announced the formation of COPWE (Committee to form the Party of the Workers of Ethiopia), intended to replace the PMAC as the ruling body of the country. Mengistu served as chairman of the executive and central committees of COPWE, whose seven-man central committee was made up of the PMAC's own central committee with Mengistu at the head. COPWE served for four years as an arm of the government which paralleled many of the functions of the Council of Ministers and which prepared the ground for the announcement of a new socialist party. Many observers felt that Mengistu and other top military officials resisted pressure from the former Soviet government to form such a party since it represented a threat to Mengistu's rule at the top.

Mengistu's foreign policy followed closely that of his allies, and he was recognized by Fidel Castro of Cuba as a true revolutionary leader. Between 1977 and 1984 Mengistu made seven visits to the former Soviet Union, and a number of other visits to political allies Cuba, Libya, South Yemen, and Mozambique. From 1983 to 1984 Mengistu served as head of the Organization of African Unity, a result of Ethiopia having served as site for the 1982 OAU meetings.

In September 1984 the celebration of the tenth anniversary of the Ethiopian revolution culminated in the formal declaration of the Party of the Workers of Ethiopia, a Marxist-Leninist party designed to take over from the PMAC. Mengistu was named head of the party, retaining his titles as commander-in-chief, chairman of the PMAC, head of the Supreme Planning Council, and head of the Council of Ministers.

Used Military Force to Maintain Authority

Beginning in 1983 Ethiopia again faced a serious famine, possibly worse than the one that helped end the imperial government of Haile Selassie. In response, Mengistu's government turned to the West for food and technical aid while retaining its strong military and diplomatic ties to the former Soviet Union. The problems of chronic famine in the north, the continued war in Eritrea, and the overall lack of growth in the Ethiopian economy forced Mengistu to rely more heavily on military authority and close political allies.

Unrest continued in the country. Mengistu maintained control through ruthless dealings with the rebellious guerrillas. Eventually rebel groups won decisive victories against his political factions. In 1991, Mengistu resigned and fled the capital city of Addis Ababa into exile.

Further Reading

Details on the life of Mengistu Haile Mariam are not readily available. A number of books and articles, however, discuss his role in the Ethiopian revolution and the policies of socialist development and diplomacy for Ethiopia. For a description of

As the program of the PMAC grew more socialist in orientation between 1974 and 1977 struggles for power ensued in which higher ranking and conservative officers were pushed out by younger and more politically radical officers. Mengistu Haile Mariam emerged as the most effective—and ruthless—of these. Under his leadership the military government of socialist Ethiopia had made a number of social and economic reforms, including a major land reform in 1975 and large-scale nationalization of foreign-owned banks, factories, insurance companies, and agricultural projects. He was promoted to lieutenant colonel in 1976 and commander-in-chief of the Ethiopian armed forces in February 1977. During 1977 and 1978 the military government withstood a major challenge from radical students and bureaucrats during the period of the "Red Terror." Many young Ethiopians were killed and imprisoned when the struggle for power between civilian and military factions erupted on the streets of the capital.

By the time Somalia invaded Ethiopia in 1977 Mengistu had become the dominant political figure in the country. When the United States refused to ship arms to the Ethiopian government to defend its eastern front with Somalia, Mengistu and the Ethiopian government turned to the former Soviet Union as their source of military hardware and political advice. After the defeat of the Somali army, Mengistu and the Ethiopian government aligned the country's foreign policy and many internal programs toward the former Soviet Union and the Eastern bloc. Internally, Mengistu called for the collectivization of agriculture along Soviet lines and continued to push for a military solution to

the Ethiopian revolution see Fred Halliday and Maxine Molyneax, *The Ethiopian Revolution* (1981) and Pliny the Middle Aged, ''The Life and Times of the Derg'' in *Northeast African Studies* 5, 3 (1984). □

Anton Raphael Mengs

The artistic theories as well as the works of the German painter Anton Raphael Mengs (1728-1779) were influential in the rejection of baroque ideas and the triumph of neoclassicism which took place in the late 18th century in Rome.

Anton Raphael Mengs was born in Aussig, Bohemia, on March 22, 1728, the son of a painter, Ismael Mengs, whose pupil he became. Taken to Rome to study with Marco Benefial and Sebastiano Conca from 1741 to 1744, Anton Raphael was said to have sometimes been locked into the Stanze of Raphael in the Vatican overnight by his father to make him copy the master's works—a stark but not untypical example of 18th-century pedagogy.

In 1744, living in Dresden, the 16-year-old artist produced pastel portraits of great accomplishment, particularly of members of the Saxon court. Appointed Saxon court painter in 1746, Mengs soon returned to Rome to continue his studies of ancient and Renaissance art. There he converted to Catholicism, married, and established himself as one of the leading painters of the city, at that time the most international artistic center of Europe. His study of ancient sculpture and of the masters of the High Renaissance, Michelangelo, Raphael, and Correggio, became the basis for his personal style. His friendship with Johann Joachim Winckelmann, the celebrated proponent of a return to the ''noble simplicity and quiet grandeur'' of ancient art, influenced most of his artistic theories. Yet, in spite of this lofty and often overly intellectualized classicism, Mengs retained some of the charming vitality and freshness of the rococo, notably in his portraits.

In both the ceiling fresco *Apotheosis of St. Eusebius* (1757) for the church of S. Eusebio, Rome, and the ceiling fresco *Parnassus* (1761) for the Villa Albani, Rome, Mengs sought to avoid baroque qualities and emphasize his classicistic doctrines, without really succeeding. Ostentatiously based on his study of classical sculpture, antibaroque in its concept, the *Parnassus* is one of his less appealing works, in spite of its tremendous fame and influence.

In 1761 Mengs was called to Madrid, where he was appointed court painter and worked feverishly, producing frescoes for the royal palaces of Madrid and Aranjuez, as well as many religious paintings, allegorical works, and portraits, all immensely successful, until total exhaustion forced him to stop for a rest in 1768. Back in Rome the following year, he painted the ceiling fresco *Allegory of History and Time* of the Camera dei Papiri in the Vatican Library, a work of much greater significance than the

Parnassus, foreshadowing, as it does, the allegorical and historical painting of the coming century.

Mengs returned to Madrid in 1774 for yet another period of work for the Spanish court. His last 2 years were spent in Rome, where he died of tuberculosis on June 29, 1779.

Further Reading

Mengs is discussed in Fritz Novotny, *Painting and Sculpture in Europe, 1780-1880* (1960), and Eberhard Hempel, *Baroque Art and Architecture in Central Europe* (1965).

Additional Sources

Pelzel, Thomas, *Anton Raphael Mengs and neoclassicism,* New York: Garland Pub., 1979. □

Menno Simons

The Dutch reformer Menno Simons (ca. 1496-1561) was one of the prominent leaders of Anabaptism in the Netherlands and northern Germany during one of the movement's most difficult periods.

enno Simons was born in the village of Witmarsum in Dutch Friesland. Nothing is known of his early background, except that he decided to become a Catholic priest and was consequently ordained in March 1524. In his new capacity, he served from 1524 to 1536 near and in his native village. His work as a priest, however, was troubled by doubts, beginning as early as 1525, about the validity of Catholic teachings. Influenced by the writings of the Protestant reformers, especially Martin Luther, and by his own reading of the Bible, he finally decided in 1536 to renounce the Catholic Church and to be baptized as an Anabaptist. In the following year, he was ordained to the office of a bishop, or overseer, of the Anabaptists.

Since the Anabaptists were considered radical revolutionaries and were being persecuted (especially after the events in Münster, Westphalia, under John of Leiden) by the other religious groups, the office was not particularly desirable. In this position, Menno preached his nonviolent type of Anabaptism in the Netherlands until 1544, by which time he had become a much pursued heretic. After 1544 he spent most of his time in Germany, first along the Rhine and then later in the north. All the while he continued to serve on behalf of his faith until his death on Jan. 31, 1561. His constant activity made possible the survival and spread of the original, peaceful Anabaptist movement when it was most threatened by persecution.

During all of his missionary activity, Menno also wrote numerous pamphlets and books explaining the Anabaptist doctrines. The most important one was *Foundation of the*

Christian Doctrine, or Foundation Book (1539). Although Menno was not a great theologian or philosopher, his writings were buttressed with quotations from Scripture and provided his followers, called Mennonites, with a good understanding of basic Anabaptist concepts. He believed that baptism and the Lord's Supper did not confer grace but reflected the inward state of the believer. The true church was composed of those who had experienced regeneration and a "new birth," thus rejecting infant baptism. Although oaths and military and government service were forbidden as contrary to Scripture, magistrates were to be obeyed in everything not prohibited by Scripture.

Further Reading

An English-language edition of Menno's works is *Complete Writings,* translated by Leonard Verduin and edited by John Christian Wenger (1956). One of the earliest biographies of Menno and still the most complete work in English is John Horsch, *Menno Simons: His Life, Labors, and Teachings* (1916). Later works on him include Harold S. Bender and John Horsch, *Menno Simons' Life and Writings* (1936), and Franklin H. Littell, *A Tribute to Menno Simons* (1961). □

Mario Garcia Menocal

Mario Garcia Menocal (1866-1941) was the third president of Cuba. An engineer and a major general of the army during Cuba's War for Independence, he became a prominent public figure during the first decades of the Cuban Republic.

ario Menocal was born in the province of Matanzas on Dec. 17, 1866. When Cuba's Ten Years War (1868-1878) against Spain broke out 2 years later, he was taken to the United States and then to Mexico, where his father settled as a sugar planter. At 13 he went to the United States to attend several schools, obtaining a degree in engineering from Cornell University in 1888.

Soon after graduation Menocal began practicing his profession. He joined an uncle in Nicaragua who was studying the feasibility of a Nicaraguan canal route. In 1891 Menocal returned to Cuba and was employed by a French company. He surveyed a proposed railway in Camagüey Province but soon got involved in Cuba's political problems.

When Cubans resumed the war against Spain in 1895, Menocal joined. He fought under Máximo Gómez, Antonio Maceo, and Calixto García, the leading generals of the war. As a soldier, he exhibited talent for military affairs and a definite aptitude for strategy, achieving the rank of general. When the United States declared war on Spain and intervened in Cuba, Menocal was promoted to major general in charge of Havana and Matanzas provinces.

During the United States military government of Cuba, Menocal was made Havana's chief of police, a post he held only briefly. He soon returned to engineering, building the

Chaparra sugar plantation for the Cuban-American Sugar Company. Under his able management, Chaparra became one of the largest sugar-producing estates of its kind in the world.

A successful businessman, a veteran of the war for independence, and his popularity increasing, Menocal turned to politics after Cuba became independent in 1902. In 1908 he ran unsuccessfully for the presidency on the Conservative party ticket, but he was elected in 1912, becoming Cuba's third president.

Menocal served two terms (1913-1921). During his first administration, education, public health, and agricultural production improved. He introduced administrative and financial reforms, particularly the establishment of a Cuban monetary system. He strengthened relations with the United States and exposed the corruption of the previous administration. As time went by, however, his administration deteriorated. Graft and corruption became widespread. Opposition and violence increased. The regime resorted to repressive measures. Menocal's reelection in 1917 caused much discontent. Opponents complained of fraud.

American Influence

Despite United States warnings that revolution would not be tolerated and that the Menocal administration would be supported, the Liberal party, led by former president José Miguel Gómez, staged an unsuccessful revolt that was harshly suppressed.

American supervision of Cuban affairs and American economic influence grew during Menocal's administration. On April 7, 1917, one day after the United States declared war on Germany, Menocal took Cuba into the war. Cuba floated loans in the United States, and marines landed on the island, supposedly for training purposes. Although Cuba's contribution to the war effort was slight, Menocal collaborated with the United States and sold Cuba's sugar production to the Allies.

This arrangement resulted in a short-lived period of great prosperity called the "Dance of the Millions." Prosperity brought corruption, speculation, and inflation. When sugar prices collapsed in 1920, Cuba plunged into depression and misery. As the 1920 elections approached, the United States sent Maj. Gen. Enoch H. Crowder to prepare an electoral code. American control of Cuban affairs was growing and with it nationalism and anti-Americanism.

After turning over the presidency to Alfredo Zayas in 1921, Menocal returned to business, but he always kept close to politics. He was defeated in the 1924 presidential elections. When President Gerardo Machado extended his presidential term, Menocal participated in an ill-fated expedition and uprising against the regime in August 1931. He made another unsuccessful bid for the presidency in 1936 and was a member of the convention that drafted the 1940 Constitution. Shortly after, in 1941, he died in Havana.

Further Reading

Information on Menocal's life and administration is in Charles E. Chapman, *A History of the Cuban Republic* (1927). □

Vengalil Krishnan Krishna Menon

Vengalil Krishnan Krishna Menon (1896-1974) was an Indian lawyer, publicisf, ambassador, foreign policy advisor, and member of India's Parliament. He was also one of the most influential men in India as the principal aide to Prime Minister Jawaharlal Nehru in foreign policy.

Krishna Menon was born on May 3, 1896, near Calicut in what is now the southern Indian state of Kerala. His father was a lawyer. After receiving a bachelor's degree at Madras Presidency College, Menon worked in the Indian Boy Scout movement for 4 years. In 1924 he left for England, where he remained for over a quarter century, ultimately serving there between 1947 and 1952 as India's high commissioner (ambassador).

In England, Menon studied at the London School of Economics (LSE), where he took a bachelor of science degree with honors and a master of science degree. He was profoundly influenced at LSE by the neo-Marxist thought of Professor Harold Laski, whose interpretation of colonialism and imperialism was to mark Menon's image of the world throughout his public life. Menon also earned a master's degree with honors from University College, London, and a law degree from Glasgow University and was subsequently called to the bar from the Middle Temple.

Work as Nationalist Abroad

But Menon's real career in England was as secretary of the India League, through which he publicized India's national interest and lobbied for independence from Britain during the years 1929 to 1947. He was particularly persuasive among Labour party members, on whom he wisely concentrated his efforts. During these years he became a member of the Labour party, was a borough councilor for Labour in St. Pancras, the first editor of Pelican Books, and editor of the 20th-Century Library of Bodley Head.

Most importantly, in the 1930s Menon met Jawaharlal Nehru, with whom he struck up a deep intellectual and personal friendship that was to last for 30 years until Nehru's death. Menon had represented Indian interests in England, but he had no experience in the nationalist movement in India itself and therefore no political base. His later influence in Indian government and politics was significantly a result of his close personal association with the Prime Minister.

Menon's second career began with his appointment as India's first high commissioner to England, in 1947. This was the first time that an Indian had held such a prestigious and high ranking political seat. From 1953 to 1962 he headed the Indian delegation to the annual sessions of the United Nations, where his outspoken advocacy of India's position and his strong ideological commitments made friends of some nations and alienated others.

During these years Menon represented Nehru at many international conferences. From late 1956 until his resignation in November 1962, following the India-China War, Menon was minister of defense. In 1957 and 1962 he was elected to the Lok Sabha, India's Parliament, as a Congress party candidate from North Bombay.

His Foreign Policy

Menon's major achievements came perhaps in his success as a negotiator and conciliator of conflicting international interests, notably at the time of the Korean armistice and at the Geneva Conference on Indochina in 1954. He has also been credited with contributing to the Suez resolution and the organization and implementation of the United Nation's Emergency Force. His greatest failure was his inability to understand the nature of India's relations with China, a failure he shared with Nehru. The India-China War of 1962 shattered many Indian hopes and misconceptions, a fact which Menon viewed after the events more with regret than with anger.

Virtually all of Menon's thoughts and actions on foreign policy were infused by a deep and pervasive distrust of the United States, which he saw as the primary agent of imperialism, racism, and capitalist exploitation in the modern world. These views were an outgrowth of Menon's political philosophy and his emotional reaction to India's colonial experience. For these reasons he also deeply hated Pakistan. He held that Pakistan was created by British imperialism and supported by United States imperialism and, as a theocratic Moslem state, was a historical threat to a secular India. Pakistan's collusion with China simply strengthened his distrust. His uncompromising position on Kashmir derived from his view of Pakistan and a fear that Kashmir might be the first step in Pakistan's effort to recontrol the subcontinent.

Although some of these positions were less than productive in serving India's interests, Menon made significant contributions to world diplomacy and to India's role in international affairs. His representation of nonalignment as an external form of India's national independence and his efforts to expand the "area of peace" in the world, to press for wider disarmament, and to encourage conciliation in and out of the United Nations were all positive efforts. They reflected Nehru's mind as much as Menon's, and in this sense Indian foreign policy in the decade 1952-1962 was a product of the unique personal understanding between the two.

After his 1962 resignation Menon's political fortunes declined. He was denied a Congress nomination in the 1967 elections, resigned from the party, and was defeated by the Congress candidate when he stood from the North Bombay (East) constituency as an independent. In 1969 he was elected in a West Bengal by-election with leftist support, and in 1971 he stood successfully as an independent from a Kerala constituency. Here too he received the support of the left Communists. His publicly stated views were

always consistent with those which he had maintained during the peak of his career.

Menon was often described as being a man of great strength, personality, and ambition. He spent his entire life serving his country. Menon died on October 6, 1974, in New Delhi, India.

Further Reading

Two biographies of Menon are Emil Lengyel, *Krishna Menon* (1962), and T. J. S. George, *Krishna Menon* (1964). The best statement of Menon's ideas is in the extensive transcribed interview by Michael Brecher, *India and World Politics: Krishna Menon's View of the World* (1968); Brecher's brief analysis of Menon's views covers the ground incisively. Additional information regarding V.K. Krishna Menon can be found in the article "Speech by Dr. Shanker Dayal Sharma President of India at the Birth Centenary Celebration of Shri V.K. Krishna Menon in the Central Hall. □

Gian Carlo Menotti

Gian Carlo Menotti (born 1911), Italian-born American composer, wrote highly melodramatic operas that mixed lyricism with atonality.

Gian Carlo Menotti, born in Cadegliano, Italy, to Alfonso and Ines (Pellini) Menotti, was brought up in a musical atmosphere and started composing as a child. He studied at the Milan Conservatory from 1923 to 1927 then came to the United States in 1928. In 1933 he finished his musical education at the Curtis Institute in Philadelphia, where in 1936 his comic opera *Amelia Goes to the Ball* was first produced. Commissioned by the National Broadcasting Company for a radio opera, he produced the humorous *The Old Maid and the Thief* (1939). In this work certain characteristics of Menotti's mature style began to appear. His effortless method of transforming the natural inflections of ordinary conversation into musical lines that remain in the memory was quite remarkable.

After the failure of his next opera Menotti turned away from the stage for a few years, but on a Guggenheim fellowship in 1946 he wrote what became his most successful work, *The Medium.* It set a precedent in the history of American opera by running on Broadway, coupled with a short curtain raiser, *The Telephone.* In 1951 the composer directed a motion picture version of the work.

Menotti's next operas never quite sustained the excitement generated by *The Medium,* even though *The Consul* (1950), which also ran on Broadway, received a Pulitzer Prize, and *The Saint of Bleecker Street* (1951) won several awards. Menotti always wrote his own librettos and preferred excessively melodramatic scenes. While ideal for a work like *The Medium* (essentially a ghost story), heavy melodrama seemed out of place in the later works, which professed to have serious social content. Musically, however, they offered some striking lyric passages.

The Christmas opera *Amahl and the Night Visitors,* written for television in 1951, was highly successful. Its simple charm has made it a perennial favorite during the holiday season. Menotti took a stand against avant-garde music in the fantasy opera *Help, Help, the Globolinks!* (1968), where the invading globolinks, representing extremist musical tendencies, are destroyed. In *The Most Important Man* (1971), with its heavy emphasis on melodrama and social significance, Menotti returned to the approach used in *The Consul* and *The Saint of Bleecker Street.* His musical style remained unchanged, relying on a natural sense of lyricism interspersed with more dissonant passages as the plot demanded.

Though known for his operatic works of the 1940s and 50s, Menotti also has composed lively orchestral music, including *Piano Concerto in F* (1945) and *Violin Concerto* (1952), as well as the ballet *Sebastian (1944).*

In addition to composing, Menotti was active in a number of related activities. He taught at the Curtis Institute of Music from 1941 to 1945, and in 1958 he established the Festival of Two Worlds in Spoleto, Italy, which was expanded in 1977 to include Charleston, South Carolina. He was also an excellent stage director, and one of his most remarkable gifts was in casting his operas. He had an almost magical sense of getting the right performer for each part; as a result, many singers appearing in his works became identified with these roles throughout their performing careers. In 1992 Menotti was named artistic director of the Rome Opera and headed two seasons. After numerous problems stemming from reported financial mismanagement by the top administrator, Menotti did not return in 1994. He is the recipient of numerous awards, including the Kennedy Center award, 1984, and the New York City Mayor's Liberty award, 1987.

Further Reading

Information on Menotti's life and work is in Joseph Machlis, *Introduction to Contemporary Music* (1961), and more extensively in David Ewen, ed., *Composers since 1900* (1969). Also see *Contemporary Composers* (1992). □

Sir Robert Gordon Menzies

Sir Robert Gordon Menzies (1894-1978) was an Australian political leader and statesman. During his term as prime minister, from 1949 to 1966, Australia underwent notable economic advance.

Robert Gordon Menzies was born at Jeparit, Victoria, on Dec. 20, 1894. His father, a storekeeper, was active in local politics and was elected to the state parliament. Menzies graduated in law from the University of Melbourne and practiced as an attorney from 1918. He was elected to the Victorian Legislative Council in 1928. Transferring to the Legislative Assembly in 1929, he held ministerial posts from 1932.

Elected to a federal seat in 1934, Menzies at once became attorney general. In a cabinet reshuffle early in 1939 he became treasurer and, on the death of Joseph Lyons in April, prime minister. Menzies drew the Country party into a coalition but was criticized for slowness in putting Australia on a full war footing, and in 1941 the disintegrating United Australia party turned from him. Slowly rebuilding a parliamentary following, he became leader of the opposition in 1943. In 1945 he was the prime mover in the creation of the Liberal party as the political voice of suburbia. Attacking the Labour party for its "doctrinaire" approach and particularly lashing the government's plan to nationalize the entire banking system, Menzies led a vigorous Liberal-Country party coalition to success in the general election of December 1949, and he became prime minister.

"Menzies' Era"

Menzies' administration eased Australia away from the United Nations-oriented policies followed by Labour and more positively identified Australia's direct association with Britain and the United States as the prime factor in foreign affairs. The ANZUS Treaty, allying Australia and New Zealand with the United States and signed in 1951, represented Menzies' ideal of a regional security arrangement. It was followed in 1954 by the multination SEATO Pact, to which Australia became a firm adherent. In the 1950s Menzies favored an accelerated industrial and economic buildup rather than greater outlays on defense hardware as the means of advancing Australia's long-range security. At the same time, he supported the economic development of Southeast Asian nations through technical training and direct aid.

In domestic affairs Menzies spoke of dismantling Labour's "socialist bureaucracy," but he set in motion a wide-ranging national development program. He expanded the large-scale immigration effort initiated by his predecessor and spurred a nationwide minerals search under federal auspices. The Snowy Mountains water conservation-hydroelectric project was supported and extended. Manufacturing was buttressed by import controls as well as by tariffs, and rural producers were given general tax aid.

Thwarted by Labour's holdover majority in the Senate, in 1951 Menzies was able to secure a "double dissolution" of Parliament on grounds of Senate obstruction of a banking bill. Public interest centered on Menzies' anti-Communist legislation—the Communist Party Dissolution Bill—which was also the subject of House-Senate differences. The election gave Menzies a majority in both houses; however, an ensuring referendum seeking federal power to legislate against the Communist party and known Communists was defeated.

Over the next 15 years Menzies remained the dominant political force in Australia, winning successive elections against a Labour party torn by disputes. His only stumble occurred in 1961, when a sharp recession in the wake of deflationary measures was reflected in a reduction of his House majority from 32 to 2. Meanwhile he had edged the Liberal party away from conservatism and strengthened its appeal to many of Labour's wavering supporters. This process included wooing the Catholic vote. The principal concession was in granting government funds to independent schools; Menzies broke with tradition when, in 1965, he backed a system of financial support for all privately run schools. He also provided liberally for universities.

Generally Menzies sought not reform but administrative proficiency. He believed in "economic climate setting" through monetary and fiscal policies and was not averse to firm action in these fields. He was able to secure wide support for government at all levels.

Foreign Policies

Menzies' stature as a world figure rested mainly on his role in the annual London conferences of Commonwealth prime ministers. In 1956, during the Suez Canal crisis, he led the canal users' mission to Egypt's president, Gamal Abdel Nasser, but failed to reach a satisfactory agreement. During a period as minister for external affairs (1960-1961) he ran into criticism for an apparent distrust of newly independent nations. In Washington he was a perennially active advocate of United States involvement in the Pacific.

From 1963 he accelerated Australia's defense preparedness sharply. He strongly supported United States policy in Vietnam; he sent military advisers to South Vietnam in 1962 and combat troops in 1965. Against some opposition Menzies signed the agreement (1963) for the U.S. Navy's communications base at North West Cape. Various United States space installations were approved as Australia became America's "reserve platform off Asia."

In 1963 Queen Elizabeth conferred the Order of the Thistle on Sir Robert, and in 1965 he was appointed to the centuries-old post of lord warden of the Cinque Ports. In 1963 he delivered the Thomas Jefferson Memorial Oration at Monticello—the first non-American to do so. Menzies' writings include *The Rule of Law during War* (1917), *The Forgotten People* (1943), *Speech is of Time* (1958), and *Afternoon Light: Some Memories of Men and Events* (1967).

On his retirement from office and from Parliament in January 1966, it was widely acknowledged that Menzies, "a massive figure forever moving restlessly on an enlarging stage," had provided a sense of stability and a background of continuity during years of rapid development of the nation's economic life and relationships with the world. That year, he became president of Dover College, a post he held for 12 years. He died in Melbourne in 1978.

Further Reading

Menzies' memoirs, *Afternoon Light: Some Memories of Men and Events* (1967), give many sidelights on his life and times. His political mastery is explained in Katharine West, *Power in the Liberal Party: A Study in Australian Politics* (1966); less complimentary views are those in Don Whitington, *The Rulers: Fifteen Years of the Liberals* (1964; rev. ed. 1965). Political background is provided in Louise Overacker, *The Australian Party System* (1952). Some intimate parliamentary background is given in Frank C. Green, *Servant of the House* (1969).
Specific aspects of the Menzies administration's policies are dealt with in H. E. Holt and others, *Australia and the Migrant*

(1953); Norman Harper and David Sissons, *Australia and the United Nations* (1959); and Gordon Greenwood and Norman Harper, eds., *Australia in World Affairs, 1956-1960* (1963). James Eayrs, ed., *The Commonwealth and Suez: A Documentary Survey* (1964), provides useful background. Defense and foreign policy issues are explained in J. D. B. Miller, *Australia and Foreign Policy* (1963), and T. B. Millar, *Australia's Defence* (1965); also useful is J. G. Starke, *The ANZUS Treaty Alliance* (1965). □

Gerhardus Mercator

The Flemish cartographer Gerhardus Mercator (1512-1594) was among the first makers of modern atlases and is best known for his great world map, or chart, using the projection that has acquired his name.

In the history of cartography the work of Gerhardus Mercator illustrated a significant departure (though by no means a complete break) with the geographical traditions of the Middle Ages and those established by the revived Ptolemaic geography. It also signaled the late Renaissance convergence of academic cartography with the practical needs of navigators, an important step in the creation of that dynamic unity between science and technology that is one of the signal characteristics of the modern world.

Mercator was born Gerhard Kremer in Rupelmonde, Flanders, on March 5, 1512. He studied with the cosmographer Gemma Phyrisius at the University of Louvain and gained practical experience as an instrument maker and surveyor. His early successes brought him into close contact with the court of Emperor Charles V; but under growing pressure for his Protestant beliefs, he emigrated to the German Rhineland in 1552. There he settled permanently with his workshop in Duisburg, and in 1564 he became cosmographer to the court of the Duke of Jülich, Cleve, and Berg.

Mercator's early works prepared the way for his world map of 1569. These included maps of the Holy Land (1537), the world (1538), Flanders (1540), Europe (1554; rev. ed. 1572), and Britain (1564). He also constructed terrestrial and celestial globes (1541 and 1551). These maps reflected the critical compilation and rendition of a growing body of data that were typical of the cartographical methods of the time. The 1554 map of Europe showed Mercator's willingness to abandon the theories of Ptolemy and other predecessors in the light of further advances in knowledge. The length of the Mediterranean was shortened by 10 degrees (though remaining disproportionately long), and the stretch of land between the Baltic and the Black seas was widened.

Others may have experimented with the "Mercator projection" before Mercator; he was the first, however, to give cartographical rendition to the solution to the problem for which the projection was designed. This was the problem of plotting loxodromes (rhumb lines, or lines of constant

GERARDI MERCATORIS RVPELMVNDANI EFFIGIEM ANNOR.
DVORVM ET SEX — AGINTA, SVI ERGA IPSVM STVDII
CAVSA DEPINGI CVRABAT FRANC. HOG. CIƆ. IƆ. LXXIV.

bearing) as straight lines on a navigator's chart. Meridians of longitude converge at the poles, but if lines of constant bearing are plotted as cutting across them at constant angles, they must appear as parallel on the flat map, or chart. This requirement in turn necessitates a proportional increase in parallels of latitude from the Equator to the poles (proportional to the increasing east-west distances between the meridians). The shape of sectional areas is preserved, and the loxodromes can now be plotted as straight lines, although this is achieved at the expense of distortion of the world map as a whole (that is, the radical increase in relative proportions from Equator to poles, hence the apparent gigantism of land masses like Australia and Greenland on a Mercator projection map). This was the solution rendered in the 1569 world map, but it was not fully accepted by navigators until small area charts based on the projection began to be published in the next century.

The rest of Mercator's life was taken up with a three-part publishing project. He planned to print maps based on Ptolemy's *Geography,* maps of the ancient world, and an atlas of modern maps. The Ptolemaic maps were published in 1578, and the modern atlas appeared in three sections between 1585 and 1595. The entire work (mainly maps of western and southern Europe), totaling 107 maps, was published in 1595. Mercator, however, had died the year before at Duisburg, on Dec. 2, 1594.

Further Reading

Mercator's place in the history of cartography is discussed in Lloyd Arnold Brown, *The Story of Maps* (1949), and Gerald

Roe Crone, *Maps and Their Makers: An Introduction to the History of Cartography* (1953; 4th rev. ed. 1968). His relation to the new geographical knowledge is examined in the appropriate chapters of Boies Penrose, *Travel and Discovery in the Renaissance, 1420-1620* (1952), and John Horace Parry, *The Age of Reconnaissance* (1963).

Additional Sources

Blondeau, R. A., *Mercator van Rupelmonde,* Tielt: Lannoo, 1993.
□

George Meredith

The English novelist and poet George Meredith (1828-1909) concentrated on detailed character development and witty intellectual discussion. His narrative style is often highly metaphorical, allusive, and aphoristic.

George Meredith was born on Feb. 12, 1828, in Portsmouth, the grandson of a prosperous naval tailor. George's father, brought up as a gentleman, was unable to manage a declining business successfully, but with the help of his wife's small fortune he was able to maintain genteel pretensions and indulged his son sufficiently to set him apart from other tradesmen's children. But in 1833 his father went bankrupt and moved to London, where half a year later he married his housekeeper. This episode no doubt contributed to Meredith's remarkable lifelong secretiveness about his social origins. After a few years at a school in Germany, he was, in 1845, articled to a London solicitor in whose circle he discovered a new world of racy intellectual and literary talk, which soon determined his aspirations. Here he also met Thomas Love Peacock's widowed daughter, a well-educated and independent woman 8 years his senior with whom he rapidly fell in love; overcoming her well-founded reluctance, he married her in 1849. A volume of poetry published at his own expense earned him a letter of recognition from Alfred, Lord Tennyson, but nothing else, and so he turned to the more lucrative medium of prose.

First Works

The Shaving of Shagpat (1855) is a quasi-allegorical Oriental tale with a fantastically complex plot and much grotesque and supernatural incident. It establishes several of the persistent themes of Meredith's fiction: the ridiculousness of many social conventions and values and the blind vanity of those who are elevated by them; the young man who must undergo a series of maturing trials precipitated by his own egoism; and the woman who, for better or worse, inspires and guides his actions. *Shagpat* did not sell, however, and the continuing financial crises compounded the strain developing in his marriage. In 1858 his wife eloped to France with a young painter. She soon returned, alone and ill, but Meredith refused to see her again until her death and tried to prevent all contact between her and their

son, to whom he became jealously devoted. These events lend a particularly personal significance to his next novel.

The Ordeal of Richard Feverel (1859) is the story of the only son of a rather too strong-minded baronet whose wife had eloped with a minor sentimental poet. His father raises him with jealous strictness according to a "system" which is thwarted when Richard, following his natural instincts, falls in love with and secretly marries a farmer's niece. But more in love with himself than either his system or his son, the baronet puts Richard through a trial of estrangement for his disobedience, and in his romantic impatience with his situation the boy demonstrates an egoism of his own that finally leads to his wife's death. The relationship of reason, natural instinct, romantic illusion, and the demands of society examined here is the theme of many of Meredith's later novels.

Evan Harrington (1860) is about a prosperous tailor's son who, having been raised as a gentleman, is forced to reenter the shop upon his father's death in order to pay his debts. The action consists of a number of ordeals through which Evan, in love with a daughter of gentry, learns to resist the temptation to pretend to the empty name of gentleman. The characters are clearly derived from Meredith's family and friends.

Middle Period

After *Sandra Belloni* (1864), *Rhoda Fleming* (1865), and *Vittoria* (1865), Meredith returned to the pattern of *Evan Harrington* in *The Adventures of Harry Richmond* (1871). Brought up under the opposing influences of his romantic,

self-deluded father, who believes he has a claim to royal blood, and a conservative country squire grandfather, Harry learns to free himself of illusion and make a rational adjustment to the realities and duties of life. *Beauchamp's Career* (1875) explores these themes further through a study of contemporary English politics. The hero stands for Parliament as a Radical, but under the rational surface his actions are motivated by passion and romantic impulse, which finally lead to his death.

Later Works

An Essay on Comedy and the Uses of the Comic Spirit (1877) analyzes the philosophy and technique of Meredith's matured art. Human civilization is maintained against barbarism by the rational "common sense" of a cultured elite, aided by the comic spirit, which uses irony to expose the basic human motive force of egoism when it degenerates into self-delusion and the empty habit of domination. Literary comedy deals with the conflict between decadent egoism and reality and concentrates upon a small number of characters in a clearly defined situation.

The Egoist (1879) perfectly embodies the principles of the *Essay* and is Meredith's most brilliant and finished work. The novel is the story of the self-defeat in love of a rich and fatuous country gentleman; its defense of the heroine's emotional and intellectual independence shows a development in Meredith's conception of women. *Diana of the Crossways* (1885), the novel which finally brought him popularity, continues the study of woman's condition. Taking a more radical situation than in *The Egoist,* Meredith has Diana run away from an incompatible husband; but this only marks the beginning of a series of trials through which she at last gains true inner independence.

Modern Love (1861), a cycle of augmented sonnets depicting the breakdown of a marriage with relentless candor, marked the final act of Meredith's early literary exorcism of his own past. Ranging in tone from cool irony to bitter pathos, it carried poetry into hitherto unexplored territory. The bulk of Meredith's verse, however, is devoted to nature.

Further Reading

A standard biography of Meredith is Lionel Stevenson, *The Ordeal of George Meredith* (1953). G. M. Trevelyan, *The Poetry and Philosophy of George Meredith* (1906), was endorsed by Meredith himself. Good studies of Meredith's work are Walter F. Wright, *Art and Substance in George Meredith* (1953), and Norman Kelvin, *A Troubled Eden: Nature and Society in the Works of George Meredith* (1961).

Additional Sources

Jerrold, Walter, *George Meredith: an essay towards appreciation,* Philadelphia: R. West, 1978; Norwood, Pa.: Norwood Editions, 1977.
Williams, David, *George Meredith: his life and lost love,* London: H. Hamilton, 1977. □

James H. Meredith

As the first black to attend the University of Mississippi, James H. Meredith (born 1933) scored one of the earliest important victories against segregation in Mississippi.

Fiercely independent and keenly intelligent, James Meredith was the great iconoclast of the civil rights movement. As the first black to attend the University of Mississippi, Meredith scored one of the earliest important victories against segregation in Mississippi. At the same time, he remained largely aloof from the established civil rights organizations. Medgar Evers and the NAACP helped Meredith win his legal battle to integrate Ole Miss, but as Meredith proudly noted, "Nobody hand picked me. I made the decision myself. I paid my own tuition."

Born on a small farm near Kosciusko, Mississippi, on June 25, 1933, Meredith was the seventh of Cap Meredith's 13 children, and the first of seven by Cap's second wife, Roxie. Meredith, baptized simply as "J.H.," inherited his independent streak from his father. The family was poor and their home lacked running water, but they were self-sufficient. "I was taught," Meredith said later, "to believe the most dishonorable thing a Meredith could do was to work in a white woman's kitchen and take care of a white man's child." Seeking a better education than he could attain in Mississippi, Meredith moved to St. Petersburg, Florida,

where he lived with an aunt, and graduated from high school in 1951. Lacking money for college, he joined the U.S. Air Force, under the name "James Howard Meredith." To the young Mississippian, attacking Jim Crow meant self-improvement, and that required money and education. In the service, Meredith saved much of his modest pay and routinely took classes at nearby schools, including the University of Kansas, Washburn University in Topeka, New Mexico Western College, and even the University of Maryland's Japan campus. After a nine-year hitch in the Air Force, Meredith returned to Mississippi and entered the all-black Jackson State University. His decision to seek admission at the all-white University of Mississippi reflected his strategy to attack a system of segregation that limited the economic opportunities open to blacks. "Before I could engage in business at the level I desired," he believed, "the system would have to be broken." Convinced that the new president, John F. Kennedy, would support his efforts, Meredith, on January 21, 1961, the day after Kennedy's inauguration, wrote Ole Miss for an application form.

Meredith's letter touched off an 18-month legal battle. Mississippi's white authorities had already demonstrated that they would try virtually anything to avoid integrating the state's colleges and universities. A black teacher, Clennon King had been committed to a mental institution in 1958 for attempting to attend summer school at Oxford. Another black man, Clyde Kennon, was sent to prison on trumped-up charges after attempting to enroll at the University of Southern Mississippi. In Meredith's case, state officials resorted to a variety of legal ploys, but in June 1962, the U.S. Court of Appeals for the Fifth Circuit ordered Meredith admitted to the university. Nevertheless, Mississippi's racist governor, Ross Barnett, personally intervened to bar Meredith physically from entering Ole Miss. In a televised address, Barnett incited white resistance and warned: "There is no case in history where the Caucasian race has survived social integration." Finally, late in September, Kennedy ordered federal troops and Justice Department officials to enforce the court order admitting Meredith to school. On Sunday afternoon, September 30, 1962, Meredith arrived on campus accompanied by a federal entourage that included over 120 U.S. marshals and Deputy Attorney General Nicholas Katzenbach. The result was a night-long riot that resulted in two deaths, 175 injuries, and 212 arrests. Despite one of the most violent challenges to federal authority since the Civil War, Meredith was quietly registered the next day. Enduring taunts and abuse from many of his fellow students, in August 1963 Meredith became the first black graduate of the University of Mississippi.

In 1964-65, Meredith studied economics at the University of Ibadan in Nigeria. The following year, he proposed to walk from Memphis, Tennessee, to Jackson, Mississippi, to encourage blacks to register to vote. The walk attracted widespread attention after a white supremacist wounded Meredith with a shotgun blast, and black leaders, including Martin Luther King, Jr., and Stokely Carmichael, flocked to Mississippi to help him complete his trek. Meredith later moved to New York City where he bought an apartment house and experienced a variety of financial and legal problems, among them a conviction for harassing his tenants.

Meredith briefly considered running for Congress against Harlem's incumbent Adam Clayton Powell. In 1968, Meredith received a law degree from Columbia University, but by the early 1970s, he had returned to Mississippi, where he continued to pursue a variety of business, political, and community activities. In 1972, Meredith ran unsuccessfully as a Republican against Mississippi Senator James O. Eastland. He served as a visiting professor at the University of Cincinnati in 1984-85, and was defeated in 1986 in a race for a position on the Cincinnati school board. In recent years, Meredith has been associated with conservative causes and candidates, but his historical significance derives from his integration of Ole Miss, which heralded the changes that would eventually come to the most racially divided state in the nation.

Further Reading

Flynn, James J., *Negroes of Achievement in Modern America,* Dodd, Mead & Co., 1970, pp. 159-167.

Lord, Walter, *The Past That Would Not Die,* Harper & Row, 1965.

Metcalf, George R., *Black Profiles,* McGraw-Hill, 1968, pp. 219-254. □

Dmitry Sergeyevich Merezhkovsky

The Russian writer and literary critic Dmitry Sergeyevich Merezhkovsky (1865-1941), a founder of the modernist movement in Russian literature, combined fervent idealism with literary innovation.

Dmitry Merezhkovsky was born in St. Petersburg on Aug. 2/14, 1865, into the family of a minor court official. Even before graduating from the university there, he began (1883) publishing in liberal magazines poems in the prevailing style and civic spirit of Semyon Y. Nadson. The appearance of Merezhkovsky's first book, *Poems,* in 1888, the year after Nadson's death, suggested that he was Nadson's successor, but in 1892 he published another book of verse provocatively entitled *Symbols* and in 1893 a small critical book, *On the Reasons for the Decline of and on New Currents in Contemporary Russian Literature.* Rejecting sociological criticism and socially oriented verse, these two books affirmed a new quasi-religious philosophy and a fresh literary manner. With his young wife, the temperamental red-haired poetess Zinaida Hippius, he served on the board of the magazine *Northern Messenger,* the first herald of the new movement.

Merezhkovsky's first popular presentation of his antithetical religious views was the trilogy *Christ and Anti-Christ,* of which volume 1, *The Death of the Gods: Julian the Apostate,* appeared in 1896, followed by *The Resurrection of the Gods: Leonardo da Vinci* in 1901 and *Anti-Christ: Peter and Alexis* in 1905. The books' persuasive power came from Merezhkovsky's success in catching currents then around him: strong contrasts between social life and spiritual values, fresh interest in the drama of pagan ancient Athens, and identification with general western European culture. His translations of *Daphnis and Chloe* and works of Pliny, Marcus Aurelius, Miguel de Cervantes, Gustave Flaubert, and Henrik Ibsen, among others, were valued contributions to Russian literary sophistication.

Merezhkovsky's application of his critical principles to Russian literature in his *Christ and Anti-Christ in Russian Literature: Tolstoy and Dostoyevsky* (1901-1903) imaginatively, if tendentiously, analyzed West versus East, flesh versus spirit, in the Russian literary tradition. Even recently, outside of the Soviet Union, critics who reject both the utilitarian attitude of the naturalist school and the structural subtleties of the formalist school have repeated Merezhkovsky's method of explaining a writer's work through biography, metaphor, and religious values.

Merezhkovsky and his wife collaborated with D. V. Filosofov, with whom, in 1903, they founded the magazine *New Way* (it was they who first published Aleksandr Blok) and the Religious-Philosophical Society, devoted to discussing issues of Slavophilism and Orthodoxy. Merezhkovsky's 1907 book, *Le tsar et la révolution,* written and published in Paris, well exemplifies the broadly cultural but conservative views of himself and his followers.

In 1906 Merezhkovsky wrote *The Coming Ham,* an attack on all forms of collectivism ("Ham," which refers to the biblical figure, is also the Russian word for "boor"), although he was "mystically" a supporter of the 1905 revolution. The failure of constitutional reform in the autumn of 1905 drove him to Paris, where he lived from 1906 to 1912 and wrote a number of works, including plays such as *Paul I* (1908). Returning to Russia, he and his wife, like most intellectuals of the time, opposed events leading up to World War I and Russian involvement in it. In 1917 he bitterly opposed the Soviets and with his wife and two friends crossed into Poland in late 1919 and encouraged intervention to overthrow the new Soviet government (as he later hoped the Germans would in 1939-1941). In 1920 he settled in Paris. There he wrote violent diatribes against the Soviets (*The Reign of Anti-Christ,* 1926) as well as many novels and essays on Classical and Christian topics but centered on the one, mystical theme of the "Unknown Jesus." He died in Paris on Dec. 9, 1941.

Further Reading

A good study of Merezhkovsky is in Marc Slonim, *Modern Russian Literature: From Chekhov to the Present* (1953). He is also discussed in Ernest J. Simmons, *An Outline of Modern Russian Literature, 1880-1940* (1943).

Additional Sources

Pachmuss, Temira, *D.S. Merezhkovsky in exile: the master of the genre of biographie romance,* New York: Peter Lang, 1990. □

Ottmar Mergenthaler

Ottmar Mergenthaler (1854-1899), the German-American inventor of the Linotype, revolutionized the printing industry with his remarkable typesetting-typecasting machine.

Ottmar Mergenthaler was born in Hachtel, Germany, on May 11, 1854. He became an apprentice watchmaker in Bietigheim at the age of 14. After 4 years there, he emigrated to the United States. He found immediate employment in the Washington, D.C., shop of August Hahl, where various types of scientific instruments, including a great many models of new inventions required for the patent application, were made. Mergenthaler's talents were soon recognized, and his services became much in demand.

Shortly after Hahl relocated his business to Baltimore in 1876, Mergenthaler was asked to correct defects in a writing machine devised by Charles T. Moore and James O. Clephane. The machine was intended to produce print by typewriting words upon a strip of paper, which would then be reproduced by a lithographic process. Mergenthaler corrected the defects in the model but became convinced that it would never perform satisfactorily. At Clephane's suggestion, Mergenthaler attempted to devise a stereotyping machine which would impress characters on a paper matrix; pouring molten metal over the assembled matrices would produce a stereotype plate for printing. By 1878 the machine was built but, as Mergenthaler had anticipated, difficulties were experienced in separating metal from matrix. The search for a reliable improvement over the laborious hand-setting of type continued.

By this time Mergenthaler was obsessed with the problem, and he pursued private efforts at a solution while continuing as a general instrument maker. In 1883 he established his own shop in Baltimore and built additional machines with paper matrices. Then he hit upon the idea of using metal matrices, casting type bars directly from them, one line at a time. After a line of matrices with indented characters was assembled and justified, molten type metal was introduced, producing a line of type ready for printing. All these processes, as well as the redistribution of the matrices, were performed by the single machine.

By July 1884 Mergenthaler had constructed the first direct-casting Linotype; it was patented in August, and in December the National Typographic Company was organized to manufacture it. On July 3, 1886, a Linotype was used to compose part of that day's issue of the *New York Tribune.* The machine's use spread quickly throughout the United States and abroad. Although Mergenthaler withdrew from the company manufacturing the Linotype in 1888, his interest in his invention remained as strong as before. He patented at least 50 improvements to it before his death.

Mergenthaler was a friendly, personable man. He delighted in his family and in his love of music. He died in Baltimore on Oct. 28, 1899, survived by his wife and four children.

Further Reading

The best sources for Mergenthaler's life and his invention are George Iles, *Leading American Inventors* (1912), and Thomas Dreier, *The Power of Print—and Men* (1936). The former contains a remarkably thorough, illustrated explanation of the Linotype in all its operations. See also Edward W. Byrn, *The Progress of Invention in the Nineteenth Century* (1900), and Waldemar B. Kaempffert, *A Popular History of American Invention* (2 vols., 1924).

Additional Sources

Bellas, R. C., *Ottmar Mergenthaler's marvel,* Baltimore: Xavier Press, 1986.

Mergenthaler, Ottmar, *The biography of Ottmar Mergenthaler, inventor of the linotype. recent findings, researched and edited by Carl Schlesinger; introduction by Elizabeth Harri,* New Castle, Del.: Oak Knoll Books, 1989. □

Prosper Mérimée

The French author Prosper Mérimée (1803-1870) was a prose writer of the romantic period in France, important for his short stories, which mark the transition from romanticism toward the more objective works of the second half of the century.

Prosper Mérimée, a Parisian born and bred, grew up with the other French romantics. Although he shared some of their traits—a love of the exotic and the violent, for instance—his skeptical, pessimistic temperament kept him from their emotional excesses. He hid his emotional sensitivity beneath a cover of ironic objectivity. As restraint and ironic objectivity were among the principal goals of the later French realists, he stands as their precursor.

Mérimée's initial writings were entertaining frauds, published as alleged translations. A more important work under his own name, *Chronique du règne de Charles IX,* brought him to serious public attention in 1829. The *Chronique* is a historical novel, but it differs from the contemporary romantic ones in its impartial stance in recounting the Protestant and Catholic positions during the Wars of Religion in 16th-century France. True to form, Mérimée refused to provide an ending and mockingly invited his readers to invent one for themselves. Like his friend Stendhal, he feared being mocked himself and never allowed himself to appear to take any of his writings seriously, posing usually as an amateur who happened for the moment to be writing a story.

A very learned man, Mérimée was appointed inspector general of historical monuments in 1831. He performed major services by saving many ancient monuments from destruction, among others the church of St-Savin with its important 12th-century frescoes. He traveled widely through France, southern Europe, and the Near East, finding there the settings for many of his short stories (*nouvelles*).

Mateo Falcone (1829) and the longer *Colomba* (1841) and *Carmen* (1845) are the principal works for which Mérimée is now remembered, typical in their settings in Spain or Corsica, their portrayal of primitive passions, and their clear, concise style. Each story is a new experiment in form. The author's position remains distant, and Mérimée usually prefers the concrete to the abstract, giving a character life by a gesture or pose alone. *Carmen* is the source for Georges Bizet's opera (1875).

Mérimée ended his career as a writer in 1848, but he was a familiar figure at the court of the Second Empire, in part owing to his long prior acquaintance with the empress Eugénie. He was also among the first in France to appreciate Russian literature, translating Aleksandr Pushkin, Ivan Turgenev, and Nikolai Gogol.

Further Reading

A thorough account of Mérimée's life is Alan William Raitt, *Prosper Mérimée* (1970). Sylvia Lyons, *The Life and Times of Prosper Mérimée* (1948), is good for placing Mérimée within his period. An excellent short section on his life, character, and works is in Albert J. George, *Short Fiction in France, 1800-50* (1964). See also G. H. Johnstone Derwent, *Prosper Mérimée: A Mask and a Face* (1926). □

Maurice Merleau-Ponty

The French philosopher Maurice Merleau-Ponty (1908-1961) was the most original and profound thinker of the postwar French movement of existential phenomenology.

Maurice Merleau-Ponty was born in Rochefort-sur-Mer (Charente-Maritime) on March 14, 1908. His father died when Maurice was still a child, and he and his sister were raised by their mother in Paris. The childhood was an unusually happy one, and Merleau-Ponty retained over the years a close and affectionate tie with his mother. In later life he ceased to practice the Catholicism which he had earlier shared with his devout mother. But apparently before his death a reconciliation had occurred, since he was buried with the solemn rites of the Church.

Merleau-Ponty was educated at the Lycée Louis-le-Grand and entered the École Normale Supérieure in 1926, graduating 4 years later. In the ensuing decade he taught at lycées in Beauvais and Chartres and, after 1935, as a junior member of the faculty at the École Normale. After the Nazi invasion of Poland he entered the army and served as a lieutenant in the infantry. With the collapse of France he was demobilized, and he returned to his teaching. During the Nazi occupation he was active in the Resistance. When the Liberation came, he joined the faculty of the University of Lyons and became coeditor with Jean Paul Sartre, an old friend from school days, of the new journal *Les Temps modernes*. In 1950 he was invited to the Sorbonne as professor of psychology and pedagogy. And 2 years later he was elected to the Collège de France to the chair formerly occupied by Henri Bergson. He was the youngest philosopher ever to hold this position, and he retained it until his death.

Merleau-Ponty's first book, *The Structure of Behavior*, was completed in his thirtieth year but, owing to the war, was first published in 1942. It is a sustained and powerful attack on behaviorism in psychology, but it also features the introduction of novel philosophical interpretations of the experimental work of the Gestalt psychologists. This study was continued in his major work, *The Phenomenology of Perception* (1945). Drawing heavily upon the phenomenological techniques of Edmund Husserl (to which, however, he added new modifications) and upon the existential strands in the thought of Gabriel Marcel and Martin Heidegger, Merleau-Ponty began to fashion a personal synthesis, an original philosophical interpretation of human experience. He is thus one of the originators of contemporary existential philosophy and, in the generous tribute of a colleague, Paul Ricoeur, "was the greatest of the French phenomenologists."

All of Merleau-Ponty's work shows a familiarity with current scientific research and with the history of philosophy. This gives his work a more balanced and solid character than that of the other existentialists. Another major concern of his was with political and social philosophy and even with the ephemeral problems of day-to-day politics. He wrote a great many newspaper articles on contemporary events and problems. More sustained essays on Marxist theory and leftist politics were gathered in two collections: *Humanism and Terror* (1947) and *The Adventures of the Dialectic* (1955). The latter work contains a powerful critique of the French Communist party, with which he had earlier sympathized. This led to an open break with Sartre and to his resignation from the editorship of *Les Temps modernes*. Nevertheless his own political views remained decisive for Sartre, as the latter freely admits in a memoir published after Merleau-Ponty's death.

Interpretations of literary works, the art of the film, and painting were also crowded into the busy final decade of Merleau-Ponty's life. In these essays, published as collections entitled *Sense and NonSense* (1948) and *Signs* (1960), he sought to work out some of the implications of his thesis on the primacy of perception. He had hoped to crown his analysis of the prereflective life of consciousness with a survey of the major modes of reflective thought in which he would seek to determine their criteria for truth and validity. But at his sudden death of a coronary thrombosis on May 3, 1961, he had written only incomplete fragments and sketches.

Merleau-Ponty was happily married to a physician and psychiatrist in Paris, and they had one child, a daughter.

Further Reading

A hundred-page memoir by Jean Paul Sartre in *Situations* (7 vols., 1947-1965) gives a very sympathetic portrait and generous account of his quarrel with Merleau-Ponty. Two excellent interpretations of Merleau-Ponty's work in English are John F. Bannan, *The Philosophy of Merleau-Ponty* (1967), and Albert Rabil, *Merleau-Ponty: Existentialist of the Social World* (1967); both are reliable, although the latter is more complete. □

Charles Edward Merriam

Charles Edward Merriam (1874-1953) was an American political scientist, critic and defender of democracy, practical politician, adviser to presidents, and a prolific writer on all phases of government and politics.

Charles E. Merriam was born in Hopkinton, Iowa, the son of a postmaster and merchant. He attended Lenox College and began the study of law at Iowa State University. Disillusioned with the legal profession, he studied social science at Columbia College, New York City. After studying in Germany, he returned to teach political science at the University of Chicago, where he remained until his death—a total of 51 years.

A Better Democracy

Merriam was preoccupied with two goals: critically examining and perfecting democracy and bridging the gap in political science between theory and practice. Democracy, he believed, was "not merely a form . . . but a means, through which the highest ideals of mankind may be achieved." In countering any attack upon democracy, he joined those who sought the cure for the ills of democracy in more democracy. He countered the argument that democracy was inefficient by holding that it did not have to be efficient, that "freedom and inefficiency are not opposites." Through scientific management, a strengthening of the executive by way of the item veto, centralized budget, and expertise, a democratically directed science could rid man of all his problems—not by creating a Marxian universal proletariat but by eliminating the oppressed proletariat if not indeed the proletariat as a class. The stronger, more efficient executive would be democratically controlled by way of initiative, referendum, and recall.

Largely because of Merriam's efforts to bring political science into touch with the real world, he is sometimes identified as the father of behavioral political science, believing that one could learn about politics only through the observation of "real" government and political behavior. He was, however, suspicious of quantification and was not, in fact, committed to the methods and techniques of what is now generally called behavioral science.

Public Office

Despite Merriam's prolific and illuminating writings, his scholarship was overshadowed by his public career. Not without some misgivings on the part of his superiors, Merriam heeded his conviction that political scientists should apply their learning by way of participation in political affairs. In 1905 he made a successful official study of the Chicago tax structure and 2 years later was appointed secretary of that city's Harbor Commission.

Since the commission was involved in studying some of the most complex and bothersome problems of Chicago politics, Merriam gained not only invaluable experience but wide political exposure that led to his election to the city council in 1909. He immediately tackled the problem of fraud and graft in the city. The council reacted by cutting off funds for his investigation, but he secured the necessary funds from a private donor and with almost flagrant disregard for his political life completed the investigation. Ironically this action contributed to his lack of success in his campaign for mayor of Chicago (on the Republican ticket). After an abortive effort to breathe life into the Progressive party, he was again elected to the city council (1913-1917).

In World War I Merriam served as the American high commissioner of public information in Italy, after which he made a futile attempt to reenter Chicago politics. The next 25 years were devoted to his professional interests. Merriam became one of the most influential members of the American Political Science Association, was influential in founding the Public Administration Clearing House, helped establish the Social Science Research Council, and interes-

ted the Rockefeller Foundation in financing faculty and study research projects.

Through his endeavors and the success of his students, such as V. O. Key and H. D. Lasswell, Merriam's influence may well have been greater and more extensive than if his university had made his lot easier. He served on presidential commissions for Herbert Hoover, Franklin Roosevelt, and Harry Truman, and he wrote and lectured extensively.

Further Reading

Reissues of three works by Merriam are particularly useful for their introductions and notes by students and analysis of his work: *Political Power,* with an introduction by Harold D. Lasswell (1964); *The Making of Citizens,* with an introduction and notes by George Z. F. Bereday (1966); and *New Aspects of Politics,* with a foreword by Barry D. Karl (1970). See also Leonard D. White, ed., *The Future of Government in the United States: Essays in Honor of Charles E. Merriam* (1942).

Additional Sources

Karl, Barry Dean, *Charles E. Merriam and the study of politics,* Chicago: University of Chicago Press, 1974.
Simon, Herbert Alexander, *Charles E. Merriam and the "Chicago School" of political science: the Edmund James lecture delivered on October 10, 1985,* Urbana, Ill.: Dept. of Political Science, University of Illinois at Urbana-Champaign, 1987. □

Charles E. Merriam

Charles E. Merriam (1885-1956) was the founder of Merrill Lynch, Pierce, Fenner and Smith, the world's largest brokerage firm. A brilliant market analyst and salesman, he reorganized the investment industry to attract small investors into the stock market.

Charles E. Merrill was born in Green Cove Springs, Florida, on October 19, 1885. The son of a physician and drugstore owner, Merrill was educated at the preparatory school of John B. Stetson University in Deland, Florida, and at Amherst College. After leaving college Merrill tried his hand at newspaper work, law school, and semiprofessional baseball before finding his niche in the business world. In 1907 Merrill took a position as office boy in the New York City branch of a textile firm. Within two years he had become a director of the company. In 1909 Merrill joined a commercial paper company, where he created and managed a bond department. After his resignation in 1913 he became a sales manager for Eastman, Dillon and Company, an established Wall Street firm.

In January 1914 Merrill decided to start his own investment banking firm and founded Charles E. Merrill and Co. in office space sublet from Eastman, Dillon. Six months later, when Merrill took on a partner named Edmund Lynch, the firm became Merrill Lynch and Company. After Merrill's successful underwriting of the McCrory Stores the firm gained a reputation as an underwriter of chain stores and grew large and profitable. Because Merrill took stock war-

rants as part of his commissions and later sold his shares when their value rose, he also amassed a personal fortune. Merrill's biggest success as an underwriter was his organization in 1926 of Safeway Stores, Inc., in which he was the largest shareholder. At the time of Merrill's death in 1956, Safeway was the second largest food retailer in the country.

In 1928 Merrill became convinced that the stock market was overpriced and advised his customers to sell their holdings; those who took his advice (the president, Calvin Coolidge, ignored his warning) were spared the ravages of the great crash of October 1929. Sure that the depression would be longlived, Merrill got out of the brokerage business in 1930, turning over $5 million of his firm's capital to E. A. Pierce and Co. and limiting his involvement to handling the equity securities of his growing list of chain stores, which by this time included First National Stores, S. S. Kresge Company, and Western Auto Supply. In addition, in 1932 he helped to found *Family Circle,* the first magazine distributed by grocery stores. For Merrill this was semi-retirement, and he spent much of the 1930s enjoying the fruits of his labor in his elegant homes in Southampton, New York, and Palm Beach, Florida.

In 1940 Merrill reentered the brokerage business, bringing about a merger of Merrill Lynch (Lynch had in the meantime died) with E. A. Pierce and Company. Another merger in 1941 created Merrill Lynch, Pierce, Fenner, and Beane—the largest brokerage house in the world, with offices in 93 cities.

In the 1940s Merrill was responsible for making vast changes in the way the investment industry operated. Adapting retailing concepts to stockbrokering, Merrill became determined to attract large numbers of small investors to the market. In 1941, using the slogan "Bring Wall Street to Main Street," Merrill started a campaign both to educate the general public about the stock market and to make changes in the structure of the business that would appeal to small investors. He accomplished the first goal by printing large advertisements and pamphlets in newspapers and magazines (and sending reprints to all who requested them) which described the workings of the investment business in simple language and by setting up a research department that would do stock analysis reports intended for, and freely distributed to, laymen.

In addition, Merrill reorganized his firm to assuage the public fear that stockbrokers were out to bilk the consumer. He insisted that his employees pass a training program so they would be at least minimally educated in the business, and he paid them on salary rather than on commission, relying on profit-sharing and bonuses as incentives. He cancelled service charges and kept commissions low. He instituted an annual report and sent it out to all his customers to assure them that their money was secure with Merrill Lynch.

Merrill's marketing strategy was extraordinarily successful; small investors responded in droves and remained loyal to the company. Although the firm's innovations were widely imitated on Wall Street, Merrill Lynch consolidated its position as the largest brokerage firm in the world. By the time of Merrill's death in 1956 the firm had 115 offices in the United States, more than 100 partners and 570 employees, and on any given day handled more than 10 percent of all the transactions on the New York Stock Exchange. In the 1980s Merrill Lynch, Pierce, Fenner and Smith (the name was changed after Merrill's death to credit a longterm partner) remained the biggest brokerage house in the world.

Merrill was not only one of the most successful stockbrokers in American history, but probably the most innovative and influential in terms of setting the course for investment brokerage. He created a conservative image for Wall Street that would attract the small investor toward acquiring shares in the country's economy and thereby made investing commonplace among the middle-class.

A firm believer in the free capital market, Merrill bequeathed his share of the limited partnership of Merrill Lynch (worth $5.5 million) to the Merrill Foundation for the Advancement of Investment Knowledge, which he had created in 1945 to give grants to institutions to study free enterprise. He donated 95 percent of his $25 million estate to colleges, churches, and hospitals. Charles E. Merrill was married and divorced three times; he had three children. He died on October 6, 1956.

Further Reading

There is no biography of Charles E. Merrill. His role in American brokerage is discussed in Martin Mayer, *Wall Street: Men and Money* (1955); Edwin Hoyt, *The Supersalesmen* (1962); and Robert Sobel, *The Big Board: A History of the New York Stock Market* (1965) and *Inside Wall Street* (1977). □

James Merrill

A lyrical and mystical poet often compared to W. H. Auden and William Butler Yeats, James Merrill (1926-1995) is best known for his series of poems inspired by the automatic writing and messages of spirit guides through the medium of an Ouija board. These poems were collected in *The Changing Light at Sandover* (1982).

While Merrill's poems are not self-confessional, he used formal poetic structures to blend autobiography with archetype and fable, creating a sense of inner tension and authenticity.

Merrill was born in New York City in 1926, the son of Charles Merrill, the founder of Merrill Lynch, the stock brokerage. Wealth brought privilege: Merrill was educated at private schools where the written word and poetry were emphasized, and he also had a multi-lingual governess as a young boy who taught him respect for languages. An appreciation for music, especially opera, came early to Merrill, and that dramatic form had a lasting influence on his poetry. Versification was encouraged in the Merrill household, so much so that in Merrill's senior year at Lawrenceville School, his father privately published his first book of poems. Merrill attended Amherst College, where he continued to write poetry, though his studies were interrupted by a year in the infantry during World War II. Returning to Amherst, he published poetry in *Poetry* and *Kenyon Review* and completed his thesis on Marcel Proust. Proust, in his fascination with the everyday and with one's own history, would have a lasting influence on Merrill's later poetry. Wealth also meant that Merrill did not have to earn his living from poetry and could live where he wanted as he wanted. Throughout his life, he travelled in Europe extensively, and made homes in Stonington, Connecticut; Athens, Greece; and New York City. With the death of his father, Merrill established the Ingram Merrill Foundation to provide grants to writers and painters. Merrill died of a heart attack in Tucson, Arizona, in 1995.

Merrill's literary product shows a gradual ripening and maturity of form from the first of his published works up through the last. The poems in *First Poems* (1951) received mixed reviews, and for the next several years, Merrill wrote short stories, a novel, and tried his hand at theater. With *The Country of a Thousand Years of Peace* (1959), Merrill came back to poetry with elegant formal poems that display a cultivated taste in things domestic and in travel. In ways, the poems here chronicle the early life of an American aristocrat, and received the same mixed reviews as his earlier poems. *Water Street* (1962) continues to chronicle Merrill's life, loves, and travels, but the language is tighter, the verse line more colloquialized. Merrill won his first National Book Award for *Nights and Days* (1966), a book that takes on Yeats's great theme of wisdom coming from age and dissolution. *Fire Screen* (1969) and *Braving the Elements* (1972) continue to demonstrate a developing maturity on

Merrill's part. The twin themes of time and eros have been established in his poetry; the formalism is still there, but does not dominate the work; and the elegance has given way to a more gritty stance. Merrill won the Bollingen Prize in 1973 for *Braving the Elements.* A smooth, conversational narrative style had been established in Merrill's poetry by the early 1970s, paving the way for his major works, *Divine Comedies* (1976) and *Mirabell: Books of Numbers* (1978). Merrill and his long-time companion, David Jackson, had been experimenting with a home-made Ouija board since 1955. Whether a *folie a deux* or a connection to a higher spiritual plane, such activities put Merrill in touch with a spirit guide, Ephraim, who led the poet to a mystical and sacred dialogue reminiscent of a blend of Yeats, Dante, Proust, Byron, and Auden. With these poems—the first of which were twenty years in the writing—Merrill became more than a lyric poet. He fused autobiography and archetype; created an epic approach to his life; and, with *Mirabell,* developed a scientific/religious metaphor for the meaning and flux of the universe. Merrill won a Pulitzer Prize for *Divine Comedies* and a second National Book Award for *Mirabell: Books of Numbers.* These poems were completed with *Scripts for the Pageant* (1980). Until his death, Merrill continued to produce poetry of note, as well as a memoir, *A Different Person* (1993), which reflected not only on his family, but on his homosexuality in relation to his writing.

The accomplishment of James Merrill was his steady growth from gentility to vision; from formal elegance to prophecy and epic poetry. Once he left mere gentility behind and dealt with themes more dramatic and personal, Merrill's poetry took on a weight and importance that brought critical acclaim from all quarters. The sacred books collected in *The Changing Light at Sandover* are regarded as a major poetic statement, and Merrill as a metaphysical poet who employed both wit and charm.

Further Reading

Contemporary Literary Criticism, Gale, Volume 2, 1974; Volume 3, 1975; Volume 6, 1976; Volume 8, 1978; Volume 13, 1980; Volume 18, 1981.
Dickey, James, *Babel to Byzantium*, Farrar, Straus, 1968.
Dictionary of Literary Biography, Volume V: *American Poets Since World War II*, Gale, 1980.
Kalstone, David, *Five Temperaments: Elizabeth Bishop, Robert Lowell, James Merrill, Adrienne Rich, John Ashbery*, Oxford University Press, 1977.
Labrie, Ross, *Merrill*, 1982.
Lehman, David, and Berger, Charles, editors, *James Merrill: Essays in Criticism*, Cornell University Press, 1982.
Moffett, Judith, *Merrill: An Introduction to the Poetry*, 1984. □

Robert K. Merton

Robert K. Merton (born 1910) was a sociologist, educator, and internationally regarded academic statesman for sociology in contemporary research and social policy. He was also a leading interpreter of responsible functional analysis, of major social factors in scientific development, and of underlying and unanticipated strains in modern society. He is considered the founder of the sociology of science.

(1983); and the first Who's Who in America Achievement Award in the field of social science and social policy (1984). In 1985 Columbia University honored him with the Doctor of Letters degree.

Born in Philadelphia on July 5, 1910, Robert Merton was educated at Temple University and received his doctorate from Harvard University in 1936. After being attracted to sociology by George E. Simpson, he studied with or was profoundly influenced by such thinkers as George Sarton, Pitirim Sorokin, Talcott Parsons, and L. J. Henderson. An instructorship at Harvard was followed by a professorship at Tulane University. From 1941 until his retirement in 1978 he was one of the key figures in the development of the Department of Sociology at Columbia University and in received national and international recognition for his contributions to sociological analysis.

Received Awards and Honors

As a consequence, Merton held a number of important positions, among them associate director of the Bureau of Applied Social Research at Columbia University, trustee of the Center for Advanced Study in the Behavioral Sciences at Stanford University (1952-1975), and president of the American Sociological Association (1957). He received several prestigious awards: one for distinguished scholarship in the humanities from the American Council of Learned Societies (1962); the Commonwealth Award for Distinguished Service to Sociology (1970); a MacArthur Prize Fellowship

Focused on Variety of Responses in Social Behavior

Though Merton studied a considerable range of social situations and social categories or groups, his basic and enduring contributions to sociological analysis consist of three complementary themes. First, human behavior can best be understood as embedded in social structures (groups, organizations, social classes, communities, nations) which simultaneously present opportunities and constraints to their members. Second, in varying degrees individuals confront differing clues and ambiguities in social demands, and thus humans develop mixed or ambivalent values and motives in their responses to others. Consequently, sociologists cannot focus on either formal, official patterns (rules, laws, etc.) or the special features of individuals to understand the course and variations in important social structures. Third, because of this pervasive complexity in social experience, normal or "routine" social behavior typically generates multiple consequences, some predictable and desirable, but others largely unanticipated and even contrary to the intentions of many persons. On the whole, then, Merton advocated careful and yet imaginative study of social phenomena and cautioned against superficial, "common sense" investigations and slavish dependence on any technique of probing human social participation.

More specifically, Merton combined study of actual (or historically significant) social organizations and groups with a focus on some limited but crucial and recurring problem in social structures—the so-called "middle range" problems and related explanations. One such focus was social specialization and related issues of differences in responsibilities, types and complexity of social contacts, and cultural interests. Merton distinguished "local" versus "cosmopolitan" types of leaders and showed how such differences underscored meaningful differences in influence. Similarly, Merton connected different levels of status with availability of different forms of personal influence ("reference groups") and linked the process of changing one's status—social mobility—with the selection of new reference groups ("anticipatory socialization") in the cases of soldiers, voters, and some nonconformists.

Studied Socialization Issues

Another cardinal issue was socialization, the process of acquiring and sustaining legitimate roles in given social organizations. In this respect Merton studied medical students, intellectuals, scientists, bureaucrats, and various professionals. He and his associates gave much attention to the conflict between ideal goals and personal status concerns, and even to the "normal" inconsistency between accepted norms in academic training and the realities of "on-the-job" training of scientists and professionals.

Concerned with Social Regulation and Deviation

Much of Merton's continuing sociological concern, however, centered on the twin sociological problems of social regulation and social deviation—each type of phenomenon necessarily conditioning the other. Merton inferentially demonstrated the basic fragility of such normal forms of social regulation as formal leadership, dominant cultural values, and professional standards. Furthermore, he pointed to such basic patterns as the variable consequences in behavior of imposing demanding objectives without providing suitable means; the fact that people often estimate their social opportunities and limitations not in objective terms, but in comparison with some desired level or with a self-selected "new" reference group ("relative deprivation"); and the special and virtually unshakable advantage of persons in favored social positions (the "Matthew Effect"), which dissipates attempts at equalization and implicitly undermines the legitimacy of those in positions of responsibility.

Demonstrated Intellectual Flexibility in Spoof

After the mid-1960s Merton immersed himself in the sociology of science, the study of major cultural and organizational factors in the work of scientists (principally in the physical and biological sciences). This involved careful analysis of the careers of Nobel laureates, the processes of competition among scientists, the connection between publication and scientific investigation, and the problematic nature of discovery and acceptance in the sacred realm of science. However, Merton also demonstrated his intellectual versatility in a delightful spoof of scholarship in his *On the Shoulders of Giants*. In retrospect, his entire intellectual career was notable for the flexibility with which he combined theoretical formulations, useful typologies and classifications, empirical investigations, and a concern for the practical implications of sociological work in modern society.

His major works include *Social Theory and Social Structure* (1949), and *The Sociology of Science* (1973). His collection of essays, *On Social Structure and Science,* was reprinted in 1996. In the introduction, the editor of the collection, Piotr Sztompka, wrote that Merton's work had "opened up fruitful areas of inquiry along lines that he and generations of others would pursue for decades."

Further Reading

The central works of Merton's early period include *Science, Technology, and Society in Seventeenth Century England* (1938), *Mass Persuasion* (1945), *Social Theory and Social Structure* (several editions from 1949 to 1968), and the edited work *Reader in Bureaucracy* (1952). Later major works dealt with the sociology of science and the professions: *The Student Physician* (1957); *Sociology of Science: Theoretical and Empirical Investigations* (1973); *Sociological Ambivalence and Other Essays* (1976); and *Social Research and the Practicing Professions* (1982). Some indication of Merton's influence is contained in a stimulating collection of essays, edited by Lewis A. Coser, in celebration of Merton's 65th birthday: *The Idea of Social Structure: Papers in Honor of Robert K. Merton* (1975).

See also *Science* November 1, 1996; Sztompka, Pi, *Robert K. Merton, An Intellectual Profile*, St. Martin's Press, 1986; and *Robert K. Merton: Consensus and Controversy*, Falmer Press, 1990. □

Thomas Merton

Thomas Merton (1915-1968), Roman Catholic writer, was a Trappist monk, social critic, and spiritual guide.

Thomas Merton was born in Prades, France, on January 31, 1915, the first-born child of an American mother, born Ruth Jenkins, and a New Zealander, Owen Merton. His parents, aspiring artists, had met at art school in Paris in 1911 and married in 1914. They seldom were able to earn their living by painting (his mother became an interior decorator and his father worked as a gardener and farmer), but art dominated their lives. Partly because of their opposition to World War I, the Mertons left France for the United States in 1916. There they were received by Ruth's parents in Queens, New York, but soon struck out on their own, trying to live by farming, journalism, and music (for a time Owen was a church organist). A second son, John Paul, was born on November 2, 1918. The profile of the Merton family at this time was one of rather poor, impractical idealists, dedicated to art and peace but not notably religious. Ruth Merton contracted stomach cancer and died in 1921, when Thomas was six.

An Unsettled Early Life

Merton's early schooling was erratic, because his father frequently withdrew the boy to have him alongside during his travels (to Cape Cod and Bermuda, among other places) to paint. Merton's father took a lover, the writer Evelyn Scott, who became young Tom's rival for his father's affections. The father's poverty, and the growing wildness of the son, led in 1923 to Tom's return to New York and the supervision of his grandparents. Owen Merton travelled to the south of France and Algeria, made a success of his painting with a London exhibit, and took Tom (as he was known in the family) back to the south of France with him in 1925. John Paul stayed in New York, while Owen (minus Evelyn Scott, who had left him) and Tom began life in St. Antonin, a rather medieval town. Tom attended a local French Catholic school, was subject to much bullying, and experienced during a reunion with his grandparents and brother in 1926 that bitterness that had become the norm in his family's relationships. He thought of his brother as a rival, and his grandparents, who had never approved of his father, were vocal in their prejudices against the Catholic schooling he was receiving.

Tom was soon moved to the secular Lycée Ingres in nearby Montauban, which he disliked because of its harsh

discipline and poor food. In 1927 he was diagnosed as having contracted tuberculosis and was placed with a couple in Auvergne to rest and recuperate. In 1928 Owen Merton had another successful art show in London and, on the advice of friends, moved Tom there for schooling. Owen had been sick periodically, and in 1931 he died, unaware that the paintings he had stored in France, on which he had rested his hopes of acquiring an artistic reputation, had been destroyed by flood.

So at age 16 Thomas Merton was a full orphan. He had been taken in three years previously by an aunt and uncle in London who were connected to the British public school system, and he was sent to Oakham public school. In 1931 his grandfather presented him with a measure of financial independence (stocks and land). London and sophistication became his enthusiasms, although at the end of 1930 he spent a brief time in Strasbourg for language studies. He did well at Oakham, becoming editor of the literary magazine, majoring in languages, and considering a future career in the British diplomatic corps.

Having won a scholarship to Cambridge, Merton finished his schoolboy career reading widely, travelling to Europe and America, and thinking romantic thoughts about poetry and young women. He also became more interested in religion, a subject he had previously approached with hostility. At Cambridge, however, he was so lured by alcohol and women (there were persistent rumors he had fathered at least one illegitimate child) that he neglected his studies and at the end of the first year did not do well enough in his examinations to renew his scholarship. On the advice—if not command—of his grandparents he returned to the United States and enrolled at Columbia University.

Turn Toward Religion

By 1935 the chief question in Merton's life was the existence of God. This dominated his years at Columbia, where he was a great success. However, at first he was more interested in writing and politics than in formal religion. In politics he felt drawn to socialist and communist political theory (more than their practice). He made good friends with a literary circle, was impressed by the English professor Mark Van Doren, and became editor of the Columbia Yearbook.

After graduation he stayed on for a master's degree in English literature (becoming much interested in William Blake), and in 1938 he was received into the Roman Catholic Church, culminating months of study of Catholic writers. Among these the philosopher Jacques Maritain was especially influential. He initially planned on a career as a writer, perhaps after a doctoral degree at Columbia, but slowly began considering a vocation in the priesthood. After various struggles, teaching at St. Bonaventure's University, and fear of being drafted, in April of 1941 he made a retreat at the Trappist Monastery in Gethsemani, Kentucky, and in December of 1941 joined the community there, entering what he expected to be a great world of silence.

Trappist Monk and Author

Thomas Merton's fame stems from the autobiography, *The Seven Storey Mountain,* that he published in 1948. In the first seven years of his life as a Trappist he had completed the novitiate and been allowed to write poetry. Indeed, his writing had become a matter about which both he and his superiors were of several minds. On the one hand, the superiors put him to writing works designed to explain the monastic life. On the other hand, both they and Merton himself feared that writing would encourage self-centeredness and eccentricity. *The Seven Storey Mountain* was a great success, being compared to *The Confessions* of St. Augustine, and it made Merton a name in households interested in religious, especially Catholic, literature.

Merton was ordained a priest in 1949, and he continued to write books, mainly on the monastic life and contemplation, that received good press. Most notable of those from the time of his ordination are *Seeds of Contemplation* and *The Sign of Jonas.* Already his concrete, readable style and his mixture of poetic and monastic sensibilities were winning him a wide audience. He was praised for being able to escape the technical vocabulary of theology and to communicate the substance of Christian experience of prayer, community life, manual work, sacramentality, and the like. At this point his spirituality was rather traditionally monastic. In later years he would win a wider audience by venturing into social questions, above all racial justice and the involvement of the United States in Vietnam. In his final years his interests broadened to Eastern religions, especially Buddhist monastic life and Taoist spirituality. But from the time of the appearance of *The Seven Storey Mountain* he was famous as the man who had been converted from a dramatic life of artistic self-indulgence to an equally dramatic life of monastic silence and penance (out of which, paradoxically, came a torrent of books).

These books helped his monastery financially in the late 1950s and they attracted more applicants to the Order. Merton assumed greater responsibilities within the monastery, serving as master of novices, but he disliked the turn toward business (dairy and food products) the monastery had taken. Through many years he was at odds with his abbot about these matters and the management of reproduction rights to his books. He became a naturalized citizen of the United States in 1951.

During the 1950s Merton continued to turn out good books on the spiritual life, and he continued to study subjects, such as psychoanalysis and zen, that he thought would help him better counsel the young monks of whom he had charge. He read widely: the fathers of the church, modern literature, Latin American history (in view of the possibility of his monastery's founding another establishment there). He also went more deeply into the Bible. In addition to his books, he wrote copiously in diaries. Some of his works on secular subjects were rejected by Church censors, and Merton felt increasingly attracted to living apart from his community as a hermit. Although he had many friends in the monastery, rules against intimacy, and increasingly conflicts with his abbot, made life there a trial.

Eventually he did win permission to live apart at Gethsemani.

Through the 1960s Merton expanded his wide correspondence with eminent figures (which already included the Zen authority D. T. Suzuki and the Russian writer Boris Pasternak). He continued to write poetry, with his major themes increasingly concerned with violence and injustice. He intensified his opposition to nuclear warfare, supported Catholic pacifists (until one burned himself in protest), and received a stream of distinguished visitors to Gethsemani. Merton was encouraged by the changes within the Catholic Church under Pope John XXIII and the Second Vatican Council. He expanded his already wide range of interests: photography, Muslim and Jewish cultures, and a deepening interest in Buddhist and Hindu monasticism.

In 1966, during a stay in the hospital, he fell in love with a student nurse and felt transformed by this wonderful yet painful experience. *Conjectures of a Guilty Bystander,* published in 1966, was one of his most influential works and won praise for illuminating the connection between monastic solitude and social conscience. His *Asian Journal* of 1968, which recorded impressions of a trip he made to give lectures and study Asian monasticism, was also influential. Merton died of accidental electrocution on December 10, 1968, in Bangkok, where he was participating in a conference on monasticism and ecumenism.

Further Reading

Of Merton's own works, *The Seven Storey Mountain, The Sign of Jonas, Conjectures of a Guilty Bystander,* and *The Asian Journal of Thomas Merton* form a representative collection. Two posthumous collections, *The Collected Poems of Thomas Merton* (1977) and *The Hidden Ground of Love: The Letters of Thomas Merton on Religious Experience and Social Concerns* (1985), complement these works. Three useful biographical studies are Elena Malits's *The Solitary Explorer: Merton's Transforming Journey* (1980), Monica Furlong's *Merton: A Biography* (1980), and Michael Mott's *The Seven Mountains of Thomas Merton* (1984).

Additional Sources

Forest, James H., *Living with wisdom: a life of Thomas Merton,* Maryknoll, N.Y.: Orbis Books, 1991.

Grayston, Donald, *Thomas Merton, the development of a spiritual theologian,* New York: E. Mellen Press, 1985.

Kountz, Peter, *Thomas Merton as writer and monk: a cultural study, 1915-1951,* Brooklyn, N.Y.: Carlson Pub., 1991.

McInerny, Dennis Q., *Thomas Merton; the man and his works,* Spencer, Mass. Cistercian Publications; distributed by Consortium Press, Washington, 1974.

Nouwen, Henri J. M., *Thomas Merton, contemplative critic,* New York, N.Y.: Triumph Books, 1991.

Woodcock, George, *Thomas Merton, monk and poet: a critical study,* Vancouver: Douglas and McIntyre, 1978. □

Claudio Merulo

The Italian composer, organist, and teacher Claudio Merulo (1533-1604) was particularly important in

the evolution of an independent style in organ composition, and he made significant contributions to the development of the keyboard toccata.

Claudio Merulo, whose real name was Merlotti, served briefly as organist of the Cathedral at Brescia. He then became second organist at St. Mark's, Venice, in 1557 and first organist, succeeding Annibale Padovano, in 1566 (at which time Andrea Gabrieli became second organist). In 1586 Merulo entered the service of the Duke of Parma, became organist in the Cathedral there the following year, and returned to the ducal service as organist in 1591. He was also active as a publisher of music, and he seems to have taken an active interest in organ building. Most of his works were published posthumously or at a long enough period after their composition to make dating of the various stylistic innovations difficult.

As yet, not enough is known about Merulo's vocal works; it is possible that he should rank with the great Venetian masters of sacred vocal polyphony. There are some Masses in the Venetian polychoral manner, as well as some motets. His four volumes of madrigals (published 1566-1604) are well within the normal style of the period.

In organ music, Merulo and his contemporaries stand at the critical point at which a distinctive idiomatic style and appropriate forms for the instrument were emerging. In his *Canzoni d'intavolatura d'organo . . . Lib. I* (published 1592) there are four pieces in keyboard tablature that appear in another source in separate part books for instrumental ensemble, showing that the idiomatic distinction was not absolute.

The toccatas of Padovano and Andrea Gabrieli take as their point of departure the rather free style of the intonation (small introductory pieces played by the organist to give pitch to singers, particularly to the celebrants). In his *Toccate d'intavolatura d'organo* (1604, two books) Merulo introduces several elements designed to tighten the form. He incorporates, between sections in the normal rhapsodic manner of the toccata, one or two sections in the imitative manner of the ricercar. He also introduces some imitative work into the opening and closing sections, achieving structural connection by using identical thematic material. Such interest in structural strength is also shown by the tendency in his ricercari (*Ricercari d'intavolatura d'organo,* 1605) toward monothematic treatment. In some cases he returns, late in the piece, to a countersubject introduced earlier and treats it imitatively.

Merulo also wrote organ canzonas, organ Masses, a few original instrumental works, and some intermezzi (stage works with incidental music, performed at the courts).

During the 16th century brilliance of performance and improvisation played an important part in the activity of the organists at St. Mark's. Merulo enjoyed such a reputation as a performer that his practice and teaching were made central in the definitive work on performance that came from the pen of his pupil Girolamo Diruta (*Il Transilvano,* part I, 1593; part II, 1608).

Further Reading

There is no definitive work on Merulo. A discussion of his works and those of his contemporaries is in Gustave Reese, *Music in the Renaissance* (1954; rev. ed. 1959). □

Franz Anton Mesmer

The German physician Franz Anton Mesmer (1734-1815) developed a healing technique called mesmerism that is the historical antecedent of hypnosis.

Franz Mesmer was born on May 23, 1734, in the village of Itznang, Switzerland. At age 15 he entered the Jesuit College at Dillingen in Bavaria, and from there he went in 1752 to the University of Ingolstadt, where he studied philosophy, theology, music, and mathematics. Eventually he decided on a medical career. In 1759 he entered the University of Vienna, receiving a medical degree in 1766.

Mesmer then settled in Vienna and began to develop his concept of an invisible fluid in the body that affected health. At first he used magnets to manipulate this fluid but gradually came to believe these were unnecessary, that, in fact, anything he touched became magnetized and that a health-giving fluid emanated from his own body. Mesmer believed a rapport with his patients was essential for cure and achieved it with diverse trappings. His treatment rooms were heavily draped, music was played, and Mesmer appeared in long, violet robes.

Mesmer's methods were frowned upon by the medical establishment in Vienna, so in 1778 he moved to Paris, hoping for a better reception for his ideas. In France he achieved overwhelming popularity, except among physicians. On the basis of medical opinion, repeated efforts were made by the French government to discredit Mesmer. At a time of political turmoil and revolution, such efforts were viewed as attempts to prevent the majority's enjoyment of health, and the popularity of mesmerism continued unabated. However, under continued pressure Mesmer retired to Switzerland at the beginning of the French Revolution, where he spent the remaining years of his life.

Critics focused attention of Mesmer's methods and insisted that cures existed only in the patient's mind. The 19th-century studies of Mesmer's work by James Braid and others in England demonstrated that the important aspect of Mesmer's treatment was the patient's reaction. Braid introduced the term "hypnotism" and insisted that hypnotic phenomena were essentially physiological and not associated with a fluid. Still later studies in France by A. A. Liebeault and Hippolyte Bernheim attributed hypnotic phenomena to psychological forces, particularly suggestion. While undergoing this scientific transformation in the 19th century, mesmerism, in other quarters, became more closely associated with occultism, spiritualism, and faith

healing, providing in the last instance the basis for Christian Science.

Further Reading

A standard history of mesmerism with biographical details is Margaret Goldsmith, *Franz Anton Mesmer: A History of Mesmerism* (1934). A definitive study of mesmerism and its relation to faith healing and the rise of Christian Science is Frank Podmore, *Mesmerism and Christian Science* (1909; repr. as *From Mesmer to Christian Science: A Short History of Mental Healing,* 1964). Also useful is Stefan Zweig, *Mental Healers* (trans. 1932).

Additional Sources

Buranelli, Vincent, *The wizard from Vienna,* London: Owen, 1976.
Wyckoff, James, *Franz Anton Mesmer: between God and Devil,* Englewood Cliffs, N.J.: Prentice-Hall, 1975. □

Messali Hadj

Messali Hadj (1898-1974) is considered the founder of the Algerian nationalist movement, having first spoken the word "independence" at an anticolonial congress in Brussels in 1927. After leading the most radical wing of Algerian nationalism for more than a quarter century, he was left behind in 1954 by the new generation of men who actually launched the Algerian revolution.

Messali Hadj was born on March 16, 1898, in the western Algerian city of Tlemcen. He was the youngest of seven children in a traditional family whose economic circumstances were extremely marginal. He attended a Qur'anic (Koranic) school and also a local French primary school. But because his parents sent him out to work during his tenth and eleventh years, Messali was 18 years old before he completed the primary curriculum. That ended his formal education.

Just before his 20th birthday, Messali Hadj was drafted into the French army, where he served three years, mostly in the Bordeaux region. In France the young man was astonished at the vastly higher living standards of French peasants and working people. Army life exposed him to the order, discipline, and relatively higher status that went with military service, while at the same time embittering him at the institutionalized prejudice to which colonial troops were subjected. It was in Bordeaux, also, that he first became acquainted with Marxist writings and with the activities of the Communist-dominated French labor movement.

Upon his discharge in February 1921, Messali returned to Tlemcen at a time when Algeria was experiencing severe economic depression. Trying his hand at five different jobs in the commercial and manufacturing sectors, Messali was appalled at the conditions imposed upon him by each of these Muslim employers. After two and a half years in which his political sensibilities grew enormously, Messali moved to Paris, joining there the largest of the North African immigrant communities in France, which then totaled some 120,000.

The new immigrant tried several industrial and service jobs but finally went into business for himself, selling stockings at weekly markets in the environs of the capital. He married Emilie Busquant, a department store clerk and member of the French Communist Party, by whom he had two children, Ali and Djanina. His wife remained loyal to him until her death in 1953.

Culturally isolated and confronted with many material problems, the Algerian workers in France discovered that only the French far left demonstrated much interest in their issues and welfare. In June 1926, with Communist logistical and moral support, North Africans created the *Etoile nord-africaine* (ENA) as a political organization to battle for their rights and for amelioration of conditions in their homelands. Messali Hadj was secretary-general of the ENA from its inception and soon came to dominate it. In February 1927 he delivered the ENA's first list of "Algerian demands" to an anticolonial congress organized by the Communist International in Brussels. Most singular among those demands was a call for the independence of Algeria. At a time when French-educated middle-class Algerians were working for assimilation of their country into the French Republic, and when Muslim reformers were calling for educational and cultural renewal, Messali's call was truly revolutionary.

Membership in the ENA grew rapidly among the émigré community. By 1928 the Communist Party terminated its financial support, partially because Messali and his colleagues demonstrated more independence than it was comfortable with and partially because the ENA's nationalistic agenda was not consistent with party priorities of the moment. When the courts outlawed the movement the next year, the ENA went underground. In 1930 Messali began publishing a newspaper, *El Ouma,* which achieved phenomenal readership and for the first time drew attention to his movement within Algeria itself. At the same time Messali was fine-tuning the rhetoric of his movement to include a blend of Marxist themes and popular Islamic themes that could resonate with the lower middle classes with whom he was most at home.

For illegally resurrecting the ENA in 1933, French courts sentenced Messali to six months in prison. When, in 1936, Islamic reformers and liberal assimilationists seemed on the point of reaching an accord with France's Popular Front government, Messali traveled back to Algeria for the first time in 13 years to register his objections. In a stirring speech delivered August 2 in the Algiers municipal stadium, Messali stunned and thrilled his audience by resoundingly rejecting assimilation. Thus he began the process of implanting the independence movement on Algerian soil. When the ENA was outlawed again in 1937, Messali founded the Party of the Algerian People (PPA). For this the authorities jailed him in August 1937, and he spent most of the next nine years in prison or under house arrest. As the 1930s advanced into the 1940s and France rejected one moderate reform initiative after another, Messali Hadj, even in prison, became the only alternative for the growing body of Algerians for whom the colonial status quo had become insupportable.

Freed in 1946, Messali founded the *Mouvement pour le triomphe des libertés démocratiques* (MTLD) as a successor to the outlawed PPA. Unusually tall, bearded, and always wearing the traditional *jalaba* with a *tarbush* or a red fez, Messali Hadj became the most potent symbol of Algerian nationalist aspirations. His organization, however, was soon riven by internal dissensions. These included divisions as to the relative merits of political as opposed to revolutionary strategies and arguments over the decision-making process and leadership, which in turn related to both ideological and generational differences. When, in 1952, Messali was ordered to house arrest in western France, intra-party communications worsened and differences between him and other party leaders grew. By 1954 disillusioned younger activists began deserting the squabbling MTLD, and by October they created the National Liberation Front (FLN), which launched the Algerian War of Independence on November 1, 1954.

The FLN called upon patriotic Algerians of all political groupings to rally to its banner. Most eventually did so, but Messali refused, going on to found his own Algerian National Movement (MNA). First in Algeria and then in France, MNA loyalists and the FLN entered into bloody, fratricidal battles, with the MNA gradually losing ground in both places. When Charles de Gaulle came to power in 1958,

Messali Hadj for the first and only time in his life urged compromise between Algerians and the French. With his effectiveness waning, he was released from house arrest in January 1959 and settled in Gouvieux, north of Paris. There he lived until he died of cancer on June 3, 1974. Messali Hadj was buried in his hometown of Tlemcen four days later.

Further Reading

The most detailed study of Messali Hadj's life and career is Benjamin Stora's *Messali Hadj, pionnier du nationalisme algérien, (1898-1974)* (1982). His career is also discussed in John Ruedy, *Modern Algeria. The Origins and Development of a Nation* (1992); Charles-Robert Ageron, *Histoire de l'Algérie contemporaine,* Vol. II (1979); and Mahfoud Kaddache, *Histoire du nationalisme algérien* and *Question nationale et politique algérienne, 1919-1951,* 2 vols. (1981). □

Olivier Messiaen

The French composer and teacher Olivier Messiaen (1908-1992), one of the most original composers and musical thinkers of his time, had a strong influence on many of the important composers of the following generation.

Olivier Messiaen was born in Avignon, France on December 10, 1908. His mother, Marie Sauvage, was a poet, and his father was a well-known translator of Shakespeare's plays into French. They encouraged their musically precocious son, who composed little pieces when he was only 7. The boy heard a performance of Claude Debussy's *Pelléas et Mélisande* when he was 10, and it made such a strong impression that he decided to become a composer. He entered the Paris Conservatory the next year and remained there for 11 years, studying theory, organ, piano, improvisation, history, esthetics of music, and composition. He was a brilliant student in all of these fields, and each played a part in his later activities.

In 1931 Messiaen became organist at the Church of the Trinity in Paris, a post he held for many years and where his brilliant organ improvisations attracted much attention. He served in the French army during World War II and spent 2 years as a prisoner of war. In 1942 he started teaching at the Paris Conservatory, and the theories he expounded in his classes in analysis and rhythm were highly stimulating to his students. They are described in his *Technique of My Musical Language* (1950). He also taught at Tanglewood in the United States and at the highly influential International Summer Course for New Music in Darmstadt, Germany.

Messiaen was an exceptional 20th-century French composer in that he was not influenced by the classicism of Igor Stravinsky, which was the predominant musical style. Messiaen believed that music was a highly expressive, romantic art. Instead of restricting the tonal resources of music, he tremendously expanded them. Drawing on his vast erudition, he found inspiration and new sounds in Japanese,

Indian, and ancient Greek music as well as in the sounds of nature, particularly bird calls. This interest is shown in such pieces as *Turangalila* (1949), *Catalogue des oiseaux* (1959; *Catalog of Birds*), and *Seven Hai-kai* (1962). Another of the bases of Messiaen's music was his mystical Catholicism, evidenced in large-scale compositions such as *Les Corps glorieux: Sept visions brèves de la vie des ressuscités* (1939; *Radiant Bodies: Seven Short Visions of the Life of the Resurrected*) and *Vingt regards sur l'enfant Jesus* (1944; *Twenty Gazes on the Child Jesus*).

It was not Messiaen's concept of programmatic music that influenced his pupils so much as his compositional techniques. For instance, he devised new scales and was one of the first to divorce rhythm from melody, usually thought to be inseparable. Messiaen conceived patterns of durations that could be manipulated and reversed in much the same way that Arnold Schoenberg manipulated tones in his twelve-tone works. Extending the idea, Messiaen saw the possibility of "serializing" dynamics (the degrees of loudness) and attacks (legato, portato, staccato), normally subservient to melody, to pursue patterns of their own. A piece for piano, *Mode de valeur et d'intensité* (1950; *Modes of Duration and Loudness*), consists of arrangements of 36 pitches, 24 durations, 7 attacks, and 7 degrees of loudness. This piece was a landmark of "totally controlled" composition, an important musical idea of the postwar period.

Messiaen composed another piece based on bird songs in 1972, titled *La Fauvette des jardins* (*The Garden Warbler*). In 1983 he saw his first opera, *St. François d'Assise*, produced at the Paris Opera. He died on April 27, 1992 in Paris. The New York Philharmonic later that year performed a posthumously published work, *Éclairs sur l'Au-Delà* (*Illuminations of the Beyond*).

Further Reading

Studies of Messiaen's life and work are in Arthur Cohn, *Twentieth-century Music in Western Europe: The Compositions and the Recordings* (1965), and David Ewen, *The World of Twentieth-century Music* (1968). For a discussion of Messiaen's place in French music see Paul Henry Lang and Nathan Broder, eds., *Contemporary Music in Europe: A Comprehensive Survey* (1966). ☐

Metacom

Metacom (1640-1676) was a Native American chief (sachem) whose tribe, the Wampanoags, waged the most devastating war against the Enghish in early American history.

King Philip/Metacom was the son of Massasoit and the younger brother of Wamsutta, all three of whom were at one time sachem (chief) of the Wampanoag tribe of southern New England. Massasoit had befriended the English settlers at Plymouth soon after their arrival, and the two communities had become allies against the traditional enemies of the Wampanoags, the Narragansett tribe. But relations between the Wampanoags and the English deteriorated gradually in the succeeding decades. The problem was simple. When the English first arrived, they offered some Native American tribes leverage against neighboring unfriendly tribes. But as the English colonies expanded, they occupied more and more land that had belonged to the area tribes. Even tribes on good terms with the English, like the Wampanoags, eventually came to see the English as a threat. In New England, these tensions resulted in King Philip's War (1675-76), one of the most serious Indian wars in all of American history.

By the 1660s, the Wampanoags, the Mohegans, and the Pequots were seen as sympathetic to the English (despite the Pequot War of 1637), while the Narragansetts were considered troublesome. When Massasoit died in the 1660s, he was succeeded by his eldest son, Wamsutta. The English bestowed new names on Wamsutta and Metacom, Alexander and Philip, respectively. Some modern writers note that this showed little respect for Native American names, but the English thought it an honor. In any case, relations with Wamsutta and Metacom soured quickly.

Plymouth held no clear charter to "their" land, and what legal authority they did possess was tied to their obligations to protect the Wampanoags. But Plymouth was also determined to expand its territory, and the younger leaders of the Wampanoags were less compliant than had been their father. In 1662, Wamsutta was summoned by the English to answer questions about a suspected Indian plot against the English. Before he could return home, he fell ill

and died. Though some Indians believed he had been poisoned, he may also have died of natural causes.

This left Metacom to become sachem, whereupon he renewed his father's alliance with the English. Rumors spread in the late 1660s that Metacom was planning an uprising, but he denied any such plans. Indeed, there were war scares linked to various tribes in 1667, 1669, and 1671, and it is impossible to determine who was planning what. In April 1671, Metacom was again questioned, this time at Taunton, about a possible Indian attack, and he was forced to surrender the weapons that various Indians had secured from the English. But Metacom may have used his influence to encourage other tribes in the area to resist. When they refused to surrender their arms, the Plymouth Colony made ready for war. A last-ditch effort to forestall fighting resulted in a meeting in September 1671, attended by the leaders of Plymouth and the Wampanoags, as well as the governors of Massachusetts and Connecticut. Metacom apparently had little choice but to accept the terms offered him: to pay a fine of £100 to the colony, to agree to follow the colony's advice before resorting to war or selling land, and to accept the authority of royal government and of Plymouth over his tribe. It is quite clear that Metacom did not take this agreement seriously, for it, in effect, ended the autonomy of his tribe in return for very little.

Most of what Metacom did in the next few years is unknown, but it is clear enough he tried to arrange alliances with other tribes, even the Narragansetts, in order to prepare to drive out the English settlers who were overwhelming his lands. Yet when war did break out in 1675, it did so before

Metacom was ready, either politically or militarily. His alliances were not yet in place, and the warriors of the region were not yet organized enough to withstand English resistance. Although the war would bear his name, it was far from under his control. By 1675, the Puritan population in New England had reached 50,000. Any Indian war designed to remove the English would require enormous cooperation between tribes which had worked against each other for years. According to historian Alden Vaughan, the Indians of the region divided, with a large minority supporting Metacom, a smaller number supporting the English, and a large group remaining neutral.

Was this war justified? Vaughan also insists that the Puritan legal system worked fairly and that the English did not abuse the tribes in their land purchases. But it is abundantly clear that the tribes had different notions of land-ownership and use than did the English. For example, if the English bought land but did not occupy it, some Indians thought the land available to them. When tribes sold land, they did not think they had renounced all hunting and fishing rights. The two cultures simply did not look upon land and its possession in the same way. Even if land disputes were not the only or even the most important issue, the tribes clearly feared that they were losing power in the face of the advancing settlers. Massasoit had allied with Plymouth to stave off the Narragansetts, but now Plymouth was the greater threat.

The events leading to the war began in 1675, with the death of John Sassamon. Sassamon was raised a Christian Indian and studied at Harvard College. For a time, he worked as Metacom's key assistant, writing many of his messages, but eventually he moved back to a Christian Indian community, finally becoming a preacher to the Indians near Middleborough. In January 1675, he warned Plymouth of Indian plans for war against the colony and suggested that his life might be forfeit because of his warning. At the end of the month, his body was found in a pond.

In June 1675, three Wampanoag warriors were convicted by an English jury (with the affirmation of a second, Indian jury) of Sassamon's murder, largely based on the testimony of one witness. Though the three protested their innocence, the trial enraged the tribe, and all three were sentenced to hang. For some reason, the third man did not die when hanged; in the terror of the moment, he claimed that the other two had actually committed the crime. He was later hanged anyway, and his "confession" only further convinced the people of Plymouth that the three had been guilty.

War Begins Between Indians, New Englanders

Reports of Indian preparations for war circulated through the community and outlying settlements throughout the early summer and fighting erupted in July. The war that followed was a Wampanoag war to be sure, but historian Francis Jennings calls it also the "Second Puritan Conquest" because New Englanders had long been preparing for an opportunity to remove the remaining major tribes.

Initially the Wampanoags and some allies (both official and clandestine) ambushed New England settlements with great success. Though some tribes did not join in (the Mohegans and Pequots remained allied to Connecticut), the Wampanoags' early successes gained assistance from tribes throughout New England. Even tribes in New York prepared for an attack, but they were first attacked themselves by the Mohawks, at the instigation of New York's governor. The attacks reached within 20 miles of Boston, the largest town in New England. Greatly feared and occupying valuable land, the Narragansetts officially remained neutral, even though many of their warriors wanted to fight. In any event, a Puritan attack in December 1675 brought them into the war officially.

But King Philip's War was not a coordinated effort; although it bore Metacom's name, its combatants did not follow his direction. He never commanded a combined Indian force. Indeed, the war followed its own path, over which he had very little control after the summer of 1675. The Indians succeeded largely through surprise and ambush. This was the first war in which they had firearms, and their New England adversaries abandoned the use of the pike. Nearly every frontier village designated a garrison house for protection in case of attack.

Despite early successes and the expansion of the war, the Indian tribes found food and weapons difficult to obtain by spring 1676. Many fled westward, others surrendered—as many as 180 on one July day in Boston. With the war nearly over, on August 1, Captain Benjamin Church spied an Indian across Taunton River and raised his gun to fire. But an Indian in Church's party called out that the man was one of theirs. Church hesitated. The Indian across the way looked up—it was Metacom—and escaped before they could shoot him. They gave chase and captured several of Metacom's party, including his wife and son, who were sent back to Boston. But Metacom got away.

No sooner had Church arrived home from this mission than he learned from Captain Roger Goulding, another veteran of the war, that Metacom had returned to his original campsite at Mount Hope. Their informant was none other than a member of Metacom's tribe, who claimed that Metacom had ordered his relative killed for suggesting a truce. This informant had escaped, he said, and would willingly lead Church's and Goulding's men back to Metacom's camp. Church believed the story, and he and Goulding and their men set out for the site.

They approached the camp just after midnight on August 12, 1676. Church posted his men—not enough to be sure of trapping the Indians—while Goulding's men moved around to attack from the other side and drive Metacom's company toward Church. There were no Indian sentries—perhaps Metacom expected to die soon. As Goulding watched and waited for his men to take up their positions, one Indian emerged from their shelter. He stopped and stared in Goulding's direction. Thinking himself discovered, Goulding fired and thus launched the attack before the trap was fully set. His men opened fire. Some Indians were hit, others ran. Metacom himself ran toward two of Church's men, one English and the other an Indian. The white man's

gun failed to fire, but the Indian felled Metacom with one shot. After the short skirmish, Church had Metacom's body decapitated and quartered; they carried his head back with them to Boston.

Although Indians were captured for months to follow, the war itself was over. In Boston, a debate raged over what to do with Metacom's son. Eventually, he and his mother were sold into slavery in the West Indies, where they disappear from the records. Although the Indian uprising had been unsuccessful, it had tremendous repercussions. Fifty-two of the 90 Puritan towns had been attacked, and 12 of these had been destroyed. Far worse damage was done to the Indian villages. As many as 1,000 colonists died from direct action; the Indian number is not known. Whole tribes practically ceased to exist. But even though New Englanders had won and their land claims were now secure, the line of frontier settlements would not achieve their pre-1675 limits until 1720. Although the New Englanders survived the most severe test of English survival in colonial history, New England's development was set back by decades.

Further Reading

Jennings, Francis. *The Invasion of America: Indians, Colonialism, and the Cant of Conquest.* Norton, 1975.

Leach, Douglas E. *Flintlock and Tomahawk: New England in King Philip's War.* Norton, 1966.

Nash, Gary B. *Red, White, and Black: The Peoples of Early America.* 2nd ed. Prentice-Hall, 1982.

Vaughan, Alden T. *The New England Frontier: Puritans and Indians, 1620-1675.* Little, Brown, 1965.

Bourne, Russell. *The Red King's Rebellion: Racial Politics in New England, 1675-1678.* Oxford University Press, 1990. □

Charles Theophilus Metcalfe

Charles Theophilus Metcalfe, 1st Baron Metcalfe (1785-1846), was a prototype of the British colonial administrator. He held successively the major responsibility for governing three of Britain's most important dependencies.

Charles Metcalfe was born in Calcutta on Jan. 30, 1785, the second son of a Bengal army officer who became a director of the East India Company and a Tory member of Parliament. Metcalfe received his early education at Eton, from which he was removed at 15 to be sent to India in the service of the company, then virtually indistinguishable from the British government of India. Metcalfe soon earned the respect of his superiors and remained abroad until 1838, rising steadily in rank and duties and finally being selected three times as provisional governor general.

Metcalfe, believing (as he wrote in 1815) that "All that rulers can do is to merit dominion by promoting the happiness of those under them," was a liberal in India, paying particular attention to financial reform and freeing the Indian press from censorship. But he never questioned whose domain should prevail in India, and he had a lively interest in the use of troops for earning merit. His liberation of the press aroused great antagonism among his colleagues, and he blamed this situation for his failure to obtain appointment as governor of Madras in 1837; he chose to retire, feeling himself in disgrace.

Back in England, where he contemplated seeking a parliamentary seat as a Whig, Metcalfe accepted the governorship of Jamaica in 1839, where he played an important part in conciliating disputes that had arisen between sugar planters and their workers who, as former slaves emancipated in 1833, were disinclined to work for others except on their own terms. The planters, for their part, were disenchanted by the quality of imperial leadership they were receiving. Metcalfe's astuteness as a reformer again came into play, and by 1841 he was satisfied that he had accomplished all that one conciliator could do, and he again retired home. In 1843 he was offered the post of governor general of Canada, which he accepted pessimistically.

Canada (then essentially referring to what is now Ontario and Quebec) was a constitutionally united colony in whose Assembly the English-and French-speaking sections had equal representation. Strife between the sections, between those who sought closer or looser ties with Britain and between those who sought responsible self-government and those who were content to let the governor from Britain have a large voice in governing, was widespread. Metcalfe naturally favored a generous view of the governor's powers, an interpretation warmly contested by many leading Canadians. Metcalfe and his supporters, though superficially more successful, failed to make their views prevail, and responsible government was finally won in 1848. But by that time Metcalfe, ravaged by cancer, was dead; he had been created a baron and retired to England in 1845; he died Sept. 5, 1846.

Further Reading

Some of Metcalfe's writings are in *Selections from the Papers of Lord Metcalfe,* edited by John William Kaye (1855). The best work on him remains Kaye's *Life and Correspondence of Charles, Lord Metcalfe* (2 vols., 1854; rev. ed. 1858), a typically uncritical 19th-century biography but one based on Metcalfe's own lucid and penetrating papers. See also Edward Thompson, *The Life of Charles, Lord Metcalfe* (1937).

Additional Sources

Bakshi, S. R. (Shiri Ram), *Ranjit Singh and Charles Metcalfe,* Malayattoor, Kerala: Vishwavidya Publishers, 1980. □

Élie Metchnikoff

The Russian physiologist and bacteriologist Élie Metchnikoff (1845-1916) is best noted for his phagocytic theory of immunity. He also made contributions to comparative pathology, evolutionary embryology, and microbiology.

On May 15, 1845, Élie Metchnikoff was born in the Ukrainian village of Ivanovka. At the age of 17 he entered Kharkov University; the following year he produced his first scientific work, "Some Facts from the Life of Infusoria"; and he completed his studies in the natural sciences by the time he was 19. In 1864 he left for Germany to expand his knowledge of zoology, studying under Rudolf Leuckart, the father of modern parasitology.

Metchnikoff went on to the universities of Göttingen and Munich. He returned to Russia in 1867, received his master's degree in zoology after presenting his thesis, *The History of the Embryonal Development of Sepiola,* and was appointed dozent at Novorossiisk University in Odessa. In 1868 he successfully defended his doctoral thesis, *The History of the Development of Nebalia,* at the University of St. Petersburg.

Metchnikoff became professor of zoology and comparative anatomy at Novorossiisk University in 1870. His interest focused on comparative embryology, intracellular digestion of simple organisms, the role of phagocytes in the digestive process, and biological methods of controlling harmful insects. After resigning his position in 1882, he pursued his experiments in his home laboratory, studying pathological microbes. Four years later Metchnikoff, along with Nikolai Fedorovich Gamaleia, organized Russia's first and the world's second bacteriological station. Its function was to prepare vaccines for diseases afflicting man and beast, including rabies, foot-and-mouth disease, anthrax, and cholera. Encountering opposition, ignorance, and animosity from Odessa doctors, St. Petersburg newspapers,

and interfering bureaucratic officials, Metchnikoff decided in 1887 to leave Russia forever.

In Paris, Metchnikoff met the ailing Louis Pasteur, and he was given the use of a personal laboratory and title of chief at the Pasteur Institute, where he began the most productive period of his career. The vaguely formulated concepts that Metchnikoff had conceived while investigating intracellular digestion eventually crystallized into his famous phagocytic theory of immunity. In 1883 he had revealed his theory of phagocytosis in "The Curative Forces of the Organism," delivered before the Seventh All-Russian Congress of Naturalists and Physicians in Odessa. The idea that phagocytes, a type of white blood cell, actually destroy living bacteria and other foreign matter and constitute a body's natural defense against infection was not favorably received by many scientists. However, by 1892 the accumulating experimental evidence supported Metchnikoff's theory of immunity. That year he also released his important work *Comparative Pathology of Inflammation,* and in 1903 his *Immunity in Infectious Diseases* appeared, soon becoming the classic text on immunology. For his many works on the processes of immunity he shared the Nobel Prize in 1908.

In 1903 Metchnikoff was appointed deputy director of the Pasteur Institute. About this time he began investigating old age. His ideas on the aging process appear in *The Nature of Man* (1903), *Studies in Optimism* (1907), and *Forty Years' Search for a Rational Outlook* (1913). He proposed the controversial theory of orthobiosis, which stressed "hygienic rules" for the prolongation of life. Despite frequent opposition to his theories, Metchnikoff became a renowned figure in the world of science and received many honors, awards, and titles. He died on July 16, 1916.

Further Reading

Still the best biography of Metchnikoff is the one by his wife, Olga Metchnikoff, *Life of Élie Metchnikoff* (trans. 1921). Biographical sketches appear in Edwin E. Slosson, *Major Prophets of Today* (1914), and Herman Bernstein, *Celebrities of Our Time: Interviews* (1924). An introductory work on immunology is Loyd Y. Quinn, *Immunological Concepts* (1968), and a fine standard text in this field is William c. Boyd, *Fundamentals of Immunology* (1943; 6th ed. 1966).

Additional Sources

Tauber, Alfred I., *Metchnikoff and the origins of immunology: from metaphor to theory,* New York: Oxford University Press, 1991. □

Klemens von Metternich

Prince Klemens von Metternich (1773-1859), Austrian politician and diplomat, suppressed nationalistic and democratic trends in Central Europe but was also the architect of a diplomatic system which kept Europe at peace for a century.

Today, more than 100 years after his death, Prince Klemens von Metternich remains a controversial figure. Many late 19th-century Europeans detested him as a foe of freedom and an obstructionist who tried to prevent the unification of the powerful nations of Germany and Italy. Yet Europeans in the late 20th century, recovering from the disasters of World War I and II, tend to see him as a perceptive visionary whose diplomatic ideas kept Europe at peace between 1815 and 1914. In this time period, Europe became the dominant economic and military power in the world. By the mid-20th century, even the future American secretary of state, Henry Kissinger, was praising Metternich's diplomacy.

The French Revolution of 1789 and its consequences were referred to by Metternich as the "hateful time." Although much of the French nobility were executed or fled the country, the French monarch Louis XVI was allowed to retain his throne as a limited "constitutional" monarch until 1793. Increasingly convinced that the king was conspiring to import a mercenary army to gain back his full power, the revolutionary government decided in 1794 to execute the king and his family. A period of bloody chaos, named the " Reign of Terror," followed.

As order was slowly restored, one of the army's generals, Napoleon Bonaparte, convinced many French citizens that he could both save the Revolution and restore order. In 1804, following a national referendum, Napoleon was crowned emperor of France. The Revolution had destroyed one monarchy; now it had created another.

Yet the rulers of the other great powers of Europe, all monarchs, did not recognize this "elected emperor" as a true monarch. From the first years of the Revolution, the other great powers had plotted to invade France and restore the family of Louis XVI. All failed; but the continuing attacks on revolutionary France gave Napoleon a justification to invade much of the rest of Europe. Between 1804 and 1807, he defeated Spain, Austria, and Prussia (a large state in northern Germany); he also pressured Russian tsar Alexander I into signing a nonaggression treaty. Napoleon portrayed such military campaigns as purely defensive—necessary to protect the French Revolution.

Metternich's family was directly affected by both the Revolution and the fighting. His father, a count who held hereditary lands in western Germany near France, was main minister in the Netherlands—which at that time was an Austrian possession. Metternich's childhood in the western German city of Koblenz, a quiet town of about 12,000, brought him into contact with French culture. His mother saw that he was fluent in both German and French; as an adult, he was often happier expressing himself in French.

After an early education by a series of private tutors, Metternich chose to attend the university at Strasbourg, a city which at various times has been part of either France or Germany. Arriving there a year before the French Revolution began, he quickly witnessed one side effect of the coming turmoil; when a mob of Strasbourg citizens attacked the city hall, a repelled Metternich described it as a "drunken mob which considers itself to be the people."

Transferring his university studies to the German city of Mainz, he met members of the French nobility fleeing the Revolution who insisted that the insurrection would quickly fail, and he believed them. But when advancing French armies destroyed much of their property and occupied their lands, Metternich and his family were forced to flee to the Austrian capital city of Vienna. He came to view revolutionaries as tyrants who used the word freedom to justify violence. He wrote that: "The word freedom has for me never had the character of a point of a departure, but a goal. . . . Order alone can produce freedom. Without order, the appeal to freedom will always in practice lead to tyranny."

Once Metternich was back in Vienna, his career as a statesman and politician advanced rapidly. His marriage in 1795 to Eleonore von Kaunitz, granddaughter of the Austrian state chancellor, gave him access to the highest social and political circles in the Austrian Empire. His wife's contacts and knowledge were important for an ambitious man who had never before lived in Austria's capital city. After serving as Austrian ambassador to Berlin and Dresden, Metternich was appointed ambassador to France in 1806.

In France when Metternich had the opportunity to study Napoleon, whom he termed "the conqueror of the world," he was not overawed; what he saw was a short, squat figure with a "negligent" appearance. In April of 1809, he appealed to the French emperor's vanity (and cemented a temporary French-Austrian alliance) by marrying Napoleon to Marie Louise, daughter of the Austrian emperor Francis I.

While in Paris, the tall, handsome, sociable, and poised Metternich began to acquire his lifelong reputation as a man who had "success with the ladies." But diplomatic success did not come as easily. He sent such optimistic reports back to Vienna—portraying a vulnerable Napoleon who was in danger of being overthrown by a resurgent revolutionary movement in France—that the Austrian government went to war against France and lost. Yet when Metternich gained favorable peace terms from Napoleon, he was rewarded by being appointed the Austrian minister of foreign affairs in October 1809. In 1813, he was given the hereditary title of prince.

Metternich was biding his time, preserving "Austria's freedom of action" while accommodating "ourselves to the victor . . . extend(ing) our existence until the day of our deliverance." He almost waited too long. When Napoleon's armies invaded Russia in 1812, Metternich ignored calls for help from Tsar Alexander I. But by late 1812, the French army was not only in retreat, pounded by a severe Russian winter, but was being pursued by the Russian army into Germany.

Belatedly, Metternich involved Austria in the struggle against Napoleon, and in 1813 Napoleon was defeated at Leipzig, Germany, by the armies of Britain, Austria, Prussia, and Russia. After Napoleon escaped from imprisonment on the island of Elbe in the Mediterranean Sea, he rallied the French army for a second time but was defeated in 1815 near Waterloo, Belgium.

The year 1815 saw Metternich at the peak of his power and popularity in Austria. In 1810, Napoleon had been master of much of Europe, and Austria had been a virtual puppet of French foreign policy; five years later, Metternich had become a key leader in the coalition of countries which defeated the French emperor twice. Now the victors held the fate of Europe in their hands.

When the victorious countries agreed to hold a diplomatic conference at Vienna (the Congress of Vienna), Metternich saw it as a personal triumph. He believed that since Austria was at the center of the European Continent, it was the logical place to "lay the foundations for a new European order." "I have," he wrote, "for a long time regarded Europe (rather than just Austria) as my homeland."

At the congress, Metternich's mastery of diplomatic maneuvering earned him the title of "the coachman of Europe." More than any other single leader, he seemed to determine the future direction of the Continent. One observer described him as "not a genius but a great talent; cold, calm, imperturbable, and a supreme calculator." Metternich's main goal at the congress was to promote the idea of the "Concert of Europe": if all the great powers acted together or in "concert," they would be able to prevent the outbreak of any large European war like the Napoleonic Wars. They might also be able to see that "the foundations of a lasting peace are secured as much as possible."

Some rulers, such as Tsar Alexander, wanted the congress to create an international "police system" to prevent future revolutions and block the emergence of new Napoleons. Metternich sympathized with this aim, but he also wanted to discourage any Russian interest in expanding into

Europe. He also was determined to frustrate Austria's main rival in Germany, Prussia.

Together with the British representative, Castlereagh, Metternich successfully worked to create a permanent alliance among the victors, envisioning grouped power that would "balance out" the ambitious or aggressive actions of any one country on the Continent. Although the Quadruple Alliance halted only a few revolutions, and Metternich was disappointed when Britain left the alliance in 1822, the "balance of power" system remained in place throughout the rest of the century. No overall European war on the scale of the Napoleonic Wars occurred until the outbreak of World War I in 1914. So influential was Metternich's diplomacy that the era from 1815 to 1848 is often referred to as the "Age of Metternich."

After 1815, Metternich devoted increasing amounts of his time to Austria's severe internal problems. The Austrian Empire was a conglomeration of 11 nationalities which had been forced under the rule of the Habsburg family by military conquests in the 17th century. The French Revolution had proved to be a threat to the multinational Habsburg Empire, since it fanned the nationalism of some groups in the Empire, such as the Hungarians. Metternich saw nationalism and liberalism as serious threats to the survival of the Austrian Empire and tried to suppress both. At the Congress of Vienna, he also worked to create confederations in both Germany (where he succeeded) and Italy (where he failed). In Metternich's time, Italy and Germany were what he called "geographic expressions"—divided into many individual governments with no national central government. Italy had more than ten governments. Until Napoleon's invasion of Germany, there were more than 300 political divisions in that country, each with its own petty monarch; the Congress of Vienna reduced this to 35, of which the two largest and most powerful were Austria and Prussia.

Metternich would have preferred a Germany united under Austrian leadership. With typical self-confidence, he worked to convince the Austrian emperor (Francis II) to allow himself to be made ruler over all of Germany. "The emperor always does what I want," he predicted, "but likewise, I say what only he should do." When the emperor rejected the idea and a loose confederation of all the German states was created instead, Metternich realized that the way was opened for the other powerful German state, Prussia, to unite Germany (which it eventually did, in 1870).

Liberalism—a 19th-century middle-class movement to weaken monarchies and create parliaments or legislatures—also threatened the Austrian monarchy. Metternich saw liberalism as a child of the French Revolution of 1789. Innately suspicious of new political systems or ideas, Metternich proudly said that "everything changes but me." He added that, "I am not one of those who think that the movement is the purpose of life."

Between 1815 and 1820, Metternich watched suspiciously as liberal revolutions weakened monarchs in western Germany. When secret student fraternities at German universities (the *Burschenschaften*) staged patriotic demonstrations, he charged that the demonstrators were really promoting liberal goals. Secret societies were "the gangrene of society," he proclaimed; "as a device for disrupting the peace, fanaticism is one of the oldest things in the world."

After a politically conservative German playwright was assassinated by a student in 1819, Metternich convinced Prussia that the two largest German states should intervene. "With God's help," he declared, "I hope to defeat the German revolutionaries as I defeated the conqueror of the world." Through the Carlsbad Decrees of 1819, Austria and Prussia forced the other German states to institute censorship of books, pamphlets, and newspapers; to allow a Central Commission and police spies to identify and hunt "subversives"; and to restrict student societies and professors in universities. For many in Germany, Metternich became a hated symbol of reaction and repression.

What Metternich feared most was that the liberal and national ideas would tear apart the multinational Habsburg Empire, causing each nationality under Habsburg rule to go its own way and establish its own separate government. In the 18th century, the Austrian emperor Joseph II had decided that the way to unify the Empire was to centralize the administrative part of the government and standardize the law. Metternich disagreed, believing that the best way to discourage independence movements was to allow each section of the Empire to have its own distinctive rules and laws.

Yet Metternich's ideas regarding Austria were rejected. Although he was appointed Austrian state chancellor in 1821, his influence was restricted to foreign affairs by Count Kolowrat, the minister of state, who had the ear of the new emperor, the mentally retarded Ferdinand. If it were not for Metternich's skills in diplomacy, his career would have been regarded as a virtual failure. At times, he himself thought that way. When word arrived that the French monarchy (which had been restored by the Congress of Vienna) had fallen victim to another revolution in 1830, Metternich collapsed at his desk, exclaiming, "My life's work is destroyed!"

When ultimately unsuccessful revolutions broke out in the Austrian Empire in 1848, Metternich, the "last great master of the principle of balance," became the target of angry mobs. Forced to resign, he went into exile in England before returning to Vienna in 1858. He died there a year later.

Metternich believed he had unfairly become a symbol of reaction and oppression. His real aim, he said, was to avoid the chaos that he believed would follow in the wake of the major political changes demanded by European revolutionaries. "Old Europe is at the beginning of the end," he proclaimed. "New Europe, however, has not as yet even begun its existence, and between the end and the beginning there will be chaos. . . . In a hundred years, historians will judge me quite differently than do all those who pass judgment on me today."

Further Reading

von Metternich, Klemens. *Memoirs of Prince Metternich, 1773-1815.* Edited by Prince Richard Metternich. Translated by Mrs. Alexander Napier. Scribner, 1880.

Milne, Andrew. *Metternich.* Rowman & Littlefield, 1975.

Palmer, Alan. *Metternich.* Harper, 1972.

de Sauvigny, G. B. *Metternich and His Times.* Darton, Longman, and Todd, 1962.

Kissinger, Henry A. *A World Restored: Metternich, Castlereagh, and the Problems of Peace, 1812-1822.* Houghton, 1957.

Kraehe, E. E., ed. *The Metternich Controversy.* Krieger Publishing, 1977.

May, Arthur J. *The Age of Metternich, 1814-1848.* H. Holt, 1933.

Schroeder, Paul W. *Metternich's Diplomacy at Its Zenith, 1820-1823.* University of Texas Press, 1962.

Schwarz, H. F. *Metternich, the Coachman of Europe: Statesman or Evil Genius?* Heath, 1962. □

Giacomo Meyerbeer

The four grand operas composed for Paris by the German composer Giacomo Meyerbeer (1791-1864) set a style that dominated the French lyric theater and exerted a powerful influence on opera production throughout Europe for a generation afterward.

Giacomo Meyerbeer began life as Jakob Liebmann Beer, later adding Meyer, the name of his maternal grandfather, and changing Jakob to Giacomo on taking up residence in Italy. Born in Berlin into a cultured Jewish family, he studied piano with Muzio Clementi and was quickly recognized as a prodigy on that instrument. He also studied music theory and composition, first with Carl Friedrich Zelter, then with the Berlin opera director Bernard Anselm Weber, and finally with the Abbé Vogler, one of the most eminent German theorists of the time. By his early 20s Meyerbeer was a sensational pianist, but his chief aim was to be a composer.

Drawn from the start to dramatic music, Meyerbeer made a moderately successful public debut in 1811 with the oratorio *Gott und die Natur.* Following that came two operas, both failures, evidently because of their overly serious, academic vein. Antonio Salieri, director of the Imperial Chapel in Vienna, advised Meyerbeer to go to Italy to see more of the world and learn how to write for the voice. He took this good counsel and studied in Venice (1815-1817).

Meyerbeer's most important model there was Gioacchino Rossini, who epitomized the abilities and qualities that Meyerbeer himself lacked. He was an apt student and by 1817 had become sufficiently Italianized to compose an Italian opera, *Romilda e Costanza,* which was produced with success that year. This turn of fortune led him to compose three more works for Italian theaters, the best being *Il Crociato in Egitto,* given in 1824. By then his eyes were already turned toward Paris, where he eventually won his greatest triumphs.

From 1824 to 1831 Meyerbeer wrote nothing for the stage. Part of that time he spent in Berlin on family affairs; otherwise he was absorbed in the observation of French life and culture. His first French opera, *Robert le Diable,* was produced in Paris in 1831. A brilliant success, it catapulted him into a ruling position in the lyric theater of France.

After *Robert,* Meyerbeer brought out three more operas on a similar model: *Les Huguenots* (1836), probably his best work; *Le Prophète* (1849); and *L'Africaine,* composed and recomposed over a period of 25 years and produced posthumously in 1865. In collaboration with the popular playwright Eugène Scribe, Meyerbeer created in these pieces a species of opera offering highly melodramatic action organized in a series of vast tableaux culminating in a striking denouement. Extraordinary virtuosity is demanded of the solo singers, but the keynote of the scores is the adroit marshaling of vocal and instrumental forces into large-scale musical developments at climatic points in the action. This is French grand opera in its gaudiest dress—massive, spectacular, and as broad in its appeal as the Cecil B. De Mille film epics.

Meyerbeer composed *L'Étoile du Nord* (1854) and *Le Pardon de Ploërmel* (1859) for the Opéra-Comique, plus a few occasional pieces written in Berlin, where for a time he held a royal appointment as general director of music. None of these added much to his reputation, which has largely vanished over the years. There is little taste now for his style of expression, but his historical position is secure as the composer who caught most fully in opera the mood of middle-class society in 19th-century France.

Further Reading

Meyerbeer's work and place in history are outlined in Donald J. Grout, *A Short History of Opera* (1947; 2d ed. 1965). An interesting defense of Meyerbeerian methods is presented in Bernard van Dieren, *Down among the Dead Men and Other Essays* (1935). For a comprehensive study of Meyerbeer and his collaborators at work in the context of 19th-century romanticism see William L. Crosten, *French Grand Opera: An Art and a Business* (1948). □

Otto Fritz Meyerhof

The German biochemist Otto Fritz Meyerhof (1884-1951) shared the Nobel Prize in Physiology or Medicine for his discovery of the fixed relationship between oxygen consumption and the metabolism of lactic acid in muscle and for establishing the cyclic character of energy transformations in the living cell.

Otto Meyerhof son of Felix Meyerhof, a merchant, was born in Hanover on April 12, 1884. His school education in Berlin was long interrupted by kidney disease, but during his period of absence his intellectual and literary interests, owing to the personal influence of his mother, developed greatly. He became a medical student in the University of Freiburg im Breisgau and also studied at the Universities of Berlin, Strasbourg, and Heidelberg. In 1909 he graduated as a doctor of medicine at Heidelberg. Thereafter he worked in the laboratory of the medical clinic at Heidelberg, where he met the young biochemist Otto Warburg, who encouraged him to use biochemical methods in his studies of the release of energy in the living cell.

Muscle Research at Kiel

In 1912 Meyerhof became an assistant in the department of physiology in the University of Kiel and in 1918 assistant professor. In 1913 he delivered a lecture on the energetics of cell phenomena which became a classic, and he published (1916-1917) three papers on energy exchanges in the nitrifying bacteria, which papers had an important influence on his own work.

Meyerhof was interested in the mechanism by which the energy of the foodstuffs is released and utilized by the living cell. He investigated muscle, because in it energy is released as heat and also as mechanical work. Louis Pasteur held that the yeast cell's need for chemical energy could be satisfied either by oxidation of sugar or by its chemical cleavage. Hence arose the theory that the yeast cell used "intramolecular oxygen," derived from the organic molecules and not from the molecular oxygen of the atmosphere. In 1867 Ludimar Hermann found that muscle can contract in the absence of oxygen, and he thought that muscle contained the hypothetical "inogen" whose molecules had the excess oxygen that was used, by a process analogous to

fermentation, for the liberation of energy during muscular activity.

In 1906-1907 (Sir) Walter Morley Fletcher and (Sir) Frederick Gowland Hopkins proved at Cambridge that, when muscle contracts under anaerobic conditions, lactic acid accumulates in it and that when oxygen is supplied the lactic acid disappears. Nothing was known of the chemical reactions involved or the way in which they release energy for contraction. No further work was done until Meyerhof entered the field at the end of World War I. But in the physical field A. V. Hill since about 1910 had been investigating the heat produced in muscle on contraction. He showed that the heat was proportional to the work performed; he also demonstrated that about half the heat appeared during the anaerobic contraction phase, while the other half was evolved during the aerobic recovery phase. Hill concluded early in his work that not enough heat was evolved during the recovery period to account for the oxidation of all the lactic acid produced during contraction.

The method for estimating lactic acid in muscle was complex and required about a week to carry out. Using a new rapid method devised by himself, Meyerhof showed in 1920 that, in anaerobic conditions, the lactic acid was derived from glycogen in the muscle and that the amount of lactic acid formed was proportional to the tension produced in the muscle. Further, in the recovery stage only between one-fifth and one-quarter of the lactic acid was oxidized, and the energy of this reaction was used to reconvert to glycogen the remainder of the lactic acid. Hopkins had this important investigation checked at Cambridge, using the older method for estimating lactic acid. Meyerhof's results were fully confirmed.

In 1917 G. Embden discovered hexose diphosphoric acid in muscle, and he thought it was an immediate precursor of lactic acid. Meyerhof confirmed this finding. He also proved that in anaerobic fermentation, for the release of a given amount of energy, more carbohydrate is used up than is the case if the carbohydrate is oxidized (the Pasteur-Meyerhof effect). He introduced the term "glycolysis" for the anaerobic degradation of glycogen to lactic acid, and he demonstrated for the first time the cyclic character of energy transformations in the living cell. He found that the difference between the combustion heats of glycogen and of lactic acid was 170 calories per gram molecule. But he found also that, when the process took place in muscle, 380 calories, and not 170, were liberated. He made many unsuccessful attempts to elucidate the source of this additional energy, namely, 210 calories. For these researches Meyerhof shared with Hill the 1922 Nobel Prize for Physiology or Medicine.

New Aspects of Muscle Research at Berlin

Shortly after receiving the Nobel Prize, Meyerhof was offered a chair of biochemistry in an important American university. To retain him in Germany, a new department was created for him in the Kaiser Wilhelm Institute for Biology at Berlin-Dahlem; to provide the accommodation, each of the heads of the five existing departments spontaneously offered to give up one of his own rooms to Meyerhof, who was head of this new department from 1924 to 1929.

In 1925 Meyerhof published the first of many joint papers with his assistant Kurt Lohmann. At that time it was thought that the ability of muscle to convert glycogen to lactic acid depended on the integrity of the muscle structure and that, if an extract showed glycolytic activity, bacterial action had probably been responsible. But in 1926 Meyerhof showed that a muscle extract, prepared with an ice-cold solution, contained the glycolytic enzyme systems and that it was active shortly after its preparation. The conclusion was that the glycolysis was not due to bacterial activity. These fundamental observations, published in 1926-1927, are regarded as the experimental foundation of the Emden-Meyerhof theory of glycolysis.

Observations had already been made by others which were inexplicable by the hitherto unchallenged lactic acid theory of muscular contraction. In 1927 P. Eggleton and G. P. Eggleton in London, and Fiske and Subbarow independently in the United States, discovered "phosphagen" in muscle. It was found to be creatine phosphate. The Eggletons showed that in muscle it decreased during the anaerobic contraction phase and that it was resynthesized during the recovery phase. They thought that it might play a part in the mechanism of contraction. In 1928 Meyerhof and Lohmann showed that 12,000 calories per gram molecule of phosphate were liberated during the hydrolysis of creatine phosphate. In 1929 Lohmann discovered in muscle the phosphate compound adenosine triphosphate (ATP). In 1932 he worked out its structure, but at that time its signifi-

cance escaped all workers. About this time too belong Meyerhof's important observations on coupled oxidations and phosphorylation in muscle extracts.

Overthrow of the Lactic Acid Theory

In 1929 Meyerhof became head of the department of physiology in a new Institute for Medical Research in the University of Heidelberg. In 1929-1930 Einaar Lundsgaard of Copenhagen, in experiments begun in Copenhagen and completed in Meyerhof's new institute, obtained results damaging to the lactic acid theory. Lundsgaard showed that, in a muscle poisoned with iodoacetate, lactic acid formation ceased although contraction still took place. In such muscles the tension produced was proportional to the breakdown of creatine phosphate. He suggested that, even in unpoisoned muscle, the role of creatine phosphate was to supply the energy for contraction, while the role of carbohydrate breakdown was to supply energy for the resynthesis of creatine phosphate. Meyerhof also produced results which discounted the lactic acid theory.

Investigations now turned toward the primary role of creatine phosphate, but there were difficulties. Meyerhof had shown that the hydrolysis of creatine phosphate is an exothermic reaction, but the actual amount of heat produced at the start of contraction did not indicate that creatine phosphate initiated the process. But in 1932 Meyerhof and Lohmann made the important discovery that liberation of the two terminal phosphate groups in ATP produced about 12,000 calories of heat per gram molecule of phosphate. There followed the significant conception of energy-rich bonds.

It was not until 1934 that the fundamental role of ATP began to be realized—5 years after the discovery of ATP itself. In that year Lohmann found that muscle extracts can liberate phosphate from creatine phosphate, but only in the presence of adenylic compounds, for example, adenosine diphosphate (ADP). The creatine phosphate reacts with ADP to give creatine and ATP; then the ATP is hydrolyzed to recreate ADP with the liberation of phosphoric acid. He also showed that the hydrolysis of ATP must precede the breakdown of creatine phosphate. Meyerhof and his coworkers then showed the sequence of chemical events in muscular contraction. They concluded that the essential event is the dephosphorylation of ATP and that both creatine phosphate breakdown and lactic acid production are necessary for the rapid resynthesis of ATP. During the next few years Meyerhof studied intermediate carbohydrate metabolism and the concept of oxidative phosphorylation.

In 1938, owing to the racial policy of the Nazis, Meyerhof and his family emigrated to Paris. He was appointed director of research at the Institut de Biologie Physico-Chimique. In June 1940, on the invasion of France, he escaped to Toulouse and thence to the United States.

Later Life

Meyerhof was appointed research professor of physiological chemistry at the School of Medicine of the University of Pennsylvania. During 10 years in the United States he published 50 papers. In 1946 he partially separated the calcium-activated enzyme adenosine-triphosphatase (ATPase), found in muscle, from myosin. In 1948 he demonstrated in muscle a new ATPase which was magnesium-activated, and he associated it with the microsomal fraction of the cell. During this period he also worked on the Harden-Young reaction and measured the equilibrium constants of the hydrolysis and synthesis of phosphate esters. He died in Philadelphia on Oct. 6, 1951.

In addition to 400 papers in scientific journals, Meyerhof published *Chemical Dynamics of Life Phenomena* (1924) and *Die Chemischen Vorgänge im Muskel* (1930), a comprehensive discussion of the subject. He received many honors in addition to his Nobel Prize. In 1937 he was elected a Foreign Member of the Royal Society, and he was a member of other learned societies in the United States, Germany, France, and Italy. He was an honorary graduate of the University of Edinburgh.

Further Reading

There is a biography of Meyerhof in *Nobel Lectures, Physiology or Medicine, 1922-1941* (1965), which also includes his Nobel Lecture. For the biochemical background see G. H. Bell, J. N. Davidson, and H. Scarborough, *Textbook of Physiology and Biochemistry* (6th ed. 1965). For a full account of Meyerhof's work on muscle see the sections by Dorothy M. Needham in G. H. Bourne, ed., *The Structure and Function of Muscle,* vol. 2 (1960), and her *Machina Carnis* (1971). □

Vsevolod Emilievich Meyerhold

The Russian director Vsevolod Emilievich Meyerhold (1874-1940/42) is noted for his stylistic experiments with nonrealistic performances in constructivist settings.

Vsevolod Meyerhold was born to German parents on Jan. 28, 1874, in Penza about 350 miles southeast of Moscow. Baptized Karl Theodore Kasimir, he changed his name in 1895, when he was converted from Lutheranism to the Orthodox Church. After a year of law at Moscow University, he studied drama at the Moscow Philharmonic Society, where one of the teachers was Vladimir Nemirovich-Danchenko, the future founder with Stanislavsky of the Moscow Art Theatre. Upon graduation in 1898 Meyerhold joined this company and in December played Treplev in the historic production of *The Seagull*. Never outstanding as an actor and opposed to Stanislavsky's naturalism, he left Moscow after 4 years to direct his own company.

Between 1908 and 1917 Meyerhold attracted international attention at the two St. Petersburg imperial theaters with his dazzling productions influenced by the conventions of commedia dell'arte and other nonrealistic theaters. Probably the most opulent spectacle ever seen on the Russian stage was his production of Mikhail Lermontov's *Mas-querade,* which opened on the very day in February 1917 when the first shots were fired in the Russian Revolution.

Early in 1918 Meyerhold joined the Bolsheviks, produced the first Soviet play, Vladimir Mayakovsky's *Mystery Bouffe,* in September, and the following year was appointed head of the Theatrical Department in the Education Commissariat. In the postrevolutionary decade of the 1920s he became the leading Soviet exponent of antirealistic theatrical experiment. Daring constructivist productions of Aleksandr Ostrovsky's *The Forest* (1924) and Nikolai Gogol's *The Inspector General* (1926) inspired a host of reinterpretations of the classics. In 1913 he had published a collection of his articles, *On the Theatre.* Expounding even more radical theories, his *Reconstruction of the Theatre* appeared in 1930.

After Mayakovksy's *The Bedbug* (1929) and *The Bathhouse* (1930) were criticized by advocates of Soviet socialist realism, Meyerhold presented *The Lady of the Camellias* (1934) and *The Queen of Spades* (1935) somewhat more realistically. Nevertheless, the official attacks on his "formalism" continued, and on Jan. 8, 1938, the Meyerhold Theatre was liquidated. On June 5, 1939, at the All-Union Conference of Stage Directors, Meyerhold made a speech apparently defending the principles he had pursued throughout his career. Immediately after the conference he was arrested. Russian sources list the date of his death in prison as 1940 or 1942.

Further Reading

Selections from Meyerhold's writings are in *Meyerhold on Theatre,* edited and translated by Edward Braun (1969). Each chapter is prefaced with an informative introduction by the translator. Contemporary accounts of Meyerhold's productions can be found in Alexander Bakshy, *The Path of the Modern Russian Stage* (1916); Huntly Carter, *The New Spirit in the Russian Theatre 1917-28,* (1929); and Norris Houghton, *Moscow Rehearsals* (1936). □

Kweisi Mfume

Kweisi Mfume (born 1948), elected president of the National Association for Advancement of Colored People (NAACP) in 1996, was the chairman of the Congressional Black Caucus. Devoted to the Civil Rights Movement, Mfume resigned from Congress because he believed that he could achieve more for civil rights in his work for the NAACP.

Former congressman Kweisi Mfume of Baltimore was one of the most prominent black politicians on Capitol Hill. Mfume, who grew up in a poor neighborhood and worked his way into the halls of power, was elected chairman of the Congressional Black Caucus in 1993, just as the number of African American representatives in Congress began to swell to record highs. According to Ron Stodghill II and Richard S. Dunham in *Business Week,*

Mfume, "the former Baltimore firebrand, represents a new generation of black leadership in Congress—a group of young pragmatists more concerned about creating economic opportunity than protest." *Baltimore Sun* reporter Susan Baer called Mfume an "up-from-the-bootstraps politician" who has become, "almost overnight, one of the nation's most visible and powerful African American lawmakers." He resigned his seat in congress to become president of the National Association for Advancement of Colored People (NAACP) in 1996.

Mfume has overcome a rough and deprived childhood on the streets of Baltimore to exhibit all the eloquence, polish, and insider know-how of a seasoned politician. His personal history serves as a classic example of a man who made the concerted decision to improve his lot in life. From a gang member and father of five children by three different women in his late teens, he became first a local radio personality then an impassioned city councilman and congressional representative for the district where he himself grew up. Today he speaks not only for the disadvantaged in urban Baltimore, but also for inner city residents in all parts of the nation. Mfume is a liberal Democrat who has achieved considerable power and prestige, especially since the arrival in the White House of President Bill Clinton. Baer noted that the four-term congressman "has earned respect as a level-headed consensus-seeker" and is well-known for his "eloquence and widespread appeal."

"Things Spun Out of Control"

Mfume was born Frizzell Gray in a working class neighborhood in Baltimore. He recalled in the *Washington Post* that he was so sickly as a youngster that his parents nicknamed him "Pee Wee." His stepfather worked as a truck driver, and his mother took odd jobs as she could find them, but the family was often desperately short of cash. Nevertheless, young Frizzell Gray was a good student who was protective of his three younger sisters. In his home, wrote a *U.S. News and World Report* correspondent, his parents emphasized "education and civil rights; Jack Kennedy and later Martin Luther King were family idols. Yet they had to watch the 1963 march on Washington on TV because the 40-mile trip cost too much. School was segregated, although the Supreme Court had outlawed such things. [Mfume] could never figure out why he passed three schools to get to his own. Still, school was fine—until his world caved in."

First Mfume's stepfather left the family. Then, when he was sixteen, his mother discovered she had cancer. She literally died in Mfume's arms quite suddenly one evening. He was devastated. Mfume told *U.S. News and World Report:* "My mother was and, even in death, probably still is the most important person in my life. After she died of cancer, things spun out of control."

Mfume quit school in his sophomore year and went to work full-time to help support his sisters. Financial troubles forced the siblings into different households. At times Mfume worked as many as three different jobs in a week— full-time in a bread factory and part-time in a local grocery and as a shoeshine boy on Sundays. The pace began to take a toll, especially since he saw so many of his peers enjoying themselves at high school dances and other social events not open to him. "After two or three years of that I just went kind of wild," he told the *Washington Post.* "I went to hell, quite frankly. I just couldn't understand why everybody else had parents, had a house to go to and had dinner on the table when I didn't have any of those things. I couldn't understand why I was being punished."

Mfume began hanging out on the street corner with friends. "Not only did I run with all the worst people, I became the leader," he recalled in *U.S. News and World Report.* "I was locked up a couple of times on suspicion of theft because I happened to be black and happened to be young. And before I knew it, I was a teenage parent, not once but twice, three times, four times, five times." Mfume did not marry the mothers of his children, but he has always taken responsibility for the boys, who are now adults.

The big change for Mfume came on a hot July night in the late 1960s. He had been loitering and drinking with his friends, when suddenly he began to feel strange. "People were standing around shooting craps and everything else, and something just came over me," he remembered in *Business Week.* "I said, 'I can't live like this anymore.' And I walked away." Mfume spent the rest of the night in prayer, then proceeded to earn his high school equivalency and pursue a college degree. "I took a lot of grief from friends, but I never went back," he told the *Washington Post.*

A New Name, a High-Profile Career

In an effort to connect with his African heritage, Mfume adopted a new name early in the 1970s. His aunt traveled to Ghana and suggested the name when she returned. "Kweisi Mfume" is a phrase of Ibo derivation that translates as "conquering son of kings." It turned out to be an appropriate choice for someone who would one day conquer the power structure in the nation's capital. *Washington Post* contributor Kent Jenkins, Jr. wrote: "For Mfume, the new name was more than an affectation. It signaled an awakening of his social consciousness and an increasing interest in politics. Like many young African Americans, he was appalled by the continuing impact of racism in America. But Mfume decided to do something about it and quickly settled on a line of attack: He would go on the radio and talk about it."

In the early 1970s, most black Baltimoreans listened to WEBB radio, a station owned by none other than the "godfather of soul," James Brown. Mfume began his tenure with the station as an unpaid volunteer, then became news reader, and finally earned a spot as an announcer. Despite pleas from management, he refused to part with his new name. Nor would he conform to the station's low-key political profile. "What Mfume had to say was not what WEBB had bargained for," noted Jenkins. "He was supposed to read commercials and introduce R and B records. But before long he was playing protest songs by jazz artist Gil Scott-Heron, reading poems by Nikki Giovanni and conducting call-in political seminars. The audience was electrified."

Concurrently, Mfume earned a bachelor's degree with honors from Morgan State University in 1976. When that college opened a noncommercial radio station, Mfume was hired as program director. Finally he had found a congenial forum for a political talk show. According to Jenkins, Mfume "became one of the strongest voices in Baltimore's black community, slamming the Democratic clubhouse organizations that dominated city politics. He aimed his most blistering remarks at [then-Baltimore mayor] William Donald Schaefer, . . . accusing him of ignoring poor neighborhoods while lavishing money on downtown redevelopment." Mfume's growing popularity as a radio personality convinced him to try his hand at politics. In 1978 he ran for Baltimore City Council.

That decision marked the occasion for another change. A seasoned political advisor told Mfume not to expect success unless he changed his attire from dashikis and jewelry to conservative suits and ties. Mfume took the advice, and he won a seat on the city council in 1978 by a mere three votes. Jenkins wrote: "On the council, Mfume moderated his dress but not his political approach, raining rhetorical fire on the city's power structure. His attacks on Schaefer were particularly poisonous . . . and the mayor's contempt for Mfume was legendary." The two men almost came to blows on several occasions.

Mfume looks back on those days now as a learning experience. Gradually he became aware that politics was a game of coalition-building and compromise, rather than confrontation. He learned the delicate art of negotiation and even eventually developed a congenial relationship with Schaefer. Mfume told *Business Week* of his former nemesis: "We could go to our graves battling each other, or we could get things done."

A Congressman with Clout

In 1986, a more temperate and polished Mfume announced his candidacy for the Seventh Congressional District, to replace retiring congressman Parren J. Mitchell. Mfume's opponents in the election tried to make an issue of his checkered past, reminding voters that the councilman had dropped out of high school and fathered illegitimate children. The strategy backfired when Mfume's sons stepped forward to praise their father and the candidate pointed to his degrees from Morgan State and the Johns Hopkins University, where he earned a master's degree in 1984. Mfume won the congressional seat with three times the vote of his next closest opponent and prepared to go to Congress in 1987. In the *Washington Post,* he recalled that many of his freshman colleagues on Capitol Hill were astounded that he had won with such an unusual name.

Jenkins wrote: "Since coming to Congress Mfume has followed a traditional path that belies his unorthodox roots." When he found himself on the House Committee on Banking, Finance, and Urban Affairs, Mfume educated himself on banking issues and economics. When his district was reapportioned to include some more rural regions of Maryland he immersed himself in farming and zoning laws so as to be able to represent his new constituents. He also developed a presence in Congress by volunteering to preside over sessions when the Speaker of the House was not present—a job that requires an understanding of arcane procedures that date to previous centuries. Mfume told the *Washington Post:* "I wanted people to get used to me real quick because I didn't plan on leaving."

At the same time, Mfume established himself as a liberal who stood solidly on the platform of expanded federal aid to inner cities. He never let a week go by that he did not return to Baltimore to deal firsthand with his constituents—a vast majority of whom are city dwellers. "I keep coming back to these communities and the lessons I learned here because that's what got me where I am," he told the *Washington Post.* "When I can't get anything moving in Washington I can always come back here. . . . Whatever I'm doing in Washington, if it doesn't matter here, it doesn't matter."

Over time Mfume became "a key player in shaping the debate and legislation aimed at curing the ills of the nation's inner cities," to quote Stodghill and Dunham. In his fourth term, Mfume had earned enough political clout to win the leadership of the Congressional Black Caucus, a body that has become increasingly important, now with 39 members in the House. An overwhelming majority of the Congressional Black Caucus members are Democratic, but Mfume has set a maverick tone for the group. Soon after his election as chairman, Mfume and the Caucus openly criticized president Clinton for withdrawing support for Justice Department nominee Lani Guinier. Later the Caucus presented a list of "non-negotiable" demands to the Clinton White House, most of them having to do with federal aid to cities and the poor. "Not too many brothers or sisters would say 'no' to the president," NAACP executive director Benjamin Chavis was quoted as saying in *Emerge*. Mfume told *Business Week:* "No longer are we going to be looked at as an addendum to the Democratic agenda. We are going to be taken seriously. . . . If that means killing an important piece of [leadership-backed] legislation, then that will be the case."

Such a strong position has assured Mfume the ear of President Clinton, as well as the respect of his fellow Caucus members. Observers note that Mfume's popularity in his congressional district is such that he can depend upon winning his seat regularly. Since that is the case, he might also be poised to earn the honor of Speaker of the House at some point in the future. Having learned through trial and error how to create coalitions and make politics work for his district, Mfume shows no sign of relinquishing his career. "I could just stand on the side and be a spectator," he told the *Baltimore Sun*. "But politics is not a spectator sport. And in Washington, it's a contact sport. And I don't play to tie, I try to play to win. But you can only win if you are in the game." He added: "I'm going to be a player in the Democratic Party . . . if they don't run me out."

On February 20, 1996, Mfume resigned his seat in Congress to become the president of the National Association for Advancement of Colored People (NAACP). He said that he could do more for civil rights than in Congress saying, "Given the polarization in the country, the levels of crime and hatred, given the despair that I see in the eyes of young people, I thought that I could do more at the NAACP." After one year of leadership, Mfume had erased the NAACP's $4.5 million debt. However, many question whether he has moved quickly enough to restore the legislative, spiritual, and moral integrity of a group that once embodied effective civil rights action. With the group's financial problems behind him, Mfume told members during a speech at the Park Plaza Hotel in April, 1997, that it is time to cement a new agenda for the group. He discussed a five-point plan that he said links today's challenges to an age-old quest for justice.

When the NAACP kicked off its six-day national convention on July 12, 1997 in Pittsburgh, Mfume said that his term as president had "gone by in the blink of an eye because the workload was so high and the challenges were so great and the possibilities were so unlimited. I'm a workaholic by nature, so the fact that all this kind of coincided together was good for me in the sense that it challenged me." Mfume will undoubtedly continue to spiritually renew his organization with his charisma and determination.

Further Reading

Baltimore Sun, August 1, 1993, p. A-20.
Boston Globe, April 6, 1997, p. B3.
Business Week, March 1, 1993, p. 72-75.
Chicago Tribune, February 13, 1997, p. Evening 2.
Detroit Free Press, July 12, 1997, p. A4.
Emerge, October 1993, pp. 24-28.
Essence, November 1993, p. 102.
Jet, August 23, 1993, p. 4.
Newsweek, July 5, 1993, p. 26.
U.S. News and World Report, August 9, 1993, p. 33-35.
Washington Post, December 8, 1992, p. D-1. □

Micah

Micah (active 8th century B.C.), a prophet of ancient Israel, is traditionally known as the author of the biblical book bearing his name. The Book of Micah is always placed sixth in the list of the 12 Minor Prophets.

Micah was a later contemporary of the prophets Hosea and Isaiah. From his book it is clear that he began to preach to the Assyrians shortly before the fall of Samaria in 721 B.C. His writings also reflect the mass transportation of Israelites from northern Palestine between 734 and 721 and the conquest of all Judean towns between that time and 701. Micah was an eyewitness of the siege of Jerusalem in 700 by the Assyrian king Sennacherib. Micah's ministry therefore took place substantially in the last 25 years of the 8th century. He was not of the priestly or aristocratic class; he came from the class of small farmers and farm laborers.

The Book of Micah falls into three distinct parts. Chapters 1-3 comment on the fall of Samaria, capital of the northern kingdom of Israel, to the Assyrian king Sargon in 721. This, Micah says, is a punishment of God for the sins of Israel. Micah then foretells the same doom for Jerusalem because the rich oppress the poor; the prophets of his time and the teachers condone this oppression; and moral cleanliness is not sought by men. Chapters 4-5 foretell the fall of Jerusalem and the restoration of its glory; he predicts that all the peoples of the earth will stream to the restored city in order to learn there how to observe the commandments of God and to attain holiness. Chapters 6-7 contain a series of oracles and denunciations. Israel's ingratitude, injustice, and cheating, the disappearance of godly behavior, and the rise of religious infidelity are all castigated by Micah. But the text ends with an expression of hope in the ultimate salvation of Israel and a petition for God's mercy and a fulfillment of God's promises to Abraham.

Although all seven chapters of the Book of Micah bear his name, serious doubts have been raised by biblical scholars as to the authorship of certain chapters. There is general agreement that chapter 1-3 come from Micah. Chapters 4-5 speak of exile, of the abolition of royalty, and of Babylon— where the later exiles were transported. All these, if taken as referring to the later fall of Jerusalem into the hands of King Nebuchadnezzar and the Babylonian exile in 597 B.C., cannot have come from the hand of Micah. Chapters 6-7 present difficulties of the same kind. One of the chief arguments against ascribing this material to Micah is the element of universalism and worldwide religious outlook. This became a conscious part of Judaism's thought and teaching only after the exile to Babylon. Indeed, in one passage of

Micah (4: 1-5) where there is mention of this universalism, we find an identical or quasi-identical, passage in the Book of Isaiah (2: 2-4). This renders scholars suspicious.

Micah's policies and his teachings were much in vogue after his death and in early Christian times. The prophet Jeremiah, 100 years later, pointed to Micah's ministry as justification for his own continual criticism and condemnation of sinners and of injustice in Israel. During the exile at Babylon, Micah's prophecies of restoration were reflected in the psalms composed in Babylon. The early Christian Gospel writers and the early theologians used Micah to establish the veracity of the Christian Church.

Further Reading

See Norman Henry Snaith, *Amos, Hosea, and Micah* (1956), and, for background, Robert H. Pfeiffer, *Introduction to the Old Testament* (1941; rev. ed. 1948). □